FEB 1 1 1999
APR 7 2000

Lawrence A. Hoffman, Ph.D., Johns Hopkins University, is Professor of Geography at The Ohio State University, where he has been a member of the faculty since 1952. Dr. Hoffman is a former Fulbright Research Scholar and has taught at Johns Hopkins University. He also served as an economist, geographer, and demographer for the United States Department of State.

ECONOMIC GEOGRAPHY

LAWRENCE A. HOFFMAN
The Ohio State University

THE RONALD PRESS COMPANY • NEW YORK

Copyright © 1965 by
THE RONALD PRESS COMPANY

All Rights Reserved

No part of this book may be reproduced
in any form without permission in writing
from the publisher.

Library of Congress Catalog Card Number: 65–21810

PRINTED IN THE UNITED STATES OF AMERICA

ONULP

Preface

This textbook deals with space, with natural resources, and with regional personality. The three aspects are viewed in a functional context; that is, they are defined relatively or practically in terms of change in habitat, man, and culture.

Where? Why? and *How viable?* are the traditional questions posed by economic geography. *Where?* can be assessed in ways that seldom wander outside the core area of geography. Satisfactory analyses of *Why?* and *How viable?* and, even more, attempts to coordinate and synthesize these questions require considerable overlapping with economic history, regional economics, regional sociology, regional social psychology, and other approaches from the social sciences and the humanities.

In the functional appraisal used throughout, three constants—space, natural resources, and regional personality—are viewed in the context of such variables as time and stage, technological and institutional changes, and changing consumption standards.

In this book, both the resources and the costs of overcoming or neutralizing negative forces (resistances) of habitat, man, and culture are compared, with attempts being made to assess net results. Location tendencies are assessed in terms of historical inertia, technological development, institutional linkages and gaps, and similar forces, rather than in terms of mathematical or highly theoretical models, which have abstracted away such considerations. The approach avoids the highly abstract and speculative location science in favor of more concrete space-adjusting tendencies evolving out of changing transport technology, larger-scale organization, and similar contexts.

Resource availability, concerned with agricultural, timber, other organic-extractive, crude mineral, and semiprocessed materials, is considered in the outer contexts of environmental, technological, economic, social, political, and other permissive and limiting factors. Land, commonly spoken of as though it were a single variable, ranging from good to marginal or bad, is actually a complex of many interacting factors. In this book, the main emphasis is on current availability, but attention is paid to possible structural changes in the variables that may affect the availability and price of the materials in the foreseeable future.

Regional examples are mainly restricted to two types: (1) more or less compact, continental-size great-regions organized around multicultural indices; and (2) economic-types of society, organized around income structure and occupational structure (high-income countries, including all countries whose national per capita income is higher than the average for mankind, and low-income countries, including all the rest). World data always refer to the entire world, with unofficial sources used to fill gaps in the official coverage when necessary. Unless otherwise identified, the statistics have been obtained from the various yearbooks and other publications of the United Nations.

Physical background from the earth science viewpoint is presented for only those aspects of resource availability where the natural elements and processes are seldom included in an introductory physical geography or general science course.

Maps of economic patterns should be consulted for precise location of individual patterns and locations. Any economic section of any general atlas is suitable. The book's graphs were prepared with the ideal of partial synthesis in the traditional commodity or product groupings; that is, to deal with aggregates such as starches, sugars, oils, fuels, metals, and many others.

Much of the material in this book is based upon nearly fifteen years of teaching economic geography at The Ohio State University to students of commerce, education, arts, agriculture, and engineering, in both thirty-hour (upperclass) and sixty-hour (underclass) courses, with changes in the order and emphasis dependent upon class composition. Where most students had no appreciable background, the regional model presented in Chapter 2 was given greater emphasis, with as much as a few weeks spent to provide concrete examples, with the use of the textual materials, supplementary regional geographies, slide-illustrated reconnaissance traverses in color, and other teaching tools to provide examples of factual and low-level generalizations that would illustrate the more abstract generalizations later on. With other classes having a somewhat better background, more time was given to systematic chapters, often with the non-text sources used in flashbacks.

Much credit is due many students and certain colleagues—S. Earl Brown, Henry L. Hunker, George P. Patten, Frank Seawall, Guy-Harold Smith, Eugene Van Cleef, and the late Alfred J. Wright—for suggestions and criticisms. The author also wishes to thank the Department of Geography of the University of Chicago for the use of the World (Abridged) Continents map from their Goode Base Map series.

LAWRENCE A. HOFFMAN

The Ohio State University
July, 1965

Contents

1 Introduction   3

The Place of Geography in Knowledge, 3   An Overview of the Geographic Viewpoint(s), 4   Resource Development and Conservation, 6   Changes in Scale of Operation, 8   Timing Problems, 9

2 Geography of Income   11

Stages in Economic Development, 14   Regional Assessments, 18   Relative Change in Economic Sectors, 48   Perspective, 57

3 Modern Economic Development: Ideology and Technology   59

Ideology, 61   Technology, 64   Perspective, 68

4 Modern Economic Development: Population and Natural Resources   69

Population, 69   Natural Resources, 89   Perspective, 91

5 Introduction to Agriculture   94

Regional Agricultural Characteristics, 95   Problems Requiring Increased Agricultural Output for Solution, 103   Increased Agricultural Supply: Grand Strategy, 110   Increased Agricultural Supply: Tactics, 122   Chief Reasons for Agricultural Poverty, 126   Perspective, 132

6 Basic Energy Foods   134

Dietary Economics, 135   Regional Starch Crops Production, 139   Food Grains, 145   Feed Grains, 153   Starchy Roots, Tubers, and Fruits, 167   Prospects, 177

7 Luxury Energy Foods   179

Sugar, 179   Oils and Fats, 193   Prospects, 212

8 Livestock and Animal Products   214

Patterns in Animal Husbandry, 219   The World's Livestock, 225   Perspective, 239

9 Fibers and Textiles — 240
Natural Fibers, 244 Man-made Fibers, 253 Textile Manufacturing, 257 Perspective, 261

10 Tree Crops and Forest Products — 263
Beverage Crops, 264 Elastomers ("Rubbers"), 279 Forests and Forest Products, 288

11 Oceanic Products — 312
Regional Productivity of Fisheries, 313 Minerals from the Sea, 323 Fresh Water from the Sea, 326 Prospects, 329

12 Introduction to Industry — 330
Regional Industrial Characteristics, 330 Industrial Subsector Characteristics, 345 Effects of Distribution and Productive Factors Forces, 358 Perspective, 371

13 Energy Resources — 373
Coal, 378 Petroleum, 385 Natural Gas, 395 Water Power and Electricity, 402 Potential Sources of Energy, 412 A Long View of Fuel and Power, 424

14 Metallurgy and Fabricating Industries — 426
Ferrous Metallurgy, 430 Non-ferrous Metallurgy, 467 Metal-transforming Industries, 480 Perspective, 494

15 Chemical Industries — 497
General Achievements, 498 Raw Materials of the Chemical Industry, 500 Location and Organization of the Chemical Industry, 523 Perspective, 527

16 Transportation, Trade, and Other Service Activities — 529
Transportation and Communications, 529 Trade and Commerce, 551 Governmental and Professional-personal Services, 568 Prospects, 569

Index — 571

ECONOMIC GEOGRAPHY

1

Introduction

The total field of knowledge may be thought of as consisting mainly of generalizations (abstractions), a mass of neutral facts (and low-level generalizations), and various techniques (tool skills: material and intellectual-intuitive), usually looked at expertly from particular points of view. The main purpose of dividing up total knowledge into various disciplines is in order that the various points of view may be more clearly seen and their relative emphasis assessed, but it can perhaps best be viewed as historical and necessary (because of the puniness of most professional competences) than of rigid ideological necessity. The real process of learning is less the memorized accumulation of facts (although some of this is inevitable, as most understand abstractions mainly in the context of concrete facts they know) than the thoughtful association of selected facts and generalizations to illustrate ideas aiding the development of critical judgment ("seeing" the gaps between reality and ideal or myth), imaginative insight (being able to put one's self in many different people's position, among other sensitivities), flexibility (being able to change quickly outer frames of reference like time, place, culture-type), and (rarest of all) creativity. Academic subjects are particular ways of looking at total knowledge, themes, or lines of interest, the main way to make knowledge continuously interesting and meaningful (especially if liberally mixed with "condiments" like agnosticism and humor).

Like most fields, geography is really a group of traditions or approaches. This chapter will preview those used in this book and indicate linkages with neighboring fields whose interests overlap.

THE PLACE OF GEOGRAPHY IN KNOWLEDGE

Geography is one of the fields interested in man's use of space and natural resources. It examines the bonds between man, culture, and land from a comparative regional viewpoint, and can initially be approached from the natural (earth science) or cultural (social science and humanities) side. Geographers contend that human societies can be fully understood only if their behavior and activities are examined against the background of (1) the space they occupy, (2) their situation (relative location in terms of both natural and cultural patterns), and (3) the present and prospective natural resources and resistances facing them.

Like history, anthropology, and some other fields, geography overlaps the traditional boundaries between physical science, biological science, social science, and humanities. It displays some of the characteristics of science, some of art, and some of philosophy, if its spectrum of traditions is surveyed. The generalist variant of geographer is suspicious of tendencies to deal with complicated human and land-use problems and prospects in exclusively natural science, social science, or humanistic contexts. The natural (physical-biological) scientists usually exclude human activities as far as they are able, and concentrate on nature as the main actor. The social scientists view problems and prospects as strictly human or cultural, and view nature either as an abstraction or as relatively passive. The humanists view problems and prospects almost exclusively in backward glances, minimizing fundamental changes brought about by dynamic science and technology. For the geographer, and others like the ecologist, man and his habitat are interdependent and separable only by feats of disciplined imagination. Each civilization has its particular view of human ecology, so there is a definite connection between culture patterns and natural patterns that are considered useful.

At various times, the geographer tries to understand and use the attitude of precision favored by the natural scientist, the attitude of tentativeness favored by the social scientist, and the attitude of appreciation favored by the humanist, but his field cannot be dominated by any one viewpoint.

Another frame of reference by which disciplines can be classified is that which is based upon the orientations about which fields can be organized: subject matter, tools, plots, contexts, theories, and problems. Some fields are clearly organized about one of these, but most fields actually combine several. The fields that engage in a wide variety of activities—ordinary teaching, extension teaching, professional training, consultive work, research—inevitably have several definitions and several orientations. Geography is mainly a context-oriented field; it is primarily concerned with relational thinking. The geographer maintains that the proportions and relations of things are as much facts as the things themselves.

While recognizing the value of thinking in the realm of validity (i.e., reasoning verifiable mainly by language, logic, and mathematics), the geographer's customary way of thinking generously illustrates validity with the realm of ordinary truth (i.e., "reality" verifiable by the senses), as the layman senses it. Geography tends to emphasize middle-level concepts and principles, often specializations of theory independently established in the systematic natural and social sciences.

AN OVERVIEW OF THE GEOGRAPHIC VIEWPOINT(S)

Even in ancient times, one can perceive different approaches in geography: a regional or area-studies approach, a spatial or location tendency approach, a man-land relationship or resource availability approach, and an earth science approach. All have yielded good geography—all have spawned extremists who have moved in name or practice outside the field to other fields or to newly emerging specialties. The regional tradition has probably somewhat less tendency than the systematic traditions to lose specialists to other fields, but has held on to the more generalist practitioners at the expense of anemic theoretical structure compared to its heavy cargoes of descriptive materials (facts and low-level generalizations).

In all the approaches, but especially in the regional approach, geography deals with combinations of things on the earth's surface as these things exist together in space in any given area. At its best, after the necessary analysis, it aims at being an integrative field, dealing with things in association, not merely with elements taken separately or items listed in inventory form. In other words, whatever its tone, geography is always concerned with regional personality (even when, as in this book, it is a secondary rather than the primary frame of reference), and with the significance of differences and similarities among places on the face of the earth.

The regional approach usually involves much description, much dependence upon history and regional aspects of social sciences for its explanations, and more dependence upon literary communication skills (than upon mathematical and formal logic ones) supplemented with graphic-portrayal (maps, pictures) languages.

Most regionalists tend to favor the unique school of thought, emphasizing differences rather than similarities, dealing with special and unique characteristics rather than comparative and general ones. In this book, a comparative school of thought has been favored, looking for parallel or analogous episodes or regularities between regions and realms (not necessarily causally related).

The spatial or space-adjusting approach abstracts away most or all of naively perceived reality, and deals with such aspects as size, shape, distance, direction, position, and other spatial aspects of reality (or simulation models of reality). In some cases, geographers favoring this approach tend to end up with aspects of geometry or other mathematics. In this book, interest in spatial aspects has tended more in the movement or circulation areas, tied in closely with changing transportation technology. The practitioners who favor the most abstract theory tend to establish hypotheses, test by striving for connecting threads or trends, with the ultimate end of gaining synthesis. Some enthusiasts attempt to achieve abiding lessons or laws in location tendencies, some basis for prediction or possible control of future behavior.

The man-land approach is favored by teachers and others mainly interested in communication with the general public. One variant of this tradition, common earlier in this century before the development of the behavioral sciences and modern culture history, was environmental determinism, one of those cosmic and panoramic ideologies so favored by philosophers (and so commonly gross oversimplifications because of their organization around simple causation rather than around multiple and interlocking causation). Recent variants of this tradition are much more cognizant of the complicated cultural buffers between man and land as simply defined in earlier days. This book is mainly organized in this man-land tradition, especially in the functional definition of resources variant pioneered by Erich Zimmermann, with spatial and regional aspects mainly used to illustrate regularities and structural changes brought out by drawing on historical parallels.

All three emphases or traditions have tendencies to misuse and degeneracy. Regional study starts with the hypothesis of a homogeneous area (one with a single or multiple similarity), which is then examined with a view to discovering its components and connections. The region is analyzed with respect to the various elements that in association give it character, and is interpreted so as to attain the greatest possible synthesis. At worst, the regional approach may degenerate into a handbook or encyclopedic description, full of sterile distributions neither functionally nor artistically coordinated. The topical approach—whether mainly concerned with space-adjusting or resource availability—usually starts with or quickly involves problems and prospects, with accompanying attempts to clarify a question of cause and effect or a question of policy underpinnings, seeking the most complete analysis possible. At worst, systematic geography can become too generalized and abstract, tending to disintegrate into overgeneralized verbalism of little use as feedback in explaining the real (confusing and chaotic) world, except at the cost of warping beyond recognition.

Three major considerations are commonly included in a geographic study of human activities in space: areal extent, areal association, and spatial interaction. (1) A study of the areal extent of any basic human activity within a given place involves observations of abstract elements (e.g., size and shape, situation, and areas of concentration and dispersal). Such a pattern is static and, while necessary as a beginning to disciplined thinking, can degenerate into sterile description if not continually fertilized with ideas of function and possible causation. In this book, little attempt at encyclopedic patterning is attempted. (2) Areal association is concerned with explaining the areal extent of a selected phenomenon in terms of the distribution of one or more additional phenomena, not in the sense of cause and effect but in terms of interrelationships. Whatsoever the region (unless it has wholly escaped human impress), it is a compound of two contrasting yet interwoven elements: a physical and biological basis, which is relatively stable; and cultural (i.e., facility, activity, institutional, ideological) patterns and distributions, which are usually changing much more rapidly. Geography studies these combinations of warp and woof (physical setting and human impress) in a characteristic sequence (observation, distribution, deduction) with the purpose of discovering (*a*) meanings in the fact that they differ from area to area, and (*b*) meanings in the togetherness, in any given area, of the natural, man-made, and human elements in the areal complex. (3) Any pattern is capable of either a static or a dynamic explanation. Spatial interaction involves the association of phenomena within a single unit of area (as contrasted with areal associations, which involve a study of the movement of phenomena from one unit area to another), with the pattern and functional organization of human occupance as focused by human enterprise and interconnected by human organization. In this book, spatial and land-use patterns will be introduced, viewed historically if that viewpoint is most meaningful in explaining present trends, and then previewed in the light of prospective changes likely in terms of changing technology, numbers, standards, and resource availability.

The economic geography favored in this book is mainly viewed in the wider perspective of economic development, which involves considerable overlapping with economic history, regional economics, regional sociology and social psychology, and other social sciences and humanities. Primarily it is a bridging-type of discipline, sharing concepts with economics but using geographic methods, testing the validity of certain economic concepts by applying them in particular places. Its core topics include production of crude materials (agricultural, stock-raising, forestry, mining), industrial development and location, transport routes and flows, market effects on commercial location, and other topics involving general location principles and the dynamics of resource development. The core topics of economics are usually quite different (e.g., activities of individual firms; competition; price movements and business cycles; taxation, finance, and fiscal policies; structure of personal and other income), although regional economics and economic geography are closely related. In the current world, political and social phenomena are intimately intertwined with economics, with the most spectacular economic progress usually powered by underlying political and social structural changes, and with economic stagnation or slow progress usually more explainable in terms of political and social roadblocks than strictly economic resistances.

The development of the patterns and organization of human occupance in the world is most understandable as the outgrowth of human choice in a frame of reference including the dynamics of space and habitat, time, technology, organization, and values. Consideration of current functions is not enough. The present pattern of form and functions usually represents a complex system inherited from the past. It was not invented by the present operators to fulfill current needs in direct response to nature, but developed by predecessors in a long sequence of historic cultural invention, innovation, and diffusion. Often brought from faraway places of origin and applied locally, possibly on foundations laid by an older system, it is still being modified in the evolving pattern of form and functions in this setting. Thus, the object of study is recognized as a pattern of occupance, functionally organized and using an old system set down in a natural environment suitable enough for its continued operation. In addition, mainly because of dynamic science and technology, the pattern changes as the developing human community transforms its habitat. With every major change that society experiences, an alteration occurs in the spatial dimensions of human affairs. The rest of this chapter explores major changes in resource development, scale of operation, and timing tactics, which will provide background concepts useful throughout the book.

RESOURCE DEVELOPMENT AND CONSERVATION

Men at each level of civilization have intermittently worried about natural resource problems. Ever since the discovery of fire and the invention of tools, men have had the ability to destroy important renewable resources. With every stagnation of technology, men have also quickly exhausted economically available mineral resources. Certain factors in modern experience have radically changed the nature of resource availability: unprecedented changes in material technology, in social technology, and in rate of population growth.

Changes in Material Technology

Since the Industrial Revolution, the interrelations between dynamic science and technology have immensely affected man's exploitation of his habitat. Acceleration of wasteful practices in the biological and related spheres has been offset by progress in the restorative and upgrading areas, but no reliable picture of the net effects is yet available, on either a continental or world scale. Apparently macro flow resources, such as radiation, tides, and wind-systems, have so far not been significantly affected by mankind's actions. However, microclimates, topsoils, and plant-animal geography have been significantly affected. For example, in producing the some 3 billion tons of food and 4 billion tons of non-food organic fuels and raw materials for industry annually, several billion tons of vital soil nutrients are consumed, but an additional 5 to 6 billion tons of these materials are removed by accelerated wind and water erosion accompanying such production.

In the area of stock resources, depletion has so far been effectively offset by increased efficiency in mining and related processing, but the increased total and per capita demands are increasing so rapidly that the fear of exhaustion of not only high-grade and medium-grade but even low-grade resources is now widespread. The ascendency of the mineral-using industries has resulted in a 5 per cent average annual increase in world tonnage consumption of minerals as compared with less than 2 per cent increase in the consumption of agricultural and related organic raw materials. At present, world annual consumption of minerals is about 25 billion tons (30 per cent fuels and ores, remainder building materials and chemical raw materials), and increasing so rapidly that prospective (long-range) use of ordinary rocks, seawater, and air as the future dominant sources of minerals is visualized by scientific dreamers.

Changes in Social Technology

The application of machine-powered techniques in the production of most goods and many services, with the resultant shift in emphasis from the self-sufficient local economy to the interregional and then to the interdependent international economy, has had major repercussions on resource availability and use.

In general, the premodern subsistence economy utilized its natural resources conservatively compared with the modern commercial economy that produces for sale in distant markets. Modern productive units are usually larger, less diversified, more affected by price fluctuations, and more subject to adverse changes from tenure, taxation, and credit disabilities.

Probably the most limiting obstacle to efficient world use of modern science and technology is the raw nationalism which is unlikely to have its dominant sovereignty formally eroded in the foreseeable future.

Changes in Population Growth

In the presently urban-industrial societies, voluntary decrease in birth rates has brought about a near equilibrium between birth and death rates after five- to tenfold increases in population, with per capita real levels of living from five to twenty times higher than before, in their previous agrarian context.

It is uncertain how similar the demographic transition (more fully treated in Chapter 4, on world population geography) in presently underdeveloped societies will duplicate Western experience. Perhaps nineteenth century European expansion of people and trade may have been unique. Also, absolute population increase in the underdeveloped societies may well be larger and be achieved faster than the Western experience, in which event new techniques and different timing will be necessary to avoid economic progress being stymied by population increase. At present, it appears that the economic progress achieved by the Newer Europeans may well be greater than that achieved by the industrialization of other segments of mankind.

CHANGES IN SCALE OF OPERATION

In mainly self-sufficient, small-scaled premodern societies, concern with situation and natural resources was mainly local, but modern urban-industrial societies' concern is more and more worldwide.

The enormous growth of population in the past several centuries has tended to aggregate itself ever more narrowly in large cities and urbanized regions, leaving the formerly "empty" quarters of the earth still relatively empty. We are witnesses of a complex and gradual process of symbiosis whereby the developing life of the city and the city-region transforms the character and subsumes the categories of rural life.

Many poorly endowed regions—especially in the mountains and forested poor-soil areas—which formerly allowed a modest level of living to a small, scattered population are now being abandoned or returned to low-grade land-use (forestry, grazing, recreation). Modern technology and standards thus often result in a withdrawal of agricultural efforts to better regions, with some abandonment of submarginal areas.

On the other hand, some regions previously considered impossible for conventional agriculture, or submarginal, are now used within the modern, commercial agriculture context. Subhumid grasslands can be extensively cultivated for grain with cheap machine power in spite of frequent crop failures or uneconomic production a large fraction of the time. Other areas enjoying superlative situation in relation to cities may use low-grade soils or short-season climates for growing perishables. Areally most spectacular, the economic mining of industrial minerals is now carried on in nearly every part of the world except the ice caps.

Increasingly, crude materials are being processed into semifinished materials near the source, in order to save weight and improve storing and shipping ability. Cheap bulk transport (by ocean and barge carriers, pipeline, heavy rail and truck carriers) allows movements of several thousand miles or more at costs less or little more than the costs of production.

Urbanized regions accessible to worldwide sources of supply and markets through use of deep-water ocean carriers have profited most from modern mechanized mobility, although the increasing importance of air-freighters make even inland cities accessible to worldwide sources of high-value materials and other goods. In general, technology and economics in water and rail shipping combine to promote volume moves of crude materials and the concentration of flows, while the introducing of trucking and air-freighting relatively favors dispersion and higher-value goods.

Scale is affected not only by transport but also by organization possibilities. Specialization, cheap communication, and governmental order and assistance have made possible modern corporate enterprise which functions effectively in continental, even worldwide, contexts under certain conditions (examined in more detail in the following section on timing). However, in spite of the progress made by private, corporate, and governmental enterprise, this factor of organization is probably the most limiting one facing modern urban-industrial mankind. Organizers able to maintain high morale in large institutions and to foresee coming problems and forestall or minimize them are rarer nuggets to find than bonanza mineral strikes. Formal education and apprenticeship training systems seem able to produce adequate numbers and quality of low-level and medium-level organizers, but really high-level organizers seem to be flukes (i.e., no good correlation with any one type of education, professional training, or class affiliation).

In premodern societies, natural resistances coupled with localized anarchy (banditry and piracy) restricted the scale advantages possible. In the modern world, the sovereign state system is probably the most limiting factor to worldwide growth of population and welfare. Technically and economically, mankind would profit from greater specialization on an areal basis, but politically there are hazards if war and preparation for war are the assumed main security frames of reference. Those countries now most dependent on outside sources of materials and markets often reflect relics of imperial patterns and associations built up during politically seemingly more secure times. In almost all cases, national protection of marginal agriculture and mining is moderate to very high, not only by the older tariff protection devices but by newer indirect devices (which often minimize heavy competition among regions within a single political unit or association). All in all, present politics are even less in tune with the realities of modern urban-industrial civilization than present economics.

TIMING PROBLEMS

Location and materials problems are better understood within a context indicating in which stage of growth an economic activity is at any specified time. A useful hypothetical growth curve may be considered in four stages: a pioneering stage, a rapid growth stage, a slow growth stage, and a stable stage (which usually evolves into decline or "reincarnation").

In the pioneering period, both the item (good or service) and the process of producing it are likely to be defective. During this experimental period, the cost of the item tends to be high and its quality poor, with the consequence that the demand is usually small, so the scale of production must be small. This is a stage in which many small enterprises may enter the field, most of them eventually failing or being absorbed. The location of facilities is often fortuitous, related to the home area of the inventor or organizer, cheap purchase or rental of old buildings, or some other chance event. Materials and other purchased factors of production are often inadequate in quality and price, but little is done about it while the technology of production and marketing problems are predominant. Examples in the United States are complete home air conditioning, color television, and most automation.

Rapid progress and growth are the hallmarks of the second stage. Eventually, both the item and process of production are materially improved, making possible price reductions and more economical servicing. The improved methods of production, distribution, and marketing are rapidly adapted, with easier financing and scale advantages accompanying the wave of profitable expansion. Better plant equipment, better location of new plant, and better sources of materials and other items represent materials-saving and transport-saving economies affected under such conditions. Giant organizations emerge, out of spectacular growth and bankruptcy of ineffective units.

Eventually, a diminished growth rate occurs, perhaps because the rate of technical progress slows down, perhaps because the expansion of markets becomes more difficult. Usually, only minor changes are made in product and process, although styling and packaging changes may be advertised as spectacular real progress. Market growth becomes smaller, since only radical social and political changes would widen the market to reach the remaining potential market segments. As in the second stage, big companies and big units have the advantages, since production and consumption is large enough to support the high fixed costs of such giants. A few good examples in the United States today would be ordinary television, refrigeration, and other consumer durables considered comforts and luxuries in the culture.

Stability, even decline, is the inevitable fourth stage. Competing activities in other regions or in foreign countries may cut down both exports and domestic sales (e.g., certain types of United States automobiles). Many goods and services valued as necessities are affected by a slowing in the rate of population growth (e.g., flour). New activities whose goods or services are substitutes may arise and cut down on the demand (e.g., TV for movies). Even when the new items are not functionally substitutes, they may replace older items in the public fancy. On the production side, new activities that do not compete for markets may compete for factors of production, making materials, labor, capital, organization, or governmental services scarcer and more costly. Sometimes even continued reduction in costs may not widen the market (e.g., drops in price of agricultural and mineral materials may not drop price of consumer's product). In other cases, technical progress in the processing industry may be impressive, but the finished product stay as costly because of higher costs of crude materials (e.g., U.S. petroleum refining). In this fourth stage, as in the first stage, smaller concerns may be relatively more important, profiting from greater flexibility of organization, lower proportion of fixed costs, and other advantages. Sometimes revolutionary changes may start another cycle of growth, either in the same general area of production, or by switching to new areas.

Most of the preceding has been mainly applicable to individual concerns, but a time perspective is equally valuable in a wider context. Differing abilities to absorb present and prospective changes in science and technology, in ideas and institutions, and in population depend as much upon what stage of economic development a society is currently in than upon any other factor. Since the bulk of this book emphasizes the importance of regional assessment of location and materials problems, the next chapter will characterize the two types of regions used: nine great-regions (general-culture regions, often with a strong geopolitical element), and two economic-realms (high-income or urban-industrial countries as one grouping and low-income or underdeveloped countries as the other grouping). Then two chapters will portray the process of modern economic development or modernization: one the more active (usually causal) factors of ideological and technological developments; the other the limiting factors of population and natural resources (both as much resistances as resources in most developing societies).

SUGGESTED READINGS

CHASE, STUART. *The Proper Study of Mankind.* (Rev. ed.) New York: Harper & Row, 1956. Pp. 327.

DEBENHAM, FRANK. *The Use of Geography.* London: English Universities Press, 1950. Pp. 206.

FREEMAN, T. W. *A Hundred Years of Geography.* Chicago: Aldine, 1961. Pp. 335.

HARTSHORNE, RICHARD. *Perspective on the Nature of Geography.* Chicago: Rand McNally (for the Association of American Geographers), 1959. Pp. 201.

HOSELITZ, BERT F. (ed.). *A Reader's Guide to the Social Sciences.* Glencoe, Ill.: The Free Press of Glencoe, 1959. Pp. 256.

JAMES, PRESTON E. (ed.). *New Viewpoints in Geography.* Washington, D.C.: National Council for the Social Studies (29th Yearbook), 1959. Pp. 260.

JAMES, PRESTON E., and JONES, CLARENCE F. (eds.). *American Geography: Inventory and Prospect.* Syracuse University Press (for the Association of American Geographers), 1954. Pp. 590.

LEARY, LEWIS (ed.). *The Unity of Knowledge.* New York: Doubleday, 1955. Pp. 306.

LEIGHLY, JOHN (ed.). *Land and Life—A Selection from the Writings of Carl Ortwin Sauer.* University of California Press, 1963. Pp. 435.

MOGEY, J. M. *The Study of Geography.* London: Oxford University Press, 1950. Pp. 164.

NEGLEY, GLENN. *The Organization of Knowledge.* Englewood Cliffs, N.J.: Prentice-Hall, 1942. Pp. 373.

RAPOPORT, ANATOL. *Operational Philosophy.* New York: Harper & Row, 1954. Pp. 258.

SIU, R. G. H. *The Tao of Science.* Massachusetts Institute of Technology, 1957. Pp. 180.

WOOLDRIDGE, S. W., and EAST, W. GORDON. *The Spirit and Purpose of Geography.* London: Hutchinson, 1951. Pp. 176.

WRIGHT, JOHN KIRTLAND. *Geography in the Making—The American Geographical Society, 1851–1951.* New York: The Society, 1952. Pp. 437.

2

Geography of Income

Although modern urban-industrial civilization evolved and developed in Britain before the end of the eighteenth century, perceptible worldwide diffusion is mainly a phenomenon of the past century. During that century, mankind's real income (excluding effects of inflation) increased over tenfold, while mankind's numbers increased some threefold. However, only a minority of mankind has greatly benefited from this vastly increased income, mainly those in the three dozen societies that substantially modernized their productive, distributive, and consumptive apparatus. About a fifth of mankind live in a score of countries whose average annual per capita income is now over $1,000 and can be considered wealthy in a world perspective, although there are usually pockets of poverty remaining if new welfare standards are applied. Another twelfth of mankind live in over a dozen countries whose average annual per capita income ranges from mankind's mean income ($450 yearly) to $1,000—these well-to-do societies tend to be among the more recently modernized or some with unusual cultural resistances (effects of war destruction or especially deep-seated social problems). Together these three dozen countries form an elite group or realm hereafter referred to as the high-income countries. They all have their economic problems, some serious from their point of view, but relatively small and manageable from the point of view of the low-income 70 per cent plus of mankind.

The countries in the low-income or underdeveloped group or realm all have per capita annual income below the world's mean for mankind, but the seven dozen or so societies (countries and dependencies) can be differentiated into several subgroupings. About a score have moderate per capita income ($250 to $450 yearly), and might be characterized as semimodernized, as they have modernized significant segments of their economies and are probably within a decade or so of reaching urban-industrial or high-income status (e.g., Mexico and Brazil in Latin America, Iberian and Balkan countries in Europe). Several dozen low-income societies might be characterized as middle-poor ($125 to $250 annual per capita income), and the remaining four dozen with annual per capita income under $125 are the poorest 55 per cent of mankind. Small groups (mainly urban-nodes or spots of modernized primary activity) in the poor societies have modernized, mainly those closely associated with the Commercial World, but such developments have not radically changed national employment structure, labor productivity, or per capita income. Table 2–1 and the graphs on pages 12, 13, and 15 indicate the world patterns of the two economic-types of society, as well as the more conventional and usually compact great-regions (culture-regions of continental size), both types of regions used

WORLD: NATIONAL INCOME (Value-added), BY GREAT-REGION AND ECONOMIC-TYPE OF SOCIETY, 1962-1964 AVERAGE-ANNUAL (U.S. $ Billion)

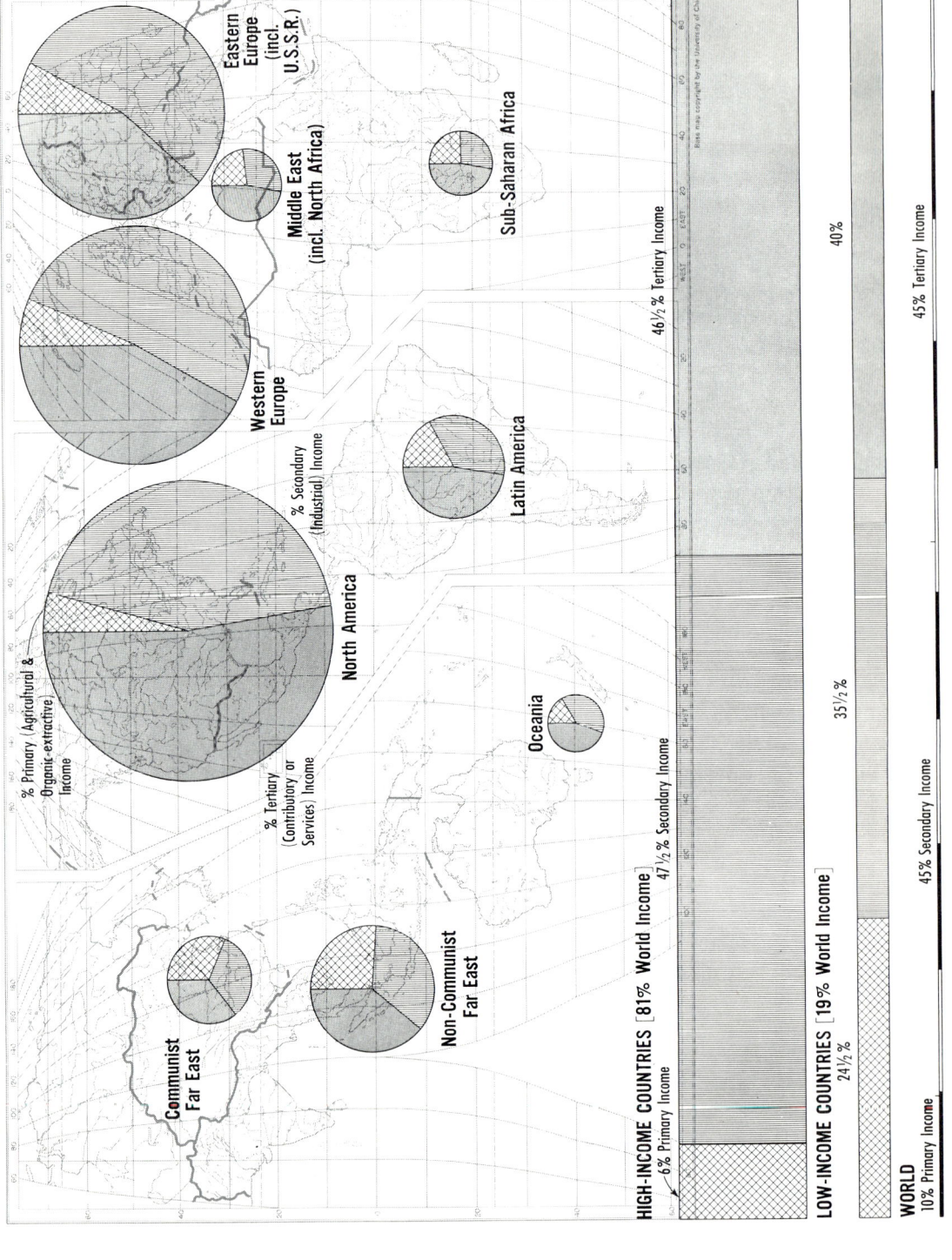

WORLD: GREAT-REGION AND ECONOMIC-TYPE OF SOCIETY SHARES OF TOTAL, PRIMARY, SECONDARY, AND TERTIARY INCOME, 1962-1964 AVERAGE-ANNUAL

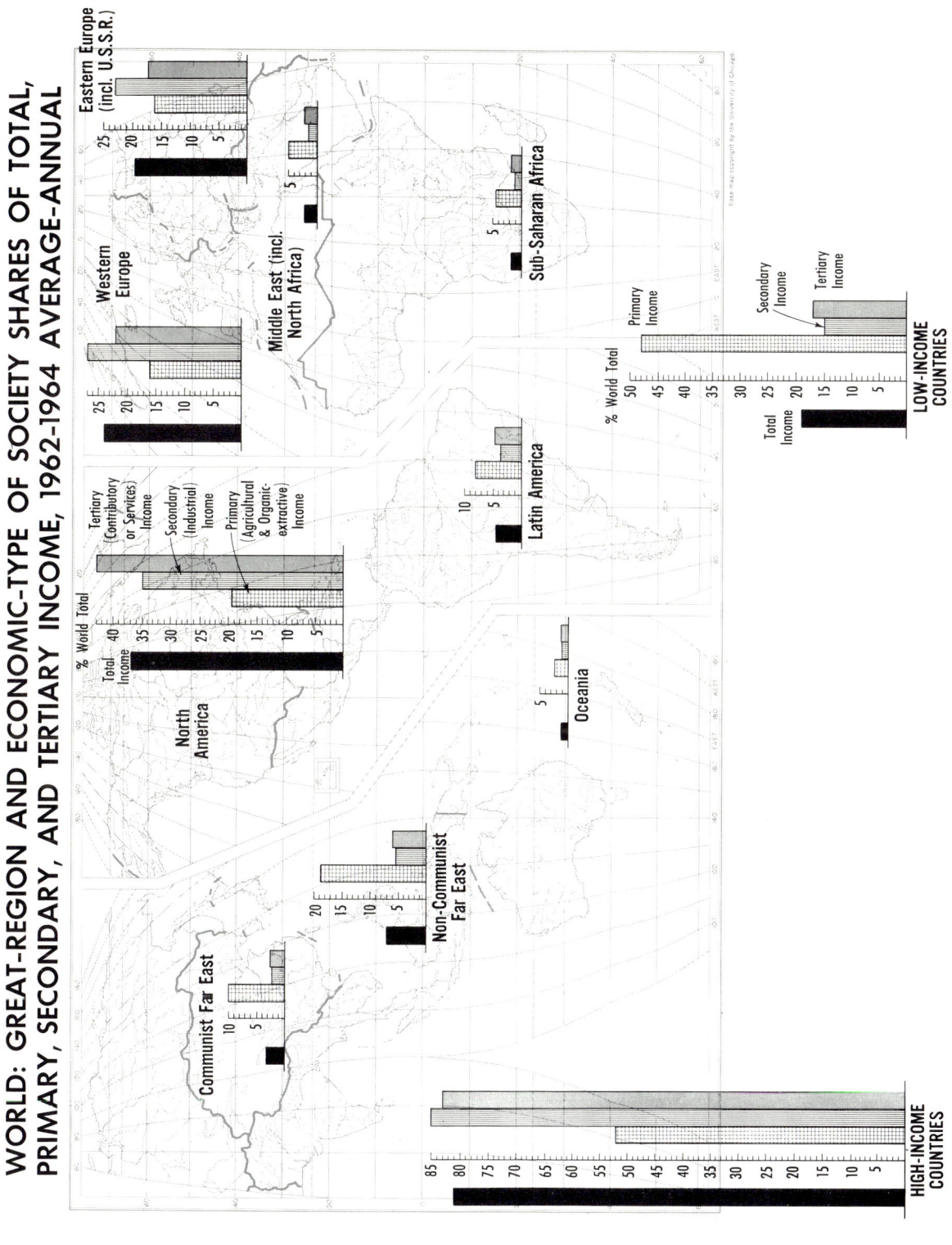

throughout the book to illustrate the meaning of things by the area they take up and to measure significance by the intensity with which an area is developed.

STAGES IN ECONOMIC DEVELOPMENT

Throughout this book, assessment of location (space-adjusting) and raw materials (resource availability) problems and prospects will mainly be done in terms of nine great-regions (i.e., the general-culture multipurpose regions of North America, Western Europe, Eastern Europe including the U.S.S.R., Oceania, Latin America, sub-Saharan Africa, the Middle East including North Africa, non-Communist Far East, and the Communist Far East) and in terms of two economic-types of society (high-income countries

TABLE 2–1

World: National Income * and Its Sector Composition, by Great-Region and Economic-Type of Society, 1962–1964 Average-Annual
(in billions of United States dollars)

	Total Income (U.S. $ billion = 100.0 per cent)	Primary (Agricultural and Organic-extractive) Sector	Secondary (Industrial) Sector	Tertiary (Contributory or Services) Sector
North America	530	5.0%	42.5%	52.5%
Western Europe	340	6.5	51.5	42.0
Eastern Europe (including the U.S.S.R.)	280	8.0	53.5	38.5
Oceania	18	16.5	39.0	44.5
Latin America	65	17.0	35.5	47.5
Sub-Saharan Africa	25	25.0	28.0	47.0
Middle East (including North Africa)	30	23.5	30.0	46.5
Non-Communist Far East	100	26.0	35.0	39.0
Communist Far East	45	31.0	33.5	35.5
World	1,433	10.0	45.0	45.0
High-income countries	1,159	6.0	47.5	46.5
Low-income countries	274	24.5	35.5	40.0
	(per cent of U.S. $1,433.0 billion)	(per cent of U.S. $138.5 billion)	(per cent of U.S. $646.0 billion)	(per cent of U.S. $648.5 billion)
North America	37.0	19.5	34.8	42.8
Western Europe	23.7	15.9	27.1	22.0
Eastern Europe (including the U.S.S.R.)	19.5	15.9	23.2	16.7
Oceania	1.2	2.3	1.1	1.2
Latin America	4.5	7.9	3.6	4.8
Sub-Saharan Africa	1.8	4.6	1.1	1.7
Middle East (including North Africa)	2.1	5.0	1.4	2.1
Non-Communist Far East	7.0	18.8	5.4	6.0
Communist Far East	3.2	10.1	2.3	2.5
World	100.0	100.0	100.0	100.0
High-income countries	81.0	52.0	85.0	83.0
Low-income countries	19.0	48.0	15.0	17.0

Source: Mainly adapted from United Nations sources, with unofficial sources used in compiling Communist (Eastern Europe/U.S.S.R. and Communist Far East) data.

* National income equals value-added by the factors of production (i.e., land, labor, capital, enterprise, and government). The primary or agricultural sector includes stock-raising, forestry, and fishing-hunting-gathering. The secondary or industrial sector includes manufacturing, handicrafts, mining, utilities, and construction activities. The tertiary or services sector includes distribution (transportation-communications and trade-commerce), non-governmental professional-personal, and governmental services.

WORLD: AVERAGE PER CAPITA INCOME, AND AVERAGE VALUE-ADDED PER WORKER, BY GREAT-REGION AND ECONOMIC-TYPE OF SOCIETY, 1962-1964 AVERAGE-ANNUAL

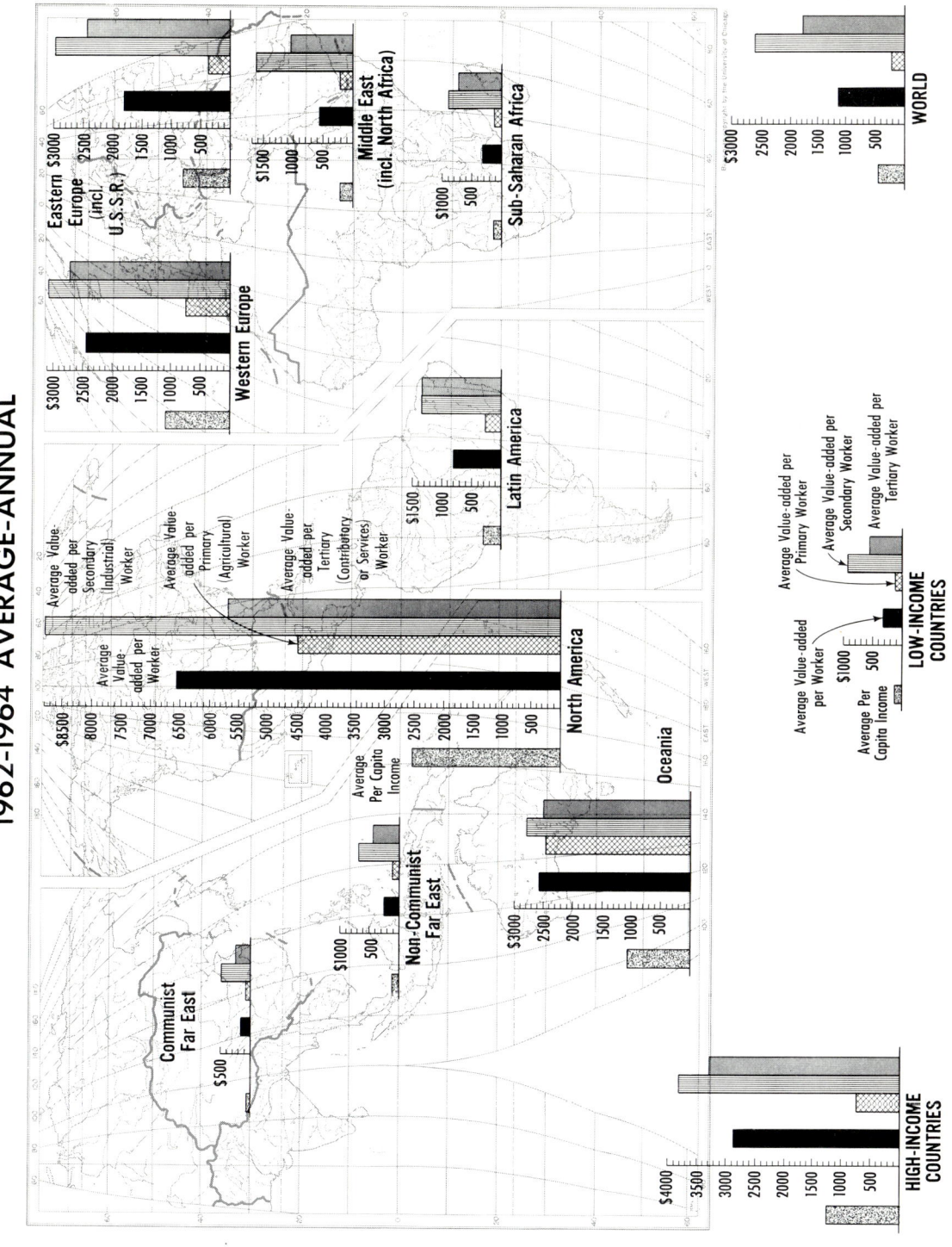

and low-income countries), both regional systems correlating with the stage of economic development or modernization reached by the early 1960's.

Although the main emphasis is on systematic analysis, the continual use of the two regional perspectives makes it useful to characterize them at this early point. The following few pages will indicate some of the differences as well as the similarities characterizing the economic types of society (each realm consists of countries that are sometimes contiguous but also sometimes widely separated by water or by other types of economies). Then both the compact or contiguous great-regions and the economic-type realms will be more realistically characterized in terms of a model incorporating generalizations organized in terms of three facets (assets-liabilities, and weighting in hierarchial form of the five pattern-complexes: natural, facility, activity, institutional, and ideological groupings).

The High-Income Urban-industrial Realm

This aggregate of highly developed economies includes those that have substantially rationalized (modernized or improved their technical efficiency) each major (primary or agricultural, secondary or industrial, and tertiary or services) sector, although most such economies will have semimodernized aspects and underdeveloped relics remaining, especially in some of their agricultural and services subsectors. Having such a status does not connote income equality with others in the urban-industrial realm. Japan and Italy have present per capita incomes perhaps five times larger than before modernizing, while the most-favored urban-industrial economies (e.g., the United States, Sweden) have per capita incomes perhaps fifteen to twenty times larger than during their premodern stage. The mass of urban-industrial nations in Europe and elsewhere are mainly ranged between the two extremes.

Differences within the urban-industrial realm can be distinguished in terms of several indices. In terms of natural resources adequacy relative to population and standards-of-living pressures, two variants can be characterized. The Newer European type includes the United States and Canada, the Soviet Union, Australia and New Zealand, and Argentina, Uruguay, and Chile (White South Africa also). All these countries have abundant per capita realized and latent natural resources, and dynamic science and technology still flexible enough to sustain continued growth in numbers and rises in the levels of living for the next generation or so, perhaps the next century. Their drain on outside natural resources is likely to be mainly in the spheres of minerals and of tropical foods and raw materials of agricultural origin. The Older European type includes most of Western and Eastern (excluding the U.S.S.R.) Europe and Japan. These countries have strong technologies but limited domestic natural resources (not only in tropical foods and non-food agricultural materials but in many mid-latitude types of such primary materials, besides great deficits in mineral materials), so there is strong pressure for attachment to foreign resources and to synthetic substitutes. Their trade position can easily degenerate into economic and political crises, although there may be no great difficulty in raising the productivity of industry, and their control over population increase is usually excellent.

Some of these high-income economies have achieved that status by highly productive specialization on a narrow front, with a surprising immaturity which only slowly yields to widening currents of diversified modernization (the bonanza mineral strikes of Kuwait, South Africa, Venezuela, and Trinidad are the most spectacular examples). Others have achieved great economic progress, but with special advantages not normally available to the average developing society (e.g., Puerto Rico's special association with the United States, Israel's special association with Jews all over the world and with certain countries). Several economies are high-income but marginally so because of unusual wartime and civil war damage (Poland and Hungary) or because of crippling communal structure (Republic of South Africa) or because of severe "overpopulation" problems (Puerto

Rico, Hong Kong). In such exceptions to the mature (diversified) urban-industrial status, additional time may bring greater per capita economic progress with diversified maturity, but in some cases they may never realize as great net profit from modernization as those elsewhere.

As indicated in Table 2–1 and on the graphs on pages 12, 13, and 15, the high-income realm produces and consumes over four-fifths of the world's income, although having under 30 per cent of mankind. Although producing slightly over half of world agricultural and related primary production, and consuming roughly the same fraction, much trade is necessary both within the realm and with the underdeveloped realm in order to achieve balance between specific surpluses and deficits. The proportion of world industrial and services production and consumption in the high-income realm approaches 85 per cent, but again with many specific imbalances.

The Low-Income Underdeveloped Realm

The countries of this economic-type remain essentially premodern in technology and economics, with all three major sectors exhibiting only slight evidences of modernization in most cases, especially in national perspective. Most workers remain in only slightly commercialized peasant agriculture, and most processing and service workers are in little-mechanized activities little changed from pre-Industrial Revolution types.

The underdeveloped realm still contains a large majority of mankind, with only a minority likely to reach urban-industrial status in the foreseeable future. Except for small groups, most of these non-industrial populations are not significantly better off than before modernization began. The benefits accruing from commercialized agriculture, from the beginnings of factory industry, and from the beginnings of modern services have mainly been absorbed by increasing population and by increasing standards of restricted elites and governmental apparatus.

These poor countries have certain basic economic characteristics: (1) Primary production predominates, with low productivity in agriculture the main immediate cause of poverty. In general, production per head of the farm population in North America and Europe appears to be ten to twenty times greater than in Latin American, African, Middle Eastern, and Far Eastern agrarian societies. (2) Population problems rank among the most troublesome, although neither density nor growth of population is entirely (in most cases, not even mainly) responsible for the poverty that besets such societies. Most such countries have heavy rural underemployment, high birth rates creating a large number of dependent children per adult, and rapidly falling death rates combined with traditionally high birth rates bringing about a rapid increase in population that absorbs one-third to one-half of new production. (3) Underdeveloped and latent natural resources, especially non-food industrial raw materials, exist everywhere (although this does not mean there are no materials problems). Without using complementary natural resources, labor and capital can make only a limited contribution to national income. (4) Paucity of organizing ability and skilled labor rank among the main problems. These poor countries in general have economically backward populations in the sense that the quality of the people as productive agents is low. (5) Capital deficiency is such that seldom does such a retarded country have as much as 10 per cent of the real capital per head as in an urban-industrial country. Not only is the capital stock extremely low, but the current rate of capital accumulation is also very low in many cases. (6) Foreign-trade-oriented economies predominate, with the ratio of exports to national income seldom less than 20 per cent. Such countries are therefore particularly susceptible to the transmission of the trade cycle from overseas.

In terms of per capita present and prospective resource adequacy, one can characterize two variants of the underdeveloped type of economy. What might be called the Brazil type includes the thinly and moderately populated underdeveloped societies so common in Latin America, Negro Africa, and Southeast Asia. Such countries are more likely to maintain a domestic orientation, and to continue providing mineral and other primary surpluses. Limitations on numbers and on standards of living are more likely to lie in the rate of application of material and social technology than in inadequate latent resources. In general, there is plenty of land available by using traditional or slightly modernized technology, so population growth presents no special short-term problem, although the simultaneous raising of the standards of living will involve raising the productivity of agriculture substantially.

The China-India type includes thickly settled underdeveloped societies including Haiti, Java, North Vietnam, Korea, and others. In spite of continuing introduction of modern technology and the conversion of latent into economic resources, such societies are likely to have continued worries over impending resource and population crises. These poor countries are unquestionably overpopulated in their present nonindustrial context. Drastic measures to increase the output of food and certain types of industrial development are required. The solution of the population problem in these countries must involve fundamental social reforms of land tenure and the introduction of birth control. Unless these measures are carried out on a vast scale, they can be expected to do little more than merely prevent already low levels of living from falling further under the pressure of population growth. These fears, akin to those faced by European urban-industrial societies not so long ago, are likely to make for continuing pressure for attachment to foreign mineral and other resources as industrialization proceeds, and may also lead to strong pressure to bring population under swifter control than was the case in the older urban-industrial economies at a comparable stage, in order that a rising standard of living might be realized.

Perspective

Modern science and technology, and other aspects of urban-industrial civilization, have a global destiny. At present, less than a third of mankind enjoy material advantages now considered anywhere near ideal. But that third has set norms of human welfare in terms of adequate food supplies, health, and other aspects of a modern standard of living of which the remaining majority of mankind is acutely aware and aspiring to achieve.

Almost all societies now wish to partake of the material benefits that urban-industrial civilization sets within the reach of the general population, although whether they are willing to pay the costs is more debatable. At least the elite, and usually most other groups in a retarded society, are determined to lift themselves out of conditions now valued as wretched and subnormal. The achievement of some variant of the urban-industrialized way of life has thus become an imperative for practically all of mankind. In many retarded regions, the political form of government and traditional social organization are of less concern than the promise of a better economic way of life, so totalitarian governmental controls are felt more acceptable than continued misery. Under a variety of political and social forms of organization, the virtual completion of the diffusion of urban-industrial civilization over almost all of mankind seems assured within the next century.

REGIONAL ASSESSMENTS

The regional assessment "model" used in this section—an adaptation of double-entry bookkeeping technique coupled with the hierarchial principle to make a more disciplined analysis leading to more perceptive coordination and synthesis—is capable of great flexibility in stressing key strengths and weaknesses facets of regional personality. Only a shorthand form is presented, but the "model" could be used as the outline for more lengthy regional monographs.

It can be used to assess areas of any size: the very-small (individual farm, mine, plant, campus); the urban-node or other small district, subnational region; continent-size large regions (like the nine regions used in this book); realms (association of regions separated by oceans or other large regions, like the high-income and low-income economic-types of realm used in this book); even to the world itself.

It can be used to implement a general regional-geographic assessment, or more restricted political-, economic-, or social-geographic approaches. It can be adapted to implement viewpoints other than the narrowly geographic one: a regional-economic one, a regional-sociological one, a regional-political-science one, or other regional perspectives. The outlines presented in this section, like the book in general, overlap the borderland where regional economic geography and regional economics are neighbors.

Like all techniques, the "model" has limitations. It does not produce complete detailed patterns such as the traditional handbook or encyclopedic surveys. But, as compensation, it points up major problems and prospects much better, even in the hands of a pedestrian manipulator. Of course, like any technique, its yield is highest when its correlations are used as an intermediate stage in an assessment combining both science and art by a manipulator exhibiting critical judgment, imaginative insight, and flexibility (ideally, in addition, creativity).

PATTERNS

The main concern of the geographer is an assessment of the habitat (i.e., natural environment) in terms of both patterns (distributions) and interrelationships (especially linkages between habitat, man, and culture in their regional context).

The main contribution of the geographer to the study of natural resources is his concern with space and resource distribution (i.e., location and raw materials problems and prospects). Among the questions always in the geographer's mind are: Where? Why? and So What? or How Viable? (i.e., the significance and dynamics). Some patterns are easily visible (to naive eyesight) and also stable (i.e., in good equilibrium with current science and technology, current standards, and other outer frame-of-reference variables). But some patterns are highly visible but relicts (i.e., slowly disappearing or becoming fossilized), and other patterns are not easily seen (except by subtle, indirect means) but are becoming important. Stable and sterile patterns are considered by the geographer, but are not his end-product (i.e., the patterns are only a halfway house to an intellectually respectable analysis, coordination, and synthesis).

In general, (1) the wider the areal coverage, the more difficulty one has in generalizing from ordinary sources (which often cover small areas in detail but do not generalize for the whole functional pattern), and (2) the more abstract the pattern, the more difficulty the average analyst has in perceiving and properly weighting.

Ideology (Allegiance-Belief) Patterns

The whole general area of functional allegiances is usually less visible to the average analyst than the formalized (institutional or mythical) affiliations, unless he has acquaintance with the behavioral sciences.

Political and economic attitudes are usually tabooed less than certain social mores (e.g., racial-religious-class prejudices) which may be just as important assets or liabilities.

Material culture is usually the least space-bound and culture-bound aspect of civilization; technological devices and ideas may pass from land to land, often ignoring political frontiers, cultural differences, linguistic diversities, and great natural barriers of mountains, deserts, rivers, swamps, and oceans. But the diffusion of ideology and institutions is more difficult, and usually either lags behind the diffusion of material culture or moves in a different package so that its profitability of use varies greatly from that in the area of original invention and development.

Institutional (Formal Human Relations) Patterns

Giant and multipurpose institutions whose formal control and communication mechanisms are spread over great stretches—for example, government, multiplant and multiproduct industry, decentralized services like a state university system or a banking or insurance complex—are difficult to see and appraise except by indirect devices, so their strengths and weaknesses are often missed.

As a general rule, in urban-industrial societies the economic institutions are often more visible to many (materialistically minded) than political or social ones, although the indirect impact of the non-economic ones on strictly economic affairs may be more important (in the long run or in a perspective involving social economics).

Activity (Goods-Services, Production-Exchange-Consumption, and Population) Patterns

Broad regional patterns or over-all assessments—for example, regional employment or income structure, quantitative overviews of the regional mix in crops or industry, and many other more abstract patterns—are difficult to obtain because the highly visible aspects of such patterns are seldom a random sample.

As a general rule, extensive agricultural patterns (many low-yield crops, ranching, and many others) and certain basic heavy-industry patterns are more visible than others (like labor-intensive engineering industry and many indoor services that may be more important in contexts like employment opportunities, value-added, or others than in naively perceived size of built-up area).

Facility (Capital Goods and Consumer-durable Goods) Patterns

Little-visible abstract patterns of scale (size) and plant-linkage tend to be overlooked more easily than physical complexes of facilities (i.e., actual buildings, machinery, transport routes, etc.).

Cultural improvements in certain patterns—for example, habitat-facility mixes like improved soils, tame forests, water storage, and many others—are more likely to be overlooked than purely artificial (entirely man-made) patterns.

Natural (Abstract-physical-biological Habitat) Patterns

Of the three natural environment subgroups—the physical, biological, and abstract elements of the landscape—the abstract elements (i.e., size, shape, situation, etc.) tend to be overlooked more easily than the physical (i.e., landforms, rocks and minerals, atmosphere, surface and underground water, littorals, oceans, and others) and biological (i.e., natural vegetation, natural animal life, microorganisms, and perhaps soils) elements. Over-all abstract assessments—for example, areawise and population-wise (per capita) perspectives—are especially prone to neglect.

Easily visible physical patterns—for example, landforms, water bodies, and others—tend to be seen and covered more adequately than the biological patterns which are extremely diverse and which link up in subtle ways with the facility and activity patterns.

Within the physical patterns, minerals tend to be covered more adequately than certain climatic elements (e.g., like reliably moist or reliably frost-free conditions) that are often more important in either their resource or resistance impact on an area.

ASSETS AND LIABILITIES

Sometimes the assets column may involve patterns entirely different than the liability column, since regional variations may be minor and there may be no other significant variations. Such an importance may indicate an important permissive pattern, and sometimes the possibility of active (even causal) forces at work in the regional dynamics.

But—more commonly—certain patterns may be found in both columns: (1) occasionally the same pattern may have the same weighting in the two columns, but this happens only when the outer frames of reference are changed (e.g., different time assumptions, or different technology assumptions, or different standards-of-consumption assumptions); (2) more often, a pattern is a major asset or liability, but a part of the pattern may be just the opposite (e.g., U.S. Eastern Seaboard has superb accessibility, but the New England portion has poorer accessibility than the Middle Atlantic portion).

The greatest value from the use of this analytical device comes from drawing up a net-accounting view, and interpreting the net assets or net liabilities in the context of regional problems and prospects.

HIERARCHIES (WEIGHTING)

Usually, a pattern that is a definite asset or liability over the entire region being assessed will be heavily weighted (number 1 or number 2), while a pattern that applies only to a small part of the region (or to a subsector portion of a major economic sector) is more lightly weighted (number 3, number 4, etc.). However, sometimes small areas (e.g., urban-region) may include almost all of the industry or certain services in a large region, and therefore the urban characteristics may determine the regional average for some sporadic patterns.

There is a tendency to often break down one pattern into several overlapping appraisals and to ignore the patterns of other major phenomena (e.g., consider several aspects of agriculture or industry, and ignore the other two major sectors or ignore the general economic matrix). A good regional appraisal in a country with a balanced economy might include an over-all view in number 1 position, with the other three points being concerned with the three major sectors (rearranged according to a hierarchy organized around problems, prospects, or other dynamic variables). The four items used in the following assessments are very arbitrary, of course: in a regional monograph, one could attempt weighting many more variables or fewer (the latter in cases of extreme specialization or underdevelopment).

A really superior regional assessment would set up the five pattern categories in a major hierarchical system, arranged according to importance in relation to some outer frame of reference like adaptation to improved political security, economic progress, or social progress goals. In the following assessments, it has been assumed that usually the more important resources and resistances are in the little-visible ideology and institutional patterns, with the more visible facility and activity patterns usually ranking in the intermediary range, and with the natural resources patterns usually being passive, permissive, or substitutable (by regional synthetic production, trade, and other aspects of a dynamic and flexible culture). While usually valid, regional specialists might well favor a different weighting (the application of the model involves more art than science and, like wise application of any technique, involves feedback of agnosticism and humor as much as professional tool-skill competence).

North America (U.S.A.-Canada-Greenland)

Assets [*]   *Liabilities* [*]

IDEOLOGY PATTERNS

1. Societies have maintained dynamic yet flexible attitudes in most areas of faith (e.g., political attitudes, economic spirit, social welfare beliefs)—experimental, undogmatic ideals hold promise of continued progress on many fronts;
2. On balance, the two societies have avoided most of gravest dangers that might have destroyed their democratic ideology (e.g., con-

1. Societies have generally rewarded action at the expense of thought, with the field of speculation being left to the critics of society (i.e., main concern with know-how rather than with know-what or know-why);
2. Most people are inclined, when they think of value judgments, to think primarily of here-and-now utility, with resultant weak-

[*] Under each type of pattern, the assets and liabilities are arranged according to their descending order of importance (i.e., most important, number 1), as far as possible (within the limits of the author's competence).

stitutional deadlock, excesses of majority rule, stiff-necked resistance to majority will, etc.);
3. This decade will see formal discrimination against Negroes and other ethnic minorities wiped out (although not all social or economic disabilities will be removed);
4. In many highly valued human characteristics —openhanded generosity, hospitality, gregariousness, justifiable confidence and self-confidence—region's populace ranks high in world perspective.

nesses (e.g., in attitudes toward intellectual and artistic trends);
3. The ideal pursuit of happiness has too often come to mean the pursuit of fun and sensual pleasure, and a carelessness and indifference to law and traditional morals;
4. Current mores overindulge youth and middle-aged and are unsympathetic to the old, and to many forms of illness, and, above all, to death (which is ignored whenever possible).

Institutional Patterns

1. Government has remained functional, without (so far) developing a pernicious bureaucracy, and without becoming a purely political or military end;
2. To some nine-tenths of its population, it is an open society, open at both ends, open all along the way, with no one ruling class but a dozen elites which shift and change;
3. Economic institutions, especially the corporate element (now dominant except if raw numbers are considered), are generally efficient along the entire management front;
4. The region's social and cultural organization is generally pluralistic, working out accommodations by compromise and concession with little reliance on fanatical or rigid doctrines.

1. Government has an enormous capacity for dodging problems rather than coming to grips with them, and developing policies that too often are watered-down compromises that can have only limited practical effect;
2. The region has become urban without coming to terms with the city, also heterogeneous without coming to terms with different races and colors (reflects lack of social maturity);
3. While 85 per cent of the whites may be considered middle and upper class in socioeconomic terms, only 30 per cent of the Negroes, Indians, and Latin Americans can be so considered (even with a generous interpretation of the term "middle class");
4. Broad diffusion of political and economic power does limit capacity of economy and society to deal with many important problems (e.g., labor, trade, transport, and oil ones).

Activity Patterns

1. Under 7 per cent of mankind produces some 37 per cent of entire world income; output per man-hour of work now some $4.00 (dozen times that of century ago in real terms);
2. Some 2 per cent of world's farmers produce 20 per cent world's primary output; 15 per cent of world's industrial workers produce 35 per cent world's secondary output; and 15 per cent of world's services workers produce 43 per cent of world's tertiary output;
3. Employment structure (7 per cent primary, 33 per cent secondary, 60 per cent tertiary) and income structure (5 per cent, 42.5 per cent, 52.5 per cent) most modern of any great-

1. About a quarter of region's families still relatively poor, in sense of having yearly incomes under $3,000 (half of average for all families)—these are mainly concentrated among minorities and among aged;
2. High-cost labor (per man-hour: $1.50 in agriculture, $3.00 in industry, $2.00 in services) makes labor-intensive agriculture (much cotton growing and haying, much horticulture) and industry (wherever meticulous assembling and inspection important) relatively expensive;
3. While the half of total distribution costs that are physical in nature (handling, storing, and delivering tasks) are generally quite efficient and cheap, much of the selling and promo-

region, but much inefficiency still exists in all three sectors;
4. The great mobility of population and work force, both domestically within the two societies and across the borders (both U.S.-Canada and U.S.-Middle American), is very important in solving both economic and social problems in North America and in adjacent parts of its Latin American neighboring societies.

tional cost can be viewed as costly, wasteful, and too often offensive to manners and morals;
4. Many small-scaled professional and personal services rank with small-scale agriculture as among the least productive (efficient) activities in the economies, and require protection to stand up to world competition.

Facility Patterns

1. Barring nuclear devastation, vast regional productive-capital and consumption-capital plant is a flexible, man-made resource which seems, with present and prospective changes, able to serve most foreseeable needs;
2. Region's land and entire stock of capital facilities probably worth about one year's world income (and including about 40 per cent of the world stock of capital);
3. Region's agricultural facilities most modernized in world, including both changes in scale as well as in physical, chemical, and biological technology;
4. Interior (roughly 500 to 1,000 miles from the sea) has world's only closely spaced transportation-communication network so situated (few seaboard areas match its accessibility in a quantity-quality-variety frame of comparison).

1. About half of all farms (but not acreage or output) substandard, having less than 10 per cent of all farm facilities (average size 20 acres compared to 225 acres for rest), unable to support full-time commercial-farming efforts;
2. Not sufficient reconstruction and new development of urban-slum areas, degraded forests and soils, contaminated water and air supplies, and other aspects of (mainly social) undercapitalization;
3. In general, inadequacies among consumer construction and private productive facilities less than in area of public social-capital facilities;
4. Transport facilities within urban regions now inadequate in relation to emerging needs (congested rail, road, airport, and other networks need enlarging and modernizing, and probably radical innovation in many cases).

Natural Patterns

1. Areawise, regional land resources moderate in relation to size: of world totals, it has 16 per cent of world area, 16 per cent of world arable land, 11 per cent of world pasture range, 19 per cent of forest land, 18 per cent of built-on land, 17 per cent of potentially arable land, and 16 per cent of wasteland;
2. Per capita land resources good: 25 acres all land-types, 2.7 acres arable, 3 acres pasture range, 9 acres forest, 1 acre potentially arable, and 9 acres waste and built-on for each of 210 million people;
3. Compactness of resources as valuable as total quantities per se in world perspective (e.g., northern and central Appalachian coal is valued as much for its location between East-

1. About two-thirds of region (mostly outside favored southeastern quadrant) is either of little use or of low-grade use except in spots (California and other spots have less than one-quarter of population-supporting capacity in entire region);
2. Region is generally poor around edges (except in accessibility), unlike other continents where best is naturally accessible to the sea, so interior resources are often poor in natural accessibility to world circulation (although better off than Siberia);
3. The high-latitude half of the region limited by cold and poor-soils and the southwestern quarter limited by semiaridity and rough topography seem precluded from present or

ern Seaboard and Lower Great Lakes markets and water-borne ores as for its quantity, quality, and variety of reserves);
4. The triangle Winnipeg-Austin-Columbus has over two-thirds of regional arable land, probably the largest block of good soils under reasonably humid climates in world.

prospective intensive land-use except in perhaps 5 per cent of area (where urban competition may be main victor for best land);
4. Increasingly, mineral resources are of medium- and lean-grades rather than of high-grade types found elsewhere (especially in underdeveloped realm).

Western (Non-Communist) Europe

Assets   *Liabilities*

IDEOLOGY PATTERNS

1. Considering all aspects of modern civilization—roots as well as current innovations—region is still heart of Western civilization, and its influence still far outweighs its small area, population, and other material indices;
2. Aspects of the "American idea" of high mass-consumption for all and the "Soviet idea" of using centralized government to accelerate economic growth are both being used to foster economic and social progress at very rapid rates;
3. Region's near universal acceptance of the small-family ideal has rendered solvable any population problems facing it in the foreseeable future;

4. Politically, the region has apparently largely outgrown its worst legacies of raw nationalism, religious and ethnic intolerances, and many deeply resented social-class inequalities.

1. Psychologically, the people of Western Europe are mainly on the defensive, and no longer wield world hegemony in political, economic, and social affairs;
2. Linguistic and religious fissures, and old nationalistic memories, still constitute real barriers between people of the region, and hinder mutual beneficial cooperation or real political and social integration;
3. Social-welfare ideals have been implemented to provide floor of material-welfare security, but effects on need for stimulation and adventure are uncertain (some think boring predictability is frustrating to many and perhaps contributes to increased juvenile and adult delinquency);
4. Region has not accepted the idea of mass-education as fully as its daughter societies (East and West), and retains essentially intact an aristocratic educational philosophy.

INSTITUTIONAL PATTERNS

1. There have been some blurrings of national boundaries (e.g., military cooperation in NATO, tariff and support prices in the Common Market, etc.), but mainly without affecting the most controversial emotional issues (e.g., ultimate sovereignty);
2. Class distinctions in living, dressing, and eating have been blurred by an affluence that, for the first time in Europe's history, reaches deep down;
3. Modern distribution institutions (e.g., retail chains, discount centers, department stores, and banks with small-town branches) are springing up, following in the North American style;

1. The movement toward political integration is a long-term and difficult process, with no assurance of substantial success in the foreseeable future;

2. There is probably a bigger break between the generations in Western Europe today than there has been at any other period since the Industrial Revolution began two centuries ago;
3. The most difficult problem of economic integration is the agricultural one: the near self-sufficiency in mid-latitude foodstuffs has been achieved at very high cost in subsidies and control rigidities;

4. Bureaucratic enterprise in new areas of government (economic development and social welfare) probably more efficient and less corrupted than elsewhere in Western world.

4. One of the factors working against a more broadly based consumer upsurge in many areas is the lack of a well-managed system of credit or installment buying.

Activity Patterns

1. Region's average per capita income now some $1,100 annually (second-highest average among great-regions), and rising rapidly, creating a broader, richer consumer market;

2. With under 5 per cent of world's primary workers, some 21 per cent of the regional labor force, the region produces 16 per cent of the world's primary products (75 per cent of its consumption of all organic crude materials by value);

3. With 10 per cent of world's industrial workers, 41 per cent of the regional labor force, region produces 27 per cent of the world's industrial output (net surplus about pays for crude materials net deficits);

4. With 15 per cent of world's service workers, some 38 per cent of regional labor force, region produces 22 per cent of the world's tertiary activities (net surplus in world trade).

1. Very-poor areas (mainly in southern Europe) and classes (mainly landless and small-holders in the 40 per cent rural population) include a third of population averaging only a third or less of the average regional income;

2. Region's primary workers include about half low-productivity labor (e.g., to obtain arable yields 75 per cent higher than North America's, region invests 4 times the labor input per unit-area);

3. Region not only deficit in crude materials (by value: 20 per cent foodstuffs, 15 per cent edible animal products, 50 per cent other agricultural materials, 65 per cent minerals imported), but much of regional production is high-cost in world context;

4. Region's distribution system still has many nineteenth century facets (although modernization is increasing, the subsector ranks second to agriculture as a haven for the underemployed).

Facility Patterns

1. Average regional rate of savings and investment high (20 per cent of annual gross national product), and well-distributed between economic sectors, and between directly productive and overhead types of capital;

2. Annual new industrial investment as large as that of North America (although industrial output is still less and per capita industrial output is only half as large);

3. Man-altered soils, pastures, forests, and controlled rivers represent world's best rural landscape for such a size of region;

4. Superb transportation-communications facilities: in either an areawise or per capita perspective, and in every type of vehicle or technique.

1. Per capita stock of capital goods and consumer-durable goods only about half of the North American average (but definitely second in world perspective);

2. Investment per man-year worked in agriculture about a fifth that in North America (but third highest in world, after North America and Oceania);

3. Larger fraction of undersized and inadequately equipped industrial and services facilities than in North America or Eastern Europe/U.S.S.R. (reflecting earlier industrial development and many small nation-units);

4. Per capita stock of consumer-durables (housing, vehicles, etc.) averages only a third that of North America (northwestern Europe about half, but southern Europe averages under a quarter).

NATURAL PATTERNS

1. Areawise (1.4 million square miles), Western Europe well-endowed: 27 per cent arable, 15 per cent pasture, 28 per cent forest, 3 per cent built-on, 2 per cent potentially arable, 25 per cent waste;
2. High proportion of land with low relative relief, rugged land trends east-west (not athwart westerlies), and the generally reliably moist climates make this 2.7 per cent of earth's land surface highly useful;
3. Excellent relative location: natural resources close to each other (little space resistance to overcome), and good natural lines of circulation cheapens cost of movement;
4. Mainly a peninsular-insular region whose seas, tidal estuaries, and rivers make for good internal and external accessibility (especially in northwest).

1. Per capita land-base small (like Far East): 2.8 acres of total land, 0.8 acre arable, 0.4 acre pasture, 0.8 acre forest, 0.1 acre potentially arable, and 0.7 acre waste and built-on;
2. Western Europe's mineral-base modest in terms of either an areawise or per capita perspective: especially in known oil and gas, in certain ores, and in certain chemical raw materials;
3. Natural soils mostly poor, as were much of original vegetation and animal life (although cultural improvements and substitutes usually high-quality);
4. Small fraction of region with subtropical and semitropical climates makes for large deficits in raw materials that require long, hot growing season (e.g., fibers, oils-fats).

Eastern or Communist Europe (including the U.S.S.R.)

Assets   *Liabilities*

IDEOLOGY PATTERNS

1. The fundamental allegiance of the population can be taken for granted, with isolated exceptions (because of opportunity for individual advancement, some improvement in levels of living, and because system works);
2. As the Communist economies have advanced, the balance between naked coercive methods and economic incentives has been decisively shifted toward the latter;
3. Compared with North America, region loses some of its potential pool of managerial and technical talent because of large rural population, but less because of financial burdens or racial and sex discrimination;
4. Old Stalinist ideal of balanced resource development (regional self-sufficiency for security reasons) giving way to regional specialization, which is economically more efficient (new tendency still anemically implemented compared with North America).

1. There is much discontent in Communist societies, but it is mostly latent and particular rather than articulate or organized (Eastern Germany probably has weakest social fabric);
2. Among whole segments of the populace, cynicism and pragmatism have replaced the idealistic fervor that kindled the populace earlier, restricting the effective implementation of plans by disciplined and devout power-elite;
3. Communist incentive system forces management to place more emphasis upon the short-run considerations than they might otherwise do ("authority breeds deception, and commands elicit simulation");
4. Criticism of fundamental doctrines, a central part of Western university life, invites social disturbances that Communist ideology will not tolerate.

INSTITUTIONAL PATTERNS

1. In terms of its ability to generate sheer growth, especially in industrial output (the question of the structure of the product-mix

1. In Communist society, control of the many by a few is the ultimate goal; coercion, rather than freedom, is the underlying instrument of

and how it is put to use being left aside), the Communist system has proved itself to be more or less the peer of the market economy, as exemplified by the United States;
2. There has been some progress in improving inflexible management: some decentralization of huge complexes, some weakening of central planning organs, some strengthening of profit motive and encouragement of managerial efficiency, some emphasis on stricter cost accounting, etc.;
3. Cities are receiving modern distribution institutions and strengthening of professional and personal-services institutions, much like Western cities;
4. In areas deemed important by the state, institutional research and development equal or superior to West.

rapid growth (wages, security, recognition —all are given by the state for the benefit of the state, fundamentally);
2. Large and important areas of weakness exist in Communist management: waste, overstandardization, overcentralization, unresponsiveness to demand, obscurity of criteria to measure efficiency, and many other defects;
3. Engineer-type managers tend to treat social technology (human relations) as just "frosting on the cake"; changes in accounting, procurement, finance, or marketing have tough sledding in gaining acceptance because of rigid system of organization;
4. Non-governmental flow of culture change generally blocked by institutions geared to block change rather than to channel it from creator to public.

ACTIVITY PATTERNS

1. Region's $280 billion income increasing some 4 per cent yearly (industrial output at a much faster rate, services output at about the average rate, agricultural output at a much slower rate), about like that of Western Europe (both higher than that of North America);
2. In all the countries, the economy has been partly rationalized, greatly expanded and diversified, and the useful portion of the land considerably extended (compared with immediate post-World War II period);
3. Region has some 20 per cent of the world's industrial workers, producing some 23 per cent of the world's industrial output, indicating above-average productivity;
4. Region has nearly 10 per cent of the world's farmers and some 12 per cent of the world's service workers, producing somewhat larger shares (16 per cent, 17 per cent) of the world's primary and tertiary income.

1. Disposable per capita consumption only a quarter that in North America, although labor productivity outside agriculture often a third to a half as great (government consumption and investment takes larger fraction of total);
2. Real agricultural output has increased little since 1958, while population and effective demand have increased considerably and consistently;
3. Region has 10 times the agricultural labor force of North America, but still does not match North America's output, although it tills half again as much arable land;
4. Net annual additions to labor force small during the 1960's, due to World War II losses, so manpower pools are getting low and greater labor productivity is needed as compensation.

FACILITY PATTERNS

1. Rate of gross investment 25–30 per cent of gross national product (half again North America's rate), mainly in heavy industry and related tertiary subsectors;

1. Much capital is wasted or poorly utilized; the unreliability of the supply system and the absence of a full charge for the use of capital motivates management to order more fixed-capital than they need and to hoard machinery and other equipment;

2. Annual new industrial investment probably larger than in North America (although per capita industrial output only a third as large);

3. Investment in basic utilities and in industrial-crop agricultural subsectors also quite adequate, especially in per capita perspective;

4. Rate of increase in consumer-durable investment rising, but majority of increase still is needed to supply the 5 per cent annual increase in the urban population (apartments have priority) rather than to raise significantly average level.

2. Capital investment in region's agriculture is still inadequate to make possible an effective use of labor and land (perhaps generation behind North America);

3. Region invests a smaller proportion of capital funds in housing, service facilities for non-governmental use, and in social-cultural facilities than North America or Western Europe;

4. A North Atlantic level of consumption of consumer-durables (either quantity-quality of housing or of other durables) restricted to small (15–20 per cent) segment of 350 million people.

NATURAL PATTERNS

1. Areawise (9 million square miles), Eastern Europe/U.S.S.R. moderately well-endowed: 13.5 per cent arable, 15 per cent range, 39 per cent forest, 1 per cent built-on, 4 per cent potentially arable, and 27.5 per cent waste (similar to North America);

2. Per capita land-base very good: 2.2 acres arable, 2.3 acres range, 6.5 acres forest, 0.7 acre potentially arable, and 4.5 acres waste and built-on (over 16 acres total land);

3. Smaller countries plus Leningrad-Odessa-Krasnoyarsk triangle of the U.S.S.R. form a subregion with good soils, relatively good climates, accessible range, accessible forests, accessible minerals, and good situation relative to world contacts;

4. Excellent forest and mineral endowments, from either areawise or per capita perspectives (equal to North America).

1. Empty half of region has only 1 per cent of population—about 90 per cent of region lies closer to the North Pole than to the equator, and half lies north of the latitude of core-area Scotland (waste + near-waste = half or more of total region);

2. Space-resistance is great: average distance from each individual to all others is about 1,000 miles (same as in North America), 5 times that in Western Europe;

3. Adverse climates (cold-dry subarctic northeastern edge of Fertile Triangle and hot-summer-dry steppes to southeast of Fertile Triangle) much more of a limiting factor in Soviet agricultural production than in North America;

4. Large fractions of mineral and forestry materials lessened in value because of poor location outside core-area (Baltic-Adriatic-southwest Siberia).

Oceania (Australia, New Zealand, Melanesia, Micronesia, Polynesia)

Assets   *Liabilities*

IDEOLOGY PATTERNS

1. Exuberant self-confidence and optimism are established traits, especially of European Oceania;

2. Traditions generally favor ethnic toleration; probably less vicious racial, caste, and class differentiations in region than in any other great-region;

1. No great ideals of politics or of humanity animate regional psychology, no visions of nobility, but mainly starker impulses of self-advancement or survival;

2. Probably nowhere in modernized parts of world do men work less hard: inefficiency is fairly general, and there is too great an inclination to leave most things important and difficult to the state;

3. Modern social-welfare security has been assured; yet people remain fiercely individualistic and independent in other areas of life;
4. Prospects seem to point toward continued progress in developing social and economic democracy (in certain areas, perhaps ahead of North Atlantic regions).

3. Remoteness has inevitably distorted Oceanic standards, pitching them sometimes absurdly high, sometimes unworthily low;
4. Highly optimistic goals set by many—e.g., vast population increase, vast industrial expansion, and others—predicate sources of immigrants, an expandable resource-base, and foreign markets of a size that may prove illusory.

Institutional Patterns

1. Political security seems assured for foreseeable future, mainly because of American commitments, both to its own territories in the central Pacific and its treaty obligations to Australia and New Zealand in the SEATO organization;
2. North Atlantic ownership and management still dominate region's economic life, especially its industry, and this association may survive radical changes in traditional trading pattern;
3. The non-European areas are evolving toward greater self-rule: ordinary political bodies, trade unions, and native councils are becoming the normal media through which the islanders express their aspirations;
4. The region is gradually organizing a distinctive culture, although there is still no recognizable intelligentsia (in spite of intelligent, educated men and women in nearly every economic class).

1. If raw nationalism should develop among non-Europeans in the region, its peace and security might easily be shattered, with involvement in Far Eastern power politics (e.g., Indonesian expansionism in near future, perhaps Indian and Chinese in the long run);
2. Although both major societies are strongly democratic, there is a long history of bad industrial relations and constant strikes—partly due to sheer bad management, partly due to bad traditions and leadership in the unions;
3. Both management and labor may be too much sheltered by the state: tariffs, export bounties, etc., for the first; basic wage protection, compulsory arbitration, etc., for the second;
4. Politics are almost wholly devoid of ideas, let alone of ideals, consisting almost entirely of the naked politics of interest groups (perhaps reflecting stage of development and working-class origin of most immigrants).

Activity Patterns

1. Only North America and Western Europe are wealthier than Oceania on a per capita basis: 0.5 per cent of the world population earns nearly triple that fraction of the world income;
2. The regional economy is fairly well-developed, in an over-all view: 16 per cent plus primary income, 44 per cent plus secondary income, and 39 per cent tertiary income (labor force breakdown: 18 per cent, 36 per cent, 46 per cent);
3. Region has probably best pastoral economy in the world: 160 million sheep, 20 million cattle, and other animals provide about two-thirds of the primary income and an even larger share of the goods exports;
4. Although the region has a rapid growth of population, it is not a serious problem, since

1. The 3 million Australoids, Melanesians, Micronesians, and Polynesians generally live poorly compared with the 12 million Europeans and 1 million Asians;
2. Foreign trade is very dependent upon a few cash crops and products (e.g., wool, meat, wheat, sugar, and copra), with result that price fluctuations in exports have disproportionate effects on the rest of the economy;
3. Lack of labor prevents areal expansion in some areas, intensification in others, and introduction of new labor-intensive activities in still other areas;
4. Some primary surpluses are declining with rapid growth of regional population and its

the resources and social flexibility seem capable of absorbing such increase for the prospective future.

continuing rapid urbanization, and with continuing large-scale development of manufacturing, necessitating structural adjustments in foreign trade.

Facility Patterns

1. Region profits not only from heavy internal investments in European Oceania, but obtains considerable additional investments from the North Atlantic regions (both because of economic and strategic significance);
2. Most agriculture that is commercial—pastoral, grain, plantation crops—is large-scale, well-capitalized, and well-organized (in world perspective);
3. Past twenty years have seen large development of fabricating industries on top of older agricultural and related processing industries (especially in Australia, but also in evidence elsewhere);
4. In areas of using superphosphate and other fertilizers and trace elements to improve cultivated and pastoral soils, region ranks ahead of North Atlantic (mainly found in Australia-New Zealand).

1. Lack of really large regional markets affects efficiency of nearly all activities that would dispose of most of their output regionally or within a single political unit;
2. Heavy cost of social welfare and certain economic-overhead types of investment make capital formation for additional development of capital-intensive directly productive activities difficult to raise regionally (so much of this is British or American);
3. Compared with size and distances, and scattered nature of territories, transportation and communication facilities are often few, far between, and inadequate;
4. In region outside of Australia and New Zealand, modernization has been anemic and usually found only in areas of direct strategic and economic interest to outsiders rather than in areas best situated to serve the local native interests.

Natural Patterns

1. Per capita supply of land probably best in world: 4.5 acres of arable, 66 acres of range, 8 acres of forest, 6.6 acres potentially arable, and 40 acres of waste and built-on (over 125 acres total land per person);
2. Region has potential for wide range of products, including almost all tropical and mid-latitude types of organic materials and a wide variety of minerals;
3. Region has moderate mineral resources: large compared with population, but modest compared with size of region—Australia has the best coal resources in the southern hemisphere and excellent ferrous and non-ferrous ore supplies;
4. Of the lands of European culture, European Oceania is the best situated for contact with the Far East, both in terms of markets for

1. Absolute land base only modest: 6 per cent of world land area has 2 per cent of world arable land, 17 per cent of world pasture rangeland (mainly low-grade), 1.5 per cent of world forest land, 3 per cent of built-on land, 8 per cent of potentially arable land, and about 6 per cent of world wasteland;
2. Few parts of the world are more cut off and isolated by the sea and sheer distance—Australia and New Zealand are center of the water hemisphere (the antipodes of the North Atlantic basin);
3. The region has high proportion of unproductive and little-productive land, due to widespread deserts, steppes, rugged uplands, poor soils, and other natural resistances;
4. Region has poorest native food plants and animals of any great-region: all commercial crops, most pasture plants, and all ordinary

Latin America

Assets | *Liabilities*

Ideology Patterns

1. Despite immense handicaps—poverty, inflation, trade imbalances, rightist-leftist subversion-revolt, and many other problems—region teems with excitement and with hope for a better future (both elites and masses usually have high morales);
2. In most of region, different races have learned to live together in harmony (especially in Brazil, but also elsewhere)—what discrimination does exist is based on economic, social, or educational grounds;
3. A favorable attitude toward birth control is evident in upper and middle classes (although a substantial effect upon regional natural increase is unlikely for another several decades);
4. Region has made a world mark in many technical and artistic fields, especially architecture, literature, painting, and music.

1. While in most presently developed societies, social reforms usually followed economic development, in most of Latin America there may have to be a reversal of that order, a very difficult feat in democratic societies;
2. There is a steady drift throughout the region toward the left in domestic politics, and toward neutralism in international affairs, even where there is no revolution in the offing, which drifts may cause great difficulty in implementing both domestic reform and international cooperation;
3. One can hardly overestimate the enormous cultural inertia and class hostility that affects landownership and the use of land, one adverse result being little rural pioneering relative to the enormous population growth;
4. There is little concern shown over issues that transcend old primary loyalty-units (e.g., the kinship system and the local community), which renders difficult the solution of modern social problems.

Institutional Patterns

1. Although seldom democratic in the British-American sense, power is increasingly shared (in fluctuating combinations among the very rich, the military, politically inclined professional men, and a growing number of variegated Marxists from all classes);
2. The beginnings of great social changes are occurring: perhaps of greatest importance, a middle class is rapidly evolving, which is revolutionizing politics, economics, and sociology;
3. Strong nationalistic spirit, in determining to modernize and become more self-sufficient in many manufactured goods and services now almost entirely imported, is providing sheltered markets without which much economic modernization would fail to develop (or would develop very slowly);

1. Region's major troubles often caused mostly by decades of neglect on the part of inefficient governments—responsible and responsive government has been rare;
2. Basic social structure seriously out of date and unlikely to endure in present form (e.g., top 10 per cent of families have nearly half of income—compared with less than 30 per cent in North America—while the poorest half of families have only 20 per cent of the regional income);
3. Raw nationalism, exhibited in harassment of private enterprise (through political instability, restrictive labor laws, government monopoly efforts, and many other inhibitions), affects development adversely, through poor economic climate for both domestic and foreign enterprise;

4. Although about half of the regional income must be devoted to support the annual population increase, the capital, enterprise, and technical knowledge being imported compensates by improving the institutional framework favoring growth.

4. All too often, governments have a high propensity for display and a still higher propensity for playing soldier, both of which play hob with budgets, credit structures, and other financial arrangements by increasing inflation.

Activity Patterns

1. The region's economy is now semimodernized, with half of the labor force and 83 per cent of the income from secondary (21 per cent and 36 per cent) and tertiary (28 per cent and 47 per cent) activities—half of political units now in high-income realm or close to it;
2. The region has had an outstanding record of economic growth: since 1925, income has increased over 4 times, with yearly increase faster than that of North America over the four decades;
3. Industrial employment and income have increased spectacularly: the 17 million workers and $23 billion value-added in the early 1960's has tripled that of the early 1940's;
4. Although agricultural output has barely kept ahead of rapid population growth, this has been quite a feat, achieved by increasing productivity as the rural labor force increase has been small.

1. Average annual per capita net product is only some $300 when measured at going exchange rates (about $550 when corrected to reflect internal purchasing power), only two-thirds of the world's average;
2. The annual population increase is close to 3 per cent and, coupled with rising aspirations, makes even a 4 per cent annual increase in total income too small for spectacular progress in per capita welfare;
3. Per capita net product varies widely by country (Haiti's is perhaps 10 per cent of Venezuela's) and by economic-sector (rural workers average a fifth the output of urban workers);
4. About a sixth of regional income is involved in world trade (triple the U.S. fraction), with most countries specialized in one or two export crops or minerals, making for great instability in both trade and general income.

Facility Patterns

1. Total economic investments are now about 10 per cent of regional income, higher than ever before, and sufficient (if income increment evenly distributed) to raise per capita levels of living 2–3 per cent yearly;
2. Industrial capacity has been rising at impressive rates (5–7 per cent annually during the period since 1950), but unevenly (spurting spectacularly in some countries, but remaining negligible in others);
3. Arterial transport-communications networks have been fairly well-developed, with inadequacies mainly in anemic regional and local complementary patterns;
4. An increasing proportion of the arable acreage is being improved (by irrigation, mechanization, chemicalization), more in export-oriented segments than in the domestically oriented segments under heavy pressure to supply more food.

1. Almost everywhere, demographic investments require half or more of all savings, leaving economic investments too low to raise labor productivity fast enough to accelerate developmental processes to the take-off stage;
2. Relative to area and population, basic utilities (accessibility-, energy-, and water-waste-types) are not expanding rapidly enough to power the accelerated general growth in other sectors of the economy;
3. Too large a proportion of enterprises—especially family-farms, -industries, and -services—are small-scaled and lacking the modern-types of capital and management needed to rapidly rationalize;
4. Rapid urbanization (over 5 per cent annually) has resulted in some of the world's worst slums, and rapid nationalization of utilities for political reasons has made largest cities inefficient in their community operations.

Natural Patterns

1. Areawise, the regional resource availability and potential is moderately good: of world totals, region has 15 per cent of total area, 10 per cent of arable land, 14 per cent of pasture rangeland, 25 per cent of forest land, 8 per cent of built-on land, 17 per cent of potentially arable land, and 9 per cent of wasteland;
2. Population-wise, resource availability also moderately good: per capita supply of 23 acres total land, 1.8 acres arable, 4.2 acres pasture, 11 acres forest, 1.2 acres potentially arable, and 5 acres waste or built-on;
3. A highly diversified habitat—in its landforms, climates, soils, etc.—means great variety in resource capabilities (e.g., tropical and mid-latitude crops and animals, forests, and fish, plus a wide range of minerals);
4. Moderate-size stock of proven minerals in considerable variety exists: in world perspective, above average in metallics, about average in petroleum, natural gas, and hydro potential.

1. Only a small proportion of region is highly useful at present: 7 per cent is arable, 18 per cent is pasture and range (mostly unimproved), 48 per cent is forest (but only a third both productive and accessible), 5 per cent is unused but potentially arable, and 22 per cent is waste or built-on;
2. Region has many superlative habitat patterns when considered separately, but they are often poorly combined, in terms of the needs of modern civilization (e.g., iron ore without coking coal, good forest land without accessibility, etc.);
3. Natural resistances—distance, rugged topography, water-swamp barriers, etc.—make most of interior isolated from favored nuclear areas along coast;
4. Region has under 1 per cent of the world's coal, and other mineralization is mainly confined to four areas (northern Mexico, northern South America, central Andes, and east-central Brazil).

Sub-Saharan Africa *

Assets   *Liabilities*

Ideology Patterns

1. Counterbalancing the various divisive features of the African heritage is the determination of most Africans to cast off old (foreign and domestic) exploitation and support a program of modernization which serves nationalist ego and purposes;
2. The newness of Africa may be its most important characteristic: the very lack of cultural luggage or of ancient prides which hold back older nations may supply a perpetual stimulus to quick modernization;
3. In over half of newly independent states, responsible leadership seems to understand that their societies are too inexperienced and disunited to modernize without outside aid;

1. Internal animosities, Balkanization, and irredentism threaten newly found freedom and a nation-building that is particularly dependent upon the presence of order;
2. Prejudice, distrust, and intolerance lurk everywhere: between the educated and the uneducated, between tribe and tribe, and between African, European, and Asian communities;
3. Despite all the popular talk of economic progress, political freedom, and emergent independent cultures, the most awesome and influential elements in African thoughts are still ancient and natural (e.g., animistic and related primitive thought and custom);

* The northern boundary of sub-Saharan Africa must be arbitrary, since the northern tier of states overlap the Middle East (in habitat, man, and culture patterns). The exclusion of Mauritania and the Sudan is especially debatable.

4. Thirst for education very strong everywhere, and this may be the way to solve many regional problems in the long run.

4. Western-style democracy (freedom combined with responsibility) has shallow roots: evidence is widespread that most Africans are apparently willing to accept governmental suppression of individual liberty and minority rights if promised nationalistic or racial goals.

Institutional Patterns

1. Vanishing colonialism and the breakdown of tribalism are shaking the foundations of the old primitive and premodern cultures, and are breaking ground for new, wider loyalty units;

2. The modernized Africans who dominate political life are agreed in wanting to minimize differences of tribe, religion, and language in their emerging societies (class differences are only just beginning to appear and are only a minor factor in politics);

3. The present is full of political intrigue, reckless ambitions, and anarchy; but there is some evidence that slowly, gradually, economic interests are hardening and a middle class is emerging, and that political activity is coalescing into forces that can be accommodated by democratic and oligarchic techniques;

4. Although hopes for a full-blown All-African political federation are unrealistic at this stage, there is a steadily growing movement toward forms of multinational cooperation in both East and West Africa.

1. Although all the new states aim at becoming nation-states, hardly any can fulfill the preconditions: unity, clearly bounded territorial basis, effective political organization, adequate economic basis to support continued existence of the state apparatus, etc.;

2. National leaders are usually determined to impose strong central governments, even though vast differences in habitat, income, education, and religion make such centralization quite inappropriate (so this aggravates internal tensions);

3. A scourge of the region is tribalism: one of the most enervating forces on the body politic of the fledgling states is the inexorable pull of such traditional elements which are usually disruptive;

4. The weakness of African political, economic, and social structures lies in the gulf between its thin upper class and the enormous native mass (in terms of institutions, civil servants, and experienced leadership, most of Africa is less well equipped for self-rule than the Asian states were).

Activity Patterns

1. The region is an important surplus raw materials supplier: about 5 per cent of world nonfood agricultural-related crude materials and 10 per cent of mineral raw materials are produced, mostly available for export;

2. There is still a relatively low pressure on resources (in world perspective), although the rate of population increase is now above the world's average;

3. There have been scattered successes in introducing improved, sedentary agricultural systems in place of the old, deteriorating, shifting-cultivation systems;

4. Important potentials still exist for improving

1. Among the poorest people in world here: nearly 7 per cent of world's population earns only 2 per cent of world's income—70 per cent of population in primary activities earns only a quarter of the total;

2. Most districts' commercial sectors are precariously organized around one cash crop or mineral, subject to violent fluctuations in output and value;

3. Much of African secondary and teritary activities in hands of outsiders or minorities (Europeans, Levantines, Indians-Pakistanis), a tempting target for agitators (both political and African economic middle class);

4. Trade unions, cooperatives, and other organi-

GEOGRAPHY OF INCOME

and expanding tree-crop and animal-husbandry activities oriented toward world markets, because of cheap land and labor and the commercial opportunities in the North Atlantic and elsewhere.

zations have been mainly led by ardent nationalists who have used them for personal political ends rather than to attain economic and social security and progress for the membership and the general public.

Facility Patterns

1. Mining and plantation agriculture, and associated distribution services, have modern facilities, mainly supplied from non-African sources of capital and organization;
2. Most of the region's 1 per cent of the world's modern industrial facilities are in the Republic of South Africa's metropolitan areas, outside of tropics;
3. In many areas, the 10-to-15-acre plots per farm family are large enough for the introduction of considerably improved agricultural technology (e.g., draft animals if area tsetse fly free);
4. The construction of expensive artificial harbors has been necessitated by the absence of natural harbors along vast stretches of faulted coastline, but have proven commercially profitable, as well as being external economies to many other economic activities.

1. The traditional agrarian economy produces little capital of the types needed for building up modern productive facilities in any sector, although it does provide its own capital (through reclamation and improvement);
2. Traditional agriculture has little operating capital (e.g., work animals) and little fixed capital (e.g., drainage, irrigation, tree crops)—"poor soil makes poor people, and poor people make poor soil worse" well illustrated;
3. Foreign capital is little interested in most investment (social overhead, economic overhead, even most forms of directly productive facilities), only in mining and plantation types providing exports;
4. Much of the most profitable investments lie in providing fairly simple soil conservation, domestic-water provision, and roads—which, however, do not attract foreign investors (or even central-government attention).

Natural Patterns

1. There are substantial natural resources for such a size of region: 18 per cent of world's area, 15 per cent of world's arable land, 20 per cent of world's rangeland, 16 per cent of world's forest land, 8 per cent of world's built-on land, 17 per cent of the world's potentially arable land, and 20 per cent of the world's wasteland;
2. Level or rolling topography and reasonably humid climates over much of the region provide favorable context for man's primary uses (in wide perspective of possibilities);
3. Some of the world's greatest remaining stores of high-grade minerals are here: especially ferrous, non-ferrous, and precious metals, but including some fossil-fuels (especially South African coal and Nigerian petroleum);
4. The region's hydro potential may be 40 per cent of the world's total (e.g., the Congo River

1. This is the world's problem region where development under tropical conditions is considered: there are some 9 million square miles of poorly accessible, tropical plateaus;

2. Much of the region suffers from water shortages (permanent, seasonal, or occasional aridity): the key to development is as much control of water as attaining greater accessibility;
3. Region is poor in good naturally rich soils, in good native grasses, in good (climax) forests, and in good native food plants—historically, the region's inaccessibility has been botanical as well as cultural;
4. Microorganisms include some of the greatest natural resistances in the region: malaria, yel-

rapids between Leopoldville and Matadi have the potential of the United States).

low fever, sleeping sickness, and many others affect humans; nagana, rinderpest, and foot-and-mouth disease affect domestic livestock; and the locust, maize stalk-borer, swollen-shoot disease of cacao, and many others affect crops.

Middle East (Southwest Asia plus North Africa)

Assets   *Liabilities*

Ideology Patterns

1. Western technology and political thinking have edged certain countries toward stability (e.g., Turkey, Lebanon), and elsewhere Arab socialism is making certain material progress (although it tends to have an authoritarian nationalist character, with scant relationship to Western parliamentary democracy and liberalism);
2. The belief is now widespread that the servitudes and miseries that have characterized the past are now escapable, which frame of mind can aid modernization if directed to necessary reform;
3. There is a substratum of unity rooted in the uniform Islamic civilization and in the centuries-long political unity of sorts maintained by the Ottoman regime, although its present evidences are mainly oral and negative (anti-foreignism);
4. Attitudes favor social mobility, with impediments due more to economic differences than to racial or ethnic prejudice.

1. Much of "nationalism" in region is xenophobic raving against Western and Israeli "imperialisms" that inflames intraregional and other international relationships without resulting in constructive effects;

2. The region is so inspired with racial, religious, economic, political, and social frenzy that it is hard to imagine establishment of even relative calm;

3. The Arabs display the double effect of wounded pride: self-exaltation and self-condemnation (the first and perhaps the best-known Arab quality is individualism: proud, touchy, volatile, generous, emotional—directed at personal honor more than at material gain);
4. The rural masses have progressively lost both the material possessions and spiritual values of an archaic society without acquiring the educational standards and technical skills of twentieth century man.

Institutional Patterns

1. In most of region, there is a broad community of language and Koranic culture, territorial contiguity, a common urge to cast off shackles of a "feudal" past, and some common political-military-economic efforts (e.g., Arab League);
2. The new middle class of salaried managers, professionals, and army officers is, in general, a cohesive, vigorous, and forward-looking element (but it lacks the entrepreneurial element familiar in the Western equivalent);
3. In the past several decades, Islam's women have achieved a greater change in status than

1. The traditional tribal order of society (particularly rigid in the Moslem world) has been disintegrating under the impact of twentieth century technical civilization, producing shattered primary loyalty-units (with accompanying psychological tensions);
2. Certain leadership unwilling to face risking their shaky position by encouraging social change, and instead favor directing public attention abroad (especially toward Israel and the West) as a substitute;
3. Many of the women still live immured behind the veil, most are pitiably ignorant,

GEOGRAPHY OF INCOME

in the preceding thousand years, although the change has mainly affected urban upper- and middle-class women (a small portion of the total);

4. Modern enterprise is gradually evolving, especially in the bigger cities and especially in the Levantine and Persian Gulf economies which have had a long history of mercantile successes.

nearly all are illiterate—this is especially true in rural and small-town areas;

4. Public-spirited citizenry and bureaucracy reasonably free from nepotism difficult to develop because of clan-tribal-community systems, which hinder fusion between non-related individuals.

Activity Patterns

1. Small parts of region have reached high-income status (Israel, Kuwait), with others close to that status (Cyprus, Lebanon, Bahrein, Qatar);
2. Over 75 per cent of the regional income comes from industry (including mining, this provides 30 per cent of all income) and services (46 per cent of all income), with per worker output 5 to 8 times greater than in the primary sector;
3. Agriculture and related primary activities support 64 per cent of the labor force (although mainly on a low level), and provides a third of the exports (actually, a much larger fraction for most countries, who do not export oil);
4. The opening-up of modern activities (especially the oil industry and related efforts) are aiding nomads, seminomads, and refugees to make a rapid adjustment to settled life under modern conditions.

1. Although the average per capita income in the region is over $200, perhaps 80 per cent of the population live on half or less that income, with only elites enjoying levels of living well above subsistence levels;
2. In region as a whole, increased income increases per capita income about 2.5 per cent yearly, after taking care of an annual population increase of 2.4 per cent, but many countries are not participating in the advance, and some classes are suffering from declining real income;
3. An extreme inequality of population to realizable resources is noticeable throughout the region, especially when comparing Egypt, Israel, and Lebanon to the rest of the region;
4. Although improving, the low levels of literacy, vocational training, and general health in much of region seriously affect economic progress and social advancement attempts.

Facility Patterns

1. The over-all rate of investment is quite high: much from oil royalties and taxes, much from foreign investments and philanthropy, but increasingly the share from indigenous modern enterprises is rising;
2. Industrial facilities for supplying local and national markets have recently been expanding rapidly: mostly consumer goods types, with little heavy industry; expansion mainly in Turkey, Egypt, Israel, and Lebanon, and in cities elsewhere;
3. Replacement of basin (flood) by perennial irrigation facilities (allowing eventual production 2 or 3 times greater) probably most im-

1. In most of region, per capita new capital investment is quite low (only a quarter that of southern Europe)—urban-nodes and a few other spots (oil field areas, especially) get the bulk of the modern investments;
2. Poor transport facilities away from international route hinders the exploitation of many local resources or the setting-up of wider markets for the new industries or other activities;
3. Apart from larger exotic rivers, facilities to tap and control water resources anemic in many areas, with surface and subsurface po-

portant avenue to solve region's food and raw materials problems;
4. Heavy investments in land-sea-air transport facilities have been and are being made, both along international trunk routes and in national networks.

tentials practically unused;
4. Highly capitalized activities based mainly on outside markets, and owned-managed by outside interests tend to get disproportionate attention, while possibilities based on local or regional markets are usually less well served.

NATURAL PATTERNS

1. Favorable situation: a corridor of unique importance between the West and an awakened Far East and sub-Saharan Africa—a middleman region of intercourse and diffusion for the Old World;
2. Phenomenal petroleum and natural-gas resources (perhaps two-thirds of world's totals) plus modest resources of coal, chrome, lead, and other ores and good resources of phosphate, potash, and other chemical and building materials;
3. Uplands provide water, summer pasture, some wood and minerals—prospects are also good for greater usefulness (in terms of prospective technology);
4. Sub- and semitropical climates permit long growing seasons provided that water and fertile soil are in juxtaposition (coastal plains and river valleys).

1. Some two-thirds of region is desert waste: only 7 per cent is arable, 18 per cent range (mostly low-grade) and 5 per cent shrubland and forest land—per capita land resources intermediate between Western Europe and Far East;
2. Great spaces coupled with rugged and infertile uplands make major obstacles to easy accessibility away from the through international routes (Gibraltar-Suez-Bosphorus);
3. Most grassland and forest land have been degraded from either natural or cultural sources (overgrazing and overcutting may be main reason for deterioration, but natural changes are also involved);
4. Problems of poor drainage are nearly as great as problems of irrigation in the alluvial areas, with large areas of alkali soils resulting from poor drainage of both cultural and natural origin.

Non-Communist Far East

Assets

Liabilities

IDEOLOGY PATTERNS

1. Morale improvements have been widespread, caused by achievements such as attainment of independence, government stability, improved internal security, and economic nationalism (although much remains to be done);
2. The "pressure of modern standards," caused by coexistence of abject material poverty and modern humanitarian ideals, which have mainly been developed elsewhere after a good deal of economic and social progress—this is the main source of motivation for change;
3. In the cities, status distinctions by hereditary occupations and caste-communal position tend

1. "People's attitudes to work and life, hardened by stagnation, isolation, ignorance, and poverty, and underpinned by tradition and often by religion, are frequently found to be inimical to change of any kind." (Gunnar Myrdal);
2. There has been a general tendency to take out general gains in the form of social amenities and redistribution of income, with adverse repercussions on the economic sinews of continued and accelerating growth;
3. Rural morale is generally poor: most of the burdens of low productivity, disguised unem-

to fade (although in the villages they remain strong and enduring);

4. There is now the existence of a value system favoring economic progress, and the availability of small but effective entrepreneurial groups basking in the sun of social approval.

ployment, and traditional social welfare are carried by the rural sector, especially the subsistence area;

4. Social changes so far have been less than the casual Western visitor to big cities tends to think—rural areas are being affected less by direct pressures of new ideas than by the indirect pressures (especially the social dissolvent accompanying rapid population growth).

Institutional Patterns

1. Governmental apparatus nearly everywhere is being strengthened: in general services (administration and defense), in social services (education, health, and housing), and in economic services (both economic-overhead and directly productive activities);
2. There is occurring a gradual creation of an influential, modern-type organizational elite that is materially or idealistically interested in modern urban-industrial enterprise;
3. Gradually, there is occurring abolition of an archaic ownership-management framework in agricultural organization, accompanied by a modest increase in the productivity of agricultural efforts;
4. The possibility of political disintegration as alien overlords withdrew in the past two decades has abated with the formation of stable successor-states—existing political dangers are related to new (Chinese Communist, North Vietnamese, and Indonesian) imperialisms.

1. Administrative machinery remains deficient outside of Japan—yet, paradoxically, inordinate demands are made upon it;

2. Only Japan is well endowed with adequate entrepreneurship (risk-taking management and capital)—other countries usually have an anemic supply, and much of that is predatory-type (super-moneylender type);

3. In many countries, a socialist orientation—calling for government-directed and -dominated development—overburden weak administration while, simultaneously, the enterprise outside the government remains underutilized;

4. Almost all institutional structures are weak in flexibility, with "education" (development of human resources in widest sense) given inadequate attention and routine actions given disproportionate attention.

Activity Patterns

1. The average per capita income—over $100 in exchange value, perhaps $300 in U.S. purchasing power equivalent—is rising some 2 per cent annually (much faster in Japan and Southeast Asia other than the Indochina and Indonesia areas—slower in other areas);
2. Industrial output has increased 15 per cent yearly over past decade (double the average rate in the rest of the non-Communist world), more than doubling output even outside Japan (although region has little more than 5 per cent of world industrial output);
3. Agricultural production (quarter of total) is increasing more rapidly than population, al-

1. The half of non-Communist mankind in the region is increasing over 2 per cent annually, thus absorbing half of the increase in income;

2. Labor productivity remains low: even with the low wages usually paid, labor costs per unit of output are not low save in Japan;

3. Increased modernization seems to have been accompanied by greater inequality of income

though not necessarily every year and not in every country;
4. The region's share of world trade (9 per cent) is a bit larger than its share of world income (7 per cent)—the third that is intraregional is increasing, with Japan as the pivot.

(industrial employers and workers, and traders have profited much more than peasants and those living on fixed incomes);
4. The region's primary exports have increased less than those of other great-regions, mainly because of increased domestic consumption of food and raw materials—manufactured exports have become more important, but not fast enough to close completely the gap, so loans, grants, and gifts have had to do so.

Facility Patterns

1. Region's annual rate of gross capital-formation some 13 per cent (net 9 per cent), perhaps half again larger than in the early 1950's, and slowly rising;
2. Infrastructure (transport, communications, energy and water-waste utilities) has been accorded highest priorities nearly everywhere, accounting for nearly a third of new investment;
3. Industry has also been fairly well supplied: about half of the 30 per cent government share and a third of the private sector's 70 per cent share have been in mining and manufacturing;
4. Agriculture has received about a quarter of all investment, less than its share of employment, but good compared with the 10 per cent shares in Latin America and sub-Saharan Africa.

1. About half of the countries save and invest at rates below the regional average (e.g., Indonesia and South Korea are very low, the Philippines just below average—only Japan has an extremely high rate, 30 per cent gross);
2. Modern facilities per capita are only from 5 per cent (e.g., Nepal) to 25 per cent (Japan) the stock in Western Europe;
3. Import of capital goods (40 per cent of all imports) has risen faster than exports—foreign aid and capital inflows (equivalent to a quarter of the exports) make up the difference;
4. Certain kinds of capital are "surplus" (some used for land and commodity speculation), while other kinds are "deficit" (new-industry "risk" types).

Natural Patterns

1. Relative to its 4 million square miles, the region is moderately well endowed with natural resources, especially the South and Southeast Asia areas;
2. The land-use pattern is quite good: over 20 per cent of the total area is arable, 10 per cent is range, 35 per cent is forest, 5 per cent may be potentially arable, 2 per cent is built-on, and 28 per cent is waste;
3. The region primarily receives its moisture during the summer growing season, an important factor in its productive agriculture (and most potential irrigation must be based on better control and redistribution of surplus monsoonal water);
4. Areawise, the region has its share of economic

1. Relative to its 950 million population, the region has a small natural resources base, although the future may disclose improvement in the area of mineral resources;
2. The per capita land-use picture is poor: 0.5 acre arable, 0.2 acre pasture, 0.9 acre of forest (much degraded to shrub), and 0.1 acre potentially arable—and these are diminishing with time and increased population;
3. Agriculture is still mainly a gamble on irregular monsoonal moisture; only 25 per cent of the cropland has an assured rainfall, with another 10 per cent having assured flooding (plus another 10 per cent having controlled irrigation);
4. Other natural resistances include about a

minerals, although in per capita perspective the picture is mediocre except in hydro, iron, ferro-alloys, and salt.

third rugged terrain, very poor immature soils, and lack of substantial fossil fuels.

Communist Far East

Assets   *Liabilities*

Ideology Patterns

1. The revival of national pride—of national "nerve"—is the most intangible and the most dynamic aspect of each (of the four) Communist regime's accomplishments;

2. Zealous, ruthless, resilient, Far Eastern Communism has reshaped the political, social, and economic contours of the most populous compact region in the world;

3. The Communist effort to orient the minds of the people toward scientific (rational) explanation of the world may prove to be one of their most significant measures in the transformation of society and culture (as in European Communist modernized societies);

4. It is still possible (for the unusually able or aggressive) to move up the social scale on the basis of merit and service to the party and government.

1. Communist social control is so pervasive that conformity (outwardly, at least) is the sole means of survival: the "people" are left with little alternative but to do what is demanded of them;

2. The states' avowed emphasis upon industrialization has created in the peasants a feeling that they have been exploited more ruthlessly than any other social group, in support of an economic program that so far has failed to bring them any substantial tangible benefits;

3. Although professedly international and socialist, the regimes have in fact drawn more strength from carefully fostered chauvinistic nationalism (antiforeign attitudes);

4. The societies have been almost completely politicized and militarized (e.g., rural communes), with familial and humanist values (at least officially) downgraded.

Institutional Patterns

1. New social structures have been created that appear to have considerable stability, as changes are largely controlled by the regimes themselves;

2. The growing cities now appear to be replacing the rural villages as the primary loyalty-units of the dynamic forces, and are now determining the mores and patterns of living for the evolving modernized societies;

3. The Communists have combined coercive power and the systematic exploitation of individual and group dissatisfactions with the old order (particularly women and youth) to inculcate a new set of basic values and related social structure which now dominate society;

4. Each state is relatively uniform in terms of

1. Despite all their faults and errors, the Communist regimes have imposed the first strong centralized governments over their countries in a century of stagnation and disorder, but at excessive cost in both economic and psychological terms to individuals and non-governmental social groupings;

2. All four regimes are totalitarian dictatorships that maintain total and rigid control over all sources of power (chief of which are the party, the armed forces, the police, and the state bureaucracy);

3. Since elections are exclusively Communist-sponsored and -conducted, and the only candidates are handpicked by the party, neither political issues nor personalities (in the Western democratic sense) are involved;

4. With further stabilization and growth in the

ethnic composition, with minorities of 5 per cent or less of the total population, with no minority a serious internal threat.

power of the Communist governments, prospects are that formalized religion and old sectional and clan loyalties will continue to decline and wither away as institutions.

Activity Patterns

1. Income (about $45 billion in an exchange-value perspective—perhaps $110 billion in a U.S. purchasing-power equivalent perspective) apparently increasing again after several years decline;
2. The 65 per cent of labor force in agriculture produces about a third of the total income, of which over half is transferred to the government, most of it being used to accelerate growth in other sectors;
3. Some increase in worker productivity has been achieved: by employing the underemployed more fully, by reducing leisure, and by raising productivity on the job (partly by eliminating many wasteful practices begun in the "Great Leap Forward" debacle);
4. The quantity, quality, and variety of industrial production have spectacularly improved in past fifteen years, although often at very high costs.

1. Regional population (perhaps 725 million) apparently increasing at about the world's average rate (extrapolated: 1.5 billion by 2000)—probably half of increase in income needed to support additional children;
2. "Overpopulation" one of greatest problems facing the region: both rural (0.4 acre arable land per person) and urban (high disguised unemployment in industry and services) types keep productivity down;
3. The favored industrial sector still adds less value than that of Japan's industrial sector, even in the heavy-industry subsector, but especially in the light-industry subsector;
4. Although small relative to total consumption, and in spite of the prevention of famine by strict control over distribution, food and agricultural raw materials deficits have wrought havoc with morale, the foreign exchange position, and other sensitive spots.

Facility Patterns

1. Annual rate of net capital investment apparently about 15 per cent (gross 20–25 per cent), half again larger than the average in underdeveloped economies outside the region;

2. Capital goods industrial capacity now over half of total industrial capacity, with some 80 per cent of needed capital goods now made within region (according to claim);
3. Major nodes of modern-type facilities exist in the Yangtze delta, southern Manchuria, the Peking-Tientsin area, and the Wuhan area (smaller nodes exist at Harbin, Taiyuan, Paotow, Lanchow, Chungking, Canton, and elsewhere);
4. About 60 per cent of cultivated land is said to be irrigated, mainly by small and medium-

1. Rate of annual investment has dropped somewhat from mid-1950's high point: expropriation, "voluntary" sales of government bonds, monopoly trading in agricultural products, and substantial European Communist credits have "dried up," and substitutes have only slowly developed;
2. In the 1959–1962 period, agriculture and industry were producing at only 75 per cent or so of capacity, after the collapse of the 1958 "Great Leap Forward";
3. Transportation and communications networks are still quite sparse for such a size of area, with poor accessibility in many areas related to distance and topography resistances not yet overcome;
4. Agriculture is starved of modern capital (only getting 10–15 per cent of new investment) at

size projects rather than by large, capital-intensive, multipurpose projects (although remaining latent possibilities require latter-type developments coupled with modern chemical technology).

a time when the traditional labor-intensive techniques have stagnated.

NATURAL PATTERNS

1. For its size (4.4 million square miles) the region is reasonably well endowed with natural resources—this is especially true of the eastern half (traditional coreland of Chinese civilization);
2. The regional situation, bordering on virtually all the mainland countries of the Far East and many of the U.S.S.R. republics, is excellent for internal development and for foreign contacts of many kinds;
3. In climatic, natural vegetation, and soils terms, the eastern half of the region is the rough equivalent of the eastern United States—the same similarity exists in minerals and waterways concentration;
4. On the whole, the region has sufficient mineral resources for a substantial development of modern heavy industry (e.g., steam-coal, tin, antimony-tungsten, and other minerals exist in large, high-grade reserves).

1. The per capita supply of natural resources is among the smallest in the world—latent resources exist, but it is unlikely that the present caput perspective will be radically changed by new finds;
2. Only about 10 per cent of the region is arable, with some 16 per cent poor range, 11 per cent poor forest, 1.5 per cent built-on, and 3 per cent potentially arable—the western half of the region is mainly waste;
3. On the whole, the eastern half of the region has a satisfactory climate, but variability in time and amount of rainfall have repeatedly brought distress (drought, flood, dust storms) to vast areas;
4. Inadequacies include: 85 per cent rugged land (over 1,500 feet elevation), severe winters in northern half (and in western high plateau), limited and poorly distributed coking coal, limited petroleum and high-grade iron ore, and other lacks.

High-Income Countries

Assets

Liabilities

IDEOLOGY PATTERNS

1. Modern man—unlike premodern man—believes in the susceptibility of man's conditions of life to rational control and salutary change: probably the main cause of continuing change and progress;
2. The worst of the sociopsychological insecurity developed while adjusting to modern civilization is mainly over (for most elements in such societies): the reattainment of justifiable confidence, respect, and balance has either been achieved or is near;
3. Economic insecurity—that accompaniment of certain facets of urban industrialization (e.g., urban congestion, which has brought on psychological strain, health hazards, wasted time, and wasted energy)—has been diminished by various forms of social welfare and security;

1. There is much psychic rootlessness in most modern societies: many old institutions and formal (ideal) values have been drained of effectiveness and prestige, with adequate substitutes not yet developed;
2. Most modern societies are still uncertain of how to convert their abundant means into morally acceptable ends, of how to choose judiciously between security and progress while still maintaining latent flexibility;
3. The restlessness of youth is exemplified by juvenile delinquency and intensified by the declining demand for unskilled labor facing those who leave school early;

4. Formal education (literacy) characteristic of 95 per cent plus of adult population, with median probably higher than in premodern society although the comparison of elites' medians must be less ego-satisfying (especially if progress in achieving wisdom and high moral stature is considered).

4. Minority groups are living in substandard conditions, often in urban or rural slums, and are usually composed largely of persons suffering from ethnic discrimination or cultural isolation.

Institutional Patterns

1. The basic problems of a high economic-growth policy are no longer technical, but political and institutional (especially a willingness of government to manage the level of over-all demand so that resources are fully utilized and recessions avoided);
2. The outstanding feature of the international economy since World War II has been the restoration of relatively free trade between the major urban-industrial countries;
3. The exceptional mobility of modern populations is obviously possible only in the larger social units characterizing the developed societies;
4. Among the social strengths of such societies: a numerous middle class, a more equal status for women, and most groups well educated.

1. Poverty is still the lot of considerable fractions of high-income societies—from a fifth to two-fifths, as a general rule—and this is probably the most formidable and most disturbing economic problem facing these wealthy societies;
2. The main question mark to continued economic progress in most areas is uncertainty how the institutionalized human factors (government, management, organized labor) will work together to make new investment productive;
3. Continued progress in many activities will be restricted in many (especially smaller) countries unless absolute national sovereignty is eroded and greater international economic flexibility is achieved;
4. In every modernized society, some aspects of organization (governmental, private or corporate enterprise, or other) have become rigid and inflexible, existing for their own sake.

Activity Patterns

1. Realm wealthy, with less than 30 per cent of mankind producing and consuming over 80 per cent of world's income—per capita income 10 times that of remainder of mankind;
2. Realm's share of world's income-sectors larger than its shares of workers: primary, 52 to 24 per cent; secondary, 85 to 36 per cent; tertiary, 83 to 40 per cent (reflecting large-scaled, efficient production);
3. Over 80 per cent of world trade is conducted by the urban-industrial realm, making for more efficient production and consumption than would be possible otherwise;
4. The population problems of such societies have been mainly solved: the processes of urbanization and closure of the demographic gap are substantially completed.

1. While most societies are 10 to 20 times better off, in a per capita income perspective, than before modernization began, there are some only 5 times or so better off (Italy, Japan);
2. Except in restricted portions of the North American, Western European, and European Oceanic regions, modernization has benefited urban activities (especially middle-class ones) more favorably than rural activities;
3. In general, the populace of wealthy societies is conservative in most fields outside of material technology and other materialistic areas—rigidities exist in coping with problems not easily solved by material means;
4. Even such wealthy societies have difficulties adjusting to the employment- and income-structural changes now necessary if the Automation Revolution is to be fully exploited.

Facility Patterns

1. All such economies save and invest about 15–20 per cent of their net income in new facilities (and about as much in human-capital investments);
2. In nearly every field of production, scale and capitalization developments have increased manyfold the productive power of each unit (e.g., resulting in increasing returns from natural resources);
3. Dynamic science and technology together have vastly increased the quantity of old-type resources, improved the quality of old-type resources, furnished new (synthetic substitutes) resources, and radically reduced the costs of production;
4. Continuing automation in both industry and in office work is more likely to be applicable and useful to these highly developed nations than to other societies (because of abundant, cheap capital and existing scale and specialization assets).

1. The attainment of proper scale and capital intensity has been less successful in agriculture and most services than in industry and mechanical transportation;
2. That mining, manufacturing, construction, and transport dating back to the late nineteenth and early twentieth centuries is usually inadequate in layout, scale, and quality of facilities (with rationalization difficult for technical reasons as well as institutional reasons);
3. Except in Western European forestry and pasture lands, and European Oceanic pasture lands, only modest capital improvement is evident in primary resources outside of commercial agriculture (and mining);
4. Capitalization of indirectly productive activities (e.g., social-overhead capital: education, health-recreation, etc.) substandard for certain areas, classes, and other groupings even in the wealthiest societies.

Natural Patterns

1. Realm's 29 per cent of mankind relatively rich in land, occupying 45 per cent of the world's land area, 48 per cent of the world's arable land, 49 per cent of the world's pasture and rangeland, 48 per cent of the world's forest land, 48 per cent of the world's potentially arable land, and 41 per cent of the world's wasteland;
2. Oceanic and riverine orientation of most of the realm (Siberia is exception) provides good physical basis for cheap and easy accessibility both within realm and with portions of the underdeveloped realm;
3. Fairly reliably humid climates coincide with most useful plains (those having above-average soils)—realm also possesses most forests and fisheries with high degrees of usefulness (solid-stands and great-schools of single species);
4. About a third of known mineral resources of high-grade exist in this realm (with larger fractions of medium- and low-grade minerals which are poorly censused).

1. About a third of the realm is wasteland: a bit under that average in the two Europes, a bit over for North America and Oceania (not counting large fractions of low-grade range and forest with little usefulness);
2. Space is a major obstacle in much of realm: about three-quarters of North America, Eastern Europe, and Oceania suffers from wide dispersal of potential resources (which reduces the value of even the high-grade resources);
3. The interiors of North American, Eastern European, and Australian portions of realm suffer from adverse continental climates both along the drier and colder edges of the ecumene;
4. The realm has only small strips of semitropical climates, so it is overwhelmingly deficit in tropical resources of food and inedible raw materials.

Low-Income Countries

Assets   *Liabilities*

Ideology Patterns

1. The revolution of rising expectations has widely permeated almost all such societies: less inhibitions about expressing desires and ambitions, more enthusiasm, initiative, and energy can be noted in the inhabitants of independent countries in the realm;
2. Leadership consciousness that economic backwardness often signifies political weakness, and a growing awareness of their social and political backwardness on the part of the general populace, both strengthen the desire for economic growth;
3. The ideological climate today in the underdeveloped countries is much more favorable to the use of the state apparatus than was the case in North America and Western Europe in the late eighteenth and the nineteenth centuries;
4. In general, economic development now enjoys a high priority throughout the underdeveloped realm (although some countries and, in particular, some ruling groups definitely prefer the status quo).

1. Compared with hospitality, generosity, or even ostentation, thrift is not a virtue, but a vice, fit only for a merchant—this inhibits the saving and investment functions so necessary for rapid modernization;
2. Realization that family limitation is necessary to consolidate economic progress in any long view is too little appreciated by elites and masses (functionless reproduction is institutionalized in most agrarian societies);
3. Economic growth is often inhibited by the cultural and psychological facts operative in such poor countries (which may be more influential than wage rates in determining the supply of labor, either in the form of additional workers or in the form of additional hours of work from the individual worker);
4. An ascribed status is common, in contrast with the achieved status found in modern societies (i.e., people are evaluated not according to what they can do but according to their position, age, sex, kin, clan, caste, and other social classification).

Institutional Patterns

1. Many of these societies have produced a new elite of reformers and innovators, ready and willing to assume the hardships and crises of modernization, and nerved with the courage to overhaul their societies and to change the ethos of their civilization;
2. Mixed economic systems—involving elements of private enterprise and central government control—are gradually assuming control in the struggle to alleviate misery (in non-Communist societies);
3. As the economy loses its characteristics of backwardness, as markets widen, as the capacity to save increases—in short, as development proceeds, individuals will acquire more of the motives and abilities for entrepreneurship, and the cultural environment will become more congenial;
4. The building of new institutions to develop

1. Leadership inadequacy—both in government and in economic management—is the main bottleneck in maintaining economic growth, much more than lack of capital or of natural resources (important as the latter may be);
2. Sweeping institutional changes are usually required—in many countries the magnitude of such change is tantamount to social revolution, and this is usually resisted;
3. Such market imperfections as factor immobility, price rigidity, ignorance of market conditions, rigid social structure, and lack of specialization have acted as frictions and impediments, preventing the achievement of an optimum allocation of resources;
4. In most of the underdeveloped realm, barren

important human resources (e.g., schools, trade unions, and employment agencies to foster character, energy, and skills) is well underway.

nationalism imperils the international cooperation so necessary to humane development in this increasingly interdependent world, besides also stifling the growth of individual freedom.

Activity Patterns

1. The realm produces 48 per cent of the world's agricultural output (61 per cent of crops, 26 per cent of edible animal products, 60 per cent of inedible raw materials), with net surpluses which pay for half of net deficits in industrial goods and services;
2. The rates of growth in annual income are mainly higher than the rates of population increase, but poverty is almost universal (economic progress is of recent origin and started from very low levels of economic and social attainment);
3. Realm is profiting from improved health and prevention of premature death at low cost: an asset in the short run, although possibly a long-term liability if a new vital balance is not reached in a generation or two;
4. The realm provides a third of non-food raw materials (organic and mineral) moving in international trade, and a quarter of manufactured goods (mainly lightly processed goods).

1. Per capita income averages $125 annually (actually three-quarters of realm's populace live in societies with averages less than that figure), which provides little above subsistence for the mass of consumers;
2. Annual population increase is about 2 per cent: almost all of realm has populations in either the early expanding or late expanding stages of the modern population cycle (population will more than double by 2000);
3. The actual and potential human talent going to waste in the underdeveloped realm is one of the greatest underutilized resources in the entire world (especially in the two-thirds of the labor force in little-productive primary activities);
4. The smallness of the cadres of skilled workers and middle-management personnel is one of the main reasons for the high costs of production in comparison to urban-industrial activities ("cheap" labor does not mean low labor costs).

Facility Patterns

1. Directly productive industrial capital needs and economic-overhead (basic utilities) capital needs are much better covered than the needs for social-overhead capital or for agricultural rationalization;
2. In countries comprising about a third of the realm's population, development has reached the stage where capital investment is at rates high enough for rapid modernization (although the stock of modern facilities is still very small);
3. Substantial amounts of capital for agricultural development and for rural social-capital development are being mobilized through community development and other cooperative projects without money savings and investments;

1. In most of realm, annual net investment runs 5–10 per cent of income, only a third to a half that needed—half to two-thirds of investments go to take care of increased population rather than to increase per capita income;
2. Much savings are sterilized in hoards, put in speculative (commodity or real estate) investments, or sent abroad for political security, rather than invested in modern productive facilities;
3. Rural activities generally have low capitalization, and there is uneconomical use of much investment due to small size and fragmentation of holdings in agriculture and to household and village scale of most crafts and services;

4. Industrial and related distribution facilities that have national-prestige status or are built by international companies are usually favored with adequate scale and modern facilities.

4. Housing and other amenities lagging behind urban growth (usually 4–5 per cent annually), producing the world's largest and worst slums, and perhaps the main reason why most inhabitants view such cities as camps rather than as homes.

NATURAL PATTERNS

1. The realm (with over 70 per cent of mankind) includes 55 per cent of the world's land area and about that same fraction of the world's land-use types: 52 per cent of arable land, 51 per cent of rangeland, 52 per cent of forest land, 48 per cent of built-on land, 59 per cent of potentially arable land, and 59 per cent of wasteland;
2. Much greater development is possible nearly everywhere on the basis of known natural resources, and the resource-base will certainly be broadened with changed technology and wider markets;
3. The per capita known natural resources of Latin America, sub-Saharan Africa, the Middle East, and Southeast Asia are quite good, perhaps as good as Western Europe at a comparable stage of development;
4. The realm has most of the world's potentialities for tropical natural resources development (flora, fauna, hydro, etc.)—which will probably be of increasing importance as knowledge of their characteristics increases and improves.

1. At present, realm does not appear to have the per capita actual and potential natural resources of the urban-industrial realm, although this may only be a reflection of inadequate knowledge;

2. The potential resources available in most of the realm are not available within present or slightly modified technology, only within radically changed (urban-industrial) technology and general culture;

3. The tropical regions of the realm generally suffer from natural resistances difficult to overcome or substitute for under present conditions: poor soils, poor vegetation, poor health conditions for man and his beasts, and many others;
4. The known per capita resource-base of most of South and East Asia, and of parts of the West Indies and the Middle East are apparently the poorest in the world, especially in known minerals.

RELATIVE CHANGE IN ECONOMIC SECTORS

Over the past century, mankind's real income has apparently increased about 3 per cent annually on the average, but since the mid-twentieth century the average annual increase has been about 5 per cent. For the entire period, industrial and services income has averaged higher rates than agricultural and related income, so the latter sector has been declining in relative importance. Such average figures obscure much variation: from region to region, from year to year, from prosperous boom period to depressed or disastrous period. Recently, for example, while the world's average increase has been about 5 per cent yearly, many countries have averaged 2 to 3 per cent while others have averaged 6 to 8 per cent, over more than a decade's perspective.

Agricultural and related production (including premodern handicrafts and services consumption by present producers) increased about $1\frac{1}{3}$ per cent annually over the past century, but has recently averaged between 2 and 3 per cent annually. Again, there is much variation; the world's average annual rate over a decade's time, and country rates in most years will show a range between 1 and 4 per cent (with decreases in country output occasionally arising from catastrophe). Spectacular increases are usually restricted to limited periods (several years to several decades) correlated with unusually favorable weather or with a concentration of borrowing new technology from outside coupled with concentrated governmental attention (Mexico since 1940 offers a good example of the latter).

Industrial output increased between 3 and 4 per cent annually over the past century, but has been about 7 per cent annually since 1950. Again, there is much variation, especially from place to place: from 4 per cent to over 10 per cent. The most spectacular reported gains may be exaggerated because of double-counting or some other inadequacy (e.g., often only large-scale and medium-scale modern industrial sub-sectors are censused, and diminished handicraft output is ignored), but there are verifiable cases of 15 per cent annually for considerable periods (West Germany and Japan are current examples), usually either with great outside aid or unusual governmental partnership with private interests. In the case of Communist economies, part of the spectacular success (even after discounting the raw claims, there is little doubt of extremely rapid rates of increase) may be accounted for by the neglect of agriculture and consumer-type services, which will soon have to be remedied at great expense.

The increased income from the tertiary or services sector has been rivaling that from industry. In the case of transportation-communication, many professional and personal services, and other contributory activities, comparison with the other sectors is fairly good, but with government and certain landlord or commercial activities the income may reflect other aspects than true value-added.

Primary (Crude Materials) Sector

Average per capita annual consumption of crude materials is now some 10 tons, for a total of over 32 billion tons of such materials (perhaps 10 cubic miles in volume). Average per capita annual consumption of nearly "invisible" natural materials is even larger, for a total of some 45 billion tons. These materials cost about 16 per cent of mankind's annual income, 10 per cent for the agricultural and other organic materials, 6 per cent for the minerals (half of that is for mining-proper and the other half is for related processing).

Observable Consumption	Billion Metric Tons	Unrecognized Consumption	Billion Metric Tons
Food [1]	3	Land [6]	13
Non-food organic industrial materials [2]	1	Water [7]	15
Fuels [3]	8	Air [8]	17
Metallic ores [4]	2	Total	45
Non-metallic minerals [5] other than fuels	18		
Total	32		

SOURCE: Mainly projections from Doane's *World Balance Sheet* (Harper & Row, 1957).

[1] Includes edible crops and edible animal products (fresh-weight) and one-third of animal feed.

[2] Include those of agricultural and forestry origin (e.g., fibers, hides, natural rubber, industrial wood, etc.).

[3] Include the mineral fuels (coal, lignite, petroleum, natural gas) and the woody fuels (fuel wood, mill wastes, agricultural wastes used for fuel).

[4] Include crude ores of all kinds, including the materials first sent through concentrating plants at the mine before shipment.

[5] Include building materials (sand, clay, gravel, stone), chemical raw materials (salt, sulfur, fertilizer minerals), and many others not previously accounted for.

[6] Includes some 6 billion tons of topsoil lost through natural and man-made erosion, soil and other fill moved by farmers and builders from place to place, and animal feed (rotational pasture's forage and permanent-range feed) not otherwise accounted for.

[7] Refers to that directly used, after some form of processing, and does not include all the water used (for navigation in canals or run through hydroelectric turbines). This figure would be enormously increased if all the water used by man's domesticated plants and semi-domesticated pasture and forests were included.

[8] Most is breathed by man or used in industrial reduction (e.g., some 3 billion tons are "mined" and processed into solids, liquids, and purified gases before being used) —again, if all the indirect uses were included, this figure could be greatly expanded.

TABLE 2–2

World: Consumption of Crude Materials, by Economic-Type of Society, 1962–1964 Average-Annual
(in millions of metric tons)

	High-Income Countries	Low-Income Countries
Foodstuffs and concentrate—one-third of animal feed	(58%)	(42%)
Starch crops (975 million metric tons cereal-equivalent basis)	51	49
Sugar (64 million metric tons brown sugar basis)	72	28
Oils-fats (35 million metric tons oil basis)	70	30
Fruits-vegetables (150 million metric tons fresh basis)	65	35
Caffeine-type beverages (5.4 million metric tons dry basis)	85	15
Wine (26 million metric tons liquid)	80	20
Edible animal products (258 million metric tons meat-equivalent basis)	75	25
Fish (48 million metric tons fresh basis)	65	35
Non-food organic industrial materials (including some "organic"-chemical ones)	(79%)	(21%)
Fibers (21.5 million metric tons)	67	33
Rubber (6 million metric tons dry basis)	93	7
Industrial wood (800 million metric tons dry basis)	90	20
Woody fuels (3,200 million metric tons forestry and agricultural fuels)	25	75
Minerals	(82%)	(18%)
Mineral fuels (5,000 million metric tons fossil fuels raw basis)	84	16
Metallic ores (2,000 million metric tons crude ore raw basis)	90	10
Non-metallic minerals other than fuels (18,000 million metric tons of building materials, chemical raw materials, etc.)	80	20
Total (32 billion metric tons)	(74%)	(26%)
Population (3.2 billion)	29½%	70½%
Annual income (U.S. $1.45 trillion)	81%	19%

As usual, "average" total world consumption data obscure the real distribution of usage, which Table 2–2 above shows is correlated with stage of economic development.

As indicated below, the cost of food is so much greater than the cost of non-food organic raw materials that its continued procurement is much more of an economic problem.

	Per Cent of World National Income [1]
Foodstuffs	
Food crops (grains, tubers, sugar, oils-fats, beverages)	5
Edible animal products (meat, eggs, fish, milk)	3½
Non-food organic industrial raw materials	
Forestry materials (logging products)	½
Inedible agricultural materials (fibers, tobacco, soap and paint materials, etc.)	1
Crude and semiprocessed organic materials	10

[1] Using other concepts of measurement than value-added, such as market value, would increase the fractions a bit.

Food. The production of food, which makes up about 85 per cent of agricultural output, can theoretically be increased nearly as quickly as non-biological crude materials, but usually personal, social, economic, and ecological hindering factors restrict the increase to modest dimensions. Land degradation and comparable phenomena are perhaps the most serious of all hindering factors in food production, and sometimes even threaten maintenance of current production. Often as important in inhibiting the expansion of agriculture to meet demand or need are cultural resistances, especially land ownership and management systems, which are exploitive (e.g., either the Communist "collective" to exploit the peasant in furthering heavy industry, or archaic landlord systems in underdeveloped countries elsewhere that exploit through rack-renting, usury, speculation, and other characteristics). In many cases, the land-tenure system prevents investment in agricultural improvement and diverts capital and savings into unproductive channels. Among the hindering factors in the realm of stable social customs are such matters as laws of inheritance and the fragmentation of land holdings, religious belief, the inability or unwillingness to work long hours with vigor, and the absence or remoteness of incentives. Even in countries that are modernizing agriculture rather swiftly, it is unusual to find it expanding at half the rate of increase achieved by industry and mechanized services.

Over 85 per cent of mankind secures a majority of nourishment from cereals and other relatively inexpensive starchy foods such as tubers and certain fruits. Nearly two-thirds of humanity derive over 80 per cent of their nutritional energy from such sources. Expansion of such plant calories is much simpler than expansion of the meat calories and protective (mineral-vitamin) foods which make up nearly half of food production by value but contribute only a tenth of the energy value. As a society modernizes, more and more of its food problems are luxury-food problems which did not exist before except for the favored elites.

Non-food materials. An overnight increase of world food production of one-quarter would theoretically bring world food supplies to a level that would provide a scientifically adequate diet for all. There is no comparable figure available of the needs of the world's people for non-edible agricultural raw materials and wood, but it would definitely be far in excess of the one-quarter increase need in foodstuffs.

In terms of value, the demand for fibers, industrial oils, tobacco, and rubber is most important, although only worth between 10 to 15 per cent of the worth of foodstuffs. In terms of areas needed for production, such industrial crops pale in comparison with the areal needs for forest land, although most timber is produced on land not suitable for cultivation.

Because so many of the producers of these industrial raw materials are large-scale and modern, and because the cash significance makes even peasant producers more flexible in their methods, usually production problems are less formidable than in the case of basic foodstuffs.

Mineral materials. About 6 per cent of mankind's national income is now spent for mineral materials, one-half of which is the value added by mining proper, with the remaining half being the value added by refineries, smelters, and energy-type utilities. Historically, minerals were considered part of primary production, although increasingly the industrial side is becoming more important, so the present tendency is usually to discuss the topic in the industrial sector of the economy.

Annual increase in consumption is nearly 5 per cent, or two to three times greater than consumption of organic (food and non-food) materials. Since mining mainly is done by modern-scaled and -equipped units of production, the need will probably be met more effectively than in the case of the agricultural materials. International commercialization of such materials is also relatively greater than in the case of non-food agricultural materials, and very much greater than in the case of foodstuffs.

The way ahead for vastly increased mineral production lies in (1) research on the origin of mineral deposits, (2) better knowledge of the distribution of elements in the earth's crust, especially those in concentrations too small to be presently worked, and (3) additional research on the basic physical and chemical properties of the minerals, with the objective of developing synthetic or substitute materials.

In regard to origin item (1), few problems are posed in minerals found in extensive layers close to the surface which are generally uniform in composition (e.g., coal, limestone, much sand and gravel, etc.). Considerable has been done and planned in a second class of minerals, those that occur as concentrations within sedimentary layers (e.g., petroleum, potash, some iron, bauxite, and magnesium ores). Little has been done but prospects are good in theory (perhaps five times as much within 1,000 feet as have already been located) for those small and erratically distributed bodies of minerals found in igneous rocks (e.g., copper, lead, zinc, tungsten, etc.).

Except possibly in the case of a few metals and other minerals, scarcities could be relieved or almost indefinitely postponed by a rise in prices. Shortages may be disturbing to restricted national economies, but the time when serious scarcities for the earth as a whole will occur is at least beyond the turn of the century.

The long view. If mankind should consume materials at the U.S. per capita rate, the resulting world need would increase to six times present consumption. Three lines of development provide the background of possible grand strategy: (1) mankind can obtain more energy and other materials from domestic resources by pushing back the scientific, technological, and economic boundaries that presently limit the supply; (2) mankind can alter patterns of materials-use by more efficient designs and processes, and by shifting the burden of use away from scarcer materials toward more abundant ones; and (3) deficit areas can get more materials through international trade (sometimes this requires lessening national and bloc attempts at self-sufficiency).

In regard to exploitation of avenue (1), there are five possibilities: (a) exploration and discovery—in most of the underdeveloped world, major mineral discoveries may still be made by following surface exposures, but in the older industrial nations increasing reliance must be placed on geophysical, geochemical, and geobiological prospecting methods to probe the hidden deposits beneath young rocks, surficial materials, and thick vegetation; (b) fuller use of known resources—physical wastes (one-half to two-thirds of food, timber, minerals not utilized) are not necessarily economic wastes, but many extractive practices need intensive improvement; (c) renewing flow resource cycles—increasingly, soil, water, and forest resources must be restored where depleted and put on a sustained yield basis; (d) finding work for presently unemployable resources—perhaps the greatest increases in our usable-resource base could be achieved by learning to tap abundant components of our total latent resource base which hitherto mankind has not known how to use—in the long run, the limits are determined by science more than anything else; (e) synthesizing new materials—additional important materials can be synthesized from abundant or renewable resources —especially in the mature industrial economies, among the most notable supplements to the materials stream are the plastics, artificial fibers, synthetic rubbers, and the like—sometimes superior to the crude natural materials replaced, they often are cheaper too.

Avenue (2) also offers several possibilities: (a) shifting from scarce to abundant materials—expanding the output and use of abundant materials might well be as important as enlarging the supply of scarce traditional materials; (b) making materials work harder and longer—vast quantities of materials have been wasted by overdesigning and overspecification, partly because of ignorance of true limits, partly because of comparative abundance leading to lavish use; (c) giving materials a second life—the latent stockpiles of potential scrap are ever growing, and better techniques and better organization for handling scrap can add vast tonnages to total economic supply.

An adequate materials policy for any nation must balance considerations of cost and security. Both concepts must increasingly be viewed in a global perspective. Several aspects of avenue (3) are important: (a) as most of mankind acquires high-consumption economies in the prospective future, domestic resource bases will increasingly become inadequate—technically and economically, such dependence on foreign resources will result in enormous advantages, but political thought will have to change radically before full advantage of this possible solution; (b) the fallacy of self-sufficiency as a basic guide to a sound materials policy is that it costs too much—not only would extreme dependence check economic growth at home and abroad, but the political consequences of self-sufficiency, with its accompanying damage to carefully established security arrangements, would prove even more serious; and (c) what happens internally in the developing nations, and to their economic and political relations with the industrially advanced nations, will largely determine whether international materials development can be used to help world progress or to feed the flames of nationalism and hinder the universal search for new patterns of political, economic, and social security.

Secondary (Industrial or Processing-fabricating) Sector

The rapid rate of growth in industrial output has raised its share of mankind's total income from little more than a third a generation ago to well over two-fifths at present, broken down into segments as follows:

	Per Cent of World National Income
Light industry (food-processing, tobacco products, textiles, furniture, and other soft and semidurable consumer goods)	13
Construction (all kinds of building, repairing, demolition)	6
Mining [1] and energy utilities	6
Heavy industry (machinery and vehicles, chemicals, and others)	20
Total industrial production	45

[1] Mining proper contributes over three-fifths of this, and is sometimes considered part of primary production (as it was so considered universally before being absorbed by modern industry).

As with organic crude materials consumption, the relative importance of industry within a country and the type of industry that predominates depends upon the economic-type of society to a very great extent (Table 2–3).

Light industry. The early stages of commercialization in most underdeveloped economies have seen the importation of processed food, clothing, and other manufactured goods including some capital goods and consumer-durable goods. These imports have thus built up a domestic market that could subsequently be transferred to domestic industries (where necessary, by sheltering such industry behind protectionist measures of different kinds).

In this way, industrialization through import substitution has had the benefit of pre-existing markets, since the early markets have not had to be created in the very process of industrialization itself. In the longer run, however, continued expansion depends upon a general rise in income in the populace coupled with continuing change in tastes preferring factory-made goods instead of home-made traditional types.

Most such industries are based upon availability of agricultural resources in the early phases of expansion, although later on many are based upon imports of foreign materials. As the processing of major crops (cereals, oilseeds, cotton, rubber, sugar, etc.) usually results in a substantial loss of weight, the industries processing these crops are almost all located in the producing countries or regions, in order to avoid the heavy cost of shipping waste matter to the place of more complicated manufacture outside the producing country or region. Owing to perishability, many agricultural products (sugarcane, tea leaves, to a lesser extent cereals) have to be processed near the producing areas. The canning and preserving industry quickly develops near the sources of supply (fruits and vegetables, marine products).

Many consumer goods industries are market-

TABLE 2–3

World: Industrial Output by Economic-Type of Society, 1962–1964 Average-Annual
(in per cents of U.S. $646 billion)

	Population	Total Industry	Light Industry	Construction	Mining [1]	Heavy Industry
High-income or urban-industrial realm	29½	85	81	84	65	94
Low-income or underdeveloped realm	70½	15	19	16	35	6
World	100	100	100	100	100	100
High-income or urban-industrial realm		100	27	14	10	49
Low-income or underdeveloped realm		100	36	15	30	19
World		100	28	14	13	45

[1] Mining and energy utilities (if the two are separated, the urban-industrial realm has only half of world mining proper but nine-tenths of utilities output).

oriented instead of materials-oriented. When the cost of transporting the finished goods exceeds the cost of transporting the raw materials and fuel, as with breweries and soft drinks, a processing or manufacturing industry is attracted to location near the market. Furniture is more bulky than the materials from which it is made, and some importance attaches to local styles and sizes, and to the fact that it is labor-intensive. Perishable commodities sold in fresh form and in small quantities for immediate consumption include both food (baked goods, dairy products, ice) and newspapers.

Necessity and comfort qualities of consumer goods tend to become relatively less important as a country becomes wealthier, and luxury-type quality goods sold more by styling and built-in servicing become relatively more important.

Construction. Commercial building and construction begins early in the process of modernization and maintains its relative importance. Housing is one of the largest items among the consumer durables of private consumption, and about half of the physical assets used for productive purposes (two-thirds or more when land, roads, and highways are included in the total) consists of immobile structures, most of which inevitably are built of local materials by local labor. A considerable fraction of this construction is not very productive directly or immediately, for example, housing in the consumer sector and land reclamation and transportation in the capital sector.

There is increasing evidence that most societies tend to underbuild and undermaintain, and that the future will see the relative importance of building and construction improve as more rapid obsolescence becomes accepted. Some think that eventually nearly half the industrial labor will be in construction, as mining and manufacturing become more automated in their production methods.

Mining. Very early in the industrialization process, industry associated with mining emerges. The processing of metallic ores and many other minerals is a substantial weight-losing process which can best be done at the mine. If cheap fuel and energy is nearby, smelting will also often be done near the mine. Continuous improvement in the utilization and transport of fuel and in the transmission of electricity has reduced the importance of proximity to fuel resources, but certain groups of industries (notably ferrous metallurgy, primary-metal-processing, cement, glass, ceramics, and heavy chemicals) are still heavily influenced by geographical differences in fuel costs.

Improvements in mining and related technology have been so spectacular in the past several generations that the cost of most minerals is usually cheaper in real terms in spite of the continuing trend toward use of leaner natural materials. This trend seems likely to continue for the prospective future, so mining is unlikely to increase its share of labor force or of income as rapidly as consumption of mineral materials.

Heavy industry. A country or region that does not have iron and steel and other basic metal industries can still develop an industry making or fabricating simple metal products or even marketing light engineering products from imported metal and non-metal parts and components. Such processed metal materials, although heavy, lose little if any of their shipping weight when made into metal products. Moreover, metal products are generally much more bulky than iron and steel and other processed metal materials in sheets or bars, and for this reason their import tends to entail much higher transport charges. Furthermore, some metal products may require special sizes and designs to suit local conditions and tastes. Thus, it is usually economical to make metal products near the market.

Vehicles and machinery of the simpler sorts or more standardized sorts tend to be diffused early from the older industrial centers to wherever markets develop. Parts are made principally in places having ready access to iron and steel and fuel, and also to capital and enterprise. Unassembled parts, compactly packed, can be shipped to plants for assembly near the market in order to save freight. This is especially economical if labor is cheap near the markets. However, as the scale of automobile or other vehicle assembly must be large to be economical, the market has also to be substantial. All these factors explain why vehicle and machinery assembly plants are proliferating all over the world. The assembly of bicycles, small pumps, and the like, is much simpler and can often be done in small workshops, so much faster spread of such industry is possible than in the larger and more complicated vehicles and machinery. Eventually, the local making of parts increases.

Mature industrialization is sometimes considered to exist when half of the industrial labor force engaged in manufacturing is found in plants making producer goods and consumer-durable goods. With the increasing tendency toward automation in manufacturing and high elasticity in consumer-durable goods evidenced in developing societies, it may well be that the share of total industry contributed by heavy industry will increase.

The long view. The development process, by increasing productive ability at the same time as it enlarges markets, virtually assures the rise of industries. This increase in the relative importance of industries, as seen in the employment and income structures, need not necessarily characterize economic development through all its stages. The services sector may very well increase, in some periods, at a faster rate than industry proper; and there may be stages in economic growth where industry ceases altogether to become relatively more important.

The advent of new labor-saving technologies, such as automation, might bring industrialization, in the employment sense, to a stopping point sooner than would otherwise be the case, but the importance of this must still be a matter of speculation at present. In terms of shares of national product, as contrasted with shares of national employment, the moment at which industrialization, strictly defined, reaches a plateau may arrive somewhat earlier, if productivity per employee thereafter increases faster in the services and primary sectors. As a general rule, those economies reasonably self-sufficient in materials are likely to develop industry to the extent of one-fourth to one-third of their total economy, with more dependent economies developing industry to the extent of one-third to one-half of their total economy to secure a surplus for export.

Tertiary (Contributory or Services) Sector

This indirectly productive sector is as important as the industrial sector, although it does not produce goods but accommodations of various sorts. Engaging between 25 to 30 per cent of the world's labor force, it accounts for well over two-fifths of all income (however measured):

	Per Cent of World National Income
Transportation and communications	6
Trade and commerce (all kinds: wholesale, retail, and others; domestic and international)	14
Government (public security, public welfare, and other branches—local, provincial, and national)	13
Other services (private professional and technical, clerical, and personal services not previously included)	12
Total services production	45

The value of services is distributed among economic-types of society in much the same proportion as industry (Table 2–4).

Transportation and communications. Agrarian societies being non-commercial and little commercial for the most part have anemic distribution compared with mature urban-industrial societies, but it often is almost as expensive, sometimes being a haven for disguised unemployment (underemployment) much like peasant agriculture. As modernization proceeds, expansion of modern-type distribution may be half a dozen times greater than the average increase in the labor force (but this is often counterbalanced by the loss of part-time distribution efforts by peasants). Not only economic progress, but the cultural, social, and moral advancement of society awaits proliferation of these place utilities (space-adjusting activities).

As mature urban-industrial status is reached, distribution generally ceases to be a growth ac-

TABLE 2–4

World: Services Output by Economic-Type of Society, 1962–1964 Average-Annual
(in per cents of U.S. $649 billion)

	Population	Total Services	Transportation and Communications	Trade and Commerce	Government	Professional and Personal
High-income or urban-industrial realm	29½	83	81	83	84	82
Low-income or underdeveloped realm	70½	17	19	17	16	18
World	100	100	100	100	100	100
High-income or urban-industrial realm		100	13	31	29	27
Low-income or underdeveloped realm		100	15	31	27	27
World		100	14	31	28	27

tivity (expanding at a faster rate than economy as a whole), and expands about the same as income in general. Much depends upon whether consumers prefer the expensive speed and flexibility of truck and airplane service over the cheaper bulk carriers favored to move package goods as well as raw materials earlier in the development process.

Trade and commerce. With increasing commercialization of an economy, especially in connection with the growth of cities and their immediate hinterlands, trade becomes one of the occupations that increases more rapidly than the average growth rate of the general population (if there exists consumer sovereignty). Together with transportation and communication, with which it is intimately related, trade promises to absorb nearly as many new workers as manufacturing activities, although this fact is often disguised by the greater attention given new factory industry in most developing economies.

Eventually, employment and income stabilize, although many modernized economies have a swollen trade sector, because of low efficiency and the tendency to shelter disguised unemployment in certain areas, especially small-scale retail outlets. Eventually, larger-scale units tend to evolve, and productivity tends to increase.

Government. Increased security risks and desire to set up welfare states have made for swiftly increasing bureaucracy and defense forces everywhere in the world. The spread of education and extensive services comes to dominate local governmental functions, while increasing control and supervision swells provincial and central bureaucracy.

In terms of employment opportunities and income, government service quickly becomes one of the fastest growing activities, although in absolute numbers usually ranking behind industry or trade in absorbing new labor. In general, the more complicated the society, the more important will be the government sector of the economy, although the prevailing ideology has some influence (but not as much as propaganda alleges). The largest question mark involves defense.

Professional and personal services. This segment of an economy is a very diverse one, including finance, insurance, and real estate services on the one hand, and hotel, amusement, medical, legal, domestic, and other services on the other. In some areas, private education is very important.

As between two countries with equal real incomes, the services here listed will be larger, the greater the urbanization, the higher the level of education, the lower the degree of inequality of income distribution, the larger the relative numbers of children and aged in the population.

In modern-type services the urban-industrial economies will have shares proportionate to their greater income, but such is not the case in domestic and certain traditional professional services. Poor societies often rate high in servants, since they often cost less than unskilled agricultural workers and the traditional emphasis on generosity in entertaining made large household staffs necessary for the well-to-do. The long-range tendency is for the proportion to fall off, as the cost of such labor goes up and urban families tend to employ less help than a rural family with the same income. Many professions widely scattered in rural areas (lawyers, doctors, ministers, etc.) tend to become more efficient in urban surroundings and do not increase rapidly, although increasing specialization may make the services increasingly costly.

The growth services in this area tend to be new developments, reflecting both the increased attention to science and technology on one hand, and the increased attention to luxury-type professional and personal services in the area of ordinary consumption on the other.

The long view. The tendency for proliferation in services which has featured the past several generations seems destined to continue during the foreseeable future. The proportions of the labor force and income derived from services will probably increase to somewhere about half again in importance (perhaps two-thirds of labor force and income from services before another generation is past).

The future "mix" of services is more difficult to assess, since the effects of automation on various professional and clerical activities has barely started, but it seems likely that productivity will change the most in those services selling standardized accommodations.

PERSPECTIVE

Mankind is following a modified but essentially similar course of economic modernization as that pioneered by Western Europeans, and practically all countries will be urban-industrial or semi-industrial by the turn of the century. But until that time, most problems involving space and resources must be surveyed and solved within a context indicating degree of modernization reached by any particular society.

During the past century, mankind's real income has increased tenfold while his numbers have increased less than threefold. At present, in spite of a doubled population growth rate, world income is still increasing twice as rapidly. But the present distribution of income may well be more uneven than at any other time in history, with the urban-industrial nations having shares as disproportionate as the elites within premodern societies. Severe pressures of population and of rising standards of living will put the remainder of mankind under heavy economic and psychological strains for the foreseeable future.

Consumption of crude materials is now increasing at a rate somewhat less than that of total income, since the increasing preference for highly fabricated goods and for services means a declining relative share of total consumption for primary products. In urban-industrial economies, an increase in production is accompanied by an increase in crude materials consumption equal to one-half to two-thirds as much by value, while in underdeveloped economies the increase is often three-fourths as much. Absolute consumption of crude materials will continue to go up, but their cost seems likely to decline to a tenth or so of total production costs within the remainder of this century.

In all economic sectors, the trend is toward greater substitution and supplementation of living energy by machinery and inanimate energy. Not only brawn but lower forms of judgment, imagination, and flexibility seem destined to be increasingly supplied by machinery when scale and standardized performance limits are permissive. The superiority of a machine-based energy economy shows up in an increasing ability to use leaner and less accessible natural resources as the supply of higher-grade materials becomes inadequate, in a great reduction of overhead costs, and in a much larger proportion of investment than was possible in premodern economies. The hourly outputs commonly found in industrial societies (50 cents to $3.00) are only possible when much of the work can be done by machines at costs per man-hour equivalent that are phenomenally low (1 to 5 cents). Since most industry, transport and routine office work can apparently be increasingly automated, the future shares of such activities in employment and income opportunities seem destined to diminish, with other activities that cannot be standardized and automatized becoming increasingly larger shares of the productive apparatus.

In both production and consumption problems and prospects, rising consumption standards and population changes are factors greatly affecting the outcome of dynamic processes. Since economic development is usually measured as increased per capita welfare and income, the next two chapters will investigate such patterns in considerable detail as a prelude to more detailed analyses of location and materials problems in the three sectors.

SUGGESTED READINGS

BARBOUR, NEVILL (ed.). *A Survey of North West Africa (The Maghrib)*. London: Oxford University Press, 1959. Pp. 406.

BERRILL, KENNETH (ed.). *Economic Development with Special Reference to East Asia*. London: Macmillan, 1964. Pp. 435.

BUTLAND, GILBERT J. *Latin America*. London: Longmans, 1960. Pp. 373.

CHURCH, R. J., CLARKE, JOHN I., CLARKE, P. J. H., and HENDERSON, H. J. R. *Africa and the Islands*. New York: Wiley, 1964. Pp. 494.

COHEN, SAUL B. *Geography and Politics in a Divided World*. New York: Random House, 1963. Pp. 347.

COLE, J. P., and GERMAN, F. C. *A Geography of the U.S.S.R.* London: Butterworths, 1961. Pp. 290.

COLE, MONICA. *South Africa*. London: Methuen, 1961. Pp. 696.

COWAN, C. D. *The Economic Development of China and Japan*. London: Allen & Unwin, 1964. Pp. 255.

COWAN, C. D. *The Economic Development of South-East Asia*. London: Allen & Unwin, 1964. Pp. 192.

CRESSEY, GEORGE B. *Crossroads—Land and Life in Southwest Asia*. New York: Lippincott, 1960. Pp. 593.

CRESSEY, GEORGE B. *Land of the 500 Million—A Geography of China*. New York: McGraw-Hill, 1955. Pp. 387.

CUMBERLAND, KENNETH B. *Southwest Pacific*. New York: McGraw-Hill, 1956. Pp. 365.

DE BLIJ, HARM J. *A Geography of Subsaharan Africa*. Chicago: Rand McNally, 1964. Pp. 435.

DEWHURST, J. FREDERICK, COPPOCK, JOHN O., YATES, P. LAMARTINE, and ASSOCIATES. *Europe's Needs and Resources*. New York: Twentieth Century Fund, 1961. Pp. 1,198.

DOBBY, E. H. G. *Monsoon Asia*. University of London Press, 1961. Pp. 381.

GINSBURG, NORTON (ed.). *The Pattern of Asia*. Englewood Cliffs, N.J.: Prentice-Hall, 1958. Pp. 929.

GOTTMANN, JEAN. *A Geography of Europe*. New York: Holt, Rinehart & Winston, 1962. Pp. 788.

HANCE, WILLIAM A. *The Geography of Modern Africa*. Columbia University Press, 1964. Pp. 653.

HOFFMAN, GEORGE W. (ed.). *A Geography of Europe*. New York: Ronald, 1961. Pp. 815.

HU, CHANG-TU, et al. *China—Its People, Its Society, Its Culture*. New Haven, Conn.: HRAF Press, 1960. Pp. 611.

JAMES, PRESTON E. *Latin America*. New York: Odyssey, 1959. Pp. 942.

KIMBLE, GEORGE H. *Land and Livelihood; Society and Polity*. Vols. I and II. *Tropical Africa*. New York: Twentieth Century Fund, 1960. Pp. 603; pp. 506.

LIU, TA-CHUNG and YEH, KUNG-CHIA. *The Economy of the Chinese Mainland: National Income and Economic Development, 1933–1959*. Princeton University Press, 1965. Pp. 771.

LONGRIGG, STEPHEN H. *The Middle East—A Social Geography*. London: Duckworth, 1963. Pp. 291.

MADDISON, ANGUS. *Economic Growth in the West—Comparative Experience in Europe and North America*. New York: Twentieth Century Fund, 1964. Pp. 246.

MURDOCK, GEORGE P. *Africa—Its Peoples and Their Culture History*. New York: McGraw-Hill, 1959. Pp. 456.

PATERSON, J. H. *North America—A Regional Geography*. London: Oxford University Press, 1960. Pp. 454.

PETERSON, A. D. C. *The Far East—A Social Geography*. London: Duckworth, 1957. Pp. 334.

ROBINSON, E. A. G. *Economic Consequences of the Size of Nations*. London: Macmillan, 1960. Pp. 447.

SHABAD, THEODORE. *China's Changing Map*. New York: Praeger, 1956. Pp. 295.

SPENCER, J. E. *Asia East by South—A Cultural Geography*. New York: Wiley, 1954. Pp. 453.

STAMP, L. DUDLEY. *Africa—A Study in Tropical Development*. New York: Wiley, 1964. Pp. 534.

TAYLOR, LEE, and JONES, ARTHUR R., JR. *Rural Life and Urbanized Society*. New York: Oxford University Press, 1964. Pp. 493.

WALKER, D. S. *The Mediterranean Lands*. London: Methuen, 1960. Pp. 524.

WATSON, J. WREFORD. *North America—Its Countries and Regions*. London: Longmans, 1963. Pp. 854.

3

Modern Economic Development: Ideology and Technology

Most major goals of a modern society—political security, economic growth, social stability with justice, conservation, and many others—are as dependent upon problems of timing in their solution as upon universal principles relating to their processes of change. Mankind is only partly through the latest change in civilization, the urban-industrial one, and national status is greatly dependent upon which stage in that transition the society has attained.

There are different ways of viewing economic development or modernization. In one sense, each country's road can be thought of as unique: depending on its peculiar natural resources and resistances, its inherited culture, its external and internal pressures during the century or more of transition, its stage in history when industrialization began, and on the nature of its power elite. In another sense, while recognizing that there are many routes to urban-industrial civilization, one can emphasize the similarities. The theory of pluralistic industrialism hypothesizes that, no matter what route a nation takes, the logic of dynamic science, technology, and social change tends to make each country more and more resemble all other modernized countries in important respects. The latter school predicts that, in time, modern technology will create in all countries somewhat similar bureaucracies and state controls, complex patterns of authority and freedom, scientific and professional middle classes, skilled-labor forces, and consumption standards. Societies would eventually all be mixtures of modern organization and modern hedonism, with more leisure, more income, and more mass culture eventually producing a culturally more homogenized world in which ideological and other differences will eventually fade and disappear.

Following are models of economic development and of resource availability in which the factors of production (e.g., land, labor, capital, enterprise, government) are arranged in hierarchial order. It is hypothesized that, in most cases of economic development, natural resources and population factors are normally passive, limiting factors that affect the timing and routing of development but are seldom causal. The dynamics of change are mainly in the realms of ideology and technology, especially in the spirit and institutions of government and other organizations, which are usually the active (causal) factors in initiating and impelling modern economic growth.

The Changing Factors in Modern Economic Development

General Cultural Changes *	*Changes in Resource Availability* *

PRIMARILY ACTIVE (I.E., USUALLY CAUSAL) FACTORS IN BOTH MODELS

The Will To Develop (i.e., standards of aspiration or of psychic insecurity)

Non-economic pressures (e.g., search for justifiable self-confidence, self-esteem, and balance, both in individuals and in institutions).

Economic pressures (e.g., search for higher total and per capita real incomes).

Changing Technology (i.e., state of arts or culture or capital)

Social technology (e.g., the routine behavior and institutional controls that are the fixed capital of men's social relationships) has widened limits of scale and specialization.

Material technology (e.g., quantity, quality, and variety of capital instruments used in agricultural, services, and industrial development) has increased labor productivity manyfold over premodern equivalent.

Dynamic Science and Technology

Stock resources (e.g., minerals) depletion has been effectively offset by advances in mining and related processing.

Flow resources (e.g., agricultural and related organic materials) status is uncertain—wasteful practices have been offset by progress in the restorative and upgrading areas, but no reliable picture of net effects is yet available for world or for large regions.

Changing Social Technology

Modern institutions (e.g., corporate units, nation-states and associated agencies) are more efficient than premodern institutions if used close to their capacity.

Raw nationalism is probably most limiting factor to man's continuing accelerated use of space and resources.

PRIMARILY PASSIVE (I.E., USUALLY LIMITING) FACTORS IN BOTH MODELS

Changing Population (i.e., redistribution and increase of humans)

Adjusting to urbanization and to demographic inflation (i.e., to modern population cycle's gap) is both very difficult and very rewarding.

Cheap attainment and maintenance of good health a boon in short run, but main drag on economic progress as widest portion of demographic gap is traversed.

Changing Resource Availability

Expanding crude materials supply within context of slightly commercialized agrarian civilization is most difficult because of rigidities.

Expanding raw materials potential within context of evolving urban industrialization (next "model" poses problems and prospects).

Changing Population Effects

Redistribution (especially urbanization) has mainly favorable effects on resource and space availability.

Effects of population growth on resource and space availability are more debatable, with main doubt relating to speed and costs of alternative ways of closing the demographic gap.

Changing Consumer Demands and Expectations (i.e., pressure of standards)

Early modernization involves heavier demands for organic materials at time when agriculture is not as flexible.

Late modernization involves increased demand for raw materials only half or so as great as total increased demand, although absolute consumption of materials continues to rise (mainly in the more easily available minerals sector of the materials field).

* Arranged in descending order of importance.

The geographer is especially interested in the resource-availability "model," but the general cultural-change "model" is useful in placing the other model in a broad perspective. Both are, like all models, extremely simplified approximations of reality and, while they are useful mental tools in assessing large "populations" (of examples), they must sometimes be altered to deal with a single unusual case. In the remainder of this chapter, a more detailed study of the primarily active factors, ideology and technology, will be given; while the primarily passive factors, population and resources, will be assessed in the next chapter.

IDEOLOGY

To revitalize a society, new and renovated ideas are required; but usually the greatest problem is to get a hearing for them. Economic development presupposes motivations, ethical standards, discipline, and skills that are lacking in most underdeveloped societies. Usually most important in mobilizing human energy is inculcating a new character (i.e., a spirit of abiding faith, a will to develop, new standards of aspiration). In order for masses of men to change radically their retarding attitudes, beliefs, and traditional habits of behavior, they must usually believe that their "golden age" lies ahead of them. A civilization expands or survives on a reservoir of abiding faith in itself, and most fundamental changes in a modernizing society must be instilled by insiders rather than by outsiders from another society (especially from one living on the residue of its age of faith). The most radical changes normally occur during the initial period when the expectation gap is wider than the possibility of satisfying. When this revolutionary ardor wanes, when the society is closest to solving its problems but is living on remnants of its age of faith, much less radical change is usually desired, although the visible facilities and skills are much more impressive than earlier.

Non-economic pressures. Historically, economic development has been inseparable from a high degree of individual and social insecurity, associated with the crumbling of old value systems and institutions, and the abandonment (at least temporarily) of the individual and traditional primary loyalty units to their own devices until revised or new substitutes are evolved. Urban-industrial civilization's developments affect the individual's relations to all social groups— the famliy, the church, the school, the labor group, the business group, the recreational agency, and others. In a period of rapid change, many historic institutions and old assumptions and beliefs are inadequate if not obsolete; and most individuals and groups feel themselves on an anemic diet of those important psychic nutrients: love, care, stimulation, and reassurance. At the social or national level, the early stage of development often involves a greater awareness of the lessened respect, status, prestige, and importance accorded a society that has slipped from a previous position of power and wealth.

Drastic change has often been the most effective vehicle to release human energy inhibited by paralysis of will. Ideas that take men outside of themselves, into ventures bigger than themselves, have usually touched off those explosions of human energy that transcend ordinary economic, military, and other professional considerations. The most potent instrument to accomplish drastic change is often an idea that releases human and institutional inhibitions and generates new vitality; but if this stimulus of change is to work itself out along the lines of constructive action, there have to be abundant opportunities, a tradition of self-reliance and social reliance, and effective leadership at every level of endeavor.

The drastic change that upsets the inner balance of most power-elites is likely to involve political or social insecurity more often than economic status, and the organizing ideals used to mobilize a society for an accelerated program of modernization involve national pride and defense more than economic incentives. Even with the mass of citizenry, the main goals are essentially non-economic: justifiable self-esteem and self-respect, the confidence of equals and superiors, a sense of balance between the need for security and the desire for change, and other goals whose attainment involves economic means but mainly other means. The grand strategy of development usually is organized around little visible social psychological forces, with tactics organized around economic and other physical incentives.

Economic pressures. Mass poverty is as old as civilization, but awareness of its social injustice and the conviction that major amelioration is possible are new. The revolution of rising expectations in the area of per capita income has been caused (1) by the example set by Western societies, who have proved that general poverty is not inevitable; and (2) by the miracles of twentieth-century mass communications, especially those not requiring literacy, which have diffused that revolutionary idea (i.e., the pressure of Western standards) more swiftly than in past centuries.

Modernization brings physical benefits too basic for any people to renounce them. Indeed, the demand for them is, nearly everywhere, among the major driving forces for change; but while everywhere happiness springs partly from improved wealth and improved health, it derives even more from mental ease, emotional spontaneity, creative will, and other causes better assayed by the behavioral than by the economic fields. To achieve joy and sanity, man needs a sense of purpose and direction, awe and wonder, deep sympathy, receptivity without prejudice, flexibility to new conditions, and other aspects of personal resourcefulness that are not illumined by the economic-man model.

As further explained in the next section, all power-elites striving for economic development (i.e., for higher total and per capita real levels of income) have economic motives in their rationalization, but political and sociopsychological motives are usually uppermost. This is easily discernible in the two great revolts of our time: that against the West's ascendancy over the rest of the world, and that against the Western middle-class ascendancy over the Western industrial class.

Even among workers, economic motivations that bring the highest satisfactions are those associated with social gains. Where economic gains are not associated with gains in social status and prestige, their translation into balanced growth is retarded, and the end product may be greater social tension than before. There are real economic incentives, especially between agriculture and industry (e.g., U.S. wage per man-hour is about $1.25 in agriculture versus about $2.50 in industry), although the higher money wages in many locations are partially a reflection of higher prices.

Not only is emotional mobilization important as a prelude to serious modernization, but maintaining high morale and high motivation is a continuing difficulty throughout the entire period of transition, which may continue from one to two centuries. The net profit that a society realizes from the process of urban-industrialization is closely correlated with its continuing willingness to undergo new change rather than aim at rigid security. There is increasing evidence that the momentum possible by exploiting modern science and technology is much greater than usually realized, because of inhibitions arising in limiting morale and institutional rigidities.

Power-elites. Modernization has been attempted by all sorts of power-elites, some traditional, some new, using a variety of techniques, and animated by a variety of goals. Some inkling of the differences is indicated below in the characterization of five types of power-elites.

Dynastic leaders are originally drawn from a landed or commercial aristocracy, a military caste, a religious hierarchy, a government bureaucracy, or from tribal chieftains. Their central strategy is usually to preserve traditional society, but they must modernize to some extent in order to guard the old order from external or internal threats. Usually, the pace of change will be no greater than is necessary to preserve the traditional elite, although military needs often dictate a more rapid pace. Normally, the preservation and protection of agriculture rates high priority, as does certain industry and construction (military, public works, paternalistic projects). Internal sources of funds are usually favored, with much use of government controls (grants, subsidies, tariffs), and diversion of agricultural rents to industrial requirements. To motivate, the main stress is likely to be on renewed loyalty to tradition, family, religion, and other old emotional ties. The educational system is also keyed to preserve old values, with higher education usually limited to elitists. The direction of change is generally toward a less elitist and less paternal approach as countervailing organized interests emerge. The German, Russian, and Japanese empires are excellent nineteenth-century examples. Present examples include much less important states: Ethiopia, several Arabian monarchies, Iran, Afghanistan, Nepal, and several Buddhist monarchies, probably destined to disappear or to be submerged by the rise of new elites.

The middle-class power-elite has historically emerged from commercial or artisan groups already in existence. This is the group that created capitalism and the ethics and mythology of individualism. Other things being equal, the central strategy has favored individual self-advancement, and the pace of change has been fitted to the mold of individual possibilities of profit-making. When unorganized, agriculture has been shaped by international competition. Profits have usually determined the sequence of industrial development in peacetime, with light industry usually favored first. Public works have often been given a low priority, except in the context of defense or organized pressure by non-elitist groups. Private sources of capital have been favored when its use was profitable, with substantial foreign capital being attracted when profits and security were assured. Money rewards have been the favored form of motivation, with the personal ethic of hard work favored. Both liberal and technical forms of education tend to be favored, since this has been the preferred source of social mobility for workers and farmers into the middle class. In general, with maturity more group and state action has emerged, mainly because of developments evolving out of defense and the rise of organized opposition. Defects of traditional capitalist economies included very unequal income distribution, a tendency to get out of control during business cycles, and instances of individual interests being served in opposition to community interests. The best historic examples were eighteenth century Britain and nineteenth century United States. Few completely middle-class dominated twentieth century societies can be identified (Hong Kong is a good one, but a minor unit), although many mixed economies have strong middle classes.

Totalitarian power-elites are mainly the revolutionary intellectuals evolving out of Marx, who first seek revolution and then an expansion of power in the name of implementing Communist ideals. However, rightist examples did exist until the end of World War II and could conceivably exist again (e.g., some would place the Republic of South Africa in such a category). The central strategy of Communist elites is forced-draft industrialization, with the fastest possible pace under an extensive set of state controls. Basic industry is given the highest priority, with agriculture, housing, and light industry receiving only selective and half-hearted support. The revolutionary ideology shows up in educational philosophy, and in methods of motivating both elite and masses. The main drawbacks of Communist systems are their excessive controls and inefficiencies, and their discouragement of quick action at the lower levels of the single factory manager or worker. With maturity, as in the Soviet Union, the system tends to become less ideological, more bureaucratic, and more sensitive to the wishes of the masses and other emerging elites besides the original one (e.g., a scientific and technological middle class). The ideal type postulated above probably fits the Communist Far East elites somewhat better than the Communist European ones.

The colonial administrator power-elite type is rapidly fading into history; but the classic cases were the British, French, Dutch, and Belgian colonizers; and the Portuguese example is perhaps the most adamant group still surviving. Mainly serving the home country was the central strategy. The pace of change tended to be slow, but depended mainly on the advantage to the mother country. Priorities were given to economic activities that furnished materials or consumption goods to the mother country, or ones that supplied foreign exchange. Funds came mainly from taxing the natives or from the mother country (with the latter source uncertain, depending on competing pressures on government and private budgets in the home country). Foreign capital is mainly found in extractive industries. Limited compulsion was the chief form of motivation, with only a limited acceptance of natives into the ruling group. The educational philosophy was usually adapted from the mother country, with higher education limited to a very few, and such training was often only given in the mother country. The direction of change was mainly toward nationalism, with occasionally a take-over by the Communists.

There is no single social base for new nationalist power-elites; their leaders may emerge from the top, bottom, or middle groups of society. Their initial central strategy is simple: to achieve national independence, which is thought to be synonymous with progress. Early unity is essentially a negative force seeking to get rid of the old group that is running society, whatever kind it is. But after the take-over, the new nationalist leaders often become confused about their solutions for problems along the troublesome route to industrialization (e.g., India, Indonesia, most African states). The pace is usually slower than expected, with high aspirations and cheap promises, but a very uncertain rate of achievement. Priority is usually given to the building of a broad industrial base, both for prestige and for economic-growth motives, with defense industry often stressed if there has been no inheritance from the colonial past. Shortages of funds are perennial; it is hard for a new nationalist elite to squeeze consumption tighter than did the previous colonial administrators, and the drive for independence often repels foreign capital when most needed (there is a tendency to seek large sums abroad either as grants or loans, but the supply is likely to be variable and short-term). Motivation is a problem; while raw nationalism is the main reliance as long as possible, its potency usually declines rapidly with the resurgence of self-interest among the diverse elements attracted to the struggle for independence. Attempts are quickly made to free the educational system from its ties with the previous colonial power, but there is soon a dilemma over whether to use the limited financial resources for general education or for special programs to produce a scientific and managerial elite. If successful, there is a tendency for more middle-class influence, as in most of the older new nationalist states in Latin America, the Middle East, and the non-Communist Far East. If unsuccessful, there is more influence for revolutionary intellectuals (e.g., the fate of Nationalist China at the end of World War II or pre-Communist Cuba in the past decade).

Generalization about power-elites is helpful if one keeps in mind that the "model" is oversimplified. Most complicated cultures have several elites, and their power-status changes with each stage of development and the problems and prospects facing the society at different times. The pluralistic school, as mentioned earlier, believes that the age of ideology will fade away with the attainment of urban industrialization along the various routes. If one includes the compromises and opportunism along with the official mythology of each ideology, there may well develop a gray zone of beliefs and attitudes that exhibit great similarity. But, by analogy with the amelioration of great political and religious ideological struggles, there will probably remain relict differences that are still important, especially as lines of potential fissure during times of troubles.

TECHNOLOGY

Technological change is a prime mover in the process of modernization. Historically, invention and innovation have generally led the process in pioneering societies already disciplined and motivated to change. Imitation by underdeveloped countries often affords a shortcut to higher levels of living.

Science and technology are morally neutral; they help impartially the needy and satiated, the tyrant and the free. Partly for this reason, they usually diffuse more easily from their region of origin than values and related institutions. Social technology, that institutional organizational structure that is needed to curb and mobilize spirit into useful disciplined energy, is usually more difficult to diffuse than material technology, especially those aspects that are substitutes for historic institutions.

Social technology. The absorption of a new level of civilization is a complex process, dependent more upon social and institutional changes than upon isolated material technological introduction. The productivity of any society is due as much to a highly developed, steadily advancing skill in human relations embodied in institutions and traditions as it is due to dynamic natural science and traditional engineering.

An urban-industrial society requires investment of the equivalent of several years' total income in social-overhead-types of capital (e.g., capital investments in human beings, such as improvements in health, education, training, and other aspects of welfare), plus about the same amount of investment in material facilities, which means that saving and investment must usually be tripled as compared with premodern societies. Such great growth of capital is not due to mechanical forces, but to the evolution of new patterns of social relationships (e.g., shifting social classes' relative positions of power and prestige, changing status of women or ethnic minorities, changed family type, and others). To save and to invest on a much larger scale, to produce and to distribute for mass markets requires many innovations in economic organizations (e.g., the introduction of the corporate form of organization, of modern bank credit, of stable monetary and fiscal systems, of institutionalized research, of mass distribution techniques, and many others).

Much diffusion of both social and material technology is best done by generalists whose technical advice is matched by their skill in human relations, who realize how much they and the people they seek to help are culture-bound. Individual flexibility, experience in cooperation, and freedom from ulterior motivations are among the indispensable qualities of good diffusers. Technicians without great imaginative adaptability, without skill in personal relations, and without sensitivity to people and situations, will not usually succeed in diffusing their skills. Techniques are animated by aims. Felt need and confidence-building must be developed hand in hand with know-how, in order to unlock receptivity and eagerness, which will eventually lead to self-starting and self-propelling forms of progress. Diffusing technology must be examined from the frames of reference both of the society into which it is being introduced, and the reference points of the urban-industrial society's science and technology where it originated (e.g., most peasants are not motivated by scientific and engineering abstractions as much as by seeing concrete results in the fields of their more venturesome neighbors). First-class extension workers are nearly as difficult to find as first-class organizers (these latter being probably the most limiting factor to rapid development). The experience of Americans and Russians is often most sought after by most underdeveloped societies, because of their power and wealth, although often their experience is less helpful than the experience of smaller countries with closer analogies in problems involving habitat, man, and culture. Ideally, the United Nations might be the best vehicle for organizing the most relevant technology to diffuse, relying upon extension workers from small states to divorce such aid from power politics, but both hegemony-seeking benefactors and play-both-sides beneficiaries avoid major use of such an alternative.

Material technology. Economic development involves significant technological advance, especially capital-deepening innovations (e.g., production becoming more capital-intensive, more roundabout, requiring major changes both in productive equipment and in the scale of operations). Improvements in the quality of capital instruments have been the most visible cutting edge of modern economic progress, the great multiplier of resources. This adding of better units of capital is a different matter from the adding of like units as assumed in many early growth models.

Modern phenomena are the worldwide pool of inventions and innovations now available, and the speed with which copying can be done as compared with earlier times. In nearly every field of production, the scientific and technical developments of the past century have increased manyfold (e.g., perhaps forty fold in the United

States) the productive power of the individual worker in the most rationalized activities, thus continually resulting in increasing returns from other factors of production (rather than the decreasing returns postulated within a context of stagnant technology by Malthus and others).

To be ideally useful in most underdeveloped societies, a new technology should be capital-saving, easily transferable, quickly productive of highly visible results, geared to the most underutilized resources, and flexible in use. However, only a small portion of the worldwide pool mentioned above would satisfy all those requirements. Since the economic policy of underdeveloped countries is generally determined by the shortages of innovating enterprisers, of risk capital, and of technicians (e.g., engineers, foremen), the difficulties in obtaining foreign exchange usually make capital-saving devices more important than labor-saving devices in those underdeveloped areas where substitutability is feasible.

Problems of agricultural development include some of the greatest difficulty in any underdeveloped society, partly because most Western experience has been with mid-latitude types of resources, resulting in an inability of tropical societies to borrow cheaply and easily much necessary technology. Mainly the reasons lie in such characteristics of traditional agriculture as undercapitalization (e.g., most peasants are too small-scale either to save enough to modernize or to use much technology developed by the Newer Europeans), lack of adaptability compared to industry (e.g., inherent difficulties of manipulating biological factors, the poor organizing ability of most small holders, and others), high fixed-costs (e.g., the costs of population growth, of support of disguised unemployment, of soil conservation, etc., bear most heavily on rural society in the early stages of development), and less elastic demand than industry and services (i.e., as income rises, agriculture tends to get a smaller share of the consumers' purchases). This lag in effecting fundamental agricultural reforms and development raises serious political and social problems as well as economic problems. Many rural groups almost inevitably are going to be among the last groups to raise significantly their levels of living.

Problems of economic-overhead types of capital investment (e.g., power, transport and communications, research establishments, and other basic facilities) also arise, but are usually solved more swiftly than retarded agriculture, mainly by government in presently developing societies. Without the quick availability of such services, the directly productive activities are poorly suited to take advantage of those aspects of modern productivity that are more dependent upon increase in size (scale) than upon increase in machine power. In poor countries just beginning modernization, sometimes three-quarters of the non-agricultural investments go into railways, roads, ports, electricity-gas-water supply, housing, schools, hospitals, and other economic and social overhead investment where the contribution of private enterprise may be marginal and inadequate.

In most underdeveloped societies, the urge toward industrialization can be viewed as the inevitable result of general economic development. With political independence and public stability, the necessary energy and other raw material resources, some initial risk capital, and the opportunity to acquire skill in modern technical and organizational methods, most countries (or even most regions within a country) tend to industrialize to some extent. Most increased income in the early stages of modern economic development comes from shifting workers in low-productivity agriculture and handicraft industry into mechanized industry and modern services, rather than from steady or spectacular increases in the productivities of already mechanized activities.

Stages in development. The economic historian Rostow hypothesizes that industrialization and other aspects of high economic development cannot escape evolving through certain stages, although it can take place under any one of a number of systems. His "model," with its traditional preconditions for take-off, take-off, drive to maturity, and high mass consumption stages, allows good analysis of changing technical and other problems with the passage of time and structural change.

Stage 1. Traditional societies live under a more or less "feudal" system (as loosely used), whose production is chiefly agricultural and limited, although it can expand. Power lies primarily in the hands of landowners, and life is not unduly invaded by modern technology. Vast areas of underdeveloped countries away from a few urban and mining or plantation nodes roughly fit this stage, although only southern Arabian countries, Bhutan, and a few others would be a good fit. From the standpoint of geographers, historians, anthropologists, and others, the differences in traditional societies would be vastly greater than the few similarities that Rostow sees.

Stage 2. This preconditions for take-off stage is one of transition. Spiritual mobilization is one of the dynamics, with the power-elite at the very least believing that there is necessity for change. Economic progress is favored, partly for economic purposes (e.g., private profit, better life for children), but even more for extraneous purposes (e.g., national power, national dignity, general social welfare, and others). There is increasing demand for a centralized state. Modern institutions rise—for mobilizing capital, for concentrating various forms (economic, social, political) of power, and for other purposes. Investment increases, although usually slowly because of competing pressures from increases in population and rising consumption standards. Most of the underdeveloped countries are probably in this stage: Ghana, Iran, Thailand, and many others.

Stage 3. The take-off stage is characterized by Rostow as involving compound-interest reaction-type change. Old blocks of resistance to steady growth are overcome. The political institutions encourage increased production. Growth becomes the normal condition and production both absolutely and per capita increases rapidly. The accelerated economic growth rapidly transforms the social and political structures. This stage, according to Rostow, usually lasts from forty to sixty years. Aggressive men are in charge (no matter what kind of power-elite), who know where they are going, and how to accumulate and to use capital. Great Britain reached this take-off stage by 1783, France and the United States by 1830, Germany about 1850, Japan about 1875, Russia and Canada about 1890, India and China perhaps by 1950 (the last two seem more doubtful examples by the early 1960's than they did in the mid-1950's).

Stage 4. The drive to maturity stage means capacity to move beyond the original economic activities that started the industrial take-off (e.g., mechanical transport, heavy industry, light industry, or others), and to turn modern technology to anything (though not everything at once) that the country chooses to produce. At this point a society can do anything it really wants to do. Power is somewhat diffused, as compared with the take-off stage, mainly because the mass of population insists on getting some benefit from the increased production called into being. Another possibility is the use of some of the surplus for international expansion: maybe foreign investment, maybe grants, maybe imperialism. The U.S.S.R., Italy, and Japan, among many, are in this stage at present.

Stage 5. Probably only the United States is well into the high mass consumption stage, although wealthy societies in northwest Europe may have recently entered it. Further extension of technology continues, but production problems are no longer the overriding consideration they were earlier. Overt aims and wants are more likely to be concerned with consumption: cheap mass automobiles, household luxury goods, social welfare and security, higher education for all children, and the like. The problems of life, according to Rostow, become more philosophical than economic.

Rostow's model, like the power-elite model viewed earlier, is useful if kept in perspective. Generalization about stages is difficult because no large society is ever entirely in any one stage. The power-elite and the middle class are likely to see their society moving more rapidly than other classes in that society. Of the 120 or so societies now existing, it is doubtful if even half could be labeled as within one or the other stage that would meet the test of consensus.

PERSPECTIVE

The spread of urban-industrial civilization over most of mankind in the next century or two seems certain, but the problems of timing, routing, and costs and the eventual (political-economic-social) consequences are not predictable with any certainty. However, it is reasonably clear that what mainly limits rapid investment and other desired change in most underdeveloped societies is not so much a lack of natural resources to develop, or of ordinary capital to invest, but a lack of confidence that the human factors (government, management, labor) will work together to make the investments productive. The dynamic elements are organizing ability and modern technology in a context of disciplined society—which have been surveyed in this chapter. The next chapter will survey the limiting factors, population, natural resources, and certain kinds of capital that need to be built into them.

SUGGESTED READINGS

ALMOND, GABRIEL A., and COLEMAN, JAMES S. (eds.). *The Politics of the Developing Areas.* Princeton University Press, 1960. Pp. 591.

BAUER, PETER T., and YAMEY, BASIL S. *The Economics of Underdeveloped Countries.* University of Chicago Press, 1957. Pp. 271.

BUCHANAN, NORMAN S., and ELLIS, HOWARD S. *Approaches to Economic Development.* New York: Twentieth Century Fund, 1955. Pp. 494.

FOURASTIE, JEAN. *The Causes of Wealth.* Glencoe, Ill.: The Free Press of Glencoe, 1960. Pp. 246.

HIGHET, GILBERT. *The Mind of Man.* New York: Oxford University Press, 1954. Pp. 183.

HIRSCHMAN, ALBERT O. *The Strategy of Economic Development.* Yale University Press, 1958. Pp. 217.

HOFFER, ERIC. *The Passionate State of Mind.* New York: Harper & Row, 1955. Pp. 151.

HOFFER, ERIC. *The True Believer.* New York: Harper & Row, 1951. Pp. 176.

HOSELITZ, BERT F. (ed.). *The Progress of Underdeveloped Areas.* University of Chicago Press, 1952. Pp. 297.

HOSELITZ, BERT F. *Sociological Aspects of Economic Growth.* Glencoe, Ill.: The Free Press of Glencoe, 1960. Pp. 250.

JANSEN, MARIUS B. (ed.). *Changing Japanese Attitudes Toward Modernization.* Princeton University Press, 1965. Pp. 546.

KERR, CLARK, DUNLOP, JOHN T., HARBISON, FREDERICK H., and MYERS, CHARLES A. *Industrialism and Industrial Man.* Harvard University Press, 1960. Pp. 331.

MEIER, GERALD M., and BALDWIN, ROBERT E. *Economic Development: Theory, History, Policy.* New York: Wiley, 1957. Pp. 588.

MEIER, RICHARD L. *Science and Economic Development.* The Technology Press of Massachusetts Institute of Technology, 1956. Pp. 266.

MOULTON, HAROLD G. *Controlling Factors in Economic Development.* Washington, D.C.: Brookings Institute, 1949. Pp. 397.

ROSTOW, W. W. *The Stages of Economic Growth: A Non-Communist Manifesto.* Cambridge University Press, 1960. Pp. 179.

SINAI, I. R. *The Challenge of Modernization.* London: Chatto & Windus, 1964. Pp. 256.

SPICER, EDWARD H. *Human Problems in Technological Change.* New York: Russell Sage Foundation, 1952. Pp. 301.

STALEY, EUGENE (ed.). *Creating an Industrial Civilization.* New York: Harper & Row, 1952. Pp. 368.

STALEY, EUGENE. *The Future of Underdeveloped Countries: Political Implications of Economic Development.* New York: Harper & Row, 1954. Pp. 410.

UNITED NATIONS, DEPARTMENT OF ECONOMIC AND SOCIAL AFFAIRS. *Processes and Problems of Industrialization in Under-developed Countries.* New York: United Nations, 1955. Pp. 152.

WEAVER, RICHARD M. *Ideas Have Consequences.* University of Chicago Press, 1948. Pp. 190.

WILLIAMSON, HAROLD F., and BUTTRICK, JOHN A. *Economic Development: Principles and Patterns.* Englewood Cliffs, N.J.: Prentice-Hall, 1954. Pp. 576.

ZOLLSCHAN, GEORGE K., and HIRSCH, WALTER. *Explorations in Social Change.* London: Routledge & Kegan Paul, 1964. Pp. 832.

4

Modern Economic Development: Population and Natural Resources

The changing standards of motivation and consumption and the changing technology briefly assessed in the last chapter are greatly important in initiating and implementing the change from agrarian to urban-industrial civilization, but are of core interest to the behavioral and engineering fields. Geographers and others interested mainly in location and raw materials problems and prospects are more interested in the primarily passive factors of population and natural resources, although they have a marginal interest in the primarily active factors because these provide an insight into the grand strategy of economic development.

Population's main interest to the geographer is not because man is his core interest, as in demography, but because of the tendency to assess resource availability, economic progress, and other generalizations in per capita perspective as much as in areawise or other absolute perspective. Population is probably the greatest obstacle (among the easily visible to naive insight) to rapid and cheap modernization, absorbing a third to a half of new income for decades during the transition to more viable patterns of high urbanization and slackened growth. To change radically population patterns and other characteristics is usually more difficult than changing facility patterns inherited from the past.

Partly because demographic obstacles are even more limiting in the short and medium run than habitat limitations, and partly because the greater part of this book is concerned with habitat resources and resistances, this chapter will examine population more carefully than natural resources.

POPULATION

Economic development is continuing to alter population structure and other characteristics throughout the world, solving some problems and creating new ones. Variations in the ways that people make their living are changing the urban-rural ratio, which reflects changes in occupational patterns. Economic well-being favors improved health and sanitation conditions, resulting in lower death rates and rapid increases until eventually reduced birth rates re-establish an equilibrium.

Of the population dynamics affecting resource-use and other aspects of development as they bankrupt Iron Age and Oceanic Age fossil patterns, accelerated urbanization and growth are most important. During the next century, the potentials and problems are much greater in continuing urbanization than in accelerated growth, although less visible to naive insight. This accelerated urbanization is mainly powered by economic change, by the faster growth of industrial and service occupations than of agricultural and related occupations.

Among the various population growth problems, most important is the closure of the demographic gap, regaining control over human reproduction, but under modern conditions of low death and birth rates instead of the premodern equilibrium opposing high death and birth rates.

World Population Distribution

The distribution of world population is markedly uneven, with over three-quarters of the 3 billion plus of present mankind concentrated in three major nodes comprising less than a fifth of the earth's land area. The largest is the humid Far East (or Monsoon Asia), where half of mankind lives on a tenth of the earth's surface. The second major human grouping includes Europe and adjacent southwestern U.S.S.R., with nearly a quarter of mankind occupying little more than 5 per cent of the earth's land surface. In the southeastern quadrant of North America is the third major cluster, with some 5 per cent of mankind living on somewhat less than that fraction of the land area.

Smaller population-nodes in Latin America, sub-Saharan Africa, and the Middle East, plus several others in the mainly empty stretches of North America, U.S.S.R., and Oceania, together add up to the equivalent of another North American cluster.

The remaining three-quarters of the earth's land surface is either sparsely inhabited or uninhabited. About a quarter of all land is desert and low-grade brushland and grassland, where aridity restricts settlement to oases. Another quarter consists of ice-covered land, tundra, and high-latitude brushland where cold and physiological aridity hampers any extensive development, but where islands of mineral and recreational resources are increasingly exploited. Most of the remaining quarter of wasteland and low-grade land-use consists either of rugged upland country limited in development by steep slopes and high altitude or of tropical forests and shrublands where development is hindered by infertile soils, excessive rainfall, and rank growth of both vegetation and micro forms of animal life.

In explaining the present pattern of world population and its inherent instability under present conditions, useful analysis can be made by viewing that pattern in the light of changing habitat, culture, and man considerations. Generalizations about population distribution and redistribution are not best analyzed in the framework of habitat (physical-environmental) associations, except in the case of those remnants of primitive society still existing. The more complex the culture under consideration, the less directly habitat factors influence population distribution, and the more important do cultural changes and demographic stage become in determining the grand strategy of redistribution.

Cultural changes. Among the cultural factors having an important bearing on the redistribution of population are occupational structure, material technology, social (institutional) technology, and social objectives.

Of the various population redistribution tendencies, most important is the phenomenal urbanization based mainly upon greater employment opportunities in industrial and services occupations than in the agricultural and extractive occupations (see Tables 4–1 and 4–2 and the graph on page 72). Under hypothetical use of prospective technology (i.e., complete factory-office automation), an ideal occupational structure might include only 5 per cent of the labor force in agriculture and related activities, perhaps 20 per cent in industrial activities (with half of these in construction and utilities), and the remaining three-quarters in distribution (transport-commerce), government, and other professional and personal services.

TABLE 4–1

World: Total and Urban Population, by Great-Region and Economic-Type of Society, 1962–1964 Average-Annual

	Total Regional Population		Population in Cities 20,000 and Over		"Officially" Urban	
	Millions	Per Cent of World Total	Millions	Per Cent of World Total	Millions	Per Cent of World Total
North America	210	6.6	100	13.6	150	14.2
Western Europe	315	9.9	140	19.0	190	18.0
Eastern Europe (including the U.S.S.R.)	350	11.0	115	15.6	171	16.0
Oceania	17	0.5	11	1.5	12	1.1
Latin America	220	6.9	55	7.5	100	9.4
Sub-Saharan Africa	210	6.6	19	2.6	25	2.4
Middle East (including North Africa)	143	4.5	28	3.9	40	3.8
Non-Communist Far East	950	29.9	175	23.8	240	22.7
Communist Far East	765	24.1	92	12.5	130	12.3
World	3,180	100.0	735	100.0	1,058	100.0
Over U.S. $1,000 per capita	672	21.1	321	43.7	470	44.5
U.S. $450–$999 per capita	265	8.3	100	13.6	118	11.1
High-income countries	937	29.4	421	57.3	588	55.6
U.S. $250–$449 per capita	241	7.6	50	6.8	70	6.6
U.S. $125–$249 per capita	243	7.7	35	4.8	48	4.5
Under U.S. $125 per capita	1,759	55.3	229	31.1	352	33.3
Low-income countries	2,243	70.6	314	42.7	470	44.4

TABLE 4–2

World: Labor Force and Sector Breakdown, by Great-Region and Economic-Type of Society, 1962–1964 Average-Annual

	Per Cent of Regional Population	Millions	Per Cent of World Total	Agriculture Sector	Industry Sector	Services [1] Sector
				(3%'s = 100.0%)		
North America	39	81	6.3	7.4	31.7	59.9
Western Europe	44	140	10.9	21.5	40.8	37.7
Eastern Europe (including the U.S.S.R.)	44	155	12.2	38.5	32.6	28.9
Oceania	40	7	0.5	18.0	35.7	46.3
Latin America	37	81	6.3	50.5	21.2	28.3
Sub-Saharan Africa	38	80	6.3	70.0	9.7	20.3
Middle East (including North Africa)	37	53	4.1	64.0	10.6	25.4
Non-Communist Far East	40	385	30.0	64.0	13.4	22.6
Communist Far East	39	300	23.4	65.0	10.2	24.8
World	40	1,282	100.0	52.2	19.3	28.5
Over U.S. $1,000 per capita	43	291	22.7	21.0	36.3	42.7
U.S. $450–$999 per capita	43	113	8.8	31.8	33.8	34.4
High-income countries	43	404	31.5	24.0	35.6	40.4
U.S. $250–$449 per capita	41	99	7.7	50.6	22.7	26.7
U.S. $125–$249 per capita	37	89	7.0	63.7	12.7	23.6
Under U.S. $125 per capita	39	690	53.8	67.5	10.2	22.3
Low-income countries	39	878	68.5	65.2	11.8	23.0

SOURCE: Adapted from United Nations data, with adjustments to fill in gaps.

[1] Includes armed forces and other "institutionalized" groups often ignored.

WORLD: RURAL-URBAN AND LABOR FORCE COMPOSITION, BY GREAT-REGION AND ECONOMIC-TYPE OF SOCIETY, 1962-1964 AVERAGE-ANNUAL

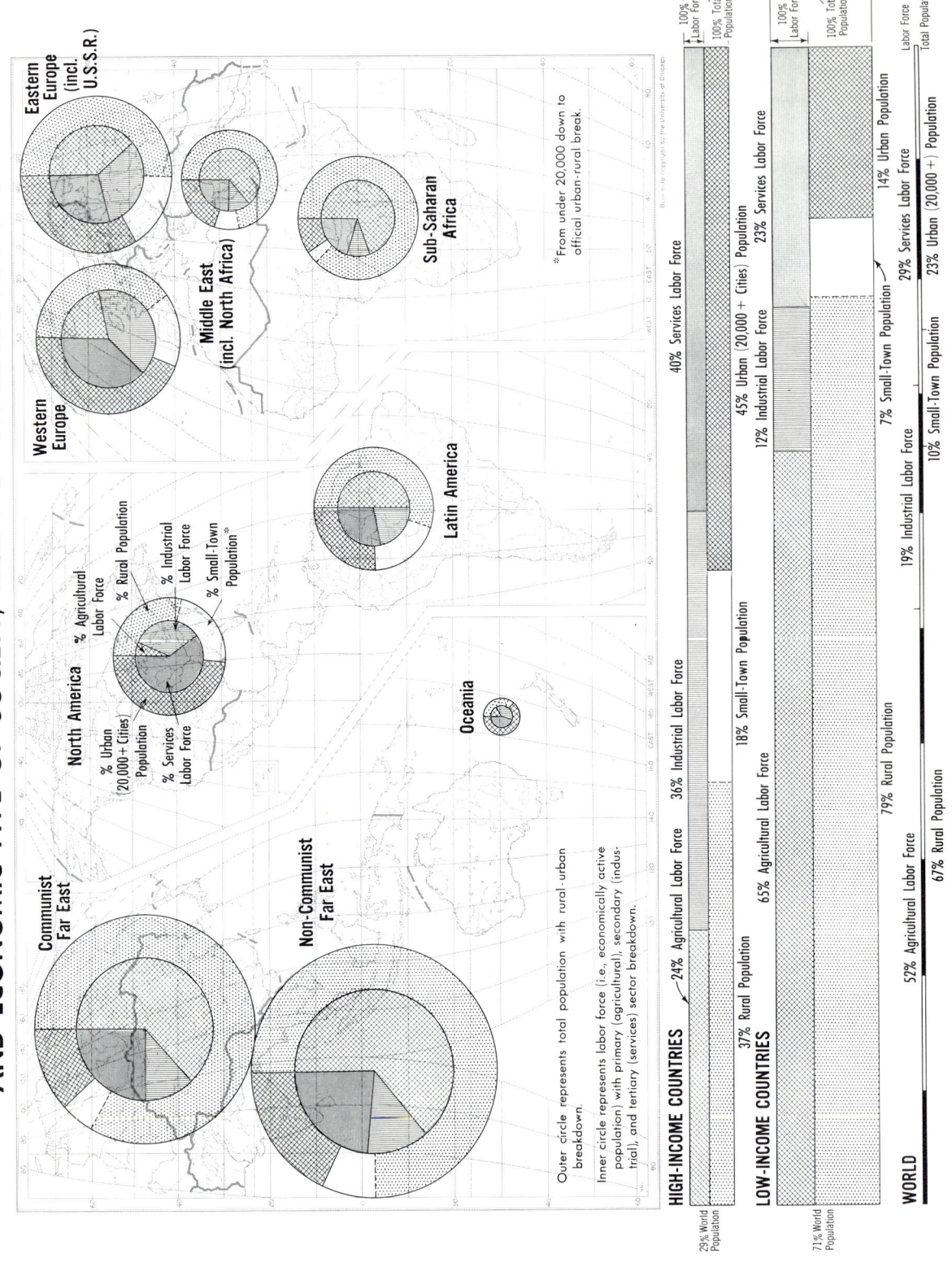

In present high-income societies considered as a group, less than one-quarter of the labor force is now engaged in primary activities, and that fraction is constantly dropping as the test of economic efficiency is increasingly applied to small-scale and medium-scale agriculture, stock-raising, forestry, and fishing. Even adding rooted or tied industries and services (i.e., allied manufacturing providing purchased factors of production and processing crude materials near their source plus allied distribution and other services in rural areas), the future rural and related small-town population will be as small a part of modern civilization as truly urban activities were in the premodern agrarian civilization.

Urban activities include practically all of the footloose-type industries and market-oriented industries and services in a mature urban-industrial society. The footloose industries and services include wholesale commerce, over three-quarters of all manufacturing, and certain specialized professional and personal services that can choose their location and attract distant clientele. In most cases such activities are free of heavy costs associated with the collection of raw materials and the marketing of cheap heavy products, so they are relatively free to locate where the combined costs of production are cheapest. Over a suitable period of time (i.e., life expectancy of facilities), such activities are almost seminomadic. With increased automation, such activities will probably require relatively less of the labor force than at present, perhaps under one-quarter of the total.

Those activities that must be located near consumers include nearly half of the workers in an urban-industrial society, including most workers in construction, retail trade, most professional and personal services, and some manufacturing. Most activities in these employment areas will probably become even more important in the future than at present, and might well furnish two-thirds of future job opportunities.

Accompanying this modern tendency to proliferate industrial and service activities is the tendency toward urbanization, both in terms of dwelling and of setting the institutional and mores patterns of modern civilization. Those effects of urbanization favorable to economic progress include: greater occupational diversification, greater opportunity for social mobility, greater readiness to adapt, the dynamic influence of technical progress which cities reflect through their contacts with other centers of technical and economic progress, and the external economies that increase productive efficiency plus the internal economies of scale made possible by units that can serve broader and easily reached markets. As usual, urbanization is a phenomenon that results in net progress, but not pure progress. Those aspects unfavorable to economic progress include: new wants being created more rapidly in cities than industrialization creates the means to satisfy them, social disorganization taking many forms (e.g., change from close primary loyalty-units to rootless existence for many, change from morally based ethics to amoral beliefs and practices, confused social stratification), and personal disorganization manifest in such conditions as juvenile delinquency, crime, and vice.

Less than 3 per cent of the world's population at the beginning of the Industrial Revolution lived in urban centers of 20,000 or more inhabitants, compared with nearly one-quarter at present. The regional concentration in such centers varies widely. The wealthy societies have nearly two-fifths of their total population in such centers, while the low-income societies average only one-sixth of their population.

Technical change. Changes in material technology since the Industrial Revolution have mainly tended toward greater concentration of population, especially in cities, but also toward dispersal of population, especially of agricultural population into areas formerly the exclusive domain of the wandering gatherers and herdsmen.

Among the determinants of urban concentration have been: improvements in mobility of cheap, bulky materials due to mechanical transport, increased mobility of labor due partly to physical, but just as much to social, accessibility, economics of scale and specialization, and increasing preference for highly fabricated goods

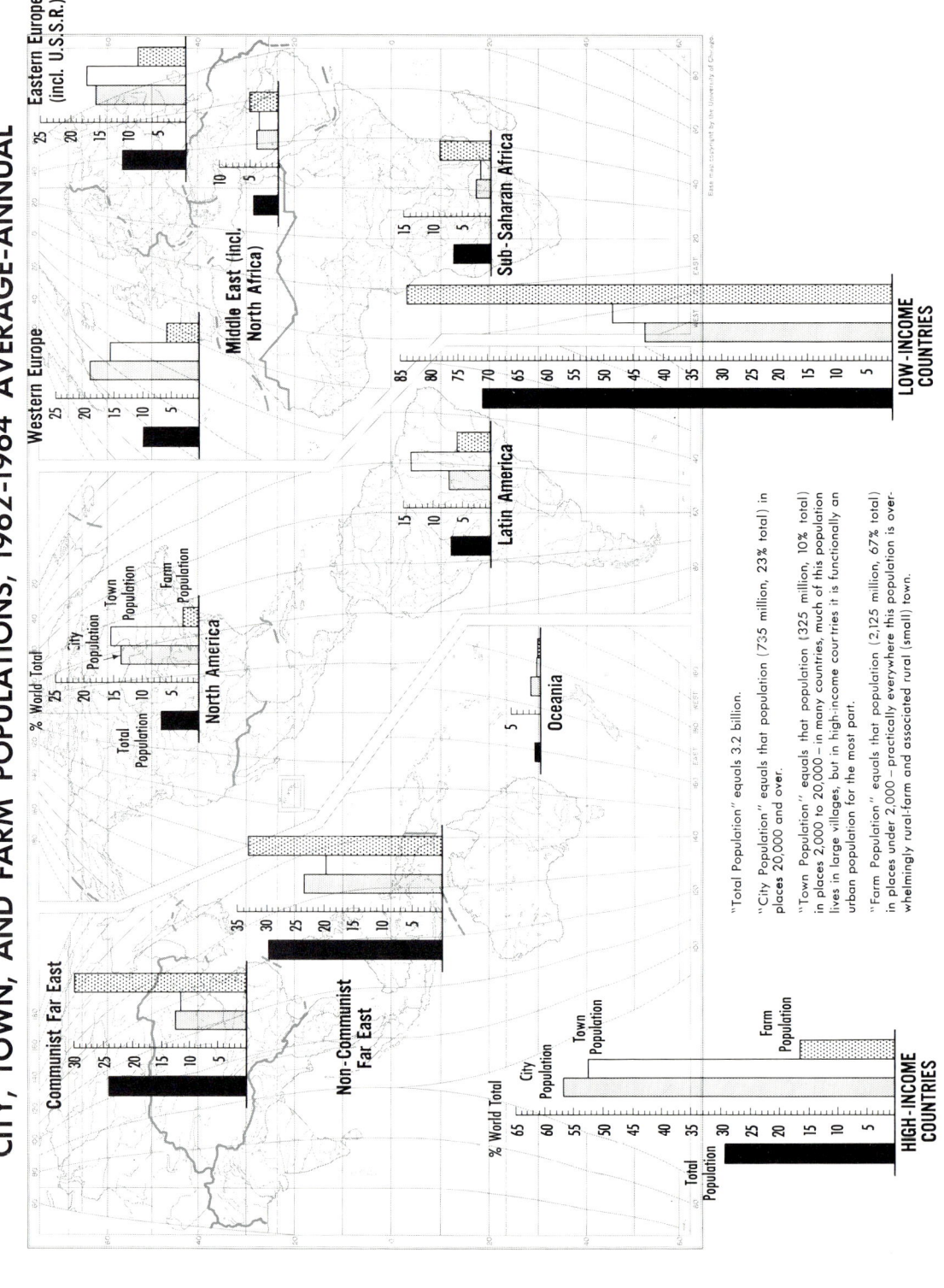

and for services, all of which have greatly diminished man's direct dependency upon land and natural resources and have greatly extended his range of choice in economic activities when he acts collectively. As a result, the more complex a culture, the less directly do habitat factors influence population distribution, and the more important do cultural changes become in determining redistribution.

Urbanization is important both to economic development and its complement, bankruptcy. By its nature (i.e., the close physical association of widely needed factors of production), urban associations bring about external economies which increase productive efficiency, and internal economies of scale made possible by broader and more easily reached markets. It is predominantly within urban centers that archaic value-systems and institutions can be drained of prestige and effectiveness and be superseded by functional substitutes of the sorts needed for modernization.

Urbanization affects natural resources availability both by its pressure of standards and by its productive contributions. Urban consumption is usually the main commercial market for most crude materials, especially of high-quality ones. Changes in occupation, class, residence, and other characteristics affect market trends continually; for example, early urbanization usually involves longer work-years so per capita energy-food intake goes up, while later developments usually increase sedentary activities, which (coupled with higher incomes) increases demand for superior protein and protective foods and for higher-quality non-food materials. The city demand for superior quality in food and non-food materials often involves urban enterprise and labor as well as capital participation in agriculture (e.g., contract-farming to produce broiler chickens, lean hogs, baby beef). Finally, ultimate success in achieving better equilibrium in agriculture and other primary activities depends as much upon what happens in cities as in the countryside; if city populations pay a "fair price," increasing production based upon permanent and more productive agriculture is better assured.

Among the determinants that have led to the expansion of resource-oriented activities into formerly marginal or inhospitable regions are such technical changes as modern irrigation, which has allowed the use of desert and low-grade steppelands for farming purposes by high-dam storage and greater command. Cheap mechanical techniques have allowed dry-farming use of subhumid grasslands and brushlands previously restricted to nomads. Cheap chemical (fertilization and pest-disease control) technology has allowed wider use of infertile soils previously left in natural vegetation or only occasionally farmed through shifting-cultivation technology. Many forms of mechanical transportation have allowed economic usage of extractive activities in high-latitude and other remote areas. When all of these technical changes leading to population dispersal are considered, they are much less important than those changes leading to urban concentration, but are more visible on a map.

Organizational changes. The existing forms of social organization have some influence upon the distribution of population. Some theorists have believed that capitalistic urban-industrial societies inevitably have excessive urban concentration as a result of worker and consumer sovereignty, leading to excessive growth of highly specialized occupations, dependence upon faraway sources of food, mechanization of agriculture, and other characteristics, while a socialistic form of industrialized society would lead to a planned relocation of population. Such a comparison was more plausible before wealthy Communist states developed; now it seems more likely to represent a lag than a fundamental ideological difference.

Attitude changes. Both political and social changes in attitude have influenced the size and distribution of population. Most important of the political efforts has been the controls over international migration, and there has been unquestionably more success in this direction during this past generation than earlier. Governments have also tried to alter the distribution of population within national boundaries, but effects are debatable and probably less important in a world context that the successful limiting of international movements. Reasons for internal redistribution include policies aiming at improved defense security, settling of sparsely populated frontier areas, attempts at greater self-sufficiency, and other measures to improve internal and external security of the state.

The proportion of national income expended for services and manufactures not heavily dependent on place-bound resources has steadily increased as per capita income has risen. Such a social attitude has been a major factor in increasing the proportion of a developed population concentrated in urban-nodes.

The institutional and attitudinal links between economic activities prevent easy relocation of population masses. This is related to the difficulty of successfully establishing a new industry until complementary and supplementary industry and services have also been established. Even the active assistance of government is often thwarted in attempts to move such industrial complexes.

Overview. The world will probably be able to support the 10 to 15 billion or more population expected within the next century if there is peace, if urban-industrial civilization diffuses throughout mankind, and if the urbanized majority of mankind will pay enough for food and other materials to permit farmers and other primary workers to make fullest use of the potentialities inherent in dynamic science and technology. This urbanization of mankind, not only in terms of residence and occupation, but also in terms of the evolution of satisfactory value-systems (e.g., new primary-loyalty groupings) and institutions, is inherently the most difficult population problem to solve because of its uniqueness, although it is less publicized than the problem of closing the demographic gap (i.e., to bring down birth rates), which has been accomplished many times in the past by many different types of cultures.

Habitat influences. While cultural factors influencing population redistribution tend to be causal, physical geographic factors tend to bulk largest in negative or limiting effects. Most important, the limitations set by climate chiefly account for the fact that about half of the earth's land area is inhabited by less than one person per square mile. About half of this adverse climatic influence is due to adverse temperature and half to adverse precipitation.

In both high and low latitudes, the indirect influences have probably had the most undesirable effects on man and his domesticates. Cold temperatures may increase susceptibility to respiratory diseases, and such characteristics as the long nights, low solar intensity even in summer, and others may have undesirable psychological effects. More important, the productive capacity of the cold regions is greatly reduced by the shortness of the growing season. Even Soviet successes show no sign that such high-latitude development adds significantly to mankind's core-ecumene regions.

Susceptibility to intestinal diseases is increased by hot climates, prickly heat may be caused by high temperatures alone, and low-latitude radiation may have some adverse effects, but one must note that large populations have resided for long periods in areas of maximum and highest average temperature. However, high temperatures are also favorable to high population density in that they promote rapid growth of vegetation, allowing multiple cropping and the production of a wider range of crops than is possible in cooler areas, and reduce requirements for shelter and clothing. The lack of a seasonal check on the growth of insects, fungi, and bacteria promotes disease among man and his plants and animals, and the lack of frost makes for certain problems in soil conservation, but modern chemistry promises more control in low latitudes than ever before.

Technological developments have tended to increase the range of temperature regimes under which man can operate effectively, and there are prospects that reduction of heat and humidity may turn out to be as cheap as control of cold in the past. However, for the present, mid-latitude climates and those of adjacent high latitudes and the subtropics with rainfall between 20 and 60 inches provide reasonable phys-

800 to 1,000 miles of land instead of the best system of inland waterways on earth.

Another important abstract asset is the association of a number of favorable physical and biological patterns. The great plain of Western Europe has a striking combination of natural accessibility, reliably humid climate, mineral resources, moderate landforms, and excellent soils. Alluvial areas in the Middle East, Far East, and elsewhere are also superlative resource-bases because of associated flatness, rich soils, abundant water, easy accessibility, and other assets. A single asset pattern is not nearly as valuable in population-supporting capacity by itself.

Overview. Urban-industrial civilization has mainly a concentrating effect upon world population redistribution. The main change is the increasing urbanization, by which the majority of mankind seems destined to clot in the 1 per cent [1] of the world's land area occupied by cities and related facilities. Even in agricultural areas, the main long-term change is toward concentration on the best land-use types. To many, this tendency is masked by the large areas that continue to be used extensively by small numbers of agriculturalists supplied with mechanical and other adjuncts, or by part-time populations. The chemical and biological innovations have favored intensification from their beginnings, while the mechanical innovations favored extensive use in the beginning but now are evolving toward variants that favor intensification as well.

Demographic change. Changes in the structure and distribution of world population take place primarily through the medium of births and deaths in various areas, and secondarily through migration between areas. In the long view, natural-increase rates and net-migration rates reflect resource change and cultural change, but in the short run demographic custom fixes such change to a very slow pace. Consequently, to reach a new equilibrium takes much time, up to now one to two centuries for a fundamental change.

[1] Perhaps double this if man-made reservoirs and man-sterilized land in the midst of facilities were included.

The inherited distribution of population is a factor of major importance in determining future population distribution, especially within a time interval of several generations. This role is much like that of natural resistances in influencing population redistribution, essentially a negative or limiting role rather than a positive one fostering structural change.

Over the long run, variations of natural-increase rates are mainly related to economic conditions, but in the short run the relationship is not necessarily such as to bring high rates of natural increase in areas where economic opportunities are plentiful, or low rates where opportunities are scarce. On the contrary, relatively large excesses of births over deaths are commonly found in areas of comparatively poor economic opportunities, often for four to six generations after economic development began.

However, in the short run, migration does act as a mechanism for partial adjustment of population imbalance in relation to the location of economic opportunities. Internal migration within countries has especially increased, so that the inherited distribution of population exercises less influence than formerly upon the areal pattern of new economic activities. It is at the international level that the influence of the distribution of the population upon the distribution of economic activities is greatest, as the international wage structure is affected sufficiently to influence the international distribution of economic activities.

An increase in trade between areas may serve in lieu of migration as a mechanism in bringing about some adjustment between population and economic activities. The feasibility of this alternative depends upon the possibility of increasing export-oriented economic opportunities in the countries of surplus labor, through the development of labor-intensive branches of agriculture, industry, and services that find wide markets abroad. This alternative is especially attractive at the international level, where the mores against freer movement of certain goods and certain services (e.g., tourism) are less restrictive than those against free movement of migrants.

The influence of existing population distribution upon the location of economic opportunities within a country includes the following aspects: (1) Since the distribution of consuming power is considerably determined by the distribution of population, and since a large fraction of economic activity is consumer-oriented, a given distribution of population (whatever its origin) will immediately dominate the distribution of consumer-oriented activities. (2) Older, more heavily settled areas are likely to have greater overpopulation and underemployment and lower wages and therefore attract labor-intensive industries (unless this labor-cost advantage is counterbalanced by disadvantages). (3) The presence of population in an area will often provide external economies which stimulate industrial development—especially important in underdeveloped regions, where supplies of labor and size of markets may be the determinants in affecting the types of early modernization.

Overview. Since the Industrial Revolution, many types of changes have interacted to alter considerably both the relative numbers of people in various regions of the world and the distribution of population within countries. Technological advances and changes in the occupational structure of the world economy have freed a large proportion of the people from their former dependency upon the land and other place-bound natural resources. The changes in technology and in consumers' wants have re-enforced the tendency for economic opportunities and population to be concentrated in certain localities, particularly in the great metropolitan agglomerations. The desires of the people and the policies of governments with reference to the growth and distribution of national populations have been shifting, and there has recently been an increased degree of governmental control over migration and natural increase, especially in the countries with planned economies. The pattern of areal variations in birth and death rates has been changing, bringing about falling natural increase rates in highly developed societies and rising natural increase rates in economically less developed countries, and also bringing about higher natural increase rates in rural areas than in the urban areas of many countries.

TABLE 4–3

World: Natural Increase Rates, by Great-Region and Economic-Type of Society, 1962–1964 Average-Annual

	Deaths per 1,000 Population	Births per 1,000 Population	Natural Increase per 1,000 Population
North America	9	24	15
Western Europe	10	18	8
Eastern Europe (including the U.S.S.R.)	9	25	16
Oceania	11	27	16
Latin America	14	40	26
Sub-Saharan Africa	25	45	20
Middle East (including North Africa)	21	45	24
Non-Communist Far East	19	40	21
Communist Far East	22	40	18
World	16	34	18
Over U.S. $1,000 per capita countries	10	22	12
U.S. $450–$999 per capita countries	12	26	14
High-income countries	11	24	13
U.S. $250–$449 per capita countries	15	40	25
U.S. $125–$249 per capita countries	22	42	20
Under U.S. $125 per capita countries	23	40	17
Low-income countries	21	41	20

Source: Mainly adapted from United Nations sources, with unofficial sources used in compiling Communist Far East data.

World Population Increase

The numerical expansion of the human race has been sporadic in any long view. In every inhabited region of the earth there have been periods when the population grew at a comparatively rapid rate, and other periods when it remained nearly stationary or decreased. The cycles of growth have not been synchronous in different areas. Diversity in the patterns of economic and social change has been matched by a diversity of population trends.

Rapid increases have been correlated with the development and diffusion of more complicated culture. Paleolithic culture probably saw only 2 to 3 million population toward the end of its nearly million-year period. The Mesolithic culture may have seen a doubling in the world population in the period of the retreat of the last great ice cap. Neolithic culture (8000 to 5500 B.C.) may have supported some 20 million by the time it had diffused over most of the world. Bronze Age civilization (5500 to 1500 B.C.) may have reached 40 million after diffusing from the Middle East over Eurasia. The early Iron Age civilization (1500 to 250 B.C.) probably passed the 100 million mark, and late Iron Age civilization (250 B.C. to A.D. 1500) reached 300 million, mainly in the early centuries when the Roman and Han Empires were at their peak. The Western-European-dominated Oceanic civilization reached about 1 billion population before it evolved into the modern urban-industrial civilization around 1800. Partial diffusion of modern civilization has already seen a tripling in mankind's numbers, and an additional doubling by the end of this century is almost assured (what additional growth may occur before relative stability in numbers is reached cannot be foreseen).

The graph on page 82 shows considerable regional differences in present annual growth rates, with the better-off regions having the lowest natural increase and the poorest regions all having rates above the world average.

Death controls. The problem of curbing population growth is more a problem of timing than of absolute difficulty. Practically all of the population growth of modern times has been caused by the decline of death rates before the decline of birth rates, that is, by the modern demographic gap or vital revolution. Before 1850, such growth was mainly caused indirectly, due to dropping death rates caused by increased wealth and order produced during the Oceanic Age by early phases of the commercial, agricultural, and industrial revolutions. Since 1850, lowering death rates have been related more to the medical, sanitary, and social welfare revolutions which have totally eliminated many diseases and reduced the incidence of others. The resulting increases in population have not been sought for as an end in itself, but have been a by-product effect of the search for improved health and the prevention of premature death. Where the mass of population lives in great poverty, the most important factors contributing to low productivity are disease and illiteracy, and probably no other types of investment will produce a larger return per unit of outlay, or pose greater long-term problems (e.g., the economics of closing the demographic gap).

Factors that have contributed to reductions of mortality in modern times include: (1) the influence of economic development and rising income levels, (2) the influence of sanitary engineering and personal hygiene (e.g., purification of water supplies, public sewage systems, increased personal use of soap and easily laundered underclothing), (3) the influence of the development of medical sciences in controlling infectious diseases, and (4) the influence of social reforms, which diffused the benefits of the above changes irrespective of economic and social status (e.g., public-health laws, factory regulations, eradication of slums and other improvement of housing conditions, and many others).

During the seventeenth, eighteenth, and early nineteenth centuries, progress in reducing Western European death rates was due more to the rising levels of living than to the development of medical sciences and sanitary engineering. Until the end of the eighteenth century, mortality conditions were little better in the region than they are in the least developed countries today. Up to 1850 and the development of the modern sanitary revolution, declines in mortality were related mainly to the increased food supply fol-

WORLD: VITAL (Birth, Death, Natural Increase) RATES, BY GREAT-REGION AND ECONOMIC-TYPE OF SOCIETY, 1962-1964 AVERAGE-ANNUAL RATES

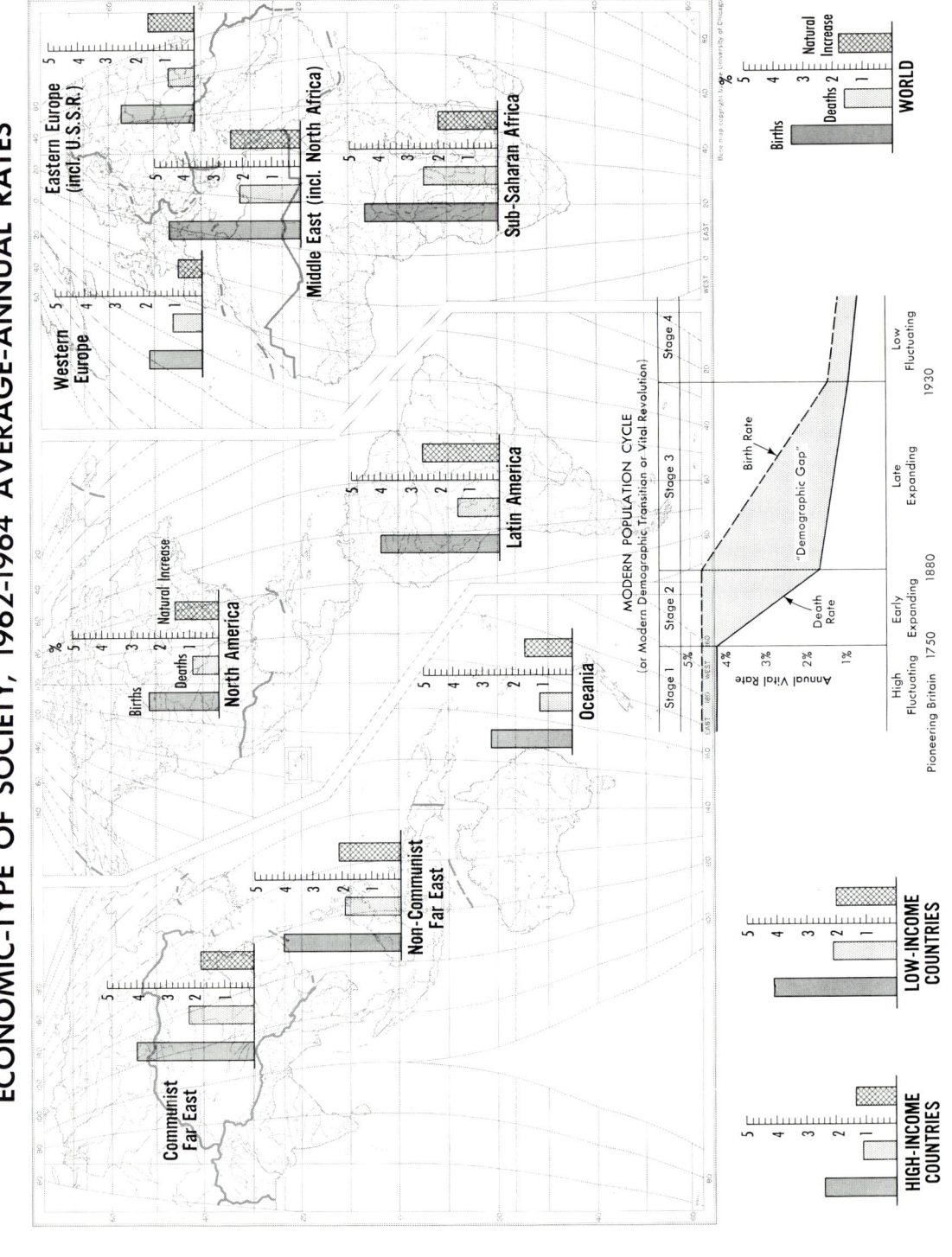

lowing the early stages of the European and colonial revolutions. New means of transportation facilitated a wider distribution of population, both overseas to newly discovered lands and internally to growing cities and areas of inner colonization, both depending as much upon Amerindian domesticates as upon Old World ones. Other technological progress insured the means of living for greater numbers of people: one series of mechanical, biological, and institutional changes began to make possible cultivation of grasslands and northern forest areas on a vast scale, and another series of changes began greatly intensified use of already cultivated areas (in Western Europe and Japan, especially).

After 1850, medical sciences and sanitary engineering became relatively more important than rising levels of living in reducing premature death. In the twentieth century, the social welfare state accelerated the tendency. Today, some of these non-economic causes of mortality decreases give rise to new problems, especially in the underdeveloped societies: (1) The newly developing countries have the benefit of techniques and other knowledge that evolved gradually in more advanced countries. (2) It has become possible to achieve a reduction in mortality in poor countries at relatively low costs (frequently personnel and facilities, and sometimes financial aid, have been provided from outside with relatively little cost to the benefiting country)—because mortality rates have been extremely high to begin with, large reductions have been possible with the application of simple and relatively inexpensive techniques. (3) There is good evidence that public health and medical techniques have provided for the maintenance and extension of human life without an accompanying improvement in economic conditions.

With the continued decline in mortality, the difference between the death rates of the upper and the lower socioeconomic strata of society has become smaller. The decline in mortality has not been uniform for all age groups, the greatest decline occurring among infants and young children. For adults in the intermediate age groups the gains, though impressive, have been less than those for children and adolescents. For the age groups over seventy-five years, only slight decreases in mortality rates have been recorded.

Internationally, there is still a large gap in the relative cost of replacing each generation and in maintaining good health. In the least developed societies, as much as 20 to 25 per cent of the income may be lost to poor health and premature death, while in the most developed societies such wastage is no more than 5 to 10 per cent.

Birth controls. The present period of rapid population growth, including perhaps another century, is not a typical one in mankind's reproductive history. For most of known human history up to the past few centuries, mankind has grown so slowly in numbers as to seem almost stationary when compared with present and prospective rates of growth. During most of this period, most women bore children near the physiological limit, but death (mainly in the form of infectious disease) was so common that only in unusual times was there any significant population increase, and this was often wiped out by periods of catastrophe. A tremendous amount of time, energy, and wealth was spent in bearing and rearing large numbers of children, a great proportion of whom died before reaching maturity. Most of the premature deaths were due to so-called natural causes (famine, disease, disorder), but some were due to deliberate human attempts to adjust numbers to the limited environment and to the pressure of standards (contraception, abortion, infanticide, exposure of the aged).

Beginning several centuries ago, among the peoples of Western Europe and their overseas and overland progeny, death rates were gradually brought under greater control than ever before, followed later by greater control over birth rates than ever before, mainly through new types of death controls but old types of birth controls. The interval was featured by large and, in some cases, tremendous increases of population. Due to productive advances made possible by the Industrial Revolution and European colonization of many regions of primitive cultures, these tremendous increments were not only supported, but at levels higher than had ever been attained before for large masses of people. Viewed in this perspective, the present population increments are the results of a significant change in human reproduction, which in the long run may be viewed among the greatest advances of mankind in this modern period. Under the new conditions, man is able to insure reproduction of himself with a fraction of the time and energy that it formerly took, with the result that he (mainly she) can devote greater attention to other aspects of life. The process of shifting from wasteful to relatively efficient replenishment of human life is called the modern population cycle (or the modern demographic transition, or the modern vital revolution).

Practically all of the population growth of modern times has been due to the decline of death rates before the decline of birth rates, to the so-called demographic gap. The reasons for the delayed decline of fertility, when the prevention or extinction of life seems physically much easier than the delaying of death, are mainly social in character. Basically, they center around the fact that many of the causes of early death can be avoided by increases in the production of material things, while the lowering of birth rates involves preliminary changes in social and family mores before the relatively simple physical prevention of conception will be effectively used by most classes of a society. Most societies are much more conservative about changing ideology, especially aspects involving religious and moral issues, than they are in changing technology. Some of the controls over mortality can be inaugurated or imposed by a small group in a society with a modicum of cooperation from the great bulk of the population: the inauguration or maintenance of public order, the extension of production when little change in the social order is involved, the extension of trade which decreases the changes of local famines by increasing the mobility of the food surplus, and the control of disease carriers to decrease the chances of epidemics. Most of the present and prospective population increase in the world is due to the inauguration or maintenance of such relatively simple mortality controls.

On the other hand, control of fertility involves changes in individual habits, which generally happen only after such controls are socially acceptable to the elite in the individual's class. In societies where high mortality historically forced high fertility to insure survival (practically all of them, most of the time), the laws, traditions, beliefs, habits, and accepted practices center about the maintenance of high birth rates. It is not that methods of preventing conception or of ending young life are unknown; practically all societies have such methods of population control and small groups in most societies do use such controls. Most techniques of contraception and abortion, as well as most of the reasons for using such methods, have been in existence for three to five millennia in complex cultures (and many primitive ones). Their use, however, was normally restricted to the relatively small upper classes, although under unusually adverse conditions their use in some premodern societies was widespread. What is modern is the almost universal attempt in the population of urban-industrial societies to use such methods as a normal and long-range method of improving individual and family status. To influence the average individual to use available or new methods of controlling fertility requires the loosening of the entire social fabric, which historically has made reproduction the easiest way for the average person to attain social prestige, and the acquiring of new interests, ambitions, and ideals. Chief among these are new interest in the pursuit of a higher standard of comfort and self-indulgence for himself and in insuring greater health, welfare, education, and prosperity for a few children rather than in rearing a large family for its own sake.

In societies that have attained modern population control, techniques have been diffused downward from the upper classes to the middle classes, and eventually to the poorer classes. The propaganda in support of new contraceptive devices and their adoption by the educated classes may have helped to spread the idea of family limitation, but cannot be considered as the main reason for its widespread adoption. The fall in the French birth rate, for example, occurred long before the modern contraceptive devices, and was apparently brought about mainly by the technique of withdrawal. However, there have been more factors promoting family limitation in cities to a greater extent than in the country. Family life in the city is less cohesive, because family members participate in other institutions and have a broader range of contacts outside the family. Children are not regarded as an economic asset in the city as they are in the country, as a smaller proportion of children, especially young children, generally contribute to the family income in the city, and those who contribute do so on a smaller scale. Status aspirations, the achievement of which may be handicapped where support of a large family is mandatory, are probably more prominent in the cities, as are the opportunities to gratify such ambitions. Finally, the spirit of rationality and independent tradition prevailing in cities is usually greater.

How long a period it will take for most of mankind to adopt the new economy in reproduction is conjectural. It has taken several centuries for the Western Europeans and their daughter societies to make the necessary psychological and social adjustments in adapting to this aspect of modern civilization. The decline has always been closely associated with the process of urbanization and industrialization and with the increasing employment of women outside the home. An unknown mix of factors, including colonialism, operating in Latin America, sub-Saharan Africa, the Middle East, and the Far East, has prevented the full application of available technical and social advances, and has so tended to prevent a new demographic balance so far. No one has yet devised universally acceptable techniques (although some believe that oral contraception may be one), or devised propaganda effective among people who have an abysmally low level of living before they urbanize. If a systematic population policy toward establishing fertility controls were pushed as rapidly and energetically as public health controls over mortality and morbidity are being pushed in many lands at present, and if the modernization of the economy and society were rapidly accomplished, the modern demographic transition in some of the retarded countries might be made in fifty to seventy-five years. However, it may take some of the retarded societies just as long a time as it took the European peoples to accomplish their vital revolution (150 to 200 years), in which cases it is doubtful if per capita gains in levels of living could be as rapid or as great as the grand visions promise.

Demographic investments. The longer that a society takes to close its demographic gap, the less its increase in real per capita levels of living, other things being equal. Demographic investments are those necessary for a growing population to maintain a constant level of living. In an underdeveloped country with a rapid population increase, demographic investments may use up most economic surplus, thus retarding the effects of economic development upon individual and social goals.

To provide the demographic investment necessary to support a 1 per cent population increase, savings from 2 per cent of the national income in a poor society up to 5 per cent in a wealthy society must be made. Thus a poor society with an annual increase of nearly 3 per cent (a common figure in many Latin American and Far Eastern societies) would find over 5 per cent of its national income absorbed by demographic investments with no rise in the level of living.

Economic investments are those that tend to raise the levels of living. With population remaining constant, the annual amount of savings necessary to produce a 1 per cent annual increase in per capita income would be about 3 to 4 per cent in most underdeveloped countries.

In underdeveloped countries just emerging from a purely agrarian form of economy, the average annual rate of savings is usually in the range from 5 to 10 per cent of its income. Assuming a capital:income ratio for normal investment of 5 to 1 and without capital import, such a savings will not yield any economic development if the rate of population growth is much over 2 per cent annually. If there were no population increase, a 2 to 3 per cent increase in per capita income might be achieved.

In underdeveloped countries that have achieved modest advances in modernization, savings often amount to 10 to 15 per cent of the national income in free societies, and are reported as from 15 to 25 per cent in centrally planned societies. Most of them must also support greater population growth than they did at an earlier stage, usually in the range of $1\frac{1}{2}$ to $2\frac{1}{2}$ per cent. Under such conditions, the less controlled societies increase their per capita income some 2 to 3 per cent annually, while the planned societies report (perhaps exaggerated) increases from 3 to 7 per cent.

Demographic stages. Changes in European vital rates in the past two centuries have followed a fairly regular pattern known as the population cycle. There is some evidence that this cycle may have universal implications, although the timing and techniques may vary considerably and the cultural resistances are more of an unknown.

1. The *high-fluctuating stage* was, presumably, the normal stage of mankind before the rise of dynamic science and technology some two centuries ago. It is hypothesized as a stage of high birth and death rates (both $3\frac{1}{2}$ to $4\frac{1}{2}$ per cent annually) and of a very slow and irregular increase of population. Even when there exists a current low rate of increase, there is a large potential growth because of the lack of secure control over either mortality or natality. Theoretically, the maximum population exists when mortality, rising as the increase of population lowers the conditions of living, fluctuates around the level of fertility. This maximum population may rise or fall with changes in the conditions of production and distribution, with major epidemics, or with changes in security. Considerable areas in sub-Saharan Africa and smaller areas elsewhere presumably are in this stage currently (lack of reliable censusing in such areas is the major uncertainty).

2. The *early-expanding stage* exists when the death rates fall rapidly, while the birth rates remain about constant (e.g., British death rate fell from $3\frac{1}{2}$ per cent in 1750 to 2 per cent in 1880, while the birth rate remained at $3\frac{1}{2}$ per cent). This results in rapid natural increase (e.g., the British natural increase rate of $1\frac{1}{2}$ per cent resulting in a tripling of the population in the 130 years). About half of mankind is today in this stage, almost all of the poorest underdeveloped regions.

3. The *late-expanding stage* occurs when the birth rates fall rapidly, with death rates also declining, but with increasing evidence that the demographic gap is beginning to close. In Britain it took fifty years for the birth rate to be halved (from $3\frac{1}{2}$ per cent in 1880 to $1\frac{1}{2}$ by 1930, with a population half again as large by the end of the period), with the death rate falling from 2 per cent to 1 per cent during the same period. In this stage, as in the previous two stages, technological advances are the prime source of support for population increase. Economic production tends to determine the size of population, but only indirectly and in relation to rising levels of living.

4. The *low-fluctuating stage* occurs when birth and death rates become fairly stable, resulting in a small and steady growth of population (e.g., British natural increase is about $\frac{1}{2}$ per cent annually, resulting from a birth rate of $1\frac{1}{2}$ per cent and a death rate of 1 per cent). This stage is characterized by limited procreation as contrasted with almost unlimited procreation early in the cycle. Technology progresses at an accelerated rate but ceases to have the same direct relationship with population changes. Population changes no longer conform to any simple population principle, and economic influences no longer determine the trend of population. The urban-industrial three-tenths of mankind is in this stage, although those societies that are offshoots of Western Europe tend to have population increase several times greater than the Narrow Seas' core-region.

Overview. An accelerated diffusion of modern technical civilization throughout most underdeveloped areas of the world will be one of the most important aspects of international relationships during the remainder of the twentieth century. Among the more significant migrating elements are dynamic science and technology, industrialization, commercialization, and population control. The need for the spread of the first three of these phenomena is generally more widely accepted than that of the fourth. That prolific breeding can be the cancer of rapid human progress in many such areas is not so widely appreciated.

Some optimists believe that the magic wand of industrialization alone is enough to solve the problems of population pressure, poverty, idleness (hidden unemployment), and ignorance. Such people generally base their hopes on modern European experience, especially on that of the Anglo-American and Russian offshoots. They forget that the exploitation of the so-called virgin resources of the newer parts of the world plus the attainment of the vital revolution in the past generation or two were just as important in bringing about the present levels of living as were the wonders of industrialization. Neither modern industrial techniques nor modern birth control techniques by themselves can solve mankind's problems. The underdeveloped societies have many potential resources that will become effective resources upon the application of modern scientific and engineering methods. But, many modern methods require huge amounts of capital, organizing talent, and highly skilled labor, most of which will have to be accumulated locally, even if much is lent or given by the more mature economies. The accumulation of such capital by Western societies was aided by the destructive exploitation of virgin land, waters, vegetation, and minerals, as well as by exploiting the advantage of a head-start in modernization over the rest of the world. It is by no means certain that ancient lands where prolific breeding presses on current production can take as great advantage of modern techniques as can those societies with greater control over their numbers. Since many underdeveloped societies will probably not enjoy such opportunities for relatively easy capital accumulation or such opportunities for mass emigration as did the Western Europeans, it is necessary that they obtain control over their numbers much more quickly and efficiently than did the luckier Europeans, if they aspire for high per capita levels of living. It should not be expected that the next stage of diffusion of modern civilization will bear a close analogy to the original European stage of that cycle.

Mankind's progress toward higher forms of civilization requires a slowing down of present population growth, and the establishment of more favorable interrelationships in every part of the world between number and quality of people, effective resources, technological advance, and realizable aspirations. It is unlikely that the unique combination of areal pioneering and commercial, agricultural, industrial, and social advances that resulted in much higher levels of living among the rapidly increasing Europeans will be repeated on the same scale in the foreseeable future among the bulk of the world's retarded peoples. It is much more likely that, in most such cases, especially the densely populated ones with small, per capita resource-bases, even moderate raises in the levels of living will depend as much upon man's ability to control population growth as upon increased production of food, energy, and other crude materials from the land, sea, and air due to prospective scientific and engineering advances.

The Long View

The goals of every society—whether freedom, peace, security, power, cohesion, prosperity, full employment, better health and education, or some others—are affected by the ability of that society to control the distribution and growth of its population. Favorable demography will not alone insure the attainment of such desired goals, of course, but it makes the problems more solvable.

The quarter of mankind that now lives in urban areas of 20,000 or more inhabitants is now increasing at a rate of some 5 per cent each year, which could mean a majority of mankind in such places by the turn of the century. In the wealthy industrial regions such urbanization is absorbing the equivalent of population growth plus diminishing the rural labor force, and on the whole this absorption is economically and socially for the betterment of society, although many short-term problems accompany the change. In the poor underdeveloped regions such urbanization is not generally absorbing the equivalent of all the population growth, so the rural population is continuing to grow in absolute numbers. And much of the urbanization in the underdeveloped regions is of a refugee nature, both in the narrow sense and in the sense of fleeing rural poverty and other miseries, meeting with little real improvement. Much urbanization is thus parasitic, either on the rural hinterland or on foreign aid.

World population is now over 3 billion. It increased by over 400 million during the 1950's, and will probably increase by over 600 million during the 1960's. At the 1960 rate, world population will double in the remainder of this century, and even a small increase in the rate would produce 7 instead of 6 billion by the year 2000.

Some 30 per cent of mankind now lives in high-income, urban-industrial, demographically stable nations: North America, Western and Eastern Europe, mid-latitude Latin America, European Oceania, Japan, and a few others. Only a fraction over two children per woman in such societies are needed to maintain a stable population; only 5 per cent of the children born die before adulthood. While moderation in population growth—either actual or incipient—is said to exist, the low-density regions (the overseas Europeans and eastern Slavs) still produce about three children per woman, which is increasing their populations at twice the rate of Europe proper, or some 50 per cent per generation.

The low-income, underdeveloped, demographically unstable countries contain some 70 per cent of mankind: tropical Latin America and sub-Saharan Africa, most of the Middle and Far East, and most of tropical Oceania. In none of them has national fertility been reduced substantially, although tiny minorities have done so. Some five to eight children are still produced per woman, although only two to three are now necessary to maintain a stable population, resulting in population increase of 50 to 100 per cent or greater per generation. The high-density regions (most of the West Indies, part of the Middle East, most of the Far East) include some three-quarters of the population in the demographically unstable realm, and are especially hampered by such conditions.

Economic development occurs only when increases in productivity and output exceed population increase. In general, although population increase may stimulate economic growth under some conditions (mainly in some of the low-density countries at certain stages in their development), it usually tends to obstruct efforts to raise per capita levels of living in less developed regions (especially in the high-density ones). Most societies that have modernized managed to increase product per head by relatively great increases in production in their early stages of economic development (mainly by accelerated expansion of those sectors having higher productivity), and to achieve later economic progress by dampening rates of population growth and aspirations. Apparently, the costs of achieving population replacement and improved health have remained at about the same proportion of total income (roughly one-quarter), with the costs of premature death predominating in the first stage of the population cycle, the costs of maintaining surplus population predominating in the second and third stages of the population cycle, and the costs of maintaining the aged and of more costly rearing of young dependents greatly increasing in the fourth stage of the population cycle.

The changes that make for increased per capita income are predominantly non-demographic in character. Population growth at best gives impetus to growth processes underway. At worst, it may help bring on an overemphasis on labor-intensive techniques of production that retards use of the most efficient organization and technology.

Modern population growth has been largely created by the uneven application of science and technology. Historically, disease and continence were the pre-eminent checks upon population growth, with the former historically the most important and now rapidly being abolished by modern medical science and sanitary engineering. In some cases a drop in the death rate of 1 per cent, which took several generations in nineteenth century European countries, can be achieved in several years. There is no prospect that there will be a sudden decline in birth rates in the next several decades. Barring nuclear warfare on a massive scale, it is likely that the death rates will decline still further, with the widest part of the demographic gap being reached by century's end, perhaps. In a view longer than that, one can only speculate, but one thing seems certain. The curve of population is an inexorable thing; either rational mankind will control it or nature will. Even with the considerable extension to be had from the application of dynamic science and technology, resources are finite; even prospective advances can but buy time to face the ultimate problem of a rational adjustment between population, standards, and resources that must sustain future consumption. As in all major problems facing mankind, the fundamental limitations are not those of science and technology, but the moral limitations of man. Morality of all great religious-moral systems stresses responsibility for all foreseeable consequences, a heavy burden when science and other disciplines enlarge the scope of vision. Problems of social psychology seem to dictate priority of economic development over any large-scale, concerted effort to spread birth control before economic modernization, but the net gain from the spread of the modern urban-industrial type of civilization to any society depends as much upon rational population control (within several generations of any rapid fall in the death rate) as upon mastery of the other variables in the transformation.

NATURAL RESOURCES

In small-scaled, premodern economies, concern with space and natural resources was mainly local, with only 1 ton or less of crude materials consumed yearly per person, at a cost of one-half to three-quarters of all economic efforts. Modern urban-industrial man's concern with both space and natural resources is more and more worldwide; economic accessibility and economic-resource patterns now correlate much more closely with dynamic science and technology and other aspects of culture than they do with natural phenomena. The superiority of a machine-based economy shows up in the much greater share of capital investment possible in an industrial society, in the ability to use lean and formerly inaccessible natural resources, in the great reduction of costs (if plant is used near capacity), and in the vastly superior degree of mobility. Present per capita yearly consumption of raw materials (other than water and air) in an urban-industrial economy ranges from 10 to 20 tons, produced at a cost of 5 to 15 per cent of all economic efforts. Within another century, such consumption may well rise to 100 to 150 tons caput yearly, costing under 5 per cent of total income.

Early-modern resource-availability. The greatest pressure on natural resources production is likely to occur during the transition from traditional to take-off status. Increased consumption during this stage usually involves demand for necessities (food, clothing, housing) from the older sectors of the economy, which are less flexible in increasing production because of rising prices than the more sensitive urban sectors which mainly service the relatively small middle-class and organized working-class markets or supply government or industrial needs.

The average peasant produces only a tenth (or even less) of the production of the average modernized farmer, and early modernization of the old agricultural sector is likely to increase output without any great increase in productivity per man-hour. The same pattern is repeated with handicraft industry and with those distributive and other service pursuits that are relics of the old village subsistence economy. Outmoded organization, scale, and equipment makes these older economic activities a series of massive obstacles to rapid economic progress. Most rural groups almost inevitably are going to be among the last groups to significantly raise their levels of living (although their psychic satisfactions may not be depressed, and certain facets of their levels of living may be better than they would have in the city).

The low degree of productivity in premodern agriculture and related pursuits and the resulting low levels of living in such activities provide the main economic and social rationale for industrialization. On the whole, agriculture becomes more efficient to the degree that the country industrializes, since so many of the necessary rural changes rest upon non-farm production, capital accumulation, and consumption (i.e., upon external economies).

Efficient production under modern conditions involves increasing the stages in the systems of productive processes in most cases (i.e., lengthening the line of production). In other words, most modern production is carried on by more roundabout ways than previously, which generally means greater labor specialization and greater capitalization. Much work formerly done on the farm and in family households is now done in factories and workshops. This is one of the reasons why modern economic development involves shifting workers from agriculture to industry and to service activities: they accompany the movement of farm and village activities to towns and cities where such production of goods and services can be concentrated and performed more efficiently and cheaply than in their former locations. In the early stage, however, urban industry and associated services do not employ all displaced village craftsmen, and they form an increasing landless labor class that is often poorer than before and often retards changes in agriculture that might increase worker productivity.

Only a minority (seldom more than a third or so) of peasants evolve quickly into efficient commercial farmers, because of advantages of scale, capital, enterprise, or others. The remainder barely produce sufficient above subsistence to pay their taxes, rent, and other cash expenses, and usually are higher-cost producers of those crude materials than the modernized producers in the same economy. As a modernizing economy approaches semi-industrial (take-off) status, an economy is likely to have more workers in agriculture than it started with, and average productivity per worker less than doubled (and most of that increase accounted for within the commercialized minority, plantation agriculture, and other innovating groups).

Although mining increases production and productivity more rapidly than agriculture, that portion oriented toward domestic markets often is inefficient in a world context, since it often is undercapitalized and has very high distribution costs because of scale and other disadvantages. That mining associated with large-scale domestic or foreign industry is usually most efficient.

Traditional societies often obtain 30 to 60 per cent of their income from the primary sector. By the time they are semimodernized, the absolute value of such production is much greater, but its relative share has dropped to 15 to 30 per cent of total income.

Late-modern resource-availability. As an economy evolves from a semi-industrial toward urban-industrial status, crude materials production becomes relatively a smaller fraction of productive effort, usually in the 10 to 25 per cent range of total income. The urban-industrial revolution does not free a society from dependence upon natural resources but, as in past levels of civilization, it broadens the supply base of such resources, both areally and in kind (quantity, quality, variety). Most important, it has liberated societies from extreme dependence upon local and regional resources. Population nodes can now be dependent upon numerous localities, some hundreds and even thousands of miles distant, supplying materials that are produced years earlier in many cases.

New resource-converting techniques turn the crude materials of the physical and biological habitat into semiprocessed materials. The most widespread changes in the natural landscape by urban-industrial man are results of the application of mechanical, chemical, and biological techniques in order to transform latent into usable resources. Such modern technology often gives value to local materials not greatly exploited previously, especially mineral fuels and other minerals. But it also removes the value of other materials, mainly those available in small amounts, in irregular quality, and at high cost. Most modern technology places a premium upon large-scale availability, even if quality is only medium-grade or even low-grade compared with premodern supplies.

Also important, new space-adjusting techniques either reduce time and cost of travel and transport distance, or permit intensification of space-use beyond that possible on the land surface (e.g., elevators, conveyor belts, pipelines, and others). By superior space-adjusting and vigorous resource-converting techniques, cities have brought the resource-bases of wider areas under their direction. In effect, trading relations can often be substituted for inadequate local or regional resources, or for inadequate national size. Because the limiting resources for an industrial society are mainly mineral or exotics from greatly different climates, and since no national unit is self-sufficient, the resource pressures of the future are almost certain to be more international, especially intercontinental.

Overview. Since human history shows a long-term trend of decreasing relative importance of physical and biological habitat factors, and increasing importance of cultural factors, increasingly those interested in location and materials problems must focus attention upon facility (fixed-capital resources and resistances, especially), activity (employment-output), institutional, and idea patterns as well as upon the traditional and more visible natural environmental patterns. The carrying capacity of the earth inherent in urban-industrial civilization opens the possibilities of a tremendous improvement in feeding and outfitting the growing population of the world but does not, in itself, solve the problems of the world's hungers. If poverty continues, the causes are less in the inadequate size of the globe or in overpopulation than in inadequate political and social value-systems and institutions which do not permit mankind to utilize the social and material technology of the most advanced nations. The earth must be constantly resurveyed in the light of changing numbers, changing culture, and changing standards, since the prospective economic-resources patterns are no more predictable than those of new knowledge and wisdom. In the foreseeable future, natural science, technological, and social science dynamics seem slated for continuing causal roles in enlarging the realm of usable resources than population-dynamics and areal expansion of the present-type resource-base.

PERSPECTIVE

Mankind must follow a modified but essentially similar avenue of economic modernization as that pioneered by Western Europeans in order to solve the world's principal economic problem of extreme poverty among a majority of its 3 billion population. The increasing discontent with present low levels of living is caused more by pressure of standards, by increasing awareness of the contrast between existing levels of living and those in the wealthier urban-industrial societies, than by deteriorating per capita production of goods and services. The only effective solution to the problems will require an immensely greater productive capacity.

Modern economic progress is characterized by increasing substitution and supplementation of living-energy with inanimate-powered machinery. The new technology requires a gradual transfer of labor and other productive factors from the older, relatively inefficient occupations (mainly peasant agriculture and related village activities of the premodern subsistence economy) into modern, specialized activities. The motivation for these occupational shifts is mainly found in the higher monetary and real income returns per worker. Most of the new, efficient activities are located in urban areas, but less than half of the new employment opportunities are in factories and related secondary industry. The majority of these new occupations are only indirectly productive, being specialized contributory (i.e., distributive-governmental-professional-personal services) activities.

When trying to predict future economic development, one quickly realizes that the greatest question marks are not geographic or economic in import. Such a factor as social rigidity is more significant in affecting the pace of further economic development than many other contributing but subsidiary hindrances: deficiencies in the natural endowment, retarding effects of vanished alien imperialism, or pressure of population increase due to a generation-or-so hiatus between the sanitary and vital revolutions. The importance of present economic resources and of current technological possibilities can be easily exaggerated in attempts to perceive along what lines economic development will proceed. Nature sets the (perhaps forever unknown) outer limits of possibility in any region, but the significant regional characteristics and values to an occupying society at any stated time are mainly determined by its technical apparatus and by the flexibility of its political and social organization. The mainsprings of civilization in any society are fundamentally rooted in the interrelationships between man and man rather than in the interrelationships between man and nature. The material level of a society rises and falls, correlated with changes in national unity, social mobility of individuals and groups, attitudes toward the future, and other little-visible aspects of man's spirit and ethics in that society. One of the important imponderables is whether the more intelligent elements among the controlling groups of that society are willing to unleash the hidden potentialities among the less powerful groups in that society, taking their chances that they themselves will change rapidly enough to avoid losing their position of wealth and influence.

When trying to visualize the "resources" needed to make a decisive difference in the perhaps century-long race between population, production, and living standards, one concludes that the most significant "resources" are in men's minds, spirits, and attitudes, not in their present liquid wealth, material paraphernalia, or latent natural-phenomena possibilities.

SUGGESTED READINGS

AHMAD, JALEEL. *Natural Resources in Low Income Countries.* University of Pittsburgh Press, 1960. Pp. 118.

THE AMERICAN ASSEMBLY, COLUMBIA UNIVERSITY. *The Population Dilemma.* Englewood Cliffs, N.J.: Prentice-Hall, 1963. Pp. 188.

BROWN, HARRISON S. *The Challenge of Man's Future.* New York: Viking Press, 1954. Pp. 290.

BROWN, HARRISON S., BONNER, JAMES, and WEIR, JOHN. *The Next Hundred Years.* New York: Viking Press, 1957. Pp. 193.

CHANDRASEKHAR, S. *Hungry People and Empty Lands: An Essay on Population Problems and International Tensions.* Baroda: Indian Institute for Population Studies, 1952. Pp. 306.

COALE, ANSLEY J., and HOOVER, EDGAR M. *Population Growth and Economic Development in Low-Income Countries.* Princeton University Press, 1958. Pp. 389.

COOK, ROBERT C. *Human Fertility: The Modern Dilemma.* London: Victor Gollancz, 1951. Pp. 351.

DARWIN, CHARLES G. *The Next Million Years.* New York: Doubleday, 1953. Pp. 210.

FISHER, JOSEPH L., and POTTER, NEAL. *World Prospects for Natural Resources.* Baltimore: Johns Hopkins Press (for Resources for the Future, Inc.), 1964. Pp. 73.

FRANCIS, ROY G. *The Population Ahead.* University of Minnesota Press, 1958. Pp. 160.

FREEDMAN, RONALD (ed.). *Population: The Vital Revolution.* New York: Doubleday (Anchor), 1964. Pp. 274.

FRIEDMANN, JOHN, and ALONZO, WILLIAM. *Regional Development and Planning: A Reader.* The Massachusetts Institute of Technology Press, 1964. Pp. 722.

GINSBURG, NORTON. *Essays on Geography and Economic Development.* University of Chicago's Department of Geography Research Paper No. 62, 1960. Pp. 173.

HATT, PAUL K. (ed.). *World Population and Future Resources.* Cincinnati: American Book Co., 1952. Pp. 262.

HAUSER, PHILIP M. (ed.). *Population and World Politics.* Glencoe, Ill.: The Free Press of Glencoe, 1958. Pp. 297.

HAUSER, PHILIP M., and DUNCAN, OTIS DUDLEY (eds.). *The Study of Population: An Inventory and Appraisal.* University of Chicago Press, 1959. Pp. 864.

HERTZLER, J. O. *The Crisis in World Population: A Sociological Examination with Special Reference to the Underdeveloped Areas.* University of Nebraska Press, 1956. Pp. 279.

HUBERTY, MARTIN R., and FLOCK, WARREN L. (eds.). *Natural Resources.* New York: McGraw-Hill, 1959. Pp. 556.

JARRETT, HENRY (ed.). *Science and Resources: Prospects and Implications of Technological Advance.* Washington, D.C.: Resources for the Future, Inc., 1959. Pp. 250.

LANDSBERG, HANS H. *Natural Resources for U.S. Growth: A Look Ahead to the Year 2000.* Baltimore: Johns Hopkins Press (for Resources for the Future, Inc.), 1964. Pp. 260.

MOORE, WILBERT E. *Industrialization and Labor: Social Aspects of Economic Development.* Cornell University Press, 1951.

Mouzon, Olin T. *International Resources and National Policy.* New York: Harper & Row, 1959. Pp. 752.

Mudd, Stuart (ed.). *The Population Crisis and the Use of World Resources.* Indiana University Press, 1964. Pp. 563.

National Bureau of Economic Research, Inc. *Demographic and Economic Change in Developed Countries.* Princeton University Press, 1960. Pp. 536.

Ogburn, William Fielding (ed.). *Technology and International Relations.* University of Chicago Press, 1949. Pp. 202.

Political & Economic Planning (PEP). *World Population and Resources.* London: Political & Economic Planning, 1955. Pp. 339.

Spicer, Edward H. *Human Problems in Technological Change.* New York: Russell Sage Foundation, 1952. Pp. 301.

Thomas, William L., Jr. (ed.). *Man's Role in Changing the Face of the Earth.* University of Chicago Press, 1956. Pp. 1,193.

Thomson, Sir George. *The Foreseeable Future.* Cambridge University Press, 1955. Pp. 166.

United Nations, Department of Social Affairs, Population Division. *The Determinants and Consequences of Population Trends.* New York: United Nations, 1953. Pp. 404.

Woytinsky, W. S., and Woytinsky, E. S. *World Population and Production: Trends and Outlook.* New York: Twentieth Century Fund, 1953. Pp. 1,268. *World Commerce and Governments: Trends and Outlook.* New York: Twentieth Century Fund, 1955. Pp. 907.

Zimmermann, Erich. *World Resources and Industries: A Functional Appraisal of the Availability of Agricultural and Industrial Materials.* New York: Harper & Row, 1951. Pp. 832.

5

Introduction to Agriculture

Agriculture and related primary activities (fishing, hunting, gathering, forestry) still employ over half of the world's labor force, although contributing only a tenth of the world's value-added by the output of all goods and services.[1] Although the agricultural sector's relative importance declines with urban industrialization, it still has vital roles to play in promoting general economic growth.

First, agriculture must supply food in increasing amounts, to supply both the increasing population still living on the land and the rapidly expanding urban population in the developing countries. If the demand is not met, there may be hunger, or food must be imported, depleting the foreign exchange needed to import industrial and distribution equipment and raw materials. Second, agricultural expansion is required to provide factors of production for the industrial and services sectors: to free labor from agriculture and make it available for industrial construction and operation and for expanding service functions, to provide food and non-food crude materials for industry, and to earn foreign exchange. Third, a rise in agricultural incomes stimulates other aspects of development: it provides much of the capital needed for further growth, either through savings or through increased taxation, and it also provides expanded markets for industry, both purchased capital goods for agricultural rationalization (improved technical efficiency) and expansion and consumers goods for the rural population.

Fully as important to economic development as its productive contributions are agriculture's problems—"overproduction," "underproduction," "underemployment," and "underconsumption"—which constitute some of the greatest resistances to general progress. Overproduction ("farm problems") is mainly found in the wealthiest urban-industrial societies, when the transfer of various factors of production (especially labor) is too slow. Causes of overproduction may be partly due to spectacular advances in technology, but are mainly due to a changed demand, induced by a slackening in the rate of population increase and the relatively low income elasticity of farm products as a people become richer. In the past decade, high-income societies as a group have increased their agricultural production several times as fast as their population growth, resulting in much storage and dumping abroad, as governments try to cope with the overabundance partly brought into being by support prices determined more by political than economic considerations. In the absence of governmental intervention, farm-product prices, land values, and rents fall, which explains the demand for such intervention; but in only a few cases have the results been a happy experience.

The problems of underproduction, underem-

---

[1] Not the same as the income of the "rural" population, which is nearly half again larger (due to non-primary income of "farmers" and "non-farm villagers").

ployment, and underconsumption in world agriculture are mainly concentrated in the low-income, underdeveloped countries. In the past decade, agricultural production has increased only a trifle faster than the population growth. Poverty characterizes the mass of subsistence and slightly commercialized peasantry, because their traditional techniques are almost stagnant and because of an unfortunate tendency to starve many agricultural subsectors of capital, enterprise, and government attention in favor of more prestigeful industrial and services developments.

A more meaningful assessment of agricultural problems and prospects can be made through great-region and country characteristics, which follows.

REGIONAL AGRICULTURAL CHARACTERISTICS

Many variables—habitat resources and resistances, man-land ratios, traditional land-use and dietary preferences, stage of modern economic development, and many others—combine to give "personality" to regional agricultural characteristics.

The graphs on pages 96–97 and Table 5–1 give relative production and breakdown into types of product.

North America

The level of per capita production of agricultural products in North America ranks only next to that in Oceania, being three times the world average. The level is now about 15 per cent higher than before World War II, owing to the large expansion during the war and in the immediate postwar years, though more recently production per capita has leveled off because of restrictions on crop areas.

North American net exports plus the accumulation of surpluses unsold amount to nearly 15 per cent of total food and feed crop production. Since 1940, grain output has increased at the same time that cultivated acreage declined, because of improved breeding, chemicalization, and mechanization.

Within the past century, the proportion of farmers in the North American labor force has dropped from 65 to 7 per cent; and within another decade or so, it will probably drop below 5 per cent. A more realistic definition of a "farm" in the next U.S. and Canadian censuses would probably eliminate two-fifths of the present total. As now defined, the dropout rate of farmers has averaged 4 per cent a year for some years. Less than a quarter of present-census farmers seem likely to survive in the long view, although the rate of dropout among the economically obsolete farmers seems likely to be determined more by political and social considerations than by purely economic ones.

Agricultural production in Canada and the United States is expected to continue at high levels, with the output limited more by restricted demand than by production difficulties.

Western Europe

Although the region has the largest agricultural deficits in the world, Western Europe produces more than three-quarters of its crop consumption, while self-sufficiency in livestock products consumption is 85 per cent (10 per cent dependent upon imported feedstuffs, with 5 per cent imported in the form of finished products). Britain requires food imports sufficient to feed about 25 million people, obtained mostly from Canada and European Oceania.

In the past decade, total agricultural production (in real terms) increased about 25 per cent, with per capita production increasing 15 per cent. The average diet has become qualitatively superior, measured in animal protein and protective foods consumption. By the late 1950's, the burgeoning market which had been able to absorb both greatly expanded domestic production and a large volume of exports was growing at a much slower rate, while home output continued to increase, resulting in pressures for greater protection.

Since World War II, Western European agriculture has become more of an "industrial" operation: the labor force has been reduced, there has been great mechanization both in fieldwork and in farm buildings, the average farm size has increased, and capital investment per farm and per worker has increased. Compared with North America, there are still significant contrasts. North American agriculture invests about

WORLD: VALUE-ADDED BY AGRICULTURE, BY GREAT-REGION AND ECONOMIC-TYPE OF SOCIETY, 1962-1964 AVERAGE-ANNUAL (U.S. $ Billion)

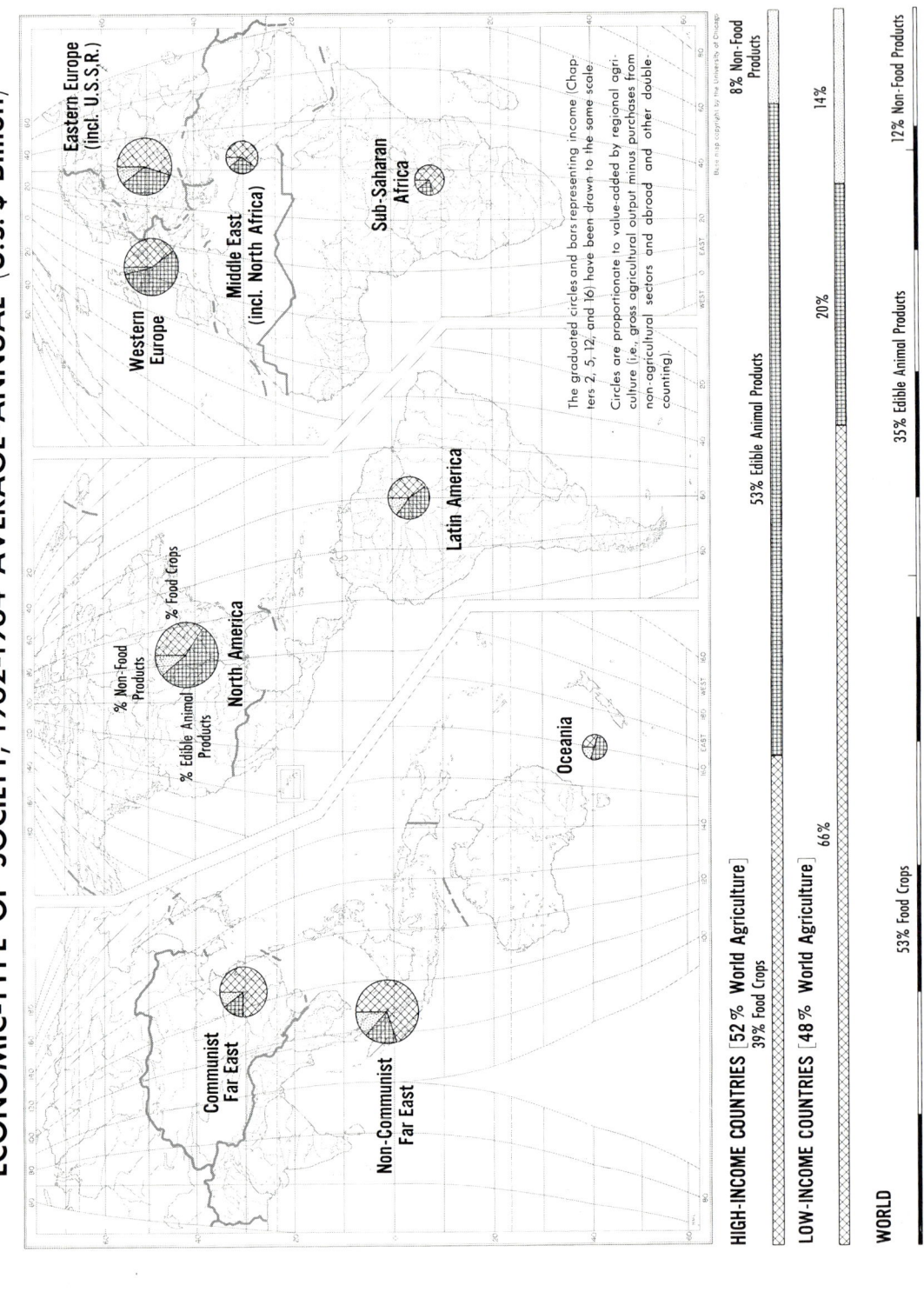

WORLD: GREAT-REGION AND ECONOMIC-TYPE OF SOCIETY SHARES OF WORLD TOTAL AGRICULTURAL OUTPUT, FOOD CROPS, EDIBLE ANIMAL PRODUCTS, AND NON-FOOD PRODUCTS, BY VALUE-ADDED, 1962-1964 AVERAGE-ANNUAL

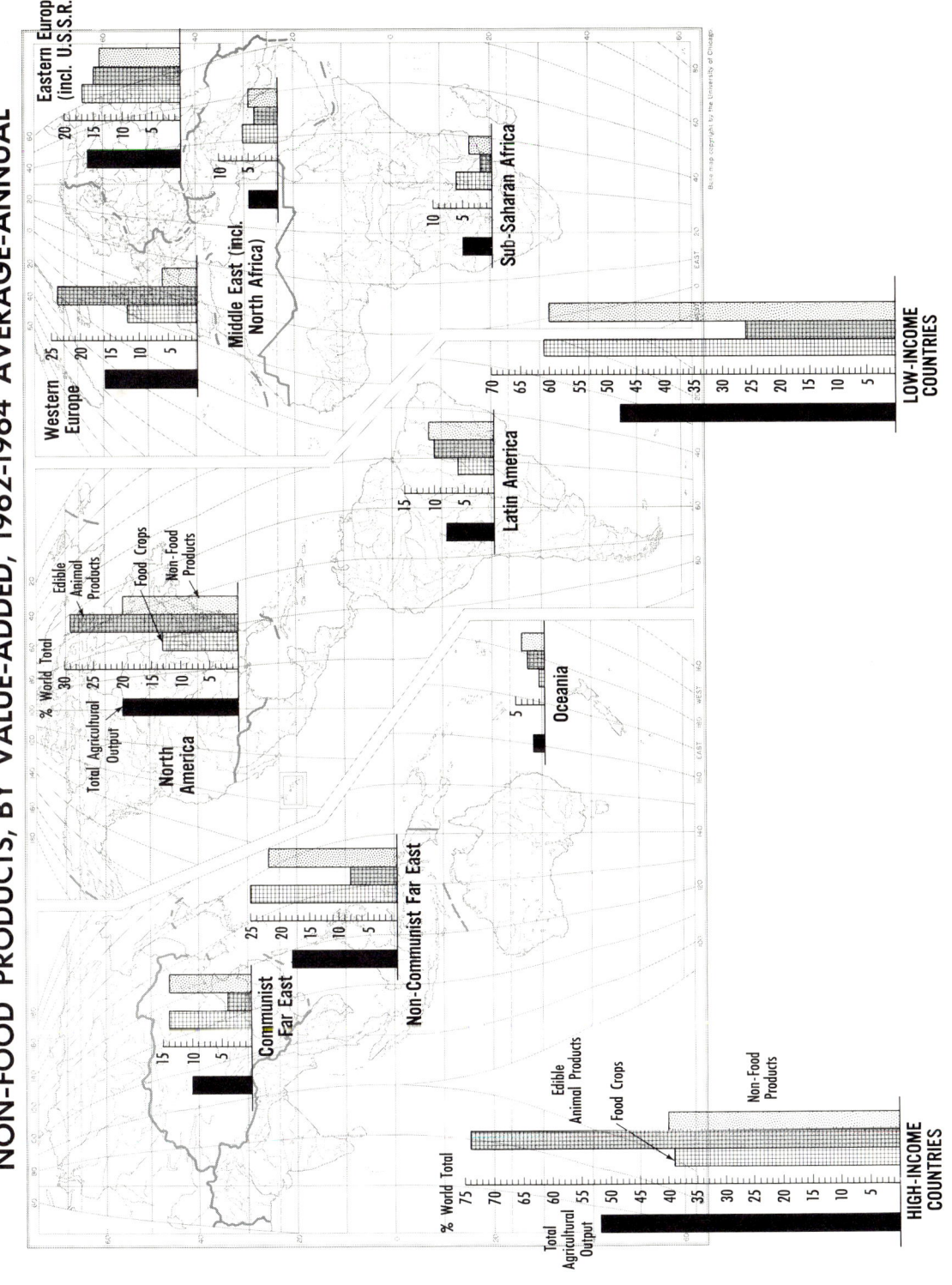

TABLE 5-1

World: Primary Production (Value-added),* by Great-Region and Economic-Type of Society, 1962–1964 Average-Annual (in billions of United States dollars)

	Primary Production		Agricultural Production				Forestry Products	Fishing-Hunting-Gathering Products
	Value	Regional Income	Total Output	Food Crops	Edible Animal Products	Non-Food Products		
North America	27	5.0%	25	34%	55%	11%	1.6	0.4
Western Europe	22	6.5	20	40	56	4	1.2	0.8
Eastern Europe (including the U.S.S.R)	22	7.8	20	55	35	10	1.6	0.4
Oceania	3	16.6	3	30	50	20	0.1	—
Latin America	11	16.9	10	40	45	15	0.6	0.4
Sub-Saharan Africa	6	25.2	6	70	20	10	0.3	0.1
Middle East (including North Africa)	7	23.3	7	60	30	10	0.1	—
Non-Communist Far East	26	26.0	23	70	17	13	1.6	1.2
Communist Far East	14	31.1	13	70	15	10	0.4	0.6
World	138½	9.7	126½	53	35	12	7.5	4.0
High-income countries	72	6.2	66	39	53	8	4.5	2.5
Low-income countries	66½	24.3	61	66	20	14	3.0	1.5

	(per cent of U.S. $138 billion)	(per cent of U.S. $126 billion)	(per cent of U.S. $66 billion)	(per cent of U.S. $47 billion)	(per cent of U.S. $14 billion)	(per cent of U.S. $4.5 billion)	(per cent of U.S. $2.5 billion)
North America	19	20	13	29	20	21	10
Western Europe	16	16	12	24	6	16	20
Eastern Europe (including the U.S.S.R)	16	16	17	15	14	21	10
Oceania	2	2	1	3	4	1	—
Latin America	8	8	6	10	11	8	10
Sub-Saharan Africa	5	5	6	2	4	4	5
Middle East (including North Africa)	5	5	6	4	5	1	—
Non-Communist Far East	19	18	25	8	22	21	30
Communist Far East	10	10	14	4	14	5	15
World	100	100	100	100	100	100	100
High-income countries	52	52	39	74	40	60	62
Low-income countries	48	48	61	26	60	40	38

SOURCE: Adapted from Food and Agriculture Organization sources.

* Value-added equals gross value of output minus purchased factors of production and other double-counting (e.g., feed).

5 million man-years of labor in a year, compared with Western Europe's 20 million. Labor input per unit of crop area is four times that in North America, while crop production per unit-area is only 75 per cent higher. Production per man-year in North America is four times that of Western Europe. The gross working capital per man-year worked in agriculture is some $1,000 in North America compared with $200 in Western Europe.

The number of larger farms is increasing very slowly in most countries, despite declines in the numbers of dwarf and small holdings. Farm consolidation is taking place mainly through acquisition of more land by farmers who already hold more than 25 acres rather than by consolidating small units to form new farms of a viable size.

Under the (politically determined) favorable price conditions that now characterize Western European agriculture, improved farm management will certainly contribute to a rise in output and probably to a significant decline in production costs. It would appear that output can easily be increased 2 per cent or more annually, almost double the anticipated rate of rise in demand. It is possible that the net demand for imported non-tropical foods and feeds would be halved by 1970 and virtually disappear during the following decade.

Eastern Europe (including the U.S.S.R.)

According to official data, total agricultural production is about 30 per cent higher than in the early 1950's, with per capita production about 15 per cent higher. Thus, per capita production would be higher than the world average, and would have been growing at a faster rate. During postwar years, increases were especially high (the official data showed a higher rate between 1953 and 1958 than for any other region), mainly because of the rapid growth of production on largely expanded areas in the U.S.S.R.

Many Western analysts question the reliability of Soviet agricultural statistics and insist on the need for downward adjustment. They feel that much outright statistical falsification occurs at every level and that not enough allowance is made for losses in storage and in transit. Samples assessing production on private plots are thought to be inadequate, thus overestimating production of potatoes, vegetables, and livestock products.

Soviet dry-farmed "New Lands" have recently averaged only 60 per cent of 1958's peak output, so some has been returned to range use, with more attention paid to irrigation and chemical fertilization elsewhere. Perennial problems plaguing Eastern European agriculture include the inferior position of agriculture in the national economy (even in Poland and Yugoslavia where the peasant is most favored), shortages of capital, inadequate producer incentives, rigid state controls, and collectivization. There is no evidence that these disadvantages will be radically altered in the near future.

In spite of the difficulties, no serious food stringencies that were widespread or of long duration have been reported, but the average diet remains a monotonous one, composed largely of cereals and potatoes. Such staples are purposely priced low by the governments, and per capita consumption is over twice that in North America. On the other hand, meat, chicken, and fresh vegetables are priced very high, so per capita consumption is only half that in North America.

Agricultural rationalization has occurred very slowly, with most occurring on state farms and collectives in the more thinly settled regions. Mechanization has been difficult and slow, especially in western U.S.S.R. and parts of other states where farms tend to be smaller.

Although intensification has been tried, it has not had the success that features Western European agriculture, except in isolated spots. In the U.S.S.R., the small plots that legally supply the free market play an important part in Soviet food production, and in themselves are far more efficient than the average state farm. Though their tilled area amounted to only 3.2 per cent of the total, the small-farm plots produce (according to official data) over 80 per cent of the eggs, 60 per cent of the potatoes, 40 per cent of the meat, and large fractions of the fruits, vegetables, and flowers.

Since nearly half of the average family budget is still spent on food, and there is still a large income elasticity for high-quality food, the great problems in Soviet agriculture in the foreseeable future seem likely to involve production and costs rather than demand.

Oceania

Food production per capita in European Oceania (Australia and New Zealand) is the highest in the world, four times the world average and eight times the level in the Far East. In recent years, there has been no upward trend in the level of per capita production in the region, however, reflecting lack of export demand more than anything else.

New Zealand has for some time realized the need for greater diversification of marketing outlets for its agricultural products and less dependence on Britain (for some 40 per cent of her exports, such as meat, butter, cheese, and fruit, Britain constitutes almost the total market). Governmental policies are being directed toward broader international marketing arrangements, particularly for dairy products and lamb. Promotion efforts are now under way to expand markets in continental Western Europe, the United States, Southeast Asia, and Japan. The narrow range of New Zealand exports can be seen in the fact that over 95 per cent of total exports are agricultural products.

Australia is better able to absorb shocks from European discrimination or serious setbacks in world market opportunities. Agricultural products still account for over 75 per cent of total exports, with wool, wheat, meat, and sugar being the chief items of trade. But only 17 per cent of Australia's export earnings could be affected adversely by Britain joining the European Common Market. Far Eastern countries now take about a third of Australian exports, compared with less than a tenth before World War II. Japan is now second to Britain and will almost certainly replace Britain as the leading market for Australian exports eventually.

The United States is the one important country that places a high duty on raw wool, thus hurting both Australia and New Zealand. Its embargoes on dairy produce also hurt both, but especially New Zealand.

Latin America

Although usually classified as one of the underdeveloped great-regions, Latin America is the most developed of them. While its rate of increase in total income is high, it promises to remain a problem as regards food, since it is in the widest part of its demographic gap, coupled with rapid urbanization and rising standards of consumption.

Agricultural production is about a third higher than a decade ago (about four-fifths from increased acreage), but population increase has been about as great, so per capita production is about the same. During the 1950's, food production and population both increased about 2.5 per cent annually, but increased commercial availability of many items had to be met from increased imports. Much of the imported food came from the United States (amounting to some 10 per cent of our total agricultural exports); on the other side of the trading, Latin America furnishes some 40 per cent of U.S. agricultural imports (mainly coffee, but including sugar, live animals, meat and meat products, and many others).

Latin America's per capita food production level is close to the world average, but retained production is considerably less because of large exports. During World War II, there was a considerable decrease, but the prewar per capita level was regained with the big expansion in output in the late 1950's. Recently, the per capita food production has fallen back again to about the prewar level.

Consumption of food varies widely among the countries, with Haiti having a dietary as poor as most in the Far East, and Argentina-Uruguay producing enough food to supply both high-quality dietaries and substantial exports. Most of the countries are in between, trying to achieve great food self-sufficiency and having some success, but not complete success. Neither the population increase nor rising dietary standards pressures on supply are likely to slacken in the foreseeable future.

As in Eastern Europe, much of the difficulty in increasing the food supply lies in the low priority given to agriculture in developmental plans, compared with industrial and service projects. Latin America has a great potential for increased agricultural output, but mainly in the context of an industrialized agriculture rather than a peasant-type agriculture. In common with many other developing regions, Latin America is going through a period of rapid social change. The existing systems of land tenure may change in the years ahead, possibly causing a temporary disruption in production. In the long view, Latin American agricultural production should prove adequate, but in the short run, the nip-and-tuck balance between supply and demand seems likely to continue.

Sub-Saharan Africa

Apparently, the region's total farm production is about a third higher than a decade back, with per capita production a bit higher than it was, but still considerably below the world average. In the 1950's, the annual rate of increase in food supply was apparently less than 2 per cent, but this will have to increase if the (apparently) more rapidly increasing population of the 1960's is to be taken care of.

Some 95 per cent of the food consumed is produced within the region, with large agricultural exports (beverages, oils-fats, cotton, and many others) being produced in addition. No country has to rely on substantial imports of food.

If the political problems of emerging statehood can be mastered quickly, the outlook for increased agricultural output per capita over the next decade or so is good. The substantial land and water resources available for development will be a great asset if capital and technical assistance are extended. Much of the arable land, pasture land, and forest land is unused or poorly used today. Generally speaking, there is relatively little of the pressure of population on land that typifies the Far East. Obstacles are also great. Soil depletion is a serious problem in most areas. Many of the native grasses have limited value for livestock feeding. Disease and pests of plants and animals restrict agricultural output. The tsetse fly alone has kept livestock out of large areas where draft animals could be effectively employed, and where animal proteins for human consumption are so badly needed. However, many of these difficulties can be overcome within the context of commercial agriculture; the great lacks are modern-type skills, enterprise, and capital.

Middle East (including North Africa)

Since the early 1950's, farm production in Southwest Asia and North Africa has increased about a third, but per capita production has remained about the same. Since the region is swiftly approaching the widest part of its demographic gap, the struggle to improve per capita position will be a difficult one.

Although irrigated agriculture is quite stable, there are rather wide fluctuations, mainly because of climatic conditions in dry-farming areas (most of Magreb, Fertile Crescent, Anatolia, northwest Iran). Recently, increased farm production has come mainly from expansion of cultivated land in such hazardous areas by reducing fallow and using pasture land, both by traditional and mechanized methods of reclamation. But in the long view, most agricultural progress will have to come from better management of currently exploited land and water resources.

As a whole, the region now produces most of the food it consumes, with only Egypt, Libya, and Algeria having substantial imports of food. Except in years of poor grain crops, the principal imports are tea, sugar, and oils-fats. Agricultural exports are some two-thirds of all exports if petroleum is excluded; cotton, fruit, wine, tobacco, nuts, wool, and hides-skins are regularly items, and in some years grains are important.

Only Israel has a fairly high-quality diet, with grain products being the mainstay of the other countries. Per capita production is somewhat below the world average, although it has been consistently maintained at more than the prewar level. The apparent self-sufficiency of calories is due to the somewhat higher level of supplies in Turkey and the Levant, with about half the population. Iran and countries in Arabia and the Magreb have daily calorie supplies of only 2,100 to 2,200. Consumption of pulses and fruits-vegetables is relatively high for most countries.

During the 1960's, agricultural production seems likely to increase slightly faster than the 2.5 per cent rate of population growth, if development measures now envisaged are implemented. Much depends on financial and technical assistance from outside the area (French and American aid in the Magreb, American and Soviet aid in Egypt and Southwest Asia).

Non-Communist Far East

Although food production has increased about a third in the past decade, and per capita production is apparently some 10 per cent higher, the region and its neighbor, the Communist Far East, have the poorest diets in the world. About 300 to 500 million people are undernourished, and an additional 500 million do not get enough food of the right kind. Throughout both regions, the people have a daily per capita calories intake (2,100) below the standard estimated by F.A.O. (Food and Agricultural Organization of the United Nations) as adequate, taking into account the climates and physical size of the inhabitants (2,300 calories). The deficits in protein and protective values represent over two-thirds of the world totals.

Once a net exporter of grain, the non-Communist Far East has become a large net importer since World War II. It still produces large export surpluses of rubber, oils-fats, jute, and other agricultural items, but increasingly their earnings go to pay for imported food and raw materials.

All the countries in the region have begun long-range development plans for agriculture. A number of obstacles threaten the successful accomplishment of these plans. There is a lack of sufficient capital for investment, especially in competition with glamorous industrial and service projects. The supply of arable land per capita is constantly declining. Soils are badly depleted in some areas by centuries of cultivation. The high illiteracy rates among farmers restrict many kinds of extension work.

In Japan and Taiwan, where agriculture is very intensively practiced, it seems doubtful whether yields will continue to increase as they did during the 1950's. The agricultural potential of the more sparsely populated countries (Burma, Thailand, Laos, Cambodia, South Vietnam) will probably languish for lack of demand for export, partly because the deficit countries attempt to become more self-sufficient, partly because of gifts and easy-credit sales from elsewhere (especially the United States). The other countries (the South Asian ones, Indonesia, Philippines, South Korea) will be hard pressed to increase farm output faster than population, especially at reasonable prices. More foreign financial and technical assistance will be necessary to achieve even modest increases in agricultural output per capita. Otherwise, foreign exchange earnings will be largely absorbed in payments for food imports, and non-agricultural development will be slowed.

Communist Far East

Official data indicated that per capita agricultural production in Mainland China steadily increased from the early 1950's until 1958, the year of "the great leap forward." However, the near-famine shortage of food reported recently, resulting from the successive bad crops of 1959 and 1960 and the lack of stocks from previous years, threw some doubts on the reliability of the high levels of per capita production reported for the late 1950's. Most outside authorities think present absolute production is no higher than it was in 1957, with the per capita level down because of presumed large population increase since then.

Mainland China is one of the best examples of what happens when the dynamic interactions between industry and agriculture are inadequately respected. In the 1950's, heavy industrialization was pushed, and the attempt was made to substitute forced labor for an inadequate level of agricultural investment (especially chemical fertilizers). In the 1959–1962 period, there was a breakdown in agricultural supplies, with the nation being forced to live at a substandard dietary and almost half of its foreign exchange being spent to buy Canadian and Australian grain to feed the coastal cities. There was also a breakdown in capacity to supply non-food industrial raw materials for domestic industry and to export for needed foreign exchange (exports are only half of their late 1950's level). Industrial production dropped, perhaps 30 per cent, mainly in the light-industry branches that processed agricultural raw materials. Private incentives have been partially restored in agriculture, but only moderate increases in production have occurred.

Overview

For the recent past, and for the near future, world agricultural production (2 per cent annual increase in calories, 3 per cent in value) will exceed world population growth. This does not mean that agriculture is a sector in the world economy without great problems. World economy, world agriculture, and similar categories are legitimate considerations in a broad overview, but they really do not exist at the level of short-run practicality. There are rather a large number of national economies more or less loosely interrelated through markets, trade, and international-aid arrangements.

Regional disparities are one of the greatest problems affecting world agriculture. In the more developed regions, the relationships between the trends in production and population reflect mainly the slow growth of population in Western Europe, the more rapid growth in European Oceania (partly from net immigration), and in North America the efforts of the United States government to restrict the expansion of production in order to check the accumulation of surplus stocks. Eastern European underproduction is mainly related to the low priority given agriculture.

The most pressing problems of food and agriculture are centered in the less developed countries. The Communist Far East has the greatest problem, again related more to governmental miscalculations than anything else. In the other underdeveloped regions, the balance is rather precarious. During the 1950's, none of them radically improved the per capita level of food production, and the early 1960's showed the same seesaw movement between demand and supply.

PROBLEMS REQUIRING INCREASED AGRICULTURAL OUTPUT FOR SOLUTION

The demand-need side of agriculture is composed of two great pressures: (1) population increase and redistribution and (2) changing consumption standards. Both are massive problems in their absolute dimensions and will require several generations for reasonable solution.

The population increase and redistribution problem is one that usually rates higher priority in a short-run perspective. Regional differentials in increase rates are most visible, but regional differentials in urbanization rates and in work loads are most important in a long-run view. Relatively, such pressures are most important in underdeveloped societies, since they can be generated without any substantial economic improvement in some cases.

The change in consumption standards is the sort of structural change that is of tremendous importance but little visible to many. Probably most visible are the traditional elite standards being adopted by other classes as they can afford them (socially superior food grains, beverages, condiments). More important, partly because they are still changing, are the newer consumption standards set by modern nutritional science, which require more superior (animal) protein, fat, and protective foods (minerals and vitamins from milk, fruits, vegetables) to satisfy. Relatively, such changes are most important in urban-industrial societies, and they usually come after considerable economic and social change.

Pressure of Population Increase and Redistribution

The low-income realm is increasing its population annually some 2 per cent at the present time, with the high-income realm increasing at about two-thirds that rate. Within each realm, there is considerable diversity. Western Europe, the Eastern European satellites, and Japan are below the average for the high-income group, with North America, Soviet Union, mid-latitude South America, and European Oceania above the average; but in no case can the rate of population increase be said to be the main reason for their agricultural problems.

Within the low-income realm, sub-Saharan Africa and the Communist Far East may be increasing at some 2 per cent annually, with the other regions at or above the average. Many individual countries are increasing 3 to 4 per cent annually, either because of reproduction near the physiological limit or because immigration is considerable in addition to natural increase.

Practically all the low-income societies belong to what is called the high food-drain type, in which a majority (often 60 per cent or more) of disposable consumer income (after taxes and savings) is spent on food. Such societies are close to fulfilling the essential conditions of the Ricardo-Malthus-Mill model in that potential increase in population is such that it can readily absorb increases in food production. They have a heavy burden of young dependents, and most of the population is at the margin of subsistence. The main effect of an increase in income is an increased demand for food: an increase of 1 per cent in income leads to an increase of some 0.7 to 0.8 per cent in demand for food (this ratio is called the income elasticity of food).

The high-income societies mainly belong to what is called the low food-drain type, in which only a quarter or less of disposable consumer income is spent on food. In such societies, the income elasticity of food is about 0.4 (for grains and starchy foodstuffs it is lower still, and even assumes a negative value in some cases). Thus, an increase in per capita incomes in these countries leads to a relative decline in demand for basic foods and contributes to the food surpluses that have appeared in some relatively advanced countries. The drain of food costs on disposable income is so low and the dependence of the population-growth variable on food availability so tenuous that the changes in population have become essentially independent. To explain population growth in such affluent societies, it is necessary to redefine the economic component to include not only food and other basic items but also medical care, prolonged education, and travel expenses involved in rearing children, and savings to be transferred to them at adulthood.

There is an intermediate food-drain type of society in which about a quarter to a half of disposable consumer income is spent on food. The Soviet Union and other high-income European Communist societies belong to this group, mainly because of inefficient (high-cost) agriculture and the heavy taxes placed upon food (comparable to those levied on liquors and tobacco products in other societies), as does Japan. There are also some of the better-off low-income societies (mostly in the $250 to $449 annual income category) that belong to the group.

The development of year-round agriculture and the increasing urbanization of most regions increase the already complicated problem of food and other agricultural inadequacies caused by increasing population. The development of irrigated or other forms of agriculture that result in multiple cropping or the increase in part-time employment (construction, seasonal industry, seasonal services) by agriculturalists often increases the per capita food requirement more rapidly than originally postulated in terms of traditional agricultural work loads. Even more complicating is the enlarging urbanization, with its increasing work-year for most occupations (as compared with the seasonal agriculture in most areas).

An increase in the supply of marketable food is needed, and this is not necessarily available with a greater amount of agricultural output. In countries where most farming is still subsistence-type, the farm population may consume much of its increased output, both because of increasing numbers and because of slight qualitative improvements in dietary. Even where rural commercial surpluses may become available, inadequate facilities for storage, preserving, and transport may result in inadequate urban supplies, especially where large year-to-year fluctuations in crops are the norm. Most of the intermittent food imports into normally self-sufficient societies are for urban consumption when rural production is low or being hoarded, and the urban population is increasing 5 per cent or more yearly.

Pressure of Consumption Standards

Although the pressure on food brought by increasing numbers and changes in occupation and residence are more visible to naive eyesight, and cause more concern in low-income societies, qualitative changes are also being made and in the long run will require as much additional production to satisfy as quantitative pressures.

In the early stages of development, changes in the quality of dietary are mainly copying the old elite preferences or some innovations now being favored by prestigeful groups. Elite dietaries generally revolve around socially prestigeful grains, with larger amounts of sweetening and other seasonings, more oil, more meat, and more exotics than the mass dietaries in the culture. As incomes rise, there is a tendency to copy certain elements, sometimes with good effects, sometimes with poor effects. The substitution of low-protein cassava with rice improves a dietary, but highly milled rice substituting for certain millets and sorghums may represent deterioration. The substitution of sugared tea for milk is usually deleterious. Rural population migrating to cities usually has an inferior dietary for some time, as protective foods (milk, fruits, vegetables) are often scarcer and more expensive, and competition with new-type petty comforts and luxuries (both food and nonfood) usually leads to their being dropped or minimized.

Much of the difficulty arises from isolated borrowings and eliminations. Originally, the rural-poor dietary may have been reasonably balanced, as well as the elite dietary. But in moving to urban areas or to other rural areas, the items eliminated may be selected with reference to unavailability or to high price, rather than to balance. Selections also are made without reference to their dietary context, thus having a different effect than among the better-off group who can afford other foods to remedy the deficiencies.

In the long run, the greatest qualitative changes in dietary consumption standards are being made because of findings by modern nutritional science. It is now known that there are two types of food "hungers": One, general hunger is energy hunger, the lack of sufficient carbohydrates (starch and sugar sources), which are the light-weight body fuel, and of the oils-fats, which are the heavy-weight body fuel. Two, there is hidden hunger or nutritional deficiencies: lack of sufficient proteins, which build and repair tissue; lack of minerals, which build the bony framework and a number of special organs and chemicals in the body (e.g., oxygen carriers of the blood); and vitamins, which, like hormones, are carried by another type of body chemical, the enzymes (biological catalysts), which perform the actual functions of both construction and energy release.

As Table 5–2 and the graph on page 106 show, average food consumption by mankind is apparently satisfactory, with the high-income societies eating somewhat more than they actually need, and the low-income societies being between 5 to 10 per cent deficit. The figures may be a bit misleading, since there is apparently more waste and feeding to animals between the retail level and actual home consumption in high-income societies than in low-income societies. The really serious calorie deficits are in the Far East.

In some areas, the calorie gap persists throughout the year, but in most areas, it is severe in the period preceding the harvests (i.e., "preharvest hunger"). Usually the deficit falls on the poorer classes (landless laborers and dwarfholders). The proportion of chronically undernourished for mankind as a whole seems to be some 10 to 15 per cent (300 to 500 million), but in the Far East it is 20 to 25 per cent, and in the other low-income regions it is only slightly less.

Malnutrition reflects the inadequacy in the nutritional quality of the diet. Diets of poor nutritional quality are common among some 60 per cent of the population in low-income societies, and small numbers in the high-income societies. Evidence can be crudely assessed from calorie intake figures showing excessive dependence on cereals and starchy roots and low con-

WORLD: DAILY PER CAPITA CALORIC INTAKE (Retail Level), BY GREAT-REGION AND ECONOMIC-TYPE OF SOCIETY, 1962-1964 AVERAGE-ANNUAL

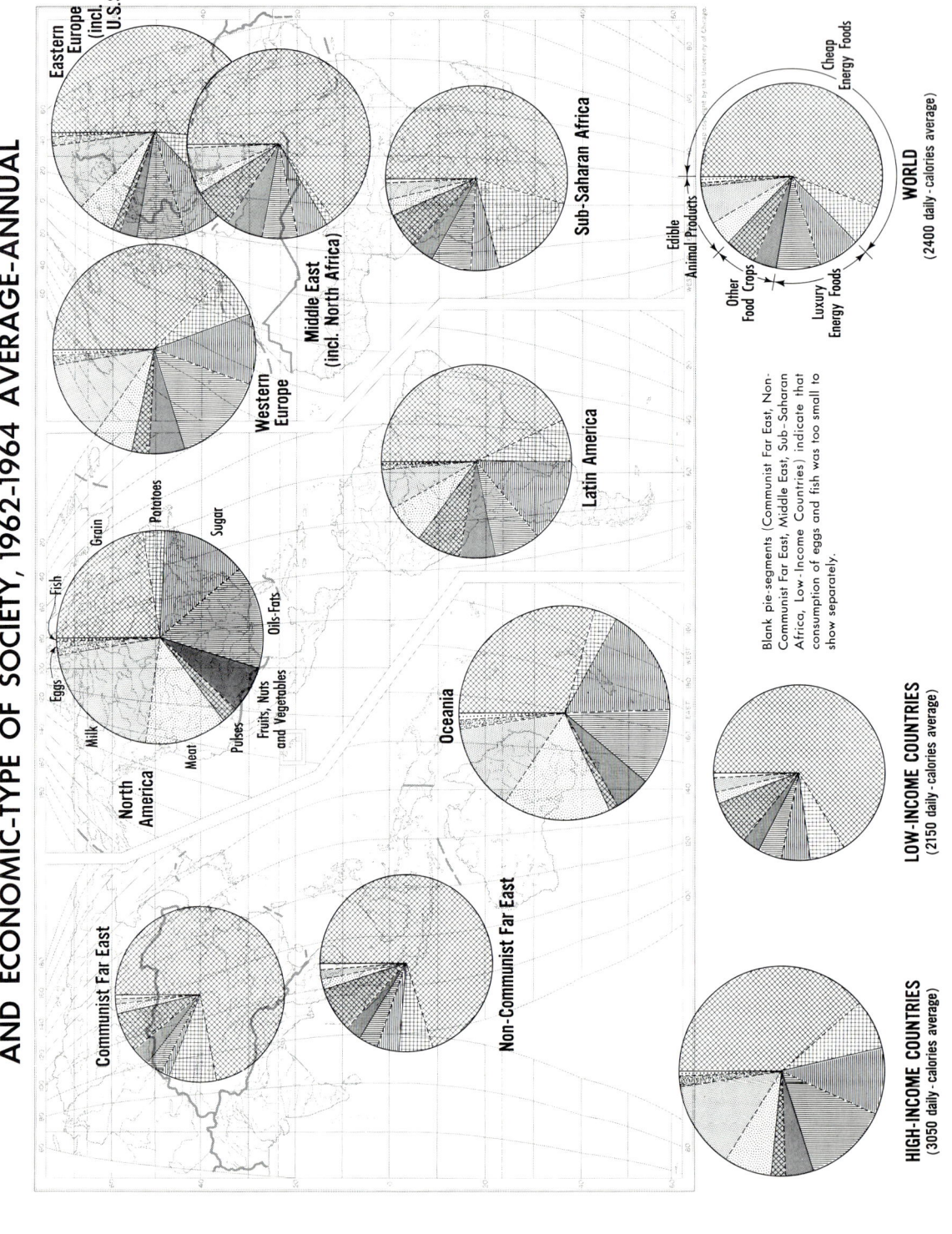

TABLE 5–2

World: Per Capita Food Consumption Levels (Retail Level), by Great-Region and Economic-Type of Society, 1962–1964 Average-Annual

	Calories per Day		Supplies as Share of Requirement	Cheap Energy Foods	
	Requirements	Supplies		Grain	Potatoes
North America	2,600	3,100	120%	21.9%	3.5%
Western Europe	2,600	3,000	115	37.3	7.3
Eastern Europe (including the U.S.S.R.)	2,600	3,200	123	50.7	11.7
Oceania	2,600	3,250	125	29.5	3.8
Latin America	2,400	2,500	104	42.8	7.3
Sub-Saharan Africa	2,350	2,400	98	54.3	16.6
Middle East (including North Africa)	2,400	2,450	103	64.5	1.3
Non-Communist Far East	2,300	2,050	90	70.0	6.3
Communist Far East	2,400	2,100	88	72.0	9.2
World	2,400	2,400	100	55.3	7.5
High-income countries	2,600	3,050	117	38.4	7.9
Low-income countries	2,300	2,150	93	66.0	7.1

	Luxury Energy Foods		Other Food Crops		Edible Animal Products			
	Sugar	Oils-Fats	Fruit, Nuts, Vegetables	Pulses	Meat	Milk	Eggs	Fish
North America	13.5%	15.7%	7.0%	2.3%	12.8%	20.0%	2.8%	0.5%
Western Europe	10.1	15.4	5.6	2.7	6.6	12.7	1.5	0.8
Eastern Europe (including the U.S.S.R.)	7.9	7.5	3.0	1.0	5.9	10.5	1.3	0.5
Oceania	16.2	12.1	5.3	1.3	16.1	13.8	1.5	0.4
Latin America	13.6	8.5	6.0	7.4	6.6	6.7	0.7	0.4
Sub-Saharan Africa	4.9	7.2	4.0	6.3	2.8	3.2	0.3	0.4
Middle East (including North Africa)	5.6	6.3	6.6	6.8	2.2	6.3	0.3	0.1
Non-Communist Far East	4.4	3.3	2.9	8.5	1.9	1.9	0.2	0.6
Communist Far East	1.5	3.2	3.4	7.1	2.8	0.2	0.2	0.4
World	7.5	7.6	4.1	5.8	4.1	6.7	0.7	0.7
High-income countries	10.3	13.4	4.9	1.9	7.6	13.4	1.6	0.6
Low-income countries	5.1	4.3	3.6	8.4	2.1	2.7	0.2	0.5

SOURCE: Adapted from Food and Agriculture Organization sources.

sumption of animal foods. In addition, consumption of other protective foods such as fresh green and yellow vegetables and fruits is inadequate. These factors, together with wrong methods of food preparation and religious taboos and traditional prejudices, are responsible for the deficiency of good-quality protein and of essential minerals and vitamins. Diets of poor nutritional quality and/or insufficient quantity are largely responsible for poor general health, listlessness, and low resistance to infections and diseases, as well as being directly responsible for the widespread occurrence of specific deficiency diseases. They also contribute to the high mortality among infants and young children and the low expectation of life in the less developed areas.

The protein-calorie deficiency is the commonest of the nutritional deficiency diseases in the world today, and probably the most important. It is especially prevalent among the eaters of corn, rice, and cassava. Natural protein is not assimilable as such, but is broken down into its fundamental building blocks, the amino acids, which are reconstituted into human tissue. Of the twenty amino acids, ten are indispensable because they cannot be synthesized by the human body from the others but must be ingested. Each meal must contain a balance of these ten superior amino acids, as there is no storage (excess is either voided or denitrogenated and used as body fuel). The balanced intake may come from either vegetable or animal sources; but all vegetable protein is incomplete protein, lacking in some of the ten varieties needed or having a shortage in some, while animal protein does contain all ten in the right proportions. Since most malnourished people are poor and cannot afford sufficient animal products, the cheapest method of supplying an adequate protein intake is to take the most adequate vegetable protein (e.g., soybean meal or some other pulse) and to fortify it with the missing amino acids from other natural sources such as "fish-flour" (and perhaps from synthetic sources, eventually).

Kwashiorkor and marasmus are childhood protein deficiency diseases that result from the provision to weaned infants of diets that lack sufficient protein of good quality and that often do not provide enough energy for the efficient utilization of this limited amount of protein. They are extremely common in the low-income societies, especially those consuming yams and cassava or maize and millets as their staples. Most Africans have apparently suffered from the disease at some time in their childhood, often with permanent aftereffects. Latin America and the Far East also have high incidence, although the increasing use of pulse in South Asia and of milk and other animal products in offshore East Asia is helping to reduce the incidence of protein malnutrition in those areas.

Mineral deficiencies that have geographical aspects include calcium, phosphorus, iron, sodium, and iodine. It is through food that soils exert an important influence on the health and vital capacity of human societies. The mineral content of a given food is extremely variable, depending on a number of factors, but principally on the local soil types.

Calcium deficiency is the most frequent and widespread mineral deficiency and is a universal phenomenon affecting all climatic zones. Calcium is the most abundant mineral in the body (some 2 per cent of the body weight) and is found in bones and in all body fluids and cells. Because of a low intake of milk and milk products, the diets consumed in many parts of the world provide much less calcium than those eaten in the more developed countries. In certain developing areas where low levels of dietary calcium are associated with lack of exposure to sunlight (vitamin D, which the body can provide itself in the presence of sunlight, is a necessary catalyst for good bone formation), because of climatic or cultural reasons, the incidence of rickets in children or bony deformities in their mothers may be high. The main belt extends across North Africa and Southwest Asia into parts of South and Southeast Asia.

Phosphorus deficiency adversely affects the synthesis of proteins, the metabolism of sugars, and the contraction of muscles. Phosphorus-poor soils and plants of certain (especially tropical) regions adversely affect human nutrition by hindering the raising of animals that supply superior proteins.

Iron deficiency is also common in tropical regions. Iron is especially important in the body as an oxygen carrier. Usually the store of iron is reused, so only wounds and menstruation cause deficiency normally. Meat products alone furnish iron in a highly available form.

Nutritional anemia, which may result from dietary deficiencies of iron, folic acid, or other nutrients accentuated by intakes of protein poor in quantity or quality, is common in areas where starchy roots are the staple foods and green leafy vegetables are eaten in only small amounts. The condition is often aggravated by chronic parasitic infestation that occurs among a high percentage of the population. Nutritional anemia affects mostly pregnant and lactating women.

Sodium deficiency is also found mainly in the tropics, because of the high rate of sweating (up to 10 quarts per day with continual heavy labor). Salt is found mainly in body fluids (especially hydrochloric acid). Apparently, imbalance between sodium and potassium is most serious.

Iodine deficiency affects the rate of using oxygen. Endemic goiter is found in areas where the soil and drinking water are low in iodine and is particularly prevalent among the inhabitants of remote granite mountains, but may also be found in certain low-lying areas. In these circumstances, the provision and use of iodized salt is the best means of eradicating the disease.

Vitamin deficiencies are numerous and the list is being continually augmented. Vitamin A deficiency is mainly due to the insufficient intake of foods like butter, eggs, milk, fish-liver oils, carotene-containing vegetable oils (e.g., red palm oil), and green and yellow vegetables. It is still widespread in many areas of the low-income realm. The importance of vitamin A deficiency is that total and incurable blindness often results, particularly among children. It also causes night blindness and skin disorders. Throughout the humid coastal zones of west Africa, supplies of carotene (a precursor of vitamin A) are ample because of the widespread use of red palm oil. Large areas in the Far East, Middle East, and Latin America have a public health problem because of a lack of vitamin A.

Among the common signs of malnutrition observed in developing societies are sore lips and sore tongues, because of the lack of vitamin B_2 (riboflavin). These result from the use of starchy staple foods that contain only traces of the vitamin and a low consumption of dairy produce, eggs, and fresh leafy vegetables.

Certain deficiency diseases have been reduced during the past decade by government programs designed to orient food production, processing, and utilization to the consumption of nutritionally satisfactory diets. For example, beriberi, which is due to the lack of vitamin B_1 (thiamine), has virtually disappeared from much of China, India, and Indonesia through the use of undermilled or parboiled rice, and the program is being adopted in parts of Africa. On the other hand, the increasing use of machine milling and consumption of highly polished rice during the same period (in south Mainland China, in Mainland Southeast Asia, and in parts of eastern South Asia) has spread the disease. In Japan, rice must be enriched with thiamine at the milling stage by law.

Indirect evidence of malnutrition is provided by vital statistics and records of growth rates of children. Infant mortality (death rate for children under one year of age) is less than 0.4 per cent yearly in high-income societies; about 10 per cent in many Latin American, Middle Eastern, and Far Eastern societies; and over 20 per cent in some African societies. Child mortality (between one and four years) is 0.1 per cent yearly in most high-income societies, and more than 2 per cent in many low-income societies.

During the last two generations, a tremendous shift has taken place in the dietary habits of many highly developed societies toward edible animal products and vegetable protective foods compared with that of cereals and other cheap energy foods. By contrast, the intake of such superior foods in many of the less developed societies, especially in the Far East, even today is much below the level in the highly developed societies two to four generations ago. While the greater part of the improvement in health and life expectancy is due to general advances in medicine and sanitary control, there is general agreement that qualitative improvements in the dietary of the high-income societies have contributed to the decrease in child mortality, increase in longevity, and greater resistance to disease. This is borne out not only among Western peoples, but also among the Japanese and others.

Overview

The world food supply available per capita, though higher than in the immediate post-World War II years, is only slightly above the prewar level. But up to half of the world's population is still hungry or malnourished or both. The progress has mainly occurred in the high-income societies.

The caloric intake in the low-income societies is only about two-thirds that in the high-income societies, on the average, and substandard even when climatic, stature, work-year, and other differences are taken into consideration (at least 20 per cent of the population in such areas is undernourished most of the year).

The nutritional quality of the diet has shown a distinct though small improvement over the pre-World War II level. However, this improvement has again mainly taken place in the developed areas, while in the less developed areas the quality of diets has barely regained the unsatisfactory prewar level. Retarded growth of children, poor physique and health in adults, low resistance to disease (particularly in children below five years), and low working efficiency, together with high mortality rates among young children and low expectations of life, are indications of widespread malnutrition in the less developed areas. In such areas, the level of animal protein is only one-fifth that in the more developed areas.

There are great differences in regional diets throughout the world, reflecting the types of crops and livestock produced, traditional food preferences, the level of living, the amount of trade, and other variables. The common pattern in most poor regions is a basic reliance on cheap starchy foods. When consumers can afford them, traditional cereal and root staples are supplemented with more expensive foods, both luxury energy foods (sugar and oil) and protective foods (edible animal products, fruits, vegetables). As incomes continue to rise, the expensive foods tend to replace the cheaper traditional foods; many of the latter continue to be produced, but for animal feed and industrial raw materials. It is generally agreed that if more than about 80 per cent of the calories in a diet are obtained from cereals, starchy roots, and sugar, there is a risk that the nutritional quality of the diet is inadequate. If this percentage is less than about 80, the diet is likely to be adequate. In well-fed countries, hardly any households have such a dietary, but some 60 per cent of the households in the low-income countries do.

The F.A.O. estimates that from 1965 to 1975 the world food supplies will have to be increased by some 35 per cent merely to sustain the world's increasing population at its present unsatisfactory levels of diet. To achieve a reasonable improvement in the levels of nutrition, world food supplies would have to be increased by more than 50 per cent, with the less developed countries needing an 80 per cent increase in total supplies and a 120 per cent increase in the production of animal products.

Since the income elasticity of the demand for food in low-income countries is some 0.7, the reasonable improvement would require a rate of growth in per capita income of nearly 3 per cent, and an increase in aggregate national income by some 5 per cent per annum. Only a minority of the low-income societies are improving their economic status at these rates at present, and they are mainly among the somewhat better-off group (more than $125 per capita income yearly).

INCREASED AGRICULTURAL SUPPLY: GRAND STRATEGY

In order to satisfy the combined pressures for additional agricultural supplies coming from increasing population and changing consumption standards, mankind needs to increase (calorie) output at a rate of some 3 per cent annually (and value output even more). The range for individual countries would run from less than 1 per cent to more than 4 per cent.

In the foreseeable future, each society must mainly solve its own agricultural problems. It is unrealistic to redistribute world population according to existing resource availability and actual production. Now, as in the past, societies under pressure to increase agricultural output have three main avenues of escape from their food and raw materials problems: intensification of yields, areal expansion, and expanding commerce. In a world perspective, their relative importance would be in the order noted.

1. Intensification of yields—improving biological and chemical technology.
   a) Most important means is still through increasing farm-produced factors of production (e.g., more fertilizer through improved crop rotations, through combining crop agriculture and animal husbandry into more productive agricultural systems, or through other innovations).

b) Most visible means to developed societies, and probably most important means if one takes a long view, is the increasing use of purchased (factory and services) factors of production (e.g., high-yielding seeds and chemical fertilizers used in highly commercial farming).
2. Areal expansion—utilization of empty and underused areas.
   a) Most important in the long run is piecemeal reclamation or inner colonization within areas already partially used (tubers, tree crops, fish ponds on poor land, hybrid animals).
   b) Most visible to naive eyesight is large-scale reclamation (clearing of forests, plowing of grasslands, major drainage and irrigation of wasteland), which usually occurs in occasional spurts.
3. Expanding commerce—increasing specialization, with greater dependence upon imports.
   a) Most difficult is the development and maintenance of foreign markets for primary specialties, highly fabricated goods, and services so as to be able to pay for food and inedible raw materials imports.
   b) Developing foreign sources may be nearly as difficult in some cases where surplus production does not already exist, requiring investment and long-run contracts as an incentive.

Intensification of Yields

Most thickly settled regions find that upping the yields of existing cropland and increasing production per animal-unit are cheaper than reclaiming the remaining slim pioneering possibilities. Most of the world's regions that are intensifying their land-use find farm-produced fertilizer and other supplies more available and cheaper than purchased supplies for most staple crops. When the latter are used, they usually find their greatest application in restricted areas and for certain (cash) crops, with the less accessible areas and subsistence crops remaining dependent upon farm sources.

Increasing the farm-produced fertilizer supply can be achieved in at least three ways: (1) through use of night soil (human excreta) and composted wastes of other local types, (2) through improved crop rotations, and (3) through combining crop agriculture and animal husbandry into more productive systems. The first is especially favored in the Far East, with the second and third finding their most intensive use in Western Europe and its cultural offshoot regions.

The use of organic waste materials from the farmyard and nearby urban centers is particularly great in the Far East, where the dense human and often dense animal populations produce immense quantities of excreta and other litter, where labor costs are low, and where distances over which the materials need to be transported are generally short. In China, about 85 per cent of the total cultivated area is annually manured through organic manures such as night soil, stable manure, compost, green-manure crops, mud from the bottom of canals and ponds rich in organic matter, oil cakes, and some chemical fertilizers. It is estimated that some 50 per cent of the manure used is night soil (about 200 million tons yearly, including stable manure), 20 to 30 per cent compost, and 10 to 15 per cent green manure. The use of chemical fertilizers is relatively small but is steadily on the increase. Korea and Japan traditionally practiced Chinese-type agriculture, but in recent decades have added the Western European system of adding mineral fertilizers to the closed cycle of compost and manure.

Even in the Far East, only partial use is made of organic waste materials. In India, an estimated 40 per cent of the animal excreta and similar waste is burned for cooking and heating because wood is scarce, and apparently about three-quarters of the nitrogen and potash in the animal excreta used for manure is lost, compared with a loss of about half under better handling. The sanitary use of human excreta has in the past been generally uneconomic under Western conditions, but it is possible that eventually algae will be grown in decomposing sewage, with the protein-rich algal cells being used for animal-feed concentrate.

In many regions, achieving permanent agriculture (i.e., soil conservation) is inseparable from the problems of intensification. Nearly ¼ billion people still live in regions of early Neolithic type (slash-and-burn or shifting cultivation), which may require up to 250 acres of forest land and brushland per capita to be sustained on a permanent basis. Recently cleared land may lose up to 300 pounds of nitrogen per year, so the second year often finds yields a fourth to a half lower than the first year. The traditional method of recuperation is to permit a forest generation to intervene between uses as cropland; but most such areas in sub-Saharan Africa, Latin America, and Southeast Asia are now too heavily populated to allow much resting, so accelerated erosion and weed infestation is rising with shorter and shorter cycles. This disintegration of the soil structure and fertility is probably sub-Saharan Africa's most serious agricultural production problem.

The first permanent agriculture (other than well-adjusted shifting cultivation) occurred in areas of new alluvium where overflowing rivers provided yearly fertilization. Over 1 billion people live in areas of new and old alluvium today, especially in the Far East. About half of these have techniques little advanced over the original Bronze Age innovations and obtain low yields from essentially residual fertility.

The most "permanent" agriculture today, supporting about 2 billion people, is in non-riverine-bottomlands, where rotations, animal manure, and mineral fertilizers insure balance between input and outgo of plant nutrients. An undeterminate proportion of such lands are probably still being mined. Some erosion is necessary to preserve good topsoil (senile soils in the tropics would sometimes be improved by more erosion), but natural erosion is very limited compared with the accelerated soil erosion now taking place in some regions, especially in the Newer European regions settled in the past several centuries. In mid-latitude regions of mature soils (e.g., American Midwest), it probably takes three centuries to form an acre-inch of topsoil weighing about 150 tons, which permits a yearly loss of half a ton per acre without destructive exploitation. Of course, soils overlying consolidated materials should be in grass or terraced, and deep loess can lose perhaps 5 tons yearly per acre. In the perhaps two-thirds of U.S. cultivated acreage subject to accelerated erosion, continuous corn sometimes results in losing 40 tons of topsoil yearly, and even rotations of corn-oats-meadow often lose 10 tons yearly, so permanent agriculture in the northwest European sense is still far from being attained. In the one-quarter of U.S. cultivated acreage seriously affected by man-induced erosion, the cost of repair averages as much cost as the first clearing of forest land.

Superlative soils everywhere in the world tend to be grassland types, since most cereals are grass relatives and require grassland-type soil structure for best growth. Continuous cultivation and crumbly soil structure are difficult to attain without rotation in which perennial grasses, legumes, and root crops are important. It is possible, theoretically, to maintain a good soil structure with the use of artificial soil conditioners, but the cost is prohibitive ($300 per acre is economical for tennis courts but not ordinary agriculture).

In general, good soil management results in higher than natural fertility, especially on forest soils. In Western Europe and Japan, per-acre yields have more than tripled since the Industrial Revolution, with some two-thirds of their plant nutrients now coming from mineral and other commercial sources. North American agriculture is still about half dependent upon farm sources, while Eastern European and Oceanic agriculture are still three-quarters dependent upon farm sources. In the underdeveloped realm, the proportion runs much higher.

Factory-produced mineral fertilizers and other agricultural chemicals are growing in importance at a fast rate, but mankind has only begun to use the potentialities. Some 40 million tons of nutrients (excluding the buffers) are now used yearly: the 10 million tons used in the low-income countries supply about 15 per cent of total requirements, while the 30 million tons used in the high-income countries supply about half of total requirements in that realm. In both realms, the artificial fertilizer is mainly used on the best land, especially that growing cash crops. Except for small spots with exceptional accessibility advantages, upgrading of mature forest soils has not yet been proven economic on a large scale. Most such soils (e.g., true podzols and latasols) are ill-supplied with humus (nitrogen) and poor in assimilable bases and phosphorus, and any large-scale improvement must be built around attainment and maintenance of a basic environment through liming, so that the nitrogen-fixing bacteria will flourish and good types of leguminous grass can be introduced.

The three expensive elements in artificial fertilizer are nitrogen, phosphorus, and potassium. Nitrogen is the element needed to support growth of stalk, stems, and leaves. Nearly a ton is in the air over every square foot of surface, but this is not available directly to plants. Most usable nitrogen comes from disintegrating humus (5 per cent N = 58 per cent C) in the topsoil. The amount of humus per acre in basic or neutral mid-latitude soils may be 2 tons, which is released by liming (liming increases the activity of soil microorganisms which disintegrate the humus, but above a certain level the liming ties up phosphorus and trace elements into insoluble forms). Fallow areas may gain 15 to 30 pounds annually by fixation of stray legumes in the vegetative cover and from rain (lightning-fixed atmospheric nitrogen), but bare land loses nitrogen at a fast rate (70 pounds per acre in mid-latitudes, often 170 to 270 pounds in the humid tropics). Some 100 to 250 pounds of nitrogen per acre can be fixed by rotating legumes with grain crops (e.g., 100 bushels of corn use 100 pounds N, 60 bushels of oats use 35 to 50 pounds N, which is recouped by two alfalfa crops giving 125 pounds N in many parts of the Midwest). If more nitrogen is desired than crop rotation can supply, artificial sources must be utilized (cost 10 to 20 cents per pound in the Corn Belt). A given unit of nitrogen usually adds 12 to 15 units of grain or hay production, or 75 units of potatoes. According to some agricultural chemists, if electrical methods to force ammonia molecules (NH_3) to give up nourishing atoms of nitrogen at the right time succeed, possible yields may be upped as much as thirty times (so far this is a dream, based upon small-scale laboratory experiment).

In many regions (especially areas of humid forest soils), phosphorus is a more critical need than nitrogen, mainly because it is linked with other elements, especially iron, into forms that are not easily available to plants. The element is needed for growth of seed, to give a good start, and to promote root development. About half of the phosphorus in the topsoil is in organic combination, which can be unlocked by the use of lime (in moderate amounts) on acid soils, or by increasing the moisture content of the soils (range and pasture plants have lower phosphorus content in dry years than in wet ones). Using granular forms of phosphate fertilizer is thought to lengthen the period before it is fixed in insoluble forms.

Potassium (potash) strengthens resistance to disease, encourages growth of plant cells, and increases the CO_2 absorbing capacity. It is less scarce than nitrogen and phosphorus but is required in large amounts during the period of most rapid growth. Topsoil often has 125 tons or more per acre, but only a few pounds are in the soil solution ready for easy use. Potassium salts do not leach away as rapidly as nitrate salts.

Practically all artificial fertilizer is still used on cropland, although experiments indicate that spectacular progress can be achieved by treatment of grassland, tree crops, forests, and fishponds. Few realize the importance of grass; for example, it provides almost two-thirds of the feed requirements of U.S. livestock (about half of it from range sources, and half from rotation meadows). Cattle fed on the native palmetto scrub range of the coastal plain South originally showed an average gain of only 5 to 15 pounds of beef per acre per year, which means an average of 20 acres needed to supply one head. An acre planted in hybrid grass (Coastal Bermuda), fertilized with 36 pounds of nitrogen, will support a steer and produce nearly 300 pounds of beef annually. With heavy fertilization—some 200 pounds of nitrogen per acre, plus phosphorus and potassium to make a 4-1-2 ratio—an acre will graze three steers for a total annual yield of 700 pounds of beef. Planter-contractors across the

South will set an acre of Coastal Bermuda, fertilizer and all, for $20, which, with some irrigation, will produce up to 16 tons of hay to the acre; rich in proteins and minerals, this is an excellent winter silage with high carotene content.

If one takes a long view of world agricultural development, there is a tendency to concentrate most production on restricted areas of superlative land (level, moist, fertile, accessible) and lavish purchased factors of production in order to intensify far beyond natural capability.[2] Although less visible than areal expansion into marginal lands, it has been more important historically and promises to be so in the future.

Areal Expansion

Mankind's major expansions of cropland have been accomplished by both intermittent large-scale and steady small-scale clearing of forest land, plowing of grasslands, drainage of swamps, and irrigation of desert land and shrubland. Historically, most cultivated land has been reclaimed from the forest, but in the past century, most additions have come from mechanized cultivation of subhumid grasslands, which historically had been the domain of the nomad and hunter.

As Table 5–3 and the graphs on pages 116–17 show, world arable acreage is now some 3½ billion acres, of which two-thirds is actually cultivated at any one time, and the remaining one-third is in current fallow, rotational meadows, and areas in tree-shrub crops. Of the total arable acreage, apparently two-thirds was originally reclaimed by clearing (mainly mid-latitude and subtropical) forests, with about one-quarter reclaimed from natural (mainly subhumid) grasslands, and the remaining tenth reclaimed by irrigation and drainage (not counting partial irrigation and drainage used to improve other soils).

There remain large possibilities of reclamation. There are some 1 billion acres of potentially arable land in the world that could be reclaimed

[2] In the past two decades, over four-fifths of the world's increased grain output have come from yield increases.

at first costs of $100 or so per acre; and if first costs several times as large are postulated, some optimists think that perhaps 3 billion or more acres might be reclaimed (about doubling the world's arable acreage). However, most of this potential is in the Americas, sub-Saharan Africa, and the U.S.S.R., while the greatest needs are in the Far East. In addition, most reclamation requires modern mechanical, chemical, and organizational technology, rather than the old-fashioned family-scale clearing used in the past. So, as in the past, large-scale additions are likely to come intermittently and not affect availability as much as other less visible forms of improvement.

Most clearing of forests for arable purposes is now a piecemeal process on the edges of the ecumene ("highly useful" realm) or an expansion in older areas (where patches of forest land, grassy swamp, etc., were left because of poor soils, poor drainage, or inaccessibility). In Quebec's colonization schemes (Clay Belts), settlers usually clear 70 acres and farm 30 of these the first seven years, with preliminary clearing and additional improvements before farming costing some $50 per acre (these expenses do not include the more than $1,000 for buildings and wells, and the homesteaded land is free). In India's Uttar Pradesh Terai (swampy Himalayan foothills), clearing farms out of the jungle has been costing $75 to $150 per acre (total costs, including buildings and wells, of which the first bulldozer clearing costs about $20 per acre). Reclamation of tropical rain forest and monsoon forest for use in paddy and other permanent cultivation has been costing $100 to $500 per acre (depending on how much drainage and contouring has to be done) in Indonesia's outer islands and elsewhere in Southeast Asia. In all such cases, except where heavily subsidized by government, such reclamation is beyond the means of the landless or small-holder peasants who most need additional land.

Practically all remaining forest land on level, well-drained ground is on poor soils, in both high and low latitudes. The problems of permanent cultivation on such soils are formidable and costly, except in paddy (wet-rice). In West Africa and Southeast Asia, more forest land has been reclaimed in recent decades by planting

TABLE 5-3

World: Land-Use, by Great-Region and Economic-Type of Society, *circa* 1963 (Estimated) *

(in billions of hectares)

	Total Area (billion hectares = 100.0 per cent)	Arable Land	Rangeland	Forest Land	Facilities	Unused But Potentially Arable	Wasteland
North America	2.15	10.5%	13.0%	35.0%	1.0%	4.5%	36.0%
Western Europe	0.37	27.0	15.0	28.0	3.0	2.0	25.0
Eastern Europe (including the U.S.S.R.)	2.37	13.5	15.0	39.0	1.0	4.0	27.5
Oceania	0.85	3.5	52.5	6.5	0.5	5.0	32.0
Latin America	2.05	7.0	18.0	48.0	0.5	5.0	21.5
Sub-Saharan Africa	2.42	8.6	21.6	25.8	0.5	4.0	39.5
Middle East (including North Africa)	1.16	7.0	17.5	4.5	0.5	5.0	65.5
Non-Communist Far East	1.00	20.0	10.0	35.0	2.0	5.0	28.0
Communist Far East	1.16	10.0	15.5	11.0	1.5	3.0	59.0
World	13.53	10.6	19.2	29.3	1.0	4.4	35.5
High-income countries	6.10	11.2	20.9	30.9	1.0	4.0	32.0
Low-income countries	7.43	10.0	18.0	28.1	0.8	4.8	38.3
	(per cent of 13.53 billion hectares)	(per cent of 1.43 billion hectares)	(per cent of 2.60 billion hectares)	(per cent of 3.96 billion hectares)	(per cent of 0.13 billion hectares)	(per cent of 0.60 billion hectares)	(per cent of 4.81 billion hectares)
North America	15.9	15.8	10.6	19.1	17.6	16.8	16.1
Western Europe	2.7	7.0	2.2	2.6	9.6	1.1	1.9
Eastern Europe (including the U.S.S.R.)	17.5	22.4	13.5	23.2	19.2	16.8	13.2
Oceania	6.3	2.1	17.3	1.4	3.2	7.5	5.6
Latin America	15.1	10.5	14.2	24.7	8.0	16.8	9.0
Sub-Saharan Africa	17.9	14.7	20.2	15.8	8.0	16.8	20.0
Middle East (including North Africa)	8.6	5.6	7.7	1.3	4.8	10.0	15.9
Non-Communist Far East	7.4	14.0	3.8	8.8	16.0	8.4	5.9
Communist Far East	8.6	7.9	10.5	3.1	13.6	5.8	12.4
World	100.0	100.0	100.0	100.0	100.0	100.0	100.0
High-income countries	45.2	47.8	49.0	47.6	52.0	40.7	40.8
Low-income countries	54.8	52.2	51.0	52.4	48.0	59.3	59.2

SOURCE: Adapted from United Nations data with unofficial estimates to fill in gaps and to bring up to date.

* Such land-use data are only roughly comparable, especially the categories "Forest Land," "Unused But Potentially Arable," and "Wasteland." "Forest Land" and "Unused But Potentially Arable" categories tend to be exaggerated in areas that are poor in high-quality possibilities. The "Wasteland" category would be greatly enlarged if Antarctica were included.

tree crops (e.g., food types like cacao and palm oil or raw material types like rubber) than by reclamation for field crops. Taking a long view, the main reclamation technique in the warmer margins of the great northern forests may well be the substitution of faster-growing hybrid pulpwoods for the present natural forest.

The plowing of grassland has been, during the past century, the cheapest reclamation in most pioneering regions. In the North American Great Plains, Siberian-Kazakhstan steppes, and southern hemisphere equivalents, $10 to $20 per acre for initial breaking of sod has been a common cost. Agriculture in such regions has high

WORLD: LAND-USE, BY GREAT-REGION AND ECONOMIC-TYPE OF SOCIETY, 1963 ESTIMATE (Billion Hectares)

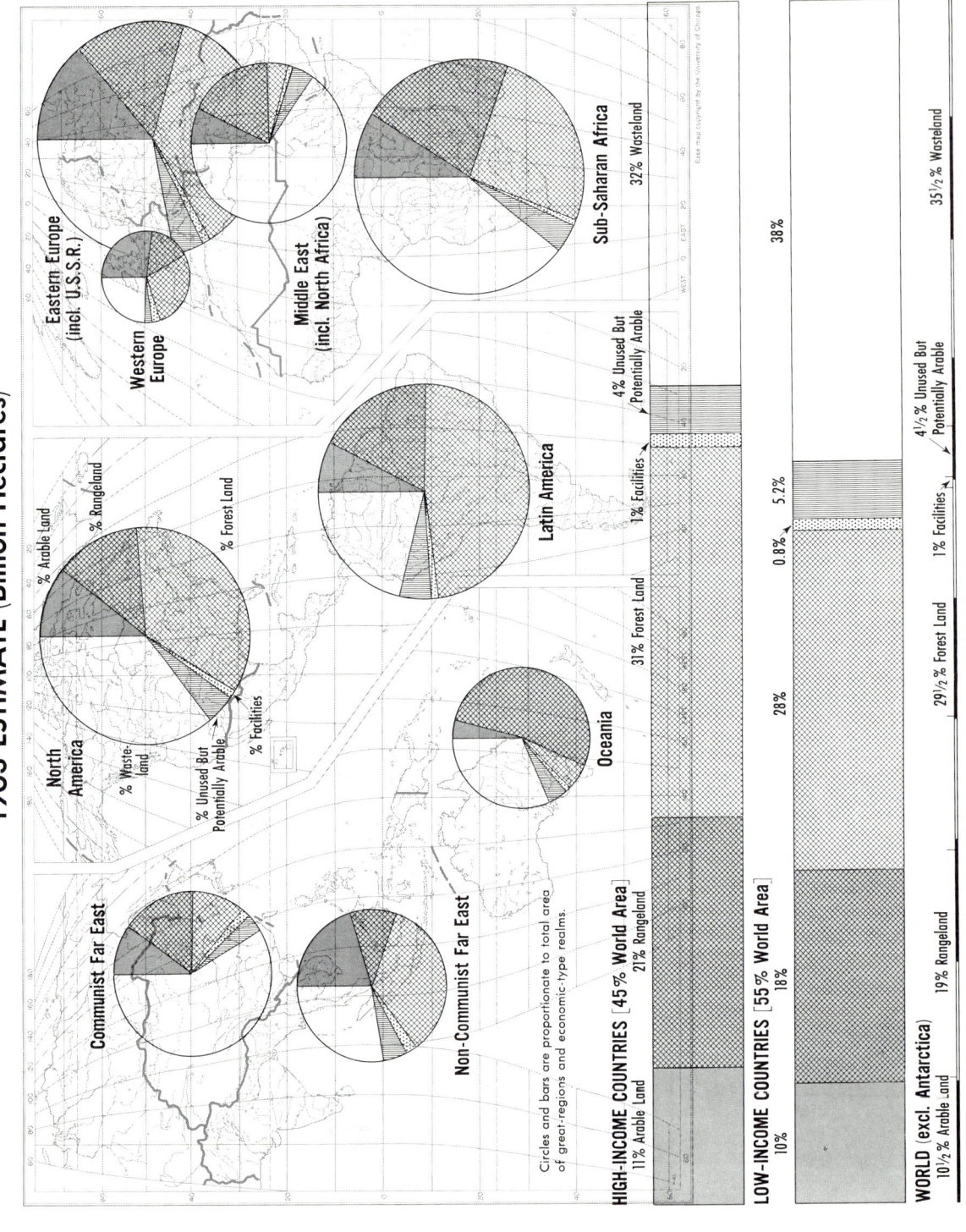

WORLD: GREAT-REGION AND ECONOMIC-TYPE OF SOCIETY SHARES OF WORLD LAND-USE TYPES, 1963 ESTIMATE

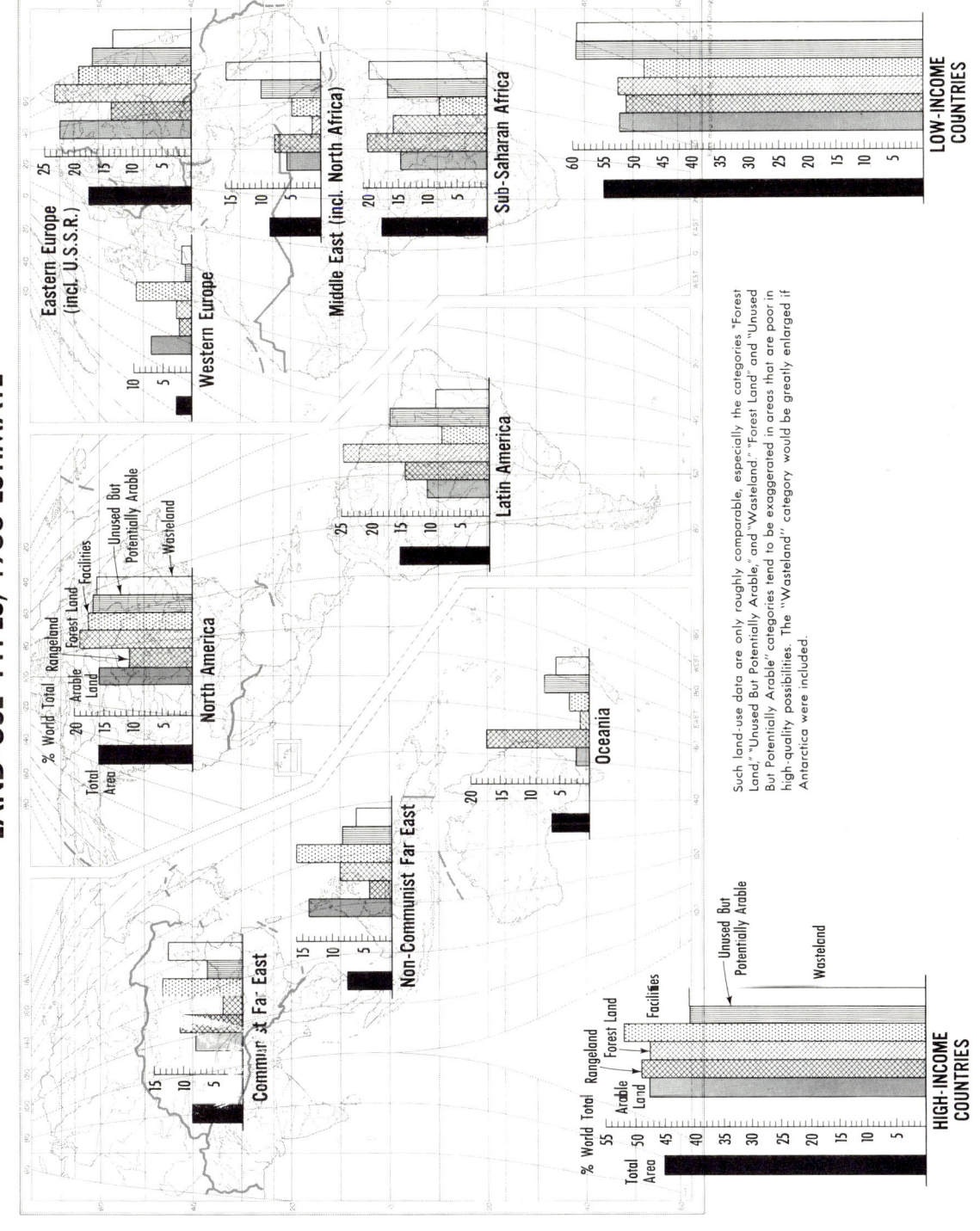

capital costs in equipment and high costs for credit during periods of drought or other catastrophe, but even so such land has provided most of the cheap surplus grain moving in commercial channels both internally and internationally. In thickly settled areas, the possibilities are mainly in small-scale reclamation of old fallow that has been so infested with weeds (e.g., Indian kans or wild sugarcane areas) that traditional techniques can no longer use such areas without an occasional assist from mechanized deep plowing and chemicalization. In the Far East, such reclamation of man-made savanna is likely to be more important than the possibilities of using the fringes of the Gobi and Thar deserts by introducing Russian or American dry-farming techniques.

In tropical grasslands of vast extent, the development of the grazing potential might add more food than extending conventional farming. At present, ranchers and nomads are using water and grazing up to the limit imposed by nature, so to become more productive they must gain control of these natural resources in order to expand and renew them. Much can be improved by developing groundwater supplies and surface-water storage, and by scientific disease control. To overcome the alternations of flood and drought, the overrapid growth and quick deterioration of the unmanaged pastures, and the provision of fodder for fattening is much more difficult, but in spots much has been done (e.g., highly improved and well-managed, but unirrigated, Lake Maracaibo pastures have tripled the carrying capacity).

In humid and subhumid areas, drainage is an effective tool for increasing crop production, since an excess of moisture in the soil hinders aeration and root growth. In the United States, some 15 per cent of the arable acreage has been added by drainage, and on about the same fraction, production has been doubled by improved drainage. Most present-day efforts are in the coastal plains of the South, where the initial costs for local drainage and flood control have been averaging about $30 per acre, with clearing and other improvements needed before use as pasture or cropland, costing another $50 to $80 per acre.

Most of the world's spectacular potentials in drainage—in the valleys of the Amazon, the Congo and upper Nile, and elsewhere—are going to cost much more, and in some cases, present technology would not be adequate. The famous Zuyder Zee projects may be more comparable in difficulty and cost (i.e., $800 to $1,200 per acre, depending on depth of water and proportion of poor soil in the reclaimed areas). Little of the remaining potentials are amenable to control exerted by subsistence peasants. Although costing more per acre initially, drained lands usually are in humid areas and have yields that fluctuate less than non-irrigated farming on the drought and frost edges of the ecumene.

In the Middle and Far East, and in other regions to a lesser extent, probably the largest reclamation and intensification potentials are through irrigation. The world's 350 million acres of irrigated land, a tenth of the total arable acreage, supports about one-quarter of the world's total population (two-thirds of them in the Far East, where over a third of the total arable acreage is irrigated). The F.A.O. estimates that another 200 million acres of steppe and desert can be economically reclaimed by regular irrigation, and that another billion acres already cultivated would profit from supplementary (5 to 6 inches) irrigation.

In the U.S. West, where good land and an adequate supply of suitable irrigation water are close to each other, an irrigation system using a gravity-type water distribution usually costs $50 to $75 per acre (not counting cost of acquiring and leveling land), while a pumped-irrigation system usually costs at least $75 to $100 per acre. In India and Pakistan, canal irrigation has recently been costing about $35 per acre (not counting the cost of colonization in formerly uninhabited regions), while tube well irrigation costs about $100 per acre in the Gangetic Plain. Quite often, the available supplies of water in the Indus Basin only irrigate adequately one-third of the commanded area during any one season, and much of the land lies fallow for one or two seasons out of every three. Perennial irrigation of the entire commanded area would require storage dams, lined canals, and other facilities that easily triple the cost per acre.

Courtesy of U.S. Department of the Interior, Bureau of Reclamation

Airview of the 550-foot-high Grand Coulee Dam and other associated Columbia Basin Project facilities in central Washington State. When upstream dams are constructed in British Columbia, Canada, regularizing the river flow, electricity-generating capacity will be increased from the present 2 to 5.6 million installed kilowatts. The area being irrigated starts 15 miles south of the Banks Lake balancing reservoir (top of photograph), or 44 miles from the Roosevelt Lake reservoir behind the dam; now half finished, eventually a million acres, about 10,000 farms, an area larger than Rhode Island, will be served. The world's six most powerful pumps (each 65,000 horsepower pump can lift 1,600 cubic feet of water per second, or as much as is needed to serve New York City) lift about 10 per cent of the average flow of the river over the 280-foot-high canyon rim to the feeder canal during the summer irrigation season. When completed, the twelve pumps will fill the Banks Lake equalizing reservoir seven to eight times a year to supply the irrigation district, the largest amount of water lifted so high to serve such a low-value use as irrigation in the world.

Although original, large-scale reclamation is more visible, improvements added gradually over two or three decades thereafter actually add more production. And piecemeal reclamation or inner colonization within areas already mainly cultivated offers continuing opportunities. During the period of primary reclamation in any region, attention is usually centered on the better soils (e.g., superior mature soils or alluvial bottomlands) and better landforms (e.g., naturally level or gently rolling spots), with the other areas left to less intensive use or to actual disuse. Later on, foreign introductions of crops, trees, and animals—or new domestic varieties from selective breeding—often allow piecemeal reclamation of the scattered lower-grade strips and patches.

Western Europe offers a good documented example. Early use of the northern plain concentrated on the alluvial and loessial soils where wheat prospered, and the sandy, acid soil main stretches were either left in forest (often furnishing feed for pigs) or were used occasionally as low-grade cropland (rye, buckwheat) or pasture. In the past few centuries, the introduction of the white potato, which tolerates acid soils, allowed caloric yields as heavy as from the better soils; and such use during the nineteenth century supplied more additional calories to Europe for food and feed than the better advertised overseas grain supplies. Sweet potatoes, yams, cassava, peanuts, and many other crops are similarly being introduced today on Far Eastern high-lands, allowing continued areal expansion after the supply of level, moist alluvium for paddy fields has become scarce.

In many paddy fields of the Far East, the diked plots are often flooded and used during the non-crop portion of the year to raise fast-growing types of fish (e.g., tilapia), the most convenient animal protein economically available in many poor, thickly settled regions. Some paddy farmers who fertilize their fishponds make more on them than when they raise grain.

Expanding Commerce

From the standpoint of technical and economic efficiency, considerably greater trade in domestic and international contexts can be justified, but politically and socially, the barriers to greater specialization weaken only slowly.

In a world perspective, now and in the foreseeable future, there will be a continuing upward trend in production of most agricultural commodities, mainly because of technological progress and national policies (some encouraging greater self-sufficiency; some, overproduction). There will continue a persistent disequilibrium of supply and demand for certain commodities, despite the continuance of inadequate nutritional levels in many regions. At present, further deterioration in the terms of trade (comparative advantage) of agricultural exporting countries seems likely. The trend toward regional economic integration may increase bloc trade, but seems likely to decrease intercontinental trade in competitive products.

In the absence of radical changes in government policies, the present surplus tendencies, already evident for certain commodity groups and in certain regions, are likely to become acute and more generalized during the remainder of the 1960's. Production in mid-latitude commodities (e.g., grain, milk, beet sugar) is likely to increase rapidly, since agricultural science and technology and the spread of such knowledge to farmers are rapidly advancing. Just as important, the need to maintain farmers' incomes at a politically and socially acceptable level in most high-income countries means that government support cannot be expected to fall drastically (although the means of protecting farm income may change). Production of most tropical agricultural commodities also appears likely to increase rapidly, as a result of large new plantings made in the mid-1950's, the spread of new knowledge (especially increased use of pesticides and other disease-control methods), and government encouragement because of the fundamental importance of export earnings to many low-income societies.

In contrast to the continuing rise in production, the outlook for consumption is conjectural. In the high-income countries, the income elasticity of demand for most products is already very low, if not negative. Increases in consumption can hardly anywhere match the likely increases in production, while population growth will be relatively slow. Only radical social change is likely to increase consumption in the small depressed groups and areas that still have low standards. Increased domestic production within Western Europe, stimulated by regional integration, is likely to make that massive market more self-sufficient in most food staples. The possibility of increased competition and further declines in world prices for most of these mid-latitude commodities is considerable.

In most low-income societies, population growth in the remainder of the 1960's will be large, but the outlook for income growth is uncertain. The most rapid growth rates have been in a few countries whose income was already relatively high for the group. The certain rapid growth of population, the present low levels of per capita consumption of most staple commodities in many countries, the high elasticity of income and demand, indicate that a considerable growth in the volume of potential demand can be expected, although the precise growth of effective demand is unknown. Much depends on the possible increases in domestic agricultural production, and on economic aid from the wealthy societies. The scope of commercial transfers of mid-latitude food supplies to low-income deficit countries appears limited. The vital need of most underdeveloped countries is for capital equipment and deficit minerals, and these are likely to receive the highest priority. The present scarcity of foreign exchange limits food imports on commercial terms, and such scarcity is not likely to vanish quickly.

Exports from the high-income countries on concessional terms or in the form of food aid are possible means of bridging the gap. The limiting factors are likely to be the continuing readiness of high-income countries to put large financial resources into food-aid programs, and the abilities of the low-income countries to absorb concessional imports without unduly disturbing domestic and normal commercial-import markets. Even the U.S. programs of the past decade have had only a small impact on the total food needs of the low-income realm, so it is unlikely that non-commercial transfers will do more than ameliorate the effects of inadequate domestic production and occasional catastrophe.

For tropical products, the demand situation in the traditional principal markets parallels that for mid-latitude products. Per capita consumption is already large, and the income elasticity remains high enough so that considerable increases in demand might still occur, especially in Western Europe and Japan. The biggest potential market is Eastern Europe (including the Soviet Union), since its consumption of tropical products is still relatively low relative to disposable income. Lower-quality tropical products are likely to be disposed at concessional price in low-income-realm domestic markets.

For agricultural raw materials, the great question mark concerns competition from synthetic materials (particularly for cotton, wool, and rubber). Low-stable price, rapidly growing productive capacity, and a widening area of substitutability in end uses characterize most of these synthetics. The market for natural textile fibers and rubber is likely to expand for the remainder of the 1960's, but competition from the synthetics is likely to set a floor price for natural products below the higher levels of the 1950's, with heavy pressure on export earnings of the tropical producers. Increasingly, a larger proportion of consumption seems likely in the producing countries of natural raw materials.

In the long view, payment for agricultural imports by presently low-income countries might be made by exporting certain industrial products or certain services. In many cases, however, no substantial comparative advantage now exists. In other cases, the advantages are in low-priced soft consumer goods or transport services which compete with depressed activities in the high-income countries, and which can be nullified by tariff or other protection (e.g., Japan and Hong Kong have great difficulty in paying for their wheat, soybean, cotton, and other imports from the United States because of pressures originating in the textile-garment and consumer electronic industries to restrict cheap exports to the United States). The difficulties placed in the path of greater agricultural trade by overprotected industry and services in high-income societies are less than the difficulties posed by overprotected agriculture, but in the future such roadblocks are likely to increase their relative importance.

INCREASED AGRICULTURAL SUPPLY: TACTICS

The tactics of agricultural development revolve around the choice of alternative technical innovations and combinations of the factors of production made by farm management, especially by those commercial enterprisers who serve domestic urban markets and the export markets. They tend to favor greater use of abundant and cheap factors of production within their reach, and a restricted use of scarce and expensive ones.

Modern farm technology can be classified according to which factor of production pays increasing returns to the farmer. In a world perspective, relative importance would be as follows.

1. Multipurpose technology: that which increases both per acre (or other unit) and labor productivities (e.g., most irrigation, chemical fertilizers and other agricultural chemicals, conservation of soil)
2. Land-saving technology: that which mainly increases the productivity per acre (or other unit) (e.g., improved rotations, improved seeds, improved animals)
3. Labor-saving technology: that which mainly increases the productivity per man-hour (e.g., application of power machines, other forms of improved farm tools).

Multipurpose Technology

The main types or forms of farm technology that increase both acre and labor productivities include the use of irrigation, the use of chemical fertilizers, the control of plant and livestock pests, and the adoption of new methods of preventing soil erosion and of maintaining soil fertility. Such technology has a universal appeal, but is especially favored by farmers who have a shortage of land and a shortage of particular kinds of labor at particular times. In regions like the Far East, such technology is as heavily favored as labor-saving technology has been favored in the Newer European societies.

In most parts of the world having both ordinary and irrigation agriculture, the value-added per acre in the irrigated areas is two to six times greater than in the dry areas. The value of supplementary irrigation as an insurance against crop failure is apparent almost immediately after the facilities are constructed (its drawback is high cost compared to benefits in humid areas where seasonal drought is slight and intermittent). Even more important are the potentialities of irrigation to act as a catalyst on methods of production. Many methods of intensification that are uneconomical on unirrigated land are highly profitable when an assured and cheap supply of soil moisture is available. In many old settled areas, both human and draft animal power, which in precanal days were tied up in expensive raising of water from wells and streams, can be cheaply displaced by gravity-flow water and be shifted into more useful activities such as weeding and tilling the better and more expensive crops now profitable to grow. It also becomes profitable to increase the operating capital employed per acre, by using more fertilizer, better seeds, improved implements, better animals, and more adequate storage facilities. In some Indian areas, the capital requirements per acre have doubled, labor requirements have tripled or quadrupled, and output has increased six times. In poor areas, an advantage is that the huge expenses are likely to be borne by government, and that the adjustments of individual farmers can be made over a long time by evolution of traditional technology.

That there are serious economic problems connected with the increased use of chemical fertilizers on a large scale (e.g., the average Japanese farmer spends over 25 per cent of his factor costs on artificial fertilizers—Japan has less than 5 per cent of China's or India's cultivated acreage, but uses more chemical fertilizers) should not obscure the fact that much of the hope for solution of the agricultural problems of thickly settled regions rests upon a greatly increased use of such manufactured plant food. The old methods of recuperating the soil—current fallow, mixed crops, crop rotation, composts, and others—are likely to remain important, but are no longer sufficient by themselves to solve the problems of greatly intensified use. Farm by-products are still important in improving soil structure, but the use of commercial fertilizers makes it possible to introduce extra supplies of nutrients into the cycle of growth and decay. A short-run difficulty is that poor farmers usually cannot afford purchased fertilizer except on their cash crops, so subsistence crops seldom show great increases in yield.

The normal recurring loss to field crops from plant diseases, weed and insect pests, vermin, wild animals, and domesticated animals may, on a conservative basis, be placed at 10 per cent of the total produce even in a relatively uneventful year (and several times that fraction in many years). Animal epidemics usually arise whenever causes can be traced back to low vitality, unclean surroundings, and polluted drinking water. Solution to these problems, although among the most profitable, is very difficult within the context of peasant agriculture. While the average peasant is fairly efficient in general farming operations, and will willingly undertake hard work in carrying them out, he is generally ignorant of measures for the control of pests and diseases, and will very often not take the simplest steps to protect his crops and animals from their ravages. One reason is that measures of crop and animal protection are recent introductions in the field of farming, and have not been stabilized as routine operations. Even in high-income societies, where most of the world's annual use of pesticides is concentrated, most farmers do not take advantage of their potentiality in upping yield and reducing labor cost per unit (Japan's farmers spend as much on pesticides as on farm implements).

Basic methods of soil conservation—designed and applied to prevent more or less permanent damage to the productive capacity of the land, such as results from bodily removal of the soil by various forms of accelerated erosion—include terracing, contour tillage, crop rotations, contour strip-cropping, rotation grazing, gully sloping and planting, and the growing of shelterbelts and windbreaks. Measures that might be called fertility methods of conservation (i.e., those methods designed and applied to prevent more or less temporary loss of productivity through cropping, leaching, waterlogging, and other forms of damage that do not remove the soil itself, but that must be controlled if the land is to be used to its maximum capacity) include drainage and irrigation, the growing of leguminous and other types of cover and green manure crops, crop rotations, and the application of manure, compost, fertilizer, and lime. Many methods used to protect or improve the fertility of the soil also aid directly or indirectly in preventing erosion while, conversely, many methods employed to protect the land against permanent loss of productivity also contribute to the fertility of the soil. The technical feasibility of these methods depends on many habitat factors (e.g., terrain, climate, natural soil type), while the economic feasibility depends on many institutional and activity factors (e.g., size of farm, ability and cooperation of the farmer in the application of remedial measures, the system of farming, financial position and status of the farmer). Since soil conservation in underdeveloped societies is essentially a form of capital investment, the rise in labor and acre productivities that usually follows makes such changes more palatable than investment which takes much longer for fruition.

Land-saving Technology

The main forms of farm technology that increase only the productivity per acre include the introduction of improved rotations, the introduction of new crop varieties, the introduction of new breeds of animals, and others. In nearly every case, more man-hours are required to take care of the innovation, so labor productivity does not increase much, although farm income usually improves because more time during the year can be devoted to productive effort. This avenue is relatively more important to regions with a relatively fixed amount of useful land.

Improved rotations are the bases of improved soil structure and higher fertility levels, but they usually require so much additional effort that increased productivity is mainly restricted to acreage yields rather than labor output. One problem in low-income societies is that the average peasant will seldom release arable land for either feed or fertilizer crops until he feels sure that he can obtain his food crops, so the extensive use of new crop rotations is likely to follow, rather than to initiate, intensification in many areas. The potentialities are enormous. In Mediterranean land, yields of wheat and other cereals can be doubled by the inclusion of fertilized annual legumes in the place of fallow. The inclusion of legumes, particularly grain legumes, in cereal rotations, can be used (apart from its favorable effect on soil fertility) to provide a more balanced diet.

Improved seeds by themselves rarely achieve permanent results, since few soils have the residual fertility to support the greater drain of soil nutrients for long. Irrigation and additional fertilization are necessary to permit the use of such higher-yielding seed on a permanent basis, and such methods of intensification are likely to be lavished only on cash crops. New varieties can also be more resistant to certain plant diseases and pests, or to extremes of weather (such as aridity or cold), than previous varieties. In the agriculturally advanced countries, where plant populations have already been well worked over, further advances will probably come mainly from hybridization. On the other hand, in underdeveloped countries, even though a large measure of selection and upgrading has been carried out by the farmers themselves over the centuries, the scope for improvement by systematic collection, testing, purification, and concentration on a limited number of varieties (each suitable to a particular set of conditions) is usually substantial. Beyond this task of selection, the production of new varieties, especially bred for resistance to specific hazards or for high-yield potentials, opens up great possibilities which have only been very partially explored in most underdeveloped societies.

Improved animals usually require better feeding and disease control, which requires additional labor, capital, and organization at such a rate that their productivities are seldom greatly increased (except the farm productivity improvement related to greater intensity of use). In the absence of such complementary changes, such improved stock usually deteriorates rapidly. In general, the greatest differences in biological capacity of animals is between high-income and low-income countries. Selective breeding—keeping careful record of performances, culling the poorer animals, and concentrating on the better ones for breeding—has been little used in most poor regions (and even among many farmers in the more advanced countries).

Labor-saving Technology

The main forms of farm technology that increase only the productivity per man-hour include the application of power machines and other forms of complicated farm equipment, but also include simpler tools. Historically, mechanization has been introduced mainly to substitute for human and draft animal labor, and so far it has greatly affected mainly high-income societies. North America performs over 90 per cent of all farm work by machinery, and in Western Europe, Eastern Europe, Oceania, and a few other countries elsewhere, the percentage is 60 per cent and up. The high-income realm operates some 95 per cent of the world's agricultural machinery.

In regions of mechanized agriculture, land is relatively less important as an agent of production than formerly. Only 2 per cent of the net costs of the U.S. economy, for example, is attributable to the cost of agricultural land, while in some low-income societies (especially those that have not undergone agrarian reform), the comparable figure is 25 per cent and sometimes higher.

The natural fertility of cultivable land is in inverse proportion to the amount of energy supporting the cultivator, as a general rule. Peasants must use the best land cultivable by their technology, but mechanized farmers can use much land that is submarginal to premodern technology. In fact, some of the most spectacular successes of mechanized farming are in the subhumid edge of the older agricultural realms, which were formerly utilized almost entirely by nomads and hunters, where large units could be set up without drastically upsetting old patterns

Combine harvesting wheat, central Great Plains. This operation is generally done by contractors, rather than by the individual farmer.

Heavy-duty row-crop tractor trailing a cultivator rig through soybeans.

Heavy tractor pulling two plows, central Great Plains. With such equipment, a family can take care of several hundred, even a thousand, acres.

Windrower working in Great Plains alfalfa.

Such large-wheeled equipment does some 80 per cent of the total work done in North American agriculture, with stationary equipment doing another 15 per cent. The human and animal labor force thus contributes only 5 per cent of all work done. In other urban-industrial regions, the proportion of mechanized work is also high, from 60 to 90 per cent.

Courtesy of J. I. Case Co.

of small holdings such as covered the old sedentary-peasant agricultural regions.

In many underdeveloped regions, if mechanization ever does spread widely, it is likely to be undertaken for different reasons than in the Newer European regions. Machine power is often useful to conserve scanty moisture, or to do tasks that man and animal power cannot do, however abundant. In much of the world, plowing hard soils before the rains come will conserve enough moisture to make the difference between poor and good yields, and this is more important than labor-saving. Even in regions of modern farming, the chief advantage of much mechanization (e.g., use of airplanes to plant, dust, spray) is often to save time rather than to save labor.

In the past several decades, the development of equipment for small holdings has progressed to the point where it is now both technically and economically suitable for many areas. The two-wheeled garden-type tractors now sell for $300 or so and can handle plots up to 3 acres, while the three-wheeled riding tractors costing about $600 (half or less of small conventional tractors) can handle from 3 to 30 acres depending on topography, soil, and other variables. Europeans and Japanese have developed much electrification for small-holders, both stationary and portable types of motorized equipment. Even so, usually small-holders use much more labor in the production of a certain quantity of agricultural produce than large-holders, since they cannot afford to acquire as much machinery as the large farmer. Also, each machine on a small farm is used for only a short time each year (so the operating cost per hour is often high), and external economies (e.g., cheap servicing) are fewer. The most recent spectacular case of farm mechanization is Japan, which now does over 60 per cent of all farm work by machine, compared with only 15 per cent or so before World War II.

CHIEF REASONS FOR AGRICULTURAL POVERTY

Everywhere in the world, agriculture is the poorest sector of the regional economy (even on

TABLE 5–4

World: Annual per Worker Output in Three Major Sectors, by Great-Region and Economic-Type of Society, 1962–1964 Average-Annual *
(in United States dollars)

	General Economy	Agricultural Sector	Industrial Sector	Services Sector
North America	6,550	4,500	8,790	5,630
Western Europe	2,430	735	3,075	2,695
Eastern Europe (including the U.S.S.R.)	1,805	365	2,970	2,425
Oceania	2,570	2,460	2,790	2,500
Latin America	800	270	1,355	1,350
Sub-Saharan Africa	315	115	900	720
Middle East (including North Africa)	565	205	1,620	1,045
Non-Communist Far East	260	105	680	445
Communist Far East	150	70	490	215
World	1,120	210	2,605	1,775
High-income countries	2,870	740	3,810	3,290
Low-income countries	310	115	935	550

* Such exchange-valued data are only roughly comparable, especially with such a concept as U.S. purchasing-power-equivalent as a frame of reference.

a country basis, only New Zealand is an exception). The chief reasons for agriculture's low showing are these: First, and most important, the capital investment per worker is usually lower than in modern industry and services, partly because return on investment is lower in absence of adequate scale, so the output per worker is accordingly lower. Second, institutional and ideological barriers hinder use of much material and social technology that is both technically and economically applicable in the context of certain reforms. Third, peasant agriculture has high fixed costs, partly due to its social welfare responsibilities inherited from the passing civilization. Fourth, agriculture is less adaptable to changes in demand than industry and services, mainly because of its biological associations which so far are less amenable to man's quick control. Fifth, in the long run, the demand for agricultural products is less elastic (expandable) than the demands for highly fabricated goods and services produced by other sectors. All these difficulties are not inevitably inherent, but are mainly the result of agriculture's long history of prior adjustment to earlier cultural stages.

Inadequate Scale

In most regions, the most important change in eventually achieving rural prosperity is the formation of economic-size holdings. The essence of efficient agriculture consists in combining four separate factors in each farm in the right proportions: an area sufficient for effective operation, flexible organization, adequate capital, and technique at a level that, in given conditions, yields the greatest economies. The first requisite is adequate area or scale. Unless a farm has sufficient area, the other factors of production usually cannot operate effectively.

Under modern conditions, in agriculture no less than in industry and services, more capital and organization are the secret of successful operation. In the long run, the main task in peasant societies is to reorganize the villages so that the two factors, capital and organization, can play their full part. Without them, there is little hope that agricultural production can be greatly increased at the same time that much labor and other factors are released. To attain a condition of competitive efficiency or profitability requires several generations of rationalization in which government and other management will face bankruptcy problems as formidable as the developmental problems involved in industrializing agriculture (i.e., "land reform" in the widest sense).

About a third of the world's agriculturalists own or operate some two-thirds of the world's arable acreage. Most of them are found in the high-income realm, although many large-scale owners and some operators (mainly plantations) are found in the low-income realm. Most peasant-agricultural societies are overpopulated in the sense that human energy exists in greater amounts than the rural economy can profitably absorb. The prevailing land-use practices require abundant seasonal labor, but do not require the whole labor force more than a third to a half of the year; although the agricultural sectors still employ more than half of the world's total labor force, actual work would probably amount to only a quarter of all work-years (standardized at the 2,000 man-hour norm). As a consequence, much of the agricultural output must go for consumption by underutilized workers (men and work animals), and savings which might be invested in modern facilities are lessened.

In the densely populated peasant-agricultural societies, which contain a majority of all farmers, usually less than a third of the land-holders are well-off or prosperous, even by local standards. Generally they are better-off because they are receiving income from other sources than their own farming efforts. In many cases, they are landlords, and have part or all of their holdings actually worked by landless laborers or by tenants. In other cases, they may be part-time farmers who have non-agricultural occupations that contribute to their total income. In any event, there are few bona fide farmers who make enough out of farming alone to satisfy their demands except on substandard levels of living (assessed by modern standards). Those who own more land than they actually cultivate themselves probably could not, in most cases, farm their entire holding by themselves unless mechanization and areal reorganization were substituted for the traditional field patterns and techniques. Often they do not have the additional capital needed to introduce the modern techniques, even if they desired to use them. In short, pressure on land is more pressure on traditional technique.

One great dilemma is that before a great deal more can be gotten out of most peasant agriculture, there must be substantially more fixed- and operating-capital investment on the land. Yet few land-holders can or will make such investment. In the case of the poorer third or so of rural families, present income is so low that not only is there no appreciable investment put into the land, but the peasant often lives by destructive exploitation of the land (and his family). For such agriculturalists, mainly landless laborers and dwarf-holders, their occupation is a sort of marginal enterprise: they take out of the land only the bare minimum, the poor gleanings of residual fertility, because they are not in a position to put anything back to improve it.

The reasons why the more solvent classes of agriculturalists do not invest more in capital improvements are many and varied. The more prosperous (e.g., the upper fifth in income) do invest, but mainly by way of buying more land, still the main rural status symbol. The middle groups, who save some years and may go into debt in unusually poor years, do not have much to invest, but probably could invest more if they wanted to. Tenants have little incentive to make permanent improvements unless they have tenure, because they may be dispossessed without having benefited from such investment. To a certain extent, social customs hinder greater investment, especially the insecure status of women. Quite often, the marriage of daughters involves considerable expense, most of which is spent on spectacular consumption rather than invested in productive enterprise. Dowries often amount to several years' family income for high-status groups. Much savings are turned into jewelry and worn or hoarded by the womenfolk. Since they sometimes do not enjoy equal rights in landed property but do own their jewelry in case of their husbands' death, they may prefer to keep the family savings in such hoards (a sort of social security reserve).

Another reason for slow capital investment lies in the poor facilities for mobilizing the small driblets of savings that do accumulate within the rural economy. The modern type of bank does not exist in most rural communities, and the cooperative societies have often failed to inspire sufficient confidence among prosperous non-members to attract their deposits. The absence of commercial farms makes investment (public as well as private) more difficult, since misuse or diversion into consumption areas is more likely in a subsistence context. Consequently, considerable amounts of potential investment funds are hoarded, spent on social events, or invested in speculative ventures.

Agrarian Reform

Part of the solution to rural poverty lies in political, economic, social, and psychological reforms within the rural societies as now constituted. The poverty of the mass of rural population is mainly a matter of premodern scale and technology, but there is also the result of such factors as obsolete land-tenure systems, fragmented holdings, rural overpopulation, indebtedness, inadequate and expensive credit, neglected physical and mental development, and other aspects of a disintegrating and obsolete social organization.

One of the most fundamental problems of peasant agriculture is to transform it from a mode of living into a business proposition for the benefit of the actual cultivators. Among necessary changes, this requires eliminating or controlling certain parasitic elements that now contribute little to agricultural development.

Political and social reasons for changes in land tenure are usually more important than strictly economic ones, but the latter are also important. Farming methods are to a considerable extent determined by the system of land ownership and control. Even if science and technology are applicable, and extension services convince the agriculturalists of the technical and economic feasibility of change, they may ignore or resist such innovations if the system under which they operate would pass on most of the profit to parasitic landlords who contribute nothing to the new order except ancient ownership rights. Where half or more of the produce must be handed over to the landlord as rent, the cultivator can seldom be expected to show eagerness to change his traditional ways.

Abolition of intermediaries is desirable, but not a panacea. Often, social inequalities will be lessened by land reform, but the economics might be virtually unchanged, as in cases where government increases the land taxes or collects payments to compensate the former owners at levels reflecting overpopulation more than actual productivity. However, tenancy legislation is important in that it mollifies powerful peasant classes, but it is only a palliative, not a cure, as far as aiding rapid economic development is concerned. Agrarian problems are much too intricate to be solved by tenancy legislation alone, even if all intermediaries could be removed at very little cost.

The most difficult problem is to determine when to reform rather than whether or not the changes are necessary. Among the educated elements in poor societies, there is a tendency to view undesirable features of the present economy and society as moral issues and yet to believe that political solutions are the real ones. Galled by the relative backwardness, many intellectuals are searching for easy solutions, which almost certainly cannot be found, except in the cheap promises of opportunists. Eventually, as the trends toward a modern economy gain momentum, most reforms will gradually be effected and will help to speed the transition. However, it is by no means certain that their urgency is such as to demand immediate solution at any price. Neither does the long-run necessity for such reforms prove the moral superiority of those most indignant and enthusiastic at an early stage. Most paper plans poured out by those demanding quick and radical reforms are worth little to the practical politician and administrator. Successful progress creeps from point to point testing each step, proceeding by devious paths when the direct route promises only disruption of existing routine without attaining more productive organization.

There is considerable economic justification for securing adequate tenure for good farmers on adequate-size holdings to provide an incentive for them to progress and profit from change. The blunt fact is, however, that real progress can be made only when huge numbers of present agriculturalists have been transferred to other occupations and modern farming methods have been quite widely introduced. Until that time, usually several generations after economic development gets under way, land reforms may achieve a barren equality but cannot banish the dwarf-holdings which are a major factor in explaining rural poverty. As a long-range goal, the prevention of further subdivision of holdings now barely economic is highly desirable, but present public opinion in most low-income areas is unwilling to condone such action as long as alternative openings in other economic activities are not available. Consolidation of holdings now widely scattered over the village area is desirable in a commercial economy where specialization can be very profitable, but too rapid a trend before accessibility and market opportunities are available can result in greater distress to many than at present. The great problem in credit is to encourage investment in forms that are significant solutions to present poverty. Eventually, diets less divergent from modern nutritional ideals will prevail, but their quick adoption is neither socially nor economically feasible at present.

If concentration on fundamental reforms were politically possible, probably public health, education, and fair employment improvements would be the most profitable long-range reforms to emphasize. Since they do not promise cheap utopias, many practical men feel that they are in the nature of social luxuries, better left until the main business of directly productive capital accumulation has been substantially achieved. As a matter of fact, to begin changing ideas in a retarded society (e.g., upgrading the cultural background and improving the social mobility of the population) is probably much more conducive to rapid progress than to change such externals as legal titles to property that has high prestige value but is declining relatively in importance as a factor in modern economic development. Make men aware of their relative status, of how others have solved common problems, of the dilemmas facing them, and eventually they will work out their own solutions.

To adapt modern organization and material technology to most peasant agricultures will probably require half a century of steady improvisation after evidence of widespread disintegration of the old agrarian civilization is apparent. Much of the lag is explainable in terms of the low priority to agricultural rationalization given by most power elites.

High Fixed Costs

In addition to outmoded scale, equipment, and organization, there are other contributing reasons why agriculture is so often little rewarding to the average farmer. In analyzing the process of economic development, too much attention is generally spent on the cost of development—the cost of building new facilities and setting up new enterprises by innovators—and too little attention is spent on the reverse side of the problem, the cost of bankruptcy—the cost of dissolving old forms of economic activity and apportioning the losses. The older economic activities, mainly agriculture and traditionally related primary activities, bear a great burden of social costs in addition to their direct-production costs. These social welfare costs can be considered as heavy-overhead costs left over from the premodern form of society, when the clan and village provided the buffers against catastrophe, which in modern societies are now the concern of central government and large-scale private philanthropy. Thus, the various economic activities (and often different organizers in the same general activity) bear unequal risks, and an accounting-book type of analysis is often of little use in trying to determine relative efficiency in adjusting to changing technological and economic conditions.

In the earliest phase of economic development, the rural areas generally subsidize the cities, although often in manners not easily determinable in money terms. Certain urban activities are able to profit from the fact that older rural activities are bearing most of the costs of maintaining society during the transitional period. This is only partly accomplished through the unequal burdens of direct taxation. More is accomplished by indirect (e.g., excise and other hidden forms) taxes, which may be paid by enterprises headquartered in cities, but whose final burden rests upon the mass of consumers, mostly in the countryside. Most important are the burdens imposed by tradition (e.g., villages providing haven for urban workers during periods of stress caused by natural or man-made catastrophe, or paying for rearing and educating of the youth who migrate to the city when about to become productive workers) and not ordinarily considered in orthodox economic analyses. Gradually this inequality is changed, as government assumes many burdens earlier assumed by the clan and the village, and as the tax structure is gradually changed so as to tap non-agricultural incomes more equitably. Someday the pendulum may swing to the other extreme, as it has in some Western societies, and certain branches of agriculture will be parasitic on the cities through variously disguised subsidization, but this occurs when societies are high-income types.

Another factor making for unequal risks in premodern societies is the unequal burden of the costs of human reproduction falling upon rural groups as compared with the economic benefits. Generally, most children who survive to adulthood in families of landless and small-holders must migrate to the cities or to other rural areas if they desire economic betterment. In one sense, the poor rural areas export human capital, for which they receive little or nothing back in return. Next to the difficulty of rapidly reorganizing the scale and technology of peasant agriculture, the proportionately greater burden placed on most rural groups by differential natural increase is most important in retarding economic progress as great and as rapid as among other groups in the populace.

Among the important corrective measures that will make for a better distributed and equipped labor force in the future are certain social investments, investments in people that enhance productivity and that make possible greater mobility. Public programs in public health, education, public nutrition, and public housing all fall into this class. A strong case can be made for greatly enlarged public grants and aids to rural farm communities and families, for such investments eventually accrue to the urban regions. For the most part it is the better equipped and more ambitious young people in rural areas who leave for the cities. Rural farm people bear a wholly disproportionate share of the cost of rearing and educating the children of a modernizing society—cost reckoned in terms of food, clothing, shelter, medical attention, and education—and this is an important reason why they are poorer than the city elements having a small-family pattern of reproduction.

Inflexibility

Although experience indicates that modern technical progress can, under favorable conditions, raise physical output per worker at about the same rate in agriculture as in industry and services, this is exceedingly difficult for the average farmer during most of the stages of general economic development. Partly this is because agriculture's basic processes are biological, rather than mechanical or chemical. The biological processes (gestation, birth, growth, maturation) take a long time, so crop and livestock products cannot be turned out or stopped at will.

Consequently, agriculture and industry are of different temperaments in committing resources to production: one is slow and gradual, and the second is sensitive and erratic. The production effort in farming is quite stable in spite of price and income variability, which fluctuations are related to bad or good crops, depression or prosperity, war or peace. The possibilities of speedup in the productive processes are limited, and the quantity and quality of the products cannot be fully controlled.

Nature largely governs the growth of crops and animals, and natural hazards often completely upset the farmer's plans and sometimes ruin him: the habitat resources and resistances have not yet been mastered and probably never will be controlled as closely and cheaply as manufacturers can control their productive environment and output. Frost, drought, floods, hail, windstorms, plant and animal diseases, and other pests, all conspire to play fast and loose with the production of a particular farm, and are a major factor in the income instability of the individual farmer. These natural risks and uncertainties determine to no small degree whether yields are large or small, whether flocks and herds increase or are decimated, whether livestock is stunted by disease or whether it gains well on feed. Over these vagaries of nature the individual farmer has relatively little control, and even in the better situated and more prosperous farming areas, the fortunes and failures of farmers are greatly influenced by these production uncertainties.

Man has not yet been able to control the macro-patterns of his habitat, especially landforms and climates. Regions on the drier and frostier edges of the ecumene (i.e., highly useful portions of the earth) are especially prone to wide fluctuations in precipitation and warmth, but even normally well-watered long-season areas have considerable local fluctuations. Some successes have been achieved in altering the soils and natural plant and animal patterns, by application of modern technology: supplementary irrigation, dry farming, drought-resistant crops, disease-resistant plants and animals, and modern pesticides are some of the important means for reducing the incidence of difficulties caused by bad weather, disease, insects, and other pests.

Even with the greater controls possible through modern science and technology, the outer limits of possibilities in agriculture are still narrower than for industry and services sectors. The natural environment sets closer limits to expansion, and the danger of resource depletion is greater than in the cases of human and man-made (synthetic) resources. With time, the substitution of leaner natural phenomena for the traditional (higher-) grade resources becomes inevitable and, unless the outer limits of technical possibilities are drastically changed, the cost will increase.

Limited Markets

Finally, agriculture's prospects are often poor because the demand for food and industrial raw materials is less elastic than for industrial products and services. Gluts of foodstuffs may be difficult to move even with drops in price. Periodically, overproduction inflicts heavy losses on agriculture, and the problem tends to become most serious when a high mass consumption stage of economic development is reached.

Engel's principle of consumption states that the poorer a family, the greater the proportion of its total expenditure on food and other necessities. With some reservations, this principle also holds for great-regions and realms: the poorer a country, a region, a continent, or realm, the larger the proportion of efforts and resources its people expend to supply themselves with necessary food.

Where people are very poor, the possibilities open to them are such that they choose farm products with little, if any, non-farm processing and servicing attached. They also are apt to consume primarily the cheaper energy foods (i.e., cereals, roots, starchy fruits) rather than animal products, to take their food as farm products rather than as retailed products, and to have a high income elasticity (0.7 to 0.8) for food.

As people become richer, they tend to consume relatively more animal products and exotic plant foods, and the non-farm services attached to the crude materials entering into retailed products become most important, with the income elasticity for farm products dropping (0.2 to 0.3) drastically. The demand for sugar, oils-fats, fruits, and vegetables, however, does maintain a greater elasticity than for other plant foods, while beef, veal, and lamb demand usually maintains a greater elasticity than the demand for fatty pork, mutton, and other less desirable meats. The most commercial farms are likely to switch products to keep servicing the most prosperous markets, while the poorer farms tend rigidly to keep producing products and qualities better suited to the markets of yesteryear.

In societies that have reached the high mass consumption stage and have made the fullest possible use of modern agricultural technology, only about 5 to 10 per cent of the employment opportunities and net income will be left in the primary sector. Even in those societies that specialize in agricultural and related exports, and in those that find labor-intensive types of modern agriculture most economical, the fractions are only a few times larger. In such societies—and in the fully urban-industrial world of the future—disguised unemployment and low productivity are just as likely to be found in certain industrial and services subsectors as in agriculture.

PERSPECTIVE

During the process of modernization, the relative importance of agriculture steadily declines. Absolute production continues to increase, but to achieve general economic progress requires an exodus of rural factors of production, especially labor. This diversion of labor into industry and services proceeds partly by an actual transfer of labor from agriculture and related activities, but even more by a long-term cityward attraction of most young adults reared in the rural society.

The main reason for the decline of agriculture's proportionate contribution to economic welfare lies in the area of changing consumption patterns under the conditions of increasing real per capita income. Changes in the class composition of income distribution are also important.

In old agrarian societies, the exodus of labor and other factors from agriculture does not usually proceed quickly enough for the increase in per capita agricultural income to keep up with the per capita industrial and services income. However, the agriculture specializing in the production of superior products (especially animal and protective foods) is likely to improve its economic status faster than the agriculture specializing in the production of inferior products (cheap starch, cheap pulse), since the demand for the superior agricultural products is more expandable.

The problem of increasing food and raw materials supply for an increasing mankind is not simply an agricultural production problem, but involves a general rise in productive efficiency, distribution efficiency, and changed consumption standards. If the food and agricultural system could be tackled in isolation, it should be relatively easy to solve. But agricultural rationalization must proceed within a context of more rapidly expanding industrial and servicing sectors, and in many newly modernizing societies much expansion in those sectors depends on important adjustments in the character of international trade (i.e., on changes in the economic life of other nations). The limiting factor most difficult to control in the long run is not so much the physical capacity of mankind to produce sufficient food and raw materials, but rather is the ability and willingness of both old and new nations to bring about the necessary economic adjustments leading to a new international division of labor.

SUGGESTED READINGS

Cauley, Troy J. *Agriculture in an Industrial Economy.* New York: Bookman Associates, 1956. Pp. 191.

Chang, Pei-kang. *Agriculture and Industrialization.* Harvard University Press, 1949. Pp. 270.

Cho, Yong-Sam. *"Disguised Unemployment" in Underdeveloped Areas.* University of California Press, 1963. Pp. 163.

Coppock, John O. *North Atlantic Policy: The Agricultural Gap.* New York: Twentieth Century Fund, 1963. Pp. 270.

Dumont, René. *Types of Rural Economy.* London: Methuen, 1957. Pp. 556.

Gerard, Ralph W. (ed.) *Food for Life.* University of Chicago Press, 1952. Pp. 306.

Higbee, Edward. *American Agriculture: Geography, Resources, Conservation.* New York: Wiley, 1958. Pp. 399.

Higbee, Edward. *Farms and Farmers in an Urban Age.* New York: Twentieth Century Fund, 1963. Pp. 183.

Ojala, E. M. *Agriculture and Economic Progress.* London: Oxford University Press, 1952. Pp. 220.

Russell, Sir E. John. *World Population and World Food Supplies.* London: Allen & Unwin, 1954. Pp. 513.

Stamp, L. Dudley. *Land for Tomorrow.* Indiana University Press, 1952. Pp. 230.

Tempany, Sir Harold, and Grist, D. H. *An Introduction to Tropical Agriculture.* New York: Wiley, 1962. Pp. 347.

United States Department of Agriculture. *Yearbooks of Agriculture. Food,* 1959. Pp. 736. *Land,* 1958. Pp. 605. *Power to Produce,* 1960. Pp. 480. Washington, D.C.

United States Department of Agriculture, Economic Research Service, Regional Analysis Division. *Man, Land, & Food.* (Foreign Agricultural Economic Report No. 11.) Washington, D.C., 1963. Pp. 153.

Van Royen, William (ed.). *Atlas of the World's Resources.* Vol. I. *The Agricultural Resources of the World.* Englewood Cliffs, N.J.: Prentice-Hall, 1954. Pp. 1–18.

Wibberley, G. P. *Agriculture and Urban Growth.* London: Michael Joseph, 1959. Pp. 240.

Woytinsky, W. S., and Woytinsky, E. S. *World Population and Production: Trends and Outlook.* New York: Twentieth Century Fund, 1953. Pp. 451–537.

Zimmermann, Erich W. *World Resources and Industries.* New York: Harper & Row, 1951. Pp. 147–75.

6

Basic Energy Foods

Although most crops contain starch, the chief starch-producing crops are the cereals and the starchy roots, tubers, and fruits, of which the cereals annually contribute nine-tenths of the some billion tons (cereal-equivalent). These basic energy foods are used for direct human consumption to the extent of 55 per cent of output, and 45 per cent enters into seed, animal feed, and various industrial uses.

In a survey of world agriculture, such crops constitute one of the most important subsectors, as illustrated from several frames of reference in Tables 6–1 and 6–2.

In a money-value—as opposed to the above caloric- or energy-value—perspective the basic energy foods category is somewhat less important, since they are relatively cheap, but they are still the most important segment of world crop agriculture (Table 6–2).

The starch crops also bulk large when considered from the point of view of several factors of production employed in agriculture. About 1.7 billion acres are annually planted to such crops, out of some 3.6 billion arable acres (about 2.5 billion of these are annually being cultivated, and the other billion are in tree crops or in rotational pasture and fallow). Of the 650 million farmers in the world, probably two-thirds devote more attention and effort to starch crops than to the other segments of agriculture, although only about one-third of all agricultural man-hours are so invested (reflecting the extensive nature of most starch production compared with many other crop and animal husbandry efforts of farmers today).

TABLE 6–1

World: Sources of Food Calories and Protein, 1962–1964 Average-Annual
(in per cents)

Calories [1]			Protein [1]
62.8		*Basic Energy Foods*	47.7
	55.3	Cereals	43.5
	7.5	Starchy non-cereals	4.2
15.1		*Luxury Energy Foods*	–
	7.5	Sugar	–
	7.6	Oils-fats	–
77.9		*All Energy Foods*	47.7
22.1		*Protective and Protein Foods*	52.3
	4.1	Fruits-nuts-vegetables	2.8
	5.8	Pulses	10.2
	4.1	Meats	20.0
	6.7	Milk and milk products	12.8
	0.7	Eggs	2.5
	0.7	Fish	4.0
100.0		TOTAL HUMAN FOOD	100.0
	2,800	Trillion calories	400

[1] Calories equal energy value in food (but not in feed or in industrial raw materials). The 14 per cent protein is included in the total caloric intake also, but is considered separately because of its unique value in growth and regeneration.

TABLE 6–2

World: Value of Agricultural Production, 1962–1964 Average-Annual
(in per cents)

Gross Value [1]		Value-added [1]
34.2	*Basic Energy Crops*	31.2
28.9	Cereals	27.2
5.3	Starchy non-cereals	4.0
7.2	*Luxury Energy Crops*	7.5
4.4	Sugar	4.5
2.8	Edible oils-fats	3.0
5.6	*Beverage Crops*	5.8
2.8	Caffeine	3.0
2.8	Alcoholic	2.8
8.0	*Fruits and Vegetables*	7.5
4.0	Fruits	3.7
4.0	Vegetables (including pulses)	3.8
55.0	Food Crops	52.0
6.7	*Industrial Crops*	8.3
1.4	Tobacco	2.1
0.6	Rubber	0.8
4.4	Fibers	5.0
0.3	Drying oils	0.4
61.7	All Crops	60.3
36.5	*Edible Animal Products*	37.1
23.5	Meats	23.7
8.5	Milk and milk products	8.7
1.8	Edible fats	1.9
2.7	Eggs	2.8
1.8	*Inedible Animal Products*	2.6
1.5	Wool-hair	2.2
0.3	Hides-skins, grease, etc.	0.4
38.3	Animal Products	39.7
100.0	Total Agricultural Products	100.0

[1] The gross value (market value) of world agricultural production is about U.S. $227 billion (exchange value), and includes considerable double-counting. The value-added by world agricultural production is about U.S. $126.5 billion—it excludes purchased factors of production and feed crops, and includes only value-added by farm factors of production (land, labor, capital, enterprise).

The farmers' income was about 70 per cent from the agricultural and related primary production, and 30 per cent from outside sources (e.g., part-time industrial and services income).

DIETARY ECONOMICS [1]

In the previous chapter, the great-region, economic-type of society, and the world dietaries

[1] Based upon *The World Food Budget, 1962 and 1966* (published in October, 1961), and *1970* (published in October, 1964), by the Economic Research Service of the U.S. Department of Agriculture.

were compared in terms of an energy-value (calorie) context, for the most part. In this section, a comparison in terms of money costs will be made, based upon the economics of three representative countries. The United States is a mature urban-industrial economy with a low-food-drain, excellent dietary. Japan is a relatively poor urban-industrial economy with an intermediate food drain (excellent dietary quantitatively, but defective in certain qualitative aspects). India is a poor, underdeveloped economy just recently at its takeoff stage, with a high-food-drain type of dietary defective both quantitatively and qualitatively from the point of view of modern nutritional science.

Food expenditures per person vary greatly from country to country. As Table 6–3 indicates, an Indian spends less than 10 per cent as much as an American or less than 30 per cent as much as a Japanese. The share of total income spent for food varies from 55 per cent in India to 28 per cent in Japan and 17 per cent in the United States.

Higher food expenditures by Americans reflect many differences: (1) a greater caloric intake, (2) more services in the form of processing, packaging, and transporting, (3) great variety, but, more than anything else, (4) a markedly larger share of costly animal products.

The food group allocated the largest share of income differs in each of the three countries. Indians spend over two-fifths on grain, Japanese use nearly a third of their food money for fish, and Americans spend well over one-quarter of their food budget on meat.

Differences in the nutritional quality of the dietaries can best be indicated by the cost of starchy staples. Americans can purchase their basic energy foods with only 12 per cent of their food budget, compared with 28 per cent in Japan and 42 per cent in India. When related to total per capita income, the contrast is even more striking: 2 per cent of American per capita income purchases the traditional food staples (largely bread and potatoes), while 8 per cent of the Japanese per capita income is required for the dietary mainstay (mostly rice), and some 23 per cent of the Indian per capita income must

TABLE 6–3

Food Expenditures, by Food Groups, 1962–1964 Average-Annual
(in United States dollars)

	India		Japan		United States	
Annual per capita income	$70		$450		$2,400	
Food expenditures per capita	$38		$125		$ 415	
Grain products		41.0%		23.5%		10.0%
Other starchy crops		1.5		5.0		2.0
Sugar		3.5		3.0		3.0
Fats and oils		5.5		3.0		4.0
Pulses (peas-beans) and nuts		8.0		3.5		13.0
Other vegetables and fruits		12.0		7.5		17.0
Meat		2.5		9.0		29.0
Fish		8.5		30.0		3.0
Eggs		0.5		6.5		4.0
Milk and milk products		17.0		9.0		15.0
Total		100.0%		100.0%		100.0%
Daily per capita food expenditures	$0.10		$0.35		$1.15	
Cost per 1,000 calories	$0.05		$0.15		$0.35	
Per cent of income spent for food	55%		28%		17%	
Crude materials' per cent of food expenditure	80%		45%		27%	

be spent for starchy staples (largely rice and wheat).

The share of food purchases involved in animal-protein foods (fish, meat, dairy products, eggs) is not as different as many would suppose: over 50 per cent in the United States and in Japan and 28 per cent in India.

Perhaps the outstanding feature in the diets from a quantitative point of view is the preponderance of starchy foods in the Indian and Japanese consumption patterns and the relative lack of starches in the American diet. Although the over-all level of food intake is much lower in both India and Japan, the per capita use of grain products is triple that of the United States (Table 6–4), providing nearly two-thirds of all calories.

TABLE 6–4

Calorie Levels per Capita, with Calorie-Intake Distribution by Food Groups, 1962–1964 Average-Annual

	India		Japan		United States	
Grain products	63.4%		63.2%		20.8%	
Wheat		11.3%		11.7%		17.4%
Rice		33.1		46.9		0.9
Other grains		19.0		4.6		2.5
Other starchy crops	2.6		7.7		3.1	
Sugar	8.2		6.7		15.7	
Fats and oils	4.2		5.0		20.5	
Pulses (peas-beans) and nuts	13.2		5.9		3.3	
Other vegetables, and fruits	2.0		4.2		6.2	
Meat, fish, and eggs	0.9		5.9		16.9	
Milk and milk products	5.5		1.4		13.5	
Daily food consumption	100.0%		100.0%		100.0%	
Number of calories	2,100		2,400		3,200	
Pounds (fresh-weight)	2		3		4.5	

In the cereals they consume, though not in most other food groups, Indians and Japanese have somewhat more variety than do Americans. Wheat accounts for most of the grain consumed in the United States, whereas in India the leading cereal—rice—accounts for about half of grain consumption, with wheat, millets, corn, and barley accounting for the remainder. In Japan, rice accounts for nearly three-quarters of total cereal intake and wheat and barley the remainder.

In the consumption of roots and tubers, the United States occupies an intermediate position between India and Japan, with its present annual per capita consumption only half what it was around the turn of the century. In Japan, white potatoes are preferred over sweet potatoes, and are becoming relatively more important, while in India, cassava ranks very low on the consumer scale of preferences, and tends to be displaced by white and sweet potatoes with economic improvement.

In the United States, four food groups other than grain products—sugar, oils and fats, meat, and dairy products—each contribute more than 400 calories per capita daily. In Japan and India, however, scarcely any group outside of grain products contributes as much as 200 calories to the daily per capita intake. Both the consumption of sugar and that of oils and fats—the luxury energy foods—are several times higher in the United States than in either of the other countries.

The calories derived from all animal products including fish amount to 135 per person per day in India and about 175 in Japan, but about 975 in the United States (more than 30 per cent of the total). The poultry consumed by an American considerably exceeds the total per capita intake of all meats in either India or Japan. The consumption of milk, like that of meat, is quite low in both India and Japan: Americans use about a quart of milk per day (much of it in the forms of butter, cheese, and ice cream), Indians only a quart every twelve days, and Japanese little more than a quart per month. In eggs, too, the differential is striking: an American eats an egg per day on the average, whereas the Japanese average is closer to one per week and the Indian only about three per year. But in the fish category, American levels compare much less favorably, being slightly less than the Indian per capita consumption, and only one-eighth as much as the Japanese average. Pulses, a rich source of vegetable protein and in part a substitute for animal protein, are used in comparatively large quantities in India and Japan, where increasing pulse consumption is associated with improved incomes. In the United States, the use of pulses (underestimated in Table 6–4, which includes only dried peas and beans, and not many types included in the "other vegetables" category) declines as incomes rise.

Fruit and vegetable consumption in the United States is about double that of India and half again as high as Japan's. Advanced methods of handling, processing, transporting, and storing such perishable foods reduce reliance on seasonal availability, and this contributes much to the greater use of these foodstuffs by Americans.

According to modern nutritional science standards—level of caloric intake, consumption of total protein (with animal, pulse, and other vegetable protein considered separately), and consumption of oils and fats—no nutritional deficits exist in the United States, but Japan is deficient in its consumption of oils and fats, and India is deficient in all categories except pulse protein. The total cost of eliminating these deficits, in terms of non-fat dried milk for animal protein, soybean oil for oils and fats, and wheat for other protein and remaining calories, amounts to about $1 per capita per year in Japan and $2.30 in India. On a national basis, Japan's only deficit—oils and fats—could be eliminated with an annual national expenditure of some $100 million. Filling the Indian deficits, however, would require nearly $1 billion, a sum approaching the value of all the products exported by the country. Given the rapid rate of growth in Japanese per capita income, the cost of filling the oils and fats deficit does not loom large. But in India, where per capita income increases slowly, the necessary financial resources are not readily available, and any immediate solution would depend in large part on external assistance.

TABLE 6–5

World: Starch Crops Production by Great-Region and Economic-Type of Society, 1962–1964 Average-Annual
(in millions of metric tons cereal-equivalent)

	North America		Western Europe		Eastern Europe (including the U.S.S.R.)		Oceania	
Cereals								
Rice (milled) [1]	2.1	1.0%	0.8	0.7%	0.3	0.1%	0.1	0.8%
Wheat	50.7	24.3	41.5	35.6	65.7	35.6	9.0	73.2
Maize (corn)	104.5	50.1	9.6	8.2	26.3	14.2	0.2	1.6
Barley	13.3	6.4	27.1	23.2	22.1	12.0	1.0	8.1
Oats	20.7	9.9	12.2	10.4	10.1	5.5	1.0	8.1
Rye	1.1	0.5	5.8	5.0	23.6	12.8	–	–
Millets-sorghums [2]	12.5	6.0	0.5	0.4	4.0	2.2	–	–
Starchy roots-tubers-fruits [1]								
White potatoes	3.6	1.7	19.1	16.4	32.6	17.6	0.2	1.6
Sweet potatoes and yams	0.2	0.1	–	–	–	–	0.3	2.5
Cassava	–	–	–	–	–	–	0.2	1.6
Bananas-plantains	–	–	0.1	0.1	–	–	0.3	2.5
Total	208.7	100.0%	116.7	100.0%	184.7	100.0%	12.3	100.0%

	Latin America		Sub-Saharan Africa		Middle East (including North Africa)		Non-Communist Far East	
Cereals								
Rice (milled) [1]	5.2	8.7%	2.4	4.1%	1.9	5.4%	91.6	58.0%
Wheat	10.7	18.0	1.4	2.4	17.1	48.9	16.9	10.7
Maize (corn)	23.9	40.1	12.6	21.5	2.9	8.3	12.6	8.0
Barley	1.7	2.8	1.0	1.7	8.8	25.2	5.2	3.3
Oats	0.9	1.8	0.1	0.2	0.5	1.4	0.1	0.1
Rye	0.2	0.3	–	–	0.6	1.7	–	–
Millets-sorghums [2]	2.5	4.2	20.0	34.1	2.5	7.1	20.0	12.7
Starchy roots-tubers-fruits [1]								
White potatoes	2.0	3.4	0.2	0.3	0.6	1.7	2.0	1.2
Sweet potatoes and yams	1.5	2.5	7.0	11.9	–	–	4.0	2.5
Cassava	7.0	11.8	10.0	17.0	–	–	4.0	2.5
Bananas-plantains	4.0	6.7	4.0	6.8	0.1	0.3	1.5	1.0
Total	59.6	100.0%	58.7	100.0%	35.0	100.0%	157.9	100.0%

	Communist Far East		World		High-Income Countries		Low-Income Countries	
Cereals								
Rice (milled) [1]	54.0	38.1%	158.4	16.2%	13.4	2.6%	145.0	31.4%
Wheat	25.0	17.6	238.0	24.4	158.0	30.7	80.0	17.3
Maize (corn)	11.4	8.0	204.0	20.9	138.0	26.9	66.0	14.3
Barley	6.8	4.8	87.0	8.9	61.5	11.9	25.5	5.5
Oats	0.9	0.6	46.5	4.8	43.3	8.4	3.2	0.7
Rye	–	–	31.3	3.2	29.7	5.8	1.6	0.3
Millets-sorghums [2]	30.0	21.1	92.0	9.4	15.0	2.9	77.0	16.8
Starchy roots-tubers-fruits [1]								
White potatoes	2.5	1.8	62.8	6.4	52.8	10.3	10.0	2.2
Sweet potatoes and yams	10.0	7.1	23.0	2.4	1.5	0.3	21.5	4.6
Cassava	1.0	0.7	22.2	2.3	0.4	0.1	21.8	4.7
Bananas-plantains	0.3	0.2	10.3	1.1	0.3	0.1	10.0	2.2
Total	141.9	100.0%	975.5	100.0%	513.9	100.0%	461.6	100.0%

The food supply of the Newer (or overseas) Europeans has been reasonably adequate for a long period, and that of northwestern Europe for a somewhat shorter period. In general, their dietaries are similar or tending in the direction of that described for the United States. Only since World War II has greatly increased production of food, or goods that can be traded for food, assured a permanently adequate diet in Mediterranean Europe, Eastern Europe and the Soviet Union, Japan, and some Latin American countries. In general, their dietary problems are minor (restricted to certain regions, classes, etc.) and, like that of Japan's described earlier, solvable with a relatively modest expenditure of effort and time. The really serious problems are in the 2 billion population of the underveloped realm. In the past generation, food production in (all) Latin America just about kept pace with population growth; sub-Saharan Africa and the Middle East apparently gained slightly; but both the non-Communist Far East and the Communist Far East lost ground slightly. The Far East's half of mankind has most of the world's major diet deficits: in calories, in animal and pulse protein, in oils and fats, and in protective foods (minerals and vitamins).

In any long view, food shortages can be overcome only by higher farm output in the deficit countries themselves. Already, some countries in the largely underdeveloped southern area of the world have achieved remarkable progress: Mexico, Costa Rica, and Brazil in Latin America; the Republic of South Africa and Rhodesia in sub-Saharan Africa; Israel, Lebanon, and Turkey in the Middle East; and Taiwan in the Far East.

REGIONAL STARCH CROPS PRODUCTION

In a century-long backward glance, world production of cereals, roots and tubers, and starchy fruits has tripled: from ⅓ billion tons in the early 1860's (recorded production ¼ billion tons, upped) to the present 1 billion tons (cereal-equivalent). Population growth in the same century more than doubled. Increases in yield have accounted for most of the increased output, although areal expansion has been extremely important in the less thickly settled regions (in general, outside Europe, South Asia, and East Asia). The heavy reliance on improved genetic and chemical science has mainly accrued to the benefit of modernizing societies. The greatest shortages are in the mainly subsistence farm economies, where traditional methods of areal expansion and intensification barely kept up with population growth.

Tables 6–5 and 6–6 and the graphs on pages 141–43 give the regional distribution and composition of starch crops production in the early 1960's.

Of the major regional producers of starch crops, North America is in the best position. Its

TABLE 6–6

World Starch Crops Production

	Million Metric Tons	Per Cent of World Total
North America	208.7	21.4
Western Europe	116.7	12.0
Eastern Europe (including the U.S.S.R.)	184.7	18.9
Oceania	12.3	1.3
Latin America	59.6	6.1
Sub-Saharan Africa	58.7	6.0
Middle East (including North Africa)	35.0	3.6
Non-Communist Far East	157.9	16.2
Communist Far East	141.9	14.5
World	975.5	100.0
High-income countries	513.9	52.7
Low-income countries	461.6	47.3

TABLE 6–5 SOURCE: Adapted from United Nations and U.S. Department of Agriculture sources, with some unofficial sources used for unrecorded and partly recorded items and areas.

[1] In order to approximate wheat-equivalent in this range of starch crops, several discounts have been applied. Since the husk of paddy is not removed in harvesting (as is true in wheat and rye), milled rice has been used by assuming 65 per cent recovery (reducing some 245 million tons of rough rice or paddy to the 158.4 million tons of milled rice). The starchy roots-tubers-fruits have been reduced 75 per cent in order to eliminate the water and waste (in excess of that 15 per cent or so found in wheat before milling): white potatoes (251 million tons fresh-weight to 62.8 million tons), sweet potatoes and yams (92:23), cassava (89:22.2), and bananas-plantains (41:10.3).

[2] Panicum and sorghum make up over nine-tenths of this miscellaneous category of cereals and seed crops used like cereals (e.g., buckwheat); highly mixed crops of cereals that are consumed without separation are also included.

share of world production is about triple its share of world population. Over three-quarters of consumption is for animal feed and industrial uses. It is a surplus producer, exporting over 15 per cent of its total production, and importing only small amounts (mainly tropical roots-tubers and starchy fruits): the region accounts for 85 per cent of all net exports of grain. In both world food grain and feed grain trade, the region accounts for about half of the total movement (being the principal supplier of every grain except rice). Exports involved over a third of regional food grain production in the past few years, and about 7 per cent of feed grain production. Subsidization is important in explaining the high fraction of food grain exports, but there is little doubt that the region has among the lowest-cost production of most cereals. Most of the crops are under acreage controls, and in the foreseeable future additional production could be obtained fairly easily if the two governments desired.

Western Europe produces about a tenth of world starch production, about the same share as it has of world population. It is deficient to the extent of nearly 20 per cent of consumption: about half of world trade in food grains and three-quarters of world trade in feed grains are destined for the region (it ranks first in every grain import except rice). Much of the existing food grain production is highly subsidized almost everywhere, especially in West Germany. About half of the consumption is for feed and industrial usage, and these segments of consumption are growing more rapidly than the direct food grain consumption.

Eastern Europe and the U.S.S.R. produce nearly as much starch as North America, with a population about half again as large. The region is roughly self-sufficient, although there are large trade movements between economies within the region, especially food grains and feed grains from the U.S.S.R. to the northern countries of Eastern Europe (East Germany, Poland, Czechoslovakia). Among the food grains, wheat is overwhelmingly important, and is rapidly displacing rye and other grains as new varieties are pushed north and south into the cold and arid limits of the ecumene. About 35 per cent of total consumption is for animal feed (much of it for work animals) and industrial usages, a considerably smaller fraction of the total consumption than in North America and Western Europe. As in North America, the cheapest production comes from the subhumid lands only recently brought under cultivation, so gradually wheat is being more heavily concentrated there, and the more humid areas are concentrating more on heavy-yielding feedstuffs (e.g., corn, barley, etc.) for the dairying and meat-finishing animal husbandry regions around the great urban-industrial nodes.

Oceania produces only 1 per cent of the world's starch, but this is double the share of world population. In certain respects, the region is like a miniature North America. The region has a surplus, due to Australian wheat shipments. Over half of total starch consumption is for animal feed and industrial usages, but this supplies a smaller proportion of animal feed than in North America and Western Europe, while the contribution of permanent pasture is much greater. Most starch consumption from tubers and fruits is in the Melanesian, Polynesian, and Micronesian portions of Oceania, as is consumption from imports (mainly central and southwestern Pacific isles).

Latin America's population is now larger than that of North America, but its starch production is less than a third as large. The region is now a net importer, especially of wheat, although it still exports some coarse grains (e.g., Argentinian flint corn to European chicken producers). The region consumes about two-thirds of its starch directly as human food, with the socially favored wheat and rice contributing only half of this, and the less favored corn and cassava most of the remaining half. With increasing per capita income (already Latin America considered as a single region is semi-industrial), the old Indian domesticates tend to be dropped or largely displaced by the Old World favorites. The region is nearly as deficient in food grains as Western Europe, but the reasons are different. Much unused potentially arable land is "sterilized" by being in large landholdings mainly devoted to

WORLD: STARCH CROPS PRODUCTION AND COMPOSITION, BY GREAT-REGION AND ECONOMIC-TYPE OF SOCIETY, 1962-1964 AVERAGE-ANNUAL (Million Metric Tons)

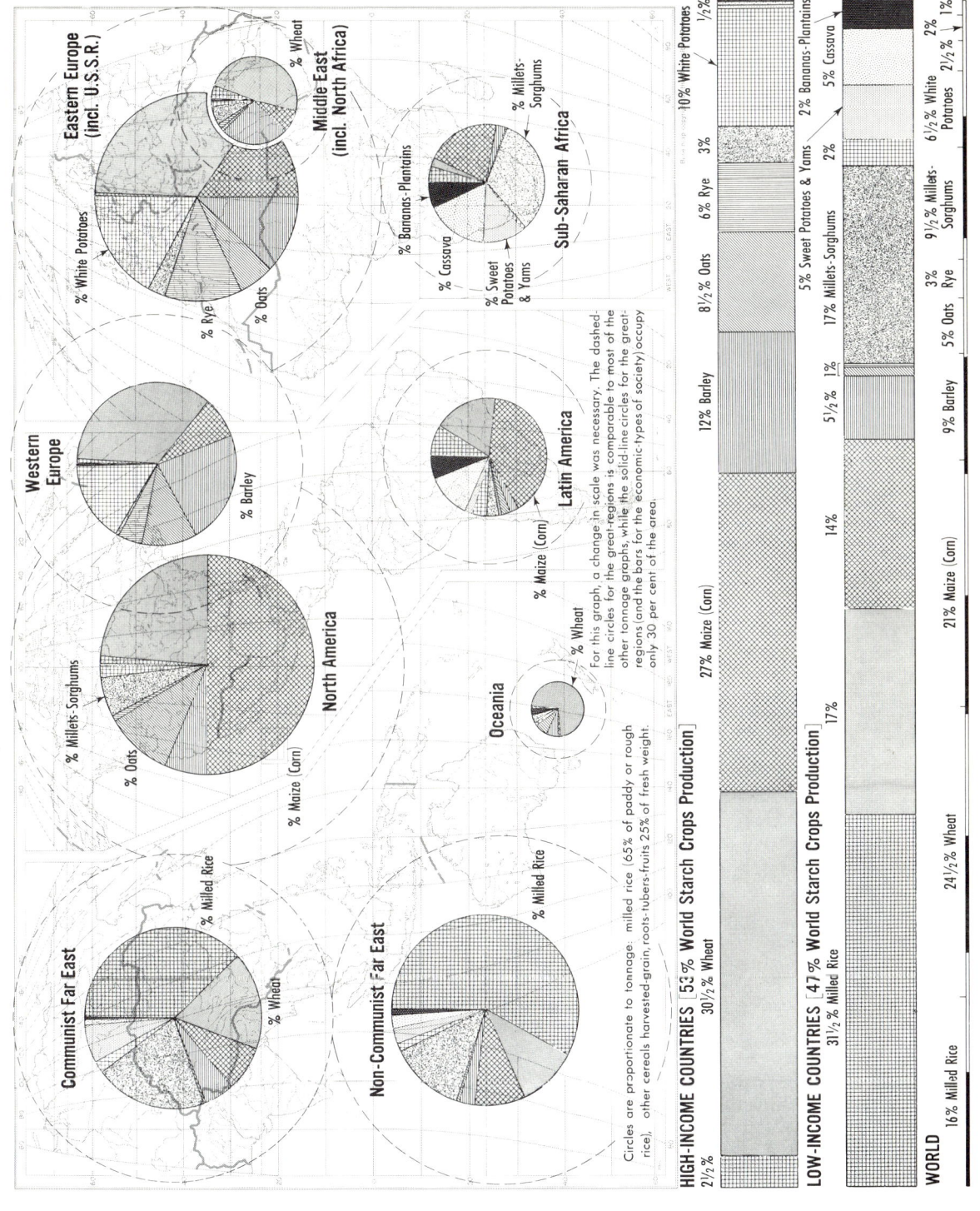

WORLD: GREAT-REGION AND ECONOMIC-TYPE OF SOCIETY SHARES OF WORLD STARCH CROPS PRODUCTION (Cereals and Cereal-Equivalent of Non-Cereals), 1962-1964 AVERAGE-ANNUAL

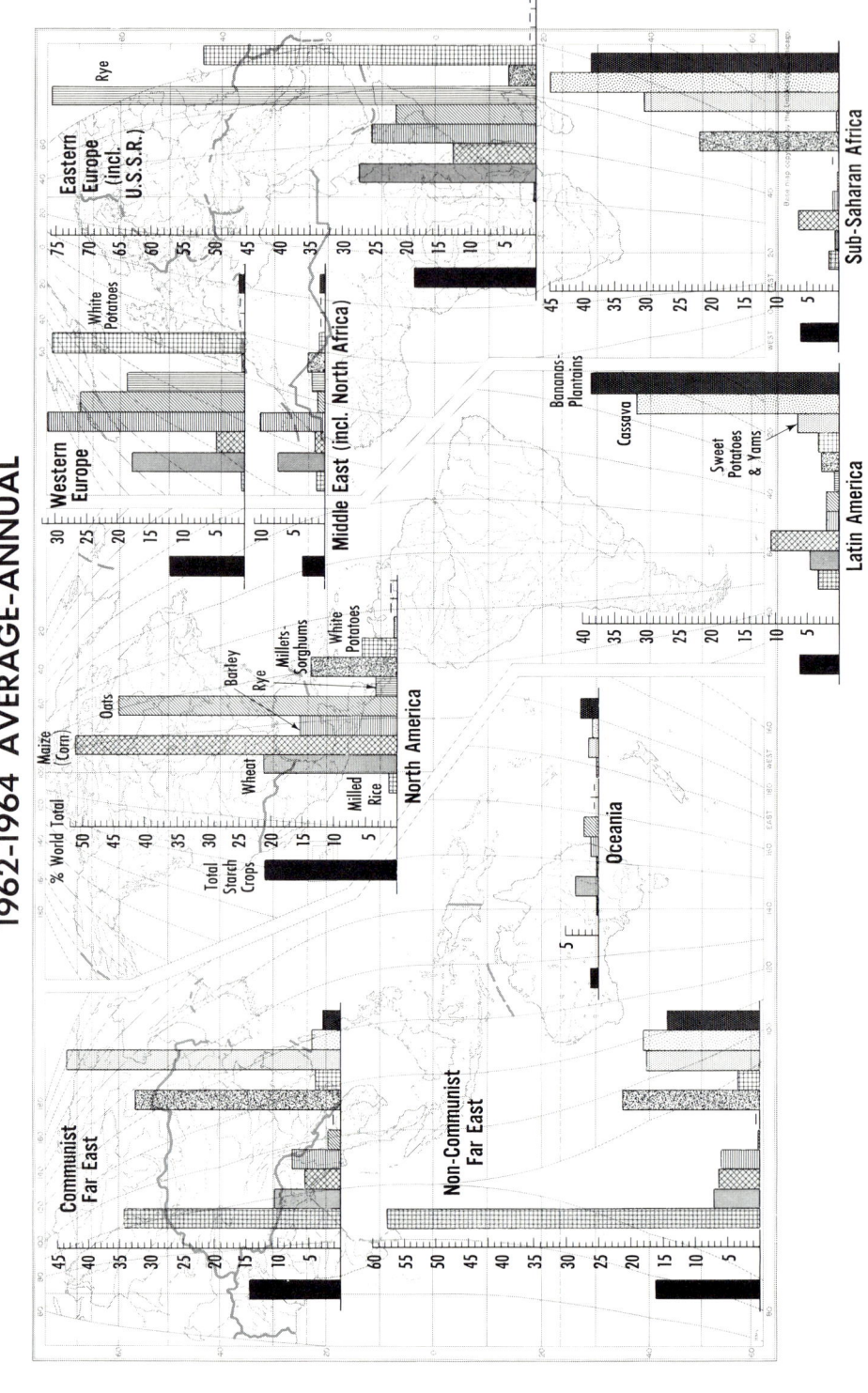

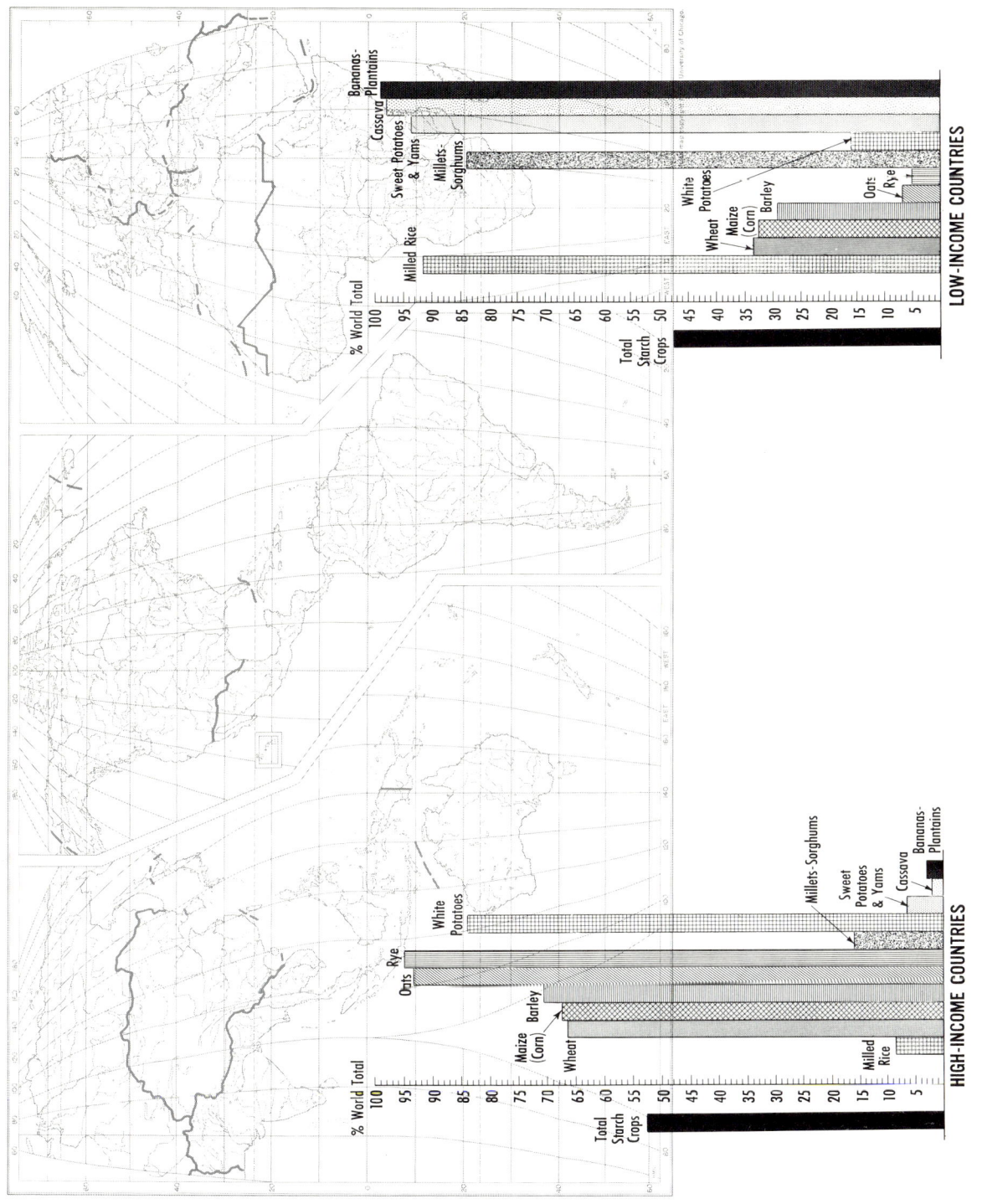

extensive pastoral activities (however, Latin America has increased grain output in the past generation mainly by making additions to the cultivated area—only a fifth of the increase has come from higher yields). Land reform is urgently needed to redistribute acreage more equitably among farmers and strengthen their incentives to produce. Another detriment is the frenzy to industrialize, often resulting in capital and other factors of production being used on prestige industrial and military facilities instead of agricultural rationalization which is more needed and often better paying in economic terms.

Sub-Saharan Africa is fairly well off, quantitatively, for an overwhelmingly underdeveloped region. It produces about the same share of world starch production as it has of world population, and since only 5 per cent is fed to animals, per capita consumption is quite good (even in oils and fats and in animal and pulse protein, only minor shortages exist). Only a tenth of consumption consists of the favored wheat and rice, with coarse grains (especially corn, millets, and sorghums) contributing over half of the dietary, and starchy roots, tubers, and fruits about a third. Although population is increasing rapidly, prospects for increased production are also bright (in the past generation, expansion has derived almost equally from additions to the planted area and from rising yields). Such technological advances as tsetse fly control and better transportation and marketing facilities are needed to expand greatly agricultural production in vast regions south of the Sahara.

The Middle East—including North Africa as well as Southwest Asia—produces a smaller share of world starch crops than its share of world population, but its dietary is better than that of the Far East. Only some 5 per cent of consumption is by animals (the vast grassland and shrubland areas provide most of the feed). The region is roughly self-sufficient, with Turkey and Syria usually producing some wheat and barley surpluses, while much of North Africa and Arabia is perennially deficient. Variability in production is great, and the surpluses are mainly correlated with good rainfall and absence of pests as the deficits are mainly correlated with poor rainfall and infestation. In an average year, the region is roughly self-sufficient. Here, as in Latin America and in sub-Saharan Africa, there are still moderate opportunities to expand arable acreage, both by dry land and irrigation technology. Most starch production is from grain, with only 2 per cent derived from roots, tubers, and fruit, as small a proportion as in North America.

The non-Communist Far East—South Asia, Southeast Asia excluding North Vietnam, and East Asia excluding Mainland China, North Korea, and Mongolia—has been favored with three successive good harvests in the early 1960's and its starch production is now about one-quarter higher than in the mid-1950's, while the rate of population growth has apparently been only half that large. The four main cereals—rice, millets-sorghums, wheat, and maize—have all reached record heights, as have both temperate and tropical tubers. The region still has a net import of about 5 per cent of its starch consumption, mainly wheat (it accounts for one-third of world imports) and rice. Livestock feed and industrial usages take about 15 per cent of total consumption, although the rate is variable correlating with size of crops and condition of forage. While the short-run view is optimistic, recently there is good evidence that population was underestimated in the 1950's, and that the region is approaching the widest portion of the demographic gap, so the future plans made earlier will have to be revised drastically upward.

The Communist Far East (the centrally planned economies) has some 15 per cent of world starch production to sustain its 23 per cent of world population. Natural calamities in the early 1960's badly affected food supplies and appear to have severely retarded the development of the whole economy. Output figures in the late 1950's were admittedly defective even by Communist account and none have been announced since 1959, so unofficial estimates have had to be used. In 1957, reported production of grain (and grain-equivalent of potatoes) was some 185 million tons for Mainland China, a figure that is thought to be reasonably accurate. In 1958, reported production was first announced at 375 million tons and then dropped to 250 million tons, while Western estimates were 200 to 210 million tons. In 1959, target production was to be some 270 million tons, but Western estimates were that production actually declined from the 1958 level. In 1960 more than half of the total farmland was affected by severe drought, typhoons, floods, insect infestation, or other damage, and there were similar disasters in 1961 and 1962. Although widespread famine appears to have been averted, many areas had near famine conditions, and almost all had great hardship. The severity of the situation is indicated by progressive reduction of the ration (said to have been 1,800 or fewer calories per person per day in the years 1959–1962, little above basal metabolism), by massive imports, and by loosening of commune discipline to allow the peasantry more effective control of field operations. The smaller Communist countries appear to have nearly as dismal an agricultural record as Mainland China, and the current production appears to be back to mid-1950's levels, with perhaps 100 million additional population since that time. In addition to the world's largest shortage of basic energy food, the Communist Far East has about half of the world's fat and animal-protein shortages.

FOOD GRAINS

The pre-eminence of cereals among foodstuffs is perhaps ten millennia old, and reflects their relative cheapness and the ease with which they can be produced, stored, and transported. Among the foodstuffs reasonably balanced nutritionally, they yield more food per acre and per man-hour than most other crops. Wheat and rice are overwhelmingly used for food—about 90 per cent being directly consumed as human food, and the remainder used for seed, feed, and industrial usages. Over three-fourths of mankind now gets most of its starch calories from one or the other, and the pressure of standards is such that practically all of mankind will do the same as soon as it can afford them.

Although the share of calories derived from starchy foods is largely a function of income, principal food staples are influenced more by physical geography. Over the years, man has learned which cereals are best suited to habitat factors such as climate and soil. Of all the grains, barley is probably grown the farthest north (in parts of Europe it is grown north of the Arctic Circle). In proceeding toward warmer climates, wherever soil conditions are favorable or can be made so, we find barley, rye, and oats, then wheat, then corn, then millets and sorghums, and finally rice, under successful cultivation.

Since the mid-1950's, global consumption of grain has increased by about 4 per cent per year, roughly double the rate of world population growth.[2] However, the consumption of food grains has increased at a 3 per cent rate, only half again as rapidly as population increase, while the coarse (feed) grains supply has increased some 5 per cent annually, about the same as that for income increase.

Although both rice and wheat are widely distributed, the overlap is quite small, as Table 6–7 indicates. Rice is overwhelmingly tropical, with only small production on the warmer edges of the mid-latitudes, while wheat is overwhelmingly mid-latitude, with only small production in the tropics (mainly uplands or cool edge during the winter).

Rice

Rice cultivation extends from latitudes 45° N. to 40° S. In effect, because of its climatic requirements, rice is limited to the tropics and subtropics. Over 90 per cent of all the world's rice is grown in the Far East (Monsoon Asia), where both the climate and the soil are highly favorable for rice growing but are poorly adapted for the raising of other grain crops except for the millets and sorghums. Over two-thirds of the entire Far Eastern grain consumption con-

[2] The annual rate of increase in grainland has been only about 1 per cent, reflecting the increasing importance of increased acreage yields in supplying this increased production.

TABLE 6–7

World: Food Grains Production, by Great-Region and Economic-Type of Society, 1962–1964 Average-Annual

(in millions of metric tons)

	Milled Rice [1]		Wheat	
North America	2.1	1.3%	50.7	21.3%
Western Europe	0.8	0.6	41.5	17.4
Eastern Europe (including the U.S.S.R.)	0.3	0.2	65.7	27.6
Oceania	0.1	0.1	9.0	3.8
Latin America	5.2	3.3	10.7	4.5
Sub-Saharan Africa	2.4	1.5	1.4	0.6
Middle East (including North Africa)	1.9	1.2	17.1	7.2
Non-Communist Far East	91.6	57.7	16.9	7.1
Communist Far East	54.0	34.1	25.0	10.5
World	158.4	100.0%	238.0	100.0%
High-income countries	13.4	8.5%	158.0	66.4%
Low-income countries	145.0	91.5	80.0	33.6

[1] The some 245 million metric tons of rough rice (paddy) have been converted to milled rice at 65 per cent in order to make it more comparable to wheat, which loses its hull in threshing and which averages less dirt, dead grain, and other extraneous matter (partly because of greater commercialization).

sists of this one cereal. Rice is not only a high-yielding cereal, and consequently highly favored by crowded populations as in the Orient, but it can be cooked with a small amount of fuel (compared with baking bread), another important consideration in parts of the Far East.

Rice is produced and consumed by subsistence farmers to a much greater extent than wheat. Half of the 250 million tons of rice grown in the world does not go beyond the farm, because the farmer and his family eat it themselves. About 5 per cent enters world trade, with the remainder mainly consumed in urban centers of the producing countries.

About half of mankind obtains the principal part of its food grain requirements from rice, or values it as the most socially desirable food grain even when unable to use it continually. Additional large numbers who depend on wheat and other cereals value it for dessert or similar uses.

Rice has been developed in numerous varieties: differing in color, shape, size, flavor, and other characteristics. Common rice comprises all the varieties whose kernels can be cooked so that they remain separate. So-called glutinous rice (which does not contain gluten) is sticky, the individual kernels losing their identity during cooking, and is used largely in making pastry and confectionery (it is most commonly found in China). In all, there are said to be more than 5,000 varieties, probably greater than for all other grains together.

International trade in rice is segregated into three specialized types, in which there is very little substitutability. About 10 per cent of rice exports consists of top-quality long-grain rice mainly sent to western hemisphere and European markets from the United States and elsewhere, recently costing about 6 cents per pound (at port of export). About 25 per cent consists of medium-quality mostly short-grain milled rice, such as the better qualities exported from Southeast Asia; competition turns more on price than with the first group, and recently it has cost about 5 cents per pound. The 65 per cent of lower-grade rice (including much broken kernel and other inferior fractions) moving in world trade mainly goes to poor countries with limited foreign exchange, and is mainly consumed by the poorer classes or used in industry; imports vary according to concessional arrangements and domestic supplies of other foods, and the price varies around 3 to 4 cents per pound.

Rice culture requires level land, heavy fertile soil, and an impervious subsoil, plenty of water, and a temperature of over 75° F. It must have no less than 40 inches of annual rainfall and is not commonly found above 3,000 feet.

Some varieties of rice require as little as three months to mature, others as much as five to seven months. Because of the large number of varieties, rice is a fairly elastic type of crop within its general area of distribution, accommodating itself to considerable differences in water supply and temperature conditions, and being able to grow on a rather wide range of soils.

There is evidently a relationship between latitude and yield, since the highest yields are re-

U.S.D.A. Photos

Rice from combine flowing into waiting hopper, in lower Mississippi alluvial area, and closeup of short-grain rice. In a world perspective, rice is restricted to a small portion of its potential habitat, and so far it has been little affected by either mechanization (less than 5 per cent is produced by large-wheeled machinery as portrayed here) or modern intensification (perhaps another 20 per cent is produced by small-wheeled machinery and heavy artificial fertilization).

corded in areas outside the zone between latitudes 30° N. and 30° S. But because many of the rice-growing countries in these areas (the United States, Spain, Italy, Korea, Japan) practice intensive cultivation, it is doubtful if latitude alone is responsible for high yields. It is possible that latitude may have an effect on yield through resultant differences in temperature and length of day.

In all the rice-growing countries of the warm temperate regions, intensive fertilization with inorganic, or with combinations of organic manures with inorganic, fertilizers is carried out, amounting on an average to 60 to 130 pounds of nitrogen, 35 to 90 pounds of phosphorus, and 50 to 100 pounds of potash per acre. This liberal use of manures and fertilizers in the warm temperate regions, and the absence of fertilizing practices in the tropics, is probably one of the major reasons for the wide disparity in yields between the two realms.

Between latitudes 20° N. and 20° S., rice is grown during the entire year so long as an adequate water supply is available; farther north and south, it is mainly a summer crop because the rice plant cannot tolerate temperatures below 70° F. Because the rice-growing season is limited to summer and early autumn in the warm temperate countries, there is little variation in the length of growing period of the varieties grown, and the growing period does not extend beyond four or five months. In the tropics, the length of growing period of varieties is from three to seven months, and the bulk of widely grown varieties requires about four and a half to five months. The longer maturity period is not linked to the heaviest yield, but because agricultural conditions—particularly lack of water control—necessitate a long growing season. The length of the growing period of varieties grown during the Far Eastern monsoon appears to depend upon the length of the rainy season and the amount of rain. There is some indication that larger yields are obtained from dry season crops than from the rainy season crops. It is clear that a distinction between growth and development can be recognized in rice. While long-day and low-temperature conditions, characteristic of the warm temperate regions, favor development, short-day and high-temperature conditions favor growth, and the former conditions are more conducive to production. Again, the response to day length is a varietal character, some varieties being extremely sensitive and others nonsensitive.

Water plays a very important role in the cultivation of paddy rice: the crop uses quantities considerably in excess of most other cultivated plants. Little rice is grown where the annual rainfall is less than 40 inches. Irrigation water requirements seem to vary from about 15 inches in the more humid tropical regions to about 20 inches in northwest India, about 25 inches in the Mediterranean regions, and perhaps 35 inches in Turkestan. The amount of water needed increases from planting time to the middle of the vegetative period and decreases thereafter. The water used on the wet-rice fields generally stands, or is in very slow motion (the latter, better oxygenated condition is considerably more favorable than the former). Generally speaking, the rice plant stands in water to an average height of approximately 1 foot for about four-fifths of its entire period of development, from the time of transplanting to that of blooming. Although it grows under swamp conditions, rice is not aquatic and needs oxygen for its root system. Fields are sometimes left dry for brief periods in order to improve aeration of the soil.

A heavy soil not completely impervious is the optimum requirement. Yields are comparatively higher in heavier rather than in lighter soils (an ideal soil should contain finer fractions of silt and clay up to 50 to 60 per cent). Rice thrives better in neutral to slightly acid soils than in definitely alkaline soils, and better in highly acid than in highly alkaline soils.

Rice crops have traditionally been divided into two broad groups, lowland and upland. Lowland rice is grown in areas where there is standing water at appropriate seasons and the soil remains saturated throughout the rice season. The rice varieties grown under such conditions generally have a longer growing period (150 to 180 days), though varieties with shorter growing periods (90 to 100 days) may also be grown where the water supply can be controlled, as in canal-irrigated areas. The least intensive type of wet-rice cultivation—found in eastern India, East Pakistan, and Burma—is characterized by the absence of seedbeds and replanting, the grain being broadcast or drilled, generally before irrigation water is applied. The incomplete preparation of the soil in broadcast fields, where it is usually difficult to break heavy soils in a dry condition with bullock-drawn plows, results in a greater proliferation of weeds. In many tropical areas, weeding is not given sufficient attention, unlike Japan where transplanted fields are weeded three to four times.

Upland rice is always rain-fed without any artificial irrigation, and all the varieties grown have short maturity periods. Not all rain-fed rice is upland rice, as much lowland rice is unirrigated in areas where the rainfall during the rice season is 60 inches or more, as in parts of eastern India, East Pakistan, and Burma. Upland rice is grown over substantial areas in Ceylon, Thailand, Indonesia, and the Philippines, but accounts for only a tenth of world rice production, and that share is decreasing. The main problem connected with upland rice is weed control but, because of the comparatively poor yield, weeding is seldom practiced. Upland soils are often poor in fertility and the fertility can be maintained only with better cultivation, manuring, and rotation practices. Some Indonesian and Japanese upland rice yields are quite good, but the yields of upland rice are usually only one-half to two-thirds those of lowland rice in the same area, even when growing on fresh fields.

Over enormous areas of South, Southeast, and East Asia, rice crop follows rice crop without interruption or fallowing. Wet rice can produce under such conditions partly because certain algae in the flooded fields are capable of fixing atmospheric nitrogen and because the linkage between iron and phosphorus is apparently weaker under such conditions than in a dry field. The rice-growing countries of the warm temperate regions practice regular crop rotation, while in the tropics there is little evidence of any systematic rotation. In large areas of some countries (e.g., India, Indonesia), it is customary to cultivate a quick-growing pulse or maize crop after rice, but since these crops are grown mainly for their grain, it is doubtful whether they benefit the soil to any extent even though they may not deplete the soil.

At harvest time, from $\frac{1}{4}$ ton of paddy per acre per crop in most of South and Southeast Asia to 2 tons in Japan are harvested.[3] The inedible fraction of paddy (rough) rice is considerably larger than the inedible fraction of threshed wheat (but about the same as the flour-extraction rate). The weight of hulled (brown) rice is usually about three-fourths that of paddy, and its volume is about one-half (in extreme cases, weight loss may reach 35 to 40 per cent; highly milled white rice is about 65 per cent of the rough paddy weight). Very little need be kept for seed, as rice is an economical crop, requiring only 3 to 5 per cent of the yield for seed (seedbeds usually are less than 5 per cent of the area to be transplanted). Some brown rice and broken white rice are fed to livestock, and broken white rice is used in brewing beer, in the making of alcohol, and in the manufacture of starch, but these uses rarely exceed the fraction used for seed, leaving 90 per cent for food.

In spite of impressive increases in production during the past decade, rice production remains in short supply and probably will continue to do so. The large population increase is continuing and still has not reached its maximum, and the overwhelming majority of rice eaters are still in the stage where increase in income results in increased consumption. Many poor people in the underdeveloped realm, who prefer rice, are living on coarse grains and on starchy roots, tubers, and fruits (e.g., sweet potatoes in south China; maize, sweet potatoes, and cassava in Java and tropical Brazil). Another interesting substitution, found in urban regions mainly, is the use of bread (e.g., in Japanese, Indian, and other cities). In Japan, present bread consumption is a dozen times larger than in prewar days, and can no longer be considered merely a substitute or supplement for rice, as it once was. A traditional Japanese breakfast is based on rice, and it is here that bread has made its biggest inroads. Its great advantage, important to city dwellers, is that it does not require cooking. Many Japanese who do not like bread will eat udon, Japanese noodles made from soft white wheat, an ingredient of many traditional dishes. Another important use for wheat is the big increase in the consumption of cakes and cookies, rarely eaten before World War II. However, one should not exaggerate the extent of the change. Heavy laborers in the cities and farmers in general still like rice three times a day. So far, the main converts to wheat have been the urban white-collar classes, and even they prefer rice for lunch and dinner. For the average Japanese, bread is not so filling as rice. Also, other foods that through the centuries have come to be associated with rice cannot be eaten with bread (e.g., raw fish, which when eaten with rice is the popular sushi, would appear ludicrous on bread).

---

[3] But, in order to achieve self-sufficiency in rice, Japan supports its price at levels two to three times as high as those of the world market.

The world's rice eaters are several generations away from the situation of the world's wheat eaters at present, where per capita consumption is dropping almost everywhere to the level of a third or less of caloric intake. Imports and substitution are important in narrow contexts, but mainly the increased demand from increasing numbers with higher incomes must be supplied from increased domestic supplies. In many areas of Latin America, sub-Saharan Africa, Southeast Asia, and tropical Oceania, the increased supplies may well come from areal expansion of paddy land. But in the largest areas of rice consumption—South and East Asia—increased output is most likely from intensified yield based on chemical fertilization. But this long-term probability would require a capacity of tremendous proportions (e.g., if fertilizer application rates in India were to reach those of Japan, India's requirements would far exceed present total world output).

Wheat

An overwhelming majority of the world's inhabitants outside of the traditionally rice-eating region (the Far East) show a decided preference for wheat bread as their principal cereal food. Wheat is the most widely distributed of all the cereals, and is the major cereal handled in grain markets. In many countries where wheat is not available for use as the principal human dietary, it is nevertheless the cereal of first choice with the result that other cereals are gradually being replaced by wheat (especially rye, maize, barley, and millets-sorghums).

Wheat's nearly worldwide popularity outside of the tropics is due to many superlative characteristics: its mild and highly acceptable flavor, to the particular quality of its protein (gluten) which makes wheat flour rank above all other flours for making leavened breads and other baked goods, to the relatively high keeping quality of its refined white flours, and to the excellent storage properties of the grain itself, enabling it to be transported long distances and to be held satisfactorily for long periods if it becomes necessary.

Wheat and rice, the dominant cereals used as food by the world's inhabitants, are both mild-flavored cereals. Their flavors blend acceptably with all other types of foods. Most people show some liking for the stronger-flavored cereals such as rye and buckwheat now and then, but for their staple cereal day in and day out the masses of the world's population turn to either wheat or rice. There seems very little likelihood that wheat or rice will ever replace one another to any large extent once either has become established as the preferred cereal of a region.

The special type of protein in wheat known as gluten is the substance that gives the soft, springy quality to bread doughs when they are being kneaded and that enables the doughs to retain the gases produced by yeast fermentation. Because of this, wheat flours can be made into soft, light, finely textured loaves of bread. Flours made from other grains do not have this type of protein and only rather heavy, solid loaves of bread can be made from them. Other flours such as rye, barley, oats, corn, millet, rice, and soy flours can be blended with wheat flour to give a fairly light loaf provided these other flours, which are lacking in gluten, are not added in high proportions.

Compared with the coarse (feed) grains, wheat is a relatively expensive cereal to produce: it is exacting in its soil requirements; it cannot be grown as far north as some of the other grains; and in most of the regions where it is grown, it is not one of the highest-yielding cereals. There are many varieties of wheat. About three-fourths of the wheat tonnage consists of winter wheats, which are sown in the fall, sprout and achieve vigorous root growth during the winter season, and proceed with vigorous stalk growth with the rising temperatures of spring and early summer. Spring wheats are sown just as soon after the frost leaves the ground, as the soil can be made ready for planting. It is important that the early growth of the wheat plant take place in cool weather.

Partly because of its many cultivated varieties, wheat can adapt itself to a fairly broad range of climatic conditions, and consequently has a wide geographic distribution. Most of the world's wheat is grown in regions with mid-latitude climates, or with dry subtropical (Mediterranean) climate. In warm, humid regions, wheat production does not pay because of susceptibility of the crop to diseases under such conditions. Therefore, practically no wheat is produced in the regions of tropical, rainy climate, nor in most regions of tropical savanna climate, although a little wheat is grown at higher altitudes where temperatures are more moderate. Little wheat is produced in areas of subpolar climate, although as a result of successful breeding of hardier varieties and vernalization treatment of wheat seed (i.e., chilling seed to shorten the growth period before blossoming) the polar limit of wheat cultivation has been moved appreciably farther north in Canada, Scandinavia, and the U.S.S.R. At higher latitudes and altitudes, oats, rye, and especially barley are more economical crops.

Wheat requires good soils in areas with a growing season of at least ninety days. Where a system of fallow in alternate years is practiced, the minimum annual rainfall is 10 to 15 inches (a small amount is grown with as little as 9 inches, when it comes in the growing season and the soils are moisture-retentive). In most wheat areas, the rainfall is less than 30 inches, but this distribution is related as much to cereal competition as to plant optimum requirements. Corn and oats require greater rainfall, while wheat survives with less and thus is often pushed to its margin. Barley is the only important grain that may be grown with less rainfall; where precipitation is considered below optimum, wheat does not yield as well as barley or millet, but as a winter crop it can be grown in many regions where it is not possible to produce winter barley.

Wheat is mostly associated with a grassland climax (occasionally a woodland climax), and is most productive on fertile, medium-textured soils with reasonable drainage. Fertile silts, silt loams, or clay loams are best, especially with certain amounts of lime and humus. Distinctly sandy soils are usually of insufficient fertility for wheat.

In general, the subhumid to semiarid regions, particularly those with soils of fairly high nitrogen content, produce the hardest wheats. Hard spring wheat and hard winter wheat have a relatively high protein content which makes for especially good bread flour when used with yeast. These hard varieties that make good bread flour grow successfully in only a few areas: the North American Great Plains, the Humid Pampas of Argentina, the Magreb (Northwest Africa), the Soviet steppes, and the Australian plains. The distinction between spring and winter wheat lies in the time of seeding, and does not necessarily indicate a difference in species, or in variety. Where frosts come early in autumn, or where average winter temperatures are low, and the snow cover is insufficient or spotty, winter killing tends to be high, and sowing generally takes place in the spring.

Where soil moisture is abundant or temperatures during the vegetative cycle are low, the growing period tends to lengthen. Starch accumulates faster than proteins, and the final percentage of the latter will tend to be lower. These soft wheats have a low protein level (as low as 9 per cent compared with a high of 20 per cent in some hard wheats), are used with chemical leaveners, and are best in cakes and pies.

Bread wheat flours are usually made from hard (spring or winter types from subhumid-semiarid areas) wheats, while the best cake and pastry flours are made of soft wheats. The strength of bread doughs must be great enough to retain the gases developed slowly by yeast fermentation, while good cake and pastry flours must provide a tender, fluffy product aerated or made porous by quick-acting leavening agents such as baking powder or soda and sour milk or cream. Durum wheat is used in the manufacture of macaroni, spaghetti, noodles, and vermicelli. Durum wheat flour has a distinct yellow or amber color that is clearly recognizable in these macaroni types of products. It also has a special type of protein, slightly tougher than the protein of bread wheat flour, which is considered highly desirable in such products. This protein gives to the cooked macaroni products their characteristic chewy textures. Durum wheat flour may or may not contain more protein than other common types of wheat flours, depending upon the conditions of growth of the durum wheat crop from year to year.

Since the end of World War II, world wheat production has increased over 50 per cent, while world population has increased less than half as fast. Both areal expansion and intensification have played a part in this expansion. Since 1945, the Soviet Union has doubled its wheat area, both by opening large new tracts for wheat growing on its semiarid southern edge and by a substantial shift from rye to wheat on its cool northern edge. Western Europe has made additional progress in intensifying acreage yields, although often at a considerable cost (from one-fourth more to one-half more than imports).

Of the world's wheat production, some 15 per cent enters world trade (20 per cent of the non-Communist realm's production). Of the 30 to 35 million tons of wheat shipped in recent years, four-fifths was exported by five countries (the United States, Canada, Argentina, Australia, and France). North America shipped two-thirds of the world's exports, roughly half from the United States, half from Canada. The exporters must have cheap wheat or heavy subsidization. In the United States, the average cost of producing wheat is about $1.50 per bushel, but the larger, more heavily mechanized Great Plains region

U.S.D.A. Photos

Dakotan wheat field near harvest-time and closeup of several wheats. Wheat, like rice, feeds about 1½ billion humans, but over 75 per cent is grown by modern mechanized and chemicalized methods, compared with 75 per cent premodern methods in rice production.

produces a bushel for half that amount in a good precipitation year, the average bushel in 1965 bringing under $2 (half again as much in Western Europe). U.S. wheat exported to Europe takes 35 to 50 cents per bushel transport costs from interior to European ports by waterway (either Great Lakes Seaway or Mississippi River routes), a bit more if railed to Eastern Seaboard ports. European protection is $1.50 or so per bushel.

Trends

When incomes pass a certain level per capita, consumption of food grains tends to decline as the general quality of diets rises with the addition of such commodities as the luxury energy foods, meat, and protective foods.

Evidence suggests that in a number of developed countries the per capita intake of food grains may already have reached the minimum level below which no further declines can be expected (20 to 25 per cent of caloric intake). The United States, the Netherlands, Denmark, and Sweden are believed close to such a minimum. In other Western European countries, as well as in Japan, Australia, and New Zealand, per capita consumption of food grains may continue to decline for some years to come, proportionately as incomes rise.

In many Latin American, Middle Eastern, and other countries now in the developing stage, wheat has gradually been replacing coarse grains as a favored cereal, as prosperity advances. In North America, wheat consumption has decreased a bit in relation to other grains, with the spread of breakfast foods processed from coarse grains (especially corn).

As a result of these various tendencies, wheat's prospects are favorable. The supply is increasing rapidly, and technical prospects for continuation of this increasing production are favorable. On the demand side, the population increase of wheat eaters is below the average of mankind, and changing consumption standards are relieving the pressure among large segments of the consumers. About a sixth of all wheat eaters now have a minimal per capita demand for the grain, and another half have a declining demand from the third of their caloric intake the grain now fills. The third of all wheat eaters who are still increasing their per capita consumption as their incomes rise are mainly in the Latin American, Middle Eastern, and Far Eastern regions of the world.

The rice eater is in a much less favorable situation, being in the approximate position that the wheat eater was around the turn of the century. The demand is increasing rapidly, fed by a population increase now above the world average, by an increasing per capita consumption where incomes are rising, and by an increasing substitution of rice for coarse grains (especially millets, corn, and barley) and starchy tropical tubers. The supply situation is favorable from a scientific and technical point of view, but the economics are difficult in the short run. Both areal expansion and intensification mainly require a switch from the traditional labor-intensive methods to modern capital-intensive techniques, a type of substitution difficult to make quickly, not only because of smallholder predominance but because of the low priority many governments place upon such agricultural rationalization in their feverish efforts to industrialize. By far the most serious roadblocks are in the Far East. There are good prospects for greater surpluses outside the Far East, but world trade on a scale now featuring wheat is unlikely in the foreseeable future, mainly for political reasons.

FEED GRAINS

In the case of wheat and rice, the portion fed to livestock is small, and mainly consists of grain so deteriorated in storage as to be unsuitable for milling into flour or polished rice. Of the total weight of such grains, much does enter into non-food uses, but it is mainly bran and germ portions going into livestock and industrial uses.

In the case of the coarse grains, the portion fed to humans directly is small and declining. In times of cheap and abundant wheat and rice, the coarse grains used directly for human food may drop to 15 to 20 per cent of total consumption. In times of shortage, the proportion may rise to about 25 per cent.

About two-thirds of the total production of feed grains is used for livestock feed and for industrial usages within the countries of production. The proportion involved in world trade is something over 5 per cent (about the same as in the case of rice). About half of world feed grains exports are from the United States, mainly because of some 60 per cent of maize exports and 80 per cent of sorghum exports. About three-quarters of the feed grains moved in world trade are destined for Western Europe (imports are a third of feed grains consumption). Japan tripled its feed grains consumption in the past decade, and now accounts for 15 per cent of the total (mainly from Thailand and the United States).

The rapid expansion of the poultry industry (some 15 per cent a year in many areas of commercial production), plus the expanding demand for feed mixtures in the other livestock branches are the chief factors explaining the rapid increase in feed grains consumption. So far, the feed grains (Table 6-8) are mainly consumed in the urban-industrial third of mankind, but similar tendencies elsewhere indicate that increasingly grain will be produced for indirect rather than direct human usage.

Maize (Corn)

Among the feed grains, maize is as pre-eminent as wheat is among the food grains in the West and rice in the East. But while wheat and rice owe their leading positions largely to preference in terms of taste and hence to the relatively high prices that they command under ordinary conditions, "corn" owes its favorable position as a general feed grain mainly to its low cost (e.g., a third to a half that of the food grains), which in turn is traceable chiefly to the large yield (2 tons per acre where climate and soil conditions favor its cultivation; half that amount in commercial production areas considered as a whole).

The United States, producing about half of the world's maize crop, feeds about 85 per cent of it to animals and uses the remaining 15 per cent for seed and industrial uses. About 5 per cent is consumed as direct human food after being processed. Some of it goes to the dry-milling industry to be converted into cornmeal, hominy, breakfast foods, and other foods. Distillers turn their share into alcohol. Feed manufacturers absorb a portion. Corn refiners and wet-millers

TABLE 6–8

World: Feed Grains Production, by Great-Region and Economic-Type of Society, 1962–1964 Average-Annual
(in millions of metric tons)

	Maize (Corn)		Barley		Oats		Rye		Millets and Sorghums	
North America	104.5	51.2%	13.3	15.3%	20.7	44.4%	1.1	3.5%	12.5	13.6%
Western Europe	9.6	4.7	27.1	31.2	12.2	26.2	5.8	18.4	0.5	0.5
Eastern Europe (including the U.S.S.R.)	26.3	12.9	22.1	25.5	10.1	21.7	23.6	75.4	4.0	4.3
Oceania	0.2	0.1	1.0	1.1	1.0	2.2	–	–	–	–
Latin America	23.9	11.7	1.7	2.0	0.9	2.0	0.2	0.7	2.5	2.7
Sub-Saharan Africa	12.6	6.2	1.0	1.0	0.1	0.2	–	–	20.0	21.8
Middle East (including North Africa)	2.9	1.4	8.8	10.1	0.5	1.1	0.6	2.0	2.5	2.7
Non-Communist Far East	12.6	6.2	5.2	6.0	0.1	0.2	–	–	20.0	21.8
Communist Far East	11.4	5.6	6.8	7.8	0.9	2.0	–	–	30.0	32.6
World	204.0	100.0%	87.0	100.0%	46.5	100.0%	31.3	100.0%	92.0	100.0%
High-income countries	138.0	67.5%	61.5	70.7%	43.3	93.2%	29.7	95.0%	15.0	16.0%
Low-income countries	66.0	32.5	25.5	29.3	3.2	6.8	1.6	5.0	77.0	84.0

take the rest, turning their corn into starch, syrup, sugar, and oil, which are then used by manufacturers whose food and non-food products reflect little of the corn origin.

Being deficient in gluten, neither cornmeal nor corn flour alone can be used to make a light bread. White cornmeal (favored in the U.S. South) and yellow cornmeal (favored in the U.S. North) is commonly employed to make corn bread, johnnycake, hoecake, or corn pone, pancakes, grits, mush, and porridge. Since corn bread is very crumbly and cannot be baked in loaves, most of the some 100 million people in the world who eat corn as their main food or as a major food consume it in the form of thin, round, unleavened cake (e.g., tortilla) or as porridge.

Nearly one-half of all U.S. corn is fed to pigs (lately pigs have brought only one-half of the price they did in the late 1940's, a severe blow to corn producers), with another third going into other livestock and into poultry. Besides the grain, the plant as a whole is an important fodder crop, being used green, dried, or as silage. For making silage, the leaves and stems are cut into small pieces and placed in silos, large receptacles with airtight sides and bottoms, where a slight fermentation produces a product more palatable for cattle. Stover, the residue after the ears have been removed, is also fed to cattle or used for silage. Recently some of the corncobs have been fed to animals. Cattle, sheep, and goats—ruminant animals with four stomachs—can convert such cheap cellulose into meat if they get plenty of protein. Urea, a nitrogen compound made from the air, provides protein at a cost of 2 cents per pound, thus permitting the wider use of agricultural wastes such as corncobs.

The varieties of cultivated corn probably reach into the thousands, differing in size, form, color, structure of the grain, and other characteristics. On the basis of grain structure, they can be classified into dent, flint, flour, sweet, pop, pod, and waxy corns. Dent or soft maize predominates in the United States and northern Mexico, while flint or hard maize predominates in most of Latin America and in Eurasia. Flint corn can be dried easily and keeps well, and lends itself better to shipment over long distances, so it is highly favored as stock feed, especially for poultry.

Each of the many varieties of corn has somewhat different minimal and optimum requirements, but varieties often appear to adapt themselves rather easily to new environmental conditions. Some general physical requirements follow. The vegetative period of corn varies from about 90 to 190 days, with optimal grain yields resulting when the growing period is at least 140 days. The crop requires considerable moisture and warmth from the time of planting to the end of the flowering period. Most crops are grown within the 25- to 40-inch range of annual rainfall but there must be adequate water available during mid-seasonal growth. Varieties vary in their temperature requirements: early maturing types will succeed when the summer temperature is 66° F. and the night temperature 55° F. or less if the growing season is cool but prolonged (e.g., much of the U.S. dairy belt). During germination, most favorable temperatures seem to be about 65° F., with temperatures below 55° F. resulting in appreciable reductions in yields. Cool nights are harmful, for they slow down vegetative growth (in regions with such nights, corn can be grown successfully only if the growing season is very long). During the last part of the growing period, particularly during the ripening of the grain, corn needs considerable amounts of warmth, combined with a great deal of sunshine. During this ripening period the optimum moisture requirements are considerably lower than during the main part of the vegetative period (often only one-third to one-half as much). Due to these climatic requirements, corn is a crop that can be grown successfully throughout the humid tropics, humid subtropics, and the warmer parts of the regions with mid-latitude climates. Probably the optimum corn-growing region in the world is the U.S. Corn Belt, providing over a third of the world's supply, so it will be described in more detail.

Corn is the most important crop in American agriculture, being grown on 1 out of every 4 acres of cropland. Currently more than 75 per cent of the nation's cropland devoted to corn production is in the Corn Belt, compared with less than 60 per cent some forty years ago (between 1920 and 1960 total corn acreage declined nearly one-fifth, all of the decline occurring outside the Corn Belt).

Corn requires a deep soil, rich in nitrogen and organic matter. The land must have a high moisture-holding capacity and be level or gently sloping to avoid serious soil erosion. Corn also requires a fairly long and warm growing season with ample rainfall. In the Corn Belt states, these factors occur in a combination that is especially favorable to the specific requirements of the crop.

The boundaries of the Corn Belt are determined on the north by the length of the frost-free season—corresponding roughly to the limit of 140 consecutive frost-free days—and on the west by rainfall. In the 1950's, development of short-seasoned hybrids enabled intensive production of corn for grain to be extended as much as 100 miles farther north in Michigan, Wisconsin, and Minnesota. While the western parts of the Corn Belt receive only 22 to 30 inches of rainfall annually compared with 30 to 40 inches in the remainder of the region, this drier section receives the bulk of its rainfall during the corn-growing season, which is supplemented by irrigation in large areas. However, in the southwestern portion of the traditional Corn Belt (especially in Kansas), farmers have steadily reduced their corn acreage since the 1930's as grain sorghum has replaced corn in areas where there is limited rainfall.

In the past, the practice of planting corn continuously without rotation invited a buildup of soil-borne diseases and insects that attacked corn seeds, roots, and stalks in addition to aggravating competition from weeds. In recent years, new hybrids have been developed that are resistant to diseases and insects, while new insecticides and soil fungicides have also aided in maintaining yields in a continuous-corn program. For example, the wireworms and cutworms that the farmer formerly killed by rotation practices now are doomed by a chemical compound that gets at the pests before they mature and eliminates two cultivations of the fields per crop season, another labor- and time-saver. Tillage costs average $10 to $15 per acre, about the same cost as the new chemicals, but the average farmer also spends about $7 per acre on labor and machinery to cultivate after the corn is up, which can be saved by such chemicalization.

Furthermore, the fertility and tilth of the soil formerly declined if legumes were not planted in rotation with corn to replenish the supply of nitrogen, loosen the soil, and add organic matter. Chemical fertilizers have been made available at a cost much less than the cost of nitrogen provided by a legume rotation crop. Some authorities say the commercial cost of 10 cents per pound for purchased nitrogen (in substantial amounts) compares with 75 cents per pound for nitrogen produced on the farm by putting land into alfalfa to get the equivalent nitrogen return. Commercial fertilizers are cleaner, easier to handle, and can be applied faster than the farmer's longtime friend, ordinary manure. Two pounds of nitrogen (20 cents) equals 1 bushel of corn, worth $1 on the farm, with only small additional costs. The growing of more plants per acre, along with high levels of chemical fertilization, has provided the organic material needed for maintaining the tilth of the soil in the absence of rotation.

Current rates of fertilizer application are considered to be well below optimum levels. One estimate is that the most profitable rate of fertilization for corn would be around 300 pounds of plant nutrients per acre, or more than twice as much as now used by Midwest farmers. On the horizon are hybrids that are tolerant of close spacing, boosting potential corn seeding rates to 50,000 plants per acre, more than double the top rates presently used and three times the typical rate. With capacity to utilize higher rates of fertilization, these hybrids would raise yields. The development of dwarf and multiple-ear corn plants may also serve to boost yields. Dwarf corn reduces the amount of nutrients that are utilized in producing the stalks and leaves of the corn plant and thus makes more nutrients

U.S.D.A. Photos

A corn picker and sheller harvesting a western Ohio field and closeup of corn kernels. Corn is favored as the most important feedgrain because of its high yield and low cost, rather than because of its nutritional advantages in producing lean meat (best use comes from half corn and half hay and oilseed-cake in the ration).

available for producing ears. Multiple-ear corn, currently undergoing limited commercial production, has a large number of small ears, which facilitates corn being planted and harvested in much the same fashion as oats and wheat, permitting capital saving by wider use of small-grains machinery and less use of expensive special machinery for corn only.

Erosion was formerly a serious problem since with steady row cropping the soil became compacted and rain ran off fields carrying the surface soil with it, instead of being absorbed by the soil. New practices of minimum tillage—which compacts the soil only in the seedbed rows, leaving the middle relatively loose—combined with chemical herbicides for weed control have reduced the problem of soil compaction associated with the many trips of heavy machinery formerly needed in planting and cultivating corn.

As a result of these changes, the amount of acreage planted to corn is no longer limited as severely as in past years by the requirements of a crop rotation. Large areas of the Corn Belt, therefore, are now suited to continuous corn planting, including most of the fertile land with gentle slopes, if special management practices such as contour plowing and cultivation are used to control erosion. For the steeper slopes, a rotation program that includes grass or legumes still must be used to minimize soil erosion caused by water runoff.

Now, as in the past, the main attractions of corn are high yields and low costs. The 62-bushel-average national yield per acre is half again as high as in the early 1950's, and technically the present yield could be increased another third. Including all operating expenses, plus depreciation, and returns to labor, capital, and land, corn is produced for 90 cents per bushel on the average (some farmers do it for 75 cents), and brings in about $1.10 per bushel on the farm ($1.50 in New York State). Efficient farmers still have substantial incentive to expand corn production. The nation's most valuable agricultural commodity, corn contributes some $4.5 billion to farm income, nearly 10 per cent from overseas sales (only soybeans and soybean products bring in more dollars). The United States now supplies some 55 per cent of world corn exports (four times those of second-place Argentina).

Obviously, not all the corn in the world is produced as efficiently as that in the U.S. Corn Belt. In much of Latin America, sub-Saharan Africa, the Middle East, and the Far East, corn is favored for reasons similar to those that made it the premier grain of Colonial America. Corn is distinctly more suited to cultivation on land only partially cleared of stones and stumps than are the smaller cereal grains and it has remained more or less the dominant cereal of isolated groups of people living in the hill country. Cutting corn by hand, whether in early America or in present Far Eastern corn areas, takes about 35 man-hours for an acre of corn (for comparison, the average U.S. farmer now has to put in only six minutes of labor to produce a bushel of corn, or six hours per acre, and the most efficient farmers put in only half that time).

In many areas of the Far East, corn is grown either because the land cannot be used for paddy (e.g., inability to irrigate) or because of a lack of labor at certain times. For example, in Java, transplanted paddy is very labor-intensive (for Southeast Asia, not compared with Japan): over 100 hours of man-labor, over 250 hours of woman-labor, and nearly 25 hours of buffalo-team-labor per acre per crop are required. In comparison, the production of an acre of maize requires only one-quarter of the number of hours of man-labor, 1 to 2 per cent of the hours of woman-labor, and roughly the same amount of animal-labor. The caloric output is roughly the same and the cost is much less (one-third to one-half as much), but the corn is much less favored and only the poor normally eat it with any regularity.

At present, American-type hybrid corn is diffusing all over the world wherever commercial production is found, upping yields and extending the areal extent. Slavic Europe is engaged in large-scale expansion as the basis of its animal husbandry (pigs, dairy cows), which is the agricultural segment with the highest elasticity of demand as urbanization proceeds. Many Latin American areas are also increasing production via the same route. The results show in the extremely rapid increase in corn production. It took a century for world corn production to double output by mid-century, and since that time production has nearly doubled again. In the foreseeable future, production will certainly equal that of wheat and rice, and the three cereals will account for three-quarters of world starch output from all sources.

Barley

Barley has the broadest limits of any of the temperate zone cereals. The crop has a wide range in the regions of mid-latitude climates, dry subtropical (Mediterranean) climate, and the adjacent areas of steppe climate.

More than half of the world's barley crop is used for livestock feed: it has a feeding value roughly 90 per cent that of corn (and usually costs about the same), with a similar carbohydrate content, about 3 per cent more protein, slightly less fat, and 5 per cent less digestible material. It is largely used as a fattening feed for cattle and hogs, and such use has been principally responsible for increased demand in Western Europe, where it is the main feed grain. Barley is particularly suitable for the production of pork and bacon of the highest quality. It produces a firmness of fat in the various products of the hog which is preferred especially in the European markets. This firmness results because barley itself contains only negligible amounts of fat. In southern Europe, the Middle East, and other areas that produce little oats, barley is a common feed for horses and other work animals.

The second largest use of barley (15 to 20 per cent of world production) is in the manufacture of beer, ale, and other alcoholic beverages. Malted barley—barley that has been allowed to sprout for a short period with further growth checked by drying the sprouted grain—is mixed with raw grain for the brewing process. Extracts of malted barley grains are also used as flavoring agents for cereal breakfast foods, for malted milk, and several other food products. Such barley must be of high quality—the grains should be of equal size, well ripened, plump, and thin-skinned, and the protein content should be low—and it brings a price like that of the highest-quality food grains. In North America and Europe, a quarter of the barley crop is used for malting, and additional amounts are imported from the Middle East.

Barley flour, because of its low gluten content, does not make a light, resilient loaf of bread. However, much barley flour is used for human food as a flat bread or a porridge, especially in North Africa and in Southwest and South Asia. However, it is doubtful if more than 25 million people now use barley as their dominant cereal, although many more use it mixed with other cereals or for occasional use. In regions where barley is commonly used as a staple cereal, there is general preference for types known as naked barley. In this type of barley, the grains are only loosely surrounded by the husk, from which they are freed in the process of threshing just as wheat is freed from the husk or chaff. Most of the barley eaten as a cereal is prepared in the form of groats—a granular product usually cooked and eaten as a porridge. Increasingly, in the areas favoring breadstuffs, barley flour is mixed with a large proportion of wheat flour. A small amount of malted-barley flour is sometimes added to wheat flour used in commercial bread making to promote more active fermentation in the bread doughs.

In many types of barley, the husk or chaff clings very tightly to the grains so that special types of milling operations are required to remove them. The name pearl barley is given to the rounded grains that have had the husks removed by coarse grinding (pearl barley used in Scotch broth and other soups is probably the most familiar form in which most Americans eat barley).

Earlier, it was mentioned that barley is often favored for its hardiness. It grows in most climates, from the subarctic through the temperate zone to the subtropics (and wintertime semi-tropics). In Scandinavia and the Soviet Union, it is cultivated near, and even within, the Arctic Circle. With a minimum of about eighty days, the growing period for spring barley is less than that of spring rye, spring oats, and spring wheat. As a result, spring barley goes far north to the polar limits of grain agriculture (partly because of the long duration of sunlight in the regions during the summer season) and is found in mountain regions as far as the upper limits for cereals (often up to 2 miles, occasionally up to 3 miles, as in Peru and Tibet). Barley's resistance to dry heat is superior to that of other small grains, and it thrives on the desert margin in North Africa and Southwest Asia, mostly as a fall-sown crop.

However hardy, barley reaches its maximum yield in the cooler, moist areas of North America and Western Europe, where the spring-sown types produce 40 to 60 bushels per acre. The varieties grown in these areas are less tolerant of moist heat than either corn or rice, or than the naked varieties of barley grown in India and Japan. Some 170 types of barley are grown in North America, varying with adaptation to soil, climate, and use. The smooth-awned, hybrid types of barley, contrasting with the bothersome bearded types, have enhanced the popularity of barley culture. Production in the United States is concentrated largely in the north central plains (Minnesota and the Dakotas) and in California. Winter barley is grown widely in the southeastern United States.

Barley and oats grown for feed are directly competitive for the land because the labor peaks for these two crops almost coincide, and the efforts required to grow the two grains do not differ very much. As a result, barley tends to be preferred where it outyields oats, and vice versa.

Barley is widely grown as a substitute crop. If a winter wheat crop fails, or conditions are too dry for corn, barley can be a valuable secondary crop. In Western Europe, barley is often a substitute crop for wheat, besides being the main feed grain grown. Increased plantings, improved disease-resistant varieties, better cultivation practices, and rapidly increasing demand for use as livestock feed have been the principal factors responsible for the larger crops in recent years. The substitution of barley in areas where acreage allotments have limited production of wheat and corn has been an important factor in increased production in the United States.

There are certain problems. Unfortunately, barley is not very winter hardy. Thus, winter barley cannot be produced advantageously over much of northern, central, and eastern Europe, so most is found in the Mediterranean region. Also, barley has a rather weak root system and, since it has a short vegetative period, it does best on porous soils, particularly fertile, well-tilled soils in which the plant foods are available in easily assimilated form. For optimum conditions of production, barley tends to need better soils than wheat. Cold and acid soils, heavy clays, poor sandy soils, and peaty soils generally are unsuitable for barley production. Feed barley, however, often is grown on soils that are considerably poorer than those required for malting barley.

Although only used about a third as much, barley's recent and prospective history is quite similar to that of corn. It, too, doubled output in the period from the mid-nineteenth to the mid-twentieth century, and during the short period since has nearly doubled output again. The cost is also about the same for feed types, although malting barley is another matter. It has shown strong competitive ability both as feed grain and as industrial raw material and promises to continue doing so.

U.S.D.A. Photos

Barley shock near Bozeman, Montana, and closeup of barley. In general, barley is favored mainly because of a combination of high nutritive value and hardiness to temperature limits. Increasingly it is used for feed and beer, but much is still used for food in poorer areas.

Oats

Oats, of all the small-grain cereals, is the highest yielding (in volume) and the cheapest to produce.[4] It is a very rapid-growing grain crop and not exacting in soil requirements, although it grows best on very heavy soils. Yet its total output today is little more than a century ago.

Although oats is the most nutritious of all cereals for human use as it has high protein, fat, and mineral content, food-use accounts for only a very small amount (4 per cent) of the annual crop-use. The protein material does not occur in the form of gluten, so oatmeal is not a good bread flour. Oatmeal has long been popular as a wintertime breakfast food, but only a few Celts and Teutons in the fringes of Europe have favored it as a dominant cereal. The highest-quality and plumpest grains of the annual oats crops are selected to be made into breakfast cereal. In preparing oats for human consumption, special milling operations are used to remove the oats hulls.

Some 90 per cent of the oats crop is consumed by domestic livestock on farms. Historically, it was especially favored for horses, but now large livestock used for meat and milk are more important, and an increasing proportion is now used in making balanced rations for pigs and poultry. The hulls of oats grains are not removed in the process of threshing the grain, and so the oats fed to livestock contains a large amount of fiber. This lightness of oats—only 32 pounds per bushel compared with 48 for barley and 56 for corn—militates against any large-scale trade, either domestically or in world trade (3 per cent); except for the small food portion, it is used on the farm where grown or nearby.

Oats is one of the late comers among the domesticated grains, and therefore is probably one of the most robust. On the whole, it needs little attention on the part of the farmer, one reason for its low cost (about half the cost of rye, little more than half that for corn).

[4] In the United States, about 42 bushels per acre, bringing about 60 to 70 cents per bushel on the farm (90 cents to $1 in New York State)—corn: 62 bushels, 90 cents to $1.10 on the farm. Oats protein is cheaper than that in wheat or corn, an advantage in animal feeding and finishing.

Courtesy of General Mills

Iowa oats field. Closeup of oats (U.S.D.A. Photo). *Oats is favored in North America and Europe because of its cheapness and the ease with which it fits into many crop rotations.*

Oats ranks high in yields among spring-planted crops, after rice and corn—yields are better than those of spring wheat and approach more nearly those of winter wheat. Oats is not very winter hardy, however, so nearly the entire crop is sown in the spring, both in North America and Europe.

Some varieties need only a vegetative period of about 80 days, although in cool and very moist regions over 110 days may be needed. Oats can be grown quite far poleward, although it does not go quite as far north as barley, nor does it go up as high in the mountains as either barley or rye.

The oats crop is less exacting than wheat, corn, and barley in its soil requirements and will, in some circumstances, withstand more alkaline or more saline conditions. It does not do well on limestone soils and dry, sandy soils. It is a crop that can stand more acid soils than other grains, and thus can be grown successfully on the leached, acid, podzolic soils of humid, cool regions where only rye is its companion.

The steady stagnation of oats production is due to many reasons. The substitution of tractors for horses has meant a drop in demand in many areas, unless there has been a compensatory increased demand for lean meat. In the U.S. Midwest, oats has traditionally been used in crop rotations or as nurse plants. Oats needs attention just before and after corn planting, so it was often grown in some variant of the corn-oats-alfalfa type of crop rotation because it fitted in well—its demands came at other times than when the dominant crops demanded attention—and provided cheap feed for work animals and other animals. Now many corn areas have abandoned such crop rotation on most of the land, and have given up or minimized oats in the process of change.

While oats has been losing ground as a feed grain, it has been increasing in importance as green forage and hay. In volume, oats ranks second only to corn as a fodder crop in North America. Oats straw has the highest feed value of any straw because the plant has more leaves than other small grains.

Rye

Before World War II, rye was the principal bread grain of the poor in northern Europe, but during the 1950's, decreasing demand—related to the increased incomes and changed standards of consumption associated with urban industrialization—and increased wheat supply—related to the northward spread of new varieties of wheat and the associated improvement of many soils that naturally were tolerated only by rye, oats, and potatoes—changed rye's status to that of a feed grain and industrial raw material. In the largest producer, the U.S.S.R., current production is only half of what it was in the 1930's, while in the rest of the world, its output is slightly less. Its production a century ago was much higher.

Some 85 per cent of the world's rye is produced in Europe and the U.S.S.R., in about as concentrated a pattern of production and consumption as in the case of rice in the Far East. In the region, rye bread had, until several decades ago, mainly been made with rye flours to which little or no white flour was added. Such bread, often called black bread, is dark colored and soggy and has a bitter flavor. In the 1930's, some 35 million Europeans still consumed rye as their dominant cereal, but the number today is much less and restricted to the poorest rural areas.

Because of the smaller degree of elasticity of the rye proteins (there is some gluten), the resulting whole-rye loaf is more dense and moist than whole-wheat bread, and less palatable. Whether it is less digestible appears to be an open question. In any event, there has been a general tendency for decades to replace rye bread with rye-wheat bread similar to the so-called rye bread most commonly used in the United States (from 10 to 30 per cent rye flour in the mixture).

In most parts of Europe and the U.S.S.R., a social stigma became attached to the exclusive use of rye bread as the staff of life, and wherever a rise in the level of living made it possible, people tended to shift from rye bread to rye-wheat bread to whole-wheat bread, and finally to white wheat bread. Thus in the Western European countries, rye bread now plays only a minor role (in many cases rye flour is now only 2 to 3 per cent of all flour consumption, as in the United States). Rye-wheat bread is still used extensively as an everyday foodstuff in northern, central, and eastern Europe, but in the cities the next step has been taken.

Rye, as one of the ingredients in various mixtures, is a useful feed grain, particularly for hogs, but on the whole it is considered inferior to barley, corn, and oats. Livestock do not relish it as an exclusive feed, as they have digestive troubles when it constitutes over half of their grain ration. Rye is used more generally as a feedstuff in Western Europe than in the United States for bacon hogs, dairy cows, and baby beef steers. High-protein ryes (about 10 per cent) are favored for bread-making purposes, while

Rye field against Nebraska sky and closeup of rye spikes. Rye has recently become a feedgrain in world perspective, with the modernization of Eastern Europe and the U.S.S.R. Types used for food come from good soils, while the types used for feed come from poor soils, for the most part.

low-protein ryes (about 6 per cent) are usually classed as feed ryes.

In North America and Western Europe, from one-fourth to one-third of the rye crop is used to make flour, whiskey, and alcohol, while in Eastern Europe and the U.S.S.R., it is nearer one-half. Rye has a longer straw than wheat and produces more straw to the acre, which is often used in the manufacture of various types of paper and cardboard.

Rye, like barley, is a hardy grain crop and grows well in cooler climates and about as far north as grains can grow. It is the most winter hardy of all the grains, and the northern limit of winter rye lies only a short distance south of that of summer barley. Rye is not as resistant to high soil-moisture content as oats, but it appears to withstand moist, cool weather better than wheat.

Rye can grow well on relatively poor soils and can stand fairly high soil acidity. Thus, it early became the principal grain crop on the sandy, podzolized soils of northern Europe, where wheat and rye were historically grown alongside each other, the former on loamy, the latter on sandy soils. In many areas, the naturally poor soils formerly in rye have been upgraded to wheat quality.

Unfortunately, rye is not as responsive to a good supply of plant nutrients as the other grains. Therefore, on better soils wheat will tend to outyield rye, and with the breeding of hardier varieties of wheat and the increased use of fertilizers, there has been a tendency in both Europe and the U.S.S.R. for wheat to expand northward at the expense of rye.

Although (food-quality) rye normally costs much less than wheat, it is worth less in terms of available nutrients. Straight flour (i.e., free of bran) can be obtained from wheat with an extraction rate of 74 per cent, while for rye it is only 68 per cent. Rye contains one-third less protein than wheat, and also somewhat less fat.

As with oats, there is a long-term tendency for rye to continue in use as a pasture grass and for other forage uses in many areas where its cultivation for grain has diminished.

Millets and Sorghums

The "millets" include a large variety of small-grain cereals: common millet, little millet, pearl millet, and great millet or sorghum. The seeds of the "millets" vary a great deal in size, shape, and color. The seeds of the common millet are rather oval in shape, about $\frac{1}{8}$ inch long, are very shiny, and may be white, yellow, red, brown, gray, or black. The seeds of some millets grow in compact heads, while others occur in loose-spreading or dropping clusters near the ends of the main plant stalk.

The "millets" properly cultivated are high-yielding cereals, but a low-yielding crop can also be grown on very poor soil with very primitive types of cultivation. This latter possibility may explain why it was more prominent than wheat or rice as a food for people in ancient times and why millet is still predominant in certain regions —especially sub-Saharan Africa, South Asia, and East Asia—where agriculture is not highly developed.

The "millets" probably originated in tropical Africa, and are the dominant cereal in parts of tropical Africa, the Deccan in India, and North China. When used in human dietaries, the grains, whole or in coarse granular form, are boiled or steamed, made into porridge, parched, or ground into flour and made into flat cakes. Increasingly, they are mixed with superior grains when economically available, and when millet eaters move into better paying jobs, they tend to switch to either rice or wheat. In years of abundant and cheap wheat and rice crops in the Far East, considerable portions are fed to work and other animals, but in years of shortage as much as 90 per cent of the crop will be used for human food. In the urban-industrial and semi-industrial realms, the "millets" are used for feed grain or industrial raw material. The pressure of population in the traditional areas of production and the spread of hybrid sorghum over many parts of the world from the United States have resulted in increasing production, apparently a doubling in the past generation.

Small "millets" include a large number of cultivated grasses with very small seeds and abundant foliage, very drought-resistant but sensitive to cold. Three are of greatest importance. Common or proso millet and foxtail millet are species of the temperate climates and are suitable for regions that are too cold for sorghums and where rainfall is low. Bulrush millet (called bajra in India) is a tropical species that is cultivated throughout South Asia and sub-Saharan Africa where rainfall averages from 16 to 24 inches; between 24 to 40 inches, sorghum increases, and where the rainfall is over 40 inches, sorghum predominates until in the tropical rainy areas first corn and then cassava become most important. The tropical millet is a rainy-season crop that has an enormous yield of forage, that is succulent when young, and that can be cut several times in a season (recently it has been introduced into the United States).

The small millets are especially favored in very hot climates where more than one crop can be produced in the same year, but only a short time is available for the second one. Sometimes they are grown intermixed with other cereals or with pulses. They are dry-regions plants, and can withstand dry heat better than any other small grain, but partly because of the marginal habitat they tend to occupy, they are usually poor yielders. The areas in which millets are predominant are diminishing, but half a billion people still use millet or millet mixes as a regular article of diet.

One millet mix in parts of the U.S.S.R. and China is a combination of millet, barley, and buckwheat. Buckwheat is not a cereal grain but is included because in method of cultivation and uses made of it, it is commonly thought of as a cereal by laymen. Actually, buckwheat belongs to the same family of plants as dock, sorrel, and black bindweed. The fruit (often incorrectly called seeds) has tough, dark-brown rinds surrounding the true seeds or kernels which are triangular in shape, with sharp angles, very similar in shape to beechnuts (*buckweizen* translated literally is beechwheat). It probably originated in mountainous central and western China. China and the U.S.S.R. are the largest producers, but there is some production throughout Europe and in North America. Buckwheat will produce a fair crop on poor soil that is poorly tilled provided the climate is not too cold, in only ten to twelve weeks. Neither buckwheat flour nor the granular buckwheat used to make porridge or to thicken soup has good keeping qualities and is particularly likely to develop rancidity in a short time during the summer season. In North America and Western Europe, much of the crop is used for livestock and poultry feeds.

Giant millet or the sorghums (as they are more commonly known) include a large number of widely cultivated grasses, among the first of the wild species to be domesticated by man, known under a confusing variety of both scientific and common names. Grain sorghums include common sorghum, durra, jowar, and kaoliang; other types include sweet sorghum and broomcorn.

All grain sorghums are very drought-resistant, and resistant to spells of quite high temperatures. They give satisfactory yields on poor soils, require only a short growing season, and need little cultivation. The root system is shallow and twice as extensive as that of corn and the leaf area is only half as great, which, together with the highly absorptive nature of the roots and the ability of the leaves to roll up in dry weather, enable the plants to withstand a great amount of heat and consequent evaporation. Their low water requirement renders them exceedingly drought-resistant, so that they are well adapted to semiarid and subhumid regions where corn will not grow reliably. Most sorghums produced for grain, however, require higher temperatures than corn, and therefore they are not grown as far poleward. The one exception is kaoliang, which is hardy and found as far north as North and Northeast China and Siberia.

The durras are the chief type of grain sorghum found in North Africa and in Southwest and South Asia, but seldom elsewhere. Kafir corn is a native of tropical Africa but has spread all over the world—its peculiar and characteristic flavor is not well received elsewhere, but it is highly nutritious and is similar to corn in composition and digestibility. The milos, also of African origin, have slightly juicy stems; compact, usually bearded heads, which are usually recurved or goosenecked; and large, soft, yellow or white seeds. The plants sucker very freely. The plants are very adaptable to moisture conditions and respond readily to irrigation. Although very drought-resistant and able to produce some crop even under severe conditions, the yield is unusually large when conditions are favorable. The kaoliangs are Chinese sorghums, and constitute one of the oldest and most important crops in that country. All parts of the plant are of some economic value, and they have furnished grain, sugar, forage, and fuel for centuries to the northern Chinese. Although they are very drought-resistant, the yield is low and so they have never become highly popular with commercial farmers.

In the southwestern part of the United States —especially the low-rainfall areas of Kansas, Nebraska, Oklahoma, and Texas—where the dry summer heat proves unsuitable to the production of corn and wheat, milo-maize is widely grown for both grain and fodder, often under irrigation. A hybrid dwarf variety that is valued for its high yield, resistance to drought and disease, and ease with which it can be harvested mechanically with ordinary small-grain machinery has spread so swiftly that some years its production is greater than that of wheat in Kansas. It is mainly used for feed in the area, costing about the same as corn (by weight) but yielding more per acre in most years. Increasing amounts are processed into high-protein livestock feeds, into starches and dextrose, and other products. Considerable amounts are exported to Western Europe (which imports over 80 per

U.S.D.A. Photos

Field of grain sorghum in South Carolina and closeup of grain sorghum. This hybrid sorghum is high yielding and is a dwarf variety that can be harvested by regular small-grains equipment. Although in wealthy societies sorghums are mainly used for feed, in the poorer societies they are favored because they give unusually good returns under the most primitive conditions.

cent of all grain sorghum moving in world trade), the bulk of the shipments being used for livestock feeding in the form of prepared feed mixtures. At 56 pounds per bushel, both corn and sorghum are more economical to ship than barley at 48 pounds or oats at 32 pounds per bushel.

In the foreseeable future, it is probable that a majority of the millets and sorghums will be consumed directly as food by the poor people of Africa and Asia. But the changes that have occurred in the urban-industrial realm indicate that in the long run they will end up mainly used as fodder, feed grain, and industrial raw material. Probably sorghum will end up as one of the big three feed grain crops, along with corn and barley, while small millet will more likely recede with oats and rye into a secondary position.

Trends

Of world grain production, which has totaled about 950 million tons in recent years, the food grains (rough rice and wheat) total a bit more than half. Probably only about 5 per cent of the starch content of these crops is fed to animals, mainly substandard qualities (much of the 25 per cent plus or minus of bran and germ tonnage removed in milling also ends up as animal feed), and there is no sign that such a distribution of present consumption will significantly alter in the foreseeable future.

Of the over 450 million tons of coarse grains produced yearly, only some 15 to 25 per cent (varying with time and the prospects of other grains) is consumed directly for human food, with another 5 per cent being consumed by industry in making beer, spirits, industrial alcohols, and for a host of starch and sugar uses. The remainder is consumed as feed by the some 3 billion large animals and perhaps 7 billion fowl in the world (more correctly by the three-fifths in the wealthier countries). The feed grains and feed tubers account for about a third of animal dietary, with another third coming from rotational pastures and agricultural wastes foraged by the animals, and the final third coming from permanent rangeland and from marginal use of other land-use types (e.g., foraging in forests and brushlands, in "waste," etc.).

It has already been indicated that, as levels of living rise, the direct consumption of cereals per capita at first rises and then falls off, as more expensive and attractive food is sought. The indirect consumption of cereals continues to rise for a long time, as many of the luxury foods are from animals. Already corn, barley, and oats are overwhelmingly used for feed, and portents are that rye and the millets-sorghums will end up similarly.

Already these coarse grains are being produced at a swifter rate than the directly consumed food grains. As urban industrialization becomes universal, a larger and larger proportion of grain production will be indirectly consumed by man as feed and non-food industrial raw material, although the 80 per cent of consumption for such purposes in the United States will probably never be reached as a world average.

STARCHY ROOTS, TUBERS, AND FRUITS

As harvested fresh, world production of starchy roots, tubers, and fruits totals nearly half a billion tons annually, about half the annual cereal production. However, some three-quarters of the fresh tonnage is water and waste so, as a general rule of thumb, the cereal-equivalent is only a quarter.

Over half of this tenth of the world's starch crop production (Table 6–9) consists of one item, the mainly mid-latitude white potato. The mainly tropical roots and tubers (sweet potatoes and yams, cassava, and many other minor tropical "potatoes") and the starchy fruits (bananas and plantains, and some other minor "tree" sources) yield the remaining 45 per cent of annual output.

White Potatoes

Potatoes are a crop of mid-latitude climates, although small amounts are grown in the subtropics and semitropics during the wintertime and in the tropics at higher altitudes. They have been adapted to so many climates and soils that they are almost universal outside the tropical lowlands. They are hardy and mature rapidly, and so can be grown as far north as 60° and at altitudes up to 2 miles. The best environment, however, is a cool, moist climate, with a mean annual temperature of 40° to 50° F., and a rich, light soil.

The largest development is in Europe and the U.S.S.R., where over 80 per cent of world pro-

TABLE 6–9

World: Starchy Roots, Tubers, and Fruits, by Great-Region and Economic-Type of Society, 1962–1964 Average-Annual *

(in millions of metric tons fresh/cereal-equivalent)

	White Potatoes			Sweet Potatoes and Yams			Cassava (manioc)			Bananas and Plantains		
North America	14.4	3.6	5.7%	0.7	0.2	0.8%	—	—	—	—	—	—
Western Europe	76.3	19.1	30.4	—	—	—	—	—	—	0.4	0.1	1.0%
Eastern Europe (including the U.S.S.R.)	130.2	32.6	51.9	—	—	—	—	—	—	—	—	—
Oceania	0.8	0.2	0.3	1.3	0.3	1.4	1.0	0.2	1.0%	1.1	0.3	2.9
Latin America	8.0	2.0	3.2	6.0	1.5	6.5	28.0	7.0	31.5	16.0	4.0	38.8
Sub-Saharan Africa	0.8	0.2	0.3	28.0	7.0	30.4	40.0	10.0	45.0	16.0	4.0	38.8
Middle East (including North Africa)	2.4	0.6	1.0	—	—	—	—	—	—	0.4	0.1	1.0
Non-Communist Far East	8.0	2.0	3.2	16.0	4.0	17.4	16.0	4.0	18.0	6.0	1.5	14.6
Communist Far East	10.0	2.5	4.0	40.0	10.0	43.5	4.0	1.0	4.5	1.1	0.3	2.9
World	251.0	62.8	100.0%	92.0	23.0	100.0%	89.0	22.2	100.0%	41.0	10.3	100.0%
High-income countries	211.0	52.8	84.0%	6.0	1.5	6.5%	1.8	0.4	2.0%	1.2	0.3	3.0%
Low-income countries	40.0	10.0	16.0	86.0	21.5	93.5	87.0	21.8	98.0	40.0	10.0	99.0

* Data on tropical items mainly non-commercial production which had to be roughly estimated on the basis of fragmentary figures. The fresh/cereal-equivalent ratio of 4:1 holds roughly true, but is also only approximate, as the moisture content varies considerably.

duction is grown, mainly for feed and industrial raw material usages. About 40 per cent of the crop is used for feed (mainly after grading has removed the better qualities for seed, food, and raw material uses); 25 to 30 per cent is directly used by humans; 20 per cent goes into starch products, industrial alcohols, and liquors; and the remaining 10 to 15 per cent is used for seed. In the rest of the world, a much larger fraction is used for direct food consumption.

In volume and weight, the world production compares with the big three among the cereals, but in more realistic terms, it is the equivalent of the barley or millets-sorghums crops in energy value. As harvested, a common breakdown would reveal nearly four-fifths water and waste (roughly 20 per cent waste, 60 per cent water), and only a bit over a fifth food value (roughly 18 per cent carbohydrates, mainly starch with a little sugar, about 2 per cent protein, 0.1 per cent fat, and 1 per cent potash). Stored potatoes generally lose 10 per cent plus of their water, upping the food value fraction a bit. A pound of food grain (wheat flour, milled rice) will have only a tenth or so water and waste and some 1,600 to 1,700 calories, while a pound of purchased potatoes has less than 300 calories.

	Area Planted (million acres)	World Production (million tons)	Average Nutritional Yield per Acre (million calories)
Wheat	500	240	1.4
Corn	260	205	2.6
Rice	340	250	2.5
Potatoes	60	250	3.8

The average acre of potatoes produces half again as many calories as the average acre of either rice or corn, and nearly three times as many calories as the average acre of wheat.

As already mentioned, potatoes require a long, cool growing season with adequate moisture throughout. The average precipitation during the growing season is one of the determining factors for a good yield: uneven distribution of rainfall usually reduces the yield, even though the total amount of rainfall may be quite enough. Heavy precipitation during the latter part of the growing season is not desirable, as it favors the development of late blight and rot, and also makes it difficult to harvest the crop. A rainfall of at least 10 inches during the growing season, or its equivalent in irrigation water, is generally required.

Growth starts at about 45° F., and if the mean maximal temperature exceeds 65° F., yields are depressed. High temperatures combined with a high humidity lead to attacks of blight (often dropping yields to half). Where the springs are mild but the summers hot (much of United States, most of India and China), the less productive early maturing types are cultivated. These can also be grown in the extreme north of Europe, and in certain highlands, where the season is short but the days long.

Potatoes, like rye, can be grown in exposed acid sandy soils, but the ideal soil is one that is naturally rich, of medium texture, friable, deep, and not highly alkaline nor yet too acid. Fine sandy loams, silt loams, and loams are among the best. Heavy, sticky clays or very light, sandy soils are not, but many such that are well worked and supplied with sufficient organic matter can produce abundant yields of potatoes that are a high-quality type.

Potatoes are usually propagated by means of tubers or parts of tubers ("seed potatoes"), although they may be grown from seed. The 500 varieties now in cultivation have been obtained by selection and hybridization, and by the utilization of mutations, which are of frequent occurrence. The most important step in increasing potato production is to rogue the inferior potato plants as well as those affected with diseases and to select the tubers from the desirable and healthy plants for seed stock for propagation. More than seventy diseases and insect pests attack the growing potato crop. The late blight of potatoes shares the notoriety of being the world's most destructive plant disease with the black-stem rust of wheat. These blights are caused by fungi: pale microscopic plants that lack chlorophyll and are obliged to live parasitically on plants that are capable of photosynthesis. The commercial potato farmer figuratively cultivates his fields with a hoe in one hand

and a spray can in the other. The late blight levies its heaviest tax in labor and cost of chemical sprays on the small farmers who can least afford to pay it. In extensive regions of the world where the climate is excellent for potatoes, including the highlands of Mexico, India, and elsewhere, people who most need this cheap, energy-rich food have had to forego it as a major staple.

Although the potato is a good source of starch and contains plenty of vitamins B and C (thus providing a better diet than the sweet potato and other tropical potatoes), there is a tendency for per capita consumption in urban-industrial societies to shrink, under pressure of changed eating habits, especially the switch from starches to proteins as income rises. The United States provides an excellent example, with per capita consumption a bit over 100 pounds per year, compared with twice that amount in 1900. In the last few years, there is evidence of stability accompanying the increasing popularity of processed products ("instant" types). Idaho, which formerly followed Maine in U.S. potato production, now leads, as she developed the processing industry at a fast clip, while Maine, New York,

Potatoes being harvested on organic muck soil in Minnesota and closeup of potatoes. The yield is some 500 bushels per acre, and the machine harvests 17 acres per day. Potatoes are dug, loaded, unloaded, washed, graded, and sacked with a minimum amount of hand labor. In Europe and the U.S.S.R., where most potatoes are grown, over half are used for feed and industrial raw material.

U.S.D.A. Photos

and Pennsylvania kept to their old pattern of supplying fresh potatoes to their accessible urban markets.

The main tendency is for an increasing usage as feed tuber and industrial raw material. The U.S.S.R. and Eastern European countries "plan" to double their potato output before the end of the 1960's, most of which will be consumed as Western Europe now uses its output, for hog feed and other livestock feed and for industrial-starch purposes.

Sweet Potatoes and Yams

The sweet potato is another American Indian domesticate, but is of present importance mainly to the Far East and sub-Saharan Africa, although it—together with the yam, taro, and cassava—is widespread in all tropics and in the humid subtropics. All these humble roots are cheap, are available throughout the year, and grow in every soil. Although of little commercial importance, they are found in every garden patch.

One of the richest tropical food plants, the sweet potato usefully supplements the big staple crops of the underdeveloped realm—corn, cassava, and rice—for it is higher in minerals and vitamins. This fact gives it an economic importance that cannot be fully measured by acreage, production, or money-value data.

China alone produces almost half of total world production. About half is consumed as human food, mainly by the poor in South China, about a third is used for livestock feed (especially hog feed), and the remainder is split between industrial-raw-material and propagation uses. It is one of the traditional famine foods, and in such times of stress the production usually increases and the proportion eaten by humans increases.

The sweet potato is a twining, trailing perennial vine with adventitious roots that end in swollen tubers containing both starch and sugar, and a little fat. The plants are grown as annuals, usually, and are propagated vegetatively by using the roots, or pieces of roots, or vine cuttings.

The plant thrives in a warm climate, but is very frost-sensitive. It is tender and requires a long, warm growing season for good growth, but is one of the most drought-resistant crops. During the early stage of growth, a comparatively larger amount of rainfall is required, but after the ground is covered by the leaves and vines, the less rainfall the better. It can be grown on a wide range of soil types, but a sandy loam with clay as subsoil is considered the best type.

It is advisable to harvest sweet potatoes at the right time to avoid heavy losses. If they are harvested too early, they will contain too much moisture, which will result in considerable shrinkage and loss in weight during storage. If they are left in the field too long, especially after frost, cold injury will start storage rot and cause heavy damage with financial loss. Chinese sweet potatoes are generally planted in June and harvested in late October or November.

Sweet potatoes easily rot when they are not stored under proper conditions. Because of a lack of adequate storage facilities, the Chinese growers suffer an average loss of about 30 per cent of their products, and even in commercial areas, spoilage is often that high (mostly due to bruised and cut tubers in times of hurried harvesting).

There are many varieties. In the United States alone, two types of sweet potatoes are grown widely: one dry-fleshed type is the dry, mealy, yellow-fleshed variety which remains firm after being cooked (favored in the North); another moist-fleshed type is the watery, soft, gelatinous-fleshed variety which remains soft after being cooked (favored in the South). Some types are favored for use as a common table vegetable, others for canning, dehydrating, flour manufacture, or for conversion into starch, glucose, syrup, or alcohol. In wealthier societies, the tuber itself and the green tops are increasingly used for animal feed.

In the Far East (Japan, South China, Java, and elsewhere), sweet potatoes allow use of hill lands when the rice-supporting capacity of the land (around 750 persons per square mile of total land) has been passed. Under such conditions, the yields are normally low, because of poor soils, lack of fertilization, and many

BASIC ENERGY FOODS

U.S.D.A. Photo

A hill of big stem Jersey sweet potatoes. Nearly 95 per cent of world production is in poor areas—half in China—where over a third is usually used for feed and industrial raw material.

other aspects of inferior culture (the culture is often more closely akin to the old shifting-cultivation technique than to the sedentary lowland cultivation), with disease being fully as detrimental in some areas.

About nine-tenths of the production from the tropical vine group of tubers comes from sweet potatoes, but there are others of considerable importance. Yams are climbing vines with large storage roots, often weighing as much as 30 to 40 pounds, and sometimes with aerial tubers as well. Probably a domesticate from Southeast Asia, they are the food of millions in the Far Eastern and Oceanic tropics and in Latin America. They are baked, boiled, ground into flour, or fed to animals (e.g., in the U.S. South, to hogs).

The true yam (in the U.S. South, the moist-fleshed sweet potato is often marketed under the name of yam) requires a deep soil, and is un-usually drought-resistant, much more than the sweet potato for which it substitutes in those areas where the very early growth period is too dry.

Taros, or dasheens, is next in importance to yams in the Orient. It apparently was domesticated long ago in the Assam–Upper Burma area (it is so old that it never flowers). Over 1,000 varieties exist in Southeast Asia and tropical Oceania, where most of the production is. The starch is considered very digestible (very little extraneous material). Requirements of very rich soil and long growing season restrict its habitat compared to the sweet potato.

There are many other examples of tropical tubers from vines. Yautias are found only in the American tropics, especially in Puerto Rico. Related to taros, they are among the least known but are probably among the oldest root crops. They are said to be twice as nutritious as the white potatoes, but again are not capable of production in as large areas.

These tropical tubers may well be produced at an accelerated scale as pressure of population in tropical areas coupled with shortages in cheap supplies of the favored food grains puts emphasis on supplementary energy food. Mainland China apparently doubled its sweet potato output during the 1950's, in spite of the low prestige value of the tuber among rice eaters.

Cassava (Manioc)

Next to the sweet potato, the cassava is the most important of the tropical root crops and furnishes the basic food for perhaps 100 million people in Latin America, sub-Saharan Africa, and the tropical Far East. A South American domesticate, acreage and production in sub-Saharan Africa now exceeds that in the Americas.

These tubers are one of the basic foodstuffs for the poorer population in many tropical regions, although it is not a well-balanced supply of energy, protein, and protective food elements, and considerable quantities enter world trade for export to the temperate regions in the form of dried manioc, manioc flour, manioc starch, and tapioca. Some of the exports are used in food, some in feed, and some are used in manufacturing inedible products.

The manioc plant is a low bush that may reach a height of from 6 to 10 feet. It is completely a tropical plant and requires a completely frost-free growing season of 9 to 18 months to reach maturity. It prefers regions with a rather moderate temperature range, ample rainfall, fairly high humidity, and considerable sunshine. It does not flourish at altitudes of over 2,500 feet, and is not grown much above 4,000 feet. Too little rainfall results in woody tubers, while too much moisture in the soils may result in rotting. Manioc, however, does have the merit of being able to withstand drought periods of considerable duration and intensity.

The underground tubers—very rich in starch, but low in protein (1 per cent more or less), fat, and vitamins—are generally harvested after ten to fifteen months, when the plant will have produced from five to ten tubers about 1 to 1½ feet long. Two-year-old plants may yield tubers over 3 feet long weighing up to 25 to 30 pounds. The yields from ordinary fields in the tropics often amount to 10 to 20 tons of tubers (3½ to 7 tons in dehydrated form), while more favored grainlands often produce only ⅓ to ½ ton of grain and seldom over 1 ton annually.

Over 150 varieties of this South American domesticate exist, some of which are poisonous and bitter, while others contain very little poison and are sometimes referred to as sweet manioc. Neither boiling nor roasting completely eliminates the prussic acid poison. The best prac-

Cassava from a single plant in a newly cleared Thailand area. Nearly all production is in poor tropical areas (about half in sub-Saharan Africa), where yields are high from disease-free areas, although the yield is mainly "empty calories" (only 1 or 2 per cent protein, with few minerals and vitamins). Tapioca is a refined product shipped to the mid-latitude countries.

U.S.D.A. Photo

tice is to use tubers with a low poison content, grate them, and soak the product in cold water. When used locally, sweet cassavas are usually boiled or meal is baked into thin cakes known as cassava bread. Much of the cassava that is exported is used in making tapioca. For this purpose, the roots are peeled and grated and the milky juices are expressed. The starchy material is then soaked in water for a few days, is kneaded, and is strained to remove any fibers and impurities. After sifting and drying in the sun, it is heated gently on hot iron plates, which partially cooks the starch and causes it to ball up into the familiar little round lumps that constitute the tapioca of commerce.

As a tuberous plant, it needs a fairly deep soil. Although it thrives best on fertile soils, rich in potash, it will still produce fairly well on some of the more leached tropical soils. The bitter variety can be left alone in outlying fields, safe from all pests except its cell-borne virus ones. It can be left in the ground for a certain period and harvested as needed, often at periods in which more favored grains are in short supply. This practice of piecemeal harvesting is partly responsible for the fact that it is frequently difficult to obtain accurate data on the production of manioc.

Bananas and Plantains

As agricultural developments first appeared in South and Southeast Asia, prehistoric man domesticated the banana, making it perhaps the first cultivated fruit. The earliest records of bananas being eaten as fruit appear in ancient Indian epics, and recorded production in the Middle East dates from 1100 B.C. In the various tropics, about 300 varieties of bananas are now grown, plus about 75 varieties of plantains. The banana is the only raw starch digestible by man, while the plantain is the cooking type especially favored by subsistence users.

The banana plant is not a true tree (it does not develop woody tissue), but is an oversized herb, a relative of the lily family. It grows from a large, bulbous rootstalk that becomes a full-grown plant in about fourteen months. At maturity, the plant stands 12 to 30 feet high and produces one large bunch of fruit that hangs from the top of the stalk. The buds and inner sheaths are used as vegetables in the growing areas. Once the stem of fruit is harvested, the plant is cut down, making way for new plants that spring from the same root.

Marketable bunches weigh from 80 to 140 pounds, and consist of from six to fifteen clusters (hands or combs). Normally, each hand contains from ten to twenty individual bananas, or fingers. Bananas are rapid growers and have a very high yield. This varies with the locality and type of culture. Subsistence producers, who account for over two-thirds of world production, generally obtain 5 to 10 tons per acre. Commercial producers generally average 10 to 20 tons, and some plantations reach 20 to 30 tons per acre. Comparison with other starch sources can be expressed thus: wheat = 1, potatoes = 3, bananas = 10 (5 to 30 range).

Served raw, dried, fried, candied, or as a flavoring, the banana is the most popular tropical fruit in the world. As noted, there are many different varieties. Some that grow in Africa are 2 feet long and as thick as a man's arm, while in Malaysia one banana has enough food value to provide three men with an adequate meal. The best-known bananas are the plantain, which is cooked before being eaten; the Cavendish and the Lacatan, favorites in Europe; and the Gros Michel ("Big Mike"), which accounts for more than 90 per cent of all the bananas imported into North America.

World production of bananas and plantains is now over 30 million tons annually, although commercial production is only some 35 per cent of total production. Some two-thirds of commercial production moves to domestic markets in the countries of production, while the remaining third moves in world trade.

The international and long-distance domestic traffic in bananas is a phenomenon of only the past two generations. Prior to 1900, bananas suffered from a double handicap. Ships were slow and refrigeration had not been developed, so the fruit spoiled en route to northern markets. There was also the hazard of growing bananas in accessible tropical jungles that had to be

Courtesy of United Fruit Co.

Airview of the United Fruit Company banana plantation at Tacamiche on the Chamelecon River, Honduras. Such an operation is a capital-intensive type of farming, presently costing around $2,500 per acre at the time of full-scale commercial production.

overcome. Once the banana trade started, however, it expanded rapidly. Prior to World War II, yearly international movements were about 2 million tons, compared with the present 4 million tons (worth over a half billion dollars a year).

Bananas can be grown in practically any tropical country, yet commercial production is limited to a few. Over 70 per cent of the bananas that enter world trade originate in eight countries: Ecuador, Brazil, Colombia, Panama, Honduras, Guatemala, Costa Rica, and the Canary Islands (all European production is from Spanish and Portuguese islands in the North Atlantic). Ecuador supplies over a fourth of the world exports. The United States tops the list of banana buyers: it purchases half of the world's supply, obtaining some 1 million tons from Central America, ¾ million tons from Ecuador, and small additional amounts elsewhere. Western Europe is nearly as important. Eastern Europe and the U.S.S.R. and Japan import small amounts, but their trade is tiny compared with the North Atlantic Basin countries.

The giant of the international banana companies is United Fruit. Until the mid-1950's it had some 40 per cent of the world banana market, but its plantations in Panama and Honduras were all but wiped out by a combination of wind, floods, and the Panama Disease (which by

One swing of the machete brings the stem of bananas down to the level of the "backer," who carries the stem to the nearest loading point, on its way to the processing plant. Plantations average 10 to 20 tons production per acre, but subsistence producers normally get 5 to 10 tons of bananas and plantains (cooking types).

Courtesy of United Fruit Co.

Courtesy of United Fruit Co.

At the plantation boxing plant, bananas are cut from the stem, washed to remove latex, graded, weighed, and boxed. The bananas remain in the box until they are placed on retailers' shelves.

infecting the soil puts banana land out of cultivation almost indefinitely). Its present share of the world market is below 30 per cent, although it has managed to hang on to its 60 per cent of U.S. banana sales.

In Guatemala, Costa Rica, and Honduras, United Fruit is the largest single private landowner, largest single business, and largest corporate employer. In Panama, only the Canal complex is a bigger business.

Growing bananas and getting them to market are not easy jobs. They are grown best on low-lying lands. They are fussy about temperature, soil, drainage, and rainfall. The plants are vulnerable even to slight flooding, moderate winds, and a wide range of diseases, as well as to insect attacks. Banana plants have, instead of a woody trunk, only a central sheaf of leaf stems. Grafting being impossible by any known techniques, and edible bananas having practically no seeds (the plants grow from a rhizome), breeding for desirable qualities is a slow and heartbreaking job.

Bananas must be picked green and shipped under controlled temperatures on a tight, fast, and costly schedule to arrive at wholesale ripening rooms a few days before they are to be eaten. Such rooms are run by jobbers or large chain-store customers in consuming areas. Banana skins are easily bruised. Careless handling or careless stowage in ships and trains, rough rides in trucks, slight abrasion by dust or gravel picked up during harvesting, fingering by a customer, these can cause black spots that interfere with sales.

United Fruit prefers the Gros Michel species of banana. It has more tolerance to temperature changes than most other species and handles relatively well because its skin is thick. But it has its drawbacks. It is more vulnerable to the dread Panama Disease, which can ruin whole areas for growing Big Mike. To control Panama Disease and Sigatoka (a leaf blight), United uses sprays, flood-fallowing techniques, and new plantings of more disease-resistant types of bananas (though these types may not sell quite so well in the United States). The methods of reclaiming infested land are very costly—the capital investment required per acre of banana plantation is now over $2,500 per acre—and only temporarily effective.

The long-range outlook for production is good, in spite of the inroads of disease. Most of the banana countries have plenty of land available, and as cultural practices improve, output per acre will increase. The main problem may be where to sell additional output. Many countries that might be good banana customers have limiting trade restrictions, and in the established markets where per capita consumption is already high, any gain will be determined largely by an increase in population. The biggest opportunities may lie in semi-industrial and recently industrialized countries where present per capita consumption is low.

Trends

Prospects for additional production of starch from roots, tubers, and fruit are excellent, although it is unlikely that their share of total world starch production will increase much above the present 10 to 15 per cent. The biggest reason for large absolute increases is that population growth in the underdeveloped realm is large and increasing, and that many such areas are running short of good grainland but still have poor soil and hill areas where these starchy substitutes for grain can be grown cheaply. In all except a few areas, production is likely to remain supplementary to grain supplies. Less than 2 per cent of production moves in world trade, mainly for use as food and industrial raw material.

On the supply side, the biggest single problem is dealing with virus diseases. In annual crops that are raised from true seeds, like the grains, virus diseases are likely to be less widespread than they are in the vegetatively propagated crops, like the roots, tubers, and fruits. Present trends in agriculture tend to encourage the development and spread of virus diseases. To gain uniformity of crop, the practice of vegetative propagation is increasing, and this encourages the perpetuation of viruses. Most of the common virus diseases of plants are spread by insects, which acquire the viruses when they feed on infected plants, and then transfer them to healthy plants on which they feed consequently. Once infected, the plant cannot be deloused without killing the cells. When annual crops are heavily infected with seed-borne pathogens, they can be eliminated by simple measures of seed disinfection. But this cannot be done with crops propagated vegetatively.

When the white potato, the sweet potato, cassava, or the banana is riddled with virus diseases, new virus-free stocks must be brought in to replace those now in cultivation. If new stocks of vegetatively propagated plants are to be provided for these countries, and that is a first essential if yields are to be raised, their introduction needs to be carefully planned, or the project will prove valueless. Only a transient and minor increase in yield will result from a piecemeal introduction with no safeguards to insure that the new stocks are isolated from existing ones. The only result would be that the viruses would soon spread from the old to the new stocks and cause their rapid degeneration. Such a controlled change is almost impossible except in the context of a commercial agriculture.

PROSPECTS

At present, the world's production of starch from grain, roots, and tubers, and fruit crops amounts to about 1 billion tons annually, grown on about 1.7 billion acres. The supply is increasing nearly twice as rapidly as the increase in world population, and, assuming peace and present technological trends, is likely to maintain this lead for the foreseeable future. However, there are problems of distribution, since two-thirds of the increased production is in the urban-industrial realm, where per capita consumption for food is declining, although feed and industrial uses are still increasing. Only some 5 per cent of annual starch production crosses international boundaries, with two-thirds destined for urban-industrial markets, so trade is not the major solution to the underdeveloped realm's problem of inadequate supply. That solution must mainly be in the area of increased domestic production.

Of the total starch production, about 55 per cent is used in the human dietary directly— about 1 pound daily for the some 3 billion population. If ideal regional dietaries are postulated, the world supply may be some 15 per cent short, with practically all of it in the thickly settled underdeveloped regions containing about one-half of mankind. The other 45 per cent of world production is used for animal feed and industrial raw materials, with over three-fourths of this consumed in the urban-industrial realm, with its third of mankind.

Increasingly, starch production and consumption are involved in industrialization. About two-thirds of the annual increase in the crude materials supply is due to intensification: upping the average acre output above the present 0.6 ton, towards the 2-ton output featured by the U.S. Corn Belt, much of Western European small-grains acreage, and Japanese grains and tuber acreage. Even more striking is the increasing industrial processing before distribution.

About a tenth of world industry is in the area of food processing, which includes about a third of so-called consumer-goods industry. Most such industry is, of course, concerned with processing crude foods other than starches: sugar, oils and fats, meat and dairy products, friuts and vegetables, beverages, and many others. The production of grain-mill products, bakery products, and other products that are mainly processed starch is a subsector of food processing that is less than a tenth of employment and value-added, but it is growing rapidly.

At present, about half of world food grains, and nine-tenths of feed grains are consumed in the crude form or in lightly processed form done by the producers themselves (handicraft alteration) or the consumers (precooking alteration). Gradually, there is a substitution of factory efforts for these farm-home efforts. The demand for high-quality milled rice and flour mixes, for breakfast foods and other preparations, for concentrated and blended feeds, and for other specialized energy foods is increasing rapidly and eventually the overwhelming majority of all starch crops probably will be factory-processed before distribution.

Milling is usually done by small- and medium-size plants that are widely scattered. There is often a heavy concentration either in the farming areas or in nearby metropolitan areas. There is less concentration in the specialized urban-industrial belts than one would expect if the industry were as market-oriented as certain other consumer-goods industries. Grain-mill products usually keep fairly well unless humidity is very high, and can be shipped about as cheaply as the crude materials (e.g., in-transit freight-rate privileges in the United States). The offal products (bran, germ, shriveled and discolored grains, etc.) may weight almost a third of the grain, so there is a tendency to process near the crude source if there is an associated animal husbandry to consume such offal by-products or feed concentrates and blends. Other locations may reflect relic tendencies from an earlier, more ruralized period, or seaboard and other locations along export routes for the crude or processed product (many such break-of-bulk locations are also well located in relation to coastal urban-regions).

Regions and countries that formerly imported mostly grain-mill products and little crude material regard the building of mills as one of the primary steps in the industrialization process. Usually a protected local market for food and feed products and local job opportunities are among the main rationales, but occasionally new areas can also build up an export business (e.g., Hong Kong exports flour made from Australian wheat). Private capital (local individuals, the international-grain-trade interests, or large milling companies of other nations) has also been attracted to such new ventures by the search for profit. Some big flour exporters have licensed new mills to produce their established brands threatened by tariffs against refined imports. Others have contracted to manage the new mills erected by others, even to the point of supplying blends of wheat (thereby maintaining quality and keeping brands before the public).

Many ventures have been unsuccessful or only partially successful. Some market orientations produce flour or milled rice of lower quality or higher price than the older sources. The amount of new employment opened up by new mills has often been smaller than expected because of automation and other modern techniques substituting for the lack of local skilled personnel. Many new mills have found it difficult to find markets for offal feeds and other by-products, or have not a sufficiently large local market to supply many specialty products.

The geographical distribution of bakeries is much more market-oriented than mills. While bread baking is a small-scale industry (even where organizational units are large), biscuit and cracker baking is often a larger-scale industry (even when small-size companies predominate), primarily because the products are less perishable than bread and related soft-dough products and (when properly packaged) can be marketed over a much larger territory than bread.

SUGGESTED READINGS

Alderfer, E. B., and Michl, H. E. *Economics of American Industry*. New York: McGraw-Hill, 1957. Pp. 500–529.

Grist, D. H. *Rice*. London: Longmans, Green, 1955. Pp. 333.

Hill, Albert F. *Economic Botany*. New York: McGraw-Hill, 1952. Pp. 560.

Jones, William O. *Manioc in Africa*. Stanford University Press, 1959. Pp. 315.

Oxford University Press. *Oxford Economic Atlas of the World*. London: Oxford University Press, 1965. Pp. 8–20.

Sheppard, Ronald, and Newton, Edward. *The Story of Bread*. London: Routledge & Kegan Paul, 1957. Pp. 189.

Van Royen, William (ed.). *Atlas of the World's Resources*. Vol. I. *The Agricultural Resources of the World*. Englewood Cliffs, N.J.: Prentice-Hall, 1954. Pp. 27–100, 139–40.

Wilson, Charles Morrow. *Empire in Green and Gold: The Story of the American Banana Trade*. New York: Holt, Rinehart & Winston, 1947. Pp. 303.

Wilson, Harold Kirby. *Grain Crops*. New York: McGraw-Hill, 1948. Pp. 384.

Wilson, Harold K., and Myers, Will M. *Field Crop Production*. New York: Lippincott, 1954. Pp. 674.

Zimmermann, Erich W. *World Resources and Industries*. New York: Harper & Row, 1951. Pp. 176–230.

7

Luxury Energy Foods

If energy intake constituted the only nutritional requirement of human beings, the average person could live by daily consuming 1.5 pounds of sugar or half that amount of oil and fat (which contains about twice as much energy per pound as do carbohydrates). Such a dietary, of course, would be inadequate, since its "empty calories" would lack protein, minerals, and vitamins.

Until recently, sugar and fat consumed in most societies totaled only 5 to 10 per cent of the dietary, and were mainly invisible (incorporated in other foods rather than being in processed, identifiable forms). But today visible supplies of both are considered necessities in the wealthier societies, and highly desirable luxuries in the poorer ones.

Dietaries in urban-industrial societies contain 10 to 20 per cent sugar and 15 to 40 per cent fat, half or more in each case being invisible.[1] Underdeveloped societies mainly consume up to 10 per cent sugar (a few sugar producers a higher per cent), and about the same fraction of fat (again, some hunting and herding peoples higher).

SUGAR

While its major role, whether within the household or in the food industry, is that of a joint ingredient, sugar has come to occupy an important position quantitatively in the modern diet. Refined sugar is consumed in annual per capita amounts ranging generally from 50 to 100 pounds or more in high-income societies, and from 5 to 30 pounds in poorer societies. Over the medium run, per capita consumption of sugar tends to move inversely with utilization of such starchy staples as bread and potatoes, which it in a sense displaces.

Less than 5 per cent of world sugar supplies now comes from bees, trees, grain, and other traditional sources. Cane and beet sugar are now dominant. Though they serve the same dietary needs, they are of different botanic, geographic, and industrial origin. When factory-processed, the products are chemically indistinguishable.

World production of centrifugal (raw value) sugar now amounts to some 60 million tons, exclusive of some 7 million tons of low-grade sugar (e.g., Indian gur, with some of molasses still in) prepared by premodern methods.[2] Nearly 60 per cent of the factory-made product is cane, and over 40 per cent is beet. A genera-

---

[1] For example, about two-thirds of U.S. sugar goes to the commercial bakers, confectioners, canners, and manufacturers of soft drinks, ice cream, and other products, while only one-third is bought by housewives. In most countries today—as in the United States a generation ago—about two-thirds of sugar consumption is bought at retail for use in the home.

[2] Gur is produced in about the same amount per unit of cane as centrifugal sugar, but ranges from 20 to 40 per cent impurities as compared with 2 to 3 per cent.

Courtesy of California & Hawaiian Sugar Refining Corp.

Typical view of one of Hawaii's twenty-six sugarcane plantations and plantation mill. The state of Hawaii produces a quarter of the sugar production of the fifty states, worth nearly $200 million annually (well over half of the total value of island products sent to the mainland).

tion ago, world production was only one-third as large, and almost three-quarters was cane. In the 1954–1964 decade, production doubled (annual increase rate was 7 per cent), with beet production increasing 10 per cent annually and cane production increasing at half that rate. The increasing importance of beet sugar reflects recent substantial gains in technological efficiency in sugar beet production coupled with heavy subsidization by mid-latitude countries—there is no evidence that it reflects improved economic efficiency compared with sugarcane production.

The gross value of raw sugar production in 1964 was some $10 billion (about two-thirds value-added by farm-produced factors of production), with the gross value to consumers being about double that amount (reflecting processing and distribution costs). Most refined white sugar retails for 15 to 25 cents per pound in small lots (50 cents in the U.S.S.R.—mostly tax), of which the U.S. farmer gets about 6 cents, and efficient tropical producers half that amount.

Big cane sugar producers (i.e., those producing 5 per cent or more of total world sugar production) include Cuba, the United States (two-thirds in Hawaii),[3] Brazil, and India (if gur is added to centrifugal sugar, India is the largest cane producer). Australia and the Philippines each produce over 3 per cent of the world's sugar.

[3] For the fifty-state United States—for purposes of sugar control, Puerto Rico and the Virgin Islands are legally domestic; fraction will be over three-quarters if they are included.

LUXURY ENERGY FOODS

Big beet sugar producers (again, those producing 5 per cent or more of total world sugar production) include the U.S.S.R. and the continental United States; France, West Germany, and Poland each produce roughly 3 per cent of the world's sugar.

The ten countries together produce some three-fifths of the world's sugar, with over eighty others producing the remainder.

World Sugar Trade

Nearly two-fifths of world sugar production moves in international trade. If long-distance domestic trade is included—shipments to metropolitan countries from offshore possessions or dependencies, or transcontinental shipments—about half of world production is consumed outside the production region. (See graphs on pp. 182–83 for regional shares of exports and imports.)

TABLE 7–1

World: Brown Sugar * Production and Trade, by Great-Region and Economic-Type of Society, 1962–1964 Average-Annual
(in millions of metric tons)

	Million Metric Tons Production (= 100.0 per cent)	Centrifugal Production		Non-centrifugal (Low-Grade) Cane Production
		Beet	Cane	
North America	5.6	58.4%	41.6%	–
Western Europe	9.0	97.8	2.2	–
Eastern Europe (including the U.S.S.R.)	11.5	100.0	–	–
Oceania	2.3	–	100.0	–
Latin America	18.0	1.0	94.8	4.2%
Sub-Saharan Africa	3.4	–	100.0	–
Middle East (including North Africa)	1.2	53.5	46.5	–
Non-Communist Far East	12.0	2.7	65.0	32.3
Communist Far East	1.2	28.7	57.4	13.9
World	64.2	39.1	53.4	7.5
High-income countries	31.3	73.0	26.8	0.2
Low-income countries	32.9	6.9	78.7	14.4

	(per cent of 64.2 million metric tons)	(per cent of 25.1 million metric tons)	(per cent of 34.3 million metric tons)	(per cent of 4.8 million metric tons)	(per cent of 22.8 million metric tons *exports*)	(per cent of 21.8 million metric tons *imports*)
North America	8.7%	13.0%	6.8%	–	–	23.9%
Western Europe	14.1	35.1	0.6	–	7.4%	20.8
Eastern Europe (including the U.S.S.R.)	17.9	45.8	–	–	12.6	21.9
Oceania	3.5	–	6.6	–	5.0	0.7
Latin America	28.0	0.7	49.7	16.0%	55.1	1.4
Sub-Saharan Africa	5.3	–	9.9	–	6.4	2.6
Middle East (including North Africa)	1.9	2.7	1.7	–	0.5	8.7
Non-Communist Far East	18.7	1.3	22.7	80.5	12.6	11.9
Communist Far East	1.9	1.4	2.0	3.5	0.4	8.1
High-income countries	48.8	91.0	24.5	1.3	26.1	73.6
Low-income countries	51.2	9.0	75.5	98.7	73.9	26.4

SOURCE: Adapted from United Nations and U.S. Department of Agriculture data.

* Centrifugal sugar includes both beet and cane brown sugar produced by the centrifugal process in modern factories (gravity separation of molasses and brown sugar which contains 2 to 3 per cent of impurities). Non-centrifugal sugar includes all types of low-grade brown sugar produced by premodern (cottage-type industry) methods: piloncillo, panela, papelon, chancaca, rapadura, jaggery, gur, muscovado, panocha, etc. The range of impurities (including the molasses) is from 20 to 40 per cent—for converting non-centrifugal production to centrifugal production equivalent (7 to 5 million metric tons), an average sugar content of 70 per cent was assumed.

WORLD: BROWN SUGAR PRODUCTION, BY GREAT-REGION AND ECONOMIC-TYPE OF SOCIETY, 1962-1964 AVERAGE-ANNUAL (Million Metric Tons)

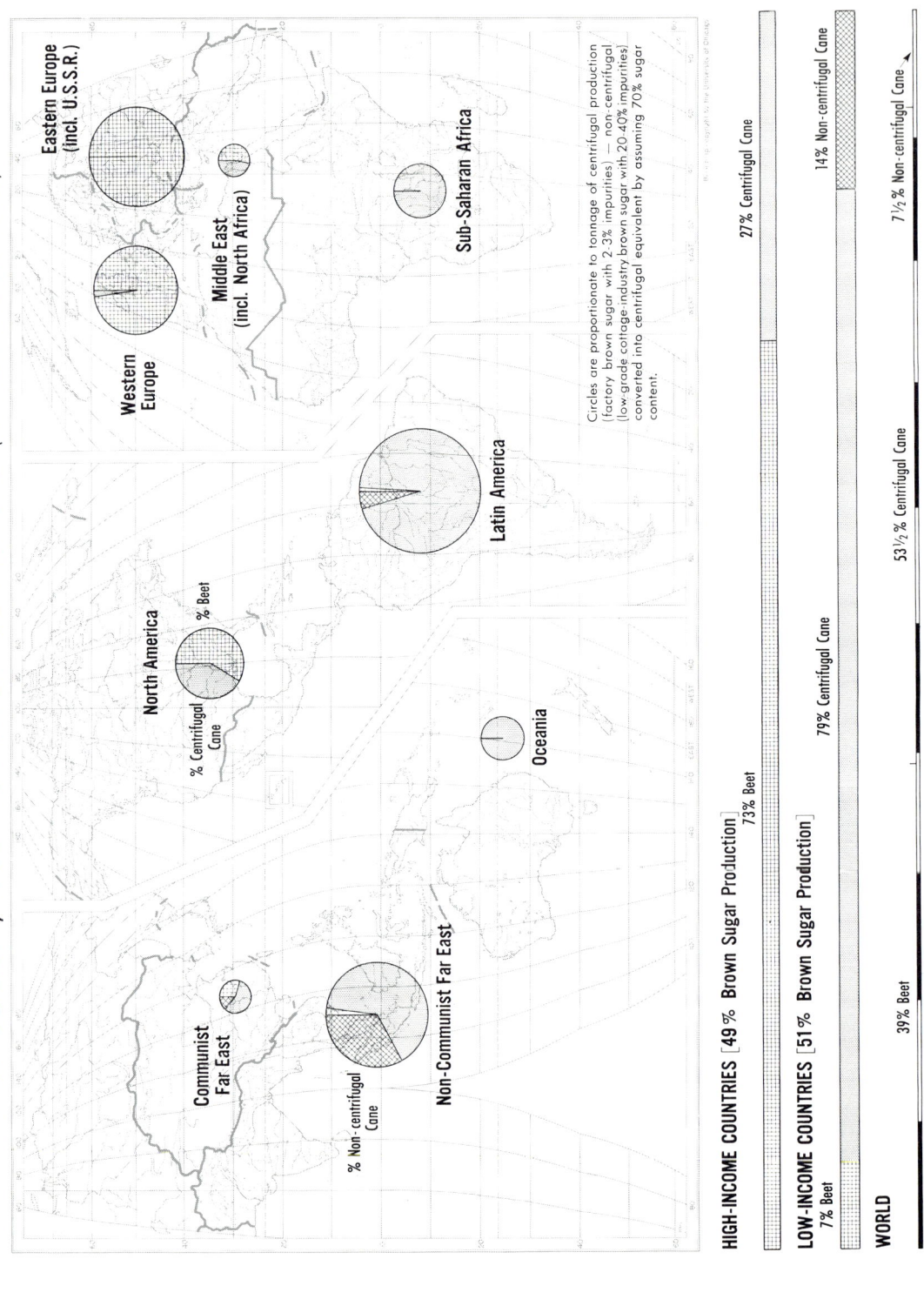

WORLD: GREAT-REGION AND ECONOMIC-TYPE OF SOCIETY SHARES OF WORLD BROWN SUGAR PRODUCTION (Centrifugal Beet and Cane; Non-centrifugal Cane) AND OF WORLD TRADE (Exports and Imports), 1962-1964 AVERAGE-ANNUAL

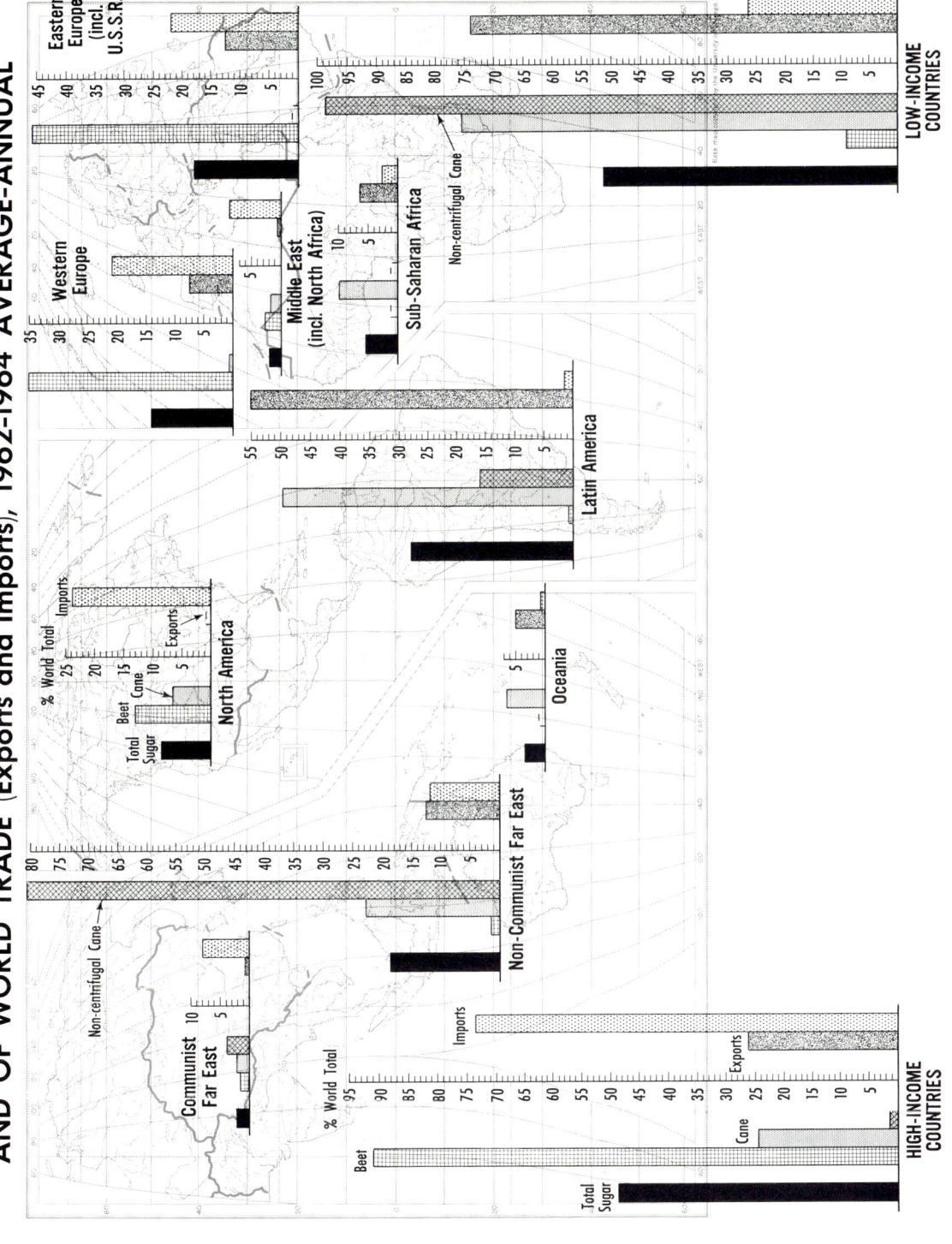

Probably no commodity in international trade is more subject to governmental control than sugar. Only about 10 per cent of the total annual world production is sold on the world ("free") market without the aid of governmental regulation, such as preferential tariffs, quotas, or other controls. Over two-thirds of the sugar moving in international trade moves under arrangements that tend to insulate it from non-quota ("free") world supplies.

For several generations, the world has generally had a chronic oversupply of sugar, except in time of war and other catastrophe.[4] Since the turn of the century, governments (both individually and collectively) have been trying to do something about it, but with limited success. The early 1960's was one of the short periods of equilibrium, but by 1965 the oversupply was 4 to 5 million tons.

There are two kinds of price for sugar moving in world trade: the world non-quota ("free") price which sags badly under the weight of a series of bumper crops in various countries (e.g., in the first months of 1965 the price dropped from over 11 cents per pound to little more than 2 cents) or rises spectacularly in the unusual periods of scarcity; and the U.S. and other national prices which hold up more evenly in markets tightly sealed off from the rest of the world by a system of quotas, controls, and allocations. Since 1950, the world "free" market price for raw sugar has ranged from 3 to 10 cents per pound (yearly averages). Generally, the U.S. price was about twice that of the world "free" market price, but in the early 1960's the two prices were fairly close together, reflecting higher U.S. prices after Cuban supplies were embargoed. In 1964, the spot or cash price for raw sugar imported into the United States under quotas was 7.4 cents, somewhat lower than the 1963 price of 8.2 cents per pound. The spot world (non-quota) sugar price in 1963 and 1964 averaged about 8.5 cents per pound (although in some months the world price was over 10 cents).

[4] The net result has been low prices for cane sugar, especially for the tenth moving in the "free" world market (such low prices have often reflected "dumping" rather than cost of production).

In 1961 and 1962, the world sugar supply dropped 10 per cent, due to a sharp decline in Cuban cane production (from 7 to 4 million tons) resulting from agricultural demoralization under "collective" enterprise, and to poor sugar beet crops in Western Europe (drop from 11 to 8 million tons) due to unfavorable weather. It took until 1964–1965 for the market to recover —both by normal Western European beet crops and by increased free-world beet and cane production elsewhere to replace the Cuban supply which now mainly goes to Communist Europe and the Communist Far East.

Prior to 1960, Cuba and the Philippines together supplied over 90 per cent of U.S. imports, with some dozen other countries supplying the balance. Since the suspension of Cuban trade, the United States has spread its foreign share of the market to a much larger number of suppliers (about twenty-five), with the Philippines being by far the most important:

CONTINENTAL UNITED STATES 1963 APPORTIONED
MARKETING QUOTAS FOR SUGAR
(THOUSAND SHORT TONS, RAW VALUE)

Source of supply		
Domestic		
Beet sugar areas	2,699	⎫
Mainland cane areas	1,010	⎬ 50 states
Hawaii	1,070	⎭
Puerto Rico	870	⎫ Dependencies
Virgin Islands	15	⎭
Subtotal, domestic	5,664	
Foreign		
25 quota countries	3,011	
Global [1] quota	1,726	
Subtotal, foreign	4,737	
Total	10,400	

[1] Legally reserved for Cuba's eventual use.

The U.S. quota price boosts costs to consumers about 2.5 cents per pound (as measured by the difference between raw sugar prices for shipment to the United States and shipment to the "free" market). In addition, a tariff of 0.5 cent per pound is levied on all raw sugar imports, boosting prices to consumers by a similar amount. On top of this, another 0.5 cent per pound is added by a processing tax on all sugar, regardless of origin. Thus, the U.S. supply management sugar program boosts prices to consumers by about 3.5 cents per pound. The program costs each consumer directly about $3.25 per year, about one-third of the total annual cost of sugar to the American householder. (This figure reflects indirect use of sugar, as well as easily identifiable personal use.)

Among the numerous countries subsidizing beet and marginal cane sugar production, the cost per pound to the U.S. consumer is near the bottom of the range. In view of heavy per capita usage, of course, the total cost of the program to the nation is very high. The U.S.S.R. program may be even more costly, but most of it reflects extremely high consumption (sales) tax rather than strictly protection costs.

Cane Sugar

There are many kinds of sugar found in many animals and plants, but the commercial product is overwhelmingly derived from sucrose found in sugarcane and sugar beet. Sugarcane is a strong, perennial grass with a round stem usually from 1 to 2 inches in diameter and 8 to 12 feet high, the sap of which is rich in sugar. Yields per acre and percentage of sugar content vary greatly, depending upon climatic (temperature and water), soil and fertilization, cultivation, and amount of replanting circumstances. By far the greatest amounts are grown within the tropics, although some is grown on the tropical edges of the subtropics. The climate should be hot and moist, with a total annual rainfall, or its equivalent by irrigation, of 40 to 100 inches, according to topography and evaporation. During its growing period, the plant is highly susceptible to drought, but too much water during the ripening period makes the juice watery and favors the spread of cane diseases. The best yields are obtained where there is a temperature of 75° to 80° F. all the year round, though the greatest sugar content is found where temperatures are somewhat cooler as the plant ripens.

As there is seldom a system of crop rotation, the soil tends to become exhausted in spite of the usual alluvial, volcanic, or limestone origin. Heavy fertilization is still uncommon (less than a fifth of cane acreage is fertilized at all), and mainly found where mid-latitude countries contain subtropical and semitropical areas. Weeding and harvesting have historically been very

Courtesy of California & Hawaiian Sugar Refining Corp.

A Matson bulk raw sugar and container ship delivers 16,000 tons of Hawaiian raw sugar to the world's largest sugar refinery at Crockett, California. At such a refinery, the final 2½ per cent of non-sugar and molasses in the raw sugar is removed. About three-quarters of Hawaiian raw sugar output is refined at Crockett and distributed throughout the western two-thirds of the United States, together with beet sugar from other C & H refineries.

labor-intensive, with mechanical equipment being important mainly in United States cane growing areas.

After the stems have been cut, they are usually crushed between heavy rollers which extract about one-quarter of the weight of the cane as juice.[5] The juice is then boiled, with the addi-

[5] A new (National Cylinder Gas Company) process handles the same amount of cane in a fraction of the space used in conventional crushers and with less than three-quarters of the power and equipment weight, and is well suited to control by automatic instruments. The big advantage of the process is that it removes nearly all of the sugar and allows a purity much higher than that achieved by conventional milling. The new equipment is cheaper in initial cost, construction, and operation, with manpower needs also lower. In operation, the process tosses aside high-pressure squeezing methods: it relies on the principle of osmosis for its results. Hot water replaces over 97 per cent of the sugarcane juice.

tion of lime to thicken it, the raw (brown) sugar crystallizing out of the thick syrup, leaving molasses as a by-product. Molasses is used to make rum, alcohol, and motor fuel (the last two usually more expensive than when made from petroleum) and, with crushed cane or other roughage, to make a nutritious cattle feed. The crushed cane (bagasse) is usually used as fuel for the boilers of the sugar mill, although increasingly it is made into board and paper.

Increases in technical and economic efficiencies have occurred in cane processing and utilization in recent decades that have more than matched changes in beet production. The sugar moving in international trade (brown sugar retaining a protective film of molasses) is usually refined in large tidewater plants that have excellent locations and facilities for handling raw sugar arriving by the shipload from offshore areas. The amount of machinery and equipment required to remove the last 2 to 3 per cent of impurities is amazing: centrifugals to separate molasses from the sugar crystals, huge melting tanks to reduce the crystals to a syrup, various types of filters to remove insoluble impurities, large char cisterns for color removal, great vacuum pans for

Hawaiian sugarcane harvesting operation. High labor cost ($22 per day—two to three times other states and territories) has led to highly mechanized operations, in which heavy machines cut the stalks or snap them off at ground level, gathering the cane as they go. Hawaiian caneland yields 10 tons of raw sugar per acre (about 7 tons per year), about two-thirds from irrigated acreage.

Courtesy of California & Hawaiian Sugar Refining Corp.

crystallization, automatic packaging machinery, and related equipment. Like other huge integrated plants, efficiency requires most capacity in use at any one time (the disruptions in supply in the early 1960's adversely affected U.S. Eastern Seaboard refineries' competitive position in the eastern Midwest compared to Western beet refineries, until new "pipelines" of raw sugar for the lost Cuban supplies were developed).

Economic improvements in cane refining include increasingly high-grade uses for by-products such as molasses and bagasse. North America and Western Europe now consume several times more molasses annually than they produce domestically. The balance is brought by tankers from overseas areas, which either wasted it or used it for low-grade uses. Both molasses and petroleum mainly move seasonally, and there is little conflict between the two: generally the major oil movement is between August and March, while the peak transport season for molasses is from February to July. There are some tankers built specifically for the molasses trade and only secondarily to carry oil. They have heavier plates in the hulls, heavier pumps, heavier pumping lines, and special liners, since a gallon of molasses weighs 12 pounds compared with 8 to 8.5 pounds for most petroleum.

Molasses is of two types: blackstrap, what is left of sugarcane juice after all commercially extractable sugar has been removed, and high-test, a molasses-type product that is processed from sugarcane juice from which no sugar has been removed. Of U.S. consumption, nearly 70 per cent ends up in the preparation of mixed feeds for cattle and for direct on-farm feeding of animals (e.g., sweetened grass silage). Some 6.5 gallons of blackstrap have the equivalent carbohydrates value of a bushel of corn and are considerably cheaper where the molasses can be moved cheaply by bulk transport. Of the remaining by-product molasses, some 17 per cent goes into industrial alcohol, 0.5 per cent into spirits and rum, and the remainder into yeast, vinegar, citric acid, table molasses, pharmaceuticals, and biologicals. High-test mainly goes into more costly edibles.

Sugar mills produce about 1 pound of dry cellulose or bagasse for each pound of sugar, which historically furnished inefficient but cheap fuel in central boilers. It takes three times as much bagasse by weight to supply as much heat as fuel oil, but the stuff is so cheap that most of the world's supply (some 65 million tons yearly) is still used for crude fuel. For a long time, bagasse was scorned as a raw material because most of its by-product uses added very little value: wallboard, wrapping paper, cattle-feed filler, etc., could not be priced higher than competitive products made from ordinary wood, wood waste, and agricultural waste.[6] Recently, however, carpentry-quality board made by new dry processing has become competitive with core lumber, high-grade lumber boards, paneling, and plywood. Bagasse costs about $2 per ton (baling, stacking, curing, and cleaning eats up 25 per cent of tonnage), with the structural board made from it costing $60 a ton (15 cents per square foot for 0.75 inch board). The 400° F. plus press temperatures are high enough to cause the lignin in the fibers to flow, one reason for the smooth skin on the board.

Many tropical sugar producers now make newsprint from bagasse, 1 ton of newsprint from 2 tons of bagasse. The Cuban and Filipino production is cheaper than the former imported supplies. A Lockport, Louisiana, plant now makes high-quality papers from bagasse (white writing, offset, mimeo, duplicator, and tablet papers). In making paper, most of the pith is removed (bagasse is 70 per cent fiber and 30 per cent pith), with the raw materials costing about $8 per ton by the time the bagasse is baled and stored.

Another promising area is the new field of sucrochemistry. A new family of detergents are digestible, bland in taste, non-irritating to the skin, unaffected by hardness of water, and low in cost compared with present detergents used in the home. Among products and processes that may make use of this more efficient emulsifier are shampoos, tooth pastes, chocolate beverages,

[6] Even today, only some 10 per cent of the U.S. bagasse is used commercially as a raw material, even including the production of insulation board and poultry litter.

Cane buggy brings up to 40 tons of harvested sugarcane from the plantation fields to the mill.

Courtesy of California & Hawaiian Sugar Refining Co.

Raw sugar is delivered from plantation mills to one of five raw sugar storage and shipping terminals in Hawaii. About 100 pounds of cane are reduced to 12 pounds of raw sugar at such a mill.

Courtesy of California & Hawaiian Sugar Refining Corp.

Courtesy of Holly Sugar Corp.

Airview of Holly Sugar Corporation's Merrill E. Shoup Plant at Hereford, Texas, newest and one of largest in world, which commenced operations on October 8, 1964. (Photo was taken on day plant was formally dedicated, September 19, 1964, as crowd began to assemble.)

salad dressings, dehydrated foods, bread softeners, cosmetics, secondary oil recovery, livestock feeds, and poultry rations. The paint industry is also interested in sucrose-linseed oil fatty-acid esters, which produce highly superior paint films both as to drying time and hardness.

The increasing use of sugarcane by-products as high-quality raw materials ranks with the mechanization and other modernization of cane production as a major avenue of cost cutting. In the foreseeable future, both avenues promise to maintain cane's competitive advantage over beet [7] in an "economic" context (not necessarily in the "political economy" of world sugar trade).

---

[7] Excluding subsidization, the average cane sugar in the world is produced for half to two-thirds of the average beet sugar (3 to 5 cents per pound compared to 6 to 8 cents).

Beet Sugar

The importance of sugar beets to Western European agriculture was understood over a century ago, particularly their role in the maintenance of rational crop rotations, which replaced the traditional, extensive three-field system dominated by cereals. It became clear very soon that sugar beets, requiring deep plowing and careful cultivation of soil, coupled with heavy chemical fertilization, contribute substantially to the increase in yields of other crops in the rotation, particularly of the only cash grain, wheat. The important role of the by-products of sugar beets (tops) and of the beet sugar industry (pulp) as a supplier of additional valuable cattle feed came to be generally recognized before 1850. European farmers understood that sugar beets not only provided them with a new cash crop, replacing other industrial crops, such as oilseeds (like rapeseed and mustard), that also were suffering at that time from overseas competition, but created the opportunity for a complete reorganization of farming on an intensive as well as diversified basis. The link with animal husbandry was particularly important at a time when prices of animal products were less depressed than those of cereals.

Sugar beets have rather exacting soil and climatic requirements. In Western and Eastern Europe, sugar beets are cultivated mainly on the same superior soils as wheat. Deep loess soils, rich in humus and lime, characteristic of relatively level to gently rolling areas on the northern edge of the central plateaus, are especially favorable for sugar beets because they are easy to work and root penetration is good. Various grades of loamy soils in the same general belt are also widely used.

In areas such as the Hereford, Texas, district and throughout the Rocky Mountains, Pacific Northwest, and the Midwest, sugar beets are stored in huge outdoor piles during the harvest season and then moved into the factory for processing as needed, with the plants operating twenty-four hours a day and seven days a week until all the beets have been processed. Here is an aerial view of a beet sugar plant at the close of the harvest season showing mountains of sugar beets stored in piles some 20 feet high. From the piles, beets are flumed into plant in water that starts the cleaning process even as it transports the roots to the refinery.

Courtesy of Holly Sugar Corp.

Mechanical harvesting of sugar beet roots on a farm near Hereford, Texas, on October 7, 1964. Lush sugar beet leaves are shown in foreground. The harvester digs, tops, and loads beets into the waiting truck for delivery to the receiving station.

Courtesy of Holly Sugar Corp.

Sugar beets require a cool climate with a sunny late summer for ripening, and summer temperatures of 60° to 70° F. Annual rainfall should be in the range of 20 to 35 inches and should fall chiefly in spring and summer. Sugar beets are mainly grown on the cooler margins of the cattle and grain areas in the North Atlantic realm, especially in the European small-holder areas where labor, though dear in relation to that of many tropical areas, is relatively cheap, for sugar beets have historically required a great deal of hand labor for planting and hoeing (twenty to thirty man-days per acre).

In the United States, the profitable use of most Western irrigated land has revolved around sugar beet cultivation. Beets yield a high gross return per acre, about twice as much as wheat for the average farmer. As the irrigated areas were usually short of labor, they first depended on Mexican braceros, and in the 1950's substituted mechanization for about 90 per cent of their labor requirements. About one hour of field work now produces enough beets to make 100 pounds of refined sugar, the lowest man-hour requirement of any sugar producing area in the world. In the 1950's, the average sugar beet yield was upped some 25 per cent, and now a new seed type promises to save costly thinning and a much higher yield also seems likely (it grows a single plant from a single germ, instead of a multiplant). More than 95 per cent of the 25-million-ton U.S. crop is now gathered mechanically, with the average harvester pulling, topping, and loading 100 tons of beets in half or less the time needed under the traditional stoop-labor system, and for about half the cost.

In the autumn, the beet tops are pulled off and the beets plowed up and sent to local refineries, where they are cleaned by machinery and cut up, the sugar being extracted with hot water. By-products include alcohol and cattle feed, and methods of extraction have improved tremendously over the past century, so much so that, weight for weight, more sugar is obtained from beet than from cane, although cane yields more sugar to the acre.

Courtesy of Holly Sugar Corp.

A pile of sugar beet roots harvested in the Hereford, Texas, area on October 7, 1964. Hat was placed in pile to give perspective of size and sugar-filled roots.

The final refining process is the same for raw sugar obtained from both beet and cane. Beet sugar and cane sugar consumed in the tropics are refined in the area of agricultural production, but the cane sugar consumed in the mid-latitudes is generally refined in the country of consumption.[8]

Prospects

In the foreseeable future, world sugar consumption will continue to rise about 2 to 3 million tons a year, due partly to world population growth (which affects even countries like the United States whose per capita consumption is stable), and partly to increased per capita demand (especially in poor societies whose per capita income is rising).

Politics are going to remain fully as important as habitat and economics in explaining patterns of sugar production, processing, distribution, and consumption. The economics of sugar beets are more complicated than those of sugarcane (because of conservation and diversification benefits hard to measure in simple economic terms) but, as in the recent past, even with indirect benefits they are not competitive without protection from their tropical rivals. Even so, they are increasing their share of world sugar production, because mid-latitude countries continue willing to subsidize their increased production.

In the long run, sugarcane holds an advantage over sugar beets as a source of supply because of its tropical environment (although some production is marginal because of situation in climatically inferior areas and in areas naturally and culturally unfavorable to large-scale production and processing). Since the largest potential sugar markets are in the poor societies of the tropical belt, sugarcane seems destined to increase its share (perhaps eventually to three-quarters or more of total world production). This could improve economic efficiency, although not inevitably so, if certain marginal sugarcane areas come to be heavily protected to insure their dominance in growing domestic markets. It is possible that eventually sugarcane may be grown as much for its cellulose as for sugar (some enthusiasts foresee the day when the latter will be a by-product).

Sugar can be made synthetically, but the chemical process is complex and costly compared with that used by the plants, and under the conditions prevailing today it would never compete economically with sugar produced so simply and abundantly by the green plants. Sugar is the basic material of the great class of carbohydrate foods: starch and cellulose are derivatives of sugar, and any attempt to make truly synthetic food would start, almost certainly, with

---

[8] In the early days, before ventilated bulk carriers, this was necessary because white sugar became lumpy while being transported. Today, white sugar can be made efficiently in the tropics and then shipped, but the relic pattern of two-step processing is maintained by inertia and by mid-latitude protection.

a synthesis of sugar. However, there is little prospect of any demand for synthetic carbohydrate in the foreseeable future; the world can produce vast quantities of extra carbohydrate more effectively by organizing its agricultural effort and rationalizing the politics and economics that control its food distribution.

OILS AND FATS

Oils and fats are the most concentrated energy food, and supply the body with long-lasting fuel. Fat is a major component of the normal body, accounting for about 15 per cent of the total weight of a young adult and a higher percentage in an older person. A healthy body maintains a constant proportion of fat, and restores this proportion if weight is lost. The body fat of an average young man represents roughly the amount of energy expended in a month of normal life.

Fat supports internal organs, provides an insulating layer beneath the skin, is essential to the skin and hair, sheathes the nerves, and helps to build resistance to infection. Some vitamins are not absorbed properly without an oily solution. Fat tissue is a living part of the body structure and not simply a tank to hold excess calories. The cells in this tissue contain some of the most active protoplasm in the body. They synthesize fat from sugar (much of the latter eaten as starch), and then release the fuel on demand. Apparently these steps are essential for a normal utilization of food energy. Carbohydrates and fat serve equally well as food for the body. The conversion of sugar to fat in the fat tissue thus enables cells in the muscle and other tissues of the body to operate on a standard fuel despite wide variations in diet.

In addition to processing starches and sugars, the fat tissue also plays a role in the metabolism of fat ingested in the diet. It stores dietary fat and mixes these molecules with fat synthesized from the carbohydrates. After mixing, the two fats appear to share a common function. The mixture leaves the tissue in response to hormonal demands, and provides fuel for the working cells.

Dietary fat is desirable for psychological as well as physiological reasons. Sedentary people in particular prefer a fatty diet, since fats are easily digested, satisfy hunger longer, and do not burden the digestive system as much as the starch foods. Fats make the bulkier energy foods more palatable, and are thought to be rich in certain vitamins.

Rich societies usually have fat intakes of 25 to 40 per cent of their total dietary, in excess of nutritional necessity. Usually half or less is from visible (refined) sources, with the rest incorporated in other energy foods and in protective foods eaten. Poor societies average only one-quarter of the intake of the wealthy societies.

The higher intakes of luxury energy foods by the wealthier societies are not unqualified advantages. The consumption of sugar in large amounts, especially in sticky forms which lodge between teeth, is correlated with increased troubles with dental caries. And the death rate from prime-of-life heart attacks goes up, roughly, with the concentration of fats in the blood. For example, atherosclerosis that narrows or closes the heart's coronary arteries with slushy, fatty deposits is the greatest killer in the United States where it claims a half million lives a year, twice as many as cancer. Most biochemists divide these circulating fatty substances into four groups: fatty acids, phospholipids, cholesterol, and triglycerides (some of these are free, some of them combined with proteins or with one another). It is not yet certain which of them are the most important in causing atherosclerosis. Cholesterol is easily measured, so it becomes a handy guide to arterial and coronary health. High levels of circulating cholesterol go with a high incidence of heart attacks in men forty-five to sixty-five (lean peasants in poor societies have half the level of well-to-do Americans). Many heart researchers believe that the triglycerides are as important, and perhaps a better clue to the risk of a heart attack. Their concentration goes up with excessive weight (no matter what the dietary), while cholesterol increases with too much dietary fat.

All natural food fats fall into one of three categories: saturated, monounsaturated, and polyunsaturated. Many heart disease doctors say that what is important is the proportion of polyunsaturated to saturated. To the chemist the term "fat" means a family of molecules formed by the union of fatty acids with glycerol, averaging 88 per cent carbon and hydrogen with only 12 per cent oxygen (therefore, only partially oxidized, which makes it approach maximum efficiency as a storage material). Chemists call a fat saturated if each carbon atom along the molecular chain has hydrogen atoms attached; it is monounsaturated if one carbon atom is free of the hydrogen bonds, and it is polyunsaturated if two or more are free. All three types of fat molecule have similar caloric values (about 265 calories per ounce, roughly double that of the same weight of starch or sugar), but each exerts a radically different influence on blood cholesterol. Saturated fats in meat, dairy products, and eggs promote production of cholesterol in quantities too large for the body to excrete (17 per cent of the average U.S. dietary is from saturated fats, with 23 per cent from unsaturated). Monounsaturated fats (predominant in olive oil and most margarines) have no apparent effect at all on blood cholesterol levels. Polyunsaturated fats (vegetable oils from corn, cottonseed, peanuts, safflower, and soybeans; fish and whale oils), on the other hand, actually lower cholesterol by increasing the excretion of bile acid. The digestion of dietary fats depends upon adequate amounts of fat utilizing factors: three of the B-complex vitamins, vitamin E, and methionine (one of scarcer superior amino acids). These vital fat utilizing factors are present in many common foods: in whole wheat bread and brown rice, in nuts, in soybeans, in many fruits and vegetables, and in animal products (meat, milk, eggs, fish). When general body functioning is healthy, and the fat utilizing factors are adequate, considerable cholesterol can be consumed and no abnormal amount appears in the blood. Controlled experiments now under way are expected to provide firmer knowledge of the links between health, total food intake, fat intake, and types of fats ingested.

Oils-Fats Processing

Important as they are, most fats and oils are coproducts and by-products, and their supply is seldom simply related to the demand for them. Lard comes from hogs, tallow from cattle; the supply of both depends not upon their demand but on the demand for meat. The supply of butter depends, to a great extent, upon the demand for fluid milk (and the kinds desired) and other milk products. The supply of fish oil now depends mainly upon the demand for fish meal in the animal husbandry branches of agriculture. In the long run, animal fats are likely to decrease in relative importance among all fats, with the increasing preference for lean meats.

About three-fifths of visible fats and oils come from the vegetable oil industry, which includes three segments: crushing, refining, and manufacturing. Crushers, who extract crude oil from oilseeds, perform a dual operation in that they produce two products from the seeds: oil and meal. Sold principally as a high-protein feed for animals, meal is a finished product ready for sale on the retail market, often bringing about as much as the crude oil. The size and location tendencies of crushers depend on the kind of oilseed grown.

Impurities are removed from crude oil in the refinery, the second step in processing fats and oils. Refineries tend to be larger than crushing mills, often one refinery handling crude oil from several mills. Some manufacturers of shortening and margarine refine the oil they use, while others buy it already refined, so the line between processing and manufacturing a finished product is difficult to determine. Manufacturing of oil products, in contrast to the crushing process, tends to be located near consuming markets.

Tremendous technological changes in the vegetable oil industry have affected its development. Premodern oil presses have disappeared almost everywhere that modern accessibility has reached. Since many oilseeds are a mixture of edible and inedible fatty acids, premodern presses did not subject oilseeds to great heat or pressure, so that the first pressing was usually edible without any further treatment (some impurities did get into the first pressing, but consumers were accustomed to certain flavor and color). Additional pressing yielded impure oil that went into soap and illuminants. Usually about half of the oil was extracted, the remainder in the cake being fed to cattle or used as fertilizer.

Early modern presses relied on the application of great heat and pressure which yielded most of the oil in the seed, but with edible and inedible fatty acids and fibrous impurities incorporated; the crude oils have disagreeable flavors and odors which had to be removed, and the various fatty acids fractions have to be separated. Before World War II, most vegetable oils were extracted from seeds by hydraulic presses: these were very labor-intensive, the heat was almost unbearable for workers, and operators were unable to regulate closely temperatures and thereby control the quality of the oil they produced. In advanced societies, hydraulic presses are not used much now, their place being taken by more efficient screw press expellers or chemical-solvent extractors. In some cases, these two machines are used together in what is called a prepress solvent extractor (these require less than a third of the labor formerly required, increase the oil yield by 10 to 20 per cent, and the quality of oil from chemical fractionation is much higher than from physical fractionation). The second phase of modern oil preparation involves many manufacturing changes, the most spectacular and controversial being hydrogenation. Most vegetable oils are usually liquid at room temperature and, as a result, are messier than the solid fats, so manufacturers of shortening and margarine usually partially hydrogenate their unsaturated oils to produce semisynthetic fat, which looks better, smells better, and keeps better. There are also other advantages to hydrogenation: a certain amount makes oil less easily oxidized and less apt to become rancid (this aspect is important in converting soybean and whale and sperm oils into fat); and a certain amount has a bleaching effect, also. Since the furor over the correlation between heavy saturated fat consumption and heart troubles, manufacturers have tried to minimize the amount of hydrogenation.

Since the commercial application of fractionation and hydrogenation in the first decade of the present century, all fats and oils have become directly or indirectly competitive with one another. Interchangeability of fats and oils tends to tie their prices together in international markets, and to make producers of oilseed crops (and other oils-fats sources) in one part of the world susceptible to developments in a far distant region. The old ideal of local or regional self-sufficiency in oils-fats has increasingly given way to the ideal of economic efficiency, involving greater interregional and international trade.

World Oils-Fats Production and Trade

Identifiable oils-fats production is now over 35 million tons annually,[9] increasing some 2 per cent annually. As Tables 7–2 and 7–3 and the graphs on pages 198–99 show, over a quarter of the world production moves in world trade. Striking regional and commodity changes have occurred in the world trade pattern in the past generation. Before World War II, the Far East was outstanding as the world's leading exporting area, with Africa second, and Latin America third, followed by Antarctica (with its whale-sperm oils) and Oceania. Western Europe was by far the leading importing area, but North America also had a substantial net import balance. Thus, the flow of trade was largely from underdeveloped to industrial countries.

Today, the situation has changed substantially. Population increases and increases in per capita consumption in the underdeveloped countries have often removed the old export surpluses, even when production has increased. The development of substitutes for fats and oils in the manufacture of inedible products (soap, detergent, and paints) and the fear of fat consumption being a possible health hazard has arrested growth in the total use of fats and oils in the importing regions with high consumption. Consumption is still quite low in underdeveloped regions, although the rate of increase in consumption is usually higher than in the industrial societies.

These medium-run trends have resulted in a severe drop in exports from the Far East (especially from India and China) and Latin America, counterbalanced by increased availability from North America and sub-Saharan Africa. The United States has changed from the largest im-

[9] Market value of crude materials is about $12 billion; retail value of refined oils-fats and manufactured edible products (margarine, shortening, salad oils) about $30 billion.

TABLE 7-2

World: Oils-Fats Production and Exports, 1962–1964 Average-Annual
(in per cents)

	Production		Exports	
	35 Million Metric Tons Output	World Value (U.S. $12 billion farm-valued)	Annual Production Exported (tonnage)	World Exports (10 million metric tons)
Soybean	12.5	6.5	41.5	17.9
Peanut (groundnut)	7.5	7.5	41.0	10.9
Cottonseed	7.3	5.9	12.0	3.1
Sunflower seed	5.7	6.4	14.2	3.2
Olive oil	4.6	9.1	5.8	0.6
Rapeseed (including mustard seed)	3.9	3.9	9.8	1.3
Sesame seed	1.7	3.9	13.4	0.8
Corn	0.7	0.8	–	–
Safflower seed	0.5	0.6	–	–
Edible vegetable oils	44.4	44.5	24.8	37.8
Coconut	6.8	5.1	60.0	15.0
Palm	4.0	3.2	41.7	6.0
Palm-kernel	1.2	1.6	97.6	4.1
Babassu-kernel	0.2	0.2	7.1	–
Palm oils	12.2	10.1	56.8	25.1
Linseed	3.2	2.8	47.9	5.4
Castor bean	0.8	1.1	66.7	1.8
Tung	0.3	0.5	36.0	0.4
Oiticica	0.1	–	84.0	0.2
Perilla	–	–	10.0	–
Industrial oils	4.4	4.4	51.3	7.8
Butter (fat content)	12.3	26.9	10.9	4.9
Lard	11.6	7.3	9.0	3.9
Tallow and grease	11.6	4.5	29.3	12.1
Animal fats	35.5	38.7	16.2	20.9
Fish (including liver)	2.4	1.1	58.0	4.2
Whale (including sperm)	1.1	1.2	97.0	4.2
Marine oils	3.5	2.3	72.5	8.4
Total	100.0	100.0	28.5	100.0

porter to the largest exporter: it now exports about a quarter of its annual production (about 60 per cent of the exports are edible oils-fats and the rest inedible types); these exports account for nearly half of the edible oils-fats that move in world trade and nearly a third of the inedible types. About a third of U.S. edible oils-fats output is exported, with about a fifth of the inedible oils-fats production, a majority through government-financed exports.

Western Europe accounts for about two-thirds of world oils-fats imports. Japan and the United States each account for little more than 5 per cent of the total, and the remainder is widely scattered.

Edible Vegetable Oils

There are several classification systems for assessing characteristics of oils and fats, from both the strict science and social science sides of knowledge. A very useful system for analyzing industrial problems is one that characterizes the chemistry of oils and fats,[10] but a more useful

---

[10] *Drying* and *semidrying* oils are of more frequent occurrence in plants of the mid-latitudes, while *non-dry-*

TABLE 7–3

World: Oils-Fats Production, by Great-Region and Economic-Type
of Society, 1962–1964 Average-Annual
(in millions of metric tons)

	Million Metric tons (= 100.0 per cent)	Edible Vegetable Oils	Palm Oils	Industrial Oils	Animal Fats	Marine Oils
North America	9.4	44.5%	–	5.1%	47.8%	2.6%
Western Europe	4.7	33.1	–	0.8	58.9	7.2
Eastern Europe (including the U.S.S.R.)	5.4	41.2	–	2.6	54.0	2.2
Oceania	0.9	0.4	20.9%	1.7	75.9	1.1
Latin America	2.8	36.2	8.5	18.8	30.4	5.8
Sub-Saharan Africa	2.6	40.7	51.0	1.6	4.6	2.1
Middle East (including North Africa)	0.8	78.9	–	2.2	17.5	1.4
Non-Communist Far East	5.9	43.9	42.3	4.1	6.5	3.2
Communist Far East	2.5	95.7	–	1.5	2.8	–
World	35.0	44.4	12.2	4.4	35.5	3.5
High-income countries	20.6	35.5	0.1	4.8	55.1	4.5
Low-income countries	14.4	57.7	29.8	3.7	7.4	1.4
	(per cent of 35.0 million metric tons)	(per cent of 15.6 million metric tons)	(per cent of 4.3 million metric tons)	(per cent of 1.5 million metric tons)	(per cent of 12.4 million metric tons)	(per cent of 1.2 million metric tons)
North America	26.3	26.8	–	31.2	36.1	21.9
Western Europe	13.2	10.0	–	2.3	22.2	29.4
Eastern Europe (including the U.S.S.R.)	15.6	14.3	–	2.6	23.6	10.5
Oceania	2.6	–	4.4	1.0	5.6	0.9
Latin America	8.0	6.5	5.6	34.3	6.8	14.9
Sub-Saharan Africa	7.5	6.9	31.6	2.8	1.0	4.8
Middle East (including North Africa)	2.2	3.9	–	1.1	1.1	0.9
Non-Communist Far East	17.3	16.6	58.4	15.7	3.1	16.7
Communist Far East	7.3	15.0	–	2.4	0.5	–
High-income countries	59.0	47.0	0.1	65.2	91.5	82.5
Low-income countries	41.0	53.0	99.9	34.8	8.5	17.5

SOURCE: Adapted from United Nations and U.S. Department of Agriculture data.

ing oils and *vegetable fats* predominate in tropical species. Animal and fish oils and fats are less well correlated with latitude.

Drying oils (soybean, linseed, tung, hemp) are able to absorb oxygen and on exposure to dry into thin elastic films. In recent years, fractionation has caused the proportion of edible oil from this group to rise spectacularly.

Semidrying oils (cottonseed, sunflower, rapeseed, sesame, corn) absorb oxygen slowly and only in limited amounts, forming a soft film only after long exposure. Some are naturally edible; others naturally inedible (again, modern chemical manipulation can greatly change such natural ratios, by increasing the edible fraction.

Non-drying oils (groundnut or peanut, olive, castor) remain liquid at ordinary temperatures and do not form a film. They are naturally edible, although some are also used in making soap and lubricants.

Vegetable fats (coconut, palm, palm kernel, babassu) are solid or semisolid at ordinary temperatures. They are naturally edible, but are also used for industrial purposes. *Animal fats* are also solid or semisolid, and *marine oils* tend to be semisolid or waxlike, and both include edible and inedible types, usually dependent on the degree of processing or age.

WORLD: OILS-FATS PRODUCTION, BY GREAT-REGION AND ECONOMIC-TYPE OF SOCIETY, 1962-1964 AVERAGE-ANNUAL (Million Metric Tons)

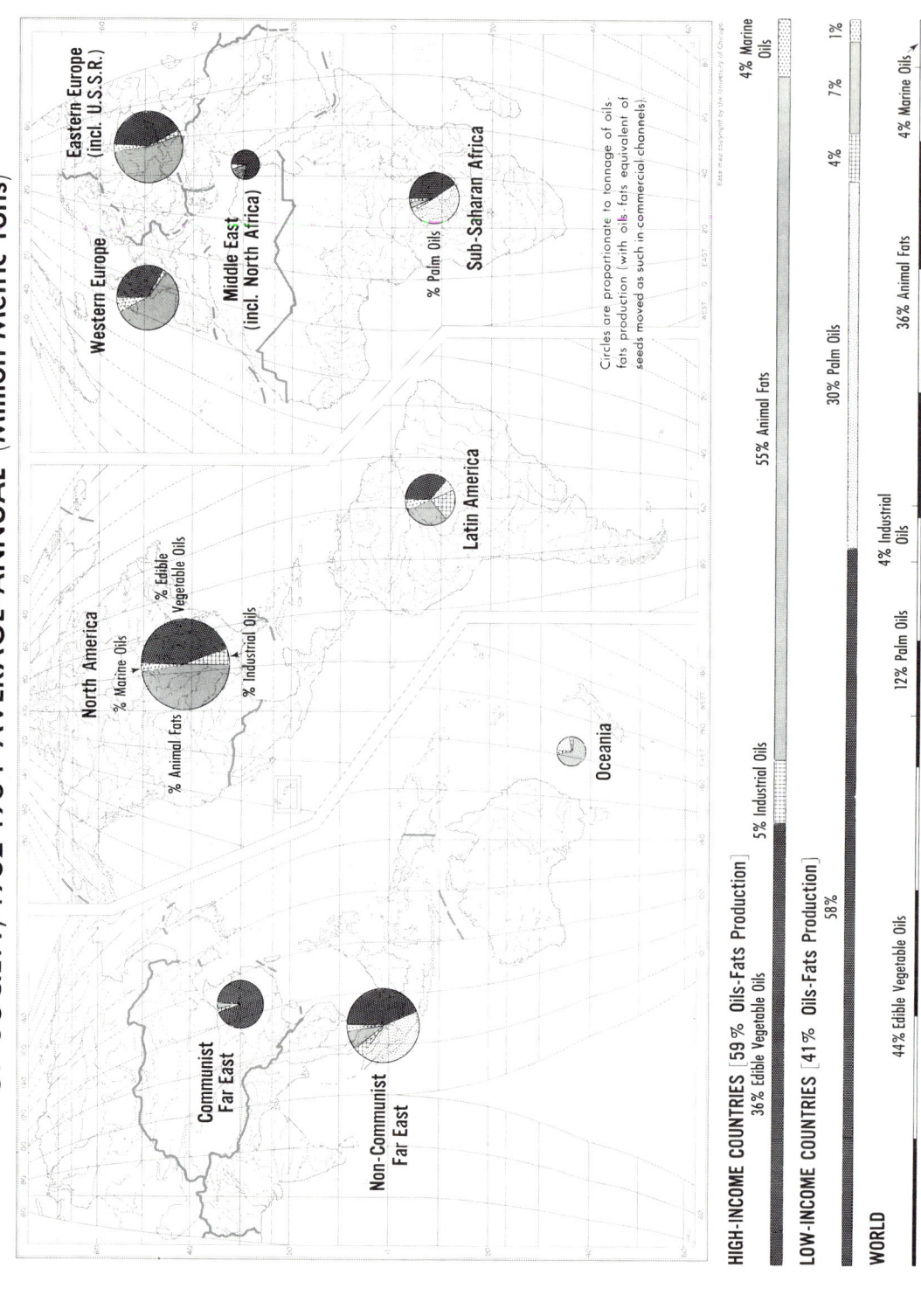

WORLD: GREAT-REGION AND ECONOMIC-TYPE OF SOCIETY SHARES OF WORLD OILS-FATS PRODUCTION (Edible Vegetable Oils, Palm Oils, Industrial Oils, Animal Fats, and Marine Oils), 1962-1964 AVERAGE-ANNUAL

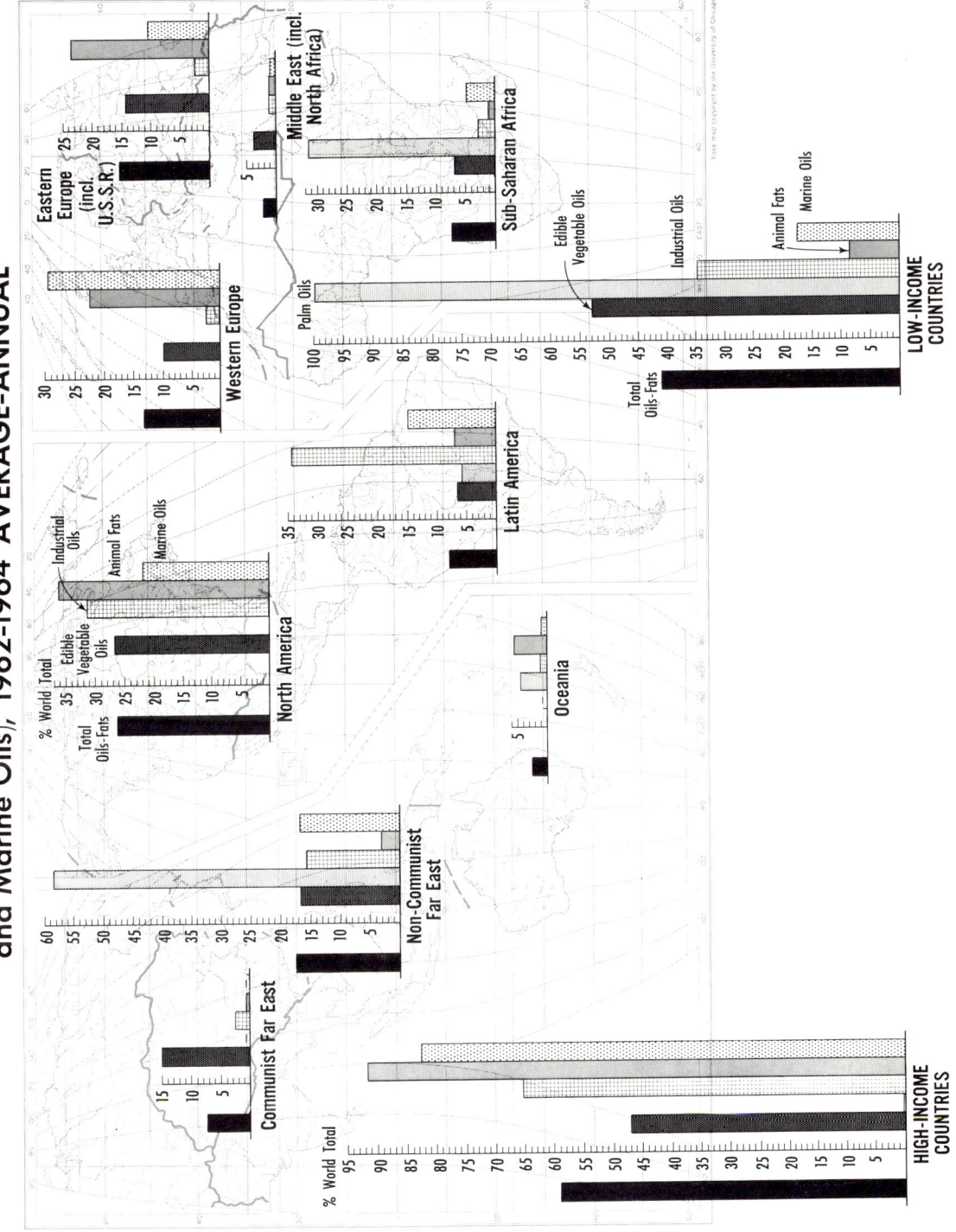

system for assessing problems of distribution and competition is one that stresses origins: edible and non-edible oilseeds, tree crops, animal, and marine sources.

The edible vegetable oils category historically has included liquid or soft oils (non-drying and semidrying ones), mainly groundnut (peanut), cottonseed, sunflower seed, olive, corn (maize germ), and safflower. These oils have a high proportion of two unsaturated fatty acids, oleic and linoleic, in their chemical structure. Soybean and rapeseed oils are soft oils from the standpoint of utilization, but they differ from the other oils of the group in their chemical constitution.

Competition among these edible oils is determined by a combination of price and other factors. For example, cottonseed oil usually sells for less than groundnut (peanut) oil, but occasionally short cotton crops coincide with bumper groundnut crops, and the ordinary price relationship is reversed. The largest substitution has been soybean oil for cottonseed or other oils, because of the spectacular rise in availability and drop in price of the former in recent decades, especially in North America.

Soybeans. The soybean is a legume that has been grown in China since prehistoric times. It was introduced into the United States early in the nineteenth century but was not widely used until the past generation, during which time per acre yield has doubled from its former 12 bushels and oil content has gone up a quarter or more from its former 15 per cent, because of better seed strains, and improvements in planting, cultivating, fertilizing, crop rotation, and harvesting systems.

North America now produces almost two-thirds of the world's soybeans, with the traditional Chinese center producing less than one-third. North American use of soybean oil is over 90 per cent food manufacturing (about a third each into margarine and shortening, and a quarter into various cooking and salad oil preparations), with industrial uses (like protective coatings) declining because of plastic and other synthetic competition. Cottonseed originally developed these markets, but now soybeans are dominant.

The $2.50 bushel of soybeans is processed into two products of roughly equal value, about 8 to 10 pounds of oil and 47 to 49 pounds of meal. The rapidly increasing supply of soybean meal has become the main component of high-protein feeds, while the output of other supplies (cottonseed, tankage, bran) has been relatively stable. A small amount of the meal is used in specialty food products (soy flour, soy sauce) and in industrial products (glues, adhesives).

In the Orient, only about one-third of the soybean production is converted into oil and meal, with the overwhelming majority being consumed directly as food. Most of the meal is also used

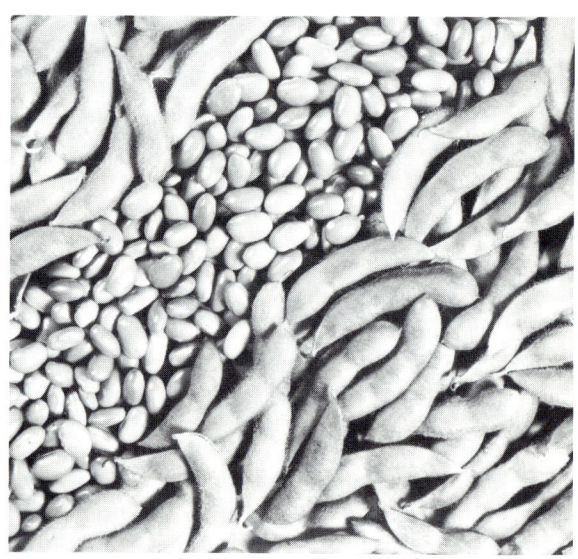

U.S.D.A. Photo

Soybeans, an annual summer legume, have been grown in China since prehistoric times, but North America now produces two-thirds of total production. The pods, which are covered with fine brown or gray hairs, usually contain two or three seeds ranging in color from very light straw through shades of gray and brown to nearly black. The oil (20 per cent by weight) and the cake or meal are each worth half the total value. The oil goes into margarine, shortening, cooking and salad oils, and into protective coatings; the meal mainly goes into high-protein feeds (except in the Orient, where most beans are consumed as food).

for human food or for industrial purposes, and little is fed to animals.

Many poor regions with poor vegetable-protein sources would like to introduce soybeans or vastly increase their output, because they are the best plant source of both ordinary and superior amino acids and because the products are worth more than from similar amounts of other oilseeds. But cultivation is difficult in low-latitude areas because of photoperiodism problems: the seed required fifteen to eighteen hours of sunlight per day to trigger germination in the original center of domestication, while many tropical areas have only twelve to fourteen hours of sunlight per day at most. It takes a long time to develop varieties that will germinate reliably under the changed conditions.

Cottonseed. Since cotton is grown primarily for the fiber, it follows that cottonseed is a by-product, bringing only 15 to 20 per cent of the value of the crop. The acreage yield of seed is only a third to a half that of other oilseeds, so in many countries producing cotton, most of the seed is fed direct to cattle or used as fuel or fertilizer, either because the necessary crushing plant is lacking or transport costs from the ginnery to the crushing plant are prohibitive, making economic oil production impossible or marginal.

The United States share of world cottonseed production has dropped to about one-quarter. Production is becoming more widespread (Eastern Europe, Latin America, the Middle East, the non-Communist Far East, and the Communist Far East each produce roughly half of the U.S. output). The product is only moderately (12 per cent) commercialized in terms of world trade. The increasing movement of oil rather than seed partly reflects the fact that cottonseed is perishable, and partly the tendency for producing countries to foster the rise or expansion of domestic crushing industry.

United States soybean and cottonseed oils face competition in world markets not only from foreign supplies in other countries, but also from other edible oils. If prices are competitive, all the soft oils are substitutable in the manufacture

U.S.D.A. Photo

Cottonseed (this is mechanically delinted) is a by-product of cotton production (bringing in 15 to 20 per cent of the value of the crop). From it is obtained a soft or edible oil, used for making margarine, shortening, and the range of salad and cooking oils.

of margarine, shortening, and the range of salad and cooking oils. Olive and sesame oils are usually too high priced, but groundnut, sunflower, rapeseed, and other soft oils are highly competitive in many of the world markets.

Groundnuts (peanuts). A legume closely related to beans and peas, but having underground pods whose shelled nuts yield 35 to 40 per cent or more oil, groundnuts are widely grown in hot countries with a moderate rainfall, especially in India, China, and West Africa, which together produce over two-thirds of the world supply. The plant itself is often used for fodder, but the nuts themselves provide as much edible oil as cottonseed, and the oil cake is also used as human food and livestock feed. Most of the nuts that enter into commerce are shelled before shipment in order to save shipping space, but the finest grades of oil come from unshelled nuts.

World production of unshelled groundnuts is now over 15 million tons, with an oil content over 2.6 million tons. Like the soybean, some 40 per cent moves in world trade. The Indian supply, the world's largest, is mainly made into vanaspati, a hydrogenated cooking oil. The Chinese use their production, the second largest, for cooking oil. The West African countries provide the largest supplies for world trade. Peanuts usually bring about 5 cents per pound (unshelled), with the oil bringing about 15 cents per pound (bulk) in export ports.

Of tropical South American origin, the groundnut does best in tropical and semitropical climates, although the warm edges of many midlatitude lands grow small amounts. It requires much sunshine, moderate rainfall, and sandy, friable soils. Since its fruits mature underground, harvesting is usually labor-intensive, although in the United States machines are used. Costs of production are about the same as for other unirrigated crops, with profits somewhat higher than alternatives, so the crop is popular. It can utilize poor sandy soils of uplands which will not support traditional cooking oils like sesame and rapeseed.

Sunflower seeds. A native of Middle America that was introduced into Europe in the sixteenth century, sunflower oil is now the main cooking oil in much of Slavic Eastern Europe. The seeds average 30 per cent oil, with the best yield about 45 per cent. The kernels are eaten roasted (like popcorn) in the Balkans and the U.S.S.R., and the stalks and leaves make fine forage and ensilage for livestock. The better quality oils are used for margarine, shortening, and cooking oils, while inferior grades are used in soaps, paints, varnishes, and lubricating oils.

The U.S.S.R. produces two-thirds of the world's annual 7 to 8 million tons of seed, with the Balkans and Turkey producing another fifth. Historically, the Ukraine and Caucasus supplied most Soviet sunflowers, but cultivation has tended to shift to the northeast, first to the middle and lower Volga areas, then to western Siberia and northern Kazakhstan. Argentina produces a tenth of the world's sunflowers, and is the exporter that supplies non-Communist markets.

Olive oil. The Mediterranean Basin produces about 95 per cent of the world's olives, with the remainder from Mediterranean-type areas in North America, Latin America, and elsewhere. The tree is quite sensitive and requires four climatic and edaphic conditions for its successful cultivation: warm temperatures, absence of severe frost, low humidity, and favorable winds. Trees bear commercially at the age of eight years, continuing to be prolific beyond the age of twenty-five years (some of them live and bear for centuries). Olives are sold mainly as cured fruit; only undersized and surplus olives go into the olive presses nowadays.

U.S.D.A. Photo

Groundnuts (peanuts) come from a legume closely related to beans and peas, but having underground pods (shells) containing the nuts. They mainly grow in tropical and semitropical climates, although small amounts grow in the subtropics (like the U.S. South) and are mainly used for cooking oil or are hydrogenated.

U.S.D.A. Photo

Sunflowers supply the main cooking oil in much of Slavic Eastern Europe (the better quality oils are used for edible oils and semisynthetic fat, while the inferior oils are used in non-food products). The seeds are roasted for human consumption, or they are used as high-protein concentrate in poultry or other animal feed. The sunflower is mainly grown under semiarid and subhumid conditions, but does extremely well under irrigation.

The olives situation is rendered very complex by the chronic instability of supplies, and the relative cheapness of substitutes, even at the domestic retail stage. Bumper or exceptionally poor crops occur at least once every five years. Imports of liquid edible oils (other than olive) into olive growing countries continue to be one of the largest but most irregular outlets for these oils in international trade. About 5 per cent of olive oil output is exported to destinations outside the Mediterranean region (another 5 per cent is sometimes traded within the region in years of imbalance).

Since the olive is a tree that can be grown on poor soils and in dry regions, its culture wrests an economically valuable crop from dry, rocky, or steep land, and has in some areas spread into land formerly totally desert. Moreover, the groves throughout the Mediterranean are worked with little mechanization and by large numbers of small growers, and olive culture and processing are labor-intensive activities in areas with large labor resources. There are a number of technical problems of major economic significance that keep productivity low, accentuate the instability of crop yields, and lead to poor quality oil: lack of water, poor cultural practices, losses from pests and diseases, and inefficiency in rural processing industries.

Olives are almost unique as an oil bearing raw material in not being to a great extent treated in modern processing industries. This is one of the important reasons for its high costs of production by comparison with other soft oils.

U.S.D.A. Photo

Fruiting olive branches are shown. The olive tree tolerates dry, rocky, and steep land, but does best under other Mediterranean conditions. Olives are sold mainly as cured fruit, with only undersized and surplus olives going into the presses. The irregular supply and high price have led to much substitution of other edible oils.

Olive milling and marketing are characterized by the large number of small and unmodernized, often primitive, crushing units, and by a relatively large number of marketing stages through which the product passes before concentration in the main consuming centers. Olive oil mills, unlike most other oilseed crushing plants, are specialized and operate normally for only a short period of the year. The cost of crushing olives is fully reflected in oil prices, since the cake has practically no value. The bulk of the oil produced is still consumed as virgin oil, but the large quantity of high-acid oils coming forward has resulted in the development of modern refining industries.[11]

Although the olive supply is still large, it is falling behind the edible oils demand. In the past generation, production growth has averaged less than 1 per cent, only about half the rate of population growth. The gap has been closed partly by mixing more abundant and cheaper substitutes with olive oil, or by manufactured products made from other oils.

Rapeseed. A member of the mustard family, the rape plant is the sixth largest source of edible vegetable oil. Its seeds average about 35 per cent oil content. About 90 per cent of world production (1.4 million tons) is used for edible products.

The crop can be grown as both a summer and a winter crop, according to locality. The Far East accounts for 70 per cent of world production, about a third in the Communist areas. The Yangtze Basin in China and the Ganges Plain in India are the two largest areas of production.

Western Europe and Eastern Europe each account for about a tenth of world output, and Canada is the most important producer in the Americas. In the Western countries, the refined oil is called colza.

Most of the world's output is crushed in premodern mills, and consumed in unrefined form by subsistent producers. In the Far East, rapeseed and mustard seed do not seem to be particularly profitable, only about as gainful as barley, winter pulse, or other secondary crops. But the particular flavors and qualities of rapeseed and mustard seed are highly desired by consumers, and this factor encourages their continued upward trend in acreage and production, although not as rapidly as the groundnut.

---

[11] Olive oil comes in two general types: (1) the sweet variety, golden or pale straw-yellow in color, delicate in flavor—favored in the United States, but not the most common type; (2) darker with more emphatic taste varieties, favored by most Mediterraneans. Through blending, olive oil packers try to achieve a standard product that always has the same taste and color.

The cheapest "olive oil" is mainly deodorized and decolorized cheaper oils of other sources, with just enough olive oil to simulate odor and flavor (in extreme cases, as little as one-quarter olive oil may be in the product).

Sesame. The six edible oilseed sources considered so far account for almost 95 per cent of the world's edible vegetable oils, but there are several other sources. Sesame is the oldest oilseed crop tilled by man, having been used in ancient Egypt and Greece. It is a small seed, high in protein, used for a cooking oil in the Far East, which accounts for over 60 per cent of current world production. In the West, it is used as a flavoring for bakery goods, candy, and in other foods; in shortening, margarine, and salad oils; and in cosmetics.

U.S.D.A. Photo

Sesame (the view shows closed and open capsules, with the tiny seeds) is the oldest oil-seed crop tilled by man. It is mainly used as a cooking oil in the Far East, and its production has been relatively static recently (like olive oil, it costs twice as much as the cheaper soft oils, and substitutes have been gaining). Attempts are being made to breed non-shattering varieties, which can be cheaply produced by mechanized methods.

In the past decade, world production and world trade have been relatively static. Production methods have remained premodern, with the result that sesame oil costs about twice as much as the cheaper soft oils. Sesame grows well in cotton-type climates. The big obstacle to expanding production in many such areas has been the fact that the seeds have had to be carefully hand-picked. This picking has had to be done just before the seed pods reach full maturity. If the harvest were delayed, many of the pods would shatter, and the seeds would be scattered.

The United States produces a small amount of sesame, mainly on irrigated land in the southern portion of the Texas Panhandle, rotated with cotton. With the development of semishattering varieties, the sesame is harvested by machine with a minimum of hand labor. In addition, it is cleaned and processed with machinery recently developed. However, it remains as costly as olive oil, and is mainly used in non-oil uses (although the oil has a pleasant flavor and a high resistance to rancidity, keeping up to twice as long as other vegetable oils). Cleaned seed is used by the bakery trade for specialty bread topping. Sesame flour also is used by the bakery trade for increasing the protein content of regular bread (the seed is half protein), as a cereal food, in baby foods, as filler in meat products.

Corn oil. The corn germ is about half oil, and is the most versatile of the vegetable oils. It is especially used in salad dressings, salad oils, and liquid shortening, after refining. The unrefined oil is also used in a wide variety of non-food products.

Some 85 per cent of the oil is produced in the United States, and has only recently become of more than minor importance. Some 85 per cent of all harvested corn is fed to livestock, and much of the remainder is processed with the germ left in before becoming part of feed mixtures. Little more than 5 per cent is processed into food and non-food products in such a way that the germ is removed. Until recently, the corn germ production was a minor by-product and often included in feed mixtures to get rid of it, with only part being processed for the oil that went into cooking oil. With the recent fear over fats in the bloodstream possibly causing heart attacks, additional germ has been processed, with the oil going into cooking oil or margarine (sometimes lightly hydrogenated).

Safflower oil. Another oilseed that has become more important as a result of cholesterol controversy is safflower. It was domesticated in

India and used there, as in the Middle East and Europe, for food, lamp fuel, medicine, and dye. The dye was made from the dried orange and yellow flowers, but the dark-red dye was not colorfast and eventually faded from popularity. The oil makes an excellent drying agent for paints, keeping white paints from turning yellow and giving a high gloss to enamels and varnish.

Recently, North American production has risen until it equals the Indian production. California-Arizona and the middle and northern Great Plains have increased output spectacularly in the past fifteen years. Safflower, a member of the thistle family, is highly resistant to rain, drought, and hail, and can be cultivated with the same equipment used for wheat and barley. This recent boom has been based upon the discovery that it is a rich source of linoleic acid.[12] The oil is manufactured into margarine, mayonnaise, and salad dressing. Much of the margarine manufacture involves mixing half liquid safflower oil with hardened oil in the finished product.

Miscellaneous oils. There are a number of minor edible oils, mainly important in the countries of production, and produced in annual amounts less than 0.2 million tons (i.e., less than the safflower output). In Western and Eastern Europe and in the Middle East, the *black poppy* is grown for both edible and industrial purposes. *Niger* is a plant indigenous to Ethiopia and other parts of tropical Africa, and also known in India. The best qualities are edible, while inferior grades are used in the soap and paint industries. *Kapok* seed comes from a fiber producing tree that grows in Southeast Asia, and the oil is similar to cottonseed oil. *Tea-seed* oil is used for edible purposes in the Far East and resembles olive oil. Small amounts of all these enter world trade, but none are staples in the worldwide sense.

Palm Oils

The competition that edible vegetable oils meet in the manufacture of margarine, shortening, and similar products—especially in the Western European market—comes from the hard oils (i.e., those that are solid at room temperature) such as the palm oils and marine oils. Such hard oils are blended with the liquid or soft oils to make a product of the desired consistency. Hence, the two groups are complementary up to a point, but because the proportions can be varied when prices encourage such substitution, they are also competitive. For example, if prices of hard oils rise far enough, hydogenated soybean oil could be used in their place.

The peculiarity of coconut and African palm oils is the presence of a high proportion of lauric acid, one of the saturated fatty acids. Lauric acid oils have a well-defined melting point around 74° F. They contribute quick-lathering qualities to soap, and have special uses in biscuit and confectionery manufacturing. The lauric acid is in increasing demand from the chemical industries. Formerly, the palm oils (and whale oils) were largely used for soap-making, but lately they have mainly been shifted to margarine manufacture since U.S. tallow is now available at relatively low prices for soap-making in those countries little touched by the detergents revolution.

Coconut oil. It is the 4 million tons of coconut kernel (copra) and the oil that is expressed from it that make the coconut of importance in world trade. The oil content of copra is high—63 per cent average, as much as 80 per cent from fresh cake—and the oil is used to manufacture food products in Western Europe and non-food products in North America, with the residue being used as cattle cake (when copra is shipped to export markets, rather than oil). Copra exports are about 1.5 million tons, with coconut oil exports about 0.3 million tons. The U.S. imports mainly from the Philippines, continental Western Europe mainly from Indonesia, Britain mainly from Malaysia and Oceania, and India and Pakistan mainly from Ceylon.

The coconut palm thrives best on sandy soils under conditions of intense heat and abundant rainfall, and hence is restricted in the main to coastal areas within 15 degrees of the equator. The palm has spread throughout the tropical islands and mainland littorals, and to Pacific

---
[12] The ratio of polyunsaturates to saturates in safflower oil is 9 to 1; in corn oil, the ratio is 5.3 to 1; in soybean oil, 3.9 to 1; in cottonseed oil, 2 to 1; and in lard, 0.3 to 1.

Ocean islanders is as important as the bananas-plantains are in the West Indies and certain African areas. One man can handle 200 acres of coconuts, if he gets occasional help in the crop periods which come about every two months. The trees bear their crop at 8 years and, when cut down, after a life of perhaps 100 years, the enormous butter-colored cabbage in the tree's heart tastes delicious, like a cross between almonds and lettuce. Owning a grove is like having a cow, a field of flax, a carbonated-water factory, a vineyard, a forest of timber, a haystack for thatch, a compost heap, sacks of feed for cattle and poultry, a field of sugarcane, and a field of groundnuts. A tree of life, providing everything from butter and milk to gin (arrack) to the cottages themselves, sugar, fiber products, palm wine, and oil, it is probably the most useful single tree in the world.

Prices of coconut oil are highly sensitive to shifts in supply and demand. Coconuts take more than a year to mature, and production is largely determined by the amount of rainfall in the year preceding harvest. Disease (especially cadang-cadang) and typhoon damage are contributing factors. Plantation operations have the best methods of cultivation and processing, and often yield 600 to 700 pounds of oil per acre in one year, but the vast majority of coconut acreage (second in extent to coffee among tree crops) is in the hands of smallholders who obtain half or less the plantation yields, and that poorer quality oil often suited better for nonfood industrial uses. The price range in recent years has been 11 to 22 cents per pound of crude oil, usually around the midpoint in average years.

Palm and palm-kernel oils. The oil palm grows wild in West and Central Africa and, until the past generation, this was the only area where the trees were commercially exploited. Plantations were established in Malaya and Sumatra after World War I and in Central America and Africa during and after World War II. But the majority of world production is still from wild oil palms.

The palm bears a fruit that yields two kinds of oil. *Palm* oil, the solid yellow or reddish fat obtained from the flesh of the palm fruit, has many uses, depending on its grade: it can be a food, a coating for iron-steel plates to be tinned, or a lubricating grease. Annual world production is some 1.4 million tons, from perhaps twice that tonnage of fibrous pulp (the oil content can range from 30 to 70 per cent). *Palm-kernel* oil is from the seed of the same fruit; a good bunch of fruit weighs about 30 pounds and full-grown trees yield four to five bunches a year. When crushed, the kernels yield about 45 per cent oil, a whitish edible fat of different composition from palm oil. Similar to coconut oil, palm-kernel oil is used in the same ways: mainly for margarine and shortening, but also for soap-making. Plantation yields some twenty years ago were only 400 pounds per acre annually, on the average; new trees now yield 2,400 to 2,800 pounds per acre annually.

Exports of palm oil are over 40 per cent of total production, coming a third from West Africa, a third from Central Africa, and a third from Southeast Asia. Production and trade are much higher than before World War II, partly because of a new process for refining and deodorizing crude palm oil, which yields a refined oil acceptable for use in margarine manufacture. Of the some 0.4 million tons of palm-kernel oil production, practically all enters world trade: Nigeria supplies almost three-fifths, the rest of West Africa and Central Africa about one-fifth each, and the remainder comes from a wide variety of other African and Southeast Asian countries.

Babassu oil. There are a number of New World wild oil bearing palms: Babassu, Cohune, Licuri, Murumuru, Oiticica, and others. Annual production of nuts is estimated at some 0.3 million tons, with oil contents in the range 60 to 70 per cent. Most of the 0.2 million tons of oil is used domestically, especially in Brazil. Two are moderately involved in world trade: Babassu oil, when refined, is much like coconut oil; Oiticica oil is much like tung oil.

Perhaps a billion babassu palms are found in northern Brazil, especially south and east of the mouth of the Amazon. The gathering process is destructive, and removing the kernels from the hard nuts is an expensive, labor-intensive process. Over 90 per cent of the oil is used within Brazil, mostly in manufacturing food products.

Industrial Oils

Industrial or drying oils are the least unsaturated of the oils that remain liquid under ordinary conditions. Linseed oil, the outstanding drying oil, contains a high proportion of linoleic acid and linolenic acid, both of which absorb oxygen and dry into thin elastic films quickly. Tung, oiticica, and some other oils contain unusual kinds of unsaturated fatty acids that also impart very rapid drying properties. Soybean oil lies between drying and soft oils in its natural properties, but with the rise of modern processing, is mainly used in manufacturing food products, although something under a tenth of its output is still used in paints, varnishes, linoleum, and other non-food products.

Production has remained stable for over a decade, and is now less than 5 per cent of the total oils-fats production. Since over half moves in world trade, they bulk larger in that perspective. Only olive oil is usually more expensive (among the major edible oils), which explains the popularity of the industrial oils in world trade. The high prices also explain the increasing substitution (treated soybean and fish oils, tall oil from the pulp paper industry, and other competitors).

Linseed oil. Historically, flax (linen) and linseed oil were produced from the same plant, with the latter being a product of the fiber production. Recently, the plant has been specialized, so the oil now comes from special varieties that are not processed for fiber. The seed-flax production is now 70 per cent concentrated in the Americas—in the northern Great Plains of North America and in the Argentinian Pampas—where its highly mechanized cultivation is carried on with small-grains equipment. The linseed oil exports are 80 per cent from Argentina and Uruguay, mainly destined for Western European markets.

The linseed oil from Eastern Europe and the non-Communist Far East (mainly India) is still partly used for edible products, the amount depending upon availability and cost of alternative cooking oils. But usually over 90 per cent of the linseed oil (over a million tons, pressed from nearly 4 million tons of seed) is used industrially, mainly in the manufacture of paints, varnishes, linoleum, and printing inks because of its special drying qualities, although small quantities are made into soft soap and certain other products.

Once dominated by linseed oil, the drying oils market now includes dehydrated castor, tung, and soybean oils, tall oils (a by-product of the sulfate pulp and paper industry that is finding many industrial uses in the form of rosin and fatty acids), and synthetic materials like alkyd flat resins. Prices are playing an increasing part in the composition of drying oil markets. Tung and castor oils are usually higher than linseed oil; refined tall oils are usually only about half as costly as linseed oil. Changes in the manufacture of both protective and non-paint products are tending to favor greater use of synthetic raw materials at the expense of drying oils, even when the prices are competitive.

Castor oil. The castor plant grows wild in most tropical and subtropical areas, and is an ideal crop for the small peasant farmer since it is perennial and grows well on refuse heaps and the borders of cultivated fields. Small amounts, about a tenth of the world production of 0.7 million tons of beans, are grown in the cooler regions, where it is usually grown as an annual. Latin America (especially Brazil) supplies about 45 per cent, and the non-Communist Far East (especially India and Thailand) another 33 per cent.

Owing to the presence of a fatty acid peculiar to itself, castor oil stands alone in a separate category. It has many industrial (soaps, paints, varnishes, plastics), military (lubricants), and other (illuminant, fertilizer) uses. Castor oil is chemically stable (it does not corrode metals or damage rubber as do many other oils), has excellent tolerance of sharp temperature changes, has unusual chemical purity in its natural state, and will spread evenly over hot metal and not drain away easily. Since the early 1930's, substantial quantities of castor oil have been used to make a drying oil similar to tung oil, by means of a chemical process called dehydration.

The United States uses some 60,000 tons of castor oil annually, about half the amount moving in world trade, mostly importing from Brazil. It is used as a source of sebacic acid as well as a drying oil in protective coatings. Since the supply and price fluctuate considerably, attempts are being made to increase domestic production (as was done in linseed oil during and after World War II). Beans are grown in California and the Southwest, and mechanical harvesters have been successfully developed, but the price has not dropped to a level where castor oil would be more competitive with linseed oil, as had been hoped. New dwarf varieties of castor bean plants only about 4 feet high have been developed, compared with the usual 8-to-12-foot height of ornamental types, and with the 30-foot-high castor trees common in the tropics. The new varieties are small enough to be harvested efficiently by machinery (the new combine harvester strips the plant mechanically and removes the beans from the hulls in a single operation), and they grow less foliage, and more beans. Castor meal is mostly used for fertilizer now (being unusable for livestock feed), but good prospects exist for its increasing use as an industrial protein (glues and adhesives). But so far, North American production of castor beans has remained less than 5 per cent of world production.

Tung oil. Also called Chinese wood oil, tung comes from a tree indigenous to central and southwest China. Chinese exports (over half of world total) often include oil from the mu tree mixed with tung oil proper. The oil is especially useful as a drying agent in paints and varnishes subject to marine and other chemical attack, but is also used in numerous other industrial products (linoleum, oilcloth, wallboards, insulation).

In the twentieth century, the tung oil tree has diffused to other parts of the world, especially to the Americas, which now produce about one-third of the world production (roughly half in North America, half in Latin America). North America's production, in the Gulf of Mexico coastal plain, is now great enough to supply almost three-quarters of North American consumption. Latin America's production, mainly in the area where Argentina, Paraguay, and Brazil come together, exports to Western Europe. Chinese exports go to Europe and the non-Communist Far East.

Miscellaneous. There are also a number of minor drying oil sources. *Oiticica* oil is much like tung oil, and comes from wild trees found in Northeast Brazil. Traditionally, it was used in Brazil for illuminant and other uses, but U.S. imports are for drying oil purposes. Supplies usually fluctuate greatly from year to year. *Perilla* oil is cultivated mainly in the Far East and produces an oil with properties similar to those of linseed and oiticica. *Hemp* seed is mainly grown in Turkey, the U.S.S.R., and China, the oil being used mainly in paints, varnishes, and certain kinds of soap. As with perilla, hemp oil exports are mainly from northeast China, and (like Chinese tung oil) apparently go to Eastern Europe.

Animal Fats

Visible animal fats (butter, hard, tallow-grease) are the second largest group of oils-fats, amounting to some 35 per cent of the total annual production. Being expensive, over nine-tenths of world production and consumption is in the high-income realm, where animal fats are a majority of all oils-fats production.

The three types of animal fats each contribute about 12 per cent of total world oils-fats production in tonnage terms, but in a value perspective, butter is more than half the total worth.

Butter. In European areas the world over, about 35 per cent of all milk produced goes into butter. However, there is a long-term tendency for the consumption of fresh milk, processed milk, ice cream, and other products to go up while the consumption of butter goes down, especially in a per capita perspective. This is especially true of the United States, where production is only two-thirds as great as before World War II (and a considerable part of that going into government-held stocks). While only a quarter of U.S. milk is manufactured into butter, another 10 per cent is manufactured into ice cream and other solid milk products that are mainly butter fat.

Of the world butter production (4.3 million tons butter fat content), 95 per cent is from high-income countries. Western Europe produces 33 per cent, Eastern Europe 27 per cent, North America 18 per cent, and Oceania 9 per cent. Of the remaining 13 per cent, well over half is from the high-income countries in the other great-regions.

Little more than a tenth of world butter production moves in world trade. Half is exported from Australia and New Zealand to Britain and the other half is mainly intra-European movements. Some 85 per cent of world imports are to one country, Britain.

In non-European areas—especially in South Asia, the Middle East, and tropical Africa—most milk is converted into ghee, pure milk fat. Ghee (clarified butter) is made by melting butter, cooling it, and pouring off the liquid portion. It is used in cooking, is mixed with rice, spread on bread, and consumed in many other ways by about a quarter of mankind. To a Westerner, ghee in its best form resembles rancid butter, but Hindus and Moslems find it delicious and call butter unpalatable. Ghee may be preserved for months without any elaborate cold storage or hermetic sealing, a great asset in hot climates.

Both butter and ghee are becoming more and more displaced by margarine, which already is produced in amounts about two-thirds as large. Margarine (invented in France in 1870), like butter, is an emulsion of fat and water. The United States, the United Kingdom, West Germany, and many other countries have per capita margarine consumption much larger than their butter consumption. In its pure form, ghee has become too expensive for most Indian families (costing from 50 cents up per pound). Ghee production in India is now some 0.7 million tons, of which two-thirds is pure ghee made from cow or water buffalo milk and the rest vanaspati (artificial ghee mainly made by hydrogenating groundnut or other vegetable oil).

Lard. Hog fat is ordinarily variable in quality and in its behavior in baked goods, but now is processed like vegetable oils to a uniform quality, such lard compounds being an American invention. Lard is used almost entirely for food, but also makes an excellent soap fat, but only exceptionally does its price drop low enough to bring it into competition with greases.

About 82 per cent of world lard production occurs in high-income countries. North America and Eastern Europe each produce 36 per cent of the total, and Western Europe 17 per cent. Of the remainder, Latin America contributes about two-thirds.

Slightly under a tenth of world lard production is involved in world trade. The United States contributes nearly three-fifths of world exports, and the United Kingdom receives over three-fifths of world imports. Of the remaining imports, Latin American countries account for over half.

Like butter, lard is fast being displaced by semisynthetic substitutes. Shortening (compounded cooking fat) is now produced in amounts equal to one-third of lard production. Even in the United States, per capita consumption of margarine is considerably larger than that of lard. Cooking oils are produced in amounts even larger than margarine output.

Tallow-grease. *Tallow* may be edible or inedible, depending on the tissues from which it is rendered and the care with which it is produced. *Greases* are inedible fats. North America accounts for 56 per cent of world production, and other high-income countries account for practically all of the remainder.

Nearly 30 per cent of the 4 million tons tallow-grease production is moved in world trade. The United States accounts for three-quarters of the total exports, exporting over half of its production. Japan is the largest single importer, taking some 20 per cent, with all Western Europe importing nearly three-fifths of the total.

Lard and greases are softer in consistency

than tallow (palm oil is intermediate in this respect but is closer to tallow than to lard or grease). Tallow, grease, lard, and palm oil, like the soft oils, contain oleic and linoleic acids, but in a considerably smaller proportion. Conversely, the proportion of saturated fatty acids (mostly stearic and palmitic) is higher than in the soft oils, though smaller than in the lauric acid groups. Inedible tallow and greases are mainly used for soap (palm oil also found its main outlet in soap-making before World War II, but now more goes into food uses than into soap),[13] but increasingly large fractions are going into animal feed (especially high-energy poultry feed) mixtures and into fatty acids supply for the chemical industry.

The use of inedible tallow and fats in poultry and livestock feed is steadily growing in the United States and abroad.[14] The innovation started in the early 1950's when the great growth of the synthetic detergent industry released many fats from soap-making. By the early 1960's, over 15 per cent of all U.S. produced animal fats (over 25 per cent of consumption) were so used, with a majority of poultry feeds and over a quarter of livestock feeds containing fat supplements. Prospects indicate increasing usage (some estimates are that feed markets in the foreseeable future could absorb two to three times as much as at present).

In Western Europe—the world's largest tallow market—detergents caused a sharp decline in imports by the early 1960's. The region's poultry and livestock activities are using more tallow in feed, but not enough to compensate for the declining use of tallow-based soap. In Japan, detergents have captured part of the soap market, but the Japanese economy is expanding so strongly that demand for tallow has increased, not only for soap, but for feed in the country's booming poultry and livestock activities.

Marine Oils

Fish and whale-sperm oils contain an unusually wide variety of fatty acids, including a rather large proportion of unsaturated acids. In their natural form, these oils are used mainly in making oilcloth, special types of paints, various other industrial products, and as low-priced fats for soaps. Most whale oil (which is actually like wax) is not used in its natural form nowadays, but is hydrogenated for use in making margarine (mainly in Europe).

Fish oil. Although little more than 2 per cent of the world's oils-fats supply, fish oils (including liver oil) have doubled in supply since 1950. Before that time, the supply was minor, with the oil and fertilizer being coproducts obtained by processing waste fish and trash fish. Since 1950, the supply of oil has increased phenomenally as a by-product of fish meal produced as a high-protein supplement in mixed feeds for the mass production poultry and livestock activities in the high-income countries.

North America and Western Europe each produce nearly a third of the world supply, but the really spectacular new production is from Latin America (Peru and Chile) and sub-Saharan Africa (Republic of South Africa, Southwest Africa, Angola) which now account for a quar-

---

[13] Tallow and coconut oil account for about 90 per cent of all oils-fats employed in soap-making. Soft vegetable oils are not especially good, because such soap is apt to waste away because it holds little water, but toilet soaps have a considerable proportion of such oils which lather freely and are perfumed. In soap-making, there is a trend away from soap to detergents made from petrochemicals. About two-thirds of U.S. per capita annual consumption of 25 pounds of soaps-detergents is now detergents, and the fraction is still rising. In Western Europe, only a third of the soaps-detergents market is now filled by detergents, but there is little doubt that the tendency is the same as in North America. Probable trends in soaps-detergents include: per capita consumption in the North Atlantic regions will remain relatively constant; synthetic detergents will ultimately take over more of the market for packaged soaps, scouring powders, liquid cleaners, and other cleaning agents; synthetics will continue to move slowly into the toilet bar field; and industrial applications, now about 15 per cent of all detergent sales, will continue to expand in the same approximate relation to household products.

[14] Fat shortens the feeding period for poultry and livestock and increases the growth rate and feed efficiency. Minor assets include cutting down dust and improving appearance and palatability, and permitting materials to be pelletized which otherwise would be difficult to use in feed mixtures. Since 1 pound of fat contains the energy value of approximately 2.5 pounds of corn, sorghum, and other feed grains, the cost of the fat should not exceed two and a half times the cost of feed grain to be strictly competitive.

ter. About three-fifths of world output moves in world trade: the third supplied by Western Europe is mainly intra-European trade, while the 28 per cent each supplied by North America and Latin America is also mainly exported to Western Europe.

Whale-sperm oils. Although modern whaling has some of the most advanced technology, fundamentally it is as fragilely based as the wild gathering of the Brazilian palm oils. Production is little more than 1 per cent of the world's oils-fats production, and the output has stagnated in recent years.

Western Europe accounts for a third of the world output, mainly Norwegian output, but in recent years Japan has been the foremost whaling nation. The U.S.S.R. has rated as third, producing over a fifth of the world total. The overwhelming output has come from the Antarctic, although the North Pacific still supplies an appreciable fraction, especially of sperm oil.

Some 97 per cent of production is from international waters. The remainder is output of shore whalers, whose catch is mainly for supplying meat to manufacturers of animal feeds (especially pet feeds). The pelagic whaling supplies meat for food and feed, but the oil output is the premier product in terms of value.

PROSPECTS

Populations with high average incomes consume more protein, sugar, and fat. The sugar and fat intake tend always to rise together: one can predict reasonably well the average consumption of fat if one knows the country's sugar consumption (this relationship is less accurate for individuals, but still correlates quite well). Many sugar containing foods (cakes, candies, cookies, chocolates, ice cream, puddings) also contain fat, and it is still not known definitively which causes problems.

Postulating increasing population and increasing economic development for decades to come, fats' share of dietaries in most of the world seems likely to increase. In some of the high-income societies, it is possible that fear of side effects might cause a drop-off in per capita consumption, although it is more likely that the composition of oils-fats consumption will be affected somewhat without radically changing the intake.

As with sugar, the rate of increase in consumption of fats tends to be little more than the rate of population increase in high-income societies, and to be several times as large as the rate of population increase in low-income societies that have begun to improve their per capita levels of living.

Fats are still the most expensive of the energy foods, but they are relatively cheaper today than in the past, because of the versatility of modern industrial processing coupled with the flexibility in supply brought into being by modern commercialization. The oils and fats market represents the prime example of commodity competition among the energy foods, primarily because modern processing (especially fractionation and hydrogenation) has greatly increased substitutability among the diverse natural varieties. Food prejudices may slow down the substitution of the cheapest oilseed or animal fat for the expensive, traditional regional source (olive, sesame, butter), but in the long run, economic rationality triumphs with most classes of consumers. In the long run, tropical vegetable oil production (and, to a lesser extent, fish oil) will probably become relatively more important among oils-fats sources, but in the short run, certain mid-latitude (especially North American) vegetable oil and animal fat sources are holding their own competitively. In addition, the increasing use of synthetics for soap- (detergent) and paint-making is increasing the proportion of oils-fats available for food-feed uses. The greater utilization of milk for drinking purposes and non-fat solid output and the increasing preference for lean-meat animals are both resulting in a long-term tendency to reduce the relative supply of animal fat.

Compared with many carbohydrates and proteins, fats are simple chemical substances. They can be made synthetically from simple natural materials, and have already been made on a modest scale for use as human food. Of the three main classes of human food they are most likely to be made synthetically in commercial quantities in the foreseeable future.

SUGGESTED READINGS

ALDERFER, E. B., and MICHL, H. E. *Economics of American Industry.* New York: McGraw-Hill, 1957. Pp. 530–52.

BOLTON, E. R. *Oils, Fats, and Fatty Foods.* Philadelphia: Blakiston, 1950. Pp. 500.

ECKEY, E. W. *Vegetable Fats and Oils.* New York: Reinhold, 1954. Pp. 836.

OXFORD UNIVERSITY PRESS. *Oxford Economic Atlas of the World.* London: Oxford University Press, 1965. Pp. 29, 32–37.

TIMOSHENKO, VLADIMIR P., and SWERLING, BORIS C. *The World's Sugar: Progress and Policy.* Stanford University Press, 1957. Pp. 364.

UNITED STATES BEET SUGAR ASSOCIATION. *The Beet Sugar Story.* Washington, D.C.: The Association, 1959. Pp. 88.

VAN ROYEN, WILLIAM (ed.). *Atlas of the World's Resources.* Vol. I. *The Agricultural Resources of the World.* Englewood Cliffs, N.J.: Prentice-Hall, 1954. Pp. 101–9, 152–70.

ZIMMERMANN, ERICH W. *World Resources and Industries.* New York: Harper & Row, 1951. Pp. 231–87.

8

Livestock and Animal Products

The world population of large animals is as numerous as that of humans. The 3.2 billion humans are in possession of 1.1. billion cattle and water buffalo, 0.5 billion swine, 1.35 billion sheep and goats, 0.2 billion draft animals (e.g., horses, mules, camels, asses, llamas), 7 billion poultry (chickens and broilers, turkeys, ducks, geese, guinea fowl), and over 5 billion miscellaneous animals in the overlapping zone between pets and economic animals (dogs, cats, rabbits, and numerous others). As shown in Table 8–1, the strictly economic animals are equivalent to some 13 billion sheep (or 2 billion cattle) when converted to a rough common denominator. They consume feed with a caloric value roughly three times that of the food directly consumed by human beings. About a third of the feed comes from permanent range, permanent meadow, and fallow land. Another third comes from hay, silage, stubble, and other sources of roughage from cultivated land. The remaining third comes from feed grains, feed tubers, and other concentrated feed that is similar to much human food.

The animal population's distribution is roughly correlated with that of the human population, considering raw numbers. The high-income countries have only a third larger fraction of the animals than of the humans. Even Western Europe has nearly as large a fraction of the world's animals as it has of humans. The other three high-income great-regions have larger shares of animals than of humans, with Oceania's ratio being 7:1. In the low-income countries, some 69 per cent of mankind possesses 63 per cent of the world's animals. The Latin American and sub-Saharan African great-regions have larger fractions of world animals than of world humans; the Middle East and the non-Communist Far East are the opposite; the Communist Far East has 24 per cent of mankind possessing less than 9 per cent of the world's animals, being the only great-region where feed calories are less than food calories.

Animal products contribute 11.5 per cent of mankind's caloric intake, including some 35 per cent of the protein intake (not including fish). Edible products include some 80 million tons of meat, 17 million tons of eggs, and 360 million tons of milk (162 million tons of dewatered milk with equivalent caloric value to meat). The value of these edible animal products amounts to some 37 per cent of the total agricultural production. Some 75 per cent of the tonnage is contributed by the high-income countries, reflecting both their more productive animals and their smaller use of draft animals. Religious and other prejudice is much less important in explaining the relative importance of animal products than is economic status, although prejudice does influence the type of meat preferred.

World trade in edible animal products involves only 5 per cent of world production (by

TABLE 8–1

World: Animal Population and Composition, by Great-Region and Economic-Type of Society, 1962–1964 Average-Annual

(in animal-units based on sheep-equivalents) *

	Million Animal-Units	Cattle-Buffalo	Swine	Sheep-Goats	Poultry	Horses-Mules-Camels	Asses-Llamas
North America	1,256	75.2%	10.2%	2.6%	8.0%	4.0%	–
Western Europe	1,051	63.2	12.7	9.4	3.8	10.5	0.4%
Eastern Europe (including the U.S.S.R.)	1,667	56.6	13.8	11.5	1.7	16.4	–
Oceania	441	47.2	1.4	48.5	0.4	2.5	–
Latin America	2,529	66.4	6.7	7.1	0.8	18.4	0.6
Sub-Saharan Africa	1,264	70.9	0.8	15.8	0.5	11.1	0.9
Middle East (including North Africa)	501	44.7	–	33.3	1.6	17.6	2.8
Non-Communist Far East	2,912	87.9	2.4	5.3	1.4	2.9	0.1
Communist Far East	1,128	50.4	22.0	8.7	3.2	13.6	2.1
World	12,749	68.1	7.8	10.5	2.2	10.8	0.6
High-income countries	4,934	64.7	9.6	11.7	3.4	10.5	0.1
Low-income countries	7,815	70.3	6.7	9.7	1.4	11.0	0.9

	(per cent of 12.75 billion animal-units)	(per cent of 1.1 billion cattle-buffalo)	(per cent of 0.5 billion swine)	(per cent of 1.35 billion sheep-goats)	(per cent of 7.0 billion poultry)	(per cent of 0.1 billion horses-mules-camels)	(per cent of 0.1 billion asses-llamas)
North America	9.9	10.9	12.8	2.5	35.7	3.7	–
Western Europe	8.3	7.6	13.5	7.4	14.3	7.9	5.5
Eastern Europe (including the U.S.S.R.)	13.1	10.9	23.1	14.3	10.0	20.0	0.5
Oceania	3.5	2.4	0.6	16.0	0.7	0.8	–
Latin America	19.8	19.3	16.9	13.5	7.2	33.8	20.0
Sub-Saharan Africa	9.9	10.3	0.9	15.0	2.2	10.1	16.4
Middle East (including North Africa)	3.9	2.6	–	12.5	2.9	6.4	19.2
Non-Communist Far East	22.8	29.5	7.2	11.5	14.2	6.1	5.5
Communist Far East	8.8	6.5	25.0	7.3	12.8	11.2	32.9
World	100.0	100.0	100.0	100.0	100.0	100.0	100.0
High-income countries	38.7	36.7	47.6	43.2	60.7	37.7	6.2
Low-income countries	61.3	63.3	52.4	56.8	39.3	62.3	93.8

SOURCE: Adapted from United Nations and U.S. Department of Agriculture sources.

* To improve comparability, a synthetic animal-unit has been devised, based upon body-weights with sheep used as the index: cattle, buffalo 8 X; swine, asses, llamas 2 X; sheep, goats 1 X; poultry 1/25 X; horses, mules, camels 15 X.

WORLD: ANIMAL POPULATION AND COMPOSITION, BY GREAT-REGION AND ECONOMIC-TYPE OF SOCIETY, 1962-1964 AVERAGE-ANNUAL (Billion Sheep-Equivalent)

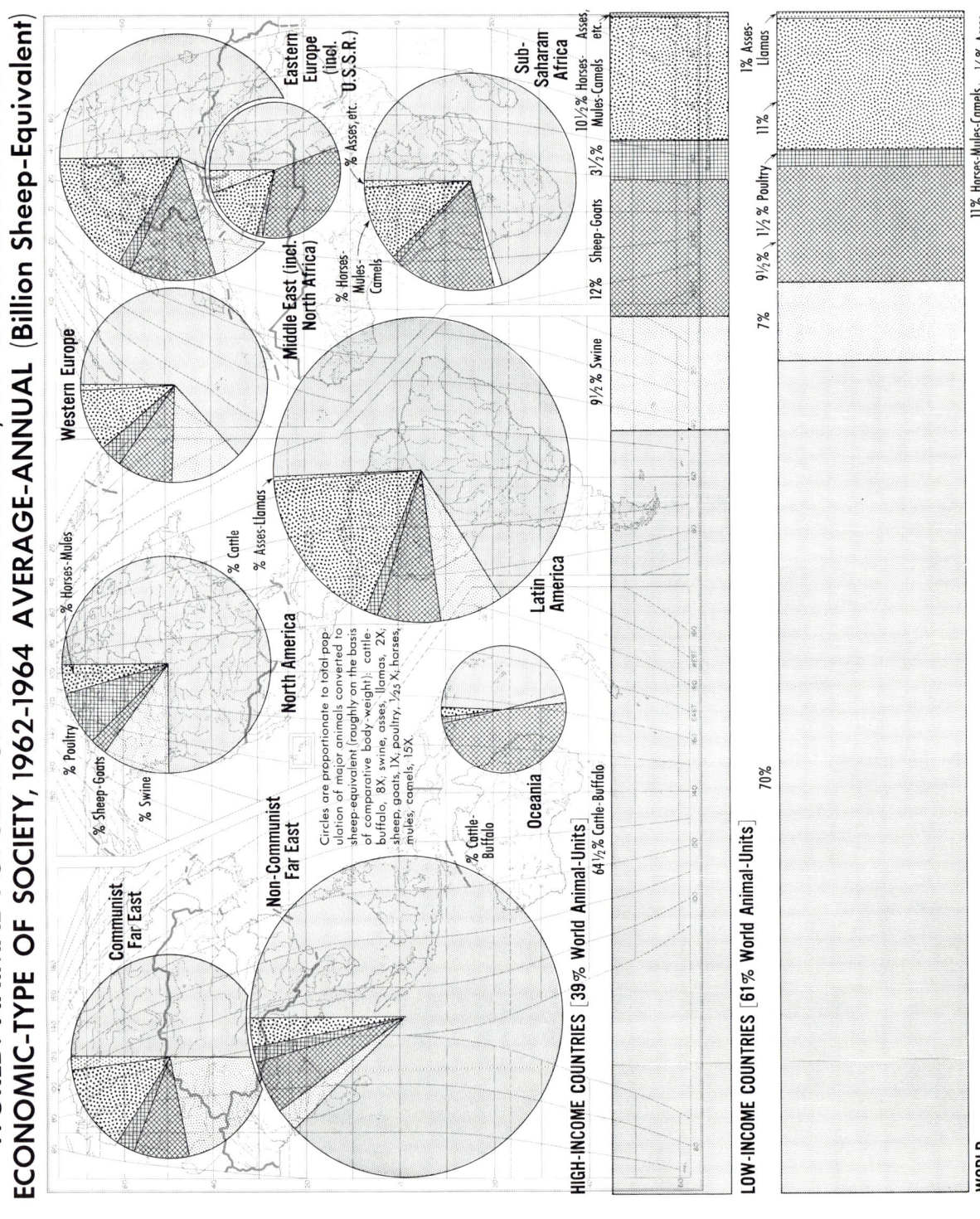

WORLD: GREAT-REGION AND ECONOMIC-TYPE OF SOCIETY SHARES OF WORLD MAJOR ANIMALS, 1962-1964 AVERAGE-ANNUAL
(Total Animal-Units Based on Sheep-Equivalents)

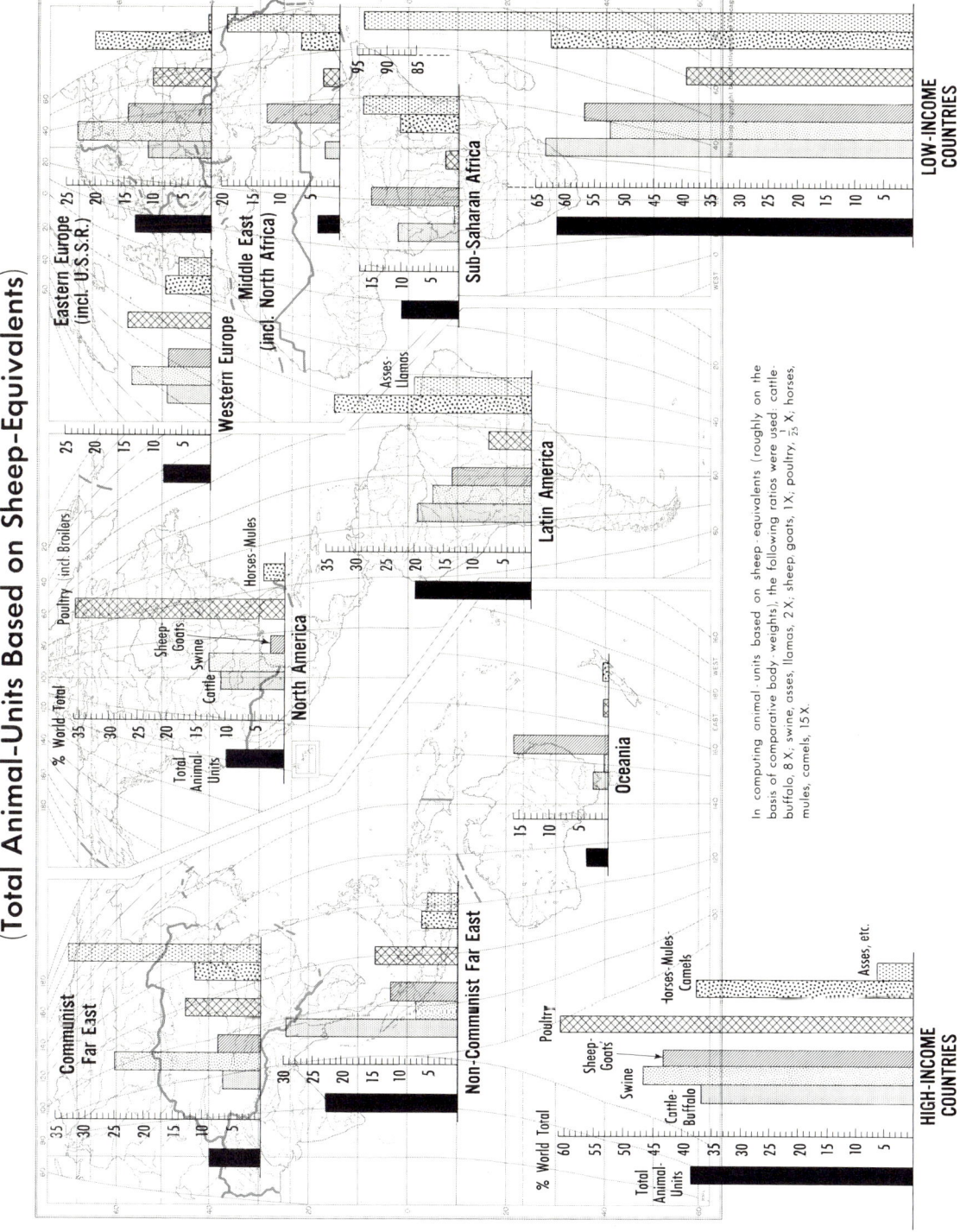

In computing animal-units based on sheep equivalents (roughly on the basis of comparative body-weights), the following ratios were used: cattle-buffalo, 8X; swine, asses, llamas, 2X; sheep, goats, 1X; poultry, $\frac{1}{25}$X; horses, mules, camels, 15X.

TABLE 8–2

World: Production and Composition of Edible Animal Products, by Great-Region and Economic-Type of Society, 1962–1964 Average-Annual

(in millions of metric tons)

	Total Edible Animal Products [1] (million metric tons = 100.0 per cent)	Beef-Veal-Buffalo Meat	Pork Meat	Mutton-Lamb-Goat Meat	Poultry Meat	Eggs	Milk
North America	54.6	16.3%	11.7%	0.7%	8.8%	7.5%	55.0%
Western Europe	68.0	10.0	10.7	1.3	2.4	5.0	70.6
Eastern Europe (including the U.S.S.R.)	57.8	6.9	10.7	2.4	2.3	5.0	72.7
Oceania	8.3	15.7	2.4	13.2	0.3	2.4	66.0
Latin America	19.5	28.7	6.1	2.6	2.6	8.7	51.3
Sub-Saharan Africa	6.6	12.1	4.5	13.7	3.0	6.1	60.6
Middle East (including North Africa)	8.3	12.1	–	6.0	3.6	6.0	72.3
Non-Communist Far East	21.9	2.7	6.9	14.6	6.0	8.2	61.6
Communist Far East	13.0	2.3	45.4	2.3	11.6	15.3	23.1
World	258.0	11.4	11.2	3.6	4.4	6.6	62.8
High-income countries	192.9	12.3	10.3	2.1	4.1	5.9	65.3
Low-income countries	65.1	8.6	14.0	7.8	5.7	8.6	55.3
	(per cent of 258.0 million metric tons)	(per cent of 29.3 million metric tons)	(per cent of 29.0 million metric tons)	(per cent of 9.2 million metric tons)	(per cent of 11.5 million metric tons)	(per cent of 17.0 million metric tons)	(per cent of 162.0 million metric tons)
North America	21.2	30.4	22.1	4.3	41.7	24.1	18.5
Western Europe	26.4	23.2	25.2	9.8	13.9	20.0	29.6
Eastern Europe (including the U.S.S.R.)	22.4	13.8	21.4	15.2	11.3	17.0	25.9
Oceania	3.2	4.4	0.7	12.0	–	1.2	3.4
Latin America	7.6	19.1	4.1	5.4	4.4	10.0	6.2
Sub-Saharan Africa	2.5	2.7	1.0	9.8	1.7	2.3	2.5
Middle East (including North Africa)	3.2	3.4	–	5.4	2.6	3.0	3.6
Non-Communist Far East	8.5	2.0	5.2	34.8	11.3	10.6	8.4
Communist Far East	5.0	1.0	20.3	3.3	13.1	11.8	1.9
World	100.0	100.0	100.0	100.0	100.0	100.0	100.0
High-income countries	74.8	80.9	68.6	44.6	67.8	67.0	77.8
Low-income countries	25.2	19.1	31.4	55.4	32.2	33.0	22.2

SOURCE: Adapted from United Nations and U.S. Department of Agriculture sources.

[1] Red meat (beef-veal-buffalo, pork, mutton-lamb-goat) and white meat (poultry) are expressed in carcass-weight, eggs are expressed in shell-weight, and milk is expressed in meat-equivalent-weight (since milk in fresh form averages only 45 per cent of the caloric value of meat, the 360 million metric tons have been dewatered to 162 million metric tons). Miscellaneous red meat sources (horse meat, rabbit meat, etc.) have been thrown in the mutton-lamb-goat category. Total milk production includes the supplies that are manufactured into butter, cheese, and other concentrated forms, as well as that consumed in fluid form.

tonnage), mainly surpluses from Newer European high-income countries in Oceania and the Americas that are traded to Western European high-income countries, especially Britain. Such trade is some 15 per cent of total agricultural trade (by value).

PATTERNS IN ANIMAL HUSBANDRY

The density of human population, the nature of the feed supply, and the possibilities for other alternate agricultural enterprises have resulted in various methods of handling animals. Some methods (e.g., nomadic herding and ranching) have high visibility but are decreasing in relative importance. Other methods (contract farming) are now less visible but contain the elements of rapid growth in a long view.

Nomadic Herding

In the utilization of grasslands and brushlands, two types of livestock activities are predominant: nomadic herding and commercial ranching. Both represent extensive use of the land (5 to 100 acres needed per animal); both are carried on in regions of sparse population (if one excludes oases in the vicinity); and in both, tending livestock far outranks the conventional production of crops. Herds and flocks in both cases graze chiefly on the natural vegetation, although control and upgrading are becoming more significant in the more advanced ranching areas.

Nomadic herding is restricted primarily to the lands marginal to the Old World deserts, with another belt in the tundra country of Arctic Eurasia. Less than 10 million nomads exist, including many seminomads who work in other activities much of the time. Roughly, one-half of the nomads live in the southwestern Asian areas, one-fourth in Soviet and Far Eastern areas, and one-fourth in north and east African areas.

The number of nomads is decreasing, and only a few countries (Saudi Arabia, Afghanistan, Mongolia) have as large a proportion of nomads in their total population as one-fourth to one-third. Dry farming and irrigation farming are encroaching on the nomadic lands, especially in the Middle East, the U.S.S.R. "New Lands" of Kazakhstan, and northwest China. Superior economic opportunities in agriculture (Fertile Crescent), ranching (U.S.S.R. "Central Asia"

TABLE 8–3

World: Types of Animal Husbandry, 1962–1964 Average-Annual

	Cattle-Buffalo	Swine	Sheep-Goats	Poultry (including broilers)	Horses-Mules-etc.
Subsistence-peasant farms [1]	40%	40%	35%	25%	40%
Nomads [2]	–	–	10	–	15
Ranches [3]	10	–	30	–	10
Commercial farms					
General [4]	35	45	20	30	30
Dairy [5]	10	10	5	5	5
Captive, contract [6]	5	5	–	40	–
Total	100%	100%	100%	100%	100%
Number in billions	1.1	0.5	1.35	7.0	0.2

[1] Subsistence-peasant farms consume 60 per cent or more of their total production.
[2] Nomads are subsistence pastoralists without permanent abode.
[3] Ranches are owned by commercial pastoralists with permanent abode.
[4] General commercial farms have a diversified output of which more than 40 per cent is for sale (the category includes semicommercialized holdings that resemble subsistence-peasant farms in general techniques).
[5] Dairy farms obtain a majority of their income from milk and milk products.
[6] Captive farms are owned by manufacturing concerns; contract farms are vertically integrated specialty farms (i.e., privately owned and organized in conjunction with manufacturing and/or commercial concerns).

WORLD: PRODUCTION AND COMPOSITION OF EDIBLE ANIMAL PRODUCTS, BY GREAT-REGION AND ECONOMIC-TYPE OF SOCIETY, 1962-1964 AVERAGE-ANNUAL
(Million Metric Tons)

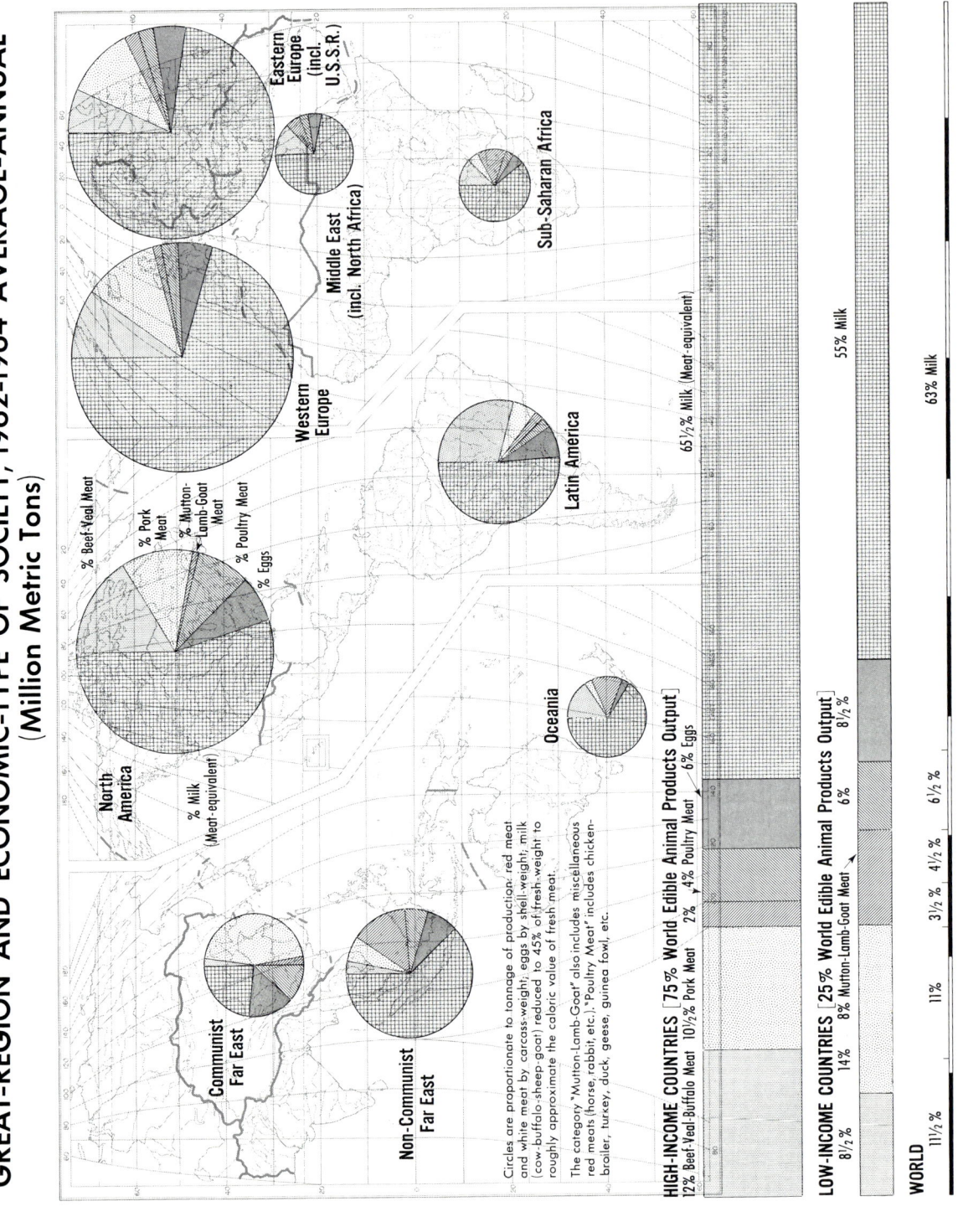

WORLD: GREAT-REGION AND ECONOMIC-TYPE OF SOCIETY SHARES OF WORLD EDIBLE ANIMAL PRODUCTS OUTPUT (Meat, Eggs, Milk), 1962-1964 AVERAGE-ANNUAL

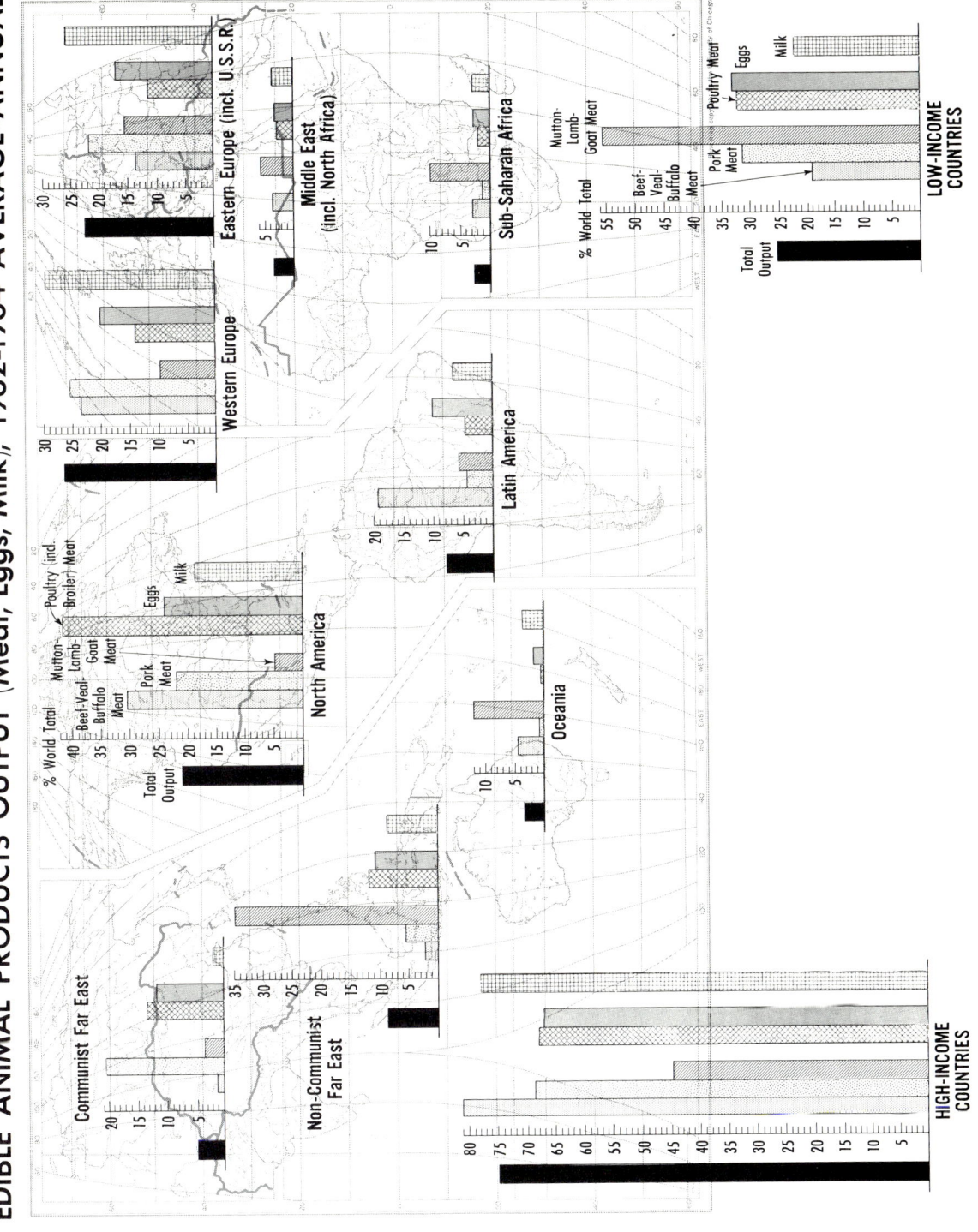

areas), mining (Saharan and Southwest Asian oil areas), and urban activities (nearly everywhere) are attracting many seminomads from going back to nomadism during climatically more favorable years. Deterioration of grazing lands and loss of supplementary sources of income from transport and protection are reducing the support-base of many nomadic areas.

Such nomadic areas have many animals per person but very light densities of both per square mile. Nomads are only ½ per cent of the world population engaged in agriculture and related activities and keep less than 5 per cent of the larger animals, mainly camels, horses, mules, sheep, and goats. Their contribution to the commercial world consists mainly of carpet wool, with most of their meat and milk production being consumed by their own people on a subsistence basis.

Commercial Ranching

Extensive ranching is the predominate animal husbandry of most mid-latitude natural grasslands inhabited by Europeans, where rainfall is too low to permit crop agriculture. The carrying capacity of such grassland is relatively low; on the average, about 10 acres of semiarid-subhumid grassland are needed to support one cow. Holdings must therefore be very large, from 2,000 acres to over 300,000 acres, with size normally increasing with a decrease in precipitation. In many regions, cattle and sheep raised on such range are moved to fattening areas before they are slaughtered.

Though they have been exploited on a large scale for less than a century, the mid-latitude grasslands have all suffered from overgrazing. In many areas, dry farming and irrigation farming have not yet reached their ultimate limits, but vast areas of these rangelands are suitable only for such grazing. To maintain their present role, these ranching areas must impove their stock, secure dependable water supplies, prevent further overgrazing, produce increasing quantities of supplementary feed through irrigation or dry farming, and provide better transport facilities.

Perhaps a tenth of world cattle and nearly one-third of world sheep and goats are kept on ranches by a human population that is only 1 per cent or so of the world's agricultural population. Except possibly in the tropical savannas, the strictly ranching population of the world is unlikely to increase.

The western U.S. grazing lands, which supply three-fourths of U.S. wool output and one-half of the lambs marketed, vary widely in productivity. In the eastern fringes, from 15 to 25 acres of Great Plains range are required to support each large animal. Grazing is possible from three to five months in the northern section and from seven to twelve months in the southern section. Farther west, in the open woodlands of the high plateau and mountain country, the carrying capacity ranges from 25 to 75 acres per large animal, with grazing restricted to two to four months. The carrying capacity of the intermontane basins and plateaus varies from 30 to 100 acres per large animal, with a two- to six-month grazing season. Perhaps two-thirds of western grazing land is not privately owned. Most grazing land has had its original carrying capacity halved by accelerated erosion, infestation with bushes, and other forms of deterioration. When a farm-unit has ten times as much pasturage acreage as that in crops, it is arbitrarily classified as a ranch by the U.S. Census Bureau.

Perhaps the best grazing lands are those in the Humid Pampas of Argentina and Uruguay, where 4 to 7 acres of native grasses will support a full-grown steer, with only 2 acres of alfalfa sufficing for the same task. Such alfalfa pasture, combined with year-round grazing, fattens steers for market a year younger than native grasses. Cost of raising animals is generally only one-third to one-half that in the United States.

The tropical grasslands are either unused (where tsetse infested) or used to support small numbers of low-grade animals. To attain a more prominent position in commercial grazing, producers in the savannas must fence much of the pasture land, provide supplementary feed or range during the dry season, eradicate or control at least some of the worst diseases and pests, improve markedly the type of cattle and quality of their products, and provide better methods of putting commodities into world commercial channels.

Diversified Farming

General or diversified farming is mainly found near the large urbanized centers of industrial countries and exhibits very heavy animal densities per square mile. In such mixed-farming areas, crop surpluses may be sold, but the main cash products are supplied by animals, a mixture of cattle, hogs, sheep, and chickens. Usually, from two-thirds to three-fourths of the farm income in the most prosperous areas of general farming will come from animal products, especially meat.

Such areas maintain about one-third of all world cattle, nearly one-half of all world hogs, nearly one-third of world poultry, and one-fifth of world sheep. Since feed accounts for 50 to 85 per cent of the cost of producing foods of animal origin, the tendency is to produce nearly all forage and feed on the farm to cut costs. In the North Atlantic areas of commercial livestock-crop farming, 1 acre of cropland or rotation pasture will feed one beef animal on the average, producing about 300 pounds of meat annually, containing 50 pounds of protein (plus 250 pounds of other food elements and wastes).

Since diversified farmers handle a variety of crops and animals, they seldom are as efficient as specialized farmers, although they also are less vulnerable to catastrophic changes in technology and economics.

Commercial Dairy Farming

In urban-industrial countries (and around large cities elsewhere), the dairy industry has been ever changing during the past century as it developed both geographically and within itself from a family-cow start to a highly concentrated and specialized industry in some areas.

The world dairy situation of the mid-1960's contrasts strikingly with that of the years since the mid-1950's. Excess stocks have practically vanished, as total demand for dairy products has been rising faster than production (partly because of rapid population increase and growing prosperity in high-income countries, partly because of the success of major exporting countries in widening world markets in the low-income countries).

Intensive dairying has very heavy animal densities per square mile, with numbers often being so large that a large fraction depends on imported feed (Eastern Seaboard area of the United States, Narrow Seas area of Western Europe). The North American Dairy Belt contains one-half of all U.S. milk cows and two-thirds of the Canadian ones. The Western European dairy region has two to three times as many cows per square mile as the densest dairy regions of the United States. In both regions, about one-fifth of all cattle are dairy cows, although many are not found on commercial dairy farms. In the United States, for example, milk is produced on over half of all farms, but commercial production is concentrated in one-third of all farms (Dairy Belt and nodes surrounding southern and western cities). The average distance that milk travels from farm to processing plant is still considerably under 50 miles, so most production is market oriented. The farms farther away tend to supply manufacturing milk for plants producing butter, cheese, condensed milk, and other milk products.

An acre of cropland or rotation pasture will produce 3,000 pounds of milk yearly in the North Atlantic area, containing 120 pounds of protein. The average (but not the poor) cow in milk, although her appetite is increased and she eats considerably more than the dry cow, is a good converter of feed energy and feed protein (a far better converter than beef-cattle or sheep), which for the most part would be hardly edible by man, into highly digestible human food.

Dairying is a labor-intensive type of farming. Feed and labor account for 80 per cent of total production costs. An average cow producing 7,000 pounds of milk per year in the U.S. Dairy Belt eats about 5,000 pounds of feed nutrients (obtained from 2,000 pounds of concentrates and 7,000 pounds of hay equivalent). The direct labor will average about 150 man-hours per cow per year, although some of the more efficient operators cut this by one-half: one man usually handles twelve to fifteen cows in the average herd, with twenty to twenty-five or more being handled by the more efficient operators.

In dairying as in diversified farming, the tendency is for farms to become larger, since economies of scale are still possible. The more efficient farms produce at some 3 cents per pound of milk (the others, 4 to 6 cents).

Contract Farming

Contract farming applies the lessons of vertical integration long practiced by other segments of the economy. By working with feedstores, packers, and other non-farm interests, farmers can develop standard products that have an assured market, while the corporations have an assured source of high-grade raw material.

In the United States, contract farming has had a long, successful history in the vegetable processing industry: about 90 per cent of the vegetables produced for canning and freezing are grown by (or under written contracts with) processors. Contract growing arrangements between farmers and processors are universal in the sugar beet industry.

The advent of contract farming into U.S. animal husbandry has been relatively most significant in poultry production, particularly in broilers (immature chickens). About 95 per cent of the commercial broilers are produced on some type of integrated basis, with turkey production about 60 per cent integrated; a smaller but still substantial (about a third) proportion of egg production is also produced under contract. Some 5 per cent of pig production is now handled by contract. Vertical integration in beef production occurs chiefly in cattle feeding, with perhaps 20 per cent of the fed cattle slaughtered today coming from integrated production programs. Such national averages obscure significant regional concentrations, as indicated herewith.

Broiler contract provisions among integrated production programs vary widely, but basically they provide the producer with credit, reduced risk, and furnish a market outlet. The broiler industry developed as a major enterprise in the South and East, although it is now common in other U.S. regions and has appeared in Britain and other Western European countries, as well as in the U.S.S.R., Israel, Japan, and in many other countries. The most spectacular progress has occurred in the South, which has a labor cost advantage (farm wage rate is 75 cents per hour compared with U.S. average of about $1— including family labor as well as hired labor). Quite often, the feedstore finances the farmer from chick to broiler sale, retaining ownership. The chicks go out to farmers on contract growing arrangements whereby the farmer furnishes the poultry house, the brooders and fuel, the feeding and watering equipment, and the litter and medicines needed, but follows the company's management directions, using its feed on credit. Payment is made to the producer on the basis of weight, feed conversion, and going market price for live broilers (early 1960's price range 14 to 16 cents per pound).

Only a third of total U.S. egg production is under contract. In some cases, the egg company keeps the farmer's henhouse full of producing chickens; pays for the feed, litter, medicines, etc.; and supplies management advice, paying 6 cents for each dozen eggs produced plus a bonus of 1 to 6 cents per dozen depending on a set of incentive performance provisions.[1]

Contract farming in swine raising is new, but both packers and feed companies are rapidly increasing its scope. Under many contracts, the packing company makes a deal with a farmer to buy all his hogs at a set premium (e.g., 2 cents per pound) over the delivery day's average market price. The packer can pay this premium because under the contract the farmer follows expert advice on breeding and feeding and thereby gets leaner pork, which brings higher retail prices and competes better with beef. Sometimes the packer leases pigs. He sends them to the farms on a schedule that will assure a fairly constant supply; damps down market fluctuations by stopping gluts and famines in supply; gives the packer and ultimately the consumer cheaper, better pork; and gives the

---

[1] The average annual price per dozen eggs in 1963 was 34 cents; in early 1965, 32 cents (a drop from 39 cents in the mid-1950's).

farmer a steady income and sometimes the financing he needs to run an efficient farm.

Contract hog raising is growing fastest in the South where farmers are ready to turn to anything that offers a more steady income because of the troubles with the declining hoe agriculture. Since they have less capital, less specialization in hog raising than in the Midwest, and are less self-sufficient in feed, they are more willing to sign contracts with meat packers and feed manufacturers. In the Corn Belt, farmers tend to be more independent, as they are already specialists in the hog business, generally have more capital than hog farmers elsewhere, and raise enough feed to fatten all their pigs with corn to spare. There is no real sign that the center of U.S. pig production is shifting, but this might eventually happen as it has, to some extent, in dairying and beef cattle production.

Integration in cattle feeding has experienced the most rapid expansion in the West, where the rapidly expanding population and the changing preference for fattened beef have been the important factors. Commercial feedlots have experienced the most rapid development where feed production has shown recent expansion (e.g., diversion of wheat and cotton acres in the Southwest to feed grain because of price support programs) and where the feeder cattle were available but there was a lack of cattle feeding know-how (e.g., Southern California).

The commercial cattle feeding industry has developed on the basis of large scale feedlots that feed 1,000 to 30,000 head at a time in a continuous operation. The contract feeding is done mainly for the cattle producers, as they hold ownership of the cattle through the feeding phase. Rates are usually based on the cost of feeds, mixing costs, and a per head daily charge of 1 to 7 cents for handling.

Perspective

In the foreseeable future, diversified farming is likely to remain the most important method of animal husbandry. In cropping regions becoming more commercialized, good farm management will find animals an important avenue to greater prosperity. The animals utilize roughage and bulky grains and tubers that may be produced in large quantities in any system of general farming. Animals are able to convert these products of comparatively low market value into meat that normally will bring a higher price. Also, they make possible the use of pasture on land not suited to crops or that is required as a rotation in the system of good farming. In a system of fairly intensive agriculture, animals and crop production are complementary, since animal rearing makes possible a more equitable distribution of farm labor because the heavier demand for feeding and care comes during the off season (e.g., winter) for crops. As industrialization diffuses, animal husbandry similar to that on the general farms of northwestern Europe and the U.S. Midwest should develop in many other crop agriculture regions.

Of the specialized forms of animal husbandry, nomadic herding and commercial ranching are likely to decrease with substitution of other types of agricultural systems or deterioration of the natural base, while dairying and contract farming are likely to increase where market conditions are especially favorable.

THE WORLD'S LIVESTOCK

For thousands of years, the three great functions performed by useful animals have been to furnish man with transport, clothing, and food.

Transport has declined most. Even in technologically backward countries, the horse as a means of transport has completely vanished from the big cities, and there is no reason to believe that he will ever reconquer his former domain. In the short span between the two world wars, the horse population of the world dropped from 150 million to half that number. The humble cousins of the horse—the mule, the hinny, and the ass—have, thanks to the technological backwardness and poverty of underdeveloped societies in warm regions, been better protected against the hegemony of the machine, and it is quite possible that they may outlast the horse as a means of transport.

The reasons underlying transformations in the second great category of animal breeding—animals bred for textile fibers—are exactly the opposite. The future of these animals is threatened because cheaper and easily manufactured synthetic and semisynthetic substitutes have been found.

The future of animals reared for meat and milk seems secure. The decisive factor will be the direction in which human taste develops. Should there be no drastic changes in income distribution or in popular custom, it is not very likely that the number of livestock raised for meat and milk will keep pace with the increase in human population. More likely, increased efficiency will provide the meat and milk necessary for the increased demand.

Cattle

Cattle are mankind's most important animals. Over one-third of the 1.1 billion cattle-buffalo are primarily engaged in the generation of brute energy for the tasks of plowing, hauling, and milling, mainly in the poor regions of the tropics and the underdeveloped mid-latitudes. The most productive third of the world's cattle are found in the highly developed European lands, because it is in these areas that the chief markets for high-quality meat and milk are found.

Breeds. Two main types of cattle exist. European cattle are found mainly in mid-latitudes, while Zebu or humped cattle are found mainly in the tropics. The former thrive best in areas where the mean monthly temperatures do not exceed 65° F., while the latter thrive best at temperatures above 70° F. In many subtropical and tropical regions, European-Zebu crosses are being developed in an attempt to combine the greater productivity of the European breed with the greater toughness of the Zebu.

Cattle are kept mainly for work, meat, and milk, or for any combination of these purposes. Work cattle are found mainly in the tropics, southern Europe, and Asia. Pure beef cattle are found mainly in the Newer European lands (the United States, Argentina, Uruguay, Australia). Specialized dairy farming takes place mainly near densely populated areas with a

Brahman bull, which is bred with shorthorn cows to get cross-breed calves. In many subtropical, semitropical, and tropical regions, European and Zebu (humped) cattle are being crossed in an attempt to combine the greater productivity of the European beef breeds with the greater toughness of the Zebu.

U.S.D.A. Photo

high level of living and is most important in the U.S. North and in Western Europe. In the United States and parts of the United Kingdom, specialized dairy breeds are important, but in most of Europe, the U.S.S.R., and other dairying areas, the cattle are mainly of dual-purpose milk-beef types.

In general, the size of the cattle in any area depends on habitat and nutritional conditions. In areas of high rainfall where soils are leached of calcium and phosphorus, the native breeds of cattle are usually small, whereas in arid areas they tend to be large in size. In specialized areas of animal husbandry, careful breeding and scientific nutritional practices obscure such natural patterns.

Considered as machines for converting vegetable matter into human food, cattle are not particularly efficient. Even in advanced regions, a dairy cow converts less than 17 per cent of what she eats into food for human consumption; a beef steer no more than 5 per cent. The cattle of poor regions are less efficient.

Cattle, however, convert feedstuffs that are otherwise useless to man, since they feed in part on certain types of cellulose, which they can digest with the help of microorganisms in their enormous stomachs. By using cattle as intermediaries, man can process the vegetation of semiarid and other grasslands that cannot be farmed in any other way. A multiple stomach and a group of microorganisms make possible the extraordinary metabolic feats of the cow: breaking down cellulose, synthesizing B vitamins, and making amino acids and proteins from simple materials (their most important feat).

Grass is the cheapest and most universal of forage crops. Cattle that can readily convert native grasses into beef or milk, while remaining immune from the ravages of insects, most cattle diseases, and high temperatures, may be the answer to those beef-hungry nations that have allowed their native cattle breeds to deteriorate. The Zebu crosses thrive on coarse salt grass, brush off insects and parasites, and are surface sweaters (like horses they do not mind the sun). Shorthorns, Herefords, and other Western European breeds do poorly in the subtropics and tropics: they lose calves, run temperatures, and look for shade when they should be grazing (so they have to be shipped for finishing).

An important possibility of enlarging the supplies of cattle fodder, especially in thickly settled underdeveloped regions, is to make wood and woody substances (pineapple foliage, sugarcane waste, and other coarse materials) available as useful feed. Lignin and cellulose form the main bulk of such plants, with the lignin imprisoning the digestible cellulose. The microbes in a ruminant's stomach make no impression on lignin, although such material can be made more digestible by grinding it to break down the lignin walls of the plant cells. If a cheap chemical or irradiation method for doing this can be found, animal husbandry based on sawdust and urea would be feasible. Corncobs, properly supplemented, are already substituting for corn in the U.S. Corn Belt at only two-thirds the cost.

Another possibility is economic production of green grass chemically (i.e., hydroponically). The grass is grown in culture tanks in which grass seeds are nourished by a chemical solution, with a heat-pump-type air conditioner and fluorescent lights providing the environmental conditions needed to coax the grass up at phenomenal rates (e.g., 6 inches in six days). A $3,000 sixty-tray unit, housed in a 10-by-12-foot building, is equivalent to 5 to 25 acres of pasture and can raise enough grass on a year-round basis for twenty to thirty head of cattle at costs from $10 to $20 per ton. Such units could provide closer control over breeding and milk production and permit dairying in some areas where climate and other conditions heretofore had been considered unfavorable. The few units now in use must be regarded more as pilot plant projects.

Cattle cycles. Historically, the number of cattle in most regions has followed a cyclical pattern with an underlying upward trend; that is, cattle inventory has risen from five to seven years and then declined for anywhere from four to nine years, following which numbers have risen again to a peak higher than the previous one.

When the cattle feeding industry developed in the nineteenth century, feed grain production was specialized geographically, and transportation systems were not highly developed. Also, feeding techniques were simple compared with those used today, and demand for grain-fed beef was concentrated in heavily populated areas (e.g., northeastern United States). Under these conditions, the industry developed rapidly in the Corn Belt and similar regions. The Corn Belt feeder would buy cattle in the fall about the time his corn crop was harvested, feed them through the winter, and market them in the spring. In this type of operation, the cattle feeding enterprise was a complementary part of the total farming operation, since the farm feeder produced his own feed and purchased the cattle to utilize this feed. Furthermore, the enterprise was adapted to the farming operation in such a way that the cattle were purchased when the feed was available and fed during the slack season for farm labor. Thus, the system can be described properly as the complementary owner-feeder system of feeding cattle. Under this system, little capital investment was needed, and each feeder handled a relatively small number of cattle. Also, the industry tended to be specialized geographically and was seasonal in nature. Fat cattle were marketed at the packing centers, which at that time were concentrated along the Missouri and Mississippi Rivers and in the Great Lakes region. Cattle were slaughtered in these packing centers, and the beef was shipped to the eastern markets in refrigerated cars.

Recently, changes in demand and in technology have influenced feeding operations in all areas. Geographical specialization is becoming less important, there is less seasonality, and the resources used are being realigned. Many of these developments result in economies of scale.

The price of beef has been increasing in relation to the price of pork. The price of beef is becoming more and more independent of the price of pork, since consumers now tend to maintain their consumption of beef even though the price of pork declines. Major reasons for the increasing demand for beef coupled with a declining demand for pork in relation to disposable consumer income are: (1) urban consumers eat much more beef per capita than farmers and are becoming a relatively more important part of the total population; (2) occupations of both urban and rural people have become more sedentary, which has caused consumers to demand more lean meats and less fatty foods; (3) with higher incomes, consumers have increased their purchases of beef relative to those of pork; (4) disposable income in the United States has become more equally distributed; and (5) vegetable oils have given increased competition to lard.

Other changes in factors that affect eating habits—age composition, occupational status, location of population, and methods of distribution—also are influencing the livestock feeding industry. Both younger and older people prefer the very tender meats. They consume substantially larger quantities of ground meats. The increased use of home freezers, population shifts from farm to city, and the geographical shifts in population that have been occurring in recent years have caused the demand for beef to increase in relation to that for most other red meats. The trend toward outdoor living has meant more outdoor cooking, which has favored an increased demand for steaks, frankfurters, and hamburgers. In recent years, consumers have been demanding more meat from grain-fed animals. Generally, however, they do not want cuts from animals that have been fed to the heavier weights. Thus, meat producers have been encouraged to emphasize feeding of younger and lighter animals. Furthermore, changing demands, along with the advent of new methods of distribution, have caused an increasing demand for more standardized meat products. Income trends need to be observed carefully because consumers, with the higher incomes enjoyed in recent years, have been more selective in their buying. They are more willing to pay a higher price if they want a particular kind and cut of meat, and they are not as willing to accept substitutes. Thus, it is important that emphasis be placed on producing the kinds and grades of meat that consumers are demanding.

Many of the major economic implications of present trends in the cattle feeding industry arise because of the substitution of one group of inputs for another. This changing composition of inputs has resulted in such changes as the substitution of capital for labor and in the use of antibiotics and synthetic hormones to encourage more efficient utilization of feed and more rapid gains.

The new systems result in the use of substantially fewer hours of man-labor per unit of gain as compared with the complementary owner-feeder system. Thus, relatively less labor and fewer feeders are needed to produce an increasing quantity of fed beef. The labor and management used under the new systems, however, must be of a high caliber because of the complexities involved in such operations. Furthermore, merchants who supply the commodities purchased by feeders need to keep well informed and supplied with the proper inputs that feeders need to produce most efficiently. This is necessary because the new techniques used in feeding are effective if properly used, but costly if used improperly. The changing input requirements significantly influence the kinds and amounts of the different items that suppliers must stock. By being informed on the proper use of the items they sell, suppliers can help promote an efficient feeding industry.

Recent developments also have resulted in a wider geographical distribution of the cattle feeding industry. Cattle feeding in the West has grown much more rapidly in the last generation than it has for the nation as a whole. In recent years, the western states accounted for one-fourth of all cattle on feed and for an even larger proportion of annual marketings of fed cattle. The cattle feeding industry is also growing in the South. Although the Corn Belt continues to be the major cattle feeding area (40 per cent of 9 million total), growth rates have been larger outside the Corn Belt.

The increasing importance of cattle raising in the more humid areas is a part of the over-all adjustment that has been taking place in agriculture since the turn of the century, particularly since the early 1940's. The adoption of mechanical power on farms and ranches has resulted in the release of considerable acreages of land formerly devoted to raising feed grains and forage for horses and mules. Since the horse and mule population was concentrated more heavily in farming areas, proportionately larger amounts of land have become available for alternative uses. The increasing size of farms also has been a factor in the development of cattle raising enterprises in humid areas.

There has been a gradual shift in the cotton producing regions from eastern humid sections to western irrigated areas. This trend has accelerated the development of livestock enterprises in the older sections of the Cotton Belt, while dampening somewhat the expansion of cattle in western sections, especially in those regions where irrigation projects have been developed from rangeland. Acreage controls on crops have intensified the search for alternatives, which often have been feed and forage production.

The carrying capacity of an acre of land in eastern areas is substantially greater than in western regions, as a result of higher rainfall. Since rainfall is less of a limiting factor, intensive pasture management practices (including fertilization, reseeding, overseeding of permanent grasses with winter grazing crops, and other pasture improvements) can be carried out more readily in humid regions. The development of breeds of cattle that are adaptable to the humid areas has been another factor promoting the growth of the humid East's cattle industry.

The feeding period has been shortened with the use of current systems and methods. Part of this reduction in length of feeding period is attributed to the reduction in popularity of highly finished beef and the increased popularity of moderately high finished beef. However, much of the reduction is accounted for by more intensive feeding and by new techniques. Much intensive feeding is done in the areas where commercial feedlots are most important.

In California, where both commercial feedlots and farmlots are important, lots are filled an average of twice each year. In the Corn Belt, the feeding period has been shortened, but it still does not average a complete second turnover during the year.

In recent years, systems for feeding cattle have been influenced substantially by the development of new techniques. Examples include the use of antibiotics, mechanical feed mixers, and semiautomatic dispensers. Proper use of these techniques results in increased efficiency, but their use often necessitates a high capital investment and a high level of managerial ability. Lack of knowledge and rapidly changing technology in the industry have resulted in a wide variation in the systems of feeding.

Transportation changes also have had a profound influence on cattle feeding. Improved highway facilities and truck transportation have had a number of different effects. They have led to decentralization of the packing industry, more ready access to feed supplies, and a more efficient dispensing of feed.

Summary. It is doubtful that a standardized system, such as exists to a large degree in the broiler industry today, will emerge in the cattle feeding industry, largely because cattle utilize a much wider variety of feeds than do broilers, and the demand for beef is much less standardized than for broilers. Frequently, gains can be made most profitably by feeding cattle while they are utilizing otherwise unmarketable roughage. In some instances, this roughage cannot be used economically under a dry-lot system operated on a year-round basis.

Cycles in cattle numbers are likely to remain a part of the general secular growth in the cattle industry, since they will act as regulators to curb excessive output in the short run. However, the basic strength in the demand for meat is likely to prevent the excessive liquidation of cattle herds that has occurred in some past cycles. The increase in cattle numbers in areas less susceptible to prolonged drought may minimize some of the sharper fluctuations in cattle inventories that have resulted when a larger proportion of the cattle population was in western range areas.

Marketings of slaughter cattle have become more stable with the development of new systems. This is advantageous to packers, wholesalers, retailers, and consumers, since supplies of grain-fed beef fluctuate less seasonally now than in the past, and facilities of related businesses can be better utilized.

The more intensive year-round type of operation also enables the cattle feeder to utilize his capital, labor, and management facilities more fully. Thus, the efficient manager can produce beef at a lower cost. The cattle feeding business is highly competitive, and profit margins are frequently narrow. Furthermore, there is substantial risk involved. These factors make capable management and familiarity with modern techniques most essential for successful operation.

Modern merchandising methods and consumer buying habits also have encouraged cattle feeders to make an effort to standardize their product. The demand for high, good, and low choice grades of beef from animals weighing less than 1,100 pounds has increased more rapidly than that for most other kinds.

Dairy Cattle

A remarkable dietary line of division runs north and south through the middle of Asia. Whereas in western and central Asiatic countries milk production has always been the chief purpose of animal husbandry, dairy products have never had much significance in East and Southeast Asia. Milk was also held in low esteem among the aborigines of the Americas on the far side of the Pacific.

Whereas the meat industry has overcome distance and meat has become an international commodity, fluid milk continues to be tied down to a limited market for the most part, since it cannot be carried long distances without drastic transformation. Less than 5 per cent of world milk production crosses national boundaries and

U.S.D.A. Photo

Mature Africander-Angus cows on the range. As with beef crosses, an important method of increasing milk production in warm and hot lands is to cross the high-yielding northwestern European breeds with the tropical breeds who are inured to low-latitude climate, disease, and feed.

that is generally in the form of cheese, evaporated and condensed milk, dry milk, and other processed products. Within countries, dewatered milk is being moved in increasing amounts to seasonally deficit centers, with the equivalent amount of water added at the consuming end before sale in fluid form.

Milk is one of the few raw products not classified in the trade according to quality. In most countries, the price is mainly based on quantity and use rather than quality.

Milk utilization. In urban-industrial societies, the average daily per capita milk consumption is under a pint per day. The Canadians and Scandinavians drink more; the Latins less. United States consumption is about average, so its use will be detailed.

Of total milk consumed, calves get less than 5 per cent; fluid milk and cream accounts for under one-half; butter, one-fourth; and the remainder includes uses as cheese (10 per cent), ice cream (5 per cent), and evaporated, condensed, and dry whole milk (5 per cent). In the past century, annual per capita consumption has declined from 800 to 700 pounds milk-equivalent, mainly because of the lessened demand for butter. Fluid milk consumption per capita has slowly declined, to some 300 pounds yearly. The 60 million tons annually consumed account for approximately 15 per cent of all retail food sales and 25 per cent of the nation's protein diet.

Prospective growth in demand seems limited by growth of population in the main, although in some smaller uses (cheese and ice cream) changing tastes are more important.

Milk production. In general, increased production comes less from increase in number of cows than from increased productivity. In the United States during the past generation, while the country's population increased by over 50 million, the country's cow population increased by only 2 million.

About half of the country's 4 million farmers derive all or part of their income from the dairy cow. Total dairy income runs over $5 billion a year. Each of the 20 plus million cows is worth from $300 to $1,200, with yearly net profit per cow ranging from $120 to $425. The pressure of overhead costs is making for larger herds.

National average annual production per cow is 5,000 pounds milk, 220 pounds butterfat. It takes thirty-three cows, each producing 5,000 pounds of milk a year, to return a labor income of $3,000. It costs $100 to feed such a cow, and the overhead costs excluding labor are about $66. The return on the milk would be $175, leaving a labor income of $9. If the same dairyman has cows with an average of 11,000 pounds of milk production annually, he would need just twenty-two cows to yield the same labor income. For the cow that produces 11,000 pounds of milk, the feed bill would amount to $167 and the overhead to $84. The milk income would be $384, with labor income $134.

Some small dairy farmers are joining cow pools, a boardinghouse arrangement that frees farmers from dairy chores and gives many of them a higher milk profit than when they did their own work. A major factor appealing to small operators in the pool is that they can be upgraded to Grade A (fluid milk) status, which pays nearly double their former Grade B (manufacturing milk) status. The pioneer pool nets 70 cents a cow per day, or $210 on a $300 cow during an average 300 milking days, more than the farmer made before when he did all his own work.

Regional economics in the Dairy Belt are important. Approximately three-fourths of milk produced in the Eastern Seaboard goes to market as fluid milk in contrast with only one-third in the great north-central dairy region. In the East, approximately one-fourth of the concentrate dairy ration is home grown, but the remainder must be purchased from the Midwest. In the north-central dairy land, three-fourths of the ration is raised on the farm and the remainder cheaply purchased nearby, but the low cost of milk production is mainly nullified by the large fraction of manufacturing milk output, which pays poorly.

Although cows are milked daily, the flow of milk is not uniform throughout the year. The flow of milk is always greater in the spring than in the fall, because dairy herds grazing on fresh green grass produce more milk. Irrigated western pastures and some southern ones favor more even growth, and eventually northern areas may use supplementary hydroponic units to achieve the same result.

A commodity likely to play a major role in eliminating animal protein and protective-food deficits in poor countries and regions is dry-milk powder. Such powdered milk is not the only source of such food elements, but is one of the most practical. It is relatively cheap (e.g., 10 to 15 cents per pound of dry skimmed milk compared with 25 to 30 cents per pound of dry whole milk), it stores well without refrigeration even in warm humid areas, it is concentrated and is therefore readily and cheaply transported and distributed, and is acceptable almost everywhere as food whereas many forms of animal protein are not acceptable. It can be used in fluid form by adding water and oil (often of vegetable origin) before consumption.

Improving breeds. Since the main avenue for increasing production is that of raising productivity, the rapid upgrading of herds is extremely important. Most economical and speedy is the increasing use of artificial insemination, now used to breed artificially nearly one-half of U.S. dairy cows (as compared with less than 5 per cent of other cows). The great advantage of the artificial method is that the sire of each calf is definitely known. That makes it possible to determine which calves really inherit a capability of higher milk yields (or of gaining weight rapidly, or of greater efficiency in turning grass or other feed into beef). Another advantage is a drop in diseases spread by bulls.

Artificial insemination is about two-thirds efficient. Theoretically, the semen collected at one time from one bull could be diluted enough to impregnate 700 cows. Under actual operating conditions, it is used for about fifteen, and the remainder discarded after several days. New techniques of preserving semen in freezers promise to make it possible to preserve viable sperms for many months if not years. Cost per commercial injection averages $6 (although some cooperatives and cow pools charge only half that much).

Superior genes can now be spread rapidly and cheaply compared to past periods, and this may mean that animals can be improved as rapidly as plants have in the past.

Swine

The distribution of world pigs is based mainly on feed supply and not on climate, as they are often kept in buildings that protect them from the rigors of northern winters. The pig, one of nature's greatest food factories, long has been the mortgage lifter on many diversified farms. He is a handy receptacle for most feed raised on farms. He can graze in a field or eat harvested grain. He enters life as a part of a large family, and he can be readied for market in a relatively short time. But this adaptability has a built-in hazard. It is easy for a farmer to increase quickly the number of hogs he raises, and when the market becomes alluring, it has been his habit to rush more pigs into the world. This tendency, in turn, has caused hog prices to fluctuate widely, as the farmer and his neighbors get into or out of pork production.

A Chester White and some Hampshire hogs in a fattening pen in Mason County, Illinois. Only about a quarter of the world's hogs are fed good grain, like these. Half are mainly fed non-commercial (off-grade) grain and potatoes, skim milk, and waste products from butter and cheese industries, as in Western Europe. The remainder are raised as scavengers, as in China and other poor countries. Only dairy cattle and broilers are more efficient in converting feedstuffs into foodstuffs than hogs.

U.S.D.A. Photo

Swine raising. About one-half of the nearly ½ billion pig population of the world is used to convert perishable by-products into human food. Small potatoes in Europe, by-products from the butter and cheese-making industries of dairy belts, shriveled grain unsuitable for milling in the great cash-grain regions, and many other similar sources provide feed for the most important system of swine raising.

About one-fourth of the world's pigs are fed on good grain, especially corn. This system is mainly found in North America and the Danubian valley of eastern Europe and has historically been favored when lard as well as pork has been in high demand.

The remaining one-fourth of the world's pigs are raised as scavengers, converting into food certain substances otherwise unfit for human consumption. China and Africa are the main regions using this system, although large cities in the urban-industrial realm often have pig farms that use garbage for feed. This is the oldest system, as the pig is often thought to be a partially self-domesticated scavenger dating from the preagricultural period of human history.

The pig is the most efficient large animal for converting vegetable matter into human food, the commercial types converting about 20 per cent of feed into food. However, the pig must subsist mainly on concentrated carbohydrates and proteins, most of which could be consumed directly by humans. Not only do hogs have high fertility and a rapid rate of growth and provide economical conversion of feed to meat, but the waste in butchering is only 25 per cent compared with an average of 55 per cent in steers and sheep.

Over the long pull, the price of hogs in the U.S. Corn Belt has averaged about twelve times the price of a bushel of corn. The old-fashioned diet, almost entirely corn, takes twice as long (75 pounds at six months) as the new diet (corn supplemented with flax, soybean, bone, antibiotics, vitamins), which results in 240 pounds at six months. Efficient producers add 100 pounds of pork for $15, which includes depreciation on implements used to raise feed and get feed to hogs. A new tendency is having farrowings spread out through the year, rather than concentrating on spring and fall pig crops.

Pork consumption. Of mankind's yearly consumption of 68 million tons of red meat, pork makes up some 43 per cent, a bit less than beef but much more than mutton (6 per cent) or miscellaneous (goat, horse, etc.) sources.

The yearly U.S. consumption of red meat is now about 170 pounds per person (not counting fish and poultry). Pork consumption averages 65 pounds per person annually, worth $4 billion. The South has the highest per capita consumption, reflecting a tendency for recently modernized regions to favor cheaper pork, which satisfies cravings for both more protein and more fat. The U.S.S.R. has reached the same stage in its development, which is the main reason for recent emphasis on feed corn and hogs. Most of continental Europe also consumes relatively more pork than beef. The Middle East and most of South and Southeast Asia differ, in that aversion to pork based on religious prejudice substitutes lamb and mutton.

Sheep

Sheep are kept mainly for meat or for wool, although in southern Europe they may also be milked for cheese production. World numbers are about 1 billion, to which might be added ⅓ billion goats, since sheep and goats are often found together.

The age at which sheep are slaughtered is affected by such factors as (1) current price of wool (if wool prices are high, the year after may see mutton and lamb production drop one-fourth, (2) amount of feed available (in many parts of the world, flocks vary by one-third, depending upon drought conditions), and (3) level of living of the producing countries (in wealthy countries, such as the United States, 90 per cent of sheep slaughtered are under one year old).

Sheep raising. Sheep need more personal care than any other livestock, since they have to be constantly protected from poison weeds and predatory animals and because of their own orneriness. This means considerable human labor of a type that does not mind loneliness. In the United States, where such labor now costs $200 to $250 per month (plus all keep except personal clothing), this high-cost factor is one of the chief reasons why the sheep population is only one-half of what it was at the turn of the century (another reason is the heavy competition from other meats coupled with substitutes for wool yarn).

Southern hemisphere mid-latitude countries (Australia, New Zealand, Republic of South Africa, Argentina, Uruguay) have some 40 per cent of the world' sheep, including a majority of the apparel-wool types. The North American and European sheep are mainly dual-purpose animals, which are valued more for meat (75 per cent) than for wool.

Being ruminants, sheep are raised cheapest when grass can be used. In much of the sheep raising world, the principal summer activity on the home ranch or farm is haymaking for winter use, while the sheep are on the mountain range. Lambs are sold in the autumn, after the sheep come off the mountain. Wool is sheared in the spring (before or after lambing) by professionals. Breeding takes place during late autumn and winter (usually twenty-five ewes to a buck). Average value of all stock sheep is about $25 per head, with good breeders worth $40. The value of good breeding is illustrated in Australia where the weight of the average wool clip has tripled (to over 8 pounds) in this century.

Poultry

Until the present generation, chickens and other fowl have been raised nearly everywhere as scavengers, as they still are in most subsistence areas. Eggs were the main product, and poultry meat a by-product.

Modern broiler raising, characterized by high efficiency in feed consumption, and helped by early determination of sex, has made it possible for poultry farmers to specialize in egg production and leave the poultry meat trade more and more to the broiler producers. These American poultry raising methods have led to steeply falling prices and rising sales, and have been widely copied, first in Western Europe, and recently in Eastern Europe and Japan.

Broiler production. Even in the United States, eggs are worth about $2 billion per year, double what chicken meat is worth. But, thanks to broiler production, the value of meat is coming up fast and may soon equal that of eggs. Per capita consumption of meat from fowl is about 40 pounds annually, one-half of that being broilers.

Broilers are young chickens of either sex marketed for meat after two to three months. United States broiler production is about ten per person yearly, while in Britain (the nearest competitor) it is one. The producer's margin of profit in the United States is only 5 cents per bird, compared with 15 to 30 cents in Britain. In the U.S. broiler industry, sizable investments are involved, and the industry is dependent upon credit extended by the feed manufacturer. Some 60 to 70 per cent of the expense in bringing a broiler to market goes for feed. The credit is of a short-term nature. Individuals commonly handle a flock of 10,000 birds, and some may handle as many as 25,000. The most efficient growers take a day-old chick and in eight to ten weeks turn it into a marketable bird of 3 pounds or more, using about 2.2 pounds of feed for every pound of live broiler (in 1930, it was 5 pounds as in the U.S.S.R. today).

Commercial egg production. United States egg production is the most efficient in the world. Today's hens lay twice as many eggs per bushel of feed as their grandmothers did, and their peak laying period has been prolonged. If a hen fails to lay at least fourteen eggs every twenty-eight days, she is sold for meat.

Eggs have gone down in price because of expansion of commercial production in the Midwest and Southeast, improved methods of breeding, the widespread use of drugs to control flock diseases, and some improper accounting. The big egg factories in the Southeast can turn out eggs for 22 cents per dozen, including production costs, interest, and depreciation on equipment. Midwest operators produce eggs for 18

U.S.D.A. Photo

A Madison, Georgia, woman working in her broiler house. She raises about 14,000 broilers every ten weeks, or four to five times a year. The raising of immature chickens for meat is a recent development and constitutes the most rapidly expanding branch of animal husbandry (more than 5 per cent yearly). It is an excellent example of vertical integration in agriculture, the farmers being associated with either feed merchants or meat-packers in a contractual relationship.

to 20 cents per dozen, since farmers there use cheaper corn and cheaper oats mixed with food concentrates than the Southeast operators, but their shipping costs are a bit more to Eastern Seaboard markets.

The Packing Industry

There has been a general tendency for the major meat packing companies to decentralize and for rapid growth in the number of smaller packers. In the United States, growth went from 1,400 plants in 1939 to double that number by 1963. The economy of the short truck haul to the decentralized slaughtering plant is one reason for the growth of the U.S. industry outside Chicago (much of the new capacity is still in the Midwest). Increasingly, both livestock and meat are shipped in larger amounts toward the Southwest and Far West from the central and northern Great Plains region. The high cost of modernizing old and often obsolete facilities in Chicago is another reason, many of them being too big for modern marketing conditions. This overcapacity is the product of the time when seasonal changes in livestock supplies were far greater than now.

The meat business is traditionally slow to change. For over a generation, trade leaders have talked about handling and distribution costs that cut profit margins without doing much to change their traditional ways of doing business. Recently, however, there have been signs of possible change. One problem that has long bothered the food industry—how to preserve meat at normal temperatures without changing its flavor—is now receiving serious attention. Meat tenderness is to a great extent dependent upon the ability of proteins to hold water. If the water in meat is lost during some stage of treatment or preparation, the meat will lose its succulence and palatability. One way is to freeze-dry, which removes water from frozen meat by sublimation under a vacuum. Another way is to wax meat so that frozen meat will keep from four to six weeks under normal refrigeration without losing any of its flavor or quality (in a freezer, indefinitely). Radiation to kill off bacteria is being experimented with and may soon allow fresh shipment.

Most meat reaches the consumer shortly after slaughter, except for several pork products that are subjected to a curing process that prolongs the marketing period. The quantities of meat products stored in cool or cold storage represent

Airview of a Swift full-line meat packing plant at Rochelle, Illinois. It illustrates the trend toward one-story facilities, with maximum use of conveyors and elimination of the moving of product in elevators and hoists, as in the older multistory buildings (where the livestock was taken or driven to the top story, and the different cuts moved by gravity through various processing steps). Both rail and truck transport are used for moving the raw material and the finished products.

Courtesy of Swift & Co.

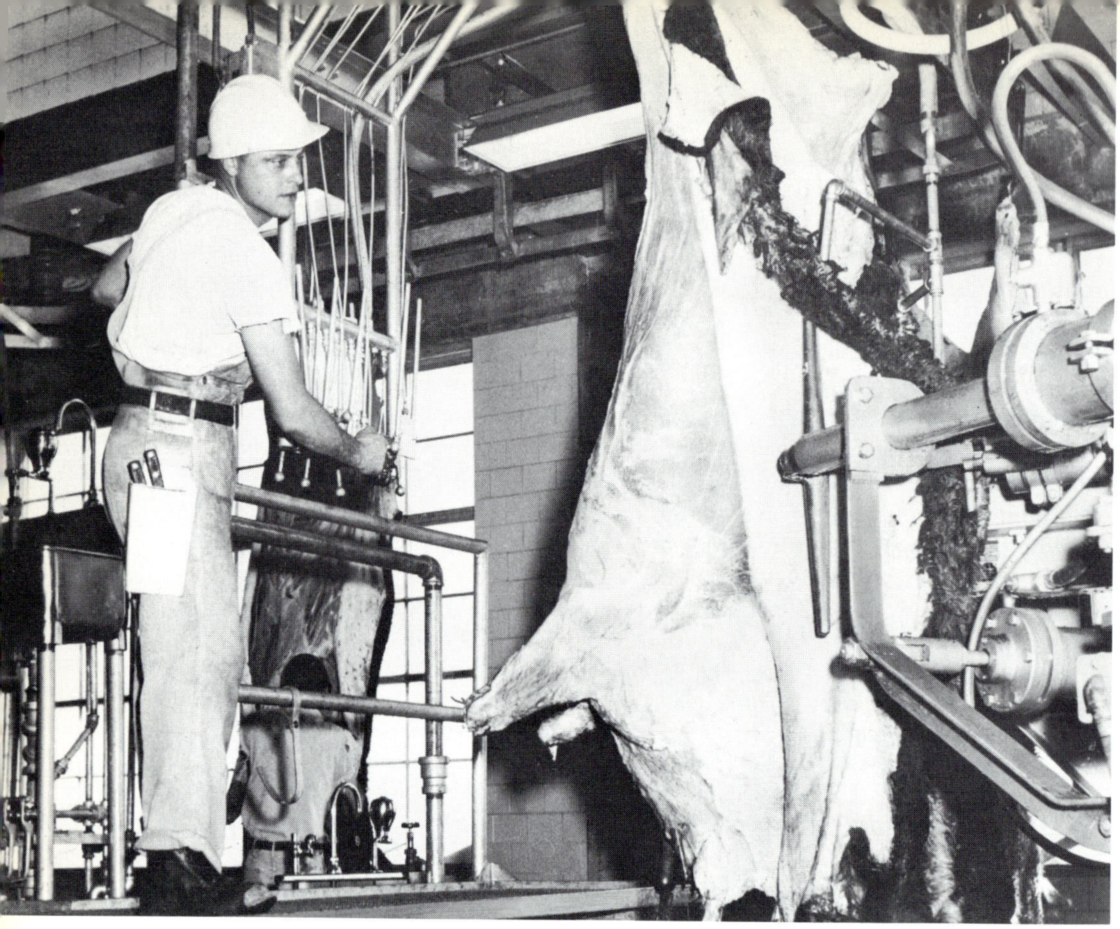

Courtesy of Swift & Co.

A typical hide-removing operation on a beef floor of the Rochelle, Illinois, plant.

Courtesy of Swift & Co.

Packages of sliced bacon are loaded on pallets in the assembly cooler of the Rochelle, Illinois, plant. The system has "tilted" conveyors, so the product moves on a first-in, first-out basis, one of the in-plant transport innovations characterizing the newer meat packing plants.

only ten to thirty days' supply. Brand-type meats (sausages, frankfurters, sandwich meats) are increasing in importance at the fastest rate.

Only about 5 per cent of all meat enters world trade and is supplied by a few countries (e.g., New Zealand and Australia, mutton and veal; Argentina, beef; Denmark, bacon and ham). Usually three-fourths of all meat in international trade moves to Britain. Technically and economically, such trade might be expanded, but it is restricted through quarantines and similar measures.

PERSPECTIVE

Perhaps the most important change in the food habits of people since the beginnings of agriculture has been the decreasing proportion of animal products in the average human diet. Animal products undoubtedly made up a substantial part of the diet of our preagricultural ancestors who lived by hunting, fishing, and gathering. The fraction of mankind that regularly consumes animal products to the extent of 20 per cent or more of its dietary is a definite minority of one-fourth or less.

To upgrade the world's average diet to reach present Western European standards would require a 20 to 30 per cent increase in per capita calorie intake, and a 40 to 50 per cent increase in total protein supply, a gigantic but not impossible feat. However, to meet the protein deficit in its qualitative as well as quantitative aspects would require an increase in animal proteins (milk, meat, eggs) of the order of 200 to 300 per cent, a task beyond present comprehension. It would seem almost inevitable that ultimate solution must involve unconventional methods (e.g., yeast and algae used to convert wastes into food and feed, microbial fermentation of petroleum, fish or plankton flours, etc.).

In the long run, it may well be that mankind will enrich his dietary with an increasing variety of synthetically produced materials and devote agriculture to the business of supplying the bulk of energy foods. However, while it is already possible to supplement diets with synthetically produced amino acids, the economics are highly unfavorable. To produce synthetically a year's supply of the three amino acids most commonly deficient in cereal diets (methionine, lysine, tryptophane) would cost about $40 per person, so it is hardly feasible for most of the world's population to supplement their diets with them.

In the foreseeable future, diets are more likely to be upgraded protein-wise by a diffusion of pulses (peas, beans, and other high-protein vegetables) and increased supplies of animal products and fish. Many land-poor countries are likely to obtain more superior proteins by the Japanese method of exploiting oceanic fisheries. In most of Latin America and Africa, conventional livestock raising will be relatively more important, as such lands are still rich in rangeland. Animal husbandry is likely to turn increasingly to new forage sources: semiprocessed agricultural waste and wood; plankton from the oceans and fish meal; and upgraded range through trace elements supplementation, pest control, and diffusion of superior grasses and shrubs.

SUGGESTED READINGS

ALDERFER, E. B., and MICHL, H. E. *Economics of American Industry.* New York: McGraw-Hill, 1957. Pp. 553–67.

CARLSON, ALBERT S. (ed.). *Economic Geography of Industrial Materials.* New York: Reinhold, 1956. Pp. 421–35.

LEWINSOHN, RICHARD. *Animals, Men and Myths.* New York: Harper & Row, 1954. Pp. 422.

LIPSON, E. *A Short History of Wool and Its Manufacture.* Harvard University Press, 1953. Pp. 205.

OXFORD UNIVERSITY PRESS. *Oxford Economic Atlas of the World.* London: Oxford University Press, 1965. Pp. 38–45.

UNITED STATES DEPARTMENT OF AGRICULTURE. *Grass.* (*Yearbooks of Agriculture.*) United States Department of Agriculture, 1948. Pp. 892.

VAN ROYEN, WILLIAM (ed.). *Atlas of the World's Resources.* Vol. I. *The Agricultural Resources of the World.* Englewood Cliffs, N.J.: Prentice-Hall, 1954. Pp. 197–256.

WILSON, CHARLES M. *Grass and People.* University of Florida Press, 1961. Pp. 233.

ZEUNER, FREDERICK E. *A History of Domesticated Animals.* London: Hutchinson, 1963. Pp. 560.

ZIMMERMANN, ERICH W. *World Resources and Industries.* New York: Harper & Row, 1951. Pp. 288–313.

9

Fibers and Textiles

Increasingly, industry prefers semisynthetic and true synthetic materials over crude natural materials.[1] One reason is cheapness, because of large-scale production, use of cheap crude materials, price stability, dynamic research, and other characteristics of twentieth-century chemical industries. The price of established synthetics (e.g., rayon) is usually less than that of traditional natural materials still produced by premodern methods. (e.g., cotton). Another reason for preference are the superior characteristics not duplicated in natural materials. Synthetics have all of the advantages of man-controlled over natural production: controlled output adjustable to demand, ability to produce to specifications, uniformity of quality, and constant improvements.

It is not inevitable that synthetics substitute entirely for their natural competitors. Many of the latter's problems are due to timing difficulties, to the lag in modernizing methods of production and related early processing. Natural materials are fighting back against the competition of the synthetics on two fronts. One counterattack is by mechanized and chemicalized production methods to lower costs of production. Usually, the natural material has lower costs of production if it is produced by modern,

[1] Some forecasters see a long-term substitution of materials, first those of vegetable origin substituting for those of animal origin, and eventually those of mineral origin becoming pre-eminent, as illustrated below:

"LAW OF DEVITALIZATION" (*after Lewinsohn*)

	Sweetening	Oils-Fats	Fibers	Containers	Light-Heat	Fertilizers	Transport
Animal	Honey Milk-sugar	Butter Lard Bacon	Silk Wool	Hides Sausage skins	Wax Tallow	Dung Guano	Pack animals
Vegetable	Cane and beet sugar	Oilseeds Margarine	Cotton Rayon-acetate	Wood Rubber	Wood Agricultural-waste	Hops Green manure	Carts Wooden boats
Mineral	Saccharin, etc.	Butter substitute (from coal) Lubricating oil	Nylon Orlon Dacron	Metals Plastics	Coal Petroleum Natural gas	Chemical fertilizers (NH_3, P_2O_5, K_2O)	Mechanical vehicles

TABLE 9-1

World: Fibers Production and Composition, by Great-Region and Economic-Type of Society, 1962–1964 Average-Annual
(in thousands of metric tons)

	Total Fibers (thousand metric tons = 100.0 per cent)	Cotton	Flax-Hemp [1]	Jute-Kenaf [2]	Hard Fibers [3]	Wool [4]	Rayon-Acetate	True Synthetics [5]
North America	4,465	74.7%	0.1%	—	—	1.7%	12.8%	10.7%
Western Europe	1,912	10.2	7.0	—	—	5.4	56.5	20.9
Eastern Europe (including the U.S.S.R.)	3,307	51.3	22.1	—	—	7.9	16.9	1.8
Oceania	630	0.6	—	—	—	97.3	1.6	0.5
Latin America	2,294	66.5	—	2.8%	16.2%	9.3	4.8	0.4
Sub-Saharan Africa	948	43.6	—	3.2	44.0	9.2	—	—
Middle East (including North Africa)	1,090	90.5	1.3	0.5	—	5.8	1.8	0.1
Non-Communist Far East	5,282	30.0	2.4	53.0	2.5	1.2	10.1	0.8
Communist Far East	1,596	68.2	3.3	25.1	—	2.8	0.6	—
World	21,524	50.3	4.9	15.3	4.3	7.1	13.5	4.6
High-income countries	10,819	47.7	7.2	—	0.1	11.7	24.2	9.1
Low-income countries	10,705	52.9	2.7	30.8	8.5	2.4	2.6	0.1
	(per cent of 21,524 thousand metric tons)	(per cent of 10,826 thousand metric tons)	(per cent of 1,060 thousand metric tons)	(per cent of 3,300 thousand metric tons)	(per cent of 923 thousand metric tons)	(per cent of 1,526 thousand metric tons)	(per cent of 2,895 thousand metric tons)	(per cent of 994 thousand metric tons)
	100.0	100.0	100.0	100.0	100.0	100.0	100.0	100.0
North America	20.7	30.8	0.6	—	—	5.0	19.7	47.8
Western Europe	8.9	1.8	12.5	—	—	6.8	37.3	40.0
Eastern Europe (including the U.S.S.R.)	15.4	15.6	68.9	—	—	17.2	19.4	6.1
Oceania	2.9	—	—	—	—	40.2	0.3	0.3
Latin America	10.7	14.1	—	2.0	40.3	14.0	3.8	1.1
Sub-Saharan Africa	4.4	3.8	—	0.9	45.2	5.8	—	—
Middle East (including North Africa)	5.1	9.1	1.3	0.2	—	4.1	0.7	0.1
Non-Communist Far East	24.5	14.7	11.7	84.8	14.5	4.0	18.5	4.6
Communist Far East	7.4	10.1	5.0	12.1	—	2.9	0.3	—
World	100.0	100.0	100.0	100.0	100.0	100.0	100.0	100.0
High-income countries	50.3	47.7	72.9	—	1.1	83.0	90.5	99.0
Low-income countries	49.7	52.3	27.1	100.0	98.9	17.0	9.5	1.0

SOURCE: Adapted from United Nations and U.S. Department of Agriculture data.
[1] "Flax-Hemp" includes ramie.
[2] "Jute-Kenaf" includes mesta.
[3] "Hard Fibers" includes sisal, henequen, abaca, and other cordage fibers.
[4] "Wool" (clean basis) includes other animal fibers (hair, silk).
[5] "True Synthetics" includes all non-cellulosic fibers (hydrocarbon-base, protein-base, glass- and asbestos-base).

WORLD: FIBERS PRODUCTION AND COMPOSITION, BY GREAT-REGION AND ECONOMIC-TYPE OF SOCIETY, 1962-1964 AVERAGE-ANNUAL (Thousand Metric Tons)

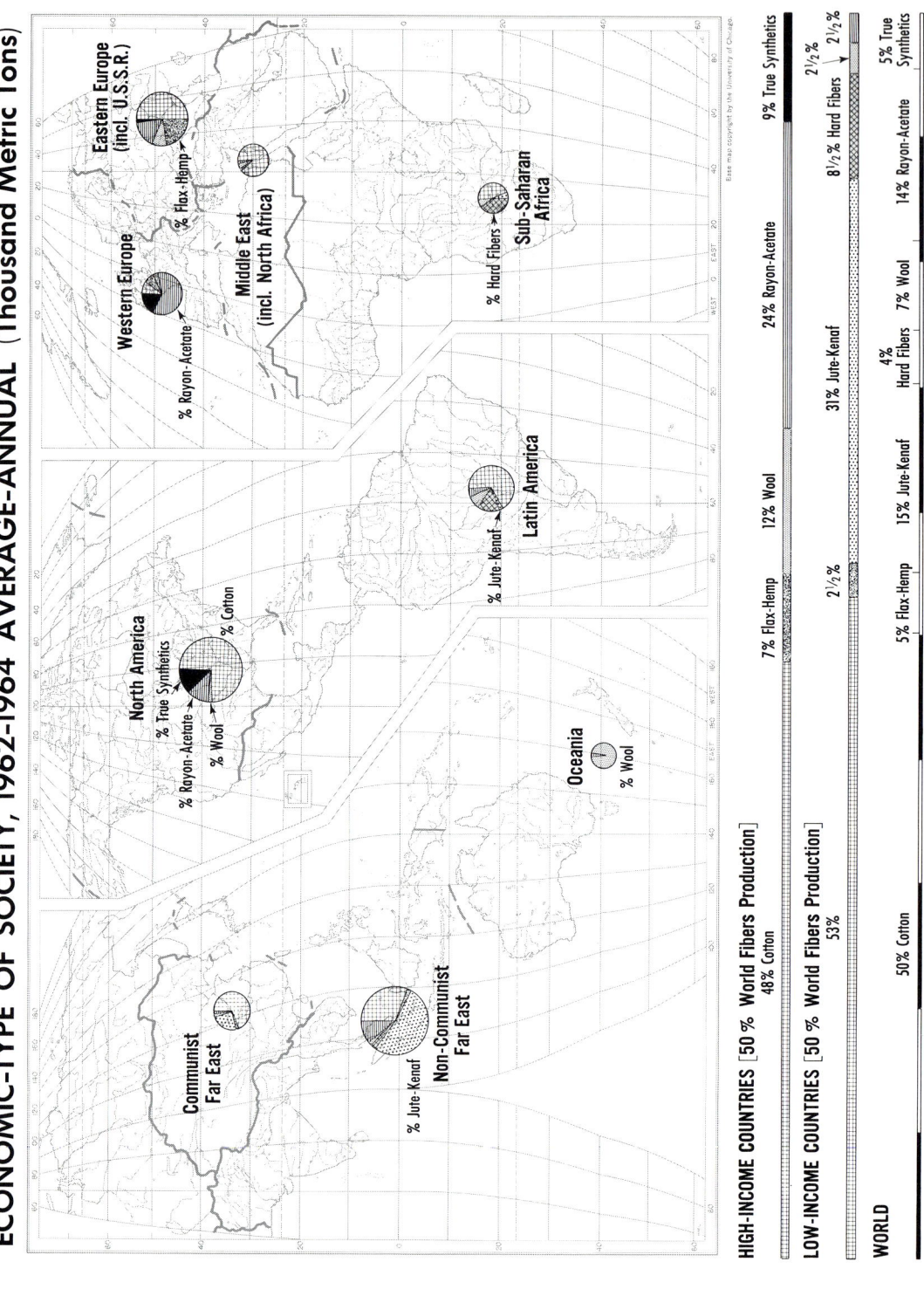

WORLD: GREAT-REGION AND ECONOMIC-TYPE OF SOCIETY SHARES OF WORLD FIBERS PRODUCTION (Vegetable, Animal, Synthetic), 1962-1964 AVERAGE-ANNUAL

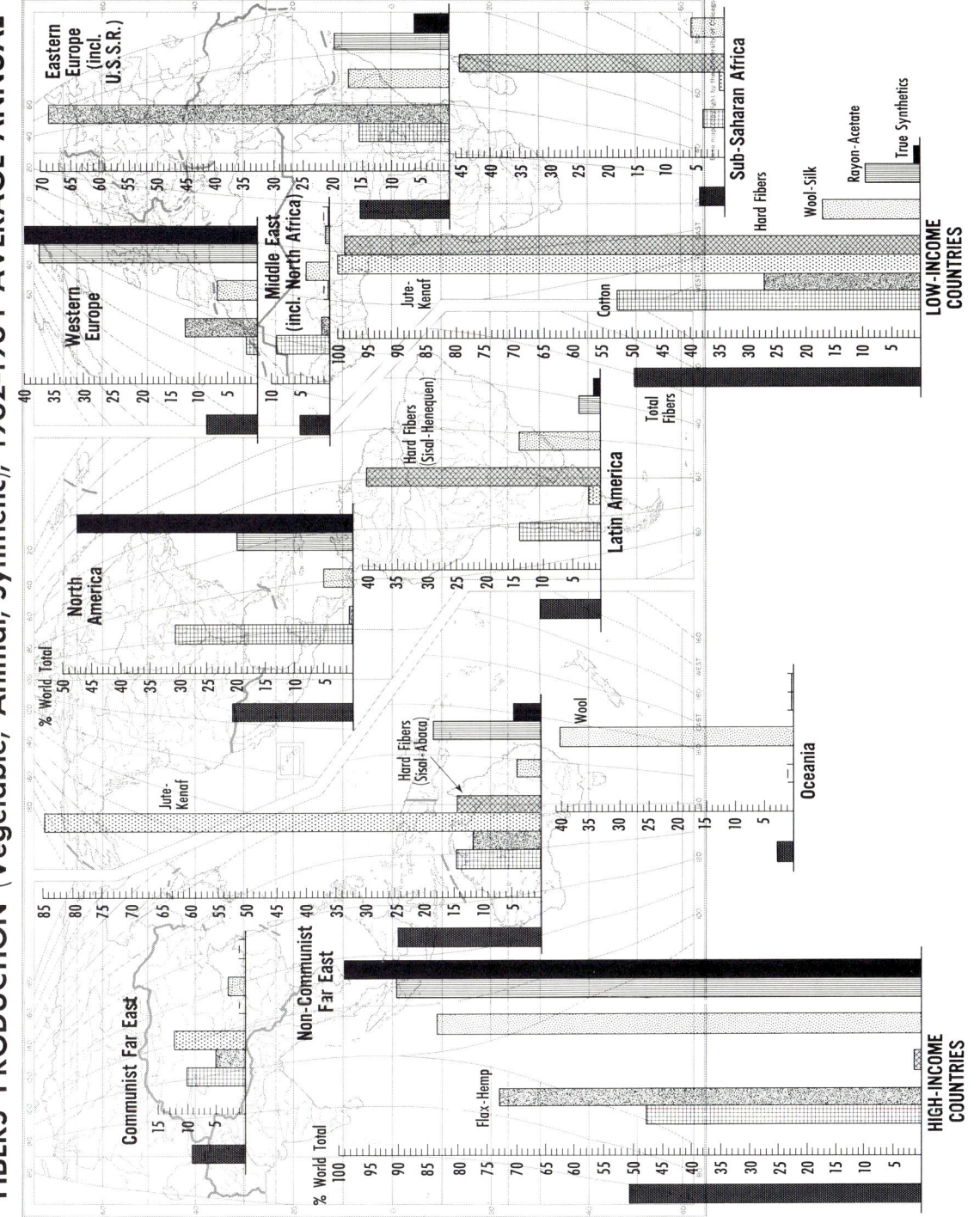

large-scale, heavily capitalized, dynamically organized units. Another counterattack is by chemicalized processing of crude materials into semifinished materials that duplicate the special characteristics of the factory-made synthetics (e.g., use of acrylonitrile on cotton, silicones on wool, etc., to add new characteristics to natural ones; use of artificial seasoning and fireproofing chemicals on wood).

Fibers offer good examples to illustrate the above frame of reference. About a fifth of world fiber consumption now consists of man-made fibers, and that proportion is still increasing, mainly at the expense of the minor fibers. Cotton and wool are still maintaining their relative shares better than silk, linen, hemp, and jute, although they are under increasing pressure. By weight, about 80 per cent of total fiber consumption is for apparel and household purposes (by value, 85 per cent), and the remainder for industrial purposes. Bulk handling and the increasing use of non-textile containers (e.g., paper) is decreasing the share of fibers used by industry. Synthetics have affected apparel textiles more by use in blends than by complete substitution.

The most useful economic classification of fibers is one organized about relative importance of factors of production. All vegetable fibers and silk are best considered as labor fibers, since they have traditionally required much cheap labor for economic production. Cotton is now under heavy pressure from synthetics and offers the best case study of counterattack against synthetic substitutes through cheapening output.

Wools of all kinds are best considered as land fibers, as traditionally cheap pasture has been the main requirement for economic production. Upgrading of sheep and pasture land and new finishing to wool cloth represent the main efforts in maintaining wool's position in the warm apparel market.

The semisynthetic rayon fibers and the true synthetic fibers are best considered as capital and organization fibers. They are the fibers now on the offensive and offer excellent examples to show present advantages over natural materials.

NATURAL FIBERS

Natural fibers are produced from a large variety of different vegetable and animal origins, and still constitute some 82 per cent of total fiber production and some 77 per cent of the total value.

	Tons	Value
Vegetable fibers	74.8%	53.7%
Cotton	50.3	40.5
Flax-hemp	4.9	4.0
Jute-kenaf	15.3	8.6
Hard fibers	4.3	0.6
Animal fibers	7.1	22.8
Wool-hair	7.0	19.4
Silk	0.1	3.4
Man-made fibers	18.1	23.4
Rayon-acetate	13.5	10.8
True synthetics	4.6	12.6

1962–1964 average-annual: 21.5 million tons, $17.5 billion gross value.

Most vegetable fibers are produced between latitudes 35° N. and 25° S. This is true of all cotton culture except some in the U.S.S.R., northern China, and northern Argentina. It applies to jute and the hard fibers, which are grown only in tropical areas. The exceptions are flax and hemp, which are mainly European crops, but which are swiftly declining in competition with tropical natural fibers and with synthetics.

Vegetable fiber production tends to be areally concentrated partly because of exacting climatic and soil requirements. The area of potential cotton culture is determined by requirements of a 200-day frost-free growing season, adequate rain or irrigation, and dry weather during harvesting. The growth of jute is partially explained by requirements of very fertile loamy soils and a continuously warm, moist, tropical climate. A further consideration in the regional concentration of these and other vegetable fibers is the necessity of abundant, cheap labor for cultivation, harvesting, and preliminary processing. Much of the future competitive position of these vegetable fibers depends upon substituting capital and organization for labor so as to drop total costs of production.

Cotton

Cotton is still the premier fiber, with 60 per cent of apparel and household textiles still being made of it. Consumption is still increasing in absolute terms, with apparel and household uses strong and severe losses only in the price-conscious industrial field—in baling and tire cords. The industrial losses were first made by paper and jute competitors, but lately synthetics have been the main competition.

In urban-industrial countries, total cotton consumption has not increased very much above pre-World War II levels. There is some evidence that once high levels of living are reached, fiber consumption is less likely to rise as consumer spending increases. Also, such highly developed countries have a larger proportion of uses in which cotton is vulnerable to competition from other materials. The displacement of cotton fibers and textiles by man-made fibers and non-textiles in industrial uses, rather than the elasticity of demand for clothing, best explains the lagging cotton consumption in North America and Western Europe.

To a large extent, the increase in cotton production and consumption has occurred in underdeveloped nations. In such countries with large available land areas and a relative abundance of labor, agriculture provides a method of utilizing underemployed resources. Cotton is a crop that can be exported and, if a country embarks upon an industrialization program, can provide the raw material for a textile industry. This desire of many countries to increase self-sufficiency in cotton production for local consumption and to achieve a more favorable balance of payment through the sale of an export crop will continue to be important. As new technologies are developed and applied in the production of cotton, a gradual increase in yields can be expected in most underdeveloped countries. These higher yields—coupled with the increases expected in acreages suitable for crops, as a result of irrigation and other land reclamation—indicate that the potential cotton producing capacities of such countries are likely to increase rather than diminish.

In the urban-industrial nations producing much cotton (the U.S.A., the U.S.S.R., and a few others produce about two-thirds of total production), changes in cotton production have been perhaps as dramatic as those that have taken place in the underdeveloped realm. The elements of change that seem particularly noteworthy are the increasing mechanization (about three-quarters of the U.S. cotton crop is now semi- and totally mechanized), shifts to irrigated acreage (U.S. West and U.S.S.R. Turkestan), and the increasing differential in yields between various regions. A continued increase in cotton production efficiency can be expected. During the past generation, mechanization and other technologies in cotton production have increased the output per man-hour, as average yields have risen with chemicalization, and as double- and four-row tractor equipment has replaced single- and double-row animal-drawn implements. Higher yields and greater output per man-hour are also resulting from the use of soil building crops, high analysis fertilizers, irrigation, and improved varieties. The improvements in ginning facilities—particularly the widespread use of lint-cleaning and lint-drying equipment—have reduced much of the former objection to mechanically harvested cotton. Since the United States produces some 30 per cent of the world cotton production, it will be used to illustrate changes occurring in the urban-industrial realm (Soviet changes are similar).

The technology of growing cotton has been so perfected that the man-hours required to grow a bale (480 pounds) of cotton have dropped since the mid-1930's from 150 hours to under 30, and the average yield per acre has risen from 157 pounds to over 500 pounds today. The most efficient producers—mechanized farms on flatlands ideally suited to irrigation and cotton culture, as in Arizona and California—can average over 2 bales per acre (and occasionally produce 6) at a labor cost of 15 man-hours per bale.

Cotton culture is now so successful and efficient that output can be maintained with only one-third of the acreage used a generation back.

U.S.D.A. Photo

The mechanical cotton picker can pick as much cotton as forty hand laborers. The half of the world's cotton production grown in the high-income countries is rapidly being mechanized, but the world's premier fiber is still primarily a labor-intensive crop.

Much of this increased efficiency is due to areal redistribution of cotton culture.

REGIONAL CHANGE IN UNITED STATES
COTTON PRODUCTION, 1924–1964
(per cent of total)

	1924	1964
Southeast	35	8
Middle South (Delta)	26	36
Southwest	38	36
West	1	20
U.S.A.	100	100

Soil conditions, technology, and sociological conditions have all been factors in the national redistribution of cotton production: (1) The large irrigated farms of the West were well adapted to mechanization, and higher yields per acre can be obtained with irrigation in the West than without irrigation in the more humid Southeast. Many farms in the Southeast have been too small either to irrigate or to mechanize economically, and, in addition, the cumulative effects of soil erosion in the Southeast began to have a telling effect on crop production in the 1930's. Even today, most of the remaining cotton production in the Southeast has high costs of production and is doomed if price supports (amounting to 6 cents per pound) are abandoned. (2) The Delta states, unlike the Southeast, had large level farm units well suited to mechanization, and the rich Delta soils were generally maintained in a high state of fertility. Cotton could be produced in the Delta with large amounts of labor as long as it was available, and as mechanization became technically and economically practicable, the land was well adapted to the change. (3) The Southwest was generally similar to the Delta but with slightly larger farms on the average and somewhat lower yields per acre. A large percentage of the farm units in the area were able to mechanize and stay in cotton production, many with the use of supplementary irrigation.

The 5-acres-and-a-mule cotton grower on the side of a southern slope still exists, but has been almost entirely displaced by his tractor-equipped neighbor. The little farms tend to be absorbed into the larger ones, since it takes about 100 acres of cotton to make full mechanization economical. A smaller tract cannot keep the machines busy enough to pay for their cost and upkeep.

A fully mechanized cotton plantation includes the following operations. The land is mechanically plowed, harrowed, fertilized, and planted. Pre-emergence spraying with herbicides controls weeds before the cotton plants sprout and until the seedlings are several inches high. The proper number of plants is assured by several different methods. Mechanical cotton planters can sow the seeds in correctly spaced clusters (stands or hills). Or thinning machines, attached to tractors, chop out surplus plants according to a preset pattern. Or some farmers simply plow at a right angle across the rows of cotton, thereby removing many of the new plants. When the cotton is seven to ten days old (3 inches high), postemergence spraying is done (1 to 3 pints per acre) on the ground and cotton stems. As the stalks of the plants become larger and stronger, some modern growers turn to miniature flame throwers for the final stages of weed control. Flaming controls all but the toughest weeds, but is a delicate job, requiring deft operation to avoid crop damage. As the cotton plants mature (2 to 6 feet high in the United States), they create enough shade to kill most weeds close by, but that is precisely the time when insects can do most damage to maturing bolls. The airplane, spraying or dusting insecticides across fields, is the best means of curbing pests over large areas just before harvest. The harvest itself is performed by monster self-powered machines that follow down the rows of plants, snatching the fleecy fiber from open bolls and blowing it into hoppers. Planters in the Southwest, where early frosts are predictable (on the high plains), can depend on winter's first touch to defoliate their cotton for harvesting. Elsewhere, growers use chemical defoliants, often sprayed or dusted by airplane, which wither leaves and cause them to drop without harming the bolls.

The revolutionary changes in cotton growing in recent decades revolve about its transformation from a small-scale Deep South business into a large-scale mechanized operation centered in the Southwest and West. Mechanization and chemicalization help keep the cost of growing cotton down. Hoe labor in cotton costs $15 to $20 per acre, while the same job done by machine and chemicals costs $10 or less. It costs $10 for fertilizer per bale and $12 per acre for poisons to burn out the grass and weeds, but increased yields make it profitable. A mechanical picker can pick 1,400 pounds of cotton per hour (a human picker perhaps 30). One family used to cultivate 10 to 12 acres of cotton by mule and manpower, but one tractor operator can cultivate 100 acres, with a little help from his family at the peak of the weeding season. It took an average of 150 man-hours of labor to grow and harvest 1 bale of cotton when using hand labor and mules, with total costs per pound of 28 cents or more. A partly mechanized farm that still does some weeding by hand requires only 30 man-hours (20 for hand hoeing) per bale, and has costs of production around 23 to 25 cents. The most efficient farms in the West, when state yields are 2 to $2\frac{1}{4}$ bales per acre, require only 10 to 15 man-hours per bale and have costs of 15 cents per pound. With present high support prices (30 cents per pound, about 6 cents per pound higher than the world market price for 1-inch staple cotton fiber), the efficient producers earn enough profit to equal returns in industry or other urban activities. They could easily produce cotton at a profit if the price dropped below that of rayon, but such a drop in price would eliminate most small- and medium-scale growers, with resultant social, economic, and political problems.

Cotton has a relative advantage in price over wool in defense against synthetics. Only a small price margin separates cotton from its man-made competitors. Although the margin remains narrow, the synthetics are now selling at the lower price instead of cotton, and probably will continue to do so if the support price remains about 30 cents per pound. The relative disadvantage to cotton lies in the greater opportunity for substitution of man-made fabrics in the cost of cotton than in the case of wool. One way of counteracting the synthetics' superior characteristics is through chemicalization of cotton yarn and cloth. Chemical modifications of cotton have been slanted toward the improvement of flame resistance (acetylated cotton makes for better heat and acid resistance), light resistance (lead-chromated), and water repellence (silicone-treated).

Acrylonitrile (a petrochemical) is the father of such synthetic fibers as orlon, acrilan, and dynel. When applied to cotton, the process is called cyanoethylation, and has the following virtues: (1) cotton's ability to resist bacteria and mildew is improved, important in making tent and tarpaulin materials; (2) cotton's resistance to acids is increased, important in work clothing and many industrial uses; (3) cotton's resistance to both wet and dry heat is improved, important in products like ironing-board covers and house awnings; (4) cotton's receptivity to dyeing is increased, as new fibers do not require such a high concentration of dyestuff in the bath as ordinary cotton does; and (5) the new fibers are more resistant to abrasion and stretch, so they will last longer than ordinary cotton. Ordinary cotton sells for 60 to 80 cents per pound of yarn, while acrylonitrile costs 31 cents per pound and treats 6 to 7 pounds of yarn, so the cost of cyanoethylation is very small in proportion to the benefits.

If cotton's price can be dropped to 20 to 25 cents per pound and its chemicalized cloth cheaply improved to compete quality-wise with rayon and other synthetics, its future seems assured as the premier fiber.

Jute

Jute is second in importance among vegetable fibers, although produced in quantity only one-third as much as cotton, and is worth only half as much as medium-staple cotton per unit. It is a fiber obtained from a tropical plant that grows from 6 to 12 feet high; is fine, soft, pliable, pale yellow or yellow-brown with silky luster; and lends itself to easy manufacture.

For economic production, a damp, hot atmosphere (75° to 80° F. throughout the year) and a large total rainfall are required, although too much rain early in the season results in shorter stalks. It is unique in being the only fiber crop that will withstand flooding. As it is used principally for cheap sacking, it must be produced more cheaply than any other fiber used in weaving, and nearly all world production comes from within a 200-mile radius of Calcutta, especially from the Ganges Delta where population is dense and wages low (5 to 10 cents per man-hour) and the fertility of the soil is renewed by the annual floods. The crop yield is extremely dependent on the weather, although normally it fluctuates around 2½ million tons.

Pakistan, which produces about 55 per cent or more of world production, manufactures about a tenth of its own production and sells the remainder in the raw state, about one-half to India and the remainder to Japan, Western Europe, and the United States. India now exports little raw jute, but does export about 1 million tons of sacking and other jute manufactures (about $100 million yearly to the United States alone).

Jute occupies an important position in the world economy because of the great demands for sacking of agricultural and other produce. About one-third of the cloth is used for other purposes. Jute enjoys its demand only because of its comparatively low price, being the least expensive of the major textile fibers. If the price is high, there is an increase in the bulk handling of agricultural produce and the wider use of such packaging substitutes as paper sacks, coarse cotton bags, and the fiber kenaf. Jute is low-strength and perishable and, even under ordinary conditions, becomes brittle, weak, and dingy in color in a short time, so its inherent characteristics are no protection from competition.

Experiments in Cuba indicate that the biggest obstacles to kenaf's development as a major commercial crop and jute substitute have been overcome. Machinery now offers cheap, profitable harvesting in place of expensive manual methods. Scientific agriculture has produced disease-resistant varieties of the plant, capable of higher yields and adaptable to several growing seasons.

Kenaf will grow in any tropical or subtropical climate with at least 5 inches of rainfall a month or the equivalent in irrigation. Its wide distribution throughout the world is indicated by the more than 120 names by which it is known. Kenaf is made from the bark of stalks of a fast-growing plant resembling the hollyhock, and will flourish in a wider range of climates than jute. It is lighter, stronger, and more durable than jute, and can be used not only for bags but also for rope, carpets, and linoleum backing, and possibly for reinforcement of molded plastics.

Kenaf can be used either as a coarse ribbon or a refined fiber. The ribbons are stronger and cheaper than jute, but rougher in texture and appearance. It is expected that kenaf's major use will be in the manufacture of bale coverings for cotton, wool, and tobacco, and bags for agricultural products.

As long as either jute or kenaf can be produced under 15 cents per pound, a mass market will be retained. If the price goes much higher, treated paper will substitute even more than now and other products will follow in the footsteps of sugar and be bulk-handled.

Linen

Flax fiber and linseed are obtained from selected types of a common parent. Their environmental and soil criteria are somewhat similar, but the production of straw with its contained fiber does require somewhat more exacting conditions.

The use of mechanical harvesters is being developed but so far produce weak fiber, and much flax is still pulled by hand. Historically, the peasants of Eastern Europe and the U.S.S.R. were the chief producers, mainly for their own handicrafts. As such populations have become commercialized and industrialized, the relative importance of flax has declined markedly. Cotton has substituted for clothing, and jute for industrial cloth.

Northern Ireland and Belgium are the main Western European centers of linen manufacturing, with the raw material coming mainly from the Low Countries and France, as Russian flax is of low grade and unsuitable for the luxury fabrics. Uncertain supplies and high prices of the raw material plus inadequate technology, marketing, and advertising methods have all contributed to decline. The United States imports have declined nearly half, and many "linen" goods now sold in the United States are actually processed cotton goods.

Hemp

True or soft hemp, like linen, is now in decline, mainly because of cotton's competition in clothing and canvas. It is now used primarily to make strong twines, ropes, and some canvas.

The hemp plant, a long stem annually growing to heights of 3 to 18 feet, can be employed for three different items: fiber from the stem, oil (similar to linseed) from the seeds, and drugs from all parts. Major cultivation is for fiber. Only in the U.S.S.R. is hemp grown for oil, and output is comparatively minor. The growing of the hemp plant for its narcotic properties is primarily restricted to Asia.

Northern hemp, about two-thirds of total acreage, is grown mainly in the U.S.S.R. and Eastern Europe. Russian attempts to cut labor costs by machine cutting and dew retting have not been very successful, taking longer and producing an inferior fiber to the traditionally water-retted product.

Southern hemp, mainly grown in Italy, Yugoslavia, and Japan, requires a longer season but has a superior fiber. Historically, it has sometimes substituted for flax, having longer, stronger, but coarser fibers. It still has special advantages for sailcloth, tarpaulins, canvas, and some twine; but it probably has lost forever its old markets for rope, binder twine, carpeting and sacking material, and fine textiles.

The U.S.S.R. consumes its one-half of world production internally, with Italy and Yugoslavia providing most of the commercial supplies moving in world trade from their one-fourth of total production.

Cordage Fibers

Hard or cordage fibers are comparatively new, being used commercially only in the past century. In contrast to soft fibers (flax, hemp, jute), which come from plant stems and are used largely in textiles, the hard fibers (agave, abaca) come from the leaves of plants and are used for cordage, with minor uses in brushes, brooms, carpets, hats, and grain bags. Cheapness and suitability for binder twines were the significant factors in the climb of these fibers to world importance—the mechanical grain binder introduced about 1880 gave the major impetus.

Today, better than 90 per cent of all binder twines are made wholly or partly from the agave fibers native to Central America: sisal, henequen, and cantala. All are grown as perennial crops in dry tropical climates, at about the same price as jute.

Sisal is the most widely adaptable agave, being more drought-resistant and having a superior fiber. Stiff, creamy white, from 2 to 5½ feet long, it is used mainly for rope, twine, and upholstery padding. New hybrid plants yield 500 to 600 leaves (200 old) twice a year (1 old), and promise considerable economies. Production is mainly in underdeveloped regions (two-thirds in East Africa and Angola-Mozambique; the remainder in Brazil, Haiti, and Indonesia), and consumption is mainly in the urban-industrial realm.

Henequen, like sisal, originated in Mexico, but unlike the latter has remained in the country. Some 85 per cent of world production still comes from there, with most of the remainder from Cuba. About half of total production comes to the United States for binding and baler twines.

Abaca is a relative of the banana and native to the Philippines. It has been the preferred rope for marine use, mining, and well-drilling, and for the better grades of large, strong cordage, but its relative share of the hard-fibers output has been declining (plant disease, wars, and competition from similar natural fibers such as sisal and henequen have contributed to the decline, but probably the most telling blow has been dealt by nylon and other synthetic materials). World production (95 per cent from the Philippines) is now only two-thirds of henequen's 150,000 tons output, and less than a fifth of sisal's 650,000 tons output.

These cordage fibers are in a stronger competitive position than the smaller soft fibers. One problem is similar to that found with other perennials. It takes two to three years for new abaca plantings to yield fiber, three to four for sisal, and four to seven for henequen. There is thus a considerable delay before supplies of hard fibers can be adjusted to changes in demand, and this accentuates price fluctuations.

Animal Fibers

Animal fibers include "land"-fibers such as sheep's wool, goat's hair, alpaca's hair, camel's hair, and others, and one "labor" fiber of decreasing importance, silk. Since the Industrial Revolution, they have declined in relative importance, and the prospective future will probably continue to see a further relative drop as wool-type and silk-type synthetics are improved and become more inexpensive.

Wool. Wool is known as the world's most versatile fiber. It has properties—warmth, resiliency, dyeability, non-flammability—that have not been completely reproduced in synthetic fibers, and it lends itself to an almost infinite variety of treatments. The special properties that wool alone possesses have generally enabled it to hold its own, but synthetics are making inroads today (especially in North America) and earning some increase in favor with the consumer.

In nearly all sheep raising countries, the num-

A closeup view shows the fleece being tied into a bundle; the hairy leg and face wool and defective belly wool is kept separate from the body wool (foreground). Wool has so far withstood synthetic competition better than the other animal fiber, silk, but in the United States wool-like synthetics and other substitutes are making significant inroads and this tendency seems likely to spread elsewhere.

U.S.D.A. Photo

ber of sheep has passed its maximum. The deficiency in the output of wool would have been much more conspicuous but for a notable increase (doubling) in the weight of fleece because of improved breeding. Even so, wool production has increased only two-thirds in this century.

Broadly speaking, there are three main categories of wool: merino, crossbred, and carpet. Merino wool, from sheep raised for wool alone, has superior fineness, softness, strength, elasticity, and felting properties. Before World War II, about one-third of the world's wool clip was merino, but it has fallen to about one-fourth now. About three-fourths of the sheep in South Africa and Australia and nearly one-half of them in the United States are merinos, but the shares are dropping.

Some 55 per cent or more of wool production is from crossbred animals, raised for meat as well as wool. Over 95 per cent of New Zealand's sheep, some 85 per cent of the sheep in Argentina and Uruguay, and over half of those in the United States are such dual-purpose animals. The value of the meat is from two-thirds to three-fourths of the value received from such animals.

The remaining 20 per cent of world wool production is coarse wool for carpets and rugs. It comes from native unimproved breeds produced chiefly in the areas of early civilization: East Asia, South Asia, and Southwest Asia. These carpet wools are the longer and coarser wools that, because of their resilience and durability, are used primarily in the manufacture of floor covering. There is a tendency for such areas to consume larger fractions of their own production, and for the urban-industrial nations to substitute natural and synthetic fibers.

Apparel wools are of finer fiber and are made into yarn and fabrics. Such wool can be spun into thread with ease, as it is light and durable, and its scales and elasticity enable cloth to be made that absorbs moisture and preserves heat. The main wool producing areas are far removed from the great textile manufacturing centers; five southern hemisphere nations (Argentina, Uruguay, South Africa, Australia, New Zealand) supply nearly two-thirds of the world's apparel fiber output.

The United States produced a tenth of the world's wool before World War II, but production is now only 5 per cent. Several factors have been involved: (1) labor shortage in the western states where large flocks are grazed on open ranges, (2) a trend toward increasing the number of small- and medium-sized flocks as supplementary enterprises to farming, which tends to increase the numbers of crossbred sheep, and (3) the condition of ranges and competition of beef cattle for rangeland influences flock size, as beef cattle and sheep compete directly for use of range resources. With high prices for beef, beef cattle herds tend to be more profitable, as they require less labor. Sheep require less initial capital, and quick returns on the investment can be expected because of the short time required to expand production, but in recent years, per capita consumption of lamb and mutton has dropped to one-half pre-World War II levels. Since wool production is a secondary source of income (only one-fourth of cash receipts from sheep has been from the sale of wool), factors affecting the production of lamb and mutton influence wool production more than the factors directly affecting the consumption of wool.

To meet the shortage, woolen manufacturers have recourse to other fibers—animal, vegetable, synthetic—to blend with wool. Animal-fiber substitutes include mohair (hair of Angora goats bred in Turkey, the United States, and South Africa), cashmere (hair of cashmere goats bred in Kashmir, Tibet and other regions of China), alpaca and vicuña (hair of animals on Peru-Bolivia plateau), and camel's hair. Reworked wool (shoddy) is also used in substantial quantities to produce cheaper wearing apparel. Cotton, rayon, and true synthetics (dacron, orlon) are also increasingly blended with wool to lower price, add special characteristics, and provide lighter-weight fabrics for informal styles.

Wool is also being chemicalized. Silicones, versatile plastic materials with tremendous life spans and a remarkable aversion for water, can give woolen and worsted fabrics many of the properties of the newer synthetic fibers without losing any of wool's own good points. The treatment lasts through countless dry cleanings. A little water will clean away almost any spot (ink and water practically bounce off) and pleats will remain even on the dampest days. The cost is minor. Normally, clean virgin wool accounts for one-third of the total cost of cloth, or some 10 to 15 per cent of the total cost of a suit or overcoat, so such chemical treatment is economical in comparison to the improvement.

Wool is unlikely to become significantly cheaper (usually in the price range 75 cents to $1.25 per pound), since pasture land is becoming scarcer with competition from crops and cattle. Upgrading of sheep seems to have leveled off in the most advanced areas. There are still some possibilities of economizing (e.g., possible chemical "shearing" substituting for the traditional mechanical type), but their effects are likely to be minor, compared with the probable price reductions in wool-type synthetics as they are improved and mass produced.

Silk. Silk was the first natural fiber to feel the competition from synthetics, because of the wide price advantage of the early synthetics and their marked similarity to the natural product. A gradually declining silk consumption, further limited by rising prices (over $5 per pound) and a virtual stoppage of imports during the World War II period, has brought per capita use of silk in the urban-industrial realm to less than 0.1 pound per year. Silk, which at its peak enjoyed a consumption of slightly less than 1 pound per capita, is the only fiber to have been almost completely replaced by the synthetics.

Silk is the lightest fiber known, natural or artificial. It is the strongest natural textile fiber, an almost invisible filament of silk being stronger than a like filament of steel. It is more complicated in its molecular composition and configuration than any other fiber, natural or artificial. It lends itself to many types of fabrics, being light-weight, crease-resistant, easy-dyeing, and possessing true luster and beauty. Being a non-conductor of electricity, it is useful for many special purposes like insulating electrical parts, making bolting (flour-sieve) cloth, etc.

Silk is obtained from the glossy thread that makes up the cocoons of silkworms and from the larvae of certain moths in the chrysalis stage. Mulberry leaves form the natural feed of the silkworm, and the heavy labor requirements of feeding and otherwise caring for the worms is responsible for the high cost of production. Certain silk growing areas have ceased production (e.g., Rhone Valley) because higher wages in other activities attracted away the labor supply. World production is small, only 30,000 tons: one-half from Japan, one-fourth from China, and the remaining one-fourth from other countries (the U.S.S.R., Italy, Turkey, India, Korea). Japan consumes most of her own raw silk, and is also the main exporter of raw silk to the North Atlantic realm. About ¾ million Japanese farm families count on silk for part of their income—some villages in the Japanese Alps have 60 to 70 per cent of such families. Chinese silk growing techniques are a generation behind Japan's, and mulberry production per acre is only 40 per cent that in Japan.

One of the major uses of silk today is in blends composed of one-third silk. Blends with cotton, wool, and linen are making the qualities of this luxury fiber available to middle-class budgets. Blended with nylon, orlon, or dacron, silk makes possible a fabric that is washable, quick-drying, crease-resistant, and can have permanent pleating features. The long-range goal is a silk wash-and-wear fabric that will do everything the synthetics do and at the same time preserve the rich feel and sheen of genuine silk. Better ways of dyeing, finishing, and printing silk fabrics are being sought. One goal is to engineer a silk cloth that lends itself to the mass-production methods of dress manufacturers turning out apparel in the moderately priced and budget lines. Present silk fabric poses some problems in manufacturers' cutting rooms and is better adapted to dresses costing upward of $100, a relatively small market.

MAN-MADE FIBERS

In the past generation, synthetic fiber production has shown substantial increases relative to the production of agricultural fibers. This fact can be attributed largely to technological advancement within the synthetic textile industry that have resulted in more favorable price relationships for the synthetic fibers. The development of better synthetics at lower prices has enabled these fibers to capture most of the increased market for fibers created by growing population and larger consumer incomes in most high-income countries.

There is little doubt that man-made fibers will continue to increase in relative importance insofar as both production and consumption of fibers are concerned. The rapidity with which technological changes have occurred in the textile industry virtually assures the development of better and less costly synthetics in the foreseeable future. Cotton production and consumption remain substantially larger than that of the synthetic fibers in spite of the phenomenal growth of the synthetic industry, however, and it is unlikely that synthetics will become more than 40 per cent of total fiber consumption within this generation.[2]

There are four classes of man-made fibers: (1) cellulose-based fibers, chiefly rayons and acetates, constituting about three-fourths of all synthetics at present; (2) protein-based fibers, such as vicara (from corn), ardil (from peanuts), and merinova (from milk), produced in very small amounts so far; (3) mineral fibers, such as asbestos and fiber glass, about a tenth of total synthetic fiber output; and (4) chemically synthetized fibers, such as nylon, dacron, the polyesters, and the vinyl and acrylic polymers (acrilan, dynel, orlon, saran, vinyon), making up about 20 per cent of synthetic fiber output. The first three classes are sometimes called regenerated or semisynthetic fibers, since the molecules are nature-made and man merely altered the polymer (chain of molecules). The fourth class is sometimes called the true synthetic group, since man made both the molecule and the

[2] Already, U.S. apparel-fiber consumption—half of total fiber consumption, with household and industrial consumption each one-quarter—is about 40 per cent man-made fibers, of which half are true synthetic and half are rayon-acetate.

polymer. In general, true synthetics cost from two to five times more per unit than the regenerated fibers, which puts them into a price group with silk as extremely expensive and more likely to be used as part of a blend than by themselves.

Synthetics are overwhelmingly produced and consumed in the urban-industrial realm. Except in the U.S.S.R., they are nearly one-third of total apparel fiber consumption, with the cellulose-based synthetics relatively more important in Europe and Japan than in North America where nearly one-half of the true synthetics are consumed.

Cellulose-based Fibers

Britain, France, Germany, Italy, and Japan—all major importers of cotton—have become major producers of rayon and acetate fibers. Wood pulp, the principal basic material from which such fibers are made, is generally available in these countries at a cost favorable to the substitution of wood fibers for cotton. Also, most of these countries have often had a shortage of foreign exchange with which to purchase cotton but have had the materials and the technical skills in their well-developed chemical industries to produce substitutes. Consumption of rayon and acetate in these countries is about equal to the equivalent of one-third of present world cotton consumption, and is still growing.

Rayon, acetate, and other similar fibers are made from cellulose, most of which comes from wood pulp, but some of which comes from cotton linters, bamboo, and other sources. In the viscose process, which is the cheapest process and accounts for 85 per cent of world production, the cellulose obtained from wood pulp is chemically treated and dissolved in a caustic soda solution. When it is sufficiently viscous or sticky, the solution is extruded through a spinneret containing a large number of holes into an acid bath where it hardens into continuous filaments, which are then twisted together to form yarn, or cut into regular lengths and spun like the natural fibers on spindles. Lately, the filament has been priced somewhat under cotton yarn, with which it competes, while the staple fiber has been priced under raw cotton.

In the acetate process, the cellulose may be derived from either wood pulp or cotton linters, and is treated with acetic acid, acetic anhydride, and sulfuric acid, and the resulting cellulose triacetate is hydrolized and dissolved in acetone. The resulting viscous solution is then fed through a spinneret into a spinning cabinet where the filaments solidify in a stream of warm air, and are then spun together on a bobbin to form yarn. Acetate is more expensive and often used as yarn to weave silklike garments, and tends to increase its share where appearance and handle are important. Acetate rayon and cuprammonium rayon (now little important) together make up only 15 per cent of world consumption.

The cheaper rayons, which mainly compete with cotton, have certain weaknesses: they do not dye well, they have low wet strength, and clothes made from them will not hold their shapes well. More expensive varieties, such as that used in tire cord, are superior in characteristics but lose much of the price advantage.

The competitive strength of rayons in the world textile market derives from such factors as these: (1) The industry uses extremely cheap raw materials (over 80 per cent wood pulp). (2) The industry has large-sized production units, with one result being continually falling prices (e.g., 1920 price $2.50 per pound, 1964 price range 28 to 41 cents per pound average grades). (3) The industry has more price stability insofar as the supply can better be adjusted to demand than in the case of the natural fibers, where violent crop and flock production and price fluctuations are common. (4) The industry has the ability to produce to specifications, with controlled output adjustable to demand, uniformity of quality, predictability of supply, and other advantages of manufacturing. (5) The industry, being a twentieth-century phenomenon, benefits from constant improvements, which the financially strong and, on the whole, progressive industry can afford to promote. (6) The industry is capital saving in that existing equipment designed for the cotton textile industry can be used.

The short-run future of rayon hangs on its own dynamic technology. Perhaps the greatest future lies in staple, a fiber that can be blended with other synthetic as well as with natural fibers. Its cotton-like qualities promise to nose out cotton from many of its present uses, unless cotton can be reduced sharply in price. Even if priced competitively with cotton, it still has an advantage, as it does not lose 6 to 7 per cent of its volume in spinning as cotton does. Recently, washable rayons have been developed. Solution-dyed filament yarn for autos and home furnishings is another bright prospect.

Rayon contributes much in the way of improved performance, beauty of texture, drapability, and hand to its textiles and to blends. But, most important, it makes possible a lower price for the finished fabric while in no way taking away from the excellence and appearance of its quality and performance.

Protein-based Fibers

Vicara is mainly made in the United States from corn; ardil is mainly made in Britain from peanut residue; lanital and merinova are mainly made in Italy and Belgium from milk casein. The production of all these fibers, which have wool-like qualities, is still quite small. They are the nearest things to wool among the synthetics, absorbing moisture and dye easily, and are mothproof, but are very weak. Costing about $1 per pound, they have little appeal pricewise, and the small production is consumed in blends. Total world production is not more than 1 per cent of total wool production.

Mineral-based Fibers

These asbestos and glass fibers are almost entirely used in industrial and household uses, although some effort has been made to adapt fiber glass for apparel uses.

Autos are using more fibrous glass every year, for insulation in the interior and for insulation and sound control in the motor. It is already used in such diverse products as skis, boat hulls, curtains and draperies, fishing rods, and truck trailers. New uses are growing in aircraft, transcontinental pipelines, and glass-reinforced plastic bodies for automobiles.

United States consumption is now approaching 100,000 tons yearly, worth $⅓ billion. Expansion seems assured if the great strength can be combined with less brittleness than at present.

True Synthetic Fibers

The wholly synthetic fibers, chiefly derived from by-products of coal and oil, have an extensive and expanding range of uses, although they are three to four times as expensive to produce as cotton even when well established. Each tends to have particular qualities for which it has been developed, but their common characteristic is strength and durability. They all are water-repellent, non-shrinking, and quick-drying. All have these disadvantages: none dye easily, all stick to you, all are non-conductive (give shocks), and all show thread holes easily. They have been introduced both in blends and in pure fabrics for such clothing as shirts, blouses, underwear, stockings, and gloves, and as suits. Industrial uses have been for beltings, awnings, and tarpaulins. (See Table 9–2.)

Even in the United States, where almost half of the true synthetics are produced and consumed, such fibers are still minority participants, as indicated below:

UNITED STATES: ANNUAL POUNDS PER CAPITA CONSUMPTION OF MAJOR FIBERS

	1924	1964
Cotton	23.0	22.0
Wool-Silk	3.5	2.0
Rayon-Acetate	0.4	6.0
True Synthetics	–	5.0
Total	27.0	35.0

U.S. total fiber consumption is expected to more than double by the end of the century, with apparel use tripling, industrial use doubling, and household use almost quadrupling. The cotton share is expected to drop to 44 per cent; natural wool, to less than 2 per cent; cellulosic (rayon-acetate) fibers, 5 per cent; and noncellulosic (true synthetics, glass fibers, etc.) fibers, 49 per cent.[3]

[3] Hans H. Landsberg. *Natural Resources for U.S. Growth—A Look Ahead to the Year 2000.* (Baltimore: Johns Hopkins Press, 1964), pp. 36–42.

TABLE 9-2
Guide to Properties of Selected Fibers

	Durability	Moisture Absorption	Moth and Mildew Effects	Reaction to Flame	Appearance	Ease of Care	Application
Natural fibers							
Cotton	Not particularly strong	Similar to rayon, vicara; shrinks unless treated	Mothproof; poor resistance to mildew unless treated	Like rayon, burns rather rapidly	More of harsh feel	Washable; needs ironing; wrinkles and spots easily	In all items; now in sheer weaves for summer wear
Wool	Has less strength than most synthetics	Fairly high; dries slowly; shrinks easily	No moth resistance unless treated; resists mildew well	Burns slowly; tends to be self-extinguishing	Soft, desirable drape that does not cling; alive and resilient	Not washable; sheds wrinkles fast; does not hold crease well	In almost every article of men's wear
Regenerated fibers							
Rayon	About same as cotton; not notably strong	Higher than most; stretches somewhat	Resistant to moths, but attacked by mildew	Burns rather rapidly; with cotton, among most inflammable	Soft feel, with tendency to cling	Washable; dry-cleans; wrinkles easily, especially when wet	In shirts, underwear, suits, ties, socks; less costly than most
Acetate	Not notably strong; loses strength at lower heat than most	Less than natural fibers, more than most synthetics	Mothproof; resists mildew, but discolors slightly	Somewhat less inflammable than rayon or cotton	Soft, lustrous look; good draping quality, but tends to cling	Washable; dry-cleans; spots rather easily	In shirts, underwear, suits; adds softness and drape
Vicara	Less strong than cotton or other synthetics	Higher than most, but shrink-resistant	Totally resistant	Burns rather easily, but less inflammable than rayon, cotton	Soft, luxurious feel like cashmere; good draping quality	Washable; dry-cleans; wrinkle-resistant	Used extensively to add drapability and softness to fabrics
True synthetic fibers							
Nylon	Ranks at top in tensile strength and resistance to friction	Very little; dries fast; will not shrink or stretch	Totally resistant	Does not support combustion; melts under heat	Soft; heat-set creases stay; wrinkles hang out quickly	Washable; needs little ironing; dry-cleans	In shirts, underwear, suits, socks; adds strength in blends
Orlon	Ranks high; better than natural and most synthetics	Almost none; dries fast; will not shrink or stretch	Totally resistant	Melts; burns only at very high temperatures	Soft, wool-like feel; drapes well	Washable; little ironing; resists spots; dry-cleans	In shirts, socks, suits; adds strength and drape in blends
Dacron	Ranks at top in strength and resistance to friction	Almost none; dries very fast; will not shrink or stretch	Totally resistant	Melts; burns only (cigarette ash will melt hole)	Fairly soft, wool-like; drapes well	Washable; spots removable with water; crease holds in rain	In socks, dress shirts, men's suits, slacks
Dynel	Among the top three or four in toughness	Very little; dries fast; will not shrink or stretch	Totally resistant	Does not support combustion, but melts at very low heat	Soft, wool-like; good draping quality	Washable; dry-cleans; resists spots; holds crease wet or dry	In socks, underwear, knit goods, sport shirts

Courtesy of J. P. Stevens & Co., Inc.

Airview of Utica-Mohawk Plant, at Clemson, South Carolina. In this Carolina Piedmont cotton plant—21 acres under one roof—Stevens Utica-Mohawk cotton sheets are produced.

TEXTILE MANUFACTURING

The world textile manufacturing industries employ perhaps 25 million people and turn out yearly products worth over $75 billion. The spearhead of industrialization in the North Atlantic realm, it is playing the same role today in the economic growth of underdeveloped countries.

Perhaps 15 million persons are employed in the cotton industry, 2 million in the woolen industry, 2 million in man-made fibers and textiles, and some 6 million in processing all other fibers (including handicraft production).

Probably as many persons are engaged in the clothing trades as in the textile industries. The net value of each segment is perhaps $25 billion yearly.

Expansion and Competition

The years since the end of World War II have seen a big growth in textile production, particularly in the underdeveloped countries, and most of it is protected from outside competition by tariffs and quotas. For countries on the road to industrialization, simple textile mills can provide employment relatively fast. They can also fill the basic need for clothing, while conserving scarce export earnings to buy "essential" goods.

As a result, world trade in textiles is down, and competition among exporting countries for a bigger share of the smaller pie is fierce.

The biggest increase in textile production since the end of the war has been in India and China. India is now one of the world's leading exporters, and a formidable competitor of the older textile exporters all over Southeast Asia and Africa. China, also, has increased its production sharply, and with India is beginning to offer sharp competition to Japan for Asian markets. The underdeveloped realm as a whole now processes about one-third of all cotton textiles, two-thirds of all jute and related cloth, less than 10 per cent of all woolen textiles, and about 10 per cent of all man-made textiles. Prospects are that expansion of textile production will mainly remain in the natural fibers area, since the underdeveloped realm retains large surpluses of raw fibers.

The urban-industrial realm makes a majority of the world's textiles, but its share is falling (in terms of quantity), and its industries are undergoing reorganization and reorientation.

Although the export markets are under increasing competition, they are still very important to European industrial countries and Japan. Britain exports 45 per cent of her cotton cloth; Japan, about 30 per cent; France and Belgium, about 25 per cent each; the United States, about 5 per cent (for comparison, the leading cotton exporter among the underdeveloped countries, India, exports about 12 per cent of her output). Britain also exports about 30 per cent of her wool textiles, with Italy and France also important, but most of the three-fourths of the

Courtesy of J. P. Stevens & Co., Inc.

The weave shed at the Utica-Mohawk Plant, showing the making of cotton sheeting.

Courtesy of J. P. Stevens & Co., Inc.

Spinning woolen thread and dyeing woolen thread at the Dublin Plant, Dublin, Georgia. Increasingly, woolen cloth is produced in the Southeast.

Courtesy of J. P. Stevens & Co., Inc.

world's wool textiles produced in the urban-industrial realm are consumed within the country of origin. About 20 per cent of man-made textiles move in international trade, mainly from Italy and Germany to the Newer European lands and to India.

Britain, once textile supplier to the world, has already lost a big part of its export market, and now faces heavy competition in its home market as well. Imports of gray cloth (from India and Hong Kong under the Imperial Preference Treaty, duty-free) are rising fast, and now imported cottons account for 10 per cent of domestic sales. In the competition for world markets, the Indians undersell the Japanese on low-price goods, and the Japanese beat the British on medium-price goods. Britain is concentrating on the quality market, where its chief competitors are limited to the Americans, Italians, Germans, Belgians, and Dutch.

Japan has regained its prewar title of the world's leading textile exporter, although its industries are still not back to prewar size. Asia and Africa are the biggest markets. Exports to the United States come to less than 10 per cent of total textile trade, and Japan buys a fifth of U.S. raw cotton exports, which amount to five times the Japanese fabric imports to the United States on an equivalent basis.

The troubles of the U.S. textile industry (producing a sixth of the world's fabrics) are part of a worldwide textile picture of rising production, increased protection, and declining trade. For almost a generation, the textile industries have shown the ability to earn a decent return on investment only during periods of unusual demand caused by wartime shortages. Despite their troubles, textile men believe that long-range prospects are good, since per capita consumption of textiles has been steadily climbing during the same period, and there is every indication that the trend will continue. But production is still outstripping sales, and thus things will probably get worse for the marginal producers—who may be forced to merge, shut down plants, or go out of business (over 800 plants have closed in the past two decades)—before they get better for the entire industry.

Unlike the automobile or steel industries, the textile industry has no real giants to set the pace in modernization. The industry is a clutter of 500 manufacturers, many of them small, inefficient, and hampered by outdated machinery (about two-thirds of the industry's machinery is overage or obsolete). The largest textile company (Burlington Mills) has only 7 per cent of the industry sales. All the manufacturers are fiercely independent and have never joined in a combined drive to promote textile sales. In general, southern mills are best off: they have lower labor costs (only 15 per cent unionization, compared with 75 per cent in the North), more efficient (newer) mills, cheaper (because closer) raw materials, lower taxes, and a faster-growing regional market.

Trends in Technology

Some of the factors that influence textile consumption are: the trend toward lighter-weight apparel in nearly all categories; the growing importance of style; the adaptation of synthetic fibers for many apparel, household, and industrial uses, especially those with a favorable price compared to natural competitors; more frequent use of casual types of business suits and other clothing; and an increasing demand for multiple-use garments.

Blends are increasingly in preference, a fact that has regional connotations, as mills in newer districts (e.g., the South) have machinery better adapted to producing blended textiles. In the long run, single-fiber fabrics may well become a rarity.

Increasingly, sales are correlated more with special finishes and styling than with economy alone. From the test tube only recently have come better dyes and finishes, plus much improved wash-and-wear qualities.

Recently, rayon has lost a big part of the market in lower-priced apparel to cotton, partly because of the new, intriguing styles in cotton and partly because of an over-all trend away from the so-called street dress and into the more casual dress. At the same time that rayon has lost ground in the lower-priced market, it has not gained in the high-price field, as cotton has been promoted into a high-fashion acceptance it has never had before, and silk has a prestige all its own.

Cotton is winning new apparel markets, largely because new finishes and dyes have made it easier to wash and iron, harder to crease, and often better to look at, with appearances ranging from the fresh crisp to the soft silky.

The true synthetics are also being greatly improved. Dyeability is being continually improved, crimped yarn is revolutionizing the hosiery industry, and acrylic fibers (orlon, dynel) resembling fur are fast absorbing cheap natural fur business.

Non-woven fabrics, now only 1 per cent of the consumption, are increasing their uses and may approach 5 per cent of consumption soon. Originally restricted to low-grade industrial wiping rags and packing materials, they now can be made to resemble anything from tissue paper to leather, and are rapidly expanding into such lines as disposable diapers, sanitary napkins, surgical dressings and bandages, electrical insulation, backing in vinyl upholstery, and as interlinings in men's suits, ties, bathing suits, foundation garments, and shoe and handbag linings. Some optimists foresee a time when disposable shirts and even suits might be sprayed or molded without the use of sewing operations. As of now, consumption is restricted by the attitude formerly accorded plastics, that the material is a cheap and shoddy substitute for the real or more traditional article.

PERSPECTIVE

Long-range lines of development in the world's fiber and textile industries can be foreseen with reasonable certainty, although not the timing.

Household spinning and weaving all over the world will have to yield to factory-made cloth, except for specialties. The organizing ability, capital, labor, and other factors of production are more easily obtained in poor countries than in the case of capital goods industries, and existing markets will absorb the simpler types of fabrics if the infant industry is protected. Those underdeveloped countries able to supply their own fibers will be especially prone to expand, and that includes a very large proportion of them. Thus, the world's textile industries are slated for rapid growth and for decentralization.

A new division of labor seems emerging, with the older textile producers orienting their production toward fine-quality goods, while the newer textile producers concentrate on staple products, even supplying the older countries with much low-count gray cloth.

Man-made fibers will continue to grow in importance, will become one-third of total world fiber consumption within the foreseeable future, and may become one-half by the end of the century. Blends will also be used increasingly, and probably become the majority of medium-price and high-price textiles in the foreseeable future.

Cotton will probably lose some ground, but seems likely to remain the most important single fiber, increasing its total consumption, and remaining about one-half of apparel-fiber consumption. Wool, the more expensive natural fiber, will be used more and more in blends to make it accessible to larger groups of consumers, and will probably drop in relative importance to one-half or less of its present status. The prospects for silk are similar to those for wool, but on a much smaller scale.

In the man-made fiber field, the regenerated fibers are unlikely to increase greatly their share of total consumption in the older industrial countries. True synthetics have a greater potential, but their known and unknown superior characteristics come at such a high price that they are likely to be used in blends, with cheaper natural and semisynthetic fibers to keep the cost down.

In the world as a whole, the textile industry will remain one of the leading segments of manufacturing, although it probably will have a decreasing share of the world's industrial labor force as automation proceeds, of total value of industrial output as consumer durables and capital goods become relatively more important, and of international trade as textile manufacturing becomes more universal.

SUGGESTED READINGS

Airov, Joseph. *The Location of the Synthetic-Fiber Industry.* Massachusetts Institute of Technology Press, 1959. Pp. 203.

Alderfer, E. B., and Michl, H. E. *Economics of American Industry.* New York: McGraw-Hill, 1957. Pp. 323–457.

Carlson, Albert S. (ed.). *Economic Geography of Industrial Materials.* New York: Reinhold, 1956. Pp. 332–91.

Kirby, Richard H. *Vegetable Fibres.* London: L. Hill, 1963. Pp. 464.

Miller, E. Williard. *A Geography of Manufacturing.* Englewood Cliffs, N.J.: Prentice-Hall, 1962. Pp. 436–57.

Oxford University Press. *Oxford Economic Atlas of the World.* London: Oxford University Press, 1965. Pp. 48–57.

Van Royen, William (ed.). *Atlas of the World's Resources.* Vol. I. *The Agricultural Resources of the World.* Englewood Cliffs, N.J.: Prentice-Hall, 1954. Pp. 182–96.

Zimmermann, Erich W. *World Resources and Industries.* New York: Harper & Row, 1951. Pp. 314–73.

10

Tree Crops and Forest Products

Hunting and gathering cultures, before the advent of agriculture, depended mainly upon tree and bush vegetable products, but since the Neolithic specialization in annual crops, tree crops have been a minority participant in mankind's agricultural efforts. When forest land was cleared, many trees from which products were gathered previously were spared and converted into tree crops. As population grew in hilly and poor-soil areas, tree crops were found to be one of the main pioneering possibilities in the marginal areas. Tree crops, as a general rule, require more water than annuals growing in the same general area, but are more tolerant of topographic and soil inadequacies. The commercialization of tropical areas in the past century has resulted in an increasing importance of tree crop agriculture, as over two-thirds of all tree crops are tropical perennials and much of the remaining fraction is from the subtropical edge of the mid-latitudes.

As indicated in the following table, an eighth of world agricultural output is from the tree crops category narrowly defined. If other products were added that are partly gathered (Brazil and other nuts, rosin-turpentine, cork, pulpwood from tree farms, and many others), the tree crops category broadly defined would be nearly half again larger than indicated.

The difference in the time factor required for production is by far the most important distinction between annuals and perennials. Various perennials take from three to ten years to start bearing, and yield from twenty to sixty or more years thereafter. The longest time requirements are generally those involved in raising woody perennials (those whose aboveground growth turns woody as in trees and shrubs). Somewhat shorter periods are involved in raising herbaceous perennials (those whose underground stems survive for years, but whose aboveground growth periodically dies down), especially when they are grown on the edge of the tropics.

Tree crops are subject to the same weather (drought, frost, hurricane) and other natural catastrophes that afflict annuals. However, the length of the production process is the main cause of the economic difficulties that tree crop growers face: pests, depressions, wars, and scien-

Tree Crops' Share of World Agricultural Production
(per cent of gross value)

Basic-energy crops (cassava, bananas-plantains)	0.8
Luxury-energy crops (cane sugar, maple and palm sugars, olive, coconut, palm, tung, and other similar oils-fats)	3.5
Fruits (deciduous types like apples, pears, cherries, etc.; tropical types like citrus, pineapple, mango, etc.)	4.0
Beverage crops (coffee, tea, cocoa; wine and other spirits)	3.5
Industrial (technical) crops (hard fibers, rubber, etc.)	0.7
	12.5

tific-technological changes all affect tree crops more seriously than annual crops, because of the longer period required for adjustment to such changed conditions. Some alleviation is possible, but no major solution. The long waiting period's economic cost can be diminished by a number of devices: the use of nurseries (common, e.g., in orchards), piecemeal plantings (common, e.g., in tropical small holding operations, by planting fields abandoned for shifting cultivation), and intertillage (e.g., using strips between trees for food-feed crops during periods of gestation or during periods of low prices).

Thus, tree crops combine the high capitalization and rather rigid overhead costs of urban industry with the traditional physical and biological risks of ordinary agriculture. Tree crops can be classified according to which category of risks accounts for most problems. Beverage crops are among those tree crops where the traditional agricultural risks—fluctuations due to natural catastrophes or to alterations of heavy and light yieldings—are the most difficult problems. Natural rubber is among those tree crops where high fixed costs and pressure from factory-made substitutes are the most difficult problems.

BEVERAGE CROPS

The most common tropical (coffee-tea-cacao) and mid-latitude (wine) beverage crops account for about one-third of the value of all tree crops. They face roughly similar problems, especially one of long-term steady growth in demand coupled with erratic growth in supply. The result is usually a wide variation in prices around a rising trend.

The demand is remarkably stable, with the main factors affecting it being price and personal disposable income. At high prices, less beverage will be demanded than at low prices. When beverages are expensive, consumers tend to cut down on the amount and strength of their beverage intake. As income rises, demand for most beverages shifts upward. Given an established taste for a beverage, changes in income tend to be a more important factor if incomes are relatively low than if they are relatively high (especially in the cases of expensive beverages such as coffee and superior wines).

Beverage supplies, on the other hand, are subject to much more variable and unpredictable factors. The weather, an inherent production cycle, and the existence of carry-overs of varying size may produce substantial short-run changes. The five to seven years required to bring trees and vines into production means that considerable time is required to effect a basic supply condition.

The response of growers and intermediaries to price change depends to a considerable extent on the length of time they have to adjust. The supply in any one year is quite inelastic, mainly dependent upon decisions made in previous years (e.g., how many trees and vines were planted, quality of such plantings, amount of fertilizer and pesticide used, care of cultivation, etc.). However, there is some elasticity. If the price is especially high, harvesting will be done with more care, those holding reserve stocks will reduce their inventories, etc. If the price is especially low, the trees or vines will not be so thoroughly stripped, some areas may not even be harvested, and those in a position to do so will place in storage to await a better market.

In the longer run, supply is much more elastic. To a large extent, growers are governed in their planting decisions by estimates of future prices. If they observe a rising trend—for example, in the decade after World War II—they tend to expect it to continue and therefore plant more. If they observe a falling trend—for example, in recent years (since the late 1950's)—they tend to foresee decreases and plant less or even abandon some producing groves and vineyards. Thus, price plays an important role in determining how much beverage is available on the market.

As the graphs on pages 266–67 indicate, coffee, tea, and cacao are essentially tropical beverages, although in sheltered spots (Japan, U.S.S.R. Transcaucasus, and elsewhere) there is some tea production in subtropical areas. Latin

TABLE 10–1

World: Beverages Production and Composition, by Great-Region and Economic-Type of Society, 1962–1964 Average-Annual
(in metric tons)

	Caffein-Base Beverages[1] (thousand metric tons = 100.0 per cent)	Coffee	Tea	Cacao [2]	Wine [1] (million metric tons)
North America	–	–	–	–	1.5
Western Europe	–	–	–	–	17.4
Eastern Europe (including the U.S.S.R.)	43	–	100.0%	–	2.2
Oceania	24	50.0%	–	50.0%	0.2
Latin America	2,673	94.0	0.6	5.4	2.2
Sub-Saharan Africa	1,486	66.8	3.8	29.4	0.3
Middle East (including North Africa)	28	17.9	82.1	–	1.9
Non-Communist Far East	981	24.2	75.4	0.4	–
Communist Far East	154	–	100.0	–	–
World	5,389	69.7	19.2	11.1	25.7
High-income countries	206	28.7	65.5	5.8	18.5
Low-income countries	5,183	71.4	17.3	11.3	7.2
	(per cent of 5,389 thousand metric tons)	(per cent of 3,759 thousand metric tons)	(per cent of 1,033 thousand metric tons)	(per cent of 1,192 thousand metric tons)	(per cent of 25.7 million metric tons)
North America	–	–	–	–	5.8
Western Europe	–	–	–	–	67.7
Eastern Europe (including the U.S.S.R.)	0.8	–	4.2	–	8.6
Oceania	0.5	0.3	–	1.9	0.8
Latin America	49.5	66.8	1.7	24.1	8.6
Sub-Saharan Africa	27.6	26.5	5.4	73.4	1.1
Middle East (including North Africa)	0.5	0.1	2.2	–	7.4
Non-Communist Far East	18.2	6.3	71.6	0.6	–
Communist Far East	2.9	–	14.9	–	–
World	100.0	100.0	100.0	100.0	100.0
High-income countries	3.7	1.6	13.0	1.9	72.0
Low-income countries	96.3	98.4	87.0	98.1	28.0

Source: Adapted from United Nations and U.S. Department of Agriculture data.

[1] Comparisons between the caffeine-base beverages and wine should take into account the fact that the former, when prepared, yield liquid tonnage about three and a half times the latter. While the coffee and tea have no caloric value (apart from the cream and sugar used with them) and cocoa has only a little (aside from other ingredients that may be used), wine has considerable caloric value.

[2] The 1.2 million metric tons of cacao have been discounted 50 per cent to approximate the portion (mainly cocoa fat) removed and used in candy and other chocolate products. The remaining cocoa powder is used in beverages.

WORLD: BEVERAGES PRODUCTION AND COMPOSITION, BY GREAT-REGION AND ECONOMIC-TYPE OF SOCIETY, 1962-1964 AVERAGE-ANNUAL (Metric Tons)

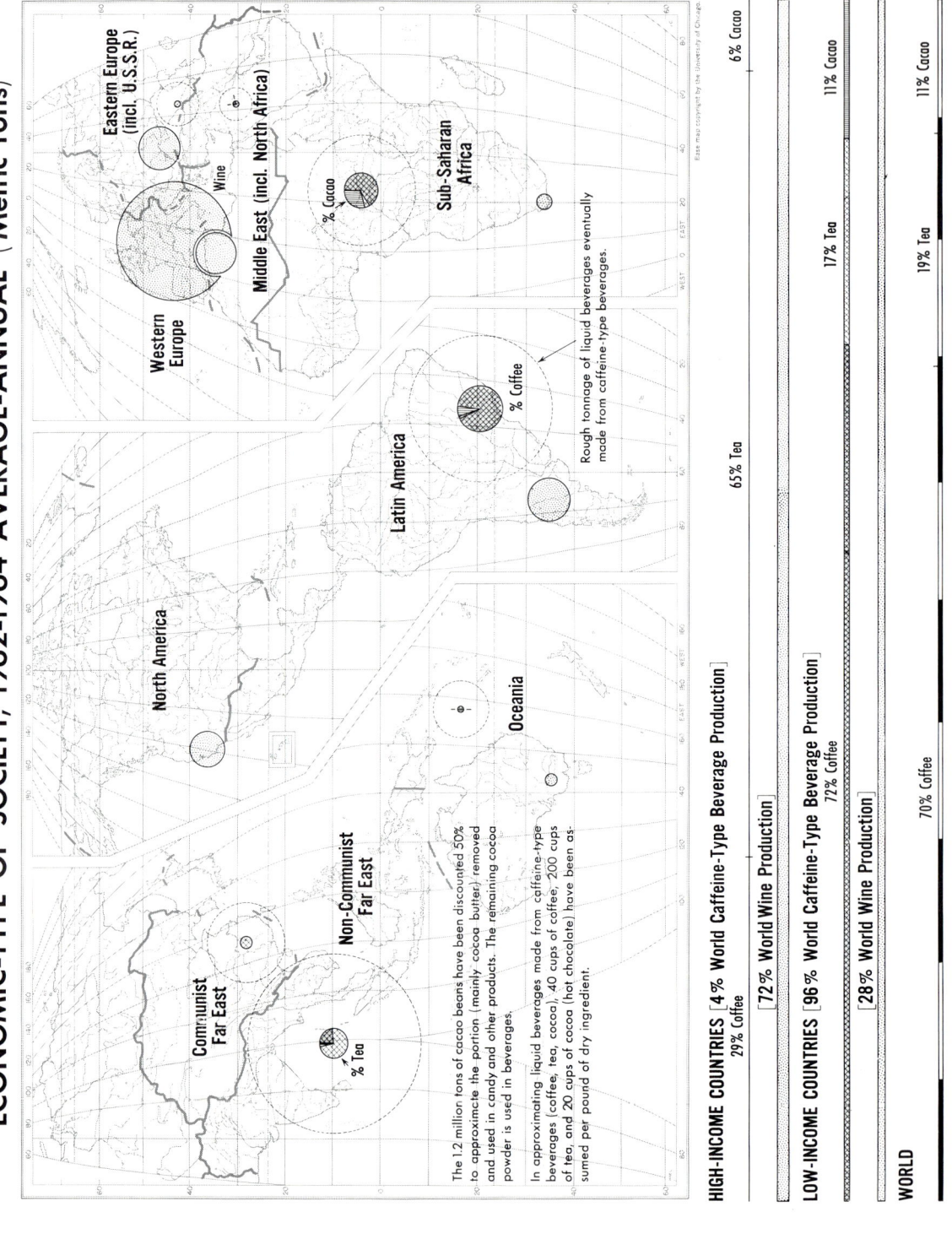

WORLD: GREAT-REGION AND ECONOMIC-TYPE OF SOCIETY SHARES OF WORLD BEVERAGES PRODUCTION (Coffee, Tea, Cacao, Wine), 1962-1964 AVERAGE-ANNUAL

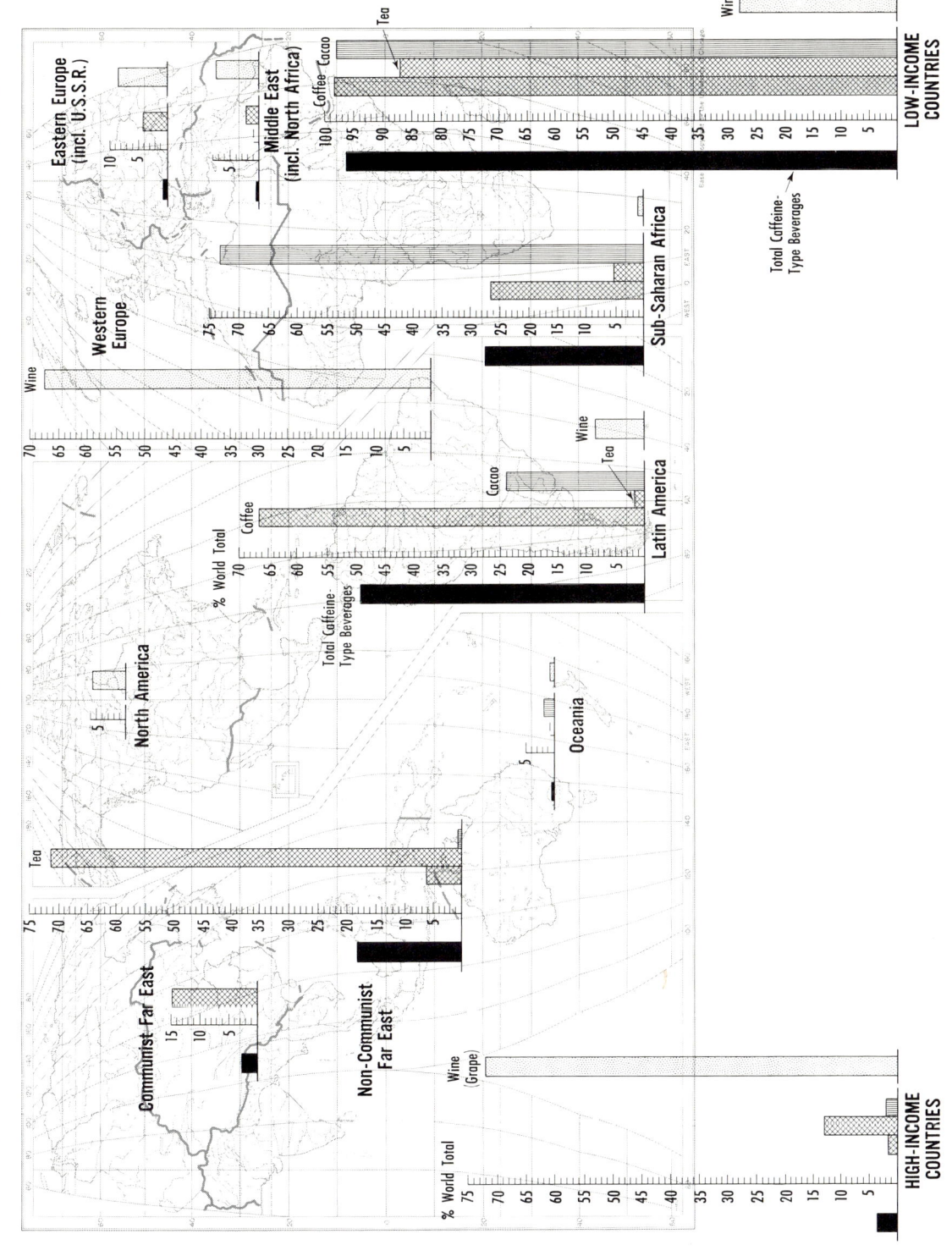

America still ranks first as a producer, mainly because of its production of two-thirds of the world's coffee, but also because of its quarter of the world's cacao. Sub-Saharan Africa is the most rapidly increasing source of exports, with its coffee production now over a quarter of the world total (practically all exported), its cacao production still nearly three-quarters of the world total, and its modest share of world tea (a twentieth of the world total) also increasing. The Far East accounts for a fifth of the world's caffeine-base beverages, practically all tea (nine-tenths of world output). Wine is an essentially mid-latitude beverage crop, the Mediterranean Basin accounting for over four-fifths of the world's supplies, and other mediterranean-type spots for almost all of the remainder.

Coffee

Coffee is the most important tropical beverage from a commercial standpoint, in spite of the possibility that more people may use tea. At least one-third of the world's population now uses coffee, spending over $6 billion annually for coffee-related goods and services:

Western hemisphere	$3.5 billion
Western Europe	2.7
Eastern Europe (including the U.S.S.R.)	0.1
Rest of world	0.1

The coffee beans entering world trade are worth some $2 billion, three-fourths coming from Latin America, and one-half destined for the U.S. market.

World coffee consumption is increasing 3 to 4 per cent annually. The U.S. increase is only half that, but Western Europe's rate of increase has recently been twice as large. Demand in the coffee producing areas is also increasing rapidly, reflecting population and income increases, as well as low prices on certain grades of dumped stocks. Currently, the average annual per capita consumption in Latin America is about 5 pounds compared with 16 pounds in the United States.

The coffee tree is an evergreen plant of African origin, occurring in a wild state wherever humid tropical conditions occur in that continent. Coffee was probably first used in Ethiopia by gathering from the extensive wild stands, and appears to have been planted first in Yemen. Production is restricted to regions lying between latitudes 25° N. and 25° S., thus being almost entirely a crop of the tropics, although in some of the tropical highlands where coffee is grown, the temperature characteristics of the climate are better described as semitropical. Temperature requirements vary with the species, but appear to lie between 60° F. and 78° F. In a few highland regions of much cloud cover, an annual rainfall of 40 inches is just sufficient when very evenly distributed, but in most areas the lower limit is 50 inches and the most favorable range is 75 to 120 inches, depending upon prevailing temperatures and distribution of the rainfall. It is preferable that the moisture be well distributed, with a minimum during the flowering season.

Coffee does best on loamy soils, deep, well drained, and rich in humus, neither very acid nor very alkaline. Coffee easily exhausts soils, as it needs fairly large quantities of both nitrogen and potash. In older coffee regions, both green manuring and chemical fertilizing are common.

The plant is very susceptible to diseases and frost is its fatal enemy. While it requires sunlight, it is so sensitive to overexposure that it is often grown partly in the shade of taller trees. Under natural conditions, the coffee tree would grow from 15 to 30 feet high, but for the convenience of the berry picker, the tree under cultivation is kept to 6 to 8 feet.

There are some twenty-five species of coffee, but only three are of commercial importance. *Coffea arabica*, the source of some 75 per cent of the world's supply, grows best in highlands. *Coffea robusta* ("Congo coffee"), supplying some 20 per cent of the world's total and *Coffea liberica* ("Liberian coffee") are primarily lowland coffees.

Arabica (called Arabian but originally Ethiopian) is the most widely cultivated species, and some fifteen varieties are grown. It occurs wild in the highlands of Ethiopia between altitudes of

U.S.D.A. Photo

Freshly picked coffee in measuring funnel.

U.S.D.A. Photo

Coffee seed and leaves.

Coffee is the most important commercial tropical beverage and, after petroleum, the most important single raw material item by value moving in world trade.

3,000 to 6,000 feet, with 4,500 feet apparently being its optimum. As it was originally a highland coffee, it requires more moderate temperatures than the other species. In regions with humid tropical conditions moderated by altitude and with a short dry season, its fruit ripens in eight months.

Robusta is a larger and more vigorous plant with thick leaves, and can be grown from sea level to considerable altitudes. It is more hardy than arabica, and is adapted to a wider range of climate. From its original Congo Basin habitat, it has spread over most of lowland and low-plateau Africa, and has been taken elsewhere in the Old World. Robusta is resistant to the most deadly coffee disease (*Hemileia*) and has substituted for both arabica and liberica plantings in parts of Africa and in Indonesia after they had succumbed to disease. Although robusta bears heavily and has high caffeine content, the quality is not as good as that of arabica, but is considerably cheaper (in 1964, arabica brought about 45 to 50 cents per pound, New York dockside, while robusta brought 6 to 8 cents per pound less).

Liberica, a native of the west coast of Africa, is the largest of the three species, reaching a natural height of 40 to 50 feet, with berries an inch in diameter. The plant is more vigorous and less susceptible to disease than arabica (which is more susceptible to the leaf-spot disease at lower elevations). However, the flavor and aroma are inferior, so it is used chiefly in blends, especially in Scandinavia.

The coffee plants generally do not begin to bear until the third or fourth year, the best yield is reached from the fifth to the eighteenth years, and production then gradually decreases for the remaining decade or so of useful life. The coffee berries are usually picked individually by hand when fully ripe, some 2,000 being required to provide enough beans for one pound of roasted coffee. In parts of Brazil and elsewhere, the bushes are stripped off or allowed to drop their berries on the ground.

After picking and winnowing (sifting to remove debris), coffee is prepared for the market by either the dry or the wet method. In the dry method, the berries are spread out on drying floors and exposed to the sun for twenty days and nights, during which they must be raked to dry evenly, and covered each night for protection against dew or rain. Eventually, the dried skin and pulp are cleaned off by machines and the parchment is removed by pounding in a mortar or by mechanical means.

In the wet or washed method, the berries are run through a pulping machine first. Depulping means removing the seeds or pits from the berries and is a very complicated job (the berry consists of an outer skin, a layer of pulpy material, a tough parchment-like inner skin, a thin silvery skin, and finally the two beans). Next, the beans are placed in vats, where the remainder of the pulp ferments and can be washed off. They are then dried by the sun or by artificial heat. The color of the finished product depends on the amount of moisture. After drying, the brittle parchment is cracked and removed by hulling machines, and the silver skin is rubbed off in polishing machines.

The wet method is the more common as it produces a more uniform coffee, but is possible only if sufficient water and fuel are available. In the dry method, water content is reduced from 60 per cent to 5 to 10 per cent in from ten to twenty days, and the final product is said to produce more aromatic coffees.

Grading—first for weight and then for size, and finally with hand inspection to remove imperfect beans—is followed by bagging for shipment. Only the beans of sufficient weight, proper size, and good, rich, olive-green color are passed for export.

Coffee cannot be stored indefinitely without loss of quality, but if ideal conditions of temperature and humidity are met, it can be kept up to five years without serious deterioration, although it is seldom held that long. While old-crop coffee usually sells at a discount, large stocks of it on hand (Brazil now has equivalent of one year's world consumption) have a strong bearing on the market.

Coffee may be held for normal business inventories by exporters, roasters, or wholesalers. Pipeline and inventory stocks between the farmer and the final consumer usually amount to some 0.4 to 0.6 million tons at any one time. In addition, stocks are held for purposes of influencing price (i.e., for speculation or for market control). Farmers, roasters, and even consumers of coffee tend to hold larger stocks when there is a general feeling that the price will rise, and to dispose of them when they feel it will fall. Of greatest importance is the coffee that is held by farmers' organizations and by governments in order to maintain or raise coffee prices. Such stocks alone were kept to the extent of some two-thirds of a year's consumption during the 1930's, and recently have been about one year's supply.

Eventually the beans are roasted, a process that results in a loss of weight but a gain in bulk, and that is accompanied by many physiological changes. The aroma, flavor, and color develop during this process. No two varieties require the same amount of roasting, and there are many differences in the temperature used and the duration of the process. The roasted coffee beans contain from $3/4$ to $1\frac{1}{2}$ per cent caffeine, the stimulating portion, and a volatile oil, caffeol, which is responsible for the aroma and flavor, besides glucose, dextrin, protein, and a fatty oil. Before coffee is sold to the consumer it is usually ground and blended. In all, there are twenty-four steps in the evolution of coffee from the tree to the cup, of which fourteen take place in the coffee producing countries. Roasting and distributing adds as much value as the cost of the green coffee. In the United States alone, there are about 1,300 highly competitive roasters who test, blend, and roast the coffee before passing it on to the consumer.

The coffee industry faces a number of major problems, most important of which is overproduction which began in the late 1950's. This overproduction brought about a precipitous drop in price, to a level lower than immediately after World War II, before international action recently brought about an upturn. In 1946, the average New York price per pound was about 50 cents, with the price advancing to a high of $1.15 in 1954 as demand outran supply. Thereafter, increased production brought the price down, from $1.03 in 1956 to 35 cents in 1962. The International Coffee Agreement which came into effect in 1963 set quotas and made other arrangements that sent prices back to about the 1946 level.

Increasing demand will not absorb the surplus in the short run. The best prospect is in Western Europe, both because of increasing prosperity and reduced import duties and taxes. The chances of increasing consumption in coffee producing countries is good, although this tends to reduce mainly the inferior grades which usually go into reserve stocks. The U.S. coffee consumption has actually fallen off—from the 24 pounds per capita annually in 1946 to under 16 pounds in 1964—although the increased population has kept absolute consumption increasing. Younger people are drinking less coffee and more of other beverages, and soluble coffees require less beans per unit.

Brazil, producing nearly one-half of the world's coffee, is engaged in a mammoth attempt to cut production by eliminating its poorest trees. The plan is eventually to eradicate nearly one-half of the present 4⅓ billion trees, thus clearing some 10 million acres now in low-yielding coffee for diversified-crop production (rice, corn, beans, soybeans, cotton). Some 0.7 million planters and farmworkers are involved, now producing almost one-third of national production. A small subsidy is the incentive to eradication.

Another partial solution is to lower the cost of production through increasing areal yields. Coffee trees have a very low yield per tree on the average. Approximately 28 ounces of coffee (finished product) per coffee tree per year is the average, with yields of bean per acre in various Latin American countries ranging from 150 to 400 pounds per acre. Nearly all major producing countries are stepping up programs to improve cultural practices: growing coffee with less (or no) shade, planting improved and higher-yielding varieties, fertilizing more heavily, and using more effective pruning practices. All of these tend to increase yields per tree. Some experimental trees have yielded as much as 8 pounds per year, and theoretically some 2,000 pounds an acre might be raised.

Another major problem—to Latin American producers—is the increasing use of cheaper African coffees to make soluble coffees. Since the end of World War II, coffee production has doubled in Africa, and its share of the world coffee trade is triple what it was before World War II. Some 15 per cent of world coffee roastings is now soluble coffee: in the United States the share is over 20 per cent; in Europe the share is about 10 per cent; elsewhere, the share is usually smaller.

The lower-priced African types (especially robusta), which generally do not suit the American taste in roasted blends, are the major ingredient of most instant coffees. The process of making instant or soluble coffee is more economical than that of producing regular grinds. Through the vacuum process of brewing and dehydration, the beans are forced to yield almost their entire essence. This results in more cups of coffee from a given amount of green beans for the instant brews (some 8,200 cups from a 132-pound bag) than for the regular types (averaging 7,100 cups from a bag).

Although soluble coffee makes more cups per pound of beans, it also increases the ease with which it can be made and dispensed—these factors may largely offset each other. Instant coffee boosts coffee consumption in countries where coffee drinking is a new thing. However, it has growing importance too in urban areas of traditional coffee drinking countries, especially among young working couples, for whom money, time, and kitchen space are prime considerations.

The United States consumer has had another disturbing effect on Latin American coffee producers, by maintaining the dilute brew which made its appearance during the high prices of the early 1950's. Some 40 to 45 cups from a pound of roasted coffee is suggested by the producers. The average U.S. family gets about 64 cups per pound, compared to less than 50 cups in 1950. The increased use of soluble coffee is not thought to be the major reason.

In the long run, coffee faces another threat. Coffee is subject to erratic fluctuations in price, due primarily to good or poor harvest, but aggravated on occasion by wrong estimates of the extent of damage caused by frost or drought. The high prices may eventually have the result of encouraging substitution. Already scientists have tracked down more than thirty of the volatile chemicals that give coffee its flavor, so synthetic coffee is well on its way. Even if the dreams of the enthusiasts are not realized (e.g., that such synthetic coffee may become available at a price only a fifth or so of the real thing), it could set a ceiling on coffee prices much like synthetic rubber's present ceiling on natural rubber price. The relationship of coffee demand and price is not perfect, but it is good enough to dispel the old notion that coffee drinkers behave irrationally in the face of price changes, or that the amount of coffee they consume is fixed only by taste and is unresponsive to price.

Tea

Tea probably originated in the general highland area where eastern India, southwestern China, and northern Burma meet. By A.D. 600 or earlier, the drinking of tea had spread to the masses of China, and by 1200 it had become the national beverage of Japan and was known over much of the remainder of the Far and Middle East. Even today, over two-thirds of the world's 2 billion tea drinkers are in Asian regions. By the middle of the seventeenth century, tea had become the national drink of England, and was commonly used in other European countries, including Russia. At present, the British are the heaviest tea drinkers in the world, while the rest of Europe makes very sparing use of the beverage (preferring coffee and wine).

Consumption of Tea, 1964
(pounds per capita annually)

United Kingdom	10.0
New Zealand	7.0
Australia	6.0
Iraq	6.0
Canada	2.7
South Africa	1.8
Netherlands	1.5
Japan	0.9
United States	0.7
India	0.6
China	0.5
U.S.S.R.	0.4

The growing acceptance of tea, particularly in lower-income countries, is reflected in its relatively recent status as the national drink of India, Pakistan, Ceylon, the U.S.S.R., and most Middle Eastern and African countries. Growth in U.S. tea imports (world's second importer) reflects both growth in population and a modest growth in individual consumption (iced tea, tea bags, and instant-tea sales are limited practically to the United States).

Tea leaves before they are brewed contain about two and a half times as much caffeine as coffee beans, pound for pound. As a result, tea is the base product from which most medicinal caffeine is extracted. A cup of coffee, however, contains about twice as much caffeine as a cup of tea. This is because a pound of coffee makes approximately 40 cupfuls of strong coffee, whereas a pound of tea will infuse about 200 cupfuls of strong tea (the United States prefers weaker brews: 65 cups of coffee and 400 cups of tea). Approximately $1\frac{1}{2}$ grains of caffeine is present in a cup of strong coffee, with $\frac{3}{4}$ grain present in a cup of strong tea (a medicinal dosage of caffeine usually ranges from 1 to 5 grains). Tea also contains vegetable tannin, a mild astringent. Like coffee, tea has practically no food value, except for the cream, sugar, and other items added.

Basically, there are three kinds of tea: black, green, and oolong. The leaves for each could come from the same plant but would vary in the finished product according to the way the leaves were cured or processed. Variations in flavor are achieved by the tea wholesalers by mixing together leaves from tea trees grown in different areas and leaves plucked under varying conditions of growth.

The tea plant (*Camellia sinensis*), although it resembles a bush when pruned for easy picking of the young shoots, properly is a tree, and will grow to 30 to 40 feet if it is not pruned. Shoots, containing two to three leaves and bud, are picked at intervals of a week to ten days. Only about one-half the foliage of the tea bush that is grown in the interval between one pruning operation and the next is taken away as crop. In the full tropics, the picking is done throughout the year, while elsewhere there is a period of rest during the cool season.

Since tea is originally a semitropical crop (the Assam-type tea grown in the full tropics is a mutation of the original Chinese-type tea), it can be grown in most areas that have a sufficiently mild winter to prevent any permanent damage to the evergreen, and a sufficiently humid climate to foster an abundant growth of young leaves. Most tea, however, is grown under tropical and semitropical conditions—from about latitudes 30° N. to 30° S.—where growth is nearly continuous. But under subtropical conditions—from latitudes 30° N. to 43° N. in Transcaucasia (U.S.S.R.), Japan, etc.—where there is a definite cold period, the plants are pruned annually and the leaves are plucked only during the warmer months. For optimum production, temperatures should be in the range of 55° F. and 90° F., and total annual rainfall should be in the range of 100 to 150 inches, well distributed through the year. However, in the subtropical areas of production, some spots exist having only 40 inches of rainfall, well distributed in the warm rainy season of growth, while at the other extreme, some tropical highlands have 350 inches or more of rainfall. However, the tea plant cannot tolerate drought or temperatures more than a few degrees below freezing. Tea is suitable as a crop in regions having moderate to high rainfalls in excess of evaporation, and that maintain equable temperatures with high humidity throughout the greater part of the growing season.

The soil requirements are critical. Teas grown in different regions have their own characteristic flavors, apparently caused by differences in soil type. Soils ideally must be acid within the proper limits, must not contain more than a trace of available calcium, must be well drained, allow of deep root penetration, and should contain plenty of available nitrogen. In practice, most tea soils—the tropical red earths form the most extensively used types—are of only moderate fertility owing to severe erosion and leaching in the hill areas. They are low in bases and phosphorus and their nitrogen content is very variable. In the commercial areas, good soils are usually favored and nitrogen fertilization comes from leguminous shade trees,

U.S.D.A. Photo

Assam tea plant. Tea drinkers number some 2 billion, about two-thirds of them in the Far East. Like coffee, tea by itself has no food value (except for the sugar, cream, and other items added for the flavoring).

manure, and chemicals. In the subsistence areas of East Asia, much tea is grown on stony soils and on steep slopes unsuitable for ordinary tilled crops, but they contribute a declining share of world production.

Some fifty-three countries now grow and process tea, a slow-growing plant that takes five years to mature. The average yield is about 1,000 pounds of black tea an acre. However, the best teas are usually from highland areas—3,000 to 6,500 feet in the South Asian commercial areas which produce one-half of the world's tea—but yields per acre may be only about one-half what they are lower down where most of the crop is produced.

The green tea, produced almost exclusively in Japan and in parts of China, is prepared by a relatively simple process of heating, rolling, and drying the fresh leaf without a process of fermentation. The preparation of black tea, grown almost exclusively in South Asia and Indonesia, is more complicated, with the leaves first withered, then rolled, then fermented, then fired, and finally graded. Oolong tea is lightly fermented and is intermediate between green tea and black tea.

Coffee and tea are alike in many ways: the better grades of both grow on mountain slopes; it takes about five years for the plants to reach maturity; new plantations in Africa are threatening traditional producers; and both beverages are competing for the American and other markets in a campaign financed in part by funds from producing countries. The similarities end when price and consumption are considered. Coffee prices fluctuate sharply, while tea quotations are relatively steady, reflecting the greater importance of plantations in commercial tea production, and the tauter organization which traditionally has kept closer control on production.

While the tea industry is not faced with the great overproduction of the coffee industry during the early 1960's, there is an overproduction problem. The surplus problem is not a simple case of too much tea, but too much plain tea—tea of medium and low grades. Since World War II, the volume of expensive blends of tea has risen only slightly, but the cheaper types have been stimulated by heavy sales in less advanced countries now experiencing minor rises in incomes.

Both quantity and quality of tea can be affected by the way in which the plant is plucked. Fine plucking means that only the bud and the two youngest leaves of the tea shoot are harvested. Coarse plucking takes not only the bud and the two young leaves but some of the larger leaves and stems as well. When tea is scarce, as in the decade after World War II, buyers will take what they can get. But when there is plenty of tea, as there is today, discriminating buyers compete for the quality tea.

Many Indian producers, when faced with the threat of surplus stocks of plain tea (mostly from North India, which produces three-fourths of the production), favor closer restriction. Ceylon producers, on the other hand, are having less trouble finding markets, as most of their production consists of fine tea, and consequently are not anxious to cut back production. India is also trying to cut back its surplus by encouraging national sales, which now account for one-third of total production, although a smaller fraction of the value, since it mainly consists of low grades.

The cost structure of East African teas is favorable as compared to that of India and, furthermore, it has the advantage of lower transport costs to North Atlantic Basin markets. While still only some 5 per cent of world production, the African competition is growing, powered by cheaper land, cheaper labor, and considerable supplies of capital and management fleeing Far Eastern nationalization or threat of it. Latin America is also increasing production rapidly, and although still furnishing less than 1 per cent of world production, the capacity of new Argentine [1] plantings is expected to triple present capacity.

As with many of the world's crops, increased production of tea is being realized from fewer acres, through improved production practices, especially the wider use of fertilizers and insecticides. Past norms of 2,000 to 3,000 bushes per acre are substantially below the optimum, and under the new intensive system, some 4,000 to 5,000 bushes per acre is advantageous. The economic advantage comes in harvesting, which is 45 per cent of the total cost of tea production. Labor productivity is greatly increased under the more intensive system.

Tea's prospects are good in the long view. It is still the cheapest of exotic beverages and

---

[1] This refers to true tea, and not to herva mate, which comes from a member of the holly family. The tree is naturally about the size of an orange tree, with a height of 25 feet and a trunk some 3 feet around. Processing consists of rendering the leaves brittle enough to be easily pulverized and dried. Potency of the drink in relieving fatigue comes from its caffeine content, much stronger than that of coffee.

its consumption in the underdeveloped countries is likely to rise correlated with improved levels of living. On the supply side, the expected yields of commercial clonal plantings is exceeding 2,000 pounds per acre after the fifth acre, or double the present yield.

Cacao [2]

Unlike coffee and tea, chocolate is a food as well as a beverage. The roasted beans contain approximately 50 per cent cocoa fat, 20 to 25 per cent carbohydrates, 15 to 20 per cent protein, up to $1\frac{1}{2}$ per cent theobromine (a stimulating alkaloid closely related to caffeine and theophylline), 5 per cent moisture, and $3\frac{1}{2}$ per cent ash (including such minerals as calcium, iron, magnesium, potassium, sodium, and a little red coloring matter). The main constituent, cacao butter, is extracted from the bean and used in candy making, while the rest of the bean forms the powder with which the chocolate drink is made.

Cacao comes from the seeds of *Theobroma cacao*, a small tree indigenous to the forests of Central America and northern South America, where it was used by the Amerindians long before the Oceanic Age. Commercial production on a large scale did not start until this century.

Cacao is a tropical crop that demands a warm, humid, and uniform environment throughout the year. It is a tree of the humid tropical lowlands, and is seldom found above 1,500 feet elevation. Most cacao is grown within 20° of the Equator, as it cannot be grown profitably where the absolute minimum drops below 50° F. In the best areas, night temperatures are about 60° F. and daytime temperatures 80° F. and over.

The plants are very sensitive to wind, drought, and frost. Shade is essential for young trees and, although some trees are grown in full sunlight, most have light shade which also provides shelter from strong wind movement (a danger that can beat off the pods). The tree is not resistant to dry weather, and areas with a dry season of over four months are not suitable.

The lower limit of annual rainfall is about 45 inches, but the distribution is very important, as prolonged dry spells are very detrimental.

While cacao can be grown on various types of soils, they should be rich in humus and minerals (especially potash) and well drained.

The tree reaches 40 feet in the wild state, but is kept pruned to 15 feet under cultivation. The tree begins to bear at five to seven years of age, reaching full bearing between the tenth and fifteenth year, producing for thirty to eighty years, although it usually yields at a low rate after twenty-five years. Thus, like coffee and tea, substantial production increases of cacao in a relatively short time are not possible. A constant program of rehabilitation, disease control, and replanting is essential to a steady annual output.

Flowers and fruits (pods) develop along the trunk and older branches of the tree, requiring about four and a half to six months to ripen. The pods are 8 to 15 inches long, about the size of large cucumbers or long, furrowed melons. The leathery looking pods, which pass through several color stages, contain twenty to fifty seeds in a gummy liquid which becomes a soft white pulp when exposed to air. Each seed or bean is enclosed in a parchment shell with two oil lobes. Two major fruiting periods occur each year, although flowers and pods may be seen on the same tree at all seasons. Two bumper cacao crops in succession are unusual. Generally, a relatively poor yield follows a large harvest, as favorable growing conditions cannot continue indefinitely.

There are about twenty species, but only two of commercial importance. *Criollo* probably originated in Central America, and produces the best quality cacao, but because of susceptibility to disease is becoming less important, and is mainly used for blending purposes. It now accounts for only a tenth of world cacao production, having been almost eliminated by witches' broom and pod rot diseases, except in restricted Middle American and northern South American areas. *Forastero* probably originated in the Guayana area, and is the major species now grown, either pure or hybridized with Criollo,

[2] *Cocoa* is an English-language corruption of *cacao*. Cocoa fat and cacao butter are the same.

especially in the African areas now producing three-fourths of world production, and in the Brazilian Hump area producing another 10 per cent or so.

Latin American cacao production, now under one-fourth of the total, is for the most part a product of estate or large-farm production. The African three-fourths is mainly a product of peasant agriculture. In Ghana, producing over one-third of the world's cacao, the average farm is about 4 acres (yielding 1 ton of dry cacao), with many farms less than 1 acre.

Both types of producer face a frustrating struggle against disease. In Latin America, the two worst diseases are witches' broom and Monilia rot; in Africa, swollen shoot causes the most trouble. Almost universal is a black pod rot that occurs wherever cacao is grown. Unfortunately, efforts to control these diseases have not met with too much success. The only reliable treatment to date for swollen shoot (a virus disease) is the removal of infected trees and some of those in the immediate vicinity. This type of treatment presents two problems. First, it is difficult to convince a backward farmer that it is to his interest to destroy an infected tree when it is still producing fruit. And, second, since treatment involves cutting out thousands of trees, the need for a supervised replanting program is most critical. The limited scale on which replanting and rehabilitation have taken place accounts, probably more than any other factor, for reduced cacao supplies in certain areas.

World cacao production since 1950 has increased about 60 per cent, from ¾ to 1.2 million tons, mainly because of the increasing use of the latest production and disease prevention (spraying) techniques in West Africa. From a 1949 average price of under 16 cents per pound, prices rose to a record 73 cents in 1954 because of short supplies. Increased supplies in the late 1950's brought the price down again to around 20 cents for four surplus years. In 1964 and early 1965, the price range per pound was in the range 17 to 24 cents. During high prices (over 30 cents per pound), candy manufacturers decrease the size of their bars and begin using synthetic flavorings and substitutes to stretch the cocoa fat supplies (e.g., compound coatings of a vegetable fat base and the much cheaper cocoa powder, instead of cocoa butter). Cocoa powder consumption also drops off if prices rise too high, especially in countries where the habit is new.

Very little cacao is consumed in the areas of production, so the condition of export markets is all important. The United States alone consumes one-fourth of world output, and even a larger fraction at times. Western Europe imports as much, and other urban-industrial markets the remainder.

U.S.D.A. Photo

Near view of cacao pods on the tree trunk. The beans inside the pods are separated into two products: the fat (cacao butter) into candy, the rest into chocolate.

Wine

The annual production of grapes is larger than that for the deciduous and citrus fruits together. However, some 85 per cent is used for making wine, and about one-half of the remaining output is dried for raisins and currants. Only some 10 per cent of fresh and dried grape production enters international trade.

Over three-fourths of the some 20 million acres devoted to viticulture are in countries bordering the Mediterranean Sea, and produce a like fraction of world wine production.

The vine has a long taproot which enables it to draw water from great depths, so that production can be carried on where total annual rainfall is small, but a long, hot, dry summer is essential. In the United States, the climatic limits are a growing season of not less than 170 days and a mean temperature between May and September of 65° F. European vines are less winter hardy than the American vines, and usually require longer seasons and mean summer temperatures of 72° F. or more, although prolonged periods of high temperature are inimical. Because some of the highest-quality wine grapes are produced fairly close to the northern commercial limit of the plant, this limit is of great importance. Little growth takes place at temperatures less than 50° F., and over 1800° F. of accumulated temperatures above 50° F. is necessary for the successful cultivation of the vine.

The grapevine needs a period of rest, without which the grapes do not ripen completely. The period of rest need not coincide with a cool winter season (e.g., grapevines can be successfully adapted to cultivation in hothouses where the period of growth is made to fall in winter, and the period of rest in summer). The equatorial limit, although much less well defined than the poleward limit, appears to be determined largely by the need of the plant for a period of rest.

Grapes require a good supply of water in the vegetative phase and dry, sunny weather during ripening and harvesting, especially raisin-type grapes. Too much moisture promotes the spread of fungi.

Grapes can be grown on many different soils, but they should be well drained. For wine grapes, the soils should not be too rich, for moderate to low production frequently is accompanied by high quality of the grapes and wine. Some rootstalks can thrive on highly calcareous soils and withstand drought.

When grapes are picked, there is a fuzz on them that consists of yeast organisms. After pressing, the yeast converts the grape sugar into ethyl alcohol and carbon dioxide, which bubbles up violently in the casks and is allowed to escape. When winter sets in, fermentation stops. But some of the sugar is left in the wine, and with the first warmth of spring the yeast starts to work on that. In champagne, the wine has been bottled and since the gas of the second slow fermentation cannot go anywhere, it gradually dissolves in the wine. It takes, meaning that the gas becomes a real and natural part of the wine, unlike the soda pop variety of sparkling wine in which carbon dioxide and a still wine are simply forced together in a tank and left to fight it out.

There is little wastage in wine production. About 70 per cent of the tonnage of grapes is converted into wine. After the juice has been squeezed from the grapes, the pomace (seeds, skins, and stems) is generally trucked back to the vineyards to be used as fertilizer. From winery laboratories come the yeast cultures that are used to activate the freshly squeezed juice.

Wine quality varies widely, and apparently the main factors are the nature of the wine, the soil's chemical composition, the climate, and the actual methods of processing adapted (e.g., extent of fermentation employed and subsequent care and handling). The first fermentation begins immediately after pressing, and continues for several days. The second fermentation, which begins in the spring, is controlled according to the type of wine required. With most wines, it is allowed to complete its course in open casks or vats, so that no carbon dioxide remains. Sparkling wines are made by bottling after the first fermentation, adding sugar, and allowing the second fermentation to take place in sealed bottles, so that the gas cannot escape until the cork is drawn. Fortified wines (port, sherry) have grape brandy added to them, which stops further fermentation.

An exceptional (vintage) year will not change the taste of most quality wines nowadays. Actually, most such wines are blends prepared carefully each year with an eye toward keeping the taste uniform. In other words, a vintage crop might change the blending pattern but not the end product.

In southern Europe, wine consumption is some ten times what it is in Britain, and U.S. consumption is only one-half that of Britain. France and Italy each produce about one-fourth of the world's wine, and other Mediterranean countries produce another fourth. France's per capita consumption is now somewhat lower than before World War II, but it is still the highest in the world, slightly over 135 quarts a year. About 80 per cent of all French wine is classified as ordinary wine (retailing at some 20 to 25 cents a bottle), and 20 per cent is superior or fine-quality wine. Exports (some 7 per cent of the volume), however, are 60 per cent fine wines by value (vermouth, brandies, champagne). Nearly one-half of the champagne and three-fourths of the cognac are exported.

France imports five to six times more wine by volume than it exports, mainly high-alcoholic-content wine from Algeria to blend with weaker domestic wines. The 300 to 400 million gallons a year of imports supply one-fourth of domestic consumption, and cost about what the quality wine exports bring. The diminished Algerian exports since independence can be made up from French surplus stocks, but their lower alcoholic content causes blending problems.

About three out of every five French farmers grow wine grapes, and some 1.5 million out of 2.2 million French farmers have vineyards. The total area in vineyards is nearly double the area in potatoes, and one-third as large as that in wheat, the main crop. The total area in vineyards is now less than two-thirds as large as it was a century ago, but improved methods and varieties have sharply increased the yields which now average about 350 gallons per acre per year.

Grapes for wine are even more valuable than wheat in terms of French farm income, in that they total nearly $¾ billion annually. To about 1 million small French farmers, vineyards are a supplemental crop that brings in some $200 to $300 of additional income a year, but they produce less than one-fourth of the total wine production. About one-half the total production comes from the 10 per cent of the growers with several acres or more of vineyards.

In the United States, California produces some 85 per cent of all wine production, and supplies some 75 per cent of national wine consumption. The national grape output is over 3 million tons, of which over 60 per cent is converted into raisins (entirely in California), 20 per cent is made into wine, and 20 per cent is sent to market as fresh fruit. Most California wine is dessert wine (sherries, ports, muscatels—mostly sweet and of 20 per cent alcoholic content), although attempts are being made to increase sales of table wines (clarets, chiantis, burgundies, chablis, sauternes, and other quality wines), an area still mainly filled by French wine importers. Most California wine is sent by railway tank car or by tank ship to the East Coast (one tankship carries 2½ million gallons of wine per trip to the Gulf Coast and the Eastern Seaboard). The California quality wines sell for little more than half the European equivalents, and are gaining in repute.

Trends

Beverage crops are economically in the nature of luxury consumption, much like the luxury-energy foods already discussed. A considerable proportion of refined sugar and milk cream is used to add palatability to the non-alcoholic beverages, and some sugar is added to certain kinds of wine.

In varying degrees, the beverages act as stimulants, and all are wanted for taste and flavor rather than nutritive value. Since they are luxuries and semiluxuries, the amounts consumed are dependent on the prosperity of the consumer. The rise in levels of living since World War II reconstruction has been accompanied by striking increases in world consumption.

Although the long-term demand for these beverages appears to be increasing at a rate of two to three times that of population growth, there are problems in the short run and medium run related to the comparatively inelastic demand. In the past decade, the increased production of wine and tea was about 3 to 4 per cent yearly, and consumption increased about the same, although there were national shortages and gluts. However, the supplies of cacao and coffee increased faster than demand—cacao supply went up an average of 5 per cent and coffee supply 7 to 8 per cent, while effective demand was going up at rates about three-fourths as fast—causing temporary gluts.

The coming decade may see greater stability in beverage supply, but this is likely to come less from control over natural resistances (occasional frost, cold, winds, droughts, microorganism outbreaks) than from international agreements to control more carefully marketable supplies by production control and storage-marketing control. Individual countries have been using such controls for a long time, but the problems in the 1960's are probably too great to be solved except by worldwide or nearly worldwide consensus between producers, intermediaries, and consumers.

ELASTOMERS ("RUBBERS")

While the beverage tree crops are affected by synthetic substitutes to only a very minor extent, natural rubber has been very hard hit. Synthetic rubber is now annually produced in amounts larger than natural rubber, and its share is increasing. Natural rubber prices (Singapore) have fallen from 49 cents per pound in 1960 to 22 cents per pound in 1964, and its supply is remaining at little more than 2 million tons (even with released stocks).

The year 1963 was the beginning of a second round in the battle between man-made and natural rubber. Up to then, styrene-butadiene synthetic (SBR) had been taking the automobile tire market away from natural rubber (over two-thirds in North America, about one-half in Western Europe, about one-third in Eastern Europe, Japan, and elsewhere). By 1963, polybutadiene and polyisoprene (stereo) rubbers, which are close in both makeup and quality to natural rubber, began making a strong bid for the heavy-tire market (bus, truck, and airplane tires). To further the substitution, stereo rubbers were priced at 25 cents per pound, about the same as delivered natural rubber and several cents above SBR rubber. Plans indicate that by 1965, world production of SBR-type synthetic rubbers will be some 3 million tons (a third in Communist countries), with stereo rubbers output over $\frac{1}{2}$ million tons in addition, mainly in the North Atlantic regions.

Historically, world rubber consumption has doubled every decade of this century, and it seems likely to repeat this doubling in the 1960's. Up to 1940, the increased supply was almost entirely natural rubber, but in the future, it is likely to consist almost entirely of synthetic and reclaimed rubbers, with natural rubber at best maintaining present output. In the synthetic rubbers, stereo types will be increasingly substituting not only for natural rubber but for the older SBR rubbers. The North American rate of increase in rubber consumption is now only half the world rate; by 1965, Western Europe's capacity to make tires will be as large as that of the United States.

Natural Rubber

Although rubber can be obtained from a number of trees and other plants, 99 per cent of all natural rubber is from one tree, *Hevea braisiliensis*, originally from the Amazon Basin, but now 99 per cent of production is from other continents. Hevea output of over 2 million tons is just under one-half of present annual production of new rubber (natural rubber plus synthetic rubber).

For optimum growth and yield, temperatures in the range of approximately 75° F. to 95° F. are best. Latex flow is inhibited by dry heat, while harvesting is troubled by excessive wetness. Some 70 inches of annual rainfall, if evenly distributed throughout the year, is satisfactory for optimum yield, but there are limited areas where 60 inches is sufficient and usually 100 to 120 inches is nearer the optimum.

Although rubber will grow under almost any soil condition, providing the climate is favorable, soil conditions do affect growth and yield. Soils rich in nitrogen are best, although the other

WORLD: ELASTOMERS ("Rubber") PRODUCTION AND COMPOSITION, AND TOBACCO PRODUCTION, BY GREAT-REGION AND ECONOMIC-TYPE OF SOCIETY, 1962-1964 AVERAGE-ANNUAL (Thousand Metric Tons)

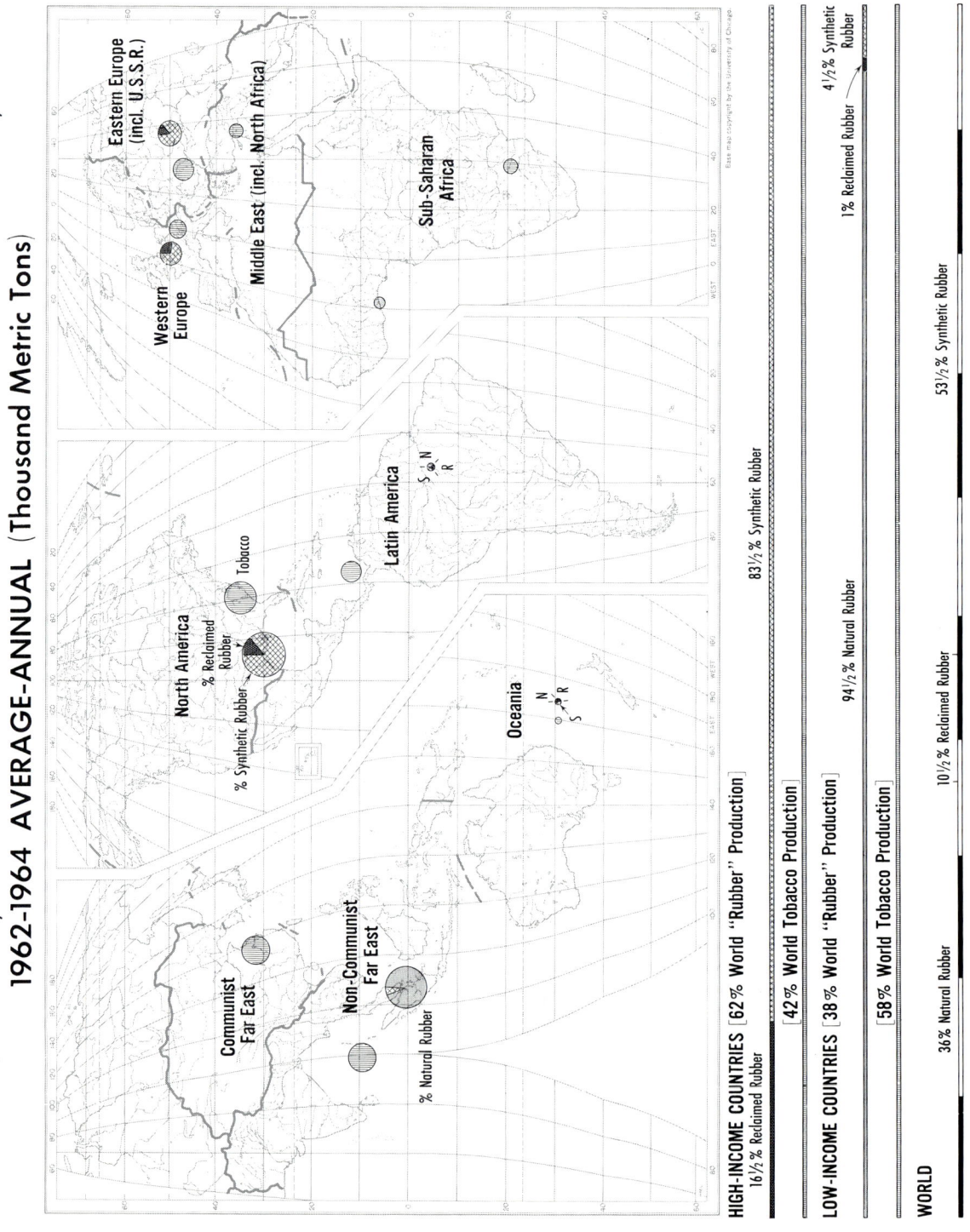

WORLD: GREAT-REGION AND ECONOMIC-TYPE OF SOCIETY SHARES OF WORLD ELASTOMERS ("Rubber") PRODUCTION (and Natural Rubber Consumption) AND TOBACCO PRODUCTION, 1962-1964 AVERAGE-ANNUAL

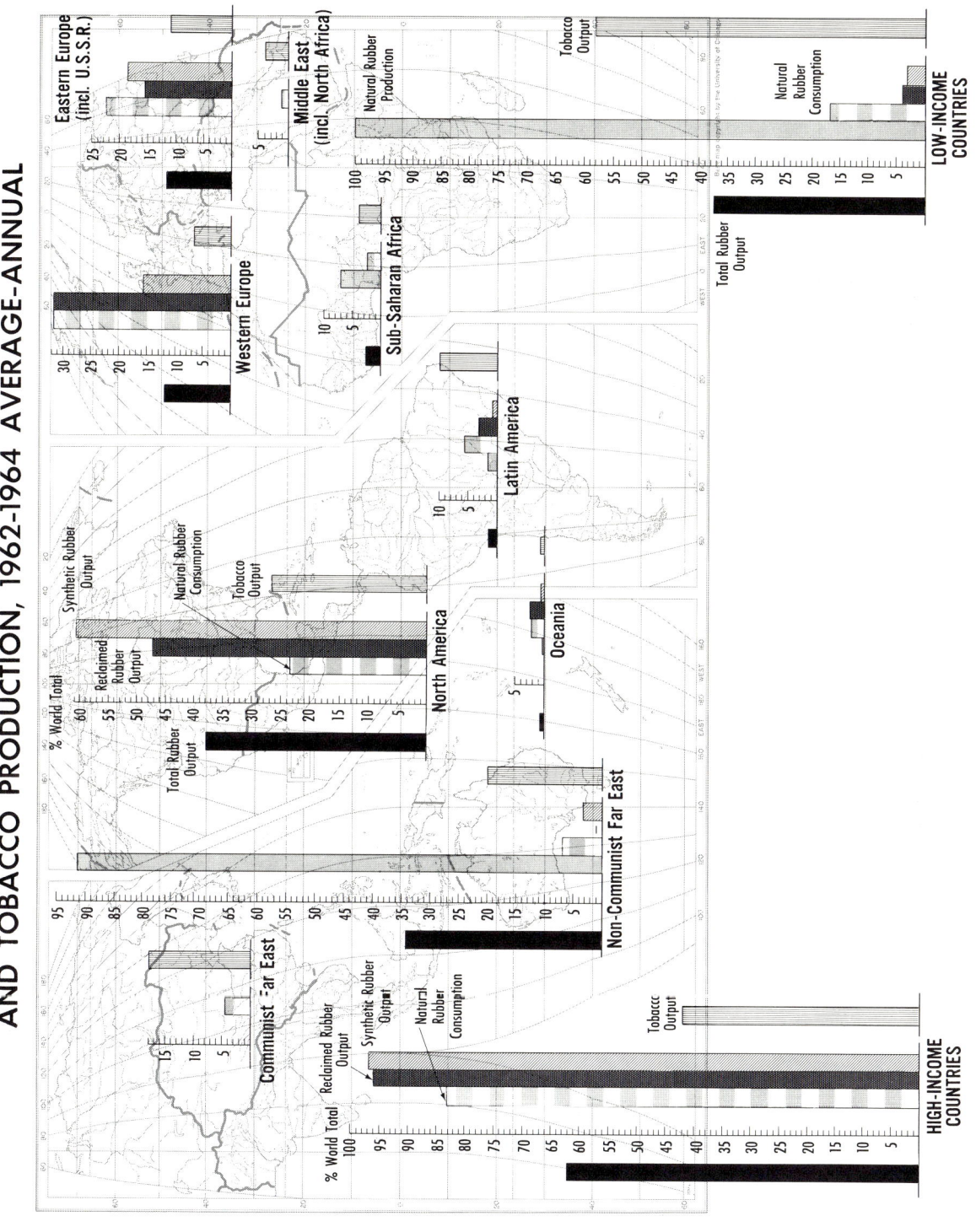

TABLE 10–2

World: Elastomers ("Rubber") Production and Composition and Natural Rubber Consumption, by Great-Region and Economic-Type of Society, 1962–1964 Average-Annual
(in thousands of metric tons)

	Total Rubber Production (thousand metric tons = 100.0 per cent)	Natural Rubber [1]	Reclaimed Rubber [2]	Synthetic Rubber [3]	Natural Rubber Consumption [4]
North America	2,250	–	13.3%	86.7%	525
Western Europe	700	–	28.5	71.4	700
Eastern Europe (including the U.S.S.R.)	700	–	14.3	85.7	500
Oceania	40	12.5%	37.5	50.0	50
Latin America	80	37.5	25.0	37.5	125
Sub-Saharan Africa	150	100.0	–	–	50
Middle East (including North Africa)	–	–	–	–	25
Non-Communist Far East	2,050	95.1	–	4.9	150
Communist Far East	–	–	–	–	100
World	5,970	35.8	10.6	53.6	2,225
High-income countries	3,710	–	16.4	83.6	1,850
Low-income countries	2,260	94.5	1.1	4.4	375

	(per cent of 5,970 thousand metric tons)	(per cent of 2,135 thousand metric tons)	(per cent of 635 thousand metric tons)	(per cent of 3,200 thousand metric tons)	(per cent of 2,225 thousand metric tons)
North America	37.7	–	47.3	60.9	23.6
Western Europe	11.7	–	31.5	15.6	31.5
Eastern Europe (including the U.S.S.R.)	11.7	–	15.7	18.9	22.5
Oceania	0.7	0.2	2.4	0.6	2.2
Latin America	1.4	1.4	3.1	0.9	5.6
Sub-Saharan Africa	2.5	7.0	–	–	2.2
Middle East (including North Africa)	–	–	–	–	1.1
Non-Communist Far East	34.3	91.4	–	3.1	6.8
Communist Far East	–	–	–	–	4.5
World	100.0	100.0	100.0	100.0	100.0
High-income countries	62.1	–	96.0	96.9	83.1
Low-income countries	37.9	100.0	4.0	3.1	16.9

SOURCE: Adapted from United Nations and U.S. Department of Agriculture and U.S. Department of Commerce data.

[1] "Natural Rubber" includes hevea but not minor shrub and other sources.

[2] "Reclaimed Rubber" includes scrap material or secondary material from both natural and synthetic original sources.

[3] "Synthetic Rubber" includes older mixture-of-plastics substitutes for rubber as well as new stereo or chemical substitutes for natural rubber.

[4] "Natural Rubber Consumption" includes a small portion from merchant and government stocks rather than from current production.

Courtesy of The Firestone Tire & Rubber Co.

A workman on Firestone's Liberian plantation prepares a young rubber tree for its first tapping. Trees usually are not tapped until they are six or seven years old. Such plantations, which have been replanted with high-yielding stock in the past decade or so, are economically efficient, having costs about half the present price. However, many small holders and some plantations have costs little lower than the present price that natural rubber brings and are marginal compared both with efficient plantations and factory-made synthetics.

major and minor nutrients are also necessary. Deep soils are preferable, as good drainage is absolutely necessary, but some shallow soils are used, when heavily fertilized by the use of nitrogen fixing cover crops and heavy chemical application.

Hevea thrives best in lowland situations, as fungus disease (root) causes trouble above 1,000 feet elevation. Bacterial disease (South American leaf disease) can and does cause trouble anywhere.

High-yielding characteristics can be passed on from generation to generation by bud grafting. The yield of rubber has been increased from some 300 pounds per acre per year on the plantations before 1920, to some 500 pounds per year on pre-World War II plantations, to some 1,000 pounds where prewar high-yielding material is now at its peak. Post-World War II acreage now in its eighth year is averaging 1,500 pounds, while some clones are producing 2,000 to 3,000 pounds for small areas (and may yield 4,000 pounds when matured). Malaya, the largest rubber producer the past few years, has now replanted about 50 per cent of its 3½ million acres with high-yielding stock (some 25 per cent of small-holders acreage, 65 per cent of estates acreage). Malaya should thus be in a position to produce more rubber at lower cost in the decade ahead, because of this replanting with improved material, but it will have its most marked effect after 1965, and because of the continued use of improved techniques which have already been introduced. Total Malayan rubber production is expected to rise from the present 0.7 million tons to over 1 million tons by 1970, when high-yielding material will occupy some 85 to 90 per cent of estate acreage (1.9 million acres yielding 0.6 million tons), and 70 per cent of small-holder acreage (2.55 million acres yielding 0.45 million tons).

Malaya's efficient rubber producers can still turn a handsome profit, because their plantings of high-yield trees have already brought the cost of production down from 23 cents per pound to 13 cents, and when all the new trees reach maturity in the mid- to late 1960's, they expect to further reduce costs to 10 cents per pound. The table on page 285 gives some indication of changing costs under the new conditions. The 1964 Singapore price per pound for natural rubber was 22 cents (New York, 26 cents).

Rubber from Firestone's Liberian rubber plantation is loaded aboard a small shuttle craft at the Harbel dock, then shipped to Monrovia, capital of the country, where it is loaded onto larger ships for shipment. Only about 35 per cent of world elastomer ("rubber") consumption is now from new natural rubber sources; the rest is from new synthetic and scrap sources.

Courtesy of The Firestone Tire & Rubber Co.

	Per Cent of 23 Cents per Pound Cost on an Estate Yielding 500 Pounds per Acre	Per Cent of 13 Cents per Pound Cost on an Estate Yielding 1,500 Pounds per Acre
Tapping	40	40
General charges [1]	30	18
Cultivation	12	7
Processing, packing, and dispatching	8	12
Replanting and research	10	23

[1] Includes repairs, depreciation, and general charges (management and office salaries, agency fees, office expenses, employee welfare benefits, rents, general transport).

Other rubber producers are also replanting, but mostly at a slower rate than Malaya. Some one-half of the 12 million acres under rubber is now replanted, but only a small fraction of this is yielding. The big, well-organized estates who replanted with improved stock in the late 1940's and early 1950's can produce rubber for 12 to 15 cents per pound. There are still many whose costs are about 18 cents. Such low-cost producers account for most of the high grades of dry rubber and nearly all the natural rubber latex (shipped liquid). The production of the small-holders—about one-half of world production—is mostly of lower grades, normally selling at discounts. Many small-holders have higher costs (e.g., 22 cents or higher), and increasingly find it difficult to compete.

Synthetic and Reclaimed Rubber

Chemically, natural rubber is a hydrocarbon $(C_5H_8)_x$. It has elasticity (much more than competitors), impermeability, softness, adhesion, toughness, and electrical resistance. No manmade substitute has all of these characteristics to the same degree, and only a tiny fraction come close (the new stereo regular rubbers just coming into large-scale production).

The old general purpose "synthetics" produced from the 1930's on are not a chemical substitute for natural rubber, but a mixture of plastics that can substitute for many of natural rubber uses. By 1963, these synthetics still accounted for 95 per cent of world production of all synthetics. No one of the four major types of these older synthetics is superior to natural rubber for general purposes, but certain types are superior for certain purposes. Over three-fourths of the total supply consists of Buna-S, used because it provides greater wearing quality than a thicker tire tread. Butyl is the least expensive, and is used almost exclusively for inner tubes, since it retains air much better than tubes of natural rubber. Neoprene resists heat, oxidation, and oil, so its uses are largely in electrical insulation. Buna-N is the most expensive type, but is favored because it blends easily with both natural and other synthetic rubbers, and is resistant to hydrocarbons (oil, gasoline, solvents) and to heat, abrasion, and age.

The average cost of producing these older synthetics in the United States is said to be about 18 cents per pound, and the average selling price is 23 cents. Such synthetic rubber capacity cost some $750 per ton in the 1950's, while the average per ton plantation rubber capacity cost some $300 for replanting and $450 for new development. However, the synthetic capacity can be created in one-third of the time required to bring new rubber trees to maturity, a great advantage at times of lagging supply.

The urban-industrial realm's pattern of rubber consumption is swiftly following in the North American lead (now some 75 per cent synthetic). Western Europe's synthetic production is picking up, as is Japan's, and other non-Communist industrial societies. In the early 1960's, the Communist bloc had the only rapidly increasing natural rubber imports, but their synthetic capacity began increasing rapidly as the mid-1960's approached, reducing their imports.

North American consumption is some 2 million tons new synthetic, ½ million tons natural, and 0.3 million tons reclaimed. About half of all rubber is used in making non-tire products (foam rubber, conveyor belting, athletic equipment, footwear, mechanical rubber goods, products for the medical and druggist professions, etc.), although tires are still the largest single use. About 60 per cent of the reclaimed rubber

Courtesy of The Firestone Tire & Rubber Co.

Airview of Firestone's Decatur, Illinois, tire plant. Opened in 1964, the plant produces passenger car tires and small truck tires.

Out of the curing molds and onto the conveyor belts, these tires are on their way to be trimmed at Firestone's Decatur, Illinois, plant. Each tire is then carefully balanced and spray painted before being sent to the warehouse for distribution to all parts of the country.

Courtesy of The Firestone Tire & Rubber Co.

is used in tires, to make sidewalls in new tires, but it is also widely used to give elasticity and protection to the coverings on playgrounds, tennis courts, racetracks, golf courses, and athletic fields. Tire manufacturers are the main reclaimers—its greatest attraction is its 12 cents per pound price, only half that of new rubber.

In 1964, the United States produced about 0.3 million tons of the new stereo synthetic rubbers, chemically very close to the natural rubber. There are two principal types: polyisoprene and polybutadiene. Polyisoprene is almost a duplicate of natural rubber and is a complete replacement, although so far its main uses have been in non-tire applications, like footwear and mechanical goods. Larger-scale production has dropped its cost of production from 23 cents per pound to 20 cents, so it sells at the natural rubber price. As far as quality and performance are concerned, it is claimed that the new polyisoprenes can replace natural rubber 100 per cent. Polybutadiene lacks the resiliency of natural rubber, but is even more resistant to heat and abrasion than polyisoprene. So far, it has mainly been used as an extender in combination with natural or older synthetic rubber, and is now capable of replacing natural rubber in about one-half of natural rubber's uses (this fraction can be increased). Polybutadiene is better adapted than polyisoprene in establishing its own market—tough and long-wearing alone and in combination, it has already developed a foothold in premium tires. Its original cost of production of 30 cents per pound has dropped, and it now sells for about the same as its stereo partner. In the 1960's, the United States will add another million tons of synthetic capacity, mostly the stereo types. About 20 per cent of United States consumption still requires either natural rubber or these new stereos.

Butadiene, one of the principal raw materials of synthetic rubber, is manufactured at Firestone's petrochemical plant at Orange, Texas. From here the butadiene is shipped to Firestone's four synthetic rubber manufacturing plants.

Courtesy of The Firestone Tire & Rubber Co.

Trends

In the 1960's, world consumption of elastomers is expected to increase at a rate averaging 7 per cent yearly, but natural rubber production is expected to increase little if at all, so its share of world consumption will soon be less than a third. Both inelastic supply and high cost of production are problems, the latter affecting estates and (especially) small holdings planted with unselected trees. Even at the price of 22 cents per pound, most natural rubber can be produced at a modest profit, and the new higher-yielding groves which will supply most natural rubber by the late 1960's will have costs in the 10- to 15-cent range, under the present cost of production of synthetic rubbers.

Malaysia, Ceylon, and India are rapidly replanting with new strains of bud-grafted or clonal seedlings by subsidizing growers ($130 to $208 per acre), and are in the best position to maintain an economically healthy natural rubber industry. Indonesia and other countries have made little or no headway in the replanting and may bear the brunt of any decreased production.

One thing is certain: the natural rubber producer must compete in terms of price in the future, not of superior quality. An added incentive to low prices, besides the competition of the synthetics, is the presence of the United States, British, and other strategic stockpiles (left over from the 1950's), which million tons of natural rubber is being sold commercially under certain conditions.

The old general purpose semisynthetics are faced with competition both from cheaper natural rubber and the new stereo regular rubbers, and they well may be the main losers in the decade ahead. In any event, with the range of technical substitutability widening, the main factor will increasingly be economic efficiency.

FORESTS AND FOREST PRODUCTS

During the last ten millennia, the area of the world's forests has probably been reduced by at least one-third, and some people think by more than one-half. Remaining forests containing timber today occupy less than 20 per cent of the world's land area, with shrub- and brushlands occupying about one-half as large an area as timberland.

About 5 per cent of the world's forests are under reasonably good management as a tree crop at the present time, with perhaps another 20 per cent handled with the idea of sustained yield as a goal (in essentially wild forests). The remaining 75 per cent of the world's forest areas are exploited with no thought for the necessity of sustained wood production or any other conservation ideal. In most populous countries, the forest receives the lowest priority in land-use, being simply relegated to residual sites not required for cultivation or grazing.

The three main reasons for the human pressure on the forest have been, and continue to be, the demands for fuel wood, construction material, and space for farms and pasture, and in all of these demands there are significant regional differences. The consensus of all reports is that destructive fuel wood cutting in the tropical forests is far more common than conservative use, but that the most potent pressure on the tropical forest comes from the third of the ancient demands, namely the need for agricultural land. The tropical forest is under increasing pressure nearly everywhere—but especially in Africa and Southeast Asia—and will not long remain intact in large blocks. The large forests in the higher latitudes—North America, northern Europe, and the northern U.S.S.R.—are in no great danger of agricultural encroachment at the present time and probably never will be, mainly because they grow in regions where neither climate nor soil is favorable to crop farming. Today, the heaviest demand for industrial wood products—lumber, pulp, plywood, etc.—is on the mid-latitude forests of North America, Western Europe, and Eastern Europe (including the U.S.S.R.). Whether or not the forest areas in the southeast of North America, in Western Europe, and in the southwestern U.S.S.R. can be permanently maintained at their present size is essentially an economic question.

As a fuel and raw material, wood has been subjected to competition from mineral substitutes. Since 1950, world roundwood removals have increased about 2 per cent annually, a little faster than the annual rate of population increase. However, that average rate obscures much reality. Fuel wood production has remained practically unchanged, with the rapid diffusion of the commercial-energy economy. Industrial-wood removals have risen about 3 per cent annually, with the world output of sawn wood increasing somewhat more slowly, and the output of paper pulp, plywood, and fiber-particle board increasing more swiftly.

The main increases in sawn wood production are in North America and Eastern Europe (including the U.S.S.R.), already the largest regional producers. In Western Europe, the sustainable limit of forest removals is being approached, and greater attention is being given

TABLE 10–3

World: Forest Land Composition,* by Great-Region and Economic-Type of Society, 1963 Estimate
(in billions of hectares)

	Forest Area (billion hectares = 100.0 per cent)	Productive-accessible [1]	Productive-inaccessible	Unproductive [2] (shrub-brush)
North America	0.76	48%	22%	30%
Western Europe	0.10	88	2	10
Eastern Europe (including the U.S.S.R.)	0.92	35	33	32
Oceania	0.06	30	33	37
Latin America	0.98	40	45	15
Sub-Saharan Africa	0.62	18	18	64
Middle East (including North Africa)	0.05	37	13	50
Non-Communist Far East	0.35	38	22	40
Communist Far East	0.12	17	36	47
World	3.96	37	30	33
High-income countries	1.84	42	26	32
Low-income countries	2.12	32	33	35

	(per cent of 3.96 billion hectares)	(per cent of 1.46 billion hectares)	(per cent of 1.2 billion hectares)	(per cent of 1.3 billion hectares)
North America	19.1	25.0	14.2	16.8
Western Europe	2.6	6.1	0.2	0.8
Eastern Europe (including the U.S.S.R.)	23.2	21.9	25.6	22.6
Oceania	1.4	1.1	1.6	1.5
Latin America	24.7	26.7	37.7	11.1
Sub-Saharan Africa	15.8	7.6	9.7	30.2
Middle East (including North Africa)	1.3	1.2	0.6	1.9
Non-Communist Far East	8.8	9.0	6.6	10.6
Communist Far East	3.1	1.4	3.8	4.5
World	100.0	100.0	100.0	100.0
High-income countries	47.6	54.4	41.5	45.6
Low-income countries	52.4	45.6	58.5	54.4

SOURCE: Adapted from United Nations data, supplemented by unofficial estimates to fill in gaps.

* *Caution:* Forest land-use data are among the less reliable categories of land-use.

[1] Productive forest land is that physically capable of producing crops of usable wood (fuel wood or industrial wood); accessible forest land is that within reach of commercial exploitation (implying mechanical transport or water transport, as well as market mechanism).

[2] Unproductive forest land is that not worth ordinary commercial exploitation, but often worth exploitation to subsistence inhabitants.

TABLE 10–4

World: Roundwood Production and Composition, by Great-Region and
Economic-Type of Society, 1962–1964 Average-Annual
(in millions of metric tons dry-weight)

	Roundwood[1] Production (million metric tons = 100.0 per cent)	Industrial Wood Production	Fuel Wood Production
North America	300	90.0%	10.0%
Western Europe	180	75.0	25.0
Eastern Europe (including the U.S.S.R.)	325	65.0	35.0
Oceania	20	75.0	25.0
Latin America	150	25.0	75.0
Sub-Saharan Africa	90	15.0	85.0
Middle East (including North Africa)	20	25.0	75.0
Non-Communist Far East	175	40.0	60.0
Communist Far East	90	45.0	55.0
World	1,350	59.0	41.0
High-income countries	825	77.0	23.0
Low-income countries	525	31.5	68.5
	(per cent of 1,350 million metric tons)	(per cent of 550 million metric tons)	(per cent of 800 million metric tons)
North America	22.2	33.7	5.4
Western Europe	13.3	16.9	8.2
Eastern Europe (including the U.S.S.R.)	24.0	26.2	21.0
Oceania	1.5	1.9	0.9
Latin America	11.1	5.0	20.0
Sub-Saharan Africa	6.7	1.9	13.6
Middle East (including North Africa)	1.5	0.6	2.7
Non-Communist Far East	13.0	8.8	19.1
Communist Far East	6.7	5.0	9.1
World	100.0	100.0	100.0
High-income countries	61.0	79.4	34.5
Low-income countries	39.0	20.6	65.5

SOURCE: Adapted from United Nations data, supplemented by unofficial estimates to fill in gaps.

[1] One cubic meter of roundwood (hardwood and softwood average) has been assumed to weigh 0.72 metric ton on an average air-dry basis.

to the utilization of mill residues and undersized wood (a trend that is slowly spreading to North America). Another substitute is a great import of tropical hardwood logs for use in furniture-making and other woodworking industries. With the harvesting of such tropical timbers becoming progressively more expensive in the main producing countries (Nigeria and Gabon in West and Central Africa, Sabah and the Philippines in Southeast Asia), especially in West Africa, the search continues for new marketable species and as yet untapped sources.

While the world sawn wood output has increased only a third in the 1950–1963 period, plywood and panel products have increased at phenomenal rates. The oldest sawn wood substitute, plywood, has tripled in output in the same period. Particle board, a newer substitute, has increased over 100 times its 1950 output (25,000 tons). Plywood production is increasing rapidly, not only in the three major urban-industrial regions but in underdeveloped regions like Latin America, sub-Saharan Africa, and the non-Communist Far East.

Pulp, paper, and paper products are other industrial-wood products that are increasing rapidly in use. Pulp and paper capacity is still increasing in North America and Western Europe, although the supply is large enough for current demand. Eastern Europe (including the U.S.S.R.) is increasing capacity very rapidly, as are other regions. Paperboard output (much of it from old newspapers and magazines) continues to increase rapidly (7 per cent annually) to meet the demand for packaging, as do the production of fine-coated and special purpose papers.

Regional Characteristics

North America. Considered as a unit, North America is roughly self-sufficient in wood. The United States is now over 10 per cent deficit (one-half in lumber, veneer, and plywood; one-half in pulpwood, wood pulp, and newsprint), but most comes from Canada. Canada produces over one-fourth of the regional cut of roundwood and could still increase its output on a sustained-yield basis. About one-fourth of all Canada is covered by productive forest land, with fully 60 per cent occupied by merchantable trees. There is still about ¼ million square miles of productive but inaccessible forest land, although the fraction of useful timber is probably only one-third.

The United States has about one-third of its continental (forty-eight state) area in forest, 25 per cent in commercial forests, and 8 per cent in non-commercial types of forest (some of the latter, like the parks and preserves, may grow merchantable timber that is not used except for watershed protection, grazing, forest recreation, and wildlife protection). The average U.S. forest acre grows about two-thirds of a ton of wood yearly, of which about one-half is cut as roundwood, and the remainder lost to insects, disease, wind, and fire or in woods waste. Nearly 60 per cent of the cut is turned into lumber, about 20 per cent into pulp, and the remainder is split between fuel wood and other uses about equally.

Over 70 per cent of the U.S. cut, and some 90 per cent of the Canadian cut are softwood, reflecting location in the great upper-latitude coniferous forest realm. The mid-latitude hardwoods are still undercut (with the greatest use still being fuel wood and farm small-stick uses), while the solid stands of softwood are more fully used.

Western Europe. About 30 per cent of the region is in forest (same fraction as for world). Of this, 90 per cent is productive forest, and almost all of this is accessible. The average acre produces nearly a ton of wood yearly (the best forests double this figure), three times the U.S.S.R. or Canadian rates, and one-half again as much as the average U.S. rate. About two-thirds of the cut is from conifers, about the same as in the United States.

Western Europe, taken as a whole, is virtually self-sufficient in forest products. However, a considerable volume of trade is carried on between the surplus and deficit countries within the region: some 25 per cent of the annual cut (40 per cent of the annual industrial-wood output, which is the type moved).

Of the 75 per cent used for industrial purposes, utilization is about as follows:

sawn wood	56%	newsprint	6%
plywood	3	paperboard	22
poles and pit props	12	fiberboard	1

Western Europe is the only great region where most of the forest land is handled like tree crops and continually on a sustained-yield basis (except temporarily during wartime).

Eastern Europe (including the U.S.S.R.). The European Communist bloc of nations has nearly one-fourth of the world's forest land. The U.S.S.R. alone has almost a fifth of the world's forest land, timber production, and timber products manufacture. As in Canada, some 15 per cent of industrial employment and output is in forestry and the closely associated lumber, pulp paper, and other industrial-wood industries (double the U.S. fraction).

Some 80 per cent of the forest acreage is in Siberia, but 70 per cent of the cut and 75 per

WORLD: ROUNDWOOD PRODUCTION AND COMPOSITION, BY GREAT-REGION AND ECONOMIC-TYPE OF SOCIETY, 1962-1964 AVERAGE-ANNUAL
(Million Metric Tons Dry-Weight)

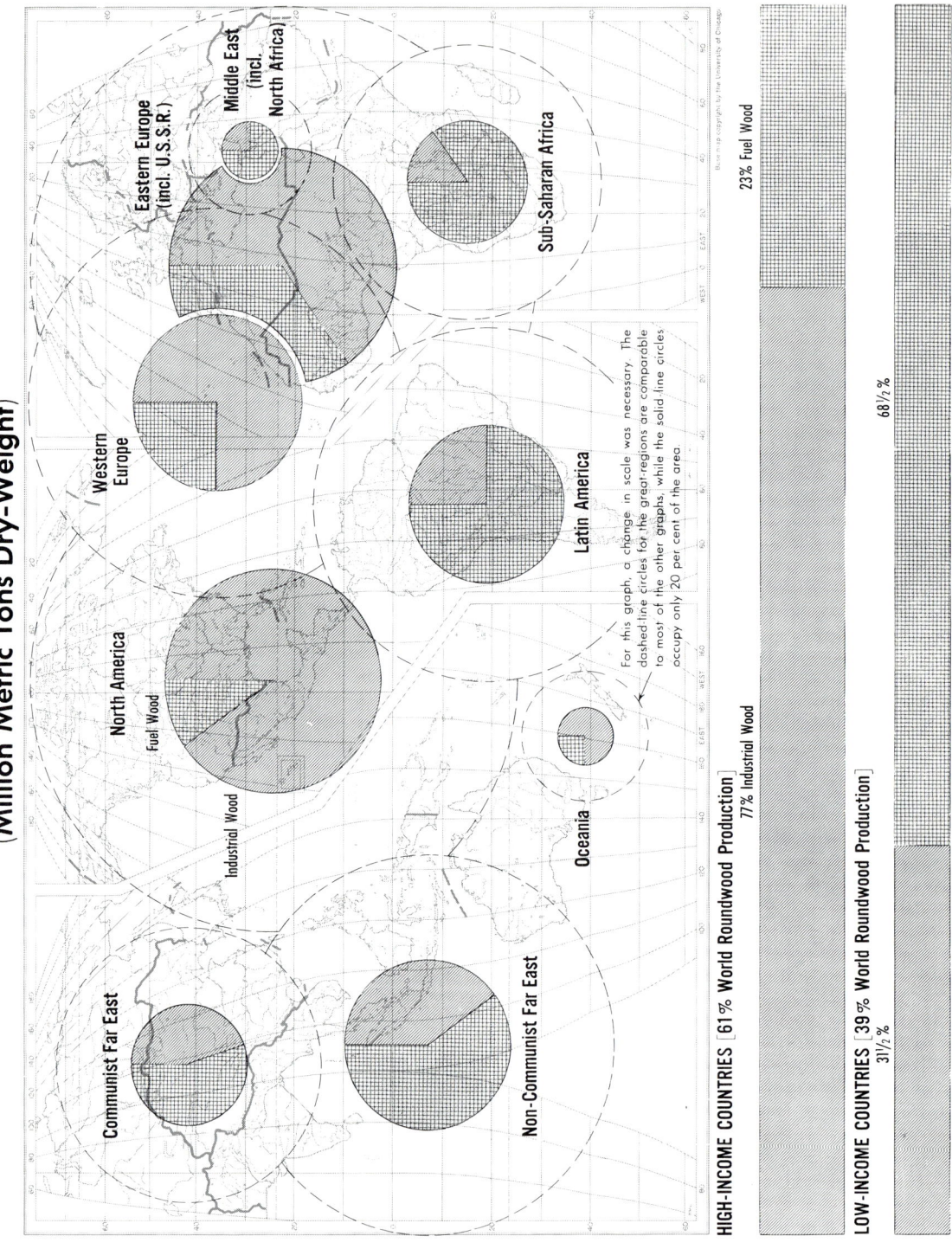

WORLD: GREAT-REGION AND ECONOMIC-TYPE OF SOCIETY SHARES OF WORLD ROUNDWOOD PRODUCTION (Industrial Wood and Fuel Wood), 1962-1964 AVERAGE-ANNUAL

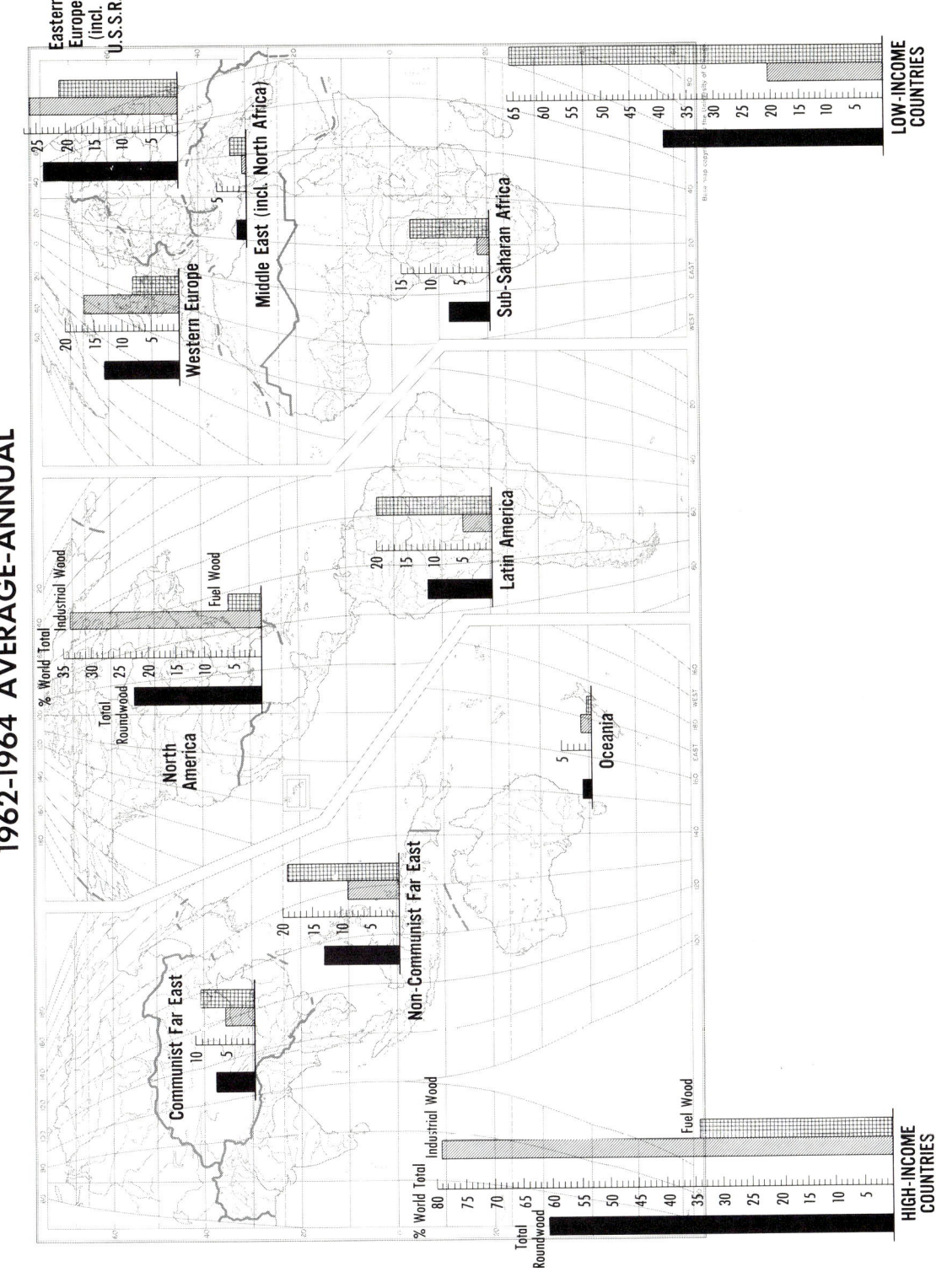

cent of the consumption is in European Russia. Some 70 per cent of the wood is still moved by water, although this fraction is likely to diminish as more and more of the cut must be made in the east.

As in Canada, while there is still considerable inaccessible productive forest land, there is increasing evidence that one-half or more of this is small-stick taiga that is unlikely to ever be useful. As the commercial fossil-fuel economy expands increasingly in the area of space heating, the large fraction of wood cut for fuel is likely to fall off.

Oceania. The Melanesian (New Guinea, Solomons, etc.) tropical forests are still used and misused mainly in a subsistence context. European Oceania is relatively poor in timberland, with commercial timber being restricted to a comparatively narrow belt of good rainfall along the eastern coasts and highlands, to Tasmania, to the small well-watered part of southwestern Australia, and to New Zealand.

Wood production is small, about the same as for Spain or Italy. The output is mainly hardwood and, while present industrial needs can mainly be met, a rapid increase in population might be difficult to serve. Considerable softwood products are now imported, so changes in technology that allow greater use of hardwoods is needed.

Latin America. Nearly 50 per cent of the region is forested, and practically all (85 per cent) consists of productive forest, but so far less than one-half of it is accessible. Middle America, because of the arid and semiarid Mexican areas, is less than one-fourth forested, while at least one-half of South America is forested. Although there are thousands of species in the vast tropical hardwood forests, about 200 species constitute the great bulk of usable timber.

The poverty in both income and commercial fuel and energy in so much of Latin America is reflected in the three-fourths of the cut still used for fuel. Lumber and similar uses now take some 10 per cent, with a variety of small-stick uses taking most of the remainder.

Latin America has the largest blocks of relatively undisturbed tropical forests left in the world. In such forests, where the various species differ greatly in commercial value, the transport distance determines the zones in which the exploitation of each category of species remains profitable. This results in concentric zones of progressive exhaustion, which are especially noticeable in the most heavily populated regions (e.g., West Indies, India, Indochina, Malaya). Consumer centers are surrounded by a first zone that is completely exhausted and where there is no longer even any firewood, then by a second zone where the timber has already been exploited, then by a third zone that still contains timber but where the valuable timber has disappeared, and finally by virgin forest, where all the resources are preserved but which has no economic value, since none of the timber is at present exploitable under profitable conditions.

As these zones are exhausted, exploitation draws farther away from the consumer centers and the cost price of various species of wood rises. Nevertheless, the opening of new routes and the development of new transport equipment have hitherto made it possible to penetrate farther and farther into the forest, without raising the cost price. Consequently, the volume of usable timber, which is usually between 6 to 12 tons per acre in the unexploited zones, nearly always exceeds the economically exploitable volume. When the forest is free from exploitation to the extent that it still contains wood for cabinet-making, the exploitation of ordinary timber is not usually considered profitable, and in places where it is still profitable, the valuable timber has already been removed. For such selective cutting, a forest concession is considered profitable when it contains about 6 tons of usable timber per acre (Western European forest land will yield thirty times as much).

This position greatly complicates the problem of the rational exploitation of tropical forests and of the extraction of their products, since contrary to the oversimple ideas sometimes put forward by new enterprises which are as yet unfamiliar with the commercial aspect of the question, it is impossible to fell all the usable species in these heterogeneous stands, and to sell them off, even at equalized prices, unless the demand for each species exceeds the quantities thus thrown on the market. It must not be forgotten that these very different species are not interchangeable and that it will be more and more difficult to strike the balance between production and consumption as larger quantities of timber are exploited.

In any case, tropical forests must be considered for a long time to come as very poor forests, requiring a much wider road network for the extraction of timber than forests of mid-latitude countries for the same tonnage extracted. The technical problems of log transportation still limit the rational utilization of world forestry resources, especially in regions remote from consumer centers, in scattered stands, and in tropical climates. Log transportation in tropical forest exploitation is characterized by four main facts: heterogeneity of the forests and their deficiency in valuable species, lack of public roads [3] and equipment in the forest regions, climatic resistances, and the lack and inferior quality of labor.

Sub-Saharan Africa. Africa south of the Sahara Desert has a sixth of the world's forest land, and over a fourth of the entire region is forested. However, most of it has been degraded by shifting cultivators and by pastoralists to brush- and shrubland. Little more than a third is now occupied by productive forest, and only about a half of that is accessible to commercial exploitation.

Of the wood cut, only about 15 per cent goes into industrial uses, and perhaps one-third of that is exported. The timber cut mainly comes from the rain forest, where the average volume of wood of all timber species is some 90 tons per acre, of which only 3 to 5 tons per acre are usually logged, and only 9 tons under the best circumstances.

It is possible that wood cut for fuel is much greater in amount that the estimated 70 million tons. The highest unofficial estimates give 50 million tons for Nigeria for each year, and possibly 250 million tons for all Africa, but it is not clear whether this includes fuel wood in the usual sense, or guesses that include the amounts used to clear grazing and arable land and to fertilize it with ashes.

Middle East. North Africa and Southwest Asia make up the poorest forested region in the world, with only 1 per cent of the world's forest land, although it has nearly 10 per cent of the entire land area of the world. Timberland is actually of very limited extent, although once much more widespread in the humid highlands. The less accessible portions of the Atlas and northern Anatolian and Iranian ranges still contain timbering operations, but elsewhere production is mainly fuel wood and other small-stick output. Thousands of square miles with rainfall over 20 inches would again have a fair forest cover if sheep and goats could be kept off, and there is the possibility of excellent commercial timber where there is 30 inches or more of rainfall.

Non-Communist Far East. Only in Southeast Asia do large areas of almost virgin forest exist, yet botanists believe primitive people even there have changed that forest slowly by cutting and burning. The thickly settled portions of South Asia have been deforested as thoroughly as much as China. Only Japan has forest land managed according to modern conservation principles.

Nearly a fifth of South Asia is covered with trees and brush of sorts, but only about half of this can be considered forest land in any meaningful sense. About two-thirds of the forest land is public property, with the remaining third being privately and cooperatively owned. If properly managed, such areas should be quite sufficient for meeting the present and prospective needs of India and Pakistan, but present forestry conditions are not uniformly satisfactory. The reserved forests, which occupy about 10 per cent of India, 5 per cent of West Pakistan, and 15 per cent of East Pakistan, are fairly well stocked and are being conserved and exploited on scientific lines, but they are not uniformly

---

[3] The construction of paved forest roads would usually not be profitable—a paved road costs approximately seven times more than a properly constructed earth road, which can be used by loaded trucks in the dry season only.

distributed. There is a broad belt of such forests along the southern slopes of the Himalayas, along the Western and Eastern Ghats, in the Satpura and Vindhyan ranges of Middle India, and along the eastern Assam-Burmese hills. Most of the merchantable forests are in these areas. But the extensive plains of northern India and West Pakistan and large areas of Peninsular India are almost completely void of reserved forests. The private forests in these tracts are generally interspersed with cultivation, but these have been very heavily felled, and most of them are now forests only in name. The so-called village wastelands have similarly been practically denuded of tree growth. Not only are these privately owned forests and village wastelands now incapable of supplying any forest produce of any consequence except fuel wood and fuel brush, but they have often become foci of erosion, which like a cancer is ruining certain areas.

It has been estimated that properly managed, accessible forest lands no larger in area than the present 10 per cent of forest land could probably supply the timber and fire wood needs of the subcontinent. Much of the existing timberland is inaccessible due to its location in the mountains, plus the fact that very few roads or railroads have been built especially for logging. In many cases, the opening up of presently inaccessible mountain forests will be less economic than reforestation in more accessible spots in the plains. This is especially likely to be true for meeting the need for fuel wood, poles, and other miscellaneous wood needs. Probably groves of quick-growing trees that can supply such village needs are the most feasible way for releasing the manure now burned as fuel so it can be used as fertilizer. Ordinary woodlots yield about $\frac{1}{2}$ ton of usable fuel wood per acre annually, but annual yields of about 5 tons can be obtained by careful forestry methods in most areas, and groves of eucalyptus have yielded as much as 12 tons per year in reserve-forest areas.

Southeast Asia still has some 60 per cent of its total area in forest and woodland, and its problems of supplying needed industrial wood and fuel wood are simpler than in most of South Asia. The tropical rain forest, which is found in the lowland equatorial areas, especially in insular Southeast Asia, has been exploited selectively for rare hardwoods, rattan, gums, and resins, but has not been commercially opened for mass production of timber. The monsoon forest, which is associated with areas of marked seasonal precipitation, is characterized by larger stands of single species than the tropical rain forest, by a more open appearance and incomplete canopy, by somewhat denser ground cover especially in the wet season, by thickets of bamboo and tropical grasses, by fires set either by men or nature, and by a greater commercial importance. The northern part of Southeast Asia's forests have often been replaced by bamboo thickets.

More than 60 per cent of Japan is covered with productive forest, not counting about 7 per cent of brushlands. About one-half of Japan's forests are broadleaved, 30 per cent are coniferous, and 20 per cent are mixed. Some 60 per cent of the broadleaved forests are coppice stands used primarily for fuel wood. The 40 per cent of Japan's roundwood cut that is industrial wood comes overwhelmingly from the coniferous forests of Hokkaido and northern Honshu. There are some imports, especially of high-grade wood pulp and veneer logs, balanced in value by exports of veneer and other manufactured items.

Communist Far East. Denudation has left little forest in China. Large remnants are found only in the Manchurian and North Korean mountains, the hills of the southeastern coastal area, and the eastern Tibetan plateau fringes, including scattered parts of Southwest China and North Vietnam. Little more than a tenth is in forest land and woodland, and probably well over one-half is shrub- and brushland.

All of China south of and including the Tsingling Mountains and its eastward extensions once was in forest, but most of this has been cut down and the slopes carry a cover of bamboo and coarse grass. Only the more inaccessible mountain reaches still support real forest. Some estimates are that the wood equivalent of grass and twigs used for fuel may be as great as the actual roundwood cut for all uses.

Of the timber stands, two-thirds by volume are in the Northeast and almost one-third are in the Southwest, leaving North, Northwest, and Central China with only 5 per cent of the total. The North and Northwest probably gets more fuel wood equivalent from agricultural waste than from trees, while South China probably gets more wood from bamboo and other grasses than from trees proper.

Fuel Wood Consumption

The heaviest single use of wood, the world over, is still for fuel, although fuel wood only constitutes about 3 to 4 per cent of the world's energy use on a caloric basis, while other non-commercial woody fuels are perhaps equal to 10 to 12 per cent of all energy consumed by mankind.

There is a long-range tendency for woody fuels to become less important, as the commercial hydrocarbons increase in relative importance. Usually, the first users to switch from fuel wood to fossil fuels are transport and utility users and mines and manufacturing users. Subsistence and slightly commercialized areas are likely, however, to continue using such fuels for household-space heating and cooking for a long time to come.

In the highly developed regions of the North Atlantic Basin, such non-commercial fuels are less than 10 per cent of the total world consumption, and contribute less than 5 per cent of regional consumption of all fuel and energy. The figures for Eastern Europe (including the U.S.S.R.) are several times as large, reflecting the less commercialized and less modernized sector of the energy economy. Eastern European tendencies are following the North Atlantic example, and the rapid spread of oil and gas pipeline networks into the coal-poor regions is seeing substitution, especially in urban areas.

The low-income countries consume three-fourths of all non-commercial fuels, with over one-half of the world's total consumed in the Far East. In most underdeveloped regions outside the urban-nodes, from one-third to two-thirds of the fuel and energy consumption is still from such sources.

The fuel wood (and that converted into charcoal) referred to in discussing roundwood production accounts for only a sixth of the total non-commercial fuels consumption, while lumber-mill waste accounts for only a bit over 8 per cent. The diverse miscellaneous category of forestry, agricultural, and construction waste is by far the most important non-commercial fuel source, accounting for three-fourths of the total.

The long-term future of fuel wood output is clear: diminishing importance. Alternate fuel is usually cheaper once development gets underway, and the commercial sources are infinitely superior in quality and ease of handling. Once pulping and other industries using small-stick roundwood develop, they can afford to pay more for such removals than those using such material as crude fuel can afford.

Lumber and Related Consumption

Forestry proper involves less than ½ per cent of the world's labor force and income, and seldom a much larger fraction even in the regions that heavily use wood. Processing into lumber and related structural materials and the making of pulp, paper, and related products, each is about triple in importance, and the making of furniture and wood fixtures is also more important.

Lumber and structural timbers consume almost one-third of the total annual wood cut of the world, and are worth many times the greater tonnage of roundwood that ends up as fuel wood.

There are three general ways in which industrial wood enters into use. One is through its use as wood itself, its physical form alone being modified to meet diverse requirements—processing into lumber, timber, and similar products. Second is through improvement of the physical properties of wood by various treatments while preserving its fundamental structure—processing into veneer, plywood, composition board, and other forms of semisynthetic structural materials.

TABLE 10-5

World: Consumption of Woody Fuels, by Great-Region and Economic-Type of Society, 1962–1964 Average-Annual
(in billions of metric tons)

	Total Woody Fuels [1] (billion metric tons = 100.0 per cent)	Fuel Wood [2]	Lumber Mill Waste	Other Wood and Agricultural Waste [3]
North America	0.11	27%	71%	2%
Western Europe	0.16	27	30	43
Eastern Europe (including the U.S.S.R.)	0.54	21	15	64
Oceania	0.02	25	25	50
Latin America	0.27	41	4	55
Sub-Saharan Africa	0.28	27	1	72
Middle East (including North Africa)	0.12	13	2	85
Non-Communist Far East	1.04	10	3	87
Communist Far East	0.66	8	1	91
World	3.20	17	8	75
High-income countries	0.80	23	27	50
Low-income countries	2.40	15	2	83

	(per cent of 3.20 billion metric tons)	(per cent of 0.55 billion metric tons)	(per cent of 0.27 billion metric tons)	(per cent of 2.38 billion metric tons)
North America	3.6	5.4	29.6	0.2
Western Europe	5.2	8.2	18.5	3.0
Eastern Europe (including the U.S.S.R.)	17.0	21.0	29.6	14.7
Oceania	0.6	0.9	1.9	0.4
Latin America	8.4	20.0	3.7	6.1
Sub-Saharan Africa	8.7	13.6	1.1	8.4
Middle East (including North Africa)	3.6	2.7	0.8	4.2
Non-Communist Far East	32.3	19.1	11.1	37.8
Communist Far East	20.6	9.1	3.7	25.2
World	100.0	100.0	100.0	100.0
High-income countries	25.3	34.5	81.5	16.8
Low-income countries	74.7	65.5	18.5	83.2

SOURCE: Adapted from United Nations data, supplemented by unofficial estimates to fill in gaps.

[1] The woody fuels converted into billion metric tons bituminous-coal-equivalent:

Fuel wood	0.23
Lumber mill waste	0.10
Other wood and agricultural waste	0.40
Total	0.73

[2] "Fuel Wood" includes wood converted into charcoal.

[3] "Other Wood and Agricultural Waste" includes large amounts of trimmings from forests and orchards, coconut shells, paddy husk, grass, straw, roots, peat, cattle and camel dung, and other materials.

Courtesy of Georgia-Pacific Corp.

A Georgia-Pacific Corporation mill-complex at Crossett, Arkansas, in the midst of its pine tree farm source of raw material. The airview shows a foodboard mill in the foreground, a kraft paper and containerboard mill to its immediate left, a flakeboard plant in the upper left (white), a chemical plant in the center (tall stack), and a lumber mill beside it. Units added or under construction since the photo was taken include a tissue mill, a grocery bag plant, a milk carton plant, a polyethylene extrusion plant, and a plywood plant.

Third is through the use of wood as a raw material in the chemical engineering industry—processing into paper and paper products or into semisynthetic fibers.

Wood is a structural material unmatched in its strength, elasticity, lightness, and beauty. Historically, it has been favored by inherent qualities that make it particularly suitable for many building purposes: good strength in relation to weight; pleasing appearance; insulation against heat and sound; ease of fastening with nails, dowels, screws, and glue; and ease of working with simple tools. It is composed of light, springy fibers of cellulose banded together and stiffened by a durable and highly stable natural plastic called lignin (coal is mainly fossilized lignin). Green wood is from one-fourth to one-third water by weight, varying by species and by season. About 60 per cent of wood after it is fully dried is cellulose. The molecular structure of cellulose is that of two joined molecules of the sugar known as dextrose (one of the sugars in honey, grapes, and corn syrup). Cellulose is naturally inedible carbo-

On a Weyerhaeuser Company tree farm, timber is managed as a crop for perpetual wood supply. Harvesting methods are based on the growth habits of the Douglas fir tree. Seedlings of this tree will not thrive in the deep shade of older and larger trees. For this reason, a system of logging called forest area selection is used. Selected blocks or strips of timber are cut, and intermittent islands of trees are left unharvested to serve as a seed source. In this way, forests are being replaced faster than they are being harvested.

Courtesy of Weyerhaeuser Co.

hydrate, but even a weak acid will split cellobiose (linked dextrose molecules) into the simpler (and edible) dextrose.

About three-fourths of the sawn timber used in the world, and an even larger proportion of wood pulp, comes from softwood. The softwoods or conifers occupy some 15 per cent of the land surface, about 95 per cent of the stands being in the northern hemisphere. The conifers predominate in cool mid-latitude climates. The northern limits are independent of the severity of the winter, but the mean summer temperature must be over 50° F. The coniferous forest (pine, fir, spruce, larch) consists of primitive trees that are tolerant of low rainfall and low soil fertility. In a more favorable environment, conifers give way to hardwoods, but they are not completely eliminated except in the wet tropics. About 85 per cent of the softwood cut goes into industrial-wood products. This reflects the occurrence in solid stands, so well adapted to mass production forestry and lumbering techniques.

The hardwood forests of the world occupy about the same fraction of the earth's land surface as the coniferous forests, but over three-fourths of the annual cut is used for fuel. The mid-latitude hardwoods (oak, elm, beech, birch, poplar) are a remnant of their original size, now occupying only 2 per cent of the land surface. Until several centuries ago, the mid-latitude hardwood forests were the main feeding grounds for hogs, but now they have been mainly eliminated by the expansion of cultivated acreage and pasture land. Mid-latitude hardwoods are the principal trees where the mean annual temperature lies between 40° F. and 65° F. The annual rainfall exceeds 20 inches, with winter being moderate with frosts and varying amounts of snow. A few hardwoods, such as birch, extend northward or upward almost as far as the conifers. The wood is often excellent, and its small industrial usage today reflects mostly scattered stands and difficulties of obtaining regular supplies and economic production.

The tropical hardwoods, occupying 12 to 13 per cent of the earth's surface, are mainly limited to regions which are frost-free and receive more than 20 inches of rainfall. For full development, a reasonably distributed rainfall of at least 80 inches is necessary, but some good timber is produced with only 30 inches if it is available in four months of the year. If the rainfall is between 20 to 30 inches, the resultant growth is brush- and shrubland, not usable for roundwood production. Only one-third of the tropical hardwoods are actually hard (ironwood, greenheart, mahogany), about one-third are actually soft (balsa is best known), and the remaining one-third are intermediate. As mentioned earlier, extreme diversity is the hallmark. For example, Philippine forests contain over 3,000 tree species that attain 1 foot and over in diameter. However, less than 60 of these species are utilized in quantity for the market. The only use that absorbs all species is for fuel, which accounts for over 80 per cent of the cut.

Timber is exceptional among industrial crude materials as it can be reproduced and can be altered during the growing period. Forestry is complicated, for many reasons, but mainly because it has the following: many end products (over 4,000 in urban-industrial societies), extremely wide geographical growing areas, the long-term nature of the growing products (many areas of woods will be harvested by individuals who were not even born when the trees were planted), the many joint uses (water and soil conservation, hunting, recreation, etc.), the few national-product markets, and the nature of forestry and mill organization (which varies widely between large, commercial corporations and owners who expend little or no effort and have little or no knowledge of the product).

In the past generation, timber has become scarce and costly in the main industrial-wood consuming areas. Even inaccessible virgin stands seldom sell under $1,500 per acre in the U.S. Pacific Northwest. When accessible, the average timber-size tree is now worth about $1,000 in the forest, and over one-third more when felled and toted to the millsite or to tidewater.

There is an increasing tendency throughout the world to move sawmills and wood products factories toward the forest as it retreats, in order

Courtesy of Weyerhaeuser Co.

Airview of Weyerhaeuser's integrated Longview, Washington, facility. To attain maximum use and value from the forest crop, tree farming, logging, sawmilling, planing, and the making of plywood, pulp, and paper are located at the same location. As an example of the economy possible, the sulfate pulp mill uses trimmings, edgings, and slabs left over from the sawmill operations to manufacture paper products.

to simplify the problem of transport or to reduce its distance and cost. Following is a table of costs for a typical northern California pine operation, handling timber that yields about 100 tons per acre, and which moves some 15 to 20 miles to the mill. The breakdown of costs per 1,000 board-feet (3¼ tons) is as follows:

Felling, limbing, and bucking		16%
Yarding (tractors) and loading		16
Road construction and maintenance	16%	
Truck operations	25	
Truck transportation		41
Supervision, technical services, and overhead		27
		100%

If the transportation hidden in the first two items is included, some 52 per cent of the total costs would be for movement. The mill cost for logs ($25 per 1,000 board-feet) is only about one-third of the finished lumber cost ready to be moved to the consuming areas.

Certain changes are taking place that affect logging technique in most urban-industrial forest areas. Large virgin timber is being replaced by young timber of smaller size. The increasing demand in certain regions for this young timber through the development of pulp mills and other wood products mills has greatly changed its economic usefulness. There is closer utilization of the large virgin timber brought about through increased demand, so that leftovers after logging can pay their way in large integrated mills (which now obtain as much as

75 per cent of the tree in the form of end products, versus 30 per cent a generation ago). The lowering of road costs due to the advent of the bulldozer has made practical the building of roads into stands of timber on steep ground. The perfecting of lightweight yet powerful machinery to meet problems of increased natural resistances, coupled with scarcity and higher wages of woods labor, has speeded the development of mechanized forestry. From the standpoint of better forest management, these improvements in logging technique are resulting in better utilization, making possible the practicing of better silviculture.

In a purely technical sense, silviculture in the forest is perhaps as bright a promise as technology at the mill, but both run into the dilemma of the small ownership and other economic problems not of their making. Such institutional and ideological dilemmas cannot be resolved by technicians, for they are not technical problems.

In the United States, about 21 per cent of the total forest land is owned by the federal government and about 6 per cent by state and local governments. The priorities of use result in little timber production. Forest industries corporations own about 13 per cent of the total (average size is 2,700 acres for some 23,000 holdings), which is handled as well as the government-owned acreage, although oriented toward wood production rather than watershed protection, recreation, grazing, etc. The big problem is the small owner. The average farm woodlot is under 50 acres, but the total forest acreage involved is some 34 per cent of the total, as there are over 3 million owners. Other small-holders number over 1 million and their combined holdings (averaging about 120 acres) total some 26 per cent of all forest land. Most of the small-holders net under $1 per acre per year, $2 to $3 is near the median profit, and $5 is very unusual, so most engage in very undesirable practices such as grazing of immature woods, letting the stand become overmature, or allowing high grading (selective cutting of certain tree types) followed by proliferation of weed-type trees, all in order to realize some

Load of logs splashes into a storage pond at a Weyerhaeuser Company installation in western Washington. Logs come from company tree farms to be sorted as to size and species by experienced boommen and directed to plants best suited to process them for maximum use and value.

Courtesy of Weyerhaeuser Co.

Courtesy of Weyerhaeuser Co.

The head sawyer is a key man in sawmill operations and an excellent example of the importance of skilled individuals in the production of quality wood products. From his booth beside the bandsaw, he directs the initial cutting of each log. He saws each log into huge rough slices called "cants" that are then transported to other manufacturing stations in the mill for further cutting and shaping. The head sawyer must know how to cut each log in a way to get the greatest value from it. A mistake in judgment here could mean an improper cut and loss of as much as 50 per cent of the log's potential value.

Courtesy of Weyerhaeuser Co.

Mechanical handling of lumber in Weyerhaeuser storage shed. By the time lumber reaches the construction industry, about half its cost represents transport charges at various stages.

A veneer peeling lathe in operation at a Georgia-Pacific, Oregon, plywood plant. The peeler logs are placed in the lathe and a blade slices off a veneer that is carried away on trays (belts) to be converted into plywood panels. Plywood's characteristics (e.g., overcoming the unidirectional strength of wood, and allowing the use of poorer quality wood in the interior of the sandwich) have made it the fastest growing segment of the wood construction materials.

Courtesy of Georgia-Pacific Corp.

short-run benefits in order to pay taxes or contribute to a substandard income.

The same problem dogs mill operations. Of the some 30,000 plus sawmills now operating in the United States, most are so-called "peckerwood" operations in the East and South, which regions together account for 45 per cent of the lumber cut. About 400 large mills in the West account for about one-third of the national lumber cut, with another 1,800 smaller mills accounting for another fifth.

Increasingly, improvements in the quality of lumber are being made by additional processing. One way is by controlled drying, sometimes to oven-dry conditions (eliminating about one-third of the weight of ordinary lumber). Another way is by seasoning with chemicals (e.g., fireproofing, termite proofing, etc.); this can now be done in a week instead of four to five years as formerly, but is too costly to use except in strategic locations. Increasing durability and overcoming dimensional instability is increasingly achieved by making plywood, laminated wood, and similar types of semisynthetic lumber. The United States alone has over 700 veneer and plywood plants whose output is now equal to some 15 per cent of the lumber output; some experts think that the fraction will increase until one-third of present lumber uses will be filled by such products. Scarfed or laminated wood is about 25 per cent stronger and 10 per cent stiffer than the same wood species in solid form; however, it costs from $250 to $600 per 1,000 board-feet, compared with the basic lumber price of some $70.

Wood and its products moving in international trade amount to some 55 million tons, about 4 per cent of total wood output or 7 per cent of industrial-wood production. About 15 per cent of world sawn softwoods, and half that fraction of sawn hardwoods, are moved (for comparison: about 10 per cent of world plywood production, and a bit more than 15 per cent of world wood pulp and world paper and paperboard production do likewise). Total trade is dominated by intra-European and intra-North American movements. The intercontinental trade involves mainly northern hemisphere sawn softwoods moving to tropical and mid-latitude southern hemisphere lands, and tropical hardwood logs moving to northern hemisphere mid-latitude lands (especially African veneer logs to Western Europe and Southeast Asian ones to Japan). Lumber is carried both in bulk by tramps and increasingly as general liner cargo. Pulp, paper, and paperboard is general cargo. Since lumber is light, it is often carried as deck cargo. Due to the freezing of Great Lakes–St. Lawrence, Scandinavian, and Soviet harbors, lumber shows the most pronounced seasonal variation in shipments and in engagement of tonnage.

Pulp and Paper

In highly developed societies, the consumption of lumber and timber tends to fall off on a per capita basis (e.g., in the United States, present use per person is only one-half what it was in 1900), partly because of increasing expense, but mainly because of the substitution of stronger and fireproof materials so important where urban living becomes dominant. The only exception

The world's largest plywood press is four stories high and an integral part of a new continuous-process method of making laminated panels from low-grade veneers. Plywood rolls continuously and automatically from the sixty-opening hot press at Georgia-Pacific's Springfield, Oregon, plant. The new type of panels has a tough, smooth built-in resin fiber surface on both sides, yet will sell in the same price range as ordinary fir plywood.

Courtesy of Georgia-Pacific Corp.

TABLE 10–6

World: Industrial Wood Output, by Great-Region and Economic-Type of Society, 1962–1964 Average-Annual
(in millions of metric tons)

	Industrial Wood Production [1] (million metric tons = 100.0 per cent)	Processed into Lumber and Timber	Processed into Pulps of All Kinds	Processed into Miscellaneous Products
North America	270	45%	22%	33%
Western Europe	135	56	22	22
Eastern Europe (including the U.S.S.R.)	210	69	5	26
Oceania	15	40	20	40
Latin America	40	30	5	65
Sub-Saharan Africa	15	27	6	67
Middle East (including North Africa)	5	40	5	55
Non-Communist Far East	70	64	13	22
Communist Far East	40	38	5	57
World	800	53	15	32
High-income countries	635	53	17	30
Low-income countries	165	54	7	39

	(per cent of 800 million metric tons)	(per cent of 425 million metric tons)	(per cent of 115 million metric tons)	(per cent of 260 million metric tons)
North America	33.7	28.3	51.3	34.8
Western Europe	16.9	17.7	25.6	11.6
Eastern Europe (including the U.S.S.R.)	26.2	34.2	8.5	21.2
Oceania	1.9	1.4	2.5	2.3
Latin America	5.0	2.8	1.7	10.0
Sub-Saharan Africa	1.9	1.0	0.8	3.9
Middle East (including North Africa)	0.6	0.5	0.2	1.2
Non-Communist Far East	8.8	10.6	7.7	6.1
Communist Far East	5.0	3.5	1.7	8.9
World	100.0	100.0	100.0	100.0
High-income countries	79.4	79.0	91.0	75.0
Low-income countries	20.6	21.0	9.0	25.0

SOURCE: Adapted from United Nations data, supplemented by unofficial estimates to fill in gaps.

[1] Of the 425 million metric tons of roundwood processed into lumber and timber and the 115 million metric tons processed into pulps, about one-third was wasted or used for a by-product use (this in terms of air-dried wood; in terms of green wood, the fraction wasted is one-half or more). Actually, some 270 million metric tons of lumber-timber and 75 million metric tons of pulps were produced. There is a bit less waste in the 260 million metric tons of miscellaneous products raw material, as much of this is used in small-stick or unaltered roundwood form (props, poles, ties, etc.) or processed into material saving types of products (e.g. various types of composition board).

to this is the vitality shown by the veneer and plywood branches.

Pulp and its products is the dynamic segment of the wood-using industry. Per capita consumption annually of paper and paper products in the United States has risen in twenty years from 200 to over 400 pounds. U.S. consumption is rising at only one-half of Western Europe's 10 per cent rate, and in some countries even higher rates are recorded.

The 300 wood pulp mills in the United States, plus the related industries—paper and paperboard, printing and publishing, rayon, and the manufacture of converted paper products—now account for 10 per cent of industrial output and nearly that share of industrial employment.

World production of pulp-based products is now some 75 million tons yearly, and is expected to double in less than two decades. New wood pulp is some two-thirds of total pulp fiber consumption, with waste paper providing nearly one-quarter, and the rest coming from rags, cotton, flax, straw, and a miscellany of minor sources. Straw is used both to make paper and paperboard, and Esparto grass is still used, to a small extent, in Europe. But the problems of collecting and storing straw and grass in the quantity needed, and the tendency of paper made from these materials to turn brittle, severely limits their use. In the United States, less than 5 per cent of all pulp is now from other than wood pulp and reclaimed wood fiber sources, while elsewhere it is triple that fraction.

One ounce of wood pulp contains over 13 million individual fibers. These threads range 0.05 to 0.15 inch in length, and their length is about 100 times their width. Glued together by another complex substance called lignin, these fibers constitute about one-half the bulk of an average tree. In the United States, normal recovery of pulp is only 75 per cent of the total cellulose (or less than 40 per cent of pulpwood logs), and elsewhere in the world it is often less.[4]

Over 5,000 different kinds of paper are now made. The pulp is obtained by four different processes—acid (sulfite), alkaline (kraft or sulfate), semichemical, and mechanical—from both softwoods and hardwoods. The softwoods or coniferous, cone bearing trees (such as pine, spruce, and fir) have loosely bonded, longer fibers. The hardwoods or broadleaf bearing deciduous trees (such as oak, maple, aspen, gum, beech, birch, poplar) have short wood fibers that form a dense, heavy wood. A cord of hardwood yields more pulp than a cord of softwood. Chemically processed softwoods yield 1 ton of pulp for 2 cords of wood used, while hardwoods yield 1 ton for $1\frac{1}{2}$ cords. The hardwood pulps are excellent for giving opacity, bulk, and good formation to fine papers, although softwood pulps are necessary to contribute sufficient strength. While hardwood pulp is now some 20 per cent of U.S. pulp, in the East and Lake states it is 30 to 50 per cent, and increasingly some paper is made from all hardwood pulp.

The acid (sulfite) process uses sulfurous acid to remove the lignin bond from spruce, fir, hemlock, and other non-resinous softwoods. The product is expensive, because of limited recycling, and there is a pitch problem (black specks on paper) that is still not solved. Sulfite paper pulp still has great importance for certain kinds of paper, where sulfate pulp is not as suitable, particularly for all kinds of greaseproof paper, tissue paper, and certain grades of fine papers. When sulfite pulp manufacturing is made more economical by the scientific recovery of waste liquors, now mainly lost in the waste water, it may gain in economic importance. At present, it accounts for only 15 per cent of U.S. pulp making, compared with 35 per cent a generation back.

Pulp for the preparation of acetate silk—dissolving pulp—has been prepared from sulfite pulp by means of suitable warm alkali treatment. By this means a pulp is obtained that shows excellent reactivity, is completely con-

---

[4] When we consider that we recover only about 75 per cent of the cellulose in a normal pulping process for paper, and must retain considerable lignin in a pulp, thereby limiting its uses, in order to increase recovery, and when we consider that the results in utilization of lignin by-products are so meager as to be disappointing, the need for fundamental research on lignin is brought out in bold relief.

verted by the acetylation process without leaving a residue, and completely dissolves in the organic solvents used in the preparation of the spinning solution.

Until the 1920's, for both technical and economic reasons, spruce was the preferred wood for pulp. By this time, however, the demand for wood pulp had reached such proportions that spruce, like rags in the earlier days, was becoming scarce and expensive. The answer was found not in a new resource but by adapting existing processes to additional species of wood, first to Western Hemlock, Douglas Fir, and Southern Pine, and then (through an adaptation, the soda process) to hardwood pulp.

At first, Western Hemlock yielded a pulp suitable for printing papers (then the most important market), but the unbleached sulfate or kraft paper originally obtained from Douglas Fir and Southern Pine, being brownish in color, could not easily be used for this purpose, although it did offer a tough fiber ideal for heavy wrapping paper and paper cartons sturdy enough to stand shipping (some 3 million tons is still used for such purposes). In time, means were found to bleach the kraft pulp, permitting the development of a host of other utility products—paper milk bottles, paper cans for cheese and ice cream, packages for butter and frozen foods, light punch cards for business machines, tough envelopes and file folders, etc. The bleached sulfate pulp costs about $150 per ton, considerably more than the kraft pulp, but can be used in making many kinds of fine papers (rag content, sulfite bond, thin papers, cover and text papers, and bristol board) formerly unavailable as markets.

In recent years, most new pulp mills have been sulfate types, whereas expansion within the sulfite industry has been insignificant. The fundamental cause of this can be found in the fact that the sulfate technique can be used for all types of wood, including hardwood fibers only one-third as long as pine fibers. Another improvement is the ability to bleach pulp to a high degree of whiteness with little or no loss of strength. Finally, the scientific method of alkali recovery, which has considerable importance in the improvement of heating economy, has made the industry self-supporting in both heat and power. The sulfate process now accounts for well over one-half of all U.S. pulp making.

Cheaper paper is made from the mechanical and semichemical processes, which were developed mainly because of the high cost and low yield of the acid and alkaline processes. The mechanical or groundwood process produces a low-quality newsprint that yellows and deteriorates quickly, since the lignin is left in when the billets are ground up. Only a tenth of U.S. paper is made by this process, but it is still widely used in Canada, which supplies over two-thirds of U.S. newsprint. It is generally applied to light-colored softwoods, but has been adapted to hardwoods, especially in the semichemical process, in which the chips are mildly cooked, then mechanically broken up. Originally used with hardwood, the semichemical process is now broadly applied, and accounts for some 15 per cent of U.S. pulp making.

There are three characteristics that distinguish wood as a raw material for chemical and chemical process industries. First, it is a perpetually renewable resource of the same kind and in the same place. Second, wood for chemical industries can be a by-product of forestry of which the principal product may be lumber or similar material. Third, the methods used in harvesting the wood crop determine the nature of future crops. Probably the major key to intensive management of the forest resource is the development of integrated utilization centers that can use more of the material brought from the woods to the sawmill, as well as permit more material to be removed from the timberland. The pulp industry and related paper products industries fit in well with such conservation. The 15 per cent of privately owned commercial timberland in the United States that is in tree farms (two-thirds in the South) is mainly held by paper companies. To speed up tree growth, such companies are developing new hybrid trees for fast growth. There are now hybrid pines, black locusts, and chestnuts, but the most spectacular is hybrid poplar. Even in Maine, the hybrid poplar has made a yield of 40 cords (70 tons) to the acre in fifteen years, which would have taken the best native trees some thirty-five years to duplicate.

Miscellaneous Industrial-Wood Uses

Use of wood in rural areas for purposes other than construction has been declining everywhere in the urban-industrial realm as a result of the rural exodus and the increasing availability of alternative materials. However, the total use of fence posts and poles is still considerable. In many isolated areas, the use of such small roundwood supplies is a substitute for lumber and metal products.

Another fairly big use is that of pit props in mining (especially coal mining). In the industrial nations, such use per ton of mined material is either stagnant or falling, as metal mesh, strips, and bolts are increasingly favored, but in less developed areas their use is still increasing.

Demand for railway ties consists mainly of renewals in most parts of the world, since no significant extensions of track are being made, but in some of the underdeveloped areas expansion is still taking place. Improvements in preservatives are also having an effect by decreasing the renewal rate.

In packaging and in woodworking industries, there is increasing consumption at a decreasing rate, since there is a tendency for declining quantities of wood used per unit produced. In these areas, there is a widespread substitution of wood composition boards of various types to substitute for lumber. Hardboard and insulation board are made from wood fibers that are pressed into sheets using the natural lignin in the fiber as the principal bonding agent, and are also known as softboard. Particle board is made from wood in the form of chips, shavings, flakes, splinters, or smaller particles, mixed with adhesives and then shaped into panels by applications of heat and pressure—the resulting product is used as core stock for furniture and doors, interior paneling, shelving, cabinets, and underlay for flooring, and for counter and sink tops. In the United States, such paperboard and fiberboard is produced in amounts equal in quantity to paper proper, while in Western Europe (where lumber is one-third to one-half more costly than in the United States) production is much larger than paper.

Trends

The ancient human pressure on the forests of the world continues at the present time, and in all probability will become more severe in the future. There are regional differences in the reasons for the pressure, but all have the same effect: the forests are losing ground, and it is generally the best and most accessible timberland that is being lost. Hence, the now inaccessible forests may become increasingly important, and the question is how much we can depend on them in the foreseeable future.

Although shrinking, the area of the accessible forest is large enough, and our technical skill, even though problems remain, is now good enough to supply all mankind with a reasonably adequate amount of wood in the near future, provided the skill is freely applied over the area and the yield of the forest is equitably distributed. But deeply entrenched cultural factors interfere with both the application of the skill and the distribution of the yield—this is the root of the forestry problem and the most difficult part of it.

Most reports—whether they deal with the United States or the world—conclude that the area of the productive forest is large enough to provide the wood needed in the future, even if the need should become two to three times as large as today, but only on two conditions: first, that much of the now inaccessible forests must be opened to utilization, and second, all forests must be placed under greatly improved sustained-yield management. These are not small conditions, and in them lies the whole forest problem.

With reasonably good management, the forests of the world can produce an annual yield of ¾ ton. The annnal natural increment in the forests of Western Europe and the United States (certainly in the southern and Pacific Coast states) runs about 1 to 1½ tons per acre annually, perhaps four to five times as much wood as that yielded by the wild forests of Canada, northern Scandinavia, and the U.S.S.R. The

1,500 million acres of inaccessible forest in the far north is not equivalent in productive capacity to more than some 200 to 300 million acres of forest land in the mid-latitudes. So, for all practical purposes, the forestry problem of the world is the problem of making the best use of the forest land within reach. The ultimate goal might be defined as the utilization of the world's forest lands in such a manner that they will permanently yield sufficient wood for all mankind at a price people can pay, while at the same time, some of the forests will provide watershed, soil, and wildlife protection, grazing opportunity, and facilities for study and recreation.

SUGGESTED READINGS

ALDERFER, E. B., and MICHL, H. E. *Economics of American Industry.* New York: McGraw-Hill, 1957. Pp. 284–321, 601–27.

ALEXANDERSSON, GUNNAR, and NORSTROM, GORAN. *World Shipping.* New York: Wiley, 1963. Pp. 106–8.

CARLSON, ALBERT S. (ed.). *Economic Geography of Industrial Materials.* New York: Reinhold, 1956. Pp. 285–331.

CHATT, EILEEN M. *Cocoa.* New York: Interscience Publishers, 1953. Pp. 302.

EDEN, T. *Tea.* London: Longmans, Green, 1958. Pp. 201.

HADEN-GUEST, STEPHEN, WRIGHT, JOHN K., and TECLAFF, EILEEN M. (eds.). *A World Geography of Forest Resources.* (American Geographical Society Special Publication No. 33.) New York: Ronald, 1956. Pp. 736.

MORTON, MAURICE (ed.). *Introduction to Rubber Technology.* New York: Reinhold, 1959. Pp. 547.

OXFORD UNIVERSITY PRESS. *Oxford Economic Atlas of the World.* London: Oxford University Press, 1965. Pp. 22–28, 30–31.

UNITED STATES PULP PRODUCERS ASSOCIATION, INC. *Wood Pulp: A Basic Fiber.* New York: The Association, 1955. Pp. 48.

VALAER, PETER JOHN. *Wines of the World.* New York: Abelard-Schuman, 1950. Pp. 576.

VAN ROYEN, WILLIAM (ed.). *Atlas of the World's Resources.* Vol. I. *The Agricultural Resources of the World.* Englewood Cliffs, N.J.: Prentice-Hall, 1954. Pp. 110–19, 129–32, 179–81.

WELLMAN, FREDERICK L. *Coffee.* London: L. Hill, 1961. Pp. 488.

WICKIZER, V. D. *Coffee, Tea, and Cocoa.* Stanford University Press, 1951. Pp. 374.

ZIMMERMANN, ERICH W. *World Resources and Industries.* New York: Harper & Row, 1951. Pp. 374–420.

11

Oceanic Products

The 71 per cent of the earth's surface covered by seawater contributes only ¼ per cent of mankind's yearly income directly. Even if generous allowance were given for the value derived from ocean lanes for transportation, the oceans would rank with the cold and dry deserts as economic barrens.

The most valuable product obtained from the sea is the 48 million tons of fish, representing about 1 per cent of mankind's food-feed supply in terms of energy supply of which about a third moves in international trade. Considering protein alone, the 2½ million tons obtained may be about 2 per cent of world supplies, or some 7 per cent of the superior protein supplied by edible animal and fish foods considered as a group.

About three-fifths of the fish landed are food-type fish, but only about a half of their weight ends up as human food. An increasing share of the remainder, plus the non-food types (mainly small or bony), is converted into animal feed, oil, and fertilizer.

Marine fish are often divided into two types: the pelagic types which swim in shoals, dwelling in the high seas near the surface; and the demersal types which are bottom-living, on the continental shelf or the upper edge of the continental slope. Most important of the pelagic types is the herring family (herring, sardines, pilchards, menhaden, anchovies, and others), followed by the mackerel family (mackerel, tuna, bonitos, and others) which are usually found in warmer waters. Most important of the demersal types is the cod family (cod, haddock, and others), followed by the flatfish (halibut, plaice, sole, and others) and by non-fish (crab, shrimp, and other crustaceans; oysters and other shellfish). The pelagic types, mainly caught by nets, are the cheapest fish: both food-type herring (often 3 to 4 cents per pound landed fresh-weight) and feed types (small herring, sardines, and anchovies; menhaden; and others) which bring in much less (around 1 cent per pound landed fresh-weight). Demersal types are mainly caught by line, trawl (a large sacklike net dragged along the sea floor), and seine (a small trawl-like net), and are usually more expensive, although cod is a comparatively inexpensive food fish in this group. Staple food fish (herring, cod, and others) are often landed and delivered fresh at about a third of the price of animal products raised on land, so superior protein is gained from fish by many regions that could not afford as much of animal protein. The lower prices reflect absence of land rental as well as the superior productivity of modern, highly capitalized fishermen (e.g., North Atlantic trawler fisheries produce 100 or more tons of bottom fish such as cod and haddock per man-year, and Pacific Coast pilchard fisheries produce about 250 or more tons per man-year, compared with Iowa's 25 tons of pork per man-year).[1] Luxury-type food fish—salmon, tuna, halibut—and crab, shrimp, and oysters are not cheap staples like herring and cod. They are usually processed ready to eat, and are often used as appetizers or side dishes, usually costing as much as freshwater food fish and crustaceans. The world's tonnage demand for food fish is increasing some 3 to 4 per cent annually, with the value increasing half again as rapidly, reflecting not only higher landed costs, but also the expensive processing and distribution that occurs before consumption. The tonnage demand for feed- and fertilizer-type fish is increasing some 6 to 8 per cent annually, but the annual increase in value is only a quarter to a third as much.

In terms of fish production per acre of water surface, the oceanic output of under 1 pound per acre pales beside the records of warm countries' freshwater pond culture: in pounds per acre per annum, south China obtains 4,000; Malaya, 3,500; Hong Kong, 3,000; Israel, 1,200; the Philippines, 600. Pond production from such areas is under 1 million tons, with other freshwater fish from rivers and lakes nearly four times as large, the total freshwater catch being about 10 per cent of the total fish catch from all sources, in terms of tonnage (share by value twice as large).

REGIONAL PRODUCTIVITY OF FISHERIES

Present Productivity

Some 20 per cent of the 48 million tons of fish caught annually in the world's waters are from southern hemisphere grounds, a spectacular fourfold increase in the fraction taken there little more than a decade ago. Most of that increase has been processed into fish meal, fish solubles, and similar feed concentrates destined for the broiler and other animal husbandry activities of the North Atlantic regions and of Japan. Since such fish bring less than the food-type fish of the traditional northern hemisphere grounds, the southern hemisphere contributes only about 5 per cent of the value of world fisheries.[2]

Since situation rather than inherent productivity delimits usability, the most valuable fisheries can be grouped as follows: (1) fishing grounds where catches exceed 10 pounds per acre and up, including the Newfoundland Banks, the North Sea, the Sea of Azov, the Sea of Japan, and the Bering Sea; (2) fishing grounds with annual catches from 5 to 10 pounds per acre, including the Gulf of Mexico, the Mediterranean Sea, the Black Sea, the Caspian Sea, the East China Sea, and the Yellow Sea; (3) fishing grounds with annual catches of a few pounds per acre, including the Baltic Sea, the Barents Sea, and the Sea of Okhotsk; (4) the least fished areas, including the open waters of the Atlantic, Pacific, Indian, Arctic, and Antarctic oceans, which yield less than 1 pound per acre annually.

The North Atlantic fishing grounds and the North Pacific fishing grounds together contribute about a half of the world's fish catch. Western European grounds and adjacent Eastern European ones contribute over 20 per cent of the total, with East Asian grounds (Communist marine plus non-Communist marine) contributing over 25 per cent. The grounds off eastern North America yield about 10 per cent of the total (nearly a third caught by Western and Eastern European craft). In both North American and Eastern European catches, over two-thirds come from Atlantic grounds. Three-fourths of the southern hemisphere's 20 per cent of the world catch comes from western South American grounds, with most of the remainder from the western portions of southern Africa.

---

[1] Total employment in fishing is over 5 million workers, of which 2 million are skilled in modern techniques, while the other part-time fishermen equal about 1 million full time equivalent workers (with labor productivity no higher than in peasant agriculture).

[2] Fish meal (representing over five times its tonnage in fresh-weight catch) cost an average of $90 a ton to produce in Peru, and sold in the range of $110 to $130 per ton at various times during 1964. Peru surpassed Japan in tonnage of fish catch in 1964 (but not in value of catch).

WORLD: FISH PRODUCTION AND COMPOSITION, BY GREAT-REGION AND ECONOMIC-TYPE OF SOCIETY, 1962-1964 AVERAGE-ANNUAL
(Million Metric Tons Fresh-Weight)

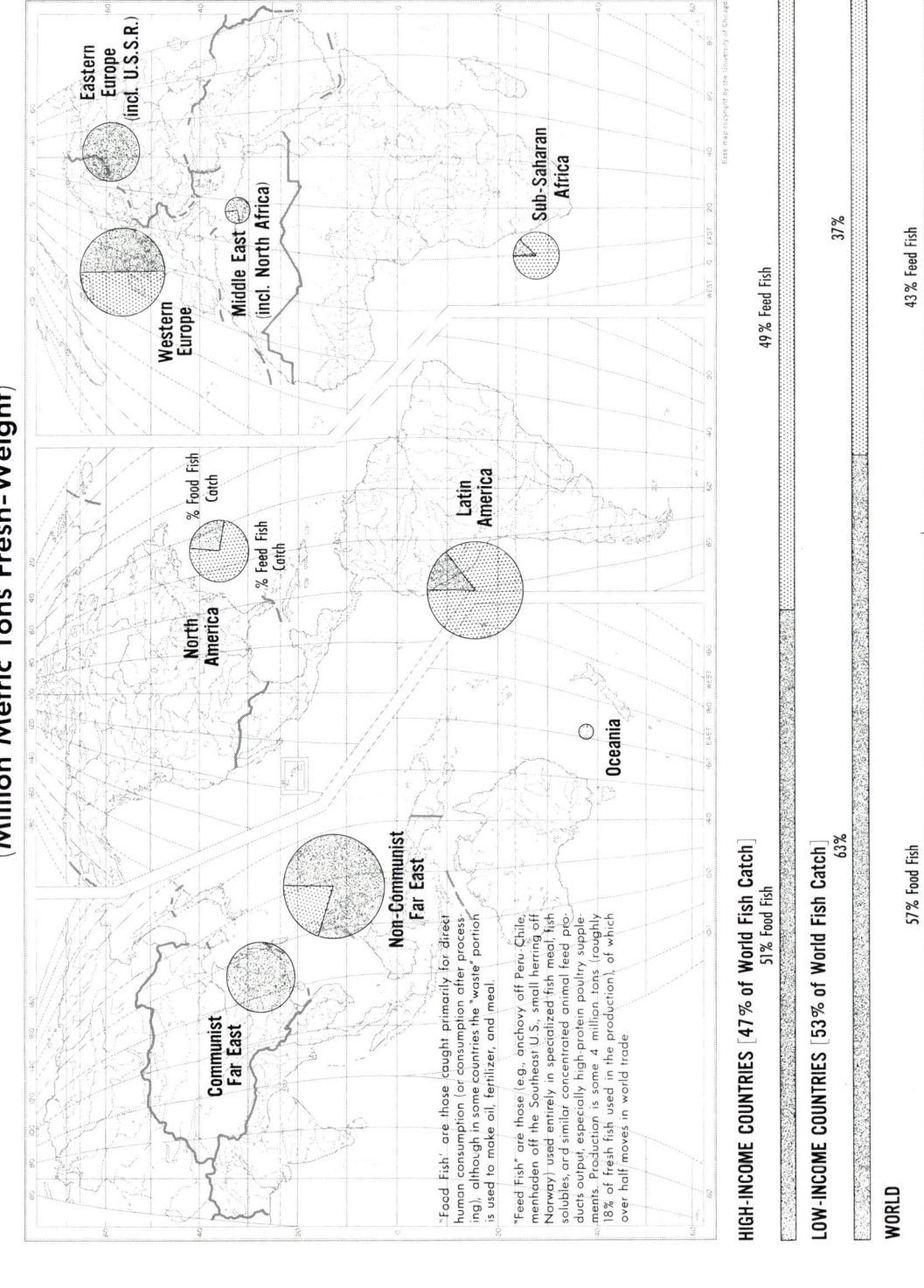

WORLD: GREAT-REGION AND ECONOMIC-TYPE OF SOCIETY SHARES OF WORLD FISH PRODUCTION, 1962-1964 AVERAGE-ANNUAL

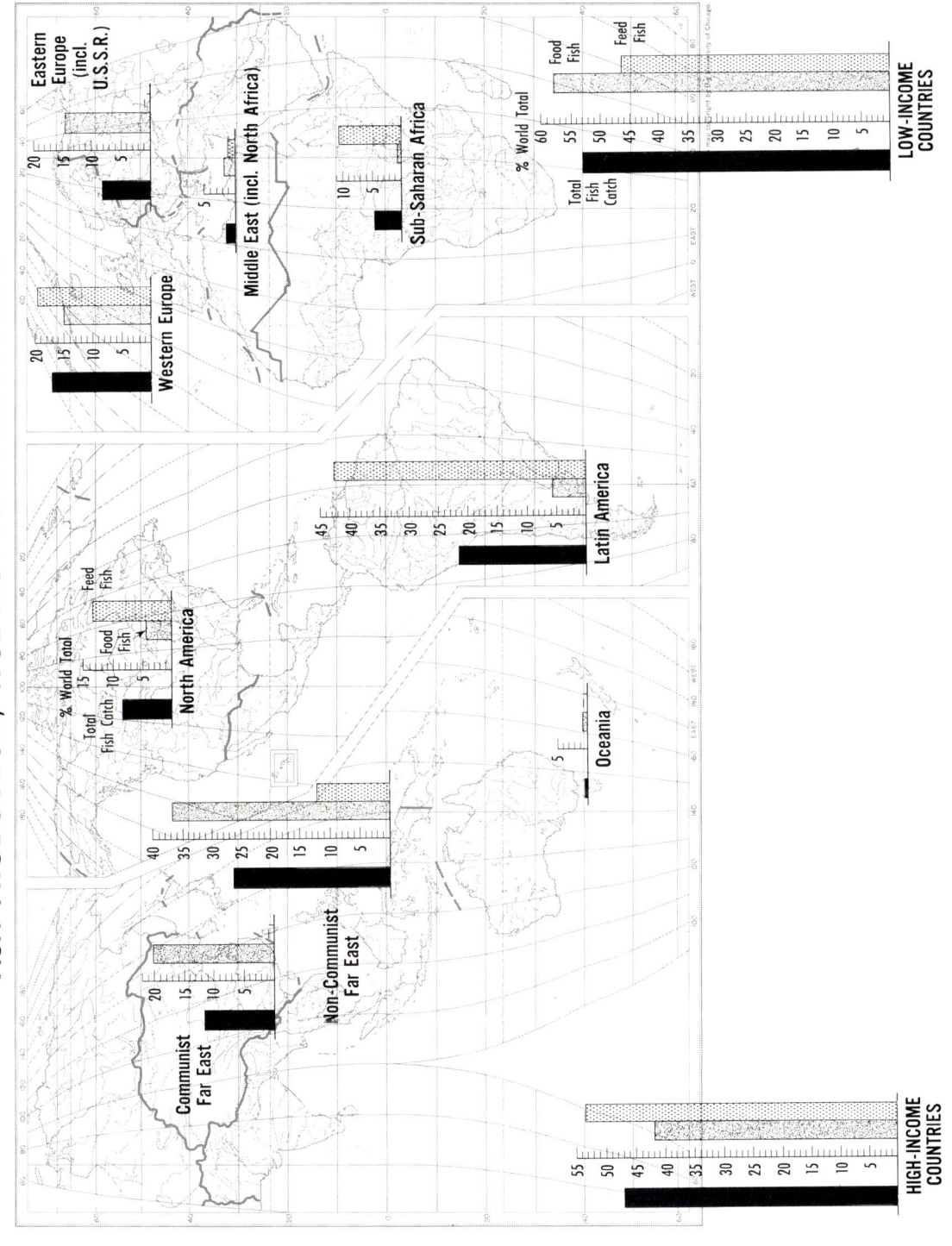

TABLE 11–1

World: Fish Production and Composition, by Great-Region and Economic-Type of Society, 1962–1964 Average-Annual *

(in millions of metric tons fresh-weight)

	Total Fish [1] (million metric tons fresh-weight = 100.0 per cent)	Food Fish [2]	Feed Fish [3]
North America	4.0	30.0%	70.0%
Western Europe	8.2	50.0	50.0
Eastern Europe (including the U.S.S.R.)	4.0	100.0	–
Oceania	0.2	100.0	–
Latin America	10.5	15.0	85.0
Sub-Saharan Africa	2.3	10.0	90.0
Middle East (including North Africa)	0.7	70.0	30.0
Non-Communist Far East	12.6	80.0	20.0
Communist Far East	5.5	100.0	–
World	48.0	57.0	43.0
High-income countries	22.5	51.0	49.0
Low-income countries	25.5	63.0	37.0

	(per cent of 48.0 million metric tons)	(per cent of 27.5 million metric tons)	(per cent of 20.5 million metric tons)
North America	8.3	4.4	13.4
Western Europe	17.1	15.0	19.8
Eastern Europe (including the U.S.S.R.)	8.3	14.6	–
Oceania	0.4	0.7	–
Latin America	21.9	5.8	42.9
Sub-Saharan Africa	4.8	0.7	10.7
Middle East (including North Africa)	1.5	1.8	1.1
Non-Communist Far East	26.2	36.9	12.1
Communist Far East	11.5	20.1	–
World	100.0	100.0	100.0
High-income countries	47.0	42.0	53.5
Low-income countries	53.0	58.0	46.5

TABLE 11–1 SOURCE: Adapted from United Nations data, with unofficial sources used to fill in gaps.

* The gross value of the annual catch is over U.S. $5 billion (perhaps U.S. $3 billion value-added), over 90 per cent from food fish and less than 10 per cent from fish meal and fish oil.

[1] "Total Fish" includes 4.5 million metric tons freshwater catch.

[2] "Food Fish" includes fish caught mainly for direct human consumption, although in some countries the waste from processing is used to make oil, fertilizer, and feed.

[3] "Feed Fish" are those specialized types (e.g., anchovy in Peru-Chile, menhaden in the United States, small herring in Norway) that are primarily processed into fish meal (some 3.75 million metric tons, about 18 per cent of the catch), a competitor with soybean meal in the concentrated animal feed markets.

Prospective Productivity

Crude estimates of the annual growth of bony fish in the oceans are from about 0.1 to 1 billion tons, or from two to twenty times greater than present production. However, if the sea is to be exploited on even a modestly larger scale (over 60 million tons), fishermen will have to have greatly improved fish catching methods and find additional fishing grounds. Little fishing is now done beyond 350- to 500-foot depths, although only 5 per cent of the oceans' areas are included in exploited shelf regions.

Recently, the fish populations beyond the continental shelves have been found to be far greater than was supposed. However, many of the fish are small and do not school, so that radically new techniques of location, capture, processing, and marketing must be developed to make the most of them commercially. There is every reason to believe that at intermediate depths fish are as abundant as at the surface or on the shallow bottom, where most commercial fishermen now cast their nets. One way of exploiting these almost untouched resources may be through new purse nets guided by improved underwater acoustic devices, for such fish can be located by sound.

As fishermen are gradually forced farther and farther from port by the depletion of nearby fishing grounds, the use of ice becomes less effective and new developments in bringing fresh fish to land must be used, based on the application of refrigeration equipment. Three

While the menhaden fish taken by the seine (or purse) boats are being pumped aboard the mother vessel, the spotter plane is seeking more schools for capture.

Courtesy of New Jersey Menhaden Products, Inc.

The seine or purse boats have completed circling the net around a school of menhaden fish, trapping them. The fish are then concentrated in a small area of the net and brought alongside the mother vessel to be pumped aboard.

Courtesy of New Jersey Menhaden Products, Inc.

broadly separate lines of development can be distinguished: (1) the use of refrigeration equipment to supplement ice, (2) the freezing at sea of only the edible portion of the fish (usually fillets) on factory ships equipped also to convert all the wastes into by-products, and (3) the freezing of whole fish at sea and their subsequent processing on land. All three lines of development are important: the first because it is in commercial use throughout the world; the second because it is helping solve the European and U.S. fresh-fish problem; and the third because it promises to afford a practical solution to many of the problems of New England's deep-sea fishing industry and may make the region's fishery more competitive (in a complex of other expensive equipment).

The operation of factory ships is very popular with all European nations and Japan, but their use by Americans is restricted by labor and management problems. American fishermen dislike long voyages (even two-week trawler voyages, although they make them), and present land-based fish processing plants dislike factory ship competition. Fresh-frozen fish satisfies the American conditions by being economical, by requiring little alteration in the fishermen's habits, and by conserving both food and non-food portions of the catch.

The tendency in commercial fisheries the world over is toward greater capitalization, with larger, more elaborately equipped boats. Japan and the U.S.S.R. are the leaders; Western European nations are close behind; the United States has lagged since 1950. The half of the some $12 billion of invested capital in the U.S. fishing industry in boats and gear has especially become less competitive; the half in processing, wholesaling, and retailing equipment has improved swiftly. Production is now about 3 million tons, of which two-fifths are food-type fish (this supplies about half of do-

The fish are being compressed in a small area and being pumped aboard the mother vessel.

Courtesy of New Jersey Menhaden Products, Inc.

Courtesy of New Jersey Menhaden Products, Inc.

An airview of a modern menhaden plant located at Wildwood, New Jersey. Dryer furnaces with automatic temperature controls and recording thermometers dry the cooked fish into fish scrap, and modern automatically controlled evaporators are used for the manufacture of condensed fish solubles.

mestic consumption).[3] Per capita annual consumption of food-type fish has remained about constant (10 pounds compared with 170 pounds of red meat), with increased use occurring mainly in the feed and raw materials categories. Nearly 2 million tons of non-food fish (mainly menhaden) and food fish remnants are converted into about 0.4 million tons of meal and 0.1 million tons of oil. The meal is mainly used as a source of protein for animal feed. It also contains an unidentified substance that accelerates growth (a substance also present in corn, wheat, and soybeans, but in much smaller quantities), and has been especially important in cutting down feed requirements and in accelerating growth in the broiler-chicken industry.

The contributions of mechanics, electronics, and chemicals to the world's commercial fishing industry continue. Salmon, tuna, herring, pilchard, and mackerel fishermen are handling nets with power-driven blocks that result in increased output with less (as much as 40 per cent less) manpower. Airplanes are increasingly used to spot surface schools of menhaden and

[3] In a value (rather than a tonnage) context, nearly half of the catch consists of crustaceans, shellfish, and freshwater food fish.

Courtesy of New Jersey Menhaden Products, Inc.

Newly processed fish scrap being aerated to cool from the dryer temperature to air temperature. The fish meal is bagged and shipped to broiler-chicken or other animal-husbandry finishers, to be used as high-protein supplement in the diet.

tuna, and their finds are radioed to fishermen. Ship-to-shore radiotelephones enable fishermen to choose a port where they can obtain the maximum return for their catches. Electric gear in tuna (line) fishing permits larger catches with less effort and also enhances the keeping quality of the meat by reducing enzyme deterioration. Resin-treated synthetic fibers are being made into nets that are lighter, easier to handle, and more durable than older types made of natural fibers. The wider application of these and other innovations now considered commercially useful could probably maintain the world's annual increase in the fish catch (6 per cent in tonnage) for the remainder of the decade. To increase that catch five to ten times, as some dream of doing, would require major advances in both science and engineering.

Outer Limits of Possibilities

Organic matter in seawater starts with microscopic floating plants (phytoplankton) which first of all require mineral salts for their growth and sufficient light intensity for photosynthesis. Since the intensity of light decreases gradually with depth, the zone in which the organic matter is synthesized is limited by turbidity and the absorption of light in seawater. Almost all of the plant life in the seas of the world is confined to depths of less than 300 feet, and in high latitudes very little lives even so far down as this.

Exhausted supplies of nutrient salts may be replenished through the movements of water masses. The circulation of water, therefore, constitutes one of the major physical factors affecting the productivity of the sea. Material drained from the land by streams is carried out and distributed in the sea by coastal currents. The upwelling of subsurface water, in which nutrient salts (especially nitrates and phosphates) are brought back to the lighted layers, is reflected in large phytoplankton (e.g., diatoms and dinoflagellates) production along the California coast, along the western South American coast (through the mechanism of the Peruvian coastal current), in regions of divergence along the equatorial countercurrents, and along the west coast of Africa.

In higher latitudes, fertilizer salts (but not plants and animals) are at their maximum in the winter months, being brought up and mixed by the winter storms—this is followed by the spring outburst, in which the phytoplankton population may increase to 10,000 times its winter value, and by a midsummer low correlated with a minimum of salts in solution (since they have been removed from solution and converted into living plant and animal tissue).

As the surface waters cool during winter in the mid-latitudes, convection currents are set up, enriching the surface waters with salts from the deep waters below, and the deep waters with oxygen for the animal life there. In addition, as underwater currents meet shallow banks or the shore, cold water is forced to the surface, bringing with it salts that maintain a vigorous plankton growth.

In the Arctic and Antarctic, the sun remains low at noon, and consequently its rays, striking the water at rather a flat angle, are mostly reflected and do not penetrate the surface—as a result, the small floating animals (e.g., plankton "grazers" like the copepods) find their optimum light level much nearer the surface than they do in lower latitudes, and consequently they tend to congregate in the top layers even by day where, too, they find the maximum crop of phytoplankton. This fact is one of the contributory causes of the extraordinary abundance of marine life, whether of whales or of fish, that is to be found in the Antarctic and in the northern seas around Iceland, Bear Island, and Spitzbergen.

In the tropics, owing largely to the amount of daylight, photosynthesis can proceed the year round. The number of phytoplankton is fairly constant and low as compared with the spring outburst in the mid-latitudes, and the number of zooplankton is likely rather constant and not very great. But since some plants and animals are reproducing at all seasons of the year, the actual amount of plankton production in coastal waters in the tropics is much the same as in regions such as the English Channel (5 to 6 tons dry-weight yearly).

There is a general absence of the annual convectional overturn that occurs in the mid-latitude and cold waters and returns an abundance of nutrient salts to the surface layers. Occasionally, local enrichment of nutrients occurs: in equatorial regions, water wells up from below to make room for the inflow of cold water from the poles (the equatorial drifts are reinforced by these vertical currents which bring supplies of cold water from the depths below); there is penetration from the south of cold currents to the South American and African coasts; local upwelling caused by the southwest monsoon on the east African and Arabian coasts sends enriched water down the west coast of India where major fisheries occur. But mainly one sees blue waters, the desert color of the sea. Far offshore, generally speaking, phytoplankton is lacking in great quantities, except for those places where diverging currents or submarine ridges cause upwelling and other necessary factors are available.

Until recently, it was believed that fish populations were less in warmer seas than in higher latitudes, but now it is thought that temperature differences may be the key. The vertical distribution of the plankton at any one place is largely controlled by light. Very few forms of life in the sea are anything like worldwide in their distribution, and the principal factor in limiting their spread is apparently temperature. Tropical plankton, for example, will have few or no species in common with mid-latitude plankton of the same salinity, simply because one type cannot survive the temperature at which another survives. The same is true of bony fish. Several bipolar species that are absent from the surface waters of the tropics can be found on the equator at a depth of 1,200 feet or so, where the temperature of the water is much the same as it is at the surface in the northern and southern parts of the Atlantic and Pacific oceans. However, although tropical water masses are enormous in extent and are now known to contain great quantities of fish in the aggregate, the catching of these economically in commercial quantities presents great difficulties. Surface fish offer the best prospects for new or greater exploitation in the foreseeable future.

Use of Plankton

Fundamentally, fishing is still hunting, not farming. Most of our commercial fish are carnivores, whereas our profitable land animals are herbivores; that is, most marine fishing is comparable to hunting for land carnivores (e.g., tigers, wolves, weasels) as a meat supply. In terms of ultimate efficiency, fishing rates extremely low: two-link food chain (man eats plants) equals 10 per cent efficiency; three-link food chain (man eats animals who ate plants) equals 1 per cent efficiency; five-link food chain (man eats carnivorous fish who ate small fish who ate animal plankton who ate vegetable plankton) equals 0.01 per cent efficiency. The average feed-food ratio in oceans is 1000:1 (whales, herring, menhaden, etc., eat krill, small marine animals, and cut down the food chain by one link), compared with that of 10:1 in ponds.

Theoretically, the possibility exists of harvesting or even directly cultivating plankton. There are those who dream of the day when seawater will be treated on a large scale, with fish and plankton filtered out and dried for food, feed, and fertilizer, minerals removed, with the fresh water pumped inland for irrigation and city uses. At present, much of the basic science and engineering is missing, so economic exploitation seems far away.

The continental shelves represent some 9 per cent of the total area of the oceans, of which about two-thirds is regularly fished. Over all the oceans, some 400 billion tons of carbon dioxide are extracted from the air each year and converted by sunlight into marine organisms. This marine biosynthesis or photosynthetic fixation of carbon is much larger than that of the land, and giving effect to both the higher rate of photosynthetic manufacture of organic matter and of the larger area, it has been estimated that 60 to 90 per cent of the total plant photosynthesis of the earth occurs at sea.

There are some 17,000 members of the algae family, but most of the experimental work has been done with chlorella, a freshwater member. Like the others, it is a microscopic plant so small that a quart of water just tinted green would contain ten times as many plants as there are people in the world today.

In its native state, growing in freshwater ponds, chlorella vulgaris utilizes about 2 per cent of the sun energy it receives.[4] In one experiment, sewage was put into a shallow pond. The organic substances were rapidly decomposed by bacteria and became feed for algae which through photosynthesis multiplied rapidly. A 2 acre pond could produce from 400 to 1,750 pounds of fresh chlorella per day, at a cost of from 1 to 10 cents a pound. About half of the pound would be protein, making the rate of protein production from 10 to 100 times that of conventional agriculture. Experiments have shown that hogs will utilize up to 10 per cent algae in their rations, while sheep will eat up to 50 per cent dried, pelleted algae with alfalfa.

Commercial production from marine plants is mainly restricted to seaweed. For over six centuries the red seaplant (Irish moss) has been gathered along the rocky coasts of Europe and New England, to make puddings, cough remedies, etc. In contrast to brown seaplants (kelp), which may extend from 75 to 100 feet, red seaplants are only 5 to 6 inches in height. Until recently, they have been gathered in areas where rakers, working from dories, could bring them in by hand. This has limited harvesting to shallow bays where, at low tide, the bottom is no more than 3 to 4 feet below the surface. On this continent, such areas are found near Scituate, Massachusetts; Rockland, Maine; Halifax, Nova Scotia; and along the windswept shores of Prince Edward Island.

Recently, a mechanical reaper has been invented, which extends economic harvesting to depths up to 35 feet, opening up countless areas of shoreline. The search for larger-scale, mechanized harvesting has arisen because of the increasing demand for mass-produced and standardized red seaplant extractives, used to produce jelling, thickening, suspending, and stabilizing agents for a host of food, drug, and cos-

---

[4] In artificial cultures, algae have utilized as much as 15 per cent of sun energy, through the provision of air enriched with carbon dioxide, and of nitrogen and certain minerals in the water in which the algae grow. For each 1⅓ ounce of nitrogen and 2 pounds of carbon dioxide, a pound of dry chlorella was harvested. There can be a harvest every day, achieved by running the water through a centrifuge to separate the chlorella. The end product is a bright-green vegetable paste, still three-fourths water, that can be used fresh, fresh-frozen, or dried. In the pilot-plant experiments, the cost of dried chlorella has been some 25 to 30 cents per pound dry-weight, but some scientists think the cost might be dropped to 10 cents under conditions of large-scale production.

metic products. Four concerns dominate the field in the United States, of which one (Seaplant Chemical) sells over $2 million yearly of extractives (at about $1.50 per pound). In Europe, where some sowing and much conservation accompany the production, seaplants are cut once a month, while in New England only two crops a season are cut.

Perspective

Mankind's entire catch of seafood today may be a mere fraction of 1 per cent of the full measure of growth in the sea. We are crude hunters in the marine biosphere, or habitable area for life, which supplies 300 times the living room offered by land and freshwater areas together. We have done little so far, in contrast to the visible achievements on land, to extend man's conquest of nature in the sea. The science of oceanography, which may unlock the major scientific problems, is perhaps two generations behind the parallel sciences of agriculture, agronomics, and animal husbandry.

MINERALS FROM THE SEA

If 1 cubic mile of seawater (weighing nearly 5 billion tons) were dried out, some fifty-four elements would be available from the $3\frac{1}{3}$ per cent salt content, weighing some 159 million tons.[5] If the salts in the entire sea were dried, they would cover the earth 200 feet deep. Besides the some 50 million billion tons of dissolved salts in all the seawater, there are about 200 billion tons of precipitated nodules on the bottom containing manganese, cobalt, nickel, copper, and other metallic minerals. However, the only products now economically taken from the seawater are ordinary salt, bromine, magnesium, iodine, and some trace elements.

Salt

About 30 per cent of the over 100 million tons of annual salt production is obtained by solar evaporation (the United States' 29 million tons comes 60 per cent from wells, 25 per cent from mines, and only 15 per cent from solar saltworks near San Francisco and the Great Salt Lake). After the salt has been removed from the seawater by solar evaporation, the remaining liquid, called bittern, contains such minerals as potassium chloride, magnesium chloride, magnesium sulfate, and calcium and sodium sulfate. Although these minerals are mined from present land deposits, some are obtained by evaporation from the sea and, if necessary, this quantity could be extended without limit.

A small production of trace element sea salt now exists, containing about 75 per cent sodium chloride and 25 per cent trace elements (iodine, iron, copper, fluorine, cobalt, magnesium, zinc, molybdenum, etc.), for use in areas where foods are grown in deficient soils. Trace element concentrate is also used in pharmaceuticals, fertilizers, and animal feed additives.

Bromine

Here is a good example of commercial production in spite of a great dilution, for bromine exists in quantities of less than a pound to a ton of seawater. Before 1933, it was obtained from mineral brine pumped from mines, or was extracted from the bitterns left from solar salt processes. The rapid increase in demand for bromine to make gasoline antiknock compounds created a scarcity, so Dow Chemical Company turned to the sea and erected a plant to extract the element from unconcentrated seawater without evaporation. Their Cape Fear, North Carolina, plant has a yearly production of 15,000 tons, from 3,000 times as much seawater.

---

[5] Approximate amount of elements in 1 cubic mile of seawater:

	Million Tons		Tons
Chlorine	92.0	Iodine	240.0
Sodium	52.0	Zinc, aluminum (each)	48.0
Magnesium	6.2		
Sulfur	4.3	Copper, lead, uranium (each)	14.4
Calcium	1.97	Silver	1.4
Potassium	1.85	Gold: varies up to	38.0
	Thousand Tons		
Bromine	312.0		
Carbon	134.0		

Courtesy of Leslie Salt Co.

Sea salt from pans in the San Francisco area being loaded onto a ship. The sea supplies about 30 per cent of the world's salt production, and over half of that moving in world trade.

Magnesium

Dow Chemical Company, which produces about 80 per cent of the present supply of bromine from seawater, also produces some 75,000 tons of magnesium from seawater (two companies in Great Britain also extract magnesium from the ocean).

Such plants make magnesium metal by electrolysis of the magnesium chloride found in brine. Total costs of production are about the same as in plants using the carbothermal process, which breaks down magnesium oxide with electricity after magnesite rock has been thermally reduced: plant costs are less, but double electricity costs reduce the capital advantage. The plants must be topographically suited to the handling, drawing-in, and emitting of vast amounts of water and close to cheap electricity, lime, and caustic soda. All three U.S. plants are on the Texas coast.

Potash and Iodine

In peacetime, there is no longer any urgent need to develop our seawater potash and iodine resources, but in wartime, there is considerable production. Some iodine is recovered from kelp in Ireland, France, and Japan during peacetime, but it is being snuffed out by cheap Chilean production from saltpeter.

Future Metal Production

A new ion exchange resin (polythiolstyrene) offers promise in the recovery of heavy metals (copper, mercury, silver, gold, uranium, etc.) from seawater. Already copper has been salvaged from dilute solutions (mine drainage). Once the metal has been picked up by the resin, it can be readily removed by treatment with strong acid (highly stable, the resin has undergone as many as twenty regeneration cycles without loss of capacity).

Seaside plants have major problems that so far have not been completely solved: (1) present-day processing costs are usually too expensive, partly because of high research costs and small-scale operation; (2) storms and hurricanes close down such plants quite frequently (e.g., Dow's Freeport plant), but the plants must necessarily be located near such hazards; (3) seawater is highly corrosive and this effect increases with the velocity of water movement; (4) pipes, drains, and condensers in the processing plants are continually being clogged with small marine life and eggs, in spite of filters and screens.

Undersea Mining

Oil, gas, coal, sulfur, tin, diamonds, and gold are mined from the sea floor or under it, and other minerals may soon be added to the list. Offshore oil and gas production is only some 1 per cent of the world totals so far, but the potential is much greater. Much of the recent offshore drilling is from ships and barges, instead of rigid man-made islands, and wellheads can now be placed on the ocean floor by means of robots controlled by sound or TV camera on shipboard. Wells have been drilled and capped some 250 feet down, and the equipment is said to have the ability to operate beneath 1,000 feet of water (which makes accessible the entire continental shelf and the upper edge of the continental slope). Over 10 million tons, some 20 per cent of Japan's annual coal production, come from undersea mines. Rock and earth islands are the sites of the shaft mines, which exploit coal seams which may extend half a mile or more under the sea floor in water depths up to 150 feet. An island has been built 7 miles off the Louisiana coast to extract sulfur from a deposit 2,000 feet below the floor of the Gulf of Mexico, which begins about 50 feet under the steel island. Japan's small iron ore production is partly from iron sands 75 or more feet down on the sea floor. Mining ships pump up the sand, magnetic separators concentrate the 3 or so per cent iron, and it is piped ashore as a slurry. Tin dredges off the Kra Peninsula of southern Thailand have been working in 50 to 75 feet of seawater for some time, as have Indonesian dredges off that country's tin islands southeast of Singapore. Off the coast of Southwest Africa, diamonds are dredged from the gravels (reportedly obtaining five times the carats per unit of gravel than dredges working the same beach deposits on land). Off Nome, Alaska, placer gold in the beaches has been followed offshore. Beach sands elsewhere are being exploited for ilmenite, rutile, monazite, and other minerals that are known to continue out into the shallow offshore waters.

Off the Southern California coast, a plan to mine phosphorite nodules (which might have been delivered to shore fertilizer plants cheaper than Idaho-Wyoming phosphate rock) was aborted because of unexploded ordnance left from a former Navy target range, which could have exploded and destroyed equipment. An even more ambitious scheme envisages the mining of nodules containing manganese, nickel, cobalt, zirconium, and copper which cover parts of the ocean floor in a concentration of 1 pound or more per square foot, at depths of 1 to 10 miles. While drag-type dredges may be able to scoop up nodules in water less than a mile deep, in deeper water a hydraulic-type dredge will have to be used (the nodules would be picked up by vacuum cleaner action and piped into the mother ship). Such equipment is now technically feasible, but the economics of such operations in the foreseeable future is more problematic.

FRESH WATER FROM THE SEA

Growth of population and industrialization are producing enormous growth in the use of water. The United States alone uses about 1 cubic mile each week (about the average flow over Niagara Falls in the same time): about 87 per cent for waterpower, 6 per cent for private industrial pumpage, 6 per cent for irrigation, and the remaining 1 per cent for domestic water usage.

U.S. municipal water utilities distribute about 80 million tons of water per day, costing about 5 cents per ton on the average. This amounts to some 150 gallons per person served by the systems (for comparison, non-irrigated farms each use about 2,400 gallons per day). In domestic usage, about ½ to 1 gallon is for drinking, 5 gallons for laundering, 4 to 8 gallons for each time a toilet is flushed, 25 gallons for each time a tub bath is taken.

Most of the water used by industry is for cooling and washing, and all but 2 to 3 per cent is returned to its source. Most of this is used by a small number of industries (e.g., 6 per cent of U.S. industrial plants use about 80 per cent of the total water used by industry), mostly those that need it for cooling. There is a tremendous difference in usage of water for the same industrial operation (e.g., Kaiser Steel's Fontana steel plant uses one-fifth as much water per ton of steel produced as the average plant).

Water delivered to irrigators by the Bureau of Reclamation costs about $4 per acre-foot (⅓ cent per ton), or one-fifteenth of the average cost of municipal water. No figures are available for the cost of water used by hydropower plants, but it is undoubtedly lower than for irrigation-quality water.

Those who suffer from occasional or continual scarcity of water have sometimes thought longingly of the inexhaustible ocean as a source of supply.[6] The difficulty has always been to find an economically practical way to get rid of the salt. Pure water can be made from ocean or brackish water in several ways, and this is being done where the high cost can be borne. But where large quantities of relatively pure water are needed, as for irrigation, currently available methods are much too expensive. At present, only 1 million of the 3.2 billion humans on earth live on fresh water converted from seawater: about half are seamen and passengers on the larger ships, and the other half are inhabitants of desert and near-desert communities in interior Australia, the U.S. South-

---

[6] The world's total water supply of some 326 million cubic miles is located as follows:

Oceans and inland seas	97.22
Ice caps and glaciers	2.15
Liquid fresh water	0.63
Atmospheric sources	0.001

The liquid freshwater fraction of some 2 million cubic miles is located in the crust as follows:

Rivers and streams	300
Surface soil and percolating downward	16,000
Lakes	30,000
Ground water less than ½ mile deep	1,000,000
Ground water more than ½ mile deep (this tends to be high in mineral content and hence less useful)	1,000,000

west, certain West Indies islands, and certain Middle East areas.

Economics of Desalting by Distillation

Within limits, science and technology already know most of the answers to desalting. The big question is how to do it cheaply enough to compete with the price of natural fresh water from streams and lakes: consumers in such areas usually pay 25 to 40 cents per 1,000 gallons (outer range: 10 to 75 cents). Natural fresh water can be moved over distances of 1,000 miles for a transport cost of about 10 cents per 1,000 gallons, so local and regional water self-sufficiency is not the only answer.

Where cost is not the controlling factor, huge conversion plants are already producing millions of gallons of desalted water daily. The larger new distillation plants can make fresh water for around $1 per 1,000 gallons.[7] There is a good possibility that in the next five to ten years the cost may be dropped to the range of 25 to 35 cents per 1,000 gallons in large plants.

Large desalting plants (capacities in excess of 1 million gallons a day) numbered about fourteen in 1964. They all used flash distillation (under low pressures, water boils at correspondingly lower temperatures) and had costs around $1 to $1.50 per 1,000 gallons. Kuwait, on the Persian Gulf, had five plants with a daily capacity of 7.5 million gallons a day, and had more plants under construction. The largest single plant was that at Aruba, a Netherlands island off the coast of Venezuela, whose capacity was 3.5 million gallons a day. Other large plants were located at Curaçao (another Netherlands possession near Aruba), in the Bahamas, in southern Italy (Taranto), in southern Israel (Elath), in Qatar (another Persian Gulf site), and in South Africa (Welcom).

Basically, distillation is quite simple: all it involves is boiling the seawater, catching the vapor, and condensing it. What runs up the cost is the large quantities of heat energy needed. To cut the cost, engineers try to get more out of every pound of fuel by building multistage systems, where the heat given off by the condensing vapor from the first stage is fed into a second "effect" to boil off more vapor, and so on down the line for as many as eleven effects. Other innovations utilize a sudden drop in pressure, rather than heat, to boil off the fresh water, or involve creating a turbulence in water at the boiling point, producing steam without as much energy as is normally required. Another great potential cost-cutter would be cheap elimination of scale, either by "snapping" or by chemical inhibitor (allowing higher temperatures).

In the next few decades, perhaps the greatest possibility of desalting by distillation is through dual-purpose nuclear projects for generating electricity and desalting seawater as a joint product. United States and Israeli engineers have recommended the erection by about 1970 of a reactor in the order of magnitude of 800 thermal megawatts (million watts) that would generate 200 megawatts of electric power and also distill between 100 and 200 million gallons of seawater daily at a cost for the fresh water of 33 to 40 cents per 1,000 gallons plus 8 cents for conveyance. The U.S. Congress was told in the summer of 1964 that by 1975 the Southern California area could have huge dual-purpose desalting and power generating plants that might turn out fresh water at a cost of 20 to 25 cents per 1,000 gallons along with 1,000 to 1,500 megawatts of electricity that might sell for from 2.3 to 2.5 mills a kilowatt-hour (the plants would produce 500 to 800 million gallons of fresh water a day). Other enthusiasts have speculated that distilling plants with a capacity of a billion gallons of fresh water a day might supply it at 10 cents per 1,000 gallons, about what New York City pays for Catskill mountains water.

Electric Membrane Desalting

Another method of desalination uses electrodialysis, a system of precipitating solids from

---

[7] A government demonstration plant at Freeport, Texas, produced 1.6 million gallons a day in 1964 at an average cost of $1.17 per 1,000 gallons (of this, 39 cents was for fuel, 25 cents for amortization of the capital, and 21 cents for labor, with the rest for incidentals). At certain times (eliminating periods of trouble), the cost dropped to 88 cents per 1,000 gallons.

solution by electric currents. It works best with brackish water averaging 1 per cent salt or less.[8] The dissolved salts break up into positively and negatively charged ions, which can be pushed by an electrical current through plastic membranes that allow passage of the charged particles but not the water, which remains in the zone between the membranes.

The U.S. Government has brackish water conversion plants at Roswell, New Mexico (a million gallons a day capacity), and at Webster, South Dakota (a quarter as large). South Africa's Orange Free State gold mining companies have the world's largest electric membrane plant, a $1 million, 3 million gallons per day plant to desalt acid mine water to a level (not that of drinking-quality water) where it is safe to dump into surface drainage channels. Cost is about 30 cents per 1,000 gallons.

The first saline water conversion plant for treating an entire municipal water supply is at Buckeye, Arizona (30 miles southwest of Phoenix). This electrodialysis plant (with a capacity of 650,000 gallons per day) filters out nearly 5 tons of minerals and salts from the water supply, cutting the mineral content from 2,200 to 500 parts per million, at a cost of 50 cents per 1,000 gallons (cost of production at plant, but not including distribution costs). When operating at 90 per cent of capacity, the cost drops to 30 cents.

Other Desalting Techniques

With sunlight free, one might think that costs would be no problem for solar stills, but such is not the case. Basically, solar stills are simply a series of evaporation basins with a glass roof. The water, evaporating under the sun's heat, condenses on the underside of the roof, and trickles down into catchment basins. Capital costs for experimental units have ranged from a low of 75 cents per 1,000 gallons daily capacity

[8] Speculated costs for large (75 million gallons per day plant) electric membrane installations are estimated as follows: $1.25 to $1.50 per 1,000 gallons of 3⅓ per cent seawater, 12 cents for brackish water of 1 per cent saltiness, 1 cent for brackish water of less than 0.1 per cent saltiness. Over 3 million Americans in more than 1,000 communities consume water that contains up to ½ per cent salt.

to ten times that amount. The arid Greek island of Simi has a solar still of 7,500 gallons of fresh water capacity a day, the gift of an anonymous American. The operating costs have been about $3 per 1,000 gallons, compared with $9 when water was hauled in.

In the United States, the sun is sufficiently strong for efficient operation only in the southwestern part. So far, only tiny solar stills have been built, from fliers' emergency kit types which produce about a quart of fresh water a day to larger stills producing up to 100 gallons of water a day. No really large-scale pilot plant has yet been built.

Another long shot, the freezing process, is also based on a theoretical advantage—the calculation that it should take much less energy (one-seventh less) to freeze water to a slush stage than to boil it. Here the big roadblocks are lack of suitable low-cost refrigeration equipment and the problem of finding an efficient way to separate the pure ice crystals from the salt solution adhering to their surface and in the spaces between them. The freeze-separation process may some day prove more economical than conventional distillation plants, but the cheapest water that it promises in the foreseeable future will cost between 50 and 80 cents per 1,000 gallons, high for municipal use and out of the question for irrigation. The Israeli have done the most with the technique.

Reuse of Sewage

Desalination of seawater has been treated with glamor recently, but from a practical engineering standpoint, sewage water renovation is more economic by a sizable margin. Sewage normally has less than 2 per cent total solids, while seawater normally has 3½ per cent. Large-scale projects in Israel and in Southern California remove about 95 per cent of foreign substances from sewage before putting it back into the soil to receive ordinary ground treatment, before drawing it out again for water supply systems.

Development of a high-temperature sterilizing process to purify water supplies and sewage has been made, which destroys harmful microorganisms through controlled heating. High-quality water from sewage would cost 25 to 30 cents per 1,000 gallons; questionable drinking water might be sterilized for as little as 15 cents.

Where the psychological barriers to quick re-use of treated sewage are difficult to overcome, the sewage effluent or a mixture of it and de-salted water might be used for certain agricultural or industrial uses.

PROSPECTS

As a vast pasture land and a limitless reservoir of minerals and water, the oceans are not to be tamed immediately. Many of the questions involving radically greater use of sea resources are still within the realm of scientific research. Since only a fraction of 1 per cent of what is spent on land in solving agricultural problems is devoted to research in the great oceanic frontier, quick answers are highly unlikely.

Next to insufficient basic knowledge of marine resources, the chief roadblock to greatly increased fish production on a permanent basis is probably the lack of international cooperation in the management of marine resources. Unfortunately, in some areas closer cooperation among the nations most directly concerned may take even longer to achieve than scientific progress.

In the foreseeable future, exploitation of latent fishery resources is most likely to be expanded by extending fishing operations to remote fishing grounds and to the middle layers of present shelf fishing grounds, both operations dependent upon improvement of certain fishing technology. Mechanization of fishing fleets in underdeveloped societies, along the lines of Japanese development, is likely to result in the greatest increase, by allowing exploitation of fishing grounds lying off present coasts beyond the 5 to 15 miles belt reached by subsistence (part-time) fishermen during their slack season. The underfished stocks in the open oceans and southern hemisphere shelf areas are destined for even greater exploitation than has occurred since 1950 in Peru, partly for nearby markets but also for meeting deficit northern hemisphere markets for fish meal and fish flour (protein concentrate).

Radically new exploitation of the seas for plankton, minerals, and fresh water may increase spectacularly in the next few decades, compared with present use, but will not be more than supplemental compared with the amount taken from present conventional sources except in spots. This is mainly because the economics are likely to be very unfavorable until the more concentrated and naturally purified land resources are depleted. This may not occur for decades.

SUGGESTED READINGS

CLAWSON, MARION. *Natural Resources and International Development.* Baltimore: Johns Hopkins Press (for Resources for the Future, Inc.), 1964. Pp. 127–51.

CROMIE, WILLIAM J. *Exploring the Secrets of the Sea.* London: Allen & Unwin, 1964. Pp. 300.

ELLIS, CECIL B. *Fresh Water from the Ocean.* New York: Ronald, 1954. Pp. 217.

HULL, SEABROOK. *The Bountiful Sea.* Englewood Cliffs, N.J.: Prentice-Hall, 1964. Pp. 340.

KING, CUCHLAINE A. M. *Oceanography for Geographers.* London: Edward Arnold Ltd., 1962. Pp. 337.

OMMANNEY, F. D. *The Ocean.* London: Oxford University Press, 1949. Pp. 238.

OXFORD UNIVERSITY PRESS. *Oxford Economic Atlas of the World.* London: Oxford University Press, 1965. Pp. 46–47.

STEWART, HARRIS B., JR. *The Global Sea.* Princeton, N.J.: Van Nostrand, 1963. Pp. 126.

UNITED NATIONS, DEPARTMENT OF ECONOMIC AND SOCIAL AFFAIRS. *Water Desalination in Developing Countries.* New York: United Nations, 1964. Pp. 325.

12

Introduction to Industry

The secondary or industrial sector of the world's economy includes factory and handicraft (artisan) manufacturing, mining, utilities (electricity, gas, etc.), and construction activities. Although employing under two-fifths as many workers as the primary or agricultural sector (0.25 billion as compared with 0.67 billion), industry contributes some four times the annual income, reflecting its greater modernization. Since 1950 (by which time the destruction of World War II had been mainly overcome), the average annual rate of increase in world industrial output has been about 7 per cent, more than doubling total industrial production and increasing the share of industrial output in total world income from 36 to 45 per cent. However, industry's share of the world labor force is not changing much, as its yearly increase of under 3 per cent is little more than the annual rate of increase in the total labor force.[1] Consequently, the indirectly productive services sector will probably have to absorb displaced agriculturalists in greater numbers than industry in the long view.

Table 12–1 and the graphs on pages 334–35 indicate that the high-income countries contribute some 85 per cent of the world's industrial output. That realm's shares of industrial subsectors are in a narrow range around that fraction (except for mining).

Labor productivity varies greatly between subsectors of industry within a single great-region and also between regions (e.g., modern subsectors may have productivity differences of 5:1 as between different regions, and the differences between the premodern subsector and its modern equivalent in the same region may be 35:1 or more). Consequently, the patterns of industrial employment often differ greatly from those of industrial output by value. Table 12–2 indicates that the underdeveloped (low-income) realm has over 40 per cent of the world's industrial labor, although it produces only some 15 per cent of the world's industrial production by value. This mainly is explained by the more than half handicrafts (artisan or cottage) "industrial" workers in its total industrial labor force, many of whom have no greater labor productivity than agricultural workers in the same vicinity.

REGIONAL INDUSTRIAL CHARACTERISTICS

In assessing industry, three frames of reference are used in this chapter. First, regional characteristics are portrayed; second, subsector characteristics are assessed in broad sweeps; third, locational tendencies in terms of relative dependence upon various factors of production are noted.

[1] Yearly increase in labor requirements in the past generation by subsector: heavy industry and construction, 3 per cent; light industry and utilities, 2 per cent; mining, 1 per cent.

North America

The United States and Canada still have over a third of the world's total industrial production, although Western Europe and Eastern Europe (including the U.S.S.R.), with 78 per cent and 67 per cent, respectively, of North America's output, are pulling abreast as a result of annual rates of increase over twice that of North America (4 per cent since 1950). North American pre-eminence holds for each of the four subsectors (manufacturing, mining, utilities, construction), both in total production and in labor productivity.

Although North America's share of world industry has been dropping recently, this has meant so far only a return to the relative position of the pre-World War II situation. The 50 per cent share of the 1940's was an abnormal situation, reflecting North American operation of its industrial capacity at near capacity while Western Europe, Eastern Europe (including the U.S.S.R.) and other regions were engaged in reconstruction from World War II damage. However, with a projection of present regional-industrial growth trends, North America's share of world industry could drop to 25 to 30 per cent in the next generation (in specific industries, like coal mining, iron and steel production, and others, this drop has already occurred).

In the early 1960's, North American industry (by value-added) was composed as follows:

Mining		7%	
Coal	0.8%		
Oil-gas	4.7		
Metallic ores	0.8		
Non-metallics other than fuels	0.7		
Energy utilities		5	
Construction		14	
Light manufacturing			30%
Food, beverages, tobacco			9%
Textiles			3
Clothing, footwear			4
Wood products, furniture			3
Printing, publishing			5
Others			6
Heavy manufacturing			44%
Paper, paper products			3%
Chemicals			9
Non-metallics			2
Metals			4
Metal products			26

The relative importance of these industries is changing. Mining and the light-manufacturing industries (especially those producing food, textiles, apparel, and lumber and associated products) are increasing at much slower rates than the utilities, construction, and heavy-manufacturing industries (especially primary metals, machinery, vehicles, instruments, and chemicals). Gradually, North American industry is becoming more like that of the most heavily industrialized countries of Western Europe (Britain, Belgium, West Germany).

About a half of North American industrial growth is occurring in regions outside the traditional manufacturing belt (U.S. Eastern Seaboard, U.S. Midwest, and southern Ontario–St. Lawrence lowland). The northern and middle Great Plains (often considered to be a westward extension of the manufacturing belt), the Southeast (Piedmont and Great Valley especially), the Southwest (western Gulf plain), and the Pacific Coast nodes are increasing relatively faster than the older industrial areas, although the newer areas still have less than one-third of all North American industry.

Gradually, a greater dependence on outside sources of minerals and other raw materials is developing, again in the Western European tradition. In terms of crude foodstuffs by value, North America is still modestly surplus, with the imports (mainly tropical items) of both the United States and Canada more than covered by the value of each country's exports (however, some of latter are due to government subsidies). At present, about 15 per cent of U.S. net consumption of inedible (including mineral) raw materials is imported. Nearly one-half of this comes from Canada and Mexico (geopolitically parts of the same region), so the inedible raw materials deficit that must come great distances from overseas is only 5 per cent of total consumption.

In mining, utilities, construction, and manufacturing, North American increased production is being accomplished with little change in employment. Automation is, of course, universal in urban-industrial societies, but is being pushed especially fast in North America because of the expensiveness of skilled labor. Where industrial employment does increase, it is likely to be in administration (including research) and as-

TABLE 12–1

World: Value-added * by Industrial Production, by Great-Region and Economic-Type of Society, 1962–1964 Average-Annual
(in billions of United States dollars)

	Total Industry (U.S. $ billion = 100.0 per cent)	Mining	Energy Utilities	Light Manufacturing	Heavy Manufacturing	Construction
North America	225	7%	5%	30%	44%	14%
Western Europe	175	7	5	28	48	13
Eastern Europe (including the U.S.S.R.)	150	8	4	23	50	15
Oceania	7	6	6	26	37	25
Latin America	23	16	5	35	28	16
Sub-Saharan Africa	7	28	3	23	32	14
Middle East (including North Africa)	9	32	3	37	12	16
Non-Communist Far East	35	10	5	36	35	14
Communist Far East	15	8	5	28	45	14
World	646	8	5	28	45	14
High-income countries	549	5	5	27	49	14
Low-income countries	97	27	3	36	19	15
	(per cent of U.S. $646 billion)	(per cent of U.S. $54 billion)	(per cent of U.S. $31 billion)	(per cent of U.S. $182 billion)	(per cent of U.S. $287 billion)	(per cent of U.S. $92 billion)
North America	34.8	29.4	36.4	37.0	34.4	34.4
Western Europe	27.1	22.8	28.7	26.9	28.6	24.9
Eastern Europe (including the U.S.S.R.)	23.2	22.4	19.5	18.9	26.1	24.5
Oceania	1.1	0.7	1.3	1.0	0.9	2.0
Latin America	3.6	6.9	3.9	4.4	2.2	4.0
Sub-Saharan Africa	1.1	3.7	0.7	0.9	0.8	1.1
Middle East (including North Africa)	1.4	5.4	1.0	1.7	0.4	1.5
Non-Communist Far East	5.4	6.5	5.9	6.9	4.3	5.3
Communist Far East	2.3	2.2	2.6	2.3	2.3	2.3
World	100.0	100.0	100.0	100.0	100.0	100.0
High-income countries	85.0	51.2	89.6	81.1	93.6	84.0
Low-income countries	15.0	48.8	10.4	18.9	6.4	16.0

SOURCE: Mainly adapted from United Nations sources, with unofficial sources used in compiling Communist (Eastern Europe including the U.S.S.R. and Communist Far East) data.

* "Value-added" equals gross value minus purchased factors of production, with elimination of internal double-counting.

sociated distribution rather than in direct production.

In its over-all industrial characteristics, North America is much like the U.S.S.R. Both great-regions have very great natural resources, and population growth coupled with increased pressure for higher levels of living present no great embarrassment, while their ability to adjust to any prospective change in industrial technology is as flexible as any other great-region on earth.

Western Europe

Western Europe was the home region of the first industrial revolution—that which mechanized industry and transport—and has participated swiftly in the second—assembly-line- and

TABLE 12-2

World: Distribution of Industrial Labor, by Great-Region and Economic-Type of Society, 1962–1964 Average-Annual

(in millions)

	Industrial Labor Force (millions = 100.0 per cent)	Manufacturing		Mining	Energy Utilities	Construction
		Factory	Handicrafts [1]			
North America	26	71%	7%	3%	4%	15%
Western Europe	57	64	10	5	2	19
Eastern Europe (including the U.S.S.R.)	51	62	5	9	2	22
Oceania	3	65	10	4	3	18
Latin America	17	42	29	3	3	23
Sub-Saharan Africa	8	20	38	19	2	21
Middle East (including North Africa)	6	28	39	7	3	23
Non-Communist Far East	52	46	33	4	2	15
Communist Far East	31	24	35	10	2	29
World	248	52	20	6	2	20
High-income countries	144	65	7	6	2	20
Low-income countries	104	34	37	7	2	20
	(per cent of 248 million)	(per cent of 128 million)	(per cent of 48 million)	(per cent of 16 million)	(per cent of 6 million)	(per cent of 50 million)
North America	10.4	14.2	3.7	5.0	17.9	8.0
Western Europe	22.9	28.3	11.6	17.5	19.6	22.0
Eastern Europe (including the U.S.S.R.)	20.3	24.4	5.6	28.7	16.0	22.0
Oceania	1.0	1.3	0.5	0.6	1.4	0.8
Latin America	6.9	5.4	10.4	3.1	9.0	8.0
Sub-Saharan Africa	3.1	1.2	6.1	9.4	2.9	3.2
Middle East (including North Africa)	2.3	1.2	4.5	2.5	2.9	2.6
Non-Communist Far East	20.8	18.3	35.3	14.4	19.6	15.4
Communist Far East	12.3	5.7	22.3	18.8	10.7	18.0
World	100.0	100.0	100.0	100.0	100.0	100.0
High-income countries	58.0	72.5	20.7	55.0	60.7	57.4
Low-income countries	42.0	27.5	79.3	45.0	39.3	42.6

SOURCE: Mainly adapted from United Nations sources, with unofficial sources used in compiling Communist (Eastern Europe including the U.S.S.R. and Communist Far East) data and handicrafts data elsewhere.

[1] "Handicrafts" includes both artisans without mechanical aids and workers with such aids in small shops.

continuous-process-type industry—and the third—automated or electronic-controlled industry—industrial revolutions that were mainly initiated in her daughter civilization to the west. At present, she is swiftly advancing at a pace fully as great as that of her totalitarian daughter civilization to the east.

In the late 1940's, Western Europe's industrial production, still staggering from World War II, was well under one-half that of North America. By the early 1960's, Western Europe's industrial capacity was 78 per cent that of North America, and her share of world production has increased so swiftly (half again as rapidly as that of North America) that within this generation she will be equaling North American capacity. With per capita industrial output still about one-half that of North America, Western Europe's annual industrial capital investment is approximately equal to North America's.

WORLD: VALUE-ADDED BY INDUSTRY, BY GREAT-REGION AND ECONOMIC-TYPE OF SOCIETY, 1962-1964 AVERAGE-ANNUAL (U.S. $ Billion)

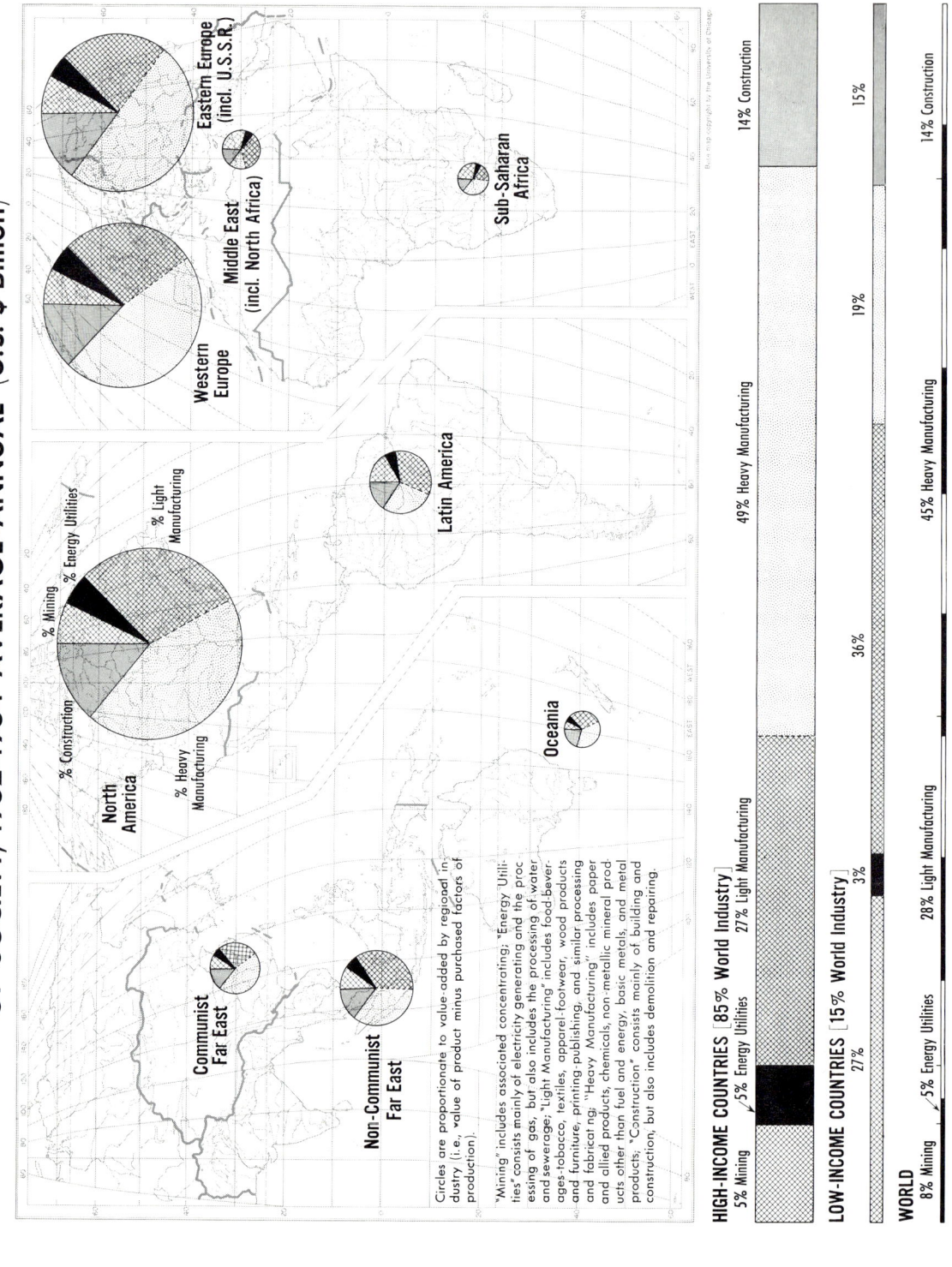

WORLD: GREAT-REGION AND ECONOMIC-TYPE OF SOCIETY SHARES OF WORLD TOTAL INDUSTRIAL, MINING, UTILITIES, LIGHT AND HEAVY MANUFACTURING, AND CONSTRUCTION OUTPUT, BY VALUE-ADDED, 1962-1964 AVERAGE-ANNUAL

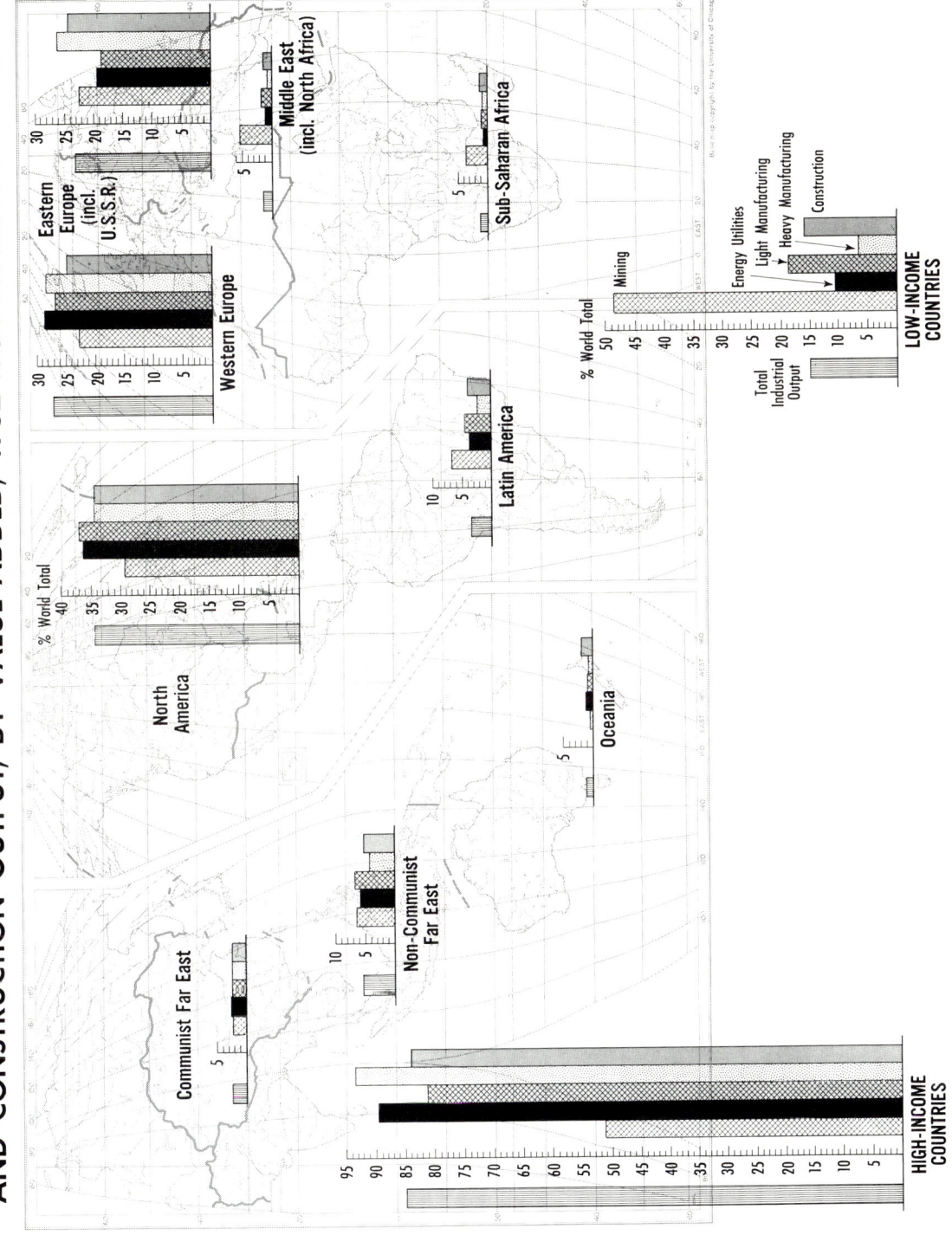

Western Europe's occupational structure is changing to one more like that of North America and other Newer European lands. Agriculture's 25 per cent share of the total in the 1950's is dropping swiftly, and will probably be only 15 to 20 per cent by 1970. The industrial labor force is increasing by ½ million each year, mainly from displaced agriculturalists, so industry's 40 per cent share of the labor force is likely to approach 45 per cent in another decade or so. The services' 35 per cent share is likely to increase somewhat, but more important is the decline in inefficient commercial and servant categories and increase in certain professional and institutionalized personal service categories. In the 1950's, Western Europe's average labor productivity increased 4 per cent annually and the continued heavy capitalization promises to maintain this increase in technical efficiency.

In the early 1960's, Western European industry (by value-added) was composed as follows:

Mining	7%	Light manufacturing	28%
Coal	4.2%	Food, beverages, tobacco	10%
Oil-gas	0.8	Textiles	6
Metallic ores	0.8	Clothing, footwear	3
Non-metallics other than fuels	1.2	Wood products, furniture	3
Energy utilities	5	Printing, publishing	3
Construction	13	Others	3
		Heavy manufacturing	48%
		Paper, paper products	3%
		Chemicals	9
		Non-metallics	4
		Metals	6
		Metal products	26

Western Europe's industry exhibits the same trends as that in North America, although the relative importance varies. There is, for example, some shift in industrial location, although it is relatively less important than in North America. The heavy industries predominate in the zone of British and central European coal fields (along the northern margin of the central European highlands). The cores of the major European industrial regions generally reflect the existence of the more productive coal fields: the South Wales, English Midlands, northeast England, northern France, Benelux, German Rhineland, East Germany brown-coal, and the Czech-Polish Silesian (the U.S.S.R. Donbass can be thought of as an extension of the same belt) fields. To the north and south, but outside the coal fields, many industrial nodes form active manufacturing concentrations that use some coal, some oil and gas, and some hydropower—they manufacture principally the lighter types of goods. Immediately north of the coal fields belt is a string of industrial centers beginning with Antwerp and the Dutch cities and continuing through Hannover, Berlin, Lodz, and Warsaw. Farther north are the industrial centers of Copenhagen, Stockholm and other central Swedish cities, and finally, Leningrad, Moscow, the middle Volga cities, and those of the central Urals. Mainly west and south of the coal fields belt are Belfast and Dublin in Ireland, Bristol and London in England, the lower Seine valley in France, the upper Rhine and south German areas, Vienna, Budapest, and other Danubian centers. In and surrounding the Alps are industrial areas in which waterpower is a factor of major importance in manufacturing: southeast France, Switzerland, Alpine Austria, and northern Italy. In Mediterranean Europe are centers of old industries that have survived the Industrial Revolution and have expanded: Barcelona in Spain, Florence and Naples in Italy, and Athens in Greece. Attempts are being made to foster industrialization in the rest of Mediterranean Europe to help solve social problems accompanying population increase in demoralized agrarian areas, but so far only ameliorative efforts have been successful.

Western Europe has a long list of strengths in its industrial structure. The long history of successful handicraft and factory industrialization gives promise of grafting any new developments without major difficulty. There is a large supply of highly skilled labor, industrial labor superior in many senses to that of North America or Eastern Europe (including the U.S.S.R.) for many labor-intensive industries. Habitat advantages include a large supply of power (mainly coal and hydro), an appreciable regional supply of raw materials, and superb accessibility. There is a large market with rapidly rising standards of consumption. Progressive policies for increased industrialization—especially helpful rapid depreciation and social welfare policies—have long provided governmental efforts equal in effectiveness to totalitarian societies without the crude coercion of the latter.

There are some disadvantages, but they are definitely less important than the advantages. There are numerous worn and frequently outmoded capital goods patterns, although most of these defects are being remedied. There are limitations on expansion of cheap power based on local resources, and local shortages of certain raw materials (especially technical crops requiring long growing seasons, and many metallic ores), but these are more likely to be geopolitical and military weaknesses than serious economic weaknesses. There is a relatively limited supply of risk capital in certain areas, but foreign and governmental efforts provide a substitute in most cases. Most seriously, historically, has been lack of economic integration, but recently the Common Market promises that in the future the political fragmentation of Western Europe will be less important in hindering certain industrial developments requiring vast-scaled capital and market aggregations.

Eastern Europe (including the U.S.S.R.)

The European Communist realm is among the fastest industrializing areas in the world, having apparently quadrupled industrial output since 1950. West Germany, Japan, and several semi-industrial economies in the mainly underdeveloped realm have higher rates of growth (which can be better verified than the Communist data), but even with large discounting of the raw Communist data by Western specialists, their growth rates in total income and industrial output are spectacular.

Even Western estimates credit the region with annual growth in national product of some 7 per cent until the early 1960's, roughly double the long-term U.S. average growth rate. The average per capita income is only about a third that in North America, and disposable per capita income much less (about a quarter) than that because of the much higher government fraction. Total regional income, stated in Soviet currency-exchange values, is approaching two-thirds of the North American goods and services output; by U.S. purchasing-power equivalent values, this might approach 80 to 85 per cent.

Up to 1958, total industrial production apparently increased some 8 to 10 per cent annually, dropping to 7 per cent since then, with capital requirements to increase output per worker doubling. In 1961, Khrushchev said that the U.S.S.R. (not including Eastern European associates) had some 20 per cent of world industrial output or some 60 per cent of the U.S. industrial output. U.S. Secretary of Commerce Hodges said in the same year that his department estimated that U.S.S.R. industrial output in 1965 would be 50 to 60 per cent that of the United States, and that by 1970, the Soviet fraction might be 60 to 75 per cent of the U.S. industrial output at that time. For this chapter, 1963 U.S.S.R. industrial production has been estimated at about 50 per cent of North American industrial production, and Eastern European industrial production has been estimated at about 17 per cent of North American industrial production.

Composition and location of Communist industrial production is also liable to a large degree of error. In the mid-1950's, about three-fourths of Eastern European industrial output was in the northwest (Czechoslovakia, East Germany, and Poland), and an even larger share of U.S.S.R. industrial output was in the "European" part:

U.S.S.R. manufacturing belt		84%
Moscow-Gorki	18%	
Eastern Ukraine	14	
Urals	12	
Volga	5	
Leningrad	5	
Five major nodes	54%	
Other western U.S.S.R. areas	30%	
	84%	
Peripheral areas		16%
Kuznetsk	4%	
Transcaucasus	4	
Central Asia	3	
North Caucasus	2	
Baikal	1	
Far East	2	

Long-term plans are to build up the peripheral areas faster than the older centers, but detail to check has not been available recently. Russia is now said to have some 65 per cent of the entire U.S.S.R. industry, with the Ukraine having 20 per cent, and all other republics the remaining 15 per cent, but this does not help determine the relative importance of the Russian east. One statement is that the triangle Leningrad-Odessa-Urals now contains about 70 per cent of Soviet manufacturing, which would seem to indicate that the other areas now have nearly twice the fraction of a decade ago. It is known that Central Asia, Kuznetsk, and Baikal have had power and metallurgy capacities that have greatly increased, but how much change this means in value-added is difficult to ascertain.

Determining industrial structure is equally difficult. Apparently, Soviet and Eastern European output (by value-added) is composed as follows:

Mining	8%	Light manufacturing	23%
Coal	4%	Food, beverages,	
Oil-gas	2	tobacco	7%
Metallic ores	1	Textiles	4
Non-metallics other than fuels	1	Clothing, footwear	3
Energy utilities	4	Wood products, furniture	4
Construction	15	Printing, publishing	3
		Others	2
Heavy manufacturing			50%
Paper, paper products			3%
Chemicals			4
Non-metallics			4
Metals			10
Metal products			29

Communist industry has a larger fraction of its output in the forms of metals and metal products than North America and Western Europe, but this will probably change gradually. Until recently, only East Germany and Czechoslovakia had well-developed chemical industries, but the U.S.S.R. and other countries are now hastily expanding this industry. Also, consumer-goods industries are slowly receiving a bit more emphasis, but for a long time they are not likely to equal their relative importance in those regions where consumer sovereignty exists to a much greater extent. There is also an increasing emphasis upon rationalization. Until recently, planned development of new manufacturing areas (e.g., the Urals, Kuznetsk, middle Volga valley, and Lake Baikal areas in the U.S.S.R. and many smaller districts in the Eastern European belt of small Communist states) was pushed irrespective of cost, with the motives of achieving greater military self-sufficiency and lessening the strain on the transport system, but lately, greater attention has been paid to comparative regional efficiency in producing specialties.

Even if American figures on Eastern European (including the U.S.S.R.) industrial output, growth-rate projections, and other variables are accepted, there is little doubt that the region, like Western Europe, is gradually approaching North America's production and could well reach equal status in absolute production before the turn of the century.

Oceania

Oceania is the fourth great-region that, considered as a whole, has reached urban-industrial status. In terms of industrial output, it has only a bit more than 1 per cent of the world output, but this is still impressive when it is noted that Australia, New Zealand, and the smaller islands have an output as great as sub-Saharan Africa with over ten times their population. The Melanesian, Polynesian, and Micronesian areas (i.e., those not "Europeanized") have as little industry as any area of comparable size and population in the world, but their population and income only drop Oceanic averages a bit.

Australia and New Zealand, since World War II, are gradually evolving into mature urban-industrial status, with greater emphasis upon producer goods and consumer-durable goods. The smaller islands have some industry, mainly processing types, except defense types on Guam and elsewhere that are tied in with the world-wide power struggle rather than economic development.

Oceanic industrial output in the early 1960's was composed as follows in terms of value-added:

Mining	6%	Light manufacturing	26%
Coal	2.0%	Food, beverages, tobacco	10%
Oil-gas	–	Textiles	3
Metallic ores	2.5	Clothing, footwear	4
Non-metallics other than fuels	1.5	Wood products, furniture	3
Energy utilities	6	Printing, publishing	3
Construction	25	Others	3

Heavy manufacturing	37%
Paper, paper products	2.5%
Chemicals	17.0
Non-metallics	2.5
Metals	5.0
Metal products	20.0

The most important industrial district is southeast Australia, which has 80 per cent of the country's industry, mainly in Sydney and Melbourne. New Zealand's industry (a fifth of Australia's) is mainly on the North Island, in Auckland. Guam (defense types), Nauru (phosphate mining), Fiji and New Caledonia (mining and plantation types) have minor industry. Australia and New Zealand are much like North America in that about a half of the industrial labor force is in large plants (100 and up), reflecting late development and government-foreign capital influences.

About 25 per cent of Oceanic consumption of all manufactured goods is imported, although this is gradually diminishing. A considerable fraction of exports are also manufactured, although these are mainly processed food and lightly processed inedible raw materials of organic and mineral origin.

The future seems likely to see little fundamental change in Oceania's industrial status. If anything, its small fraction of world industrial output is likely to diminish a bit. The two industrial countries are likely to become more mature (i.e., with greater emphasis on complicated industry), and the little-industrialized areas may develop some processing types. Most changes are likely to be of regional, rather than of world, importance.

Latin America

Although many think of Latin America as an underdeveloped region like sub-Saharan Africa, actually it is better assessed as semi-industrial. While only the Republic of South Africa in sub-Saharan Africa is well on its way to mature urban-industrial status, in Latin America the list of countries is much longer (Mexico, Cuba, Puerto Rico, Venezuela, Brazil, Uruguay, Argentina, Chile) and contains three-fourths of the population. In comparison with the behemoths of the northern hemisphere, Latin America's 3½ per cent of the world's industrial output is tiny, but it is as large as that of sub-Saharan Africa, the Middle East, and Oceania combined (with twice the population of Latin America) and growing rapidly, with many countries having growth rates among the highest in the world. For the region as a whole, annual average growth in gross national product has been some 5 per cent since 1950, with the annual increase in per capita income being some 2 per cent. Increasing the per capita income is particularly difficult, as the regional population increase is nearly 3 per cent annually (by 1975, Latin America will have well over 300 million population).

The 90 million Latin Americans who now live in officially urban areas (some 45 per cent of the total population) have annual incomes averaging three times the rural average. Of the 18 million urban families, about 6 million have annual incomes of $500 or less, another 5 million are in the $500 to $1,000 range, another 5 million are in the $1,000 to $4,000 range, and the last 2 million families average over $4,000. The last three groups are capable of buying good housing and manufactures consistently—they are about two-thirds of the half of the Latin American population who definitely live in the commercial world. Most manufacturing tends to be in such urban areas. São Paulo has nearly one-half of Brazil's industry (nearly 60 per cent of that country's manufacturing is still food processing and textiles). Some two-thirds of Argentina's manufacturing labor force of about 1 million are in Greater Buenos Aires. Some three-fourths of Chile's industrial output is in the Santiago-Valparaiso area. About 40 per cent of Mexico's 1½ million industrial workers are in Greater Mexico City. The same pattern holds true of most other Latin American industry.

Latin America's industrial output (by value-added in the early 1960's was composed as follows:

Mining		16%	Light manufacturing	35%
Coal	0.4%		Food, beverages,	
Oil-gas	12.1		tobacco	19.0%
Metallic ores	2.7		Textiles	6.5
Non-metallics			Clothing, foot-	
other than			wear	2.5
fuels	0.8		Wood products,	
Energy utilities		5	furniture	2.0
Construction		16	Printing, pub-	
			lishing	3.0
			Others	2.0
Heavy manufacturing				28%
Paper, paper products		2.0%		
Chemicals		11.0		
Non-metallics		3.5		
Metals		4.5		
Metal products		7.0		

The future of Latin American industrialization seems bright, but there are great problems. Most important is the lack of market: probably only fundamental social reforms will add many groups now in the non-commercial half of the total population as important purchasers. The same holds true for the poorest third of the urban population. Another resistance is the habit of the wealthy in many countries to prefer land owning, speculation in commerce and urban real estate, and foreign accounts in which to invest their savings rather than in local industry. Only gradually will the risk capital now supplied by the governments and by foreigners come from private internal interests. The lack of external economies—especially transportation, communication, and banking services—makes expansion of the market area from most nodes extremely difficult. The raw nationalism which insists on national self-sufficiency in prestigeful areas—mining, heavy industry, utilities—makes economic production difficult in many of the smaller countries.

Sub-Saharan Africa

Africa south of the Sahara is the poorest and least industrialized great-region of the world,[2] especially when South Africa (the only high-income country in the whole region) is excluded—only about 10 per cent of the income of tropical Africa is derived from industry, and half of that is from a few mining nodes (especially the Katanga–northern Zambia mineralized belt and several smaller West African districts).

The Republic of South Africa accounts for one-half of the total sub-Saharan African income, and nearly two-thirds of the employment and value-added coming from mining and factory industry. About a fourth of the national income is from manufacturing, and some 13 per cent is from mining (as large a percentage as from agriculture). The Pretoria-Witwatersrand-Vereeniging area—1 per cent of the republic's area with 20 per cent of the total population—is the main industrial region, with over one-half of the total industrial labor force of over 1 million. The food processing industries were among the first manufacturing to become established and, although no longer the most important in terms of employment and net value of output, they have nevertheless shown a striking growth during the present century. During and since World War II, producer goods and consumer-durable goods industries have increased in relative importance, although the republic does not have as mature an industrial economy as Australia because of the one-third of the Bantu majority still in tribal areas and the one-third of Bantus working as unskilled labor on European farms. The European and urbanized Colored, Bantu, and Asian portions of the total population—considered separately—would have an urban-industrial structure.

Modern industry of any kind is rare outside the areas mentioned. Very little cheap power is available over large areas of tropical Africa. Coal is expensive, most hydro is just a latent resource, and most imported oil is used for transport and to produce thermal electricity. Fuel wood, charcoal, and waste is the fuel for some surprisingly large mines and factories.

Some new industry is raw material oriented: rice hulling, starch (cassava) making, fruit canning, rubber processing, some cloth production (still mainly imported), charcoal making, lumber and plywood production, and many others. Others are market oriented: vegetable oils (although most oilseeds are exported to the North

---

[2] Per capita industrial output is only 5 per cent of the high-income realm's average.

Atlantic, a small peanut crushing industry is developing in Senegal, Nigeria, and elsewhere), beer, cigarettes, furniture (mainly steel), bricks and tiles, printing, and many servicing types. Peasant industries—mainly spinning, weaving, and dyeing of cloth; tailoring; leather working; distilling; blacksmithing—are still important in less accessible areas (e.g., one-third of the consumption of industrial products in northern Nigeria is still estimated to be supplied by such handicrafts).

Sub-Saharan Africa's industrial output (by value-added) in the early 1960's was composed as follows:

Mining	28%	Light manufacturing	23%
Coal	2.2%	Food, beverages, tobacco	9.0%
Oil-gas	0.7		
Metallic ores	17.5	Textiles	3.5
Non-metallics other than fuels	7.6	Clothing, footwear	4.5
		Wood products, furniture	2.0
Energy utilities	3		
Construction	14	Printing, publishing	2.0
		Others	2.0
		Heavy manufacturing	32%
		Paper, paper products	2%
		Chemicals	7
		Non-metallics	3
		Metals	12
		Metal products	8

Even today, agricultural exports account for over 60 per cent of the total value of sub-Saharan exports (agricultural imports are some 15 per cent of all imports), and most modern industry in many areas is likely to remain processing of such products on their way to world markets or processing of agricultural imports for local markets. Gradually, new market-oriented industries that exploit established markets formerly filled by imports are being developed. Foreign capital, in the foreseeable future as in the past, is likely to be most attracted by mining and plantation-associated industry. Modern industry is likely to diffuse gradually all over the continent, but for the foreseeable future, about a half is likely to remain in the South African and Rhodesian areas dominated by Europeans. Elsewhere, only locally is heavy industry likely to emerge, although certain light manufacturing is springing up in some cities.

Middle East (including North Africa)

North Africa and Southwest Asia have among the least industry of the nine great-regions, although its oil production—contributing 10 per cent of the total regional income—is of major interest both to the region and most of the remainder of the world.

Both the larger part of present oil production and factory manufacturing are phenomena of the past two decades. There was important oil production in Iraq and Iran before World War II, but the Arabian (Kuwait, Saudi Arabia, Qatar, and other Persian Gulf) and North African (Algeria, Libya) production is overwhelmingly from the 1950's. Factory manufacturing other than light processing of agricultural crude materials before export is also recent. Israel is the only state that is substantially modernized—about a third of its employment and income is from the industrial sector. Egypt, Lebanon, Turkey, and Iran have considerable manufacturing dating mainly from World War II shortages, but their economy has been much less affected in a relative sense. Import processing and market-oriented consumer-goods industry is increasing in nearly every big city in the region: Casablanca, Algiers, Tunis, Alexandria, Cairo, Haifa, Beirut, Damascus, Aleppo, Bagdad, Istanbul, Ankara, and Tehran being among the more important and are where major utilities and construction efforts are found.

The Middle East's industrial output (by value-added) in the early 1960's was composed as follows:

Mining	32%	Light manufacturing	37%
Coal	1.0%	Food, beverages, tobacco	17%
Oil-gas	27.0		
Metallic ores	1.5	Textiles	11
Non-metallics other than fuels	2.5	Clothing, footwear	3
		Wood products, furniture	2
Energy utilities	3		
Construction	16	Printing, publishing	2
		Others	2
		Heavy manufacturing	12%
		Paper, paper products	1%
		Chemicals	3
		Non-metallics	3
		Metals	1
		Metal products	4

Probably Middle Eastern oil and gas production will greatly increase in the foreseeable future as a fraction of the world production, from the present 25 per cent to 35 per cent or higher in the next decade. The income from oil and gas is important since much of that portion is invested in the industrial sector. Manufacturing is likely to increase, with the main emphasis continuing to be in the light-manufacturing area, although the heavy-manufacturing area may become more important than its present one-fourth of all manufacturing. However, the Middle East does not have the solid fuel and other minerals needed for a really large primary metals production, although small oil-gas-electric furnaces are feasible. Metal products production will increase, although much will be as at present, from imported metals or parts. The petrochemicals have a good raw materials base, as do the non-metallic mineral products.

Non-Communist Far East

South Asia, Southeast Asia (excluding North Vietnam), and non-Communist East Asia (Japan, South Korea, Okinawa, and Taiwan, Hong Kong, Macau) have nearly one-third of mankind but only 5½ per cent of the world's industrial output by value. About half of that industrial output is from the two urban-industrial units, Japan and Hong Kong, where the contribution of industrial output is more than one-third of the national product. Another third of that industrial output is from countries like India, the Philippines, and Taiwan, where the share from the industrial sector is 20 to 25 per cent of national product. Elsewhere, the relative position of industry is still of rather minor importance as compared with the dominant role of agriculture. Regional industrial output has quadrupled since 1950, perhaps the greatest increase of any great-region.

The region has 21 per cent of the world's industrial labor force, compared with its 5½ per cent of world industrial output by value. This reflects the huge number of handicraft workers in handicraft manufacturing and construction. As a general rule, labor productivity in small modern industry is only one-third to one-half that in large industry, and that in cottage industry only a tenth or so as productive as that in large industry. In India, for example, large industry and small-factory industry account for 2 per cent of total employment but nearly 90 per cent of all manufacturing by value, while the 10 per cent in cottage industries (13 million as compared with 3 million in modern manufacturing) turn out the remaining small fraction.

Whereas agricultural production has been increasing annually only about as fast as population growth, industrial production has been increasing some four times faster. During the 1950's, the output of foods, textiles, tobacco, and beverages doubled, while the output of energy, chemicals, and basic metals more than trebled. By the early 1960's, industrial output (by value-added) was composed as follows:

Mining	10%	Light manufacturing	36%
Coal	3.8	Food, beverages,	
Oil-gas	3.2	tobacco	9%
Metallic ores	2.1	Textiles	12
Non-metallics other than fuels	0.9	Clothing, footwear	4
Energy utilities	5	Wood products, furniture	5
Construction	14	Printing, publishing	3
		Others	3
		Heavy manufacturing	35%
		Paper, paper products	2%
		Chemicals	9
		Non-metallics	3
		Metals	4
		Metal products	17

The early stage of industrial development in most countries is reflected in the structure of manufacturing, in which generally light consumer-goods industry—especially food processing and textiles—predominates. Taken together, the food and textile industries account for between 45 and 75 per cent of total employment in manufacturing in most countries of the region. The pattern is equally striking in terms of output. The food and textile industries account for about 60 per cent of value-added in manufacturing in India, Pakistan, the Philippines, Taiwan, and South Korea, and the share for most other countries is much higher. For Japan, this contribution is less than 30 per cent.

In the 1950's, a number of countries—such as Pakistan, Thailand, the Philippines, Hong Kong, and Taiwan—attempted to diversify their economies by concentrating on the production of consumer goods, especially labor-intensive industries with modest capital requirements, standardized machinery, plentiful raw materials, and a ready domestic market. In certain instances, the lack of raw materials has not prevented the growth of these industries when a sufficient local or export market exists (e.g., the rise of the cotton textile industry in Taiwan and Hong Kong, following Japan's early example).

The Philippines, Taiwan, and South Korea have industries mainly oriented to the domestically available crude-food raw materials, much like New Zealand in the 1920's or Belgium in the 1840's. India and Pakistan mainly have textiles in their consumer-goods industry, much like Britain in the 1870's or Japan around 1900.

The metallurgical and engineering industries generally constitute a much less important part in the industrial structure of the region, employing less than 10 per cent of the labor force in manufacturing. Japan's fraction is over one-third, and its producer-goods industry is now as important as its consumer-goods industry, the only such example of a mature industrial nation in the region. India, the Philippines, Taiwan, and South Korea are in an intermediate category, with a ratio of 2:1 between consumer-goods and producer-goods industry. The other countries are more immature. India is emphasizing the growth of heavy industry in order to provide a strong industrial base for future development and may reach Japan's status in the next decade.

Communist Far East

Mainland China, North Vietnam, North Korea, and Mongolia considered as a unit have some 23 per cent of mankind but only some $2\frac{1}{3}$ per cent of the world's industrial output by value, although over five times that fraction of the world's industrial labor force. Some 3 to 4 per cent of the population, income, and industrial effort is found in the minor Communist states, so in most contexts, Mainland China's distinguishing characteristics are those for the whole block of centralized ("planned") East Asian economies.

Communist determination to industrialize their Far Eastern states—reflected in the two Chinese five-year plans (1953–1957 and 1958–1962)—is motivated by both ideological and economic factors. From the Communist takeover until 1958, progress in reconstruction and development was impressive. By the end of 1952, gross industrial production had reached about two and a half times the 1949 value, surpassing the pre-1949 peak in most key products. By 1957, modern industry was to account for 36 per cent of the aggregate value of agricultural and industrial output, compared to less than 27 per cent in 1952. Industrial output was given as two and a half times the 1952 level by the end of the first five-year plan. Present industrial capacity is thought to exceed the 1957 level, but by what margin is not clear. The iron and steel industry, coal mining, and electricity generation have apparently developed much further. What has happened in the light-manufacturing fields, where raw materials have (like crops in general) probably fallen back to the 1957 level as a result of four years of disaster, is not clear, but many think that such industry may be a fifth or so under the targets reached by the end of the first five-year plan.

The pre-World War II industrial structure of China was characterized by a heavy concentration of modern industry in coastal and riverine ports, by a preponderance of consumer-goods industry (especially textiles, like India), by a striking importance of foreign-owned and -managed industry, and by an external orientation of much manufacturing with respect to raw materials.

During World War II, industrial development in Southwest China through the relocation of old coastal enterprises and the establishment of new enterprises, and similar developments in Japanese-controlled North and Northeast China, led to some modification of the prewar distribution of modern industry. Although Shanghai was still the major industrial center at the end of World War II (with perhaps one-fourth of all modern industrial capacity), there were other developments that have been expanded since the Communists started their accelerated industrialization: the Tientsin-Tangshan-Shihchingshan industrial triangle around Peking, the Taiyuan (Shansi) metallurgical and machinery industrial node, and the Chungking and Wuhan iron-steel industries of the middle Yangtze. The most important modification of the distribution of Chinese industry in the past generation, however, was undoubtedly the development of southern "Manchuria," particularly the Luta (Dairen), Anshan, Fushun, Mukden, and Harbin areas, as a huge industrial complex of the metallurgical, machinery, chemical, and processed-energy industries by the Japanese.

On the whole, China has sufficient mineral resources for a substantial development of modern industries, but is not as well endowed with known per capita resources as other areas of equal size now modernized. Though China is relatively rich in coal and iron, its iron ore deposits are of comparatively low quality and most of its coal deposits are not of the coking variety. On the other hand, since vast areas of China have not been explored for mineral deposits, it is difficult to predict what the country's industrial potential is.

Generally speaking, distribution of minerals falls into two major regional divisions: coal, iron, and petroleum in the Northwest, North, and Northeast; the non-ferrous metals and ferroalloys in the South and Southwest. The loess region of Shensi-Shansi (possessing almost 70 per cent of all Chinese coal reserves), Manchuria (the Northeast), and North Korea are natural districts for heavy-industry development. The Manchurian basin with 70 per cent of China's accessible better-grade iron ore, together with some good coking-coal fields nearby, has become the leading center of iron and steel works, and will probably be equaled by the Northwest and North in the near future. The lower Yangtze valley, with its convenient water transport and proximity to the South China metalliferous belt, is most promising for the mixing of consumer-goods and producer-goods industries serving the ⅓ billion market of central China. The Southwest's plateaus, rich in latent hydropower and some uncommon minerals, would make a likely center for light metallurgical industries with the improvement of transportation.

The stagnation of Communist Far Eastern agriculture for half a decade has reduced its share of total income to less than a third, while industry provides a third, and all services slightly more. As in Communist Europe, mining-utilities and heavy industry are a substantial majority of all industry. Also, again as in Communist Europe, engineering and chemicals subsectors are being developed to supply agriculture with improved technology (since farm-produced factors of production have failed to substantially increase output since the late 1950's). Rationalization (improving technical efficiency) is eliminating much of the uneconomic "backyard" efforts of the late 1950's.

Trends

There are considerable differences in regional-industrial growth rates. In a generation-long backward glance, North America and Latin America increased their value of industrial production some 5 per cent annually, but in a view restricted to the 1950's, North America's annual rate of increase was lower, while Latin America's rate of increase was 7 per cent (and many countries had even higher rates). In a generation-long backward glance, Western Europe and Oceania, in the urban-industrial realm, and sub-Saharan Africa, Middle East, and non-Communist Far East, in the predominantly underdeveloped realm, increased their volume of industrial production at a somewhat slower rate (around 4 to 5 per cent), but their production rate was stagnant or down during the 1940's and very much higher in the 1950's period of reconstruction and resurgence, around 8 to 10 per cent annually (again, 15 per cent rates of increase were not unknown for individual countries in this period). The Communist realm, both European and Far Eastern, had experiences much like the second group alluded to: wartime slump in industry considered as a single sector, with accelerated recovery and development since—the European Communist region doubled its industrial production during the 1950's and the Far Eastern Communist region may have increased its output by six times from the post-World War II low of the late 1940's (light industry may have increased four times and heavy industry ten times in the decade).

Looking ahead, it is possible that North America's share of world industrial output will continue to slip for the next generation, dropping to somewhere between one-fourth and one-third of the total, while Western Europe and Eastern Europe (including the U.S.S.R.) may slightly increase their shares to near equality with North America. The other great regions may increase their relative shares, but their combined totals seem unlikely to do more than equal the share of one of the big three regions in the medium-long view ahead. In the long view, there may be a more radical change, with the Far East likely to bulk largest in an absolute (but not necessarily in a per capita) context.

INDUSTRIAL SUBSECTOR CHARACTERISTICS

In this section, attention will be focused on the world's industrial sector and its subsectors, with the aim of obtaining an over-all view of composition in terms of employment and value of output and in terms of relative rates of growth. First, composition of industrial output (by value-added) is given:

Mining	8%	Light manufacturing	28%
Coal	1.5%	Food, beverages,	
Oil-gas	4.0	tobacco	9.0%
Metallic ores	1.5	Textiles	5.0
Non-metallics other than fuels	1.0	Clothing, footwear	4.0
Energy utilities	5	Wood products, furniture	3.5
Construction	14	Printing, publishing	3.5
		Others	3.0
Heavy manufacturing			45%
Paper, paper products			3%
Chemicals			9
Non-metallics			3
Metals			5
Metal products			25

Second, composition of the labor force brings out how much construction and certain light manufacturing is still carried out by handicraft-type industrial labor, while mining, utilities, and heavy industry have much less of this premodern factor of production.

Mining	6%	Light manufacturing	38%
Coal	3.0%	Food, beverages,	
Oil-gas	0.5	tobacco	10%
Metallic ores	1.5	Textiles	10
Non-metallics other than fuels	1.0	Clothing, footwear	7
Energy utilities	2	Wood products, furniture	6
Construction	20	Printing, publishing	2
		Others	3
Heavy manufacturing			34%
Paper, paper products			1.5%
Chemicals			4.0
Non-metallics			3.5
Metals			5.0
Metal products			20.0

Third, some concept of changing composition in the world industry sector is given by comparing average annual growth rates in employment and in value, in a generation-long backward view. This generation includes over a decade in the late 1930's and 1940's during which the Great Depression and World War II resulted in a depressing effect and the nearly two decades since the end of World War II which has seen extremely rapid growth rates in most parts of the world. If the advances of the 1950's are maintained, growth rates in the 1960's could average considerably higher than the ones given. (See Table 12–3.)

Food processing, printing, and construction—like the majority of services—are ubiquitous, found in all cities and most towns. In such industries, large-scale production for a regional, national, or international market is, as a rule, of subordinate importance in comparison with production for the city itself and its trade hinterland. There are, of course, exceptions. And, the ubiquitousness of such industry does not mean that they are of equal importance in all cities. There are significant variations between cities of different size and different functional type as well as regional variations.

TABLE 12–3

World Industry: Average-Annual Growth Rates, by Subsectors, 1937–1963

(in per cents)

	Number of Workers	Volume of Production (value-added)
Mining	1	4
Coal	1	1
Oil-gas	2	6
Metallic ores	1	3
Non-metallics other than fuels	1	3
Energy utilities	2	4
Construction	3	5
Manufacturing	(3)	(5)
Light manufacturing	2	3
Food, beverages, and tobacco	2	3
Textiles	1	2
Clothing and footwear	1	2
Wood products and furniture	3	3
Printing and publishing	3	5
Others	2	4
Heavy manufacturing	3	6
Paper and paper products	3	5
Chemicals and chemical products	3	7
Non-metallic mineral products	2	5
Basic metals	3	5
Metal products	4	7
World industrial sector	3	5

The other subsectors are mainly sporadic (concentrated) types.

Light Industry

Food, beverages, and tobacco. Food processing and associated industry is a diverse subsector, with numerous locational and scale tendencies. Flour milling is a rather unimportant industry from the standpoint of employment, as it is highly mechanized and has a low value-added (e.g., in the United States, labor costs are 3 per cent of sales value, as compared with 70 per cent for direct raw materials).

In general, bakeries form a large and ubiquitous industry, with those plants turning out soft goods setting the general pattern. However, increasingly, the cookie and cracker branch is characterized by large plants located in the principal centers of population.

Canning plants are generally very seasonal, with housewives or other casual labor forming one-half to two-thirds of the labor force. Most canning is a typical example of a raw-material-oriented industry. A large share of the requirements of the canneries is grown and sold on a contract basis by local farmers. In many areas of suitable soil and climate, receipts from the canneries make up a considerable share of the total farm income. The perishable nature of most of the raw materials is responsible not only for the raw materials orientation but for the typically small scale of individual plants (the larger ones tend to be located in subtropical areas where both summer- and winter-type crops are available).

Several changes in food processing technology may have the effect in the next few decades of increasing the sporadic location of larger-scale plants. One is the process of dehydrating food without sacrificing shape—big drawbacks are cost (cheapest freeze-drying is 2 to 3 cents per pound) and the unattractive appearance of the product. Second is nuclear irradiation, which may make it possible to keep some foods (particularly meat and fish) longer than ever before, often even without use of refrigeration. Both, when perfected, will cut transport and storage costs.

Sugar refining is mainly found near the raw material or near port cities. Confectionary making, which is a closely related industry, is widely scattered, with a heavy concentration in densely populated areas.

Both breweries and soft drink plants have a more or less ubiquitous distribution, although there is a tendency for larger and fewer breweries when highway transport is well developed. New continuous-flow brewing can be utilized, and concentrated beer (75 per cent dewatered) can be shipped long distances. The cheap soft drinks are even more sensitive to transportation costs than beer. Wineries and the distilling industry are more sporadic than the brewing and

Courtesy of General Foods Corp.

Post Division plant of General Foods Corporation at Battle Creek, Michigan, which produces Post cereals (Post Toasties, Grape-Nuts, Grape-Nuts Flakes, Bran Flakes, Raisin Bran Flakes, Sugar Crisp, Alpha-Bits, Oat Flakes, Crispy Critters, Bran and Prune Flakes, Sugar Sparkled Corn Flakes, Sugar Sparkled Krinkles, Post-Tens, and Treat Pak) and Tang, Instant Postum, and Coffee-Flavor Instant Postum. The raw materials are almost all from the Corn Belt and Dairy Belt; the market is mainly national.

Courtesy of General Foods Corp.

A quality control technician takes a sampling of Post Toasties that flow over a cooling screen after leaving the roasting oven at the Post Division plant of General Foods Corporation at Battle Creek, Michigan. The cereal samples are checked for color, uniformity, moisture content, and other factors of importance to the consumer.

Courtesy of General Foods Corp.

Post Division plant of General Foods Corporation at Kankakee, Illinois, which produces Corn Grits, Brewer's Flakes, Confectioner's Flakes, Corn Oil, Core Binder, Corn Meal, and other corn products—and dog foods marketed under the Gaines-burgers, Gravy Train, Gaines Bits, Gaines Biscuits, and Gaines Meal brand names. Located in the middle of the Corn Belt, the plant is also well situated for national distribution.

soft drink branches. Whiskey, especially, is an expensive product that can stand long transport charges.

In most parts of the world, meat packing is a fairly ubiquitous industry, but in the United States it is becoming more so. Contrary to most other American industries, there is a considerable recent increase in the number of plants, reflecting decentralization toward the source of animals. Fresh milk, cream, ice cream, and similar dairy products generally have a ubiquitous distribution, but the manufacturing of the less perishable dairy products is often highly concentrated where supplies of cheap industrial-grade milk is available. Milk is not shipped any farther than is absolutely necessary to obtain an adequate supply, being low in value per unit of weight and perishable, so each city is the center of a milk producing area, and as much of the production as can be marketed fresh is done so. Butter, cheese, dried milk and dried cream, and other concentrated milk and butterfat products tend to be mainly produced in the less urbanized milk-surplus areas, such as the western part of the U.S. Dairy Belt or in New Zealand.

Tobacco processing has been traditionally bracketed with the food and beverage industries, although the product has no food value. In many states, cigarette and cigar making employ about the same number of people, but the cigarette industry is by far the largest when measured by tobacco consumption or value-added. In the United States, the cigarette industry is concentrated in the Piedmont region, with Louisville a secondary center. In countries where most tobacco is imported, the industry tends to be more ubiquitous. Handmade cigars are mainly made where cheap labor is plentiful,

Courtesy of General Foods Corp.

Post Division plant of General Foods Corporation at Evansville, Indiana, which produces Swans Down Flours, Cake Mixes, and Bakery Donut mixes. The soft winter wheat, which is the main raw material, comes from the surrounding region, and the hard winter wheat and the spring wheat, which are part of certain flour blends, come from the Great Plains Wheat Belt.

but in the United States, more are now machine made, the industry centered in Philadelphia.

Textiles. Textile manufacturing—like the apparel industry—is a low-wage industry and employs a large share of women. However, the two industries differ considerably in their distribution. Textile manufacturing tends to dominate many towns, but the apparel industry (its world employment total equalling that of textile manufacturing) does not dominate any city, often being in locational tendency a parasite industry that occurs in places with male-dominated industries.

Coarse cotton fabrics have a wide market even in poor countries, and can be produced by semiautomatic machines imported from older centers and manned by unskilled or semiskilled laborers, so they are among the industries that lead the process of industrialization in hitherto non-industrialized countries.

Knitting mills have a wider distribution than the other textile branches. The finer the cloth, the more likely that distribution will be sporadic (generally found in the older centers, with more skilled labor).

In poorer regions, vast numbers of handicraftsmen are still found making textiles, although their efficiency is very low. In India, handicraft weavers may number 3 million (full-time equivalent) workers, in comparison with 1 million factory (mill) workers, but their cloth production is less than 20 per cent of the total (practically all use thread that is spun by the mills).

Apparel and footwear. In the poorer parts of the world, apparel is still mainly made at home or by local tailors, rather than from factory industry. Apparel manufacturing is a big-city industry and a low-wage industry, for the most part. The industry is dominated by rapidly shifting fashions, so it has not been mechanized in a way comparable with other manufacturing industries.

In modernized economies, the apparel industry is increasing labor productivity quite rapidly, but in a world view, this is counteracted by increasing clothing employment in countries with less efficient clothing industries.

In poor societies, shoes are made at home or by local craftsmen, and the rise of factory industry has not reduced the widespread pattern of production very much. From the turn of the century, a stronger emphasis on style helped to preserve the specialized, moderate-size plant as a characteristic of the industry and helped strengthen the market orientation. Very high-priced and specialty shoes tend to have a more sporadic pattern of plant location than cheap and medium-priced shoe manufacture (like Bata-type shoes).

Wood products and furniture. This subsector includes all wood processing except the pulp and paper industry, which, because of its large-scale plants, huge capitalization, and heavy power consumption, is normally considered a heavy industry.

Logging, sawmills, and related factories (veneer mills, plywood plants, box factories, etc.) employ about two-thirds of the people in wood manufacturing, with the furniture industry employing the remaining third. These plants are usually located in small towns and rural districts, in general following the distribution of forests or of intermediate points accessible both to forests and to markets (e.g., cheap riverine or tidewater linkage).

In most countries, the furniture industry is composed of small units (e.g., in the United States, there are over 3,000 manufacturers and more than 30,000 retailers). Big factories are not markedly more efficient than plants of moderate size, since the industry turns out a bulky and relatively cheap product that, in general, cannot very well carry the costs of long-distance transportation. As a result of these two characteristics, furniture manufacturing is widely spread over great-regions, but the factories tend to cluster in furniture towns and there is a certain specialization among them (e.g., in terms of different pieces of furniture). Big cities have some furniture making that is market oriented: some custom-work wooden furniture, but mainly upholstered and metal products.

Printing and publishing. Newspapers are published nearly everywhere, being one of the most ubiquitous industries. In highly urbanized societies, however, there is a tendency toward local monopoly, monopolistic competition, and more sporadic location.

On the average, a daily newspaper pays out for newsprint about one-third of its revenues, roughly the fraction it receives from subscriptions. The larger users profit by carload lots and long-term contracts, and by more efficient utilization of personnel and equipment. In fact, the scale of operation over which decreasing costs prevail is far beyond the needs of the largest communities. In Britain, Japan, and other small countries, the largest newspapers have almost national circulation, and there is a tendency in that direction even in giant countries like the United States and the U.S.S.R.

Periodicals and books are almost exclusively published and, to a large extent, also printed in a few of the biggest cities. Strictly governmental centers often develop as their largest factory industry the printing of government materials (e.g., Washington, Madrid, Rome). Publishing of commercial materials tends to concentrate in the largest cities (e.g., in the United States, New York and Chicago are the two largest centers).

Other light manufacturing. This is a very miscellaneous grouping, so only a few examples will be given. Rubber products is an industry where an original sporadic location has gradually given way to considerable decentralization, chiefly resulting from the need for economy in distribution.

Instruments and related products—jewelry,

silverware, watches and clocks, photographic equipment, and a host of similar products—is generally high labor cost and low raw materials cost industry. Transport costs for raw materials and finished products play a rather insignificant role for the localization of such industry, which is often located in traditional areas (e.g., in the United States, in southern New England and upper New York State). In countries where such manufacturing is new, the largest city may be favored (e.g., in Japan, Tokyo).

Heavy Industry

Paper and allied products. Integrated mills, mainly those making newsprint, wrapping paper, and paperboard in large quantities from only one or two types of pulp, tend to be raw material oriented, and are largely located in the peripheral regions (e.g., in the United States, the South, Pacific Northwest, Upper Great Lakes, and the New England highlands). For many products in which different types and grades of pulp are used, a location close to the market is more essential.

Pulp may be transported to the paper mill by pipeline in water suspension, as wet laps (sheets formed by pressing out most of the water), or in dry form (sheets or rolls). The amount of water left in the pulp is dependent on the distance the pulp must be transported and the preference and needs of the customer.

Mills depending extensively on wastepaper for raw material are generally located close to market as the source of the wastepaper and the purchaser of his product are at the same general location. Non-integrated mills generally make a large number of small items calling for shipments in less than car- or truckload quantities, need a wide variety of fibrous materials, and must ship on short notice, so they too must be close to markets.

Chemicals. Heavy or industrial chemicals, selling at low prices relative to weight and bulk, cannot carry the costs of long transportation, so they are manufactured near sources of raw materials or in port cities in the market areas (the first illustrated by the western U.S. Gulf Coast, the second by the Narrows Seas littoral of Western Europe). The plant location considerations for the basic manufacturer include important ones like proximity to raw materials, fuel and power, transportation, labor supply, water supply, and waste disposal; and less important considerations such as market location, living conditions, nearness to suppliers, and nearness to equipment and plant maintenance services.

Light chemical industries take basic chemicals and convert them into materials useful to the rest of industry and often to the consuming public. They generally make expensive products relative to weight (e.g., pharmaceuticals), and can locate themselves with regard to the national market. For them, the locational factors include important ones like market location, labor supply, waste disposal, fuel and power, living conditions, and nearness to equipment and plant maintenance services; and less important factors such as transportation, water supply, nearness to suppliers, and proximity to raw materials. This second group adds two-thirds or more of the value-added by the entire chemical industry, so the main manufacturing belts tend to contain most chemical manufacturing (e.g., in the United States, Greater New York City is the largest center).

Nearly everywhere in the world, the chemical manufacturing industry is a growth industry, usually doubling every decade, and as its relative importance increases, its distribution is becoming more ubiquitous.

Non-metallic mineral products. This subsector is an extremely diverse one, with the biggest tonnage items being building materials and similar items. Cheap brick and tile plants tend to be widely distributed (as low-quality clay is widespread), a wide variety of fuel can be used, and transport is very expensive for such cheap and bulky products. The pottery branch, however, produces items with a rather high unit value, in which there is high labor cost, marketed over a wide area, so its locational pattern is more sporadic. Fuel is important, but high-quality clay is easily shipped.

Like brick- and tile-making, cement plants are scattered in rough proportion to the population distribution. Ideally, the sites of plants are raw material oriented and the regional location of plants is market oriented. Of the raw materials, limestone exerts the greatest influence on plant location. The clay or shale used is more widely distributed, and the amount used is only one-third of the limestone tonnage. The fuel—usually coal for the kiln and electricity for grinding—usually moves to the limestone. Nearly 2 tons of raw materials and fuel must be assembled to produce 1 ton of cement. Many large plants are now located on the outskirts of cities where navigable waterways or other bulk-type transport provide cheap transport to the nearest raw materials and fuel. Cement plants are examples of continuous-process industry, in which operation at full capacity is often more important than an ideal site and situation.

Airview of the Union Bridge Plant of the Lehigh Portland Cement Company, located northwest of Baltimore, Maryland. The limestone is taken from the main quarry site near the crushing plant, while the sandstone and shale are obtained from smaller quarries nearby. Portland Cement is composed principally of the oxides of calcium, silicon, aluminum, and iron in various mineral combinations; the first two of these, in the form of calcium silicates, are mainly responsible for its capacity to harden after being mixed with water. The product from this plant is mainly used in the Baltimore and Washington, D.C., urban areas.

Courtesy of Lehigh Portland Cement Co.

Courtesy of Lehigh Portland Cement Co.

Airview of the Miami, Florida, plant of the Lehigh Portland Cement Company. The principal raw material for this plant is coral rock, which underlies hundreds of square miles of the Everglades, and which is being quarried in the background of the photo. This is one of the most modern cement plants in the world, with an annual capacity of 2½ million barrels of cement, and embodies many of the latest concrete techniques in its buildings.

Courtesy of Lehigh Portland Cement Co.

View of raw grinding mills (note the prestressed and precast structural system of concrete columns, beams, and roof members). These mills use steel balls as grinding media; and, as the mills rotate, the tumbling action of these balls pulverizes the raw materials. The water that is added makes a slurry, which has such fineness that over 92 per cent will pass through a wire mesh containing 40,000 holes to the square inch.

View of rotary kilns and coolers. Slurry enters the higher end of the kiln, is dried and calcined as it moves forward until it reaches the intense white heat of the burning zone (temperatures higher than the melting point of steel). Here the constituents of slurry combine to form a completely new set of compounds, and the nodulized raw material that enters the burning zone is transformed into hard, glassy balls of Portland cement clinker.

Courtesy of Lehigh Portland Cement Co.

Undersilo loading of bulk tank trucks and rail hopper cars. From each of thirty locations, a truck or car may be loaded, weighed, and ready to roll in twelve to fifteen minutes. Most truck movements are in the metropolitan region.

Courtesy of Lehigh Portland Cement Co.

The glass industry comprises three distinct branches with the same fundamental technology but with different products and markets: pressed and blown glassware, glass containers, and flat glass. Within the wide area having a favorable market location, the industry seems always to have chosen sites with access to cheap fuel, especially in regard to the first two branches. The flat glass branch is characterized by very large plants, so economy of large scale explains concentration in spite of bulk and relatively cheap product made from scattered fuel and raw materials.

Basic metals. The metal-making industries tend to be the substance of major manufacturing nodes. The three major locational factors include: fuel and energy, ores, and the market for primary metal or slightly altered mill products. In a long view, the relative advantages of raw materials orientation have been reduced, as the transport costs have been cut by increasing efficiency in fuel and energy use, the increasing use of highly concentrated ores, the heavy use of scrap, and increased on-site efficiency by such developments as oxygen production.

The growing demand for high-quality metals and alloys, and a need to be in close contact with many fabricators have increased the advantages of market-oriented sites. Coastal sites lying between inland fuel sources and foreign ore sources, and in proximity to great markets, have been increasing in relative importance in recent decades. Some great metropolitan ports have located capacity based almost entirely on foreign fuel and raw materials, especially in Japan and South America. Many older smelting districts are located on fuel lying between the ore fields and the ultimate market or (more rarely) are located on the ore lying between the market and the fuel.

Increasingly, smelting and refining are separated. The older non-ferrous metals tend to be smelted near the mines, but refined close to the market (e.g., copper). In older ferrous metal centers, some of the highly concentrated ore pellets are so pure that they can be used, at least in part, as scrap equivalent without ever passing through iron furnaces.

Heavy fabrication tends to be near primary metal-making, especially the production of structural metal products, of metal stamping and coating, of fabricated wire products, of heating and plumbing equipment, of tin cans, of cutlery, hand tools, and hardware, of lighting fixtures, and of miscellaneous metal products. Often this will be done by the integrated primary-metal producer, or by other plants who locate alongside or nearby.

Metal products. This is probably the most diverse subsector, with machinery and vehicles being among the largest branches. With proper allowance for the interdependence of locational factors and general industrial distribution patterns, the market stands out as the single most important factor for the location of the machine manufacturing industry. Such market orientation in machinery does not only minimize transport costs, but also provides for personal contact between the men who produce the machines and those who use them in their factories, which contact gives impulses to improvements and inventions. The strongest market orientation is evident for factories supplying specific, sporadic industries with machinery: in the United States, textile machinery in the Eastern Seaboard, shoe machinery in New England, oil field machinery and tools in the Southwest and Southern California, printing machinery in New York and Chicago, and automobile machinery in southern Michigan and northern Ohio. Factories making machinery with a more ubiquitous demand, such as office machines and agricultural implements, generally have a favorable location with regard to the national market (e.g., downstate Illinois or southwest Ohio).

Mass-produced motor vehicles are just the type of metal product for which a marked geographic concentration can be expected, especially in making parts and subassemblies. In this industry, very large production units are more efficient than smaller ones. The increases in distribution costs of the bulky product, which result from a regional concentration of production, are not large enough to offset the savings in production costs, especially since they can be reduced by a system of well-located assembly plants to which parts can be shipped in bulk from the manufacturing plants at a fraction of the cost for transportation of the assembled product. For a heavy steel consuming industry like automotive manufacturing, a central location with regard to the steel industry is essential, and this can be illustrated both in the Midwest and in the major Western European industries.

Other vehicle-making—aircraft and missile manufacturing, shipbuilding, and diesel-electric railway rolling stock—is essentially an assembly industry, with much less vertical and horizontal integration than in the case of the automotive industry. Parts and subassemblies—airframes, engines, instruments, etc.—are seldom produced at the same plant or even by the same company. The final assembly plants obtain from other sources completely assembled subassemblies and actually add only a quarter or so of the value-added in manufacturing the entire vehicles from the crude materials on.

Other Secondary Subsectors

Building and construction.[3] Most building and construction is a ubiquitous activity. Much is done by peasants or even urban dwellers for themselves. In developing societies, often the first "industrial" jobs obtained by landless laborers or small-holders in their non-agricultural season are in building and construction, either in nearby road, dam, and similar construction or in urban building developments.

Cities grow at different rates. In the United States, only in about 10 per cent of all cities are less than 4 per cent of the work force engaged in building and construction; about the same fraction of cities have 10 per cent or more of their labor force so engaged. In fast-modernizing economies, building and construction tends to be a larger fraction than in more stable economies. In the United States, the fast-growing cities west of the Mississippi and in the South, low in manufacturing, have a higher building and construction percentage in their work force than the slow-growing manufacturing cities of the main manufacturing belt. Some Latin American, Middle Eastern, and Far Eastern cities—increasing from 7 to 10 per cent yearly—have as large as 20 to 25 per cent of their labor force in building and construction.

Building contractors often operate on a large scale, building homes, factories, dams, roads, and other items even at considerable distances from their home towns. In the case of highly specialized capital goods—especially high dams, protected harbors on exposed coasts, and very high buildings—there are American, British, Italian, and other companies who build for a nearly worldwide market. But the local and regional scale is far more common.

Mining. The mining industry is the least urbanized of all industry groupings. Only a minority of miners live in cities, while the majority live in small towns. Before the Industrial Revolution, most mining was so separated from smelting, refining, and other processing that it was considered a primary activity and often grouped together with the smaller ones added to agriculture and stock raising. Most mining today has been absorbed into closely associated concentrating, smelting, and refining operations, so that the extractive aspects occupy only a minority of labor, capital, and other productive elements organized into the "mining" enterprise.

In the past generation, mining has diffused more rapidly into the underdeveloped and semi-industrialized realms than manufacturing proper. The mature urban-industrial regions—North America and Western Europe—increased their mining output (value-added) at a rate little more than one-half of the world average (4 per cent), while the other regions had rates of 5 per cent or higher.

In that quarter century, the volume of world activity in petroleum and natural gas extraction more than quadrupled, and such mining increased in importance until it composed one-half of the total by value. Coal mining increased some 1 to 2 per cent per year, and most of that was in Eastern Europe (including the U.S.S.R.), the Communist Far East (for the non-Communist urban-industrial world, output was stag-

---

[3] Includes demolition and repair, roughly a third of the value-added (this is why some analysts place this subsector in the services sector).

nant or declining), and in the non-Communist underdeveloped realm. Mining of metallic ores and of non-metallic minerals other than fuels expanded at rates intermediate between those of coal mining and oil-gas extraction, and the shifts in distribution were less drastic. While metallic ores were being mined at a growth rate averaging some 3 per cent annually, the output of primary metals was going up at nearly twice that rate, reflecting greatly improved furnace efficiency, wider use of scrap, and other economies in the metallurgical and associated fabricating industries.

Public utilities. The processing of water and sewerage, the manufacture and mixing of gas, and the generation of electricity form a group of utilities that are growing rapidly with the urban industrialization of mankind. In terms of the weight of raw material processed, water filtration plants would rank as the most important manufacturing branch (e.g., in the United States, about 1 cubic mile of water is treated bimonthly, not counting that going through hydroplants, compared with several cubic miles of raw materials and fuel as normally defined used by all other industry in the course of a year). As time goes on, more and more water must be used many times in one hydrologic cycle, so the quantity, quality, and variety of treatment given sewerage and other waste water and that given raw water before distributing for consumption is becoming more complicated and expensive. If large amounts eventually must come from desalting brackish water and sea water, this utility may well become tremendously more important in terms of employment and value-added.

At present, with an increasing proportion of gas coming from natural rather than city gas, the gas utility industry is adding more value by distribution efforts than by manufacturing efforts. However, if natural gas becomes scarce and more expensive, and recourse is made to low-grade coal and oil shale for future supplies, the manufacturing efforts may increase in relative importance.

Generation of electricity is a growth industry almost everywhere in the world, with doubling of production every decade commonplace. Even in mature urban-industrial economies, the appetite for this secondary form of energy is phenomenal (e.g., in the United States, requirements for electrical energy by the year 2000 may be nearly seven times what they were in the early 1960's because of increasing population and greater use of this energy in industrial processes and other consumption). Employment is not increasing as rapidly, because of great increases in technical efficiency of generation, but this trend could be slowed down if nuclear generation (with the accompanying need to protect workers and nearby urban regions from radiation hazards) should become dominant.

Trends. Among the manufacturing industries, the heavy-goods branches (paper, chemical, non-metallic, and metal products) made the greatest gains in output during the past generation and are the main growth industries of the present and foreseeable future. In general, this is true by great-region and by economic-type of society as well as for the world economy. At a growth rate double that of the light-goods branches, the heavy-goods branches will soon be relatively more important in the world economy, just as they are now in the mature urban-industrial great regions.

Coupled with expansion in the heavy-goods industries greater than that in light-goods processing has been variation in year-to-year change in the level of output that is greater for the former group than the latter group. Increases in the productivity of labor have been more rapid for the heavy-goods industries than for light-goods manufacturing, in the case of each great-region and economic-type of society as well as for the world.

The average rate of growth in the output of light manufactures is higher in regions with high rates of population growth and recent high rates of disposable consumer-income increase. For the world as a whole, food manufacturing has the highest average rate of expansion in output among the larger subsectors, although this is not the case in every great-region. For the world as a whole, the volume of clothing manufacturing expanded less than the output of other light-goods processing, partly because the average rate of increase in labor productivity was very high in those regions with mechanized clothing industries. The net effect of the changes in the volume of activity and labor productivity is that wood processing shows a greater increase in employment than any of the other larger light-goods industries, both for the world as a whole and in nearly every great-region.

The basic processing of metals, the making of paper, and the making of building and related products have lower rates of annual increase than the chemicals and metal products subsectors, although higher than any of the larger subsectors of light-goods industry. The lower rate of growth in the output of primary metals relative to the expansion in the volume of metal products reflects economies realized in the use of metals and the increased degree of fabrication occurring in the making of machinery, vehicles, and other metal products. The high growth rate in chemicals reflects the increasing chemicalization of nearly every aspect of modern society—agricultural and industrial production, public health and medicine, and many other areas—while the average gain in labor productivity is greater than in other heavy-goods branches, both for the world as a whole and most great-regions.

Mining is increasing labor productivity at very rapid rates nearly everywhere in the world. The increasing importance of oil-gas extraction as a fraction of world mining output is one reason, for its labor productivity is extremely high. In the other branches—coal, metallic ores, and non-metallics other than fuels—the increasing technical efficiency is related to larger-scale and higher degrees of mechanization per worker than in the past.

Mainly because of increasing efficiency, the utilities are not growth industries in terms of employment and value of output. Their physical output, both in absolute and in per capita terms, is increasing at very rapid rates, both in the world as a whole and in every great-region.

The average annual rate of increase in the volume of building and construction is as large as that for the industrial sector as a whole, and so is its increase in labor requirements. Although labor productivity in certain types of construction has been increasing rapidly with greater mechanization and electrification, this branch of industry is one of the least rationalized branches taking a broad view over its many subtypes and over the world as a whole. Probably some two-thirds of the 50 million building and construction workers in the world are either handicraftsmen or only slightly mechanized workers. Since this is one industrial subsector where unskilled labor from overpopulated agriculture can be used as a substitute for more efficient technique, the average labor productivity for the world as a whole is likely to lag for a long time to come.

EFFECTS OF DISTRIBUTION AND PRODUCTIVE FACTORS FORCES

In this section, attention will again be focused on the world's industrial sector and subsectors, with the aim of assessing how transfer costs and other distribution costs between production and consumption and relative costs of the factors of production (land, labor, capital, enterprise, and government) affect the location of industry, its technology, and growth rate.

Increasingly, governmental policies are a major determinant in the selection of industries for establishment, expansion, or maintenance. While most easily seen in Communist economies, this is becoming more common in all types of economic systems. While used sparingly in free enterprise economies except during war or other stress, in the past generation and in the decades ahead there has been so much occasion for intervention that the old mythology of government providing only security and general rules is honored mainly in the mythology.

In the absence of government policies, demand and the relative scarcity in the supply of factors of production are the two major determinants in the pattern of industrial development. In an isolated (closed) economy, manufacturing industries produce goods to satisfy the demand of people inside the system, and the demand pattern plays a dominant role in determining the kind (structure) of manufacturing. The various branches—in the absence of non-economic frictions—tend to be located in places where the supply of factors of production is relatively abundant and cheap, and where the assembly of such factors—including transport and other distribution costs—will, under the given scale and production technique, result in the lowest unit cost of production.

Actually, international trade as a complicating variable must always be considered, even in centrally planned economies. All countries import some goods that are produced more cheaply or more flexibly elsewhere, and export other goods that they can produce at lower cost or more flexibly (e.g., faster). The larger the economy, the less likelihood that international trade will be a dominant interest either in market or factor supply.

Market-oriented Industries

More and more, many manufacturing industries locate new capacity where the minimum costs of a combination of both production and distribution costs is found. Since transfer costs of finished (packaged) goods tend to be higher than the cost of moving factors of production—because of the use of more expensive quality transport—there is an increasing tendency for market-oriented capacity.

A high degree of perishability in the commodities produced makes a market location necessary. Many foodstuffs sold in fresh form and in small quantities—fresh milk and butter, ice cream, bread, cakes, and numerous other items—are manufactured locally or at least within a small regional radius. Ice is another, as is a local newspaper (time and dialect may be components in the latter's perishability). All these industries are found, or can be developed, in almost every city of any size in any region or any type of economy.

An increase in weight, bulk, or fragility in the product also tends to market orientation. When the cost of transporting the finished goods exceeds the cost of transporting the raw materials and fuel, a processing or fabricating industry is attracted to location near the market. This is especially likely when water is added to a cheap product like soft drinks and beer. The making of bulky containers—boxes, barrels, cans, etc.—is generally done near the main customers. Many soft consumer goods that are sold in small packages—household chemicals such as detergents and medication—prefer a market orientation even when bulky raw materials are used, if cheap bulk transport is available for supply purposes. Another example of market orientation manufacturing is the assembly of bicycles, motorcycles, and automobiles from compactly packed unassembled parts imported or brought in from other regions. Making or fabricating simple metal products or even light engineering products from imported metals is also common (e.g., making frames and bars for windows, doors, and staircases, or making furniture from knocked-down wood or metal components).

The production of a relatively cheap commodity whose distribution costs are high, even though the product is not perishable, also makes a location near the market attractive. This is true of many building materials such as brick, cement, tile, and many similar heavy, low-value products.

A market location is also desirable where personal contact between producer and consumer is necessary. Most maintenance services need a market location. Where some importance attaches to local styles and sizes—garments, furniture, even certain complicated engineering products—the factory gains by proximity to its customers. Many machinery manufacturers prefer a market orientation not only to lower transfer costs on the finished products, but also to make easier personal contact between maker and user, with its tendency toward more frequent improvement and invention.

Another consideration is the size of the market area, which is affected by the nature of the product. Industries face very different locational problems, depending upon whether the extent of their market is local, regional, national, or international. For firms with a substantial overseas, as well as national, market, a port location may be attractive, even if off center in relation to domestic distribution. For firms with mainly a national market, location is often with relation to the best market area, even if minor segments of the market must be supplied at high transfer costs (e.g., electrical machinery in the U.S. Northeast supplying national market).

Market capacity is an especially important consideration when locating continuous-process or automated plants such as primary metals, chemicals, and metal parts. Even when supplying a large regional or national market, it is often important to have a local market sufficient to cover the high fixed costs.

Since most manufacturing plants—three-fourths or more in a mature urban-industrial nation—use the products or waste products of other industries instead of raw materials in the usual sense, market location may be imported in an indirect sense. Many non-integrated steel, paper, and similar plants which use waste and scrap locate in a large market because only there is cheap accessibility. Also, external economies in other factors—varied types of labor, varied servicing, etc.—are mainly available in large-market areas.

In economies where the market—either other industries or final consumers—is demanding high-quality distribution and fast styling changes, the market location is becoming the norm, and other locations are to be explained mainly in terms of historical terms or in non-economic decentralization (e.g., defense, depressed area resuscitation, avoidance of poor labor relations or public relations, etc.). Most sites become a derived market even if the original location was for other purposes (e.g., a concentration of industry at any point creates a market and a raw materials location can quickly become a market location too). The importance of market locations has been augumented by the near-universal practice of charging higher freight rates on finished products than on raw materials.

Natural Resources and Raw-Materials-oriented Industries

The pattern of natural resources does determine, to a considerable extent, the pattern of industrial development in most countries, although absence does not preclude industry (e.g., Japan, Hong Kong) and presence does not guarantee much manufacturing (e.g., most processing and fabricating of rubber, tin, and copra does not take place where the main surpluses are located). The factor of production "land" includes natural resources of all kinds (agricultural, forestry, fishery, fuel and mineral resources, potential water power) as well as other natural phenomena that are a combination of resources and resistances (e.g., terrain, climate, abstract elements of habitat).

In processing agricultural materials, loss of weight is an important consideration. Grain milling usually results in a loss of one-third or more of the weight, sugar refining eliminates 85 to 90 per cent of the fresh beet or cane, oil pressing eliminates from 40 to 90 per cent of the weight of the oilseeds (depending on the type), concentrated milk products (butter, cheese, dried milk) lose 80 to 85 per cent of the fresh milk weight, dried and processed tea-leaf is only one-fourth of the green-leaf weight, ginned cotton is only 35 per cent of the unginned cotton weight, clean wool is 55 per cent of the greasy wool weight, jute fiber is only 8 per cent of green jute, etc. Sometimes other considerations are more important: waste products that can be used (e.g., as an animal feed) or that can be eliminated cheaply (e.g., waste water can be dumped raw some places and must be processed to a certain level of purity elsewhere), economies of scale may be achieved by linking processing and fabricating together in an integrated plant some distance away from the place of production, or the structure of freight rates may favor the transport of the crude material to a regional rather than local processing plant.

The degree of perishability of the agricultural material is also of importance in assessing the strength of its attraction for manufacturing. The canning and preserving of fruits, vegetables, fresh milk, fish, and many other materials that are highly perishable or that travel badly are often found very near the sources of supply.

Weight reduction is also important in the processing and fabricating of forestry products. Lumber processing usually takes place near the timber stands, since the bark, sawdust, and other waste left behind totals 55 to 60 per cent of the timber that reaches the sawmill (not counting waste in forestry operations). Pulp and paper usually weigh some 35 to 40 per cent of the weight of pulpwood used.

Sometimes weight reduction is done elsewhere than near the source of supply because the value of the raw material is sufficient to bear the costs of transport. Greasy wool is often shipped as such because it can afford the cost, and because clean wool often mats in shipment (i.e., forms felt).

In modern urban-industrial civilization, minerals are increasing in relative importance to total crude-materials consumption. In certain areas, food especially, there is as yet little substitutability by mineral-based synthetics; but in the inedible raw materials and fuel energy areas, minerals and minerals-based materials are increasingly preferred, because of cheaper cost, superior characteristics, and greater flexibility and reliability in expanding supplies. Following is an estimated century-long backward view of visible (direct) crude-materials consumption (billion metric tons):

	1863	1963
Agricultural and other foodstuffs	1.0	2.85
Inedible agricultural raw materials	0.1	0.15
Industrial roundwood	0.3	0.8
Woody fuels of agricultural and forestry origin	2.0	3.2
Organic materials	3.4	7.0
	1863	1963
Mineral fuels	0.4	5.0
Metallic ores (before concentration)	0.1	2.0
Non-metallic minerals other than fuels	3.5	18.0
Mineral materials	4.0	25.0

The annual rate of consumption of organic materials has been little higher than the annual rate of population growth, while the rate of consumption of mineral materials has been several times as rapid (like the increase in income).

Besides the phenomenal long-term rate of increase in minerals production, the shift from selective-mining technology to mass mining is perhaps the most outstanding development. With this increasing industrialization of mining has come a radical shift in mining methods and in related processing to reduce bulk and upgrade in other ways. Open-pit operations have greater relative importance, with bigger equipment (shovels, trucks, locomotives) being used, and with rubber tire trucks being preferred over tracked vehicles, resulting in more powerful, lower slung, faster, and more flexible loading and hauling units. Shaft-mining technology is also being radically changed: trend is toward light, more portable drilling equipment; mine-roof and mine-wall bolting practices are spreading (increasing safety and cutting costs over timbering); concrete is being increasingly used for shoring-up tunnels or headframes, sometimes being transported deep into mines through pipelines; more ore is being crushed underground, and then transported to the hoisting shafts or elevated clear to the surface by conveyor belts; and television is often employed for remote control of hazardous operations or for centralizing control of several simultaneous jobs being done by semiautomatic facilities. Lean ores and other minerals require far more elaborate treatment and far more expensive equipment than the rich ores of yesterday: ore-dressing or concentrating changes include using controlled temperature and alkalinity in froth flotation, extension of the coal industry's sink-and-float process to ores of ever more kinds of metal, use of centrifugal force in radically new mill hardware, perfection of electromagnetism and electrostatics for huge tonnage operations, use of gamma rays to dress uranium ore, and a means of speeding solids out of slimes by high-frequency sound waves. Extractive metallurgy is also changing: still most important is fire (pyrometallurgy), but it is increasingly supplemented by leaching (hydrometallurgy) and electrolysis (electrometallurgy) in separating target minerals into their constituents through chemical change; radioactive separation is still largely in the laboratory stage, but promises to become a fourth major branch of metallurgy in the foreseeable future.

The degree of mineral concentrating and the place where it occurs depend on the nature of the specific mineral. In comparison with organic materials, minerals are peculiar in a number of ways. First in importance is the fact that deposits are exhaustible; the continued exploitation of a mineral deposit is frequently accompanied by increasing difficulties that may be temporarily or partly neutralized by improved technology, but in the long-view, the end is preordained. The problems are most visible in the area of expendable minerals, especially fugitive mineral fuels such as oil and gas, but many other minerals disappear in use, although that characteristic may not be extremely important if availability is common, as in the construction minerals. Second most frustrating is the hidden nature of most minerals. Their discovery is still a matter of chance to a large extent, although the increasing use of indirect detection (geophysical, geochemical, and geobiological) devices reduces the area of uncertainty somewhat. This characteristic goes far toward explaining the speculative character of much mining, and the uncertainty that besets the discovery of new (supplementary or rival) deposits, as well as the extent and persistence of known deposits. Petroleum, natural gas, and primary-ore deposits are among the minerals most affected. A third peculiarity is strictly limited areal availability. Minerals are highly localized in occurrence, only a few covering large areas, and many of world importance cover only a few square miles. In an economic context, because of trade, this sporadic pattern is not very important, but in a geopolitical context, it is the main reason for government support of strategic mining and for maintenance of stockpiles. The final peculiarity is that most metals are durable with an accompanying tendency toward accumulation of secondary metals. There is some scrap in organic materials (e.g., scrap lumber, shoddy wool, etc.), but recycling is actually of as much importance in determining the supply and cost of many metals as new-metal mining.

Crude materials may be divided into two major categories: those used on a large scale as the basic production ingredients of modern industrial society, and those used very little if at all. These two categories may be further subdivided into materials that are plentiful when comparing the rate of use with known reserves, and those that are scarce by the same criterion.

Each of these four categories has its technological problems, which differ in kind and importance.

First, there are present production materials that are plentiful in relation to use. This includes three basic minerals (coal, iron ore, and bauxite ore), the non-metallic building materials (water, clay, stone, sand, gypsum, limestone), chemical raw materials (sulfur and pyrites, salt, potash, phosphates, air, boron), and certain others (e.g., bromine, iodine). Because of the large-scale use and basic importance of these materials, even slight increases in cost can have tremendous effects on the whole economy of the country; therefore, technology has the task of holding costs down. Ample resources of varying concentrations exist for all these materials in a world perspective (and usually in a great-region perspective), so techniques of discovery, while important, are not the chief problem. With this group as a whole, the chief concern is to develop techniques for processing lower-grade resources without permitting costs to throttle development. Much of the coal now mined would have been marginal several decades ago, as it has 30 to 40 per cent impurities, most of which have to be removed in huge preparation plants before market-quality grades are available. Increasingly, crude iron ore is of such low grade (20 to 40 per cent iron content) that it must be upgraded to 60 to 65 per cent pellets before it is worth shipping any distance. The same type of weight loss and upgrading of quality is becoming nearly universal in all the minerals of this group.

Second, there are present production materials that are scarce in relation to their use. Petroleum and natural gas, and certain forest products are two groups of major importance to the United States and most other regions. The group also includes older non-ferrous metals (copper, lead, zinc, tin), ferro alloys (manganese, chromium, nickel, molybdenum, tungsten, vanadium, cobalt, and many others), and numerous uncommon metals (the noble metals, the fissionable metals, mercury, antimony, bismuth, germanium, beryllium, and many others). In this group, the main problem is availability, and cost, though vital, is secondary. These substances are now absolutely necessary and their supply is limited. In the short run, technology must find new deposits and increase the amount of recycling. In the long run, technology must find ways of utilizing extremely lean sources, or substituting more abundant materials or using non-metallics (e.g., new plastics) for some of the group.

Third, there are potential materials that are plentiful. This includes the alkaline-earth metals (calcium, magnesium), the alkali metals (sodium, potassium), and other metals (silicon, titanium, zirconium), and the polymeric materials. These materials are abundant in nature but, compared to that abundance, little used. The problem is essentially one of learning how to produce and to use them in larger quantities and at lower cost. These are the materials from which substitutes for our problem materials (the second group) could come. Recently, small-scale use of many has begun (e.g., silicon, titanium, zirconium), but mainly for airspace, nuclear power, and other uses where expense is no great concern.

Fourth, there are potential materials that are both scarce and undeveloped. This includes a varied list of little-known materials (e.g., lithium, used a bit as industrial catalyst and as copper alloy; indium, used as an alloy in precious metals; hafnium, used in nuclear-reactor controls; rhenium, used as an alloy with tungsten; the "rare earths" like germanium and selenium). Here the main job is to study every property of these materials and to use them as far as possible only where they are essential.

The demands that mineral development and conservation place upon technology are these: to foster new techniques of discovery (especially to probe deep and under thick layers of masking materials), to bring into the stream of use dilute materials that so far evade our efforts (ordinary rock, seawater, air), to apply the principle of recycling more and more broadly, to learn how to deal with lower-grade concentrations of useful materials, to lessen or eliminate the need for a scarce material by substituting one that exists in greater abundance, and to develop and use more economically the renewable resources in nature. Few of these demands lie in any realm of high scientific difficulty. The realm of difficulty lies in costs. An absolute shortage of anything is most unlikely and is not the threat that faces world industry. The threat is of slowly fading supplies that, if not compensated, could produce a rise in costs to the point of arresting those increases in the real level of living that have up until now constituted industrialization's major contribution to modern civilization.

Compared with the nineteenth century, this century has seen a movement away from industrial location right on mineral deposits. The possibility of using substitute materials has vastly increased. In locating a steel-making plant, the fact that either pig iron or scrap can form the main charge into the open hearth or other steel furnace is of prime importance. Even more important has been the possibility of substitution in energy supplies, for many processes can meet their energy requirements from a variety of sources. Less and less energy is employed as a crude fuel, either on the site of exploitation or at a point to which the primary energy source can be brought economically. The primary-energy sources are increasingly used indirectly, after being converted into secondary-energy forms (refined-oil products, purified gases, electricity), which may be either more convenient or cheaper to transport or use. Cost is becoming the main consideration in what energy is used: electric-generation plants, cement kilns, steel mills, and many other industries are increasingly set up to switch swiftly from one source to another, in line with small changes in price. This is especially common when the main demand is for heat, as in metal smelting, in many food processes, and in many industrial heat treatments; newly industrializing regions tend to depend relatively more upon oil, gas, and hydroelectricity than the older industrial regions that leaned mostly on coal. Another major demand is energy for motive power, either to drive machinery—in which case electricity is about the only form now used—or to move materials and products—in which case refined oil is preferred except in cases where electrified trucks or conveyor belts can be used. Another demand for energy is that required for chemical and electrolytic processing; oil and gas tend to be preferred in chemical processing, as they are also the favored raw materials. No large-scale economic substitution is yet possible for coking coal in blast furnaces, and little is possible where transport is based on the internal-combustion engine, but such areas are much smaller than the larger areas of energy demand where substitution is the norm.

The pull of materials will depend on the number of materials involved and their relative importance. In general, as the number of materials used increases, the influence of any one will decline, unless it is one that loses much weight. The electronic and fine-chemicals industries use numerous materials, but none is significantly weight losing or perishable, and most are required in relatively small quantities, so in such industries materials exert little, if any, influence on the location decision.

The connecting link that mainly determines whether or not materials attraction is an important factor in industrial location lies in the transport characteristics (availability, cost, quality of service). Material-supply considerations tend to play a greater place in location decisions during times and in places when transport facilities are limited. In mature urban-industrial regions—furnished with a transport complex featuring both bulk carriers and package-goods carriers in variety and abundance—only a one-fourth or less of manufacturing (that directly concerned with reducing bulk, waste content, and perishability in agricultural and extractive materials) need be seriously concerned with material-supply considerations as the primary locational factor. In the other three-fourths or more of manufacturing, costs of materials procurement are usually much smaller than those of procuring labor and other factors of production.

The Labor Influence on Industrial Activity

Labor is required in all manufacturing, even automated and continuous-flow types, but its importance in influencing location decisions varies widely. It has already been indicated that, where transport costs exert a significant influence, they afford some sort of natural protection to several kinds of industry: (1) the industries for processing or refining locally produced raw materials that lose much weight in the operation, and (2) industries for manufacturing (often with simple processes) those commodities for the local market that gain weight or bulk in the operation. Such industries become more advantageous if they require, in addition, limited capital and heavy labor outlay, since in many newly industrializing regions, capital is scarce and labor is relatively abundant.

Cheap labor is so important that, even where transport costs exert little influence, it may be advantageous for underdeveloped regions to establish highly labor-intensive industries. Where products can be produced by differing combinations—combining capital and labor in varying proportions—some regions may also be in a good competitive position to establish industries using labor-intensive techniques for the production of commodities produced elsewhere by capital-intensive methods.

In most countries with a mature industrial sector, workers' wages form from 35 to 45 per cent of the total factor cost of manufacturing. Usually, labor costs are low in the industries already discussed under materials orientation: flour and meal, sugar refining, meat packing, petroleum refining, basic chemicals, pulp mills, primary metals, and many others. The labor input is usually relatively high in the textile industries, the clothing and shoe industries, and some metal fabricating industries. Establishments in the latter industries are often relatively small and tend to employ a high proportion of women. In branches of clothing and shoes manufacturing where fashion is important, the location may be forced to stay in centers of relatively high wages, while the branches turning out ready-to-wear clothes and ordinary-quality shoes will migrate out to cheaper labor. Luxury goods of other kinds may not be capable of mass-production methods (e.g., jewelry, fine sports equipment). Products that still require manual skill, such as the old craftsmen standards, or which are ordered in small batches for single customers also have a high labor component. New England, the Sheffield area, Berlin, Leningrad, and Tokyo are examples of industrial districts with high proportions of labor-intensive manufacturing.

Even when not the dominant locational factor, all industrial enterprises must be aware of areal differences in labor costs, labor supply, and specific skills availability. Labor costs are sometimes confused with the wage rate. In fact, a low wage rate does not necessarily result in a low labor cost, or a high wage rate in a high labor cost, since the productivity of the worker also has to be taken into account. In underdeveloped countries and regions, cheap and abundant labor usually refers only to the unskilled kind, and technical personnel and skilled labor are usually scarce and comparatively dear in relation to their productivity. Skill-oriented manufacturing is not among the industrial branches in which underdeveloped countries are in a favorable position to develop.

The impediments to labor mobility are usually much less serious in advanced than in underdeveloped areas, but everywhere labor is relatively immobile in the short run. This is less true in local mobility, which may reach out from 20 to 50 or more miles, depending upon the kind of transport network. Interregional mobility, which requires the uprooting of homes and severance from local social connections as well as job changes, is normally a slow change. Large-scale, interregional migrations do not usually occur unless there is some social, economic, or political upheaval, and such major movements are restricted to the short term.

Labor mobility between economic activities, including that between subsectors in industry, is also an important feature of an industrial society. Ideally, stagnant and dying industries might release labor that would be absorbed by new growth industries, but there is a great deal of friction in this kind of adjustment. Not only differences in wages but differences in job prestige and fringe benefits hinder rapid movement. Coal miners, textile workers, and many other workers in industries that are declining in employment opportunities are noted for resistance to job change.

A firm will normally wish to find an adequate pool of the kinds of labor it requires already existing in a prospective location. By locating in an area already provided with a suitable labor pool, the employer also finds additional external economies in the economic overhead (transport, communication, power, research) and social overhead (education, health, general welfare) areas that save both capital and operating expenses. Many industries locating in an entirely undeveloped area have found greater expense for such overhead facilities than for their directly productive facilities. Consequently, there is a tendency for new firms in an industry to locate in older areas—unless they have a need for market orientation greater than cheaper factor costs—which have developed complementary and supplementary goods and services.

Labor-supply considerations involve not only the physical presence of labor, but age and sex structure, general education and technical training, level of specific industrial capability, and general attitudes toward management, increased productivity, and flexibility. Thus, an area with industries employing a high proportion of males may be a favorable place to establish an industry needing mainly women workers. In older industrial areas, the general atmosphere for industrial work is good, and workers can quickly understand and operate new machines and adopt new processes. The situation is greatly different, however, in the underdeveloped areas where there is a very limited supply of skilled factory labor. Factory work calls for a different kind of expertness than the instinct for workmanship (expertness, adroitness, and care in the use of materials) shown by many artisans in such societies. It requires more consistent regular exertion, endurance, repetitive work, submission to factory discipline, use of machinery rather than hand tools, and reliance on teamwork; in short, it demands the exercise of skill under controlled conditions. Transition from agrarian to industrial employment brings an impressive array of social, psychological, and economic problems; and while the development of a supply of skilled industrial labor is interwoven with society-wide problems, it can at the same time be identified as a special problem. There is a gradation of skills extending from the semiskilled to skilled labor, to foremen and supervisors to management technicians, which can be distinguished in terms of length, type, and costs of education and training. Alleviating the shortage of skilled labor may be less difficult in individual cases than easing the shortage of supervisors and foremen, since the length of training is shorter and training costs are lower, but the former is a considerably larger problem in terms of total magnitude.

Some underdeveloped regions have new industrial plants with more automation than plants in the older industrial regions. The explanation lies in the fact that the supply of skilled labor and foremen is so short that labor-saving techniques are economic, especially in countries that are establishing rather high minimum wages and legally compelling the firm to provide housing and other expensive amenities. Legal restrictions on the use of labor, the hours of work, the standards of safety and work pace, the minimum age for employment, and other legal requirements greatly affect labor supply, as do labor union activities (e.g., closed shop, rigid apprenticeship system).

The need for special skills is a factor of importance in influencing the location of much industry. Some industries still call for a high degree of manual skill, and such processes often tend to concentrate at the point where the industry first grew up. Wherever individuality still counts and the product of an individual's specialized skill and taste still commands a market, centers of special labor skills remain. But the range of such products is declining in the age of automated parts making, subassembling, and final assembling, and the influence of special manual skills in new location decisions is similarly declining. All labor-oriented industries have an incentive to reduce their dependence on labor by developing and increasing mechanization, greater labor specialization on a routine-repetitive basis, closer supervision, and in other ways, but this incentive is particularly strong for firms oriented to special labor skills. Less and less of modern manufacturing output is dependent on craftsmen's ability, as methods of production are perfected that can substitute the machine for the worker's skill.

Regional advantages in labor costs, labor supply, and special labor skills are usually short run. In the long term, most variations are modified, removed, or compensated by migration of people and skills, by the development of new technology, by changing attitudes, etc. Relative to other considerations, labor considerations are becoming of less importance with increasing mechanization and automation. Labor does have some adaptability, compared with a fully automated plant, and this is likely to retain it some influence as a locating factor where flexibility is needed. But the label "highly skilled" is likely to be increasingly narrowed to a maintenance-engineer type of skill, and most industrial labor will be semiskilled.

Capital-Availability Influences

Capital requirements also affect the location of industry and the kind and costs of processing and fabricating at various locations. The availability of capital varies regionally—more important, internationally—and categories of capital have varying degrees of mobility. Regional differences in the cost of capital are not necessarily of the same order or even in the same direction as variations in the price of labor. Skillful management uses the cheaper factor in any area to offset the disadvantage imposed by the dearer factor.

Two kinds of capital may be distinguished: capital goods or facilities on the one hand, and money capital on the other. The two are closely connected, for the ultimate objective of money capital is to procure equipment, working stocks, plant and land; loans negotiated in money terms are often in fact provided in the form of equipment or other material goods. But there is a significant difference between the two. Capital equipment in place is relatively immobile, and this is especially true of buildings and heavy, fixed equipment. Its value lies in its output or as second-hand facilities or scrap. This is a major reason for areal inertia: heavy investment in fixed capital is not willingly written off until its useful term of life has been served. Another reason is that old capital is nearly costless, having been amortized long ago—even if not as economical in terms of operating costs as new equipment, it is worth maintaining on a standby basis for use when the more efficient new facilities are fully in use.

By contrast, money capital is much more mobile, especially within a country and within an industrial subsector. Other things being equal, the quantity available for any particular use depends on the price offered (assumptions include security of the investment and certainty of returns). In advanced economies, "risk capital" is usually quite readily available for the promotion of new enterprises or the development of promising new internal areas, as investors feel secure and thus risk capital is quite mobile. In underdeveloped economies, risk capital may be available in certain areas—e.g., grain or land speculation, investment in old established industries, or to organizers in the same primary loyalty units—but it is very rare elsewhere. Money capital is not so mobile across national boundaries, for the risks are usually greater. Much depends on the type of economic system, the medium- and long-run prospects, and the governmental stability in the country of projected investment. In the non-Communist regions of the world, usually any move that improves the prospects for industrial development in a country or region will result in increased investment from foreign sources, especially in areas that complement production in the investing country or where established export markets are threatened by increased protection or other barriers. Ofttimes the amount of capital involved in international movements is important all out of proportion to its money value, as it moves in a package deal with catalyst types of enterprise, technical and marketing skill, and other factors of production that would not be available otherwise.

International migration of capital—like international migration of other factors of production—is increasingly circumscribed by political controls. Popular and governmental attitudes toward private capital is generally unfavorable in underdeveloped areas. Increases in private foreign investment are often from reinvested profits rather than from new investment. In the foreseeable future, more and more international capital flow seems likely to be governmental loans and grants. While useful, this type of investment is not guided by consistent economic reasoning—as is most private capital movement—and is more likely to be poorly invested or wasted because of primary motivation directed toward political or social change.

Technology establishes a set of alternative combinations of capital and labor that must then, among other things, be weighted by the relative factor prices before the proper choice of technology can be made. In a long view, manufacturing has evolved through the following phases: household manufactures, village handicrafts, town artisan's workshops, primitive factories, integrated assembly lines, continuous-flow processes, and the automated factory. This sequence reflects a rising ratio of captial inputs to labor inputs and assumes an increasingly complex organization of the productive process. While household manufactures, village handicrafts, and town artisan's workshops are of great significance in underdeveloped regions today, it is impossible to rely on these comparatively inefficient methods of processing and fabricating for rapid economic growth, although some can be transformed by increasing their technical efficiency, scale of production, and interdependence with larger factories through subcontracting. On the other hand, the tremendous amounts of capital required for automatic factories (from $100,000 to $1,000,000 per worker—at least 100 times that needed per worker in primitive factories), the inflexibility of operations, and the obstacles to the transfer from one cultural setting to another of such an intricate and mature technology and production organization would seem to argue against any widespread immediate automation in most parts of the world.

Most widespread factory industry can be divided into continuous-flow processes and mechanical processes. The former includes the modern methods applicable to heavy chemicals, paper, sugar, liquid fuels, cement, fertilizers, beer, electric power, and many other manufactures. In such industries, the differentials in productivity between the modern continuous-flow process and the alternatives of production by a batch process, or by hand, are so substantial that the modern methods are clearly to be preferred. The capital requirements per worker are high for these modern processes, and there is little possibility of tampering with the production flow proper with a view to substituting labor for capital. There are, however, considerable opportunities for employing labor-intensive methods in various auxiliary operations in internal transport, materials handling, packaging, and administration. In India, the capital per worker employed in modern continuous-flow industry will be only one-third to one-half that in the United States.

In industries where mechanical processes dominate, there are greater prospects for substitution of labor for capital without loss in efficiency. Metal working, textiles, furniture, transport, and construction are examples. Again, the auxiliary operations within these plants show the most promise for employment administration and clerical work, materials handling, inspection, repair, and shipping. But, on the production line proper as well, there are opportunities for expanded labor utilization (e.g., multipurpose tools instead of specialized machine tools, slower speeds). Again, Indian factories in these areas often have only 10 to 20 per cent as much capital per worker employed as the U.S. equivalents.

Since industrial facilities have a life usually measured in decades, it is important that they be chosen not just on the basis of factor proportions now existing, but with an eye to the capital-labor combination to be expected a decade or more hence, and emphasis should be placed on flexibility. Much capital is wasted or poorly used because too rigid a facility is set up at the beginning.

Management-Availability Influences

The efficient application of capital, labor, and other factors of production in a modern productive enterprise depends on the general level of business organization and management in the region concerned. A complex modern industrial economy demands an adequate supply of men with skills and experience in management of risk and uncertainty (board of directors, top managers, principal shareholders), in planning and innovation (research, engineering, marketing), in coordination, administration, and control (comptroller, cost and quality control, work study, production planning, personnel and industrial relations), and in routine supervision (supervisors and foremen). The high-level management in large industries—who must be capable of policy formation and planning, the setting of objectives and standards, and interpreting a variety of data from all the downsloping levels of the bureaucracy—is probably the shortest factor of production in modern industrial society. Theoretically, such men can effectively direct four major management areas: planning or initiation, organization, motivation (the question of inducements to work), and control (which provides the data from which a further round of planning can begin).

Established industrial districts usually possess a good supply of men in the managerial class and men receiving the necessary training and experience in the art of management. This plays a part in location decisions, although managerial ability is usually fairly mobile, especially within national boundaries, and an area with good prospects can usually attract men of ability. But imported managerial and executive personnel are not always enough. Local participation in management may be immediately necessary (especially in routine supervision and in personnel and industrial relations), and in the long run essential. In an advanced economy, minor executive posts can usually be filled with only a short period of training of available local talent.

However, neither mobility nor relatively quickly developed local ability are characteristics in less-developed regions. There one of the greatest obstacles to industrial development is the general lack of trained and experienced men of high executive and managerial talents. Such an obstacle cannot be quickly removed, for many managerial types require not only formal education but practical experience or they can do much harm to an enterprise. The mobility of managerial and enterprise abilities across international boundaries is as difficult as the movement of capital. The rates offered must be competitive, and that often includes attractions and amenities usually described as non-economic. Often, foreign management is regarded with suspicion, distrust, and dislike—hostile attitudes that detract any large flow even if the financial rewards are adequate.

In the case of the small-scale firms that dominate the industrial picture in underdeveloped regions, the enterpriser must be assessed in more personal and less functional terms than in developed regions, although he may be carrying out all the theoretical functions noted earlier. Often, he must depend on his personal ability rather than subordinates. Improvement in the quantity and quality of enterprisers in small firms is extremely difficult to effect, more so than alleviation of the shortage of management skills in the large-scale firm, since the latter shortage can be tackled by direct and large-scale measures (e.g., training abroad, importing foreign personnel). Yet the small establishments are important for their own sake and because they may act as a seedbed for enterpriser talent (if not for technical management skills) for medium- and large-scale firms in the future.

The average enterpriser is usually a hardworking, harassed individual, operating under many personal, firm, and societal handicaps, but still getting things done. He may not be efficient in an ideal sense, may not have adequate knowledge, may even be headed in the wrong direction, but he is an active, aggressive element in an otherwise placid community or industry or firm. Quite often, his value may be just as great to society if he fails (e.g., sometimes he tries to force change when the timing is wrong, but he was right in a medium-view rather than a short-view context).

The need for first-class organizational ability is even greater where resources are scarce than where they are abundant, for there skill, ingenuity, and innovation must offset the lack of a good resource base. Poor management puts a region with material deficiencies into an impossible position commercially. The essence of good management is to capitalize on favorable natural, human, and cultural resources, and to offset adverse environmental and human resistances.

Government Influences

The policies and measures that governments can adopt in order to promote industrialization range from the efficient performance of primary functions, through various measures that are indirect in the sense that they act by encouraging, guiding, or controlling the private sector, to central direction and participation in the management of industry. Governmental action affecting the location and efficiency of industry is not confined to totalitarian societies, but is prevalent in all economies today, although the methods can be more direct in totalitarian states than democracies. Intervention by governments in the location of manufacturing activity may be incidental or deliberate, encouraging or inhibiting, partially influential or wholly causal.

Maintenance of law, order, and justice; national defense; roads and communications; health and education services—these and others are primary functions of government. They affect industry indirectly, usually favorably, for the most part, in terms of creating external economies, but sometimes adversely by lack of needed information or lack of planning in the areas mentioned.

Government has the critical problem of reconciling credit needs and maintaining reasonable price stability in the economy. If easy credit leads to inflation, this may adversely affect development by creating social tension, reducing the incentives to save, and resulting in the misdirection of resources. A poor monetary framework is most characteristic of underdeveloped economies trying short cuts to an accelerated rate of economic growth.

Industrialization requires changes in social institutions, laws, and customs that profoundly influence the functioning of the economic system. The task of creating new institutions, passing new laws, and giving authority to new customs and traditions devolves upon the government more than upon any other institution.

The wide range of measures and policies involved begins with the reform of taxation, inheritance, and tenancy laws, and extends to the introduction of new laws relating to factory operation (hours of work, minimum wages, safety and health requirements, minimum ages of working force, etc.), organization of companies, and creation of special institutions to insure better marketing conditions and to encourage new enterprise, research, and innovation.

Government influences in the marketing area involve the introduction of industrial standards, the setting-up of government-sponsored selling organizations, and government efforts to expand international trade (negotiating new trade and financial agreements, setting-up state-trading corporations, etc.).

Governments also encourage invention and induce enterprisers to venture into new fields by a variety of measures, including geological and other earth-materials surveys, industrial-research coordination, patent acts, regulation of monopoly, creating industrial development corporations, and many others.

Apart from providing a general economic framework conducive to industrialization, governments may adopt a series of specific measures designed to promote industrial development by means of protection and incentives. Quite often, the only substantial market for manufactured goods is that served by imports, and this is tapped or monopolized by protective tariffs or by quota systems. Sometimes the new industry eventually improves its competitive position to the point where it can progress on its own, but the world is full of industrial enterprises that have remained infants for decades, even a century, without improving their cost advantage.

Tax concessions for encouraging new enterprises have usually taken the form of total exemption from taxes and duties for a certain period, or of an income tax concession (higher rates of depreciation allowed, lower rates of tax on reinvested profits, carryover of business losses for a period of years, etc.). Only occasionally is this tied in with location specification.

Financial and credit assistance to industry by governments involves both loans and subsidies. Government loans are usually for a longer duration and at an artificially low interest rate, compared with the commercial alternative. Subsidies are less common, although disguised subsidization is often very important (e.g., government plant being sold for a fraction of actual cost, subsidized rents in industrial estates, subsidized services aimed at increasing the attractiveness of selected areas).

Government can also indirectly affect industrial activity and location by its unemployment policies, by its control of land use (zoning), and by its system of taxation. Taxes have much less influence on industrial location than often assumed. They generally form a small fraction of total costs, and often industry gets better services for its taxes than it could possibly get by any purchase from the private sector. In the industries where taxes are a majority of manufacturing costs—cigarettes, liquors, and similar luxuries—they tend to be the same everywhere in the country and therefore are not likely to affect industrial location (where bootlegging occurs, there may be an effect). But excessive taxation may have an indirect effect by holding down the rate of consumption so that the market will not support the scale and economy needed for efficient production methods. Finally, if government revenue is mainly spent in new industry areas, the older industry areas may suffer by general stagnation accelerated by selective governmental purchases.

Trends

Increasingly, governmental and corporate decisions on industrial location are becoming relatively more important than materials-oriented and labor-oriented location. The net result is a larger proportion of new-plant locations either market oriented or in intermediate locations serving a number of major market areas.

Although most crude and raw materials are not available to industry at equal cost irrespective of location, sites away from the manufacturing of parts and components are not so natural-resources bound. The increasing upgrading of crude materials at or near the place of origin, increasing transportability, and the increasing efficiency in use in manufacturing plants are all reducing the cost of materials fraction of the total costs of production.

Labor considerations are also becoming of less importance, relative to other factors-of-production considerations, as a result of increasing plant efficiency via mechanization, automation, and other rationalization. The upgrading of national standards of general and technical education, coupled with other social welfare improvements, is resulting in easier labor mobility, which decreases that factor's role in industrial location or in determining "labor" productivity.

Within countries—even within ideological blocs to a certain extent—most capital is increasingly mobile, so its direct influence on industrial location and on industrial efficiency is less than in the past. Government loans or other institutional credit makes for capital that is much less placebound than in the old days of individual enterprise. The main effect is in the international diffusion of cheap capital, and even here political loans are making for more equality.

The influence of business management on location has mainly affected only the precise points of production within generally suitable regions. The main influence is probably in more heavily weighting short-run site advantages than would happen otherwise. "Location science" has not become a major management tool skill.

Next to the increasing importance of market as an industrial location factor, government has probably increased its role the most among the factors of production. Some of this is direct and visible, but most influence is subtle, by setting up and implementing national standards paid for by differential taxation that falls the heaviest on the older industrial districts that would be in the best situation to progress without governmental transfusions. Even such industrial diffusion outside the traditional manufacturing belts and older nodes is likely to be mainly limited to new market possibilities and is not likely to significantly reduce the absolute predominance of the older regions except in very special cases.

PERSPECTIVE

Industrialization in the broadest sense means an absolute and relative growth in the importance of manufacturing and closely related activities (especially activities involved in the building and operation of a modern economic infrastructure, or economic and social overhead capital). This growth may be measured in terms of employment; in the long-run, the employment structure of most nations will be the opposite of what it was in the agrarian level of civilization (i.e., 80 per cent or more in industry and services instead of 80 per cent or more in agriculture and related activities). The same long-term tendency can be expected in national-product shifts.

Industrialization may be viewed as both a cause and a result of economic development. Economic development requires and implies higher productivity per capita. As productivity increases and incomes rise, the consumption pattern gradually changes: the demand for manufactured consumer goods rises more rapidly than the demand for agricultural and related organic materials. Increased productivity in the industrial sector as well as closely associated subsectors in the agricultural and services sectors will call for an increased demand for manufactured producer goods. The modernization process, by increasing productive ability at the same time as it enlarges markets, virtually assures the rise of industries. However, this increase in the relative importance of industries —as seen in the employment structure, especially—need not necessarily characterize economic development through all its stages.

In many ways, industrialization depends on higher productivity in certain areas of agriculture (e.g., export crops) and of services (the areas concerned with the geography of circulation). It is also true that there is a bootstrap element in the process of industrialization. Since the net value of output per worker in industry tends to be higher than in agriculture (especially in overpopulated countries), any successful transfer of labor from agriculture to industry soon contributes to higher productivity, so that a certain cumulative element is introduced into the process that can be utilized by good developmental planning. In industry, the scope for internal and external economies is greater than in other sectors (especially compared to agriculture). As industrialization proceeds, economies of scale and interindustrial linkages (vertical, horizontal, diagonal, areal complex) become more pronounced, and here again good development planning can take advantage of such developments. Industrialization is associated with the development of scientific and engineering research, training of labor and management, and with other attributes of a modern society that, in turn, are beneficial to the growth of productivity in agriculture, distribution, and other related areas of the economy. There is also a valid infant-industry argument: the productivity basis for industrialization may latently be there, but obscured by a late beginning, with its young industries appearing inefficient because they have to face the competition of firmly established competitors enjoying internal and external economies of scale and historical experience. The growth of such immature industries and the acquisition of experience may then create the initially lacking productivity, but such evolution is not preordained.

That such bootstrap aspects exist in the process of industrialization in no way alters the fact that there must also be a growth of productivity in the other sectors of the economy. The feedback effects in industrialization proper are helpful in making the process cumulative, but they do not make it possible to modernize the entire economy and society by themselves. The need for healthy foreign trade is a case in point: an export crop or export mineral not only provides foreign exchange, but raises some incomes and creates an actual demand for imports of both consumer and producer goods. That domestic market has usually been subsequently transferred to domestic industries, in the shelter of protectionist measures, if necessary. Thus, industrialization profits by the benefit of pre-existing markets. Equally important, by encouraging a country to specialize in the things in which it is relatively more efficient, foreign trade helps it to lay the productivity basis for a subsequent sound cumulative industrialization.

SUGGESTED READINGS

Adams, Walter. *The Structure of American Industry*. New York: Macmillan, 1954. Pp. 590.

Alderfer, E. B., and Michl, H. E. *Economics of American Industry*. New York: McGraw-Hill, 1957. Pp. 710.

Alexandersson, Gunnar. *The Industrial Structure of American Cities*. University of Nebraska Press, 1956. Pp. 134.

Doane, Robert R. *World Balance Sheet*. New York: Harper & Row, 1957. Pp. 260.

Estall, R. C., and Buchanan, R. Ogilvie. *Industrial Activity and Economic Geography*. London: Hutchinson, 1961. Pp. 232.

Miller, E. Willard. *A Geography of Manufacturing*. Englewood Cliffs, N.J.: Prentice-Hall, 1962. Pp. 490.

United Nations. *Economic Bulletin for Asia and the Far East*, Vol. IX, No. 3 (December 1958 issue on industrialization). Pp. 95.

United Nations, Department of Economic and Social Affairs. *Patterns of Industrial Growth, 1938–1958*. New York: United Nations, 1960. Pp. 471.

United States Government Printing Office. A Report to the President by The President's Materials Policy Commission, June 1952. *Resources for Freedom*. Five volumes.

Woytinsky, W. S., and Woytinsky, E. S. *World Population and Production: Trends and Outlook*. New York: Twentieth Century Fund, 1953. Pp. 1,268.

Zimmermann, Erich W. *World Resources and Industries*. New York: Harper & Row, 1951. Pp. 832.

13

Energy Resources

About a quarter of mankind's 32 billion tons of annual earth materials consumption consists of energy resources, mainly 5 billion tons of fossil fuels (coal-lignite, crude petroleum, natural gas, and some minor sources) that contribute over 87 per cent of the total inanimate energy consumption. Mankind still consumes some 3.2 billion tons of wood and agricultural wastes—the total amounting to some 13 per cent of the total when reduced to coal-equivalent basis. This energy costs about 5 per cent of mankind's income, somewhat over half for the crude fuel and energy, and nearly half for the refining into processed energies that are consumed.

At present, the annual increase in world energy consumption is about 5 per cent, twice the average during the past century. In terms of value, the increase rate is even higher, as the tendency is toward greater relative consumption of the more expensive sources of energy, and toward ever more complicated processing into secondary forms of energy before actual use. This rate of increase will probably accelerate, as an increasing share of mankind urban-industrializes, as ever leaner earth materials are utilized, and as ever more complicated fabricating becomes the norm.

The rate of increase in commercial energy production is higher in the underdeveloped (low-income) realm than in the urban-industrial (high-income) realm. This partly reflects the tendency for early industrialization and related primary and tertiary developments to be especially high energy using, but it also reflects energy surpluses that are exported to the deficit wealthy countries. The low-income realm produces over 22 per cent of the production of commercial (fossil fuel and hydro) energy, but consumes only 16 per cent. The difference represents 5 per cent of the energy consumption of the high-income realm, or nearly 45 per cent of the commercial energy production of the low-income realm. About half of this international trade is accounted for by Western European deficits (20 per cent of world consumption, $11\frac{1}{2}$ per cent of world production) and Middle Eastern surpluses ($10\frac{1}{2}$ per cent of world production, 1 per cent of world consumption), with most of the remainder accounted for by Latin American surpluses (over 7 per cent of world production; less than 2 per cent of world consumption), which move to North America and Western Europe. Eastern Europe's surpluses (modest in world perspective) mainly move to Western Europe. Japan's consumption is double its production and is made up by Middle Eastern and North American supplies for the most part (Eastern Europe and Oceania are minor sources).

The greatest movement is petroleum. The Middle East produces twelve times its needs,

TABLE 13-1

World: Production and Composition of Commercial Fuel and Energy, by Great-Region and Economic-Type of Society, 1962–1964 Average-Annual
(in billions of metric tons coal-equivalent)

	Total Production (billion metric tons coal-equivalent = 100.0 per cent)	Coal-Lignite	Crude Petroleum	Natural Gas	Hydro-electricity
North America	1.60	26.3%	34.3%	37.1%	2.3%
Western Europe	0.57	86.6	3.9	4.0	5.5
Eastern Europe (including the U.S.S.R.)	1.16	61.8	25.1	12.0	1.1
Oceania	0.04	94.3	–	–	5.7
Latin America	0.35	2.6	87.9	8.0	1.5
Sub-Saharan Africa	0.06	84.6	12.7	–	2.7
Middle East (including North Africa)	0.51	1.0	97.5	1.4	0.1
Non-Communist Far East	0.20	70.0	20.3	4.1	5.6
Communist Far East	0.41	97.2	2.1	–	0.7
World	4.90	46.2	35.3	16.4	2.1
High-income countries	3.80	45.0	32.7	20.0	2.3
Low-income countries	1.10	50.2	44.5	3.7	1.6
	(per cent of 4.90 billion metric tons coal-equivalent)	(per cent of 2.26 billion metric tons coal-equivalent)	(per cent of 1.73 billion metric tons coal-equivalent)	(per cent of 0.80 billion metric tons coal-equivalent)	(per cent of 0.11 billion metric tons coal-equivalent)
North America	32.8	18.7	31.9	74.4	35.1
Western Europe	11.6	21.8	1.3	2.8	29.8
Eastern Europe (including the U.S.S.R.)	23.7	31.7	16.9	17.4	12.5
Oceania	0.7	1.5	–	–	1.9
Latin America	7.3	0.4	18.0	3.5	5.2
Sub-Saharan Africa	1.1	2.1	0.4	–	1.5
Middle East (including North Africa)	10.4	0.2	28.7	0.9	0.5
Non-Communist Far East	4.1	6.1	2.3	1.0	10.6
Communist Far East	8.3	17.5	0.5	–	2.9
World	100.0	100.0	100.0	100.0	100.0
High-income countries	77.7	75.8	72.1	94.9	83.7
Low-income countries	22.3	24.2	27.9	5.1	16.3

SOURCE: Adapted from Statistical Papers Series J, Statistical Office of the United Nations (Department of Economic and Social Affairs).

and Latin America produces over five times its needs, while Western Europe produces only 6 per cent of its requirements. Eastern Europe produces a fifth surplus; all other great-regions are deficit (North America 22 per cent; the others mainly 35 to 65 per cent deficit except Oceania, which is over 99 per cent deficit). Coal movements are important mainly in that the Western European and Japanese needs are for coking coal.

This chapter shows how energy resources may be increased in four broad ways, countering the effect of the factors leading to an ever greater consumption of energy: better methods of recovery of conventional energy sources, the discovery of additional supplies of such conventional sources, more effective uses of available energy, and the exploitation of new sources of energy in the prospective future. In the next generation, the first three ways are inevitably

TABLE 13-2

World: Consumption * and Composition of Commercial Fuel and Energy, by Great-Region and Economic-Type of Society, 1962–1964 Average-Annual
(in billions of metric tons coal-equivalent)

	Total Consumption (billion metric tons coal-equivalent = 100.0 per cent)	Solid Fuels	Liquid Fuels	Natural and Imported Gas	Hydro- and Imported Electricity
North America	1.73	22.8%	40.8%	34.3%	2.1%
Western Europe	0.96	55.9	38.5	2.3	3.3
Eastern Euorpe (including the U.S.S.R.)	1.09	63.8	22.2	12.8	1.2
Oceania	0.05	56.9	39.2	–	3.9
Latin American	0.08	8.0	77.4	9.3	5.3
Sub-Saharan Africa	0.06	73.8	23.0	0.8	2.4
Middle East (including North Africa)	0.05	10.9	76.4	11.8	0.9
Non-Communist Far East	0.34	44.4	31.6	20.9	3.1
Communist Far East	0.41	96.1	3.2	–	0.7
World	4.77	47.2	33.0	17.6	2.2
High-income countries	4.00	42.7	36.1	19.0	2.2
Low-income countries	0.77	71.1	16.4	10.7	1.8
	(per cent of 4.77 billion metric tons coal-equivalent)	(per cent of 2.25 billion metric tons coal-equivalent)	(per cent of 1.57 billion metric tons coal-equivalent)	(per cent of 0.85 billion metric tons coal-equivalent)	(per cent of 0.11 billion metric tons coal-equivalent)
North America	36.3	17.5	45.0	70.7	35.9
Western Europe	20.1	23.7	23.4	2.7	30.6
Eastern Euorpe (including the U.S.S.R.)	22.8	30.7	15.4	16.5	12.6
Oceania	1.1	1.3	1.3	–	2.0
Latin American	1.6	0.3	3.7	0.8	3.9
Sub-Saharan Africa	1.3	2.0	0.9	0.1	1.4
Middle East (including North Africa)	1.1	0.3	2.7	0.8	0.5
Non-Communist Far East	7.1	6.7	6.8	8.4	10.2
Communist Far East	8.6	17.5	0.8	–	2.9
World	100.0	100.0	100.0	100.0	100.0
High-income countries	84.0	76.0	92.0	90.4	86.9
Low-income countries	16.0	24.0	8.0	9.6	13.1

SOURCE: Adapted from Statistical Papers Series J, Statistical Office of the United Nations (Department of Economic and Social Affairs).

* The difference between world fuel and energy production (4.90 billion metric tons coal-equivalent) and world fuel and energy consumption (4.77 billion metric tons coal-equivalent)—0.13 billion metric tons coal-equivalent—is mainly explained by bunker and other storage.

going to be most important, so attention is first concentrated on them. The fourth way, which will be increasingly used by the turn of the century, will be considered toward the end of the chapter.

Fossil fuel reserves are conjectural. Perhaps 8 trillion tons, some 1,500 cubic miles, are "known"—enough hydrocarbon material to fill in the Great Lakes (or the Grand Canyon twice over), but small when compared with the 317 million cubic miles of water in the oceans, or even with the 9,000 cubic miles of water that runs off the land into the seas every year. About 90 per cent of the fossil fuel reserve is coal. It is doubtful if more than a third of this reserve could be technically minded, even if prices were

WORLD: PRODUCTION AND COMPOSITION OF COMMERCIAL FUEL AND ENERGY, BY GREAT-REGION AND ECONOMIC-TYPE OF SOCIETY, 1962-1964 AVERAGE-ANNUAL
(Billion Metric Tons Coal-Equivalent)

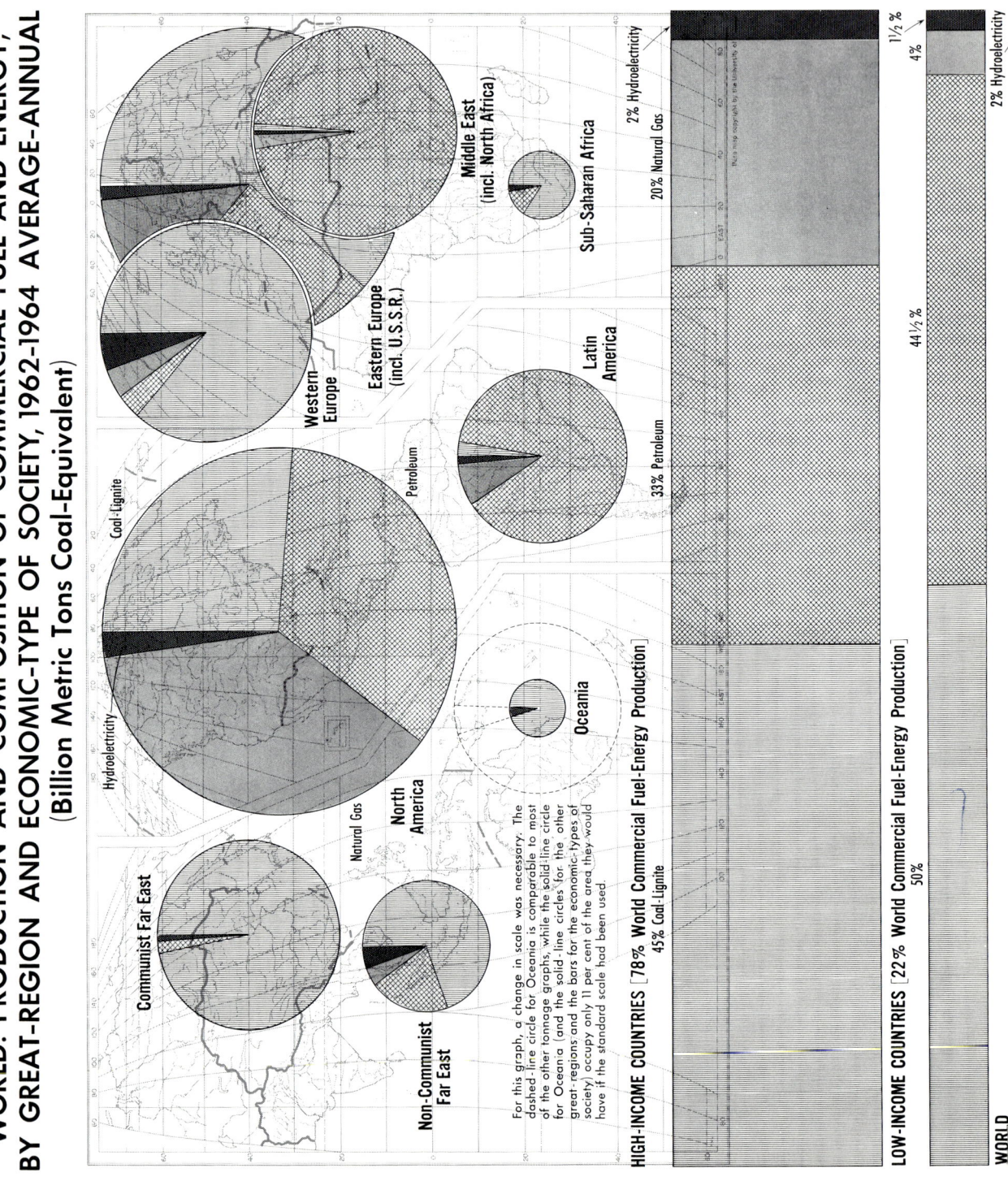

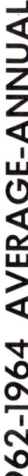

[illegible] REGION AND ECONOMIC-TYPE OF SOCIETY SHA[illegible]S OF WORLD COMMERCIAL FUEL AND ENERGY PRODUCTION AND CONSUMPTION, 1962-1964 AVERAGE-ANNUAL

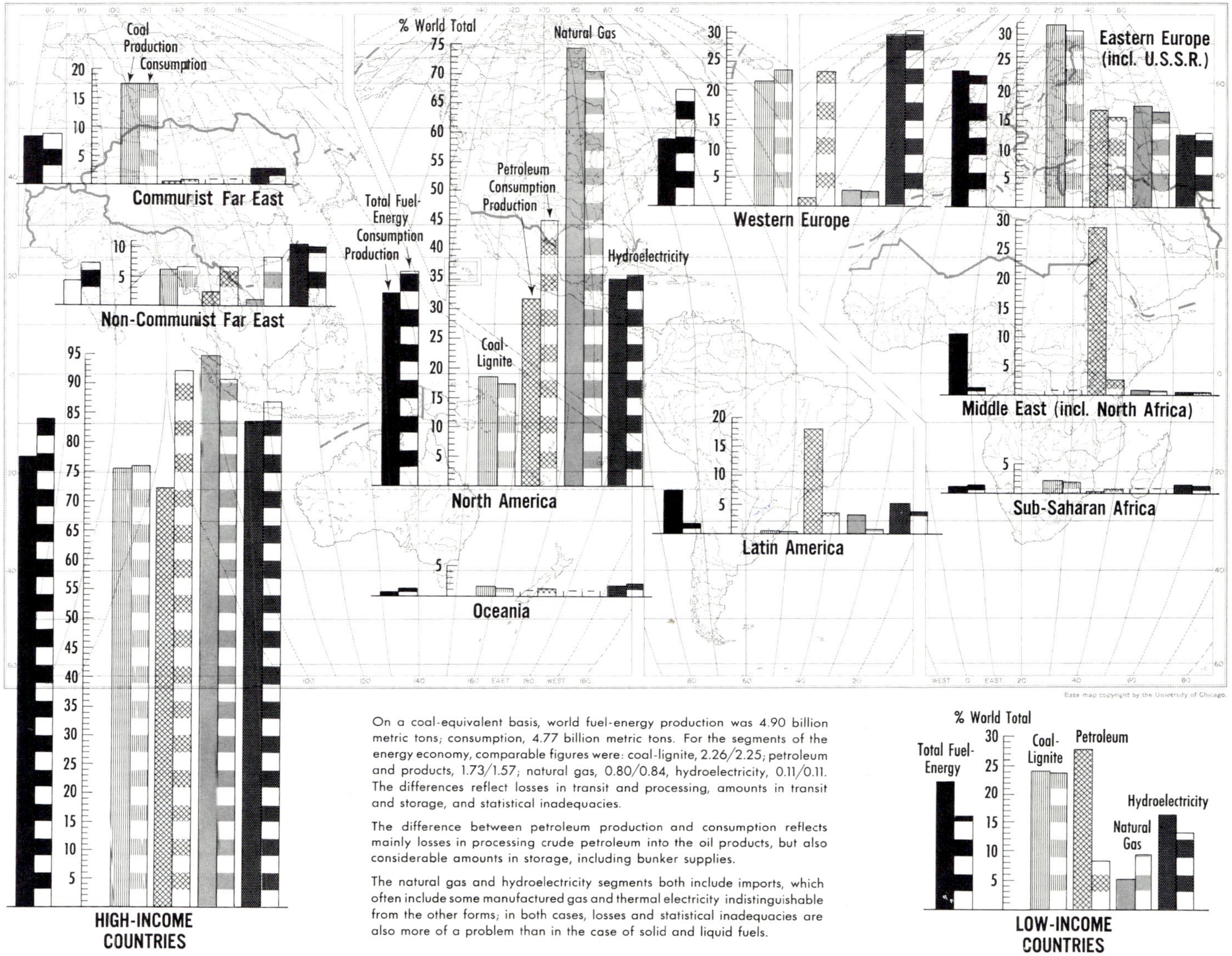

On a coal-equivalent basis, world fuel-energy production was 4.90 billion metric tons; consumption, 4.77 billion metric tons. For the segments of the energy economy, comparable figures were: coal-lignite, 2.26/2.25; petroleum and products, 1.73/1.57; natural gas, 0.80/0.84, hydroelectricity, 0.11/0.11. The differences reflect losses in transit and processing, amounts in transit and storage, and statistical inadequacies.

The difference between petroleum production and consumption reflects mainly losses in processing crude petroleum into the oil products, but also considerable amounts in storage, including bunker supplies.

The natural gas and hydroelectricity segments both include imports, which often include some manufactured gas and thermal electricity indistinguishable from the other forms; in both cases, losses and statistical inadequacies are also more of a problem than in the case of solid and liquid fuels.

favorable—economic reserves may be a tenth or less of the total. Current annual production of all fossil fuels is under 1 cubic mile, or under 1 per cent of the economically available reserve.

COAL

Coal is still the major commercial fuel (in terms of tonnage or caloric production), but is declining in relative importance, although its total production is continually rising and its reserves include over two-thirds of recoverable hydrocarbon energy. Of the major industrial nations, the United States was first to experience drastic absolute as well as relative declines in the use of coal (although the United Kingdom, West Germany, and Belgium are now undergoing the same evolution). Both bituminous coal and anthracite coal are consumed in smaller amounts now than in 1920, and combined they now contribute little more than one-fourth of the U.S. energy economy. Outside the United States, coal still supplies 56 per cent of energy requirements, although in most countries there is a tendency for petroleum and natural gas to increase their relative shares at the expense of coal.

There is a worldwide tendency for coal industries to largely liquidate that part of their markets vulnerable to technological progress and retreat to a market consisting principally of customers with increasing fuel demands for which coal is suited, such as electricity and primary-metallurgy. In the United States, the bituminous coal industry expects consumption in the next generation to increase over 3 per cent annually, with the portion used for electricity generation increasing from the present one-half to two-thirds. Most of the remaining demand will be for coking-coal and fuel for producing cheap process steam.

Reserve Problems

The difficulties of the older coal industries relate mainly to poor geology and low labor efficiency, especially in Western Europe and Japan. However, in the case of the United States, retarded technology and organization and severe competition from other hydrocarbons are the main causes of economic difficulties.

In the earth's crust, carbon is not a common element, being only 0.2 per cent at most. If this were uniformly distributed, industrial civilization as we know it today, with its dependence on concentrated forms of energy, would be impossible. However, a large proportion is found in concentrated deposits of various kinds of hydrocarbons, possibly 90 per cent in the form of coal. Even in terms of estimated technically recoverable potential, coal still accounts for perhaps 70 per cent of available fossil fuel, with petroleum and natural gas accounting for about 15 per cent, and all the others (oil shale, tar sand, etc.) accounting for the final 15 per cent.

Coal resources are distributed unevenly throughout the world, as seen in Table 13–3. About 97 per cent of the resources are in the northern hemisphere, with over three-fourths being in three states: the United States, U.S.S.R., and China. Vast regions have only modest or insignificant resources.

In accessible areas, perhaps half of the coal resources are technically recoverable, but only a small portion economically. For example, the U.S. coal resource is at least 2 trillion tons. However, less than 5 per cent of this amount exists in beds 28 inches or more thick at depths of no more than 1,000 feet—the type of coal resource now being exploited. Another 20 per cent is estimated to lie in beds of such thickness at depths between 1,000 and 2,000 feet. The half of this coal (in thick seams under 2,000 feet thick) that is mineable amounts to less than 10 per cent of our total coal resource.

Considering coal as worth about $4⅔ per "average" ton at the mine, perhaps an eighth of U.S. coal reserves can be mined at or near such costs, another eighth at costs one and a fourth to one and a half times such cost, and another quarter at costs one and a half to four times such cost. The remaining half of U.S. coal resource is not to be considered an economic reserve under foreseeable conditions.

General availability obscures difficulty in obtaining specific grades of coal. The grades of bituminous coal important in the manufacture

TABLE 13-3

Probable World Coal Reserves *

(in per cents)

	Coal Reserves (5 trillion metric tons)	Lignite Reserves (1⅓ trillion metric tons)	Peat Reserves (120 billion metric tons)
North America	43	74	8
Western Europe	9	5	8
Eastern Europe	2	1	25
U.S.S.R.	20	16	59
Oceania	1	1	–
Latin America	–a	–	–
Sub-Saharan Africa	2	1	–
Middle East (including North Africa)	–	–	–
Non-Communist Far East	3	1	–
Communist Far East	19	–	–
High-income countries	78	97	98
Low-income countries	22	3	2

* In seams at least 1.2 feet thick, to a depth of 4,000 feet, according to van Krevelen and Schuyer (Communist claims run much higher for their two regions, but their methods of estimating are more speculative).

a Dash equals under ½ per cent.

of metallurgical coke will amount to only a few hundred million tons until we dig deeper than 1,000 feet, where most of the tenth of our coal that is considered cokable is found. Of our fuel-grade bituminous coal, some 27 billion tons can be produced at something like present costs. Another 21 billion tons of sub-bituminous and lignite coal can be mined economically, but much of it contains too much moisture and ash to be used efficiently as boiler fuel in raw form; however, low-temperature carbonization of such coals yields a char that is often an excellent boiler fuel and a tar that can be converted to motor fuel.

Comparable data are not available for other countries, but a crude extrapolation indicates that perhaps not more than a tenth or so of the world's coal resource is economically available at present. Even postulating substantial changes in technology and economics, it is difficult to imagine more than one-fourth to one-third of the coal resource ever being mined for fuel use.

Production Problems

World bituminous and anthracite coal production is nearly 1.9 billion tons annually, with lignite production adding over 0.9 billion tons (about half that amount in coal-equivalent terms). Production of coal is increasing under 3 per cent annually, and the production of lignite is about stable, so the solid fuels have the lowest rate of increase of any major segment of the world's commercial energy economy. Most of the increased coal production is concentrated in North America and Eastern Europe (including U.S.S.R.), with the Communist Far East another potential source of increase when it resumes rapid economic growth. In Western Europe and in many other coal-producing areas, production is stable, even declining, as other fuel (especially imported petroleum and natural gas) fills most of the increased demand for energy.

The United States and Communist China are the largest producers of coal proper, with the U.S.S.R. having about the same coal equivalent when its lignite production is reduced to that basis (in raw tonnage of coal and lignite, it ranks first). Britain, West Germany, and Poland are in the second rank of producers.

Coal is much more a place-bound fuel than petroleum, with only some 5 per cent of the world's annual production moving across international boundaries, and only half of that is

TABLE 13–4

World: Great-Region and Economic-Type of Society Shares of World Coal, Lignite, and Coke Production, 1962–1964 Average-Annual

(in per cents)

	2,255 Million Metric Tons Coal-Equivalent of Coal and Lignite	1,855 Million Metric Tons of Coal	915 Million Metric Tons of Lignite	280 Million Metric Tons of Metallurgical Coke [1]
North America	18.7	22.6	0.6	19.3
Western Europe	21.8	24.1	14.2	33.9
Eastern Europe (including the U.S.S.R.)	31.7	20.1	81.8	30.0
Oceania	1.5	1.4	2.2	1.1
Latin America	0.4	0.5	–	0.7
Sub-Saharan Africa	2.1	2.5	–	0.7
Middle East (including North Africa)	0.2	0.3	0.2	0.3
Non-Communist Far East	6.1	7.4	0.2	7.2
Communist Far East	17.5	21.1	0.8	6.8
World	100.0	100.0	100.0	100.0
High-income countries	75.8	72.5	93.0	87.5
Low-income countries	24.2	27.5	7.0	12.5

Source: Adapted from United Nations data.

[1] The metallurgical coke is a secondary product manufactured from selected types and blends of bituminous coal, so its raw material is also included in the coal column.

intercontinental traffic. In terms of great-regions, North America is 7 per cent surplus; Eastern Europe and sub-Saharan Africa, 3 per cent each; and Oceania, 14 per cent. More specifically, the surplus coal fields are the United States' central Appalachian (West Virginia) one, Poland's Slask (Silesian) one, Australia's Queensland ones, and South Africa's Natal one. The deficit great-regions in world trade are Western Europe and the non-Communist Far East (8 to 9 per cent), and the Middle East (12 per cent). Japan's imports of coking coal from West Virginia are the largest long-distance traffic.

Coal's diminished rate of growth has been mainly due to loss of markets (especially space heating, railroads, and some industrial uses) to petroleum and natural gas because of lesser convenience and lesser efficiency (due mainly to older coal-using equipment). A second cause of substitution is cost, especially when transportation cost is added to production cost. High cost is of primary importance in Western Europe and Japan, where the average ton of coal costs double the U.S. price, and some marginal mines now being eliminated rapidly have costs three to four times the average U.S. coal mine price.

The high cost of coal is mainly related to the 70 per cent labor cost (compared with 25 per cent in petroleum and 10 per cent in natural gas). The U.S. coal industry's success in dropping its average price per ton by $1.50 is mainly a result of the dropping of the proportion of labor costs from 70 per cent in the mid-1930's to about 50 per cent (some of the most efficient mines have 40 per cent labor cost).

This increasing efficiency has been achieved by increased mechanization both in open pit and shaft mines. About one-fourth of U.S. coal production now comes from stripping operations, where the average mine removes over 40 feet of overburden to reach less than 5 feet of coal (some mines remove 80 to 100 feet of overburden), at an average cost of $4 per ton (some produce coal at less than $3¼ per ton). The larger shovels will strip a cubic yard of over-

The Bucyrus-Erie strip mine shovel operating at the Peabody Coal Company's River King mine about 30 miles east of St. Louis, Missouri, moves 140 cubic yards of earth (about 250 tons) at one bite. The stripping shovel is traveling on the coal seam that it uncovered.

Courtesy of Peabody Coal Co.

burden (1½ tons or so) for 5 cents (of which 3 cents is capital charge, 1 cent labor charge, and the other 1 cent power and all other charges). Most stripped coal is of low grade, with triple the fraction of impurities in underground coal (30 to 35 per cent ash and sulfur content is common), so it must be upgraded in coal preparation plants before moving to the consumer. It is non-coking and mainly ends in electric generating plants and other steam-raising uses.

Now, and probably even more in the future, most coal must come from shaft mines, since little of the total reserves are stripable, even if the limit of overburden that can be economically removed should be tripled. Most U.S. underground coal production [1] is still only semi-mechanized, but about one-fourth is now ac-

[1] Underground mines account for about three-quarters of world coal production, mainly from vertical-shaft mines. United States underground mines account for two-thirds of total coal production, but are mainly horizontal mines.

counted for by the continuous miner (introduced around 1950). A continuous miner can mine up to 8 tons a minute (as much coal as the average underground miner can mine in a day).

Localizing factors are of little significance in the distribution of high-efficiency strip mines. In contrast, a combination of factors has influenced the location of high-efficiency underground mines, especially thickness of coal seam, size of mine, location of major markets, and availability of water transportation. Thickness of seam is increasingly important, for unlike stripping, underground mining costs bear a direct relationship to the vertical dimension of the seam.

The cost of developing a completely mechanized mine is estimated at $6 to $12 a ton of annual output, compared with about $2 a ton for facilities in which hand loading predominate. With stagnant market conditions, there is little incentive to replace capacity. The average new U.S. mine has a life of about thirty years, but the average life of all existing mines will be over fifteen years because capacity has not been maintained in recent years. Probably a fifth of U.S. coal mining capacity should be replaced within the next five years, but that would require over $1 billion (for building 100 million tons of new capacity), which is likely to be forthcoming only if industrial (especially utility) demand increases rapidly.

Gradually, the increased capital requirements of high-efficiency mines are resulting in the elimination of the weakest units. Since 1950, some 2,000 mines have been eliminated, leaving about 7,000 operating bituminous mines, while employment has dropped from 415,000 to 140,000.

In Western Europe and Japan, both geological and organizational difficulties stand in the way of rationalization. Most coal seams are thin, irregular, and deep, so that wholesale mechanization on the U.S. pattern is out of the question. When old seams are worked out, new shafts must be sunk 1,000 feet or more to the coal face (average depth of existing mines is 2,500 feet). The nationalization of coal mining in many countries was dictated less by ideology than by inadequacy of private ownership to supply adequate capital for rationalization and expansion.

Courtesy of Peabody Coal Co.

In the foreground, a 9-cubic-yard coal loading machine loads from the seam into the pit haulage truck, which moves 60 tons to the coal preparation plant where one-third waste is removed. In the background is a Marion 70-cubic-yard stripping machine.

Courtesy of Joy Manufacturing Co.

The 45-foot-high Joy Pushbutton Miner mines coal from under the high wall without removing overburden or sending men underground. Seen here is the boring machine on its way down the launching ramp toward the coal seam, followed by interconnected conveyors stored on the winding roadway of the Helitrack. Crossed cylinders synchronize steering of the two rear crawler trucks of the structure. The entire system is controlled by an operator in a control cab hung under the structure beside the launching platform.

Courtesy of Joy Manufacturing Co.

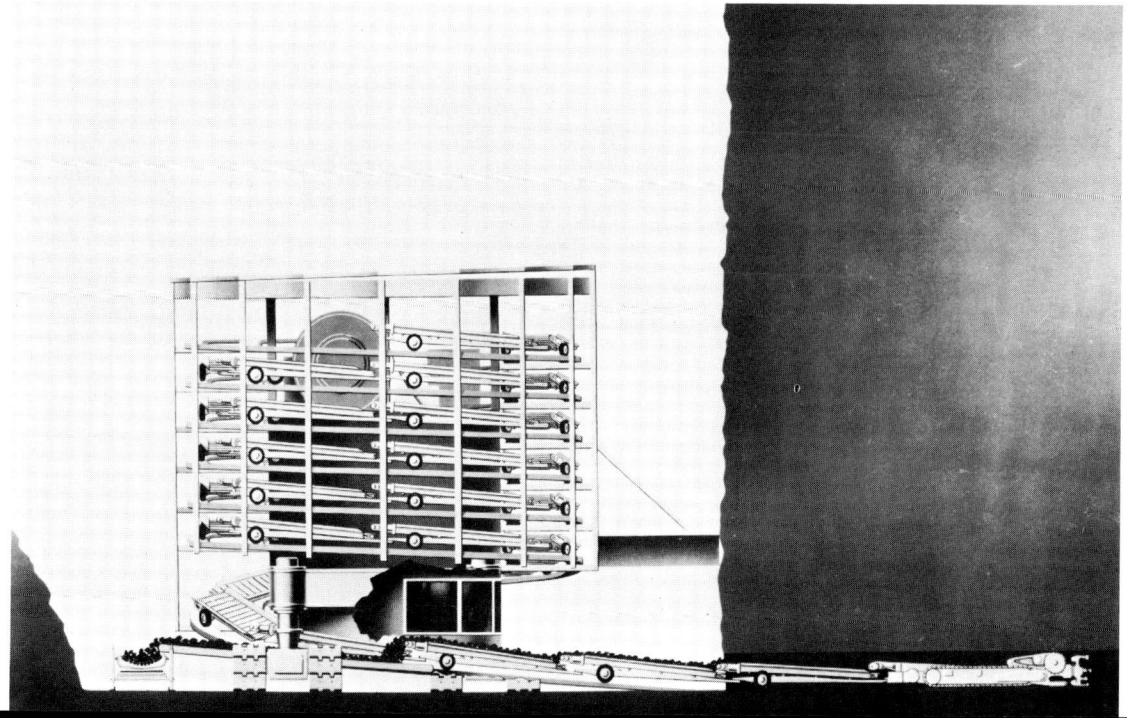

Courtesy of Peabody Coal Co.

A continuous mining machine in operation at a Peabody underground coal mine near Springfield, Illinois.

Coal Conversion

The future demand for coal depends mainly upon changes in petroleum and natural gas supplies, as well as upon technological progress in nuclear electricity.

Gas manufactured in coke ovens and water-gas machines cannot compete with natural gas, and this would be true even if coal were available at the point of use for $2 to $3 per ton. In addition, manufactured gas has only about half the heating value on a cubic foot basis, which makes it much less satisfactory for transmission and distribution. Extensive calculations have indicated that enriched gas manufactured by the Lurgi process, even from relatively low-cost coal, would be in the range of 75 cents to $1 per 1,000 cubic feet. This could not compete with natural gas, which is available at the pipeline to most cities at less than 50 cents per 1,000 cubic feet.

It will be years before oil from coal will replace petroleum in countries whose crude oil production is nearly adequate, although such nations may have coal in abundance. The world's largest oil from coal plant is near Johannesburg, South Africa, and is proving commercially attractive, but has the benefit of unusually favorable circumstances. What made the project attractive was the large low-grade coal deposits particularly adaptable to modern mechanical mining methods. The lack of oil production and the fact that Johannesburg, the largest gasoline consuming area in the country, is some 400 miles from the nearest coastal port are other important factors in the economics of the plant. From a ton of coal, which costs 60 cents to mine (probably the world's cheapest coal), the plant produces a barrel of products with a value of $12. The first step is the gasification of the coal; raw gas costs 7 cents for 1,000 cubic feet, and purified gas costs 12 cents. The rest of the operation is not unlike that of a modern oil refinery. Except in such unusual cases, however, such plants are likely to remain uneconomic where cheap petroleum is readily accessible.

Much more feasible in the short run is expansion of coal chemicals, which are worth several times as much as liquid fuels from the same amount of coal. This trend is occasioned by the inability of coke ovens in many areas to adequately supply coal-tar chemicals.

Coal Transportation

The average ton of coal now costs half as much to transport as to produce. About three-fourths of the world's coal moves by rail, with the movement of individual carloads costing around 3 cents a ton-mile for short distances (100 miles or so) and a third to a half that cost on long hauls. In attempts to cut down on this high transport and handling charges, substitutions of new forms of transport are increasingly being made. Barge-trains (on the Ohio, Illinois, Rhine, Dnieper, and other rivers) can move coal for as little as $\frac{1}{3}$ to $\frac{1}{2}$ cent per ton-mile, nearly as cheaply as the average collier carriage on the open seas, but its availability is limited. Slurry pipelines, mechanized (unit) trains, and long-distance power transmission are all technically feasible, and one of these (or a combination) is likely to be the main remedy in keeping coal a major contender in the battle for the utility market, both against natural gas and residual fuel oil, and against atomic energy.

Many electric utility companies are building new plants near the mouth of coal mines, or so close that short conveyor belt systems are the only transportation required. For somewhat longer distances, coal pipelines are apparently feasible. The prototype Cadiz-Cleveland (Ohio) coal-slurry pipeline has been "mothballed" after driving down the rail rate, but other ones (e.g., Utah–southern California, West Virginia–New York metropolitan area) are being projected. The railway answer has been the integral-train or unit-train development—shuttle trains that sharply reduce the turnabout time and effects savings of more than 30 per cent on operating costs. Each train carries more than 7,000 tons of coal each trip, and in full operation travels more than 80,000 miles a year (six times that traveled by average hopper cars), carrying over a million tons per year. Since 1962, coordinated programs for building high-voltage transmission lines and putting power plants right in the coal fields have been begun. One transmission system, more than 600 miles of 500,000-volt lines, will tie new power plants near Johnstown, Pa., and Morgantown, W. Va., with Wheeling, Philadelphia, Northern New Jersey, and metropolitan New York. Locating the plants at the mines is expected to cut fuel costs by up to $2 per ton by 1967 when the first part becomes operational, compared with the present $4 to $5 per ton rail costs.

Perspective

Markets hold the key to coal's future, both domestically and internationally. The dominant growth factor is in increasing industrial activity. Short-run problems are those of inadequate returns from labor-intensive mines and continuing pressure from conventional competitive fuels. The medium view (a generation ahead) is good, as reserves are adequate to meet even accelerated requirements. The long view (past the turn of the century) is problematical, mainly because the degree of substitution by new energy sources (especially nuclear energy) is only dimly perceived. In 1964, the medium-view outlook for conventional energy sources looked better than it did in 1950.

PETROLEUM

Despite the development of nuclear energy, petroleum will remain the world's second energy source for the immediate future, and could become first (especially in caloric value of production or in work-done contexts). Consumption of 1.31 billion metric tons at present is likely to double within another decade, and the share of petroleum in the world's total energy consumption will rise from 35 to 40 per cent or more.

Per capita consumption of petroleum products is now about 20 barrels (nearly 3 tons) annually in the United States, only one-fourth as great in other industrial nations, and only a few gallons in most underdeveloped nations. In the foreseeable future, oil consumption will probably increase less than 5 per cent annually in the U.S., but outside the United States a growth rate of 8 per cent or more appears more likely. This means that the 1975 oil demand will be 75 per cent greater in the United States, and likely to be trebled in the rest of the world.

Before World War II, United States demand for oil products was 4 per cent annually. After World War II until 1955, it went up to 6 per cent annually; since then it has gone down below 4 per cent because of complete dieselization of the railroads being completed, the renewed competition from coal (especially in the

TABLE 13-5

World: Crude Petroleum Production, Trade,* and Consumption, by Great-Region and Economic-Type of Society, 1962–1964 Average-Annual
(in millions of metric tons)

	Crude Petroleum Production	Net Imports	Crude Petroleum Consumption
North America	423	64.0	487.0
Western Europe	17	234.0	251.0
Eastern Europe (including the U.S.S.R.)	224	−18.0 [a]	206.0
Oceania	–	14.0	14.0
Latin America	240	−54.0	186.0
Sub-Saharan Africa	6	−3.5	2.5
Middle East (including North Africa)	382	−292.5	89.5
Non-Communist Far East	32	38.0	70.0
Communist Far East	7	–	7.0
World	1,331	−18.0	1,313.0
High-income countries	962	147.0	1,109.0
Low-income countries	369	−165.0	204.0

	(per cent of 1,331 million metric tons production)	(per cent of 350 million metric tons net imports)	(per cent of 368 million metric tons net exports)	(per cent of 1,313 million metric tons consumption)
North America	31.9	18.3	–	37.1
Western Europe	1.3	66.8	–	19.1
Eastern Europe (including the U.S.S.R.)	16.9	–	4.9	15.7
Oceania	–	4.0	–	1.1
Latin America	18.0	–	14.7	14.2
Sub-Saharan Africa	0.4	–	1.0	0.2
Middle East (including North Africa)	28.7	–	79.4	6.8
Non-Communist Far East	2.3	10.9	–	5.3
Communist Far East	0.5	–	–	0.5
World	100.0	100.0	100.0	100.0
High-income countries	72.1	42.0	55.2	84.5
Low-income countries	27.9	58.0	44.8	15.5

SOURCE: Adapted from United Nations data.

* The small difference between exports and imports is the amount in transit and storage. Total international trade in crude petroleum involves some 46 per cent of total world production, but much of this is intraregional and intra-realm trade (both overland and oceanic movements included).

[a] Minus sign equals net exports.

utility industry), the increased use of natural gas, and increasingly efficient machines.

The most substantial oil consumption increase will take place in Western Europe, which, like the United States in 1919, is in the midst of a great growth in its use of automotive fuels and other major products of petroleum. If the present annual rate of increase continues, by the early 1970's over half of the regional energy economy will be oil.

In the underdeveloped realm, the rate of growth in oil demand will probably surpass even that in Europe shortly, since coal is seldom available in great amounts, most hydro possibilities are poorly situated, and nuclear developments are seldom feasible to fill the booming needs (mainly transportation and industrial power).

Nearly 46 per cent of world crude-petroleum production moves across international borders;

it is worth over 10 per cent of the value of the world's goods trade, being the most important single item moved. Of the 0.6 billion tons moved, about one-third is intraregional and two-thirds moves between the great-regions, mainly in intercontinental flows. Western European imports are the largest, some 250 million tons; United States imports are about 100 million tons (including residual fuel oil) and Japanese imports are nearly half as large (Japan has the third largest national refinery capacity).

On the world's sea-lanes (coastal and intercontinental), petroleum makes up over one-third of the total weight of all goods moved, and it accounts for about half of the total ton-miles of movement. Although pipeline movement of crude oil is important in world trade (mainly in United States–Canada and U.S.S.R.–Eastern Europe traffic), as a rule overland transport is complementary to and not competitive with tanker transport. The tendency to favor supertankers (over 40,000 tons) in recent years has strengthened the cost advantage of market-oriented refineries.

Four major problems faced the oil industry at the beginning of the 1960's. The world now has a far greater supply of known oil reserves in relation to demand (forty years' supply) than in any time in recent history, and this may be continued for some time, if the Saharan and other recent discoveries are as rich as they appear. Geographic separation of supply and consuming areas results in a continuing tug of war between producers and consumers over the terms on which oil should be supplied. The competing economic interests of the participants in international oil affairs, the links in the chain between producers and consumers (producing countries, consuming countries, and the commercial oil industry), are becoming sharper. Conflicting national interests over the availability of oil supplies for security purposes are producing more restraints on movements.

Reserve Problems

Petroleum's share of the world's energy economy is still rising, but its long-term prospects are doubtful because of limited reserves compared with coal. The U.S. prospects are especially poor, as she is still producing over one-third of the world's oil with little more than a tenth of the proven reserves, and prospects for large new finds mainly rest on offshore and extremely deep (more than 4 miles down) possibilities.

At present, only one-third of the oil actually found in place can, on the average, be recovered economically. Thus, the 330 billion barrels (over 45 billion metric tons) of presently proven world petroleum reserves count only one-third of the petroleum discovered; the other two-thirds is only occasionally technically or economically recoverable, although much will eventually be recovered as methods improve and costs decline.

TABLE 13–6

World: Proven (Recoverable) Petroleum Reserves, by Great-Region and Economic-Type of Society, 1962–1964 Average-Annual

	Billion Metric Tons	Per Cent
North America	6.0	13.3
Western Europe	0.3	0.7
Eastern Europe (including the U.S.S.R.)	5.5	12.2
Oceania	–	–
Latin America	3.5	7.8
Sub-Saharan Africa	0.3	0.7
Middle East (including North Africa)	27.6	61.3
Non-Communist Far East	1.5	3.3
Communist Far East	0.3	0.7
World	45.0	100.0
High-income countries	24.5	54.5
Low-income countries	20.5	45.5

The total crude oil awaiting (potentially available for) future recovery in the United States can be inferred from expert opinion to be on the order of 500 billion barrels (70 billion tons), as compared with present proven reserves of about 37 billion barrels (5+ billion tons). The inferred total figure includes present proven reserves, the currently unrecoverable content of known reservoirs, and crude estimates of the total content of undiscovered reservoirs, without regard to present or future technologic feasibility of discovery and recovery.

In the sedimentary areas of the United States, there are some thirty well-defined structural basins from which the greater part of this country's future oil production is expected to come. Between these structural basins there are uplifts or arches, from which a large part of the nation's past production has been obtained. Since these have been heavily eroded, producing horizons were found at a much shallower depth than in the basins. Since the arches and uplifts have been developed rather intensively, attention is now centered largely in the basins. This has been possible only by improved drilling technology, which permitted going to greater depths. Although the thickness of the sediment is not known in many of these basins, some geologists maintain that it ranges up to 50,000 feet in southern California.

Probably 80 per cent of all producing fields have deeper possibilities (65,000 feet in sandstone; 51,000 feet in limestone theoretical lower limits). Some companies now are becoming interested in the oil prospects of the deeper horizons throughout the Appalachian Basin, the oldest producing area in the United States. Nearly all the old wells there have been shallow; most of them have been less than 1,000 feet deep.

The average depth of all wells drilled in the United States is now about 4,500 feet and is increasing by some 50 to 100 feet each year. Some oil is coming from 18,000 feet. Perhaps 10-mile deep oil wells will be drilled by 1975; these are now technically possible, but the cost would be about $5 million per well.

Very small fields—under a million barrels—have increasingly dominated onshore operations; their proportion has risen from 70 per cent in the early 1940's to over 85 per cent in 1964. We seem to be in the mature phase and approaching the end of a cycle in discovery technology, in the sense that the dramatic early results of geophysical techniques are no longer being duplicated. However, slightly more than half of proven reserves are in giant fields (those with ultimate reserves of 100 million barrels or more). The vast bulk of reserves are in fields comprising roughly 1,900 square miles, or only 0.2 per cent of the favorable area.

Of the 750,000 square miles of shelves bordering the United States, only 300 square miles off California and 20,000 square miles off Louisiana and Texas are being prospected. But already the experts guess that the Gulf waters hide some 12 billion barrels of oil and at least 70 trillion cubic feet of gas (equal to one-third of the proven oil and gas reserves in the United States). Half of all this lies off the coast of Louisiana.

Two elements make the Gulf of Mexico fruitful for oil development. One is the presence of salt domes, the same formations that are found in the 1,000 or more oil fields stretching along the Gulf Coast ashore, that are such a helpful guide to oil deposits. Another is the thickness of the sedimentary beds in which oil may occur, often running in this part of the continental shelf to depths of from 20,000 to 30,000 feet.

The U.S.S.R. has about 14 per cent of the world's land area and 20 per cent of the world's sedimentary area (United States has 5 per cent and 12 per cent, respectively); reserves so far have proven to be about the same size as those of the United States. Production is rapidly increasing (205 million tons in 1963, 390 million tons expected by 1970, perhaps 700 million tons by 1980). The Urals-Volga region has about 100 large deposits, 70 being exploited, accounting for a majority of Soviet proven and indicated reserves. Its fields are spread over an area as large as the British Isles, with usually only two or three productive horizons. In the Baku region, there are twenty-two oil horizons capable of production, accounting for the high and continual output (since 1873) and for the relatively small number of wells.

The most spectacular oil reserves are found in Caribbean and Middle Eastern (including North African) areas, which account for three-fourths of the world's proven reserves. Most are located in a few large fields, with most of the available crude located at depths less than a mile. Most horizons are very thick (30 to 300 feet being very common, some much thicker, including one 1,200 feet thick), compared with those in the United States (many 2 to 3 feet thick being exploited).

Courtesy of Arabian American Oil Co.

Airview of the Arabian American Oil Company's Manifa rig. As typical in the Middle Eastern oilfields, proper well-spacing places wells several miles apart to get maximum ultimate recovery from their reservoirs. The average well produces over 700 tons of oil daily (compared with less than 2 in the United States) at an average cost of under $3 per ton (compared with $16 in the United States) before taxes and royalties.

In Southwest Asia and North Africa, especially, geological structures are unusually favorable to oil occurrences. The average daily output per well is very much higher than in the United States, and since many areas have not yet been intensively explored, eventual production can be expected to exceed present proven reserves by manyfold. The annual rate of withdrawal relative to proven reserves is only 0.8 per cent for the Middle East, compared with 7.5 per cent for the United States and 2.5 per cent for the world as a whole.

Production Problems

The U.S. petroleum industry is plagued with serious problems: economically much of it is marginal compared with newer producers, and its long-run prospects are uncertain because of limited reserves that are very expensive to find and to produce.

The price paid for crude oil is the largest factor in the final price of refined products. Integrated oil companies can import foreign crude delivered at coastal refineries for about $1 per barrel cheaper than average U.S. costs, and without quota control, they would import much more than the present 14 per cent of consumption, perhaps as much as half of the total.

In the early 1960's, the average U.S. crude oil price per barrel was $2.90, on which the producer received 75 cents free of the federal income tax through the 27½ per cent depletion allowance. It cost some 80 cents to find that average barrel, some 60 cents to develop the facilities to produce, and some 75 cents to operate the well. Many domestic producers make profits of 50 cents or so per barrel, as their wellhead costs run higher than average.

In comparison, overseas producers make from 75 cents to $1.40 per barrel from producing and transporting; this barrel costs them perhaps 35 cents to produce.[2] Much foreign production is cheaper. For example, Kuwait's Burgan field produces some 1.3 million barrels of oil per day, more than one-third of the output of Texas, at about 10 cents a barrel. Lifting that much additional oil in Texas from already existing facilities only partially used would cost on an average of about $1 a barrel "out-of-pocket" expenses.

The reasons for such high American costs are easy to explain. Most important oil fields in the United States were opened before 1940, and nearly all of those tapped before 1945 have now passed their peak. The average annual output per U.S. well of all 40,000 oil fields (of which 200 are considered major fields) is some 600 tons, compared with about 430,000 tons in the Middle East (if "strippers" were eliminated, the U.S. average would increase to some 2,500 tons). The average well in Kuwait and Arabia produces more oil in one month than the typical well now being developed in the United States will produce during its life of 20 to 30 years.

Not only does the small scale of U.S. wells and fields result in heavier production costs, but only a small minority (10 per cent) are flowing wells. In the Middle East and most other foreign fields, natural earth pressures (gas, water, or a combination of these) cheaply bring the oil to the surface, while in the United States most output is pumped or must be artificially pressurized to produce.

There are some 1,400 new oil discoveries each year in the United States, but most of them are expensive primary producers. For example, great hopes are held for the vast offshore Gulf area, where geologists believe that at least as much oil and gas exist as has been found along the coast onshore in the past half-century. Of the more than 2,500 offshore wells drilled in the Gulf Coast areas from 1947 to 1960, only about one-third were barren (on land, the ratio of success usually runs to one producitve well in nine drilled). When they hit, discoveries have added eight to nine times as much hydrocarbon reserve as the average onshore well. However, the costs of such offshore oil operations are reckoned at between two to seven times those on dry land. Even capital-saving innovations are likely to remain very expensive compared with land operations of similar depth. An off-

---

[2] Persian Gulf crude listed at $1.80 a barrel in 1964 was being sold for as low as $1.35 after discounts. Libyan oil listed at $2.20 a barrel (both because of high quality and proximity to Western Europe) was going for as little as $1.55 per barrel. The countries are now getting 60 to 70 per cent of the profits on production, as the companies must absorb the discounts. Venezuelan crude costs about twice as much to produce, but sells at a competitive price.

shore well drilled down through as much as 300 feet of water and 16,000 feet of mud and shale costs as much as $3 million, about six times the cost of a similar dry-land operation. The newest "floaters" rigs (costing $8 million or more, with daily expenses of $10,000 or more) can now drill as far down as 25,000 feet in 600 feet of water; if a good productive well is brought in, it may either be capped and held in reserve or hooked up to tankers or an undersea pipeline, while the big rig moves on to another job. Up to 1965, oil companies have invested $6 billion in offshore operations and have recovered $3 billion of it.

Additional oil can be obtained either by exploration or by improved recovery methods. In the United States, oil finding costs are rising so swiftly that secondary recovery is becoming increasingly important, and tertiary recovery is beginning. The average total cost of finding, developing, and producing oil rose over six times in the past generation (from 50 cents per barrel in the mid-1930's to over $3 in the early 1960's). The cost of finding oil (only a part of the average total cost of recovering oil) in the same period increased over twenty-five fold (from 6 cents to $1.65 per barrel), while developing and producing costs both increased about three times.

Secondary recovery of oil (injected fluids such as natural gas, air, water, or steam to sweep additional oil from the porous spaces of the reservoirs) now accounts for over one-fifth of the crude oil produced in the United States. Gas is usually the less efficient displacing agent, compared with water, but about 10 per cent of the national output is being used for repressuring purposes. It is also more expensive; natural gas or air may cost on the order of 5 to 20 cents per reservoir barrel, depending upon the pressure to which it must be compressed. Water generally can be obtained even after purification at from several cents to perhaps 10 cents per barrel (sometimes carbon dioxide is added to form chemicals after combining with certain hydrocarbons that in effect serve as a detergent to release the oil and gas). In typical reservoirs, from 5 to 20 per cent of the oil may be displaced by the gas phase in a solution gas drive; then it is possible to introduce additional gas through an injection well, but recoveries associated with such an operation will usually not exceed 30 per cent of the oil in place (because of capillary or surface forces, the gas enters the larger pores of the porous medium and leaves residual oil in all the smaller openings). Water preferentially enters the smaller pores. The capillary forces pull the water into the porous medium and displace the oil. The pull is greater in the smaller openings, so the water preferentially enters the smaller pores, displacing as much as half the oil. Superheated steam (500° F.) is being used in California and elsewhere to melt asphaltic or paraffin deposits that sometimes clog wells, helping to stimulate the movement of oil. Steaming works particularly well where shallow formations hold thick, spongy masses of heavy oil in reservoirs of limited size; in large deposits of tightly compacted formation, "steam-soak" methods have been much less effective. In 1964, 3 per cent of California's production came from steaming projects, and that fraction is expected to double in 1965. Some enthusiastic producers (steam recovery has boosted initial production by three to ten times in some cases) predict that over-all recovery of heavy crudes can be increased from about 20 per cent to about 40 per cent. Recovery by both primary and secondary techniques has averaged only 40 to 60 per cent of the total original oil. Unrecoverable oil (impossible to remove by conventional primary and secondary techniques) amounts to about six times the proven (recoverable) reserves.

More recently developed methods, such as the use of solvents and the application of heat, can be used to yield even more of the remaining oil and are known as tertiary recovery. The challenging part of the problem is the severe limitation imposed because of the low price of crude oil ($1.65 to $4 range per barrel), depending upon the composition of the crude and its location. Since tertiary recovery costs from 50 to 150 per cent more to operate than conventional production techniques, only special circumstances make it economical at present. "Fire-flooding" thins the oil underground so that it flows ahead of the blaze to another well, but

Courtesy of Arabian American Oil Co.

Lineup of tankers at the Arabian American Oil Company's Ras Tanura North Pier. The largest tankers (over 50,000 tons) can pass south through the Suez Canal (to the Persian Gulf) when empty, but when fully loaded go around Africa's Cape of Good Hope to reach their North Atlantic destinations. Middle East crude can be landed on the U.S. Eastern Seaboard for $1 to $1.50 a barrel less than Texas crude, and sells at about $1.25 less (within the quota limit).

such thermal recovery of oil costs from 50 cents to $1.50 per barrel of oil produced, so the economic picture is uncertain so far as large-scale application in the near future. Miscible-phase displacement uses a solvent (propane or butane gas) to wash the oil out of the rock and sand, moving it to a producing well; it promises nearly complete recovery in abandoned fields, if the gas is available at cheap rates.

The comparative economics of oil availability is very complicated, dependent upon comparative technological progress in discovery, development, and refining, and upon satisfactory international politics as it affects prices and barriers to movement of cheap foreign oil. Some 80 per cent of oil has been found in anticlinal traps (40 per cent of present finds), yet some authorities believe that three-fourths of ultimate finds will be in stratigraphic traps, much of it in shallow, cheaply exploitable horizons. If the new flow of Soviet and North African oil is as vast as some predict, it might involve a break in the price structure of world oil. A spectacular breakthrough in tertiary oil recovery—some imagine phenomenally cheap liquidification through ultrasonics or nuclear alteration—might alter costs in favor of greater recovery from old fields. The delayed advent of competitive atomic power, especially in transportation, would lengthen the period in which oil is dominant in international energy movements, probably by a few decades.

Oil Transport

As transportation costs are an extremely important item in the delivered price of petroleum products, oil companies, from the inception of the industry, have sought methods to secure low-cost transportation. In most situations, tankers, pipelines, and barges are the most economical crude oil carriers, and there are few areas in which they are not used almost exclusively.

Oil accounts for nearly half of the cargoes moved by sea. Tankers represent one-third of the world's merchant fleet tonnage, and provide the cheapest transport of any crude material, from one-third of a mill (10 mills equal 1 U.S. cent) per ton-mile on the largest tankers used continually to several mills on the smaller tankers (or others used below capacity). In 1964, a 50,000-ton tanker (the largest that can come through the Suez Canal fully loaded) charged about 66 cents per barrel plus 12 cents Suez tolls to move Persian Gulf oil to the U.S. Eastern Seaboard; while from Venezuela it was about 16 cents.

The largest movement of crude oil in the world is some 250 million tons moved to Western Europe, some 90 per cent from the Middle East, and most of the remainder from Venezuela. This European market is the most rapidly growing one and seems probable to more than double in the present decade. The Saharan oil boom can offer cheaper oil and gas, and leverage in negotiations between oil companies and the governments of Persian Gulf area oil-producing countries. North African production is expected to reach 2 to 3 million barrels daily in the 1960's decade (equal to two-thirds the present output in the Middle East), which can be delivered some 20 to 50 cents per barrel cheaper than in the case of Persian Gulf area crude (which has a longer tanker trip and either heavy pipeline or Suez charges). The United States is the second largest importer of oil, most of it imported from Venezuela (especially the residual fuel oil that makes up 40 per cent of U.S. imports), but an increasing fraction is coming from the Middle East (to the Eastern Seaboard) and Sumatra (to California). The Japanese market is supplied by Persian Gulf sources through supertanker transport via Sunda Strait. Other tanker movements are small in comparison.

Pipelines rate next in importance to tanker movements of oil, both in ton-miles moved and in cheapness. Crude oil pipelines in the United States are the nation's third largest handlers of freight, carrying over three-fourths of the crude oil products and nearly a quarter of the refined products, amounting to a sixth of all the intercity freight traffic in the country. Crude oil

Courtesy of Arabian American Oil Co.

The 30–31 inch crude oil pipeline that reaches more than 1,000 miles from producing fields in Saudi Arabia to Tapline's Sidon terminal in Lebanon is an alternative to the route around southern Arabia and through the Suez Canal. By either route, Persian Gulf oil is some $3 per ton (about 40 cents per barrel) more costly to deliver to the Narrow Seas ports than Libyan oil from Gulf of Sirte ports.

moved via pipelines 20 inches in diameter and over (that are full) costs ¾ to 1 mill per ton-mile (normal tariffs of most common carrier lines are 1½ to 3 mills on long hauls and 3 to 4 mills on short hauls). Normal tariffs on products (gasoline, jet fuel, distillates, etc.) moved via ordinary common carrier lines are 3½ to 7 mills per ton-mile.[3] Pipeline systems are spreading rapidly in many parts of the world. The U.S.S.R. is tying together its Volga-Urals fields with its own and Eastern European market centers. Argentinian pipelines from Patagonia and the Chaco now supply the Humid Pampas market. European pipelines are expanding rapidly, some of them being international to move oil from South European ports to Northwest European refineries and depots.

Barges are the third cheap oil carrier, moving crude and refined products for 1.5 to 3 mills per ton-mile on common carriers (1 to 2 mills on captive tows). The Mississippi, Volga, and Rhine rivers carry the greatest traffic. With the growth of a large-scale regular traffic, inland-waterways movement of oil may be displaced by pipeline, which has less flexibility but is cheaper if fully utilized.

Only about 5 per cent of oil movement is by expensive rail and truck transport. Truck transport is so expensive (2 to 4 cents per ton-mile in the United States) that movement from refinery or depot to city retailer is usually as expensive as the crude movement from oil field to refinery even when separated by thousands of miles. Rail movement is somewhat cheaper, usually 1 to 2 cents per ton-mile.

Oil Refining

There is a continuing trend for refining capacities to locate in areas of petroleum products consumption rather than crude oil production. Among the reasons are the pressure exerted by industrial markets with their need of highly refined products and a widening range of petrochemical products, the rapid multiplication of sources of crude, the awareness by foreign companies of the political risks inherent in large fixed investments in underdeveloped countries, and the saving in distribution costs by market-oriented sites. As an example, the Middle East, which had 10 per cent of the world's refinery capacity in 1950, now has only about half that fraction (it refines about one-fourth of its crude production).

Within the great market areas, there is a trend toward fewer but larger oil refineries. The United States had 459 in 1940, but has only 300 today. A similar trend in European refineries exists. This is in spite of the fact that recent advances in refining technology now make it possible to construct small but efficient processing units (such plants tend to be located in rather sparsely inhabited regions such as the U.S. West).

The great bulk of U.S. refinery capital outlays in recent years have gone to add new products, upgrade quality, and raise the value of total output through fuller utilization of chemical by-products, not to expand capacity. The intensification of competition, with its squeeze on refining profit margins (now only 55 cents per barrel in the United States), is increasing the pressure for modernization, and rising output will soon pick up what little excess capacity the refineries have.

Perspective

The center of the question of what happens to world energy prices over the next several decades lies in what happens to the geographical distribution and to the f.o.b. price of oil from the really low-cost areas with their superabundant reserves.

Venezuela and the Middle East are low-cost sources on any full-cost-of-supply basis, and the principal problem with respect to these areas that concerns users is the price problem. On the other hand, the costs of domestic oil in the United States are relatively high and may be rising. Total domestic availability of crude oil in another decade or so, at no appreciable increase in constant dollar costs, may be less than today (with perhaps one-third from secondary production). Each foot of exploratory drilling

---

[3] The most efficient lines carry a gallon of oil more than 1,000 miles for under a cent, less than one-quarter the cost of other land transportation.

has located only about 20 barrels in the United States, about 700 barrels in Venezuela, and more than 13,000 barrels in the Middle East.

There are many groups, possessing great economic and political weight, who are not at all interested in a low-cost energy supply. In the United States, gas producers would like to be able to charge into the cost of gas the price of the oil that gas is displacing from the market. The 20,000 or so domestic oil producers, accounting for slightly over half of domestic crude output, maintain that without price increases, the increasing cost of domestic oil exploration and development will soon cease to be covered. The score of importers, who produce almost half of U.S. crude, are interested in drawing a larger part of their oil, for sale in the domestic market, from lower-cost foreign sources, but have not expressed a desire to pass these cost advantages on to consumers. The interest in low energy cost is a diffuse consumer interest that, like all consumer manifestations, is disorganized and relatively impotent.

The situation in Western Europe is not too dissimilar. Although oil from the Middle East can now be landed in most of Western Europe at prices that tend to make the high-cost domestic coal output non-competitive, strong forces are arrayed against a rapid displacement.[4] Nearly everywhere there are subsidies (differential taxes on oil, and others) to protect the high-cost, high-employment coal industries.

Neither the producing companies nor the owning governments in the principal centers of overseas oil production, Venezuela and the Middle East, are interested in any substantial break in the world price structure. They are in favor of a lowering of barriers to oil imports in the West, which would lower the average costs of European energy use and arrest a tendency toward increasing energy costs in the future in the United States. Such price-lowering influences as may be brought to bear by increasing competition and overabundant supplies may well be offset by the effects of increasing pressure by owning governments for a larger share in the proceeds.

NATURAL GAS

Natural gas has evolved as an autonomous industry in the United States in the past generation, but is still a by-product associate of the petroleum industry in most countries. The separate gas public utility industry in the United States has matured in the sense of complete national and activity coverage, supplying 30 per cent of the national energy economy in the form of gas and another 3 per cent in the form of liquefied natural gases (which is usually included in petroleum data). About 11 per cent of natural gas production is by the gas utility industry, and the other 89 per cent by independents, mainly oil companies.

The natural gas public utility industry in its broadest sense involves some 8,000 independent producers (the 25 largest producers account for 59 per cent of the total production of natural gas; at the other extreme, some 6,000 small producers account for under 10 per cent of the output); about 108 pipeline companies (with over 60,000 miles of field and gathering mains and over 200,000 miles of transmission pipeline), of which 28 were engaged in interstate movements; and some 1,495 gas distributing utilities, who served nearly 40 million customers (including liquefied gas users) through some 450,000 miles of distribution mains.

Public Utility Sales of U.S. Natural Gas, 1963 *

	Per Cent of 15 Trillion Cubic Feet Dry Gas	Per Cent of $6½ Billion Gross Value
33.0 million residential users	34	55
2.7 million commercial users	10	14
0.2 million industrial users	51	28
0.1 million other users	5	3
36.0 million total users	100	100

* The data do not include usage of natural gas by the oil and gas producers themselves (for any purpose, including repressuring) nor do they include the sales of liquefied (wet) gases.

---

[4] If oil could be freely brought in, only about 90 of the current 250 million tons of annual coal production might survive.

The householders who use natural gas solely for residential heating and cooling number over 24 million and are increasing by about 1 million each year (the number of gas-heated homes has quadrupled since 1950). Another 9 million householders use gas for other purposes, mainly cooking. Such residential users pay about three times more per unit for their gas consumption, because of the relatively small use per household. Commercial users are also increasing rapidly with gas being used mainly for space and water heating, cooking, refrigeration and air conditioning, clothes drying, and incineration. Industrial users, who consume over half of total gas (by energy value), are able to get the product at a much lower cost, not only because the cost of local distribution is lower, but also because their consumption is often complementary to that of other users.

Gas is a highly favored fuel, possessing many superior characteristics that will favor its continued use after the early phase in which its main attraction may have been its low price. It is convenient, requiring no handling or storage space. It is delivered ready to burn, can be ignited with exceptional ease and speed, and requires no large investment in equipment. On ignition, it immediately develops its maximum heating capacity, and its quality gives it a constant heating value. It is the most easily controlled fuel in regard to both temperature and combustible atmosphere, responding instantly to thermostatic control, making it especially desirable in many heating and metallurgical operations. It is completely combustible, leaving no ashes and creating no dust.

The gas industry's main consumer problem is the electrical industry's problem in reverse. Electric utilities, faced with peak demands for power to run air conditioning systems in the summer, are fostering use of the heat pump to consume electricity in the winter. Gas utilities, faced with peak cold weather heating demands, are pushing gas-consuming appliances that are used in both summer and winter (air conditioners, clothes driers, refrigerators, water heaters) and uses that are high in summer (irrigation pumps, seasonal industry).

The factor most likely to retard future growth of the natural gas market will be the rapidly rising cost of gas in comparison with the prices of coal and fuel oil, its chief competitors. In 1945, the average wellhead price per 1,000 cubic feet of natural gas was under 5 cents; by 1963, this had risen to nearly 16 cents. In many areas, by the time gas is sold (especially to industrial users), it is more expensive than its competitors on an energy-equivalent basis.

Reserve Problems

Like the other hydrocarbons, natural gas is a complicated mixture of numerous different hydrocarbon molecules plus other types of molecules, as indicated below:

Dry gases are those molecules that remain in gaseous state under usual conditions of temperature and pressure: Methane or marsh gas, CH_4, is usually 80 to 90 per cent of the average natural gas mixture; Ethane, C_2H_6, is the other dry or lean gas and is usually 5 to 10 per cent.

Liquefied petroleum gases are those molecules that are extracted and handled in the liquid state, but consumed in the gaseous state: Propane, C_3H_8, is usually 3 to 5 per cent of the average mixture and is the L.P.G. usually sold in bottled or tank form in the North; Butane, C_4H_{10} (and an isomer, Isobutane), is usually 1 to 2 per cent of the average mixture and is the L.P.G. mainly sold in the South (it has 3,270 B.t.u. per cubic foot, compared with Propane's 2,520).

Natural gasoline is normally liquid gasoline molecules of low octane number, making up 1 to 2 per cent of the average mixture (to distinguish natural gas liquids from crude petroleum, Pentane is commonly considered the heaviest of the natural gas liquids, although natural gasolines may contain hydrocarbons of higher molecular weight): Pentane, C_5H_{12} (and an isomer, Isopentane); Hexane, C_6H_{14}; Heptane, C_7H_{16}; and Octane, C_8H_{18}.

Non-hydrocarbons mainly consist of Helium (when found, usually ½ to ¾ per cent, with richest about 2 per cent He), Nitrogen, Carbon Dioxide, Hydrogen Sulfide (some deposits have as much as 35 per cent H_2SO_4), and Sulfur, in greatly varying amounts.

Proven (economically recoverable) reserves of natural gas in the United States amounted to some 276 trillion cubic feet in 1963, or some eighteen times current annual consumption. In recent years, additions have been about twice the annual withdrawal rate. Recent estimates of total ultimate recoverable natural gas reserves have been in the neighborhood of 1,400 to 1,700 trillion cubic feet, or about 100 times current annual rate of production.

Thus, in the medium run (one to two generations), sufficient U.S. natural gas reserves are at hand and are expected to be discovered to supply even consumption rising at the present rate (doubling each decade). In addition, there is Canadian and Mexican gas upon which we are already drawing to a minor extent (in early 1960's, 0.3 per cent of net consumption).

Over 70 per cent of present U.S. proven reserves are made up of the great stores of non-associated gas (that from dry or straight natural gas wells) first discovered about thirty years ago. Relatively little non-associated gas has been found in this country since the 1920's. Such primary gas production usually lasts about twenty years or so after exploitation is begun. The discovery of gas associated with oil (casing-head gas) has provided almost all our recent additions to proven reserves, such residual gas production usually lasting about ten to twelve years after exploitation is begun. Some production is from condensate gas wells, from the gas left after liquid hydrocarbons have been removed upon reduction of the natural well pressure. Because drillers have been going deeper for oil, the ratio of gas found with oil has been increasing. About half of U.S. uncommitted gas reserves are now controlled by four of the biggest oil and gas companies, over two-thirds by the eight largest, reflecting this tendency.

Gas wildcatting is mainly (80 per cent) done by small producers in some 30,000 square miles (1 per cent of the United States). Pipeline companies purchase gas from over 100,000 wells (about 5,000 new gas wells are added each year), most of which have been drilled by the 5,000 independents. Gas has been found in thirty-one states so far, but nearly 90 per cent of the reserves are found in five states: Texas 45 per cent, Louisiana 22 per cent, Kansas–New Mexico–Oklahoma 23 per cent.

In the long run (after the turn of this century), it is problematical what reserves will be available. With substantially present technology, future reserves to be discovered can only be done at increasing costs and by a continued intensive exploration deeper in the earth and farther out to sea. Perhaps the largest remaining supplies will be from the continental shelf and slope and from foreign deposits. If, as some believe, gas consumption around 2000 will be triple the present rate, important supplemental supplies may be synthetic methane, chemically identifiable with natural gas, made from low-grade coals and oil shales. Cost of producing such synthetic gas is now too high in most areas, but only slightly higher than the present cost of natural gas in the more remote sections of the country. Lurgi machines, using non-coking and relatively cheap coals to produce a gas of 400 to 500 B.t.u. per cubic foot, which can be processed to a gas of 800 to 900 B.t.u., have costs of 75 cents to $1 per 1,000 cubic feet, even using very cheap coal. This cannot compete with natural gas, which is available at the pipeline in most cities at 50 to 75 cents per 1,000 cubic feet. Slight changes in technology or price may well see important substitution of synthetic gas for natural gas, although complete replacement seems unlikely within the coming century.

Much less is known of natural gas reserves outside the United States, but the chances are that ultimately the United States will be found to have no larger a fraction of the world's natural gas than of the world's oil, perhaps 10 to 15 per cent. About two-thirds of Middle Eastern and Venezuelan casing-head gas is still being vented (released into air) and flared (burned), compared with less than 5 per cent in the United States, but increasing amounts are being used for consumption or for repressurizing.

Eastern Europe (including U.S.S.R.) produces 17.5 per cent of the world's natural gas, and it makes up some 13 per cent of the regional energy economy. Soviet gas fields have been found in the Ukraine, the Volga Basin, in western and eastern Siberia, and in Central Asia, while the Transylvanian Basin is expected to supply not only Romania but other Eastern European countries. Soviet plans call for a fifteen fold increase of consumption between 1960 and 1975.

Latin America produces some 3.5 per cent of the world's natural gas, and it provides nearly a tenth of the regional energy economy. Venezuela, Mexico, and Argentina are developing pipeline networks similar to that of the United States.

Western Europe's 3 per cent of world production (even with imports, only 2.5 per cent of regional energy consumption) mainly comes from Po Valley (Italy), southwestern France, and northern Netherlands deposits (the latter containing three-quarters of Western Europe's reserves, larger than those of Canada). These supplies, plus imported liquefied gas from Algeria, Libya, and elsewhere, are expected to raise Western European natural gas consumption to 10 per cent of the regional energy consumption by the mid-1970's, probably at the expense of coal's present 48 per cent. If North Sea probes find even larger deposits, the fraction will likely be much higher.

The Middle East produces only 1 per cent of the world's commercial natural gas, providing some 12 per cent of energy consumption (after oil exports are eliminated), mainly used in the oil field areas or shipped in liquefied fractions to nearby cities.

The non-Communist Far East produces about the same quantity of natural gas as the Middle East, with the Malaysian-Indonesian supplies being used about the same way. Pakistan has exploited its northeastern Baluchistan's Sui and other fields to supply the Indus Basin. Japan supplements its modest national production by imports of liquefied gas from its Middle Eastern oil-gas concessions.

Natural Gas Transport

The techniques used to tie together gas supply and gas demand—long distance pipelines coupled with summer storage systems near the market—have been the driving forces behind the rapid expansion of the U.S. gas utility industry to the nation's fifth largest.

The Southwest produces about 80 per cent of U.S. natural gas production, with the remainder split between California, the Mountain States, and the central Manufacturing Belt States. Both the Southwest and the Mountain States use about half of their production and send the other half to deficit areas. The Southwest and the Northeast (Manufacturing Belt) consume about 40 per cent each of all gas consumed in the country, with California consuming most of the remainder (the Pacific Northwest, the Mountain States, and the Southeast together consume little more than 5 per cent of the national total).

The some 60 per cent of U.S. natural gas that moves in interstate commerce has as its main incentive the great price differential between producing and consuming regions. Of $1¼ (about 1,000 cubic feet in the average Manufacturing Belt city) of gas sold to the ordinary householder, 10 per cent represents well-cost, 20 to 30 per cent long-distance pipeline charges, and the remaining 60 to 70 per cent the cost of local distribution. Natural gas fields now produce some 40 billion cubic feet daily, of which some 25 billion cubic feet are daily moved over the 710,000-mile pipeline system. The great era of U.S. pipeline expansion has nearly ended; from now on, expansion will be mainly a matter of keeping pace with population growth and its redistribution in areas already served.

In 1963, about 280 underground storage pools in twenty-three states had the capacity to store some 3.7 trillion cubic feet of natural gas, an amount equal to one-fourth of the total annual gas consumption (or equal to gas consumption for the two coldest months). Most are renovated depleted oil-gas fields, but increasingly many are natural formations of porous earth and rock never used naturally. Such balancing reservoirs are necessary in order to cover the high fixed costs of pipeline (e.g., new lines must be used 60 to 70 per cent of all the hours in the year to cover such fixed costs) by providing peak-load reserves. It costs about $4,000 per inch of diameter to lay a mile of pipe across normal terrain (i.e., about $100,000 per mile of main transmission line in rural areas), and sometimes ten times as much in traversing a metropolitan area. Operating costs are much less of a problem (e.g., 1½ to 1¾ cents per 1,000 cubic feet moved 100 miles).

Another method of handling the excess gas received during the summer (often the August demand is only a tenth of the January demand) is selling gas to utilities or other industrial users on an interruptible basis. Usually such sales are at little above cost, but some have been at little more than the cost of such gas at well-head (i.e., letting other gas users absorb the transmission costs).

In serving continental markets, the U.S. prototype is easily copied, but in supplying a market like Western Europe's, the problem is much more complicated. If transport is available, the market potential is great, since present use is only 10 cubic feet per person per day, a tenth of U.S. consumption. A Kirkuk to Paris pipeline would be 2,500 miles long and, with branch lines averaging 300 miles, could supply natural gas to a population half again that of North America. Such an overland route might deliver gas at a price similar to that in the Boston area, but would be geopolitically vulnerable. The average cost of producing "city gas" in London, Paris, and Berlin is about $1 per 1,000 cubic

This methane-liquefication plant at Arzew, Algeria, is the first commercial plant of many that will soon be shipping products all over the world. The conversion of natural gas into a world energy, like petroleum, instead of the continental energy it has been until recently may be a more important development in the next several decades than the more advertised approach of nuclear electricity to an economic-competitive position with conventionally generated electricity.

Courtesy of Continental Oil Co.

Courtesy of Continental Oil Co.

The new liquid-methane tanker "Methane Princess" entering the Algerian port of Arzew (near Oran). A United States–British–French combine has a $64 million plant to liquefy methane gas (at −285° F.) and ship it to Britain in such insulated tankers. The natural gas comes from central Sahara Desert gas fields to Arzew by pipeline where its volume is reduced 600:1 before it is shipped out.

feet, with household users paying about $2.50. The average cost of equivalent energy from coal is 65 cents to $1.75, depending upon nearness to coalfields. Saharan gas might be delivered by pipeline across the Mediterranean, either at the Strait of Gibraltar or farther east between Oran and Cartagena, but the technical problems of construction are immense and the geopolitical problems may be nearly as great as on the route across Eastern Europe.

An alternative to the use of such long international pipelines is the tanker movement of liquefied gas. The importance of liquefied butane, propane, and methane derives from the potential to make natural gas an international commodity like petroleum, and to make an economic fuel out of the over 1 trillion cubic feet of natural gas being flared annually in the Middle East, Venezuela, and elsewhere. Methane, the most abundant natural gas fraction, contracts in the ratio of 600:1 when liquefied at − 285° F., with a barrel of liquid methane being equivalent in heating value to 3,500 cubic feet of dry gas. In 1964, a plant at Arzew, Algeria, began liquefying methane which was shipped to Britain in two special tankers to supply some 10 per cent of the cooking gas used by British housewives.[5] Algerian methane will also be delivered to France as soon as its methane tanker

[5] Reportedly, the delivered price in Britain was 88 cents for the equivalent of 1,000 cubic feet of methane. Bigger tankers are expected to drop the transport costs.

is finished. An even larger facility is being constructed at Marsa El Brega, Libya, to liquefy methane that will be shipped by tanker to Barcelona, Spain, and terminals in northern Italy. The expansion of such facilities depends on several factors, especially the size of new gas finds under the North Sea.

The Federal Power Commissioner believes that liquefied methane will soon find its way into the United States, and that large volumes of the natural gas consumed in Eastern Seaboard and West Coast population centers by 1970 will come from outside continental North America. With the price at the wellhead and costs of transportation both increasing, Eastern Seaboard distributing companies are losing or soon will lose many of the markets into which valley sales used to be made. Until such time as gas-fired air conditioning or some other off-peak use is found, the high cost of incremental additions to the load curve of the average distributing company actually threatens the growth rate of the gas industry. Here is where liquefied methane holds the greatest promise. But as the technique progresses and volume grows, the inherent economies of transoceanic transportation (the cheapest type of transportation known) will soon reduce the unit cost per 1,000 cubic feet of natural gas brought in by tanker to where it might well compete with firm loads or even interruptible loads. Speculative estimates as to costs of moving liquefied methane include 25 to 50 cents per 1,000 cubic feet of dry gas equivalent from Venezuela to Eastern Seaboard ports.

Since peakloads in the northern hemisphere occur at directly opposite times of the year as in the southern hemisphere, the possibilities of peaking in northern and southern hemisphere cities with the same tanker equipment are good. This extreme flexibility of transportation is one of the great advantages of transporting liquefied methane by tanker.

Petrochemicals

About 2 per cent of the oil and gas now consumed in the United States is used as raw material in the petrochemical industry. In 1964, total chemical industry output was 150 million tons, 30 per cent of which were petrochemicals. Total value-added was $18 billion, about 30 per cent from petrochemical intermediaries. Yearly increase is expected to average near 10 per cent for quite a while; some experts think that gas may eventually price itself out of the industrial market, but not for twenty years at least.

Of 10,000 chemicals sold, some 3,000 are petrochemicals. They are normally considered as consisting of three main families. The largest family, Aliphatics, that of straight chain hydrocarbons, makes up nearly 90 per cent by value of all petrochemicals and is almost entirely made from petroleum. Detergents, synthetic rubber, and squeeze-bottle plastics are products from this family. The Aromatics family is made more from gas than from petroleum and ends up as synthetic rubber and explosives. The "Inorganics" family is usually made from natural gas, and its tonnage products include carbon black and synthetic ammonia fertilizer.

A non-hydrocarbon found in natural gas, and in increasing demand, is helium. The government produces the present supply from the richest wells ever found, containing about 2 per cent He and sells it at $15 per 1,000 cubic feet. These wells will soon be exhausted, and future production will have to come from leaner deposits. Much is wasted in wells with $1/2$ to $3/4$ per cent He, but costs would be about $45 m.c.f.

An associated industry is the production of natural gas liquids (L.P.), which now accounts for over 3 per cent of the U.S. energy economy, more than twice the energy content consumed from anthracite. Of such L.P. consumption, half is for heating and half is for use in vehicles and in manufacturing synthetic rubber.

Perspective

Natural gas is truly a growth industry, the ultimate expansion of which is limited in terms of available supplies. The principal problems of the U.S. industry arise out of the basic economic problem of the allocation of scarce economic resources. Elsewhere, the main problem seems to be the same as that dominant in the United States a generation back—economic accessibility of known and probable supplies.

Future increases in natural gas reserves are likely to be associated with discoveries of new oil wells, unless experience with offshore drilling should prove the contrary. Estimates of world reserves are not reliable.

Natural gas is a continental fuel at present. Unlike coal and oil, it cannot be stored readily, and its use is limited to those areas that can be economically reached by pipeline, the only practical mode for its transportation. The greatest potential change in consumption is likely to be made when natural gas can be liquefied and moved by tanker in large volume economically, thus converting this segment of the energy economy to an international fuel such as oil.

WATER POWER AND ELECTRICITY

The last segment of the world's primary energy economy, hydro- or water-power, is the smallest. Hydroelectricity is some 2 per cent of primary energy consumed in the world, assuming a kilowatt-hour is equated with the amount of coal giving the same amount of heat, some 0.125 tons per 1,000 kilowatt-hours (some sources equate a kilowatt-hour of hydroelectricity with the amount of coal necessary to produce a kilowatt-hour in a thermal plant, some 0.6 tons per 1,000 kilowatt-hours).[6] Since practically all hydropower is converted into electricity (although only one-third of all electricity generated), it is convenient to consider the two together.

The modern significance of water power is that it is a valuable by-product of the electrical industry. Electricity's main contribution to man's energy supply is that it has made the transmission of power easy, flexible, and highly divisible. Nearly as important, because of its qualitative superiority, electricity has made possible whole new industries unthinkable without it (e.g., electrochemical and electrometallurgical industries). Finally, electricity has emancipated water power from the tyranny of the primary power sites; sites now 300 to 400 miles from main load centers can now be economically used, and we are within sight of continental grids.

Water power's importance in the world's energy economy is much greater than its small share, as usually calculated, indicates. Most important, transformation of falling water into electricity in new plants occurs with less than 10 per cent loss (national averages are in the range 5 to 20 per cent), while mineral fuels are converted into electricity with 60 to 75 per cent loss. Operating costs of hydroelectricity stations are generally lower than operating costs of thermal-electricity stations, so most of the cheapest electricity in the world comes from water power developments. In many areas of poor mineral fuels (e.g., shield areas and areas of mineral-poor highland), water power is the mainspring of the energy economy. Water power is continuously renewable, a great advantage in conservation but usually not a major consideration in economics.

A trend line of 7 per cent growth per year, or a doubling every decade, is a good representation of the growth of electric energy in the world as a whole and in a wide variety of countries ranging from the most highly industrialized to the least developed. However, in most countries, the thermal segment of the electricity generation is increasing at the expense of the hydrosegment (e.g., in the United States, water power is growing about 5 per cent annually, with thermal capacity growing at nearly double that rate).

Such an increase in consumption makes the electrical industry one of the growth industries. In the United States, as in most other industrial societies, total industrial electricity consumption (including that supplied from industry's own plants) is about three times as great as residential consumption.[7] Consumption is uneven, with some 20,000 industrial establishments out of a total of around 250,000 accounting for better than 90 per cent of over-all requirements. Three major industries—primary metals, chemicals, and pulp paper—account for roughly three-fourths of total industrial generation, which in turn amounts to about one-fourth of the total electric power used by industry. Electric energy sales to commercial customers represent about a sixth of total utility sales; some 8 million customers in

---

[6] First measure is used by the United Nations (and in this book's tables and graphs); the second measure is used by the *Oxford Economic Atlas of the World*.

[7] Including half of utility sales.

Courtesy of American Electric Power System

The Philip Sporn Plant, a 1.1-million-kilowatt power plant of the American Electric Power System, is located at New Haven, West Virginia, and receives its coal supply principally by barge. Such plants generate base-load electricity at costs around 2.5 to 3 mills per kilowatt-hour, using steam-coal that costs 15 to 20 cents per million B.t.u. (roughly $3 per ton).

1964 had an average annual use of about 21,000 kilowatt-hours (five times the average residential usage). Within another generation, there are expected to be some 10 million commercial customers, each consuming at about twice the present rate. It is anticipated that residential use (now a third of utility sales) will increase from 4,500 kilowatt-hours per home at present to at least 7,000 in another generation. It could be much more if all-electric homes become popular (the typical fully electrified home, of which there are nearly 2½ million today, consumes from 20,000 to 25,000 kilowatt-hours per year).[8] The

[8] The national Electric Heating Association expects 19 million or more such homes by 1980.

average selling price of U.S. electricity today is about 1.7 cents per kilowatt-hour: residential users pay about 2.3 cents, commercial users a bit less, and industrial users about 1 cent.

In general, the use of electric energy is determined by complex economic and non-economic factors, only one of which is the cost of electric energy and the primary fuel for its generation. The cost of energy-consuming equipment far exceeds the cost of the electric energy required for its operation and the capital cost of the energy-producing facilities. Much more important factors in determining the establishment and expansion of energy-consuming industries are markets, transportation costs, location of raw materials for processing, etc. Rarely is it true to say that the cost of electric energy determines the character of an economy.

Reserve Problems

The world has some 200 million installed kilowatts in developed water power, generating over 950 billion kilowatt-hours of electricity yearly. This is perhaps 13 per cent of the world's potential at mean flow (estimated at some $1\frac{1}{2}$ billion installed kilowatts with 7 to 8 trillion kilowatt-hours generating potential). However, such global estimates of potential water power must be accepted with great caution. The total flow of rivers during the year can be divided into several categories on the basis of the portion of the year during which it is available; very few rivers can be developed for water power if only the year-round flow is utilized, and to what extent it pays to regularize the natural flow is a complex engineering and economic question. Mean flow (i.e., flow available half of the time) is a much more reliable basis upon which to measure potentialities than the ordinary minimum flow usually found in published sources.

In estimating potential water power, the custom is to disregard the effect of storage, except for constructed reservoir sites, the potential power being based on the existing flow. The amount of developed power by countries is

Coal barges waiting to be unloaded at an American Electric Power System power plant on the Ohio River. The cost of movement per ton-mile is 3 to 4 mills. This is the cheapest inland movement of coal, and it is only a third of what it would cost to move the same coal by rail.

Courtesy of American Electric Power System

based on the installed capacity of water power at constructed plants, which averages two to four times, and may be as much as ten times, the potential power at low flow at the same sites. Thus, potential power may be considerably understated, particularly when compared with developed power. This fact should be considered in comparing potential power with developed power and also in estimating the percentage of a nation's water power resources that are utilized.

As in the development of most potential resources, the urban-industrial realm has made much greater relative use of its possibilities. Although endowed with little more than a third of the world's potential water power, such countries have over four-fifths of the world's installed water power facilities. And, again, as usual when breaking down the urban-industrial realm into regional components, Western Europe has made the greatest relative use, as compared to her daughter civilizations to the east or west or in the antipodes. However, changing perspective, the underdeveloped realm gets more than half of its total electricity from developed water power, while the urban-industrial realm gets only about a quarter from that source. Among the poor regions, Latin America and the non-Communist Far East have made the greatest relative use of water power.

Coal preparation plant at Muskingum Mine and beginning of the 4½-mile overland coal conveyor system leading directly to the Muskingum River plant. Both conveyor and 0.9-million-kilowatt electric plant are owned by the Ohio Power Company of the American Electric Power System. Such giant power plants at or near coal mines are increasingly common (e.g., soon Philadelphia will receive electricity via a 500,000-volt AC line from two 1.8-million-kilowatt stations near Johnstown, Pennsylvania).

Courtesy of American Electric Power System

TABLE 13-7

World: Electricity Generating Capacity and Potential Water Power, by Great-Region and Economic-Type of Society, 1962–1964 Average-Annual *

(in millions of kilowatts)

	Total Capacity [1] (million kilowatts = 100.0 per cent)	Steam Power Capacity [1]	Water Power Capacity [1]	Potential Water Power	
				Minimum Flow [2]	Mean Flow [3]
North America	263	78%	22%	53	150
Western Europe	190	64	36	31	80
Eastern Europe (including the U.S.S.R.)	125	80	20	68	300
Oceania	9	61	39	9	25
Latin America	23	54	46	53	175
Sub-Saharan Africa	9	78	22	201	500
Middle East (including North Africa)	6	67	33	3	15
Non-Communist Far East	42	43	57	52	175
Communist Far East	18	61	39	20	80
World	685	71	29	490	1,500
High-income countries	618	74	26	166	580
Low-income countries	67	47	53	324	920

	(per cent of 685 million kilowatts)	(per cent of 485 million kilowatts)	(per cent of 200 million kilowatts)	(per cent of 490 million potential kilowatts)	(per cent of 1,500 million potential kilowatts)
North America	38.4	42.2	29.0	10.8	10.0
Western Europe	27.7	25.2	34.0	6.4	5.4
Eastern Europe (including the U.S.S.R.)	18.2	20.6	12.5	13.9	20.0
Oceania	1.3	1.1	1.8	1.8	1.6
Latin America	3.4	2.6	5.2	10.8	11.7
Sub-Saharan Africa	1.3	1.5	1.0	41.0	33.3
Middle East (including North Africa)	0.8	0.8	1.0	0.6	1.0
Non-Communist Far East	6.2	3.7	12.0	10.6	11.7
Communist Far East	2.6	2.3	3.5	4.1	5.3
World	100.0	100.0	100.0	100.0	100.0
High-income countries	90.0	92.6	81.7	34.0	38.6
Low-income countries	10.0	7.4	18.3	66.0	61.4

* In North American, Western European, and a few other countries, such estimates are based on known sites, but elsewhere the estimates are based mostly on rainfall and topography and therefore are not so reliable.

[1] "Capacity" includes that installed in industrial plants as well as in public utilities.

[2] "Minimum Flow" includes that available for 95 per cent of the time and 100 per cent efficiency assumed.

[3] "Mean Flow" includes that available for 50 per cent of the time and an over-all efficiency of 80 per cent (from reservoir level to station bus bar) assumed.

The greatest concentrations of water power potential are in four restricted belts: Largest is the Congo River and its tributaries, especially its great rapids over the edge of the plateau, equal to triple the entire North American potential. Next largest are the streams in northern India and southwest China, and along the southern and eastern edges of the Tibetan highlands, with at least the equal to Europe's potential (and perhaps much more, as this belt is poorly inventoried). Northwestern North America, especially the Columbia-Yukon systems, has half of the entire North American potential. Northwestern South America, especially the Andean headwaters of the Amazonian and Orinoco systems, probably has a potential equal to that of the United States or Canada. Very little of these potentials has been developed or seems likely to be developed in the near future. Most of the potentials await either urban-industrialization of the surrounding regions or development of massive electrochemical and electrometallurgical industries by outside capital for outside markets. In many cases, the hydrodevelopment will not be for its own sake but as part of multipurpose river development, with water supply, irrigation, navigation, and other goals fully as important.

Water Power's Prospects

In most parts of the world, the share of hydropower in total electricity generation seems likely to decline, even in the short term before nuclear electricity becomes economically competitive (although hydro's share of peak-load output may increase). This is especially probable in urban-industrial economies. An important reason is that most of the possible technical efficiency in hydroelectricity generation has already been realized, while thermal plants may be able to double their efficiency in the next generation. The electrical utility industry has been averaging approximately a 2 per cent improvement in power generation efficiency over the past twenty years, and this seems likely to continue for several more decades. One possibility is magneto-hydrodynamics (MHD), which promises an efficiency of 55 to 60 per cent (fuel costs of 1.78 mills per kilowatt-hour) compared with the 40 per cent in the best conventional plants (fuel costs of 2.12 mills per kilowatt-hour). Basic difference between the two systems is that the armature, which is rotated through a magnetic field in the conventional generator, is replaced by high-temperature gas in the MHD (with part of the boiler, steam piping, steam turbine, steam condenser, boiler feed pumps, and other equipment being eliminated). A major problem is to develop materials that can withstand great extremes of temperature: the gas may be heated to more than 5,000° F., while the magnetic apparatus is close to absolute zero.

Even ignoring such radical change, much progress is being achieved along conventional lines. Much progress is currently being made in thermal plants by cutting down fuel costs, which account for about 80 per cent of total operating costs (fuel for a good size boiler for just one year can run close to the cost of the boiler itself). The newest steam plants burn somewhere between ½ to ¾ pound of coal for each kilowatt-hour of electricity produced (depending on the coal used), compared with the national average of 0.9 pound per kilowatt-hour. In a 275,000-kilowatt unit (the largest are nearly twice this size), some 1½ million pounds of steam pass through the turbine each hour. It expands to a volume 2,600 times its original form in the fraction of a second and blasts through the turbine at about ten times the velocity of a hurricane. In a snap of the fingers, steam is cooled from 1,100° F. to 80° F. The top speed on some of the larger turbine blades will reach 1,070 miles per hour, well over the speed of sound. There will be a centrifugal pull of more than 50 tons on each such blade. Efficiency increases with higher temperatures and faster speeds. However, above 1,050° F., stainless steel piping is required, and that increases costs 50 per cent. So the cost factor will keep temperatures at about 1,050° F., thus limiting pressures to about 3,500 pounds per square inch for the foreseeable future in most areas, except in areas where fuel costs are extremely high (some plants operate at 5,000 pounds per square inch and 1,200° F.).

Another reason for the declining prospects for

water power in many areas is that most of the cheaply harnessed hydrosites have already been used, and many areas face higher costs of development, no matter whether public or private organizations are in charge. For example, in the Pacific Northwest, utility men figure that the region needs about ½ million kilowatts of new capacity each year to keep pace with growth in demand. In effect, this means one major new power dam each year at a cost of $¼ billion or more. The best sites have already been taken up by the federal government. Any new generation will be higher-cost power. Even the output from the latest federal projects now under construction will cost more, though it will be mixed with the cheapest power from earlier dams to delay a price hike. One Bonneville Power Administration industrial rate of $17.50 per kilowatt-year is unrealistically low and cannot be maintained. Apparently, the era of very cheap power is fast coming to an end in the Northwest.

With many of the more favorable hydrosites already developed, a trend toward more economic methods of dam construction is an important factor in extending the economic feasibility of remaining sites. In particular, two types of construction are increasingly favored: the rockfill construction in which the waterproofing is obtained by means of a deck on the upper face made of asphaltic cement to give it the necessary degree of flexibility without cracking, and a combination rock and earth fill, the latter comprising a core of well-packed clay soil in between rockfill on both upstream and downstream sides. Such cheap methods are increasingly favored not only in industrial areas but in underdeveloped areas with limited steel and cement supplies.

In spite of such progress, the extreme diversity of water power sites, which requires that construction remain a craftsman-like operation, makes the reduction of capital costs less likely than in thermal or nuclear plants. The extreme diversity relates to the reliability of flow, the source of water, topography, manner of flow, manner of use, and situation.

Water power at most sites is quite undependable, a defect that seriously interferes with its full utilization for the generation of electrical energy. Even primary-power, or firm-power, sites are much more variable than usually realized. The flow of water through the Great Lakes–Niagara–St. Lawrence drainage basin is the most constant of any river system in the world, with the high water volume each year being only twice what it is in low water seasons. The Columbia's flow is thirty-five times greater in high water seasons than in low. Most rivers in strongly seasonal climates have differences ranging from hundreds to thousands, requiring tremendous storage capacity if anything like median flow is to be harnessed.

Most streams are rain fed and have their greatest volume shortly after their highest seasonal rainfall. Some are glacier fed, which afford almost costless storage, and discharge during the season of least cloud cover and warmest weather. In certain areas, such as northern Italy, hydroplants on both types of river are tied together: the Apennine streams carrying the base load during the winter (rainy) season, the Alpine streams being the main reliance during the summer (drought) season. Most valley glaciers in mid-latitude mountain regions are diminishing in size, reducing the advantage to be gained from such natural storage.

The manner of flow affects facility costs greatly. Run-of-river plants are usually cheap, requiring little expensive construction, but utilizing only 30 to 40 per cent of the river flow. Storage-type plants are usually very expensive, sometimes (such as Hoover Dam) requiring big enough reservoirs to hold two to four years' flow of the river, but are able to utilize 50 to 75 per cent of the entire flow (most of the remainder being lost by evaporation and percolation).

Topography affects the type of hydroinstallation that is technically feasible. Low-heads are common, but only occasionally used, although the French-developed system of submersible units promises greater use of such low falls (often 20 to 30 feet or so). Moderate-head plants (mainly 75 to 100 feet, such as many of the TVA main stem plants) are more common; the average usable head on rivers is estimated at about 450 feet, usually used in several successive power plants on the same river. High-head plants generate much electricity with very little water; a few ½-mile heads are harnessed in North America (mainly on the sharp eastern slope of Sierra Nevadas), but most such plants are found in the European Alps, some of which have a fall of over a mile. The new cheap methods of dam construction are obviously less suited to the higher moderate-head and high-head sites.

The manner of use involves consideration of public versus private harnessing of rivers. It is often less politics, however, than technology that determines the relative roles of public and private power. There has been, apparently, inexorable forces at work that have made evolving electrical technology and ever-changing energy-resource base (from steam and diesel to atomic energy) more receptive to public enterprise than has been the case in other utilities. Approximately 47 per cent of U.S. hydroelectric capacity is owned by the federal government, 11 per cent by non-federal governmental bodies, and 42 per cent by private owners, reflecting the increasing importance of federal multipurpose projects in the West and TVA areas. However, total electrical-distributing business is only 25 per cent publicly owned (public-power agencies and Rural Electrification Agency Co-ops together).

Situation, or relative location, affects the comparative economics of electricity generation. A hydropotential located in a fuel-rich area has a different comparative economics than one in a shield area where competition is less rigorous.

Increasingly, in regions of heavy electricity consumption other than fuel-less shields and uplands, hydropower is becoming supplementary to steam plants. For example, the TVA area's original dependence upon hydropower has become changed to an electricity supply over three-fourths steam generated. In areas of mature economy, one type of hydroelectric development is still a growth activity—pumped-storage projects. A pumped-storage development requires a steady supply of water in one reservoir and a second one at a higher elevation than the first. In such a power generation system, water is pumped from the lower reservoir to the higher during periods when electric power demands are at their lowest. The water is stored in the upper reservoir until an especially heavy demand for electricity develops. Then it is allowed to flow downhill to its original source after passing through turbine blades in a generating station between the two reservoirs. The power that is generated is only two-thirds that fed in originally, but it represents a saving over the former waste that is especially useful for peak loads. Western Europe now has 3 million kilowatts capacity, and North America has about the same amount built and building.

Data on hydroelectric generation indicate that, with the possible exception of the Pacific and Mountain regions, the extent of availability of hydroelectric generation has had little effect on kilowatt-hour sales per capita. In the Pacific and Mountain regions, hydro has undoubtedly affected kilowatt-hour per capita upward. The greatest per capita sales of kilowatt-hours of electricity are scored in states boasting huge public power projects or where governmental agencies are major power users.

Regional Economics of Electricity Generation

A relatively balanced demand for electricity, with resultant high load factor (usage) and low cost, usually results only where all major sectors of the economy consume electricity. This is usually found only in highly developed (urban-industrial) economies.[9]

Whereas in developed countries more than half the electricity is sold to industry (U.S.S.R. consumes nearly 80 per cent in its industry), in the underdeveloped countries, there are four different patterns. First, there are countries in which the bulk of all electricity produced is consumed in mining export industries. Second, there are countries in which the bulk is used for urban-residential purposes. Third, there are

[9] Annual plant-utilization factors for mature urban-industrial countries usually are in the range of one-third to two-thirds (the United States normally has a factor in the 50 to 55 per cent range). The gap between the actual electricity generated and that theoretically capable of generation at full rated capacity reflects non-use of certain facilities, part-time use of other facilities, and some waste.

countries in which local industries consume the overwhelming part of all available electricity. Fourth, there are countries in which agriculture and industry consume the bulk of the electricity produced. Of the categories, only the last one appears satisfactory, and it is found in only a very few underdeveloped countries; these show a relatively balanced electricity demand, with roughly one-third consumed in industry, another third in agriculture, and the remaining third in households and commercial establishments. Those underdeveloped countries in which two-thirds to three-fourths of all electricity is consumed by local industry show, as a rule, a very low load factor because of the fact that most industries are single shift.

Rural electrification in underdeveloped areas is at the same time a more important and a more complicated task than that in the developed countries. Whereas in the underdeveloped areas the vast majority of the population is in the rural areas, the bulk of the population in the industrial countries is not living in the rural areas; thus, rural electrification represents quantitatively a far more complicated problem than in industrial countries. Also, whereas nearly all industrial countries are situated in areas of moderate climate where irrigation is not as a rule necessary, where food does not spoil rapidly, etc., most of the underdeveloped countries are in warmer or tropical areas where the introduction of electricity might bring about structural changes in agriculture and a considerable improvement of agricultural returns. There are also social reasons of considerable importance that make it advisable to introduce electricity in the villages as quickly as possible in order to permit changes in the traditional pattern of village life. In industrial countries, one of the main tasks of rural electrification is to replace human labor by electric power. In many underdeveloped countries, this cannot be the aim. Rather, the main tasks of rural electrification are higher output, employment in dead season, lower production costs by replacing animal labor but not human labor by electric power, improvement in food preservation and in social conditions, and modernization of village industries. Thus, underdeveloped countries will have to undertake their own research in all fields from equipment to finance. Cooperation in such research and pooling of experience among underdeveloped countries will become necessary in the future. In some underdeveloped countries where rural electrification will have to be based on isolated production, in the absence of country-wide transmission lines, it would be desirable to design cheap small generating stations to be fueled by agricultural by-products cheaply available in the villages. The stress in all such equipment should be on cheapness in capital cost and simplicity in operation rather than on fuel efficiency. Similar efforts are required in respect to cheap distribution lines and cheap consumption equipment.

Industrial countries, because of the huge amounts involved and rapid changes in substitutability, must pay more attention to economics. Costs of power from several selected types of power installations range from less than 1 to 30 cents per kilowatt-hour. Most residential consumers of electricity in North America pay 2 to 3 cents per kilowatt-hour for power from central plants. Power from some small central installations is more expensive, ranging up to 3½ cents per kilowatt-hour, and that from gasoline- or diesel-powered generator sets used on non-electrified farms for pumping irrigation water, etc., costs in the range of 4 to 8 cents per kilowatt-hour. In some foreign locations, much higher costs prevail, even in central stations. Not many regions in Europe, for example, have sufficient traditional sources of energy such as low-grade coal or hydropower to meet the increasing demands of consumption at present costs. During the next ten to twenty years, widely scattered lignite fields (Western Germany, Poland, Czechoslovakia, Austria, Yugoslavia) may be increasingly tapped. The hydroelectric potential is very unevenly distributed and is relatively small in most highly industrialized countries of Western Europe; the greatest potential for the next twenty to thirty years is available in Norway, Austria, and Yugoslavia. Looking ahead, a new relationship must be developed in the energy production of Europe. Increased international cooperation will become an absolute necessity if the price of power is kept at the present level. It is becoming an absolute necessity for the progressive economic development of Europe to find new sources of energy and at the same time facilitate a more even balance of power production (both thermal and hydro supply) within both the national and international levels.

Another method of increasing efficiency and thus lowering costs is to enlarge grid systems. Some electrical engineers dream of continental grids of extra-high-voltage (EHV) lines tying together all the great and small power systems, allowing full use of generating capacity and full efficiency of transmission lines and distribution systems.

Already, local and regional grids have greatly increased efficiency over the past generation. A single utility needs to keep in reserve generators that will turn out 25 per cent of its usual capacity to insure uninterrupted power in case of a breakdown; but when three or more utilities are linked in a pool, chances of simultaneous failure are so small that reserve units can be cut to between 5 and 10 per cent of capacity. About 80 per cent of the 160,000 miles of transmission lines in the United States are still operating at voltages of 138,000 and below. In many areas, this is enough, but it is too low for peak loads in some areas, and definitely too low in others to make high-priced rights of way yield efficient returns.

To carry prospective loads, power companies must either double the number of existing lines and operate them at the voltages now used, or up the voltage to provide more power over fewer lines. There are about 2,500 miles of 345,000-volt lines, most of which are in the eastern part of the Midwest. For the next fifteen to twenty years, such 345,000-volt lines will be ample to carry the loads needed by most companies. By 1970, such EHV lines will be the backbone transmission lines of the utility industry in the East, Midwest, and South. The higher cost of EHV lines is more than offset by the increase in capacity (e.g., a 345,000-volt line costs four or five times as much to build as a standard 115,000-volt line, but it can carry nine times more power, at roughly half the cost per kilowatt-hour).

Lines of even higher voltage are feasible, by converting alternating current to direct current for long-distance transmission and then reconverting back to alternating current for local usage. Uneconomical for short-distance transmission, direct-current lines begin to pay off at distances over 400 miles by eliminating serious loss of current along the way. Hydro-Quebec is constructing a system of 735,000-volt lines (the first commercial installation of such high voltage in the Western world) to carry power from the vicinity of Labrador to the Montreal area. Ontario's Hydroelectric Commission has a 460,000-volt line from the Hudson (James) Bay vicinity to southern Ontario. Consolidated Edison Company of New York is planning to bring a huge block of Labrador hydroelectricity over 700,000-volt (or higher) lines, either via Quebec or across the Maritimes. In the U.S. West, ten private utilities and five public systems are planning a network of 750,000-volt lines between the Pacific Northwest, California, and the Colorado Plateau areas.

The U.S.S.R. is now operating a 500,000-volt line between the Kubyshev hydroplant and the Moscow area, and an 800,000-volt line between Volgograd (on the lower Volga River) and the Donets Basin 300 miles to the west. Eventually, the Soviets plan to transfer 50 billion kilowatt-hours a year from the giant hydroelectric plants on the Angara and Yenisei rivers and from the Siberian coal-fed thermal power plants westward to "European" Russia, transmitted over a 1,500,000-volt direct-current line.

With such extra-high voltage, generating plants can be located near the source of power, and the power sent to the areas of consumption by wire more cheaply than coal, for example, can be transported. Such interconnected systems provide the cheapest electricity, with large steam units (or nuclear units in the future) best suited to carry base loads, and hydroplants (except in shield and alpine areas) or older steam units best used for peak loads. Pumped-storage plants in such grids decrease losses resulting from the extreme perishability; off-peak power from thermal or nuclear stations is sent to hydroplants where special reversible turbines pump water from below the dam up into the reservoir for use at some other time.

Perspective

Past trends of generating capacity have indicated a more rapid increase in fuel-generated electric power than in hydrogenerating capacity. Except for coal, there are upward pressures in the real costs of production for hydropower and thermal-produced power by oil and natural gas. Increased demands for coal by electric power industries in most mature industrial countries are expected to help coal out of its doldrums. New types of gas turbines using coal might have not only the advantages of greater efficiency and lower capital investment, but also they will not require large quantities of cooling water, a tightening commodity in many areas.

The average cost of electricity from water power is usually less than for thermal generation, but the advantage of these lower costs is concentrated in special areas. Even in areas with considerable remaining potential, another generation is likely to see only 10 per cent or less of electricity generation coming from hydroplants, perhaps less than from nuclear plants in many countries. Most of the hydrodevelopment is likely to be used for peak-load flexibility, either conventionally or via pumped-storage auxiliary, in systems dominated by coal and nuclear facilities.

POTENTIAL SOURCES OF ENERGY

During the first eighteen and a half centuries of the Christian era, some 9 Q [10] of energy are estimated to have been consumed by mankind,

[10] The large energy unit Q may be expressed in several different ways: either as 1.0×10^{18} B.t.u. or as the equivalent of 38 billion tons of bituminous coal (which is equal to about fifteen times the present annual world coal production or to about 2/3 per cent of the world's proven/probable bituminous coal reserves). Total economically recoverable world reserves of conventional fuels are estimated by various sources between 40 Q and 100 Q. The figures will change, of course, with changes in technology and economics.

corresponding to an average rate of under 1/2 Q per century. After the Industrial Revolution began, the rate of consumption accelerated, so that by 1850 the actual rate was about 1 Q per century. If the entire present population of the world were to consume energy per capita at the same rate as in the United States at present, total world energy consumption would be over 5 1/2 Q per decade, instead of the present 1 Q per decade, and all known reserves of economically recoverable conventional fossil fuels would be exhausted in less than a century. Even if the present annual demand for primary fuels (5 per cent) is projected, such fuel reserves would be exhausted in about two centuries, even in favored regions such as North America.

Actually, changing technology and changing economics may well increase the ultimate recovery to several times such present estimates. However, estimated consumption rates could also increase more rapidly than projected. Regional energy contexts also differ greatly. Consequently, substitution of non-conventional energy sources is inevitable; in fact, they are already occurring on a small scale in certain areas.

Other Hydrocarbons

Of the fossil fuels, liquid petroleum and natural gas are the most convenient for production and use, while coal is by far the most abundant. However, there are other fossil fuels that are not unimportant, although they are still either less desirable as fuel sources, or less accessible, or in smaller supply.

Ultimate recovery is unlikely to be as great as conventional fossil fuels now being exploited, but for certain types of fuel and for certain regions, they may well be of major importance in the future.

Gilsonite. A very minor hydrocarbon in a world perspective, but one recently added to the rank of fossil fuels currently being exploited, is gilsonite (Uintaite), a petroleum-like substance that through geologic accident failed to liquefy. Some 60 per cent of all the world's known gilsonite (at least 16 million tons, or the equivalent of 100 million barrels of oil) is near Bonanza, Colorado. This natural pitch is found in long fissures that sometimes run close to the surface. The veins run up to 22 feet wide, from 100 to 1,500 feet deep, and up to 40 miles long. It is mined by hydraulic methods that literally sluice the shiny black material out of the narrow vertical seams by means of a drilling machine mounting two high-pressure jet nozzles. Daily some 700 tons of slurry (65 per cent water, 35 per cent gilsonite) is moved through a 72-mile-long pipeline to the refinery near Grand Junction, Colorado. The refinery turns out 1,330 barrels of gasoline and 275 tons of low-sulfur-content coke (mainly for the aluminum companies in the Pacific Northwest). The crude is produced for $1½ to $2 per barrel, which is competitive with low-grade natural petroleum.

Oil shale. Originally, oil shale was lake sediment, much like the material often turned into petroleum, but not subjected to the pressure and heat that occurred elsewhere. Strictly speaking, oil shale is not shale, but a combination of marlstone (a cousin of limestone) and kerogen (a yellow waxlike substance similar to gelatin in consistency). Heating "cracks" the kerogen and releases shale oil, a sticky, smelly, evil-looking jelly that can be substituted for petroleum (although refining difficulties are like those associated with high-sulfur-content crude oil).

The measured quantities of oil shale are staggering in size, and they grow larger as more information becomes available. Actually, we have resources several times the amount given in published figures. Estimates of total economically recoverable petroleum and oil shale resources in areas outside the Communist bloc were recently estimated as follows (after Miller and Cameron):

	Liquid Hydrocarbons	Oil Shale
	(billions of barrels)	
United States	170	2,000
Rest of Free World	730	2,000
	900	4,000

In addition, the U.S.S.R., China, and other Communist nations have huge reserves (and currently they have the largest production of oil and gas from such oil shale).

Oil shale technology, as we now know it, is straightforward. The shale must be mined, then subjected to a heating process (retorting) to distill from it a crude oil, and finally the oil must be refined to usable products. Rock quarry operations applied to underground mining of Colorado shale have dropped costs to under 50 cents per ton (or $1 to $1.30 per barrel of oil). Up to 150 tons of oil shale per man-shift of underground labor has been achieved (compared with 25 tons in most mechanized underground mines). New retorting methods derive all process fuel from the shale itself and require no water for condensing and cooling the product oil (important in the arid West and northeast Brazil, where the largest known reserves are found); the retorting costs are now about $1 per barrel. Raw shale oil, as it flows from the retort, is a black, highly viscous oil with a high nitrogen and sulfur content. Most of the sulfur and nitrogen must be removed, and the wax-forming compounds also must be rearranged or eliminated if shale oil is to be upgraded to the crude-petroleum level. Shale oil refining has been aided greatly by new processes developed to refine high sulfur crude petroleum. Coking, a form of thermal cracking, and hydrogenation, the adding of hydrogen molecules to the coked shale oil in the presence of a catalyst under high temperatures and pressures, are the steps needed to upgrade the shale oil to the free-flowing marketable crude.

Careful engineering and economic studies of the large-scale application of the new methods developed for oil shale utilization indicate that Colorado shale oil may cost no more, and perhaps less, than new domestic petroleum. It is estimated that crude shale oil could be produced and sold profitably for a wellhead price of no more than $2½ per barrel (favorable economics depend, to a large extent, on sales of by-products: ethylene and olefinics, plus ammonia, sulfur, and coke). It is probable that a change in market conditions must take place before shale oil will be produced in quantity. As long as there is shut-in petroleum production capacity that can be made available at no additional investment, there would seem to be little incentive in bringing in new oil supplies that require substantial investment.

A recent suggestion is to attempt mining oil shale by using atomic explosions. The only purpose of the explosion would be to create a permeable matrix. The shale then would be ignited underground and a portion of its organic matter burned. This heat of combustion would release the oil and allow it to be pumped to the surface in a manner analogous to petroleum production. There is no certainty that oil produced in this manner will cost any less than that produced from favorable locations by conventional methods. There is no assurance yet that the method will even work, but if found feasible, the most likely application will be deep-lying oil shale strata and perhaps some of the leaner shale deposits.

Another suggestion is to convert oil shale into gas instead of into oil (the Soviets are reported to be doing this to Estonian oil shale to produce gas for the Leningrad market). The process of conversion is called "hydrogasification" because it uses hydrogen as a reagent to gasify the organic matter in oil shale. If the Colorado oil shale deposits were used for gas production instead of oil, 6,000 trillion cubic feet could be produced (present proven reserves of natural gas are 250 trillion cubic feet; ultimate reserves might be 3,000 trillion cubic feet). Gas will be produced from oil shale when demand exceeds our ability to produce gas economically from natural reservoirs. The oil shales of the West and probably those of the East, because of their proximity to the large population centers, may become an important fuel-gas supply for our cities and towns as well as raw material for the petrochemicals industry.

Tar sands. Naturally occurring tars are called by many different names: tar sands, bituminous sands or sandstones, asphalt rock, pitches, etc. Little is known about origin; some think that they are residues from natural evaporation of crude petroleum, and others think they may represent early stages in the formation of crude petroleum. Ignorance of reserves is even greater. The largest known deposit of tar sand is in the northern part of Alberta, Canada, extending along and back from the Athabaska River and its tributaries. Other large subterranean deposits of tar are believed to exist in Venezuela and in Iraq, and some believe deposits may be located along the fringes of many petroleum basins elsewhere.

The known minimum area of the Alberta tar sands stratum is some 1,500 square miles; estimated maximum extent is 30,000 square miles. The thickness of the deposit ranges from a few feet to 200 feet. Less than 2 per cent of the stratum is exposed at the surface, and an additional but lesser fraction lends itself to open-pit methods. As to the remainder, it is buried beneath 500 to 1,800 feet of shale, sandstone, and glacial drift, and defies the ordinary techniques of underground mining. The mass is neither static enough to provide supporting columns for underground tunnels and drifts nor sufficiently fluid to be forced-pumped by gravity, so the mechanics of removing the tar sands from beneath an overburden too deep for open-pit methods has thus far discouraged the most seasoned production men.

A typical square mile of the Alberta tar sands will contain 1 barrel of crude tar per cubic yard; if 175 feet thick and assuming 15 per cent recovery, yield from 15,000 square miles could be 300 billion barrels. Some estimates are much higher, 700 billion barrels or more (twice the world's proven oil reserves).

Several processes to separate the oil from the sands have been developed and tested, including centrifugal, electrostatic, and hot water washing methods. The Great Canadian Oil Sands, Ltd., company will quarry 100,000 tons of sand a day and move it by a conveyor system to a separation plant where the 31,500 barrels a day of oil will be separated from the sand by hot water or low-pressure steam, after which it will be hydrogenated so that it can be shipped through a pipeline to the Sun Oil, Ltd., refinery at Sarnia, Ontario. Coke and sulfur will be by-products when the facility begins producing in 1967. Strip mining can reach perhaps 5 per cent of the sand.

Shell Oil Co. of Canada, Ltd., aims at producing 100,000 barrels of oil per day by injections of steam and chemicals, with a push-pull pumping technique. In a 2-acre square, there will be one production well with injection wells on the corners through which a recipe of hot water, steam, and sodium hydroxide will circulate, forming an emulsion of water and tar that can be drawn up by pumping. Each 130,000 barrels of tar will yield 100,000 barrels of oil when run through a still at the well site, which will be piped to an Edmonton refinery, with the residual pitch being used as fuel for making more steam and hot water. From 50 per cent to perhaps 70 per cent of the potential oil may be reached by this process. The Alberta government says it agrees with Shell's prediction of need for tar sands production before 1980, but it is reluctant to allow big production that may injure the province's $4 billion investment in conventional oil production.

Peat. Peat is a product of the natural decomposition of such aquatic plants as reeds, rushes, sedges, and mosses. These plants show luxuriant growth under favorable conditions in fairly still but not stagnant water. The peat or turf used for fuel is the accumulated mass of bog vegetation made carbonaceous through decay.

Peat is a very young fossil material, so young that it is being formed today at a rate that almost removes it from the classification of unrenewable resources. The rate of accumulation of peat is doubtful, but poor bogs accumulate at an average rate something like that of timber, with average accumulation probably several times greater than that. George Kazakov, a Russian peat expert now living in the United States, computes that there are 223 billion dry tons of peat available on earth, more than half of it in the U.S.S.R. The reserve is equal to about 1 per cent of the world's coal reserve in energy value.

Raised (high) bogs, with only minor ash and about half the B.t.u. value of good coal, are being drained and dug extensively in northern Europe and the U.S.S.R. The U.S.S.R. produces over 160 million tons of peat, some 92 per cent of world production. Ireland is the second producer, about two-thirds of its 4 million tons being used for electricity generation. West Germany is third, and the United States is fourth, with 0.6 million tons production and 0.3 million tons imports (about 94 per cent of the consumption being for general soil improvement). Besides power generation and briquetted types for household consumption, in Europe and the U.S.S.R. some is distilled like wood to form gas, semicoke, liquid fuels, ammonium sulfate, calcium acetate, methanol, creosote, and other products.

Peat has been proposed as a raw product for the manufacture of liquid fuel. The various coal-conversion processes can be applied to peat; but technologically, bituminous coal is the best raw product, followed by subbituminous coal, lignite, then peat. Little is known about the economics of such conversion, but with Europe's increasing use of imported petroleum and the U.S.S.R.'s spreading oil pipeline network into its peat areas, the likelihood of widespread conversion seems unlikely.

Perspective. The miscellaneous fossil fuels (oil shale, tar, peat) are small in size compared with coal (maximum estimates 1:20; minimum estimates 1:10), but substantial when compared to petroleum and natural gas (maximum estimates 5:1; minimum estimates 1½:1). Their rate of use will probably be determined by trends in petroleum and natural gas and nuclear applications to transportation. If nuclear application to small vehicles becomes feasible, marginal fossil fuels may not be competitive, so far as energy use is concerned. If, as now seems likely, nuclear applications are restricted to large vehicles (ships, locomotives, large planes) and small vehicles remain dependent on liquid fuels, then the potential use of marginal petroleum deposits and of other (coal and the unconventional) fossil fuels that can be converted into acceptable liquid fuels becomes more likely. Large-scale use of oil shale, the most likely new source, seems slated for inauguration as soon as heavy pressure is put on domestic crude production, providing that protection from cheap imports is not completely eliminated.

Nuclear Power

Nuclear power is more expensive than competitive fuels almost everywhere and may remain so for a long time. The development period will last through most of the 1960's, with economic substitution mainly occurring in the 1970's in restricted areas such as electricity generation and production of low-pressure steam. The chief advantage of nuclear power lies in its comparatively low fuel cost; the chief economic disadvantage of the nuclear plant is the relatively high capital costs.

Nuclear power improves its comparative advantage with respect to fuel costs in proportion to the increase in transport costs, so its first economical applications are likely to be in relatively inaccessible areas. Also, the installation must have a high load factor or utilization factor to justify the high capital cost, so the first economical applications will probably be for base-load purposes.

Reserve problems. Uranium is widely distributed through practically all rocks all over the world, but it usually is in very low concentration, something like 1 to 2 ounces of uranium for 30 tons of rock. It is widely distributed because it is chemically active; it forms compounds with other elements, and the compounds formed dissolve readily in water. Throughout the earth's history, then, most of the uranium has been spread evenly at low concentration. Uranium is a major constituent of about 100 types of mineral and is about as plentiful in the earth's crust as lead and zinc, but there are few places where the concentration is sufficiently rich to justify exploitation.

The presently economically recoverable deposits are of two types. Veins containing mostly pitchblende (with uranium in unoxidized form) have been found principally in the Congo (now worked out), Canada, and Portugal; such deposits range between 1 and 4 per cent uranium and are found mainly deep in the earth. Much more common are replacement deposits, such as those in the U.S. Colorado Plateau, Australia, and elsewhere; these are lower grade (0.1 to 1 per cent of uranium oxide) and are found where uranium-bearing minerals have been deposited in the pores of sandstones and conglomerates.

Non-Communist Uranium Oxide (U_3O_8)
Reserves and Production, 1962 *
(thousand tons)

	Reserves	Production
United States	250	17.6
Canada	380	8.37
South Africa	370	4.8
France	} 100	1.6
Australia		1.4
		33.8
Probable additions		
Extensions of existing ore zones	400	
New ore bodies in present and adjacent districts	500	
Total	2,000	

* Assuming $8 (U.S.) to $10 (foreign) value per pound of U_3O_8.

The 2 million tons of uranium oxide available at the U.S. high purchase prices (in other markets, the price per pound of uranium oxide is $5) is only a small portion of known resources. If higher-cost ($20 to $100 per pound of U_3O_8) uranium in phosphates, shales, and lignites is considered, the inferred reserves might be increased ten times. In addition, there are enormous quantities of uranium that theoretically are recoverable from granite and other common rock, and from sea water.

Considering the United States alone, the some 90 million tons of known uranium ore, containing less than 0.3 per cent uranium oxide or some ¼ million tons, is less than half the inferred uranium resources. In addition, some 90 million tons of low-grade thorium are known, but it is not yet an economic resource. Eventually, it is planned to develop thorium breeder reactors, which will use uranium fuel encased in thorium-232, which will be converted into uranium-233, a useful fuel, by the slow-moving

Courtesy of Union Carbide Corp.

Union Carbide's Nuclear Division plant at Uravan, Colorado. Here low-grade uranium ore from mines in the Colorado Plateau is concentrated and refined to reduce bulk before shipping to other plants that produce the various grades of uranium oxide or uranium metal.

(thermal) neutron particles emitted in the pile.

If assumptions of recovery costs four to five times present ones are made (or if spectacular technological advances are made), the reserves might be increased twenty to thirty times in the long run. Such increased needs hardly seem possible in terms of reactor-fuel requirements in the foreseeable future, especially with breeder-reactor developments.

Nuclear power production problems. Electricity generated in nuclear reactor systems is not yet economically competitive with the latest conventional generating plants in the United States, but may be so by 1967. At the end of 1963, fourteen nuclear plants, with more than 1 million kilowatts capacity, were generating electricity, enough to supply the domestic needs of 1.5 million people. By the end of 1965, the capacity will be doubled, but even then it will be less than 1 per cent of total generating capacity. But the United States Atomic Energy Commission predicts that by the year 2000 nuclear power will be supplying half the nation's electricity.

The 1957 Shippingport, Pa., plant had costs of 60.15 mills per kilowatt-hour; the 1959 Dresden, Ill., plant, 9 mills; the 1960 Yankee, Mass., plant, 11 mills; the 1962 Indian Point, N.Y., plant, 14.7 mills; the 1963 Humboldt Bay, Calif., plant, 8 mills; and the Oyster Creek, N.J., plant (when completed in mid-1967) is expected to have costs between 3.79 and 4.25 mills, which is cheaper than a conventional plant in the same area. Such a plant as the last named will be more economical than conventional plants in New England, California, and Florida, where fuel costs to power companies are 34 to 36 cents per million British thermal units. In much of Appalachia and the Southwest, where fuel costs to power companies run from 15 to 25 cents per million B.t.u., conventional plants would still be cheaper in supplying regional markets, although only those areas with costs under 20 cents seem safe for several decades to come.

In Western Europe, also, large-scale nuclear power stations would seem to be economically justifiable by 1968 to 1970 (but will provide less than 5 per cent of all electricity generated). Present power production costs of nuclear plants already in the European Atomic Energy Community (Euratom) are about 50 per cent above power costs of conventional plants of the same size. The latest conventional plants have costs between 5 and 7 mills a kilowatt-hour, while the most efficient nuclear plants have costs of 9.5 mills. But plants under construction today for operation in 1968 to 1970 are expected to produce electricity at the same cost as conventionally produced power today.

The manufacturers of generating equipment expect orders for nuclear power plants to double between 1964 and 1966, with about 20 per cent of power generation sales in 1966 being nuclear capacity. Between 1958 and 1964, the cost of such nuclear power plants has dropped from more than $300 per installed kilowatt capacity to less than $130 a kilowatt (conventional equipment in large packets dropped from $150 to $100 a kilowatt in roughly the same period). Such companies as General Electric, Westinghouse, and Babcock & Wilcox now stand ready to quote firm prices on plant. By about 1970, many believe that a majority of all new base-load generating capacity will be nuclear.

Operating costs are also falling. General Electric expects large (50,000 up to 1 million kilowatts) boiling water reactors to have fuel costs below 1.5 mills per kilowatt-hour (averaged over the life of such a plant) and to have total generating costs under 5 mills in almost all cases.

The cost of nuclear fuel accounts for about a third of the cost of nuclear electricity. Part of the cost comes in the expense of fabricating the fuel rods to the fine tolerances and high standards required for a reactor (five years ago, the fabricating costs ran to $60 to $70 per pound, but now the cost is less than $50 and still dropping), part in the enriched uranium fuel that is burned, and part in the reprocessing to remove the unburned uranium and newly created plutonium from the spent fuel. Uranium oxide fuels have been found to last considerably longer than had been predicted. Only a few years ago, nuclear engineers were expecting some 10,000 megawatt-days of power for each ton of uranium fuel (1 megawatt-day equals 1 million watts of energy produced in one day). By 1963, the estimated lifetime had been raised to the range 18,000 to 20,000 megawatt-days, and in the relatively near future, the figure will rise to 25,000.

Most spectacularly, the Atomic Energy Commission now has developed a fast breeder reactor at the National Reactor Testing Station, Idaho Falls, Idaho. The sodium-cooled reactor utilizes 100 per cent of the energy produced by the fission of uranium-235, compared with only 2 per cent at most of the energy put to use in conventional reactors. The first-generation thermal reactors used only the 1 per cent of natural uranium that is uranium-235 to produce electricity. The remaining 99 per cent, uranium-238, was wasted. With fast breeders, however, one neutron is added to each uranium-238 atom to produce plutonium-239, a fissionable material, all of which can be used to produce electrical power. Thus, while producing electricity, the fast breeder produces more nuclear fuel (of another type) than it consumes. The conventional nuclear plants could produce only twice the electricity that fossil fuels could, but the more efficient breeders could mean that existing sources of uranium could produce 100 times as much electricity as the world's remaining stores of fossil fuels—each ton of uranium fuel yielding more than 250,000 megawatt-days of power.

It should be kept in mind that less than a tenth of the total commercial fuel and energy is converted into electricity at present, so nuclear reactors' eventual dominance of the electricity-generating industry has a limited substitutability in terms of the entire energy consumption. But there are additional possibilities, one of them being the nuclear production of process steam. The industries that are the major users of low-pressure steam are petroleum refining, pulp and paper, chemicals, and food processing. Over 80 per cent of the total energy used in such industries is used in the form of low-pressure steam; only 20 per cent is used as electricity. In addition, the use of process steam is growing at a faster rate than the use of electricity. Since 70 cents per 1,000 pounds of steam is well within the realm of possibility of even the older nuclear reactors, this use of nuclear power (heat) may be the largest use in high fossil fuel cost areas, rather than the more spectacular electricity generation.

Nuclear power and location theory. The chief obstacle to bringing electric power to most of the earth today is more a matter of demand than of supply. It is erroneous to assume geographic uniformity of power costs because the cost of transporting the fissionable material to any part of the globe will be negligible. If nuclear power does become competitive nearly everywhere, it is not likely to replace all other power sources. A more probable assumption is that it will gradually replace those conventional sources that are relatively high in cost, subject to fluctuation in amount, or likely to become exhausted; and that, at the same time, it will be used simultaneously with the superior alternative sources of fuel and power.

Any lowering of power costs based on nuclear energy will hardly be of sufficient importance to nullify other locational factors. Any wholesale relocation of industry is unlikely. In the same way, any rapid, general, and marked increase in the levels of living of the various peoples of the world (and especially of those whose current levels are lowest) is unlikely to result from the advent of nuclear power alone.

For industries with high fuel and power orientation, cheap nuclear power would offer the greatest potentialities for the relocation of existing capacity. Any marked reduction in power cost based on nuclear electricity should serve to increase electric-furnace capacity, particularly if the demand for electric-grade steel rises, as it well may. If nuclear power could be marketed at a price that compared favorably with that of other cheap sources of power, it could have far-reaching consequences for the aluminum industry. It could remove one of the major obstacles to the growth of competition in the industry by expanding the now limited number of locations at which cheap power would be available. However, nuclear electricity would have to be sold commercially at a cost not to exceed 4 mills per kilowatt-hour in the New York City area and 3¼ to 3½ mills at Chicago, or it would be too expensive to allow successful competition with existing capacity. All the evidence available indicates that the introduction of nuclear power is unlikely to result in any major change in primary metallurgy, and even less in fabricating industries.

The common insistence that the development of nuclear power spells an equalization of economic strength among nations is another instance of contemporary mythology. The utilization of nuclear power requires large amounts of capital and extensive technical resources. Until these are made available to the economically backward and underdeveloped areas of the globe, the benefits of nuclear power seem likely to remain for them largely hypothetical, or, at best, indirect. If nuclear power does prove to be commercially feasible, it is likely to be restricted for some time to the already highly industrialized nations because of the severe economic and cultural limitations to its utilization elsewhere; if this is true, the discrepancy between developed and underdeveloped areas may well be accentuated rather than diminished.

Obviously, the absolute position of any nation may be bettered by the addition of new energy sources. Great Britain, France, Belgium, Japan, etc., will probably make the greatest relative use of nuclear power, while the United States appears least likely to improve its relative economic status through economic development of such an energy source.

Perspective. The impact of nuclear energy upon the world's energy resources is greatest in the area of increasing life expectancy. The potential energy in fissile form may be 1,000 times greater than the potential energy in fossil fuels. Technically recoverable reserves are estimated at from 20 to 30 up to 100 times greater than the equivalent mineable fossil fuels; the great difference in estimates of exploitable uranium and thorium reflects the lack of precise geological information on many deposits and the rapid changes occurring in mining and concentrating technology. Economically recoverable nuclear materials used with present reactor technology have much less available power than that available from similar quality fossil fuel, but this will soon radically change when present experimental breeder reactor technology is commercialized and diffused.

No essential difference exists between the arrangements that make use of the heat from the nuclear reactor and that from the everyday fossil fuel burning boiler. The economics are still in favor of conventional plants located in the midst of cheap coal, lignite, petroleum, and natural gas, mainly because capital charges for nuclear plants are still higher than for conventional plants and because certain operating charges ("insurance" in both the narrow and broad senses) still are much higher. Within the decade ahead, new nuclear plants will increase their competitive advantage, especially versus older conventional facilities; and within another generation or so, nuclear plants will probably provide cheaper base-load power (when plant-utilization factor is 75 per cent or higher) except in very special areas. Within the next century, nuclear electricity will dominate nearly everywhere in the world, with other sources being minor and complementary (e.g., useful for maintaining peak-load flexibility).

Solar Energy

On a single day, the land areas of the earth are flooded with more energy from the sun than the human race has utilized in the form of fuel, falling water, and muscle power since it evolved perhaps a million years ago. The whole amount of fossil fuels left in the earth on the most optimistic guess is the energy equivalent of only 100 days of sunshine. Such is the energy potential of solar energy from a nonfunctional point of view.

However, in sharp contrast with practically all our conventional sources, solar energy is of immense quantity, universal availability, very low concentration, and extreme variability. Possibly the greatest problem in solar energy utilization is its intermittent nature. Not only is there the regular variability from day to night and season to season, but there is fluctuation due to cloudiness. The use of solar energy must therefore depend on there being (1) no need for continuous energy supply, or (2) supplementary energy use, or (3) some form of solar energy storage.

At least within the next few decades, solar energy cannot be expected to furnish an appreciable fraction of the energy needs of any country; perhaps 1 per cent in the year 2000 would appear to be an optimistic estimate. Most of this supply would be for space heating, as the outlook for its utilization in industry does not appear bright at present.

In an over-all view of the potential of residential heating and cooling with solar energy, the following factors are of particular importance: (1) these uses represent a sizable segment of the total energy demand, (2) the cost of heating and cooling with conventional energy is likely to continue its rise, and (3) the quantity of solar energy available in winter and summer in most areas of the country is adequate for most of the house heating and cooling requirements.

Solar heat collectors. Houses designed to be heated by sunlight have been built experimentally, and the system holds promise for those regions in the middle and lower latitudes where fuel costs are high and likely to go higher.

The amount of solar energy available is not a simple function of latitude, but as a first approximation, that factor is important. In general, the solar energy that reaches horizontal surfaces in the lower middle latitudes is equivalent to about 1,000 tons of coal per acre per year, or nearly 3 tons per day. In summer, in the arid subtropics, the average daily rate is equivalent to nearly 4 tons of coal per acre per day, and a rate of 5 tons is reached on a clear, dry day in June. The daily U.S. solar energy supply is about 1,700 times as great as all our present uses for energy.

To make solar energy usable, some sort of surface must be provided to intercept the radiation and convert it to another form such as heat, electricity, or chemical compounds. Conventional energy exchange surfaces, such as in a boiler furnace, may transfer heat at hourly rates of 100,000 B.t.u. per square foot of area; solar energy, however, has a maximum intensity of only about 350 B.t.u. per hour. This means that very large surfaces must be used for the recovery of appreciable quantities of energy.

Flat-plate heat collectors are essentially multi-paned "windows" (usually two to three sheets of glass) permanently curtained with a black sheet of copper, which serve the purpose of accumulating energy from the sun. All the heat is absorbed by the copper backing, from which the heat can be carried into more effective storage than is provided by normal furnishings. Such flat-plate collectors, properly disposed, are capable of trapping about one-third of the sunshine falling upon them (this is a mean value, taking into account periods of highest solar intensity and other periods when the rate of collection is lower than the rate of heat loss). In Boston, houses with an area of solar collectors a fifth of the total house envelope, and house walls of conventionally good insulating properties, can be solar heated completely without fuel when the mean atmospheric transmissivity is above 55 per cent (100 per cent is defined as no atmospheric interference).

Heat storage is the central problem. Many types of storage systems are possible. An M.I.T. house (Boston area) uses water (250 pounds per square foot of collector area) to take care of the house-heating load for two average sunless winter days in that area (if the water storage is put in the living area instead of in the attic, the heat leakage would be in the area where it is needed). A Denver, Colorado, house uses 10 tons of gravel, packed inside several columns that are an integral part of the house's interior design, which stores heat collected from sun-absorbing glass panels that fit flat on the roof in full harmony with the architectural design (together with an auxiliary gas-heating unit for extreme weather, this solar-heating system costs $2,100 compared with $1,300 for a conventional system; taking care of three-fourths of heating needs, the operating cost is about $150 yearly, or about the same as a conventional system's costs). Other houses use salts (hydrated sodium sulfate, disodium phosphate, etc.) that have a high heat of fusion (can absorb and release four to eight times as much heat as conventional construction materials), which can store enough heat to tide over two weeks of cold, sunless weather in about 1 per cent of the space to be heated (located in small sealed cans put in an insulated tank, concrete floor, or in walls or ceiling).

With heat collection by 1 square foot of a flat-plate solar-heat exchanger at a rate of 150,000 to 300,000 B.t.u. per annual heating season (variable with the length of the heating season), the value of the output per square foot of exchanger would range from 11 to 60 cents, based on a value of delivered heat of 75 cents to $2 per million B.t.u. At a fixed cost of 10 per cent per year, an expenditure of $1.10 to $6 per square foot could be justified for the collector and associated equipment. It appears that collectors and associated equipment can be built, in quantity, for costs within this range ($1 to $6 per square foot), and development of solar space-heating systems appears attractive. There are regional differences in the feasibility of heating houses by solar energy. The coastal South and Southwest are parts of a zone of maximum feasibility, where houses can be comfortably warmed by solar energy alone without difficulty. The upper South and middle Mountain and Pacific Coast regions are parts of a zone of engineering feasibility, where houses could receive at least the major portion of their heating from the sun, but economic feasibility would depend upon future technical progress and the comparative cost of other systems of space heating. Northern New England, the Great Lakes region, the northern Great Plains and Rocky Mountain regions, and the Pacific Northwest are parts of a zone of minimum feasibility, where only a minor part of space heating could be obtained from the sun, and economic application seems unlikely in the foreseeable future.

Solar energy equipment now being manufactured and sold falls into four groups: water heaters, solar-electric converters (solar batteries), solar cookers, and toys and novelties. Water heaters are common even in the subtropics, with about 25,000 being used in Florida; they comprise simply a glass-covered, blackened metal sheet in contact with tubing through which water circulates to an insulated storage tank (a 50-square-foot unit on a house roof in southern Florida can supply enough warm water for the average family, but at a cost greater than conventional water heating systems). Solar batteries are now mainly used on space probes and on experimental isolated rural telephone circuits; at present, prices of silicon metal and solar cells generating capacity would cost over $50,000 per kilowatt, compared with operated plant costs of below $200. In most parts of the low latitudes, the solar cooker may be used nearly every day in the year, from mid-morning to mid-afternoon, taking perhaps twenty minutes to prepare a meal. It consists of an anodized aluminum reflector, about 10 square feet in area, that concentrates the reflected solar energy directly to the blackened bottom of a cooking pot or of an insulated pressure cooker. The $15 cost is prohibitive for most potential users.

In both space heating and the other uses, development is still in the experimental stage, and economics are highly unfavorable. Commercial applicability remains in the unforeseeable future, but interest will probably be maintained because (1) the temperatures required are low enough (100° to 150° F.) to permit the use of flat-plate collectors, (2) the solar energy incident on a dwelling during the winter in most temperature climates is more than the energy needed for comfortable heating, (3) there is no requirement for conversion of thermal to other forms of energy, and (4) comfort heating is a major user of conventional fuels.

Heat pumps. The heat pump operates on principles identical with those of the household refrigerator: by the circulation of a substance that is gaseous under ordinary pressures but liquid at higher pressures, it is possible to pump heat from a low-temperature level to a higher one. The familiar refrigerator removes heat from food at relatively low temperatures and delivers this heat at higher temperatures to the room in which the refrigerator is placed. The heat pump does the same thing in the same way on a larger scale, except that instead of cooling food it cools water, air, or earth; the amount of heat that can be efficiently delivered to the house depends upon an ample supply of material to be cooled (obviously, if the supply is too limited, the temperature of the supply will be lowered, and more energy will be required to raise the heat to the relatively high level of house heating). A heat pump is a sort of mechanical miner of solar energy—the energy stored up in the water supply, the air, or the ground—but while the coefficient of performance of the mechanical coal miner is 20:1, that of the heat pump is usually 3:1 to 4:1.

The energy that is "mined" by the heat pump may be used for heating in winter or for air conditioning in summer. Both are accomplished without combustion, and so without odors, dirt, soot, or chimney. The heating cycle may also be used for making hot water, or for industrial processes such as drying evaporation, and distillation.

Despite their brief modern history, the heat pumps in use at the beginning of 1965 numbered about 400,000 (only central types, not including room air-conditioners), with annual sales now at 75,000 units. Heat pumps work best where the weather is temperate (no extremes of cold and hot), or where heating and cooling needs are fairly evenly balanced, as in the South and Southwest. Their use is increasing in the North, but there units usually have a built-in supplemental heating element that generates additional heat automatically when the temperature outside drops to around 20° F. In average climate locations, a heat pump costs from 5 to 20 per cent more to install than a conventional packaged gas heating and electrical cooling system. For a well-insulated house of 3,000 square feet (eight to ten rooms) in Kansas City, an adequate heat pump will cost at least $3,500 installed. Operating costs vary, of course, depending on climate and the local rate for electricity. In hot climates, the cost can be about the same as for a combination heating and cooling system; in colder climates, the month-to-month outlay can run 20 to 40 per cent more. Although the heat pump has a promising future, its net effect on the energy system will doubtless be to stimulate the per capita demand for energy, rather than to conserve energy, because of the encouragement to year-round air conditioning.

Industrial sunpower. In addition to operation without fuel, the solar furnace has two other advantages: the possibility of heating bodies to extreme temperatures, and perfectly clean operation. In France, the U.S.S.R., and the United States, experimental solar furnaces have achieved temperatures over 3,000° C. by using a plane mirror as a heliostat moving with the sun and deflecting the sun's rays so that they strike a parabolic concave mirror in the axial direction, whatever the position of the sun may be. Although higher temperatures have been reached in the electric arc, and still higher ones in electric sparks, the solar furnace is superior as regards the spatial extension of the hottest zone, so that larger bodies can be heated to extreme temperatures. Besides, there is no contact with, or interference from, any electrodes, so that chemical processes with high purity standards can be performed, or the melting of highly refractory substances can be achieved. In contrast to the application for house heating or cooking, however, the fuel saving as a result of the use of solar energy for industrial furnaces is scarcely worth mentioning in the proportion to total world energy consumption.

A serious difficulty in producing industrial power from solar energy is the intermittent supply of energy. No power is available during the night, and little or no power at all, according to the latitude, is available during the winter months in places beyond the 40th parallel. Solar power supply would therefore require the construction of plants not only for power generation, but also for storage of energy. Within the tropical zone, storage for the daily demand would suffice; in higher latitudes, storage for a half-year's supply of energy would be necessary. Even at latitudes as low as 30°, the winter supply of energy drops to about 43 per cent of the maximum rate; and at 45° latitude, the contribution in the winter months is so small that a continuous power supply could be upheld only at the cost of building storage plants with a capacity holding at least a three to four months' load.

Production of power from solar energy can be performed in several different ways. Indirectly, by using photosynthesis for growing vegetation (especially algae), fuel for thermal power plants can be produced. Semi-indirectly, by heating boilers or air heaters of conventional thermal power plants with sunshine concentrated by collecting mirrors, electricity could be generated. Directly, by converting radiation into electric voltage by means of thermocouples or photovoltaic cells, electricity could be generated in giant solar batteries. Another possibility is photolysis, the photochemical breakdown of water under exposure to sunlight, with the production of hydrogen that can either be combined with hydrogen and oxygen to form liquid fuel or used in fuel cells to produce electricity.

Perspective. Man already knows how to harness the sun's energy, although seldom efficiently even from a technical viewpoint. He does not know how to harness it economically on any important scale. It is the present-day low efficiencies and high costs that stand in the way of large-scale substitution of conventional energy. When it is learned how to raise the efficiency or lower the cost, or both, man will have at hand an inexhaustible source of power for the service of mankind. This does not seem likely to occur during the remainder of this century, with the intervention of the nuclear power age between the decline of the fossil fuel age and the rise of a solar power one.

A LONG VIEW OF FUEL AND POWER

The drain on the world's finite supply of fossil fuels is becoming immense and shows every sign of continuing acceleration. The two outstanding pressures that have accelerated fuel demand during the past half-century have come from the popularity of electric power and the internal-combustion engine. These have increased mineral-fuels consumption more rapidly than expected, so that a projection of present rates of use for several more generations will see the exhaustion of cheaply mined reserves almost everywhere. In a practical sense, after another century fossil fuels will probably cease to exist except as raw materials for chemical synthesis.

Peak production of coal for fuel may be a century or more off in the favored United States, U.S.S.R., and China; but in most of the world, peaks are likely in this century. Peak production of petroleum and natural gas may be half a century or more off in the favored Middle Eastern and other zones, but in the United States and many other marginal areas, economic peaks are also likely in this century. Oil shale will provide additional fossil fuel, but apparently only in a few areas such as the United States and Brazil, and on a large scale only when the petroleum and natural gas production becomes more expensive. Tar sands will also provide much additional fossil fuel, in Canada for certain, perhaps in many other areas as tertiary methods become common in the world's petroleum and natural gas zones.

What will follow the fossil fuel age is not perceivable with any accuracy. For the foreseeable future, nuclear power from essentially conventional plants producing steam and electricity seems probable. Perhaps, eventually, power may be obtained from chemical and nuclear reactions without the intermediate generation of heat with attendant losses, but the technology for such heatless power hardly exists at present.

The use of fusion is even more hypothetical. Fusion is the building-up, rather than the splitting, of atoms; in fusion, several light-weight atoms are squeezed together, the result being a slightly more stable atom near the center of the list of elements. The heavy hydrogen in the oceans' waters could theoretically provide enough fuel for 1,000 times the world's present power needs over the next million years, but no usable technology is known, and scientific minds have not reached a consensus on the feasibility. The same scientific uncertainty faces large-scale use of solar energy. Attempts to utilize this vast heat resource, now wasted except for minor indirect use via natural avenues, have been made for two centuries, thus far without notable success. The substitution of either fusion or solar energy for conventional or fission energy thus remains almost entirely speculative.

SUGGESTED READINGS

AYRES, EUGENE, and SCARLOTT, CHARLES A. *Energy Sources—The Wealth of the World.* New York: McGraw-Hill, 1952. Pp. 344.

CLAWSON, MARION (ed.). *Natural Resources and International Development.* Baltimore: Johns Hopkins Press (for Resources for the Future, Inc.), 1964. Pp. 27–125.

COTTRELL, FRED. *Energy and Society.* New York: McGraw-Hill, 1955. Pp. 330.

ISARD, WALTER. *Atomic Power.* New York: Blakiston, 1952. Pp. 235.

MANNERS, GERALD. *The Geography of Energy.* London: Hutchinson, 1964. Pp. 205.

MARCUS, ABRAHAM, and MARCUS, REBECCA B. *Power Unlimited.* Englewood Cliffs, N.J.: Prentice-Hall, 1959. Pp. 152.

ODELL, PETER R. *An Economic Geography of Oil.* London: G. Bell & Sons, 1963. Pp. 219.

Oxford University Press. *Oxford Economic Atlas of the World*. London: Oxford University Press, 1965. Pp. 58–69.

Pratt, Wallace E., and Good, Dorothy. *World Geography of Petroleum*. Princeton University Press and American Geographical Society of New York, 1950. Pp. 464.

Schurr, Sam H., and Netschert, Bruce C. (with others). *Energy in the American Economy, 1850–1975*. Baltimore: Johns Hopkins Press (for Resources for the Future, Inc.), 1960. Pp. 774.

Thirring, Hans. *Energy for Man*. Indiana University Press, 1958. Pp. 409.

Ubbelohde, A. R. *Man and Energy*. New York: Braziller, 1955. Pp. 247.

United States Government Printing Office. "Hearings Before The Subcommittee On Automation And Energy Resources Of The Joint Economic Committee, Congress Of The United States, Eighty-Sixth Congress, First Session. Pursuant to Sect. 5(a) of Public Law 304, 79th Congress. Oct. 12–16, 1959. Washington, D.C., 1959, 352 pp."

Van Royen, William, and Bowles, Oliver (eds.). *Atlas of the World's Resources*. Vol. II. *The Mineral Resources of the World*. Englewood Cliffs, N.J.: Prentice-Hall, 1952. Pp. 8–55.

Wu, Yuan-Li. *Economic Development and the Use of Energy Resources in Communist China*. New York: Praeger (for the Hoover Institution on War, Revolution, and Peace), 1963. Pp. 275.

Zimmermann, Erich W. *World Resources and Industries*. New York: Harper & Row, 1951. Pp. 454–612.

14

Metallurgy and Fabricating Industries

The processing of metallic ores and scrap in the 1962–1964 period produced an average annual metal output of some 440 million tons, with some 90 per cent of this production being steel, and the remainder roughly divided between merchant pig iron (used in making iron castings and wrought iron) and all other metals. Table 14–1 and the graphs on pages 428–29 indicate relative regional importance, broken down by ferrous and non-ferrous fractions.

	Primary and Secondary Production (million metric tons)
Crude steel	395.0
Merchant pig iron	25.0
Older non-ferrous metals	
Copper	5.4
Lead	3.1
Zinc	3.7
Tin	0.2
Light metals	
Aluminum	6.4
Magnesium	0.16
Others	0.01
Others (not included above, directly or indirectly)	0.01

About 15 per cent of mankind's fuel and energy is consumed in producing these primary metals, and about twice as much more in transforming them into fabricated products. Metallurgy proper involves only several per cent of world income, but the metal transforming industries using the metals account for some 15 per cent of world income.

Metallurgy is a growth activity in most of the world, adding over 5 per cent to capacity each year. However, the growth in the decade or so ahead is not expected to approach the rate that prevailed in the 1950's, as there is already a considerable amount of excess capacity in some countries. In many high-income countries, the principal motivating force behind the drive to raise metals production continues to be the desire to satisfy the demand for more consumer goods (automobiles, refrigerators, small appliances and household items of all types) by expanding populations with rising levels of living. Equally important in some parts of the world, and the prime consideration in most low-income countries, is the desire of nations to become self-sufficient in these key industrial materials or to cut down the drain of foreign exchange used to import metals.

Ferrous (iron-steel) metallurgy accounts for 95 per cent of world metals production, and about three-quarters of the value of fabricated or engineered metal products. However, there is a tendency for these overwhelming figures to diminish a bit as, in the balance, steel has been deeply hurt by substitute materials (non-ferrous

TABLE 14-1

World: Metals Production and Composition, by Great-Region and Economic-Type of Society, 1962–1964 Average-Annual
(in millions of metric tons)

	Total Metals (million metric tons = 100.0 per cent)	Crude Steel [1]	Merchant Pig Iron [2]	Older Non-ferrous Metals [3]	Light Metals [4]
North America	130	89.4%	4.9%	3.2%	2.5%
Western Europe	116	91.2	5.2	2.3	1.3
Eastern Europe (including the U.S.S.R.)	119	92.5	4.6	1.9	1.0
Oceania	5	84.9	3.8	11.3	—[a]
Latin America	7	84.5	4.2	11.3	–
Sub-Saharan Africa	4	68.2	11.3	18.2	2.3
Middle East (including North Africa)	1	71.4	14.3	14.3	–
Non-Communist Far East	38	89.0	7.9	2.1	1.0
Communist Far East	18	81.1	16.2	2.1	0.6
World	440	90.0	5.7	2.8	1.5
High-income countries	396	91.4	4.4	2.6	1.6
Low-income countries	44	76.4	17.4	5.3	0.9

	(per cent of 440 million metric tons)	(per cent of 395 million metric tons)	(per cent of 25 million metric tons)	(per cent of 13 million metric tons)	(per cent of 7 million metric tons)
North America	29.6	29.4	25.6	32.8	50.0
Western Europe	26.4	26.8	24.0	21.6	22.7
Eastern Europe (including the U.S.S.R.)	27.1	27.9	22.0	17.6	18.2
Oceania	1.2	1.1	0.8	4.8	–
Latin America	1.6	1.5	1.2	6.4	–
Sub-Saharan Africa	1.0	0.8	2.0	6.4	1.5
Middle East (including North Africa)	0.2	0.1	0.4	0.8	–
Non-Communist Far East	8.7	8.6	12.0	6.4	6.1
Communist Far East	4.2	3.8	12.0	3.2	1.5
World	100.0	100.0	100.0	100.0	100.0
High-income countries	90.2	91.7	70.0	81.6	94.0
Low-income countries	9.8	8.3	30.0	18.4	6.0

SOURCE: Adapted from United Nations and U.S. Bureau of Mines data.

[1] "Crude Steel" includes some 265 million metric tons of iron (usually molten metal), some half that amount of scrap, and some 8 million metric tons of ferro alloys (not including cladding materials from the older non-ferrous and light metals groupings).

[2] "Merchant Pig Iron" includes wrought iron, sponge iron, and similar forms of iron used without conversion into steel.

[3] "Older Non-ferrous Metals" includes mainly primary and secondary output of copper, lead, zinc, and tin.

[4] "Light Metals" includes mainly primary and secondary output of aluminum and magnesium, as well as tiny amounts of exotic space metals.

[a] Equals less than 0.1 per cent.

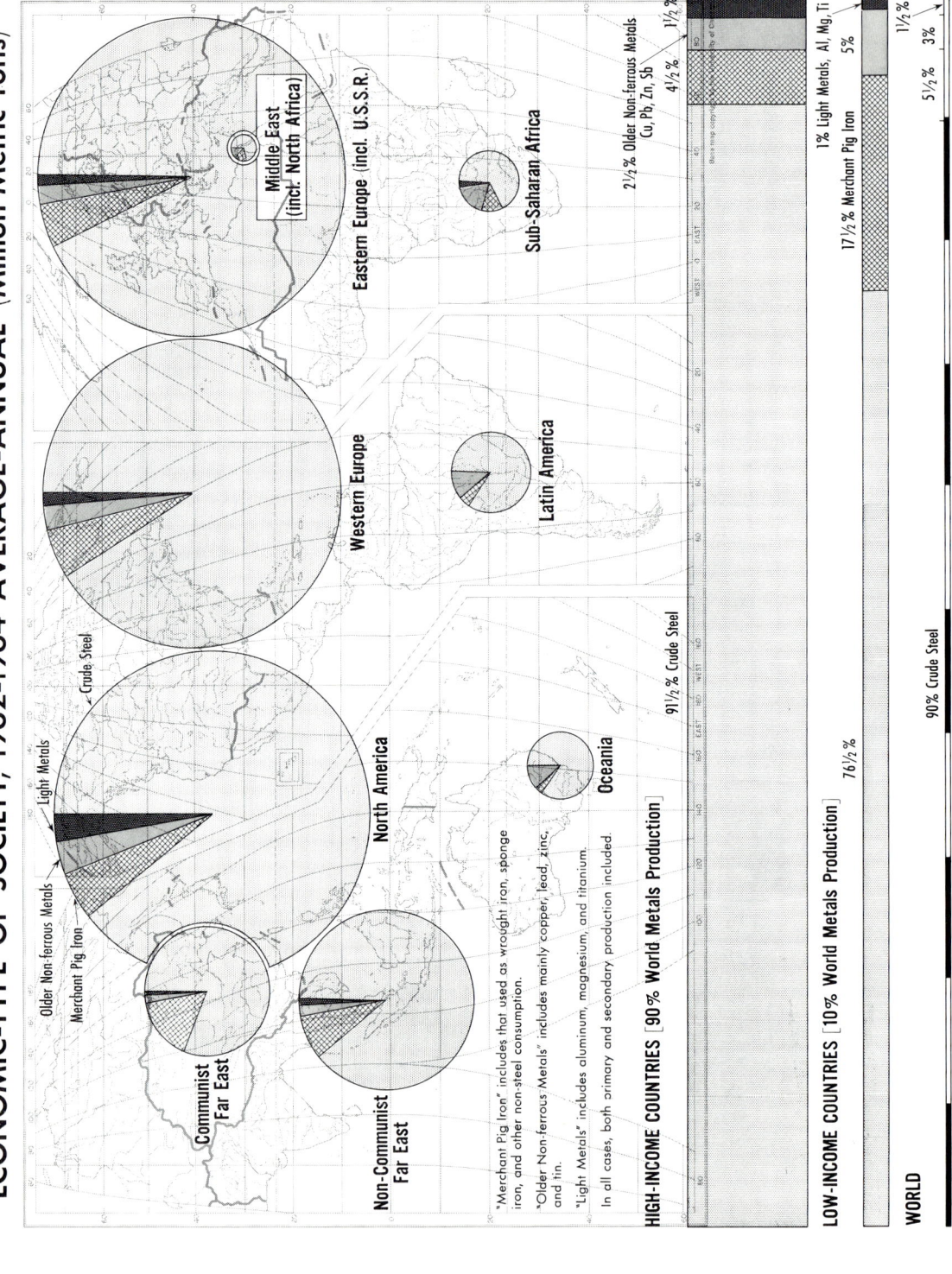

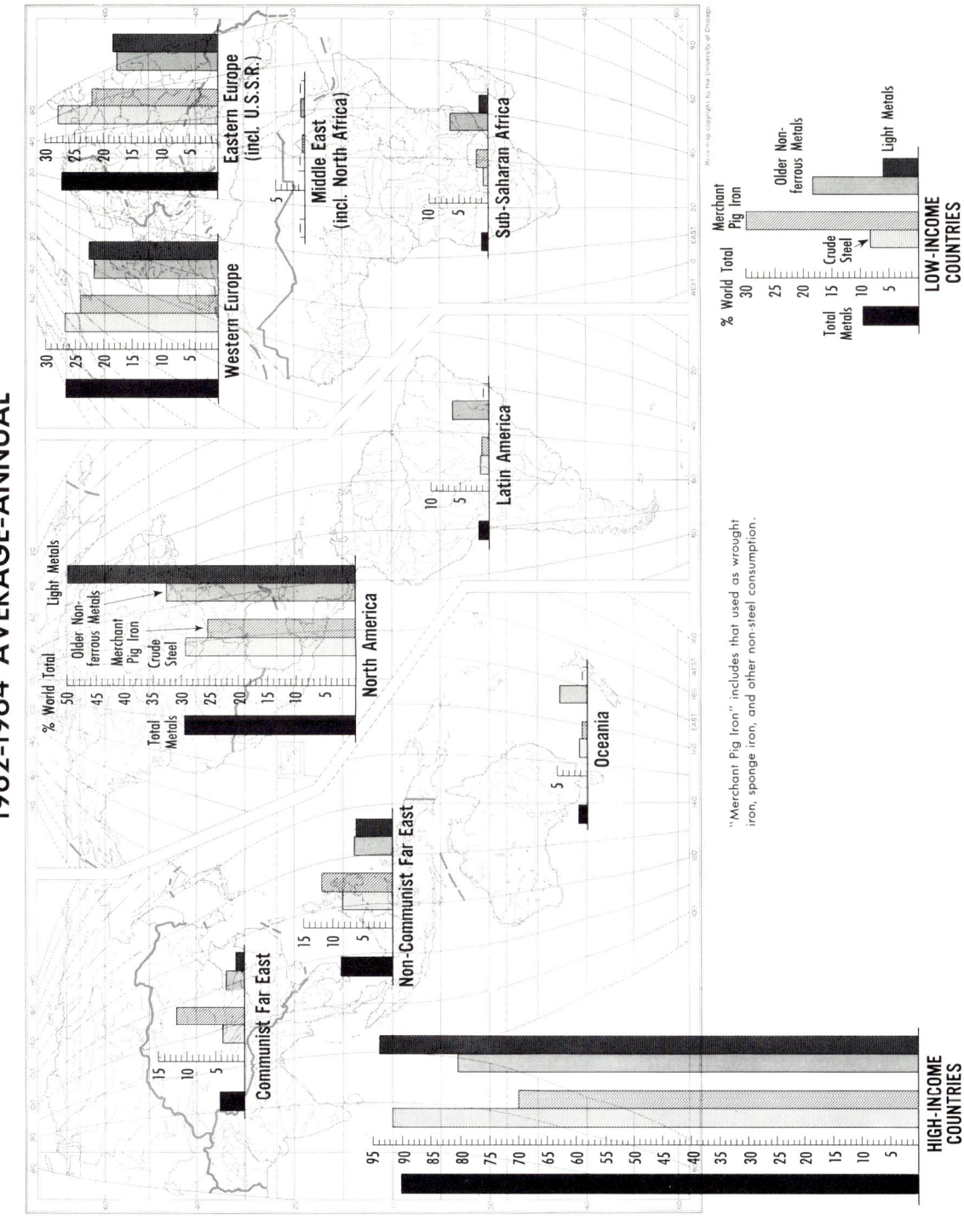

metals, plastics, concrete):[1] they are resistant to corrosion, easier to process, lighter in weight and therefore more easily and more cheaply transported; in general, they are simpler to maintain and to repair.

FERROUS METALLURGY

In the foreseeable future, the world picture of steel production is not likely to change radically, despite large absolute and relative increases in some countries. If more countries can be expected to approach self-sufficiency in tonnage steels, deficits in specialty types are likely to grow in many other countries now roughly self-sufficient.

In the generation ahead, the expected average annual rate of increase in world crude steel production is over 5 per cent, with per capita increase nearly 4 per cent. North America and Western Europe are expected to show growth rates below the world averages in both perspectives, with Eastern Europe (including the U.S.S.R.) and Oceania expected to show growth rates moderately above the world averages, and the other great-regions expected to show growth rates twice the world averages (with the Middle East and the Communist Far East perhaps tripling or quadrupling the world averages).

These differentials will change regional shares of world steel production, but not radically. The big three regions—North America, Western Europe, and Eastern Europe (including the U.S.S.R.)—each with a fraction of present world output between 25 per cent and 30 per cent, are likely to slip to the lower edge of that range, while the other great-regions will increase their fractions (doubled in the cases of the two Far Easts, a third-larger fraction or less in the case of the others). Absolute world steel production will more than double in the quarter century, but in spite of the considerable increases expected in the crude steel output of traditional deficit regions, demand is likely to rise still faster in some of them, and the gap to widen in absolute terms.

[1] In the period 1950–1964, U.S. plastics production more than tripled, aluminum production more than doubled, cement production increased nearly three-fifths, while steel production increased by only an eighth.

The one region that is expected to change from a net importer into a net exporter is Oceania. In the Far East, Latin America, and the Middle East, absolute deficits are likely, in that order, to be higher at the end of the period, although relative deficits will diminish (in the Far East, from a fifth to a tenth; in Latin America, from three-fifths to a sixth; in the Middle East, from over nine-tenths to about half). There may be a smaller deficit in sub-Saharan Africa, in both perspectives. The other regions—the big three —are expected to remain surplus regions, but to less than a twentieth of their production in all cases.

Over-all, in the presently underdeveloped regions, the long-term tendency is for apparent deficits to shrink in relative terms and for the deficit areas to become less dependent on outside sources of supply, especially in tonnage steel.

Raw Materials Consumption

The doubling of world steel production in the past decade, and the expected doubling again in little more than another decade, is putting strain on the raw materials base of the industry. Most raw materials problems of metallurgical industries (ferrous and non-ferrous) are solved by progress along four avenues: (1) beneficiation (upgrading) of lean, domestic materials (ores, flux, fuel), usually at higher cost than mining depleted higher-grade materials—especially favored by inland sites not serviced by cheap water transport; (2) increasing dependence on imports of foreign high-grade materials (especially ore, coke, and scrap), cheaper than comparable domestic materials but less dependable in wartime —especially favored by tidewater sites or other waterfront sites; (3) increasing use of substitutes (scrap or other metals most common, but concrete, plastics, and cermets also important)— especially favored by older centers with greatest scrap mobilizing opportunities and greatest range of competing suppliers; and (4) improvements of metal quality through increasing use of alloys, usually diminishing the amounts of metal needed for specific purposes—as in the third avenue, especially favored by the older centers with the more sophisticated producers and users.

TABLE 14-2

World: Great-Region and Economic-Type of Society Shares of World Iron Ore, Pig Iron, and Crude Steel Production, 1962–1964 Average-Annual (in per cents)

	287 Million Metric Tons Iron Ore [1] (Fe-content)	292 Million Metric Tons Pig Iron [2]	395 Million Metric Tons Crude Steel [3]
North America	23.7	23.7	29.4
Western Europe	18.4	27.7	26.8
Eastern Europe (including the U.S.S.R.)	29.6	27.7	27.9
Oceania	1.2	1.4	1.1
Latin America	9.1	1.4	1.5
Sub-Saharan Africa	3.5	0.9	0.8
Middle East (including North Africa)	1.2	0.2	0.1
Non-Communist Far East	5.6	9.9	8.6
Communist Far East	7.7	7.1	3.8
World	100.0	100.0	100.0
High-income countries	76.7	87.3	91.7
Low-income countries	23.3	12.7	8.3

SOURCE: Adapted from United Nations and U.S. Bureau of Mines data.

[1] Crude iron ore production over 600 million metric tons is concentrated before shipping, especially in North America, but increasingly elsewhere.

[2] Pig iron production includes about nine-tenths molten metal or actual pig iron that is made into steel, with under a tenth made into various kinds of iron products.

[3] Crude steel production is about two-thirds from molten metal and pig iron and one-third from scrap.

Iron ore production. Iron ore production is increasing at a very rapid rate, not only because of the rapid increase in steelmaking, but because of the lowering quality of ore in most parts of the world, and because of the tendency to make less steel from scrap (partly because of the increasing importance of the oxygen converter in steelmaking, partly because of capacity increases in areas of little and expensive scrap).

Even considering Fe-content, iron ore production in the past decade increased some 7 per cent annually, and in the generation ahead, it will be even larger. North American output may be half again as large as now; Western European, doubled; Eastern European, Oceanic, and sub-Saharan African, tripled; and Latin American, Middle Eastern, and Far Eastern, quadrupled. In the case of the big three steelmaking regions, crude ore production will increase at very rapid rates, as their ore quality is dropping fast.

Estimates of world iron ore resources vary widely and are probably greatly underestimated. Much of the world has not yet been geologically surveyed adequately, and the basis of assessment varies widely, with little consensus as to the break between science and economic limits of what constitutes an ore. The increasing industrialization of mining is rendering many small deposits economically useless at the same time that large deposits of ironstone are being brought within range of profitable mining even when low in iron content and high in impurities. The distribution of reserves and other resources is likely to be greatly modified in the long run, but the basic pattern of relative poverty in high-grade ores in the actual great metallurgical districts and relative wealth in many underdeveloped countries and portions of developed countries is likely to persist for a long time.

TABLE 14-3

Unofficial Estimates of Iron Ore and Ironstone Reserves and Resources in the Early 1960's (in billions of metric tons)

	High-Grade (50%+ to 70% Fe) Ores [1]	Medium- and Low-Grade (20% to 50% Fe) Ores and Ironstones [2]
North America	15	150
Western Europe	16	20
Eastern Europe (including the U.S.S.R.)	30	300
Oceania	3	10
Latin America	25	60
Sub-Saharan Africa	10	30
Middle East (including North Africa)	1	5
Non-Communist Far East	15	45
Communist Far East	5	10
World	120	630
High-income countries	63	480
Low-income countries	57	150

[1] Informed guesses.
[2] Speculative guesses.

Reliable coverage is much less available. In the recent past, the U.S. Department of the Interior estimated some 11 billion tons of crude ore reserves usable under present technical and economic conditions, with some 73 billion tons of potential ore likely to become available under more favorable conditions:

	Economic Ores	Potential Ores
	(billions of tons)	
Lake Superior area	8	56
Southeastern area	1	12
Northeastern area	1	4
Central, Gulf, and Western areas	1	1

Some 3 billion tons of ore have been shipped from the upper Great Lakes iron ore ranges, with over half of the high-grade ore removed (including some two-thirds of the high-grade open-pit ore). What ore is left is either covered by deeper layers of glacial drift or else is of quality too low for direct shipment.

In 1963, U.S. iron ore consumption including agglomerates totaled some 116.5 million tons (nearly 80 per cent from captive mines) of which 28.5 per cent was imported (mainly high-grade direct-shipping ores), 8 per cent was high-grade domestic direct-shipping ores unprocessed before blast furnace use, and the remaining 63.5 per cent was beneficiated domestic ores (36 per cent sintered or fused-fines, and 27.5 per cent pellets, briquettes, nodules, and similarly highly concentrated products). Within a few years, the proportions of pellets and similar products will surpass that of sintered (semi-processed) agglomerate.

Essentially, beneficiation and other treatment of ore are a massive invasion of the mine site by modern technology. Steelmen have found that the cheapest way to get more iron to feed their furnaces is to have better raw materials, and with ore this is done in two ways: (1) increasing the iron content of the ore, and lowering the amount of undesirable impurities such as silica; and (2) processing the pieces of ore to sizes that permit the blast furnace to "breathe" better through its charge of ore, coke, and limestone. From now on, even the best Mesabi ores will have to be treated to improve their structure, size, or chemical analysis—or all three—before they meet the new standards of quality the industry is setting up. Ores with more than half iron content are improved by screening out finer particles and crushing large pieces to blast furnace size. Ores with under half iron content are washed at the

Interior of the concentrator building at Reserve Mining Company, Silver Bay, Minnesota. Magnetic separators (center) attract particles of magnetic iron ore and reject useless sand. Hydroseparators (right) wash clinging sand away from iron ore particles. Filters (left) remove water from concentrate.

Courtesy of Reserve Mining Co.

Courtesy of Reserve Mining Co.

Airview of the Reserve Mining Company's taconite processing plant on Lake Superior northeast of Duluth, Minnesota. The village of Silver Bay, Minnesota, can be seen in the background. Additional level land is made by filling in spots along the lake front with waste from the plant. Pellets and similar high-concentrate iron supplies are now almost 40 per cent of U.S. (domestic) iron ore supplies and will be 70 per cent of the 1970 output.

mine site, to remove clay, loose sand, and other easily removed impurities, or dried to remove excess moisture. Hard-to-handle ores (even high-grade ores will contain portions of only 35 per cent iron content) require high-density concentration equipment after washing. Such upgrading seldom costs more than half a dollar per ton, compared with the $3 per ton cost of beneficiating the lean taconite and jasper by electrical and chemical methods. About a third of the 27 per cent iron content taconite is magnetic ore suitable for conversion into 61.5 per cent iron content pellets by the electrical method. The remainder will eventually be processed either by artificially converting it into magnetite or by chemical (froth flotation) beneficiation such as is now used on some of the upper Michigan jasper ironstone. The magnetic taconite is available in enough quantity to supply about four times more iron content than that already removed in the form of high-grade direct-shipping (51.5 per cent iron content) ore. With tax stability assured for twenty-five years as a result of the late-1964 passage of the Minnesota Taconite Amendment, the 17 million tons annual capacity is expected to increase to 60 million tons. By 1970, about 70 per cent of the state's "iron ore" shipments will be taconite pellets.

Jet piercers generating 4,300° F. jet flames sink blast holes into hard taconite. Water in contact with the heat forms steam that carries small particles of rock up and out of the hole.

Courtesy of Reserve Mining Co.

Interior of Reserve Mining Company car dumper building at Silver Bay, Minnesota. Unique rotary dumper dumps two cars of taconite at one time without uncoupling.

Courtesy of Reserve Mining Co.

Interior of concentrator building at Reserve Mining Company, Silver Bay, Minnesota. Taconite, ¾ inch in size, is fed to rod mills at the left and ball mills that grind it to the fineness of flour. Rods and balls tumbling freely inside the rotating mills grind the rock.

Courtesy of Reserve Mining Co.

The southern Appalachian mountains (northern Alabama and adjoining parts of Georgia and Tennessee) contain vast tonnages of medium-grade (31 to 39 per cent Fe), medium phosphoric, bedded oolitic ores very similar to the sedimentary ores of western Europe. The commercial Birmingham ore can still be economically furnaced without costly beneficiation, although its costs have risen sharply. Potential ore in beds of Clinton (Silurian) age outside the area immediately tributary to Birmingham probably totals at least 5 billion tons, but most of this is in beds only 3 feet thick, contrasted to an average thickness of about 8 feet in Birmingham ore now being mined.

Small amounts of high-grade ore still remain in the Adirondacks, but most of the Northeast ore is medium-grade and must be beneficiated before use, mainly by cheap techniques. The predominant ore is magnetite and mining is mainly by underground methods.

Iron deposits are widely distributed throughout the western United States, with the principal production restricted to southeastern California, southwestern Utah, and eastern Wyoming. There are large reserves compared with the small present use.

Canada has large reserves of the Lake Superior type in western Ontario (e.g., Steep Rock has more than 1 billion tons down to 3,000 feet) and along the Quebec-Labrador boundary (a half-billion tons proved, probably 2 billion in all—53 per cent shipping ore), and very large reserves of oolitic ore on Belle Isle, Newfoundland, well sited for export. Within this decade, the Labrador Trough (from the north bank of the lower St. Lawrence to Ungava Bay) should be exporting some 40 million or more tons yearly, or two-thirds of the current production of the Minnesota ranges.

Bedded Jurassic ores in England, France, Germany, and elsewhere account for most of Western Europe's iron ore production. The English deposits (East Midlands, Lincolnshire, Yorkshire) are abundant but low-grade (25 per cent iron on average), have a high phosphorus content, are rarely self-fluxing, and are commonly required to be sintered before use. Most of the

French minette ore is obtained from underground Lorraine workings with slightly higher costs than the British ores (much of which is open-pit mined), but the possibilities of blending siliceous and calcareous ores into a self-fluxing blended ore, and the lack of conservation costs (compared with the British need for reconstitution of land surface) counteract the slight difference in costs. The 1960 reserves were given at over 6 billion tons of economic ore (3.6 billion tons of calcareous ore and 2.5 billion tons of siliceous ore), with lower-grade material totaling another 10 billion tons or more. German reserves are considerably less than the British or French, but their mining and concentration pose similar problems. The large Swedish Lapland deposits of high-grade magnetite ore (some 3 billion tons, 2 billion at Kiruna) are the only ones able to pay for transport to Narrow Seas and other markets. A large part of the West German smelting industry and smaller portions of the British and French industries have been tailored to fit the needs of Swedish ores. Some 15 million tons are usually exported annually (two-thirds from Kiruna). About half of the production is still from open pits, but the share is declining as the walls are getting too high. The other high-grade Western European ore deposits—in both northwestern and southern Europe—are small and either uneconomic to exploit or of mainly national importance (e.g., Spanish Biscayan coastland).

Deposits of worthwhile ore in Eastern Europe are small and few. Poland and Czechoslovakia must import much of their present requirements, and as their smelting industry expands, they will increase their dependence on Soviet deposits. Hungary, Romania, and Bulgaria have deposits of very small economic value, and Yugoslavia has modest deposits adequate for only a small industry.

The U.S.S.R. possesses high-grade reserves mainly in southern European Russia, including the Urals, and the Asiatic Russian areas have no large high-grade deposits. The traditional high-grade deposits are fast being depleted, and reliance is increasingly on upgrading lower-grade ores. The Krivoi Rog ores (a 35-by-5-mile deposit in the great bend of the Dnieper River) of the southcentral Ukraine are still the most important producer in the country: mainly phosphoric hematite of fairly high grade, the easy-to-work friable deposit must be sintered before smelting, and the high silica content necessitates much lime before use. Besides the 1 billion tons of high-grade ore, Krivoi Rog has some 50 billion tons of low-grade potential ore. Second in importance is Magnitogorsk in the southern Urals—its fifth of U.S.S.R. output is about half of the Krivoi Rog output. Here, open-pit production of diminishing quality magnetite will be increasingly for local use instead of long-distance use. Other deposits that may increasingly be used include the abundant but low-grade and highly phosphoric and highly siliceous powdery Kerch deposits of the eastern Crimea, and the huge, deeply buried Kursk magnetite deposit. Recent guesses on the latter claim some 30 billion tons of high-grade ore (56 to 69 per cent iron content, with few impurities) and some 170 billion tons of low-grade ferrous quartzites. Present Soviet iron ore production is about 120 million tons annually, some 60 per cent from the Ukraine. Over half of the current output must be sintered, and large-scale pelletizing of the lean quartzite has begun. Siberian ores being mined are low-grade, not abundant, and contain considerable impurities (silica, sulfur, zinc, etc.)—recently, by accident, huge iron ore deposits were discovered at Bakchar in the Tomsk region some 130 miles north of Novosibirsk (one estimate is that they contain 110 billion tons, of which 40 billion could be mined by surface methods), and these may supply the expected Siberian steel increase from 8 to 27 million tons by 1980.

In the period 1960–1963, Australian proven and indicated reserves of iron ore increased more than twenty fold, to more than 10 billion tons. Some 8 billion tons are in Western Australia—one 3-billion deposit at Pilbara, 750 miles north of Perth, and others in the same vicinity, are to be exploited by an Australian–United States consortium, with some 4 million tons exported each year by the late 1960's, mainly to Japan. Hammersley Mine, 650 miles north of Perth, will supply 65 million tons over twenty-two years, starting delivery in late 1966, while the Mount Goldsworthy Mine, about 100 miles farther south, will supply 16 million tons beginning in early 1966. The Japanese mills will pay between $9 and $10 a ton for the ore, about $900 million in the two-decade period. Additional huge deposits have been found in the Northern Territory, Queensland, and Tasmania. The older deposit in South Australia is the reliance of the Australian iron-steel industry near the Iron Knob mining area and in the Sydney region.

Latin American iron ore reserves and potential resources are immense. Brazil may have the largest high-grade iron ore reserves in the world, with massive low-silica, high-grade sedimentary hematites in Minas Gerais totaling nearly 20 billion tons of proven and probable reserves, with perhaps twice that amount of potential ores. Exports are now 8 million tons (about 7 per cent of world trade), slated to rise to 20 million tons annually when the Ponta do Tubarao port (which will handle ships up to 150,000 tons) is completed. Venezuela has similar leached-enriched sedimentary deposits in the Guiana highlands —Cerro Bolivar has some 1 billion tons of proved ore, with other nearby deposits about equal— considerable amounts are worked in the soft, easily mined deposits some 300 miles inland, mainly exported to the United States. Chile has more modest reserves, but they are high grade, relatively free of harmful impurities, close to the coast, and cheaply mined and moved either to the steel plant in south Chile or to Baltimore. Middle America also has considerable reserves; some Mexican deposits (e.g., Durango) are high grade, while the extensive deposits of Cuba and other West Indies islands are lower grade but easily upgraded in iron content, although often the nickel and chromium content poses such difficulties in smelting that they are little used.

Mainly a tableland of ancient rocks, with great areas of pre-Cambrian sedimentaries, Africa has many large deposits like those of Lake Superior or Australia. Ore is mined and smelted locally in both the Republic of South Africa and in Southern Rhodesia, but elsewhere ores are mined for export only. Extensive surface deposits of laterite (e.g., Guinea) and beds of pre-Cambrian ore (e.g., Liberia, Sierra Leone) are being increasingly inventoried and exploited. In just the past several years, prospecting inland has found that the Liberian sector of the Nimba range contains at least a quarter billion tons of proven high-grade ore, with the Guinea sector of the same mountains containing as much, and other Guinea deposits nearby some two to three times as much as the Nimba area. When interior mines are fully operative, Liberia's ore exports are expected to rise from 4 to 25 million tons annually. Gabon is expected to be exporting 15 million tons when its 400-mile inland Mekambo deposit can rail output to the sea near Libreville.

The iron ore inventory of the Middle East exhibits only modest reserves, but this could mainly reflect lack of information. Modest to small deposits are known in most countries of southwest Asia, with very small production to supply the local smelting industries in Turkey and elsewhere. Egypt has a modest deposit near Aswan that produces for the Helwan (Cairo) mill. Northwest Africa has some half billion tons of known iron ore in the three Maghreb countries, with a yearly export of several million tons of high-grade ore to Northwest Europe. Recent findings in northern Mauritania (the most Saharan country in sub-Saharan Africa) suggest the possibility of additional finds in the Saharan portions of Morocco, Algeria, and elsewhere.

The Far East is comparatively rich in iron ore, especially India, which may rival Brazil in size and quality of reserves and inferred resources. The most important Indian deposits are high-grade hematite of the Lake Superior type along the Bihar-Orissa boundary and westward across central India, low in sulfur but high in phosphorus. Some 10 billion tons of workable high-grade ore are known, with several times that amount of medium-grade ore, and vast deposits of the original jasper formations that are just the subject of speculation. Lateritic ores are also widespread, but because of their low-grade and high impurities are not likely to receive attention in the decades ahead. Southeast Asia also has substantial deposits, although only the small high-grade deposits of Malaysia, southeast Luzon, and a few other places are worked for exports. Vast low-grade and contaminated resources are known. Indonesia has vast lateritic deposits, mainly in the lakes district of central Celebes and in southeast Borneo; the nickel content (making smelting difficult), the inaccessibility, and scarcity of coking coal in the region have resulted in a lack of exploitation. Similar potentials exist in northeast Mindanao, northern Laos, and elsewhere.

The iron ore reserves and resources of the Communist Far East are much better than formerly thought, but comparison with the past or with other areas is difficult because of the unreliability of data collected in the 1950's. Before the Communist takeover, China was not thought to be rich in iron ore of high quality, although large quantities (4 billion tons) of low-grade 25 to 40 per cent highly siliceous ores were known in the pre-Cambrian sedimentaries of Northeast China (Manchuria), together with small high-grade deposits high in sulfur. Other small deposits were found widely scattered in the rugged country of central and southern China, without good bulk carrier transport. The Japanese exploited a modest sized high-grade deposit on Hainan Island. Apparently, some good ore (50 per cent Fe) has been found in north China —perhaps 7 billion tons in Shansi and 3 billion more in Honan southeast of there. Communist sources claim high-grade workable reserves of 12 to 15 billion tons (the U.S. Bureau of Mines accepts 5 or more billion tons). North Korea has ½ billion tons of low-grade ore in the Musan area of the northeast near Vladivostok, and North Vietnam has some potentials.

Trade in iron ore. Ores constitute one of the largest tonnage movements in world trade, ranking with petroleum, coal, and grain. Movement of iron ore by deep-sea shipping alone involves about 115 million tons of ore and agglomerates, about a fifth of total world production of crude ore (and about a quarter of world production of Fe-content, since higher-grade materials predominate in such long-distance movements). Such deep-sea movement of iron ore is growing at an average annual rate of 10 per cent.

The United States is the world's largest importer of iron ore, taking over 35 million tons of high-grade ore and agglomerates (about a third of the Fe-content going into pig iron production). Well over 80 per cent of the imports come from Canada and Venezuela, with Chile, Brazil, and Liberia also contributing important amounts.

Japan, which depends on Latin America (Peru, Brazil, Chile), India, and Malaysia as its main sources of imported iron ore, is in second place in world standings, with imports of around 25 million tons. Since Japan imports over 90 per cent of its ore, it is possible that she could become the largest importer by the late 1960's.

West Germany, which imports over 20 million tons, principally from Scandinavian, Brazilian, and West African mines, is in third place. There are also numerous other European importers, since only France and Sweden are net exporters of importance. In recent years, Eastern European countries have emerged as importers of seaborne ore on a small scale.

The world's ore carrier fleet is being added to rapidly, with some 375 ships of 7 million deadweight tons in 1964. Many new ships are in the 50,000 to 70,000 tons range, and plans involve ships rivaling supertankers of more than 100,000 tons capacity.

In the case of the United States, the supersized, specialized ore carrier has eliminated small tramp ships and taken over the job of keeping the United States supplied with iron ore imports; about half of present imports are carried in specialized carriers exceeding 30,000 tons (mainly foreign built and under foreign flags of convenience, but U.S. steel company owned). However, less than a tenth of the ore imports of continental Western Europe and even less of British imports are carried in the large specialized carrier (some 90 per cent of British imports are carried in specialized ore carriers, but half are carried in small vessels of less than 15,000 tons). The relatively short trips from Scandinavian and Mediterranean ports account for this European lag; on imports from Latin America, West Africa, and Canada, larger ships are used. The Japanese are more like the United States. Their bulk carrier fleet has increased from 1 to 2 million tons annually between 1960 and 1965; some thirty-eight ore carriers and thirty-seven coal carriers are built or are being built, most of them heavyweights ranging in capacity from 45,000 to 65,000 tons. By the late 1960's, Japanese imports of iron ore are expected to be 40 million tons a year, and coal imports are expected to be 20 million tons a year, both items mostly from very great distances (a third to a half world away).

The United States is now engaged in catching up with Western European superiority in certain phases of converting raw materials into steel, but it is superior in rapidity of materials handling (U.S. mills move materials from three to five times faster than in Western Europe). Transport costs (freight and dock charges) range from one-third to two-thirds of the delivered price of ore at U.S. steel mills. The grade of the ore, the distance of deposits from steel-producing centers, and the mode of transportation (including whether commercial or captive vehicles are used) are primary factors in this cost. Since transportation costs are based on tonnage, they are less per unit of natural iron on richer than on leaner ores, as less waste material need be transported. In a ton of taconite pellet with an analysis of 61.5 per cent natural iron, some 20 per cent more iron content is transported than in a ton of standard grade Lake Superior direct shipping ore that has 51.5 per cent natural iron. In a ton of rich foreign ore with 67 per cent natural iron, 30 per cent more iron content is transported than in a ton of Lake Superior standard grade ore.

Iron ore is being transformed into an international commodity, with its price and supply movements determined not merely by domestic conditions but by international politics, price policies, and climatic conditions. Eventually more than half of American iron ore requirements will come from abroad, putting it into the group that includes most Western European countries and the Japanese smelting industry. The situation of Eastern European (including U.S.S.R.) smelting districts is somewhat less favorable for dependence upon high-grade imports because of poorer waterway availability, but mainly because of government policy that stresses resource self-sufficiency.

Iron ore shipments clearly show seasonal variations, largely caused by export variations from Sweden and Canada. The freezing of the St. Lawrence River and Gulf and the Baltic Sea results in a pronounced winter minimum (in spite of 60 per cent of Swedish ore shipped via ice-free Narvik in Norway and increased North American rail shipments in the winter).

The large steel-producing countries of Western and Eastern Europe, like the United States, have large iron ore resources of their own, but these are mainly of medium and low grade. While the French metallurgical industry is based mainly on domestic low-grade ore, West Germany, Belgium, Luxembourg, and Britain get most of their ore from abroad. Belgium and Luxembourg still depend mainly on French low-grade ore brought over short distances by rail or barge; the others depend more on high-grade ore brought from more distant sources. Sweden is still the largest supplier; its northern district exports through Narvik in Norway and Lulea on the Gulf of Bothnia, while its older ore districts in central Sweden ship small amounts through a variety of smaller ports. Other high-grade imports come from other Scandinavian countries, from Iberia, and from the Maghreb. The future will see vast increases in ore imports from other continents.

The Soviet Union, the world's second largest iron-steel producer, covers her requirements from domestic ore fields: 60 per cent from the Ukraine, and the rest from the Urals and Siberian fields. The U.S.S.R. also supplies the smaller Eastern European countries with the bulk of their ore imports. Both movement within the Soviet Union and the exports are predominantly overland by rail and barge, and not by world shipping—very similar to the internal and external movements of French minette ore.

Shipments of iron ore and agglomerates from United States mines, which still supply two-thirds of ore consumption, are over 80 million tons valued at some $0.7 billion (average value is some $10 per ton at nearest shipping center, such as Minnesota lakeside port). Some three-quarters of this domestic production comes from the Lake Superior district, whose regular unscreened Mesabi natural blast furnace ore (51.5 per cent natural iron content) brings about $12 delivered at Lower Great Lakes ports and whose pellets bring about $15 (such commercial prices are higher than production from captive mines, which actually supply most of the movements).

Over 15 million tons of high-grade ore imports come from Canada, with a similar amount from Venezuela, and additional supplies from a variety of sources. The U.S. Eastern Seaboard is especially well situated to receive ore imports by large ore carrier (Bethlehem Steel Company imports well over half of its ore), although the Midwest also participates. Iron ore moved by big ore carriers costs only a seventh to a fifth as much as by land, or some 2 to 3 mills per ton-mile compared with 10 to 15 by rail (again, these are commercial rates; captive vehicles often cost only a third to half as much). Following are commercial rates:

	Lower Lakes Ports	Eastern Seaboard	Pittsburgh
	(United States dollars)		
From Lake Superior iron ranges to	$3–$4		$6.50
From Labrador-Quebec via St. Lawrence Seaway to	$5.25		$8.30
From Venezuela via Atlantic Ocean to		$5.50	$10.80

Even though captive fleets on the Great Lakes tend to hold transportation costs below the $2 per ton listed as the going commercial rate from Duluth-Superior to Lower Lakes ports (it costs $1 to $2 to rail the ton from the iron ranges to lakeside port), the costs per ton-mile are definitely higher on lake ore carriers than on oceanic ore carriers. On the Great Lakes, iron ore is only two-fifths of total freight (the rest being mainly coal, flux, and grain), but it is a majority of the ton-miles of freight movement, since ore carriers tend to travel farther per trip. Most of the movement is by older, smaller ships with high labor costs (e.g., 10,000-ton lake ships haul ore using 230 man-days, while 25,000 tonners use but 175 man-days). Imports (both on the Canadian run via the Seaway and on the open ocean) not only travel on larger (therefore cheaper) ships, but on foreign ships whose original and operating costs are much lower than for American-flag ships of comparable size. Including transportation costs, imported iron ore is some 10 to 20 per cent cheaper than domestic ore (per iron point), a respectable saving when one considers that from 15 to 25 per cent of the total cost of making a ton of steel is that of the iron ore.

Steel companies plan about a generation ahead for their prospective ore supplies, so an approximate trade pattern for 1975 or thereabout can be glimpsed. Western Europe's ore deficit is expected to be four times its present one, with Africa, North America, and Latin America being, in that order, the expected sources of its 30 million tons (Fe-content) of ore imports. The second great deficit area will be the United States, with its expected 25 or more million tons (Fe-content) of ore imports coming nearly two-thirds from Canada, a quarter from Latin America, and the remainder from Africa and elsewhere. Japan's expected deficit will be about as great as that of the United States, with Latin America (mainly Brazil and Peru) supplying three-fifths, and the North American West Coast and other parts of the non-Communist Far East each supplying a sixth, and Africa the remainder.

North America is expected to have a small net surplus in ore supplies, practically all due to Canada's surplus of 30 million tons (Fe-content), over half of which will go to the United States, a third going to Western Europe, and the remainder to Japan. Latin America's surplus will be about the same as that of Canada, with half going to Japan, and a quarter each to the United States and to Western Europe. Sub-Saharan Africa's surplus will be half that of Canada or Latin America, with practically all destined for Western European markets and only small amounts for Japan and the United States.

Iron and steel scrap. The two principal steel-making raw materials are pig iron (usually in molten-metal form), made by a complex and expensive process of production from iron ore and service materials (coke and other fuel, flux, air), and scrap, which can be cheaper (usually in mature economies). In most forms, scrap has a superior metal content than pig iron (which usually has 7 to 8 per cent impurities). Scrap requires a much smaller investment in fixed facilities or in working capital.

Historically, up to a decade ago, scrap made possible more adjustments of steel output to sudden spurts in demand. Until the late 1950's, only that part of the metal input for crude steelmaking that could not be covered by scrap would be in the form of pig iron. However, at the present time, changes in steel technology are reducing the need for scrap. Some scrap men say the mills are pushing this further than need be, but steelmakers feel they have no alternative in the face of historically violent fluctuations in both the price and the quality of the scrap they purchased.

Steel mills have been reducing their need for scrap mainly by two methods: one is to increase the amount of hot metal produced by existing blast furnaces (the speedup with tailor-made raw materials has accomplished this), and the other is to increase the proportion of hot metal to scrap that can be put into the open hearth furnaces to make steel (historically, 70 per cent was the top economical charge, but this is now 80 to 85 per cent). Of increasing importance is the rise of steelmaking by oxygen converters, which can only utilize 25 to 30 per cent scrap from a technical viewpoint.

About 35 per cent of all iron and steel is irretrievably lost by rusting [2] or burial or is abandoned as worthless. The other 65 per cent returns to the steel mills for remelting and reuse, about a quarter in a short time, the rest within a generation or so.

Scrap arises from four sources: (1) the iron and steel industry itself supplies circulating scrap, usually from a fifth to a third of steel output, depending upon the nature of the steel mill and the composition of its semiprocessed shipments; (2) industries consuming iron and steel as a raw material produce scrap, often 15 to 20 per cent of the regional supply in areas with varied engineering industries (e.g., the type generated when an auto manufacturer punches out fenders from steel sheets or when a foundry casts a base for a machine tool); (3) worn-out or obsolescent iron and steel products (capital goods or consumer durables scrap) often provide half the supply in older regions of complicated industry and wealthy consumers, but is unimportant in underdeveloped regions; and (4) imported scrap, which is less than 5 per cent of the amount consumed in the world (mainly from the United States to Western Europe and Japan).

The total amounts of potential scrap are increasing rapidly, especially in North America and Western Europe. Several factors account for this faster recycling. The lifetimes of metal products in use are shorter in countries with high rates of steel utilization; the degree of motorization, the consumption of other durable consumer goods, and the degree of specialization on light, rather than heavy, engineering industries—these and other factors tend to shorten average lifetimes. In the remainder of the world, scrap availability as a share of metal in use is smaller. In most Communist and underdeveloped countries, relatively more steel is used for basic investment in dams, roads, and public utilities, which have a longer lifetime than motor vehicles or other consumer durables of increasing importance in high-income countries with higher levels of utilization of steel and other metals.

Both scrap-dealers and steelmen suspect that improving and standardizing scrap quality will help stabilize the market and make the steel mills more willing to use scrap. Scrap is now moving across the oceans in large bulk carriers, halving the cost of movement by small ships used up to 1962.

In the United States, the increasing supply of, and slipping demand for, auto scrap has cut prices by almost 50 per cent since 1958 (to some $30 per ton, about the price for molten metal in efficient integrated steel mills), and sparked a shakeout among scrap processors. A number of smaller yards have closed their doors, and larger dealers have increasingly mechanized their operations. In the process, the $2 billion yearly scrap business—historically characterized by small business, big profit margins, and a low mortality

---

[2] In the United States alone, the cost of corrosion (rusting) is about $8 billion annually.

rate—is shifting toward big companies, small profits, and a steady elimination of marginal operators. Accompanying this is the first major change in basic scrap technology since presses and shears. The trend is toward ever bigger, fancier, and costlier crunchers and cutters, and more of a volume approach to scrap handling and preparation. There are now mammoth presses that can squash two cars, side by side, into a bundle the size of a filing cabinet. Giant shears can slice through more than 30 tons of metal an hour. Push-button grinders can shred scrap into a fine slaw. In the offing are pelletizers that will munch its metal up into tiny shrapnel. All these changes are helping guarantee quality, yield, and handling qualities of a given load of scrap.

There is good evidence that scrap may well start becoming more important again, after a decade of depression. While the first-generation (L-D) oxygen converter is limited to around 25 to 30 per cent scrap in its charge, the new Stora-Kaldo process can go up to 40 to 45 per cent scrap, approaching the open hearth range. The decentralization of the steel industry also bodes well for scrap; more and more small electric furnaces, using a 100 per cent scrap charge, are starting up wherever there is a good supply of scrap and cheap electric power. In the United States, these furnaces now account for 8 per cent of the steel output, mainly small structurals and reinforcing bars.

Ferro alloys. The third class of raw materials to actually enter and remain in the steel is the diverse and growing group called ferro alloys, most of which go into the growing fraction of alloy-steels production. At present, some three-quarters of world steel production consists of carbon or tonnage steels, with a fifth being ordinary alloy steels and the remaining 5 per cent jewelry (stainless and other very high-grade) steels.[3]

Ferro alloys are multipurpose materials, being used for some three or four reasons: (1) Some ferro alloys are used because of the specific properties that they impart to steel when they come alloyed with it (i.e., when they dissolve in the iron, or form carbide compounds)—examples would include manganese (15+ per cent) for hard, abrasive-resisting steel with ductility; chromium, nickel, and molybdenum for tough, shock-, corrosion- and oxidation-resistant, ductile steels; tungsten and cobalt for tool steels; vanadium for spring steels; silicon for high-magnetic and high electrical-resistant steels; lead for easily machinable steels; and many others. (2) Some ferro alloys are used to counteract harmful gases or harmful oxides in the steel—examples would include manganese (in small amounts), silicon, aluminum, vanadium, zirconium, and others for deoxidizers and to remove other harmful gases and oxides; this use includes all steels, tonnage as well as strictly alloy types. (3) A relatively recent use (mainly since World War II) is as an additive or economizer—examples would include the use of boron, zirconium, titanium, tantalum, and others to cut down requirements of scarcer or more expensive ferro alloys (e.g., substituting for chromium, nickel, and molybdenum in making stainless steels). (4) A more debatable class would be metals used because of their beneficial effects in ridding steel of impurities or in rendering impurities harmless—examples would include the use of considerable zinc, tin, lead, copper, and other metals to form rust-resisting coatings, the use of small amounts of manganese to counteract sulfur, and other uses that many would not consider ferro-alloy types. World production of ferro alloys narrowly defined (first three uses) is some 8 million tons metal content. About half that metal content from the categories of older non-ferrous and light metals is used to clad and otherwise protect iron and steel (i.e., implement the fourth category of uses).

The United States mines ore deposits of most ferro alloys, but is a major producer of only a few small-tonnage items (95 per cent of world boron mine output, 90 per cent of molybdenum, 85 per cent of vanadium, 35 per cent of titanium) and must import most of the bigger tonnage

---

[3] A typical stainless steel might include 74 per cent iron, 18 per cent chromium, and 8 per cent nickel. The Inconel used in atomic reactors includes 78 per cent nickel, 15 per cent chromium, and 7 per cent iron (and costs twice as much).

items (manganese, chromium, nickel). About fifty foreign countries send one or more ferro alloys.

Manganese is produced in amounts equal to some 6 million tons metal content, although, like most ferro alloys, little is ever reduced to pure form. Over half comes from the production of the U.S.S.R. and mainland China, but little of this moves out of the Communist realm. India, South Africa, and Brazil are the largest sources elsewhere, although many smaller producers also exist. Some ten Latin American sources provide nearly half of U.S. imports, which in turn are some 90 per cent of total U.S. needs. In the largest use of manganese, some 11 to 14 pounds go into every ton of steel (whether produced by Bessemer, open hearth, oxygen, or electric furnace) to minimize the deleterious effects of oxygen and sulfur in steel and to improve the rollability and surface finish. In larger amounts (over 15 per cent in ferro-manganese form), it confers on steel a tough sort of hardness that makes the finished product suitable for power shovel teeth, frogs and switches on railway trackage, and many parts of agricultural machinery. It also has an economizer effect, as the nickel requirements of standard alloys can be dropped from 8 to 4 per cent by substituting manganese. Technically, the manganese oxide and sulfide in slag can be recovered and recycled, but the product is not now economically competitive with imported manganese under peacetime conditions.

About 2 million tons of chromium (metal content) are produced, over three-quarters outside the Communist Bloc, with South Africa, Rhodesia, the Philippines, and Turkey being large producers. United States production is less than 10 per cent of its needs, and western hemisphere imports are also small. Chemical-grade chromium salts are used to give paints more brilliance, leather more durability, and bleaching, dyeing, and oxidizing of cloth and other materials that extra something that spells process improvement. Refractory-grade chromite is widely used to endow chrome bricks and chrome cement for furnace linings and roofs with high melting points, chemical stability, and stubborn resistance to alkali or acid. Metallurgical-grade chromium goes into an array of alloy steels: less than 2 per cent added to medium and high carbon steels used in bearings and on wearing surfaces increases their hardness and toughness; from 1 to 5 per cent introduced into permanent magnet steels sharpens their ability to concentrate a magnetic field; some 4 per cent upward in high-speed tool steels stiffens their resistance to wear. Medium or high carbon steels with 12 to 18 per cent chromium are used in cutlery, valve parts, and dies requiring minimum distortion in heat treatment and maximum life in cutting edge; stainless steels have a minimum of 12 per cent chromium. Usually, over half of the chromium consumption of an industrial society will be metallurgical-grade forms.

About two-fifths of a million tons of nickel (metal content) is used annually in the world, with some 60 per cent from Canada, and with the U.S.S.R., Cuba, and New Caledonia also being major producers. Non-Communist capacity is over 350,000 tons (two-thirds supplied by Canada's Inco), with consumption a bit lower. Nickel, like copper, is added to molten steel in metallic form to increase toughness, strength, and ductility, and in large amounts to increase resistance to heat and acids. With chromium, it is one of the principal alloying elements used in making stainless steels. Because of its comparatively high price (some 75 cents a pound), reflecting lean ores and refining difficulties, it is economized when that is feasible.

The other ferro alloys—excluding those used for cladding—are produced in amounts smaller than 100,000 tons yearly. Tungsten's annual output is some 60,000 tons, a majority from the Communist realm. The United States consumes about 35 per cent of world production, two-thirds imported from South Korea, Bolivia, Portugal, and other sources. Tungsten helps impart hardness and toughness to steels at high temperatures and is therefore found in many high-speed tool steels.

Molybdenum is produced to the extent of some 40,000 tons (metal content). Colorado has some 90 per cent of the world's known reserves, and the U.S. share of Free World production is some 85 per cent. Because of its very high (4,748° F.) melting point and great strength at high temperatures, it is enjoying wide use in missiles and other space age devices, and this is expected to lead to a doubling of consumption within a decade or two. Its role of imparting hardness and resistance to impact, in addition to the high-temperature strength mentioned, makes for wide use in stainless, heat-resisting, and tool steels, in spite of high cost (some $1.25 per pound). It also plays an economizer role, as the addition of only 0.2 per cent to a special steel can drop nickel need from 1.25 to 0.65 per cent and chromium need from 0.8 to 0.5 per cent.

Cobalt is another small-output (some 20,000 tons metal content produced annually), high-cost ($1.50 per pound) ferro alloy that is rapidly increasing in use. About half of the Free World's production (over 45 per cent of the entire world's production) is from the Congo, with Zambia, Morocco, the United States, and Canada also being important producers. The United States consumes some two-thirds of the world's total (about 85 per cent imported). Combined with nickel and aluminum, cobalt makes efficient magnets. Its hardness at high temperatures and abrasion resistance enhance its usefulness in high-speed cutting tools and in gun barrels and rockets. It is a necessary ingredient in certain steel alloys required to withstand the fierce heat of jet engines and gas turbines without warping, corroding, or disintegrating.

Vanadium is produced in a small amount, about 5,000 tons metal content yearly—about two-thirds in the United States, with important production in southwestern Africa, Finland, and Peru. As little as 0.4 per cent greatly increases the elastic limit and tensile strength of steel without materially lowering its ductility, making it highly useful in producing spring steel. Vanadium steel also has remarkable resistance to fatigue under alternating stresses (e.g., steel forgings or castings required to stand up in difficult service under high stresses, as in engine and motor parts).

When proper metallurgical techniques are used, boron can improve the capacity of low- and medium-carbon steels to harden without adversely affecting the physical properties or safe performance of the alloy. Boron steels, furthermore, are less sensitive to shatter cracks and flakes than some of the steels they replace. The amount of boron used is remarkably small, from about 0.001 to 0.006 per cent. Its economizing role is fabulous; in making stainless steel, 1,800 pounds of boron save 656,000 pounds of nickel, 119,000 pounds of chromium, 52,000 pounds of molybdenum, and 9,100 pounds of manganese.

Columbium is used in some stainless steels designed to be welded or used at high temperatures. It controls the size of the grains, the minute crystalline structures of steel that affect its strength and workability (usually the finer the grain, the better the strength and other mechanical properties of steel). In effect, columbium doubles the strength of new steels without making it harder to work. Most production is a by-product of Nigerian tin mines; most consumption is in the U.S. aircraft-missile industry.

Copper is mainly used in cladding steel, but it is used as a strictly alloying element, serving to retard corrosion in some steels. The addition of copper is usually made in metallic form. The same is true of lead, which is used to improve the machinability of some steels.

Silicon improves the magnetic characteristics of steel, making the product desirable for some electrical equipment. The crude material (sand) is universal, but production of metal is expensive.

Titanium is used in steels designed for high-temperature applications to prevent unwanted changes in crystalline structure, particularly of stainless steels. Only a tiny amount is used as an alloying material, compared with that going into light-metal production or (in oxide form) into white paint.

Zirconium reacts with sulfur, nitrogen, and oxygen to cleanse steel of such impurities. Steels containing zirconium in various quantities are used in some tough, high-strength parts such as axles, crankshafts, and rock drills. United States annual capacity is some 2,500 tons, most of it high-grade metal ($6.50 per pound) used in nuclear-reactor construction. A lower grade ($3.50 per pound) is used as ferro alloy and for other uses.

Considered separately, the ferro-alloy industry of a major metallurgical nation has an impressive output. That of the United States puts out over $½ billion worth of products yearly (2 million tons, including the iron content of its various ferro alloys), and production is slated to increase by half again by the mid-1960's. The catalyst value in upping the value of steel industry products is equally impressive. A standard stainless steel may contain 18 per cent chromium, 8 per cent nickel, plus some other elements; it may cost up to ten times the price of ordinary carbon steel (U.S. stainless steel output was only 0.2 per cent of total steel output in 1940, 0.6 per cent in 1950, but 1.2 per cent in 1960, and is still rising in relative importance).

Service materials. This category includes materials necessary for iron and steel production that disappear or are removed. Probably most important is coking coal. About 15 per cent of world coal production is used to make metallurgical coke for pig iron and blast furnace ferro-alloy smelting alone. Specific coke consumption will decrease in different countries by 15 to 30 per cent in the foreseeable future, depending mainly on the rate of increase in iron content in the blast furnace burden and on the degree of raw material preparation. Even so, total coke consumption will increase substantially.

The use of coal to make metallurgical coke requires certain physical properties and qualities so as to produce coke with size uniformity, absence of dust, and with low sulfur and ash content. The prime determinant of whether a coal is suitable for conversion to coke is the property of caking. A caking coal becomes plastic when heated, and through further heating in the range of 1,650° to 2,000° F. in the absence of air, the contained volatile material is driven off, leaving a porous, carbonaceous mass of coke. The coals having the best caking qualities are those of bituminous rank with a moderate percentage of contained volatile material, or medium-volatile bituminous. Specific reserve data on caking coal are lacking, but the general magnitude of such reserves is known to be small, probably only 5 per cent or so of all coal reserves.

Modern blast furnaces require a strong, but not brittle, coke that is able to support the heavy weight of the furnace charge without crushing. The structure of the coke, which provides these properties, is in turn determined by the expansion characteristics of the coal charged to the coking oven. The dimensional behavior of coal in the coking process is complex, and it is variable not only among coals of different volatile categories, but among coals of the same volatile category from different fields. Economic operation of the blast furnace requires uniformity of charge, with blending or mixing of the coal charge to the coke oven being common practice. In the United States, recently the average proportions were approximately 67 per cent of the more abundant high-volatile type, 20 per cent low-volatile (range 4 to 40 per cent), and 13 per cent medium-volatile.[4] The drain on known areas of low-volatile bituminous reserves has been severe, chiefly because of their highly localized occurrence. In the United States, two-thirds of all coal delivered to coke ovens came from Pennsylvania and West Virginia, but over 90 per cent of the low-volatile coal came from the two. One cannot equate coking reserves too closely with low-volatile bituminous, as there is a limit, because of the expansion characteristics of this type of coal, to the gain in quality and yield that can be obtained through its use in the charge.

Sulfur, which is present in measurable amounts in almost all coals, is an annoying source of corrosive gas when coal is burned for any purpose and is a critical impurity in metal smelting. About three-quarters of the sulfur present in the coal remains in the coke, and in the blast furnace it is carried over into the metal product, where it constitutes a deleterious impurity that is difficult and expensive to remove. Sulfur can be removed from run-of-mine coal, the cost and degree of success depending on the mode of occurrence of the sulfur (whether organic or

---

[4] The U.S. steel industry now consumes only 20 per cent of the total coal production, about 60 per cent coming from captive mines (by comparison, only 10 per cent of coal consumption by electric utilities is from captive mines).

pyritic, finely disseminated or in nodules). At present, very finely disseminated pyrite cannot be removed during coal preparation because the coal must be reduced to too small a size for economic processing, and organic sulfur cannot be removed since it is combined with the coal substance. The technique of chemical desulfurization of coal is available, but economics are unfavorable.

A third problem is ash content in coking coals, which lowers the productivity of the blast furnace. The average ash content in coal charged to coke ovens is 10 per cent or less. A reduction of 1 per cent in ash content increases the rate of pig iron production by 3 to 6 per cent. Just as blending makes possible the use of coals whose volatility differs from the ideal, so the use of coals with high ash and sulfur content is made possible through preparation, which utilizes various techniques to separate certain proportions of the impurities from the mined coal and thus provides a higher quality product.

A decline in coke quality does not necessarily pose an insurmountable difficulty to the smelting industry. The economic efficiency of coke from poor quality coals is not necessarily inferior. High ash is not always harmful, and a higher sulfur content can be tolerated under certain conditions. The quality of any individual coal for use in the coking charge is less significant than consistency. In the short run, the increasing use of pelletizing and other techniques leading to a richer blast furnace charge will mean a decline in the amount of coke required to produce a ton of pig iron. In the long run, it is possible that the entire question of coking coal could become academic through realization of the possibility of a continuous large-scale process to win iron from its ore without the use of coke (e.g., the reduction with hydrogen or carbon monoxide from any fuel source).

Another type of service materials is the group of fluxing and refractory materials. Vast tonnages of limestone are utilized for fluxstone in metallurgical furnaces, particularly those of iron and non-ferrous metals.[5] Such flux serves to offset silica, to yield a thin slag, and to produce a basic slag that collects and retains impurities separating from the metal. About 5 pounds of fluorspar are used in making every ton of steel (e.g., about 250,000 tons of metallurgical grade material in the United States) to insure proper oxidizing conditions in open hearth and electric furnaces—added to the bath, it makes more fluid the molten limestone floating on top of the liquid steel, thus allowing for quicker elimination of impurities and faster transfer of heat through the slag blanket to promote furnace efficiency. These and others of this type of service materials are generally widely distributed and reasonably priced compared with coke and other fuel.

A relative newcomer to the service materials category is oxygen. Present oxygen consumption trends in the U.S. steel industry indicate its use at the rate of about 1,000 cubic feet a ton by 1964, used as indicated:

Blast furnace	10%	Oxygen introduced to speed pig iron production and decrease coke requirement
Open hearth steel-making	44	Pure oxygen injected directly onto molten bath to speed refining process, to reduce carbon content of pig iron, and, mixed with fuel oil or gas, to raise combustion temperature and speed melting of iron, steel scrap, and limestone
Basic oxygen process, electric furnace, and miscellaneous metallurgical uses	8	Oxygen used to speed refining of steel (oxygen converter uses 1,650 cubic feet of gas per ton of steel)
Scarfing Hand Machine	14 13	Oxygen-torch equipment used to burn defects from surface of steel to prepare it for further processing
Scrap preparation	5	Oxygen torch used to cut scrap to desired sizes
Construction and maintenance	6	Oxygen-burning gear used in cutting of steel structures, heavy production equipment, etc.

Most steel companies purchase their oxygen as they do electricity or gas. Its cost depends on the amount used: 100 tons a day costs about $15 per ton; 500 tons daily, about $10 per ton. The steel industry accounts for some 45 per cent of

---

[5] Of the some 40 million tons of limestone and other fluxes, 80 per cent is from captive quarries.

the on-site oxygen capacity in the United States (chemical industry 41 per cent, missilery 13 per cent, and all other industries 1 per cent). The phenomenal rate of increase—from 3 to 10 million tons in the 1959–1965 period—has been accompanied by a precipitous drop in price (during the 1950's, the price per ton dropped from $100 to $10 to $15).

The foreseeable future seems to promise a continuation of the recent tendency toward better preparation of raw materials. In North America, Western Europe, and Eastern Europe (including the U.S.S.R.), the share of sinter and pellets in the blast furnace burden seems likely to increase to nearly 100 per cent. Specific coke consumption will decrease by 15 to 30 per cent, depending mainly on the rate of increase in iron content in the blast furnace burden and on the degree of raw material preparation. Intensification of all metallurgical processes, particularly by the widespread use of oxygen, is probable, and this will require improvements in other service materials, such as fluxes, refractory brick, and coolants.

Iron and Steel Furnaces

The underlying aims of technical development in pig iron production are higher productivity of blast furnaces and labor, a lower specific consumption of coke and other raw materials, and a lower over-all cost of iron.[6] To economize coke is the main concern. The blast furnace is essentially a tower-type chemical retort, which uses hot carbon-monoxide gas from burning coke to remove chemically bound oxygen from ore and flux to fluidize the mechanically mixed impurities into slag.

By far the most important method of improving pig iron production lies in the better preparation of raw materials, in the first instance through iron ore enrichment (previously discussed), mainly done at the mine or associated beneficiation plant. The use of such enriched (pelletized) ore lowers slag volume and can raise production rate 10 per cent or more. Larger ore size (agglomeration) encourages an even, rapid flow of reducing gas through the furnace; it also prevents loss of fine particles. Sintering (baking with fine coke) is costly, but higher ore costs warrant the expense, since less ore is lost as stack fines and deoxidation is improved. Sintering conserves iron ore by converting the growing proportion of fine particles into superior blast furnace feed. Sintering half the ore charged into blast furnaces increases pig iron production by 10 to 20 per cent, while at the same time it reduces coke and limestone consumption per ton of iron produced by about 10 to 20 per cent. Also, fewer costly blast furnaces need be built if more sintering equipment is installed (in the early 1960's, adding a blast furnace to an exist-

---

[6] Approximate distribution of costs* in making steel:

	United States		United Kingdom	
	Percentage of Subtotal	Percentage of Grand Total	Percentage of Subtotal	Percentage of Grand Total
Ore, scrap, and other materials	43	14	40	11
Fuel (mainly coke)	38	12½	41	11½
Labor	4	1½	6	2
Balance	15	5	13	3½
Total for iron	100	(33)	100	(28)
Iron	41	(33)	35	(28)
Scrap, ferro alloys, and other materials	37	29½	35	28
Fuel	3	2½	9	7
Labor	6	4½	8	6½
Balance	13	10½	13	10½
Total for steel ingots	100	(80)	100	(80)
Ingots used		(80)		(80)
Circulation scrap credit		−12		−7
Fuel		1		2
Labor		11		9
Transport (delivery)		8		5
Balance		12		11
Total for heavy steel products		100		100

* "Costs" is used here to include taxes and return on capital.

Productivity Team Report, Anglo-American Council of Productivity, *Iron and Steel*. Although the data are from the 1950's, and a similar table for the early 1960's is not available, a partial check indicates that the distribution of costs has not been radically changed, as rationalization (improved technical efficiency) has been roughly similar across the board (in iron and in steel furnaces, and in associated mill operations). In real terms (excluding inflation effects), molten iron and ingot steel have become about a quarter cheaper in each country.

Courtesy of Inland Steel Co.

Inside view of the sintering plant, Indiana Harbor Works, Inland Steel Company. Of the total U.S. iron ore consumption, over 35 per cent consists of sintered- or fused-fines such as these, to improve size, porosity, and composition, which permit faster furnace operations.

ing plant cost about $15 million; at a new location, about $25 million—in either case, the necessary supporting coke ovens would cost an additional $25 million; a large, modern sintering plant to help add the equivalent hot metal output would cost only $5 million to $10 million). Another refinement—grinding limestone fine and incorporating it into the iron sinter to make it self-fluxing—has proven to increase efficiency as much as the clinkering of blended and roasted ore fines. In the United States, about nine-tenths of all iron ore (excluding pellets and similar products) was sintered at mills before use by 1964, as against 20 per cent in 1950.

Improvements in blast furnace operation have been achieved partly by larger size (elimination of small, old units has raised the average nearly everywhere in the world, but especially in Western Europe), but even more by new ways of running the furnaces and with new raw materials to feed them. It took about 15 per cent less ore, limestone, and coke to make a ton of iron in a blast furnace in 1964 than it did in 1958. Swifter production schedules have upped furnace productivity; in the early 1950's, the best blast furnaces produced about 2,000 tons of iron a day, while the most efficient ones produced 3,000 tons daily in 1964 (for the same capacity). In the late 1940's, the United States had some 200 blast furnaces producing 60 million tons of pig iron. By 1964, about 140 blast furnaces turned out 86 million tons of pig iron. The same changes have been occurring in Western Europe, in Eastern Europe, in the Far East, and elsewhere.

Experiments have been made on the smelting of pig iron in low-shaft blast furnaces (20 to 30 feet high instead of the 100 feet or more in the regular-size ones), and it has been claimed that ore preparation could thereby be obviated. However, most of the evidence shows that ore preparation is as necessary as in conventional blast furnaces, and that the only advantage is the possibility of using poor coking coals. It would appear that low-shaft blast furnaces can be used economically only in regions without high-grade metallurgical coke or ample resources of cheap electricity.

Another substitute for the blast furnace that has seen considerable experimentation and some adoption is direct reduction of ore, or the removal of chemically bound oxygen by heating to temperatures below the melting point of iron, while leaving gangue (mechanically mixed impurities) in the sponge iron that is produced.

Sponge iron contains more impurities than pig iron (which usually contains some 4 per cent carbon and about the same fraction of slag), and these must be poured off when the iron is melted in the steelmaking process. Whereas the blast furnace is tied to coke, a direct-reduction plant can be located wherever there is natural gas, petroleum, or non-coking coals.

A 500-ton-daily-capacity plant at Monterrey, Mexico, turns out sponge iron as a charge for electric furnaces, and is the only commercially successful plant in the world, although many pilot plants also exist, and other commercial plants are projected (in Mexico, Brazil, Saudi Arabia, Taiwan, and the Philippines). Such underdeveloped countries must process small amounts of iron at the lowest possible cost. Conventional blast furnaces have to produce 1,500 tons per day to be economically feasible (with accompanying coking and other ovens, a new site requires an original investment of $20,000 to $30,000 per ton of capacity). The Monterrey plant cost some $12,000 per ton of capacity, and at full capacity, iron production is 20 to 30 per cent cheaper than in a small blast furnace of equal capacity.

Direct reduction runs hydrogen and carbon monoxide gases through the ore under heat and pressure to carry away the oxygen and sulfur (some 90 to 95 per cent of the oxygen and 60 per cent of the sulfur in the Monterrey plant, while incorporating $1\frac{1}{2}$ to 2 per cent of carbon). Giant heating towers break down methane (or oil or poor-grade coal), which is used both as reducing agent and as fuel for the process. Water and heat are added to the methane to produce hydrogen and carbon monoxide, which are then forced through a reaction chamber filled with 100 tons of ore for twelve hours to produce about 63 tons of the clinker-like cakes of sponge iron. The sponge iron is different physically and chemically from pig iron, but the quality of the steel made from either is about equal. About 10 per cent of Mexican steel production is now made from sponge iron made in the Monterrey area, and other plants are projected for Mexico City and Vera Cruz.

While direct-reduction plants are likely to proliferate in underdeveloped countries with cheap oil and gas and a wish for modest-scale steel production, the vast increase in productivity of blast furnaces since 1950 has drastically reduced the steelmakers' urgency for finding efficient direct-reduction methods as a substitute in urban-industrial countries. Such plants at best can offer only slight challenge to the improved blast furnaces. For one thing, practically all existing steelmaking in old metallurgical districts is geared to a fuel supply from the gases given off in blast furnaces and coke ovens, so replacing the blast furnace with a direct-reduction process that consumes rather than produces fuel would go against the economic grain of established smelting facilities. Fuel costs in gas-rich Texas might provide reducing gases cheaper than from coke brought from either the Eastern or Western Interior Highlands, but in the Manufacturing Belt, the costs per ton of iron produced would be similar ($5 to $10). Larger integrated steelworks now have lower capital costs and lower operating costs per ton of capacity than the largest direct-reduction plants now contemplated.

Steel is a form of iron that contains from 0.06 to 1.8 per cent carbon in chemical or molecular combination (not graphite or free carbon as in cast iron). The shares of different steelmaking processes in a given region depend on many factors: the kind of ore and amount of scrap available, the product mix of steel products required, the time and stage of capacity expansion, and many others. The first modern steelmaking furnace, the Bessemer converter, is now less than 10 per cent of world steelmaking capacity and is of major importance mainly in Western Europe. The backbone of world steelmaking is still the open hearth, which accounts for about half of all capacity, although its days of great expansion are over, and much of the capacity consists of small and old units that are marginal producers and used only under special conditions. The third steelmaking furnace, the electric one, is still under 10 per cent of world capacity and not likely to radically change that fraction. The fourth steel furnace, the oxygen converter, developed in the early 1940's in Austria, is the current favorite; together with continuous casting and vacuum degassing, it represents the wave of the future, although as of 1964 it constituted under 15 per cent of world capacity (about 40 per cent in Japan, 20 per cent in Western Europe, 12 per cent in North America, and under 5 per cent elsewhere).

The acid Bessemer process can be used only for processing very low-phosphorus iron ore; it was widely used in some countries several decades ago, but has declined to 2 per cent or so of world steel production. The basic Bessemer process is used for high-phosphorus pig iron and is therefore of particular importance within continental Western Europe (France, Belgium, Luxembourg, Western Germany), but its role even in countries where it predominates has been threatened since World War II by the growing demand on the part of wide-strip mills for steel of deep-drawing qualities. To produce basic Bessemer steel with a nitrogen content at least as low as, or even lower than, that of open hearth steel, two processes have been introduced: bottom blowing with a mixture of oxygen and steam, or oxygen and carbon dioxide. These

Floorside of a seven-unit open hearth shop (335-ton furnaces). Most U.S. steel is still made by such open hearths that have been adapted to use heavily oxygenated air, although new capacity is usually the oxygen converter, which uses pure oxygen.

Courtesy of Inland Steel Co.

Courtesy of Jones & Laughlin Steel Corp.

The basic oxygen furnace produced only 12 per cent of the U.S. steel production in 1964, but comprises nearly all new furnace capacity being built, as its capital costs are less than half those per ton capacity of new open hearth furnaces, its operating costs are 5 to 20 per cent cheaper than existing open hearth operating costs, and its speed per "heat" averages five times that of existing open hearths. Here the 70 per cent molten iron is being poured into the tilted vessel that already contains the 30 per cent finely chopped scrap, resulting in the bright orange aura (the reaction is similar to that when water is poured into hot grease). After being tilted upright, the vessel will receive its charge of burnt lime and a "jet" of some 1,500 cubic feet of oxygen. Temperatures will rise to 2,900° F., and in forty to fifty minutes the heat will be ready for tapping.

uses of enriched air (30 to 36 per cent oxygen) make it possible to decrease the nitrogen content of steel, to increase the quantity of steel scrap that can be remelted in converters, and to increase the productivity of the converter, but the nitrogen content still remains higher than in the best quality open hearth steel.

Open hearth furnaces have been increasing in size steadily in recent years (as have blast furnaces, electric furnaces, and oxygen converters). In the United States, U.S.S.R., and Mainland China, the largest fixed open hearth furnaces are about 500 to 600 tons capacity (with some of 800 to 900 tons being planned), while in Western Europe, sizes tend to be somewhat smaller (200 tons average, about 400 tons tops). The future position of open hearth furnaces is especially doubtful in the field of steel production in non-integrated steelworks (i.e., those using a cold burden), as it is now quite fully established that in such cases both investment cost and operational expenses are much less for electric furnaces than for open hearth furnaces. The basic oxygen converter represents a capital investment of $15 a year per ingot ton capacity, compared with some $40 for new open hearth facilities. In old centers, with almost costless facilities (inherited from the past), the operating costs may still favor open hearth production, but in the case of new capacity, the oxygen converter has cheaper costs (often $5 per ton).

The use of oxygen increases the productivity of an open hearth furnace by 20 to 60 per cent, depending on the amount of oxygen used (industry has yet to find the point of diminishing returns from oxygen use). The introduction of oxygen onto or into a steel bath for direct oxidation accelerates carbon removal and thus increases open hearth furnace productivity. It also decreases the time required for a heat. This use of oxygen for direct oxidation of steel has three disadvantages: it shortens the life of the roof, it gives rise to a large volume of brown iron oxide fumes (incurring municipal regulation), and it decreases the steel yield; ways of overcoming these difficulties, in particular the use of steam for cooling the zone of reaction, are now being worked out. In 1960, some 25 per cent of United States open hearth capacity was equipped with oxygen roof-jets; by 1964, it was well over 75 per cent.

Electric furnaces are becoming increasingly important, particularly in countries with cheap electric power. Oxygen is now regularly used in electric furnaces, where it increases productivity and, at the same time, substantially reduces specific consumption of electric energy and the cost of steel. One use is in the production of carbon or low-alloy steel (e.g., the type used in automobile trim), where its purpose is the same as for direct insertion into the open hearth furnace bath; that is, to accelerate the melting of scrap, and for direct oxidation. The second use is in the remelting, in electric arc furnaces, of stainless or other high-alloy scrap. One of the known drawbacks of electric furnaces, especially for mass production of regular carbon steel, is that until recently their charge consisted almost entirely of steel scrap and that hot iron could not be effectively used in them. During recent years, success in using a burden of 50 per cent scrap and 50 per cent pretreated (desiliconized and partially decarbonized) hot metal has been achieved.

The basic oxygen furnace (an Austrian development, often called "L-D" from the Linz and Donawitz centers where it was developed) can make steel better and cheaper and averages five times faster than its open hearth competitor. The L-D version is first tilted on its side and then charged with steel scrap (up to 28 per cent of the total charge). Then in goes a load of molten iron from the blast furnace, after which a load of flux, slag-forming materials, is put into the now molten mixture in the furnace. From oxygen lance, a jet of 99+ per cent of pure oxygen is blasted into the mixture, raising the temperature to over 2,900° F. and quickly burning off the impurities. The finished steel is made in about an hour, compared to six to nine hours in an open hearth. The L-D is the most popular oxygen furnace, but there is a Swedish (Kaldo) method in which the vessel, instead of standing still and vertical during the oxygen blow, is horizontal and rotates continually.

Tremendous quantities of high-purity oxygen

are obviously essential to the process; the usage runs 1,500 to 2,000 cubic feet of oxygen per ton of steel, compared with 900 cubic feet per open hearth ton. The greatest appeal of basic oxygen steelmaking lies in the lower capital costs (less than half as much a ton as open hearths), lower operating costs (maybe $1 to $3 a ton below efficient open hearths, and up to $10 a ton below outmoded units), and the faster operating rate, ranging from four to eight times faster. The latest units are 300 tons or so, ten times the size of the original Austrian prototypes. Total U.S. oxygen steel capacity at the beginning of 1965 was about 21 million tons, is expected to reach about 40 million tons by the beginning of 1967, and may reach 65 or more million tons by 1970.

The semifinishing of steel (turning the output of the metal into slabs, billets, and bars for subsequent rolling into sheet and other finished products) is today a batch process. The furnace output is cast into ingots, which are later heated in soaking pits, and then rolled on a primary rolling mill into slabs, billets, and bars. A process used for some years by non-ferrous metal producers (and some European steelmakers)—continuous casting—is now proving that these batch-type steps can be smoothed into a continuous production line.

From huge ladles, purified steel pours into a funnel (tundish) at the top of a tower, which directs it into the opening of the mold. Inside the mold and cooling chamber, steel takes shape and begins to harden. Rollers pull the steel (on which a hard skin has now formed) from the mold, then curve it into a horizontal plane, after which torches cut the still hot, but now solid, length of steel into slabs, bars, or billets.

Continuous casting results in a tremendous increase in yield over the traditional way of making semifinished products, as well as being capital saving by eliminating ingot molding, soaking, and primary rolling steps. In the conventional processing, 1 ton of molten metal will produce 80 to 86 per cent of its ingot weight in semifinished products (most of the remainder is trimming and scaling of the ingot, which scrap is returned to the steel furnace). Continuous casting, on the other hand, yields 94 to 98 per cent of its molten-metal charge in semifinished product. Makers of continuous casting equipment claim a 30 to 50 per cent savings in capital costs and average operating savings of $4 to $6 a ton over today's standard techniques.

Most of the technical problems associated with continuous casting of billets and bars have been solved, but the making of slabs is still troublesome. In conventional steelmaking, the gas and other impurities in rimmed steel (the variety used for rolling into plates and sheets) collect at the top of the ingot, which end is cut off before the ingot is rolled into slabs. But in the continuous caster, there is no place for the gas and impurities to go, so bubbles often form inside the cast pieces, leaving holes that make rolling smooth sheets impractical. The answer so far appears to be a third major innovation, vacuum degassing, which uses a vacuum vessel to suck the gas impurities out of molten steel. Ladles of molten steel, holding up to 350 tons, roll into place atop a movable platform that can be raised or lowered by jacks. A snorkel attached to the base of the degassing vessel dips into the molten metal each time the platform is raised (some forty times for a 350-ton load). The molten steel that is sucked up into the evacuated chamber of the degassing vessel boils off the gases and other impurities. Aside from its probable use in making continuous casting more workable, vacuum degassing possesses a tremendous potential for making better and more uniform steel (better ductility, impact strength, fatigue strength, and rupture and magnetic properties), a boon not only to the specialty steelmakers who have been using it for some time, but throughout the industry now that it has been adapted to big-scale operations. One estimate is that three-quarters of all steel produced will be vacuum degassed by 1975 or thereabouts, by one or another of a variety of methods.

The teaming of vacuum degassing with continuous casting may well assume rank with expansion of basic oxygen furnaces to revolutionize the steel mill in the next two decades. So far the continuous casting facilities have been relatively small units that turn out billets, but in the future larger units making slabs are likely. Koppers Company estimates that by 1975 some 135 million tons of continuous casting capacity will be in operation, making perhaps 60 per cent of all steel worked in the United States at that time.

The revolutionary changes sweeping the steel industry affect not only the making of semifinished steel so far discussed, but also the finishing processes (chiefly rolling). Since steel customers want larger and longer weld-free sheet and plate, ever bigger rolling mills to meet this demand are being built or planned. More significant than increased size of such mills are the computerized controls that are operating some of the new hot-strip mills. As the speed of the rolling mill increases, so does the likelihood of error by human operators, and eventually a point is reached where manual operation becomes uneconomical, or even impossible. So computer control is fast becoming an inseparable part of the steel mill, not only for the strip mill (maintaining gauge, changing rolling pressures, and other tasks), but in the foreseeable future also controlling the blast furnace.

Besides superior quality control, costs can be dropped by a combination of these revolutionary new processes. Some experts predict that the price of steel (1964 average about $152 a ton) will be cut 30 to 40 per cent by 1970 (in terms of present prices).

Location of Iron and Steel Production

Steel mills can be classified according to location: (1) near the source of ore—Britain's works on its Jurassic ores, Lorraine (northeastern France) and Lower Saxony (central Germany), Duluth and Sault Ste Marie works in the Upper Great Lakes; (2) near the source of fuel—Ruhr and southern Belgium industries, Pittsburgh and Birmingham districts in the United States, New South Wales industries in Australia; (3) close to the market—Eastern Seaboard and Lower Great Lakes districts in the United States, Kinki (Osaka) and Kanto (Tokyo) districts in Japan; (4) at some intermediate point—most tidewater British sites, new French and German Narrow Seas plants, Brazilian and Argentinian plants.

In spite of cheap bulk carrying, one-third of the cost of pig iron and two-fifths of the price of steel mill products represent the transport charges on materials. Between 60 and 90 per cent of all man-hours directly involved in making steel are related to handling, lifting, and carrying the 3 to 5 tons of consumable raw materials (excluding gases) that go into the making of each ton of steel and the pig iron used in its manufacture.

In the location of new capacity, several general locational tendencies can be distinguished. Older smelting districts, with leaner materials that have to be processed before using, and with cheap bulk carriage of raw materias coupled with expensive distribution of mill products, tend to locate new capacity in or near markets and bring in upgraded materials. Newer smelting districts, with good-quality, cheap raw materials but considerable transport problems in moving bulky items cheaply, tend to locate capacity on or near materials and then try to attract steel-finishing plants to the site. The latter tendency predominates in most of the world except North America and the Narrow Seas area of Western Europe.

North America. The United States has nearly a third of the world's steelmaking capacity, about 170 million tons in 1964, although a large fraction is inefficient and capable of producing types of products for which there is a slackened demand (e.g., rails and accessories, pipe, and wire). Flat-rolled demand has increased rapidly, and finishing facilities for such products are being added. Ingot production in 1964 was some 127 million tons, with mill products shipped some 85 million tons. The shifting product mix has raised questions whether ingot capacity is a reliable measure (some feel that even shipments are not very reliable for measuring steel's operating rate).

In 1964, open hearth output was 98 million tons, basic-oxygen output some 15 million tons (a fourfold increase in four years), electric furnace output some 12.5 million tons, and a small output was still from Bessemer furnaces (although the last-named is declining rapidly).

Some 85 per cent of the production and 80 per cent of the consumption are still concentrated in the Manufacturing Belt, roughly north of the Ohio and east of the Mississippi rivers, although there is a long-term tendency for the South and West to increase their shares. Approximately, distribution of steel production and consumption in the early 1960's was as follows:

	Production	Consumption
Eastern Seaboard (Megalopolis)	15%	13%
Pittsburgh (including Upper Ohio River Valley)	30	15
Erie Lakeshore	15	22
Chicago (including St. Louis, Duluth, etc.)	25	30
Manufacturing Belt	85%	80%
South (Southeast and Southwest)	8%	11%
West (Pacific Coast and Mountain States)	7	9
United States	100%	100%

Eastern Seaboard. Most plants in this Atlantic coastal plain and nearby Appalachian uplands district are market oriented, relying on cheap metropolitan scrap and cheap local and seaboard accessibility to counteract the costs of bringing in fuel, ore, and flux. Most ore is imported at moderate cost, but coking coal has considerable land movement from the central and western Appalachian mines. The district's steel products mix is made up of some half heavy products (going into construction, shipbuilding, and other heavy-industry uses), with half light products (going into parts, containers, tools, and the like). Much of Bethlehem's Sparrows Point (Baltimore) and U.S. Steel's Fairless (Philadelphia) production goes by sea to other coasts of the United States or to foreign markets, while many special steels are brought in from the Pittsburgh district or imported. Additional capacity is likely to be built, but one problem is that areas like New England that might seem to consume enough steel to support an integrated plant have such a varied consumption that no mill of such size could afford such a products mix economically.

Pittsburgh. The impetus of early growth, immense capital assets, proximity to Eastern Seaboard and Lower Great Lakes markets by rail and truck and to Southwest markets by barge, and local coking coal (cheaply mined and cheaply barged) are likely to perpetuate Pittsburgh's importance (although its share of national production has been dropping since 1900). Only the problem of expensive iron ore ($2 to $3 per ton higher than the Eastern Seaboard or Lower Great Lakes plants) constitutes an assembly costs problem, and this is partially counteracted by the fact that this is the only U.S. district making every kind of steel sold in the country. Gradually, steel-using industries are increasing in importance, but about half of the mill products still moves out.

Erie Lakeshore. The Detroit area deficit is partly filled by lake shipments from Buffalo's Lackawanna plant, but much comes in from the Pittsburgh and Chicago districts and from foreign areas. If steel consumption in the automobile and other consumer-durable industries did not fluctuate so greatly, more capacity would probably be built in the Detroit or Toledo areas.

Chicago. The Greater Chicago urban region (with a population of 8 million, including Milwaukee and northwestern Indiana) produces and consumes about a quarter of U.S. steel (as much as consumed by Britain). Capacity increases of a third will soon make the district about as important as West Germany or Japan. The giant plants at South Chicago, Indiana Harbor, Gary, Hammond, and Burns Harbor are low-cost producers, having every advantage except that of cheap fuel supply (mainly supplied from the Upper Ohio River Valley). Unlike the Pittsburgh district, there is an abundance of level land (partly slag-filled shallow portions of Lake Michigan), over which plant expansions or new facilities can spread in whatever manner is best suited to their own internal organization. Most distribution is short-range: half of the output is trucked to users within 50 miles of the plants, three-quarters is used within 200 miles, with most of the remainder going to users within 400 miles (some goes by barge down the Illinois and Mississippi rivers). The district's products

Courtesy of Inland Steel Co.

Airview of the East Chicago, Indiana, steelworks complex taken during the 1960 strike (the only time a good airview of such a complex can be taken). The view is looking north. To the left of the Indiana Harbor Canal is the Youngstown Sheet and Tube Company plant; to the right of the canal is the Indiana Harbor Works of the Inland Steel Company. A good example of a market-oriented location: the coking coal and iron ore are from the southeastern and northwestern edges of the Middle West; the mill products are shipped by truck in the metropolitan region, by rail and inland waterway to markets farther away.

mix is well suited to supply both the Midwest's construction industry and the machinery and vehicle industries (including the sheet and strip users within 250 miles who consume two-thirds of the national supply). The areas farthest away are supplied partly by smaller facilities, and partly from the Greater Chicago center by mainline railway or by barge (the latter movement will be improved with new connections between Lake Michigan and the Illinois River). Capacity is increasing along the Illinois River.

South. The Southeast has its main integrated-plant production in the Birmingham area, but there is considerable non-integrated capacity elsewhere. The coal, ore, and flux in the Birmingham area are close together, but problems arise from the low-grade ore which must be shaft-mined and expensively processed to remove the high silica and phosphorus content. A considerable portion of the molten iron is cast; that made into steel is first sent through Bessemer converters to burn off carbon and silica, with the

Courtesy of Inland Steel Co.

An airview of the Indiana Harbor Works plant of the Inland Steel Company, taken when the plant was operating at near capacity. The view is looking northeast at Plant 2 (beyond the tracks) and Plant 1 (short of the tracks).

elimination of phosphorus done in open hearths. A greater problem is the relatively low per capita consumption of steel in the Southeast, with much of that coming in from the Manufacturing Belt in the form of fabricated items.

The Texas plants profit from ready accessibility to nearby oil-gas and other markets, but most of their materials must come considerable distances. Houston has an integrated plant which is in competition with Midwestern pipe and other items barged down the interior inland waterways from the Chicago and Pittsburgh centers.

West. Considered as a whole, this district has a large market, but one thinly spread over a very large area, except for the Los Angeles urban region (7 million population) whose Fontana (Kaiser) plant disposes of two-thirds of its output in the metropolitan area. The coking coal supplies of central Utah and the Colorado-New Mexico borderland are adequate for the foreseeable future, although only the Geneva (Utah) and Pueblo (Colorado) plants have cheap coal; the coastal plants must bear rail hauls of 600 to 800 or more miles.

There are sizable deposits of ore, relative to present demand. Eagle Mountain supplies Kaiser's Fontana steel complex in the Los Angeles area, after a relatively short rail haul. United States Steel's Geneva Works near Provo, Utah, has been getting a diminishing share of its ore from open-pit mines near Cedar City in southwestern Utah, and now obtains over half of its supply from a new taconite operation in the South Pass area of Wyoming over 350 miles away (the newly opened ore body of magnetic taconite averages less than 30 per cent iron, which is upgraded to 60 per cent before being shipped from the 8,300 feet high mine). About half of California's steel consumption is served by steel mills within the state, with the other half supplied by other U.S. mills (e.g., railed from Geneva, or shipped from the Eastern Seaboard mills via the Panama Canal) or from Japan.

Overview. United States steelmakers have modest advantages over most foreign steel mills when assembly costs of raw materials are considered: in the early 1960's, the average advantage was about 5 per cent as compared with Northwest Europe's mills, and about 10 to 15 per cent advantage as compared with Japanese mills.[7] However, higher labor costs quickly nullify the materials' advantage as additional processing is done. The average U.S. steelworker is paid well over three times as much as his counterpart in West Germany (fringe benefits included in both cases), while his labor productivity is about two and a half times as much as the German steelworker's. This large differential in wages, coupled with a much more modest differential in productive efficiency, finds immediate expression in the lower selling prices of some Western European mill products and some fabricated items in the U.S. market.[8]

The pattern of steel demand is changing; the United States is using relatively less heavy, low-priced tonnage steels like rails and merchant bars and is using more and more special, high-priced steels. Although special steels are more vulnerable to the competition of light metals and plastics than heavy steels, it is nevertheless possible that steel consumption in tons will increase by roughly 3 per cent a year, or nearly twice the population growth rate, and that dollar sales,

---

[7] U.S. steel industry: distribution of sales proceeds, 1963:

Costs	
Employment costs	38.0%
Products and services bought	42.0
Wear and exhaustion of facilities	7.0
Interest and other costs on debt	1.0
Income and other taxes	6.5
Total	94.5%
Profit	5.5%

The $14.6 billion of total sales included those receipts from associated activities (e.g., bridge-building, shipbuilding, etc.) owned by the steel companies and their subsidiaries.

Annual Statistical Reports, American Iron and Steel Institute.

[8] This disadvantage can be easily exaggerated. Imports of foreign mill products have been larger than exports of U.S. mill products for the years after 1959. However, if such items are considered together with the steel in fabricated goods imports and exports, the U.S. net exports are still large. Also, export tonnage of iron and steel scrap is larger than U.S. exports of both mill products and indirect exports together.

owing to the growing importance of special steels, will increase by more than 3 per cent a year. However, most other important steel consuming nations will be increasing their use at a faster rate, so the U.S. fractions of world steel production and consumption are likely to diminish even further.

Canada. The main steel industry problem historically has been the smallness of market. The country is rich in high-grade iron ore reserves, but these are generally difficult to get and their exploitation is only just beginning, mainly for use in the United States and Western Europe. In contrast with its abundance of ore, Canada is sadly deficient in coking coal, with the only significant deposit at Sydney on Cape Breton Island. Sydney is well located in relation to all its raw materials, but it is remote from its markets, so it is the least important producer and has the lowest rate of expansion. Hamilton, near Toronto, has about half of the national capacity (6½ million tons in 1964) and has the same assets as the Lower Great Lakes districts in the United States. New facilities near Montreal are also market oriented. Sault Ste Marie has local ore and flux, but depends on Appalachian coal; it is marginal to Ontario-Quebec markets, and being somewhat closer to the expanding markets of Canada's Prairie Provinces is a doubtful advantage.

Western Europe. Steel production in recent years has been about as large in Western Europe as in North America or in Eastern Europe (including the U.S.S.R.). If the fuel and other crude materials base of the industry is included, some 2 per cent of employment and 8 per cent of gross national product are involved. The location of capacity reflects the early development; over half of all steel production is near coal, and less than a fifth each is near ore or near the market.

Fuels and raw materials (coal and coke, other fuels, iron ore, purchased scrap, and ferro alloys) account for about half of the sales value of production in the Western European steel industry (including depreciation, interest, and profit before income taxes). The comparable figure for the U.S. industry would be some 5 per cent less. However, the sum of labor costs and materials costs in the United States and that of the major Western European producers is approximately equal (but comparisons are misleading unless they are based on the same products). Raw labor costs in the United States are 3.2 times those in Germany and 3.8 times those in the United Kingdom; although American labor is about 2.5 times as efficient, labor costs per ton in the United States are some 1.3 times those in Germany and some 1.7 times those in the United Kingdom.

West Germany. In 1962–1964, the average annual steel production was 33 million tons (a bit under Japan's). Some 80 per cent of the steel is made in the Ruhr, that spectacular 30- by 15- to-20-mile area (half the size of Rhode Island) whose annual industrial output is some $25 billion, a quarter each from coal and steel (both stagnant), and half from fabricating industry. The Ruhr coalfield is the largest in Western Europe, and its coking coal output is the Common Market's main supply. Water transport (via North Sea ports, the Rhine Basin's rivers, and canals linking with other areas) allows Rhineland imports of high-grade ore, exports of steel products, and intradistrict movements. Reserves of iron ore are not very large and are almost restricted to low-grade, phosphoric deposits, upon which Thomas steel production is based. Open hearth and basic-oxygen plants use imported high-grade ores and local scrap. The Ruhr area consumes about 60 per cent of its own steel in local transforming industries, ships about a quarter to the rest of Germany, and exports the remainder, mainly to other Western European markets. The rest of West German production is located on Saar coal, Hannover ore, and the Bremen market-oriented site on the North Sea coast.

United Kingdom. Recently, Japan has passed Britain in steel production, but Britain's 25 million tons or so of annual output place it fifth in world perspective. Some 60 per cent of capacity is at tidewater. The industry as a whole enjoys some outstanding advantages: (1) Coking coal reserves are good though not abundant; not all fields produce coke of metallurgical quality, but this type of coal is available from the South Wales, Yorkshire, and Durham fields. (2) The availability of scrap plus low-phosphorus ores allow 85 per cent open hearth steel output; the country is one of the most richly endowed Western European iron ore sources, although the reserves are made up largely of low-grade, phosphoric ores of the oolitic belt, whose output is blended with about half foreign ores (Fe-content). (3) The steel plants are well located; home-produced coal is available both to tidewater plants (with their advantages for assemblage of foreign materials and export) and to inland sites based on local ore (East Midland and Lincolnshire areas). (4) Steel plants are rarely far from internal markets, so scrap supplies are readily available, and outbound freight costs are low. (5) The metal-transforming industries are well developed and expanding, enabling the United Kingdom (like West Germany) to concentrate on indirect exports of steel. The British steel industry is characterized by a large number of operating units, only a few of which are modern, integrated works, and is widely dispersed, but the compensating advantages permit an output cheaper than that of the United States on the average.

France. The some 20 million tons of annual steel output in France put her in sixth position in the world (ahead of Mainland China, Poland, and Czechoslovakia). The Northeast (Lorraine) district produces about three-quarters of French pig iron, and about two-thirds of the French steel (mainly in basic furnaces to get rid of the high phosphorus content of the minette ores). The Lorraine district has very large reserves of low-grade phosphoric ore, but little of high-grade quality, and only a small part of its coal makes high-grade metallurgical coke. The coke produced is made from a blend of roughly one-third Ruhr coking coal imports, another third of Saar and Aachen imports (also from Germany), and the final third consists of Lorraine and other low-grade coking coals (recent experiments indicate that as much as 85 per cent usable metallurgical coke can be made from Lorraine coal, but it would be more costly, so apparently large-scale dependence on strictly French coal is unlikely). The recently completed canalization of the Moselle River will allow cheaper inbound German coking coal, and cheaper French steel export.

The North district is a sort of French Ruhr, with a more balanced and self-contained production and consumption than Lorraine; its 20 to 25 per cent of French steel production and consumption consists of more specialized products (e.g., tubes, flat products, and cold-rolled sheet), rather than the more competitive, low-profit products that Lorraine specializes in.

Dunkerque has an integrated steelworks dependent upon imported ore. There is also some specialty steel production from electric furnace capacity in the Massif Central and the French Alps.

The markets for French steel are fairly scattered, and not as concentrated as the German markets. The Paris area consumes about a third, the North about a fifth, the Northeast an eighth, and the remainder is widely scattered elsewhere in France or exported (the internal markets and the exports are both supplied mainly from the Northeast surplus).

Belgium and Luxembourg. The some 12 million tons of steel produced yearly in these two countries are mostly exported. Of Luxembourg's production, less than 5 per cent is retained, about 35 per cent goes to Belgian markets, and another 40 per cent to Antwerp for export by maritime transport. The Belgium steel industry is somewhat more financially integrated with end-product customers, but large segments are also primarily for export. Luxembourg produces Thomas-quality steel from its own low-grade ore and a slightly higher grade from Lorraine; all of its coke is from the Ruhr and Aachen fields in Germany. Belgium is largely dependent on Lorraine ore (90 per cent of its steel is also Thomas type). Only 20 per cent of its coke is imported, but the domestic coal is so expensive that the high cost has led to a high scrap use.

Italy. A complete lack of metallurgical-quality coal, limited ore (only 40 per cent domestically supplied, mainly from Elba), and limited scrap (over half imported) have not prevented Italy from developing a relatively large steel production of some 10 million tons annually. About half of the steel is from electric furnaces (90 per cent located in the inland north, where cheap Alpine electricity is available at sites with considerable local scrap). The very large use of scrap, in order to minimize the need for imported coking coal, is met by imports from North America. The limited but intensive use of local iron ore is mainly along the Tuscan and Ligurian coasts, and in the Aosta valley (which has an integrated plant in the Alpine area). Italy has five large integrated plants at coastal sites: Genoa, Trieste, Piombino, Naples, and Taranto (the last a recent addition, a part of the program to revitalize the backward south of the country).

Others. The other countries of Western Europe account for some 15 million tons of steel production annually (as much as Latin America, sub-Saharan Africa, the Middle East, and South and Southeast Asia put together). The Netherlands produces steel at the intermediate site of Ijmuiden, where ore is imported from Sweden and North Africa, with coking coal barged from the Limburg field. The Scandinavian countries (especially Sweden) mainly depend on electric-steel production, with Norway and Sweden using their own hydropower and high-grade iron ore, and Denmark using mainly scrap and imported metal. Switzerland imports over 80 per cent of its iron ore to make its specialty steels in electric furnaces. Austria is self-sufficient in good quality iron ore, but must import much coal for its steel industry. Spain is not well endowed for the modern practice of steelmaking, but has a modest production in the North; its rich iron ores are mainly exhausted, with the remaining reserves either poor in quality (low grade, highly siliceous) or difficult of access; it has poor-quality coal, little of it coking quality, so imports are necessary. Portugal is just starting a steel mill near Lisbon, using local coal and ore supplemented by imports.

Overview. In the next several decades, Western Europe's steel industry will probably increase at a faster rate than that of North America, but still below the average world rate of increase. It will probably increase its dependence on imported iron ore. In many other respects, Western Europe's changing scale and technology seem to follow the past generation's evolution of North American ferrous metallurgy and related transforming industry. Increasingly, her exports will be indirect types (machinery, vehicles, and other metal products).

Eastern Europe. Although producing about 25 million tons of steel annually, the region as a whole is poorly endowed with resources for ferrous metallurgy. Except for the Silesian field, which only has modest coking coal reserves, other coal basins are small in total resources and none produces high-quality coking coal. Iron ore deposits are numerous but small, too small in most instances for economical exploitation.

Poland. The 100-billion-ton Upper Silesian coal reserve yields most of the annual 100-million-ton coal production, but its coal yields a friable coke that could be used only in small stacks. The best coking coal comes from the small Walbrzych field in Lower Silesia, which is blended with the Upper Silesian product to produce a suitable metallurgical coke. Local reserves of iron ore (30 to 35 per cent iron content) are almost exhausted and costly; iron ore is imported from Krivoi Rog, Sweden, and elsewhere in exchange for Upper Silesian coal to the extent of about 85 per cent of ore requirements. Attempts are being made to provide water transport to the Upper Silesian field, but its situation on the divide between the Odra and Vistula makes provision difficult. Most of Poland's third of Eastern European steel production is located in Upper Silesia, but there are plants at Warsaw and Szczecin.

Czechoslovakia. Production is roughly the same as in Poland, with both countries aiming at an annual output of 11 or more million tons by the early 1970's. Czechoslovakia has only one-quarter of the Upper Silesian coal basin, but its share of coking coal is larger than in the Polish section. The other coal basins do not produce coking coal. Iron ore deposits are small in size but of good quality, and the country produces one-third of its ore requirements. A new integrated iron and steel plant at Kosice in eastern Slovakia will use Krivoi Rog iron ore and Czech coking coal from Ostrava.

East Germany. Although probably larger than the Balkans' supplies, East Germany's coking coal and iron ore resources are small compared with either present or prospective needs. The integrated works on the Oder (Polish Odra) River near Frankfurt uses Upper Silesian coke and barged ore. Consumption is about double the 3 million tons annual production.

Hungary. Most of the country's coal is lignite, but some of the 10 per cent that comes from the Pecs field supplies a usable coke. There is very little iron ore; Russian ore is brought in via the Black Sea and the Danube. Consumption and production are about equal at some 2 million tons yearly.

Romania and Bulgaria. With modest crude materials bases, both countries plan substantial increases. By 1970, Romania's 1 million tons production will increase to 5 million tons when its Galati plant is operative. Bulgaria's present and prospective outputs are about a quarter of Romania's.

Yugoslavia. Iron ore resources are among the largest in Eastern Europe, but coal is poor in quality and inadequate in quantity. Most of the raw materials and smelting capacity is in the Bosnian-Herzegovinan region, although the older industry is in the north.

Overview. In Poland and Czechoslovakia, current expansion is justified by their long tradition in ironmaking, by their reserves of some of the needed raw materials, by their possession of technical skills, and by the size of their metal-using industries that provide a ready-made market. East Germany's expansion would not take place in a united Germany. Elsewhere in Eastern Europe, the expansion has been forced in the face of a poverty of resources and a lack of metallurgical skills, with the four metal-producing countries heavily dependent on imported raw materials and costly processes needed to adapt local materials to at least some of their requirements.

U.S.S.R. In 1963, steel production in the U.S.S.R. was about 80 million tons. The planned 1980 goal announced in the late 1950's of some 250 million tons may not be reached, as there is evidence of the same evolution as in the United States toward greater quality and greater substitution by other materials. Preliminary 1965 data indicate a slackening rate of increase.

In the United States, steel investment is as close as possible to the center of mill distribution, but in the U.S.S.R., they look for a substantial ore deposit and build a mill around it; then with steel available, they seek to induce steel-using industries to locate there. Usually, some 65 per cent hot metal and 35 per cent scrap is charged in the open hearths. Mills use 25 to 50 per cent more man-hours per ton of like product than U.S. steel mills, but mainly in materials handling and administration rather than shop production. They have better performance from their iron-smelting plant than the United States, have par in steelmaking, do a bit poorer in steel rolling and finishing, and are distinctly behind in large-scale high-alloy output, according to U.S. steelmen. As in the United States and Western Europe, there is a trend to poorer ores, indicated by the fact that raw iron ore production in the next fifteen years is slated to increase some 50 per cent faster than their pig iron production. Unlike the United States and Western Europe, there is no readily available high-grade foreign ore, while they must export to Eastern Europe if the present degree of autarchy is to be maintained.

Ukraine. About half of Soviet pig iron and two-fifths of Soviet steel are produced in the Ukraine, either on Donbass coal or on Krivoi Rog ore, or at intermediate sites on the Dnieper River or on the Sea of Azov shore. Over half of Soviet coke, over half of Soviet iron ore, and large amounts of other materials are produced. Costs are often higher than in the Urals or at Kuznetz, partly because of more costly crude materials, but partly because of a larger fraction of old facilities.

European Russia other than the Ukraine is noteworthy more for its steel and rolling mills than for its integrated works (e.g., about 5 per cent of Soviet steel production is in the Moscow area and 2 per cent each in the Leningrad area, Volga area, and North Caucasus area). Many of these minor areas depend upon Donbass coke, although the Leningrad area now uses coking coal from the Pechora basin near the Arctic Ocean (where severe climatic conditions increase production costs by 50 per cent over more favored basins).

Urals. About one-third each of Soviet iron and steel is produced in the southern and central Urals district. The better Magnitogorsk ores (enriched by the leaching away of the silica) are almost exhausted, and future reliance will be placed on the lower-grade ores of the area and on other ore bodies farther north in the Urals. The Urals district makes about a third of Soviet coke, but almost all from Kuzbass and Karaganda coal. The Karaganda coalfield is the closest supply and it is easily worked, but its coal has a high sulfur and ash content and is not really suited for high-grade coking coal; the same is true of the Kizel coal basin in the northern Urals (and the East Siberian field near Irkutsk).

Kuzbass. The Kuzbass smelting district provides about a tenth each of Soviet iron and steel production. The Kuznetsk coal basin has large coal reserves, and a small part of them are high-quality coking coal, but local iron ore deposits are small and low grade, although increasingly used (70 per cent of needs). Relatively, the Kuzbass seems slated to have eventually its share of Soviet fuel and metals output substantially increased to perhaps half the Donbass output.

Overview. Present Soviet plans in ferrous metallurgy assume an increase in production that will double output within the coming decade, and triple present production by about 1980. If the political framework remains permissive to these goals, there is little doubt of the Soviet capabilities in technology and resource availability to implement the political goals. The biggest question mark would be the possibility that the political-economic goals would be changed, that Soviet consumers would have a chance to choose and might elect an evolution in consumption standards such as Western Europe is now undergoing, with a greater emphasis on highly fabricated consumer durables and on personal services.

Oceania. Australia's nearly 5 million tons of annual steel production is the only important output in Oceania, although a small production also exists in New Zealand. Australian iron ore resources are immense, mainly located in easily accessible locations in the northcentral, northwestern, southcentral (these South Australian iron ranges are the main supply for the national steel industry), and southeastern (Tasmania) edges of the continent. The New South Wales coalfields are not large in total coal reserves, but they do contain a high proportion of coking coal. Steel plants—at Newcastle and Port Kembla on coal, and at Whyalla, some 40 miles from the South Australia iron ranges (getting coking coal by returning ore boats)—are modern and highly efficient, producing the cheapest steel in the world in recent years. The limiting factor to future growth is likely to be in the market area, rather than in the materials base of the metallurgical industry. New Zealand is building a small steel plant that will reduce ore from black beach sands.

Latin America. Relatively rich in reserves of high-grade iron ore—in Brazil, in Venezuela, and elsewhere—Latin America is the most poorly endowed great-region in coal resources. Some of the coal of Chile and Colombia is of coking quality; Brazilian coal is poor but can be blended; but in the rest of South America, it is doubtful if coking coal exists. In the whole of Latin America, only Mexico has good-quality hard fuel available in quantity for a domestically based metallurgical industry. In 1964, with over ten times the population, Latin America had a steel production little larger than Canada's.

Brazil. With the most extensive deposits of high-grade iron ore in the region, if not in the whole world, and a considerable fraction of all Latin American coal, Brazil is moderately endowed for supporting the 10 million tons annual production of steel ultimately projected for the core area. The largest steel plant—Volta Redonda in the Paraiba Valley between Rio de Janeiro and Sao Paulo—is expected to approach 3 million tons output by the mid-1960's. Brazilian coal is mixed with two-thirds West Virginian coal to make the coke, while the iron and manganese ores and the flux and electricity are from the core area that consumes three-quarters of the steel.

Argentina. Recently, the country finished the first portion of an integrated iron and steel mill at San Nicolas on the Parana River below Rosario, which is expected to turn out steel competitive with imported products. Iron ore will come from the Corboda area to the northwest, but coke will be imported, as Argentinian coal in the Andean piedmont belt along the Chilean border (best in southern Patagonia) is poor quality, non-coking, and economical only close to the mines. The intermediate site will be favorable for scrap collection and distribution of the products.

Chile. At Huachipato, an industrial suburb of the south Chilean city of Concepcion, there is a small but modern steel plant that supplies most of the country's steel requirements. Iron ore is brought from Cruz Grande, 500 miles to the north, by sea to ore docks at the plant. Coal comes by rail from Lota on the northern side of the Lebu Peninsula southwest of the plant; the coal is poor but usable when blended. Limestone is shipped in some 900 miles from an island off southern Chile. The natural resources base is better than the plant in Argentina, but distribution costs are higher.

Peru. At Chimbote (southern edge of northern oases group) a new steel mill has been built. Using low-shaft electric furnaces, it is supplied with iron ore by ship from San Juan, 500 miles to the south, with local hydroelectricity, limestone, and anthracite coal. The tiny plant (under 100,000 tons) has high costs of production and distribution.

Colombia. At Paz del Rio, northeast of Bogota, there is a small integrated works using local supplies of iron ore, limestone, and coal, and serving as the nucleus of several associated industries such as wire, rails, and fertilizers.

Venezuela. A government electric steel plant at the confluence of the Orinoco and Caroni rivers (Guayana region of southeastern Venezuela) will produce some 0.4 million tons of reinforcing rods, seamless tubes, rails, and other products during its initial phase, perhaps three times as much eventually. The neighborhood of the steel plant supplies high-grade iron ore and cheap hydroelectricity; natural gas and low-grade coal are available from the eastern Llanos; coal can be cheaply obtained from the ore carriers that transport Guayana ore to the Eastern Seaboard.

Mexico. Plants at Monterrey and Monclova make use of coking coal from nearby Sabinas—Mexico has the best coking coal reserves in Latin America, although they will be inadequate in the long run—iron ore from Durango to the southwest, local limestone, and manganese from northwestern Chihuahua. The other third of Mexico's million ton production comes from non-integrated production in Mexico City and elsewhere. The natural resources base is quite good, although the poor transport facilities between materials and works and between works and markets are high in cost, partly because of the great distances involved.

Overview. Latin America is not richly endowed with balanced raw materials or capital to create a major steel industry. The region has only 1 per cent of world coal reserves and an almost complete lack of good coking coal. The iron ore picture is most satisfactory, but some countries must depend on imports of high-grade ore, pig iron, and scrap. Even more formidable are the small markets, which are due mainly to the high degree of political fragmentation and the low average purchasing power. The additional problems of low labor skills and general inexperience with industrial problems are likely to deter capital, except that furnished by governments with non-economic goals in mind.

Sub-Saharan Africa. Much like Latin America, Africa is relatively rich in iron ore and poor in coal. Most of the known high-quality ore is in West Africa and South Africa, but indications point to potential resources rivaling Latin America. The Republic of South Africa has almost all the 3 million tons steel production. A private plant near Newcastle, using local ore and coking coal, produces the cheapest pig iron, much of which is shipped to the Vaal River steelworks near Johannesburg. A largely governmentally financed plant near Pretoria uses local coking coal and high-grade ore from northwest of the site. There are large coal, high-grade iron, limestone, and ferro-alloys reserves; the main limiting factors are the small market and the modest scale of production which that market can support. There is a small steelworks at Que Que, in Southern Rhodesia, using Wankie coal and nearby ore, but its output is very small.

Middle East (including North Africa). Southwest Asia and North Africa have negligible coal resources and are poorly endowed with iron ore, in a world perspective. At present, there are only two small integrated works. Egypt has one in the Cairo area, dependent on Western European coke and on ore railed from the Aswan area. Turkey has the small Karabuk plant in northwestern Anatolia, using nearby coking coal and ore from Divrik 600 miles to the southeast (small in amount, distant, and not of a high grade). Many other places have tiny electric steel capacity, but all works together result in an annual capacity of less than ½ million tons in the entire Middle East.

Non-Communist Far East. There are only two countries with important steel production in this region: Japan, whose 40 million tons output in 1964 placed it third among world producers, and India, whose 6 million tons output will be tripled by 1970 or thereabouts.

Japan. The country has fourteen integrated mills with four more being built, practically all tidewater plants. There are sixty-two steelmakers, but four account for 55 per cent of the output. Per capita steel production is some 550 pounds annually (about one-half of Western European consumption). The 1966 output is expected to be 50 million tons, and eventual output twice that. The natural resource base is not only inferior to that of India, but among the poorest in the world. Ore reserves are small and widely scattered, with a large proportion being iron-sands; over 90 per cent of ore requirements and half of the scrap requirements are imported. Coal is mainly tertiary in age and contains a high proportion of ash and volatile matter; about a third of the coking coal blend is imported from West Virginia. Only the works in northern Honshu (the Kamaishi works use local iron-sands supplemented by imported ores) and southern Hokkaido (the Muroran works smelt local limonite with fuel from a nearby field) use local materials for the most part. The Kobe-Osaka area has about one-quarter of Japan's steel capacity, both integrated plants and many non-integrated steelmaking and rolling works. The Tokyo (Kanto) area is now equally important, with several integrated works (including a new one at Chiba) and a large number of semi- or non-integrated steel and rolling works. Northern Kyushu—the oldest smelting district—has facilities close to tidewater and uses imported ore and coke prepared by blending local with imported coal. Other works are found at Nagoya and elsewhere. The recent phenomenal expansions have mainly been in the Kinki and Kanto nodes, where the big coal and ore carriers can unload at the deep-water Kobe and Yokohama ports, and where market-oriented sites have most of their customers within trucking distance.

India. Industrial prospects are probably better for India than for any other non-Communist underdeveloped country, including heavy industry prospects. The reserves of high-grade iron ore are large, perhaps rivaling those of Brazil, but coal reserves are not proportionate (known coking coal would perhaps smelt 1 per cent of known high-grade ore). The most abundant coking coal is only 100 miles or so north of the largest ore reserves in the Chota Nagpur iron ore belt along the Bihar-Orissa border. Unless inferior qualities of coal can be used, shortage of fuel poses a serious restriction to indefinite large-scale expansion, but this will not be a serious limiting factor for the immediate decades. The industry has great advantages: a large market, economical large-scale production, good resource base, and the knowledge that it has already achieved technical and financial success with a minimum of outside help. The older smelting centers at Jamshedpur and Asansol, and the new center of Durgapur, use cheap Damodar coal (pockets of Gondwana coal-bearing sedimentaries are strung along the river where structural troughs protect strata from erosion) and high-grade (65 per cent) iron ores from the 40-mile-long Singhbum deposit on the northern flanks of the Orissa hills. Patches of the same ore belt extend westward to Chattisgarh and southern Madhya Pradesh, in the vicinity of which new integrated steelworks have been constructed (Rourkela, Bhilai), still dependent upon Damodar coke but using local coal for other purposes. Capacity will soon reach 6 million tons, and 10 million tons is projected for the late 1960's.

Southeast Asia. In most of the region, iron ore resources are small, and many of them are either difficult of access or of poor quality; only the Philippines is an exception. Fuel for blast furnace use is rare throughout the region. Non-integrated works are common in the larger cities, and Indonesia is building a small integrated works, but prospects for a major smelting industry in the foreseeable future are poor.

Communist Far East. In the late 1950's, the region may have reached a production of 20 million tons of ferrous metal, but apparently much of the output from backyard and low-shaft furnaces was substandard and has been abandoned. Present production for mainland China is apparently about 13 million tons, with North Korea having about 2 million tons and North Vietnam a very small output.

China. Chinese resources for steelmaking are much like those of the Soviet Union; only a few deposits both of ore and of coking coal are large enough to justify the building of large-scale works in their vicinity, but there are also many small deposits scattered throughout the rest of the country. About two-thirds of the modest reserves of high-grade iron ore are in southern Manchuria; good quality hematite and magnetite are nearly exhausted, with the remaining reserves being low-grade, highly siliceous ores. Coke for the Manchurian plants comes from long distances. North China is rich in coal, but the proportion of coal that makes a satisfactory metallurgical coke is not high. Numerous small ore deposits are found within or on the fringes of the immense North China coal deposits. The Yangtze Valley has numerous small ore deposits, some local coking coal, and cheap water transport. Modern facilities have been built in the upper, middle, and lower basins of the Yangtze, while many of the small fuel and ore resources have been exploited with the aid of cheap labor using low-shaft furnaces. As a matter of fact, about half of the entire Chinese steel output is said to be from premodern-type facilities.

North Korea. The area has a number of ore deposits, with the largest one being the Musan low-grade deposit near the Soviet border. Coal reserves are more modest and are non-coking.

Projected steel output for 1965 is some 5 million tons.

North Vietnam. This Communist state has an endowment for steelmaking that is much poorer than that of North Korea. There are numerous small ore deposits, and the largest coal reserves in Southeast Asia provide several million tons of anthracite coal yearly. At Thainguyen, 30 miles north of Hanoi, the capital, there are two small blast furnaces with an annual production of 0.1 million tons of iron (but apparently no steel output up to early 1965).

Prospects. During the expected doubling in world steel production by the mid-1970's, the present regional pattern is expected to change in detail but not radically. North America, Western Europe, and Eastern Europe (including the U.S.S.R.) will then have nearly 75 per cent of world production, instead of nearly 85 per cent as in the late 1950's. The difference will mainly be accounted for by North America's drop in relative importance by 10 per cent, resulting in each of the three regions having roughly a 25 per cent share of world production.

The main regional change will be in the position of the Far East, which will have 20 per cent of world production or double its late 1950's position. This will be achieved by large shifts in the positions of India and China, and a maintenance of Japan's relative status. Oceania, the Middle East, and sub-Saharan Africa will roughly maintain their present relative shares, with Latin America increasing her share modestly.

Interregional trade in steel mill products seems likely to maintain present absolute dimensions of about 20 million tons annually, but the relative importance of such trade will decline as production increases rapidly and more countries reach approximate self-sufficiency. Western Europe will continue to supply about half of the world surplus, but the U.S.S.R. will supply over twice the North American exports, representing a substantial change in position. The Far East will take about half of the imports, with Latin America having a deficit almost as large as sub-Saharan Africa and the Middle East combined.

NON-FERROUS METALLURGY

While steel is essentially modern urban-industrial civilization's only cheap, multipurpose metal, and while the non-ferrous metals are essentially expensive, single-purpose metals, the competition is increasing and the distinction is blurring. It is not expected that iron and steel will lose the primate position, but the non-ferrous share will probably increase in the foreseeable future to some 10 per cent of world metals consumption.

The older non-ferrous metals—copper, lead, zinc, and tin—are only slowly increasing their production and consumption. The light metals—aluminum, magnesium, titanium, and others—are a more rapidly changing group. The older non-ferrous metals all suffer from reserve problems, with the older mining districts also generally suffering from lower-cost competition from the newer mining districts. The light metals have only minor reserve problems, but only aluminum is in a very favorable position at present, combining rapid growth with a low and stable price. The newest light metals—especially titanium and beryllium—suffer from inadequate technology and high prices, which mainly limits them to defense needs and prevents any large-scale substitution for the scarce older metals.

Copper

Being a high-priced (36 cents per pound in mid-1965, delivered in London), special-purpose (electrical uses) metal, copper is much different from steel. Competition turns more sharply on price, because essentially only one grade (electrolytic) is sold. World trade in ore concentrates, metal, and finished products is much greater, as no industrial country is self-sufficient. About a third of world copper production (over 5 million tons annual production of refined metal) is a by-product of other mining activities, with the remaining two-thirds from lean ores and complex ores unavailable until modern selective froth-flotation concentration was available. The industry's feast-or-famine supply cycles, with their accompanying price gyrations, have helped aluminum, plastics, and other ma-

TABLE 14-4

World: Great-Region and Economic-Type of Society Shares of World Older Non-ferrous Ores and Metals Production,* 1962–1964 Average-Annual
(in per cents)

	5.1 Million Metric Tons Copper Ore (Cu-content)	4.9 Million Metric Tons Smelter Copper	5.4 Million Metric Tons Refined Copper	190 Thousand Metric Tons Tin Ore (Sn-content)	195 Thousand Metric Tons Refined Tin
North America	31.4	33.0	39.0	0.2	2.9
Western Europe	2.0	3.6	18.6	1.3	18.0
Eastern Europe (including the U.S.S.R.)	17.6	17.8	15.0	9.2	10.8
Oceania	2.4	2.0	1.9	1.5	1.5
Latin America	19.6	16.0	6.2	12.7	2.6
Sub-Saharan Africa	19.6	19.3	11.1	11.1	5.3
Middle East (including North Africa)	1.5	1.0	0.4	–	–
Non-Communist Far East	2.0	5.3	5.9	51.2	46.4
Communist Far East	3.9	2.0	1.9	12.8	12.5
World	100.0	100.0	100.0	100.0	100.0
High-income countries	70.6	72.3	83.0	13.5	33.9
Low-income countries	29.4	27.7	17.0	86.5	66.1

	2.8 Million Metric Tons Lead Ore (Pb-content)	3.1 Million Metric Tons Lead Metal	3.9 Million Metric Tons Zinc Ore (Zn-content)	3.7 Million Metric Tons Refined Zinc
North America	14.8	26.5	25.5	31.0
Western Europe	10.1	23.0	13.5	26.3
Eastern Europe (including the U.S.S.R.)	24.6	20.5	18.1	20.0
Oceania	16.9	10.8	9.5	5.4
Latin America	16.9	9.7	25.3	3.1
Sub-Saharan Africa	3.5	0.5	4.3	2.8
Middle East (including North Africa)	4.6	1.3	2.8	–
Non-Communist Far East	3.4	3.7	6.1	7.4
Communist Far East	5.2	4.0	4.9	4.0
World	100.0	100.0	100.0	100.0
High-income countries	75.6	76.9	67.1	87.3
Low-income countries	24.4	23.1	32.9	12.7

Source: Adapted from United Nations and U.S. Bureau of Mines data.

* Crude ore production was approximately as follows: copper, 350 million metric tons; tin, 4 million metric tons; lead, 80 million metric tons; zinc, 60 million metric tons. Metal production includes both primary and secondary forms of output; the final copper, tin, and zinc production is mainly electrolytic, while lead production is mainly smelter output.

terials to invade many of copper's traditional markets.

Only the precious metals come from lower-grade ores than copper. Of the 85 per cent of the world's copper produced in the non-Communist areas in the early 1960's, about 27 per cent came from ores with less than 1 per cent copper, 33 per cent ran 1 to 2 per cent, and 40 per cent above 2 per cent. Scrap is increasingly important, with new (copper smelter) and old scrap together now accounting for a third of primary copper production. Copper has a use cycle of about 40 years, and because of its permanent nature (particularly its resistance to corrosion) and high cost, about 60 per cent of the copper put into use is recoverable as old scrap. Copper is also increasingly alloyed (with beryllium and other metals) to improve its qualities and cut down on specific quantities needed.

About 90 per cent of the world's mineable copper lies in four districts—Western United States, Peru-Chile, Central Africa, and Soviet Kazakhstan—all of them outside the major consuming areas. Three-quarters of the output is carried across the seas (even most of the U.S. domestic traffic).

Western United States. The United States has extremely low-grade ore, with the present production—some 1.3 million tons production or about 25 per cent of world production—coming from ore with an average content of 0.7 per cent and with over 80 per cent of mine output coming from ores with less than 1 per cent copper. Copper reserves (i.e., proven inventory) total some 35 million tons metal content, enough to last about one generation at the present production rate. Additional large tonnages with 0.25 to 0.50 per cent metal are known, but are not economic reserves at present.

About a quarter of present mine capacity is marginal at the present price range, and perhaps as much is only modestly profitable because of low-cost capital, integrated operations, and protection. However, compared with lead-zinc mining, most copper mining is still economically healthy, with the large, shallow open-pit and new block-caving shaft production fairly low cost and able to successfully compete with foreign areas having higher-grade ore and cheaper labor.

Southern Arizona has about a third of the U.S. mining production, with other basin and range areas in the vicinity also important. Central Utah and neighboring Nevadan areas are nearly as important. The northern Rockies are much less important, and the output from Upper Michigan and other eastern mines is now very small, although potential resources are still large.

Copper smelting (blister copper) capacity is almost all in the West, but a majority of copper refining (electrolytic copper) capacity is on the Eastern Seaboard (the New Jersey part of Greater New York and in Baltimore).

Latin America. Chile now produces nearly 15 per cent of world copper production, ranking third after the United States and Northern Rhodesia. She has about 1 billion tons of proven ore averaging 2 per cent metal content. The Braden mine southeast of Santiago in central Chile is the largest underground mine of any kind in the world. Chuquicamata has the largest copper ore body known in the world. Another recent Atacama addition is the new El Salvador mine, with some 375 million tons of 1.5 per cent ore (the ore concentrates are shipped in slurry form by pipeline to the smelter seventeen miles away).

Peru also has about 1 billion tons of ore, but its 1 per cent content is somewhat poorer than the Chilean ore. The new Toquepala mine, some fifty miles inland from the south coast and 11,000 feet in elevation, has some 400 million tons of ore under the 130 million tons of overburden.

The recent additions are all open pits with cheap costs of production (e.g., Toquepala is reputed to have the world's lowest cost of production, about 11 cents per pound), because of shallow overburden and modern equipment, so increasingly Latin American copper will have an advantage over North American copper, whose open pits are getting so deep that more and more shaft mining will be necessary. Politically, however, there are hazards affecting economics although compromises are possible (e.g., in early 1965, Chile's government persuaded its U.S. copper companies—Kennecott and Anaconda—to sell part interest, and to invest over $400 million by 1970, doubling production and refining a larger share within Chile).

Central Africa. Northern Zambia, which produces two-thirds of Central Africa's more than one-fifth of the world's copper (Congo's Katanga producing the other third), has some 850 million tons of 3.5 per cent ore. The lure of the Copperbelt, despite habitat obstacles and present political risks, lies in the fact that its mineable reserves are in the 3 to 5 per cent copper content area (besides other minerals, such as cobalt), although underground mining is necessary. Royalty charges of 3 to 4 cents per pound, plus heavy transport charges to the sea, spell costs of 20 cents per pound before the main distribution costs and profit have been added, which is only moderately cheap in a world context. The Union Minière (Belgian mining company) in Katanga produced about 0.3 million tons of copper in the early 1960's, making it the third largest copper company in the world (both open-pit and shaft mining techniques are used). As in Latin America, the greatest question marks are political.

U.S.S.R. Soviet copper production is some 0.6 million tons and is increasing, but the deficit of some 0.2 million tons is likely to be maintained. About 55 per cent of production is from Kazakhstan (Dzhezkazgan and Kounrad areas in east), with some 20 per cent each from the Urals and the far north (Norilsk), and the remaining 5 per cent from Armenia. Reserves are as low grade as in the United States.

Overview. Copper is not among the rapid growth industries, although the average annual rate of increase in production and consumption is about 4 per cent. The greatest increases in production are likely to occur in the Central Andean and Central African regions, which have relatively low-cost production based on superior reserves and cheaper labor costs. The greatest increases in consumption are outside the United States, especially in Western Europe and Japan.

Lead and Zinc

The fortunes of lead and zinc are tied closely with progress in many other industries: lead with auto batteries, cable coverings, pigments, pipe, radiation shields, etc.; zinc with galvanized steel, brass, die-casting parts for automobiles, and household appliances. Zinc's position is much better than that of lead in recent years: (1) zinc is still one of the best all-round materials for corrosion-resistant coatings on steel; (2) the heavy volume of construction in recent years has kept demand growing for galvanized steel, either as siding and roofing for cheap buildings or for duct work in air conditioned expensive buildings; and (3) most important, the continuous galvanizing process both cuts costs and improves quality, with continuous galvanizing keeping prices competitive in zinc's older markets, and the sheets produced by continuous galvanizing so improved as to gain new markets (e.g., their ability to withstand severe bending without breaking the zinc coating, plus their availability in coils as well as sheets, makes the material useful in roll-fed, high-production stamping plants). On the other hand, lead during the 1950's was hard hit by the loss to plastics and aluminum of two-thirds of the market for telephone and utility line cable sheathing, besides losing out in the storage battery field (although it still takes over a quarter of lead consumed). Prospective world annual rates of increased consumption are 4 per cent for zinc and 3 per cent for lead.

United States. Domestic production of lead and zinc has suffered much more from foreign competition than domestic production of copper. Partly this has been due to high labor costs ($20 to $30 daily, versus $2 to $5), but even more to leaner ores.[9] In the early 1950's, the United States produced about 25 per cent of

[9] Average metal content of world lead ores is about 7 to 8 per cent, compared with 2 per cent in the U.S. ores; for zinc ores, the world average is about 15 per cent, compared with 5 per cent in the U.S. ores.

world zinc ore and 20 per cent of world lead ore; by the early 1960's, the fractions were around 10 per cent (under for lead, over for zinc). By that time, domestic mines met about 40 per cent of total lead requirements, with imports (20 per cent) and scrap (40 per cent) supplying the remainder. Domestic mines met about half of total zinc requirements, with imports much more important than scrap in supplying the remainder. From a security viewpoint, it is significant that more than 75 per cent of the zinc imports and 50 per cent of the lead imports are from neighbors, Canada and Mexico.

Although lead and zinc mines are mainly in the hands of fairly big companies, the occurrence of the metals in veins has prevented use of mining techniques as efficient as those used by the copper industry to overcome high labor costs and lean ores. Southeast Missouri, which now produces about a third of U.S. lead, has ore that averages 2 per cent metal (without silver content, which helps defray part of costs in many other lead mining areas). The Tri-State (southwestern Missouri/southeastern Kansas/northeastern Oklahoma) lead-zinc district still has large reserves, but they only average about 1 per cent combined metal content. Recent price increases (from 13 to 16 cents per pound of lead, and from 13 to 15 cents per pound of zinc) have helped marginal mines.

High capital using U.S. smelting companies have a better chance of competing with their opposite numbers abroad than do the U.S. mining companies. They do well in zinc processing, of which over 40 per cent of consumption is used in galvanizing (some 6 to 7 per cent of the total weight of galvanized sheet consists of zinc) and another 40 per cent is used in die casting, both areas of American technical superiority.

Australia. The disadvantages that domestic mining labors under can be shown by comparing its lean ores with the rich ores mined in Australia. Mount Isa in Queensland is owned by an American company and has the same labor costs as U.S. mines, but the ores average 4.5 per cent copper, 8.4 per cent lead, and 6.2 per cent zinc (the copper lodes lie alongside the silver-lead-zinc deposits). The Broken Hill lead-zinc area in western New South Wales has ore just as rich. Australia is already as important as the United States in mining lead and zinc and has a much more economically healthy industry.

Canada. Zinc production is already as important as in the United States, most of it by-product output from gold, copper, and other mines. Lead is much less important. In both cases, recent finds augur well for additional discoveries, as only a small portion of the Shield and Mountain regions have been carefully prospected. The recent extension of the railway in western Canada into the sub-Arctic will permit exploitation of known lead-zinc deposits that could not bear the expense of air and winter sled-train transport.

Mexico. Both lead and zinc production are nearly as important as U.S. output. The industry has troubles that are due more to political uncertainty than to geological and other technical problems. Fear of nationalization or other forms of Mexicanization has affected the industry in many ways. Little basic prospecting has been done outside existing mining areas, although there is evidence of additional resources. The combined metal content of the old mines has dropped from some 25 per cent a generation back to 10 per cent or less now. There has been little modernization, while organized labor has upped labor costs to where, on a productivity basis, it is not the great asset of earlier days.

U.S.S.R. The Soviet lead ore output is the largest of any country, and its zinc ore output is among the largest, although there is some evidence that its non-ferrous industry has high costs. The largest production is in the Altai, along the Chinese border, with other production in the mountainous southern and eastern border regions and in the Urals.

Others. Half of the world's lead and over a third of the world's zinc are produced in other countries than those mentioned. Western Europe's lead mining output is no larger than before World War I and only supplies a quarter of the region's consumption, but zinc mining output is larger and supplies a larger fraction of smelter needs. The deficits are coming from the booming Central Africa and Australia mining districts.

Overview. Unless no alternative to lead shielding for nuclear reactors is found, lead consumption seems destined for very small growth in the foreseeable future. Increasingly, secondary lead will become an important element in smelter production. Zinc's prospects seem brighter, because of the metal's importance in cladding steel and in die casting. World trade seems likely to involve an increasing proportion of world lead and zinc production, and increasingly the trade will involve metal more than ore and concentrates.

Tin

The laggard among the major non-ferrous metals in modern urban-industrial society is tin. It still remains an indispensable metal for a limited number of uses, but improved and more economical uses of tin and better techniques for the recovery of scrap have lessened the demand for metal relative to the tin-plate output. World tin production is now greater than a generation ago, with consumption forging ahead of production in the early 1960's (the prospective annual rate of increase in the foreseeable future is 2 per cent). During 1964, the price went up to the highest levels since the Korean War; even the 1965 $1.85 per pound price is encouraging marginal mine production and increased usage of scrap.

A ton of tin-plate contains only 12 pounds of tin, about half of the amount used before electrolytic plating was substituted for hot dipping. Other metals (aluminum and lead) and other materials (glass, plastics, and paperboard) are substituting in the containers industry, and scrap tin (40 per cent of U.S. consumption) increasingly is used in making bronze, brass, and solder.

The market problems have partially disguised the fact that known high-grade tin reserves are relatively scarce, with the world total not more than a generation's supply at current annual production rates (some ¼ million tons new metal).

Malaysia. No new mines have been opened for some time, and the remaining reserves and resources are lower grade and will require more efficient dredges, excavators, and pumps. In the past decade, Malaysian production has dropped from a third to a quarter of world output. The piedmont tin belt extends into Thailand.

Indonesia. In the islands southeast of Singapore, Indonesia has the continuation of placer deposits now worked in Malaysia. It also has similar problems, with perhaps even greater organizational difficulties since it nationalized the industry. Refining is at Arnheim, Netherlands.

China. In recent years, Communist China's tin output has been second to that of Malaysia. Its Yunnan deposits are the northern edge of the great tin belt that extends through North Vietnam, Thailand, Malaysia, and Indonesia, and produces two-thirds of the tin ore produced annually in the world. Production—apparently mainly from lodes—was upped during the 1950's in order to provide foreign exchange. Sales to the U.S.S.R. (mostly re-exported) in the late 1950's were from 15,000 to 20,000 tons yearly, but in 1964 such sales had dropped to some 4,000 tons. Chinese sales to the West are now some 7,000 tons annually.

U.S.S.R. Soviet annual consumption of tin is estimated in the range of 30,000 to 40,000 tons, of which about three-fourths is believed to originate in Siberian lode mines. Import requirements are some 10,000 tons annually, not counting stockpile needs. The smaller Eastern European countries now import their own tin requirements.

Africa. Nigeria and Katanga (Congo) have placer production that has the same asset (low-cost production) and liability (low reserves) pattern of Southeast Asia's alluvial tin.

Bolivia. The 15 per cent of world tin production from Bolivia is the only substantial output from western hemisphere sources. Economically, it is the sickest tin mining industry in the world and would drastically diminish if U.S. subsidies for geopolitical reasons were not maintained. The tin belt is some 500 miles long and 60 miles wide in the eastern Andes, with mines some 12,000 to 16,000 feet above sea level, in an area of no local labor and little fuel or other resources. The ore is mainly in narrow veins that are mined much the same as coal; originally, the ore had metal content of 1.5 to 5 per cent, but the average is now under 1.5 per cent. The lean ore coupled with high labor costs since nationalization have pushed costs of production above the world price of tin much of the time (but not in 1964 and 1965), with the government (with indirect U.S. aid) subsidizing continued exploitation during periods of low prices (under $1.40 per pound).

Overview. With secondary tin meeting an increasing part of North American and Western European consumption, their demand is likely to remain stable at best. Consequently, an increase in world production is likely to be restricted to increased consumption in other parts of the world, which in turn awaits the development of other (food-processing, brass-bronze) industry.

Aluminum

With the brightest future among the nonferrous metals, aluminum consumption is expected to double by 1970 to 12 million tons,

This is a typical bauxite mining area as operated by the Kaiser Bauxite Company on the island of Jamaica. The bauxite is found in relatively shallow pits close to the surface of the interior plateau. In mining, the top soil is first scraped away, and then shovels scoop up the red bauxite. When a particular area is mined out, the top soil is replaced and the land rehabilitated.

Courtesy of Kaiser Aluminum & Chemical Corp.

Courtesy of Kaiser Aluminum & Chemical Corp.

Bauxite storage, drying, and shipping facilities of Kaiser Bauxite Company at Port Kaiser on the southern coast of the island of Jamaica. In the foreground is a 35,000-ton ore carrier being loaded with bauxite for shipment to the alumina plants of Kaiser Aluminum and Chemical Corporation located on the Mississippi River at Baton Rouge and Gramercy, Louisiana.

even assuming an average-annual rate of increase of 7 per cent (down from the more than 10 per cent in the 1950's). Although aluminum is losing out in its traditional aviation field to other light metals, more aluminum is being used in automobiles, homes, commercial and industrial structures, oil field equipment, highway facilities, cans, foil, and many other products, so its long-term demand seems assured.

Because of the distribution of bauxite deposits—mainly in underdeveloped countries—in relation to the industrial nations with smelting capacity, there is a heavy movement of bauxite and, more recently, aluminum in international trade. Over 90 per cent of world bauxite consumption is used for aluminum production, and some 85 per cent is from captive mines.

Aluminum reduction plants can be divided into two types: those that locate near the cheapest power and bear very heavy distribution costs, and those that locate near moderate-priced energy sites closer to their markets in order to cut down on distribution costs. The first tendency accounts for the overwhelming proportion of capacity at present, but the second is important in explaining the location of most new U.S. capacity since World War II. It could become very important if nuclear electricity eventually brings 3- or 4-mills-per-kilowatt-hour electricity to the great metropolitan areas of the world.

North America. In 1964, the United States had nearly 3 million tons of primary aluminum capacity,[10] and Canada had well over a million tons, together some three-fifths of world capacity. The United States consumed about half of the world's output, while Canada exported most of her metal to the United States, Britain, and elsewhere. Per capita U.S. consumption is some 30 pounds yearly, three times that of Canada or Western Europe and six times that of Japan.

North America has energy and markets, but practically no rich ore. Some 2 million tons of bauxite are mined (practically all in Arkansas), but imports are over five times as great (half from Jamaica, another quarter from Surinam, and the remainder from British Guiana, Haiti, and the Dominican Republic). Canada has no domestic production of bauxite, importing mainly from British Guiana and Jamaica. While

[10] In addition, there is 0.5 million tons of secondary capacity.

Airview of Chalmette, Louisiana, Works of Kaiser Aluminum and Chemical Corporation. Located on the Mississippi River a few miles south of New Orleans, Chalmette is the largest aluminum reduction plant in the United States with an annual capacity of 247,500 tons of primary aluminum. The southwest's cheap natural gas supplies are used in alumina-making (hot lye cooks bauxite to rid it of mechanically mixed impurities) and in the thermo-electric plants that provide the current to fission the alumina (aluminum oxide) and produce the aluminum metal.

Courtesy of Kaiser Aluminum & Chemical Corp.

Courtesy of Kaiser Aluminum & Chemical Corp.

Airview of Ravenswood, West Virginia, Works of Kaiser Aluminum and Chemical Corporation. Ravenswood Works is made up of two plants: a reduction plant (left), which has an annual capacity of 145,000 tons of primary aluminum, and a sheet, plate, and foil rolling mill (right). The plants are located on a 3,000-acre site along the Ohio River, within easy reach of enormous steam coal reserves and the largest markets for aluminum mill products.

North America has only tiny reserves of high-grade bauxite (50 per cent alumina minimum, 13 per cent silica maximum), there are tremendous resources of aluminous clays with about 44 per cent each of alumina and silica that may someday be ore.

In recent years, the cost of producing primary metal worth 24 to 25 cents per pound has averaged about 15 cents; it is somewhat cheaper in the Pacific Northwest where plants use 2 mills current, somewhat higher in the Southwest with 4 mills current and in the Ohio Valley with 3 to 4 mills current. Fixed costs (e.g., the cost of not producing from capacity) are some 4 to 6 cents per pound, fuel and energy some 3 to 4 cents per pound, raw materials about the same, with transport several cents, and other costs (especially labor) the rest. Metal sold overseas sells for 22 cents, while that sold domestically brings 24 cents.

The mathematical center of the U.S. aluminum market is around Terre Haute, Indiana, with some 70 per cent of total sales within 500 miles of that center. More new capacity has been built in the Ohio Valley in recent years than anywhere else. Increasingly, the new inter-

TABLE 14–5

World: Great-Region and Economic-Type of Society Shares of World Bauxite, Aluminum, and Magnesium Production, 1962–1964 Average-Annual
(in per cents)

	34.4 Million Metric Tons Crude Bauxite	6.4 Million Metric Tons Aluminum Metal [2]	160 Thousand Metric Tons Magnesium Metal [2]
North America	5.3	50.0	55.0
Western Europe	11.2	23.4	20.0
Eastern Europe (including the U.S.S.R.) [1]	20.4	18.2	21.3
Oceania	0.2	0.3	–
Latin America	51.0	0.3	–
Sub-Saharan Africa	5.8	0.9	–
Middle East (including North Africa)	–	–	–
Non-Communist Far East	5.0	5.2	3.1
Communist Far East	1.1	1.7	0.6
World	100.0	100.0	100.0
High-income countries	28.7	94.0	99.4
Low-income countries	71.3	6.0	0.6

SOURCE: Adapted from United Nations and U.S. Bureau of Mines data.

[1] Soviet production of aluminum-bearing materials includes nephelite and alunite as well as bauxite.

[2] Aluminum and magnesium metal production includes primary and secondary supplies.

mediate and market-oriented aluminum plants tend to have more and more in common with a steel industry complex; some 80 per cent of primary metal production goes to market as wrought metal (foil, sheet, strip, plate, extrusions, and forgings).

Western Europe. This region produces nearly half as much aluminum as North America and, while it produces twice as much bauxite, must still import half its ore. Continental Western Europe has considerable metal exports, but the large British imports make the region a net deficit one over-all.

France, Italy, and Greece have industries based on domestic bauxite. South European bauxite also moves to German coal and lignite for initial processing, with the alumina being reduced by Alpine hydropower or in Norway. Since electricity tends to be more expensive in Western Europe than in many other places, it is expected that the rapidly increasing consumption will more and more depend upon imported ingot from Africa and elsewhere.

Eastern Europe. The U.S.S.R. now has over 1 million tons aluminum capacity, with other Communist European countries having about a quarter as much. The region is roughly self-sufficient in ore, with Hungarian and Yugoslavian bauxite mines supplying the western countries of the bloc, and the U.S.S.R. using mainly Urals bauxite, Azerbaijani alunite, and Siberian nephelite (the last two high-cost sources).

Most Soviet expansion is taking place in the Urals and in Siberia, with over three-fourths of the country's capacity eventually due to be located there. In addition to old plants near Leningrad (using local low-grade bauxite), Zaporozhye on the Dnieper in the Ukraine (using Greek bauxite), and Transcaucasia (Sumgait near Baku and Erevan, the capital of Armenia), the Soviets have large new plants on the Volga and in the Urals, in the Kuznetsk Basin, at Krasnoyarsk, and near Irkutsk. Krasnoyarsk now uses Bratsk electricity, but will soon have its own supply, and Bratsk will have a new aluminum plant to absorb most of its own power.

Oceania. Australia now has the world's largest high-grade bauxite resources, some 3 billion tons in northern Queensland and in the Northern Territory. Metal-making capacity is also increasing rapidly, already being 0.1 million tons, and soon to be triple that when Western Australian and New Zealand plants are built.

Latin America. Jamaica alone produces over a fifth of the world's annual bauxite production of some 35 million tons, with Surinam, British Guiana, and other producers bringing the regional share to about half. Since practically all is exported, the Latin American countries supply two-thirds of the bauxite moving in world trade.

Proven reserves for Jamaica are given at 550

million tons, with those for Surinam at over 100 million tons, and those for British Guiana at somewhat less. However, recent finds promise huge additions, and raw material availability is a minor problem in maintaining or increasing present output.

Aluminum reduction is minor, but plans for large-scale production exist. Brazil plans to build a plant to use Paulo Afonso power and local bauxite in its Northeast. Aluminium of Canada is building a hydroelectric plant with accompanying refinery in British Guiana. Even when completed, the capacity will be small compared with raw material and hydro potentials.

Africa. Guinea has some 600 million tons of bauxite known, with several times that amount in inferred resources. Ghana and other areas also have large reserves and potential resources. But actual bauxite production has recently been only 1 to 2 per cent of the world total, and actual metal production (from a Cameroon plant) was also only 1 per cent of world ingot production.

However, there are plans to greatly increase both ore production and metal reduction, mainly for Western European markets. The largest project that seems closest to actual building is the Volta River project in Ghana, which would use local ore and 2.6-mill electricity to produce 120,000 tons of aluminum initially (and nearly double that amount ultimately).

Far East. India and China have modest bauxite deposits, and they plus many other countries have large inferred resources, but in recent years, actual production has only been 3 per cent of the world total. There are reduction plants in Japan, China, and India, but output is only some 5 per cent of the world ingot production. Substantial increases in ore and metal output are projected, but for domestic consumption. What trade in ore and metal does evolve is likely to be intraregional.

Prospects for a wider dispersion of aluminum industry in the Far East seem better than for ferrous metallurgy.

Overview. On balance, the prospects for increased aluminum consumption are quite good. New and expanding uses are probable if the metal maintains its present low current price relative to competing metals. Greater substitution of aluminum for steel appears to depend mainly on cost rather than upon aluminum's qualitative superiority. If and when very cheap electricity becomes available—either by spectacular progress in the nuclear-electricity field or by a large-scale development of smelting capacity in certain highland areas of the humid tropics with most remaining 2- to 3-mill hydropotentials left in the world—the cost of producing aluminum may decrease relative to that of steel. However, this seems unlikely to happen during the next decade or so.

Europe and Japan are undergoing the same revolution in the use of aluminum as the United States, but have had a later start. This will change the relative regional distribution of metal smelting, both by greater development of capacity in those areas and in certain overseas areas favored by them.

Magnesium

This metal is almost the only structural metal for which any area could find domestic crude materials (magnesite, brucite, dolomite, olivine, salt water). It has a long list of desirable characteristics. Magnesium weighs only two-thirds as much as aluminum and one-quarter as much as zinc or steel. Volume-wise, it is cheaper than any other virgin metal except cast iron. Metal-working tools cut magnesium like butter; it is the easiest machining metal known, and can take deep, fast cuts and yield an excellent surface finish, and it is amenable to casting and extrusion. Because it is so malleable under heat, magnesium sheet can be formed on presses in deeper single draws than just about any other material.

Magnesium has long been heralded as the major competitor of aluminum, but after a generation of use, it is still a minor factor in the metals market (0.16 million tons annual production), because of the fact that even though it can be obtained at moderate cost (magnesium pig is 35 cents per pound, ingot 36 cents per pound), its large-scale use awaits technical improvement in alloying, fabricating, and coating. Impediments to greater use include these: although its most promising uses are in fields where lightness and rigidity offer economies over heavier metals, its relative weakness is a problem; magnesium also suffers from corrosion and inflammability problems (development of an alloy with better corrosion resistance or the discovery of a satisfactory coating for magnesium could lead to a rapid increase in consumption).

North America. The United States now produces about 70,000 tons of primary magnesium and 10,000 tons of secondary magnesium, while Canada produces about 10,000 tons of primary magnesium. Some nine-tenths of U.S. primary capacity is in Dow seawater plants on the Texas coast, with the rest of the production from magnesite-using plants owned by smaller companies. Consumption is half again as large as production, the difference made up by withdrawals from inventoried metal. Aluminum producers take some 30 per cent of magnesium production, while other metallic ore reduction (titanium, zirconium, hafnium, uranium, and beryllium) takes another 16 per cent. Automobile use is now the largest non-metallurgical use (mainly in die casting); some 16 per cent is used in aircraft and missiles (all defense uses some 20 per cent).

Others. Western Europe and Eastern Europe each produce nearly two-fifths of North American magnesium production, with the U.S.S.R. producing practically all of Communist Europe's output, and Norway half of Western Europe's output.

Magnesium has been produced in the U.S.S.R. since the 1930's, both in the Urals industrial area and at Zaporozhe on the Dnieper River in the Ukraine. The ore used has been carnallite (also a major source of potash), produced in the area of Solikamsk and Berezniki on the western slopes of the Ural Mountains. About 10 to 12 tons of carnallite are required to produce 1 ton of magnesium metal by the electrolytic process and uses up 20,000 to 24,000 kilowatt-hours of electricity for each ton of metal. A new plant to produce both magnesium and titanium was opened in early 1965 at Ust-Kamenogorsk, an industrial center of eastern Kazakhstan, at the western foot of the Altai Mountains whose streams provide the low-cost hydroelectric power. Token amounts of titanium were previously produced in the Ukraine (from ilmenite ore found in rich sandy placer deposits along two right-bank tributaries of the Dnieper River), but the new plant is the first large-scale output.

Other Light Metals

Titanium is light (40 per cent less than stainless steel), strong, highly corrosion resistant, and resistant to moderately high temperatures (maintaining useful strength up to 1,000° F., whereas aluminum begins to weaken above 300° F.), but its drawbacks, especially its high cost (composite mill products price is some $6 per pound; on a volume basis, the metal sells at four to five times the price of competitive stainless steels) and the difficulties in fabricating the metal (so far, titanium cannot be easily cast), have kept it an essentially military metal (military aircraft take half of the consumption; missiles and other space hardware a third; and of the civilian 17 per cent usage, about two-thirds goes into civilian aircraft). Mill products consumption of 7,500 tons yearly is expected to be doubled by 1970.

Titanium ores are common. Rutile is the richer but less abundant ore, with 90 per cent of the current 180,000 tons being recovered from Australian beach sands, although increasingly future production will come from the world's largest deposit located in Sierra Leone. Mexico's Oaxaca province has another large deposit. Ilmenite is the commoner ore, but it only runs 25 to 30 per cent titanium oxide (rutile, 60 per cent) and is mainly used for paint pigment.

Beryllium is almost as light as magnesium, but has three times the strength of steel, and has a melting point twice as high as alumnium or magnesium. It is costly to mine, has to be refined under vacuum to keep out the impurities that make the metal brittle, and is even more difficult to shape than titanium is. Aircraft and missile parts cost $75 to $100 per pound (compared with $20 to $40 for aluminum parts; titanium parts cost are between the two).

Lithium, the lightest metal, is being used as an alloy more and more (e.g., in titanium). The metal is only one-fifth the weight of aluminum and so light that it will float on water for a few moments before it vanishes in a chemical reaction. Lithium carbonate runs about $1 a pound, with the metal costing about $13 per pound. North America has the bulk of production and consumption, with ore coming from lithium ores in the Black Hills of South Dakota, the Kings Mountain region of North Carolina, Canada (northwestern Quebec and Manitoba), and Southern Rhodesia (the largest high-grade body in the world is found at Bikita). Most lithium is used in chemical rather than metallic form.

Prospects. One of the fundamental forces at work has been a decline in the ability of urban-industrial economies' mines to compete with mines elsewhere without protection. This is especially true of the U.S. mining industry's competitive position, in almost all ores except the very newest ones to be exploited.

Assuming relatively free movement of ores, concentrates, and metals, such deficits need not be economically disadvantageous. But in cases where industrial countries have excess capacity—even though uneconomic or only marginally economic—the temptation to protect such sources under the guise of defense excuses is likely to remain strong so long as international tension remains high.

The difficulties are especially great in the older non-ferrous metals—copper, lead, zinc, and tin—whose ultimate resources total less than 0.2 per cent of the earth's outer crust, and whose higher-grade deposits are almost entirely in underdeveloped and semi-industrial countries, although much of the mining capacity is in older mining districts with lean ores, inadequate scale, older technology, and other difficulties. The difficulties are much less in the newer light-metals group, whose ultimate resources are 550 times greater than in the older non-ferrous group, and where relatively high-grade ores are much more widely distributed over the earth, with less contrast in geographic competitiveness.

METAL-TRANSFORMING INDUSTRIES

In the period 1962–1964, the average annual world metal-making capacity was some 550 million tons, with world production about 440 million tons of ingot production. Shipment of semi-finished (mill) products was about 325 million tons, apparently destined to fabricating industries and other users as follows:

Capital Goods		*Consumer Goods*	
Construction	20%	Automobiles	15%
Industrial machinery	20	Containers	5
Railroads	10	Appliances	5
Mining equipment	10	Other consumer goods	5
Other capital goods	10		30%
	70%		

There are significant regional differences in how metals are consumed. In the United States, capital goods absorb less than 65 per cent of all metal (construction, industrial machinery, and others absorb relatively larger fractions than in world perspective indicated above), and consumer goods over 35 per cent of all metal (automobiles taking over 20 per cent of all metals). Western Europe is following in U.S. footsteps, but the Communist realm and the underdeveloped realm have a different pattern of consumption, with some 90 per cent of their metals used in capital goods construction and manufacturing.

United States. Over 3 billion tons of iron and steel have been produced in the United States in this century, with two-thirds of it—some 10 tons per capita—still in use. Current production and consumption are roughly in balance; steel-mill products exported are now less than steel-mill products imported, but the metal in indirect net exports more than compensates.

The use of steel in metal-fabricating plants in the Eastern Seaboard and the Midwest still far overshadows that of the outlying states, but the latter now consume about a fifth of total steel consumption, and a bit more of all metals.

Western Europe. In Western Europe, the consumption pattern is, on the whole, similar to that of the United States, with some differences. There is a difference in the individual shares of products in total metals consumption (e.g., the shares of flats and tubes are appreciably lower than in the United States, while that of sections are much higher). The most marked difference is for tubes, since in the absence of an oil and gas industry comparable to that of the United States, the machinery industry is the largest consumer, followed by building and civil engineering.

The share of Western European trade in the world metals market is over half of world exports, even if intra-Western European trade is excluded. Although in modern times no single Western European country has had within its own borders a balanced supply of iron ore and coking coal, for the most part Western Europe considered as a whole produced its 28 per cent of the world's crude steel from primary materials extracted from its own subsoil (in the early 1960's, about 15 per cent of iron ore, 10 per cent of scrap, 10 per cent of coking coal, and over 95 per cent of ferro alloys were imported from outside region). However, the tendency is toward greater imports. By 1970, more than one-quarter of Western European pig iron will be produced from imported ores; perhaps three-quarters of its zinc and even more of its lead will come from abroad in the form of ores, concentrates, and refined metal; virtually all of regional consumption of copper and tin will be based on outside suppliers, as will its consumption of nearly all the ferro alloys; and perhaps half of the aluminum consumed will come from sources abroad in the form of alumina or finished metal.

Both North America and Western Europe are expected to increase their metals consumption at a slower pace than the rest of the world, as can be seen below in estimates prepared by the Economic Commission for Europe.

TABLE 14–6

Expected Percentage Increase in Steel Consumption Between 1957 and 1972–1975
(in per cents)

	Absolute Increase	Per Capita Increase
North America	52	27
Western Europe	92	79
Eastern Europe (including the U.S.S.R.)	124	99
Oceania	122	174
Latin America	173	112
Sub-Saharan Africa	133	111
Middle East (including North Africa)	216	150
Non-Communist Far East	266	192
Communist Far East	430	313
World	212	162

Construction

It is in construction that steel faces the broadest range of competitive materials. Prestressed concrete has already displaced millions of tons of heavy steel products (high buildings in Latin America, Latin Europe, and elsewhere; overpass bridges in U.S. highway construction). Copper and plastics—and to a much smaller extent, aluminum—have displaced much steel in the manufacture of standard pipe used for plumbing and heating, water supply, and other purposes.

In the long run, however, steel may be threatened less by displacement by other materials than by displacement by air; by engineering and design innovations that reduce the total weight of material, whatever material is used. Because of the relative slowness with which labor productivity has advanced in construction, architects and structural engineers are designing buildings that permit use of lighter materials or fewer structural members.

Machinery

Nearly everywhere, the manufacturing of machinery tends to be concentrated geographically more than most other industries. Quite often, an old manufacturing district gradually specializes in the machinery used in that branch of industry

Courtesy of Allis-Chalmers Manufacturing Co.

Airview of the West Allis Works of the Allis-Chalmers Manufacturing Company in the Milwaukee, Wisconsin, area. The Lower Great Lakes from Milwaukee to Buffalo is the greatest machinery manufacturing region in the world and accounts for half the North American output.

as its share of production declines. Western Europe produces about a third of the world's production of all machinery, with the United States second with about a quarter, and the U.S.S.R. third with nearly a seventh of all machinery produced (but with a quarter of machinery going into its favored heavy industry). Japan produces nearly 5 per cent, and the remaining fifth of world production is widely scattered, not only among other urban-industrial societies, but in many underdeveloped societies, where simple machinery or a narrow branch of machinery building is often represented.

Immediately after World War II, the United States produced over a third of the world's machinery and electrical apparatus and led in almost every kind. It also contributed about a third of world export as much as all of Western Europe. Although such goods were only a tenth of national machinery production—compared with about a third of Western European production exported—U.S. exports were very important in determining the level of profits in many branches of the industry.

By the early 1960's, the American share of world machinery production and world machinery exports had dropped substantially. Direct machinery exports were down, machinery imports were up, and net exports were less than 5 per cent of national machinery output. Labor costs were not in balance with productivity, and such labor costs are the largest factor of production in most machinery (e.g., the price for custom-built equipment made in the United States includes up to 55 per cent labor cost). Average hourly employment costs (wages plus fringe benefits) in machinery-making industries in the early 1960's were as follows: United States, $4; Britain, West Germany, Netherlands, $1.50; Belgium, France, $1.25; Italy, $1.10; Japan, $0.75. The U.S. employment costs were so high that, in general, U.S. machinery-making industry could consistently undersell their competitors in only two general areas: (1) mass-produced items where labor-input is low (e.g., some types of equipment where most assembling and most testing can be done by machine); and (2) new items of advanced design, where the heavy research investment of U.S. business and government provides technological leadership. If the United States is to maintain its position in the world's machinery exports, it must develop and promote growth in the new fields of technology—in automation, electronic gadgetry of other kinds, nuclear energy, etc.—since there is increasing difficulty in maintaining many traditional export lines where much skilled tooling and inspection is necessary. Production of run-of-the-mill machinery for export is rarely a real assembly line operation. Individual buyers want special gadgets and gimmicks, and many export orders are tailor-made. This tends to give an advantage to machinery exporters abroad—Western Europe and Japan especially—who have lower costs.

The U.S. machine tool industry—some 300 companies in contrast with 1,500 in Western Europe—is counterattacking against its foreign competition on two fronts: (1) U.S. machinery-makers are seeking to win back their dwindling foreign markets by moving to Western Europe

Combining the generator shaft and turbine shaft on a hydroelectric unit destined for the Pacific Northwest.

Courtesy of Allis-Chalmers Manufacturing Co.

Courtesy of Allis-Chalmers Manufacturing Co.

Machining the rotor for a 146,000-kilowatt steam turbine-generator.

Machining a nuclear-reactor pressure-vessel.

Courtesy of Allis-Chalmers Manufacturing Co.

themselves—companies representing three-quarters of U.S. cutting tool volume have arrangements to produce machine tools abroad; and (2) on the production front, U.S. toolmakers are busily engaged in cutting costs to meet lower foreign prices by standardizing parts, redesigning machines for greater simplicity and customer appeal, and putting more emphasis on the machines U.S. factories can turn out better than overseas makers.

United States imports are coming from two sources: (1) American-owned manufacturing plants in Western Europe—one machine-tool maker says he can make identical machines in his 100 per cent owned Western European subsidiary 35 per cent cheaper than in his U.S. plant, and sell them to advantage, costwise, in the U.S. market; and (2) Western European manufacturers who are selling to U.S. manufacturers in the same lines (usually standardized machine tools that tend to be similar in any industrial society).

The competitive struggle for international machinery markets—now mainly restricted to the older North Atlantic Basin countries—is bound to get more complicated as Communist countries, Japan, and other newcomers begin to export on a larger scale. Japan, especially, with its need to develop along the same lines as the Western European Narrow Seas' countries, will increasingly be exporting machinery to Far Eastern and other markets where American and Western European machinery has hitherto had little competition.

Motor Vehicles

United States predominance in the motor vehicles industry has been lessening in the past generation, as the industry has diffused throughout the world. Since 1958, less than half of the

Airview of a new tractor plant at Aurora, Illinois, which is about 40 miles west of the Chicago lakefront and well situated with relation to nationwide rail and superhighways routes and to international routes via the Chicago Lake Calumet port and the St. Lawrence Seaway.

Courtesy of Caterpillar Tractor Co.

world production of automobiles and commercial vehicles (trucks and buses) has been manufactured in the United States. In 1964, the United States and Western Europe each assembled some 8 million automobiles and some 2 million commercial vehicles (by value, the U.S. output was still larger, because of greater average weight and power). Japan, Canada, and the U.S.S.R. contributed most of the remainder of world production, but the number of countries who assemble and partially manufacture vehicles is continually rising.

Excluding the aerospace (aircraft and missile) industry, the motor vehicles industry is the branch of transport equipment manufacturing where the United States maintains the greatest comparative advantage in a world perspective. Integration (forward and backward), standardization of essential parts and components, multiple lines of cars (so far as styling selling points are concerned), and regional assembly plants have yielded great economies, and maintained the domestic industry's hold on the national market. But increasingly the main American impact on the world market is from foreign subsidiaries of U.S. companies. The imports of foreign cars and parts about equal in value the exports of American cars, other motor vehicles, and parts.

Historically, the industry has had a very strong tendency toward geographical concentration, although that tendency is now beginning to weaken somewhat. Great economies of scale have been possible in making the engine, gearbox, axles, suspension and other components, and in assembling body and components, as well as in distribution. The manufacture of individual parts (pistons, piston rings, engine blocks, valves, springs, etc.) and the assembly of these separate parts into units or subunits (e.g., the engine) require considerable skilled labor and capital-intensive automated facilities, and therefore tend to remain in the older centers (e.g., in the United States, about two-thirds of the workers and value added [11] by the industry are still

[11] Value added by the motor vehicles and equipment industry is less than 30 per cent of the gross value of output, in spite of relatively high wage rates and profits. Over 4 per cent of national income is involved.

Courtesy of Caterpillar Tractor Co.

Decals being put on finished tractors. The Caterpillar plants at Peoria, Decatur, and Aurora, Illinois, manufacture tractors, engines, motor graders, and earth-moving equipment.

Courtesy of The White Motor Co.

Airview of the main truck assembly plant, Cleveland, Ohio, of The White Motor Company. This company is one of the world's largest producers of heavy-duty trucks.

in Michigan, Indiana, and Ohio). However, the final assembly of the whole vehicle no longer requires much skilled labor (e.g., labor costs are only 20 to 25 per cent of total costs, with materials and components some 50 to 60 per cent),[12]

[12] Despite the inroads made by newer materials, the American automobile is still basically an iron and steel product, as illustrated by the materials in a 1964 Plymouth (3,350 pounds):

	Pounds
Iron and steel used (75.6%)	
Plain carbon steel	1,874.0
Cast iron	392.0
Alloy steel	118.0
Malleable iron	64.0
Galvanized steel	57.7
Aluminized steel	24.0
Stainless steel	7.5
Other materials used (24.4%)	
Plastics, etc.	641.8
Aluminum	76.7
Copper and brass	35.8
Lead	32.2
Zinc	24.8
Magnesium	1.4

New York Times, January 3, 1965, p. 12.

but transport costs of assembled vehicles are high, so the pattern of assembly plants has more widely diffused (e.g., in the United States, about two-thirds of all cars are now assembled outside Michigan). This market orientation also features the Western European assembly plants.

The type of motor vehicle manufactured reflects habitat, man, and culture. The large American car developed because there were bad roads here, great distances to be traveled, an abundance of raw materials, cheap gasoline, and no particularly restrictive taxes. The European car, small and maneuverable, developed because there were good roads (but narrow and congested ones), a poor supply of raw materials, and high taxes. To these factors one can add high income and suburban living in America and low income in Europe, and the conspicuous consumption of Americans, who want their cars to reflect their progress in life. The European car is showing better marketability in other parts of the world than the American car, which is one

Courtesy of The White Motor Co.

Airview of The White Motor Company's diesel engine assembly plant, Springfield, Ohio.

The White 4000 receives final inspection and adjustment of such items as fenders, hood, bumper, battery box, and engine dog house cover at this point near the end of the Cleveland assembly line. Following still more inspection stops, it will be given exhaustive tests on the chassis dynamometer before being released for delivery to the customer.

Courtesy of The White Motor Co.

Guided missile destroyer being fitted out in the graving dock.

Courtesy of New York Shipbuilding Corp.

reason for the faster rate of growth of the industry there.

American trucks and other industrial vehicles are relatively more favored abroad than American cars because of their size, ruggedness, and dependability. The proportion of trucks and buses in the automotive industries of the underdeveloped and semi-industrial countries and in the Communist countries is much larger than in the urban-industrial North Atlantic, where motor vehicles are more consumer durables than productive-capital facilities.

Shipbuilding

Ships are built by the main maritime, trading, and steel-producing nations, but the pattern is greatly different from those in other vehicle industries. Of the 1,700 new ships under construction at mid-1965 (tankers constituting nearly half the 11 million deadweight tons), Japan accounted for 40 per cent (four times its nearest competitor), and all Western Europe about half. The United States ranked tenth among the world's shipbuilding nations; only half of its shipbuilding capacity was being used, and more value was added by ship repair and modernization than by new-ship construction. Only a score of private yards and half that many navy yards are still operating (little more than half the World War II number), and their continued existence is mainly related to U.S. Navy and Maritime Commission work.

Japan. The capacity of the Japanese shipyards is some 4.3 to 5 million deadweight tons a year, depending on what kinds of ships are being built and how much repairing and conversion is being done. In 1965, nearly 4.5 million tons of ships were under construction, of which about 2 million tons of new ships were for export (ships are the largest single export). Tankers of 150,000 to 160,000 deadweight tons are under construction, while new yards can build 200,000 tonners (182 feet in width), and 250,000 tonners are projected.

Japanese shipbuilding is concentrated in twen-

Courtesy of New York Shipbuilding Corp.

A 60,000-ton aircraft carrier, the first to be armed with guided missiles, under construction in the graving dock at Camden, New Jersey. American shipyards mainly build Navy ships and Maritime Commission ships, while most American owned and managed industrial bulk carriers are built abroad and operated under foreign "flags of convenience." About two-thirds of the work done at American shipyards is ship repair and ship rebuilding.

Courtesy of New York Shipbuilding Corp.

Airview of the 237-acre yard of the New York Shipbuilding Corporation on the Delaware at Camden, New Jersey, opposite Philadelphia. Facilities include five large covered shipbuilding ways, the only ones of their kind in the United States, and a graving dock, 1,100 feet long by 150 feet wide, the largest privately owned facility of this type in the United States.

ty-four dockyards owned by nineteen companies. The nine largest companies account for 80 per cent of the new ships built and about 75 per cent of the ship-repair work. Their fifty-four ways employ some 75,000 men, half of the total, and can build tankers and other bulk carriers for about $100 per ton, compared to $175 in Western Europe and $270 in the United States.

One Japanese advantage is cheaper labor. Even with fringe benefits included, the average man-hour costs about 80 cents, compared with as much as twice that in Western Europe, and nearly triple that in the United States. The Japanese industry is also technically more efficient (e.g., prefabricated blocks weighing up to 200 tons welded together on one side), and offers easier credit terms than its competitors.

Aircraft and Missiles

The aerospace industry turns out few units compared with the automotive industry, but the value added per pound of metal used is from $50 (fighters) to $100 up for bombers and missiles, compared with only $1 to $2 for automobiles. In the United States, the value added by the automotive industry is about the same as in the aircraft and missiles industry, while in the U.S.S.R., the latter is much more important. Reliable information on the distribution of the world's aircraft and missiles industry is lacking, but apparently almost half is in the United States, with nearly a quarter each in Western Europe and in Eastern Europe (including the U.S.S.R.). Within the United States, the location of assembly plants is more widely dispersed than in most industry; only one-third is in the northeastern industrial belt, with another one-third in southern California, and most of the remainder split between the states of Washington, Kansas, Texas, and Georgia. Much of this dispersal of assembly plants reflects government policy during World War II.

In this industry, which is mostly an armaments industry, and where costs of design and development are so huge that only the two giants seem able to bear them, it is almost impossible to know what economic production is. Some evidence shows that Western European and Japanese manufacture of American-type planes is cheaper than in the United States, but it is fragmentary and inconclusive. British and French production of jet air liners is small compared with the American output, and is apparently as much for national prestige as for economic profitability purposes. Soviet jet liners, adaptations of military aircraft, have had such high operating costs that they, too, have posed little competition to American domination of the world market.

Gradually, there is a shift in production and procurement from aircraft and missiles to space vehicles and related space projects. This is not yet a sharp trend, but it may be indicative of the aerospace industry's future course. If one includes companies engaged in the manufacture of military and commercial aircraft—missiles, space craft, rocket engines, and integral communications and electronic equipment—the U.S. aerospace industry now has 1.3 million employees (only slightly over half production workers), and an annual payroll of over $9 billion. It accounts for 3.5 per cent of the gross national product, 5.4 per cent of all exports, and more than 17 per cent of federal expenditures. Of the $21 billion of sales, about $8.5 billion are for aircraft, $5.5 billion for missiles, some $5 billion for space vehicles, and nearly $2 billion for non-aerospace products.

Railway Equipment

For the past generation, this has been a relatively stagnant industry in most urban-industrial nations, partly because of improved efficiency in use of new diesel-electric and electric equipment, but mainly because of cessation of large-scale expansion in rail networks. Building of steam-powered equipment is still important in Western Europe, Eastern Europe (including the U.S.S.R.), and elsewhere; but in the United States, the only important demand is for diesel-electric locomotives. Concern over "sick" coal industries has inhibited dieselization in many areas.

Of world production of locomotives and rolling stock, apparently about one-quarter each is in the three northern hemisphere great-regions, with Communist China and India also important. Almost universally, the trend is toward standardization in locomotive manufacture, a great change from the tradition of custom-building in this oldest of the heavy-engineering industries in the world.

In the U.S. locomotive market, the Electro-Motive Division of General Motors has recently supplied some three-quarters of the total, with General Electric being its main competitor. Capacity is probably half again larger than necessary, since mergers and the tendency to rely on fewer but more powerful locomotives seems likely to cut replacement needs down 20 per cent or more for the 29,000 diesel locomotives on U.S. railroads today. Railway management seems now to favor long trains instead of many short trains with high-cost crews, which favors 2,500-horsepower locomotives over the early 1,500-horsepower models.

The world export market is dominated by Western European countries, partly because so many nations' networks were originally financed and equipped by European capital. Many underdeveloped countries, however, are building assembly and overhaul facilities, and dispersion of capacity seems likely to continue. Since most railways are nationalized, problems of market and capital availability are less likely to hinder the development of new capacity than in many other heavy-engineering industries.

Light Engineering

The radio-television, typewriter, washing machine, and other light-engineering industries employ over 10 million workers, use about a tenth of all metals consumed, and add about a third of the value that is added by all engineering industries (the heavy-engineering—machinery and vehicles—branch employs some 25 million workers and uses about half of all metals consumed, adding several times as much value).

If all such light consumer durables (excluding automobiles) are grouped together, North America still has the largest share of production, although its share of world output has dropped from two-thirds just after World War II to only two-fifths at present. Western Europe has about one-third of the capacity, and Japan and the Eastern Europe (including the U.S.S.R.) areas contribute most of the remainder.

Western Europe and Japan have excellent market prospects for such products, because only 10 to 20 per cent of their potential markets for the various products have been saturated, while in the United States, 90 per cent or more has been saturated and only the replacement market is available.

Hand tools. Hand tools produced in the United States (e.g., hammers, screwdrivers, pliers, wrenches, and other gear common to a carpenter's kit) cost some 50 to 55 per cent more than their functional counterparts made abroad and marketed here. The largest single cost in the manufacture of a hand tool is labor, about 45 per cent of the total. The average total employment cost (straight-time wage plus fringe benefit costs) in the United States runs from two to six times that of foreign competitors (1963 per man-hour: over $3 in the United States, $1 to $1.50 in Europe, and 50 cents in Japan). Labor-cost discrepancies are not the whole story; two other factors contribute notably to the competitive handicap facing domestic hand tool producers: trade and other design and sales deception practiced by foreign producers, and impulse price buying by consumers that tends to obscure such quality advantages that American tools have over imports. But the main advantage is cheap labor in producing a standardized product.

Typewriters. Between the early and late 1950's, American typewriter imports increased from 31,000 machines to 470,000, while exports dropped from 198,000 to 36,000. Foreign production costs run from two-thirds to three-quarters of those in the United States. The industry's hourly wage is just over $2 per hour, well below the average for U.S. metal-working trades, but three times the hour wages paid in West Germany, the main exporter.

Imports (mostly portables, with some manual standards) are up from 15 per cent of U.S. sales in the mid-1950's to 35 per cent in the early 1960's. In the 1950's, manual standard sales dropped 40 per cent, with most of this market shifting over to electrics, with the U.S. companies getting practically all because foreign electrics were not being produced in large numbers (IBM took over half of the electrics market). But foreign competition in electrics is now increasing, and the same comparative advantages remain. To stay in a narrow budget and to get the needed fine tolerances, the traditional four (Royal, Remington, Smith-Corona, Underwood) now make 85 to 90 per cent of their parts. There is almost no automatic assembly, so labor runs over 60 per cent of manufacturing cost. For parts fabrication, assembly, and packaging, a single portable takes about seven to eight hours to build; an electric requires twenty-five hours.

Other mechanical products. Sewing machines, cameras, watches, and many other light-engineering products would show the same tendencies as the typewriter industry. A Japanese sewing machine can be laid down in Cleveland, competitive with White's best products, to retail at a price lower than the cost of purchased parts for the machines made by White's, so the American company is now a distributive organization for production from its foreign subsidiaries. Direct and indirect labor costs are half or more of total costs in making fine cameras or fine watches, so American production in these areas is increasingly restricted to cheap lines, assembly of cheaper foreign parts, or specialty items where research and early luxury-market exploitation allows relative advantage.

Electronic products. The $5 billion plus annual sales of the U.S. electronic industry are primarily a combination of two disparate yet related types of industrial activity: (1) about half is accounted for by mass-produced consumer durables (e.g., radios, television sets, tape recorders, and a host of other gadgets); and (2) the remainder consists of products that are capital goods, still mostly aerospace and other "defense" items but increasingly computers and related components of automation systems, both types made up of numerous small "runs" of specialized equipment. The industry is still concentrated in the Manufacturing Belt, the ordinary consumer types mainly from centers like Chicago and Philadelphia, but some of the specialty items (close to research and development) are from the Boston urban region. Sizable fractions of the military and industrial-automation systems are produced in the South (Texas and Florida aerospace centers) and the West (Greater Los Angeles, San Francisco, and Phoenix urban regions).

For the electronics industry as a whole, the elimination of handwork in the final assembly is, by itself, only a minor accomplishment. Mass producers of radio and television sets figure that no more than 15 per cent of their factory costs is chargeable to labor. Even on low-volume military equipment, literally assembled by hand, labor cost rarely exceeds 30 per cent. Stated another way, 70 to 85 per cent of the cost of electronics is already built into most equipment in the form of components—resistors, capacitors, vacuum tubes, etc.—before a single wire is soldered. In some of these components, cheap labor is the main item of cost, especially Japanese-made transistors, found in a majority of American-used transistor radios (whether imported or U.S. assembled).

Prospects

Engineering production usually involves two production stages: (1) the production of parts, tools, and particular types of metal—this has traditionally involved highly skilled workmanship, but there is a distinct tendency to substitute metal extrusion and powder metallurgy for the skilled labor usually necessary for the precision-machining operations, or to have the machining operations done by automatic batteries of machines; followed by (2) their assembly into finished articles, often by mass-production methods using semiskilled labor.

The second stage is diffusing rapidly throughout the world wherever a market develops, either in less-developed regions of older industrial economies or in accessible cities of underdeveloped economies. The first stage is still mainly in the older centers, and it is still too soon to see clearly whether it will also diffuse universally. Some of the new technology—such as automation—which theoretically might favor less-developed areas with a scarcity of skilled labor, has such high capital and technician levels of intensity that high fixed costs might hinder diffusion in some areas and thus prevent the theoretical short cut to a more balanced complex of engineering industries.

In the long run, the high labor costs of most fabricating industry is likely to favor a wide dispersal of most types of heavy- and light-engineering industries, especially into countries with adequate scale (market) and government encouragement.

PERSPECTIVE

In the foreseeable future (several decades), steel will certainly not be displaced from its position of hegemony in the metallurgical industry, although the relative shares of non-ferrous metals and non-metallic substitutes will increase a bit. Probably the greatest long-range competitive challenge to steel is the combination of materials.

Distribution of metallurgical capacity will continue to diffuse universally, with direct trade in metal becoming a smaller share of world production and consumption, and with indirect trade (in fabricated-metal products) becoming the most important avenue of metal movement in world trade.

Practically everywhere, the metallurgical and related industries will be growth industries, but even more in newly industrializing economies than in the mature urban-industrial economies of North America and Europe. Even in the United States, alloy steels and the light metals are likely to increase capacity rapidly, although the carbon steel and older non-ferrous metals' capacities may increase slowly.

Upgrading of medium-grade and low-grade crude materials (fuel, ore, flux, service materials) will be the main avenue along which progress in solving raw materials problems of the metallurgical industry will be made. Long-distance trade in remaining high-grade crude materials will be important for some time, but increasingly even newer metallurgical districts will be using materials that will need to be beneficiated before shipment, so both internal and international trade will increasingly involve processed rather than raw materials.

Scrap seems likely to become more important in some areas than at present, as integrated plants become relatively more important, and as more countries begin to possess large accumulations of capital goods and durable consumer goods that will need replacement. In the older industrial economies, scrap will regain its older popularity as the scrap industry becomes more efficient with rationalization, as improved oxygen converters are developed, and as the new team of electric furnace and continuous casting becomes widespread.

In all metals, the tendency will be for integrated producers (those smelting, refining, and semifabricating in one plant) to become increasingly important, to more completely control their basic materials, and to increase technical efficiency of furnaces by more thorough preparation of crude materials into semiprocessed forms. Increased furnace efficiency will also come from economies of even larger scale than at present, and by making metal-making even more of a continuous-process operation than at present. New types of facilities—oxygen converters, continuous casting machines, and others—will become increasingly important. Oxygen furnaces will probably be a quarter of world steelmaking capacity in the next generation, and eventually predominant. Continuous casting machines may sweep milling operations as swiftly.

Increasingly, market-oriented and intermediate sites—especially tidewater, lakeside, and deep riverine ports—will be favored for integrated mills, and crude materials oriented facilities will be mainly the concentrating works integrated with mining (e.g., making screened, sintered, and pelletized ore). At the same time, a minor trend toward decentralization is visible; small electric furnaces using a scrap charge (some with continuous casting operations) are turning out small structurals and reinforcing rods for the widely diffused construction activity, but this is a small share of the total market.

Metal fabricating industries seem destined for worldwide diffusion, nearly as swiftly as primary metallurgy. Greater regional and metropolitan assembling operations seem certain, but the tendency in production of more complicated components is more clouded. The skilling of labor forces in more new industrial areas, plus certain tendencies in automated manufacture, might diffuse production of parts widely, but the necessary scale and huge capitalization demands may be so high that such production may remain much more concentrated than assembly operations.

World exports of machinery, now some dozen per cent of all trade, are increasing in relative importance. The United States, West Germany, and Britain, now supply about 70 per cent of such heavy engineering exports, but will probably see their shares decline somewhat as other countries expand such exports. The present half of such exports moving to underdeveloped countries will probably increase as the pace of industrialization in such areas of the world increases. In exchange, such underdeveloped countries will probably increase their exports of the simpler metal products (for the same reasons that their exports of standardized semidurable products also will increase).

In general, distribution of heavy-engineering capacity tends to approximate the market potential. There is a wider diffusion of those branches (e.g., shipbuilding) in which semiskilled labor is relatively most important, with a greater concentration of those branches (e.g., sophisticated electronics) in which technician and skilled labor is relatively most important in factor costs.

SUGGESTED READINGS

ALDERFER, E. B., and MICHL, H. E. *Economics of American Industry.* New York: McGraw-Hill, 1957. Pp. 25–180.

CUNNINGHAM, WILLIAM G. *The Aircraft Industry: A Study in Industrial Location.* Privately printed, 1951. Pp. 247.

ESTALL, R. C., and BUCHANAN, R. OGILVIE. *Industrial Activity and Economic Geography.* London: Hutchinson, 1961. Pp. 232.

FISHER, JOSEPH L., and POTTER, NEAL. *World Prospects for Natural Resources.* Baltimore: Johns Hopkins Press (for Resources for the Future, Inc.), 1964. Pp. 73.

HEDGES, ERNEST S. *Tin in Social and Economic History.* London: Edward Arnold, 1964. Pp. 194.

HERFINDAHL, ORRIS C. *Three Studies in Minerals Economics.* Washington, D.C.: Resources for the Future, Inc., 1961. Pp. 63.

LANDSBERG, HANS H. *Natural Resources for U.S. Growth.* Baltimore: Johns Hopkins Press (for Resources for the Future, Inc.), 1964. Pp. 257.

LISTER, LOUIS. *Europe's Coal and Steel Community.* New York: Twentieth Century Fund, 1960. Pp. 495.

MILLER, E. WILLARD. *A Geography of Manufacturing.* Englewood Cliffs, N.J.: Prentice-Hall, 1962. Pp. 281–400.

OXFORD UNIVERSITY PRESS. *Oxford Economic Atlas of the World.* London: Oxford University Press, 1965. Pp. 70–93.

POUNDS, NORMAN J. G. *The Geography of Iron and Steel.* London: Hutchinson, 1959. Pp. 192.

UNITED NATIONS, ECONOMIC COMMISSION FOR EUROPE. *Long-Term Trends and Problems of the European Steel Industry.* Geneva: United Nations, 1959. Pp. 176.

VAN ROYEN, WILLIAM, and BOWLES, OLIVER (eds.). *Atlas of the World's Resources.* Vol. II. *The Mineral Resources of the World.* Englewood Cliffs, N.J.: Prentice-Hall, 1952. Pp. 56–120.

VOSKUIL, WALTER. *Minerals in World Industry.* New York: McGraw-Hill, 1955. Pp. 10–138, 205–37.

15

Chemical Industries

Chemistry is the science of transforming matter, the science of materials, and the science of the ceaseless change and interchange of natural phenomena, without which no life, no product, no mechanism, no feature of the universe can be embodied or perceived.

Chemical change is one of the great universal forces of nature. Man has consciously used chemical change since the time he discovered fire, for combustion is one of the basic chemical actions. Through the centuries, he learned to use chemistry, without understanding why it worked, to fertilize his crops, produce metals from stone, make glass, cook and preserve food, and make wine and beer, gunpowder, dyes, medicines, and hundreds of other things in common use. Chemical products play an important part in the making or functioning of nearly every material thing man uses.

Modern chemical technology penetrates all areas of an industrial economy. Its products have a role in satisfying the six basic needs of mankind: food, clothing, shelter, transportation and communication, medication, and machinery and other equipment with which to work. No other major technology is so close to a basic science. It is the only technology bearing the name of a scientific discipline. The science of chemistry opens to chemical technology an endless frontier. Already the alteration and substitution of nature's building blocks, which is modern chemistry's domain, has changed man's use of earth materials as much as the mechanical and electrical revolutions. However, uncomprehensible terminology, heterogeneous raw materials, products and processes, and even the hazy history of the industry's development tend to make the industry a question mark to the public.

The very scope of the industry is debatable. A distinction is usually made between chemical manufacturing industries (a combination of purely chemical concerns and allied-process industries) and the chemical process industries, which use chemicals at one or more stages of their operations but not as the dominant factor cost. The purely chemical concerns manufacture basic or primary chemicals—heavy chemicals such as acids and alkalies, alcohols, plastic ingredients, tanning materials, drug and dye ingredients—and usually account for about one-third of the value added by chemical manufacturing as a whole in a mature industrial society. Allied process industries, which produce fertilizers, paints, plastics, synthetic fibers, soaps and detergents, and many other products in which the value of basic chemicals is the dominant factor cost, account for the other two-thirds of value added by all chemical manufacturing.

Chemical process industries include semisynthetic (rayon-acetate) and true synthetic textiles, rubber products, paper products, leather products, fuel products, ceramic products, most primary metals, and many others. The distinction between chemical manufacturing industries and chemical process industries is often not a sharp one, and many sources maintain that both groups are fast merging and must soon be considered as one.[1] If the chemical and chemical process industries are rolled into one, they would account for about one-fourth of all manufacturing in an urban-industrial society.

In this discussion, however, chemical industries will be defined as those making basic chemicals and those using such basic chemicals to manufacture ultimate (consumer-type) chemicals. The U.S. chemical industry, thus defined, employs some ¾ million persons (under 5 per cent of manufacturing employment), operates over 13,000 plants in all fifty states, and sells more than 10,000 different products worth some $40 billion gross (about $18 billion value-added), over 10 per cent of the entire industrial income. Although it is the world's largest chemical industry, with over a third of the world's total chemical production, its relative importance is similar to that in other mature urban-industrial societies in Western Europe (Communist Europe is aiming at a similar mix by the end of the 1960's).

United States Chemical Industry, 1963
(in per cents)

¾ Million Workers		U.S. $18 Billion Value-added
33.3	Basic chemicals	35.5
18.0	Fibers, plastics, rubbers	16.4
14.1	Drugs	16.4
11.5	Cleaning and toilet goods	15.7
8.3	Paints and varnishes	5.8
5.9	Agricultural chemicals	3.3
8.9	Miscellaneous	6.9
100.0	Total chemical industry	100.0

The pace of growth in the chemical industry has been faster than any other industry (except electronics in recent years) for over a generation. Between World War I and World War II, the U.S. rate of growth for the chemical industry was some 300 per cent, while other industry grew some 160 per cent. From then until the early 1960's, the chemical industry increased some 350 per cent, with other industry growing 200 per cent.

The chemical industry produces products worth about $125 billion for the world, with value-added probably 45 per cent of that. The North American share is some 35 per cent (95 per cent United States), with Western Europe nearly 25 per cent, and Eastern Europe (including U.S.S.R.) some 20 per cent. Japan has a rapidly growing chemical industry, with under 5 per cent of the world's total, which leaves 15 per cent for the remainder of the world, half of that in urban-industrial nations other than those mentioned.

GENERAL ACHIEVEMENTS

Geographical interest in the chemical industries is not so much in chemical processes proper, but in the indirect influences on space and resource availability. The quantity, quality, and variety of raw materials have been vastly increased by the growth of modern chemical technology. Similarly, chemical developments have had the general effect of reducing prices of crude materials and curbing monopolistic tendencies based on natural products. Many modern industries exist only because of chemical processes, since they would be inconceivable with only mechanical or electrical tools. Finally, although the major long-run tendency is toward lessened regional and national self-sufficiency, the short-run and medium-run improvements in self-sufficiency that do occur are almost entirely due to changes in resource availability brought about by chemical technology.

Increased Raw Materials Availability

The chemical industry differs from other industries chiefly in the fact that it has tremendous flexibility, both in the raw materials it utilizes and in its processing techniques. It has a unique facility for processing abundant crude materials not only into products suitable as substitutes for

---

[1] A good example is the recent appearance of leather substitutes (e.g., Du Pont's Corfam), which are waterproof, shape-retaining, scuff-resistant, porous, and long-wearing. By early 1965, over a million pairs of shoes made of such materials were sold, and a quarter or more of the U.S. shoe output by 1985 may be made of such synthetic leathers (world shoe output by that date is expected to exceed world hides output by about half).

other materials, but also into new materials having new properties and superior to anything previously known.

Much of the increased raw materials supply has been achieved by the competition of new chemical sources with the older natural sources. In the foods area, some true synthetics (e.g., vitamins, amino acids) and many semisynthetics (e.g., hydrogenated oils, concentrated purified proteins) compete with natural foods. In the textiles area, many semisynthetic and true synthetic fibers compete with natural fibers (e.g., nylon with silk, rayon with cotton). In the construction area, plastics compete with both metals and wood, and new (light, alloy) metals compete with older base metals. In the industrial materials area, methanol competes with natural wood alcohol, synthetic rubber with natural rubber, and coal-tar dyes with natural plant and animal dyes. In the agricultural area, synthetic fertilizers compete with manure, nitrate, and by-product sulfate of ammonia. The list could be extended greatly.

Chemical sources pitted against each other already account for many raw materials, and this type of competition promises even greater success in the future. Benzene and naphthalene are made both from by-product coking of coal and from petroleum refining. The basic petrochemicals—ethylene, propylene, butylene, isobutylene—are made from either crude oil or natural gas processing.

Thus, chemical technology is a powerful extender of the resource base. Products that are quite different in composition can be derived from different starting materials or can be synthesized by different processes from the same starting materials.

Price Reductions and Weakened Control by Natural Monopolies

These forms of progress have been achieved both by greater technical efficiency and by larger scale-of-production advantages. Originally, xylene for Dacron was made from coal tar, but now it can be more cheaply produced by freezing out high-purity xylene from naphtha, so over three-fourths now is from that source. Originally, glycerin was a by-product of soap-making, but over half of it is now made from by-product propylene, accompanied by a drop in price from 41 to 29 cents per pound. Natural rubber now sells for about 25 to 27 cents per pound; its price was driven down almost half in a decade by the lowering prices of first generation (semisynthetic) and new true synthetic rubbers. Currently, most acetylene is derived from calcium carbide (an inorganic material), but soon it will be made from natural gas for 10 per cent or more below the present price, and this will probably encourage wider use of acetylene-based chemical products.

Natural monopolies broken or weakened by chemical substitutes are as common as examples of spectacular price reductions caused by changing chemical technology. The use of modern coal-tar dyes has almost entirely displaced natural dyes (e.g., "purple snail," Brazilwood, indigo). Synthetic ammonia has reduced to minor significance the nineteenth-century Peruvian guano, Chilean saltpeter, and Indian saltpeter holds on the nitrogen market. The modern drug industry is continually weakening natural sources by synthesizing drugs that are in short supply or too expensive.

As the whole of mankind industrializes and as high- and medium-grade resources are increasingly displaced by upgraded lean materials, the role of evolving chemistry will probably be the main tool in effecting such substitution at reasonable price shifts. Perhaps all industry not considered part of chemical manufacturing will at least become chemical process industry.

Creation of New Industries

Just as the electrical age produced many industries (e.g., light metals) that were unthinkable in the context of purely thermal or other processes, so the chemical age has produced many industries unthinkable in the context of purely mechanical or electrical processes. Goodrich's discovery of vulcanized natural rubber made a dependable industrial raw material. The development of polymerization, in which simple molecules are linked in long chains or rings to form giant molecules or polymers, produced the category of plastics and recently a true substitute for natural rubber. Nuclear chemistry is probably the most tremendous frontier of the future, and it promises entirely new substances as man learns how to alter atoms in ways that nature did not. Present experimentation in linking inorganics into organics (e.g., plastics including silicon or fluorine) promises new, more stable construction substances. Protein chemistry (the building of the most complicated molecule assemblages) may evolve through biochemistry breakthroughs to possibly direct photosynthesis.

Chemical technology plays two unique roles in advancing the conservation of natural resources. Among all forms of technology, it has done the most toward finding substitutes for the resources that are rapidly being depleted; these substitutes are being synthesized from the more abundant resources whose exhaustion seems much more remote. Also, chemical technology is capable of reforming the molecular structures that go into ultimate products in such a fashion as to fit ever more closely the uses to which these products are put, thus achieving substantial reductions in the strain upon the resources that are needed to maintain a given level of living.

Geopolitical Influences

Chemical technology has played an important, although subsidiary, role in implementing both peacetime and wartime attempts at greater self-sufficiency. The basic process of steel-making, allowing use of acidic iron ores, made Germany potentially self-sufficient in iron ore by transforming Lorraine minette (high-phosphorus, low-grade iron ore) into economic reserves. The synthetic ammonia process (the direct combination of hydrogen and nitrogen under the influence of a catalyst to form ammonia, NH_3) of the German chemists Haber and Bosch furnished a substitute for imported Chilean nitrate during World War I and to a great extent nullified the British blockade of Germany. During World War II, the Fischer-Tropsch process of making synthetic gasoline (coal oxidized to CO gas, then recombined into such mixed compounds as gasoline and straight aliphatics) allowed Nazi Germany to again greatly nullify the blockade of petroleum imports from overseas.

The image of an exploding population that presses on a fixed resource base is essentially a myth in the long run. Economic growth will not be seriously limited by a shortage of natural resources. To hoard resources unthinkingly in the name of conservation is to misunderstand completely the nature and scope of technological change. In the short run, to be sure, specific shortages may impede growth in a given country, but over longer periods, such problems will be solved efficiently, mainly through the diffusion and development of modern chemical technology.

Molecular engineering will accelerate worldwide economic growth substantially if the underdeveloped countries can import modern chemical techniques for deriving useful products from their low-grade resources, rather than trying to duplicate exactly the existing technologies of present industrial societies, which have been shaped by the history of specific economic development and by specific resource endowment. Engineers and economists would be well advised to study the possibilities of adapting chemical technology to the production needs and resource characteristics of the underdeveloped countries. That might prove to be their most valuable import, much more important than imported conventional equipment.

RAW MATERIALS OF THE CHEMICAL INDUSTRY

In their investigations into the nature of matter, physicists and chemists have found that all complex materials are built from about 100 fundamental substances known as elements. These 100 basic building blocks of nature cannot be transformed one into the other at will, but are fixed and stable under ordinary conditions. By combining these elements in various ways and in varying proportions, chemists have made over half a million compounds, some 10,000 of them now in regular production. Nature also performs similar building operations, but her syntheses are frequently so complex that man so far cannot duplicate them.

Since elements cannot be created at will, when the chemical industry demands a certain element, it must be sought in nature. Hundreds of natural materials are utilized, but the basic crude materials used in the greatest amounts are the hydrocarbons (coal, oil, gas), cellulose (wood, plant materials), salt, sulfur, limestone, air, and water. From these crude materials (and many others), the purely chemical concerns make intermediaries: basic petrochemicals from crude oil and natural gas, chemical pulps from wood, chlorine and caustic soda from salt, acids from sulfur, quicklime from limestone, nitrogen and oxygen from air, hydrogen and oxygen from water, and numerous others. The allied process industries take most of these intermediates and combine them in unlimited alterations and substitutions to make the end products of chemistry that are ultimately consumed by the public.[2]

Hydrocarbon Materials

The synthetic organic chemical industry is that portion of the chemical industry dealing primarily with the manufacture of products con-

[2] Average annual per capita "consumption" in the United States is about 60 pounds each of ammonia and caustic soda, about 80 pounds of chlorine, and 200 pounds of sulfuric acid.

Allied Chemical's Plastics Division Plant (foreground in airview) at Ironton, Ohio, produces coal-tar chemicals, including refined tars and oils, naphthalene, and phthalic anhydride. In the background is an adjacent plant for coke and by-products operated by the Company's Semet-Solvay Division. Barges and trains are involved in the main transport efforts, with conveyors and pipelines involved in the plant-complex movements.

Courtesy of Allied Chemical Corp.

Courtesy of National Distillers and Chemical Corp.

Dehydrators, light and heavy oil absorption towers, and heavy oil stills of the extraction unit at the Tuscola, Illinois, plant of U.S. Industrial Chemicals Company, remove heavy hydrocarbons from more than 500 million cubic feet of natural gas each day, which are then processed into Petrothene pellets and other organic chemicals products. Organic chemicals' output is increasing at a rate over twice that of other chemicals.

taining carbon derived from coal, petroleum, and natural gas. Starting with coal tar, the carbon base most readily available to the nineteenth-century's coal economy, and moving to other hydrocarbons, the chemist has poured his basic materials into reactors and, by the application of heat, pressure, and catalysts in endless combinations, has drawn out a stream of compounds now totaling over half a million, only a small part of which so far has found use. The more typical organic chemicals would include such products as ethyl alcohol, ethylene glycol, carbon tetrachloride, plastics, dyes, pharmaceutical chemicals, and thousands of other products ranging from aspirin to xanthates. Of the two branches of the chemical industry, the organic is much larger in terms of value of product, and is faster growing. The reactive and widely distributed carbon-based compounds have provided the chemist with seemingly endless building blocks.

Although now less dominant, because of the rise of the petrochemicals, coal chemicals are still tremendously important. In the by-product coking process, coal is heated in the absence of air. The volatile materials are then treated to yield gas, tar, ammonia liquor, ammonium sulfate, and light oil. Further refinement yields the intermediaries. United States coke-making yields each year some $300 million worth of benzene, naphthalene, and other chemicals used in the making of paints, medicines, perfumes, explosives, plastics, and innumerable other products. The trend is for petrochemicals and coal chemicals to become more competitive. Benzene from petroleum has surpassed coke-oven output, so chemical companies that make styrene, phenol, insecticides, and other benzene derivatives are no longer alarmed by a drop in steel production. In the case of naphthalene, however, the chemical industry is still largely dependent upon the steel-makers' coke ovens, although some naphthalene from petroleum is available.

The petrochemical business basically consists of the upgrading of hydrocarbons from petroleum and natural gas into a variety of increasingly important chemicals. More than 3,000 different petrochemical products are now sold. In 1964, U.S. petrochemical intermediaries (nearly half of the world's total) amounted to 45 million tons worth nearly $5 billion, and petrochemical's growth rate was still among the fastest of the chemical subgroupings. By volume, petrochemicals constitute only 30 per cent of the some 150 million tons of U.S. chemicals, but in value, they represent nearly 60 per cent of the total sales volume of intermediaries. About 50 of the 3,000 petrochemicals now being produced are considered big tonnage items, with the rest selling in small quantities ranging down to a few pounds annually.

Basic Petrochemicals

From Crude Oil	From Natural Gas	From Both Crude Oil and Natural Gas
Kerosene	Carbon black	Ethylene
Cyclohexane (benzene)	Methane	Propylene
Methylcyclohexane	Ethane	Butylene
Dimethylcyclohexane	Propane	Isobutylene
Sulfonates	Propane-butane	
Naphthenic acids	Butane	
Cresols		

Most analysts are currently predicting a U.S. annual growth rate of 7 to 9 per cent in the petrochemical industry, contrasted with an average of well over 10 per cent in the 1950's. Much of the rapid postwar development of petrochemicals was based upon the exploitation of previously unused refinery gases (about 5 per cent of what can be extracted from each barrel of crude oil), which now provide about half of the industry's feedstock requirements. Much of the expansion in the 1960's must be based upon exploitation of alternative raw material sources, which are often much more expensive. For example, ethylene (presently the most important petrochemical intermediate) can be up to twice as costly to manufacture from natural gas liquids as from refinery off-gas.

Another significant change in the petrochemical industry that may make the future appear less bright than earlier is increased international competition. In the past, foreign producers (Western Europe and Japan) have often been dependent upon relatively high-cost hydrocarbon raw materials, but the recent completion of many refineries abroad has made large quantities of refinery off-gas available. Many foreign countries beginning natural gas exploitation are able to supply their new petrochemical industry with cheap wet gas feedstock.

Intensified sales efforts by alternative chemical sources bring the fear of overproduction to many old-time petrochemical concerns in the United States. Most feared is new capacity built and projected by the petroleum industry, which sees profit from further manipulation of its own increasingly expensive crude oil and natural gas. Crude liquid hydrocarbons are generally priced in the vicinity of 1 cent per pound. By conversion to gasoline or some other fuel, an oil company is able to add about 1 cent to their original value. But by conversion to a petrochemical, it can boost the sales price per pound of the original hydrocarbon feedstock material an average of 10 to 15 cents (conversion of natural gas into ethylene and then into polyethylene represents a twenty-eight-fold upgrading of the raw material stock).

Of the major petrochemical groups, the "aliphatics" (ethylene-, propylene-, butylene- and acetylene-based chemicals), which now represent over half of total petrochemical production, appear likely to account for at least two-thirds of the projected growth of petroleum-based chemicals in the next decade. It is expected that the "inorganics" (ammonia, sulfur, and carbon

Courtesy of National Distillers and Chemical Corp.

Airview of the Tuscola, Illinois, plant, U.S. Industrial Chemicals Company Division, National Distillers and Chemical Corporation. Petrochemical plants are now more widespread than formerly and are located near oil refineries and their by-product gas supply or near a gas pipeline supply, as in this case.

black) and the "aromatics" (benzene, toluene, and xylene) will make only relatively small contributions to the over-all growth of the U.S. chemical industry.

Competition is expected to change the relative preferences in the aliphatics group. Ethylene is now the favorite, some 3 million tons yearly now being produced. About one-fourth is used in manufacturing the plastic polyethylene, with other end uses being the manufacturing of ethylene glycol (for antifreeze), acrylonitrile (for synthetic rubber), polyglycols (for water soluble lubricants), and ethanolamines (solvents for fats and oils). Ethylene oxide, first used in the manufacture of ethylene glycol (antifreeze), is finding increasing use as a building block from which to construct more complex molecules (e.g., wetting agents and detergents are among the other outlets for this basic material).

Propylene chemicals are booming because they are 40 per cent cheaper than ethylene. At present, propylene chiefly goes into the thermoplastic, polypropylene, with other end uses being isopropanol (an intermediate material of many uses), acrolein (used in making plastics, perfumes, and colloidal forms of metals), and cumene.

Butylene is mainly used as a blending stock for high-octane fuels. Isoprene now gives promise of becoming a petrochemical of major commercial stature. It is now a by-product of gas oil cracking, but processes will be developed for synthesizing it from other hydrocarbons. The goal is a product that will have the same properties as natural rubber and compete with it in cost. In like manner, new synthetic lubricants are making their appearance to meet the extreme operating conditions encountered in jet engines, rockets, and missiles.

Many important petrochemicals can be made from either ethylene or acetylene. Ethylene (also propylene and butylene) has been usually derived from the cracking of hydrocarbon gases or as a by-product from the cracking of crude oil to produce various distillates, notably gasoline. Acetylene is usually derived today from calcium carbide for which the requirements are limestone, coal, and electrical energy; but in the future, acetylene is expected to be increasingly derived from the cracking of hydrocarbon gases, thus putting it at the disposal of the chemical industry at a relatively low cost in areas where carbide-derived acetylene has been relatively expensive. Acetylene is still used widely as an illuminant and for welding, but increasingly it is important in the production of acetic acid, acetaldehyde, polyvinyl chloride, aniline dyes, and synthetic rubber. Since acetylene has been cheapened, the plastic material polyvinyl chloride has dropped in price from 38 cents per pound to 19 cents.

The U.S. petrochemical industry—intermediate plus allied processing—is highly concentrated:

Southwest	45%
Northeast	20
Midwest	15
Pacific Coast	10
Southeast	5
Mountain and the rest	5

If one considers only the manufacture of basic petrochemicals, the production is even more concentrated. The "Golden Crescent"—a strip of the Gulf of Mexico coast running 700 miles from New Orleans to Brownsville—contains more than 80 per cent of all U.S. basic petrochemical producing capacity, and is the largest concentration of petrochemical production in the world. Houston and Beaumont together account for more than 30 per cent of total U.S. petrochemical capacity. The attractions of this Golden Crescent are many. Up to 75 per cent of all claimed petroleum and natural gas reserves in the country lie within easy pipeline reach of the area. Because about 35 per cent of the nation's refinery capacity is located in the Southwest, area users have found abundant quantities of very low-cost petrochemical feedstock in the form of refinery off-gas. The average delivered cost of natural gas used in industrial quantities in the early 1960's was about 17 cents per 1,000 cubic feet in Texas, compared with over 65 cents in New York, a leading northeast chemical producing state. Fresh water and salt domes are immediately available. The flat Texas-Louisiana terrain is ideally suited for the construction of underground pipelines that are necessary to move petrochemical raw materials and intermediates easily from plant to plant. Specialization in the manufacture of basic chemicals to supply many users has produced significant scale economies, and the firms now engaged in petrochemical production on the Gulf Coast are perhaps more interdependent than those in any other major industry in the United States. Finally, water transportation is immediately available to ship products to lucrative markets in the eastern United States or abroad, or by Intercoastal Canal and the Mississippi system to Chicago and the Midwest.

Not all the U.S. petrochemical complexes are confined to the Gulf Coast. There are several big concentrations elsewhere. Generally, however, these facilities are self-contained, with little interchange of products between them. The dispersal will continue. Unskilled or semiskilled labor costs are a comparatively small percentage of manufacturing costs in the petrochemical industry, and plant construction and maintenance costs have been nearly equalized throughout the nation, following the development of construction techniques that permit outdoor chemical processing facilities in northern states. Raw material costs are much more important (e.g., two-thirds of basic ethylene chemicals capacity is on the Gulf Coast, although the main markets are in the northeast and are likely to remain there since the cost is 20 per cent more or less).

Cellulose Materials

About 75 million tons of wood pulps (small amounts of straw, coarse fiber, and grass pulps included) are produced and consumed yearly in the world: over 50 per cent in North America (two-thirds in the United States), some 25 per cent in Western Europe (nearly two-thirds in Scandinavia), nearly 9 per cent in Eastern Europe (two-thirds in U.S.S.R.), nearly 5 per cent in Japan, and 10 per cent in the rest of the world. However, most cellulose is not used in purely chemical or allied processing industry, but in chemical process industries (e.g., pulp-paper, rayon-acetate).

About one-fourth of world pulp is made mechanically, and this goes into newsprint and other cheap paper almost entirely. Chemical pulp (soda, sulfite, sulfate) also mainly goes into paper and paper products. Semichemical pulp mainly goes into fiber boxes, although some goes into making high-quality paper. A relatively small but growing use for chemical wood pulps is for the production of highly purified pulps called dissolving pulps or high alpha-cellulose pulps. They are used in the manufacture of such products as rayon products and tire cord, cellophane, absorbent tissue, lacquers, smokeless powder, photographic film, plastics, and a variety of cellulose chemicals. Several million tons of dissolving wood pulp are produced annually in North America, and nearly as much in the rest of the urban-industrial realm.

Cellulose threads range from one-twentieth to one-sixth of an inch in length, and their length, in all cases, is approximately 100 times their width. One ounce of wood pulp contains over 13 million individual fibers. To produce 1 ton of ordinary chemical pulp requires 2.6 tons of dry wood, 130 pounds of salt cake, 55 pounds of lime, 95 pounds of burnt lime, 220 pounds of chlorine, and 75 pounds of caustic soda, plus 18 million B.t.u.'s of steam, 535 kilowatt-hours of electricity, 20 gallons of fuel oil, and 65,000 gallons of filtered water.

Chemical cellulose is used in the production of nitrocellulose, a standard explosive. More than half of the explosives produced during World War II were made from wood pulp, and most explosives used for mining and construction and for sporting ammunition are also derived from chemical cellulose.

Chemical cellulose is the basic processing material for photographic film and photographic paper. The rapidly growing plastics industry requires more and more cellulose each year for items like telephones, television cabinets, counter tops, plastic walls and tiles, kitchen utensils, containers, etc.

One of the newer uses of chemical cellulose is in the production of fine chemicals. There are many new compounds in daily use; e.g., CMC (carboxymethylcellulose) which is now used in cosmetics, ice cream, tooth paste, and laundry preparations.

As with coal chemicals, chemical cellulose is now under heavy competitive attacks from petrochemicals. For example, the more expensive cellophane is losing ground to the newest and cheapest of the petroleum plastics, polypropylene, which can also be produced as a fiber to make an excellent no-ironing blend of cloth and also to be used in making plastic furniture. If cellulose stages a large-scale comeback, it may well be by processing into sugar and (through the transformation of certain yeasts and molds) protein feedstuffs and by developing lignin chemistry to use the cementing material that binds the wood fibers together. For the foreseeable future, larger use of cellulose in chemical process industries seems more likely than spectacular expansion of purely chemical and allied process uses.

Salt Materials

The older inorganic branch of the purely chemical industry—comprising alkalies and acids—has merely paralleled industrial growth in recent decades and has not spectacular growth-industry characteristics like the petrochemicals. Inorganic chemistry involves all the elements outside the carbon compounds, including that two-thirds of the atomic table labeled "metals." Here, curiously enough, more progress is being made by industrial research elsewhere (e.g., the development of semiconductor and solid-state materials) than by pure chemical research.

Sodium chloride, or common salt, is distributed

widely over the globe. The salt contained in oceans, inland seas, and salt lakes (around 5 million cubic miles) would blanket the entire earth with a white mantle some 200 feet deep. Huge additional resources also lie beneath the earth. The largest known chunk of salt on earth is a 10-mile-long mountain in the Dominican Republic which holds ½ billion tons of salt. Rock salt deposits exist in every continent. One Midwestern deposit (running under New York, Pennsylvania, West Virginia, Ohio, Michigan, and southern Ontario) covers some 70,000 square miles, and central Europe contains deposits totaling as large.

World production of salt is now over 100 million tons annually, nearly 30 per cent of which is used for dietary purposes and the remainder for industrial and other purposes. The human body tends to maintain an even balance of 0.88 per cent salt, which requires an average consumption of about 12 pounds annually for each of the 3 billion human population. Domestic animals also consume huge amounts of processed salt.

There are three major ways of obtaining salt: solar evaporation, man-made brine, and mining rock salt. Most of the pure crystal salt for food uses comes from solar evaporation. A gallon of seawater contains a little over ¼ pound of salt (it is estimated that if all the oceans dried up, they would leave about 4½ million cubic miles of rock salt, a pile about fifteen times the volume of Europe above sea level). Seawater is usually spread out in large fields where the sun will evaporate the water, after which the salt is scooped up and further purified. The best sites are in parts of the oceans having either a desert climate or a near-desert climate seasonably (e.g., Mediterranean, Steppe, and similar regions). Tropical and semitropical coasts mainly depend on evaporation, although quality often is poor. During the dry season, many coastal fishponds are diverted to salt-making. In the Philippines, for example, such ponds average about 15 tons per acre per dry season; it is inferior in quality, having only 80 to 90 per cent sodium chloride, with much magnesium sulfate (epsom salts), gypsum, magnesium chloride (poison), and varying amounts of sand and filth. Japan imports some 2½ million tons of sea salt annually, mainly from mainland China and Formosa, but also from India, Aden, Egypt, and Spain. As a rule, ships are not chartered for the trade, but the salt is carried back in ballast when the ships might otherwise sail empty (prices are $5 to $10 f.o.b., or about $15 per ton c.i.f. Japan).[3]

Another way of making table salt—although most production goes into chemicals—is to drill a well to a salt bed, pump water down to the salt, and pump the brine solution up, where it is processed in vacuum pans where the water boils off and leaves pure crystal salt. In one type of operation, hydraulic fracturing, two holes (as far apart as 1,000 feet) are drilled deep into a salt bed. Water is forced down one hole under high pressure (up to 5,000 pounds per square inch). The salt bed fractures rapidly toward the second hole (the target well), and under continuing pressure, brine is forced horizontally along this fracture into the target well and is then pumped to the surface for evaporation. Another type of operation uses wells consisting of two tubes (one inside the other), some extending more than ½ mile into the earth through various layers of shale and stone to the salt beds. Clear water is pumped down the outside tube to dissolve the salt, then it is brought to the surface again through the inside tube by pump or air lift.

Rock salt is the same chemical as the table sale used to season food, but is not refined and purified as is the table product.[4] Rock salt is used just as it is found in nature—crushed and screened to desirable size but without further processing. More than 7 million tons of rock salt are used in the United States alone each year, with the largest quantities used for deicing roads and in the manufacture of chlorine, but it has literally thousands of additional uses. There are five large and expanding outlets for rock salt: chemical industries (chlorine, caustic soda, soda ash), deicing of highways and sidewalks

---

[3] The term "f.o.b." means free on board (i.e., a price f.o.b. is a price that does not include carriage charges from seller to buyer). The term "c.i.f." means that cost, insurance, and freight are included in the price quoted.

[4] By the ton, such rock salt costs under 0.4 cents per pound, compared with 10 cents per pound for table salt bought in small quantities.

TABLE 15–1

World: Great-Region and Economic-Type of Society Shares of World Salt, Alkalies, Sulfur, and Acids Production, 1962–1964 Average-Annual
(in per cents)

	103.0 Million Metric Tons Salt (NaCl) Production [1]	12.2 Million Metric Tons Caustic Soda (NaOH) Production	14.9 Million Metric Tons Soda Ash (Na_2CO_3) Production	19.1 Million Metric Tons Sulfur (S) Production [2]	57.4 Million Metric Tons Sulfuric Acid (100 per cent H_2SO_4) Production
North America	31.5	48.5	31.6	32.5	35.8
Western Europe	23.4	14.4	24.9	26.1	28.3
Eastern Europe (including the U.S.S.R.)	16.0	16.8	29.8	15.0	18.0
Oceania	0.6	0.4	0.5	0.6	2.1
Latin America	4.0	2.5	1.0	8.9	1.8
Sub-Saharan Africa	1.0	0.2	1.0	1.5	1.1
Middle East (including North Africa)	2.0	0.2	0.3	2.3	0.5
Non-Communist Far East	8.4	12.9	6.1	10.5	10.0
Communist Far East	13.1	4.1	4.7	2.6	2.4
World	100.0	100.0	100.0	100.0	100.0
High-income countries	69.7	94.1	85.3	80.0	89.1
Low-income countries	30.3	5.9	14.7	20.0	10.9

Source: Adapted from United Nations and U.S. Bureau of Mines data.

[1] Of the 103.0 million metric tons of salt production, some 30 per cent is from the ocean and salt lakes, and the rest from man-made brine (wells) and rock-salt mines. Some 30 million metric tons are used in human and animal nutrition, with the other 70 per cent used in industries, mainly in manufacturing alkalies (caustic soda or sodium hydroxide, soda ash or sodium carbonate, and chlorine) but also in numerous non-chemical industries.

[2] Of the 19.1 million metric tons of sulfur, about half is native or elemental sulfur from brimstone (Frasch wells) and sour fuel (especially sour gas) sources, and about half from pyrites (sulfide ores, especially iron types and copper types). Most sulfur goes into the production of various acids, although small amounts are used without being put through the chemical industry.

(it reduces clogging of drains compared with sand or a mixture of sand and salt), metal processing and ceramics (to increase hardness of products in electric and reverbatory furnaces and as a descaler in hot-rolling of steel billets— to make the brine used as electrolyte to precipitate uranium from its ores), hides and leather industry, and other manufacturing areas.

The poorest countries consume little more salt than dietary requirements, usually some 10 to 15 pounds per person annually. Industrial countries consume eight to twelve times as much. In the United States, only about 2 per cent of the salt consumed is for dietary use (this supplies half the total dietary salt requirements, with the other half being contained in natural foods). The average American family spends about $2 a year for its table salt. The chemical industry consumes 65 per cent of the U.S. 29 million tons, more than half being used to make chlorine. The second largest user group includes highway departments and others, who use it to deice roads (this usage has doubled in the past five years). Agriculture is third in consumption, and meat packing is next, with other industries (textiles, glass, metals, rubber, oil, cosmetics, and pulp-paper) also being important. Over half of total production is delivered to customers in brine form (chiefly to the chemical industry), which costs about $2 per ton. In bulk carloads to industrial firms, evaporated granulated salt costs about $13 to $14 per ton, and rock salt costs $7.50 per ton or so at mine or refinery. Wells now produce 60 per cent of all U.S. salt; mines,

25 per cent; and solar salt works, 15 per cent. Texas produces 19 per cent of the total; Louisiana, 18 per cent; New York, Michigan, and Ohio account for about 15 per cent each; California, 6 per cent; Kansas, 5 per cent; and about twenty other states produce the remaining 7 per cent.

Industrial salt is mainly used for making alkalies: soda ash (sodium carbonate), caustic soda (sodium hydroxide or lye), and chlorine gas. Alkali plants tend to be market oriented, but also as close to cheap salt, cheap limestone, and cheap fuel and energy in such urban nodes as possible. Soda ash is used in large tonnages (about 15 million) in making soaps, glass, and in the manufacture of other chemicals. Most soda ash is produced by the Solvay process in which brine is saturated with ammonia gas (catalyst), then carbon dioxide gas is introduced to yield sodium bicarbonate, which is heated to produce soda ash. Pulp and paper producers and textile mills increasingly produce their own chlorine (for bleaching materials) by the electrolytic breaking down of brine; the caustic soda they produce as a by-product (roughly in equal amount to the chlorine) is sold commercially. A minor source of soda ash is by recovery from trona (natural soda).

Caustic soda (lye) is mainly used in the making of rayon, soap, dye, petroleum products, textiles, and paper. The older method of production treated a solution of sodium carbonate with slaked lime to form calcium carbonate precipitate and caustic soda solution. The newer method of brine electrolysis is becoming more

Allied Chemical's manufacturing center at Syracuse, New York, makes soda ash and related alkalies and chlorine from salt by the Company's Solvay Process Division.

Courtesy of Allied Chemical Corp.

WORLD: PRODUCTION OF BASIC CHEMICALS AND FERTILIZERS, BY GREAT-REGION AND ECONOMIC-TYPE OF SOCIETY, 1962-1964 AVERAGE-ANNUAL
(Million Metric Tons)

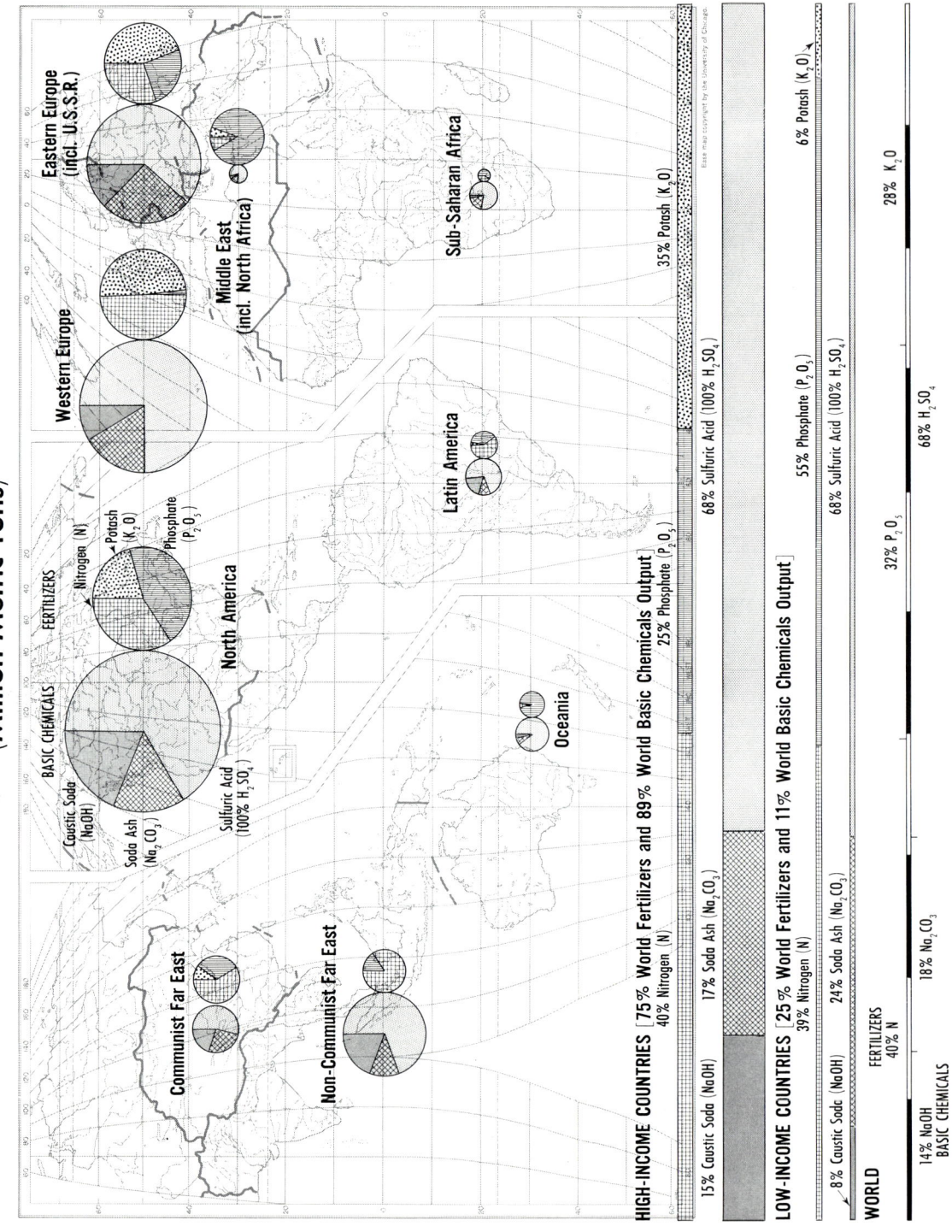

WORLD: GREAT-REGION AND ECONOMIC-TYPE OF SOCIETY SHARES OF WORLD BASIC CHEMICALS PRODUCTION AND FERTILIZER PRODUCTION AND CONSUMPTION, 1962-1964 AVERAGE-ANNUAL

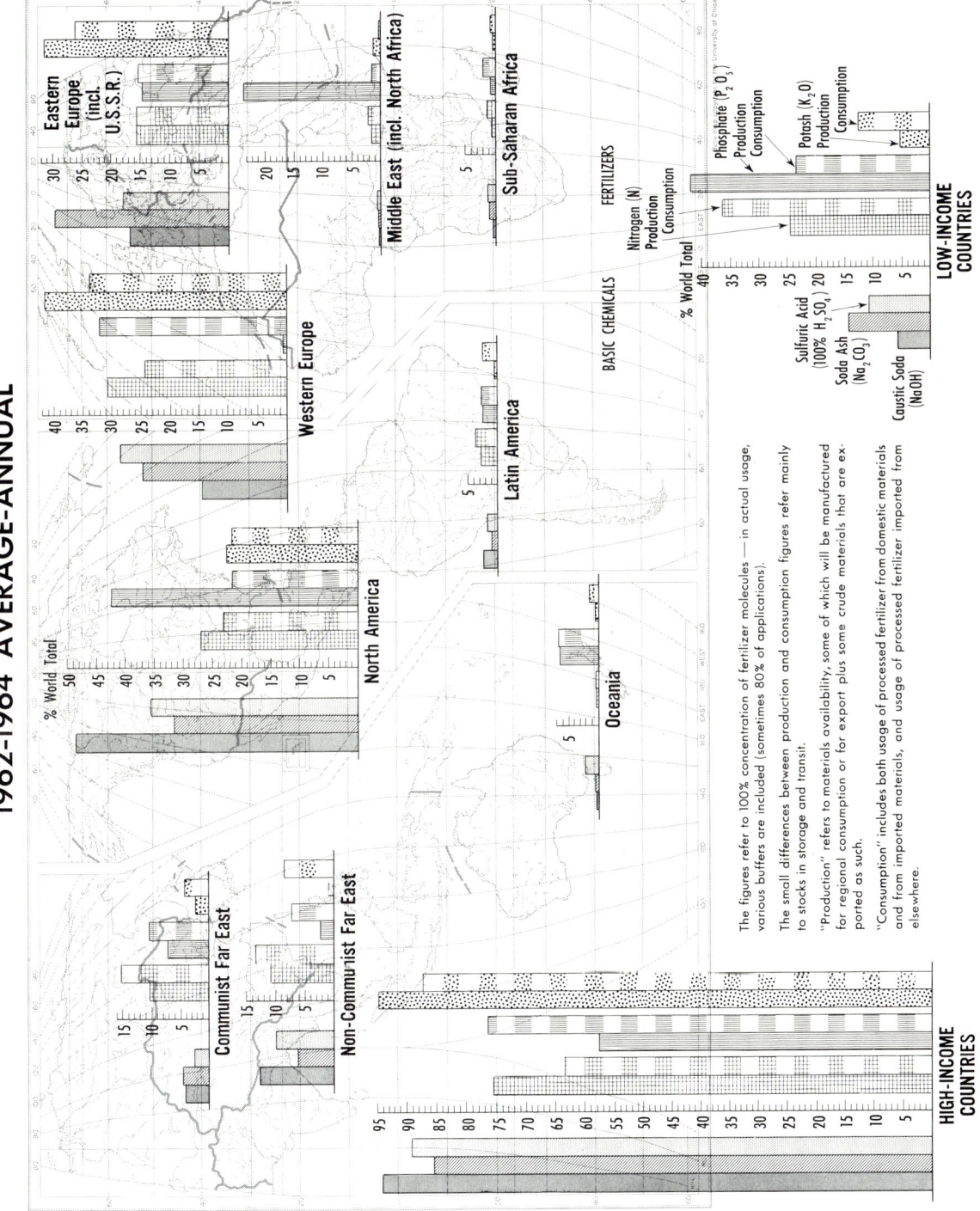

important. Caustic soda production follows the same general pattern as soda ash, but is somewhat more scattered (due to electrolytic production by textile, soap, paper, and petroleum refining plants).

Sulfur Materials

Sulfur is often considered the most important basic chemical, and its consumption is used as a barometer of general industrial activity. World consumption (1964) is about 20 million tons annually, increasing about 5 per cent annually. About three-fourths of the sulfur is burned and the sulfur oxide gases converted into sulfuric acid, which is then used in making fertilizer (one-third in treating phosphates), refining petroleum, leaching and refining ores, cleaning iron and steel mill-products, refining sugar, making explosives, finishing textiles, and in many other industrial processes. The other one-fourth of sulfur consumption is mainly in making digester liquors for chemical pulp mills, in making pesticides, in vulcanizing rubber, and in making many other industrial products. In the United States, annual per capita consumption is now over 80 pounds; in other industrial countries, from one-fourth to one-half as much.

Sulfur constitutes only 0.1 per cent of the outer crust (like barium), but it is highly concentrated in a few deposits (mainly in pyrite, gypsum, and hydrocarbon deposits, with some in native sulfur deposits), and there is no possibility of ultimate exhaustion in the foreseeable future. The high-grade, low-cost brimstone deposits are by no means inexhaustible, however, and may soon decline in relative importance. At present, about 9 million tons of elemental sulfur (brimstone) is produced yearly, mainly from underground salt domes along the U.S. and Mexican Gulf coasts, but also from underground mines in Italy, Japan, the U.S.S.R., and elsewhere. About as much production comes from sulfide ores mined for sulfur (chiefly pyrites, or fool's gold). Several million tons come from miscellaneous sources: by-product recovery from smelting sulfide (copper, lead, zinc) ores, desulfurizing fossil fuels (coal, petroleum, natural gas), and using gypsum (anhydrite).

Only one in twenty of the hundreds of salt domes along the Gulf of Mexico's Louisiana, Texas, and Mexico coastlands possesses commercial sulfur deposits. The 5 million ton U.S. brimstone production provides three-fourths of the raw materials used in making sulfuric acid, with pyrites and desulfurization splitting the other one-fourth about equally. Brimstone is found in limestone formations capping or flanking the salt domes at depths from 500 to 1,000 feet below the surface. Superheated water (330° F. is forced down into the 25- to 300-foot-thick formations to melt the sulfur (sulfur is fluid at 240° to 280° F., will revert to stone at 240° F. or lower or again at more than 100° F. above its melting point) in the outermost of three concentric pipes (often 10 inches in diameter). The melted sulfur rises part way up the middle pipe, and compressed air (sent down the inner pipe) forces the sulfur to the surface. At the surface, some of the molten brimstone is sprayed into storage vats to cool and solidify, but most is shipped as a liquid (a transporting method that is becoming more common). The amount of water needed to mine a ton of sulfur (ranging from 1,000 to 15,000 gallons) determines the efficiency of the operation. One well will remove sulfur from less than a single underground acre, so new holes must be drilled continually (the reason is that hot water will not penetrate limestone effectively for more than 200 feet). Low-cost (around $10 per ton dockside) domes are close to the surface, have excellent porosity of limestone, and good slopes of the contours (insuring escape of the mine water, after it has done its work, to the bleed wells); such an operation uses only 1,000 to 2,000 gallons of hot water to produce 1 ton of sulfur. The average U.S. dome requires more than 3,000 gallons, with average production cost about $20, for a ton of sulfur selling at about $26. Mexican producers are getting a foothold in the U.S. sulfur market because there is no sulfur tariff, they can ship the brimstone in non-U.S. ships at lower rates, and they can produce at the relatively low cost of $10 or so a ton at the dock. All Mexican producers together have at least 50 million tons of reserves, about one-fourth of U.S. Frasch-available reserves. United States and Mexican brimstone is available in other countries of elemental sulfur production at two-thirds the cost of the local product (excluding protection).

European production of sulfur and pyrites amounts to well over 3 million tons, besides which about $\frac{2}{3}$ million tons are imported annually from the United States and elsewhere. About 7 million tons of pyrites (averaging 45 per cent sulfur content) are produced, plus over 1 million tons of sulfur from desulfurizing natural gas (especially southwest France) and another $\frac{1}{4}$ million tons from Sicilian brimstone. Pyrites include all iron sulfides (mainly pyrite, pyrrhotite, and marcasite), which are used, after mining and concentration, for the production of sulfuric acid. In almost all cases, European pyrites can readily compete with U.S. sulfur as a source material for sulfuric acid because the mining of the ore is done on a large scale and because important by-products are obtained from the ore, including such metals as copper, lead, zinc, gold, and silver, and such non-metallic minerals as barite. In some areas (especially in Britain), acid is being produced from anhydrite (gypsum). It costs nearly $3 a ton more than that produced from sulfur, but roughly the same amount cheaper than that from pyrites (capital cost of an anhydrite plant is about half as much again as that of a pyrites plant of similar capacity).

Recovered sulfur from sour natural gas is less expensive to mine than Frasch-produced brimstone. Desulfurizing in the Peace River area of Alberta produces sour gas sulfur (the purest[5] available) at $2 per ton. Ultimately, the Canadian gas fields are expected to yield a tremendous 260 million tons of sulfur (as large a supply as that expected from all U.S. and Mexican Frasch production). However, transportation is a costly problem, for most Canadian gas fields are in isolated areas located far from sulfur markets,

and the sulfur will not be economical to extract until markets open up for the gas itself.

The production of sulfuric acid is a strongly market oriented process, with all the markets for the product intermediate ones (in the United States, 35 per cent fertilizer, 20 per cent other chemicals, 10 per cent petroleum, 35 per cent all other industrial users). The acid equivalent in crude sulfur has only about one-third the weight of an equivalent amount of sulfuric acid. In addition, the freight rate on crude sulfur is much cheaper. So the 45 to 50 million tons annual acid production is overwhelmingly market oriented. Some 80 per cent of crude sulfur is now moved in liquid form.

In the foreseeable future, elemental sulfur from salt domes and sour gas sulfur seem the comers at the expense of old-fashioned pyrite sulfur. However, because the two types are chemically different, they are not interchangeable. Most long-time sulfur users have facilities suited only for pyrite sulfur. But elemental and sour gas sulfur have enough advantages over the pyrite type to bring them almost all the new business.

Fertilizer Materials

Higher agricultural production seems more likely from higher yields because of greater use of fertilizer and water than from areal expansion relying on tractors and other mechanization. Expanded use of commercial fertilizers[6] seems likely as the main avenue to vastly increased fertilization. About 40 million tons of chemical fertilizer (excluding buffers) are now sold in commercial mixes each year: about 40 per cent nitrogen (N), and around 30 per cent each of phosphate (P_2O_5) and potash (K_2O). The world's most intensively farmed regions depend upon such commercial fertilizer sources for one-third to two-thirds of their total plant nutrients, and the fraction is growing larger. Mankind's solution of food and related material problems

---

[5] About 60 per cent of Frasch sulfur is dark (the bright yellow variety brings the highest price) because of petroleum contamination. It brings a lower price because it cannot be used for certain purposes (e.g., paper production) and causes "stack mist" (type of smog), which can get the acid manufacturer in trouble in many localities. The contaminants can be removed, but it costs $1 to $2 per ton to brighten it up.

[6] The U.S. National Fertilizer Association estimates that, on the average, $1 spent on fertilizer produces crops worth nearly $4, with 1 ton of fertilizer properly used producing 125 bushels of corn, 2 bales of cotton, 85 bushels of wheat, 185 bushels of potatoes, or 1,375 pounds of tobacco.

Courtesy of Olin Mathieson Chemical Corp.

Airview of Olin's Pasadena high-analysis fertilizer plant on the Houston Ship Canal. The large pile in the background is gypsum. A sulfuric acid plant is just out of the picture to the left.

Both in the United States and in the world as a whole, the chemical fertilizer industry is expected to triple production by 1980. World use is expected to be for the following purposes: 24 per cent to help feed the population increase, 16 per cent to help improve the quality of diets, 18 per cent to replace plant nutrients removed or wasted, 24 per cent to reduce costs, and 18 per cent to implement new farm technology and government policies.

rests more upon the contribution of the chemical fertilizer industry than upon any other factor.

Nitrogen. Nitrogen fixation still ranks as one of the most underexploited discoveries of this century, in spite of an annual 15 million ton annual production. In 1900, over 90 per cent of commercial nitrogen fertilizer came from natural sources (saltpeter, guano, various animal and vegetable wastes from food processing industries), with the remainder mainly from the by-product coke ovens. In 1964, Chilean and other nitrates provided only 2 per cent of the world's commercial nitrogen supply, and organic materials (guano, slaughterhouse wastes, and sewage) supplied about the same small fraction, with over 80 per cent of nitrogen obtained by fixing atmospheric sources, and about 15 per cent obtained from the by-product coke ovens.

The air is thought to contain 4,650 trillion tons of nitrogen, of which perhaps 100 million tons are thought to be fixed annually by lightning and washed down to earth and ocean. This atmospheric supply is practically limitless, providing a source limited only by the plants' capacity to use it. Two older methods are now of minor importance. The electric arc method (the original Haber-Bosch process) passes air through the arc to form oxides of nitrogen that are absorbed in water to form dilute nitric acid. A little is still produced in Norway but the high electricity costs have made the method uneconomic. The

TABLE 15-2

World: Great-Region and Economic-Type of Society Shares of World Fertilizer (Nitrogen, Phosphate, Potash) Production and Consumption, 1962–1964 Average-Annual *
(in per cents)

	15.4 Million Metric Tons Nitrogen (N) Production	15.6 Million Metric Tons Nitrogen (N) Consumption	12.8 Million Metric Tons Phosphate (P_2O_5) Production	12.5 Million Metric Tons Phosphate (P_2O_5) Consumption	11.1 Million Metric Tons Potash (K_2O) Production	11.5 Million Metric Tons Potash (K_2O) Consumption
North America	27.0	23.2	42.2	21.6	22.7	21.8
Western Europe	30.8	24.4	0.4	32.1	41.7	34.0
Eastern Europe (including the U.S.S.R.)	15.7	15.7	14.9	15.3	31.7	26.2
Oceania	0.2	0.3	6.6	6.9	–	1.4
Latin America	2.9	3.8	2.3	2.8	0.2	2.6
Sub-Saharan Africa	0.5	1.3	0.8	2.0	–	0.7
Middle East (including North Africa)	1.7	2.2	23.4	1.6	1.4	0.3
Non-Communist Far East	10.9	13.5	2.3	7.2	–	8.7
Communist Far East	10.3	15.6	7.1	10.5	2.3	4.3
World	100.0	100.0	100.0	100.0	100.0	100.0
High-income countries	75.5	63.5	57.8	76.5	94.9	87.2
Low-income countries	24.5	36.5	42.2	23.5	5.1	12.8

SOURCE: Adapted from United Nations, U.S. Bureau of Mines, and U.S. Department of Agriculture data.

* The figures refer to 100 per cent concentration of fertilizer molecules—in actual usage, various buffers are included (sometimes 80 per cent of applications). The differences between production and consumption figures refer mainly to stocks in storage and transit.

"Production" refers to materials availability, some of which will be manufactured for regional consumption or for export plus some crude materials that are exported as such (e.g., only a small fraction of the Middle Eastern phosphate rock production is processed into phosphatic fertilizers in the region; most is moved to Western Europe where it is processed for use there).

"Consumption" includes both usage of processed fertilizer from domestic materials and from imported materials, and usage of processed fertilizer imported from elsewhere (e.g., most underdeveloped regions import large amounts of processed fertilizer from North America and Western Europe because they either lack fertilizer-making capacity or have a shortage of such capacity).

cyanamide method combines nitrogen gas from the atmosphere with calcium carbide at high temperatures to produce calcium cyanamide. Although it uses only one-fourth as much power as the arc process, it still is too expensive to compete with synthetic ammonia made from natural gas, although there are a few old facilities that still use it.

The synthesis of ammonia process involves combining 3 hydrogen atoms and 1 nitrogen atom under great pressure in the presence of a catalyst to form synthetic ammonia. The hydrogen is obtained from the decomposition of natural gas (especially in the United States), coke oven gas, water gas, or water (the last three sources mainly used in Europe and Japan). The nitrogen is obtained from a liquefied-air fraction or from burning gas high in nitrogen. In the United States, it costs between $35 and $50 a ton (at 100 per cent capacity operation) to produce a ton of ammonia, which sells at $75 a ton (the price to the farmer in the ground is much higher, some $150 to $200 per ton).

In the distillation of coal, the nitrogen gas fraction is combined with hydrogen to form ammonia, which is usually treated with sulfuric acid to form ammonium sulfate (21 per cent N compared with the 82 per cent N in anhydrous ammonia). It can also be recovered by absorption in water as aqua ammonia.

In most industrial nations, from two-thirds to three-fourths of chemical nitrogen is used for fertilizer purposes. The remainder is used in making explosives, synthetic resins, printing ink, refrigeration fluid, and other products, and for other uses such as metal treating. The potential fertilizer markets are also very large. Aerial fertilization of forests has increased tree growth by 40 to 65 per cent. Other pilot-plant experimentation in some lakes and ponds has so increased their plant growth as to boost the weight of fish caught per acre some fourfold. Other trials indicate that fertilized pasture acres support more animals and make the land ready for grazing much earlier.

The importance of nitrogen to agricultural productivity and to war potential has encouraged industrial nations to assure domestic supplies even at high cost in some cases where older techniques are still used. World trade involves about 20 per cent of production. The United States, although producing nearly 25 per cent of the world supply, imports some Chilean nitrate and exports other types. Europe and Japan export surpluses to deficit (mainly underdeveloped) areas, although some of the latter (India, China, etc.) are building capacity rapidly.

Phosphate. Phosphate is mainly used in commercial fertilizers, although about 10 per cent is used for other purposes. Elemental phosphorus is used for making phosphoric acid, phosphorus

Allied Chemical's plant at Omaha, Nebraska, which makes synthetic ammonia, nitrogen, and urea from natural gas and air. The products are mainly used for fertilizer.

Courtesy of Allied Chemical Corp.

compounds for metal alloys, matches, flares, and lubricating oils. Phosphoric acid is used in drug, food, metal, and textile manufacturing. Various phosphates are used in detergents and cleaning compounds, chemical processing, animal feeds, oil well drilling muds, and paper and bleaches. About 12 million tons of P_2O_5 (phosphorus pentoxide) is used in ordinary superphosphate, concentrated superphosphate, nitrophosphate, and other types of commercial fertilizer.

Phosphate deposits are found in igneous, metamorphic, and sedimentary rocks. Some is distinctly crystalline material of inorganic origin (e.g., apatite) occurring in veins; some occurs in consolidated and partially disintegrated sedimentary strata several inches to 6 feet or more in thickness; and some occurs in the form of individual nodules or pebbles imbedded in a matrix of sand, clay, and soft phosphatic material. Most is of organic (animal) origin, formed originally either on the land or under the sea. In color, it ranges from nearly pure white, through various shades of gray and brown, to almost jet black.

Reserves are not known with certainty, but are very large and increasing rapidly. In the early 1960's, estimates of proven reserves approached 75 billion tons, of which the Middle East (including North Africa) had over half (Morocco, with 30 billion tons some 125 miles inland from Casablanca and Safi, has the world's largest exports, chiefly because it is near Western Europe). North America has a fifth of the world's proven reserves: two-thirds on the Pamlico River 50 miles inland from the North Carolina coast in Beaufort County (these were found in the 1960 to 1963 period and are not yet the source of important production), about a fifth low-grade ore in the Rocky Mountain States of Utah, Idaho, Montana, and Wyoming (high freight rates restrict the area of use), and the remainder in Florida and Tennessee (which provide most production). The Soviet Union has phosphate and other reserves that are about a tenth of the total, and are the source of Eastern European requirements. There are smaller reserves in Oceania (many coral islands, especially Nauru), in Latin America (mainly Peru), in sub-Saharan Africa (mainly Senegal, Togo, and South Africa), and elsewhere. Recent metallurgical developments have brought lower-grade phosphates and former wastes (from past mining and concentrating efforts) into the economic category.

The U.S.S.R. has the world's largest production of inorganic phosphate, its most important production coming from Kola Peninsula apatite deposits at Kirovsk (south of Murmansk). The rock is mined underground and concentrated by flotation. North Africa has the world's largest production of underground mining of sedimentary (organic) phosphate rock, which is mainly shipped off to Europe, the greatest deficit region, as soon as it is dried. The United States has the world's largest production of open-pit pebble phosphate, with Oceanic islands also mainly producing by surface methods.

The Florida pebble field accounts for nearly 75 per cent of the entire 20 million tons U.S. production (the Northern Rockies, with 20 per cent of the reserves, account for only 13 per cent of production; and Tennessee accounts for the remainder). High-grade phosphate pebble rock deposits lie about 25 miles east of Tampa, in a shield-shaped area about 50 miles long and 40 miles wide. The phosphate beds were formed in the late Miocene or Pliocene Age some 10 to 15 million years ago. The original source of the phosphorus was the primitive rock of the earth's crust. Through erosion, the phosphorus found its way into sedimentary rocks formed at the bottom of the sea (including much of organic origin). When the land that is now Florida finally emerged from the sea, large lakes and pools remained, and subsequent erosion carried phosphate pebbles of various sizes, together with sand and clay, to the lakes and pools where the material settled to the bottom as a conglomerate. These pebble phosphate beds are irregular in shape and are found in strata from 5 to 20 feet thick containing from 10 to 50 per cent phosphate material. Some 5 to 40 feet of overburden covers the phosphate-bearing matrix and is removed by dragline buckets that can pick up 17 cubic yards of earth (20 to 25 tons of material) in one bite. After being uncovered, hydraulic guns, spraying 2,000 gallons of water a minute, break the matrix down into a slurry. A 16-inch pipeline carries the slurry to the processing plant (usually no farther than 2 to 3 miles from the dragline and sump). The processing plant consists of two units: a washer and a recovery operation. Washing is primarily a screening operation to separate the larger sizes of pebble phosphate rock from the slurry. The fine portion of the slurry is pumped into the recovery unit where the smaller phosphate particles are separated from the sand and clay by hydraulic sizing. Some of the ground phosphate rock is packed in bags for movement to agricultural areas where it will be applied directly to the soil. But most of the ground rock is shipped in bulk to fertilizer and other manufacturers. To produce a ton of ordinary superphosphate containing 16 per cent P_2O_5 requires about ½ ton of rock and ⅛ ton of sulfur (to produce ½ ton of 70 per cent sulfuric acid). Since the total weight of both is less than the weight of the final product, and since the transportation rate on each of the two raw materials is less than on the fertilizer, production locations close to market are desirable. Concentrated (triple) superphosphate containing 42 to 50 per cent phosphoric acid is produced by treating rock with phosphoric acid instead of sulfuric acid. Ammonium phosphate is manufactured by treating phosphoric acid with ammonia and contains 15 per cent ammonia and 52 per cent phosphoric acid (it usually is produced at nitrogen plants). The most concentrated form, calcium metaphosphate, containing about 65 per cent phosphoric acid, is produced by passing hot phosphoric gas through hot phosphate rock. Annual production of Florida pebble phosphate rock is about 15 million tons a year, with another 5 million tons coming from Tennessee, Wyoming, Utah, and Idaho. In the case of rock ranging in grade from 68 to 78 per cent bone phosphate of lime (BPL), the wet process (sulfuric acid) is mainly used. Phosphate rock containing as little as 50 to 55 per cent BPL may be employed locally for the manufacture of elemental phosphorus, where long hauls are not involved and the ratio of lime to silica is favorable; in a blast furnace or electric furnace, the phosphorus vapor is collected as elemental phosphorus or phosphoric acid.

Half of world phosphate-rock production moves in world trade, mainly from North America, the Middle East (mainly Northwest Africa), and Oceania. Western Europe depends mainly upon Northwest Africa and Florida; Australia and New Zealand depend upon coral atolls in the southwest and central Pacific Ocean; and Japan receives supplies from all three surplus sources.

Potassium. Potassium is the third major fertilizer mineral; annual production approaches 11 million tons. About 90 per cent of production is consumed by agriculture, with the remainder used in industry. Caustic potash (KOH) and potassium carbonate (K_2CO_3) are used in the making of soft soaps, crystal glass, tableware and colored glass, and many other products. Potassium chlorate is used in making matches, fireworks, and explosives.

Potassium salts are widely distributed and found associated with many other materials. They occur in seawater and in salt lakes. Beneath the surface of the earth are deposits of the chlorides and sulfates of potassium that originated from the evaporation in past geological times, under arid conditions, of seawater in enclosed but extensive basins. World resources are immense, but not known with precision. The range of estimates is from some 15 billion tons (proven) to over 60 billion tons (estimated total resources). When the more speculative higher estimates are used, Germany, the U.S.S.R., and Canada are at the top, with Israel-Jordan (Dead Sea), Spain, and France also having large resources.

The United States has very small reserves, but has been producing about a fifth of world production recently. Some 90 per cent of U.S. potash production comes from Carlsbad Mines (southeastern New Mexico), with the remainder from lake beds in California and Utah. The Carlsbad high-grade deposits are becoming depleted, and Germany (both West and East) and France, with cheaper labor, can underprice the U.S. producers and have in recent years exported increasing amounts to this country. United States companies are interested in the western Canada deposits. Under the plains of central Saskatchewan lies estimated potash reserves of 6 to 7 billion tons about 3,000 feet below the surface. The main mining problem is a 300-foot layer of water-soaked sands between the potash and the surface. Mining (both conventional and solution types) has already begun at several spots along the 450-mile-long and 50-mile-wide arch across the province. By the mid-1960's, annual production of nearly 2 million tons is indicated; by 1970, it will be over 4 million tons of K_2O annually; and by 1975, some 6 million tons (over half of present world production).

German, French, Spanish, and Soviet deposits are also shaft-mined, like the U.S. Carlsbad deposit. The German (Stassfurt) deposits are 1,000 to 3,000 feet deep; the Soviet (Solikamsk area, northern Urals) are shallower. Underground potash salts are low grade, so only a small fraction is prepared for market by grinding. Higher grades (30 to 50 per cent K_2O) are obtained by refining.

The largest brine operations are those operated by Israel and Jordan on the Dead Sea. The water contains over 2 billion tons of potassium chloride. The Israeli are diking some 36 square miles of their third of the Dead Sea to create a vast artificial evaporation lake. They hope to increase output from some 160,000 tons to 800,000 tons by 1970, mainly for export (third in importance after citrus and polished diamonds). The output of ordinary salt (mainly shipped to Japan) and other salts like bromides and bromine is also increasing.

World trade in potash has a long history of original dependence on Germany, which has rapidly decreased in the past generation. After World War I and the Communist takeover of Russia, the United States, the Soviet Union, France, Spain, and several other countries became self-sufficient. Recently, the Dead Sea producers and Canada began planning large increases in their exports, which will further decrease Germany's relative share of world trade.

Although by custom the contents of plant nutrients in fertilizers are measured by N (nitrogen), P_2O_5 (phosphorus pentoxide), and K_2O (potassium oxide), the fertilizers do not in fact contain those ingredients, or do not contain them in those particular chemical combinations. Frequently, the plant nutrients are combined and marketed as mixed or complete fertilizer. The composition of such fertilizer is stated by a formula in which the percentage of the three minerals in alphabetical order is indicated (e.g., 6-8-10 means 6 per cent nitrogen, 8 per cent phosphoric acid, 10 per cent potash, and 76 per cent diluting filler material). The large proportion of filler material limits the range of shipment, so most fertilizer plants are market oriented close to cheap bulk-shipment access to raw materials. In recent years, there is a tendency to manufacture concentrated fertilizer compounds that are then shipped long distances to where they are diluted either by a commercial outlet or on the farm (e.g., in irrigation water) before application.

Lime Materials

The element calcium is over 3 per cent of the earth's crust, between iron and sodium in relative abundance. Under present technology, probably 100 billion tons of reserves are available. The most usual forms of this element are limestone and gypsum. Limestone is more or less a pure form of calcium carbonate ($CaCO_3$) in which the impurities consist principally of silica, alumina, iron, gypsum, alkalies, and carbonaceous matter. Dolomitic limestone, sometimes containing more than 20 per cent magnesium oxide (MgO), is also found and is used for soil improvement as well as for fertilizer (although its main uses are as flux and ore). Gypsum is dihydrate calcium sulfate ($CaSO_4 2H_2O$) and is used more for building material (plaster) than for chemical use.

No reliable data on world production of all limestone are available, since many of the uses are by non-commercial and other producers. Much is used as building stone, but even more as crushed stone (for road construction, concrete making, and other purposes). Limestone with silica impurities is favored for highway and other construction. About 800 pounds of silica-free, sulfur-free, phosphorus-free limestone is required as flux for each ton of steel produced. Lime has also become a foremost raw material for the chemical industry, and in point of tonnage lags only behind carbon, salt, and sulfuric acid.

Lime is obtained by calcining or cooking limestone, a rock chiefly consisting of calcium carbonate, usually an accumulation of organic remains, such as shells. Most lime companies quarry their own stone. The ledges are often 10 to 40 feet thick, with some over 100 feet. Overburden may range from a few inches to over 100 feet, but that over 10 feet becomes too expensive to remove (even 10 feet of earth costs $5,000 per acre). After the strippers and bulldozers remove the overburden, electric drills put in holes for dynamite. The power of the blast is exerted horizontally, so as to lessen the danger of debris being spread over a large area. Dump-type trucks carry 20 to 25 tons of cracked rock to the crusher, which is usually about 15 feet in diameter by 20 feet deep (it operates similar to mortar and pestle). After being crushed and screened, the limestone is conveyed to rotary or vertical kilns where it is calcined into quicklime (calcium oxide) at 2200° F. In effect, the heat causes carbon dioxide to be removed as a gas, with 100 pounds of pure limestone yielding 56 pounds of quicklime. About 80 per cent of the quicklime is then sold in pebble or pulverized form. The remaining 20 per cent is treated with water to form hydrated lime, a fine white powder used to make mortar or plastic. The 80 per cent of lime sold for chemical purposes ranks it as the second largest basic chemical, outstripping such basic items as soda ash, caustic soda, chlorine, and alum.

In the United States, about 10 million tons of lime are used yearly, about one-third of the output being captive production (only sulfuric acid exceeds it in the matter of captive production). The trend during the past several decades has been toward greater mechanization and larger producing units. There are now some 65 concerns with 110 plants in 31 states, only half the number in the mid-1930's. Alkali manufacturers and pulp and paper companies each use about one-fourth of total consumption, with other industrial users being the processors of calcium carbide, cyanamide, glass, leather, pesticides, and many others. Purification of water and building are also large-scale consumers.

Lime is the lowest cost chemical, when compared with alkalies and acids, on an equivalent reactivity basis (E.U.R.). The replacement of lime with such other chemicals would be unusual, whereas the replacement of other chemicals with lime is common. The following rather startling comparisons were made on this basis for lime and eight chemicals with production in excess of 1 million tons a year:

	Cents per Pound	E.U.R. Price
Lime (100%)	0.6	0.17
Caustic (98%)	2.7	1.08
Ammonia	4.2	0.71
Soda ash	1.8	0.93
Sulfuric acid	1.2	0.58
Phosphoric acid	7.1	2.34
Nitric acid	3.9	2.45
Sodium sulfate	1.4	0.99
Chlorine	3.0	1.06

Air Materials

Roughly, air is composed of 78 per cent nitrogen, 21 per cent oxygen, and 1 per cent argon and the rare gases. The easiest way to separate them is distillation of the fractions after the air is liquefied at −313° F. The nitrogen boils at a lower temperature than oxygen, so it passes off first and, after being freed of oxygen impurities (*ca.* 7 per cent), it is passed over calcium carbide heated to a temperature of 1832° to 2015° F. so as to form calcium cyanamide (fertilizer). The oxygen (practically pure) boils off at −297.3° F.

Sales of all industrial gases now gross $0.5 billion a year in the United States, with an annual growth rate of about 15 per cent. The largest item is some 10 million tons of oxygen. Nearly half is used by the metallurgical and related industries, two-fifths by the chemical industries, over a tenth by the missile and space industries, and the rest by other industries. Steel's oxygen consumption is headed up a steep curve, now that the industry is using oxygen for combustion, rather than principally for surface preparation and plant maintenance. About 1,000 cubic feet of oxygen is now used per ton of steel, and it is still rising swiftly.

Until recently, oxygen was made centrally and distributed in tanks. Distributing even big loads of gases from central plants was very expensive, but the present tendency of on-site production and storage in liquid form has dropped oxygen from $100 per ton to $10 to $15 per ton. On-site plants, the cheapest way for a big user to get oxygen, have tripled in five years. This type of plant, which is usually operated by an oxygen company rather than by the user, came into vogue a decade ago. At that time, installations ranged in capacity from 2 to 25 tons a day, but now they often run into the hundreds of tons.

The idea of an oxygen plant for each factory is relatively young, but it is already threatened with an even new one. That is the concept of a large central oxygen plant, hooked by pipeline to a number of companies lying in one industrial complex. The advantage claimed for the central supplier is that it can smooth out the zigs and zags of the demand graph.

Many mid-1960 contracts of on-site plants call for a price of 5 cents per 100 cubic feet of oxygen, perhaps a sixth of the cost for the gas that would have been required several years ago. At such a low cost, many new users are expected in the next decade.

Other Raw Materials

Many other raw materials are used by the chemical industry, in addition to the tonnage items already discussed, and the list and relative use is continually changing, with evolving chemical technology and changing price structure. As an example of a material that seems slated for much greater importance, we consider boron

Airview of an open-pit borate mine and adjacent processing plants owned and operated by U.S. Borax & Chemical Corporation at Boron, California, some 135 miles northeast of Los Angeles. This is the only open-pit borate mine in the world. The pit is currently 400 feet deep, 3,000 feet long, and 2,000 feet wide. Ore is moved out of the pit by a 1,300-foot mechanized conveyor belt system visible in the center foreground.

Courtesy of U.S. Borax & Chemical Corp.

Courtesy of U.S. Borax & Chemical Corp.

Partial view of U.S. Borax's Boron, California, facilities. Rotating kilns or calciners (foreground) partially dehydrate certain kinds of borax products. A row of driers can be seen beyond the calciners; a cooling tower is at the left; six-story-high crystallizers and four huge, covered thickeners can be seen in the background. Borax, boric acid, and other boron compounds go into glass and ceramic-making, fertilizers, detergents, and numerous other products.

(the close neighbor of carbon in the periodic table). The source of boron is borax, and nowhere in the world are there deposits as rich as those in California's Mohave Desert region and the dry lakes near Death Valley. Three U.S. companies now supply 95 per cent of the free world's borax needs. Two of them (West End Chemical Corporation and American Potash & Chemical Corporation) get their borax from rich brine deposits under the dry crust of Searles Lake near Death Valley, together with soda ash, sodium sulfate, potash, bromine, and lithium compounds. The new open-pit mine of U.S. Borax & Chemical Corporation taps a unique deposit of kernite, a concentrated form of crystalline borax. The only deposit of its type in the world, the mine is expected to contain well over 100 years' supply of ore at current depletion rates. It is from this mine that most of the basic increase in borax output will come. Until recently, U.S. Borax dug its ore by underground room and pillar cutting, which allowed it a maximum ore recovery of only 40 per cent. Primarily, it was to get 100 per cent ore recovery that the company decided to strip the 150- to 200-foot-thick overburden off the ore deposit and change to open-pit mining. The switch also cuts labor and equipment costs. But the company expects to get even greater economies from its new refining plant. More than 47 per cent of the weight of common borax is made of water. Driving off this water is the first step in processing borax to upgraded chemicals. And since it does not pay to ship water even the smallest distance, U.S. Borax is putting its new refining plant as close as possible to the edge of the open pit. Because it is a simple pumping operation, there is no question that getting brine to the surface is cheaper than U.S. Borax's mineral mining operation. But the Searles Lake brines contain so many mineral salts that separation—a complex procedure of continuous evaporations and crystallizations—is a much more critical and expensive refining process. Because of this, costs of the three producers probably even out.

The most common boron compounds, such as refined borax and boric acid, turn up in dozens of uses that consume tonnage quantities (crude borax costs about 2 cents a pound). Glass- and ceramic-makers still buy the largest proportion of all borax sold in the United States, about 40 per cent of the nearly 1 million tons annual consumption, using it especially in Pyrex glass, glass fibers for plastics and insulation, and enamels and porcelains. Another third goes into fertilizers, weed killers, gasoline additives, and welding fluxes. The fastest growing use is in exotic fuels; the organo-boron compounds are expected to lift the demand for borax to 2 to 3 million tons by the late 1960's. Chemists explain boron's function in such fuels as essentially threefold: it locks hydrogen, the perfect fuel, into a liquid or solid form, making it easier and safer to handle and transport; it is, along with lithium, the lightest element to which hydrogen can be attached; and it contributes itself to the total release of energy when the fuel is ignited. So far, of course, the cost restricts use mainly to military applications. While commercial-grade borax costs only $40 per ton, the rich side of the family brings very different prices (ranging from over $70 per ton for anhydrous borax to $26,000 to $40,000 per ton for elemental boron).[7]

LOCATION AND ORGANIZATION OF THE CHEMICAL INDUSTRY

The chemical industry as we know it today is essentially a twentieth-century phenomenon. It began in Western Europe, but now the largest segment of the world industry is in the United States (about one-third of the total, a decline from nearly one-half immediately after World War II when the Western European industry was prostrate). Japan is of increasing importance, while the Soviet bloc is trying to build up capacity after a comparatively late start (except in East Germany).

Taken as a whole, the chemical industry tends to be market oriented, although much of the purely chemical segment is raw materials oriented. In allied process industries, quite often know-how (technology) is as important as the market and materials factors, and an area with few raw materials and only a small market may rate high in expensive chemicals (e.g., Switzerland in many drugs).

The chemical industry is generally characterized by the concentration of control and major share of production by a few large companies. Cartelization is common, perhaps reflecting the central European origin of modern chemistry. Competition comes more from dynamic technology than from the structure of the industry.

Location Tendencies

The purely chemical group has several traits in common, which heavily influence its pattern of location. The commodity is invariably bulky, necessitating movement in carload lots. The industry, considering the bulkiness of the product, tends to locate near the source of the raw material. The value added at this stage of production is usually rather small per unit of output.

[7] The hard boron-resin-fiberglass upper stages of the Minuteman and Polaris missiles are reported to cost over $200 a pound of finished product.

The price per unit is relatively low (e.g., even after the inflationary spiral of the last several decades, the wholesale price of sulfuric acid and caustic soda is only 1 to 2 cents per pound). The bulky product, low value-added, and low unit-value necessitate large-scale operation. Product differentiation is at a minimum (e.g., the rigid standards set by government or chemical engineering societies prevent significant deviations from the established quality norm). Most of these basic chemicals are used as raw materials in allied process and chemical process industries, so demand is relatively inelastic, with demand roughly paralleling the general industrial production curve in mature industrial economies.

The plant location considerations for the basic-chemical manufacturer might be broken down as follows. Most important are proximity to fuel and power and raw material. Labor supply and transportation availability are of somewhat less importance, but still major considerations. Water supply and waste disposal are unusually important, compared with most industry, and often are so important as to become area considerations as well as site considerations. Alkali plants are usually near salt, limestone, and coke (especially deposits in the vicinity of urban areas); acid plants tend to be even more market oriented because of the problems of handling and shipping such corrosive materials. Fertilizer plants must pay great attention to cheap unskilled labor and cheap bulk transport. The concentration of the carbon-black industry in northern Texas is an example of location near raw material and also isolation to reduce subjection to air pollution of large populations. The problem of obtaining clean, soft, cooling water supplies in adequate quantity at low cost is fast increasing; in many cases, it is being accentuated by the waste from older plants.

The allied process concerns, who take basic chemicals and convert them into materials useful to industrial consumers and often to the general consuming public, use the same criteria in locating new plants as the purely chemical concerns, but must place different emphasis on various of these criteria. Market location is very important to this type of chemical manufacturer, inasmuch as his packaged products ordinarily carry a higher freight rate than his raw materials and many of the shipments are l.c.l. (less than carload lots). The labor supply is important because a higher percentage of employees is usually required in this type of operation than in the basic manufacture of chemicals. Waste disposal and fuel and power are also very important, although the relative weighting will depend on the specific industry. Living conditions and nearness to equipment and plant maintenance services are important because the allied processor is generally smaller than the basic producer and external economies are relatively more important. Less important considerations include transportation, water supply, nearness to suppliers, and proximity to raw materials. Product transportation is not as important inasmuch as the manufacturer has deliberately located near his market and most of the shipments will go by truck. Water supply, while important, is often provided by the city or is readily available from streams or ground water. Nearness to suppliers is not of great significance because supplier requirements other than containers are limited. Proximity to raw material is of less consequence because suppliers of raw material will usually equalize or allow freight regardless of where they are located.

Site conditions are always important for both types of manufacturer since they have a profound influence on both original investment and operating costs. Topography (flat, cheap, or zoned land; sea, lake, or river location) is always a consideration of major importance. Soil conditions must be considered for many reasons (foundation aspect, often water supply and waste disposal aspects). Position of plant to local transport facilities is especially important to those manufacturers who combine both functions; they usually try to combine bulk-carrying routes on one side of the plant with package-goods carriers (mainly highways) on another side. Waste disposal problems vary with the specific operation; the large basic-chemical manufacturer will almost always create more of an odor nuisance than the allied processors, and some of the latter are located adjacent to or even in residential areas. Availability of homes for workers seldom is much of a problem to allied processors, but the basic producers who are raw material oriented may have to encourage or even build its own community for its personnel. Local ordinances (including sanitation, air and stream pollution, zoning, and other factors) are stricter in favored areas (e.g., Pittsburgh-Cincinnati Ohio River section, Delaware River from Phillipsburg to Delaware Bay, Susquehanna River from Harrisburg to Chesapeake Bay, Cleveland area of Lake Erie, Houston Ship Canal) than elsewhere. Living conditions for labor and management (climate, scenery, recreational facilities, quality of schools, churches, bus transport, etc.) must be considered always, but they vary so widely that easy generalization in terms of types of the chemical industry does not suffice. Community directives for zoning land use and community attitude toward manufacturing activities tend to be similar to those toward heavy industry in general (i.e., upper- and middle-class neighborhoods spurn plants).

Distribution

In low-cost tonnage chemicals, such as acids and alkalies, transport is about 8 to 10 per cent of the sales dollar; this rises in high-cost fine chemicals, such as drugs and dyes, to 25 per cent. This does not include container costs that, for most chemical producers, run from 4 to 8 per cent of the sales dollar. Selling costs, including advertising (often 10 per cent and over), are even more variable; in fine chemicals sold to ultimate consumers, such costs run higher than production costs plus transportation.

In the United States, some 70 to 75 million tons of intermediary chemicals are moved by common carrier transportation companies: 60 per cent by railroads, 25 per cent by truck, and 15 per cent by water. Additional volume is moved by chemical companies themselves, mainly by barges and pipelines owned by the producers.

Approximately 168,000 tank cars are in commercial freight service on U.S. railroads. About 28 per cent of these, or approximately 47,000, are in chemical service. However, more than 43 per cent of railroad revenues from tank cars are earned in transporting chemicals. Over 6 per cent of the total gross revenues of U.S. railroads are derived from transporting chemical products.

According to the Interstate Commerce Commission, some 20 to 25 per cent of the tank-truck revenues of interstate "for hire" carriers is earned in transporting chemical products. This does not include movement by company trucks.

Up to now, barges have carried most of the chemicals shipped by water; they do a fair job on the inland routes, but they are slow and capacity is not large. Recently, converted and special tankers have been carrying shiploads of intermediaries in coastal runs. In the design of such chemical ships, special linings and pumping systems have been installed at costs of about $200 a deadweight ton. Balsam wood, glass, cofferdams, and double bottoms (tanks within tanks) are installed to insure freedom from contamination and resistance to explosion.

Pipelines are increasingly used to move chemicals. Today, the petrochemical companies in the Houston-Beaumont areas are virtually locked together by a maze of underground pipelines, commonly known as the "Spaghetti Bowl." The key material in the network is ethylene, of which the major supplier is Gulf Oil Company; Gulf pumps over 200,000 tons of it into the Spaghetti Bowl every year. But there are also hundreds of miles of other pipelines connecting the plants and carrying not only brine, natural gas, and crude oil, but such things as acetylene, hydrogen chloride, sodium hydroxide, and methyl isobutyl carbinol.

The transportation difficulty in the U.S. chemical industry arises mainly because of the geographic split in the industry. Chemical production plants are going up in the Southwest and Deep South near the fuel and raw material sources, while chemical finishing plants mainly remain close to ultimate consumers in the industrial North. If this split continues, large fleets of special chemical tankers and long-distance intermediary pipelines may be the most economical means of connecting the two segments of the U.S. chemical industry.

Organization

The chemical manufacturing industry is, by and large, an orderly type of industry, especially if its extremely rapid growth rate and influx of newcomers are considered. There is a trend toward organizational concentration or integration. Assurance of raw materials is the major reason for "backward integration." Since most crude materials of the industry (cellulose, hydrocarbon, salt, sulfur, limestone, air, water) are abundant, and since prices of intermediaries are low due both to cheapness of the materials and to newcomers bringing new capacity into production, integration backward does not assume major importance. When it does occur, it is often motivated to assure not only cheap supplies, but also products precisely tailored to meet the quality requirements of the company's allied-processing plants. More important is "forward integration," becoming more and more the marketer, by raising the product line beyond the tonnage intermediaries that the newcomers can readily make to finished products that are less susceptible to price erosion. While such company marketing is increasing, it is still uncommon (e.g., Du Pont now sells only 5 per cent of its products directly). The most apparent form of integration is circular or complex integration, leading toward diversification. In turn, the chemicals field is being invaded by petroleum, rubber, liquor, meat packing, and other manufacturers, some of whom may eventually become more chemical industry than other types. Decentralization of basic-chemicals plants closer to consumers has partly been motivated by the traditional attempt to lower the heavy transport charges but also, to a lesser extent, to try and lessen the tendency by industrial consumers to make their own basic chemicals in attached or nearby plants (e.g., pulp and paper, textile, and other chemical-process industries making their own acids and alkalies).

In price competition, chemicals has always been a gentlemanly industry. Except in one or two natural products (e.g., ethyl alcohol), there has rarely been really cutthroat competition in prices. However, there is constant struggle among chemical companies to excel in new and better products at low prices, but exchange of information, cross-licensing of patents, and co-ordinated research are common practices. The best indication of existing competition is the trend toward lower prices. Some questionable aspects of competition include the dominance of a few producers in certain specialized fields. On the whole, friendly relations are the result of the nature of the business. The great breadth of the chemical field allowed companies to stake out areas only partly in direct competition with one another. The complexity of the field puts most major companies in the odd position of being both competitors and customers of one another, and this tendency is increasing.

Even more conducive to good manners has been chemicals' capital investment, among the highest in industry, whether looked at per worker (around $20,000) or per ton of capacity (about $1,000 per yearly ton of the cheapest plastic, as against under $300 per yearly ton of steel). Up to the end of World War II, the industry managed to finance expansion without resorting to borrowing, with reinvestment of earnings accounting for more than half of new capital needed for growth purposes. Since that time, the industry's continued and immediate expansion has come more and more from borrowing and the issuance of preferred stock.

Labor requirements in the chemical industry are becoming more skilled and technical. About 3 to 4 per cent of all workers are in research (there are probably more chemistry Ph.D.'s in industry than in all colleges and universities). There are only 0.2 per cent of all workers in iron-steel in research, and only 0.03 per cent of all textile workers in research, in comparison. Partly because of unskilled workers in basic chemicals, partly because of the large fraction of technical workers, the pull of unionism has not been as irresistible as in most industries. Industry-wide bargaining is unknown. No single union dominates at the bargaining table. Many chemical plants either are non-union or prefer independent unions.

Over-all, the chemical industry is one of the few major manufacturing industries that leans to the protectionist side. Moreover, it is one of the most modern and most dynamic industries, unlike the majority of high-tariff industries, which tend to be high-cost, small-scale operations. However, not all chemical manufacturers are alarmists about foreign competition. The makers of cheap, bulk chemicals—caustic soda, sulfuric acid, phosphates, etc.—do not believe foreigners can compete, because of high freight charges for low-unit-price products. Generally, the ones who fear competition are the makers of synthetic organics: plastics, resins, dyes, medicinals, rubber processing chemicals, agricultural chemicals, etc. Many of these are not mass-production chemicals, but batch ("pot and kettle") process chemicals that are expensive and require skilled labor and costly (hand-made or hand-altered) facilities.

While sensitive to imports, the chemical industry is continually increasing its foreign investments, both in industrial and underdeveloped economies. Relatively, the underdeveloped realm's chemical picture is changing the most rapidly. Existing industry is puny and concentrated mainly on the manufacture of traditional consumer goods—toiletries, soaps, matches, oils and fats—with little output of intermediaries. There are numerous increasing demands as development gains momentum: agricultural chemicals (synthetic fertilizers, insecticides, fungicides), motor vehicle and tire chemicals (synthetic rubber, carbon black, paints and enamels), textile chemicals (detergents, dyes), metal-transforming materials (abrasives), mining materials (explosives), and general chemicals (alkalies and basic acids). Most chemical intermediaries can be manufactured cheaper than present imports if the scale of production can be keyed to regional rather than small-nation markets. In restricted cases, intermediaries can be produced in the underdeveloped realm more cheaply than in the urban-industrial realm, and exports might be developed, provided relatively free trade exists. Possibly, larger versions of the chemical tankers now engaged in U.S. coastal traffic may some day ply the oceans like present-day oil tankers, gas tankers, and ore carriers, as international specialization increases.

PERSPECTIVE

Since the mid-1920's, the rate of growth of the chemical industry in the urban-industrial realm has been nearly 10 per cent per year, as against about half that for most other industry. In addition, many other industries have become chemical process industries, and this tendency seems likely to continue in the foreseeable future.

The ability to make chemical changes in the materials provided by nature could well serve as a measure of man's development. Man ceased to be an animal and became human at the stage when he learned to make his first chemical change, fire. The era that started with the reduction of copper ores might be called the age of empirical chemistry. This age continued for about 6,000 years, ending in the latter years of the eighteenth century, when mankind entered what can be called the age of electronic chemistry. The main limitation to the age of empirical chemistry lay in the fact that each invention had to be made by chance. Since the chemistry of the various reactions was not understood, no real research could be undertaken. Mankind was groping in the dark, although the progress made was enormous compared with that of the previous era of fire and stone tools. Thus, man merely scratched the surface of the natural wealth that was surrounding him.

The rapidity of progress during the age of electronic chemistry (all chemical reactions involving only an exchange of electrons between the atoms, the atoms' nucleii remaining unchanged) is as astonishing as its slowness in the preceding age. The accomplishments of this short one and a half centuries outdo all that man could boast of for the entire procession of the millennia of his recorded and unrecorded history. Once the foundations of scientific chemistry were laid (by Lavoisier, Dalton, Avogadro, Galvani, and Volta), all the resources of nature became potentially available to man. Man was able to discover the rest of the chemical elements and to understand and undertake chemical synthesis, the most creative of all man's endeavors. Identical end products could be produced by different processes starting with the same raw materials or, more importantly, from entirely different raw material bases.

The age of nuclear chemistry (since 1945, when man began to perform reactions involving changes in the nucleus of the atom) is too young to foresee its main results. Some think reactors themselves will be used to produce chemical reactions and nuclear power simultaneously. For example, a sodium-cooled reactor will have its coolant sodium become radioactive when it is irradiated with neutrons. Therefore, the sodium that carries the heat out of the reactor after going through the heat exchanger to form steam still is intensely radioactive with 15-hour half-life radiosodium. A suggestion has been made to put the radioactive sodium through a series of piping in an adjoining room in which wheat, meat, and other foodstuffs could be irradiated, pasteurizing cheaply. Another suggestion is to produce nitric acid by the irradiation of air in an air-cooled type of reactor; the air forming nitrogen oxide would be further processed into nitrogen dioxide and nitric acid. There may be other instances of where chemical reactions may be profitably catalyzed by the intense radiation in atomic reactors.

The days of easy geographical quest for more food, fuel, and other materials are over, and our urban-industrial civilization's frontiers now mainly lie in science and technology. Chemistry offers many potentials to displace materials now supplied by agriculture, mining, and industry with semisynthetic and true synthetic substitutes. For the present, however, nature has supplied man with such abundant sources of fuel and food that he will not be pushed toward large-scale true-synthetic substitutes for some time unless there continues to be unequal distribution among the nations of the world because of war and political shortsightedness. Science must go forward, regardless of immediate practical applications, accumulating a reserve stock of knowledge that can be used in any emergency or to supply an entirely urban-industrial mankind of perhaps 10 to 15 or more billion in another century or so.

SUGGESTED READINGS

Adams, Walter. *The Structure of American Industry.* New York: Macmillan, 1954. Pp. 199–235.

Alderfer, E. B., and Michl, H. E. *Economics of American Industry.* New York: McGraw-Hill, 1957. Pp. 239–58.

Carlson, Albert S. (ed.). *Economic Geography of Industrial Materials.* New York: Reinhold, 1956. Pp. 222–53, 392–402.

Oxford University Press. *Oxford Economic Atlas of the World.* London: Oxford University Press, 1965. Pp. 84–85, 94–95.

Van Royen, William, and Bowles, Oliver (eds.). *Atlas of the World's Resources.* Vol. II. *The Mineral Resources of the World.* Englewood Cliffs, N.J.: Prentice-Hall, 1952. Pp. 141–61.

Zimmermann, Erich W. *World Resources and Industries.* New York: Harper & Row, 1951. Pp. 776–96.

16

Transportation, Trade, and Other Service Activities

The tertiary or contributory (indirectly productive) or services sector of the world's economy does not produce goods but accommodations of various sorts. About 28 per cent of the world's total labor force is now engaged in the services sector, and about 45 per cent of the value-added by world income is thereby derived.

	Per Cent of 1.3 Billion World Labor Force	Per Cent of $U.S. 1.45 Trillion World Income (value-added)
Distribution services	12	20
Transportation and communications	4	6
Trade and commerce (wholesale, retail, and others—domestic and foreign)	8	14
Governmental, professional, and personal services	16½	25
Governmental (public security, public welfare, and other branches—local, provincial, and national)	8½	13
Other services (private professional and technical, clerical, and personal services not previously included)	8	12
World services sector	28½	45

As the graphs in earlier chapters showed, the services sectors of the most advanced regions tend to have about half of their total labor force and total income involved therein, or as much of their economic efforts as the directly productive primary and secondary sectors together. The high-income realm accounts for over four-fifths of the world's services and of each major subsector.

While it is useful for certain purposes to isolate artificially economic activities into primary, secondary, and tertiary, in practice it is necessary to consider economic-activity complexes in which all three are interdependent. This has been done in earlier chapters, so following are certain facets of services that are best analyzed in isolation.

TRANSPORTATION AND COMMUNICATIONS

The development of transportation and communications not only adds to national income by its own services, but—far more important than this—it makes an indirect contribution to the national income and general economic development through the expansion of almost all sectors of the economy.

Improvement of accessibility contributes to economic development in a number of important ways. First, it enlarges the market and thereby stimulates economic specialization.

TABLE 16–1

World: Value-added * by Services Production, by Great-Region and Economic-Type of Society, 1962–1964 Average-Annual
(in billions of U.S. dollars)

	Total Services (U.S. $ billion = 100.0 per cent)	Transportation and Communications Services	Trade and Commerce Services	Professional and Personal Services	Governmental (Civil and Defense) Services
North America	278	12%	36%	30%	22%
Western Europe	143	16	28	26	30
Eastern Europe (including the U.S.S.R.)	108	11	24	20	45
Oceania	8	19	26	25	30
Latin America	31	13	32	32	23
Sub-Saharan Africa	12	21	30	33	16
Middle East (including North Africa)	14	14	32	29	25
Non-Communist Far East	39	15	33	26	26
Communist Far East	16	12	25	16	47
World	649	14	31	27	28
High-income countries	537	13	31	27	29
Low-income countries	112	15	31	27	27
	(per cent of U.S. $649 billion)	(per cent of U.S. $88 billion)	(per cent of U.S. $203 billion)	(per cent of U.S. $173 billion)	(per cent of U.S. $185 billion)
North America	42.8	40.0	49.2	48.0	32.4
Western Europe	22.0	26.1	19.7	21.4	23.3
Eastern Europe (including the U.S.S.R.)	16.7	13.6	12.8	11.6	27.0
Oceania	1.3	1.7	1.0	1.2	1.4
Latin America	4.8	4.6	5.0	5.8	3.7
Sub-Saharan Africa	1.7	2.8	1.7	2.3	1.0
Middle East (including North Africa)	2.2	2.2	2.2	2.3	1.8
Non-Communist Far East	6.0	6.8	6.4	5.8	5.4
Communist Far East	2.5	2.2	2.0	1.5	4.0
World	100.0	100.0	100.0	100.0	100.0
High-income countries	82.7	81.2	82.8	82.3	83.9
Low-income countries	17.3	18.8	17.2	17.7	16.1

SOURCE: Mainly adapted from United Nations data, with unofficial sources used in compiling Communist (Eastern Europe including the U.S.S.R. and Communist Far East) data.

* "Value-added" equals gross value minus purchased factors of production, with elimination of internal double-counting. The services sector is especially difficult to evaluate, since so many subsectors (government, exploitive landlords and money lenders, etc.) are able to set monopoly prices that may have little relevance to reasonable costs of such "service."

With the availability of cheap, speedy, and far-reaching transportation and communications, farms or industries formerly distributing to relatively scattered and nearby markets find that they can now service a larger market area just as well by forming larger and more efficient production units. Increased political unification, increased urbanization, the development of a more sophisticated culture and more diversified consumption, and many other marketing changes are also permissive to enlarged scale of production and to increased specialization.

Second, greater accessibility helps increase the supply of various factors of production (e.g., supplies of materials and labor) by permitting their mobilization from larger areas without excessive increase in the cost of shipment. Industries collecting energy and other raw materials from nearby sources now find it possible to obtain them from a larger supply area without substantially increased shipment costs. Vastly changed value of land, more equalized prices of materials, and other changes permit the improved location of agriculture and industry on sites that minimize combined production and distribution costs. Cheaper communication permits great mobility of labor, management, and capital as contrasted with previous accessibility patterns.

Third, improvements in the geography of circulation help by leading to the establishment or expansion of related economic activities (i.e., by providing external economies). Communities or regions so connected and integrated become less self-sufficient and more productive, and interregional trade grows on the basis of specialization according to comparative advantage. Economies are realized by increasing the input of purchased factors (goods and services) from outside suppliers wherever they are cheaper or superior to in-plant supplies.

For most countries in the early stages of development, the value of freight and passenger transportation increases at a much higher rate than increases in income (often three or four times faster). In developed societies, the subsector ceases to be a growth activity and expands a bit slower than total income, although areas like road transport and aviation may still grow at rates faster than national income.

Transportation Availability

Users of transportation and similar services generally compare competing forms in terms of availability, cost, and quality of service. Under the category of availability are considerations such as (1) nature of route, (2) traffic density, (3) length of haul, (4) weight of consignment, and (5) loadability.

Nature of route. Some routes are direct, that is, between places on main trunk lines (railway, road, waterway), while others are indirect or cross-country between places not connected by any main routes. The cost and quality positions of railways are likely to be favorable on their trunk lines between major metropolitan areas, or in private-siding to private-siding operations—that is, where consignments are carried direct from an agricultural collection point, mine, or factory to their ultimate destination without transshipment. However, railways are at a considerable disadvantage for cross-country routes where freight cars need to be shunted through several marshaling yards.[1] The operation of pickup trains collecting freight cars loaded at a number of small separate stations is also very costly. The same advantages and disadvantages apply to large deep-sea ships, large airliners, and large-diameter pipelines.

Road vehicles are favored on cross-country routes, mainly because the total length of roads (over 12 million miles in the world, of which about a third is hard surfaced and open the year round) is much greater than that of railroads (about 1 million miles in the world), and increasing more rapidly. This greater mileage, plus the greater flexibility in size of vehicles used, means that road vehicles are likely to have a relative advantage in handling cross-country traffic because they make fewer transshipments. In some delta areas (e.g., Low

---

[1] "Piggyback" movement—the hauling of truck trailers on railway flatcars—is one way of reducing this handicap. Now under 5 per cent of U.S. intercity rail ton-miles, it may be 20 per cent by 1970 if present trends continue.

WORLD: VALUE-ADDED BY SERVICES, BY GREAT-REGION AND ECONOMIC-TYPE OF SOCIETY, 1962-1964 AVERAGE-ANNUAL (U.S. $ Billion)

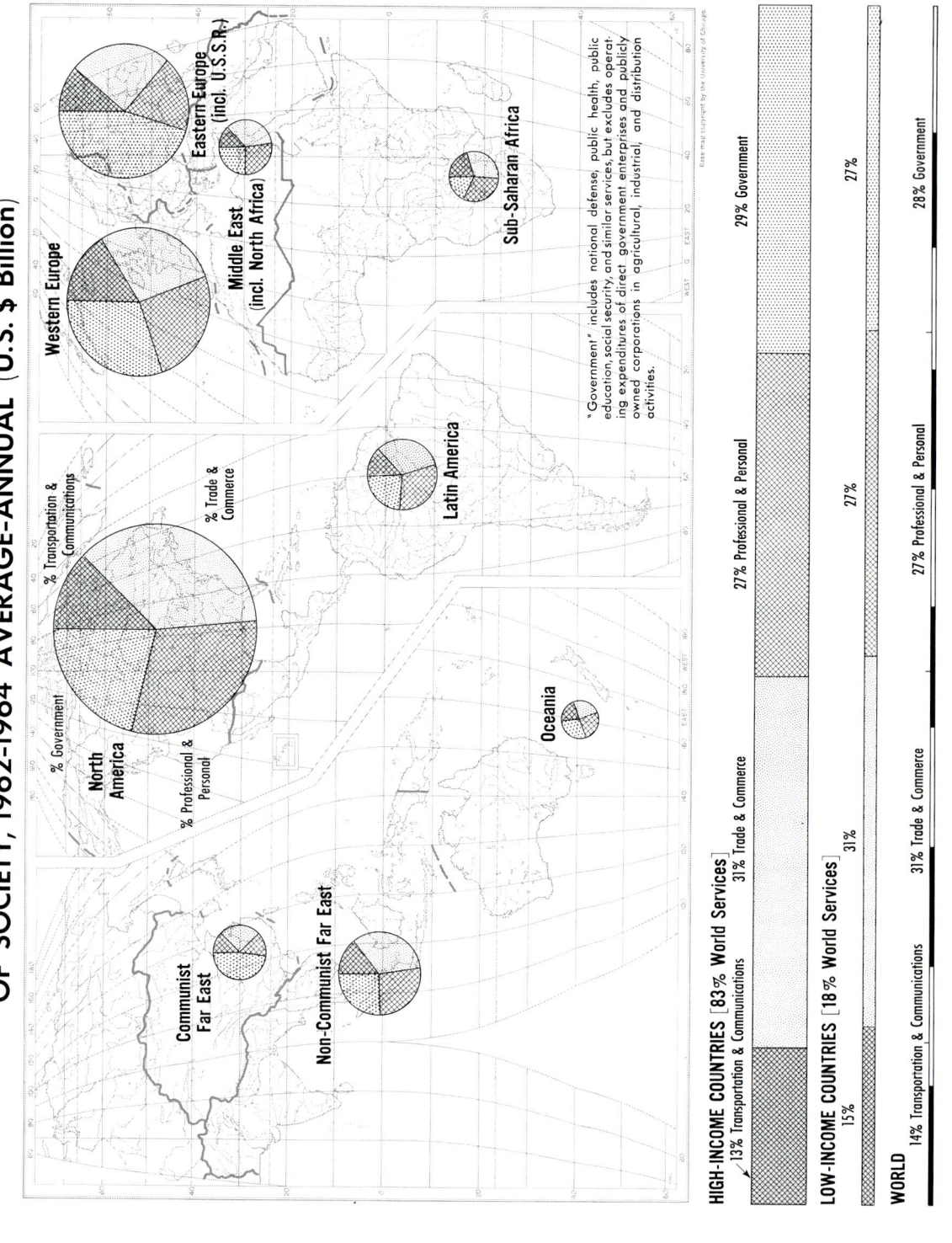

WORLD: GREAT-REGION AND ECONOMIC-TYPE OF SOCIETY SHARES OF WORLD TOTAL SERVICES, TRANSPORT, COMMERCE, PROFESSIONAL-PERSONAL SERVICES, AND GOVERNMENT SERVICES OUTPUT, BY VALUE-ADDED, 1962-1964 AVERAGE-ANNUAL

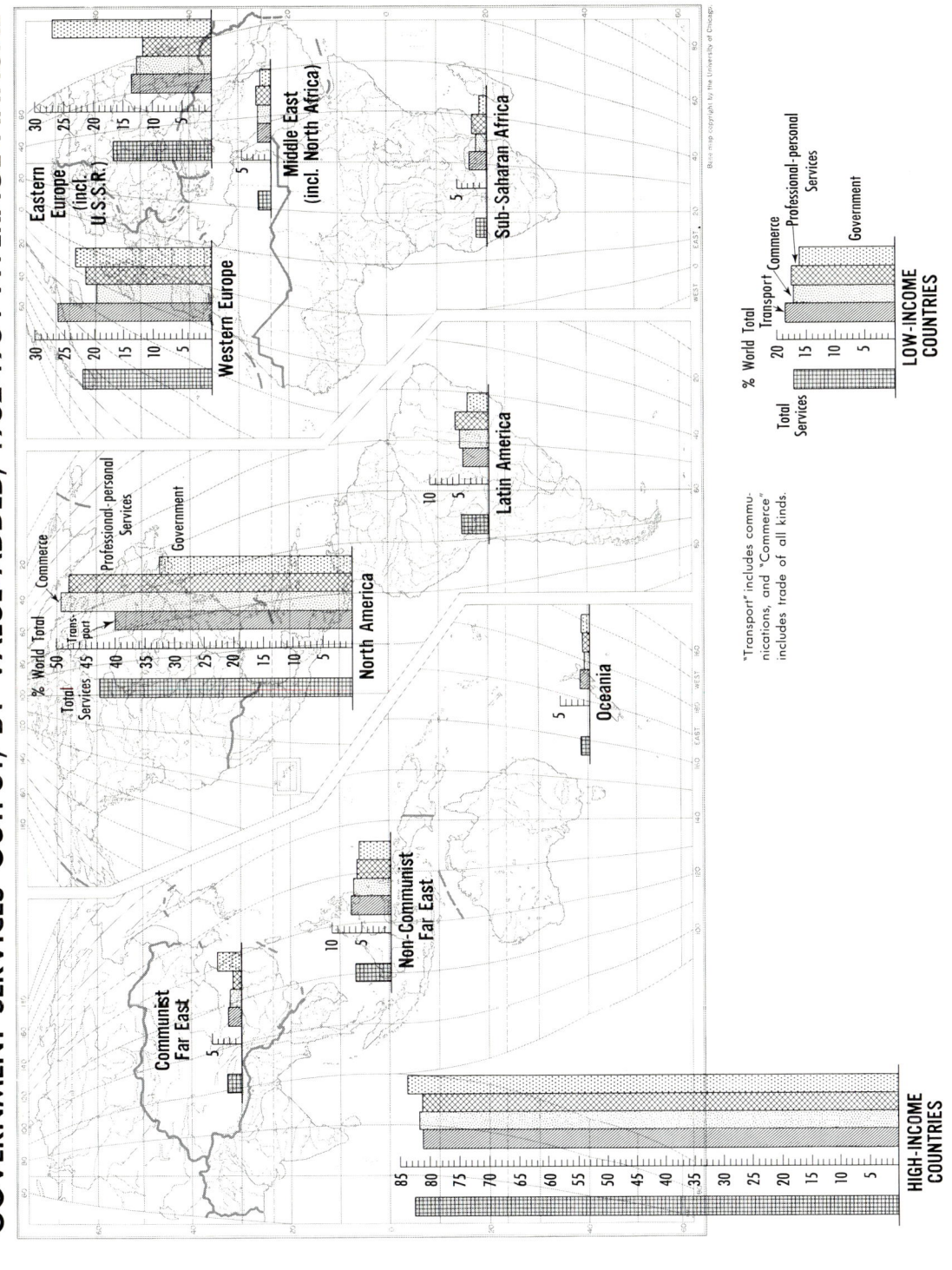

"Transport" includes communications, and "Commerce" includes trade of all kinds.

Courtesy of Pennsylvania Railroad Co.

Eastbound and westbound piggyback trains passing on Horseshoe Curve, west of Altoona, Pennsylvania. The tremendous growth of piggyback freight has resulted in expanded operation of solid trains for this business, as this picture illustrates, although some still moves in regular mixed freight trains to various points. Piggybacking is just one phase of the containerization revolution sweeping the package goods movement, whether on land, sea, or in the air.

Countries, East Pakistan) that have a dense network of waterways, the best carrier for cross-country traffic may be water vehicles; but in most hinterland areas, the roads have the advantage of greater availability. The more rapid expansion of the road network is also important; across the United States, some 25,000 communities not being served by any other transport system are entirely dependent upon highway transport (four out of five new plants located in the United States since World War II have been situated in out-of-town areas).

A pipeline is usually a one-way thoroughfare that operates around the clock, every day of the year, and almost always at peak capacity. It can get into, and out of, places that stop most other conveyances. The maximum grade (incline) on freight-carrying railways is 3 per cent; on highways, usually the maximum inclines are 6 per cent (occasionally 12 per cent); but for a pipeline, a 45 per cent grade is commonplace and 70 per cent is not considered startling.

Sometimes availability problems arise because of an embarrassing wealth of competing networks. The United States has provided itself with four practically complete systems—rail, road, pipeline, air—plus impressive sets of inland waterways and electricity-transmission grids. Almost any one of the basic systems is capable of doing far more than it usually is doing, but no two are capable of doing it all. The area of overlap is so great that somebody is usually getting hurt in the competitive scuffle. Problems arise because of the continued existence of marginal lines (e.g., some 30 per cent of the U.S. trackage handles only 2 per cent of the rail traffic, but political and social considerations slow down the consent of regulatory commissions to drastic pruning).

Sometimes availability problems arise because

of lack of complete networks. Africa has only fragments of a rail network and, unlike parts of Latin America and the Far East, lacks continuously navigable waterways to supplement the rail routes. On account of the varying gauges, the Australian rail network is not nearly as effective as a map suggests; and, again, there are no perennially navigable waterways to supplement the rails.

So far, deep-sea ships have been the most insulated from severe competition. The bulk traffic across the wide oceans has been unaffected, although passenger traffic has mainly passed to the airliner. Coastwise package-goods traffic and considerable coastwise bulk traffic have been lost to competing overland transport forms. About three-fifths of the world's ton-miles of commercial intercity freight movement is still by deep-sea ship (the average ton of 1.5 billion tons moved at sea travels some 4,000 miles), which is likely to remain pre-eminent in intercontinental bulk-traffic movements.

Traffic density. The size of the traffic flow, in both directions, between two places, is one of the main influences determining the availability, cost, and quality of service. The railways are less suited for routes with light traffic where it is impossible to achieve a good over-all load factor, perhaps the main reason why underdeveloped societies now modernizing often place earliest reliance upon road and air development.

Although a good load factor is desirable for road vehicles, road costs will not be as high as rail costs on routes with a sparse traffic flow. The possibility of using smaller and more cheaply

The SS "United States" arriving at its New York City pier. Liners now carry less than half of all passengers crossing the wide oceans, but still carry over 95 per cent of the high-value, low-bulk package goods moved intercontinentally. The bulk carriers have had little competition from land transport, except in coastal waters. United States flag carriers carry only 8.5 per cent of U.S. foreign trade (over 300 million by tonnage): liners, 4.4 per cent; tramps, 2.3 per cent; tankers, 1.8 per cent.

Courtesy of United States Lines Co.

operated road vehicles gives road operation a flexibility not possessed by the railways. The relatively short turnabout time of a truck reduces storage requirements, and the plant installations needed for loading and unloading are less costly than for other means of transportation. Moreover, trucks frequently enable the shipper to bypass the warehouse and deliver directly to the retailer or large consumer, thus avoiding double handling of a product. This prime advantage of motor-truck transportation in having flexibility as to where it can go and the ability to adapt itself to changes in source of supply and in markets makes for increasing dominance in short- and medium-distance package-goods movement. However, trucking's costs make it notoriously difficult to develop a solid two-way flow of traffic on costly long hauls.

Barges are inflexible, except in comparison with pipelines, as their movements to shift within the confines of navigable water limits to meet changes in markets and in sources of supply are quite restricted. Their use in some places at certain times of the year may be limited by the freezing over of rivers and waterways. Also, the depth and breadth of channels and locks of some inland waterways may prevent the use of some of the larger, more efficient barges.

Foremost among the disadvantages of pipelines is their inflexibility. A pipeline is a relatively permanent installation, which cannot be moved readily to meet changes in markets or in sources of supply. They are costly to construct, involving heavy fixed investments; and their economical operation requires a sustained, near-capacity volume of oil moving through the lines. Furthermore, pipelines are not practical for the transportation of very heavy, viscous oils and greases and, of course, cannot carry packaged oil products.

Insofar as competition exists between tankers and pipelines, the former have an advantage in their greater degree of flexibility. If the market falls off in one area, tankers can be moved to other trade routes, whereas the pipeline is committed to its existing source of supply and market. If traffic is large enough to justify supertankers, one-way traffic may still be highly efficient. The more than 4,000 oceangoing oil tankers, somewhere between production and consumption, move over three-fifths of all oil used. Every day some 25 million tons of petroleum and its products are traveling at sea, enough for about ten days' world consumption. About two-fifths of the absolute movement is international, with the rest being national coastwise traffic. Tankers constitute one-third of the 150 million tons of oceanic carriers.

Length of haul. Railways have a relative advantage over the roads for the longer hauls. This is because the costs of a rail haul tend to taper with increasing distance. As the fixed costs per shipment—more important for railways than for roads—are spread over a longer distance, the cost per ton-mile will fall. Just when a haul becomes sufficiently long distance for the railway advantage depends upon a number of other variables, but in most of the world, it probably begins for hauls of about 100 miles (although this may be extended under special circumstances, as in the United States, to several times that distance). The nature of future transport demand is also clearly influenced by the size of the country (e.g., Ceylon's low average length of haul favors new roads rather than more railways, while the opposite tendency is found in the U.S.S.R. with its long hauls).

Road vehicles' costs do not show the marked tapering off with increasing distance that is found on the railways. The overhead costs borne by the roads are relatively much less important. Also, there is an increase of costs for road transport beyond certain mileages (e.g., when the vehicle cannot get back to its home base in the same day, resulting in poor vehicle utilization and increased labor costs when the driver must be maintained overnight away from home). The maximum outward and return journey that can be performed in one day will vary with permitted driving hours, loading and unloading time, and the average speed obtainable, but is not likely to exceed 200 miles in most parts of the world, and often is much less. The relative advantage of trucks is particularly marked for shorter hauls (e.g., around metropolitan areas).

Inland waterways craft and coasting vessels

are in an intermediate position between railways and roads. Overhead costs will be less important than on railways, but on the other hand, the returning-to-base problem of trucks is not normally encountered. In competition with railways, craft and small vessels may be expected to carry consignments for the shorter hauls. Small inland waterway craft may be under no disadvantage, compared with roads, for very short hauls (such as local transport within an urban region covered with a network of waterways) where no transshipment is required.

Since the power plant of a plane cannot be detached during loading and unloading, like the engine of a train or the truck to which trailers are attached, cargo planes can fly only a short time daily (although increasing use of detachable containers may increase flying time). Loss of time in loading, pickup, and delivery outweighs the advantage of air cargo transport except on long hauls (e.g., in the United States, air cargo hauls are, on the average, three times longer than rail shipments of less-than-carload lots and more than five times as long as highway cargo consignments).

The most spectacular long hauls are on or across the oceans. The world average round trip of supertankers and ore-carriers is about 10,000 miles. The average round trip of a U.S. oil tanker, even though most are engaged in coastal traffic, is still some 5,000 miles. The largest jet airliners can also make one-stop oceanic hops, which is reflected in their carrying of some three-quarters of all passenger traffic on the northern routes across the Atlantic and Pacific Oceans.

Weight of consignment. The chief advantage of rail transport is for very heavy overland consignments. In much of the world, most motortrucks carry only 5 tons or so, and even on surfaced, public roads 15 to 25 tons is average, while a trainload of mineral traffic often amounts to 1,000 tons and ore trains of 10,000 tons or more are common. Mixed package goods traffic is much less, often in the 100- to 500-ton range (often part of a passenger train movement).

The railways will therefore have a considerable relative advantage, particularly over road transport, for bulk primary (agricultural, timber, crude mineral) consignments weighing hundreds or thousands of tons. The cost per ton carried on a train, river-tow, or ship will continue to decline with increasing weight of the load, as fuel, labor, and terminal costs are spread over a greater tonnage. The cost of adding extra freight cars, barges, and compartmented ship space, up to the pulling capacity, will obviously be very small.

On the other hand, railways are at a relative disadvantage in carrying small consignments of one or several tons, or less, which cannot easily (except at high cost) be amalgamated in the normal conditions of railway operation and which will mean that many freight cars with a capacity of 15 to 40 tons will be filled with loads of only several tons. An important weight distinction for the railways is between carload and less-than-carload consignments, with most railway systems losing on their less-than-carload traffic.

The optimum weight of consignment by road (the load that will just fill a truck) will vary with the carrying capacity of the trucks used but will of course be very much smaller than a trainload. Road vehicles will be at a relative advantage for consignments in the several hundred pounds to several tons range, as these can be amalgamated on a truck and give a good load factor. For example, where the demand is for the conveyance of agricultural products in relatively small consignments, mainly from villages to nearby towns, the relative advantages will be mostly in favor of roads (e.g., Turkish and Iranian wheat) and natural waterways where they exist (e.g., Thai rice). The advantages of composite loading usually keep road costs below rail costs even for hauls of over 200 miles.

The roads will also have an important relative advantage over rail for consignments in the 1- to 5-ton weight range, which must be transshipped when sent by rail (being collected and delivered by road vehicles) but which can be collected, carried on the trunk run, and delivered all by the same road vehicle without any transshipment at all. This particular advantage does not exist for smaller consignments weighing less than 1 ton. Parcels (several to several

Courtesy of Pennsylvania Railroad Co.

A 101-car unitized coal train, handling more than 7,000 tons of coal, powered with four 1,800-horsepower diesel units, enroute to a large eastern electric generating station. Such shuttle operations, although restricted to large mines and large users who can load or unload within the short time limit, offer the cheapest wheeled movement (often half to two-thirds the cost of individual carloads). Some authorities predict that, in a decade or two, nuclear-powered locomotives may pull strings of 100-to-150-ton freight cars at 75 to 100 miles per hour.

hundred pounds) and small (up to 1 ton) consignments must normally be transshipped from collection to trunk vehicles (and into delivery vehicles) on road as well as on rail. The cost of amalgamating the small parcels is not necessarily higher on the railways than on the roads. Where road vehicles carrying loads of 15 tons or more are in use, they will usually have lower costs for a full load of 15 tons than the railways.

The range of carrying capacities of inland waterway craft is wider than that of either road vehicle or trains. While there are numerous very small boats and barges, some individual craft may carry up to a thousand tons and integrated-tows can have a capacity of 3,000 to 20,000 or more tons. The very considerable capacity of the larger craft gives them an important advantage in carrying very large tonnage of bulk consignments that may be as great as that of the railways. Inland waterways are still used largely for shipment of bulk commodities, and some non-navigable rivers are used to float timber. Moreover, waterways offer facilities for storage (e.g., coal or grain in barges, especially when rivers are frozen over).

Coastwise traffic and oceanic traffic consist mostly of bulky and heavy commodities (e.g., coal, oil, clay, lumber, steel), which are usually moved in ships especially adapted to them. A substantial proportion is carried by industrial firms in their own carriers. The carrying capacity of deep-sea shipping is limited mainly by port facilities and depth of anchorage. The 45 per cent of all tonnage moved by ship that is oil mainly moves in tankers of 10,000 to 130,000 tons capacity.

Air freight generally consists mostly of articles of high value, small size, and low weight. The few exceptions are mostly of a military or other necessity, where cost is of little importance, and even such shipments are in truck-size consignments for the most part.

Loadability. The loadability of a consignment is measured by the relation of its weight to its bulk. The carrying capacity of both road vehicles and railway freight cars can be measured either as the maximum possible axle load or as the weight of the maximum volume of traffic of standard loadability that they can carry. Traffic of standard loadability may be defined as occupying 100 cubic feet per ton. If consignments are heavier than this, in relation to bulk, then a 100 per cent load factor is more likely to be obtained, although unfilled cubic capacity may remain. Consignments of less-than-average loadability will give a less than 100 per cent load factor, because the freight car or road vehicle will be filled with a load lighter than either axle load capacity or a full load of traffic of standard loadability.

There are two important ways in which load-

The "Queen Elizabeth," longest luxury liner on the high seas, is shorter than the largest integrated tows on America's inland waterways, as shown in this composite photograph. This particular tow of eight tank barges carries more petroleum than the average tanker in the coastal and transoceanic trades. The larger tows on the Ohio and Mississippi rivers often have twenty or more barges, carrying 20,000 to 25,000 tons of coal or other merchandise. Even relatively small tows on smaller waterways carry cargo equivalent to two to ten average railroad freight trains. Special tows barge automobiles, motor trucks, and military vehicles on the Ohio, Tennessee, and Mississippi rivers. This American innovation is now spreading overseas, as it represents a labor-saving, lower-cost substitute for the older methods of barging.

Courtesy of The American Waterways Operators, Inc.

ability may affect a comparison of road and rail costs. First, it is very important to remember that, for traffic of standard loadability or less, railways have a built-in disadvantage in that they will normally achieve much poorer load factors than road vehicles. Comparisons of road and rail costs based on capacity ton-mile figures can therefore be very misleading. Second, road vehicles have a relative advantage for traffic of poor loadability in that they show more flexibility in the relationship of axle load to cubic capacity.[2] Smaller vehicles generally have a higher ratio of standard capacity tons to axle load capacity than larger ones. This means that traffic of poor loadability can be carried more cheaply in smaller vehicles with lower operating costs than in larger ones (e.g., a 6-ton consignment of 50 per cent loadability could be accommodated in two 4-ton capacity vehicles). Railways usually do not possess this flexibility.

To operate properly, a pipeline must be completely full all the time, from one end to the other. In a crude oil pipeline extending 1,000 miles, even a shipment of 100,000 barrels would occupy only a small portion of the pipeline's total length. So most crude oil and all refined petroleum products pipelines normally will have a number of different items in transit at one time, sometimes ten to twenty-five different products.

Barges are more economical for commodities needed in units of 500 to 1,000 tons, the usual capacity of a big barge.[3] Both barges and ships have some of the same difficulties in handling package-goods traffic as the railways do. Containerization may remedy some of the difficulty; on coastal craft and on big ocean ships, it has been found that craft can make two round trips with containers compared to one with conventional loading.

Transportation Cost

Transport by water is generally cheaper than by rail, chiefly because of two factors. One, little tractive power is required to move heavy loads slowly over water (e.g., one ordinary power unit can move more freight in a single row of barges than can be handled in several freight trains). Two, waterways are provided by nature or at public expense and are improved and maintained from public funds. Bulk movements by U.S. barge-tows average about 3 mills per ton-mile, or about a third of the average rail cost. Many rail movements of bulk goods move at lower rates because of a partial waterway link or the possibility of substituting waterway vehicles.

The supertankers and giant coal and ore carriers offer the cheapest freight movement of all, from a third of a mill to a few mills (0.03 cent to 0.2 and 0.3 cent) per ton-mile on trunk-line routes. The movement of package goods on liners is more expensive, partly because of the poor loadability and emphasis on speed, but even more because of port expenses. United States' liners often find over half of the cost of operating their ships goes to the handling of cargo (e.g., in New York, it costs $8 or $9 to handle Venezuela-bound cargo, whereas in European ports, costs range from $2 to $4 a ton). Containerization (packages and small consignments in 10- to 20-ton containers) has halved cargo-handling costs where it has been applied, by reducing time spent in port from a quarter to a half. The actual ocean movement of package goods usually costs about 1 to 5 cents per ton-mile on long hauls, but several times as much on shorter coastal hauls.

Most of the world's bulk traffic by railways moves at rates from 1 cent to 3 cents per ton-mile. The larger countries (United States, Soviet Union, India) tend to have lower rates than the smaller countries (Britain, Japan), because of the longer hauls and evening out of handling costs. The cheapest rates are those on minerals (5 to 7 mills per ton-mile), which are often

---

[2] United States railroads are partially countering this traditional handicap by emphasizing specialized rolling stock in their new equipment purchases, and by encouraging "piggyback" and other containerization movement.

[3] True of inland waterways' barges, but oceanic barges are much larger (e.g., the Eastern Seaboard coal run from Hampton Roads, Virginia, to New York includes four 11,000-ton former coastal colliers converted into 13,000-ton unmanned barges hauled by oceangoing tugs).

Courtesy of Chesapeake & Ohio Railway Co.

Airview of colliers loading at Newport News, Virginia, Pier 14. The cheapest movement of coal is by 20,000- to 60,000-ton colliers, which carry coal a third to a half of the way around the world for less than it costs at the pithead. Steam coal is under heavy pressure from residual fuel oil competition, but coking coal is indispensable to steel production and the pattern of world steel production would be significantly different without oceanic movement of West Virginian metallurgical coking coal.

subsidized (e.g., coal on Western European and Indian railways) or carried at near cost because of alternative transportation available to shippers (coal and ore in American Midwest).

Road vehicles vary widely in cost around the world, much more than rail rates. Traditional pack animal and wagon transportation costs around $1 to $2 per ton-mile. Early road motorization on unimproved roads drops the cost to about a quarter or half the previous rate, while motor haulage on improved roads drops to a tenth or less of the premodern road movement's cost. The United States' 6 cents or so per ton-mile is probably the world's lowest rate for a large chunk of varied traffic; European and Soviet rates are higher on the average. Large U.S. oil trucks have costs of 2 to 4 cents per ton-mile.

Air freight rates per ton-mile average between 20 to 25 cents in the United States, and about 35 cents or more elsewhere. Less than a tenth of 1 per cent of world freight traffic moves by this most expensive of all modern vehicles.[4]

[4] One reason for the high cost of air transport can be illustrated thus: 1 gallon of aviation fuel will move 10 to 15 ton-miles on the largest planes; 1 gallon of ship fuel oil costing about half as much, will move 250 ton-miles on an average-size freighter.

Quality of Transportation

Speed. Besides availability and cost of transport, users are concerned with the quality of transport, especially in such characteristics as speed, reliability, and level of damages. Speed, to transport consumers, measures the time between notification that a consignment is ready for collection and its delivery to the consignee. Generalizations about the speed of different transport services are somewhat dangerous, since there are so many variable factors.

Railways lose time on terminal and marshaling operations, but are quicker on trunk journeys when compared with road. This means that the longer the direct trunk haul, the more likely is rail to be quicker than road (e.g., piggyback and unit-trains average 70 miles per hour in the United States). Rail is likely to become the faster service for direct hauls of more than 250

Airview of a Pacific Intermountain Express terminal. Trucking is a rapid growth segment of transport economies, having almost become a part of the assembly line in manufacturing and a part of the inventory pipeline in distribution. Road vehicles are especially favored on shorter hauls, on cross-country routes, and on routes with sparse traffic having poor load factors. Package goods, especially in the 1- to 15-ton range, particularly those consignments needing urgent delivery, profit most from truck movement. Expensive in a crude ton-mile cost perspective, trucking is usually much cheaper in an indirect perspective in which its speed, reliability, and inventory-saving characteristics are also considered. Some authorities predict that, in ten to fifteen years, three-bottom 80-ton tractor-trailers will be in common highway use.

Courtesy of American Trucking Associations, Inc.

miles, though this figure may vary considerably in different areas.

A special advantage of road vehicles is their flexibility in timing. On the other hand, as railway operations demand adherence to fixed timetables, it is more difficult to carry a rush consignment at short notice or to wait for an important consignment that has been delayed. Because they carry smaller loads than freight cars, trucks offer more frequent schedules. They can depart immediately and lose less time waiting for the assemblage of freight. The speedier service permits faster turnover of stock and reduces the amount of capital tied up in inventories, which may, in certain circumstances, deteriorate or decrease in value if delayed.

Water transportation is slow and subject to weather uncertainties. Much freight therefore has been diverted to the railroads (which offer many auxiliary services in addition to the advantages of speed and established schedules). For example, New Orleans to Pittsburgh barge time is up to twenty-one days, while the rail run is four days.

Oil pipelines move products at some 3 or 4 miles per hour, so that many movements take a week or more (e.g., three weeks from Houston to New York; one week from Utah to Pasco, Washington). Somewhat faster movement requires expensive pumping under higher pressures.

The advantages of high-speed planes (nearly 600 miles per hour on big jets) are greatly affected by airport conditions. On short-haul flights (e.g., Boston–New York, New York–Washington, D.C.) and some medium-distance routes (e.g., New York–Cleveland), delays on runways and in over-the-airport traffic patterns wipe out the advantages of speed in the air.[5] As with trucks, there are indirect benefits from speed. Because of its speed as a long-range conveyor belt, the airplane does not demand a long lead time between the placing and fulfillment of an order, so inventories can be reduced, cutting warehousing costs. Because of speed, too, changes in the design of the product, either because of buyer demands or development of better specifications, can be effected and introduced to the market more readily.

Reliability. Reliability depends mainly upon the managerial efficiency of a particular transport organization, and it is not possible to make any general comparisons between different services in this respect. Trucks—the road "tramps"—can provide many individual and specialized services, beyond the capacities of mass transportation facilities. Such services often involve small and light, but high-rated, freight that used to provide net income to railroads. A truck can accept an urgent shipment at any time and can change the route and schedule and adjust its services to the desires of the customer. A phone call brings the truck to the shipper's door, and in no time the loaded truck is on its way. A special train cannot be charted, but a special truck can be hired. If the shipment is not ready, the truck can be held, but the train cannot. This difference is of special importance when goods are for export; a hauler may be able to delay his departure if the goods are not ready and still reach the port before the ship leaves, while similar delay in shipment by rail may mean that both the train and the ship are missed. In the past generation, the truck has become almost a part of the assembly line in manufacturing and of the inventory "pipeline" in distribution; it carries raw materials to processing plants, finished parts to subassembly shops, assembled units to the main production plant, and the completed products to wholesalers, then to retailers and finally to the consumers.

Pipeline advantages include dependability, continuity of movement in all types of weather, small evaporation losses in handling oil, and less vulnerability in time of war.

The dependability of waterways and air vehicles depends, to a large extent, in what region and in what season they are operating. Winter conditions, especially, affect them adversely (e.g., intermittently frozen channels and ports, fogged-in airports).

---

[5] The new Japanese express train service between Tokyo and Osaka has cut deeply into air travel, by averaging around 100 miles per hour on the 320-mile run. Similar speedy rail passenger movement is afforded in Western Europe by the Rheingold Express and other elite trains (and will be afforded by the projected U.S. Eastern Seaboard fast-train).

Level of damages. Other things being equal, the level of damages will depend upon the nature of the journey and the number of transshipments required. Damage is most likely to happen during transshipment, and roads usually gain over railways here. Damage in transit is least likely to occur by inland water transport, which has a real advantage for carrying certain fragile commodities. Road transport is likely to be smoother than rail, except where road surfaces are very poor, or where individually braked freight cars are used on the railways. Ordinarily, less damage is done in shipment by truck than by rail, particularly when goods are fragile or are difficult to load and unload (e.g., large pieces of machinery). Yet packaging is simpler and less costly, so goods often can be sent unpacked or in cartons and light crates, while rail transport requires heavier and more elaborate packing. Truck service is a door-to-door service; and, in addition to saving time, this feature is a major reason why damage claims in the trucking service are low in comparison with other forms of transportation.

Lighter packaging may often suffice in air transport, and shipments are less frequently damaged. For perishables, there is less waste from spoilage, which otherwise may be as high as 20 or 30 per cent for slower land vehicles. Because shocks can be avoided, delicate precision instruments and fragile articles (e.g., electronic devices, photographic equipment, telescopes, watches, glassware) are increasingly air-freighted. Speed of delivery permits lower inventories and faster turnover, which lessens the risk of style and market changes, thereby releasing otherwise tied-up capital and cutting warehouse expenses.

Freight Traffic Summary

The appearance of motor vehicles and airplanes has challenged the railroads' hegemony in urban-industrial areas and raised questions about their merits in many underdeveloped areas. However, although the railroads no longer dominate land transport, they remain the backbone of the transportation system in advanced countries with highly developed transport competition. They carry freight in all weather, and in long-distance bulk-transport, their services have not been matched by any other means of transportation. A railway can normally be justified only if there is a basic flow of bulk commodities and a minimum traffic flow (e.g., minimum flow of 600 to 1,000 tons per day, at least 70 per cent by weight being bulk traffic sent out in consignments of 20 tons or more). The construction of rail networks as intensive as those developed in Western Europe and northeast United States in the nineteenth century seems unjustified under present-day conditions. Railroads will continue to be favored in handling bulk-goods movement in continental areas, especially in handling heavy traffic between main centers having good load factors and avoiding intermediate marshaling. They will continue to offer their best service in regular traffic flows from private siding to private siding (i.e., where road-to-rail transshipments are avoided). The rail advantage be-

TABLE 16–2

World: Commercial Freight Traffic, 1962–1964 Average-Annual

Intercity Vehicle Movements [1]	Per Cent of 4,150 Billion Ton-Miles of Overland Traffic	Per Cent of 10,000 Billion Ton-Miles of Land-Sea Traffic	Approximate Average Length of Haul (miles)
Railroads	62	26	250
Inland waterways	14	6	100
Pipelines	12	5	250
Roads [2]	12	5	150
Air	–	–	500
Overland	100		165
Oceans (deep-water coastal and oceanic shipping)		58	4,000
Total		100	400

SOURCE: Adapted from United Nations data, with unofficial sources used to close gaps.

[1] "Intercity Vehicle Movements" includes captive—as well as strictly commercial traffic.

[2] "Roads" includes premodern commercial (porters, pack animals, carts and wagons) road traffic, perhaps a quarter in sub-Saharan Africa, the Middle East, and the Far East, but mainly mechanical vehicles traffic.

Courtesy of Norfolk & Western Railway

The most important rationalization of rail movement in the past decade has involved dieselization, centralized electronic control of movement, and customized transportation vehicles. The thirty-six special cars now available compare with seven types a decade ago. There are special cars for various commodities, cushioned underframe cars for moving fragile shipments, and special equipment to save time and effort by facilitating more rapid loading and unloading. It is hoped that such improved service will maintain the railroad's 40 per cent of total intercity ton-miles of freight in the face of heavy competition.

comes marked in long-distance hauls (less than 50 miles usually not practical except in certain mining areas): after 100 miles or so in small countries or where road facilities are anemic, after 300 or 400 miles even in large countries where highway networks are superb. The best competitive position occurs in moving bulk consignments, beginning with shipments of 15 tons or more and becoming marked with shipments of several hundred or more tons.

Freight transportation across the oceans has not been challenged and no effective rival is in sight, so it is likely to grow as industrialization spreads and international trade expands. Inland waterways have lost some of their importance in countries well provided with other means of bulk transport, but they still account for a substantial part of all land freight traffic. More and more restriction of many natural waterways routes is likely as irrigation and other water withdrawals in drier areas increase, but some expansion will accompany wider acceptance of the multiple-purpose concept in water projects. Consignments that can complete the whole transit by water are especially favored, even if such routes have a poor over-all load factor; since the medium not only supports the weight of watercraft, but also is relatively frictionless, two-way traffic is less important than with most competing vehicles. Low-grade bulk cargo with a low price relative to weight predominates, since it is less concerned with speedy, reliable service. Large bulk consignments (from 100 to 2,500 or more tons) are favored, and fragile consignments are better handled than by competing bulk carriers. The great advantage of natural waterways is that there are no construction costs except perhaps some dredging. Where the main traffic flow is of bulk goods, this will be carried most economically where a waterway exists that connects the appropriate places and that can accommodate craft of a reasonable size. A canal is now most likely to be justified as a secondary and specialized means of transport for solid minerals, liquids, and agricultural bulk consignments. For collection, seasonal roads may be necessary to link agricultural producing areas with the waterway. Under such conditions, a parallel railway would be difficult to justify.

For the foreseeable future, highway transport has the brightest prospects of all means of overland transportation, especially in terms of a value context. In advanced countries, motor traffic is growing both by generating new traffic and by substituting for rail or water traffic. In underdeveloped countries, highway traffic will grow even more rapidly, as the market is growing at an extremely fast rate (as much as 20 per cent yearly in some instances); and with the gradual removal of facility and financial obstacles, rapid expansion can be taken for granted. Roads provide a flexible form of transport, capable of meeting a variety of traffic needs, such as small consignments of mixed traffic, traffic below the density required for railroads (or below standard loadability), and for consignments sent on short hauls, or requiring speedy or door-to-door delivery. The kind of traffic for which road transport is most suitable—consumer goods sent to a large number of destinations in small consignments—is likely to grow greatly in volume and importance with the development of a country's economy. The truck has also become almost a part of the assembly line in manufacturing. Truck hauling over a short distance is usually more convenient than shipment by rail and requires less handling. The truck picks up the product from the platform of the consignor and delivers it at the door of the consignee. Since the truck drivers usually load and unload, no extra expenditures for handling arise, which lessens the gap in total costs that exist in terms of crude ton-mile cost comparisons with rail. Road vehicles are especially favored on shorter hauls (50 or 100 miles in most areas), on cross-country routes, and on routes with sparse traffic having poor load factors. Package goods, especially in the 1- to 15-ton weight range, particularly those consignments needing urgent delivery, profit most from truck and bus movement. Consignments of poor loadability, those in which the ratio of space to weight varies greatly, are also best handled by road vehicles, since these vehicles are normally available in a greater variety of sizes than their

TABLE 16–3

World: Overland Commercial * Freight Movement, by Great-Region and Economic-Type of Society, 1962–1964 Average-Annual
(in billions of ton-miles intercity traffic)

	Billion Ton-Miles Intercity Traffic (= 100.0 per cent)	Rail	River-Canal [1]	Pipeline	Road [2]
North America	1,700	45%	15%	20%	20%
Western Europe	250	60	20	5	15
Eastern Europe (including the U.S.S.R.)	1,500	80	10	5	5
Oceania	15	85	–	–	15
Latin America	80	60	5	30	5
Sub-Saharan Africa	60	85	5	–	10
Middle East (including North Africa)	80	20	5	60	15
Non-Communist Far East	235	70	20	5	5
Communist Far East	215	75	20	–	5
World	4,135	62	13½	12½	12
High-income countries	3,355	60	13	13½	13½
Low-income countries	780	70	16	8	6

	(per cent of 4,135 billion ton-miles)	(per cent of 2,570 billion ton-miles)	(per cent of 555 billion ton-miles)	(per cent of 510 billion ton-miles)	(per cent of 500 billion ton-miles)
North America	41.1	29.8	45.9	66.5	68.1
Western Europe	6.0	5.8	9.0	2.4	7.5
Eastern Europe (including the U.S.S.R.)	36.3	46.7	27.0	14.7	15.0
Oceania	0.4	0.5	–	–	0.4
Latin America	1.9	1.9	0.7	4.7	0.8
Sub-Saharan Africa	1.5	2.0	0.5	–	1.2
Middle East (including North Africa)	1.9	0.6	0.7	9.4	2.6
Non-Communist Far East	5.7	6.4	8.5	2.3	2.3
Communist Far East	5.2	6.3	7.7	–	2.2
World	100.0	100.0	100.0	100.0	100.0
High-income countries	81.1	78.8	77.3	88.1	90.0
Low-income countries	18.9	21.2	22.7	11.9	10.0

SOURCE: Adapted from United Nations data as far as possible, with crude private estimates to close gaps in published information.

* "Commercial" includes captive subsidiaries of commercial enterprises.

[1] "River-Canal" includes barge and boat traffic on rivers, canals, and lakes, but does not include deep-sea ship movements, either coastwise or intercontinental.

[2] "Road" traffic is by motor vehicles, for the most part, but includes commercial premodern (pack animal, cart, porter) movements also (perhaps a third in sub-Saharan Africa, the Middle East, and the Far East).

WORLD: OVERLAND COMMERCIAL FREIGHT MOVEMENT, BY GREAT-REGION AND ECONOMIC-TYPE OF SOCIETY, 1962-1964 AVERAGE-ANNUAL
(Billion Ton-Miles Intercity Traffic)

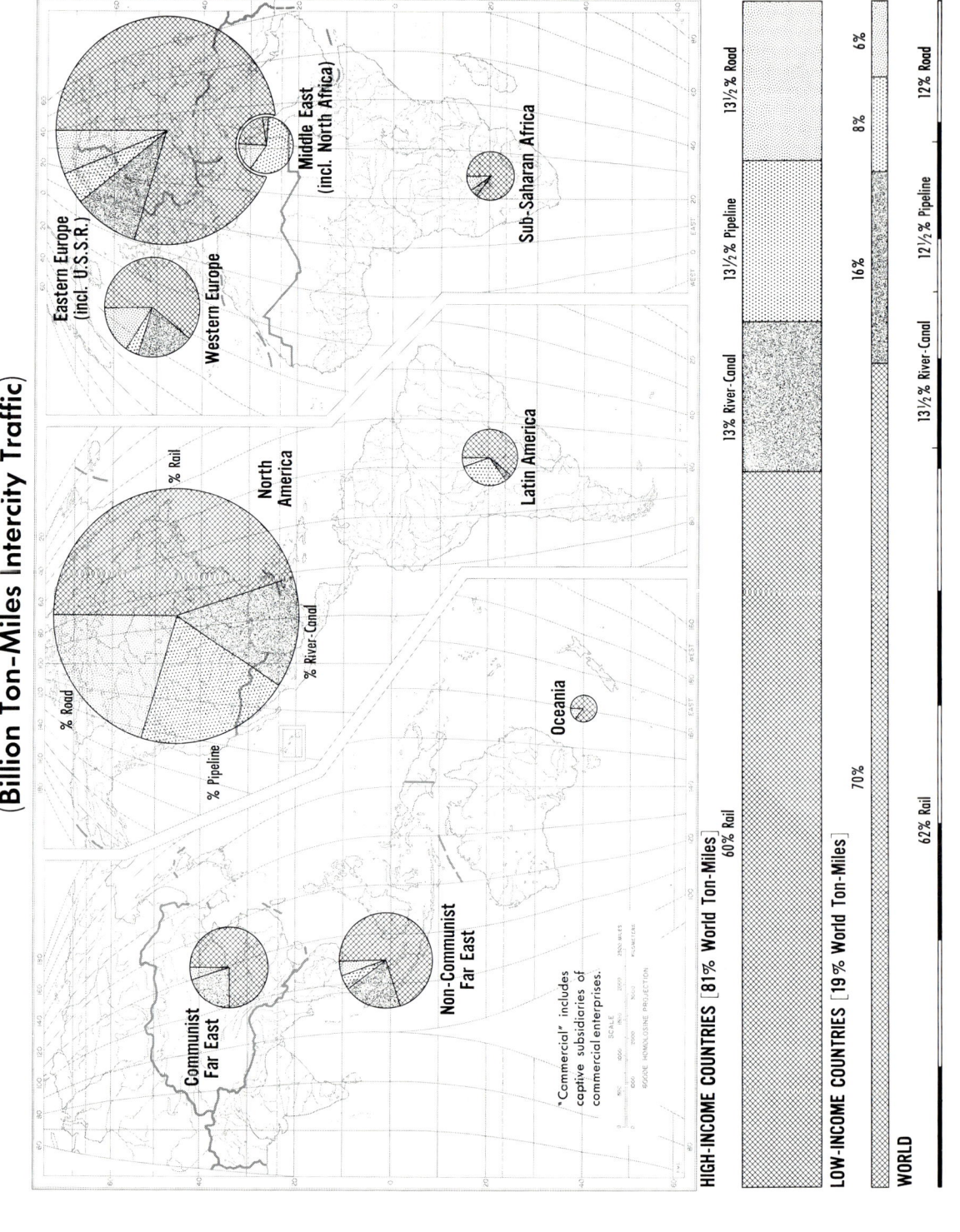

WORLD: GREAT-REGION AND ECONOMIC-TYPE OF SOCIETY SHARES OF WORLD OVERLAND COMMERCIAL FREIGHT MOVEMENT, 1962-1964 AVERAGE-ANNUAL

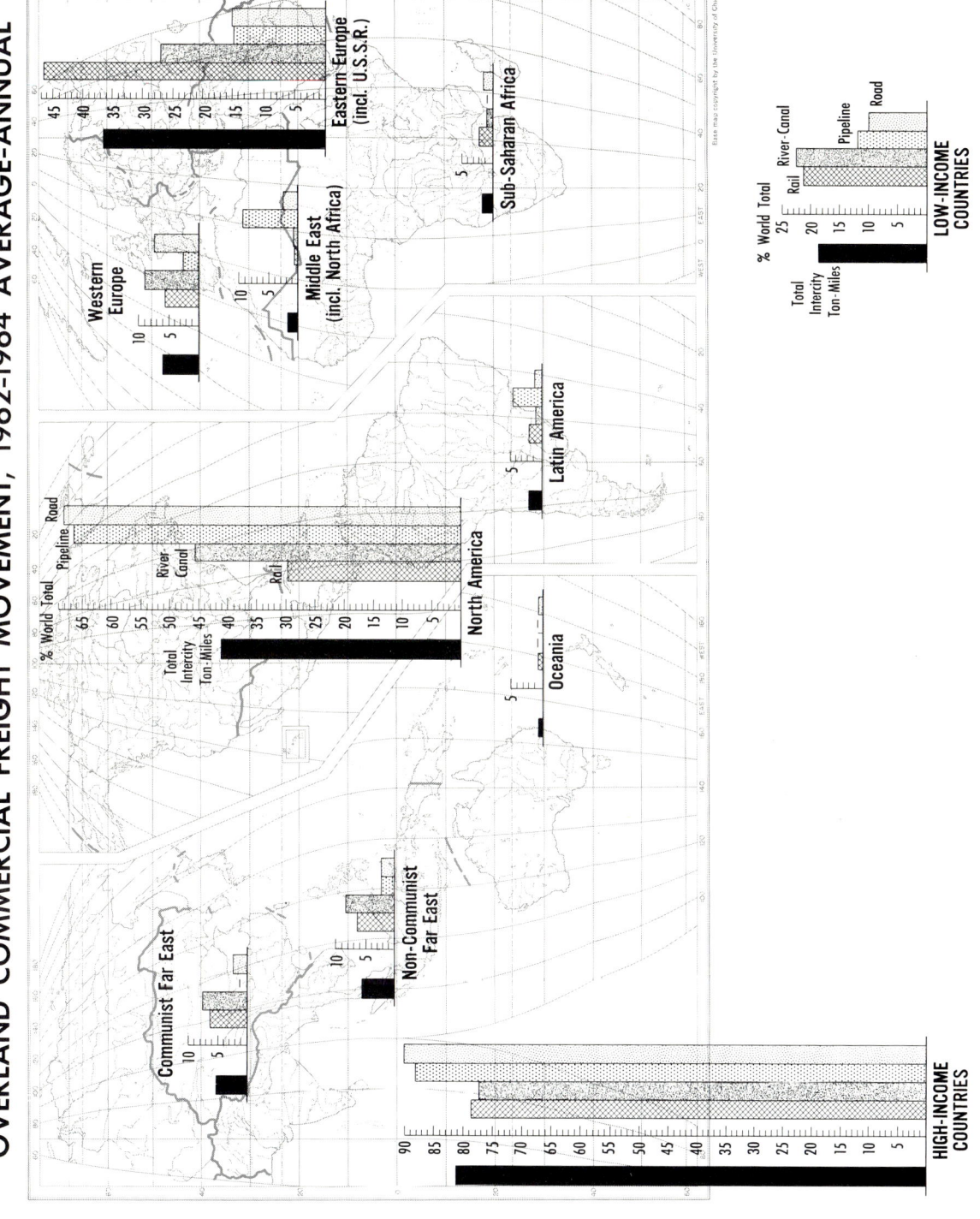

competitors. Demands for passenger transportation by car, bus, and motorcycle mean that it is almost inevitable that all countries must eventually develop a road network, whether or not commercial road transport seems justified economically as the best means of carrying the freight traffic of the area. Since roads generally remain free to all users, road freight competition greater than could be justified if it had to bear its full share of costs must be expected.

Pipelines are economical if three prerequisites are satisfied: a commodity (liquid, gas, slurry) that can be sent through a pipeline; an assured, immense source of supply of that commodity; and a long-term market for it. With those conditions satisfied, no cheaper form of overland transport exists. A barrel of gasoline moving from Tulsa to Chicago costs less than 60 cents by pipeline; it would cost almost three times as much by rail tank-car. On a short trip, the gap would be even wider (e.g., from Philadelphia to New York, a barrel of gasoline moves for less than a dime by pipeline, but over a dollar by rail). Only the largest tankers offer cheaper movement; even here, labor and other operating costs are relatively higher for tankers than for pipelines, so tankers are more vulnerable to the rising trend in labor costs. The Persian Gulf to the Eastern Seaboard supertankers around Africa haul a barrel of oil halfway around the world for about $1.25.

Passenger Traffic

Railroads offer the most dependable and among the cheapest overland mass transportation service. In many areas—especially the Communist bloc countries and in most of the underdeveloped realm—where cars and buses are few, railroads are the most important means of transport, both commuter and long distance. Commuter trains offer the cheapest mass local movement of urbanites (partly because they seldom are operated at a profit), while the long-distance trains offer comforts and luxuries seldom possible on buses.

Among the urban-industrial regions, there is a great difference in how people are moved. Passenger traffic on Western European railways far exceeds (by four times) the volume of rail travel in the United States, whereas rail freight traffic in Western Europe is only a third that of the United States. Passenger traffic on Soviet railways is also several times greater than the intercity United States rail traffic (now less than 3 per cent of intercity passenger-mile movement).

Private cars offer the most comfortable form of personal travel, but as mass media they are restricted to the wealthier societies, especially the United States, where nine-tenths of all passenger miles are now by car. They allow direct departure from home, without a rigid timetable and without need to pack as carefully and economically in terms of weight and space as when traveling commercially, and freedom to stop at any desired place. They are cheaper (when car is loaded) and allow cheaper family accommodations at overnight stops, as well as more privacy.

Bus traffic is increasing phenomenally in most parts of the world, especially in commuter movement and in feeder-route traffic to long-distance rail and air trunk lines. Fastest expansion is in areas with little rail competition, but buses are cutting into rail transport even in countries where the railroads are publicly owned and also are discouraging motor competition.

Broadly, the highways of the air have been superimposed upon the old long-distance routes of land transportation. Speed and frequency in schedule are the chief advantages that airlines offer in passenger traffic. Because of the remoteness of airports from old city cores, the time savings are mainly found on long trips. Passenger service will continue to be the mainstay of air operations in the foreseeable future. Helicopters and other air-taxi services will increasingly compete in commuter traffic, but the main substitution will be in medium- and long-distance passenger movement. On practically all oceanic routes, air service is increasing its share of total movement, even on routes where tourist-type water traffic predominates.

The high visibility of air traffic should not obscure its limited use, even in the United States, where nearly half of commercial intercity passenger miles of movement is now by air. Of all United States' trips of 200 miles or more, less than 10 per cent are made on commercial airlines, while over 75 per cent are made by car. Less than one-quarter of the American population has ever traveled on a domestic airline, and some 15 per cent of the flying public account for nearly two-thirds of all air trips. Only 2 per cent of mankind has been up in a plane.

Communications

From the standpoint of fundamental importance in modern civilization, the postal, telegraph, telephone, radio, and television services are comparable to the transport services. The effects may be seen in business organizations, in decentralized management and production, in the establishment of warehouse and factory branches, in long-distance control of sales forces, in close control over inventory changes, and in organization setups dependent for their workability upon fast interchange of orders and reports. Public security and welfare services are as intimately dependent upon such rapid and cheap communications as business. Increasingly, the telephone enters into all phases of private life, and its tie-in with television has begun.

The high-income, urban-industrial societies dominate world communications just as they do transport as may be seen in Table 16–4.

Most villages and small towns in the underdeveloped societies lack even the most elemental form of modern communication, the postal service. Many countries push radio contact first, because it does not require literacy. As the full complement of communications evolves, it has been the experience of developed societies that they require from ten to twenty times more workers in the field of communications than they did in a slightly commercialized underdeveloped context.

TRADE AND COMMERCE

Of mankind's annual income—nearly $1½ trillion computed according to exchange value, perhaps a third larger computed in terms of the United States' purchasing-power value—about a sixth is not traded, consisting of goods and services consumed by the producers or distributed without money or commercial exchange being involved. This subsistence sector (see the graphs on pages 556–57) is relatively small in the highly commercialized North Atlantic Basin re-

TABLE 16–4

World: Great-Region and Economic-Type of Society Shares of World Telephones, Radios, and Television Sets, 1962–1964 Average-Annual

	Telephone Instruments		Radio Sets		Television Sets	
	Per Cent of 158.0 Million	Per 100 Population	Per Cent of 525.0 Million	Per 100 Population	Per Cent of 136.5 Million	Per 100 Population
North America	54.7	41.0	38.1	95.0	45.4	30.0
Western Europe	25.3	13.0	21.9	36.5	27.1	12.0
Eastern Europe (including the U.S.S.R.)	6.3	3.0	19.0	28.5	10.3	4.0
Oceania	2.2	21.0	2.9	88.0	1.2	10.0
Latin America	3.5	2.5	7.6	18.0	3.7	2.0
Sub-Saharan Africa	1.0	0.7	2.0	5.0	0.1	0.1
Middle East (including North Africa)	1.0	1.0	2.0	7.0	0.4	0.4
Non-Communist Far East	5.7	0.9	5.5	3.0	11.7	1.7
Communist Far East	0.3	0.1	1.0	0.7	0.1	0.01
World	100.0	5.0	100.0	16.5	100.0	4.0
High-income countries	93.7	16.0	85.7	48.0	94.8	14.0
Low-income countries	6.3	0.4	14.3	3.3	5.2	0.3

SOURCE: Adapted from American Telephone and Telegraph Company and United States Information Agency data.

gions, but is over a third of the regional incomes of Africa and the Far East.

The total value of goods and services sold and bought annually in the least modernized societies is likely to be less than the national income. In highly developed societies, it greatly exceeds national income, by a factor of three or four times; retail sales of goods alone are about half the value of national income, intermediate (jobber-wholesaler to retail outlets) sales are even larger, and manufacturers' sales (to wholesale and retail outlets, to other factories, to overseas concerns, and directly to ultimate consumers) may total even larger than intermediate sales. Only a small proportion of such sales are, of course, value-added by trade, since the gross values include multiple counting.

Considering the world economy as a whole, about 8 per cent of the 1.3 billion labor force are engaged in trade and commerce, and some 14 per cent of the nearly $1½ trillion income is earned from organized trade. Underdeveloped countries tend to have from 5 to 10 per cent of their labor force in trade, and to earn from 10 to 15 per cent of their income from trade (both types of data are highly suspect, since much activity is by part-time labor whose efforts are censused as being more specialized than they really are). Urban-industrial societies tend to have from 10 to 20 per cent of their labor force in trade, and from 15 to 20 per cent of their income earned in that subsector (even in such societies, there is much underemployment and much doubt as to the real value accruing from the commercial subsector).

International trade is only 12 per cent of the world's income—double that figure if both exports and imports are added together—with North America and Eastern Europe (including the U.S.S.R.) being the great-regions whose economies are least involved, and the Latin American and sub-Saharan African great-regions being the economies most involved relative to their income. As modernization ("industrialization") diffuses universally, there is a tendency for international trade to decrease as a share of total income, with industrial and service trade becoming more domestic than earlier, although much of primary trade (especially agricultural inedible crude materials and much minerals trade) is somewhat more inclined to maintain the international specialization which featured it in an earlier stage of economic development.

Requisites for Trade

The basic conditions necessary in order that people may trade with one another include mutual accessibility, surpluses of goods and services, and some differences in the surpluses. As trade increases, there is a feedback relationship with these variables, since they must constantly change as the quantity, quality, and variety of commercialization changes.

In local-exchange or barter economies, contact means actual physical touch; habitat resistances often make for high-cost transport, and the economies have small trade radii. In money or exchange economies, haulage is for the most part highly mechanized, and an increasing share of trade is indirect—generally the potential trade is not realized less because of inadequacies in the facility patterns of transportation and communication than because of political and other cultural barriers to easy intercourse.

Surpluses of goods and services include many that are only local and temporary, but the backbone of trading relationships are the long-term surpluses. Some reflect favorable habitat, but many more reflect cultural superiority (e.g., facility, activity, institutional, and ideological advantages). However, in this unsettled age, numerous changes are occurring in patterns that were stable for generations, partly because real changes in technical and economic efficiency are accompanying worldwide industrialization and partly because heavy subsidization of exports and heavy controls over imports obscure real advantages and disadvantages.

Differences in commodities and services take many forms. Different varieties come easiest to mind, but different grades of the same general material or differences in the stage of processing or fabrication of a basic substance are increasingly even more important in initiating or increasing the flow of trade. Mutual accessibility and surpluses of goods and services are permissive factors more easily obtainable than whether the degree of difference is sufficient to cause really large trade flows.

Differences in commodities and services spring from causes such as habitat dissimilarities, cultural peculiarities, and economic-stage status. The natural resources patterns are little changing and will continue to remain a paramount reason for heavy trade flows, especially differences in mineral endowment and in latitudinal contrasts. The major change in the relative importance of this factor is likely to be the future role of synthetic materials substituting for natural materials. Cultural peculiarities never were as important in causing trade currents as their high visibility might indicate; if the market does increase, some other country than the original innovator usually evolves cheaper or more flexible production. Now, as since the inauguration of the Industrial Revolution, much trade reflects differences in the stage of economic development, but gradually the older division of labor between a few industrial regions in Western Europe and North America and a predominantly agrarian world elsewhere is changing as urban-industrialization continues on its path to universality. More often than not, newer regions have cheaper production than the former imports into their home market. Gradually, a new division of labor is evolving—both internationally and internally within countries—with new comparative advantages evolving because of different costs among modernized regions, which is due to cheaper skilled labor, cheaper capital, cheaper management, or cheaper governmental security and social capital. Even if all mankind should evolve mature urban-industrial economies (not likely), there will be the bases for even larger amounts of domestic and international trade than now occur, but perhaps even more vulnerable to political manipulation than now, since the technical possibilities of substitution will be greater than at present.

International Commercialization of Major Economic Sectors

World trade involves about 12 per cent by value of mankind's annual production of goods and services. Merchandise exports plus merchandise imports, plus the two-way traffic in services (including capital, gift-grant, and monetary-metals flows), involve a total movement equal to a quarter of the yearly $1.7+ trillion gross national product. Domestic trade is much larger; including multiple counting, the total flow of trade is probably well over double the value of total yearly income.

Agriculture. Primary production (agricultural crops, stock raising, forestry, and fishing-hunting-gathering) brings in yearly about 14 per cent of the world's gross national product (about 10 per cent of value-added by all economic activity).[6] About half of this production is not traded, while the other half is traded one or more times. In the low-income countries, most farmers are still self-sufficient in the sense that only a third or so of production is sold, mainly to pay rent, taxes, and interest, but also to finance some consumption expenditures from commercial channels. The crops and animal products that pass into town and urban markets tend to be the higher-quality foodstuffs and inedible raw materials. Even in highly commercial societies, there is heavy use of farm-produced supplies (factors of production and consumption goods-services); for example, feedstuffs that are only indirectly marketed (as meat, milk, and inedible raw materials). The most commercialized products are beverages, fibers, and natural rubber; about nine-tenths of world production is sold, with a majority crossing international frontiers. In the necessity- and comfort-type foods—starch crops, sugar, oils-fats, and edible animal products—a majority of world production is traded, but only a tenth or so internationally. In forestry and fishery products, over two-thirds of world production is sold, but domestic trade is responsible for all except a sixth or so. Gradually, as urban-industrialization eliminates marginal farmers and increases specialization among commercial farmers, agriculture is increasingly commercialized,

---

[6] The income of farmers and other primary workers is about half again as large, as it includes income from secondary and services activities (from part-time work, interest-profits-grants, and similar earnings).

although the fraction that moves in international trade is decreasing while domestic trade absorbs an increasing share of world production. At present, under 15 per cent of total primary production moves across international frontiers (some 13 per cent of edible products output, plus a third of the much smaller output of inedible products); such primary products are now only 16 per cent of world trade (two-thirds of the fraction before World War II). Both self-sufficiency policies (especially in regard to expensive edibles that can be produced nationally) and the increasing importance of synthetic substitutes for inedibles explain the downward tendency.

Industry. Secondary production (three-quarters manufacturing; one-quarter mining, energy utilities, and construction) is annually worth some $750 billion (gross national product valued—some $650 billion in terms of value-added), which is roughly 45 per cent of all income. This sector is relatively more commercialized than the agricultural one, with about nine-tenths of the annual production of all processed and fabricated goods being traded one or more times. Some 15 per cent of the secondary production moves across international production (such manufactured and other secondary goods make up 54 per cent of world trade), but the shares by subsectors vary widely. The products of construction and energy utilities are the least involved in world trade. Mineral production is almost completely commercialized, with nearly half involved in world trade (about a third of mineral fuel production by value—some three-fifths of other minerals), while under 5 per cent of the output of the construction and energy-utilities industries moves in world trade. Manufacturing is now about 95 per cent commercialized (artisan or handicraft output is still subsistent to a considerable extent), with over 15 per cent moving in world trade (about 20 per cent of machinery-vehicle output and of light-manufacturing output—half that fraction of other manufacturing such as chemicals). With increasing industrialization of mankind and increasing demand for consumer-durable goods, there are tendencies for both capital goods and consumer-durable goods output to increase more rapidly than other secondary subsectors and for their shares traded internationally also to increase.

Services. The tertiary sector that produces services annually brings in some $725 billion (gross national product valued—some $650 billion in terms of value-added), which is roughly 42 to 45 per cent of all income (depending upon which system of valuing output is used). Only about a seventh is non-commercial (an inadequate figure, because the services of most women at home are usually ignored in calculating income), and less than a tenth (7 per cent of gross national product value) crosses international frontiers, mainly transportation and commercial services involved in moving goods and services across international boundaries, although there is an increasing international trade in governmental and other professional services.[7] Distribution (transportation and commerce) is almost completely commercial, even in agrarian societies where much of it is generated on a part-time basis (e.g., the transport efforts of agriculturists and their work animals during the non-agricultural season, or their womenfolk's trading efforts on village and town market days). Governmental services are also almost completely commercialized in one sense of that term, since only a tiny part of local governmental services in underdeveloped societies is obtained through traditional redistribution systems not involving taxes. The same is true of professional and personal services; even in mainly subsistent areas, such services are mainly purchased, although in isolated areas relics of non-commercial distribution of certain services still survive. Since even in highly developed societies most services are purchased from local and regional sources, the continuing urban-industrialization of mankind is likely to see the vastly increased output of services consumed within urban regions and within

---

[7] Services moving in world trade now constitute 30 per cent of the total, nearly double the value of agricultural and other primary products crossing international frontiers.

TABLE 16–5

World: "Subsistence" (Producer) Consumption * and International Trade, Relative to Gross National Product, by Great-Region and Economic-Type of Society, 1962–1964 Average-Annual
(in billions of United States dollars)

	Gross National Product (U.S. $ billion = 100.0 per cent)	Regional Income Involved in "Subsistence" (Non-commercial) Sector	Regional Income Involved in International Trade [1]		
			Total	Merchandise	"Invisible" (Services)
North America	630	7%	6%	4.5%	1.5%
Western Europe	400	10	21	15.0	6.0
Eastern Europe (including the U.S.S.R.)	350	20	7	5.8	1.3
Oceania	20	25	20	17.5	2.5
Latin America	80	25	16	15.0	1.2
Sub-Saharan Africa	30	40	20	17.0	3.3
Middle East (including North Africa)	40	25	20	14.4	5.0
Non-Communist Far East	120	35	15	11.3	3.8
Communist Far East	50	40	8	4.0	4.0
World	1,720	15	12	8.8	2.8
High-income countries	1,390	11	12	8.8	3.1
Low-income countries	330	36	10	8.5	1.8

	(per cent of U.S. $1,720 billion)	(per cent of U.S. $269 billion)	(per cent of U.S. $200 billion)	(per cent of U.S. $151 billion)	(per cent of U.S. $49 billion)
North America	36.7	18.5	19.0	18.7	20.4
Western Europe	23.2	15.0	42.0	40.0	48.0
Eastern Europe (including the U.S.S.R.)	20.3	26.0	12.5	13.6	9.2
Oceania	1.2	1.9	2.0	2.3	1.0
Latin America	4.7	7.4	6.5	8.0	2.0
Sub-Saharan Africa	1.7	4.5	3.0	3.4	2.0
Middle East (including North Africa)	2.3	3.7	4.0	3.7	4.1
Non-Communist Far East	7.0	15.6	9.0	9.0	9.2
Communist Far East	2.9	7.4	2.0	1.0	4.1
World	100.0	100.0	100.0	100.0	100.0
High-income countries	81.0	55.8	83.0	81.5	87.8
Low-income countries	19.0	44.2	17.0	18.5	12.2

SOURCE: Adapted from United Nations data, for the most part, but with much other (unofficial) data used.

* "Subsistence" consumption (i.e., non-commercial redistribution) refers to the production of goods and services that is consumed by the producers themselves and their families and similar associates (the remainder of production is traded once or more through commercial channels, both domestic and foreign, before final consumption). Such estimates are necessarily crude, and may well be underestimated, since much self-production and self-consumption is not counted as income or counted at nominal value.

[1] The merchandise portion of international trade is the export of goods (f.o.b.), while the "invisible" portion is the average income from the sale of transportation, communications, and commercial (i.e., distribution) services, the sale of professional and personal services, the income from foreign investments, the income from private and official donations, and the sale of monetary metals. The degree of error in the movement of services and other "invisible" items can be high, for many reasons (short-run imbalances covered by credit, smuggling of monetary metals, and many others).

WORLD: "SUBSISTENCE" (Producer) CONSUMPTION AND INTERNATIONAL TRADE, RELATIVE TO GROSS NATIONAL PRODUCT, BY GREAT-REGION AND ECONOMIC-TYPE OF SOCIETY, 1962-1964 AVERAGE-ANNUAL (U.S. $ Billion)

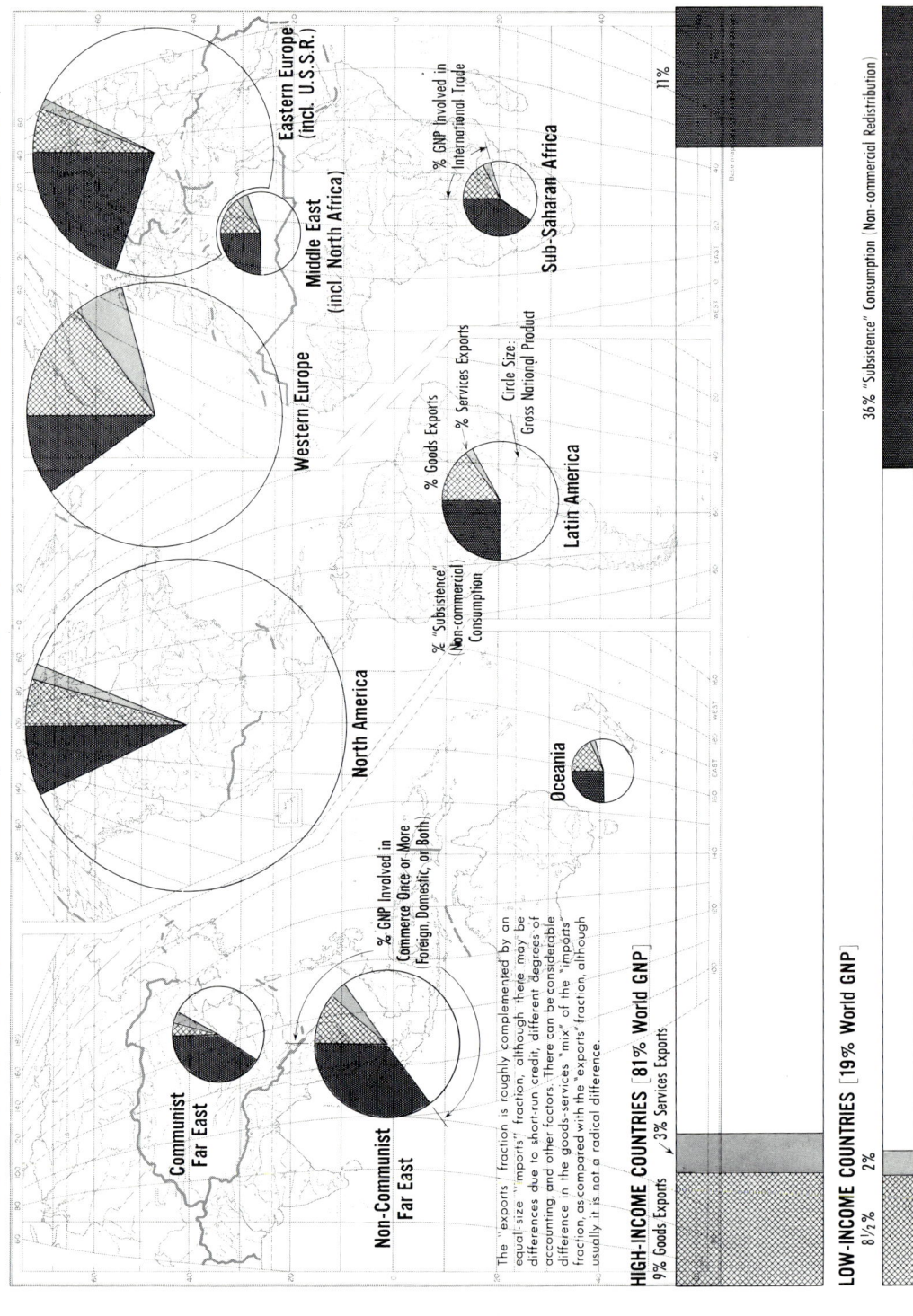

GROSS NATIONAL PRODUCT, INTERNATIONAL TRADE [Total Exports, Goods Exports, "Invisible" (Services) Exports], AND "SUBSISTENCE" (Non-commercial Redistribution) CONSUMPTION, 1962-1964 AVERAGE-ANNUAL

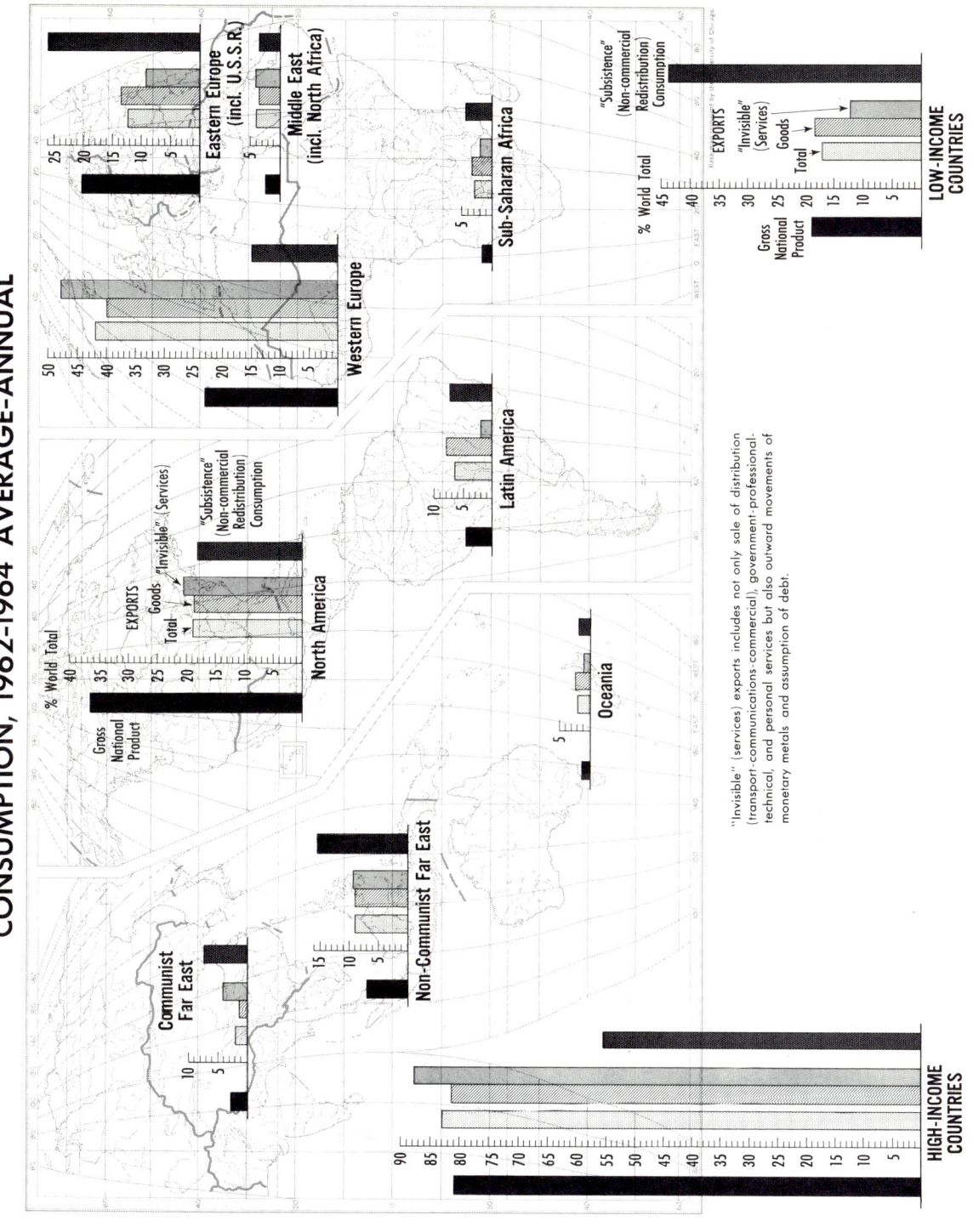

national boundaries, with only a small fraction crossing great distances or international frontiers.

Commercialization of Great-Regions

About two-thirds of the $3½ trillion of gross trade in the world is carried on in the North American and Western European regions, inhabited by the most commercialized half-billion people in the world. The Communist realm may account for a fourth, overwhelmingly in Eastern Europe and the Soviet Union. The remaining half of mankind accounts for only a tenth of world commerce, which reflects the subsistent and slightly commercialized economies in most of Latin America, sub-Saharan Africa, the Middle East, and the non-Communist Far East (although certain areas, countries, and economic activities within the realm are much more commercialized than the average). There are considerable differences in the commercial characteristics of the various regions (see the graphs on pages 556–57 and 562–63), some of which are herewith indicated.

North America. The United States and Canada are the most commercialized great-region in the world, with total trade (including much multiple counting) about three times the over half-trillion dollars income. North America has rationalized (improved the technical efficiency) its three major economic sectors more than any other region and has led the world in the development of mass merchandising, just as Western Europe has led the world in intensifying use of medium- and low-grade natural resources, and the Soviet Union has led in rapid and sustained growth of heavy industry. Trade developments in North America tend to diffuse throughout the world after the initial period, not only to other urban-industrial regions but elsewhere, wherever American concerns are important.

Characteristics of modern merchandising include the following: style, speed, and other status-associated factors are often as important to consumers as price; continual change—sometimes real progress, sometimes petty innovation that is essentially just change for its own sake—is a major spur to buying; consumer credit permits people to borrow from future income in order to buy goods—often expensive ones—that they might not otherwise afford; and advertising has assumed a major role as the stimulator of people's appetites for goods that they may not have known about or felt a need for. These and similar changes have mainly added to the costs of distribution, but other changes have helped cut costs.

In some areas of distribution, costs have been cut by eliminating the middleman between factory and consumer, thus saving the profits that wholesalers and jobbers exact along the route. Many makers of industrial goods have already done this, with more than three-quarters of industrial purchases now going direct from factory to users. However, bypassing the middleman is not so promising for makers of consumer goods, since most appliance makers could not afford the heavy cost of reaching their mass market.

To cut costs of handling, many merchants pin their hopes on greater mechanization of warehouses. By merely loading and stacking goods on pallets and moving them by fork-lift, the cost of hand loading is cut by as much as half, and the capacity of warehouses is more than doubled. Some automation enthusiasts foresee the day when electronic brains will do most of the paper work now done by store managers and robots will do most of the labor of stock clerks.

The biggest chance to cut distribution costs is at the retailer's level. Two of the most promising developments have been the spread of self-service selling even to department and drugstores and the rapid increase in automatic vending machines. The self-service supermarkets (now handling nine-tenths of the $62 billion yearly food and grocery trade) have not only trimmed distribution costs enough to cut average markup (now some 19 to 20 per cent for the most part; 14 to 15 per cent in the case of the food discounters who handle less than 5 per cent of total food business), but they have done much to change the manufacturer's selling methods, so that many non-food items now move through such centers. Many businessmen, notably appliance makers, are concentrating on fewer but bigger dealers, while the small retailer is more and more forced into organizations that pool their buying power and shipping needs in order to get the same savings as big retailers do from carload purchases, centralized warehouses, and mechanized handling.

Manufacturers have learned an important lesson: that overconcentration of production often merely buys factory efficiency at the expense of economic distribution. More and more, manufacturers are building smaller plants designed to serve individual regional markets. On both ends of the distribution chain, manufacturers and merchants are coming to realize the same thing: that the only way to cut down distribution expense is to organize it on the same large-volume, low-profit principle as production.

Within urban regions—now containing some 70 per cent of the American population—shopping is being redistributed areally, and the relative importance of different types of retailing is changing. Increasingly, downtown areas are concentrating on comfort and luxury types of goods and services. Shoppers like downtown areas because of the wide array of goods offered there, the range of sizes and colors, and the range of prices. In the main, the more style is involved, the more the downtown area is preferred. Shoppers tend to go to their local shopping districts or centers for convenience items (such as food) and to downtown areas for so-called shopping items (such as furniture), which people like to mull over before buying.

The old-time department store is becoming more and more a regional chain, in which a number of small units cluster around a big central store that handles warehousing, administration, and other services for them. In spite of this suburb and exurb (satellite town) drift, department stores are filling a diminishing share of the total market. Specialty stores (e.g., appliance, family shoe and clothing, and floor-covering stores) are often more attractive for many reasons, including the concentration (layout of goods) that specialization permits, sometimes better salesmanship and servicing, and other assets (or presumed assets). The growing importance of consumer hard goods sometimes means that manufacturing company outlets or licensed specialty outlets seem to be more reliable servicing agents in fulfilling guarantees, although in such hard goods, national brands can usually be obtained in many stores in a city. The emphasis on price in soft goods has also put the department store on the defensive in many places, as its credit policies; its broad selection of goods in many sizes, colors, and brands; its many services of other types, and its personal flavor are generally very costly.

North American retailing is overwhelmingly oriented to distributing North American goods and services. Less than 10 per cent of products coming into the region find their way in recognizable shape onto retail shelves; the other 90+ per cent go into agriculture and industry as factors of production. Imported goods are between 2 and 5 per cent of over-all store volume in most departmental and specialty stores, and there is little indication that this ratio between domestic and foreign goods in regional retailing will significantly change in the foreseeable future.

Western Europe. Retail trade is characterized in Western Europe by overcrowding and low productivity. The region has over four million retail shops (over half in food trade) and some ten million employed, but roughly half of these shops account for only 15 per cent of their combined sales. The typical owner of the little family foodshop is a sort of urban peasant who has independence, but little else except hard work, long hours, and a low level of living for himself and his family. Western Europe has five to eight food stores per thousand population, depending on the country, compared with less than two for the United States. In spite of the relatively backward organization of food retailing in Western Europe, the costs of the service are less than might be expected, from less than 15 to highs of less than 25 per cent markups, depending on the country.

Among the most promising developments in retail trade since World War II are the rapid growth of self-service shops and some tendency toward breaking down the boundaries between the traditional retail lines, especially in the large

TABLE 16-6

World: Exports and Their Composition, by Great-Region and Economic-Type of Society, 1962–1964 Average-Annual *
(in billions of United States dollars)

	Exports F.O.B.[1] (U.S. $ billion = 100.0 per cent)	Food, Beverages, and Tobacco Products	Crude Materials Excluding Fuels	Mineral Fuels	Chemicals	Machinery and Transport Equipment	Other Manufactured Goods
North America	28.2	18%	16%	4%	8%	32%	22%
Western Europe	60.5	11	8	5	8	33	35
Eastern Europe (including the U.S.S.R.)	20.5	13	13	12	5	27	30
Oceania	3.5	40	41	2	2	3	12
Latin America	12.0	40	22	29	1	–	8
Sub-Saharan Africa	5.1	38	36	3	1	–	22
Middle East (including North Africa)	5.7	8	21	65	–	–	6
Non-Communist Far East	13.5	20	24	4	3	11	38
Communist Far East	2.0	19	26	–	–	–	51
World	151.0	17	15	10	6	24	28
High-income countries	123.0	15	13	6	6	29	31
Low-income countries	28.0	20	24	26	3	2	16
	(per cent of U.S. $151.0 billion)	(per cent of U.S. $26.2 billion)	(per cent of U.S. $22.8 billion)	(per cent of U.S. $14.6 billion)	(per cent of U.S. $8.9 billion)	(per cent of U.S. $36.1 billion)	(per cent of U.S. $42.4 billion)
North America	18.7	19.6	19.8	7.5	26.0	24.9	14.6
Western Europe	40.0	25.6	21.0	20.5	54.3	55.4	50.0
Eastern Europe (including the U.S.S.R.)	13.6	10.3	11.9	17.1	11.3	15.2	14.4
Oceania	2.3	5.3	6.1	0.7	1.1	0.3	0.9
Latin America	8.0	18.3	11.4	24.0	1.1	–	2.4
Sub-Saharan Africa	3.4	7.2	7.9	1.3	1.1	–	2.6
Middle East (including North Africa)	3.7	1.9	5.3	25.3	–	–	0.7
Non-Communist Far East	9.0	10.3	14.4	3.4	4.5	4.2	12.0
Communist Far East	1.3	1.5	2.2	0.2	0.6	–	2.4
World	100.0	100.0	100.0	100.0	100.0	100.0	100.0
High-income countries	81.5	68.7	70.2	51.3	90.4	98.3	89.6
Low-income countries	18.5	31.3	29.8	48.7	9.6	1.7	10.4

Source: Adapted from United Nations data.

* Data refer to total international trade, both intraregional (e.g., across Western European borders, often only short distances) and intercontinental across oceans or other vast distances. Composition data approximate (definitions vary). Military goods and services are usually not reported, or else are given a nominal value.

[1] "F.O.B." equals transaction value (i.e., exports valued at frontiers of exporting countries) including value paid exporter plus (a) transportation and insurance to frontier but excluding (b) international transportation and insurance charges.

TABLE 16-7

World: Imports and Their Composition, by Great-Region and Economic-Type of Society, 1962–1964 Average-Annual *
(in billions of United States dollars)

	Imports C.I.F.[1] (U.S. $ billion = 100.0 per cent)	Food, Beverages, and Tobacco Products	Crude Materials Excluding Fuels	Mineral Fuels	Chemicals	Machinery and Transport Equipment	Other Manufactured Goods
North America	24.0	20%	16%	11%	4%	18%	31%
Western Europe	70.0	20	16	11	6	21	26
Eastern Europe (including the U.S.S.R.)	18.0	15	15	7	4	27	32
Oceania	3.5	6	8	10	8	34	34
Latin America	11.5	11	6	8	11	40	24
Sub-Saharan Africa	5.5	16	4	8	7	30	35
Middle East (including North Africa)	6.0	17	8	9	8	28	30
Non-Communist Far East	16.0	17	20	11	8	22	22
Communist Far East	3.5	32	17	14	8	16	13
World	158.0	17	15	10	6	24	28
High-income countries	128.6	16	13	6	7	28	30
Low-income countries	29.4	29	24	26	3	3	15
	(per cent of U.S. $158.0 billion)	(per cent of U.S. $28.6 billion)	(per cent of U.S. $23.2 billion)	(per cent of U.S. $16.0 billion)	(per cent of U.S. $9.8 billion)	(per cent of U.S. $37.2 billion)	(per cent of U.S. $43.2 billion)
North America	15.2	16.8	16.4	16.3	10.1	11.6	17.3
Western Europe	44.3	49.0	48.4	48.1	42.7	39.5	42.1
Eastern Europe (including the U.S.S.R.)	11.4	9.4	11.7	7.5	7.1	13.2	13.4
Oceania	2.2	0.7	1.1	2.5	2.6	3.3	2.8
Latin America	7.3	4.2	3.0	5.6	12.2	12.5	6.7
Sub-Saharan Africa	3.5	3.2	0.9	2.5	4.0	4.5	4.4
Middle East (including North Africa)	3.8	3.5	2.1	3.1	5.1	4.5	4.2
Non-Communist Far East	10.1	9.4	13.8	11.3	13.2	9.4	8.1
Communist Far East	2.2	3.8	2.6	3.1	3.0	1.5	1.0
World	100.0	100.0	100.0	100.0	100.0	100.0	100.0
High-income countries	81.4	70.0	70.0	51.7	89.8	98.0	90.0
Low-income countries	18.6	30.0	30.0	48.1	10.2	2.0	10.0

Source: Adapted from United Nations data.

* Data refer to total international trade, both intraregional (e.g., across Western European borders, often only short distances) and intercontinental across oceans or other vast distances. Composition data approximate (definitions vary).

[1] "C.I.F." equals value of imports at frontier of importing country (i.e., export value at frontiers of exporting countries plus international transportation and insurance charges). Because of revaluing and many other reasons, the difference between f.o.b. and c.i.f. is often only a rough approximation of the real cost of transportation and insurance.

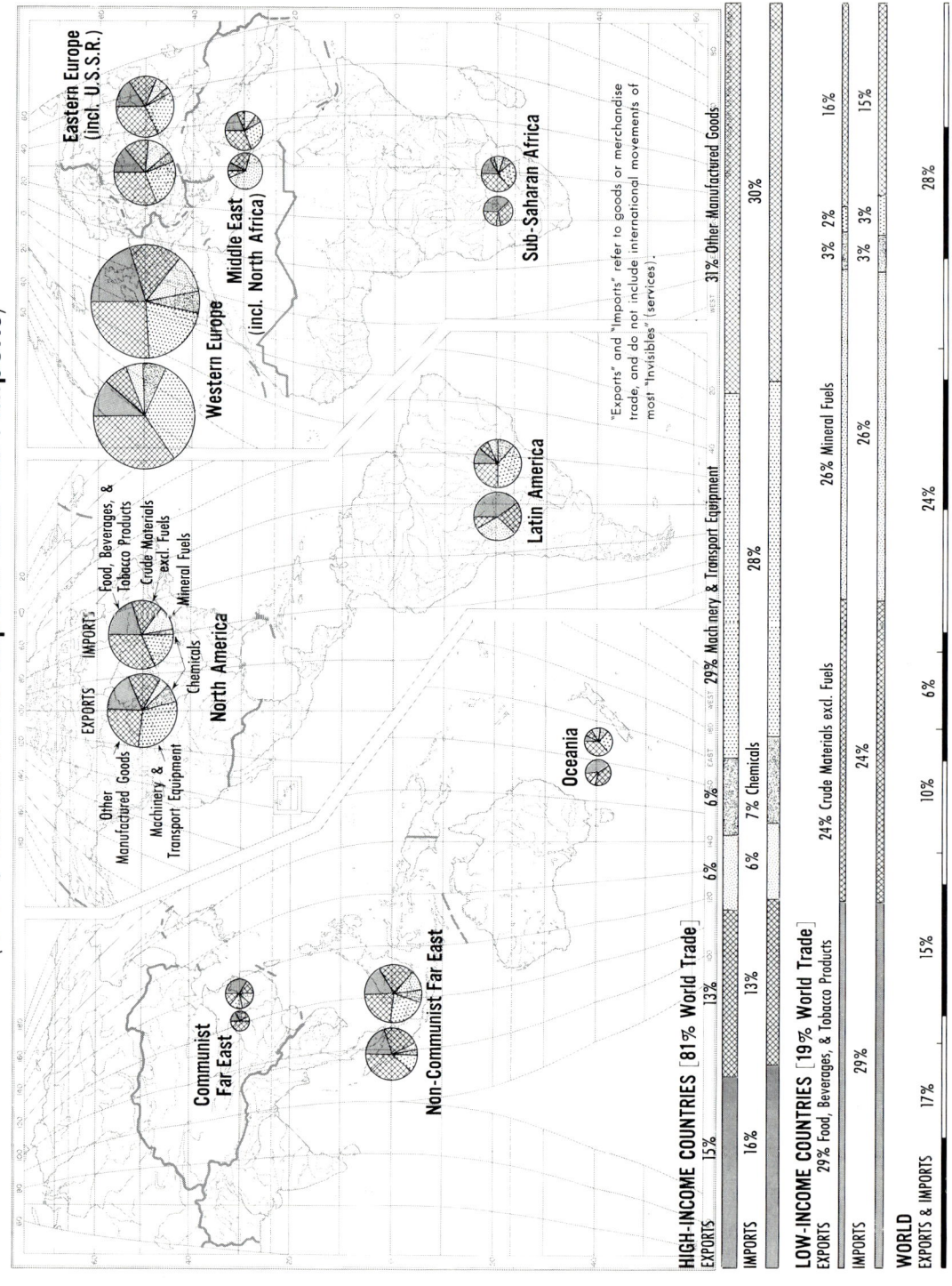

WORLD: GREAT-REGION AND ECONOMIC-TYPE OF SOCIETY SHARES OF WORLD EXPORTS AND IMPORTS BY MAJOR GROUPINGS, 1962-1964 AVERAGE-ANNUAL (U.S. $ Valued)

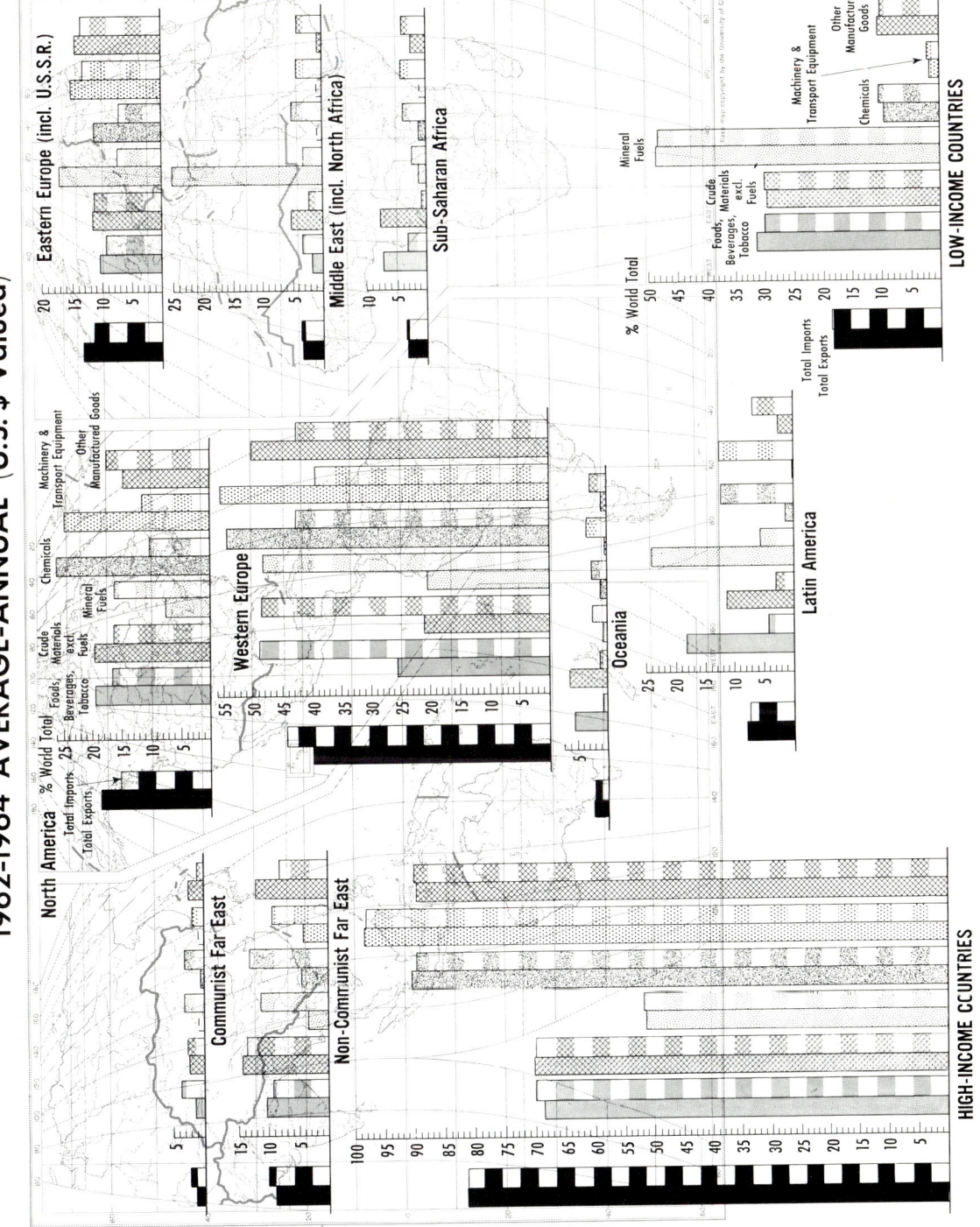

cities. Self-service should result in a saving of manpower and lower costs and prices, and the resulting competitive pressure on the independents should promote the development of voluntary chains to effect collective purchasing and other economies. Whatever pioneering changes may be in prospect, the size and organizational structure of retail trade have not fundamentally changed in the past generation. Although retailing, like agriculture, has long been an overcrowded activity, there is little evidence of a massive shift of workers from this field into less crowded and more productive activities.

While total trade in Western Europe is less than in North America, foreign trade is much greater, both absolutely and relatively. With 10 per cent of the world's population, Western Europe produces about a fifth of the world's income and accounts for two-fifths of the world's merchandise trade and nearly half of the world's invisible trade.[8] The region's visible and invisible imports, on the one hand, and its exports, on the other, each amount to about 20 per cent of gross national product (about 12 per cent without intra-European trade). Raw materials and lightly processed materials make up over four-fifths of imports from outside Europe (food-feed about one-quarter, inedible agricultural raw materials same, minerals and base metals about one-third), while Western European exports to the rest of the world are about three-quarters fabricated goods. Most earth materials are produced domestically; taking food, drink, and tobacco together, the region produces some four-fifths of its requirements at home (over 90 per cent for continental Western Europe); for inedible agricultural materials, the figure is over two-thirds; for fuel and energy, three-quarters.

Eastern Europe (including the U.S.S.R.). Except for those trade activities serving industry and the Communist elite, many of the merchandising activities of Soviet Europe are among the most backward in the world for a region of such urban-industrial development. There are two types of retail outlets: government stores with fixed prices and the farmers' markets where prices fluctuate according to the principle of supply and demand. Not all government stores are equally well stocked, and shortages are common, except in the most ordinary staples (e.g., bread, cabbage). Meat, milk, eggs, and fresh vegetables are among the most scarce items in government stores and often cost two to three times the government store price if available in the farmers' markets.

In the larger cities, better-off housewives can shortcut traditional marketing by going to order bureaus of big grocery and department stores and simply give a clerk a list of what they require. The next day groceries are delivered to the apartment door. However, traditional personal shopping is still preferred by the majority of housewives. There are no supermarkets in the American sense. In the new apartment house areas on the outskirts of Moscow and other large cities, there are some self-service grocery stores, but they are conventional, modest-sized grocery stores with checkout counters at the exit. And they handle for the most part only packaged groceries and canned goods. The multipurpose supermarket dealing in every kind of food and household supply has not yet made its appearance. Department stores are also comparatively rare compared to Western Europe and North America.

Total trade is apparently equal to about twice the gross national product, with non-retail (factory to factory and other types) trade being relatively more important compared with total trade than in the North Atlantic regions. Foreign trade is also relatively less important; only some 5 per cent of gross national income is exported (or imported), an even smaller proportion than for North America. Less than a third of this is with non-Communist countries. Exports and imports are dominated by crude and lightly processed materials, with manufactures being mainly capital goods or their components.

Oceania. European Oceania (Australia and New Zealand) has urban-industrial economies and merchandising characteristics much like

---

[8] For example, some two-thirds of the 80 million foreign vacationers are entertained in Western Europe, bringing in about $6 billion gross (two-thirds of international tourism). World tourism grosses $30 billion yearly, two-thirds domestic.

those of North America and Western Europe, while the Melanesian, Micronesian, and Polynesian archipelagos include many underdeveloped areas still subsistent or slightly commercialized. Foreign trade is very important, with the per capita foreign trade being the largest of any great-region. Over 85 per cent of the exports are food and other crude materials, while about 60 per cent of total imports are machinery and manufactured consumer goods. Domestic trade in European Oceania is more modern than that in Western Europe as a whole; this is because of the higher average income and more specialized occupational structure (less semi-modernized sectors).

Latin America. Although usually grouped with the underdeveloped realm, Latin America is better characterized as semi-industrialized, as only half of its present labor force is now agricultural, and almost half of the population now lives in urban places. The average per capita income of about $300 is considerably higher than that for sub-Saharan Africa, the Middle East, or the Far East. In some respects, the region shows signs of its transitional economic status. Foreign investments are especially important; direct investments by American companies in the recent past have contributed between 5 and 10 per cent of the region's total net capital investment, but their contributions to economic growth were more important (over a third of the mining and industrial production comes from such companies; about a third of all Latin American exports originate with those companies, and about a fifth of all taxes, including a third of the income taxes, are paid by the American companies). Agriculture represents a declining share of the value of all goods and services produced: from nearly half of gross national income before World War II to only one-quarter at present. About two-fifths of agricultural output is in the form of crops harvested for export (coffee, sugar, cacao, bananas, henequen), and these plus mineral exports account for 90 per cent of all Latin American exports.

Along with the spread of other American marketing techniques, self-service merchandising is catching on in Latin America (although not as quickly as in Western Europe). American oil industry commissaries have spread the institutions in much of Latin America (and in the Middle East). Sellers of business machines have also been a powerful stimulus. Although some 20,000 self-service stores now exist outside North America, supermarketing in Latin America and elsewhere is unlikely to spread as rapidly as in the United States and Canada. For one thing, it is difficult to get the space necessary for an American-type operation in the crowded cities of old settled areas. And most retailers cannot move to the suburbs (as American merchants might) until their customers become motorized. Perhaps the biggest deterrent to expansion is the low average income of customers. There is no Saturday night stocking up for the week, and even when customers are moderately well off, most homes do not have refrigeration to store enough perishables for once-a-week shopping. Another big problem is the difficulty of importing refrigeration, office machines, and other equipment, or starting local production of standardized products. Latin America (and European) processors prefer to sell in bulk, but attractive packaging is a cornerstone of self-service merchandizing. Allied to this problem is the limited use of brand names, which are still in their infancy abroad.

In the foreseeable future, more and more Latin American countries are going to reach semi-industrial and urban-industrial status. Income and trade are going up, but a greater proportion will be domestic. The value of farm output has kept pace with population growth over the past several decades, but meanwhile the per capita value of industrial production nearly doubled. The gain in exports in the past decade was only one-quarter (if Venezuela is excluded, less than one-tenth); this was the smallest increase of any of the world's great-regions. More and more, other tropical agricultural and other mining areas are increasing their exports at a faster rate (e.g., in the past decade, Latin America's share of world coffee exports dropped from almost 85 per cent to less than 75 per cent).

Sub-Saharan Africa. Tropical Africa (excluding the Republic of South Africa) is probably the least developed area of its size and has the lowest per capita income and the largest share of subsistent income. Marketing has developed along two parallel lines: one based on European methods (although many large retail food and department stores are owned and managed by Levantines and South Asians), and the other based on the traditional African village markets and roadside stalls. The customer uses whichever type of facility happens to be handiest to him at the time. In either type, he can buy a surprising variety of consumer goods from almost any part of the world. The main difference is that the African markets have no fixed prices; the buyer arrives at a price through bargaining with the seller. In the department stores, prices are fixed, as a general rule. Many of the old, established import firms are depending more and more on wholesale trade and have restricted their retail outlets to the large urban centers. The rising African middle class is increasing its share of domestic trade and is putting heavy pressure on Levantine and South Asian traders in the process.

Foreign trade involves a very large share (20 per cent) of sub-Saharan Africa gross national product, and much of it leaves the region without being serviced by intermediary traders (e.g., plantations and mines shipping direct to the North Atlantic Basin countries). Some 90 per cent of the international trade is with countries outside of the region, with the largest volume of intraregional trade being in southern Africa. Some 75 per cent of imports are fabricated manufactured goods, with about half of such imports being capital goods and parts for such goods. An even larger fraction of the region's exports are crude materials, with the "manufactured" exports being mainly lightly processed goods such as smelted and refined metals. The relatively large fraction of "invisibles" reflects exports of much gold and interest profits, and imports of capital and gifts-grants.

Middle East (including North Africa). Although still fundamentally underdeveloped, the Middle East is more commercialized and modernized than sub-Saharan Africa, being more comparable to Latin America. Several small countries are high income: Israel (a special type of urban-industrial society because of its imbalanced imports of refugees and gifts-grants); Kuwait (a very large portion of whose income from oil royalties is invested abroad by the government rather than being used domestically); and Lebanon, Cyprus, and Bahrein (all special examples because of mineral royalties, entrepôt trade, and haven for capital). None of the larger countries are in the group, although Egypt and Turkey have made considerable progress and others have had modest success in modernization. The tremendous petroleum and natural-gas reserves and rapidly increasing production already yield over $3 billion royalties and taxes each year to the oil-rich states (and it is increasing rapidly), plus external economies in the form of related industry and services that aid other modernization. Domestic trade is well developed, overwhelmingly in the hands of indigenous merchants, and increasing at a rate faster than that of general income. Food exports (now 8 per cent of total exports) and even inedible raw materials exports (now 21 per cent) seem likely to decline in relative importance with increasing population and development of more consumer-goods industry, with mineral exports providing the steadiest source of foreign exchange.

Non-Communist Far East. Of the third of mankind living in this region, only the 100 million in Japan live in a mature urban-industrial economy whose commercialization is like that of the North Atlantic Basin economies, although urban-nodes elsewhere (e.g., million and multimillion city-regions such as Bombay, Karachi, Delhi, Calcutta, Singapore, Manila, Hong Kong) show similar tendencies, as do other areas (especially the plantation belts of Ceylon, Malaysia, the Philippines, and elsewhere). Excluding Japan, the proportion of non-commercial redistribution (producer-consumption) runs as high as in sub-Saharan Africa or the Communist Far East; even including Japan, the proportion runs very high.

The large domestic markets and policies toward self-sufficiency in many areas of the economy characterizing such large countries as India,

Pakistan, and Indonesia result in international trade involving a smaller share of the total income than in such regions as sub-Saharan Africa or the Middle East, but it is still almost as large a share as in Latin America.

About a third of the nearly $20 billion of goods and services exports is traded within the region; this is a larger share than in the case of the other underdeveloped regions and mainly reflects Japan's trade with other countries in the region. Of the other international trade, roughly a quarter each is with Western Europe, North America, and Eastern Europe (including U.S.S.R.), and the last quarter is widely distributed with other great-regions. Of the goods exported, about a quarter consist of food and aromatic crops (e.g., tea, spices), about half consist of crude materials of agricultural origin (e.g., jute, natural rubber), about a tenth are minerals, and some 15 per cent are highly fabricated goods mainly shipped out of Japan (the last figure does not count processed goods, as three-quarters of the value of the rubber and oils, half of the value of the cotton, and tin, and a third of the value of the jute exported consist of processing done on the crude materials before shipping them out). Japan's export pattern is unique in the region: two-fifths capital goods, two-fifths consumer goods, with crude materials the remaining fifth.

The imports again reflect a great difference between Japan and the rest of the region:

	Japan	Rest of Region
Consumption goods		
Food	12.5%	15.9%
Others	2.4	16.3
Materials chiefly		
for consumption goods	45.4	25.8
Capital goods	14.9	33.0
Materials chiefly		
for capital goods	24.8	9.0

Communist Far East. Since the Communist takeovers in the Far East (except in Mongolia, since World War II), foreign-trade developments have been as erratic as have been general economic development and political associations.

In the early 1950's, the Communist Far East's trade with Communist Europe expanded spectacularly from a quarter of the total in 1950 to triple that fraction by 1952. For much of the decade, the exports remained the historic ones: foodstuffs such as soybeans, tea, and dried eggs; inedible agricultural raw materials such as hides, raw silk, tung-oil, and hides; minerals such as coal, antimony, and tungsten; and some handicrafts. The change was that they moved to Communist Europe rather than to the West (although some eventually reached the West through Communist Europe).

There was much greater change in the import pattern. Historically, these imports have mainly been raw cotton, tobacco, petroleum products, and some consumer goods (soft and hard). The imports of cotton and tobacco stopped quickly, as regional production was expanded. So did imports of consumer goods. Petroleum now came from Communist Europe. The main imports quickly became machinery, trucks, metals, and precision instruments—roughly half from the U.S.S.R. and half from smaller Communist European nations.

By the late 1950's, the Communist Far East began augmenting its historic exports with cotton textiles, bicycles, hardware, aluminum ware, and other light consumer goods from its expanding industrial output. Apparently, these exports were sometimes made for prestige purposes as much as for purely commercial purposes.

Much of Mainland China's trade with the non-Communist world remained like the pre-Communist pattern. Imports from abroad were small and mainly came direct to Chinese ports, but over a quarter of Chinese exports went to Hong Kong (about two-thirds stayed in that British colony, mainly food and other products consumed locally, but the other third were trans-shipped overseas).

Most Chinese purchases from the U.S.S.R. were paid for at the time that they were bought, with only $½ billion commercial credit extended by the U.S.S.R. in the early 1950's.[9] After 1955, until the 1959 ideological rupture, the U.S.S.R.

---

[9] Military aid was apparently much greater, but was treated separately.

imported more from China than she sent China, apparently being paid back earlier credits and interest. The imports were mainly raw materials (meat products, vegetable oils, raw tobacco, wool, and non-ferrous ores and metals), with some textiles and clothing to supply the rapidly expanding Soviet demand for soft consumer goods. What the U.S.S.R. exported to China were complete industrial plants, iron and steel, and petroleum.

Between 1959 and 1962, Chinese trade with the U.S.S.R. fell 67 per cent and that with other Communist European countries over 50 per cent, as a result of the ideological break. In the same three years, poor food crops caused cutbacks in most imports to pay for foodgrain imports from Canada and Australia, and for chemical fertilizer.

In 1964, total Chinese foreign trade was some $2½ billion (a figure that a medium-size Western European nation could match). Goods exports did not cover the cost of imports, so silver bullion shipments and short term credit were necessary to balance. The other countries—Mongolia, North Korea, and North Vietnam—also had imbalanced trade, but were able to use Communist European credit to a considerable extent, in spite of the latter two countries' support of China in its feud with the U.S.S.R.

By 1964, Mainland China was conducting three-quarters of its foreign trade with the non-Communist world. Of the quarter still conducted with Communist Europe, most was still with the U.S.S.R. (some of it was re-exports from other Eastern European states or from Cuba), mainly petroleum, sugar, and other crude materials, as capital goods and military hardware are now little involved.

Summary

Trade and commerce is a growth activity in the present world economy, and seems likely to remain so for the foreseeable future. The increasing specialization and commercialization of national economies everywhere is adding full-time employment at rates as great (often greater) as those in industry. Part-time workers in marketing were historically mainly from among the peasantry; now they usually are students and housewives from urban centers. With increasing urbanization—from well over a quarter of mankind in cities 20,000 and over at the present time to perhaps double that figure before the end of the century—the commercial sector is also becoming as urbanized as the industrial sector.

GOVERNMENTAL AND PROFESSIONAL-PERSONAL SERVICES

About a sixth of the world's labor force, and half again that fraction of the world's income, comes from services other than distribution. Most urban-industrial societies have much larger fractions, but the proportions vary widely, depending upon many considerations (e.g., feeling of need for defense and internal security, degree of social welfare, policy of rewarding public servants, and unionization or other job-security organization).

Governmental Services

Almost everywhere, increased political-security risks and the desire to set up welfare societies have made for swiftly increasing defense-security forces and civilian bureaucracies. In the least developed societies, this group of activities employs only 1 to 2 per cent of the total labor force (plus fractions of time of the less specialized labor force); but in most urban-industrial societies, it rises to much higher figures, often 10 to 15 per cent (excluding employment in government-owned industry and distribution).

Police and armed forces increase rapidly, partly because of the fragility of most new states that are only beginning to be nations, and partly because of great-power insecurity attending the radical ideological divisions in the world. The pressure for universal literacy and vocational training makes the teaching force among the largest professions in any society. The pressure for governmental economic guidance and control swells the bureaucracy, even in societies that do not put centralized government planning high among their ideals (often to repay the literate elite who helped found independence). The distribution of government activities varies widely with the ideology and power-politics involvement of states; urban-industrial societies commonly spend 5 per cent of gross national product on military and 10 per cent on civilian activities (but the United States and the U.S.S.R. spend double that military fraction). There is a tendency for governmental activities to be more urbanized than the general populace, but quite evenly distributed within that context.

Professional and Personal Services

Non-governmental professional and technical specialties are anemic in underdeveloped societies; usually they are less than 1 per cent of the labor force, even if full-time religious personnel is included. In mature urban-industrial societies, the increased demand for secular professions and subprofessions, excluding government, will usually reach 5 to 10 per cent of the labor force. Proportionately, religious personnel usually drops off, partly because of difficulty in recruiting in an increasingly secular society but mainly because so many services formerly associated with religion are done by government or private professional services. After extremely rapid growth during early modernization, the numbers in certain professions may drop off without any decrease in efficiency of service (e.g., with increased urbanization and motorization, fewer doctors are needed for a given population than formerly in a more rural immobile setting).

In the personal services, household servants decline in relative importance as urban-industrialization proceeds, partly because the supply of cheap labor drops and partly because more specialized commercial substitutes (e.g., grooming services) or industrial substitutes (e.g., "built-in maid services" in preprepared foods, better-fitting factory-made clothing) are more efficient in servicing wider markets. In a modernized society, tourism may employ about 5 per cent of the working population when the working class is well off in income and leisure.

The distribution of service activities varies with the quality and cost. For ordinary services (e.g., doctor, minister), people are usually willing to go about as far as they will go for staple goods or to participate in neighborhood institutions. Less frequently used specialists (lawyers, medical specialists, university teachers) are typically found in the luxury-goods centers, usually the nearest city or the core area of a large urban-region. In a small minority of cases, prestige specialists may have a national market and locate almost where they will (provided suitable institutional surroundings are available, such as medical centers to service medical specialists), but more usually the supply of services must be ubiquitous.

PROSPECTS

In all mature urban-industrial societies, more of the labor force released by agricultural rationalization or provided by population increase has been absorbed by the services sector than by the strictly industrial sector. If both agriculture and industry are rationalized according to present technical feasibilities, an ideal occupational and income structure might find only 5 to 10 per cent in agriculture, 20 to 25 per cent in industry (with about half in construction and energy utilities), and the remaining majority of 65 to 75 per cent in the services sector. Such a "projection" is, of course, not a precise "prediction."

This ideal breakdown could alter. The urban-industrial world is still in the infancy of automation, and it is still not clear in what areas automation will increase efficiency the most. Possibly, many services will prove amenable to greater automation than many facets of industry, with the consequence that the directly productive sectors may bulk larger than now seems likely. Whatever the composition of the labor force and income, nothing short of nuclear destruction would seem to be capable of halting the increasing urbanization of population, of almost all industrial and service activity, and perhaps of substitution for present agricultural and other primary materials.

SUGGESTED READINGS

ALEXANDERSSON, GUNNAR, and NORSTROM, GORAN. *World Shipping*. New York: Wiley, 1963. Pp. 507.

BARACH, ARNOLD B. *The New Europe and Its Economic Future*. New York: Macmillan, 1964. Pp. 148.

BARACH, ARNOLD B. *U.S.A. and Its Economic Future*. New York: Macmillan, 1964. Pp. 148.

MEYER, JOHN R., PECK, MERTON J., STENASON, JOHN, and ZWICK, CHARLES. *The Economics of Competition in the Transportation Industries*. Harvard University Press, 1959. Pp. 359.

O'DELL, ANDREW C. *Railways and Geography*. London: Hutchinson, 1956. Pp. 198.

RENNER, GEORGE T., DURAND, LOYAL, JR., WHITE, C. LANGDON, and GIBSON, WELDON B. *World Economic Geography*. New York: Crowell, 1951. Pp. 758.

SEALY, KENNETH R. *The Geography of Air Transport*. London: Hutchinson, 1957. Pp. 207.

WARD, RICHARD J., and HOFFMAN, LAWRENCE A. (eds.). *Readings in Economic Geography from* Fortune. New York: Holt, Rinehart & Winston, 1960. Pp. 130.

WOYTINSKY, W. S., and WOYTINSKY, E. S. *World Commerce and Governments*. New York: Twentieth Century Fund, 1955. Pp. 907.

Index

Acetates, 254–55, 256, 308
Acid soils, 148, 160
Acids
  amino, 108, 201, 227, 239
  fatty, 193, 194, 195, 200, 206, 208, 211
  industrial, 508, 514, 516–17, 518
Activity patterns, regional, 20, 22–23, 25, 27, 29–30, 32, 34–35, 37, 39–40, 42, 44–45, 47
Aden, 507
Afghanistan, 63, 219
Africa, 17, 33, 195, 234, 272, 274, 276, 288, 320, 437, 472; *see also specific countries and areas*
Africa, Central, 207, 470
Africa, East, 250
Africa, North; *see* North Africa
Africa, sub-Saharan
  agriculture, 35, 101, 104, 112, 114, 138, 154, 167, 341
  beverage crops, 265, 268
  chemical industry, 508, 515, 517
  colonialism, 34
  commerce, 565–66
  energy resources, 374–424 *passim*
  exports, 341, 560
  fiber production, 241
  fishing industry, 316
  food consumption, 107, 164, 170, 171
  forest products, 289, 290, 291, 295, 298, 307
  grain production, 154, 158
  ideologies, 33–34
  imports, 386, 561
  income, 14, 555
  industry, general, 332, 333, 340–41, 344
  land resources, 114, 115
  livestock, 215, 218
  metallurgy, 427, 430, 431, 468, 481
  minerals, 35
  modernization, 33
  natural resistances, 35–36
  population, 70, 85, 86, 88
  raw materials, 34–36
  rubber production, 282
  service output, 530, 547, 551
  starch crops, 138, 139, 144
  steel industry, 465
  sugar production, 181
  tribalism, 34
  water power, 406
Africa, West, 438
  fats-oils production, 201, 202, 207
Agglomerates, 438, 439
Agrarian reform, 128–29, 144
Agriculture, 6–9, 45; *see also specific crops*
  animal products, 214–39 *passim*
  areal expansion, 110, 111, 114–20, 139, 152, 153
  capital investment, 28, 30, 42–43, 47, 49, 66, 95, 115–18, 124, 126, 127–29, 244, 245
  chemicalization, 30, 32, 95, 118, 156, 157, 227, 245, 513–19
  expansion of commerce, 110, 111, 120–22
  food supply, 99–110 *passim*, 134–212 *passim*
  income, 14, 48, 120, 123, 132
  intensification of yields, 110–14, 152, 153
  labor, 22, 24, 37, 42, 57, 70, 73, 95, 104, 127, 158, 224, 228, 244, 245, 249, 336
  markets, 131–32
  mechanization, 32, 95, 99, 101, 124–26, 208, 209, 245, 246–47, 250, 513
  modernization, 23, 25, 30, 32, 76–80, 89, 113, 114, 153, 227
  output, 22, 25, 30, 32, 42, 48, 53, 66, 75, 90, 94–212 *passim*
  overhead, 22, 130–31, 152–53, 232, 246
  patterns, visibility, 20, 219
  plantation, 35, 67, 207, 341
  poverty of, 126–32
  premodern, 17, 32, 66, 90, 91, 101, 123, 126, 127–29, 130, 219
  raw materials, 358–71 *passim*
  technology, 35, 113, 114, 120, 122–26, 129, 130, 132
  tree crops, 288–311
Air cargo transport, 533, 537, 543
Air supplies, 23, 49; *see also* Gases
  production, 520–21
Aircraft manufacturing, 356, 444, 491–92
Airlines, commercial, 550–51
Alabama, 435
Alaska, 326
Alcohol, 149
  industrial, 166, 168, 187
  potable, 101, 154, 159, 163, 168, 277–78, 346
Algae, 111, 149, 322
Algeria, 101, 341, 398, 400, 437
Alkaline soil, 38, 148, 168
Alkalis, 309, 508–12
Aluminum, 442, 473–78
Amazon River (and Basin), 118, 207, 279, 407
Amino acids, 108, 201, 227, 239
Ammonia, 515–16
Anatolia, 101
Andes Mountains, 33
Angola, 211, 250
Animal feed, 110, 120, 124, 134, 140, 144, 153–67 *passim*, 186, 189, 191, 194, 201, 209, 211, 212, 225, 227–30, 235, 312, 319, 322, 517
Animal husbandry, 194, 219–25, 227, 230, 239, 251
Animal products; *see also* Livestock

571

Animal products (*Continued*)
  edible, 25, 47, 132, 135, 137, 214–39 *passim*
  fiber, 250–53
Animals, work, 35, 124, 126, 214, 225
Antarctic Ocean, 313
Antarctica, 212, 321
Antibiotics, 229, 230
Antimony, 43, 567
Appalachian Mountains, 78, 388, 435
Apparel, 349–50; *see also* Garment industry; Textile industry
  cotton, 245, 249, 260
  ready-to-wear, 364
  synthetics, 253, 254, 255, 260
  wool, 251, 252
Arabia, 144, 390
Arctic Ocean, 313
Arctic region, 159, 219, 321
Areal association, 5–6
Argentina, 16, 151
  agriculture, 244, 274
  exports, 152, 239
  fuels, 394, 398
  industry, 339, 464
  livestock, 222, 226, 251
  oils-fats production, 202, 208
Arizona, 206, 245, 328
Armenia, 470
Asia; *see specific countries and areas*
Asia, Central, 338
Asia, East, 48, 164, 273; *see also* Far East
Asia, South, 48, 149, 164, 173, 273, 342, 566
Asia, Southeast, 17, 39, 100, 112, 114, 288, 295, 342, 437, 466
  agriculture, 104, 144, 149, 158, 173, 296
Asia, Southwest, 341
Assam, 171, 296
Assembly lines, integrated, 367
Aswan, 347
Athabaska River, 414
Atlantic Ocean, 313, 321
Atomic Energy Commission, 417, 418
Auckland, 339
Australia, 16, 28–31, 45, 100, 103, 178, 180, 326
  diet, 153
  exports, 152, 210, 239, 472
  industry, 180, 336, 338, 339, 380
  livestock, 251
  mineral deposits, 436–37, 463, 471, 477, 479, 518
Austria, 410
  steelmaking, 450, 452, 453
Automation, 44, 45, 54, 55, 57, 58, 73, 261, 331, 366, 367

Automotive industry, 54, 67, 255, 470, 485–89

Babassu oil, 207–8
Bagasse (crushed cane), 186, 187
Bahrein, 37, 566
Baku region, 388
Balkan region, 11, 202
Baltic Sea, 28, 313
Bananas, 138, 167, 173–76, 250
Banking services, 340
Bantus, 340
Barley, 137, 138, 145, 150, 151, 153
  animal feed, 158–62
  surplus, 144
Bauxite, 51, 473–78 *passim*
Beef, 162, 223, 224, 228–30; *see also* Meat industry
Belgium, 63, 420
  industry, 249, 255, 450, 460, 482
  international trade, 258, 439
Benelux, 336
Beriberi, 109
Beryllium, 467, 479–80
Bessemer processes (iron and steel), 449, 450, 456
Beverage industry, 331, 336, 338, 340, 341, 342, 345, 346–47
  crops, 264–79
Bhutan, 67
Biological innovations, 76, 78, 79
Biologicals, 187
Birmingham (Alabama) iron ore, 435, 456
Birth control, 18, 31, 83–85, 87, 89
Birth rates, 84
  vs. death rates, 7, 17, 70, 80, 86
Blast furnaces; *see* Steelmaking furnaces
Bolivia, 252, 443
  tin production, 472, 473
Borax, 522–23
Borneo, 438
Brazil, 31, 149
  agriculture, 139, 174, 250, 276
  coffee production, 269, 271
  economic growth, 11, 339
  industry, 180, 207, 208, 339, 413, 424, 464
  natural resources, 17, 33, 437, 438, 443
Bread, 149, 151, 155, 159, 162, 178
Breweries, 54, 346
Brimstone; *see* Sulfur
British Guiana, 475, 477
Broiler industry, 224, 230, 235, 319
Bromine, 323
Buckwheat, 164–65
Building materials, 38, 49 n., 300, 310

Bulgaria, 436, 462
Buna-S, 285
Bureaucracy, 25, 59, 368
Burma, 102, 148, 171, 296
Butane gas, 400
Butter, 209–10
Butyl, 285
Butylene, 504–5

Cacao (and cocoa), 263, 265, 275–76
Calcium, 108
California, 302, 388, 398, 411, 418
  agriculture, 159, 206, 209, 245
  industry, 327, 328, 391
  land resources, 23, 230
  mineral deposits, 435, 509, 518, 522
  wine production, 278–79
Calories, 51, 105, 107, 108, 110, 120, 135, 158, 168, 214
  deficits, 136, 137, 139
  per capita levels, 136, 137, 145, 153, 239
  sources, 134, 194
Cambodia, 102
Camel products, 222, 252
Canada, 16, 103, 204, 331
  agriculture, 95, 151, 224
  chemical industry, 518, 519
  commerce, 557
  economic development, 67
  energy resources, 407, 414, 415
  exports, 152, 309, 438, 439, 440, 443, 471, 486, 519
  metals production, 475
  milk consumption, 231
  ore deposits, 435, 438, 439, 440, 471, 478
  steel industry, 458
  tea consumption, 272
  wood products, 291, 294
Canals, 118, 546, 547
Canary Islands, 174
Canning industry, 170, 340, 346, 360
Capital and capitalization, 9, 17, 23, 25, 28, 32, 37, 47, 67, 318, 326, 350, 452, 491, 495, 526
  accumulation, 87, 90
  agriculture, 28, 30, 42–43, 47, 49, 66, 95, 102, 115–18, 124, 126, 127–29, 178, 230, 244, 245
  availability, 366–68
  modernization, 61–64, 407
  money, 366–67
  risk-taking, 39, 66, 337, 367
  shortages, 99
  social overhead, 45, 65
  substitute for labor, 229, 244
  waste, 27

INDEX

Capital goods, 20, 42, 337, 366–67, 480, 494
Capital-intensive techniques, 30, 43, 45, 65, 153
Capitalism, 63
Carbohydrates, 158, 168, 187, 191, 192, 193, 234
Carotene, 109, 114
Cartelization, 523
Cassava (manioc), 105, 108, 120, 137, 138, 140, 149, 167, 171–73, 340
Castor oil, 208–9
Cattle feeding industry, 225, 227, 228, 229
Cattle industry, 223–33 passim, 251
Caucasus region, 202
Caustic soda, 509–12
Cellulose, 191, 227, 300–301, 506
 fiber production, 253, 254–55
Cement plants, 352, 363
Central America, agriculture, 174, 250, 275; see also Latin America
Cereals, 51, 53, 99, 105, 110, 124, 134, 135, 137, 138, 153–67 passim, 164, 166, 189, 190
 starch crops production, 138–45
Ceylon, 148, 206, 272, 274, 288
Chemicals and chemical industry, 26, 38, 49 n., 78, 90, 139, 194, 309, 331, 336, 338, 340, 341, 342, 344, 345, 346, 351, 358, 401, 497
 geopolitical influences, 500
 location, 523–25
 organization, 526–28
 raw materials, 498–99, 500–523
 synthetic fibers, 253–56
Chicago, 236, 419, 494
 steel industry, 455–56
Chile, 16
 chemical resources, 499, 500, 514, 516
 industry, 339, 464
 ore deposits, 437, 438, 469
China, Mainland (Communist), 18, 29, 39, 109, 200, 313
 agriculture, 102–3, 111, 122, 144–45, 164–65, 170, 171, 234, 253
 economic growth plans, 42, 102
 forests, 295, 296, 297
 fuel production, 378, 379, 407, 413, 424
 industrialization, 67, 258, 343–44, 466, 507
 livestock, 244, 252
 oils-fats production, 200, 201, 202, 209
 ore deposits, 438, 443, 472
 tea consumption, 272
 trade with U.S.S.R., 567–68

China, Nationalist, 64; see also Taiwan
Chocolate, 275–76; see also Cacao
Cholesterol, 193, 194, 205
Chrome, 38, 443
Chromium, 437, 442, 443, 445
Cigarette industry, 348
Climate, 28, 33, 43, 45, 46, 91, 151, 163, 170, 185, 250, 279
 and fibers, 244, 248, 250
 humid, 24, 70, 79, 229, 232, 246
 and population, 76–79
 rice-growing, 146–48
 and technology, 76–77
 tropical, 151, 167, 244, 250
Coal, 30, 33, 35, 38, 51, 78, 255, 331, 336, 338, 340, 341, 342, 344, 345, 346, 352, 361, 362, 477, 502, 567
 anthracite, 378, 379
 bituminous, 378, 379, 415, 445
 conversion of, 383
 production, 379–83
 reserves, 378–79
 steelmaking, 447–67
 transportation, 383–85
 undersea, 325
Coal-tars, 499, 502
Cobalt, 326, 442, 444, 470
Coconut oil, 206–7
Coffee, 263, 265, 268–72, 274
Coke, metallurgical, 380, 381, 413, 415, 432, 440, 445, 446, 447, 449
Coking, 413, 445, 446, 448, 449, 455, 481, 502
Colombia, 174, 464
Colonialism, 64, 85
Colonization, 83, 114
Colorado, 413
Columbia River, 407, 408
Commerce, 6, 56, 530, 551–68
Common Market, 24, 100, 337
Communications, 8, 19, 23, 25, 32, 40, 42, 55–56, 340, 530, 551
Communism, 26–27, 41–42, 63, 75, 343, 344, 358, 564
Congo River, 35–36, 118, 107, 444
Conservation, 6
 forests, 288–311 passim
Consignments; see also Transportation
 loadability, 539–40, 546
 weight, 537–39
Construction industry, 53, 54, 331, 336, 338, 340, 341, 342, 345, 346, 356, 481
Consumer goods, 20, 25, 28, 37, 53, 55, 177, 338, 341, 344, 480
Consumption, 23, 55, 90
 animal products, 218
 bananas, 173–77
 barley, 158–62

 coal, 378–80, 445
 coffee, 268–71
 cotton, 245, 253, 254
 crude materials, 49, 57, 561
 dairy products, 230–32
 electricity, 402, 407–9
 feed, livestock, 110, 120, 124, 134, 140, 144, 153–67 passim
 fertilizer materials, 513–19 passim
 fibers, 245, 251–55
 fish, 312, 319
 food, general, 50, 51, 94–212 passim, 228–34, 312
 fuel, 375
 meats, 228, 234, 252
 metals, 431–47 passim, 480–94
 natural gas, 395–401 passim
 oils-fats, 193–212 passim
 paper, 308–9
 per capita, 27, 99, 176, 210, 252, 268, 308, 319, 385, 412
 petroleum, 385–95 passim
 raw materials, 430–47, 500–523
 rice, 145–50 passim
 rubber, 279, 282
 rye, 162–64
 salt, 507–12
 starches, 167–76 passim
 sugar, 187–92 passim
 sulfur, 512–13
 tea, 272
 wheat, 151–53
 wine, 278
Containers, 240; see also Packaging
Continuous-flow processes, 367–68
Copper, 51, 326, 426, 442, 444, 467–70, 480, 481
Copra, 29, 206–7
Cordage fibers, 250
Corn, 108, 137, 138, 140, 144, 150, 153–57, 165, 194, 205, 319
Corn Belt, U.S., 155–56, 157, 158, 177, 225, 227, 228, 229, 230, 234
Cornmeal, 155
Cosmetics, 189, 322–23
Costa Rica, 139, 174
Cottage industries, 342, 367
Cotton, 22, 53, 101, 121, 229, 244, 245–48, 249, 253, 254, 255, 256, 258, 261, 349
Cotton Belt, U.S., 229
Cottonseed oil, 194, 201
Credit, 32, 370
Crop dusting, 247
Crop rotation, 77, 111, 113, 122, 123, 124, 134, 149, 156, 157, 185, 189, 225
Crops
 beverage, 263, 264–68, 278–79
 cacao, 275–76
 coffee, 268–72

Crops (*Continued*)
  beverage (*Continued*)
    tea, 272–75
    wine, 101, 277–78
  cash, 34, 111, 189
  subsistence, 111
  tree, 134, 263–88
Crude materials, 34, 362–64; *see also* Raw materials
  consumption, 49–52, 57
  deficits, 25
Cuba, 64, 180, 443
  agriculture, 249, 250
  industry, 339
  sugar production, 184
Culture, 3–6, 19, 22, 36–37, 91
  economic growth, 11, 48
  population redistribution, 70–73, 75–76, 81
Curaçao, 327
Cyanamide, 514–15
Cyprus, 37, 566
Czechoslovakia, 140, 337, 338, 410, 436, 462

Dacron, 253, 256
Dairy Belt, U.S., 223, 232, 348
Dairy farming, 100; *see also* Milk, products
  commercial, 223–24
  specialized, 226–27
Dam construction, 408
Dead Sea, 519
Death rates, 81, 83, 88–89, 193
  vs. birth rates, 7, 17, 70, 80, 86
  child, 109
Dehydrating, 170, 189, 209, 346
Delta region, U.S., 246–47
Democracy, 21, 29, 31, 33
Demography, 32, 44; *see also* Population
  changes, 79–80
  economic development, 69–89
  investments, 85–86
Denmark, 153, 239
Depression, Great, 345
Desalination, 326
  economics of distillation, 327
  electric membrane method, 327–28
Deserts, 30, 38, 77, 219
Detergents, 211, 212, 401, 517; *see also* Soap and soap-making industries
Dextrose, 165, 301
Diet, 95, 99, 100, 239; *see also* Nutrition and nutrients
  basic energy foods, 134–78
  beverages, 268–72
  dairy products, 230–31
  fats, 193–95, 205, 228
  luxury energy foods, 179–212

underdeveloped societies, 104–7, 135–39, 149, 170, 179
Dietary economics, 135–39
Discrimination, ethnic, racial, 22, 26, 31
Disease resistance, 176, 249
Diseases, 35–36, 101, 130
  animal, 36, 123, 222, 235
  diet, 108–10, 193–95
  plant, 123, 156, 168, 174–76, 250, 268, 269, 276, 283
  population check, 76, 81–84, 88
  viruses, 176–77
Distilling industry, 154, 159, 163, 168, 186, 187, 191, 346–47
Dnieper River, 463, 477, 479
Dominican Republic, 507
Donets Basin, 411
Dow Chemical Company, 323, 325
Drainage, 38, 114, 118, 123, 176
Drought, 145
  plant resistance, 165, 170, 171
Drugs, 130, 229, 230, 235, 249, 322
Dry farming, 118, 130, 219, 222
Dry-milling industry, 154
Dyeing, 248, 252, 253, 255, 261, 509
Dynel, 248, 253, 256, 261

East China Sea, 313
East Pakistan, 148
Ecology, 4, 50
Economic cycles, 48, 63
Economic development, 10, 24, 59–61
  agriculture, 126–32
  economic sectors, change in, 48–58 *passim*
  ideology, 61–64
  industry, 330–72 *passim*
  inhibitions of inhabitants, 46, 48
  natural resources, 89–91
  population, 69–89
  stages, 14–18, 66–68
  technology, 64–68, 122–24
"Economic geography," 6
Economic history, 6, 16
Economic management, 46
Ecuador, 174
Education, 24, 36, 39, 65, 67, 130
  colonialism, 63, 64
Eggs, 109, 134, 135, 136, 137, 194, 224
  production, 235–36
Egypt, 37, 102, 437, 566
  industry, 341, 507
  oils-fats production, 205
Elastomers, 279–87; *see also* Rubber
Electricity, 54, 126, 352, 358, 363, 375, 396, 423

nuclear power, 417–20
transmission, 78, 410–11
water power, 402–12
Electronic industry, 121, 494
Elites, 18, 22, 26, 44, 46, 51, 61, 62
Employment; *see also* Labor and labor force
  national structure, 11, 55
  opportunities, 20, 56–57, 70, 91, 132, 178
Energy resources, 363, 373–424; *see also specific resources*
Engineering industry, 20, 343, 493–94
English Channel, 321
Entrepreneurship, 39
Erosion, 7, 49 n., 77, 112, 123, 156, 246, 273, 296, 517
Ethiopia, 63, 268
Ethnic minorities, 22, 44, 65
Eurasia, 155
Europe, 7–8, 16; *see also specific countries and areas*
  agriculture, 17
  industrial regions, 336
  population, 88, 89
Europe, Eastern (Communist), 16, 45
  agriculture, 28, 99, 112, 124, 138, 163, 167, 174, 249
  beverage production, 265
  chemical industry, 508, 515
  commerce, 563
  energy resources, 373–424 *passim*
  fiber production, 241
  fishing industry, 313, 316
  food consumption, 107, 139
  forest production, 289, 290, 291–94, 298, 307
  grain production, 154
  ideologies, 26
  imports, 184, 186, 561
  income, 14, 337, 555
  industry, 332, 333, 337–38
  investments, 27–28
  land resources, 115
  livestock, 215, 218
  market, 121
  metallurgy, 427, 430, 431, 436, 439, 468, 477, 481
  natural gas production, 398
  oils-fats production, 197, 208, 210
  population, 282
  services, 530, 547, 559
  starch crops, 138, 139, 140
  steelmaking, 461–63
  sugar production, 181
  technology, 406
Europe, northern, 162
Europe, southern, 25, 159

INDEX

Europe, Western (non-Communist)
  agriculture, 25, 95–99, 112, 124, 138, 154, 174
  animal products, 215, 218
  beverage products, 265
  cattle industry, 227
  chemical industry, 508
  commerce, 559–64
  consumption
    animal fats, 210
    cotton, 245
    food, 107
    starch crops, 140
    synthetic rubber, 285
    tropical products, 121
  energy resources, 373–424 *passim*
  exports, 560
  fiber production, 241
  fishing industry, 316, 318
  forest products, 288, 289, 290, 291, 298, 307
  grain production, 154
  ideology, 165, 248, 276, 561
  income, 14, 25, 555
  industry, 332–37, 344, 345
  labor force, 25
  land resources, 115
  metallurgy, 427, 430, 431, 435–36, 468, 481
  natural gas production, 398
  natural patterns, 26, 79
  oils-fats production, 197, 210, 212
  population, 83, 85, 86, 88, 103
  productivity, 25
  rubber output, 282, 287
  service output, 530, 547, 551
  starch crops, 138, 139, 140
  steel industry, 459–61
  sugar production, 181
European Atomic Energy Community (Euratom), 418
Expansionism, 29, 39
Explosives, 401, 516
Export bounties, 29
Exports; *see* Trade, international
Extra-high-voltage (EHV), 411

Fabrics, 251, 252, 253, 255, 260, 261, 349; *see also* Fibers; Textile industry
Facility patterns, regional, 20, 23, 25, 27–28, 32, 35, 37, 40, 42–43, 47–48
Fallowing, 149, 214
Famine, 145
Far East, Communist; *see also* specific countries
  agriculture, 17, 42, 102–3, 104, 120, 138, 154, 167, 344
  beverage production, 265, 268
  chemical industry, 508, 515
  commerce, 567–68
  energy resources, 374–424 *passim*
  exports, 560
  fiber production, 241
  fishing industry, 316
  food consumption, 107, 170, 171
  forest products, 289, 290, 296–97, 298, 307
  grain production, 154
  ideologies, 41
  imports, 184, 386, 561
  income, 14, 555
  industry, 42, 102–3, 332, 333, 343–44
  institutions, 41–42
  land resources, 115, 118
  livestock, 215, 218
  metallurgy, 427, 430, 431, 438, 468, 478, 481
  natural resources, 43
  oils-fats production, 197, 208
  rubber production, 282
  service production, 530, 547, 551
  starch crops production, 138, 139, 144
  steel industry, 466–67
  sugar output, 181
  water power, 406
Far East, general, 70, 79, 85, 153
  diet, 105, 108, 146, 170–71
  population, 85, 88
Far East, non-Communist; *see also* specific countries
  agriculture, 39–40, 102, 114, 138, 167
  beverage production, 265
  chemical industry, 508, 515
  commerce, 566–67
  energy resources, 374–424 *passim*
  exports, 560
  fiber production, 241
  fishing industry, 313, 316
  food consumption, 170, 171
  forest products, 289, 290, 295–96, 298, 307
  grain production, 154, 158
  ideologies, 38–39
  imports, 386, 561
  income, 14, 39, 555
  industry, 39, 102, 332, 333, 342–43
  institutions, 39
  land resources, 115, 118
  livestock, 214, 215, 218
  metallurgy, 427, 431, 437–38, 468, 478, 481
  morale, 38–39
  oils-fats production, 197
  rubber output, 282
  service production, 530, 547, 551
  starch crops output, 138, 139, 144, 145
  steel industry, 465–66
  sugar production, 181
  water power, 406
  world trade, 40
Fats, 102, 105, 109, 132, 134, 135, 136, 137, 158, 179, 209–12, 240
  monounsaturated, 193, 194
  polyunsaturated, 193–94
  processing, 194–95
  production, 195–97
Fatty acids, 193, 194, 195, 200, 206, 208, 211
Federal Power Commission, 401
Ferro alloys, 442–45
Fertilizers, 30, 77, 112–14, 120, 122, 123, 147, 150, 156, 163–64, 170, 185, 189, 201, 208, 209, 229, 240, 245, 247, 264, 273
  production, 111, 273, 312, 320, 323, 326, 401, 512, 513–19
Feudalism, 36, 67
Fibers, 51, 225
  animal, 250–53
  cordage, 250
  cotton, 245–48
  flax, 249
  glass, 255
  hemp, 249–50
  jute, 248–49
  production, 240–56 *passim*
  synthetic, 240, 248, 253–55, 256
  textile manufacturing, 257–61
  vegetable, 244–50
Fiji, 339
Fish
  by-products, 318–22
  as food, 120, 134, 135, 136, 137, 211, 239, 312–23
  oil, 194
  types, 312–13
Fishing grounds, 313, 316
Fishing industry and fisheries, 45, 73, 94, 239
  productivity, 313–23 *passim*
Flax, 208, 234, 249, 250
Florida, 418
  phosphate deposits, 517–18
Flour, 155, 171, 205
  rye, 163, 164
  wheat, 150, 151, 159, 164
Food and Agriculture Organization of the United Nations (F.A.O.), 102, 110, 118
Food and foodstuffs, 30, 45, 49; *see also specific foodstuffs*
  animal products, 214–39 *passim*
  basic energy, 134–78
  consumption, 50, 94–212 *passim*
  fish, 120, 134–37, 312–23 *passim*
  luxury energy, 137, 179–212
  production, 50–51, 100–110 *passim*, 132–33, 346–48
  retailing, 563

Food and foodstuffs (*Continued*)
  world trade, 121, 152, 154, 158, 174, 181–85, 195–96, 202, 203, 210, 268–72
Food freezing, 237, 318, 346
Food industry, 331, 336, 338, 340, 341, 342, 345, 346–49
Food processing, 177–78, 187–88, 207, 208–10, 212, 309, 346
  coffee, 270
  dairy, 223
  fish, 211, 318
  meats, 236–39
  oils, 194–95
  sugar, 187–89, 191–92
Footwear, 349–50
Forced labor, 102
Foreign aid, 88, 102, 103
Forests, 20, 23, 25, 26, 30, 33, 35, 38, 45, 51
  clearing, 114–15
  forest products, 288–311, 360, 362
  forestry, 6, 73, 94, 297, 301
Formosa; *see* Taiwan
France, 63, 102, 254, 483
  birth rate, 84–85
  chemical industry, 518, 519
  economic growth, 67
  exports, 152, 249, 258, 439
  fuel production, 398, 420
  industry, 336, 477
  ore deposits, 435, 436, 438, 439
  productivity, 181, 278
  steel industry, 450, 460
Freighting, 54, 153, 346, 351, 393, 416, 440, 544–50; *see also* Transportation
Fruits, 99, 101, 103, 107, 110, 132, 134, 144, 149, 167–76, 263, 277
Fuels, 7, 49, 54, 90, 165, 186, 201, 297, 336, 338, 340, 341, 342, 345, 346, 351, 362, 375, 449
Fungicides, 156
Furnaces; *see* Steelmaking furnaces
Furniture industry, 54, 310, 350
Fusion (power), 424

Gabon, 437
Ganges River, 118, 204
Garment industry, 121, 245, 331, 336, 338, 340, 341, 342, 345, 346, 349–50; *see also* Apparel
Gases, 331, 336, 338, 340, 341, 342, 345, 346, 391; *see also* Natural gas
  industrial, 400, 445, 446, 447, 449, 514–15, 520–21
  manufactured, 383, 397
Gasoline, 413; *see also* Petroleum
Geography, 3–6
Geology, 51, 78
  fuels, 378–79, 390

Georgia, 435
Germany, East, 26, 140
  industry, 336, 337, 338, 462
Germany, Empire of, 63, 67
Germany, West, 49, 140, 181
  exports, 260
  fuels, 379, 410
  imports, 254, 438
  industry, 336, 337
  labor costs, 483
  mineral deposits, 435, 436, 439, 500, 519
  steel industry, 450, 459
Ghana, 67, 276
Ghee, 210
Gilsonite, 412–13
Glass industry, 255, 355, 523
Glucose, 170
Gluten, 155, 159, 161, 162
Glycerol, 194
Goats, 222, 234
Gobi Desert, 118
Gold, 78
Government, 22, 49, 56, 184
  centralized, 24, 67
  and industry, 369–70
  as service, 568–69
Grains, 102, 105, 136, 137, 140–44; *see also* specific grain foods
  animal feed, 153–67, 177, 225, 228
  food, 145–53
  production, 145–46
  surpluses, 118
Grapes, 277–78
Grass and grasslands, 77–78, 83, 112, 114, 115, 118, 151, 219, 227, 232, 239
  commercial ranching, 222–23
Grazing, 222–23, 232
Great Britain; *see* United Kingdom
Great Canadian Oil Sands, Ltd., 414
Great Lakes, and region of, 78, 153, 228, 408, 422, 432, 440, 455–56
"Great Leap Forward," 42, 102
Great Plains, North American, 151, 153, 206, 208, 222, 236, 331, 422
Great-regions, 11–16
  assessments, 18–48
Greece, 205, 336, 477
Greenland, 21; *see also* North America
Gross national product, 27, 555
Groundnuts; *see* Peanuts
Guam, 338, 339
Guatemala, 174
Guinea, 437
Gulf of Mexico, and coast, 313, 325, 388, 390, 511
Gur (sugar), 179

Habitat, 6, 19, 20, 33, 70, 90
  influencing population redistribution, 76–79
Haiti, 18, 32, 100, 250, 475
Han Empire, 81
Hand-tool industry, 493
Handicrafts, 48, 49, 66, 336
Hay and haymaking, 22, 214, 235
Health conditions, 48, 65, 81, 83, 88, 130, 195; *see also* Diseases; Nutrition and nutrients
  food consumption, 105–10, 193–95
Hemp, 244, 249–50
Hemp oil, 209
Henequen, 250
Herbicides, 157, 247
Herding, nomadic, 219–22
High-income countries, 11, 16–17
  agriculture, 94, 103–4, 112, 120, 124, 138, 167
  aid programs, 121
  animal products, 214, 215, 218
  beverage production, 265
  capitalization, 45
  chemical industry, 508, 515
  energy resources, 374–424 *passim*
  fiber production, 241
  fishing industry, 316
  food consumption, 104, 105, 107, 109, 179
  forest products, 289, 290, 298, 307
  grain production, 154
  ideologies, 43–44
  imports, 386, 561
  income, 104, 555
  industrial labor, 333
  industrial output, 53, 332
  institutions, 44
  land resources, 115
  metallurgy, 426, 427, 431, 468, 481
  modernization, 44
  oils-fats production, 197, 209, 210, 223
  population, 44, 71, 78, 212, 223
  service production, 56–57, 530, 547, 551
  starch crops production, 138, 139
  sugar production, 181
  technology, 44, 124
  water power, 406
Hindus, 210
Hogs; *see* Pork and pork products
Homogeneous area, hypothesis of, 5
Honduras, 174
Hong Kong, 17, 63, 121, 178, 260, 313, 567
  industry, 342, 343

Horses, 222, 225, 229
Horticulture, 22
Housing, 28, 48, 54, 76, 130
Hudson Bay, 411
Humus, 113, 151, 190, 275
Hungary, 16, 436, 462, 477
Hunting, 94, 124, 239, 263
Hybridization, 124, 156, 159, 164, 165, 250, 309
Hydroelectric power, 374, 375, 402–12
  potentials, 33, 35
Hydrogenation, 195, 210, 211, 212, 414

Iberia, 11
Iceland, 321
Idaho, 169, 517, 518
Ideologies, 5, 19, 56, 59, 303
  Eastern Europe, 26
  economic development, 61–64
  Far East, Communist, 41
  Far East, non-Communist, 38–39
  high-income countries, 43–44
  Latin America, 31
  low-income countries, 46
  Middle East, 36
  North America, 21–22
  Oceania, 28–29
  sub-Saharan Africa, 33–34
  Western Europe, 24
Illiteracy, 81, 102
Immigration, 103, 104
Imperialism, 36, 39, 67, 92
Imports; see Trade, international
Income
  food consumption, 104, 110
  modernization, 39, 44
  national, 14, 16, 17
  per capita, 11, 25, 29, 39, 44, 47, 85, 132, 135, 137, 337, 339
  population, 85–86
  real, 11, 48, 91, 132
  regional, 11–58 passim
  rise in levels of, 81, 104, 105, 121, 268
India, 18, 29, 109, 288
  agriculture, 111, 114, 148, 150, 164, 180
  diet, 135, 136, 137, 149, 169, 272
  economic development, 67, 137, 368
  exports, 248, 253, 258, 438
  imports, 206
  industrialization, 64, 258, 342, 343, 507
  natural resources, 118, 122, 407
  oils-fats production, 201, 206, 208
  ore deposits, 437, 438, 443

Indian Ocean, 313
Indiana, 476
Indians, North American, 22, 170–71
Individualism, 29, 36, 63
Indochina, 39
Indonesia, 40, 64, 102, 109, 288, 325, 438, 472
  agriculture, 114, 148, 149, 250, 274
  expansionism, 29, 39
Indus River, 118, 398
Industrial development, 6, 7, 8, 18, 32, 53–55, 87, 144, 153, 176, 245, 326, 552
  economic growth, 358–72 passim
  and ideology, 61–64, 369
Industrial location, 6, 9, 54–55, 336, 358, 369, 419–20, 523–25
  labor-oriented, 364–68
    vs. materials-oriented, 370–71
  market-oriented, 53–54, 73, 178, 341, 350, 359–60, 365, 387, 477, 486
  materials-oriented, 360–64
Industrial Revolution, 7, 24, 73, 78, 80, 83, 112, 250, 332, 336, 412
Industry; see also specific industries
  and agriculture, 102–3, 360–64
  capital availability, 366–68
  decentralized, 27, 348, 442
  and government, 369–70
  and heavy manufacturing, 20, 27, 37, 43, 54–55, 78, 331, 336–45, 351–56
  and labor, 364–66
  and light manufacturing, 53–54, 331, 336, 338, 340, 341, 342, 345, 346–51
  locational tendencies, 6, 9, 54–55, 358–71, 523–25
  management availability, 368–69
  markets, 53–54, 73, 178, 341, 350, 359–60, 365, 387, 477, 486
  multiproduct, 19–20
  national income, 37, 53–55
  raw materials, 103, 110, 168, 170, 254, 337, 339, 340, 346–56 passim, 360–64
  subsector characteristics, 345–58
Insects, 145, 146
Institutions and institutional patterns, 19–20, 21, 67
  Eastern Europe, Communist, 26–27
  Far East, Communist, 41
  Far East, non-Communist, 39

high-income countries, **44**
  Latin America, 31–32
  low-income countries, 46–47
  Middle East, 36–37
  North America, 22
  Oceania, 29
  sub-Saharan Africa, 34
  Western Europe, 24–25
Integration, economic, 120, 121, 337, 526
  vertical, 224
International Coffee Agreement, 270
International trade; see Trade, international
Iodine, 108, 109, 325
Iran, 63, 67, 101, 341
Iraq, 272
  oil production, 341, 414
Ireland, 249, 325, 415
Iron, 51, 54, 78, 148, 426, 449; see also Steel industry
  alloys, 442–45
  furnace techniques, 447–54
  industrial location, 454–67
  international trade, 438–40
  mining, 430–38 passim
  ore, 30, 33, 325, 344, 363, 431–38
  pig, 427, 430, 431, 440, 447, 448, 450, 481
  scrap, 440–42
Iron, dietary, 108
Irredentism, 33
Irrigation, 32, 38, 40, 114, 118, 122, 144, 148, 165, 168, 185, 191, 219, 227, 229, 245, 249
Islam, 36–38
Israel, 16, 101, 139, 313, 327, 328, 566
  Arab nations vs., 36
  income status, 37, 341
  industry, 224, 341, 519
Italy, 254, 294, 327, 398, 483
  agriculture, 147, 249
  exports, 250, 260

Jamaica, bauxite production, 477
Japan, 39, 49, 63, 83, 104, 295, 325, 566
  agriculture, 102, 111, 112, 122, 123, 147, 148, 149, 150, 158, 212, 249, 253
  consumption
    feed grains, 154
    synthetics, 254
    tea, 272
    tropical products, 121
  diet, 135, 136, 137, 139, 149, 153, 272
  exports, 258, 260, 485, 486, 516
  fish production, 313, 318
  food expenditures, 135, 136

Japan (*Continued*)
  fuel production, 378, 382, 398, 420
  imports, 100, 121, 210, 248, 254, 436–39, 440, 465, 507, 518
  industry, 67, 224, 285, 296, 337, 342, 344, 350, 355, 450, 465, 466, 482, 489, 493
  international trade, 40, 258, 260, 566, 567
  mineral deposits, 438, 440, 511
  per capita income, 16, 44
  population, 88, 103
  shipbuilding, 488–91
  silk industry, 253
  tea, 272–74
Java, 18, 149, 158
Jordan, 519
Jute, 102, 244, 248–49, 250

Kansas, 156, 165, 397, 509
Kaoliangs; *see* Sorghums
Kashmir, 252
Katanga, 340, 470, 472
Kazakhstan, 202, 219, 470
Kazakov, George, 415
Kelp, 325
Kenaf, 249
Khrushchev, Nikita, 337
Koppers Company, 453–54
Korea, 18, 111, 147, 253
Kuwait, 16, 37, 327
  oil production, 341, 390
Kuzbass, 463
Kuznetz industrial region, 337, 338, 463

Labor and labor force; *see also* Employment
  agricultural, 22, 24, 37, 42, 57, 70, 73, 95, 104, 127, 158, 224, 228, 232, 244, 245, 249, 336
  vs. capital, 229, 244
  cost, 22, 35, 39, 54–55, 130, 157, 224, 232, 235, 244, 249, 351, 364, 365, 458, 459, 482–83, 491, 494, 536
  industrial, 22, 25, 27, 32, 42, 54, 330, 332, 336, 364–68
  location, 364–68, 370–71
  mobility, 73, 365
  productivity, 11, 32, 39, 90, 123, 158, 229, 232, 274, 330, 336
  service, 22, 25, 56-57, 132, 529, 531, 536, 552, 568, 569
  skilled, 87, 331, 486, 526
  technology, 55, 66, 122, 124–26, 526
  unemployment, 42, 56, 66, 87
  unskilled, 43, 47, 526
Labor-intensive techniques, 43, 54, 79, 132, 153, 158, 185, 195, 202, 203, 208, 223, 274, 336, 343, 364, 365, 368
Labrador, 411
Lake Baikal, 337, 338
Lake Erie, 455
Lake Maracaibo, 118
Lake Superior, 439–40
Lambs, 235, 252
Land resources, arable, 23–24, 30, 33, 35, 40, 43, 45, 48, 77, 214
  reclamation, 111–20 *passim*, 245
  technology, 123–24
Land tenancy, 128–29
Land tenure, 18, 50, 128
Land use, 31, 77
  areal expansion, 114–20
  intensive, 24
Land values, 94
Landforms, 33, 77, 79, 120
Landownership, 31
  agrarian reform, 128–29
  landlord systems, 49, 50, 128
Laos, 102, 438
Lard, 210
Lateritic ores, 437–38
Latin America, 22, 23; *see also* specific countries
  agriculture, 17, 31, 32, 33, 40, 100–101, 112, 138, 154, 155, 167
  beverage crop production, 265, 269, 271, 274, 276
  chemical industry, 508, 515, 517
  commerce, 565
  diet, 139, 153, 171
  economic growth, 31, 32
  energy resources, 373–424 *passim*
  exports, 195, 208, 560
  fiber production, 241
  fishing industry, 316
  food consumption, 107, 108, 268
  forest products, 289, 290, 291, 294–95, 298, 307
  grain production, 154, 158
  ideologies, 31
  imports, 386, 561
  income, 14, 32, 100, 339, 555
  industry, 32, 332, 333, 339–40, 344
  investments, 32
  land resources, 115
  landownership, 31
  livestock, 214, 215, 218
  metallurgy, 427, 430, 431, 438, 443, 468, 469–70, 477–78, 481
  nationalism, 31, 64
  natural resources, 33, 398, 406, 437, 443
  oils-fats production, 31, 32, 70, 85, 88, 100, 339
  services, 530, 547, 551
  starch crops production, 138, 139
  steel industry, 463–65
  sugar production, 181
  urbanization, 100
"Law of Devitalization," 240
Laws and legislation, 369–70
Lead, 38, 51, 426, 442, 470–72, 480
Leadership, 46, 61, 62–63
Lebanon, 36, 37, 139, 341
Legumes, 124, 157, 200
Leningrad, 28, 336, 337, 338
Leopoldville, 36
Levantine states, 37, 101, 566; *see also* Middle East
Liberia, 437, 438
Liberica, 269
Libya, 341, 398, 401
Lignin, 227, 300, 308, 309
Lignite, 379–80, 410, 415, 416, 477
Lime, 190, 509, 518
  production, 519–20
Limestone, 51, 352, 432, 446, 448, 509, 512, 519–20
Linen, 244, 249
Linseed oil, 208
Literacy, 37, 44; *see also* Education
Lithium, 480, 523
Littorals, 20
Livestock, 29, 31, 95, 99, 110, 113, 130; *see also* specific animals
  breeding, 124, 219–25 *passim*, 227, 230, 232, 239
  diseases, 36, 123, 124, 222, 235
  feeding, 101, 110, 124, 134, 140, 153–67, 225, 227–30
Loams, 151, 190, 244, 268
Logging, 295, 302–6
Louisiana, 388, 397, 512
Low-income countries, 11, 17–18; *see also* Underdeveloped societies
  agriculture, 104, 120, 138, 167
  beverage production, 265
  chemical industry, 508, 515
  consumption
    crude materials, 50
    food, 104, 105, 107, 108, 109, 110
  diet, 104–7, 179
  economic growth, 46, 48
  energy resources, 373, 374, 379, 380
  exports, 560
  fiber production, 241
  fishing industry, 316
  forest products, 289, 290, 298, 307
  ideologies, 46
  imports, 386, 561
  income, 47, 104, 555
  industrial labor, 333

industrial output, 53, 332
institutions, 46–47
investments, 47
land resources, 115
livestock, 215, 218
metallurgy, 427, 431, 468, 481
natural resources, 48
oils-fats production, 197, 208, 209
population, 71, 73, 88, 121, 212
rubber production, 282
services, 56–57, 530, 547, 551
starch crops production, 138, 139
sugar production, 181
technology, 48
water power, 406
Lumber, 187, 297–300, 340, 360; see also Forests
Luxembourg, 439, 450, 460

Machine tools, 483–85
Machinery, 20, 54, 57
 manufacture of, 359, 481–85
Maghreb, 101, 151, 437, 439
Magnesium, 51, 325, 478–79
Magnetite, 433, 436
Magnetohydrodynamics, 407
Maine, 169, 309
Maize, 108, 149, 150; see also Corn
 feed grain, 154–58
Malaysia, 173, 206, 207, 313, 398, 437, 438, 472
 rubber production, 283–85, 288
Malthus, T. R., 66
Management, 27, 29, 32, 39, 47, 63, 368
 availability, 368–69
Managerial ability, 230, 369
Manchuria, 42, 344, 438, 466
Manganese, 326, 442, 443
Manioc; see Cassava
Manufacturing, 40, 45, 53–55, 56, 194, 208–10; see also Industry
Manure, 111, 112, 123, 147, 149, 156, 273; see also Fertilizers
Margarine, 205, 206, 210, 211
Marine oils, 211
Maritime Provinces, 411
Market-orientation, 53–54, 73, 178, 341, 350, 359–60, 387, 477
Marketing, 9, 228–29, 230
Markets, 6, 9, 31, 46, 53, 54, 55, 249, 343, 407
 "free," 184
 limited, 131–32
 location, 359–61
Mass consumption, 24, 66, 67
Mauritania, 437
Meat industry, 29, 99, 105, 108, 134, 135, 136, 137, 222–23, 224–30

Meat-packing industry, 224–25, 236–39, 348
Mechanical processes, factory, 367–68
Mediterranean region, 124, 139, 148, 203, 268, 313
Melanesia, 28–31 passim, 140, 294, 338; see also Oceania
Merchandising, 230, 557
Mesabi iron mines, 432, 440
Metal-making industries, 355, 364, 480–94; see also Metals and metal products
Metal refining, 355
Metal smelting, 355, 436, 440, 448
Metallics, 33, 331, 336, 338, 340, 341, 342, 345, 346
Metallurgy, 33, 78, 338, 343, 361–64
 ferrous (iron-steel), 430–67
 non-ferrous, 467–80
Metals and metal products, 35, 54, 78, 331, 336, 338, 340, 341, 342, 345, 346, 355–56, 358, 359
 fabricating industries, 480–94
 future production, 325
 non-ferrous, 362–63
Methane gas, 400, 401
Mexico, 49, 169, 191, 398
 agriculture, 139, 250
 chemicals, 512, 513
 economic growth, 11, 339
 exports, 331, 471
 metallurgy, 33, 437, 471, 479
 ore deposits, 437, 471, 512
 steel industry, 449, 464
Mexico City, 339, 449
Michigan, 156, 509
Micronesia, 28–31 passim, 140, 338; see also Oceania
Microorganisms, 20, 35, 70, 76, 113, 227, 248
 in sewage, 328–29
Middle class, 22, 36, 37
 ideology, 62–64
 influence, 59–68 passim
Middle East (including North Africa), 17, 79, 81
 agriculture, 37, 38, 101–2, 138, 154, 159, 167, 173; see also specific countries
 beverage crop production, 265
 chemical industry, 508, 515, 517, 518
 commerce, 566
 culture, 36–37
 energy resources, 373–424 passim
 exports, 560
 fiber production, 241
 fishing industry, 316
 food consumption, 107, 153, 173, 272

 forest products, 289, 290, 295, 298, 307
 grain production, 154, 158
 ideologies, 36
 imports, 386, 561
 income, 14, 37, 555
 industry, 332, 333, 341–42, 344
 institutions, 36–37
 land resources, 115, 118
 livestock, 214, 215
 metallurgy, 427, 430, 431, 437, 468, 481
 nationalism, 36, 63
 natural gas production, 398
 natural resources, 37–38, 48
 oils-fats production, 197
 petroleum industry, 386, 387, 390, 393, 394, 395
 population, 70, 85, 88
 services, 530, 547, 551
 starch crops production, 138, 139, 144
 steel industry, 181
 water power, 406
Migration, 79, 87, 103, 104
Milk, 103, 108, 134, 136, 137, 210, 223, 348
 consumption, 231–32
 products, 100, 108–9, 134, 136, 137, 194, 210, 223–24, 230–33, 348
Millets, 137, 138, 144, 145, 150, 151, 153, 164–67
Mindanao, 438
Minerals, dietary, 108–9, 139
Minerals and mineral products, 7, 8, 18, 20, 24, 25, 28, 30, 32, 33, 35, 40–41, 43, 48, 114, 121, 344
 consumption, 49, 50, 87
 exploitation, 90, 362
 and fibers, 253, 255
 national income, 51
 non-metallic, 351–55
 production, 51–52, 54, 78
 salts, 320–21
 sea, derived from, 323–26
Mining, 6, 8, 35, 40, 45, 49, 54, 67, 78, 331, 336, 338, 340, 341, 342, 345, 346, 356–57, 361–62
 chemical, 507, 508, 512–23 passim
 coal, 378–85 passim
 ferro alloy, 442–45
 iron, 430–38 passim
 non-ferrous metal, 467–80 passim
 undersea, 325–26
Minnesota, 156, 159, 433
Missile manufacturing, 356, 444, 491–92
Mississippi, 228

Mississippi River, 153
Missouri, 228, 471
Modernization, 11, 30, 44, 45, 55, 371, 394, 566–69
   agriculture, 23, 25, 32, 94–133 *passim*
   economic growth, 14–16, 31, 48–58
   food problems, 51, 105–10
   international trade, 552
   population, 69–89 *passim*
   science, 139
Molasses, 186, 187
Molybdenum, 442, 443–44
Mongolia, 219, 343, 569
Montana, 517
Morocco, 437, 444
Mortality rates; *see* Death rates
Moslems, 210; *see also* Islam
Motor vehicles, 485–89; *see also* Automotive industry
Mozambique, 250
Mules, 222, 229
Myrdal, Gunnar, 38

Nationalism, 24, 29, 31, 34, 36, 52, 60, 64, 340
Nationalization, 32, 274
Natural gas, 33, 38, 78, 363, 374, 375, 378, 395–96, 449, 503
   reserves, 396–98
   transport, 398–401
Natural monopolies, 499
Natural patterns, regional, 20, 23–24, 26, 28, 30–31, 35–36, 38, 40–41, 43, 45, 48
Natural resistances, 33, 35–36, 40–41, 48
Natural resources, 3, 8, 10; *see also* Raw materials
   availability, 5, 6, 89–91
   distribution, 19, 23–48 *passim*
   and economic growth, 89–91
   exploitation, 87
   and industry, 360–64
   per capita supply, 43, 87
   underdeveloped, 43, 87
   underwater, 323–26, 398
Natural science, 3, 4
Nauru, 339
Nepal, 40, 63
Netherlands, 63, 327, 398
   food consumption, 153, 272
   labor costs, 482
New Caledonia, 339, 443
New England, 21, 318, 323, 418, 422
New Mexico, 328, 397
New York, 169, 270, 327, 419, 509
New Zealand, 16, 28–31 *passim*, 100, 251
   diet, 153, 272
   exports, 210, 239

industry, 338, 339, 348
   mineral deposits, 463, 477, 518
Newsprint, 309
Niagara, 408
Nickel, 326, 437, 442, 443, 445
Nigeria, 35, 341
   mining, 444, 472
Night soil, 111; *see also* Fertilizers
Nile River, 118
Nitrates, 320
Nitrogen, 111, 112, 113, 147, 149
   production, 513, 514–16
   in soils, 151, 156, 273, 279, 283
Nomadism, 37, 118, 124, 219–22
North Africa, 101–2, 392, 393; *see also* Middle East
North America; *see also* specific countries
   agriculture, 17, 22–23, 25, 95, 96, 103, 112, 124, 138, 154, 167
   beverage production, 265
   chemical industry, 508, 515, 517–18
   commerce, 557–59
   consumption
      cordage fibers, 250
      cotton, 245
      food, 107
      per capita, 27, 99
      rubber, 282, 285
      synthetics, 254
   energy resources, 373–424 *passim*
   exports, 195, 560
   fiber production, 241
   fishing industry, 313, 316
   forest products, 288, 289, 290, 298, 307
   grain production, 154
   ideology, 21–22, 46
   imports, 386, 561
   income, 14, 22, 31, 337, 555
   industry, 331–32, 337, 344, 345
   institutions, 22
   labor costs, 22
   land resources, 23–24, 115
   livestock, 215, 218
   metallurgy, 427, 430, 431, 468, 475–77, 479, 481
   minerals, 24
   oils-fats production, 197, 209, 210, 212
   population, 70, 88, 104
   rubber production, 282
   service output, 530, 547, 551
   starch crops production, 138, 139
   steel industry, 454–59
   sugar production, 181
   technology, 124
   water power, 406, 407–9, 410
North Atlantic region, 29, 30, 35, 191, 274, 279, 551, 564

fisheries, 312, 313
   imports, 253
   livestock farming, 223
North Atlantic Treaty Organization (NATO), 24
North Korea, 343, 344, 438, 466–67, 568
North Sea, 313, 398, 401
North Vietnam, 18, 39, 343, 438, 467, 568
Norway, 212, 439, 479, 514
Nova Scotia, 322
Nuclear projects and nuclear energy, 327, 385, 408, 416
   location theory, 419–20
   production, 417–19
Nutrition and nutrients, 51, 130, 135–39, 164; *see also* Calories; Diet; Vitamins
   deficiency, 105–10
   fat consumption, 193–95, 205, 228
   ocean products, 320–22
Nuts, 134, 263
Nylon, 250, 253, 256

Oases, 77, 219
Oats, 138, 145, 150, 159, 164
   animal feed, 161–62
Oceania; *see also* specific countries and areas
   agriculture, 25, 30, 95, 100, 112, 124, 138, 154, 167
   beverage production, 265
   chemical industry, 508, 515, 517
   commerce, 564–65
   consumption
      food, 107
      manufactured goods, 339
      yams, 171
   energy resources, 373–424 *passim*
   exports, 560
   fiber production, 241
   fishing industry, 316
   forest products, 289, 290, 298, 307
   grain production, 154
   ideologies, 28–29
   imports, 386, 561
   income, 14, 29, 555
   industry, 332, 333, 338–39, 344
   institutions, 29
   land resources, 115
   livestock, 215, 218, 219
   metallurgy, 427, 430, 431, 463, 468, 477, 481
   natural resources, 30–31
   oils-fats production, 197, 210
   population, 70, 88, 103
   rubber production, 282
   services, 530, 547, 551

starch crops production, 138, 139, 140
steel industry, 463
sugar production, 181
water power, 406
Oceans and oceanography, 20, 45, 78
products, 312–29
salt production, 507
Odessa, 28, 388
Oil cakes, 201
Oil shale, 413–14, 415–16, 424
Oils
edible, 102, 105, 109, 132, 134, 135, 136, 137, 144, 179, 193–94, 240
processing, 194–95
production, 195–97
vegetable, 195, 196–209, 340
fuel, 331, 336, 338, 340, 341, 342, 345, 346
offshore, 390–91
industrial, 51, 208–9, 240, 341
by-products, 255
paint industry, 189, 208
paper industry, 208
price, 394, 395
refineries, 394
Oilseeds, 53, 340
Oiticica oil, 208, 209
Okinawa, 342
Oklahoma, 165, 397
Olive oil, 202–4
Orange Free State, 328
Ores, 49
ferrous, 30, 33, 325, 344, 362, 426, 427, 431–38
non-ferrous, 30, 426, 427, 442
Organization, 9–10, 44
social, 18, 92
Orinoco River, 407
Orlon, 248, 252, 253, 256, 261
Ottoman Empire, 36
Outdoor living, 228
Oxygen, 445, 446, 447, 449, 520–21

Pacific Northwest region, U.S., 407, 408, 413
Pacific Ocean, 313, 321, 518
Packaging, 187, 249, 309, 359
Paint industry, 189, 194, 206, 208, 212
Pakistan, 148, 206, 272, 295, 296, 398
industry, 248, 342, 343
Palm oils, 206, 207
Pampas (Argentina), 151, 208, 222
Panama, 174
Panama disease, 174, 176
Paper industry, 208, 331, 336, 338, 340, 341, 342, 345, 346, 351
pulp, 291, 306–10 *passim*

Pastry products, 150–51
Pasture ranges, 23, 25, 26, 29, 30, 33, 35, 38, 43, 45, 101, 115, 118, 164, 222, 229, 232, 244, 252
rotational, 134, 166, 223
Peanuts (groundnuts), 120, 194, 201–2, 341
Peasantry, 65, 66, 95, 118, 249, 568
Peat, 160, 415
Peking, 42, 344
Pennsylvania, 170, 445
Per capita consumption; *see* Consumption, per capita
Perilla oil, 209
Persian Gulf, 327, 341, 390, 393, 550
Peru, ore deposits, 438, 444, 464, 469
Pest control and pesticides, 123, 239, 247, 263
Petrochemicals, 401, 502–5, 525
Petroleum, 33, 35, 37, 38, 43, 51, 78, 187, 341, 344, 362, 374, 378, 385–87, 413, 566, 567
production, 390–92
refining, 394–95
reserves, 387–90
transport, 393–94
Pharmaceuticals, 187, 351, 502
Philippines, 40, 102, 148, 206, 301, 313, 507
agriculture, 250
industry, 342, 343
ore deposits, 437, 438, 443
sugar production, 184
Phosphates, 38, 320, 326, 416
production, 513, 516–18
Phosphoric acid, 516–17, 518
Phosphorus, 108, 113, 147, 273
Photosynthesis, 320, 321, 322, 423
Pigs; *see* Pork and pork products
Pipeline systems, 393–94, 398, 399, 400, 414, 415, 525, 531, 536, 540, 547, 549
Pittsburgh, 455
Plankton, 320 23
Plantains, 167, 173–76; *see also* Bananas
Plantations, 35, 67, 207, 341
Plastics, 261, 401, 504
Podzols, 77–78, 113, 163
Poland, 16, 99, 140, 181
fuels, 380, 410
imports, 436
industry, 337, 461
Polyethylene, 504
Polymers; *see* Fibers, synthetic
Polynesia, 28–31 *passim*, 140, 338; *see also* Oceania
Population, 20, 24, 44; *see also* Demography
animal, 214, 215, 225

death controls, 81–83
density, 17, 42, 77, 219, 223
economic development, 69–89
food production, 103–5, 121, 226, 228
growth, 7–8, 18, 27, 31, 32, 47, 60, 80, 81–87, 95, 101, 102, 103–5, 121, 139, 195, 212, 263, 268, 326, 339
shifts, 23, 79–80, 103–4, 228
urban, 94
world distribution, 70–80
Pork and pork products, 155, 161, 162, 210, 223, 224–25, 228, 233–34
Portugal, 63, 443
Potash (potassium), 38, 51, 108, 111, 113, 147, 268, 325
production, 513, 518–19
Potatoes
sweet, 120, 137, 138, 149, 167, 170–71
white, 99, 120, 137, 138, 162, 167–70
Poultry, 137, 154, 155, 214, 223, 224, 235–36
Poverty, 11, 44, 47, 81, 92, 95; *see also* Low-income countries
agricultural, 126–32
economic pressures, 62
family income, 22
Power-elites and economic growth, 61–67; *see also* Elites
Precipitation; *see* Rainfall
Premodern societies, 8, 11
Price supports, cotton, 246, 248; *see also* Subsidies
Prices and pricing, 245
chemicals, 518, 520, 521
commodities, general, 184, 200, 206, 207, 228, 247, 248, 252, 270, 271, 272, 274, 279, 390, 394, 416, 508
fluctuation, 7, 9, 130, 250, 254, 271
"free" market, 184
raw materials, 249, 437, 499
rigidity, 46
rises, 51–52, 252
rubber, 284, 288
steel, 441–42
synthetics, 248, 253, 254–55
Prince Edward Island, 322
Printing industry, 308, 331, 336, 338, 340, 341, 342, 345, 346, 350
Producer goods industry, 338, 343, 344
Product-mix, 26–27, 449
Production, commodity
aircraft, 491–92
alloys, 442–45
animal products, 214–39 *passim*
barley, 158–60

INDEX

Production, commodity (*Continued*)
  beverages, 265–78 *passim*
  cacao, 275–76
  coal, 379–83
  corn, 154–58 *passim*
  cotton, 245–48
  dairy, 223–24, 227
  eggs, 224
  electronic products, 494
  fertilizers, 513–19
  fibers, 241, 244–56 *passim*
  fish, 312–23 *passim*
  forest products, 288–311 *passim*
  grain, 145–46
  industrial oils, 208–11
  iron, 447–67
    ore, 431–38
  lime, 519–20
  livestock feed, 153–67 *passim*
  machinery, 481–85
  marine oils, 211–12
  millets, 164–67
  motor vehicles, 485–89
  oats, 161–62
  oils-fats, 195–212
  paper, 306–11
  petroleum, 390–92
  rice, 145–50 *passim*
  rubber, 279–88
  rye, 162–64
  salt, 507–9
  silk, 252–53
  starch crops, 138, 139, 140, 144, 145
  steel, 430, 447–67 *passim*
  sugar, 179–81
  synthetic fibers, 253–56
  tea, 272–75
  tools, 493
  wine, 277–78
  wool, 250–52
Production and productivity, 9, 20, 87
  agricultural, 22, 25, 27, 30, 32, 42, 48, 53, 66, 75, 90, 94–212 *passim*
  economic growth, 67, 90, 95, 99
  food, 50–51, 94–212 *passim*
  industrial, 27, 49, 53–55, 330–528 *passim*
  labor, 11, 32, 39, 90, 123, 158, 229, 232, 274, 330, 336
  modernization, 48–58 *passim*
  services, 56–57, 530, 547, 551
Production costs, 57
  chemicals, 514, 515, 526–27
  energy resources, 390–91, 399, 403, 407, 410
  machinery manufacturing, 482–83
  metals, 433, 440, 449, 452, 476
  steelmaking, 458
Professions, 23, 49, 56–57, 336, 530, 569

Propane gas, 400
Propylene, 504
Proteins, 105, 108, 114, 134, 136, 151, 155, 194, 212, 214, 239
  animal, 137, 145, 223, 232, 312, 319, 322
  and fibers, 253, 255
  vegetable, 137, 162, 201
Publishing, 350
Puerto Rico, 16, 17, 171
  industrialization, 339
Pulp and pulp products, 254, 306–10
Purchasing power, 337, 551

Qatar, 327, 341
Quebec, 114, 411
Queensland, 437, 471, 477
Quotas, 184, 370

Race, 22, 34
  prejudice, 26, 31, 36
Radio, 551
Railroads, 394, 525, 531, 536–47 *passim*, 550; *see also* Transportation
Railway equipment industry, 492
Rainfall, 40, 43, 70, 126, 168, 170, 172, 176, 185, 201, 202, 275, 277, 301
  coffee, 268
  fibers, 244, 248, 249
  forest products, 295
  grain growth, 151, 155, 156, 165
  livestock feed, 227
  rice growing, 146
  rubber, 279
  tea, 273
Ranching, 20, 219
  commercial, 222–23
Rapeseed oil, 204
Raw materials, 14, 49–52, 57, 89, 121, 132, 133, 567; *see also* Natural resources
  chemical, 500–523
  industrial, 103, 110, 168, 170, 254, 337, 339, 340, 346–56 *passim*, 360–64
  location, 17, 351, 360–64
  metallurgical, 430–47, 467–80
Rayon, 244, 248, 252, 254, 255, 256, 260, 509
Real income, 11, 48; *see also* Income
Recycling, 360, 362, 363
Refrigeration, 173, 239, 318, 328
Refugees, 37
Regional approach, 4–5, 11–16, 18–48; *see also* Great-regions
Rents, 94
Research, 4, 370
Retailing, 557, 558, 559, 564, 565
Rhineland (Germany), 336
Rhodesia, 139, 341, 437, 443

Rice, 105, 108, 137, 138, 144, 153, 164, 177, 178
  cultivation, 145–50
Rickets, 108
Rivers, 25, 38, 45, 79, 407, 408
Rocky Mountain region, 422
Romania, 436, 462
Roots, edible, 138, 139, 144, 149, 167–76
Rostow, W. W., 66–67
Rotation grazing, 123
Rubber, 51, 53, 102, 135, 288
  natural, 279–85
  processing industry, 340, 350
  synthetic, 285–87, 401
Ruhr-Lorraine industrial region, 459–60
Rum, 186, 187
Rural electrification, 410
Rye, 138, 145, 150, 159, 162–64

Safflower oil, 194, 205–6
Sahara, 399–400, 437
St. Lawrence River, 408, 439
St. Lawrence Seaway, 440
Salt, 41, 108, 323, 506–12
Sanitation, 81–83, 88, 92
Saturated fats; *see* Fats
Saudi Arabia, 219
  oil production, 341
Savings, 47, 128
Scale of operation, 8–9
Scandinavia, 151, 159, 438, 439
  milk consumption, 231
Science, 19, 64, 87, 89
Scotland, 28
Scrap, iron and steel, 440–42, 495
Seeds and seeding, 124, 134, 168
Senegal, 341, 517
Services, 47, 57, 90
  contributory, 14, 49
  decentralized, 20
  governmental, 530, 568–69
  labor, 22, 25, 56–57, 132, 529, 531, 536, 552, 568, 569
  output, 55–56, 530, 547, 551
  professional and personal, 23, 49, 56–57, 336, 530, 569
  trade, 551–68
Sesame oil, 205
Sewage, reuse, 328–29
Sewing machines, 493
Shales, 416
  oil, 413–14, 415–16
Sheep and sheep-raising, 222, 223, 234–35, 250–51
Shell Oil Company of Canada, 415
Shelter; *see* Housing
Shipbuilding, 489–91
Shipping, 187, 536, 537, 540; *see also* Transportation
  fuels, 393, 400, 401
  ores, 439–40

INDEX

Siberia, 23, 45, 99, 115, 411
   fats-oils production, 202
   ore deposits, 436, 439, 472
Sierra Leone, 437, 479
Sigatoka disease, 176
Silage, 155
Silicones, 252, 442, 444
Silk, 244, 250, 252–53, 254, 567
Silviculture, 303; see also Forests
Sisal, 250; see also Fibers
Slum areas, 23, 44, 48, 81; see also Housing
Soap and soap-making industries, 194, 206, 208, 209, 211, 212, 509
Social mobility, 36, 73, 92
Social mores, 19, 22
Social psychology, 6, 89
Social science, 3, 4
Soft drinks; see Beverage industry
Soil conservation, 66, 76, 123
Soils, 7, 20, 23, 24, 28, 30, 33, 38, 41, 45, 48, 70, 108, 145, 151, 165, 173, 176, 246, 263, 273, 275, 277, 279, 283, 517, 518
   acid, 148, 160
   alkaline, 38, 148, 168
   alluvial, 120, 185
   depletion, 101, 102, 112, 149, 156, 268
   development, 25, 78, 111–14, 122
   laterite, 78
   limestone, 162, 185
   loamy, 190, 244, 268
   loessial, 120, 190
   podzolized, 77–78, 113, 163
   and population redistribution, 76–77
   sandy, 160, 163, 168, 170, 202
Solar energy, 420–24
Sorghums (giant millet), 138, 144, 145, 150, 154, 156, 164–67
South, U.S., 456–58, 525
South Africa, Republic of, 16, 327, 328
   agriculture, 139
   fuels, 380, 383
   ideology, 63
   industry, 35, 340
   livestock, 251, 252
   mineral deposits, 437, 443, 517
   tea consumption, 272
South America; see also Latin America
   agriculture, 172, 275
   fishing grounds, 313, 321
   industry, 355
   mineralization, 33
   population, 104
South Dakota, 328
South Korea, 40, 102, 342, 343, 443

South Vietnam, 102
Southeast Asia Treaty Organization (SEATO), 29
Southern Rhodesia, 437
Southwest, U.S., 246, 247, 421
Soviet Union, 16, 28, 43, 63, 65, 87; see also Europe, Eastern
   agriculture, 99–100, 104, 114, 140, 151, 159, 162, 174, 181, 249, 250
   aircraft and missile industry, 491–92
   chemical industry, 512, 517, 518, 519
   coal production, 377, 379
   consumption, 250, 272
   diet, 139, 162, 164, 165
   energy production, 409, 411, 413, 414, 415, 417, 418, 423
   fishing industry, 318
   foreign aid, 102
   income, 104
   industry, 67, 332, 337–38, 350
   livestock, 227
   metal fabricating, 482
   oils-fats production, 202, 209, 212
   ore deposits, 436, 439, 471, 472, 479
   petroleum industry, 388, 392, 394
   population, 70, 104
   steel industry, 462–63
   trade, 563, 567–68
     with Communist China, 567–68
Soybeans, 121, 137, 194, 200, 319
Space, spatial approach, 3, 4, 5, 19
Spain, 146, 294, 336, 401, 507, 518, 519
Spatial interaction, 5, 6
Specialization, 8–9, 57, 73, 90, 531
Spitzbergen, 321
Starches and starch crops, 105, 108, 110, 132, 134, 149, 155, 165, 167–76, 179, 191
   industrial use, 170
   production, 138–45
Steam power, 406
Steel industry, 54, 343, 363; see also Iron
   continuous casting process, 453–54
   crude steel, 427, 430, 431, 440, 441
   furnaces, 447–54
   international trade, 438–40
   iron ore production, 431–38
   "L-D" process, 452–53
   location, 454–67
   scrap, 440–42
   service materials, 445–47
   stainless steel, 445, 452

Steelmaking furnaces
   blast, 441, 445, 446, 447–54 passim, 518
   continuous casting, 453–54
   electric, 446, 450, 452, 495, 518
   open hearth, 450, 452, 459
   oxygen converter, 450, 452–53, 459, 495
Steppes, Siberian-Kazakhstan, 115
Stockholm, 336
Storage, agricultural product, 168, 170, 239, 270
Subsidies, 552
   coffee, 271
   farm, 130, 140, 180, 185
   fuels, 395
Sucrochemistry, 187–89
Suez Canal, 393
Sugar, 29, 53, 110, 132, 135, 136, 137, 165, 168, 212
   beet, 179, 189–93, 240
   by-products, 187–89, 192
   cane, 179, 185–89, 240
   centrifugal (raw value), 179, 181, 186
   refining, 191, 194, 346
   world trade, 181–85
Sugar refineries, 191, 194, 346
Sulfur, 444, 445, 508, 511–13
Sumatra, 207, 393
Sun Oil Ltd., 414
Sunflower seed oil, 202
Surinam, 475, 477
Sweden, 16, 153, 438, 439, 491
Switzerland, 386
Sydney, Australia, 339, 437
Synthetics, 52, 300, 320, 397
   fibers, 240–44, 248, 250, 253–55, 256
   food, 212, 240
   vs. natural materials, 240–44, 250, 251
   rubber, 279, 285–87, 401
Syria, 144
Syrup, 170, 186, 187

Taboos, 107
Taconite, 433, 439
Taiwan
   agriculture, 102, 139
   industry, 342, 343, 507
Tallow-grease, 210–11
Tapioca, 171, 173
Tar sands, 414–15
Tariffs, 29, 121, 184, 370
Taros (dasheens), 171
Tasmania, 437
Taxation, 6, 7, 37, 63, 104, 130, 184, 370, 433, 487, 565
Tea, 53, 263, 265
   climate, 273
   production, 272–75
Technicians, 64–66

Technology, 4, 5, 6, 19, 44, 45, 54, 225
  capital, 367
  changes, 7, 8, 9, 48, 73–75
  chemical, 497, 498, 499, 500, 521, 526–28
  crude materials, 361–63
  economic development, 64–68, 245
  energy resources, 388, 390–91, 407–9
  farm, 122–23, 130
  labor-saving, 55, 66, 122, 124–26, 229, 244
  land-saving, 123–24
  material, 60, 63–66, 91
  metallurgy, 430–33, 441, 442
  modernization, 18, 23, 44, 90–91
  population, 76, 79–89 passim
  premodern, 17
  social, 18, 27, 60, 64, 65
  textiles, 253–56, 260–61
Teeth, 193
Telephones, 551
Television, 551
Temperature, 76, 155, 165, 167, 172, 176, 227, 268, 273, 275, 277, 301; see also Climate
Tennessee, 517, 518
Tennessee Valley Authority, 408–9
Terracing, 123
Texas, 165, 205, 388, 390, 397, 449, 512
Textile industry, 121, 225, 517
  chemicalization, 248, 252, 253, 255
  fiber production, 240–56
  manufacturing, 257–61, 331, 336, 338, 340, 341, 345, 346, 349
  technology, 253–56, 260–61
Thailand, 67, 102, 148, 154, 208, 325, 343
Thar Desert, 118
Tibet, 252, 407
Tientsin, 42, 344
Timber, 288–306 passim
Timing problems, 8, 9–10
Tin, 43, 426, 442, 472–73, 480
Titanium, 442, 444, 467, 479
Tobacco, 5, 104, 135
Togo, 517
Tomsk region, 436
Topography, 23–24, 33, 35, 42, 77, 408, 524
Totalitarianism, 18, 41, 336, 369
Tourism, 79; see also Travel, personal
Trade, international, 29, 30, 32, 47, 52, 132, 146, 152, 173–74, 359, 551–52
  agriculture, 553–54
  animal products, 214–19, 239
  bananas, 174
  chemicals, 519
  coffee, 268–72
  fishing industry, 312–23 passim
  fuels, 386–87
  grains, 178
  hemp, 249–50
  industry, 554
  iron ore, 438–40
  oils-fats, 195–96, 202, 203, 210
  services, 554–58
  sugar, 181–85
  textiles, 258–60
  wheat, 152
  wood, 306
Trade unions, 29, 34, 47, 526
Transport routes and flows, 6, 20, 38, 531–35
Transportation, 5, 23, 25, 32, 37, 40, 42, 45, 49, 55–56, 77, 78, 83, 338, 340, 359, 364, 525–32
  air, 533, 537, 543, 550–51
  animal, 225, 240, 245
  availability, 531–40
  costs, 54, 153, 346, 351, 393, 416, 440, 526, 540–41, 544, 550
  freight traffic, 544–50
  of fuels, 383–85, 393–94, 398–401, 415, 525
  passenger, 550–51
  quality, 542–44
  rail, 394, 531, 535–40 passim, 544, 547, 550
  road and truck, 230, 346, 394, 531, 536, 537, 540–41, 543, 544, 546, 547
  routes, 20, 38, 531–35
  water, 240, 531, 533, 536–37, 538, 539, 540, 543, 546
Travel, personal, 550–51
Tribalism, 34, 37
Trinidad, 16
Tropics, 151, 167, 171, 185, 208, 263, 268, 273, 275, 288, 294, 321
Tsetse fly, 101, 144, 222
Tubers, 134, 137, 138, 139, 144, 149, 153, 167–76
Tung oil, 208, 209, 567
Tungsten, 43, 51, 442, 443, 567
Turkey, 36, 101, 144, 341, 566
  agriculture, 139, 252, 253
  oils-fats production, 202, 209
Typewriter manufacturing, 493

Ukraine
  industry, 337, 338
  oils-fats production, 202
  ore deposits, 436, 439, 477, 479
Undercapitalization, 23, 66
Underdeveloped societies; see also Low-income countries
  agriculture, 124, 126, 170, 245
  capital, 121, 367
  diet, 104–7, 135–39, 149, 170, 179
  electricity, 410, 419
  fuels, 385
  industrialization, 64–68 passim, 257–58, 330, 339–44 passim, 364, 365–66, 441, 482
  labor, 330
  livestock, 226
  mechanization, 245
  monetary policies, 369
  population changes, 85–86
  transportation, 225
  urbanization, 88
Unemployment, 42, 56, 66, 87
Union Minière Mining Company, 470
Union of Soviet Socialist Republics; see Soviet Union
United Fruit Company, 174–76
United Kingdom, 227, 255, 272
  capitalism, 63
  exports, 258
  fuels, 379, 420
  imports, 100, 210, 239, 278, 438, 439
  industrialization, 11, 67, 336, 343, 350
  ore deposits, 435, 436
  steel industry, 459–60
United Nations, 65
United States, 9, 16, 21, 36, 39, 43, 65
  agriculture, 147, 154, 155–56, 158, 159, 160, 168, 184, 185, 191, 224–25, 303
  aircraft manufacturing, 491–92
  cane production, 180
  capitalism, 63
  cattle industry, 223–28 passim
  chemical industry, 498, 503, 506, 518, 519, 520, 525
  coal production, 377, 379, 380, 382, 385
  consumption
    coffee, 268
    fibers, 255
    inedible raw materials, 331
    iron ore, 432
    mass, 67
    meat, 228
    milk, 231
    per capita, 52
    potato, 169
    sugar, 192
    sulfur, 512
    wine, 278
  corn crop, 155–56, 177
  cotton culture, 245–48
  dairy farming, 223, 232, 233

diet, 135, 136, 137, 153, 162, 169, 193, 194, 231, 271, 508
economic growth, 67
exports, 100, 121, 152, 154, 158, 165, 210, 258, 482, 486
fishing industry, 318
foreign aid, 102, 121
forest products, 291, 301–9 *passim*
imports, 174, 184, 206, 248, 249, 250, 260, 270, 331, 387, 393, 432, 437, 438, 443, 485, 493
industry, general, 331, 355, 439, 444, 480–81
land resources, 118, 124
livestock, 113, 215, 222–36 *passim*, 251
meat-packing industry, 236–37, 348
metal fabricating, 480–81, 482, 483
metallurgy, 433, 435, 442–45, 469, 470–71
motor vehicle manufacturing, 486–87
natural gas industry, 397, 398, 401
oils-fats production, 201, 205, 210
petroleum industry, 385–91 *passim*, 393, 394, 395
production, 180, 181, 184, 185, 263–68
shipbuilding, 489–90
steel industry, 439, 440, 441, 442, 448, 452, 454–59
transportation, 533, 543, 544, 550
water resources, 326, 327, 328, 402, 407, 411
wool production, 251, 252
U.S. Borax and Chemical Corporation, 522–23
U.S. Steel Company, 455, 458
Ural Mountains, 78
energy resources, 388, 394
industry, 336, 337, 338
metallurgy, 436, 439, 463, 470, 477, 479
Uranium, 416, 418
Urban-industrial societies, 11, 16–18, 20, 22, 43, 44, 48, 53, 57, 73, 76, 132, 177, 178, 285, 302, 310, 331, 338, 339, 356, 357, 360, 361, 528, 549, 569
agriculture, 94, 164
commerce, 557, 558, 559
consumption
cotton, 245
grain production, 167

millets and sorghums, 166
rye, 162
silk, 252
synthetics, 254
wool, 251
distribution, 55–56
economic development, 59–64 *passim*, 69, 91
energy resources, 405, 407
food drain, 135
imports, 252, 276
industry, 258, 482
population, 84, 86, 89
production, 254, 258, 482
transportation, 550
Urbanization, 30, 32, 43, 44, 60, 61, 103, 158, 531, 569
food supply, 104
population, 73–76, 79
Urea, 155
Uruguay, 16, 208, 222, 251, 339
Utah, 435, 517, 518
Utilities, energy, 40, 331, 336, 338, 340, 341, 342, 346, 357, 395
Uttar Pradesh Terai (India), 114

Values, 6, 21, 91
Vanadium, 442, 444
Vegetable oils; *see* Oils, edible
Vegetables, 99, 103, 107, 108, 109, 110, 132, 134, 136, 170, 194; *see also specific vegetables*
Venezuela, 16, 32, 327, 339
exports, 438, 440
ore deposits, 437, 438, 440
petroleum industry, 394, 395, 397, 398
steel industry, 464
Vicara, 253, 255, 256
Village handicrafts, 367
Vinyl, 253, 261
Vitamins, 103, 105, 108–9, 139, 169, 170, 193, 194
Volga Valley region, 337, 338, 411

Wages, 364–65, 370; *see also* Labor and labor force
War, 11, 16, 27, 250, 516
Wasteland, 23, 30, 33, 35, 45, 48, 70, 296
reclamation, 114–20 *passim*
Wastes, 7, 27, 42, 53, 239, 360
agricultural, 167, 170, 187, 277, 360
economic vs. physical, 552
fertilizer, 11, 517
Water resources, 37, 38, 49, 77, 79, 87, 122, 147, 148
contaminated, 23

desalination, 326–28
power, 402–12
technology, 407–9
underground, 20
Waterways, 43, 78, 153, 394
Weed control, 157, 247
Weight losses of agricultural materials, 360–61
Welfare and security, 8, 65, 551
material, 24
social, 24, 29, 39, 43, 52, 67
West Indies, 48, 206, 437
West Pakistan, 295; *see also* Pakistan
West Virginia, 445
Western societies, 24, 77, 130
Wet-milling, 154–55
Whale oil, 194, 195, 211
sperm, 195, 212
Wheat, 29, 121, 137, 138, 144, 145, 149, 150, 153, 162, 319
durum, 151–52
spring, 159
Wine and wineries, 101, 268, 277–78, 346
Winnipeg-Austin-Columbus triangle, 24
Wisconsin, 156
Women, 65, 365
Islam, 36–38
Wood products, 331, 336, 338, 340, 341, 342, 345, 346, 350
Woodworking industries, 310, 350
Wool, 29, 135, 222, 234, 235, 244, 248, 250–52, 256, 261
Workshops, town artisans', 367
World War II, 27, 63, 100, 330, 331, 340, 343, 345
Wuhan, 42, 344
Wyoming, 435, 517, 518

Yams, 108, 120, 167, 170–71
Yangtze Basin, 42, 204, 344, 466
Yautias, 171
Yeast fermentation, 150
Yellow Sea, 313
Yemen, 268
Yugoslavia, 99, 249
exports, 250
fuel production, 410
ore deposits, 436, 477
Yukon River, 407

Zambia, northern, 340, 444, 470
Zinc, 51, 426, 442, 470–72, 480, 481
Zirconium, 326, 442, 444
Zooplankton; *see* Plankton
Zuyder Zee, 118